THE BLITZ
THEN AND NOW

History with its flickering lamp stumbles along the trail of the past,
trying to reconstruct its scenes, to revive its echoes,
and kindle with pale gleams the passion of former days.

WINSTON CHURCHILL, NOVEMBER 12, 1940

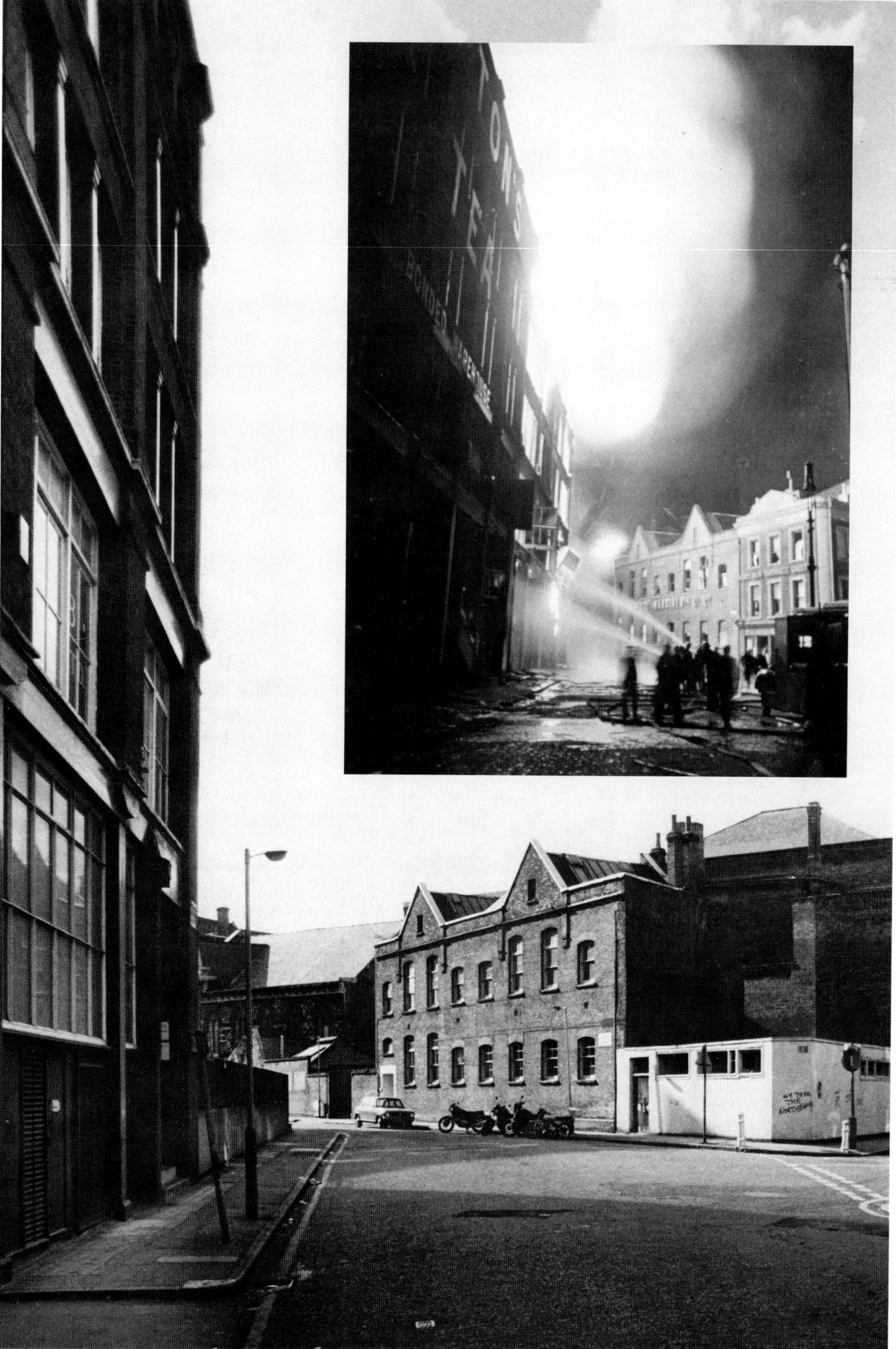

THE BLITZ
THEN AND NOW

VOLUME 2

The Night Blitz
KEN WAKEFIELD

The Aircraft Losses
PETER CORNWELL SIMON PARRY

The Photographs
ANDREW HYDE

The Eyewitnesses
HARRY ANDERSON
JIM BARKER
CYRIL DEMARNE
JACK DYER
ROBERT GÖTZ
ALAN SEYMOUR

Additional Contributors
HARRY ANDERSON CHRISTOPHER BARKER DENIS BATEMAN
PETER CHAMBERLAIN MAJOR A. S. HOGBEN ROY HUMPHREYS
REGINALD KING ANDY SAUNDERS DAVID J. SMITH

The Researchers
MICHAEL OCKENDEN COLONEL ROY M. STANLEY II JEAN PAUL PALLUD

Assistant Editor
GORDON RAMSEY

Editor
WINSTON G. RAMSEY

Tribute to a nation's civilian war dead. At Rose Hill Cemetery, Doncaster, individual headstones mark the graves of those killed, 16 of whom died in the town's worst incident on May 9, 1941 (see page 605).

Credits Volume 2

THE BLITZ THEN AND NOW

ISBN: 0 900913 54 1

Designed and edited by:
Winston G. Ramsey
Editor *After the Battle* magazine

PUBLISHERS
Battle of Britain Prints International Limited
Church House, Church Street,
London, E15 3JA

PRINTERS
Plaistow Press Limited
Church House, Church Street, E15 3JA

PHOTOGRAPHS
Where the copyright of photographs is clear, this has been indicated on the last page. The Editor is indebted to many individuals for the loan or supply of additional contemporary pictures, or copies of photographs, for which it has not been possible to determine the true provenance. All present day comparisons copyright of *After the Battle*.

COVER
From a painting by George A. Campbell.

REAR COVER
A sculpture created by John Mills and unveiled by Cyril Demarne in the Hall of Remembrance at London Fire Brigade Headquarters, Lambeth, on November 10, 1985, as a memorial to all those wartime Fire Service comrades who died as a result of enemy action.

FRONT ENDPAPER
Albert, Prince Consort, in Holborn Circus silhouetted against the backdrop of Wallis's store on the night of one of the heaviest raids of the war on April 16-17, 1941 — the reprisal raid on London in response to the RAF's attack on Berlin on April 9-10. (See also page 534.)

REAR ENDPAPER
'At least dolly's safe.' Just where we do not know, but a scene familiar in every corner of the British Isles during the Blitz.

FRONTISPIECE
Firefighters in action during one of the big raids on London on the night of January 11-12, 1941. Lipton's Tea bonded warehouse survived the blaze, as did Warriner's warehouse on the opposite side of Tabernacle Street. Nos. 74-76 on the corner were not so fortunate. (See also pages 394–395.)

PAGE 18-19
Date: September 7, 1940. Time: 6.48 p.m. German Standard Time. Place: London. To Londoners this was the beginning of the infamous Black Saturday raid when the Luftwaffe turned its attention from Royal Air Force ground targets to industrial and commercial premises marking the turning point in the Luftschlacht um England.

ACKNOWLEDGEMENTS
The Editor is indebted to the following for their help, assistance and advice in the preparation of this volume:
'Bud' Abbott; Perry Adams; Herr Albinus, Dr Hofmann, Herr Meyer, Dr Trumpp and staff of the Bundesarchiv; Rupert Allason; Mervyn Amundson; Patrick Baird, Local Studies, City of Birmingham; D. T. Barriskill Esq., Guildhall Library; Jim Beedle; Revd Philip Blewett, British Film Institute; Howard Bloch, Newham Central Library; Paul Bookbinder; Keith Braybrooke; Alan Brown; Eddie Browne; A. de Bruin Esq.; Pat Burgess; David Burgess-Wise of Ford of Europe Incorporated; Frau Busekow of the Deutsche Dienststelle; Mrs Peggy Campbell; Steve Caseley; C. S. Caspers Esq.; E. Chumley Esq.; Joe Collier of the Wartime Aircraft Recovery Group; Bob Collis of the Norfolk & Suffolk Aviation Museum; Mrs L. Cooperwhite, Central Library, Greenock; M. Costello Esq., Irish Lights; J. S. Cox of the Air Historical Branch; J. I. Cross Esq., Snowdonia Aviation Historical Group; Jill Crowther, Local Studies, Kingston-upon-Hull; Peter Danter of Aerofilms Ltd; David Davies; Miss K. Dee; Captain John Deverall; Nigel Douglas; Bryn Elliott; Christopher Elliott; John Ellis; A. W. Evans Esq.; Mark Evans of the Midland Aircraft Recovery Group; Brian Evelin, Fire Brigade Museum; Peter Felix of the Derbyshire Historical Aviation Society; James D. Ferguson; Robin Fletcher of the Humberside Aircraft Preservation Society; Peter Foote; John Frost of the Historical Newspaper Service; Adolf Galland; Ron Gammage; S. Gaskell Esq., Central Library, Liverpool; Gerd E. Gerhard; T. Graham, Central Library, South Shields; Robbie Gribben of Skyfotos Ltd; Delwyn Griffith; David Hale; C. G. Hall Esq.; Steve Hall; Jim Halley; Peter Halliday; Barry Hammerton; T. N. Hancock Esq.; Mrs R. A. Hands; Roland Hautefeuille; Ian Henderson; David Higham Ltd; Robin Hill of the Essex Historical Aviation Society; Philippa Hodgkiss; Robin Hood of the Devon Aircraft Research & Recovery Team; Roy Humphreys; Dewi Jones of the Gwalia Aviation Research Group; Maurice Kanarek; George Karger; A. R. Kemp Esq.; Barry Kemp of the Lincolnshire Aircraft Recovery Group; Paul Kemp and staff of the Imperial War Museum; Bill Kerr; Alex King; David King of the Booker Aircraft Museum; Mrs Hazel Kissoon and staff of the Commonwealth War Graves Commission; Dennis Knight; Captain Roger Lewis, OBE, DSO, RN; London Transport Museum; Norman Longmate; Alistair Macdonald, MBE, MC, BA; Mrs Mairi MacKay, British Alcan Highland Smelters Ltd; Miss Patricia Malcolm, Central Library, Clydebank; Karel Margry; Mrs P. Marshall; S. McCann Esq.; G. F. Miles Esq.; John Molyneux of the Warplane Wreck Investigation Group; George Morely of the South West Aircraft Recovery Group; Roger Morgan; Mrs Ruth Nicoll; Geoff Nutkins of the Shoreham Aircraft Preservation Society; Martin Olive, Local Studies, Sheffield City Library; Commander J. G. D. Ouvry, DSO, RN, JP; Nigel Parker of the Thames Valley Aircraft Recovery Group; Terry Parsons; Michael Payne; John Penny of the Fishponds Local History Society, Bristol; Paul Piratin; Dr Alfred Price; Phil Reed; Major-General D. H. G. Rice, Central Chancery, Orders of Knighthood; Bruce Robertson; Brian Sadler; Frank Sainsbury; Michael Schmeelke; Vernon Scott, The Western Telegraph; Mick Skeels of the Essex Aviation Group; E. W. Skerry Esq., Severn Trent Water; David Stansfield of the Pennine Aviation Museum; G. Stevenson Esq.; Sun Life of Canada; J. Thurston Esq.; Alan Tomkins; Fritz Trenkle; Ullstein Bilderdienst; Steve Vizard; the staff of the Volksbund Deutsche Kriegsgräberfürsorge; Dick Walker; Mrs A. D. Walton of the University of Keele Air Photo Library; J. D. Walton of the North East Aircraft Museum; Bill Welbourne of the Fenland Aircraft Preservation Society; Alan White of the Severnside Aviation Society; Alan Williams; Henry Wills; Tom Wylie, Ulster Museum.

Contents

Dedication

In the phraseology of the time, the Blitz placed ordinary people 'in the Front Line'. As the number of civilian casualties continued to rise, it was therefore only fitting that the National Government should have decided to initiate some form of permanent memorial in honour of those killed as a result of enemy action. Thus on February 7, 1941, a Royal Charter entrusted the duty of compiling the names of civilian war dead to the Imperial War Graves Commission, and an Advisory Committee was formed, consisting of Viscountess Davidson, Lady Megan Lloyd George, Dr J. J. Mallon and Mr Harold Clay, in order to determine the exact form that such a record should take as a memorial and where this should be sited.

In obtaining the necessary information, the Imperial War Graves Commission relied primarily upon that furnished by the Registrar-Generals of England, Scotland, Wales and Northern Ireland, to which further details were added as a result of correspondence between the IWGC and relatives of the deceased. In the case of members of the Civil Defence, these details included rank, number and name of service. For England, Wales and Northern Ireland the lists of names were arranged by counties, first by county boroughs and then by boroughs and other districts, these divisions being in alphabetical order. The names were entered according to the place of death; not home address. The same system applied to Scotland except that the cities of Aberdeen, Dundee, Edinburgh and Glasgow came first in their respective counties.

An initial record of those killed between the outbreak of war and September 30, 1941 comprised over 42,000 people, about half of whom had died in the London Civil Defence Region, and this formed a Roll of Honour, provisionally entered in three bound volumes, placed in the trust of the Dean of Westminster in December 1942. A further volume, added later, contained a list of the 1,005 civilians killed in Cyprus, East Africa, Gibraltar, Iran, Malta, Nigeria, Palestine and Turkey, and those who had lost their lives at sea.

On February 24, 1943, King George VI inspected the bound volumes at Westminster Abbey and work started in September of that year on a Memorial Case to house the complete Roll of Honour on the west wall of St George's Chapel, close to the tablet commemorating the million dead of the British armed forces of the First World War. The memorial was designed by Sir Charles Peers, the Surveyor to the Abbey, who described it as . . . 'of oak, carved and panelled, with hollywood inlay in the panels, and a frieze and cornice above, enriched with colour and gilding.' However, due to shortages of skilled labour and materials, it was not completed until May 1945.

In the autumn of 1945 another volume was added containing the names of the further 18,000 civilian war dead killed since the end of September 1941.

As late as 1947 it was not possible to forsee when a date would be arrived at to clearly define the end of the Second World War. Men serving in the Commonwealth armed forces were still losing their lives in many parts of the world, or dying of wounds received prior to the cessation of hostilities. Others were being killed in Palestine, or in bomb and mine clearance. Following the precedent established after the First World War, the Imperial War Graves Commission (the name was changed to 'Commonwealth' in March 1960) sought a Supplemental Charter for the purpose of commemorating all war deaths, both military and civil, occurring prior to December 31, 1947.

After the checking and correction of the temporary wartime lists had been finalised, arrangements were made for the complete record of names to be printed and bound. The Roll was set in the classic Bembo typeface, printed on hand-made paper from mills in Kent, and bound in red Nigerian goatskin, native cured and dyed especially for the purpose, with lettering hand-tooled in 22-carat gold.

On February 21, 1956, the Duke of Gloucester, as President of the Imperial War Graves Commission, handed over the Roll of Honour to the Dean and Chapter of Westminster in the Jerusalem Chamber. One volume, over which a light is kept burning, lies open in the Memorial Case, and every day a single page is turned.

The names therein recorded embrace both commoner and peer. They span the deaths of new-born babes to a Chelsea Pensioner in his hundredth year. The pages record whole families wiped out; elsewhere perhaps an only child, or a child's parents. While some died alone others lost their lives in the company of dozens, even sometimes over a hundred, of their countrymen. The first were nearly 100 passengers on the SS *Athenia*, torpedoed by a U-Boat on the day that war was declared. By the end of nearly six years of war, their number comprised part of a worldwide total estimated at some 40,000,000 civilian war dead, of which about 600,000 were citizens of the Third Reich.

To those 60,000 British civilians who died and the 86,000 who were injured, this project, spread over three volumes, is dedicated.

CIVILIAN CASUALTIES — MINISTRY OF HOME SECURITY STATISTICS (COMPILED FROM POLICE AND MEDICAL REPORTS)

(Source: *Civil Defence* (O'Brien), HMSO, Official War History Series)

	KILLED			*ADMITTED TO HOSPITAL (Mostly Seriously Injured)*		
	London	*Elsewhere*	*Total*	*London*	*Elsewhere*	*Total*
3.9.39–6.9.40.	257	1,441	1,698	441	1,848	2,289
7.9.40–31.12.40	13,339	8,730	22,069	17,937	10,303	28,240
1941	6,487	13,431	19,918	7,641	13,524	21,165
1942	27	3,209	3,236	52	4,096	4,148
1943	542	1,830	2,327	989	2,461	3,450
1944	7,533	942	8,475	19,611	2,378	21,989
1.1.45–9.5.45	1,705	155	1,860	3,836	387	4,223
Northern Ireland	–	967	967	–	678	678
	29,890	30,705	60,595	50,507	35,675	86,182

Note: In addition 150,833 civilians were slightly injured.

CIVILIAN CASUALTIES BY BOMBING AND VARIOUS FORMS OF LONG-RANGE BOMBARDMENT

(Source: *The Defence of the United Kingdom* (Collier) HMSO, Official War History Series)

	Killed	*Seriously Injured*	*Total*
Bombing	51,509	61,423	112,932
Flying Bombs	6,148	17,981	24,165
Rockets	2,754	6,523	9,277
Cross-Channel guns	148	255	403
Totals	60,595	86,182	146,777

Of these 146,777 casualties, 80,397 (including about nine-tenths of those caused by flying bombs and roughly the same proportion of those caused by rockets) occurred in the London Civil Defence Region, and 66,380 elsewhere. Casualties to service personnel are not included.

Foreword

The Editor has selected for publication in this volume several articles based on my firefighting experiences during World War II. The action takes place mainly in the East End of London, for that is where I served, but the events I describe are typical of what took place in other heavily bombed towns and cities throughout Britain.

When, in September 1938, Prime Minister Neville Chamberlain returned to London from his meeting in Munich with Adolf Hitler, he waved aloft the latest of the Führer's worthless pledges as a symbol that Britain and Germany would never again go to war with each other. The Prime Minister's faith in the integrity of the German dictator, however, was not shared by those responsible for the safety of the civilian population. The Air Raid Precautions Act of 1938 had been promulgated and, among a flurry of circulars sent out by the Home Office following Munich, was one instructing Local Authorities to proceed with recruitment for an Auxiliary Fire Service, under which the strength of the regular fire brigades would be increased fifteen-fold.

Accordingly, a vigorous campaign calling for volunteers for the AFS was initiated and thousands of men and women came forward to offer their services. In West Ham, as elsewhere, a number of schools became vacant under plans for evacuating children to safer areas; these were taken over for use as training centres for the AFS, or earmarked for future use as emergency fire stations.

The Home Office Circular set out a training schedule under which auxiliaries were to be given sixty hours instruction, mainly of a practical nature. Volunteers reported to their training centre where instructors were on hand to receive a typical cross-section of the local male population; dock workers, musicians, bus drivers, office and factory workers, butchers and bakers but, so far as I am aware, no candlestick maker. Many were men who had served in the Armed Forces in the first World War and these proved invaluable stiffeners of morale later, when units came under heavy attack. The vast majority of auxiliary firemen saw their first fire on September 7, 1940, when the Luftwaffe commenced its bombardment of London.

Some of the events of the eight months' ordeal by explosion and fire endured by the citizens of London are set out in the following pages. We experienced the blood, tears, toil and sweat we had been promised. We in the Fire Service witnessed the agony of civilian men and women and were inspired by their fortitude and undaunted spirit. The terrifying, sleepless nights did not deter them from the daily business of producing the paraphernalia of war or the no less vital task of sustaining the family unit.

Firemen, regular and auxiliary, were force-fed with the firefighting experiences of a lifetime, crammed into the space of eight months. In pre-Blitz training sessions we had endeavoured to prepare the auxiliaries for an ordeal they, or we, could not envisage for one has to experience the horror of exposure to aerial bombardment in order to comprehend its shattering effect. We witnessed greater fires than any had seen or could possibly have imagined, yet morale remained high and camaraderie flourished.

The colours of the Women's Section of the AFS flew high. Firewomen took on any job short of handling the branches and performed their duties efficiently and with valour. Theirs was a vital contribution to the war effort.

I hope I may be pardoned for adding what I consider to be a justifiable expression of pride in the achievements of Fire Services throughout the country in combatting the enemy attack.

In London, of all the buildings that survived the Blitz, St Paul's Cathedral is the supreme example of a portion of the nation's heritage that bombs failed to efface or flames consume. Yet it is but one of the London fireman's many battle honours. It remains a matter of regret that no recognition of the work of the wartime fire services is to be found in the heart of the City of London, where many firemen died in the battle against the flames.

Whenever I see that symbol of a nation's endurance, the famous photograph of St Paul's, taken on the night of December 29, 1940, its majestic dome glimpsed through drifting smoke as it stood amid the glare of the burning city, I am struck by the vision and aptness of those lines lines penned by the nineteenth-century poet, John Davidson:

> . . . Swung in space of heaven's grace
> Dissolving, dimly reappearing,
> Afloat upon ethereal tides,
> St Paul's above the city rides.

As in 1893, so in 1940. As then, so now.

CYRIL DEMARNE, 1988

From the Editor

The period covered by this volume forms the core of our trilogy on the Blitz. It spans the complete Night Blitz of the winter of 1940-41, traditionally known as *the* Blitz, and runs until German interests turned Eastwards, after the great raid on London on May 10-11, 1941; the climax of eight months of gradually escalating attacks.

If we adopt the German viewpoint, the victory achieved by RAF Fighter Command at the end of the big daylight battles in 1940 was but a phase in the overall 'Luftschlacht um England' — the air attack on Britain. Mounting losses had begun to make daylight operations prohibitive and, as autumn turned to winter, the lengthening hours of darkness turned also in the Germans' favour, swinging the advantage gained by the RAF back to the Luftwaffe.

As we shall see, for night after night hundreds of German bombers were able to range over the whole country at will, with minimum risk of detection or of being brought down. Suddenly 'the Few' were blind, and I have tried to illustrate both the frustration of failure and the sensation of success as electronic aids began to swing the pendulum back — if not all the way, at least as far as it caused Luftwaffe crews much anxiety at what the darkness held in store.

During the Battle of Britain, with its great emphasis of machine against machine, man against man, the aircraft losses played a major part in our story on a day-by-day basis. As these losses diminish in November, after the switch from day to night battle, so the story of the Night Blitz is taken up in this volume by Ken Wakefield with his detailed account of operations. The day-by-day record of events thus changes to night-by-night from November 14-15. Also as we progress through the winter and spring of 1941 I have been a little more liberal in including details of aircraft brought down during this period which would not normally have fulfilled the criteria we used for the summer combats where we strictly listed only those down on land or from which bodies or prisoners were taken. I thought it important to fully detail the gradually increasing number of bombers brought down by night fighters, even though some of these were at sea around our shores, otherwise the pattern of the changing fortunes of the RAF night flyers would have been lost.

Obviously we shall have to adopt a different approach again when we come to deal in Volume 3 with the years that follow — May 1941 to May 1945 — to complete our coverage of the air offensive in the various forms in which it reappeared and ended with a vengeance.

I have attempted to complement Ken's facts and figures with descriptive captioning covering other aspects which I hope help colour the scene and set the events against a wider background. Churchill's frustration at not being able to retaliate measure for measure; the vital long-term importance of the Lend-Lease agreement by the USA; ARP and Civil Defence, and the real heroes of this book — the firefighters — are just a few of the themes I felt important to relate as the Night Blitz unfolds. Unfortunately we are limited on some incidents by what photographs are available, and I have been frustrated on many occasions where we have not been able to find illustrations to cover a particular raid or event. We must realise that not all incidents were photographed and not all places; we therefore get too much on some raids and nothing on others. Another problem is caused by some pictures lacking a precise date, the puzzle to pinpoint the correct incident being compounded in some cases by the release of photographs several months or even years after the event. Censored captions have also not helped identify a particular raid and I have made frequent reference throughout the book to the work of the Press and Censorship Bureau.

A London News Agency picture just captioned 'Debris near London Bridge Station'. As it was stopped by the censor on April 24, 1941, it most probably shows the aftermath of the special 1,000-tonne attack mounted on the night of April 19-20 to mark Hitler's birthday (see page 555). However the picture is even more significant as the large archway, mid-way along the station behind the lorry, is the entrance to Stainer Street, used as a shelter by thousands of Londoners. It had received a direct hit two months previously causing one of London's worst incidents with nearly 100 killed (see pages 434-435 and 656).

VOLUME 1

THE PHONEY WAR
September 3, 1939 — May 9, 1940
Exploratory raids, minelaying and reconnaissance

BLITZKRIEG
May 10, 1940 — June 22, 1940
Attack on France and the Low Countries up to the surrender of France

THE AIR ATTACK ON ENGLAND BEGINS
Contact Phase June 23 — August 7, 1940
Fighter sweeps and attacks on convoys

BATTLE FOR COMMAND OF THE AIR
Stage I August 8 — August 23
Attacks on coastal targets, airfields and aircraft industry

Stage II August 24 — September 6
Airfield attacks and fighter battles increase

VOLUME 2

ATTACKS ON ECONOMIC TARGETS
Stage I September 7 — September 19
Day and night bombing of Greater London

Stage II September 20 — November 13
Daylight fighter-bomber sorties and night bombing

Stage III November 14, 1940 — June 21, 1941
Night bombing raids on targets throughout Britain

VOLUME 3

INTERREGNUM
June 22, 1941 — April 22, 1942
Isolated attacks on shipping and coastal towns

THE BAEDEKER RAIDS
April 23, 1942 — October 31, 1942
Attacks on provincial towns

TIP-AND-RUN
November 1, 1942 — January 20, 1944
Intruder raids, often by single aircraft

THE STEINBOCK RAIDS
January 21, 1944 — May 29, 1944
The so-called Baby Blitz

THE V-WEAPON CAMPAIGN
Vergeltungswaffe 1
June 13, 1944 — March 29, 1945
Vergeltungswaffe 2
September 8, 1944 — March 27, 1945

THE DEFECTORS
Ends VE-Day May 8, 1945

The air offensive against Great Britain — the various phases of the campaign as complied from British and German sources.

As I have worked for the first six months of 1988 putting everything together, I was very conscious of — and tried to guard against — becoming conditioned to casualty figures just becoming statistics. Unfortunately, human nature being what it is, one tends to emphasise the worst cases, the biggest raids, etc., but I have tried to balance this with various incidents in the smaller towns or villages. Inevitably though, coverage of the major raids occupies our thoughts most of the time as one attack exceeds another in size, damage or deaths. Casualty figures compiled at the time by the Ministry of Home Security can only be taken as a rough guide as many victims were not recovered for days or, indeed, in some cases, for some months. Rarely did Home Security issue updates and when they did they could sometimes be the source of further confusion as in the Belfast raid (see page 529). For the major raids or incidents I have included the post-war figures as given in the official Civil Defence history but these do not correspond in many cases with the Civilian War Dead Roll (for further detail of which the reader is referred to page 6). The latter, because it was dependent on the accuracy of returns from each borough, is also not one hundred per cent reliable as casualties taken to hospitals outside the location under attack are listed as dying in that other area. Therefore it is often difficult to establish precise numbers for a particular raid. Suffice it to say that by the time you come to the end of this book 40,000 people will have died, over a hundred deaths every time you turn a page. It is a thought I have tried to keep in the forefront of my mind as I have worked to achieve our intention of dedicating the project to all those who lost their lives.

WINSTON G. RAMSEY, 1988

KEN WAKEFIELD, MRAeS

Ken Wakefield was born in Bristol in 1928 and became an aviation enthusiast at a very early age. His interest in air operations over the United Kingdom developed during the Battle of Britain, and as a 12-year-old schoolboy he experienced at first hand — and has vivid recollections of — the Blitz on his home city. His interest eventually led to a detailed study of Luftwaffe operations over the UK, in the course of which, in addition to extensive research into original British and German records, personal contact was made with many former members of the German Air Force. Arising from this and other research Ken Wakefield has written two books (*Luftwaffe Encore* and *The First Pathfinders*) and he is the author of many articles on historical civil and military aviation.

Ken is married, has three grown-up children, and has spent his entire working life in aviation. He trained as a pilot with the Royal Air Force Volunteer Reserve and took up airline flying in 1951, becoming a Training Captain on various types of aircraft; at the time of his recent retirement from British Airways he was a Route Check Captain on TriStars. He was elected a Member of the Royal Aeronautical Society in 1974 and in 1977 was awarded the Master Air Pilot Certificate of the Guild of Air Pilots and Air Navigators. In retirement Ken has continued writing on historical civil and military aviation and is active in the restoration and flying of vintage aircraft.

Ken Wakefield's fifteen-year study of the air attacks on the UK has resulted in the creation of the 150,000-word daily synopsis for the period November 1940 to May 1941 which forms the major part of this volume. The intimate detail with which each day is recorded, from the phases of the moon — a vital factor in night bombing — to the weather, the units participating and the targets hit, is the most thorough study of the period ever undertaken. Ken firmly believes that 'the old adage that history told from one side alone is not history at all is, surely, unquestionably true', and he explains that 'accordingly my account of the Night Blitz on Britain is based very largely on both British and German official records.'

'The British records, held in the Public Record Office and the Air Historical Branch of the Ministry of Defence, included Royal Air Force Fighter Command Forms 'Y' (daily summaries of operations), Fighter Command Combat and Casualty Returns, Air Ministry and Fighter Command Intelligence Summaries and Command, Group, Wing, Squadron and Station Operations Record Books. Countless other files were consulted, mostly in the AIR series in the PRO, containing correspondence, minutes, studies and reviews of the period under research.

'German records, made available to me unhesitatingly by the Bundesarchiv at Freiburg, included the daily operations reports compiled at the time by the Operations Staff of the Luftwaffe. The records of Luftflotte 3, one of the two principal air fleets engaged in the Blitz, were also made available and proved of inestimable value; unfortunately the parallel records of Luftflotte 2 did not survive the war but as this air fleet played a lesser rôle their loss is not vital. Their absence, in any event, is offset to some degree by the availability of other supporting records including a Staff Study of the bombing of Britain, written in 1944 by Hauptmann Otto Bechtle and a complete listing of German aircraft and crew losses for the period under review. In addition, German official records have been augmented by diary accounts, personal flying log books and other documentation kindly supplied by former Luftwaffe aircrew members who participated in the campaign.

'Much of the text of my contribution is taken up with Daily Summaries of Operations and the following explanatory notes also indicate the sources used in their compilation:

(1) The period covered by each Summary is from dawn of one day to dawn of the next. Thus, 'Sunday, November 24-25' covers the period from dawn on November 24 to dawn on November 25.

(2) Times for sunset and sunrise are given in local British time for a position in central southern England. British Summer Time (BST) was in force for the winter of 1940-41 (GMT + 1 hour), changing to Double BST (DBST) on May 4, 1941 (GMT + 2 hours). All times in both German and British records have been adjusted in my account to the local time currently in use for the particular date. Adjustments of sunset/sunrise times for other locations are as follows (approximations for mid-winter): Newcastle, −9 minutes; Glasgow, −2 minutes; Derby, as given; London, as given; Manchester, +1 minute; Birmingham, +3 minutes; Bristol, +10 minutes; Belfast, +11 minutes; Plymouth, +20 minutes.

(3) Moon data includes the phase and the times during which the moon was above the horizon for an observer in central southern England. 'Dusk' and 'Dawn' indicates the rising or setting of the moon before or after the hours of full darkness. (It should be borne in mind, of course, that cloud or other meteorological conditions could prevent sight of either the sun or the moon. Conditions could also affect the twilight periods and bring on early darkness, for example).

(4) Weather conditions for the UK and the Continent have been summarised from Fighter Command Forms 'Y', Air Staff Operations Summaries and Command Operations Record Books. The statement refers to conditions experienced during the hours of darkness.

(5) The main text of my summary for each day is based on the following:

(a) The brief statement of daylight activity is derived from Fighter Command Forms 'Y'.

(b) The initial summary of German operations is a synopsis of the daily Luftwaffe Lagebericht (Luftwaffe High Command Situation Report).

(c) The German account of each attack (including unit details, bomb loads, bombing times (start and finish), special observations, etc.), is based on the daily Lagebericht and Luftflotte 3 operations reports.

(d) The British acccount of the attack including details of damage, casualties, etc., is based on Ministry of Home Security Periodic Summaries.

(e) Information on British defence claims and other action by Fighter, Anti-Aircraft and Balloon Commands, is taken from Fighter Command Forms 'Y', Combat Reports, Fighter Command Combat and Casualty Returns. Air Ministry and Fighter Command Intelligence Summaries and various Operations Record Books. Some additional material came from personal flying log books and diaries.

(6) The additional combat details which appear at the end of some of the Daily Summaries have been compiled from Intelligence Summaries, German Quartermaster (Abteilung 6) returns and personal accounts, diaries and log books. I have selected the incidents for their particular interest and they are not always the result of British defensive action.'

Ken's home town, Bristol, under attack on November 24, 1940.

DENIS BATEMAN

Denis Bateman, who retired recently from the Air Historical Branch of the Ministry of Defence, was Editor of the Branch's histories, controller of the Photographic Library, and researcher. Twenty-eight of his forty-four years in Government Service have been spent in the AHB, where he was the longest serving member. He is married with two children and lives in Middlesex. He has written a number of RAF-related articles, including several for *After the Battle* magazine. Apart from checking numerous queries, it has been Denis's primary task to compile the index.

PETER CHAMBERLAIN

Born in East London, Pete was called-up in October 1940 to join the Royal Engineers and, after basic training, was posted in early 1941 to the 20th Bomb Disposal Company, RE, stationed in Tunbridge Wells, Kent. There he joined a Bomb Disposal Section operating in Kent and Sussex. Early in 1945 Pete was transferred to the 4th Bomb Disposal Company, RE, based at Balham and served in South London. Demobbed in June 1946 he is now widely recognised as a leading expert on weapons of the Second World War and on the development of armoured fighting vehicles. He is author and co-author of over sixty publications on these subjects, and was for twenty years a consultant to the photo library of the Imperial War Museum. Pete would like to place on record his thanks to Herr K. R. Pawlas, editor of *Waffen Revue*, and Major Arthur Hogben, RE, of the Explosive Ordnance Disposal Technical Information Centre for assistance in the preparation of his contribution.

PETER CORNWELL

Born in 1942, Peter was evacuated to London to escape the bombing of Swansea and still has a vivid memory of being carried by his mother downstairs to the cellar of their home in Brockley during one particularly heavy raid on London in 1944. This, and watching the victory flypast from the kitchen window, are his only personal memories of the air war over Britain — a subject he has studied in depth since schooldays.

Well known for his research into the events of 1940, a period which has held his interest for over 25 years, he has contributed to many articles and books on the subject and was major co-author of *The Battle of Britain — Then and Now*. His extensive records of Luftwaffe losses, covering the period May to December 1940, form the main basis for his contribution. Employed as a Regional Training and Development Manager for Prudential Assurance, he lives with his wife and two sons in Girton, outside Cambridge.

'As an ardent chronicler of 1940 events, the invitation to contribute to this project provided me with a most welcome opportunity to once again consider in depth the losses suffered by the Luftwaffe during the 'Luftschlacht um England'. Following as it does relatively swiftly on my earlier work for *The Battle of Britain — Then and Now*, this new project offers an ideal vehicle to cover German losses over Great Britain in as much detail as possible and in light of the additional information which has come to hand since publication of that earlier work — itself since up-dated.

'The criteria adopted here for including specific Luftwaffe losses was simple: either the aircraft in question came down on land in the UK or alternatively, fell in waters surrounding the British Isles and resulted in dead or captured Luftwaffe personnel coming under British authority. Most of the casualties fall into these categories, though it must be admitted that the known circumstances of certain losses has not always permitted a rigid application of these guidelines. In such cases, where the criteria for inclusion has been exceeded or ignored, brief explanatory notes have been included to assist the reader whenever possible.

'Like most researchers in the field, I rely heavily upon contemporary Luftwaffe documentary sources which survive. These are ably described by Ken Wakefield and Simon Parry in their own introductory remarks. However, for the period covered by my own research, even such prime sources as the Namentliche Verlustmeldungen and the Verlustlisten of the Genst.Gen.Qu.6 Abt.(Ic) have had to be widely supplemented with often vital missing detail. In most instances, this has been culled from a wide variety of alternative sources including the Dienstalterliste der Offizieren der Deutschen Luftwaffe and the extensive records of the Volksbund Deutsche Kriegsgräberfürsorge — the German War Graves Commission.

'RAF Intelligence reports on Luftwaffe casualties for the period are held by the Air Historical Branch of the Ministry of Defence. These detailed reports can often contain information of a sensitive nature and, as a result, access to them is not permitted under English statute. They will remain closed for 75 years and have not, therefore, been consulted during preparation of this work. However, certain extracts from them, dealing largely with technical aspects of crashed enemy aircraft, have been released into the public sector and can be freely consulted at the Public Record Office. It follows, therefore, that certain events described by me are my own interpretation of the known facts. I have not found it necessary to consult the Ministry of Defence, Air Historical Branch in connection with any entry in my text so any comments offered

should not be taken to reflect any form of 'official' view.

'Many good friends and correspondents have contributed over the years to my fund of knowledge on this subject. They are far too numerous to mention but all deserve my thanks — I hope they find these results worthwhile, interesting and possibly even useful. A small coterie of those who contributed directly to this current work, deserve special mention:

'John Vasco, a meticulous researcher into Luftwaffe operations during the last war, proved indispensable during regular motoring sorties throughout Germany and Austria to interview ex-Luftwaffe aircrew on their experiences. For his continued stimulus, infectious good humour and enthusiasm I am most grateful. My thanks are also due to Herr Schönemann and Frau Busekow of the Deutsche Dienststelle (WASt) in Berlin for their continued interest in my research into Luftwaffe losses during 1940. To Karl-Fritz Schröder, himself a youthfully vigorous veteran of many a "Feindflug", I express my particular appreciation and I am particularly grateful for his help in researching on my behalf details of Luftwaffe casualties of the period and for clarifying many of the inconsistencies which abound in surviving contemporary records. Without his valuable contribution this work would be the poorer — for this and for his warm hospitality during recent visits to Germany I am indebted to both Karl and his wife Gerda. Also, my sincere thanks to Ann, Simon and Alex who continue to support and sustain my curious obsession with events now long past. Without their enduring patience and good-natured tolerance throughout the punishing period of draft preparation imposed upon an already demanding work schedule, this particular project would have proved impossible for me to complete.'

CYRIL DEMARNE

Cyril was born in Poplar in 1905 and joined West Ham Fire Brigade in April 1925. He was a Sub Officer instructing the Auxiliary Fire Service when war was declared and spent the period from September 1940 to May 1941 serving in West Ham, one of the worst blitzed areas in the country.

In October 1941 he was appointed Company Officer at Whitechapel in the newly formed National Fire Service and was twice promoted in 1943. In January 1944, as Divisional Officer, he was transferred back to West Ham in time for the 'Baby' Blitz and flying bomb attacks.

In November came a further transfer to the City and Central London where he was involved in three of the most deadly V2 incidents in which more than three hundred people were killed. After two years service in

the West End based on Manchester Square Station, he was promoted to Chief Fire Officer West Ham and in 1952 received the Order of the British Empire. He retired from the Fire Service in 1955.

In 1980 he published his memoirs of his wartime service in *The London Blitz — A Fireman's Tale*. 'To the best of my knowledge', wrote Cyril in his introduction, 'this is the first account which presents a fireman's-eye-view of those memorable days and nights . . . I write mainly about London simply because I was there. Nevertheless my stories about fire-fighting in the Royal Docks for instance differ only in detail from operations in other ports throughout the country. The indomitable spirit displayed by ordinary people in London's East End will be familiar to observers in other blitzed areas.'

Cyril is a natural writer and gifted story-teller and has put pen to paper to produce colourful accounts of the period, many of which have been specially written for us.

JACK DYER

In 1939 Jack Dyer was an 11-year old schoolboy living in Ilford on the eastern outskirts of London, together with his mother and father and two elder sisters, Hilda and Joan. September 2, the day before was was declared, found him on Ilford railway station with hundreds of other local schoolchildren, all ready labelled up for evacuation. For the next seven months his home was to be in Sidegate Lane West in Ipswich but in May 1940 it was decided that eastern England would not be the safest of places and he was re-evacuated to Wales for the duration of the Battle of Britain and the night Blitz.

By 1944, back in Ilford in his final year at Ilford County High School, Jack, though shy and introverted, had a strong perception way beyond his sixteen years of the momentous events then taking place. Activity in the air was constant as the Allied air forces built up their strength for the coming invasion of Europe, and it was at this stage that he decided to begin an 'Air Diary'. Written in pencil in a school exercise book, interspersed with newspaper cuttings, the pages became a living history and now stand as a unique record from which Jack has allowed us to include extracts for Volume 3.

ROBERT GÖTZ

Robert Götz was just 18 years old when he undertook his first mission in the air offensive against Britain. All told he flew on 39 flights to England, the first eleven as a Bordschütze (air gunner), thereafter as an observer/navigator (Beobachter) before transferring to the Eastern Front in May 1941, where he undertook about 290 sorties against Soviet forces, mostly in the He 111.

Throughout his youth he kept a personal diary from his schooldays in Würzburg during the early days of Hitler until the last desperate attacks on the Russian assault bridges over the River Oder in April 1945. He managed to hold on to the diaries through six years of battle and to bring them safely through the lines. Avoiding capture, he reached Würzburg only to find the city totally destroyed but on one wall of his house he found a crayoned address of his mother, still alive, but living in the country.

As Editor I realised that Robert Götz's recollections, since prepared in an unpublished manuscript with the title *Bestrafte Traume (Punished Dreams)*, were exactly what was required to balance our appreciation of what it was like to be on 'the other side'. Yet initially when I approached him he was wary lest our motives were simply to portray his actions as just another 'Nazi airman'. In his reply to me he explained that his account included 'unpleasant personal political events during my youth, and also the collapse of our country. It contains contemporary historical altercations and events unconnected with operational flights; together with letters, records of conversations, and observations — all of which I have combined into a TOTAL PICTURE. Portions extracted from it would by themselves provide a very lop-sided picture, and that is something I don't want.'

Nevertheless, after written assurances that his extracts would be treated with the respect due to them as historical documents, he agreed to selected passages being included.

ANDREW P. HYDE

Andrew was born at home in his father's shoe shop in Dagenham Essex in 1961, but has lived most of his life in Basildon where his family moved in 1970. He left school in 1977 and after a variety of jobs joined British Telecom in 1979. He has been interested in history and the Second World War all his life, and this led to his first work for *After the Battle* covering Pearl Harbor being published in 1982.

Andrew recalls that 'When I embarked upon this project I had no idea that it would grow from a modest idea to write an article for *After The Battle* into the mammoth work it has become, and one which would involve such specialised knowledge that I could not complete it alone. Now, some nine years after its conception, is a work so vast that it has actually taken longer to complete than that period in our history which it covers!

'It has been my task to cover the civilian's war and to take most of the comparison photographs — both in this and the other two volumes — necessitating numerous journeys to every corner of the United Kingdom. I have attempted to illustrate every important aspect of the Blitz on Britain, dealing not only with the 1940-41 period to which the word 'Blitz' is more often associated, but the Baedeker Raids, the 'Baby Blitz', and the V-weapon campaign. My travels have taken me not only to the 'big names' of the Blitz — the cities which suffered widespread damage and casualties — but also to small towns and villages, where individual tragedies were just as harrowing to those who experienced them.

'Many people asked me why someone of my age has developed such an interest in this period. I feel that the answer lies in the fact that I was born to parents who lived through every year of the war, and from them I have absorbed the folklore — and the mythology — of the Blitz. Their's was a frugal wartime wedding in 1943, but it was one which set them off on forty-two years of marriage, the first of which were the most frightening but the most exciting they had to endure. My mother spent much of her war years engaged in war work, and to this day has not the faintest idea what it was she was helping to make! She lived in the East End of London during the war, was bombed-out three times, and even buried alive in an air raid shelter which received a direct hit and in which she remained trapped with her younger sister for nine hours. My elder sister is a 'war baby', and my mother gave birth to her during the height of the V2 rocket campaign. She vividly recalls bringing her into the world at the very moment that one exploded a short distance away, clouds of dust obscuring the delicate proceedings. A family therefore rich in nostalgia, our photograph album is packed full of pictures showing a family at war, and that plus my own imagination filled my head with curiousity and interest in a chapter of history so close to home.

'Without doubt, however, it is my late father who has influenced me far beyond anyone else. As a child he would enthral me with war stories seen from the civilian front line — like his and my mother's wedding night being spent with an unexploded land mine in the garden, or an uncle home on leave from North Africa who declared that he could not wait to go back on active service where it was a darned sight safer! My father spent the war years continuing the trade he had learnt at a home for crippled boys after contracting polio at the age of eighteen months, that of a cobbler, repairing army boots for British and American servicemen. He had to go everywhere using walking sticks, and one night during a raid he found himself negotiating miles of hose pipe, being shouted at by wardens, firemen and police alike to get to a shelter. He spurned the idea; he would far rather be killed at home if anywhere. He spent one night in a flooded Anderson and no more, at least it was warmer indoors, he told me, and you could die more comfortably. He was just an ordinary bloke, and if his attitude to the Blitz was as carefree as this, then I am certain that so too was the overwhelming majority of other people's. His sense of history and love of the past fed my own, and in a way I like to feel that, until his sudden death on May 4, 1985, we worked on this project together, as a team. Often he would travel with me on my trips to towns for research work and to take comparison photographs. His unerring enthusiasm, and his support is the one major factor which sustained me when it seemed that the task would never reach completion, and indeed it would be the greatest failing on my part had I not seen it through to the end.'

MICHAEL OCKENDEN

Michael Ockenden served in the Royal Air Force for five years as an Air Electronics Officer on Nos. 617 and 50 Squadrons and also qualified as a linguist in German and French. Since leaving the RAF, he has been engaged in the teaching of English to overseas students and is Co-Principal of a recognised English language school in Eastbourne. His other interests include local history and genealogy.

Michael's task has been to research and translate specific German Luftwaffe records which are now preserved at the Bundesarchiv, Freiburg im Breisgau.

JEAN PAUL PALLUD

Jean Paul Pallud was born in Annecy in south-eastern France in 1949 and graduated from Grenoble University as a Physicist Engineer. He currently works for the French telecommunications organisation, devoting much of his leisure activities to his hobbies of mountaineering and the study of the history of the Second World War. His first book *The Battle of the Bulge — Then and Now* was published by *After the Battle* in 1984 to which magazine he is a regular contributor.

An operations map was completed for every Luftwaffe raid over Britain and, from those that have survived, Jean Paul has selected examples of the best from the Bundesarchiv files for inclusion. He has also selected many Luftwaffe photographs from the French Army collection of captured enemy material at Fort d'Ivry, Paris.

SIMON PARRY

Simon Parry was born in 1958 in Kingston, Surrey, and currently works in telecommunications. Simon has an abiding dedication to the study of the air war over Britain during World War II; a founder member of the Air Historical Group in 1977, he has attended many notable aircraft recoveries in recent years

When approached to compile the record of the Luftwaffe losses in the air attacks against Great Britain, Simon responded with enthusiasm, sharing the task with Peter Cornwell who has contributed the details for the period July 10 — October 31, 1940.

'In compiling the casualties sustained by the Luftwaffe, many fundamental terms of reference had first to be established in order to give the reader, be he (or she) casual or academic, an informative yet readable text. Paramount amongst these was a decision as to what constituted 'the Blitz'. Eventually it was concluded that it could not properly be restricted by any arbitrary chronology inasmuch that any loss sustained by the enemy in an attack on Britain's industry, population or trade, would necessarily have had to be incorporated. To have listed each loss encompassed by these parameters in detail would have entailed the publication of a book of prohibitive size so it has been decided to chronicle fully only those aircraft and crews which fell in or in close proximity to Britain, or whose crews were recovered from the sea off the coast.

'In each introductory paragraph, a résumé of other operational losses is given. The majority of these aircraft will have fallen into the seas surrounding Britain and it is doubtful whether their exact fates were ever established. The crews of many of them remain listed as missing, there being no known grave. Any reader wishing to pursue further details of these losses is referred to the Luftwaffe Quartermaster General's Returns (Oberbefehlshaber der Luftwaffe Genst. Gen. Qu./6 Abteilung/40.g.Kdos.IC), a microfilm copy of which is held by the document department of the Imperial War Museum, London.

'In many of the combats which come within the scope of this project, it has been possible to identify the individual RAF pilot or crew responsible for the destruction of the aircraft detailed. This is made possible by the isolated, often one-to-one nature, of the engagements, and is particularly true of those occurring at night when a night fighter was directed onto a 'Bandit' by an operator at a Ground Control Interception Station who tracked and plotted the combat. Matching victors to victims, even after more than forty years has elapsed, can still be an emotive subject and is something which was seldom ever done on any organised basis during the war. If his claim was allowed, any claimant was credited simply with an enemy aircraft destroyed.

'The method I have used to tackle this vastly complex subject was to compile a full listing of claimants for aircraft destroyed over and around Britain on a day-to-day basis. Having completed this laborious task, each claim was examined clinically, taking into account many factors such as location and time, yet making allowances for errors that may have been due to operational conditions. After all this had been taken into account, there appeared one inescapable conclusion: that there were far more claims submitted than aircraft destroyed! This came as no surprise and the reasoning behind it is plain to see if one considers the conditions prevailing at the time. For instance, in daylight, several pilots may attack aircraft in a formation and, seeing one fall away from the rest to crash, assume it to have been their victim. At night, when at best only fleeting glimpses of an enemy were caught, a fighter pilot could often be dazzled by brilliant flashes from his foe and believe the machine to have been fatally hit by his attack. However, these might well have been flashes from return gunfire or exhaust flames as throttle settings were adjusted abruptly during evasive action. Often jettisoned bombs exploding on the ground were mistaken for crashing aircraft and there seems little doubt that many similar occurrences led pilots to file claims in good faith and in the belief that an enemy had been destroyed. I am indebted to John Foreman for making available to me copious files on fighter claims and for his work in verifying many of the statements made in this work. Copies of Fighter Command combat reports are available for inspection in Class AIR50 at the Public Record Office, London.

'The Luftwaffe Quartermaster General's Returns form the basis for my compilation of the German losses. Although the original records are undoubtedly riddled with errors and omissions, they remain the standard reference for this subject. A significant problem is the absence of the returns for the entire year of 1944. It has been established that they were captured and sent to Britain but were not returned to the Bundesarchiv along with other similar files when these were given back to Germany in the 1960s. In order to overcome this, reference has been made to other contemporary reports from many sources. Notable amongst these are those submitted by the officers attached to Air Intelligence 1(g) who reported on the wreck of each enemy aircraft brought down in Britain. Summaries of these reports can be found in the Public Record Office files references AIR22/266 and 267, AIR40/45, AVIA15/737 and others in the class AIR40. Also of great assistance were the files relating to dead and captured enemy aircrew. These are held in Public Record Office files AIR2/6387, 8735, 8736 and 8739. My thanks go to Nicholas Pointer of the Public Record Office for his valuable and professional advice on the documents in their possession. I am also very grateful to Mr. J. S. Cox of the Ministry of Defence Air Historical Branch for providing answers to many specific questions where the information was unavailable from other sources.

'Records of the Wehrmacht were originally stored in temporary hutted accommodation in Berlin after hostilities but in 1949 an attempt was made to burn them. Although many were destroyed or badly damaged, use has been made of many of the documents that survived. Of note are the Namentlichen Verlustlisten of units participating in Operation 'Steinbock' which were obtained from the Deutsche Dienststelle (WASt) in Berlin.

'An essential feature of the research for this work has been the examination and cross-checking of the burial register of the Deutsche Soldatenfriedhof at Cannock Chase and the Namenbuch Über Deutsche Kriegstote in Grossbritannien.

'A typical example of how information from many of the sources mentioned above has been pieced together is given by the case of a Junkers Ju 188 wreck which was located off the Essex coast. Public Record Office file AIR40/45 contains the following:

Report No. 8/22 Ju 188

"In the early hours of 4th January, 1944, the remains of an aircraft were seen on Maplin Sands, Foulness Island. These were found to be portions of a Ju 188. It is believed that the aircraft had been shot down by A.A. fire on 28th January, 1944. The machine had dived steeply into the sand and disintegrated, and it was only just visible at low water."

'Certainly a Junkers Ju 188 was claimed destroyed by an AA battery at Clacton (PRO Ref AIR16/173) but no loss could be attributed to the wreck.

'Another document in the Public Record Office, AIR2/8735, stated that small portions of flesh had been discovered in the wreck on Maplin Sands and that the identification number 58215/198 had been found. This number is known to have been related to crews of 6/KG6 and provided the first firm clue to the identity of the wreck.

'Police records held in the Essex County Records Office make reference to another aircraft claimed by the Clacton AA guns at 0540 hours on February 4 which fell south of Clacton where, later that day, wreckage was found. A note contained in some ARP Air Raid Damage Reports which had been rescued from a Council dump in 1985 read:

"Foulness. Crashed Aircraft. German aircraft, make not known, struck sands ½ mile SE of Eastwick Head MR 457098 and disintegrated. Parts of bodies recovered with German AF uniform. Number of crew not known." Perhaps it is this aircraft that RAF Air Intelligence had reported on and assumed to have crashed almost a week previously?

'A copy of the Namentlichen Verlustlisten for II/KG2 had by this time been obtained from the Deutsche Dienststelle (WASt) in Berlin. Examination of the entries for February 4, 1944, proved revealing for there, on the singed page, the number 58 215/198 appeared. The number belonged to Obergefr. Werner Zwintschert, the Bordfunker aboard Ju 188E–1 (260216) U5+KP of 6/KG6. Presumably insufficient remains of the crew were located to warrant their burial and they remain listed as missing.

'On a personal note, I would like to express my gratitude to the small team who assisted in the compilation of my contribution, each of whom gave selflessly of their time and knowledge to check thousands of names, numbers and facts. My thanks are due to Brian Bines for making available his files on Operation 'Steinbock' and to Stephen Burns, who combed every last syllable of the early drafts for errors. Stephen's tireless efforts examining the Luftwaffe Quartermaster's Returns and burial records deserves special mention. Peter Foote also spent many hours examining the early drafts and checking them against his files which cover a lifetime's research into the air war over Britain. Philippa Hodgkiss was rarely at a loss for an answer and delved deeply into her files on Luftwaffe wrecks in the West Country. A long term stalwart was Frank Marshall, who spent many days helping me transcribe Luftwaffe records long before this work was proposed and whose help was never more than a telephone call away. Among others who gave invaluable help in the early stages were Dennis Knight, Stephen Pickett, Peter Rushen and Guy Smith. John Ellingworth also contributed from his detailed files. In Europe, Winfried Bock, Ab Jansen and Emil Nonnenmacher provided assistance in their specialist areas.

'The Editor felt, as with *The Battle of Britain — Then and Now*, that details should be included of aircraft excavated or wreckage recovered in recent years. Certainly the investigation of crash sites has on many occasions uncovered a vital clue in the identification of the aircraft concerned. The community of aviation archaeologists in Britain have often been maligned for their cavalier attitudes towards the more scholarly aspects of their hobby. Certainly it is true that, in the early years, much information was lost to the historian in poorly recorded excavations and this is to be regretted.

'A long-standing personality in aviation and archaeology circles, Alan Brown, was able to furnish much material from his files which provide coverage of every corner of the British Isles. Perry Adams always extended a helping hand and treated me with great hospitality during my researches in the Dorset area. Terry Parsons was always happy to discuss the countless excavations that he has participated in, and filled in details of many others which would otherwise have gone unrecorded. Valuable support in this project was provided by Nigel Parker, whose genial manner could be guaranteed to brighten the most depressing of days.

'The following groups provided information from their files: David Stansfield, Pennine Aviation Museum; Peter Felix, Derbyshire Historical Aviation Society; Alan White, Severnside Aviation Society; Bill Welbourne, Fenland Aircraft Preservation Society; Paul Kiddel, Thames Valley Aircraft Recovery Group; Mark Evans, Midland Warplane Museum; Mr. J. D. Walton, North East Aircraft Museum; Brian Sadler, Essex Historical Aviation Society; George Morley, South West Aircraft Recovery Group, and Steven Laing of the Scotland West Aircraft Investigation Group. Others who provided assistance were Pat Burgess, Alf Batt, Colin Brown, Colin Pratley, Ron Gamage, David Smith, Nigel Douglas, Dick Walker and Barry Hammerton.

'Particular thanks are due to Steve Vizard and John Ellis, who have never been at a loss for a word of encouragement and whose advice on crash sites and relics is much appreciated. Sitting in a restaurant with John and Steve, drinking coffee whilst discussing crash sites far into the night, is an unfading memory of the early days of the research.

'Several museums which specialise in exhibiting the remains of crashed aircraft have become established in recent years. All provided valued assistance and are listed here:

Tangmere Military Aviation Museum, Tangmere Airfield, Chichester, Sussex. Andy Saunders and Peter Dimond, directors of the museum and themselves experts in their fields, were especially helpful. Kent Battle of Britain Museum, Hawkinge Airfield, Folkestone, Kent. Many thanks go to Mike Llewellyn and Dave Buchanan for their assistance. Norfolk and Suffolk Aviation Museum, Flixton, Suffolk. Bob Collis provided copious and detailed notes on the museum's work and on crashes in their area. Wartime Aircraft Recovery Group, RAF Cosford, Shropshire. Bomber County Aviation Museum and the Humberside Aircraft Preservation Society, Cleethorpes, Humberside. Booker Aircraft Museum, Booker Airfield, High Wycombe, Buckinghamshire. Essex Aviation Group Museum, Duxford Airfield, Duxford, Cambridgeshire, and the Warplane Wreck Investigation Group.

'The list of those to whom my sincerest thanks is due would not be complete without mention of the people who have become as much a part of this work as myself. They are my family, who have gamely tolerated my obsession over the years, and Jan Harman, without whose support and assistance this work would never have been completed. Finally I must mention Martine Harman, to whose generation the events detailed will seem but far distant history.'

ANDY SAUNDERS

Andy Saunders was born in 1955, long after the war ended, but was inspired at an early age by tales of the Battle of Britain as told him by his parents, both of whom had witnessed many of the dramatic events of 1940 in the skies around his Sussex home. In the 1960s he was fascinated by the wooden marker crosses on the graves of a number of German airmen in the cemetery near his Hailsham home. In later years, he discovered that these airmen were involved in some of the incidents witnessed by his parents, and a growing interest in aviation and local history led to a natural progression of interest in the Battle of Britain and related subjects; with a particular emphasis on events in Sussex. During 1969 he discovered a propeller from a crashed B-25 protruding from a river near Pevensey and this lead to an immediate interest in, not only the research of wartime air crashes, but the recovery of artefacts from such incidents.

In 1971 he became a founder member of the Wealden Aviation Archaeological Group which became very active during the 1970s, with recoveries of wartime aircraft throughout the UK, but more particularly in Sussex and Kent. During 1974, conscious of the need for the long-term security and preservation of the recovered items, he made moves to secure Museum premises at the disused RAF airfield at Tangmere. Although initially thwarted in his efforts, he persevered with the plan and, with a team of like-minded and dedicated enthusiasts, set up the Tangmere Military Aviation Museum project which was formally launched on September 15, 1980. Two years later the Museum opened and has since become a thriving collection, of which Andy has been a Curator and Director since its inception.

Apart from his involvement with Tangmere Museum, Andy remains fully involved in the aircraft recovery scene and also the research of various aspects of the 1939-45 air war. His home in Hastings is filled with the fruits of years of research and recovery work and is within easy reach of much of the activity which interested him and which, were it not for the moderating influence of his tolerant wife, would, he says, become an 'all consuming passion'. Apart from his spare time interests his full time occupation is Health and Safety Officer to the local Council.

ALAN SEYMOUR

Alan Seymour was born in Kentish Town in 1902 as the eldest of five children. His father died when he was only 11 (from rheumatic fever brought on by injuries he had sustained in trying to stop a runaway horse) and his mother struggled to bring up her children against a background of poverty and ill fortune. Alan had a passion for art, with a natural talent to go with it, and while working at a variety of jobs, went to evening classes and won a Slade scholarship. On the outbreak of war, he joined the Civil Defence serving as a mortuary attendant and later as a draughtsman at the Ministry of Aircraft Production. After the war he continued his varied career and practised homeopathy and osteopathy before becoming a chiropodist. His account of his traumatic experiences in North London during the Blitz was prepared for us in 1982; sadly he died in March 1985 before seeing his contribution in print. He was 82 . . . and still working!

DAVID J. SMITH

Born in Birkenhead, Cheshire, in 1943, David Smith has been an aviation enthusiast since the age of 10. He entered an insurance company as a trainee in 1962 but decided that this was not the career he wanted, and in 1965 joined the Ministry of Aviation as an Air Traffic Control Assistant and served at Preston Air Traffic Control Centre. Promoted to Air Traffic Control Officer Cadet in 1967, he trained at Bournemouth-Hurn, Edinburgh and Prestwick. Subsequently he worked as an Air Traffic Controller at Coventry Airport and, from 1982 to date, at Liverpool Airport. He began writing for aviation magazines in 1972, originally on wreck investigation and recovery, and has written several articles on this theme for *After the Battle*. He has also produced a long-running column, 'Wreckovery' for *Aviation News* from 1974 to date and later became interested in airfield histories and wrote two volumes of PSL's *Action Stations* series, plus regular potted histories in *Flypast* magazine. He also wrote the *Airband Radio Handbook* explaining Air Traffic Control procedures to those who listen in to the air traffic frequencies. He is married with three sons and lives on the Wirral.

ROY M. STANLEY II

Born in 1936, Roy Stanley received a BA in history and geography at De Pauw University, Greencastle, Indiana, and an MA in geography at the Northwestern University, Evanston, Illinois. After he joined the USAF in 1959, Roy Stanley was trained as an Air Force photo interpreter and from 1959 he served on the Air Staff in the US Strategic Air Command and with the Defense Intelligence Agency. In the late 1960s he was instrumental in devising human and computer readable photo interpretation reporting techniques and formats that are still used throughout the US Department of Defense and by several other NATO nations. During the same period he headed the computer branch that pioneered special databases, computer assistance, and coverage prediction techniques to improve the imagery exploitation potential of the SR–71 Blackbird reconnaissance aircraft when it first became operational. On one of his two tours in South-East Asia he was the Chief of the Indications Center at the control HQ for the 1975 evacuations of Phnom Phen and Saigon, and the recovery of the crew of the SS *Mayaguez*. In his last position, he was responsible for management, formulation and defence of the $3 billion USAF intelligence budget. By the time he retired from the US Air Force in July 1985, he had been awarded the Air Force Commendation Medal, the Joint Service Commendation Medal, the Meritorious Service Medal (twice), the Defense Meritorious Service Medal, the Bronze Star, and Legion of Merit.

Having worked with Combat Intelligence, Colonel Stanley was assigned in 1975 to the organisation responsible for (among other things) all US Department of Defense holdings of intelligence and mapping photography — over one hundred-thousand 10-inch-high cans, each containing roll negatives of up to three hundred exposures of US and British aerial photography. More important the holdings included original German prints captured at the end of the war — material for which I as Editor had searched for years to no avail. To me it was a mystery why the Luftwaffe photographic reconnaissance material taken of British targets appeared to have disappeared without trace, but exhaustive enquiries both in this country and Germany proved fruitless. Colonel Stanley advised me that he believed German material did still exist in the UK but the question was where? The obvious repository was JARIC, the Joint Air Reconnaissance Intelligence Centre at RAF Brampton, but previous enquiries there had proved negative. Then in 1985 I managed to get an admission that the captured German photography *was*, or rather had been, at Brampton but as no one had ever asked to see it, it was destroyed in 1980!

Colonel Stanley came to the rescue. After three year's work, and after screening over a million negatives, he realised that he was sitting on a gold mine of World War II history and he began to select material for transfer to the National Archives in Washington. On his retirement from active service he agreed to undertake a search for photographic cover taken by Luftwaffe Aufklärungs units over Britain — the first time such material has appeared specifically relating to the Blitz.

Die Wehrmacht
IN DIESEM HEFT:
Kampf und Ende des Kreuzers „Blücher"
USGEGEBEN VOM OBERKOMMANDO DER WEHRMACHT
4. Jahrgang · Nummer 19 · Berlin, den 11. September 1940 · Einzelpreis 25 Rpf. und Bestellgeld · Erscheint vierzehntäglich
Luftalarm in London –
Deutsche Flieger kommen!

The Luftwaffe

The following explanatory notes are intended as a simple aid to readers unfamiliar with the various forms and style of unit designations and codings employed by the Luftwaffe during 1939–40.

Aufklärungsverbände *(Reconnaissance units)*
Generally deployed in Gruppe strength and operating in either a Fernaufklärungs (long-range reconnaissance) role or Nah-Heeres-Aufklärungs (close Army co-operation).

Examples: 3/Aufklärungsgruppe Ob.d.L. = No. 3 Staffel of the Luftwaffe High Command reconnaissance Gruppe.
3(F)/123 = No. 3 (long-range) Staffel of reconnaissance Gruppe 123.
4(H)/31 = No. 4 Staffel of Army reconnaissance Gruppe 31.

Ausbildungs Staffeln *(Training squadrons)*
Attached to various Jagdgeschwader and Kampfgeschwader in order to maintain an adequate level of replacements for losses suffered by their respective 'parent' units. They undertook basic operational training.

Example: Ausbildungs Staffel KG40.

Ergänzungs Staffeln *(Replacement training squadrons)*
Organised along similar lines as the Ausbildungs Staffeln and attached to both Jagdgeschwader and Kampfgeschwader, these units provided a nucleus of replacement crews fully operationally trained.

Example: Ergänzungs Staffel JG54.

Erprobungsgruppe 210 *(Experimental test wing 210)*
Theoretically engaged on the operational evaluation of the still-experimental Messerschmitt Me 210, this specialist unit was actually deployed operationally as a single Gruppe flying Messerschmitt Bf 109s and Bf 110s. The daring, often brilliant precision attacks flown by this unit reflected the expertise of its aircrews who suffered some heavy casualties.

Jagdverbände *(Fighter units)*
Messerschmitt Bf 109 equipped, these formations were normally deployed in Geschwader strength but often operated as independent Jagdgruppen for tactical purposes. During 1940, the first Nachtjagdgeschwader (NJGs) were established as a night-fighter force in defence of Reich territory and for night intruder sorties over Britain.

Examples: 2/JG26 = No. 2 Staffel of Jagdgeschwader 26.
1/NJG2 = No. 1 Staffel of Nachtjagdgeschwader 2.

NORMAL GESCHWADER ESTABLISHMENT

Geschwader Stab Schwarm
(Group HQ Staff Flight)

Stab I Gruppe	Stab II Gruppe	Stab III Gruppe
(I Wing HQ Staff)	*(II Wing HQ Staff)*	*(III Wing HQ Staff)*
1 Staffel *(Squadron)*	4 Staffel *(Squadron)*	7 Staffel *(Squadron)*
2 Staffel *(Squadron)*	5 Staffel *(Squadron)*	8 Staffel *(Squadron)*
3 Staffel *(Squadron)*	6 Staffel *(Squadron)*	9 Staffel *(Squadron)*

Normal Geschwader comprised three Gruppen as above. Any additional Gruppen constituted as follows:

Stab IV Gruppe	Stab V Gruppe
(IV Wing HQ Staff)	*(V Wing HQ Staff)*
10 Staffel *(Squadron)*	13 Staffel *(Squadron)*
11 Staffel *(Squadron)*	14 Staffel *(Squadron)*
12 Staffel *(Squadron)*	15 Staffel *(Squadron)*

Note: Gruppen always indicated by Roman numbers — Staffeln by Arabic

Examples: Stab KG2 = HQ Staff of Bomber Group 2
Stab II/JG27 = HQ Staff of II Wing, Fighter Group 27
I/ZG26 = I Wing, Long-Range Fighter Group 26
5/StG77 = No. 5 Squadron of Dive-bombing Group 77

Kampfverbände *(Bomber units)*
Conventional long-range bomber units generally deployed as a Geschwader but often single independent Gruppen operated. Some constituent elements specialised in low-level raids whilst others concentrated on purely night attacks.

Examples: 9/KG76 = No. 9 Staffel of Kampfgeschwader 76.
2/KGr100 = No. 2 Staffel of independent Kampfgruppe 100.
I/KG.z.b.V.172 = First Gruppe of Kampfgeschwader 172 on special assignment (zur besondern Verwendung).

Küstenfliegerverbände *(Maritime Luftwaffe units)*
Largely engaged on coastal reconnaissance and minelaying duties and deployed in Gruppe strength. Operated under Luftwaffe command but in close co-operation with the German Navy who provided most of the crews. Some formations later absorbed into Luftwaffe command structure and operated as conventional bombing units.

Examples: 1/196 = No. 1 Staffel of Küstenfliegergruppe 196.
3/506 = No. 3 Staffel of Küstenfliegergruppe 506.

Lehrgeschwader *(Instructional/operational development groups)*
Operationally deployed during 1940, these formations were originally conceived as operational development units, separate Gruppen within each Geschwader often having different functions and equipment. Absorbed into the Luftwaffe command structure they largely flew conventional attack missions.

Examples: V(Z)/LG1 = Fifth (Zerstörer) Gruppe of Lehrgeschwader 1 (Bf 110s).
II(S)/LG2 = Second (Schlacht i.e. ground attack) Gruppe of Lehrgeschwader 2 (Bf 109s).
7(F)/LG2 = No. 7 (Fernaufklärungs) Staffel of Lehrgeschwader 2 (Bf 110s).

Seenotflug Kommando *(Air-sea rescue unit)*
Engaged on search and rescue missions and subject to tactical deployment in small complements of generally less than Staffel strength.

Stukageschwader *(Dive-bombing groups)*
From the German 'Sturzkampf-flugzeug' i.e. dive-bombing aircraft. A generic term but synonymous with the Junkers Ju 87 with which these units were principally equipped during 1940.

Example: 6/StG77 = No. 6 Staffel of Stukageschwader 77.

Wettererkundungs Staffeln *(Weather reconnaissance squadrons)*
Ostensibly engaged on long-range weather reconnaissance and information gathering flights over enemy territory these units were often attached to regular reconnaissance formations and employed on armed incursion raids.

Zerstörergeschwader *(Long-range fighter groups)*
'Destroyer' units, principally Bf 110 equipped during 1940, and engaged on bomber escort duties or long-range free-lance fighter missions.

Example: II/ZG26 = Second Gruppe of Zerstörergeschwader 26.

JAGDVERBÄNDE

Stab Schwarm	*Geschwader Markings*	*Gruppe Markings*
OC	<−+−	⋖ or ≪
ADJUTANT	<I	<
IA	<I−	<− or <←
TO	<I○	<○ or <●
NO	<‖	<I

Gruppe	*I*	*II*	*III*	*IV*	*Staffel Colour*
Staffel	1	4	7	10	White
Staffel	2	5	8	11	Red or Black
Staffel	3	6	9	12	Yellow
Gruppe Symbol	None	−	∿ or I	+ or ●	▲ Ground Attack

KAMPFVERBÄNDE

Stab	*Last Letter of Code*	*Colour of Aircraft Letter*
GESCHWADER	A	
GRUPPE I	B	
GRUPPE II	C	Predominantly Green
GRUPPE III	D	
GRUPPE IV	E	
GRUPPE V	F	

Gruppe	*I*	*II*	*III*	*IV*	*V*	*Staffel Colour*
Staffel Code	1	4	7	10	13	White
Last Letter of Code	H	M	R	U	X	
Staffel Code	2	5	8	11	14	Red
Last Letter of Code	K	N	S	V	Y	
Staffel Code	3	6	9	12	15	Yellow
Last Letter of Code	L	P	T	W	Z	

VOLUME 2
BLITZ!
September 1940–May 1941

Saturday, September 7, 1940: When a day became night . . . and night was turned into day. A westerly breeze pushes smoke from the docks out across the East End.

Introduction

On Saturday, September 7, 1940, the Germans changed the direction of their air war against Britain and in so doing, many historians believe, changed the course and eventual outcome of the Second World War.

Until now the Battle of Britain, as it was to become known, had been primarily directed at the destruction of the Royal Air Force as an essential prerequisite to airborne and seaborne landings. Without gaining and maintaining air superiority over southern England the prospects of a successful invasion were slim, but, despite massed attacks against RAF stations, backed by strikes against factories of the British aircraft industry, the resistance offered by Fighter Command seemed as resolute as ever. However, German Intelligence was certain that the last reserves of Fighter Command could be drawn into battle and destroyed if their bomber arm turned to London as a primary target. Thus, on September 7, the day on which Reichsmarschall Hermann Göring, the Commander-in-Chief of the Luftwaffe, assumed direct command of the air offensive against Britain, the full weight of the attack was directed at London, Britain's capital city and the very heart of the British Commonwealth and Empire.

The assault on London had tactical, strategical and political implications, for, in addition to luring Fighter Command's supposedly last reserves to destruction, the attacks were meant to destroy the all important Port of London and to disrupt the workings of Government by eradicating its administrative quarter around Westminster from where, it was assumed, the conduct of the war was directed. Finally, as a bonus, it seemed more than likely that the heavy bombing of the docks would have a far reaching effect on the residents of East London; sustained heavy attacks, by day and night, were bound to lay waste much of the East End with, inevitably, heavy casualties, and it was hoped that public reaction might force the British Government to sue for peace. In none of these quests, however, were the Germans to succeed.

The London Blitz, as the assault on the capital became known, was to continue unabated for more than two months. Initially, day and night attacks took place, but as German daylight losses continued to be prohibitively high, there was a change to predominantly night raids by long-range bombers with minor fighter-bomber strikes by day.

Although the London Blitz opened on the evening of September 7, bombs had actually fallen on the capital for the first time during the night of August 24/25. On that occasion several aircraft engaged in attacks on the Short Brothers aircraft factory at Rochester, Kent, and oil storage installations at Thameshaven inadvertently dropped their bombs too far up river. In Britain the bombing was seen as an extension to London of the indiscriminate bombing already experienced in the provinces and the next night Berlin was bombed by the RAF on Churchill's instructions. This retaliation did not meet with the approval of an Air Staff whose members preferred to continue with attacks against military targets connected with the still possible invasion. Eighty-one RAF bombers were dispatched to Berlin where, in fact, they were ordered to bomb military and industrial targets, but only about one quarter of this number actually reached the German capital because of thick cloud. Their bombing was scattered and failed to do any military damage, but succeeded in injuring Göring's personal pride, for it was the Reichsmarschall who had once proclaimed: 'No enemy aircraft will fly over the Reich.' The attack also led Hitler to withdraw his embargo on attacks on London; incensed at what he called the 'nightly piracy' of the British, he finally gave way to his own Air Force leaders and, after consulting them on September 2, announced in a speech to the Reichstag two days later that the time for reprisals had come. For months, Hitler declared, British bombers had been killing German civilians (which was true, for RAF attempts to bomb legitimate targets in Germany were no more successful than the Luftwaffe's night operations over Britain, where many civilians, too, were killed). Hitler continued: 'They [the British] will understand now as, night by night, we give them the answer — when they declare they will attack our towns on a large scale, then we will erase theirs.' With these words the Führer was to unleash a bombing offensive which, before the war was ended, was to have unimagined repercussions for the German people, culminating with the destruction of Dresden in 1945.

The night of September 5/6 brought the first intended attack on London when 68 long-range bombers of Luftflotte 2, one of the three air fleets engaged in the Battle of Britain, attempted to bomb the London docks. For most of the crews taking part it was a new departure. Unlike some elements of Luftflotte 3, the second major air fleet attacking Britain and the one with considerable night operational experience, the crews of Luftflotte 2, although trained in night flying, generally lacked operational experience in this type of work. They were now faced with different techniques; instead of mass daylight formation attacks to which they were accustomed, crews were called upon to make their own way to the target in darkness, locate and bomb their objectives individually, and then find their way back to base. However, London was a big target and the broad ribbon of the Thames running through it simplified navigation so that the crews of Luftflotte 2 found little difficulty in delivering 60 metric tonnes of high explosive bombs in and around London's dockland, causing several large and numerous smaller fires.

Crews of Luftflotte 3 were engaged in attacks against other targets that night and in order to launch the London raid the Luftwaffe was forced to press every available aircraft into use, for large scale daylight operations were still being pursued at this stage. To facilitate this, and subsequent operations, Luftflotte 5, the third air fleet engaged in the air offensive against Britain and operating from Scandinavian bases, lost its only two long-range bomber Gruppen or Wings when I and II Gruppen of Kampfgeschwader (Bomber Group) 26 transferred from Norway to bases in Belgium. Within a few days of their arrival they were pressed into participation in the first night attack on London. Similarly, a few days later, a coastal reconnaissance unit, Küstenfliegergruppe 606, moved into Brest/Lanvéoc naval air base and was almost immediately dispatched to bomb London.

On the fateful September 7, with Hermann Göring personally in command of the offensive according to a communiqué issued to the German people, the great 'reprisal' began. That Saturday evening London experienced a devastating attack, but the Luftwaffe suffered heavy losses. Although unfortunate for the citizens of London, the new offensive almost certainly saved the Royal Air Force for, largely unknown to the Germans, their recent attacks on British airfields — and particularly the attacks on the fighter-controlling sector stations — had Fighter Command reeling. Had they continued, the German attacks might well have had an extremely serious effect on the ability of the RAF to continue its heroic defence of the homeland. And without serious air opposition the intended invasion would undoubtedly have succeeded.

As the German daylight raiders retreated they left many fires burning in the East End dock areas, where, despite the legitimacy of the enemy's target, damage to residential property was extensive. Many Londoners lost their lives and hundreds were injured, but this was of little concern to the German leaders; the slightest crack in the morale of the British people could well lead to a massive reaction by the population against the Churchill Government and this, in turn, might bring about capitulation. But it was not to be. Later on, when it was the turn of the German people to suffer air attacks of even greater magnitude, the Allied leaders found the same resolute stance by the proverbial public at large. And they should have expected this from the experience of London.

The fires started by the evening raiders of Luftflotte 2 on September 7 continued to burn after nightfall and served to guide the 247 aircraft of both Luftflotten 2 and 3 which continued the attack throughout the night. They dropped a further 330 tonnes of high explosive and 440 incendiary bomb cannisters (each of which contained 36 one-kilogramme incendiaries) on Silvertown and adjoining districts along the banks of the Thames. Battersea and West Ham power stations were hit, together with railway and dock installations, but the densely packed rows of terraced houses in the city's East End suffered, again, most of all.

The defences, so supreme by day, were totally ineffective at night. The anti-aircraft guns, struggling with failing communications and an out-dated fire control system, could do little to stem the seven-hours-long onslaught. A few night fighters of the wholly inadequate force available flew patrols over north-east London but failed to intercept any of the attackers. In short, the defences of the biggest target in the world were swamped and rendered helpless by their own inadequacy and the sheer weight and length of the attack. Only 92 guns were on sites in the London area and even some of this feeble number failed to engage the enemy because of a breakdown in communications.

Within 48 hours the AA guns were doubled in strength, at the expense of other areas, but no greater success followed. The raids, by day and night, continued in this manner until the night of September 11/12 when the gunners were given a free hand. The resultant barrage of wild shooting was music to the ears of Londoners — and the spectacle must have appeared daunting at first to participating German crews — but in fact did little or nothing to stem the attacks, which continued unabated.

From September 7 to 15 the day and night assaults on London continued, but thereafter heavy daylight raids by bombers were almost entirely replaced by high-flying fighter-bomber attacks which, although harrassing, achieved little in military terms. For another two months the heavy night

Albert E. Creffield took both photos for the *New York Times* from London Bridge. The first picture was taken early evening while the raid was still in progress; the second when the Luftwaffe returned that night.

attacks continued, with bombs falling on nearly every borough, but most of the damage occurred in the same riverside districts that took the brunt of the initial attacks. Residential, commercial and industrial premises all suffered, as did the docks, railways and public utility (gas, electricity and water) services. Many were made homeless and, although casualties were heavy, they were alleviated to some degree by the availability of deep shelters in the form of London Transport's underground railway stations. Without these, made available only after some initial reluctance, the casualty list for September and October — 13,000 civilians killed and 20,000 injured — might well have been higher.

Despite the tremendous amount of damage inflicted on London it gradually became evident that unless key installations — power stations, gas works, railway stations, bridges and essential communications facilities — were destroyed, the Luftwaffe could not possibly succeed in bringing London to its knees. Its attempt to destroy, disrupt and demoralise the city was doomed to failure unless it could permanently destroy these key installations; in addition, the sheer size of London almost certainly ensured its survival against a bomber force unable to deliver a truly collosal weight of bombs, and this the Luftwaffe, almost entirely dependent on twin-engined medium bombers and single-engined dive-bombers, was unable to do. London, covering many square miles, was well able to absorb raids by an average of 160 long-range bombers per night; to erase it, as Hitler had promised, was beyond the capability of the German or any other air arm at that time with the weapons then available. Nor did the attacks, mainly centred on one part of London, break the morale of its citizens. On the contrary, the raids served to bind the people even more closely together and, from the very outset, there was little possibility of the British Government being forced to succumb and seek surrender by a broken, rebellious people.

The accuracy of bombing in 1940 was minimal and hits such as this one on the District Line tunnel at Blackfriars in September were more by luck than judgement. The cut-and-cover method of constructing the older lines just below the roadway (unlike the later deep bored system) meant that they were particularly vulnerable to surface breakthrough.

Forty years later it is virtually another world. When Blackfriars was opened in 1886 it was originally called St Paul's until 1937 when the name was transferred to the new Central Line station. It was completely rebuilt in 1977 and the bridge realigned.

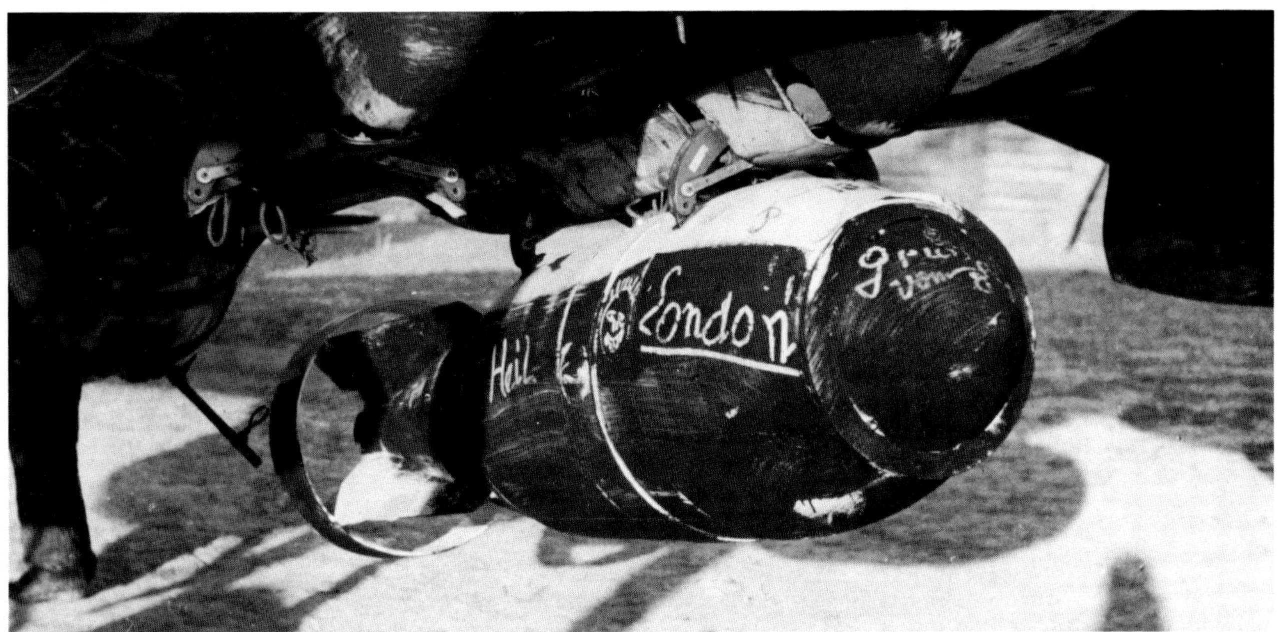

TARGETS

The question of whether or not the Germans were engaged in reprisals, indiscriminate area bombing, or attempted attacks on legitimate targets important to the country's war effort, has long been argued. Clearly the results were little more than one would expect from indiscriminate area bombing, and in the beginning there was certainly a reprisal

An SC 1000 HE bomb in position on the port external PVC bomb carrier of an He 111H-5. Painted Hellblau 65 during manufacture, large calibre bombs were treated to a coat of matt black distemper when required to be carried at night. Various 'Greetings', an indication of 'London' as its destination, and other inscriptions have been made by scraping this easily removed black distemper. The Kopfring on the nose of the bomb was to prevent deep penetration into the ground.

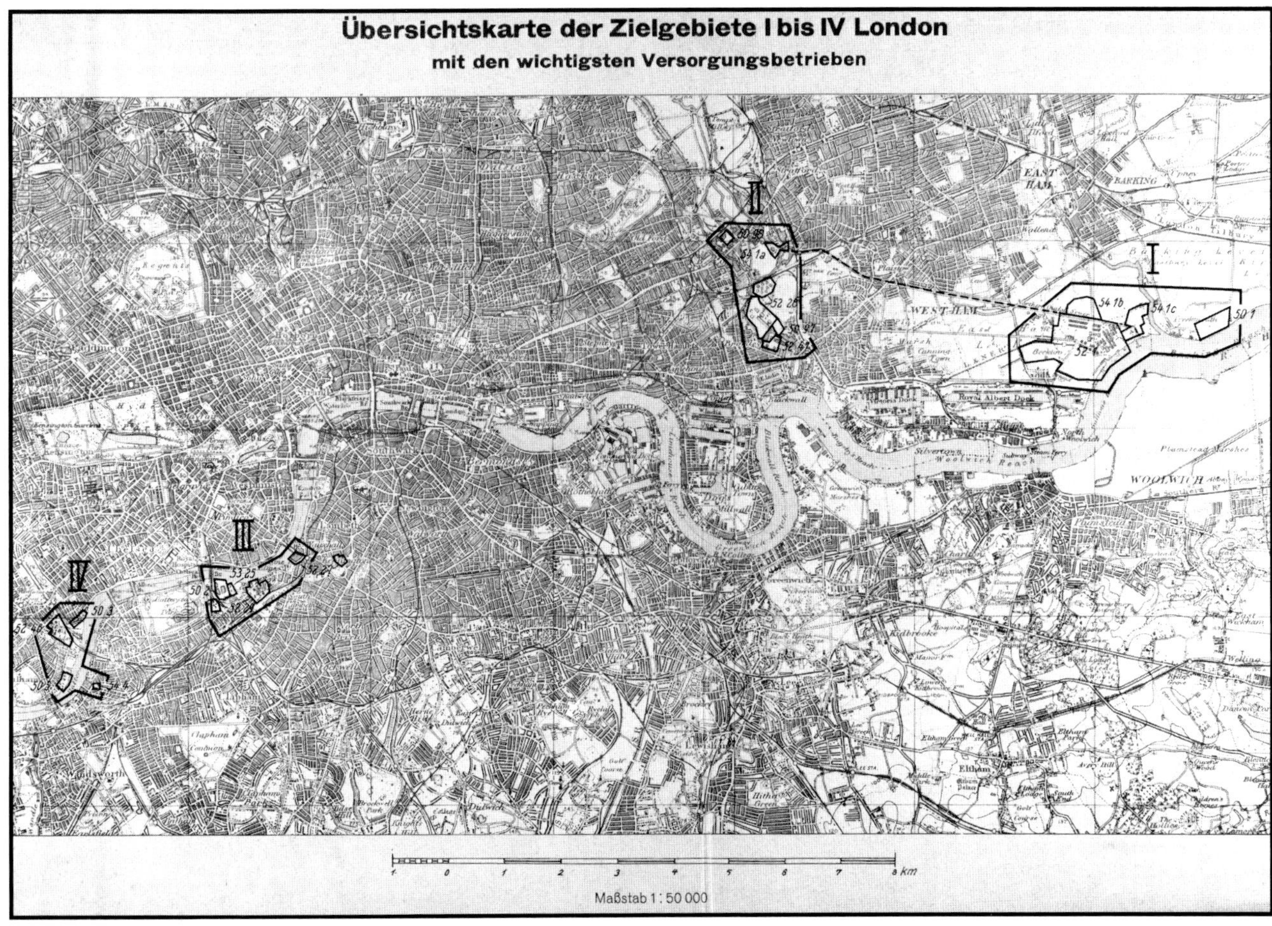

Being on the receiving end of so much of the bombing, civilians must understandably have felt that the Germans had adopted a policy of indiscriminate bombing. However the Luftwaffe force would have been hopelessly inadequate had London 'in toto' been the target and the basic intention was initially to single out key points — Zielgebiete — for attack. Only after the difficulty of hitting even large targets covering a square kilometre or more like those illustrated here was appreciated, were larger Zielräume covering several square miles introduced.

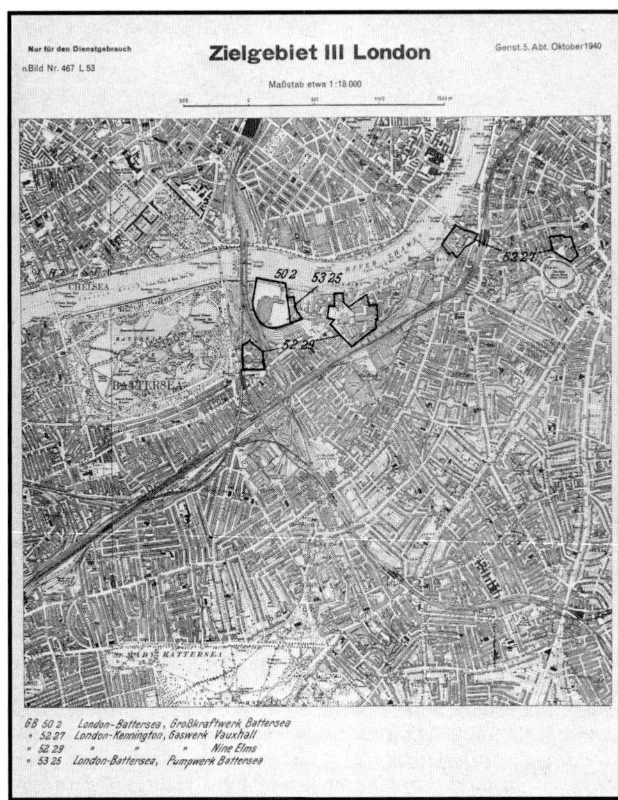

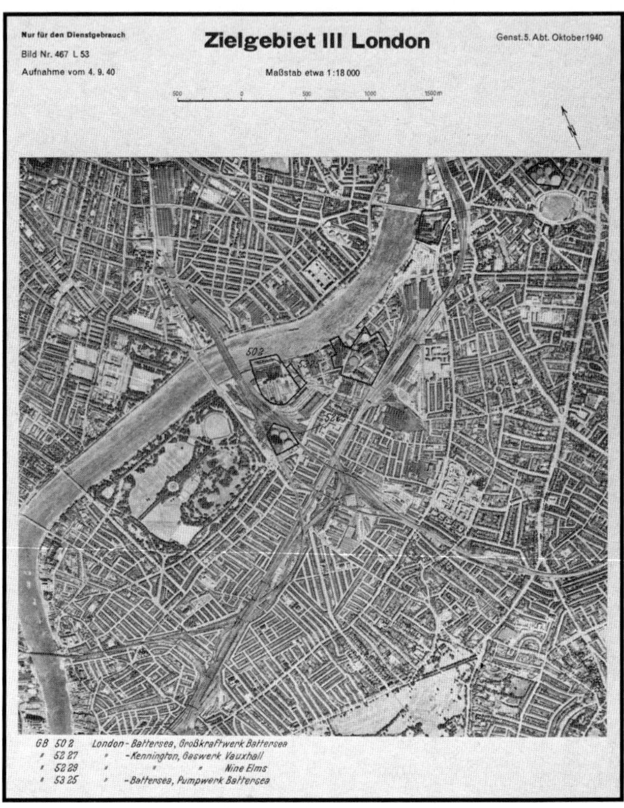

Nur für den Dienstgebrauch
Zielgebiet III London
Genst.5. Abt. Oktober 1940
Bild Nr. 467 L 53
Aufnahme vom 4. 9. 40
Maßstab etwa 1:18 000
GB 50 2 London-Battersea, Großkraftwerk Battersea
" 52 27 " -Kennington, Gaswerk Vauxhall
" 52 29 " " " Nine Elms
" 53 25 " -Battersea, Pumpwerk Battersea

Crews were briefed with target maps on which the individual buildings were identified within each Zielgebiet. A standardised system of prefixes denoted the purpose of each building: 50 for instance standing for a power station; 52 for a gasworks etc. Targets were overlaid on both street maps, copied from British Ordnance Survey sheets, and photographs taken on photo-reconnaissance sorties. ***Above:*** **Here GB 502 is Battersea power station, with 53 25 the pump house, 52 27 Vauxhall Gasworks and 52 29 Nine Elms Gasworks. The photo was taken three days before the London raid but not issued until October.** ***Below:*** **Within each target set, oblique shots were included to help identify salient features, the twin chimneys of Battersea power station making it known to German crews as the 'packet of Woodbines'.**

element, but Luftwaffe records leave no real doubt that the intention was to devastate London's vitally important docks and destroy Government offices in central London from where the war against Germany was being directed. At first bomber units were allocated specific targets such as the West India Docks or Battersea power station, but soon came the realisation that such accuracy was not possible at night (or indeed, as often as not, by day). From the night of October 8-9, therefore, crews were allocated industrial or dock Target Areas (i.e. a prescribed area within which lay a variable number of specific targets) and London (and, later, other cities) were divided into a number of such areas. Thus, Luftflotte 3 operations reports for attacks subsequent to October 8 refer, for example, to Zielräum or Target Area 'G' (the area inside the 'U-loop' of the Thames). Zielräum 'E' (the area north of the Thames covering part of west and north-west London) and Zielräum 'A' (encompassing the Elephant and Castle to Blackfriars Bridge district and part of the East End). Within these laid down Zielräume, crews were invariably given a Schwerpunkt or Concentration Point upon which to aim, and often this took the form of a well defined specific objective such as the Battersea power station (with its large chimneys known to German crews for obvious reasons as the 'Packet of Woodbines'). However, despite the introduction of Target Areas, units continued to be allocated specific targets and for the entire period of the London Blitz Luftwaffe operations reports mention the Victoria, East India, Wapping and West India Docks, the gasworks at Beckton, Bromley and elsewhere, various railway termini and certain bridges over the Thames. It appears, therefore, that when conditions of moonlight and visibility permitted, many crews were allocated specific targets; otherwise they were instructed to bomb laid down Zielräume. German crews knew full well, however, that their chances of hitting the specific targets by visual bomb aiming at night were extremely slight. Their chances on nights of little moonlight were even less, and on cloudy nights, nil. In practice, therefore, on occasions when crews were unable to make out their assigned objectives — and with no desire to return to base with their bombs still on board — they invariably aimed their bombs in the general direction of their Target Area, using whatever fires were already visible as a rough and ready aiming point.

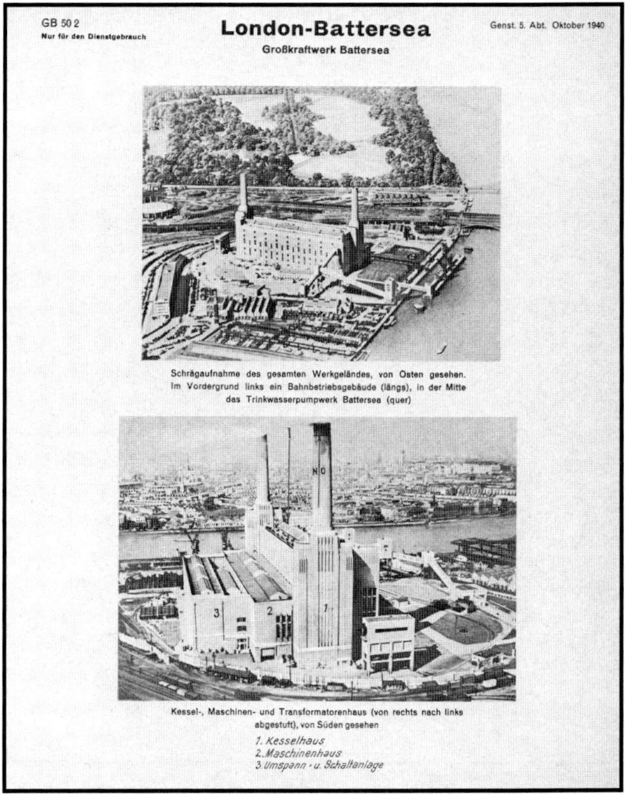
GB 50 2
Nur für den Dienstgebrauch
London-Battersea
Großkraftwerk Battersea
Genst. 5. Abt. Oktober 1940

Schrägaufnahme des gesamten Werkgeländes, von Osten gesehen. Im Vordergrund links ein Bahnbetriebsgebäude (längs), in der Mitte das Trinkwasserpumpwerk Battersea (quer)

Kessel-, Maschinen- und Transformatorenhaus (von rechts nach links abgestuft), von Süden gesehen
1. Kesselhaus
2. Maschinenhaus
3. Umspann- u. Schaltanlage

The partnership of pilot and navigator — personified here by Leutnant Ebbehard Wüllenweber and Feldwebel Emil Ebert. Their Heinkel came down at Sherborne on May 7, 1941.

NAVIGATION

In essence the Luftwaffe was a tactical air force, but as the Blitz continued it assumed a progressively more strategic rôle and coped remarkably well with it, from an operating point of view. The British defences, so supreme by day, were woefully inadequate by night, so the biggest problem facing German bomber crews was a navigational one — finding their targets and then locating their bases upon return.

The basis of navigation in the German Air Force, as in all air forces, was based on 'Dead Reckoning' or DR procedures, sometimes termed 'clock and compass' navigation. With a knowledge of his aircraft's climb/cruise performance and given a forecast wind velocity and details of the track(s) to the target, the navigator was able to calculate the headings to fly and time to reach his objective. A number of factors could upset this arrangement, however, not the least being an inaccurately forecast upper wind. It was essential, therefore, for the navigator to check his progress along his desired track or route and this was accomplished, whenever possible, by map reading. By visually fixing his position from time to time it was possible for the navigator to adjust his headings and correct his estimated arrival time; further, by finding the wind actually experienced he could correct his calculations for the rest of the flight, including his return leg to base. However, at night or when in or above cloud, map reading was not always possible and, in such conditions, recourse was taken to 'fixing position' by means of radio aids.

One method of fixing position was by the use of radio beacons. By the late summer of 1940 the Signals Branch of the Luftwaffe had set up a large number of radio beacons, arranged in a large arc that swept around Britain from Brittany to Norway. In addition to these high powered beacons, many of which were in coastal locations, most German airfields possessed lower powered beacons to assist 'homing'. All German long-range bombers carried Direction Finding (D/F) equipment and by taking a bearing, or series of bearings, on suitably located beacons it was possible for the navigator to plot his position with reasonable accuracy. The system was not without its shortcomings, however, and at certain times — particularly dusk and dawn — and in conditions of atmospheric static, the accuracy of positions so found left much to be desired.

German bombers in flight maintained two-way communication with their Control Stations by means of Wireless Telegraphy (W/T), using Morse and various Luftwaffe codes to maintain secrecy. The German ground W/T stations also possessed a D/F capability so that it was possible to obtain bearings on aircraft in flight. Should, therefore, an aircraft suffer an in-flight failure of its own D/F equipment, it could request bearings from one or more ground stations and again plot its position with a fair degree of accuracy. There was, however, a serious drawback which tended to inhibit the use of this method — British W/T stations could also monitor the transmissions from German aircraft and by 'D/F-ing' them could fix the bomber's position. There was, in view of this, a reluctance on the part of German crews to transmit for D/F purposes unless they were well on their way home or desperately lost in an emergency situation.

The direction-finding loop aerial on an early Do 17Z-1; on later variants the aerial was replaced by a different type housed in a small, streamlined plexiglas blister.

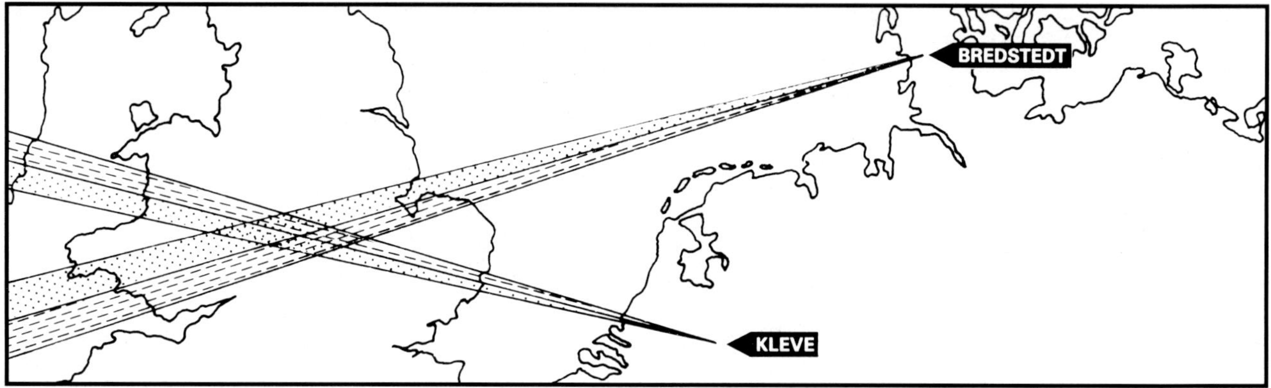

BOMBING AIDS

Knickebein used the signals from two transmitters in occupied territory to pinpoint the target with intersecting beams. However the system was really only accurate enough for locating a town — not a particular target within it. To do that the X-Verfahren system was developed which could bring an aircraft to within a 1000 feet of its target at a range of 180 miles. A further refinement — the Y-Verfahren system — was accurate enough to pick out a largish building at over 100 miles.

Perhaps rather surprisingly, in view of its mainly tactical rôle, the German Air Force also had several other, highly secret radio aids to navigation. Rejecting astro-navigation as a bomber navigational aid, the Luftwaffe instead had invested in several precision radio beam systems working on very high frequencies (VHF). The first of these, known as Knickebein, was available to the entire bomber force as the signals were received by the same equipment fitted as standard in all German bombers for the so-called 'blind' (or beam) approach-to-land system devised by the Lorenz company before the war and adopted, among others, by the German national airline Luft Hansa, the Luftwaffe and the RAF.

Knickebein was intended for blind bombing, using two VHF transmitters which formed a beam intersection over the prescribed target. The pilot aurally tracked along the approach beam (which passed over the target) and, when well established, switched to the 'cross' beam. At the intersection, which was offset as required by the ground stations to allow for any wind or drift effect, the bombs were manually released with no need whatsoever for visual contact with the ground. The accuracy of the system was good; very narrow beams were used (0.33°) although, of course, the beam widened with increased distance from the transmitter and at a distance of 180 miles the beam 'on course' steady note was one mile wide (deviation to left or right of the beam was indicated aurally by the Morse characteristics E (·) or T (—) respectively). It could be said, therefore, that at distances up to about 180 miles, Knickebein offered a potential bombing accuracy of about one mile. Its principal limitation, as with all VHF aids, was one of range; at the height at which German bombers could operate, this was limited, for all practical purposes, to about 150 to 180 miles. By the time the London Blitz got under way there were five Knickebein transmitters in service (numbered Kn I to Kn V) and positioned from Bredstedt (Kn I) in Denmark to Morlaix in Brittany (Kn V.)

A Heinkel He 111H-3x and personnel of Kampfgruppe 100, taken at Vannes in 1940. On the extreme left is Oberleutnant Gerd-Hermann Franke, an officer involved from the beginning with the proving and development flying of X-Verfahren. He was shot down and taken prisoner near Lymington, Hampshire, on July 8, 1941, during an attack on Southampton. Hauptmann Kurd Aschenbrenner, Gruppenkomandeur of KGr100, is facing the camera, wearing a white-topped (summer style) peaked cap. Third from the right is Hauptmann Hermann Schmidt, the Staffelkapitän of 1/KGr100. Note night-flying black distemper on the side and lower surfaces of the Heinkel; also clearly visible are the two additional radio masts required by the X-system receivers. An aircraft so fitted was called a 'He Dreimaster' (Heinkel Three-master) by the personnel of KGr100.

The second beam system was called the X-Verfahren or X-System, and was available only to one Gruppe in the Luftwaffe (Kampfgruppe 100) trained and equipped to use it. More complex and more accurate than Knickebein, X-Verfahren called for aircraft especially equipped to receive the intricate signals (the on-board equipment, which included two special receivers, was collectively known as X-Gerät) and its operational effectiveness demanded sound training and excellent crew co-operation. In simple terms X-Verfahren was a multi-beam system working in the frequency range 66.0 to 77.0 megacycles compared to Knickebein's 30.0 to 33.0 megacycles. It made use of multiple transmitters (named Wotan Is) to provide a fine approach beam set in a coarse approach beam, and three cross-beam intersections in the Target Area. The Wotan Is transmitted 180 directional signals per minute and part of the X-Gerät was an electronic analyser or decoder, necessary to resolve the signals and produce both visual and aural 'on course' signals to the pilot and navigator. Another, vital part of the X-Gerät was the X-Uhr (X-Clock), used to time the run (and thus the ground speed) of the bomber as it crossed two of the beam intersections (the first being a 'forewarning signal') while tracking in towards the target on the main approach beam. Activation of the X-Clock, as required by crew operating procedures, led to the automatic release of the bombs at precisely the right moment. Again, totally blind bombing was the aim but, much more accurate than Knickebein, an accuracy to within about 300 metres (980 feet) was possible for an aircraft flying at 20,000 feet and about 180 miles from the 'main course' transmitter.

The third, and most accurate precision system of all, was Y-Verfahren, also known as Y-Verfahren (Kampf) or Ypsillon. This incredibly advanced system was even more ahead of its time and provided an automatic beam tracking capability to the target through the aircraft's auto-pilot. Only one unit in the Luftwaffe was equipped with Y-Verfahren, the III Gruppe of Kampfgeschwader 26 (III/KG26), and although operational trials with the new system commenced in September, it was not ready to play its full part until October.

Y-Verfahren employed one approach beam only, along which, after a manually flown interception, the aircraft automatically flew. As the German bomber tracked towards its target, it received further signals from another ground station and 'triggered' or re-radiated these back, giving a ground controller the aircraft's 'distance out' along the beams by means of the distance measuring properties of radio wave propagation. Further, D/F-ing of the aircraft enabled beam azimuth corrections to be made at the transmitter (called Wotan II), ensuring that the aircraft adhered to a precise track over the target. As the bomber neared its target, warnings were passed to the crew by VHF communications (sometimes by code-words, sometimes by Morse characteristics), the bomb doors were opened and, at the appropriate moment, the bomb release command was given by the ground controller. (This usually took the form of a nine-second Morse Code signal, 'VB', ie, ···———···, and the bombs were released upon receipt of the last 'dot'.) Like Knickebein and X-Verfahren, the new system was limited in range and required participating aircraft to fly at the great height, for those days, of about 20,000 feet. Under average conditions Y-Verfahren was expected to be very precise indeed and was capable of hitting a building the size of a power station at a range of about 120 miles.

Major Viktor von Lossberg, Gruppenkommandeur of III/KG26, the Y-Verfahren specialist bomber unit which played a leading rôle in the 1940–41 night Blitz on Britain, He is seen *below* in the observer's hatch of a He 111H-5y of III/KG26. Note the Gruppenkommandeur's pennant and the large additional antenna mast associated with this special Y-Verfahren-equipped version of the He 111 and located immediately behind the forward crew compartment. Also clearly visible is an SC 1000 externally slung on a PVC bomb carrier.

Less accurate but intended for en route navigation rather than precision bombing were two further German radio aids, one of which, also available to U-Boats and other shipping, was known as Elektra. The other system, a forerunner of Knickebein called Karussell, was less used, but neither of these aids played a significant part in German operations over Britain in 1940.

From the foregoing it can be seen that as a night bombing force the Luftwaffe was apparently well equipped in a navigational sense. Night operations also helped to offset the defensive armament shortcomings that daylight operations in the Battle of Britain had revealed. Flame damping exhausts were already fitted to most German bombers so that the only additional work required to fit them for night flying was the application of a coat of matt black distemper to their pale blue undersides to reduce the effectiveness of searchlight beams.

While groundcrew personnel manhandle a Do 17Z-3 its crew members pose, rather self-consciously, for the photographer. The Do 17Z, prominent during the Battle of Britain and well liked by pilots for its superb handling qualities, played a minor part only during the Blitz. Restrictions on the size of bomb it could carry, imposed by the physical dimensions of its bomb-bay, and its limited range and load carrying capability, all served to expedite the Do 17s departure.

AIRFIELDS AND AIRCRAFT

German airfields, many of them former French, Belgian or Dutch air force bases, were variable in standard but most offered reasonable night flying facilities. However, with typical German thoroughness, a massive improvement and expansion plan was implemented without delay, and before long most Luftwaffe bomber bases could boast hard surface runways, approach and runway lighting and adequate radio communications and navigational aids (including the Lorenz beam approach system at many airfields and a 'ZZ' — D/F let-down — system at others). Most bases were linked by teleprinter to their respective Fliegerkorps or air fleet headquarters, but considerable use was also made of ground-to-ground W/T radio to pass operational orders and generally maintain communications with airfields in extreme north-west France where teleprinter links did not exist. In such cases messages were passed in Morse, use being made of the now well known Enigma machine to mechanically decode and encode secret or classified information.

Without heavy four-engined bombers in its inventory, the German Air Force was incapable of lifting an enormous weight of bombs in one night. Nevertheless, it was not realised in the autumn of 1940 just what weight of bombs was necessary to make strategic bombing effective. It was assumed in Britain that the Germans had something like 1,000 long-range bombers in the medium classification with each capable of carrying, over short to medium ranges, a bomb load in the region of one tonne; and assuming a serviceability factor of, say, 50 per cent (a not unreasonable

TONNES OF HIGH EXPLOSIVE AIMED AT BRITISH CITIES, NIGHT OF SEPTEMBER 7, 1940–NIGHT OF MAY 16, 1941 MAJOR* ATTACKS ONLY

Target Area	*Number of Major Raids*	*Metric Tonnes*
London (entire period)	71	18,800
London (after November 14)	14	5,149
Liverpool–Birkenhead	8	1,957
Birmingham	8	1,852
Glasgow–Clydeside	5	1,329
Plymouth–Devonport	8	1,228
Bristol–Avonmouth	6	919
Coventry	2	818
Portsmouth	3	687
Southampton	4	647
Hull	3	593
Manchester	3	578
Belfast	2	440
Sheffield	1	355
Newcastle–Tyneside	1	152
Nottingham	1	137
Cardiff	1	115

* Major attacks are those in which 100 tonnes or more of high-explosive were aimed. The table above, compiled from German statistics, does not take into consideration the weight of incendiary bombs aimed.

One of 75 Fiat BR 20M bombers of the Italian Air Force — the Corpo Aereo Italiano — attached to Luftflotte 2 in the autumn of 1940. This aircraft of the 242 Squadriglia, 99 Gruppo, 43 Stormo, was based at Chièvres, Belgium, from September 27.

figure), it seemed more than likely that the Luftwaffe could deliver, with few problems, 500 tonnes of bombs on any one night. In practice, this weight was seldom delivered, but the offensive launched against London in September 1940 was not inconsequential, despite the use of medium bombers only, and by the middle of November the Germans could claim to have dropped 13,651 tonnes of HE and 12,596 IB cannisters on the British capital.

At the start of the Blitz the Luftwaffe was using three principal types of bomber: the Dornier Do 17, the Heinkel He 111 and the Junkers Ju 88, though a few other types, including the Focke-Wulf FW 200 maritime reconnaissance aircraft, appeared from time to time. By the end of 1940 the obsolescent Do 17 was largely phased out and, from then on, the Ju 88 and He 111 carried on almost exclusively, though joined on occasion by light bombers of the Bf 110 type and, rarely, by the Ju 87 single-engined dive-bomber.

In October the German bomber force was augmented by 75 Fiat BR 20 medium bombers of the Italian Air Force, sent to Belgium by Mussolini to take part in the 'final part of the war against England'. Known as the Corpo Aereo Italiano (CAI) this force established its headquarters at Brussels with a Bomber HQ (Comando Bombardamento CAI) at Chièvres and two operational Wings (13° Stormo BT, later re-designated KG13, and 43° Stormo BT, to become KG43 in German Air Force terminology) at Melsbroek and Chièvres. In practice, this force was to play only a very minor part in the air war over Britain and after only three months, because of operational and administrative problems, it returned to Italy, somewhat to the relief of the Luftwaffe; its aircraft, ancilliary equipment and crew training and standards were not compatible with North-West European requirements in wintertime.

At first the majority of German HE bombs were of small calibre, with those of 50 kilogrammes (112 pounds) predominant. Also widely used was the 250kg (560lb) HE, but gradually bombs of increasing size and weight came into service, culminating with the enormous 'Max' of 2500kg (5,600lb). However, perhaps the most potent of German bombs remained the tiny one-kilogramme incendiary which, dropped in profusion, caused millions of pounds worth of fire damage and virtually burnt out whole districts. Mention must also be made of the use of so-called landmines; intended originally for marine use, a change in detonator rendered them suitable for use against land targets where their tremendous blast effect, heightened by their slow, parachute retarded descent, caused enormous damage in built-up areas. Unexploded (UXB) or delayed-action (DA) bombs also caused severe dislocation at times and presented numerous problems for the bomb disposal units of the Royal Engineers, Royal Navy and Royal Air Force.

The most potent of all the weapons in the Luftwaffe's armoury (fully detailed in Volume 1) was the little 1kg incendiary. Thousands were dropped from containers and it had the ability to cause far more damage for its size than either the huge Max or the Luftmine. Here armourers load B 1 E incendiaries into a BSB 1000 non-expendable container.

Albert Kesselring had commanded Luftflotte 1 in the invasion of Poland, and Luftflotte 2 during the battle of France.

Hugo Sperrle, who had formerly led the Condor Legion in the Spanish Civil War, now commanded Luftflotte 3.

Hans-Jürgen Stumpff had commanded Luftflotte 5 in the campaign in Norway and Denmark.

ORGANISATION

As Supreme Commander of the Wehrmacht, the German Armed Forces, Adolf Hitler was theoretically in overall command of the Luftwaffe and he did, in fact, control its broad direction. For all practical purposes, however, he exercised his command through Göring, the Commander-in-Chief of the Air Force (Oberbefehlshaber der Luftwaffe), but as the Blitz progressed Göring turned more to politics, affairs of State and hunting. His disenchantment with his Air Force, following what he saw as its failure during the Battle of Britain, was reciprocated and by the late autumn of 1940 it was with some relief that senior Air Force officers found that Göring was leaving the day to day control of the Luftwaffe to Generalfeldmarschall Erhard Milch. State Secretary in the Air Ministry (Reichsluftfahrtministerium or RLM) and Inspector General of the Air Force, Milch was both a competent technical man and first class administrator. He combined considerable energy with great drive and personal ambition, but seemingly had a penchant for making enemies among certain factions of the Wehrmacht's hierarchy. He was highly respected by many senior Air Force officers, however.

From a magnificent new building on the corner of Leipzigerstrasse and Wilhelmstrasse in Berlin, the RLM exercised operational control and administrative authority over the Air Force through the Oberkommando der Luftwaffe (OKL), the High Command of the Air Force. In practice then, while Hitler through Göring and, later, Milch directed the broad rôle of the Luftwaffe, operational control was exercised through the OKL with day-to-day operations managed by the Luftwaffe General Staff, the Führungsstab.

German long-range bombers did not come under a central command, as in the RAF with its Bomber Command, but with other types, such as reconnaissance aircraft and fighters, were allocated to Air Fleets or Luftflotten. As previously indicated, three such Luftflotten were engaged in the air war against Britain; they were of varying size, but each comprised a number of subsidiary commands known as Fliegerkorps which exercised operational control over their respective Kampfgeschwader or Bomber Groups. In turn, each Kampfgeschwader comprised three Wings or Gruppen of three Staffeln or Squadrons.

Luftflotte 2 had its Headquarters in Brussels and was commanded by Generalfeldmarschall Albert Kesselring. In September 1940 its long-range bombers were attached to I and II Fliegerkorps and IX Fliegerdivision (shortly to be retitled IX Fliegerkorps) and were based on airfields in Belgium, Holland, North Germany and that part of France north of the Seine. Although used as part of the normal bomber force, elements of IX Fliegerkorps were also largely engaged in the laying of sea mines around Britain's coastline; Luftflotte 2's other bomber units were primarily concerned with operations against targets in the eastern half of the UK, but such territorial limitations were not rigidly enforced. Kesselring, the air fleet commander, was an officer of great ability and experience; a veteran of the Great War he subsequently served in the Reichswehr and transferred to the newly forming Luftwaffe in 1933.

Luftflotte 3, the second major air fleet ranged against Britain, had its Headquarters at Saint-Cloud near Paris. Its bombers were divided between IV and V Fliegerkorps on airfields in occupied France south of the Seine and, to a lesser extent, in southern Germany. It was commanded by Generalfeldmarschall Hugo Sperrle, the well known leader of the Condor Legion during the Spanish Civil War. An airman in the First World War, Sperrle also later served with the Reichswehr, commanding an infantry regiment until transferring to the Luftwaffe in 1934. A fearsome-looking man, the monocled Sperrle was every Englishman's idea of a 'typical Nazi'; it was even said in Germany, jokingly, that Sperrle was put in command of Luftflotte 3 to frighten the British into submission, but in fact he was a scrupulously fair man who was highly regarded by subordinates of all ranks. He was an efficient commander who demanded and received the utmost from all who served under him. Generally speaking, Luftflotte 3 covered targets in the western half of Britain.

Smallest of the three air fleets was Luftflotte 5, commanded by Generaloberst Hans-Jürgen Stumpff, a man of long military experience who transferred to the Luftwaffe in 1933. From its Headquarters in Kristiansund, Denmark, Luftflotte 5 controlled bombers attached to X Fliegerkorps during the early part of the air war over Britain, but in August they were transferred to other commands. A single bomber Gruppe returned to X Fliegerkorps in October, but for the remainder of the winter of 1940-41 only a small number of long-range bombers remained on Scandinavian bases and these were mainly engaged in anti-shipping duties; they did, however, join with Luftflotten 2 and 3 in attacks on Scottish targets from time to time, working closely with Luftflotte 2.

The German bomber force, in addition to the normal Kampfgeschwader, also included a number of independent Kampfgruppen (Bomber Wings) not attached to any particular Kampfgeschwader. There were also the Lehrgeschwader (LG) and Küstenfliegergruppen (KüFlGr), both formerly with specialist (flight development and coastal reconnaissance) functions but used as part of the normal long-range bomber force during the Blitz.

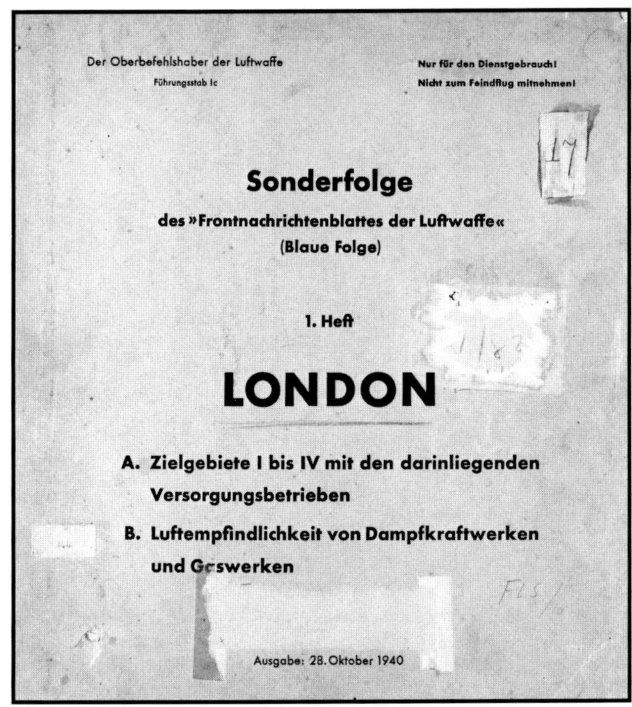

Der Oberbefehlshaber der Luftwaffe
Führungsstab Ic

Nur für den Dienstgebrauch!
Nicht zum Feindflug mitnehmen!

Sonderfolge

des »Frontnachrichtenblattes der Luftwaffe«
(Blaue Folge)

1. Heft

LONDON

A. Zielgebiete I bis IV mit den darinliegenden Versorgungsbetrieben

B. Luftempfindlichkeit von Dampfkraftwerken und Gaswerken

Ausgabe: 28. Oktober 1940

INTELLIGENCE

Backing the bomber-equipped units of the Luftwaffe were highly trained Signals, Intelligence, Meteorological, Administrative and Servicing organisations. Airfields came under various Air District Commands for administrative and logistics purposes and attached to each airfield were aircraft servicing units. This system accounted for the extreme mobility of the German Air Force; operational flying units consisted of little more than crews and aircraft, so when they moved base the transfer of large numbers of ground staff was not involved. Upon arrival at their new base or area of operations they would find administrative, servicing and support personnel awaiting them, together with stocks of bombs, fuel and other essentials. Maps and target documentation were also readily available, enabling flying units to go into action immediately upon arrival.

The Luftwaffe Intelligence system worked well at higher levels, in an organisation sense, but did not include the provision of specialist Intelligence officers at flying unit level where Gruppe or Staffel leaders undertook such duties, briefing and debriefing crews before and after missions. They were aided in these tasks, however, by the availability in good measure of books, maps and other documentation dealing with British targets, defence systems, and so on. Typically, in 1939 the Luftwaffe General Staff had produced a publication dealing in detail with the British Isles; this covered every town of note, giving information on its industrial and strategic importance, with maps and photographs as appropriate. Also included was a thorough appreciation of the weather conditions to be expected in the various regions of the British Isles at different times of the year, with much more information likely to be of use to airmen.

Similar but more detailed information was prepared before the war by the Luftwaffe's 5 Abteilung (5th Branch, Foreign Powers Section) of the Operations Staff which compiled 'Target Files' covering every significant target in Britain. Each target was allocated a number prefixed by GB (for Grossbritannien); the first part of this number included the particular target group (e.g., airfields were coded GB 10, docks were GB 45, power stations GB 50, and so on) and the second part of the number identified the specific target in its group. Thus, for example, GB 45 3 was the target number for London's Millwall Docks. By mid-1940 Luftwaffe Intelligence was in possession of a vast amount of target material and this was updated and revised that summer following intensive photographic reconnaissance activity over much of Britain.

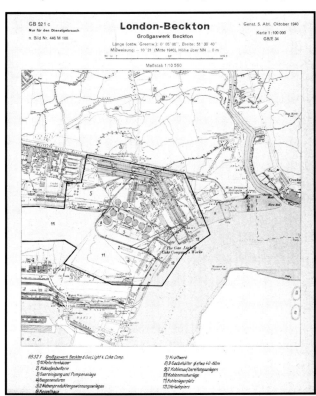

GB 521 c
Nur für den Dienstgebrauch
n. Bild Nr. 446 M 108

London-Beckton
Großgaswerk Beckton
Länge (ostw. Greenw.): 0° 05' 00'', Breite: 51° 30' 40''
Mißweisung: – 10° 21' (Mitte 1940), Höhe über NN ... 0 m

Genst. 5. Abt. Oktober 1940
Karte 1:100 000
GB/E 34

Maßstab 1:10 560

GB 521 Großgaswerk Beckton d. Gas Light & Coke Comp.
1) 12 Retortenhäuser
2) Koksofenbatterie
3) Gasreinigung und Pumpenanlage
4) Gasgeneratoren
5) 2 Nebenproduktengewinnungsanlagen
6) Kesselhaus
7) Kraftwerk
8) 9 Gasbehälter ⌀ etwa 40-60m
9) 2 Kohlenaufbereitungsanlagen
10) Kohlenmischanlage
11) Kohlenlagerplatz
12) 2 Verladepiers

The prime industrial target in the London area was the Beckton Gasworks which produced the supply for central London. The entire gas output left the plant in large trunk mains which ran from the works side by side to the centre of London from where it was distributed on a grid system over the City. The Key Points Intelligence Branch of the Home Office stated in its 1940 report on damage to those targets affecting the national war effort published on June 30, 1941 that 'if the enemy had continued his attacks on this works the London gas supply would inevitably have been cut off for a considerable period'. As it was, when the supply was stopped for some days, it was due to the severing of the main lines leading from the gasworks rather than hits on the plant itself. On September 7 the gas supply was cut off in eight boroughs.

BRITISH COUNTER-MEASURES

In matters of Intelligence the Royal Air Force had no equal and, by the time the Germans launched their attack on London, British Air Intelligence (AI) knew a great deal about its adversary. The various branches of AI obtained information from a variety of sources, but much of it came through captured German airmen interrogated by the Branch known as AI1(k) at Cockfosters, London, and AI1(g) Branch, which carried out the detailed examination and technical analysis of crashed German aircraft. Other Branches specialised in the examination of captured maps, navigational logs and associated documentation, and signals material. Few prisoners-of-war willingly gave away information, but the cunning interrogation methods employed by Squadron Leader Denys Felkin's AI1(k), supported by hidden microphones and other subtleties, together with the material found on them and gathered by other departments (diaries, maps, bus tickets — which revealed base locations —leave passes, letters, etc.), all served to complete the picture and enabled the RAF to acquire a very full knowledge of the Luftwaffe Order of Battle, equipment, bases and operating procedures and personnel.

At Trent Park, Cockfosters, under Squadron Leader S. D. Felkin, the Combined Services Detailed Interrogation Centre (CSDIC) developed sophisticated interrogation techniques for prising information from German Air Force prisoners . . .

Scientific research amply played its part, too, including the brilliant investigative rôle played by Dr R. V. Jones, the young physicist who was head of Scientific Intelligence on the Air Staff. Suffice to say that as a result of clever anticipation, aided by a report leaked to Britain and information supplied by the French before the capitulation, British AI discovered the secrets of Knickebein and, to a lesser degree, the X- and Y-Verfahren precision bombing systems. Accordingly, a radio counter-measures section came into being under the control of the Deputy Director of Signals 'Y', but before long essential expansion led to the formation of No. 80 Wing commanded by Wing Commander E. B. Addison, OBE. With its Headquarters at Garston, Hertfordshire, No. 80 Wing quickly became a large radio counter-measures and signals monitoring organisation, working in close association with the Wireless Intelligence Development Unit (WIDU).

. . . while 15 miles to the west, No. 80 Wing established itself in the Aldenham Country Club prepared to do battle over the ether.

Today, unfortunately, the building, then known also as the Aldenham Lodge Hotel, where the RAF's wireless war was masterminded, is no more. It lay here off The Drive where now the houses of Regents Close and Lodge End have been built.

The Knickebein beams were code-named 'Headache' — not inappropriately — by the British and the 'jammers' used to interfere with the German transmissions were suitably named 'Aspirins'. Jamming was to be a last resort, however, and, more subtly, plans were made to transmit false beam signals and interject these over the German signals to lead bomber crews astray. By October, by which time No. 80 Wing was established in new premises at the Aldenham Country Club at Radlett, Hertfordshire, fifteen Lorenz-type beam Aspirin sites were in operation.

Earlier, an examination of the German use of the internationally well known radio beacon navigational aid brought about the brilliant decision to re-radiate rather than jam them. With the invaluable help of a Research Establishment run by the BBC and the General Post Office, a number of re-radiating transmitters were erected and, intended to 'mask' the enemy transmissions, were known as Masked Beacons or 'Meacons'. As a result, attempts by German aircraft to obtain D/F bearings from radio beacons were usually frustrated — over Britain the bearings were totally unreliable and, unknown to German crews, usually indicated the bearing to the Meacon site; over the Channel the bearings were usually vague and ill-defined and only close in to the genuine beacon could bearings begin to serve any useful purpose. As the Meacons picked up and simply re-broadcast the original German beacon signal, it was impossible for crews to differentiate between the two. By late August nine Meacons were in use and they continued to multiply through the autumn.

Monitoring from mobile vans, watcher stations and aircraft of the WIDU ultimately revealed the existence of the second German beam system, X-Verfahren, although it was in use for some time by the Luftwaffe before it was identified and linked to Kampfgruppe (KGr) 100. The linking of X-Verfahren to KGr100 was accomplished in association with the RAF's 'Y' Service, an organisation charged with monitoring all German Air Force W/T and R/T (radio telephone) communications. Manned very largely by pre-war radio amateurs or 'hams', the 'Y' Service was aware of the radio callsigns of all Luftwaffe units, monitored aircraft movements (operational and training) and operational messages and was instrumental in building up and updating the RAF's knowledge of the German Order of Battle. Mainly through the 'Y' Service the RAF knew the location and strength of every enemy unit in the West and, indeed, in Europe and the Mediterranean. With the discovery of X-Verfahren, therefore, it did not take the 'Y' Service long to link it with the Vannes-based KGr100.

The belated discovery of X-Verfahren — it had first been used experimentally over London and the Thames Estuary in October 1939, then withdrawn and re-introduced on August 13, 1940 — resulted in the introduction of a jamming system improvised by the Metropolitan-Vickers company, under the direction of an ex-BBC technical expert, and by the beginning of November the first such set was installed at Hagley. The X-Verfahren beams were known as 'Rivers' to the RAF (following the Luftwaffe practice of code-naming the X-System's Wotan I transmitters after rivers in Germany, a practice known to the 'Y' Service) and the British jammers were code-named 'Bromide'. Unfortunately for the British, the Bromides were not very effective in countering X-Verfahren. In fact, the claims of the effectiveness of British radio counter-measures have been generally overstated in Britain by authors and historians who have taken only British wartime reports into consideration. Extant Luftwaffe records and information obtained by the author from former aircrew personnel of KGr100 and III/KG26 fully support this statement. Too much credence has been placed on British claims which, because they were made in wartime reports, do not take the German view into consideration. For example, X-Verfahren remained largely unhindered throughout the winter of 1940-41 and the interruption to Y-Verfahren signals later on were not as complete as British Intelligence reports would have one believe. On the other hand, the Meaconing of radio beacons and interference to Knickebein signals were undoubtedly effective, as was the relaying of false D/F bearings to German aircraft requesting W/T assistance. But even with Knickebein, interference was successful only over land and Luftwaffe crews continued to use it as a track-keeping aid up to and sometimes beyond the British coasts. As a precision bombing aid, however, British counter-measures rendered it largely unuseable.

In spite of the strenuous efforts made to negate the German navigational bombing aids, X- and Y-Verfahren remained effective throughout the night Blitz of 1940–41 — contrary to what has often been claimed in Britain — and borne out by surviving Luftwaffe records and interviews with former members of the two 'Pathfinder' units, KGr100 and III/KG26. Here officers of the latter unit take time to relax between sorties at Poix Castle (von Lossberg is below the right-hand window).

The first pathfinders. An He 111H-1x (coded 6N+EK) of 2/KGr 100. One of the two additional masts associated with X-Gerät is visible to the rear of the normal W/T communications mast. The protuberance under the nose is the housing of the Lofte 7c periscopic bombsight, used for conventional bombing.

TACTICS

From the earliest days of the Battle of Britain, German long-range bombers had operated over many parts of the country at night, attempting harassing attacks (known as Störangriffe) on specific targets (Störziele) such as aircraft factories and dock installations. Only small forces of German aircraft were so employed and, apart from keeping a large part of the population awake and interfering with night shift production, they achieved little. Few of the targets they sought were hit and most of the damage was confined to residential premises. The Germans soon learned, however, that unlike daylight operations, in which they sustained heavy losses, they could operate almost at will during the hours of darkness; true, there had been some early night losses, but once the Luftwaffe learned to fly above 12,000 feet — the limit of searchlight effectiveness — or on cloudy nights (which rendered searchlights useless), their losses were almost nil. This was further borne out in late August when Luftflotte 3 attempted several heavy night raids on Liverpool; however, although their losses were minimal, the results were not particularly good as the bombing lacked concentration. London, on the other hand, was nearer at hand and easier to find than Liverpool and, when the Luftwaffe launched its night Blitz on London, there was every confidence that greater concentration of bombing would be achieved with the low losses that experience led them to expect.

However, on dark and cloudy nights even London was difficult to find, for, quite early in the offensive, it became clear to the Germans that the RAF was interfering with its radio beacons and Knickebein. Accordingly, the decision was taken to relieve KGr100 of other tasks — mainly X-Verfahren guided attacks on aircraft factories upon which it had been engaged since August 13 — and use it to start fires in London to guide other, less well-equipped units. Thus was born the idea of a 'Beleuchter-' or 'Firelighter-' gruppe (sometimes called an 'Anzündergruppe') to serve as 'Pfadfinder' (Pathfinders) for the rank and file main bomber force. Unlike the later British Pathfinder Force, however, KGr100 did not mark the target with flares or other pyrotechnics, but always by means of fires started with incendiaries or small calibre HE bombs. Further, KGr100 was not always the first Gruppe to arrive over the target, nor were its aircraft concentrated over the target in time — they usually bombed with intervals of two to five minutes between each so that, on average, it could take up to an hour for, say, twelve aircraft to bomb. Invariably, during this time, other units joined in the bombing so there was a marked difference in the German and later British methods of 'pathfinding'. British Pathfinders, when they came into being, always provided target marking by means of pyrotechnic ground and sky markers upon which the main force bombed; they always opened the attack and provided pyrotechnic back-up, if required, throughout the raid.

In its new rôle KGr100 was always allocated a specific target, generally in central London and usually a power station, gasworks or dock installation, but on the night of September 17/18 its X-beams were aligned on Piccadilly Circus and over the Handley Page aircraft factory at Cricklewood in north London on the night of 22/23rd.

It was about this time that, again, the RAF's 'Y' Service achieved a major breakthrough. Based at Vannes in Brittany, KGr100 was not in teleprinter connection with its Fliegerkorps or Luftflotte headquarters and consequently it received its operations orders by means of Enigma-coded W/T messages. In turn, the Operations Command Post of KGr100 passed instructions for X-beam alignment, times of transmission, etc., to the Wotan I beam stations which it controlled, again using Enigma-coded W/T messages. And all these transmissions were monitored and recorded by the RAF's 'Y' Service. To the 'Y' Service operators they meant little, but gradually the secrets of the Enigma code were laid bare by the Government Code and Cypher School (GC and CS) at Bletchley Park and this led to the now well known 'Ultra' warnings. However, some time was yet to pass before GC and GS could regularly and speedily decode Luftwaffe Enigma messages and give advance warning of impending attacks. Meantime the 'Y' Service noted everything and passed it all on to Bletchley Park for attention.

The 'Fire Control' method of bombing, as the Germans called the KGr100-led attacks on dark or cloudy nights, was a success from the outset and gained for the Beleuchtergruppe a certain prestige among bomber units. However, the Fire-raiser rôle was not to be theirs alone for, expanding the system, the decision was soon taken to use II/KG55 and III/KG26 in a similar capacity. Although not equipped with any form of special radio aid, II/KG55 had considerable night operational experience and by the use of Knickebein and other conventional aids had displayed particular skill at finding targets at night, illuminating them by means of parachute flares and bombing them visually with very heavy HEs carried externally on their latest He 111P-4 aircraft. The third Beleuchtergruppe, III/KG26, had only recently regained operational status since re-equipping and re-training on special He 111H-5y aircraft equipped to use the Y-Verfahren precision bombing aid. Since then it had carried out a few special operations from its new base at Poix, including attacks by two aircraft on the Crown Tube Works at Birmingham on the night of October 9/10, and on October 12/13 against the Beckton Gasworks (by three aircraft), the Rover Motor Works at Coventry (one aircraft) and Aluminium Castings, Ltd., at Birmingham (another single aircraft). Neither No. 80 Wing nor the 'Y' Service picked up any signals concerned with these Y-Verfahren guided missions but this situation was not to last for long. From hereon, though, III/KG26 was to assist with target marking, but like KGr100 it was always allocated specific targets.

On Friday, September 6 — the eve of the London attack — a War Office photographer visited the 155th Anti-Aircraft Battery at Chadwell Heath, Essex which lay right in the path that the bombers would take less than 24 hours later. First picture in the sequence shows the personnel of the battery marching past the Gun Laying (GL) radar transmitter on the right.

BRITISH DEFENCES

The successful outcome of the daylight Battle of Britain owed much to the British early warning radar system, allied to a superior method of fighter control. The early warning enabled Fighter Controllers to put fighters in the right place at the right time, vectoring the interceptors into a position from where the airborne fighter leader could take over and complete the interception visually. The radar system, however, scanned only the sea approaches and over land the eyes and ears of the Observer (later Royal Observer) Corps took over. Nevertheless, despite its shortcomings, the system — at that time unique and in service only with the British — worked well. At night, however, it was a totally different matter. Even in bright moonlight it was impossible to bring night fighters into sufficiently close proximity for their crews to see the raiders. What was needed was an improved ground radar control system, directing night fighters into fairly close range from where airborne radar in the fighter could take over and complete the interception until, at very close range, visual contact and combat ensued. It was necessary, too, to have over-land radar in addition to scanning and controlling the over-sea approaches.

These basic requirements were well known to Air Chief Marshal Sir Hugh Dowding, the Air Officer Commanding-in-Chief Fighter Command, a far-sighted officer to whom goes much of the credit for the successful outcome of the Battle of Britain. His unstinting efforts had ensured for his Command an organisation, with men and equipment second to none, with which to meet the massed German daylight attacks of 1940. A brilliant officer he also anticipated the requirements necessary to defeat the night bomber, but until the scientists and engineers could produce the right equipment — production versions of experimental apparatus already in existence — he was forced to compromise. Fortunately the AOC-in-C Fighter Command, with other senior RAF officers, had rejected in time the pre-war philosophy that searchlights, directed by sound locators, were sufficient for the guidance of both fighters and AA guns alike. Early versions of a ground control radar, known as Ground Controlled Interception (GCI), had materialised on an experimental basis and an airborne radar (Airborne Interception or AI) had been tried, but by the summer of 1940 both, although full of promise, fell short of being operationally ready.

Also urgently required were small radar sets able to direct both AA guns and searchlights and here quicker progress had been made. Gun laying (GL) radar was already in service on a small scale and a searchlight control radar, otherwise known as SLC or 'Elsie', was also coming into use.

Although an Army Command, manned largely by Territorial units, AA Command, under General Sir Frederick Pile, came under the operational control of Dowding. Pile, although senior to Dowding, accepted this with good grace and, indeed, enthusiasm and as a result he was invariably consulted by Dowding as an equal rather than a subordinate. In consequence a high degree of understanding developed between the two men and their Commands, to the benefit of all.

The newly built 4.5in battery formed part of the 52nd Heavy 'Ack Ack' Regiment located at Chadwell Heath and Barking.

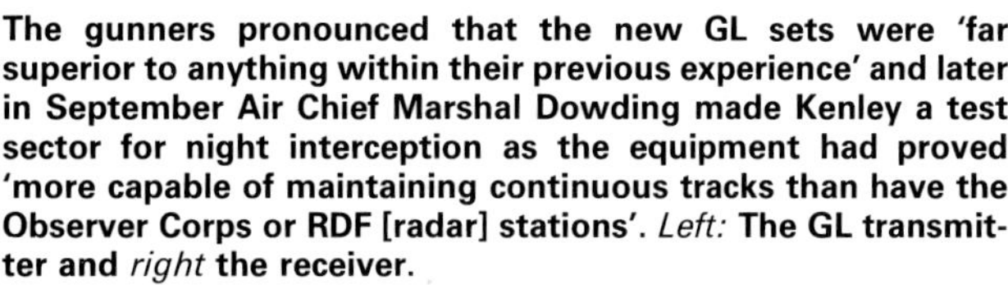

The gunners pronounced that the new GL sets were 'far superior to anything within their previous experience' and later in September Air Chief Marshal Dowding made Kenley a test sector for night interception as the equipment had proved 'more capable of maintaining continuous tracks than have the Observer Corps or RDF [radar] stations'. *Left:* **The GL transmitter and** *right* **the receiver.**

The British night defences suffered from a lack of basic equipment as well as deficiences in technology. At the outbreak of war AA Command had only 695 of an agreed establishment of 2,232 heavy guns, and many of those in service were of the obsolete 3-inch variety. Light AA guns were in similar short supply with only 253 of the planned 1,200 in use; searchlights, too, with 2,700 in service, were well below the required 4,700. As war production got under way these deficiences were slowly remedied, but even by July 1940, when air raids began in earnest, there were still only 1,200 heavy guns, 549 light guns and 3,932 searchlights in use. Action was possible only against 'seen' targets; otherwise blind, geographical 'barrages' were adopted by the guns. By mid-1940, however, many of the newer 3.7-inch and 4.5-inch guns were entering service.

Working closely with Fighter and AA Commands was Balloon Command. Its barrage balloons, largely manned by pre-war part-time airmen of the Auxiliary (later Royal

Right: **The Chadwell Heath battery was also equipped with the Mk VII sound locator — the old fashioned method of tracking targets but already acknowledged as being a failure.** *Below:* **The site of the battery today — compare with the views at the top of the page.**

The balloon barrage was manned by RAF personnel of Balloon Command created in November 1938 under the auspices of Fighter Command. This 'pig' is protecting an industrial site, 'somewhere in the north of England'.

Auxiliary) Air Force, served to force enemy aircraft to fly at a height at which they could best be engaged by AA gun-fire. They also prevented low flying or dive-bombing attacks and were an important, integrated part of the air defence scheme. Balloon Command also suffered a shortage of equipment, but this was the experience of every Command in the Royal Air Force including Fighter Command upon which the basic air defence of the country depended.

Before the war there had been no specialist night fighters and most of Fighter Command's units were designated day and night Squadrons. Experience soon showed, however, that a two-crew aircraft carrying AI radar and possessed of an extremely heavy armament was necessary and, with these requirements in mind, the Bristol Beaufighter was evolved. As an interim measure, an adaptation of the Bristol Blenheim Mk I light bomber entered service; with increased armament and an early form of AI the Blenheim Mk IF fighter was a step in the right direction but it was barely fast enough to do the job. Pressed into night fighter service, too, was the two-seat turret-equipped Boulton Paul Defiant Mk I, hopelessly outclassed by day during the Battle of Britain but expected to fulfil a non-radar equipped so-called 'Cat's Eyes' rôle until replaced by the Beaufighter. Also impressed in a Cat's Eyes rôle was the superb single-seat Hawker Hurricane Mk I, slightly inferior in performance to its Supermarine Spitfire counterpart but considered more suitable for night flying on account of its wide track undercarriage, robust construction and excellent reputation as a gun platform. Spitfires also flew by night, as did Gloster Gladiator biplane fighters, but normally only as day squadron aircraft flown by the more experienced squadron pilots and not as regular night fighters.

By late August 1940 six twin-engine night fighter squadrons were equipped with Blenheims but they were achieving little success. The vagaries of early AI sets, lack of proper night fighting training and the absence of GCI Stations all contributed to their failure and single-engine Cat's Eyes fighters, wandering around trying to find enemy aircraft caught in the beams of searchlights, achieved little more. The

A Boulton Paul Defiant Mk I night fighter. Defiant squadrons suffered disastrous losses in August and, relegated to night operations, the aircraft achieved only limited success as a 'cat's eye' or radar-less fighter, but with the Airborne Interception (AI) radar-equipped Bristol Blenheim Mk IF, bore the brunt of night fighting until the Beaufighter Mk IF entered service in numbers.

first Beaufighter was handed over to the RAF in late July, but it was not until September that the first five aircraft, equipped with AI and IFF (Identification, Friend or Foe, a transponder device that identified it as a friendly aircraft to ground radar stations) were issued to squadrons. Single aircraft went to Nos. 25, 29, 219, 600 and 604 Squadrons, but teething troubles and a production delay occasioned by a heavy daylight attack on the Filton factory in September further slowed deliveries. Gradually, however, matters improved and a big step forward occurred when, as an interim measure awaiting the arrival of ground GCI Stations to direct night fighters, use was made of the GL radar (intended for the guns of AA Command) for this purpose. A few GL sets were positioned on the approaches to London and brought new hope to Fighter Controllers literally struggling in the dark.

About the middle of October the first experimental GCI Station came into operation near Ford in Sussex. This equipment provided the GCI Controller with a Plan Position Indicator (PPI), a display upon which the positions of both the night fighter and the raider could be seen and which greatly facilitated the interception of the latter by the former.

To keep abreast of developments at first hand Dowding paid a visit to the Tangmere Sector on October 28 to see Elsie, the searchlight control radar, in action, but like so

A Hawker Hurricane Mk I night fighter of No. 87 Squadron. In addition to forming the equipment of several night fighter squadrons, Hurricanes of some day fighter units, flown by selected pilots, took part in Fighter Night patrols over certain target cities. In general, however, single seat fighters with no form of AI radar were of very limited value in the night air war over Britain during the winter of 1940–41.

The combination of Ground Controlled Interception (GCI) radar and the Bristol Beaufighter Mk I, fitted with AI radar and an unparalleled armament of four 20mm cannon and six .303in machine guns, revolutionised night fighting. Production delays, in part caused by a heavy German attack on Filton during the Battle of Britain, slowed the introduction of the Beaufighter into squadron service, but by the late spring of 1941 its success rate against German night raiders was mounting rapidly. This photograph of a new Beaufighter Mk IF, at the Bristol Aeroplane Company's factory airfield at Filton, clearly shows the nose 'barbed-arrow' and wing-mounted dipole antennae of its AI Mk IV radar.

many of the early trials the demonstration was not a success. Greater things were expected of the production version, however, and Dowding was confident of its eventual success.

Fighter Command had more than mere equipment worries, though, and a sharp reminder occurred on the night of October 30 when a sudden deterioration in the weather left four fighters on patrol in conditions of very low cloud. One managed to land safely at North Weald and a Defiant crash landed at Biggin Hill without injury to its crew but the others, a Blenheim and a Beaufighter of No. 219 Squadron, crashed with five fatal casualties.

Despite all the efforts of AA and Fighter Commands, German bombers continued to parade over London each night, largely unscathed and creating dreadful havoc. But Dowding and the scientists working with his Command left no stone unturned in their bid to defeat the night bomber; while the AI/GCI combination retained top priority other devices were tried including star shells fired from the ground to illuminate enemy aircraft and searchlights mounted in aircraft. Two other ideas gained Dowding's support and both were tried out by No. 219 Squadron; firstly, a Lorenz beam approach receiver was fitted in a Beaufighter of that squadron with the intention of 'hunting in the beam' for raiders using Knickebein for their approach to London. Secondly, it was decided to fit an infra-red viewer, a product of EMI, in another Beaufighter to examine the possibility of locating the hot engines, or exhaust gases generated by the engines, of enemy aircraft. Other schemes were the launching of a free balloon barrage (with explosive cannisters attached thereto on wires) in the path of approaching bombers, and the sowing of an aerial minefield (explosive cannisters suspended on long wires from parachutes and known as the Long Aerial Mine or LAM), again in front of approaching raiders. These last two proposals, known respectively under the code names 'Pegasus' and 'Mutton', involved the Command in a great deal of time and effort but failed as effective weapons.

London answers back. 'Keep on shooting away regardless' were Winston Churchill's instructions to Pile, even though the reassuring pounding deprived Londoners of a night's sleep. These are the guns of Hyde Park in action in 1940.

THE NIGHT BLITZ WIDENS

By early November there was little reason for the German war leaders to imagine that their assault on London was going to achieve the results expected. Invasion could not now be contemplated until the summer of 1941 at the earliest, but in any event by early winter Hitler was looking with some distrust at Russia, an enemy of old with whom, at that time, he shared an uneasy alliance. Fearing what he saw as an inevitable attack from the East, despite a non-aggression pact, Hitler decided to strike first. Expecting a quick victory in the spring he could then turn again to Britain; in the meantime, while he prepared for his Eastern Campaign in the utmost secrecy, Hitler ordered a widening of the air offensive against Britain. From hereon attacks were to be extended to major industrial centres and the great commercial ports upon which Britain depended for her very survival. London, as both a port and industrial centre, still qualified for the target list, but the overall aim was to prevent the country as a whole from expanding its war effort and recuperating from recent losses. The entire war economy of Britain was to be destroyed, and with it the morale of its people. Thus weakened, and with Russia vanquished in a short, sharp offensive in the spring, Britain would surely capitulate when the might of the Wehrmacht was again turned against her.

And so it came about that, for the first time in history, one nation prepared to subject another to a strategic bombing offensive of some length and magnitude. It was not a new concept but one that the disciples of Douhet, the renowned Italian theorist on strategic bombing, had advocated for years. Whether or not it would work in practice remained to be seen, but it was generally felt throughout the world, except in Great Britain, that if any country could make it work then that country was Germany.

KEN WAKEFIELD, 1988

LUFTWAFFE OPERATIONS AGAINST GREAT BRITAIN

Many of the former Armée de l'Air bases used by German bombers were grass airfields which became unsafe or unusable in wet weather. During the winter of 1940–41 much was done to improve them, sometimes using French civilian labour to lay concrete or tarmac runways, taxiways and dispersals. This picture shows such work in progress while mechanics are servicing the engines of the He 111P-4 in the foreground. One aircraft is seen to have a large high-explosive bomb slung externally beneath its fuselage centre section. The aircraft are believed to belong to KG55, the Griffon Geschwader based at Villacoublay, Chartres and Dreux.

After the Western campaign had been successfully concluded the aim of the Oberkommando der Wehrmacht (OKW) was a speedy decision in the war against Britain. This it hoped to achieve by an invasion of Britain which was to be preceded by German mastery of the air over the British Isles. Whereas, up to the conclusion of the Western campaign, the air war against Great Britain was restricted to very weak forces combating enemy merchant shipping and the enemy navy with bombs, torpedoes and mines along the East Coast, under the new circumstances which arose the total force of the Luftwaffe could be employed on a strategic offensive against Britain since the occupation of all areas opposite Britain with their airfields and their installations provided every facility for an enveloping strategic concentration. In spite of such a favourable position, the achievement of air mastery by the Luftwaffe presented a formidable task, even though the latter was superior in numbers and frequently also in quality of material.

Previously every opponent had been quickly and thoroughly beaten in so-called 'Blitz' campaigns. The opening of an offensive by the Luftwaffe coincided with the march into, or occupation of, the territory of the enemy state, as, for example, in the case of Norway. In all previous campaigns the Luftwaffe had been employed primarily in support of the Heer or Kriegsmarine. For the first time in military history an air force was going to conduct, independent of operations by other services, an offensive which aimed at decisively smashing the enemy air force.

With its brilliant achievements during the earlier part of the war, the Luftwaffe had now to attempt to answer the question of whether it is at all possible to destroy a modern air force solely through operational air warfare — as maintained by the Italian General Douhet — and what is more, to undermine the general fighting power of the enemy by massed air attack until he is ready to sue for peace.

Of all the enemy air forces operating in 1940, the British Air Force was the most formidable in battle. Encounters of German units with British Spitfire and Hurricane formations during the Western campaign, and above all along the Channel at the time of the British retreat to Dunkirk, had been the hardest so far.

In supporting the British Expeditionary Force and also their French ally in France, the British had brought only parts of their Royal Air Force into operation.

No attack worth mentioning had been undertaken by the enemy against Reich territory up to the summer of 1940. But wherever the enemy went on an offensive sweep, as for instance in the attack on the cruisers at Wilhelmshaven on September 4, and the thrust into the Heligoland Bight on December 19, 1939, the attacker distinguished himself by his tenacious courage in the face of grave losses.

It was to be expected that, having learnt the lessons of the campaigns to date which had been so powerfully influenced by the Luftwaffe, Britain would mobilise all her forces to meet the coming air war against her islands. Until 1940 the emphasis in the British aircraft industry lay in the expansion of a defensive air weapon which was at about the same technical level as that of the Germans.

Apart from this, the insular position of Britain makes it more difficult to attack. To reach targets, long distances had to be flown over sea, and the majority of aircrews lacked experience in this type of flying. Pilots of single-engined aircraft in particular had to overcome many misgivings when flying over the sea.

THE AIR WAR AGAINST GREAT BRITAIN JULY 1940–JUNE 1941

Until the opening of the German air offensive, enemy shipping in the Channel was attacked by limited forces of the Kanalkampfführer [Channel Command] *and by Fliegerkorps VIII, and off the East Coast of England by aircraft of Luftflotte 5.*

In addition, single aircraft in the course of a sustained armed reconnaissance attacked airfields, harbour installations and armament works in southern England and the Midlands, mostly by night, and in daytime only with the aid of suitable cloud cover. No important new information on the strength of the British defences could be gained during that period.

Masked by these operations which were not intended to bring about a decision of themselves, the strategic deployment of the Luftwaffe was completed in July 1940. Since the Norwegian campaign Luftflotte 5 (Generaloberst Stumpf) had been deployed in Norway and Denmark, Luftflotte 2 (Generalfeldmarschall Kesselring) in Holland, Belgium and Northern France, and to the south in France was Luftflotte 3 (Generalfeldmarschall Sperrle).

The invasion was scheduled to take place four weeks after the start of planned air attacks against the mainland of Britain, which were to be inaugurated on 'Adlertag' [Eagle Day]. *Preparations for the crossing had to be completed by September 20, 1940. It was planned to cross with the 6 and 9 Armee to various points on the south and south-east coasts of Britain, the centre of the attack lying between Dover and the Isle of Wight. The code-name for the invasion was 'Seelöwe'* [Sea-Lion].

Luftflotten 2 and 3 were to secure air superiority over southern England by operations against:

(a) Enemy aircraft, especially fighters in the air and on the ground.

(b) Bases and supply installations, especially those of night bomber units.

(c) R.A.F. ground units in the London area.

Luftflotte 5 was to pin down enemy defence forces by attacks on airfields in the Newcastle area.

The Command hoped that it would not require more than four days to smash the enemy fighter defences in southern England. Once this goal was reached the offensive was to be extended northwards, sector by sector, across the line King's Lynn–Leicester until all England was covered by day attacks.

The code-word 'Adlertag' was announced as applying to August 13. During the two previous days, air battles had developed over the Channel and off the English south coast in connection with bomber and fighter-bomber attacks on the harbour installations of Portland and Portsmouth and their neighbouring airfields, and these surpassed all previous air combats in the war against Britain both in scope and in intensity. The decisive battle for air mastery had begun. The 'Adlertag' did not bring the success hoped for. Because of unfavourable weather only a proportion of the attacks planned could be carried out. For the same reason the necessary fighter escort for the bomber units proved very inadequate. Losses for that day were very high. Not until August 15 was it possible to bring all forces into operation. The targets for attack by Luftflotten 2 and 5 were again the airfields in southern England and in the region of London. For the first time Luftflotte 5 attacked the combat area as ordered. Of the 801 bombers and dive-bombers and 1,149 single and twin-engined fighter aircraft of Luftflotten 2 and 3 employed, 73 were lost. The total losses by the enemy were given as at least 143 aircraft.

At the beginning of the daylight attacks the principle of giving bomber formations the minimum necessary fighter escort only so as to leave the majority of the fighters free to pursue their real task of destroying the enemy in open combat, was generally accepted. In the very first days of the air war, however, it became evident that the numerous dogged British fighter pilots who were supplemented by formations of volunteers from nations conquered by Germany, made operations by bomber and Stuka units so difficult that it was necessary to have as escort two and even three times the strength of the formation which was to be escorted. The attack and escort tactics of each German fighter Geschwader was specified by its Kommodore. There was no standard tactical procedure. The tactical unit of the bomber and Stuka Geschwader was the Gruppe, which was employed on the same principles as during the Western campaign.

In spite of strong German fighter escorts, the British fighter defence caused the Stuka formations unusually heavy losses, so that further use by day of the Ju 87 against targets on the British mainland had to be abandoned after a few attacks. The performance of the Me 110 also failed to satisfy expectations.

In comparison with other theatres of war, reconnaissance proved very difficult. Heer reconnaissance aircraft formations hardly ever reached the British coast.

The first German aircraft to come down on British soil during the Second World War scattered itself over this valley in the Orkneys. The Junkers Ju 88A-1 of I/KG30 was hit by anti-aircraft fire during an air raid on Scapa Flow on October 17, 1940 and exploded over the island of Hoy. ***(See Volume 1, page 39)***

After the first week of this decisive battle, the German official communiqué reported for the period August 12–19, 624 British aircraft destroyed, 174 German aircraft missing.

Destruction effected on enemy airfields subjected to repeated attacks was considerable by current standards. Yet during the following weeks, mastery of the air over southern England could not be achieved.

On August 20 the battle order of the Oberbefelshaber der Luftwaffe was as follows: 'Continue the fight against the British Air Force until further notice with the aim of weakening British fighter strength. The enemy is to be forced by ceaseless attacks to bring his fighter formations into operation. In addition, aircraft factories . . . and R.A.F. ground units are to be attacked by single aircraft by day and night when the weather does not permit larger formations to operate.'

The battle against the British Air Force was continued on the lines of this directive without a decision being obtained. Recognising this fact, the Oberkommando der Wehrmacht decided in September to switch the main weight of the air offensive to London, the heart of the enemy power. Incomparably greater success than hitherto could be anticipated from this policy. For while the main objective of wearing down the British fighter forces was not abandoned, economic war from the air could be embarked upon with full fury, and the morale of the civilian population subjected at the same time to a heavy strain.

The enemy himself provided the necessary justification in international law for this phase of the war.

During the month of August nightly penetrations by the British Air Force into Reich territory had increased. For the first time since the beginning of the war Berlin was attacked on August 26. In view of the systematic attacks by Britain on non-military targets in the hinterland during the Western campaign, the Führer announced on September 4 that he intended the Luftwaffe to carry out counter-measures. In his speech the Führer stated: 'You will understand that we are now giving our reply night after night, and with increasing force . . . If they [the British] *declare that they will attack our cities on a large scale, then we will wipe out their cities!'*

Three days after this speech, on September 7, the air war began on London, which was the target for the following weeks. For this the bomber units of Luftflotte 5 had been moved to the zone of Luftflotte 2. (Luftflotte 5 did not carry out any further bomber operations against Britain during the war.) The Oberbefehlshaber der Luftwaffe had personally taken over command, as was announced in the war communiqué of September 8.

The few daylight attacks by strong bomber formations (200–300 bombers of all types were over the target every time) achieved good results against dock and supply installations along the Thames. Major conflagrations caused extensive devastation. These attacks were continued until September 27. Losses suffered by formations led thereafter to a reduction of the forces engaged on any single daylight attack to one Ju 88 Gruppe, and from the beginning of October to the use of fighter-bomber formations, only (Me 109s each carrying one SC 250 bomb). The individual bomber Gruppe as well as the fighter-bomber formations, with a strength of up to 120 aircraft, was escorted in its outward and return flights by 2–3 fighter Geschwader. When the weather situation did not permit attacks by regular formations in the prescribed form, use was made of cloud cover for nuisance raids by single aircraft. The month of October saw the continuation of the war of attrition against London and the final shifting of the main weight of attack from daylight to night raids. In September, these had been carried on simultaneously with daylight attacks.

From the middle of November the massed night attacks were extended to the industrial cities and ports of the Midlands. The central feature of the prosecution of the war remained the attack on London, however, attacks by day being continued as already described. The tactics of air war by night developed during the ensuing winter months. Only those details of tactics which differ from those now applied will be mentioned here.

Concentration of attack in one place and at one time was not necessary because of the weak defences. The individual units proceeded to the targets along separate courses. To increase the strain on the morale of the population, the duration of the attack was prolonged as much as possible. Only the weather rendered it necessary to concentrate the attack. On the other hand, attacking those parts of the target area where the most important economic and industrial targets were sited was already being attempted. For this purpose specific targets were allocated to units in each attack. To facilitate locating of targets and the individual objectives within the target areas themselves, the major attacks were carried out by moonlight. London, offering a large target area, was attacked chiefly during moonless nights.

TONNES OF BOMBS (ALL TYPES) AIMED AT BRITISH CITIES IN NIGHT ATTACKS AUGUST 12, 1940–JUNE 26, 1941

Target Area	*Weight in Tonnes*			*Number of Significant Attacks**
	High Explosive	*Incend-iaries*	*Total Weight*	
London	14,754	1,135	15,919	79
Liverpool–Birkenhead	2,796	304	3,100	14
Birmingham	2,057	225	2,282	11
Bristol	1,237	248	1,485	10
Plymouth	1,125	207	1,332	8
Portsmouth	1,091	180	1,271	5
Southampton	971	88	1,059	7
Glasgow	748	176	924	4
Coventry	797	69	866	2
Manchester	703	106	809	4
Sheffield	587	70	657	3
Hull	474	57	531	3
Swansea	363	103	466	4
Cardiff	273	63	336	3
Belfast	180	25	205	2
Other targets	550	60	610	–
Totals:	28,736	3,116	31,852	159

Note: The above statistics are taken from this Staff Study prepared by Hauptmann Otto Bechtle and entitled 'Der Einsatz der Luftwaffe gegen England, ihre Taktik und die Lehren 1940–43' (published 2.4.44 in Berlin-Gatow). However, a comparison of the weight of high-explosive figures contained in this Study with those given on page 28 (compiled from Luftwaffe High Command Situation Reports) reveals a number of discrepancies.

* 'Significant Attacks', for the purpose of this Table, are those in which approximately 50 tonnes or more of high-explosive were aimed at target cities. It should be borne in mind, however, that the above figures do not necessarily reflect the true weight of bombs that actually fell on the target area indicated (because of navigational errors, etc.).

The dropping of numerous incendiary bombs at the start of the attack had proved its value as a method of target marking. He 111s of Kampfgruppe 100, the so-called Anzündergruppe [Fire-Raiser Group] *had taken over this special task. This Gruppe made the fullest use of specially narrow beams* [X and Y beams], *which at that time could not be jammed, to help locate the target. Bombs were dropped with the aid of the GörzVisier 219 or the Lofte bomb-sight in high altitude attacks of 2000–6000 metres. The majority of the HEs were of 250 to 500kg calibre. In addition, very heavy bombs up to a calibre of 2500kg and aircraft mines were used sporadically. The ratio of HEs to incendiaries was usually 1:1.*

As compared with today [1944], *the enemy defence was poor. Single and twin-engined night fighters appeared only sporadically over the mainland and the Channel, but during the winter of 1940–41 numerous long-range night fighters interfered quite effectively in some cases with take-offs and landings. The night fighter defence became more effective from the middle of March 1941 only. From that time the importance of the AA defence was less than that of the night fighters.*

From time to time the enemy succeeded in diverting crews from their prescribed targets by cleverly designed dummy installations. As an example of a major attack diverted by decoy artifices, mention must be made of the attack on Liverpool on the night of November 29–30. Major conflagrations had been faked by pouring burning oil on the Dee estuary west of Birkenhead and the majority of the crews had taken these for fires in Liverpool.

Apart from these concentrated attacks, nuisance raids on aircraft industry and on the ground establishments, etc., of British night fighter units were accorded increased importance. A few selected and experienced crews carried these out during the night and in poor weather conditions, taking advantage of the element of surprise.

The unfavourable weather associated with this season restricted the activity of fighter units, but the air superiority of the Luftwaffe over the Channel and almost as far as the English coast was maintained.

The month of November saw 23 major Luftwaffe attacks on vital British centres. In each attack 100–600 tonnes of bombs were dropped on these targets. During the period November 1–15, 1940, 1,800 bombers dropped 1900 tonnes of HEs and 17,500 incendiary bombs on London alone. Of the towns attacked, Coventry, a centre of the British aircraft industry, must be mentioned. During the night of November 14–15, 454 aircraft raided this town, dropping 600 tonnes of HE and incendiary bombs. Coventry has become a by-word wherever operational air-war is discussed as a result of the extensive damage caused by this raid.

The enemy's hopes of a slackening in the attacks under autumn and winter weather conditions were not fulfilled. When at all possible, sorties were carried out, the peculiarities of the various aircraft types being taken into account. If, for instance, Ju 88 and He 111 Gruppen could not operate because they needed a longer runway for take-off and had a higher landing speed, Do 17s took off in Gruppen on their own. As a result of these tactics, losses due to bad weather conditions (such as faulty landing, icing-up, bailing out when badly off course) outnumbered those due to enemy action.

However, this tempo could not be maintained during the following three months. Apart from the numerous QBI weather reports [QBI=bad weather and visibility], *the condition of many airfields prevented flying (taxi-ing areas waterlogged). At that time only a few airfields in the West had runways and concrete taxi-ing lanes.*

Not until March 1941 did it become possible to resume the previous battle tactics with heavy new offensive blows. The Balkan campaign and a division of forces in support of Italy in the Mediterranean area brought about no noticeable decline in the number of aircraft in operation as compared with the autumn months, because not only had the units been brought up to strength, but new ones re-equipped with new aircraft types had been supplied from Germany.

The heaviest night attack on London was made in April, with a total of 711 aircraft over the target (the operation consisted of a double attack), dropping a bomb load of 1026 tonnes of HE and 150 tonnes of incendiary bombs. Also worthy of mention are the two heavy attacks on Glasgow in May 1941.

On May 22, HQ of Luftflotte 2 was moved to Poznan. At the beginning of June the units belonging to this Luftflotte also moved to the East. In the West, Luftflotte 3 took over command of all Luftwaffe forces remaining there.

HAUPTMANN OTTO BECHTLE,
BERLIN-GATOW, FEBRUARY 2, 1944

Unteroffizier Ambrosius, parachuted to safety and became one of the most talkative of prisoners at CSDIC (page 32). The other three crewmen, Oberleutnant Flaemig, Unteroffizier Attenburger and Obergefreiter Faust are officially listed as missing; what remains were found after the explosion of what one presumes was the bomb load were buried in these two graves in Lyness cemetery — the German word 'Soldat' being used as a generic term for 'serviceman'.

SATURDAY, SEPTEMBER 7

The enemy activity was very slight during the morning with only about 30 aircraft crossing the coast, when Dover and Hawkinge were attacked. At 1635 a large attack developed in which some 350 aircraft made for the Thames Estuary, East London and aerodromes, North and South London. By 1815 all raiders were proceeding home.

In the afternoon attacks considerable major damage was done and many large fires started. Reconnaissance flights were also made over Liverpool, Manchester, Bristol

In September 1940 Hermann Göring, created Reichsmarschall on July 19 following the defeat of France, travelled to the Channel coast to take personal charge of the attack on London. From September 6–8 his forward headquarters was established in the Hague (Netherlands), moving to Ronce (Belgium) from the 8th to 15th, and Boulogne (France) from the 15th to 17th. On the 18th it was located at Coudraix, near Beauvais. On the day the new phase in the battle commenced, Saturday, September 7, the Reichsmarschall's personal train 'Robinson' took him to the Pas de Calais where he proceeded with Generalfeldmarschall Kesselring, General der Flieger Bruno Lörzer, commander of II Fliegerkorps, and others to Cap Griz Nez to watch the aircraft set out for Britain. This rather well-worn photograph — of poor quality as German archives do not hold the original print and everyone has to use a copy held at the Imperial War Museum in London — supposedly taken on the 7th, shows Göring (sixth from right) flanked by Lörzer (in the forage cap or Fliegermütze), Kesselring and what appears to be General der Flieger Kastner, Chief of Personnel in the RLM.

Forty years later the smashed remains of the Grosser Kurfürst cross-Channel battery lie amid patches of scrub behind the grey nose of France — the closest the Reichsmarschall came to a Britain he attempted to bomb into submission.

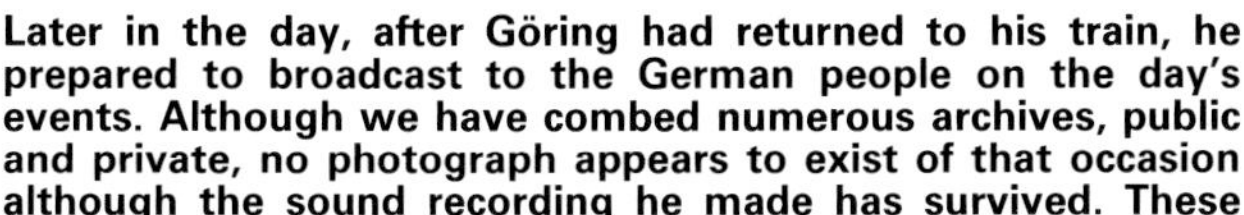

Later in the day, after Göring had returned to his train, he prepared to broadcast to the German people on the day's events. Although we have combed numerous archives, public and private, no photograph appears to exist of that occasion although the sound recording he made has survived. These pictures found in the French Armée collection in Paris, although again of poor quality, are obviously of the same era as Lörzer and Kastner are again prominent. The Reichsmarschall wears his newly-awarded Grand Cross of the Iron Cross, another special creation just for him.

Channel, Norfolk, Harwich, Yorkshire, Lowestoft and Biggin Hill during the morning.

No. of bombs dropped: not available.

Following the mass attack on London during the afternoon, enemy activity by night commenced at 2010 and the country was not clear until 0500 the following morning. Between five and eight raids were continuously in progress over the Greater London area up till 0430 hours on the 8th. Areas mainly affected were West Ham, Poplar, Stepney, Southwark and Bermondsey. The main objectives were docks, oil, road and rail communications and industrial establishments in the Thames Estuary and Northolt aerodrome. Approximately 120 aircraft working singly were used in these operations. Large fires developed on the banks of the Thames which were seen from a very great distance and greatly assisted the enemy's activities.

A few minor incidents occurred during the night in eastern and south-eastern counties, but apart from these enemy activity appears to have been concentrated solely on London.

No. of bombs dropped: not yet available. Enemy aircraft casualties: destroyed 88, probable 22, damaged 33.

Some evacuation in Thurrock, Tilbury, Purfleet. Reinforcements of the Fire Services have been despatched to London from various places including Birmingham and Nottingham, and the latter have also been reinforced, in case of emergency, from Manchester. All London Fire Services will be at full strength tonight.

A determined attack was made on the London Dock at 1635 hours, starting many fires which attracted considerable bombing during the night. This attack was the heaviest yet made and combined with the fact that there is a considerable concentration of barges on the French coast, suggests that it may be a preliminary to an attempted invasion. If this is so, further bombing on a large scale, probably directed at ports, must be expected. There was practically no activity during the night over the rest of England which may mean that the enemy is beginning to feel the heavy loss of personnel which he has suffered, or is conserving his reserves.

Given the issuing of the chilling Invasion Alert 'Imminent' on this day, it was paradoxical (and to the British no doubt ominous) that, despite the fine weather and beyond some early 'sparring', no large German raids materialised until late afternoon. Then, as Luftwaffe aircraft formed-up over Calais, where Göring and his entourage were assembled to witness events, it became clear to RAF Fighter Controllers, through the RDF network, that this was the largest raid yet mounted. Shortly after 4.15 p.m. almost 1,000 German aircraft, stepped-up in ranks from 14,000 to 23,000 feet, were crossing the English coast between Deal and Margate; a single huge phalanx forging on towards its target — London. 20 British squadrons rose to meet them and the vast vault of sky above the eastern approaches to London and the capital itself witnessed furious combat the like of which had never before been realised in the history of aerial warfare. Through sheer weight of numbers many bombers reached and bombed their targets in London's dockland starting huge fires and leaving vast areas devastated. Nearly 1,800 Londoners were killed or seriously injured. As conflagrations raged through tracts of eastern London's dockland, a second wave of bombers dumped their loads onto the flames in raids lasting throughout the night and on into the early morning. The attack on London and the subsequent night bombing of the capital were to provide the let-up that was needed by the RAF exhausted by the assault on its infrastructure, and tired British squadrons were able to gain some respite and gather themselves afresh. As events were later to prove, this momentous day, which witnessed the first and last mass daylight attack on London, was a turning point in the eventual outcome of the Battle of Britain. It cost the Luftwaffe the loss of 40 aircraft, 14 more being damaged on operations. Another machine was destroyed and 4 more damaged in accidents. Many fell in Britain:

ANNOUNCER: *The moment facing each of us here in this place again is one which we shall never forget. This hour has seen our own plane crews assembled within a few kilometres of the English capital, and striking for the first time at the enemy's heart . . . The Reichsmarschall is leaving his train and coming past us. He sees us. Is this what he was intending? Is he really coming? Yes. He is coming! The Reichsmarschall is coming from his train and is coming to the microphone.*

GÖRING: *I now want to take this opportunity of speaking to you, to say this moment is a historic one. As a result of the provocative British attacks on Berlin on recent nights the Führer has decided to order a mighty blow to be struck in revenge against the capital of the British Empire. I personally have assumed the leadership of this attack, and today I have heard above me the roaring of the victorious German squadrons which now, for the first time, are driving towards the heart of the enemy in full daylight, accompanied by countless fighter squadrons. Enemy defences were as we expected beaten down and the target reached, and I am certain that our successes have been as massive as the boldness of our plan of attack and the fighting spirit of our crews deserve. In any event this is an historic hour, in which for the first time the German Luftwaffe has struck at the heart of the enemy.*

GERMAN WIRELESS BROADCAST, SEPTEMBER 7, 1940

4(F)/14 Messerschmitt Bf 110C-5 (2208). Shot down by Red Section of No. 602 Squadron (Flying Officer P. C. Webb, Pilot Officer S. N. Rose and Pilot Officer A. Lyall) during photo-reconnaissance sortie over the south coast of England. Exploded under attack and fell into the sea 10 miles south of Bembridge 9.55 a.m. Lt. H. Goedsche killed. Oberlt. G. Russell missing. Aircraft 5F+MM lost.

The body of the pilot from this aircraft, Hans Goedsche, was later washed ashore and buried at Shoreham on November 22.

1/JG2 Messerschmitt Bf 109E-4 (3909). Suffered engine failure during escort sortie to London and forced-landed at St. Radegund's Abbey, near Dover 6.30 p.m. Oberlt. A. Götz captured unhurt. Aircraft 8+ a write-off.

Site investigated by the Brenzett Aeronautical Museum but no relics discovered. Site later re-examined by Steve Vizard and John Ellis and surface relics including 20mm ammunition discovered.

5/JG2 Messerschmitt Bf 109E-1 (3320). Engine damaged in fighter attack during escort sortie over London. Pursued south at low level by Flying Officer W. J. Scott of No. 41 Squadron and eventually crashed in the Channel off Folkestone 6.00 p.m. Uffz. W. Melchert captured unhurt. Aircraft 6+— lost.

4/JG26 Messerschmitt Bf 109E-4 (5385). Sortied to cover withdrawal of bombers returning from attack on London. Engaged by fighters and hit in petrol tank and oil cooler so forced-landed at Sheerlands Farm, Pluckley 6.00 p.m. Oberlt. H. Krug (Staffelkapitän) captured unhurt. Aircraft 12+— a write-off.

'Tiger's-head' staffel insignia removed by troops in 1940 and donated to Kent Battle of Britain Museum by local landowner, now in the Hawkinge Aeronautical Trust collection.

6/JG26 Messerschmitt Bf 109E-4 (735). Both radiators severely damaged in fighter attack during escort sortie over London. Retired south but finally abandoned over the Channel off Shakespeare Cliff, Dover 7.00 p.m. Uffz. E. Braun baled out and captured unhurt. Aircraft lost.

1/JG27 Messerschmitt Bf 109E-4 (5390). Shot down in combat with fighters during escort sortie over London. Probably that attacked by Flight Lieutenant G. ff. Powell-Shedden of No. 242 Squadron. Crashed and burned out at Park Corner Farm, Hacton Lane, Cranham 5.10 p.m. Lt. G. Genske baled out and captured unhurt. Aircraft a write-off.

3/JG51 Messerschmitt Bf 109E-1 (4840). Reported hit by AA fire during escort sortie to London but possibly that attacked by Pilot Officer J. W. Broadhurst of No. 222 Squadron. Crashed at Oad Street, Borden, near Sittingbourne 5.45 p.m. Gefr. H. Werner baled out and captured unhurt. Aircraft 9+ a write-off.

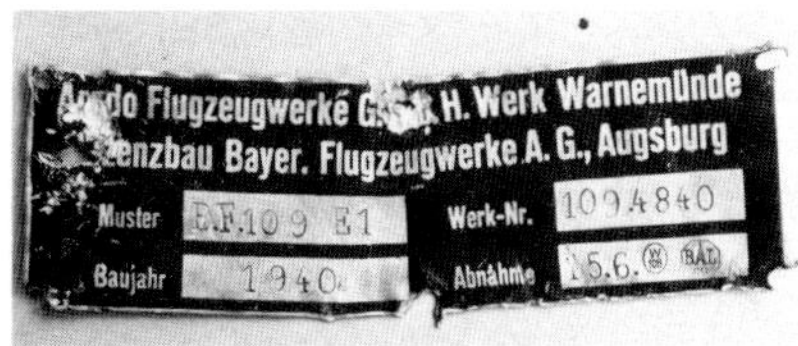

Site excavated by Steve Vizard in 1982 and Daimler-Benz DB 601 engine unearthed together with aircraft maker's plate confirming identity '4840', flare pistol and many other interesting items.

GERMAN LONG-RANGE RECONNAISSANCE AND LONG-RANGE BOMBER UNITS IN THE WEST, SEPTEMBER 7, 1940

Unit	*Commanding Officer*	*Equipment*	*Strength*	*No. of aircraft serviceable*	*Base*
LUFTFLOTTE 2 (Brussels) (Generalfeldmarschall Albert Kesselring)					
1(F)/22	–	Do 17			
		Bf 110	13	9	Lille
2(F)/122	–	Ju 88			
		He 111	10	9	Brussels/Melsbroek
4(F)/122	–	Ju 88			
		He 111			
		Bf 110	13	9	Brussels
I Fliegerkorps (Beauvais) (Generaloberst Ulrich Grauert)					
5(F)/122	Hptm Boehm	Ju 88			
		He 111	11	11	Haute-Fontaine
Stab/KG76	Obstltn Fröhlich	Do 17	6	3	Cormeilles-en-Vexin
I/KG76	Hptm Lindeiner	Do 17	26	19	Beauvais/Tille
II/KG76	–	Ju 88	27	21	Creil
III/KG76	Obstltn Genth	Do 17	24	17	Cormeilles-en-Vexin
Stab/KG77	Obstltn von Wühlisch	Ju 88	1	1	Laon
I/KG77	–	Ju 88	36	31	Laon
II/KG77	–	Ju 88	32	25	Asch-Nord
III/KG77	Maj Kless	Ju 88	30	19	Laon
Stab/KG1	Obstltn Exss	He 111	7	5	Rosiéres-en-Santerre
I/KG1	Maj Maier	He 111	36	22	Montdidier and Clairmont
II/KG1	Obstln Kosch	He 111	36	23	Montdidier and Nijmegen
III/KG1	Maj Fanelsa	Ju 88	9	–	Rosiéres-en-Santerre
Stab/KG30	Obstltn Loebel	Ju 88	1	1	Brussels
I/KG30	Maj Dönsch	Ju 88	10	1	Brussels
II/KG30	Hptmn Hinkelbein	Ju 88	30	24	Gilze-Rijen
Stab/KG26	Obstltn Fuchs	He 111	6	3	Gilze-Rijen
I/KG26	Maj Busch	He 111	25	7	Moerbeke and Courtrai
II/KG26	–	He 111	26	7	Gilze-Rijen
II Fliegerkorps (Ghent) (General Bruno Lörzer)					
1(F)/122	–	Ju 88	5	3	Holland
7(F)/LG2	–	Bf 110	14	9	–
Stab/KG2	Oberst Fink	Do 17	6	6	Saint-Leger
I/KG2	Maj Gutzmann	Do 17	19	12	Cambrai
II/KG2	Maj Weitkus	Do 17	31	20	Saint-Leger
III/KG2	Maj Fuchs	Do 17	30	20	Cambrai
Stab/KG53	Oberst Stahl	He 111	5	3	Lille
I/KG53	Maj Kauffmann	He 111	23	19	Lille
II/KG53	Maj Gruber	He 111	29	7	Lille
III/KG53	Maj Edler von Braun	He 111	19	4	Lille
Stab/KG3	Oberst von Chamier-Glisczinski	Do 17	6	5	Le Culot
I/KG3	Obstltn Gabelmann	Do 17	29	25	Le Culot
II/KG3	Hptm Pilger	Do 17	27	23	Antwerp/Deurne
III/KG3	Hptm Rathmann	Do 17	28	19	Saint-Trond
ErproGr210	Hptm Lutz	Bf 110			
		Bf 109	26	17	Denain/Valenciennes
IX Fliegerdivision (IX. Fliegerkorps from 16.10.40) (Soesterberg) (Generalleutnant Joachim Coeler)					
3(F)/122	–	Ju 88			
		He 111	11	10	Eindhoven
Stab/KG4	Obstltn Rath	He 111	5	5	Soesterberg
I/KG4	Hptm Meissner	He 111	37	16	Soesterberg
II/KG4	Maj Dr Wolff	He 111	37	30	Eindhoven
III/KG4	Hptm Bloedorn	Ju 88	30	14	Amsterdam/Schipol
KGr126	Maj Schellmann	He 111	33	26	Nantes
Stab/KG40	Obstltn Geisse	Ju 88	2	1	Bordeaux/Merignac
KüFlGr106	–	He 115			
		Do 18	28	16	Brittany and Borkum
LUFTFLOTTE 3 (Saint-Cloud) (Generalfeldmarschall Hugo Sperrle)					
1(F)/123	–	Ju 88			
		Do 17	10	7	Paris
2(F)/123	Maj von Obernitz	Ju 88			
		Do 17	10	8	Paris
3(F)/123	–	Ju 88			
		Do 17	12	9	Paris/Buc

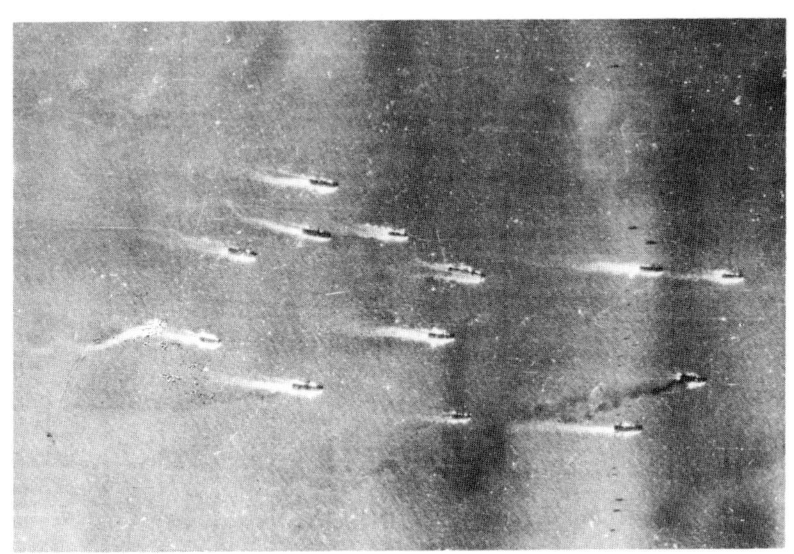

The Aufklärungsverbände were the units carrying out photo-reconnaissance, the 'F' (for Fern) denoting its use in the long-range rôle. This picture taken in September off Clacton-on-Sea shows an East Coast convoy with one of the vessels burning.

IV Fliegerkorps (Sèvres with forward HQ at Dinard) (General Kurt Pflugbeil)

3(F)/121	–	Do 17	10	6	NW France
Stab/LG1	Oberst Bülowius	Ju 88	3	3	Orléans/Bricy
I/LG1	Hptm Kern	Ju 88	27	13	Orléans/Bricy
II/LG1	Maj Cramer	Ju 88	31	19	Orléans/Bricy
III/LG1	Maj Dr Bormann	Ju 88	30	19	Châteaudun
KGr806	–	Ju 88	27	18	Nantes and Caen/Carpiquet
Stab/KG27	Oberst Behrendt	He 111	7	4	Tours
I/KG27	Maj Ulbricht	He 111	35	13	Tours
II/KG27	Hptmn Eschenauer	He 111	32	15	Dinard and Bourges
III/KG27	Maj Freiherr von Sternburg	He 111	20	13	Rennes/Saint-Jaques
KGr100	Hptm Aschenbrenner	He 111	28	7	Vannes/Meucon
KGr606	Maj Hahn	Do 17	33	29	Brest/Lanveoc-Poulmic and Cherbourg
3(F)/31	–	Do 17 Bf 110	9	5	Saint-Brieuc
I/KG40	Maj Petersen	FW 200	7	4	Bordeaux/Merignac

V Fliegerkorps (Villacoublay) (General Ritter von Greim)

4(F)/121	–	Ju 88 Do 17	13	5	Normandy
4(F)/14	–	Bf 110 Do 17	12	9	Normandy
Stab/KG51	Obstltn Schulz-Heyn	Ju 88	1	–	Orly
I/KG51	Hptmn von Greiff	Ju 88	33	13	Melun/Villaroche
II/KG51	Maj Winkler	Ju 88	34	17	Orly
III/KG51	Maj Marienfeld	Ju 88	34	27	Etampes
Stab/KG54	Obstltn Höhne	Ju 88	1	–	Evreux
I/KG54	Hptm von Heydebreck	Ju 88	30	18	Evreux
II/KG54	Obstltn Köster	Ju 88	26	14	St André-de-l'Eure
Stab/KG55	Obstltn Korte	He 111	6	6	Villacoublay
I/KG55	Maj Roeber	He 111	27	20	Dreux
II/KG55	Maj Kless	He 111	30	22	Chartres
III/KG55	Maj Schlemmell	He 111	25	20	Villacoublay

LUFTFLOTTE 5 (Kristiansund) (Generaloberst Hans-Jürgen Stumpff)

X Fliegerkorps (Stavanger) (General Hans Geisler)

2(F)/22	–	Do 17	9	5	Stavanger
3(F)/22	–	Do 17	9	5	Stavanger
1(F)/120	–	He 111 Ju 88	13	2	Stavanger
1(F)/121	–	He 111 Ju 88	7	2	Stavanger and Aalborg
1/506	–	He 115	8	6	Stavanger
2/506	–	He 115	8	5	Trondheim and Tromsö
3/506	Hptm Bergmann	He 115	8	6	List

3/JG51 Messerschmitt Bf 109E-3 (5091). Hit in petrol tank during combat with fighters following escort sortie over London. Abandoned aircraft crashed and burned out at Bethersden 5.45 p.m. Uffz. H. zur Lage baled out and captured unhurt. Aircraft 7+ a write-off.

Site excavated by Steve Vizard and surviving remains unearthed.

9/JG51 Messerschmitt Bf 109E-4 (4097). Radiator damaged in fighter attack during escort sortie over London. Abandoned aircraft crashed at Little Clacton 4.59 p.m. Uffz. K. Koch baled out and captured unhurt. Aircraft 11+I a write-off.

1/JG77 Messerschmitt Bf 109E-4 (5811). Engaged by fighters, probably Spitfires of No. 602 Squadron, and oil cooler damaged in combat during fighter-bomber sortie. Possibly that attacked by Squadron Leader A. V. R. Johnstone. Forced-landed at Rolvenden 5.45 p.m. Oberfw. G. Goltzsche captured unhurt. Aircraft 11+ a write-off.

6/KG4 Heinkel He 111P-4 (3078). Hit by AA and one engine disabled during bombing sortie over London. Abandoned aircraft believed crashed in the Thames Estuary off the Isle of Grain 10.40 p.m. Uffz. R. Klein and Gefr. H. Backmann baled out and captured unhurt. Oberlt. W. Klotz and Uffz. W. Wolf killed. Uffz. A. Knoll missing. Aircraft 5J+JP lost.

Stab I/KG53 Heinkel He 111H-3 (6912). Both engines disabled in attacks by fighters during weather reconnaissance sortie over East Anglia. Probably that claimed by Pilot Officer A. C. Cochrane of No. 257 Squadron. Ditched in the sea off Harwich 6.00 p.m. Oberlt. A. Weber, Oberfw. M. Winter and Fw. F. Kempgens took to their dinghy and captured unhurt. Oberfw. G. Müller and Flgr. H. Hönig missing believed drowned. Aircraft A1+AB lost.

5/KG53 Heinkel He 111H-2 (2777). Attacked by fighters, probably Flight Lieutenant G. R. Edge and Flying Officer L. C. Murch of No. 253 Squadron, following bombing attack on Thameshaven. Then port engine disabled in attack by Flight Lieutenant D. G. Parnall of No. 249 Squadron and hit by ground-fire prior to forced-landing at Old Marsh, Isle of Grain 5.30 p.m. Crew set fire to aircraft. Oberlt. H. Bräuer and Oberfw. A. Pitzka captured unhurt. Gefr. E. Urich and Uffz. F. Bergmann captured wounded. Obergefr. P. Neumann killed. Aircraft A1+DN a write-off.

4/KG54 Junkers Ju 88A-1 (6032). Crashed in the North Sea during night sortie to London — exact cause unknown. Oberfw. H. Schmitz, Oberfw. H. Bremer and Fw. E. Kalucza killed. Fw. H. Lieberknecht missing. Aircraft B3+AM lost.

The body of Heinrich Schmitz was washed ashore at Southwold on October 25 and buried in Ipswich cemetery. Reinterred after the war in the Soldatenfriedhof at Cannock Chase, his date of death is there recorded as September 8.

The deaths of Hans Bremer and Erwin Kalucza were also confirmed in German records in a report dated 7.11.1941. As no mention of them has been found in British records consulted, it is assumed that they were recovered by German authorities.

Apart from the odd early morning Aufklärungs sorties to report on the effectiveness of the previous day's attacks, the plotting tables in Britain on Saturday, September 7 remained ominously bare of any major activity. Not until 4.00 p.m. (5.00 p.m. by German Central European Time in France) did the first radar contact indicate that something was afoot over the Pas de Calais. Quickly the plots built up to massive proportions as wave after wave appeared on the flickering screens and the Observer Corps began confirming raids of 20+ ... 30+ ... and 50+ ... crossing the coastline on a twenty-mile front. At the mouth of the Thames, the Shell Mex BP Works on the northern bank at Thames Haven was high on the priority list of Luftwaffe industrial targets and had already been hit two days before. Now it was to be struck again together with Thames Board Mills and Jurgens Margarine Works. ***Top and right:*** **The same fire seen through different eyes.**

Post-war modernisation has meant that all the old wartime 2,000-gallon tanks have been replaced and the house beside the railway line, formerly the Pig and Whistle pub but latterly used for the plant manager's accommodation, demolished.

Meanwhile another recce aircraft on Sortie GB1066 was busy recording the progress of I Fliegerkorps on its flight across Kent. The aircraft was flying at 30,000 feet and the 200mm focal length of the lens has resulted in a very small scale negative covering a swathe some 12 kilometres wide. Consequently the formations flying some 10,000 feet lower are minute and without enlarging a section the aircraft would have ended up on the page as specs of dirt! Three fighters (ringed) are closing on a converging course. The large fire in Seal Chart Wood is a mystery as it is unlikely that any bombs would have been jettisoned this early in the raid and no aircraft crashed there. Picture taken at 6.53 pm. German time.

OPERATIONAL ORDERS OF I FLIEGERKORPS FOR THE FIRST ATTACK ON LONDON, SEPTEMBER 7, 1940

From G.O.C. I Fliegerkorps — Corps HQ 6.9.40
Ia Br.B.Nr. 10285 g.Kdos. N.f.K.

1. In the evening of 7.9. Luftflotte 2 will conduct major strike against target Loge. [code-name for London]
   To this end the following units will operate in succession:
   For the Initial Attack: at 18.00 one KG of II Fliegerkorps
   For the Main Attack: at 18.40 II Fliegerkorps
   at 18.45 I Fliegerkorps, reinforced by KG 30

2. *Disposition of I Fliegerkorps Units:*
   KG30 (Plus II/KG 76): on right
   KG 1 central
   KG 76 (less II/KG 76): on left
   For target see general Appendix.

3. *Fighter Cover*
   (a) Purpose of Initial Attack is to force English fighters into the air so that they will have reached end of endurance at time of Main Attack.
   (b) Fighter escort will be provided by Jafü 2 in the proportion of one fighter Geschwader for each bomber Geschwader.
   (c) ZG 76 (for this operation under I Fliegerkorps command) will as from 18.40 clear the air of enemy fighters over I Fliegerkorps targets, thereby covering attack and retreat of bomber formations.
   (d) Jafü 2 guarantees two fighter Geschwader to cover I and II Fliegerkorps.

4. *Execution*
   (a) Rendezvous:
   To be made with Fighter Escort before crossing coast. Bombers will proceed in direct flight.
   (b) Courses:
   KG 30: St. Omer—just south of Cap Gris Nez—railway fork north of 'Sevenoaks'—target.
   KG 1: St. Pol—'mouth of la Slack'—Riverhead—target.
   KG 76: Hesdin—north perimeter of Boulogne—Westerham—target.
   (c) Fighter escort:
   JG 26 for KG 30
   JG 54 for KG 1
   JG 27 for KG 76
   In view of the fact that the fighters will be operating at the limit of their endurance, it is essential that direct courses be flown and the attack completed in minimum time.
   (d) Flying altitudes after RV with fighters:
   KG 30: 15,000–17,000 ft.
   KG 1: 18,000–20,000 ft.
   KG 76: 15,000–17,000 ft.
   To stagger heights as above will provide maximum concentration of attacking force. On return flight some loss of altitude is permissible, in order to cross English coast at approximately 4000 metres.
   (e) The intention is to complete the operation by a single attack. In the event of units failing to arrive directly over target, other suitable objectives in Loge may be bombed from altitude of approach.
   (f) Return flight:
   After releasing bombs formation will turn to starboard. KG 76 will do so with care after first establishing that starboard units have already attacked. Return course will then be Maidstone—Dymchurch—escort fighter bases.
   (g) Bomb-loads:
   He 111 and Ju 88: No 50kg bombs
   20 per cent incendiaries
   30 per cent delayed-action bombs of 2–4 hours and 10–14 hours (the latter without concussion fuses)
   Do 17: 25 per cent disintegrating containers with B 1 E Z and no SD 50.
   Load only to be limited by security of aircraft against enemy flak. Fuel sufficient for completion of operation and for marginal safety to be carried only.

5. To achieve the necessary maximum effect it is essential that units fly as a highly concentrated force—during approach, attack, and especially on return. The main objective of the operation is to prove that the Luftwaffe can achieve this.

6. I Fliegerkorps Operational Order No. 10285/40 is hereby superseded.

By order of the G.O.C.
(signed) Grauert.

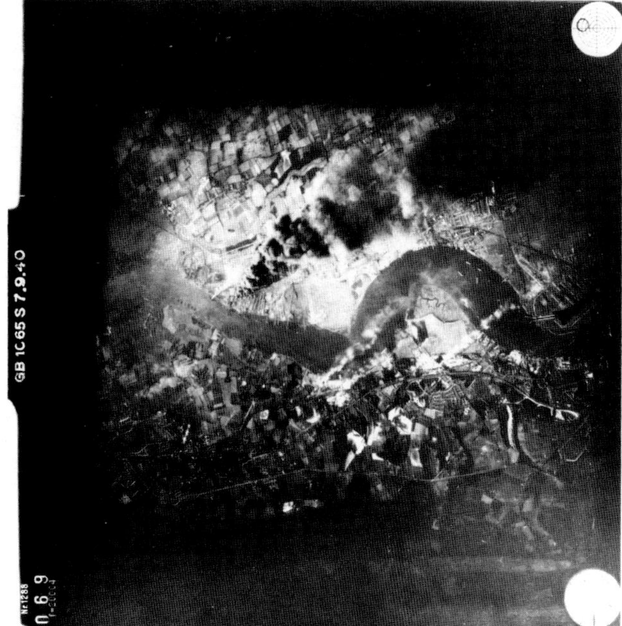

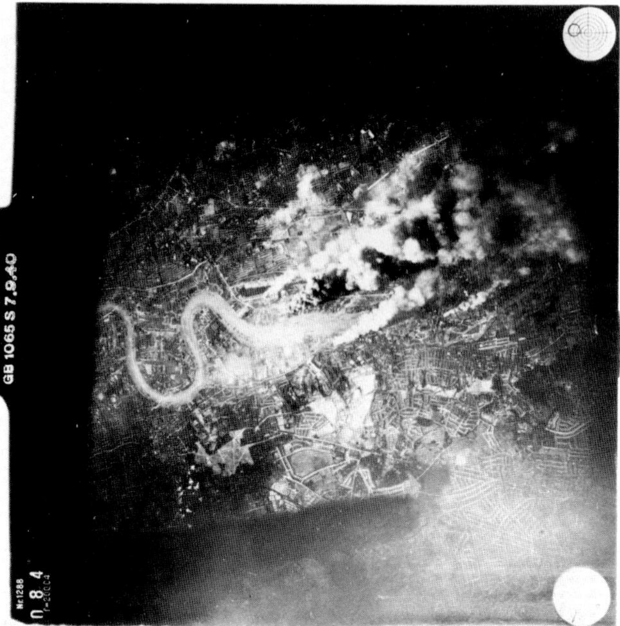

However the photography from the machine on the more northerly route along the Thames (Sortie 1065) was far more dramatic and pictures have survived from two of its cameras. Because each Rb 75/30 camera and film cassette weighed about 200lbs, a large aircraft would have had to be used, probably an He 111, borne out by the shadow of the gondola gun barrel on the left of the print. The camera serial number, the frame count and focal length was automatically recorded on each exposure, as was the time and attitude of aircraft (the spirit level on the lower right). We can also tell that the cameras are old models as later ones did not have the ability to record the sortie number and date on the film (via a data chamber in the camera magazine). We have turned the prints round to be able to view them from the more natural position with north at the top. *Above left:* Frame 69. The Anglo American Oil Works on fire at Purfleet. This blaze burned all night and Home Security reported that at 1.00 p.m. on Sunday, 18 to 20 tanks were still ablaze with 20 firemen trapped. It had still not been extinguished by the 13th. *Above right:* Accounts are conflicting as to the time the first bombs fell on London but Home Security, after a typing correction on the original, give it as 1635 hours — 4.35 p.m. Frame 84 taken at 5.48 p.m. British time shows the conflagration developing in the docks where Tate and Lyle's sugar factory, Loders and Noculine's fat refinery and Millenium and the Empire flour mills suffered major damage. *Below:* This frame, taken two minutes later, shows bomb bursts right across Stepney and West Ham. The explosions and the departing formation (top left) are arrowed on the original.

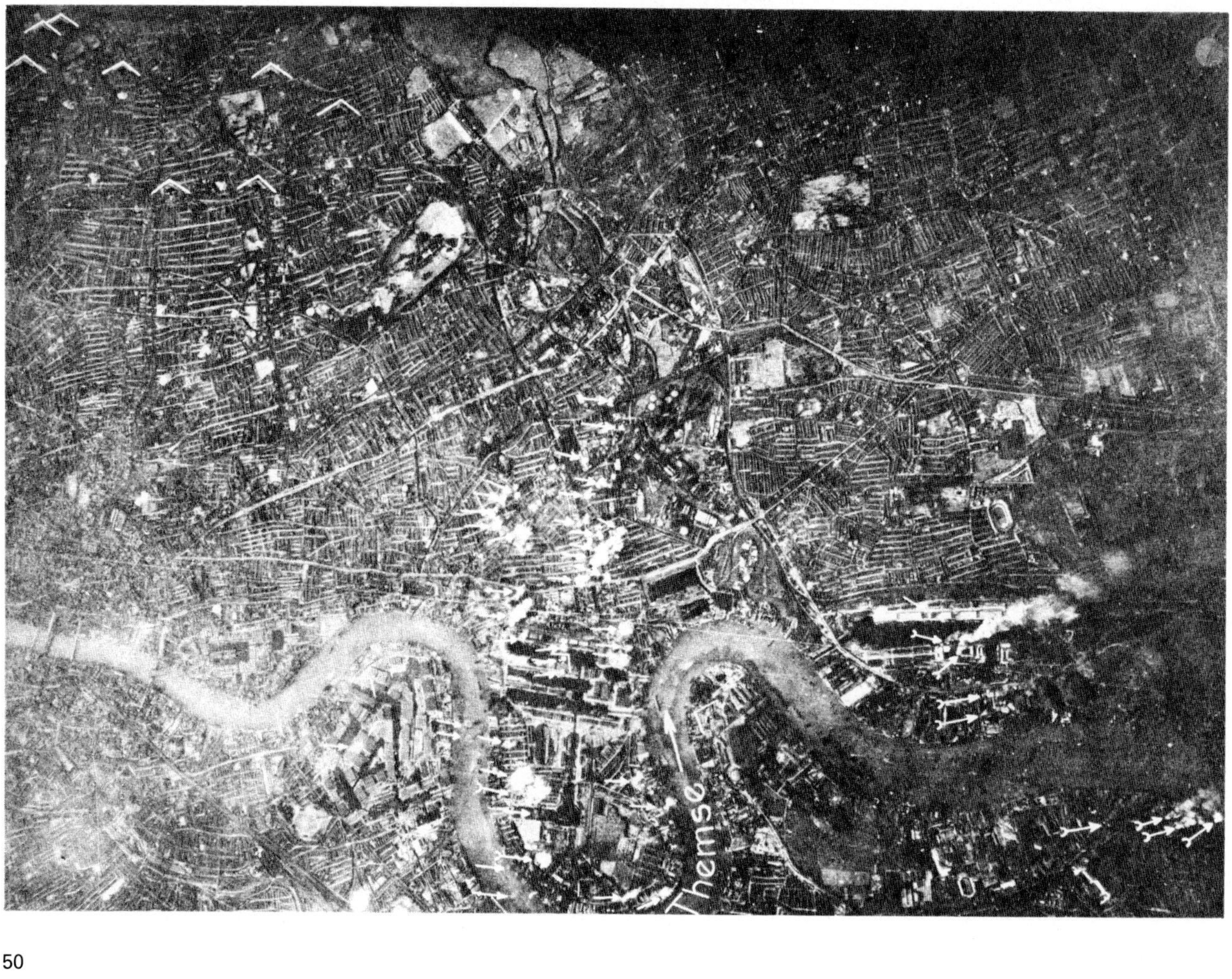

Above: **Compare this print taken from the left camera (denoted by the suffix 'L') of a pair of split-verticals having a focal length over three times as great (752mm) — hence the larger scale. The fire in Woolwich dockyard can be seen in greater detail and careful examination reveals five barrage balloons flying over the area. Time 5.46 p.m. (British time)**

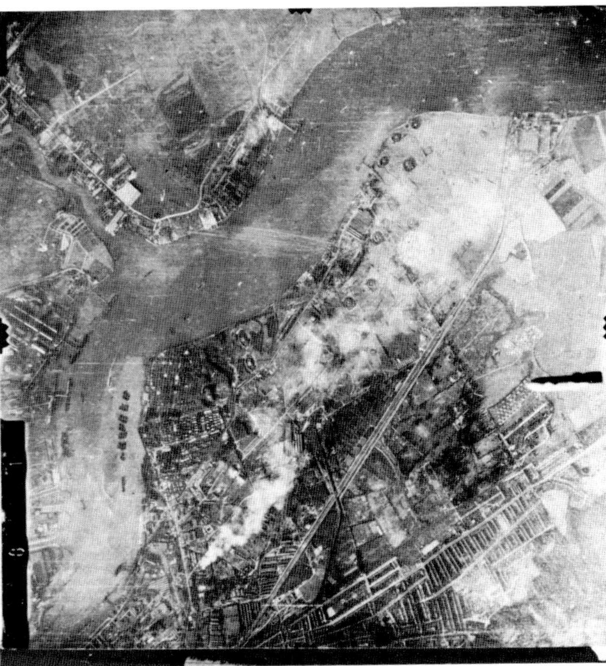

Just to the north these two shots, this time taken from one of the Dorniers, show three of the aircraft on their bombing run up to West Ham. Bombs are falling towards the Beckton Gasworks just out of the pictures to the left.

With RAF defensive measures being primarily designed to protect the vital sector aerodromes (Northolt, Duxford, Debden, North Weald, Hornchurch, Biggin Hill, Kenley, Tangmere and Middle Wallop), the change in German tactics found the majority of No. 11 Group squadrons thinly spread and unable to meet the incoming aircraft in strength near the coast. For the greater part of the day the lull before the storm had kept most squadrons on the ground, these pilots of No. 43 Squadron even having time to have their photos taken relaxing in the sunshine outside the Officers' Mess at Tangmere. L-R, standing: Pilot Officer H. C. Upton, Pilot Officer A. E. A. van den Hove d'Ertsenrijck and Pilot Officer D. Gorrie. L-R, seated: Pilot Officer S. Cary (Squadron Adjutant), Flight Lieutenant J. I. Kilmartin, Squadron Leader C. G. Lott, Flight Lieutenant R. C. Reynell and Squadron Leader C. B. Hull. (George Lott, just released from hospital, had been blinded in one eye during an earlier combat on July 9.)

In the defence of London that afternoon, Ceasar Hull and Dick Reynell were the first to fall — around 4.45 p.m. They were followed in quick succession by another ten of 'The Few': Reg Lovett of 73 Squadron, John Benzie of 242, Bob Fleming of 249 and Kenneth Wendel of 504 all being shot down around five o'clock. Half an hour later four more pilots had gone: Hugh Beresford and Lancelot Mitchell of 257 and Hugh Coverley and Henry Moody of 602. Then, just before six-thirty p.m., Joseph O'Brien of 234 crashed near Biggin Hill. ***Below:*** **Tangmere closed in 1970 and by 1985 many of the station buildings had been demolished for a new housing estate, including the old Officers' Mess.**

Stab KG76 Dornier Do 17Z (2596). Attacked by Spitfires of No. 602 Squadron, including Pilot Officer E. W. Aries, during photo-reconnaisance sortie over London Docks. Probably also attacked by Flying Officer G. C. B. Peters of No. 79 Squadron. Went out of control and collided with Flight Lieutenant P. C. Hughes of No. 234 Squadron. Crashed into a stream at Sundridge near Sevenoaks 6.00 p.m. Lt. G. Schneider, Oberfw. K. Schneider and Uffz. W. Rupprecht killed. Fw. E. Rosche baled out slightly wounded and captured. Aircraft F1+BA a write-off.

Crash site on a waterworks excavated by the Kent Battle of Britain Museum and one propeller blade and an oil pump, plus various fragments and a machine gun cleaning kit extricated under extremely difficult conditions. Oxygen mask donated by Sevenoaks resident bearing the name 'ROSCHE' on leather trim. Items now in the Hawkinge Aeronautical Trust. Maps in the Vizard collection. Site re-excavated by Chris Bennett in June 1984 and many interesting relics unearthed including Bramo Fafnir engine, propeller boss with bullet-holed blade still attached, undercarriage, MG15 machine gun and numerous maker's labels bearing '2596' confirming identity. Flying helmet bearing name 'ROSCHE', together with gunner's tool kit and syringe from first-aid kit in the After the Battle collection.

The last pilot to die in the battle that day was Australian Pat Hughes. Flight Lieutenant Hughes, based with No. 234 Squadron at Middle Wallop was typical of the pilots of Fighter Command facing overwhelming odds that day as they attempted to break up the German formations. One of the Luftwaffe aircraft on photo-reconnaissance that day was the Dornier 17 of Leutnant Gottfried Schneider detailed to record the scene over the London Docks. Attacked by a succession of RAF fighters, as Pat Hughes closed on the bomber it suddenly went out of control and collided with his Spitfire, bringing it to earth at Bessels Green west of Sevenoaks. Six days later Kay, his young British wife of five weeks, was present as the RAF laid him to rest in St James's Church Sutton-in-Holderness, Hull — her home town. On his headstone the immortal words first spoken by Winston Churchill on August 16: 'Never in the field of human conflict was so much owed by so many to so few.' The picture shows Pat earlier in 1940 with his dog 'Flying Officer Butch'.

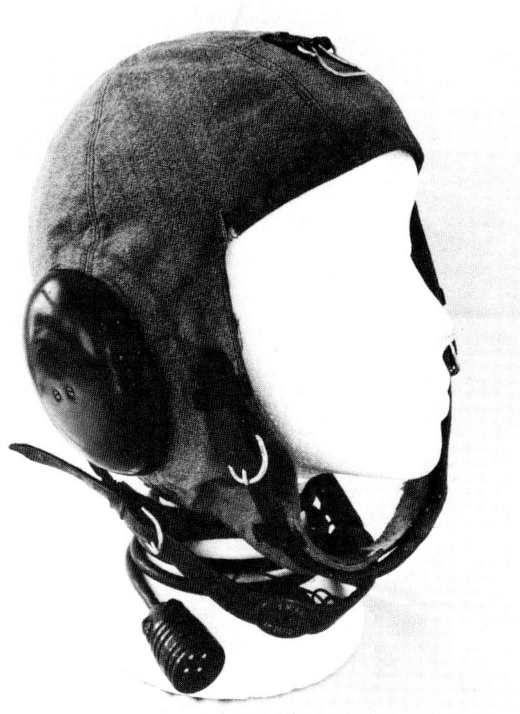

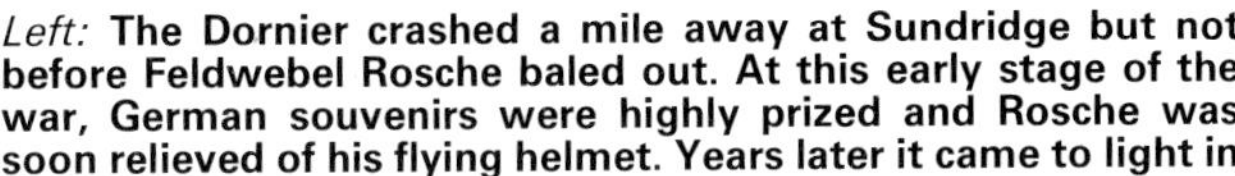

Left: The Dornier crashed a mile away at Sundridge but not before Feldwebel Rosche baled out. At this early stage of the war, German souvenirs were highly prized and Rosche was soon relieved of his flying helmet. Years later it came to light in the possession of a Sevenoaks resident and has since found its way into the *After the Battle* collection. *Right:* Another relic knocked off in the collision and found some distance away was one of the tail fins; now owned by Dennis Knight.

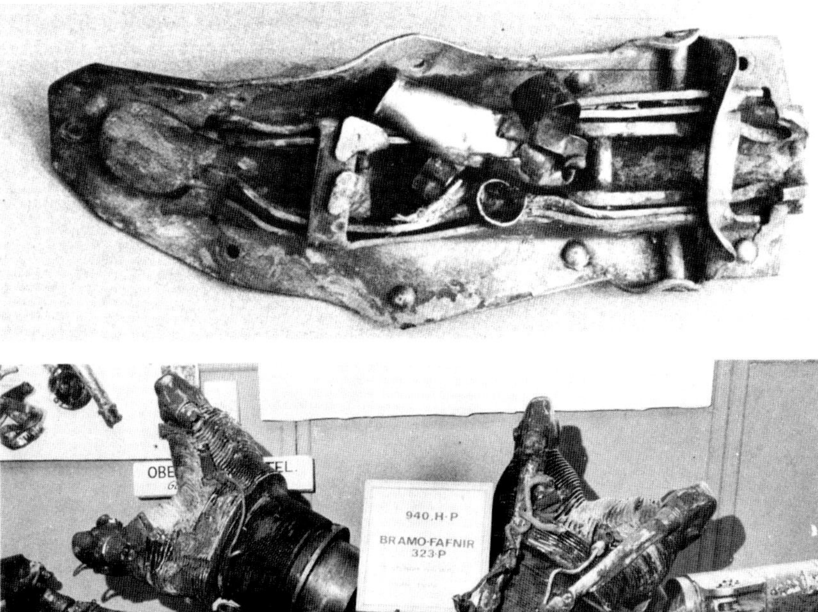

Years later Englishmen of another generation found that German war souvenirs had an equal attraction. *Above:* Prised from its forty-year earthen grave — the gunner's battered tool kit still in its leather case. *Centre:* An incredible piece of evidence of the collision — a British .303in cartridge case jammed in one of the cowling fasteners of the Dornier! *Right:* One of the engines can now be viewed during the summer months at the Military Aviation Museum at Tangmere. And there in the village churchyard can also be found the last resting place of the first Royal Air Force pilot to die in the battle that day: South African Squadron Leader Caesar Barrand Hull.

1/LG2 Messerschmitt Bf 109E. Shot down by Sergeant B. Furst of No. 310 Squadron in combat over Canterbury. Exploded in mid-air and crashed at Wickhambreux 5.35 p.m. Uffz. W. Götting baled out and captured unhurt. Aircraft 11+ a write-off.

Site excavated by the Kent Battle of Britain Museum which recovered the control column, signal pistol, radio mast, Swastika marking from the tail, and complete belts of 7.92mm ammunition. Later re-excavated for the benefit of the surviving pilot who attended recovery operations. Propeller boss and blades, complete armour, armament, pilot's maps and compressed fuselage panels unearthed. Items now held by the Hawkinge Aeronautical Trust. First-aid kit in Steve Vizard collection and relics also held by the Southern Area Wartime Aircraft Preservation Society.

Casualties on the ground were difficult to establish but Home Security estimated that 400 had been killed and 1,300 seriously wounded. Of these 200 were believed to have lost their lives in the East End, and 800 wounded, although many people were still trapped.

Above: **The rising pall of smoke and flame over the East End as seen from a position overlooking Fleet Street.** *Below:* **As the original vantage point has since been demolished, Andrew Hyde's comparison has been taken a little further back from the roof of the National Insurance and Guarantee Corporation.**

Since the end of the war the Pool of London has undergone radical change. Gone are the forests of riverside cranes, moved downstream to Tilbury where larger ships have easier access; gone are the huge warehouses, demolished for redevelopment or conversion into up-market accommodation; gone are the barges, tugs and lighters but in are the pleasure craft . . . and HMS *Belfast* preserved as a permanent feature of the river.

Stab I/ZG2 Messerschmitt Bf 110C-4 (3246). Attacked by Flying Officer J. R. Hardacre of No. 504 Squadron and Pilot Officer H. J. S. Beazley of No. 249 Squadron during escort sortie for KG53 Heinkels attacking Thameshaven. Possibly also that attacked by Sub Lt. R. J. Cork of No. 242 Squadron. Tail shot off in further attack by Squadron Leader M. L. ff. Beytagh of No. 73 Squadron and crashed and exploded at Noak Hill, Billericay 5.30 p.m. Oberlt. G. Granz (Gruppe Adjutant) and Fw. W. Schutel baled out and captured unhurt. Aircraft 3M+BB a write-off.

Home Security claimed 88 aircraft destroyed; in actual fact the Luftwaffe's losses were less than half this total. (Readers must bear in mind that we only detail those down on land or from which prisoners were taken.) Of the 24 lost over the UK only 4 were bombers on the London raid. Rather more fighters were shot down, which would seem to indicate that the RAF was diverted from the raiders by their escorts. One of those machines was Oberleutnant Granz's Bf 110 which crashed near Billericay. Where, other than in England's green and pleasant land, could such a marvellous scene have been enacted? The wreckage is still smoking . . . the battle is still being waged . . . yet the inferno in Dockland could be a million miles away instead of less than twenty . . . and everything stops to help a young Eve collect her fruit.

Major recovery undertaken by No. 2393 (Billericay) Squadron ATC in the summer of 1971. Complete Daimler-Benz DB 601 engine excavated plus propeller boss with two blades attached, both undercarriage legs, cannon blast tubes, intact magazine of 7.92mm ammunition, two oil coolers, four compressed air bottles and several manufacturer's plates. Relics held by the Essex Aviation Group and the After the Battle collection. Pilot presented with propeller boss and one blade subsequently donated by him to the Buckerbing Helicopter Museum, West Germany.

A well-used picture but always poorly captioned. There has even been some doubt about when it was taken as most people use the copy print (C5422) in the Imperial War Museum which simply states: 'A Heinkel III aircraft over the Thames-side Silvertown district of London, as seen from another German aircraft'. This is the original German photograph which was taken at 6.48 p.m. German time. The actual aircraft can be seen on page 50. The aircraft is also over Wapping not Silvertown which is four miles to the east — the area within the characteristic U-bend of the river being designated by the Luftwaffe as Zielräum G (see page 24).

BLACK SATURDAY

September 7 was a glorious summer day with the sun shining from a clear blue sky fringed with a few fleecy clouds. The activity of the previous evening, when a few isolated bombers dropped fire and explosive bombs on Silvertown and Custom House, kept me busy until four o'clock in the morning and there was time for only a few hours sleep before the daily routine began at seven o'clock.

I tried to get my head down after lunch but felt uneasy and couldn't rest. Everybody who could be spared crept away to catch up on sleep and there was little activity at Abbey Road School in West Ham, the London Fire Regions' J District Control that Saturday afternoon, that is until shortly before five o'clock when the Air Raid Warning Red message was received and the sirens began their wail. I was in the yard and heard the drone of approaching aircraft rapidly swelling to a roar. Suddenly, squadrons of bombers appeared all over the eastern sky, flying very high and escorted by hundreds of fighter aircraft, glinting in the sunlight as they weaved and turned over the bomber formations. Rosettes of black smoke from exploding anti-aircraft shells spread across the sky as the menacing roar of aircraft engines combined, in a devilish symphony, with the bark of anti-aircraft gun-fire, the scream of falling bombs and the earth-shaking thump as they exploded.

I dived for the safety of the Control Room, where calls for assistance were already flowing in from Dagenham, Barking, East and West Ham. The electricity mains were damaged in the first minutes of the raid and the fire control operated by the light of candles, set in jam jars.

The Nazi airmen had no difficulty in identifying their targets in the clear afternoon light. The first bombs fell on the Ford Motor works at Dagenham, closely followed by a rain of high explosive and fire bombs on Beckton Gas Works, the largest in Europe. Below them now lay the great Thames bight at Woolwich Reach enclosing the three Royal Docks, their warehouses and sheds stacked with foodstuff and materials vital to the war effort. Large cargo vessels lay moored at the quayside, sitting-duck targets for the bomb aimers.

Now came an avalanche of bombs raining on the East End of London from an estimated 300 bombers. Flames erupted from the great factories and warehouses lining the River Thames from Woolwich to Tower Bridge. In the crowded dockland streets, massive warehouses and tiny dwellings alike came crashing down under the impact of high explosives, burying under the debris their occupants and any luckless passer-by. Much of West Ham's dockland area was ablaze, the flames reaching out to encompass adjoining buildings.

Columns of fire pumps, six hundred of them ordered to West Ham alone, sped eastwards to attend fires in ships and warehouses, in sugar refineries, in oil depots, paint and varnish works, chemical works, the humble little homes of the workers and hundreds of other fires, any one of which in peacetime would have made headline news.

Two hundred acres of tall timber stacks blazed out of control in the Surrey Commercial Docks. The rum quay buildings in West India Docks, alight from end to end, gushed flaming spirit from their doors. An army of rats ran from a burning Silvertown soap works; a short distance further along North Woolwich Road, molten pitch from a stricken tar distillery flooded the road, bringing to a halt all emergency vehicles. On the riverside, blazing barges threatened wharves. They were set adrift by well-intentioned people, only to be swept by the tide broadside downstream to the peril of fireboats, manoeuvring to pump water ashore to feed the land pumps.

It was a scene of horror and chaos as Civil Defence workers, themselves shocked and terrified by their first experience of the Blitzkrieg, dug into demolished buildings in search of casualties buried in the debris. Others shepherded dazed and shocked men, women and children, rendered homeless but thankful to have escaped with their lives, to rest centres in schools and church halls, where they were given shelter whilst arrangements were made for their more permanent accommodation elsewhere.

At six o'clock the raiders had gone but the All Clear brought no relief to firemen striving against odds to contain the great conflagrations that blazed all around them. Others laboured to prevent smaller fires from combining to create more conflagrations. The street water mains, totally inadequate to carry the vast quantities of water needed to control fires of such magnitude, were further depleted when sections fractured under the pounding of high explosive bombs. Those firemen working on dockside fires were fortunate in having an almost unlimited supply of water to draw on but watched their powerful jets bore in to the mass of flames without visible effect. Some of the regulars had encountered fires of equal ferocity in peacetime, but never on such an overwhelming scale. The choking fumes of burning rubber and tar; the blistering heat and blinding sparks were merely unpleasant incidentals. Fear was the overpowering emotion that drew branchmen together in small groups, each gaining comfort from the presence of the other.

Many feared their last hour had come but they carried on, encouraged by the example of comrades slogging away at blazing buildings, their heads down to shield faces from the scorching heat and flying sparks. They yelled warnings to unwary crews, as slabs of masonry and coping stones from collapsing buildings began to topple. All around them lay a maze of twisting, snaking fire hose whilst the whine of dozens of pumps, running at full power, added their quota to the general din. Clouds of greasy black smoke rose high into the sky, dimming the golden sunlight but billowing orange and yellow flames provided a weird substitute.

This *is* Silvertown, with Silvertown Way curving round at the bottom where it becomes North Woolwich Road. Below the Dorniers — the bar possibly denotes they are from the I Gruppe — lies West Ham speedway stadium in Canning Town. Ironically the large bomb burst between the road and the river is virtually slap-bang on the spot where Brunner Mond's works stood in the First World War — the TNT purification plant which blew up in January 1917 in the 'Silvertown explosion'. Fires have started either side of the Royal Victoria Dock but the worst is yet to come. The 'J' District Control Room where Cyril Demarne was on duty lay in Abbey Road — off the top left-hand corner of the picture.

At half past seven the bombers were back, about 250 of them, to drive home the attack. Succeeding squadrons of Heinkels and Dorniers queued to deliver their cargoes of destruction on a target still blazing from the afternoon raid. East Londoners had been severely punished, none more so than those living in the Tidal Basin area. Their houses had been built in the 1850s to accommodate the thousands of workers engaged in building the Royal Victoria Dock and those who worked in the large factories at Silvertown. Part of the plan was to house the workpeople within a short walk of their place of employment.

With the Blitz came the inevitable overspill of bombs aimed at docks and warehouses. The closely packed streets were no match for even the smallest of the German bombs. Great gaps were torn in the terraces, leaving piles of debris where neat little homes once stood. Still, grotesque figures, sprawling in the roadway, splayed against a

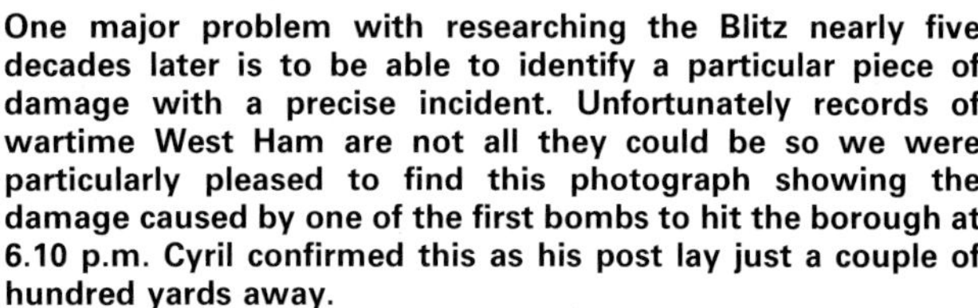

One major problem with researching the Blitz nearly five decades later is to be able to identify a particular piece of damage with a precise incident. Unfortunately records of wartime West Ham are not all they could be so we were particularly pleased to find this photograph showing the damage caused by one of the first bombs to hit the borough at 6.10 p.m. Cyril confirmed this as his post lay just a couple of hundred yards away.

Eight people are reported killed in the incident. Nurse Annie Bond, Nurse Agatha Credland and six patients. All told 114 'West Hammers' are given in the Civilian War Dead Roll as losing their lives on the 7th, which accounted for 10 per cent of the borough's wartime casualties. For at least 20 years the yawning gap remained to be seen on Bryant Street while the rest of the hospital went about its daily business; your Editor snapped this picture sometime in the early 1960s.

mall or tossed in a corner like a rag doll, were camouflaged by mortar dust, merging with surrounding rubble. Bricks and tiles, roofing timbers and shattered glass littered the road together with remnants of cherished items of furniture that once made a home.

Many families were buried in the rubble of their homes and had to be dug out by rescue squads. Those lightly buried freed themselves and immediately began digging frantically for their nearest and dearest. Some were beyond aid and scenes of heartrending grief were witnessed as survivors uncovered the torn and mutilated bodies of loved ones. First aid and rescue parties moved in, treating the injured and covering the dead with a blanket or whatever came to hand, leaving the body stretched out on the rubble to await collection by a mortuary van.

Hour after hour the bombs rained down, demolishing yet more buildings and starting fresh fires. Great blazing embers, carried aloft in the terrific heat upcast, spread fire over the heads of the firemen. Powerful jets of water seemed to be turned to steam and all the effort appeared to be in vain; the task was overwhelming.

Against the glare of the flames parachutes could be seen floating down, carrying a land mine resembling a small boiler and packed with a ton of high explosive. When it landed, there would be a flash of blinding pink light which seemed to persist for seconds, then, what appeared to be a whole street would go flying in the air in a great gust of smoke, dust and flame, scattering bricks and roofing slates, furniture and bodies. The blast flung firemen off their feet and drove the air from their lungs. After a time, the scream of falling bombs and the thunder of explosions became just a background to the brain-

Remembering that I still had the photo I thought it would be a good example to include to illustrate an original, authenticated piece of 'Black Saturday' bomb damage and I earmarked it to use in this project. Alas when I came to take a modern comparison in 1987, although the breach still remained, albeit tidied up, the hospital itself had closed and was boarded up pending disposal.

Within three months all had gone . . . swept away far more efficiently than by Göring's demolition company.

numbing din but, always, one was aware of tortured eyes and the dry mouth, the scorching heat and the rumble of collapsing buildings. The fearful dread of impending doom receded as time passed and the imagination dulled. Many who felt that they were engaged in a hopeless task battled on, taking heart as neighbouring crews stuck to their task.

Meanwhile, Civil Defence workers led the homeless to rest centres in neighbouring halls. Many had superficial cuts and abrasions and were caked with dried blood; all were smothered in plaster dust from walls and ceilings. They had lost everything they possessed but cared nothing other than that the family had been spared. All window glass was shattered by blast and many reached the rest centre with tiny splinters of glass embedded in face and hands.

During the evening I received word that my close friend Wally Turley, with two members of his crew had been buried when a bombed building collapsed during firefighting operations. Two fire pumps had arrived and Sub-Officers Turley and Webb together ran into the burning building with their crews. A quick reconnaissance and Wally shouted: 'You take the back, Harry; I'll look after this side'. Webb and his crew ran out of the building with the intention of attacking the fire from the rear when, to quote Harry Webb, 'the whole bloody guts of the building fell in, burying the lot'. The shocked survivors tore at the great slab of concrete that buried their comrades but found it far beyond their ability to move. Heavy lifting gear had to be brought in to recover the bodies.

The corporation depot in Abbey Road was used as an ARP Cleansing and Ambulance station and here the West Ham Civil Defence organisation was struck a grievous blow right at the beginning. At 7.15 p.m. a direct hit led to the collapse of the building and the deaths of 13 men; ARP Rescue Squad Leader Alf Bridgman; Fred Chilvers, Auxiliary Fireman Hugh Dicken; Ted Dunn of the ARP Demolition Squad; Matthew Fenwick of the ARP and Fred Jones; Auxiliary Fireman Bill Long and the Squad Leader of the Light Rescue Service Sid Lowings; George Odell; Wally Porter of the ARP Rescue Service and Frank Swift ARP Messenger; Sub Officer Wally Turley and ARP stretcher bearer Bill Willis. This is the scene which met the eyes of Cyril Demarne when he reached the spot just a couple of hundred yards from Fire Brigade Control. Protruding from beneath the huge slab was an arm — that of his friend and colleague Wally Turley and gently he removed his wristwatch which he retained as a keepsake of a gallant comrade. Today all those firemen killed in West Ham are remembered by the roads which bear their names, Turley Close standing on the exact site of the Fire Control building in Abbey Road School *(See Volume 1, page 238)*.

The sun slowly dipped below the western horizon but thousands living to the west of London observed the phenomenon of a crimson sunset in the east! Strangely, as night descended over the blazing city, it brought not darkness but simply changed the colour of the sky from blue to varying shades of pink and red as the glare from hundreds and hundreds of fires reflected on clouds of smoke drifting across the East End.

Still the squadrons droned overhead and the bombs screamed down. Not only water mains were fractured by the

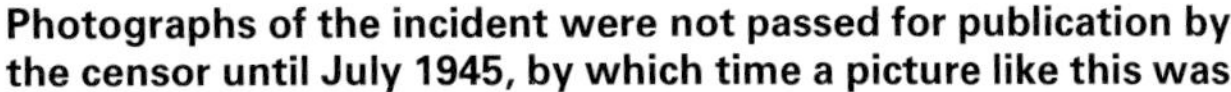

Photographs of the incident were not passed for publication by the censor until July 1945, by which time a picture like this was nothing compared to the huge devastation wrought by flying bombs and rockets.

pounding HE; power and telephone cables and gas mains were equally vulnerable. These were days before radio was available to the Service. Fire Officers, unable to telephone situation reports or calls for assistance, relied upon motor-cycle dispatch riders or the heroic teenage messenger boys with their bicycles, to maintain communications. It was no fault of the DRs and messengers that Controls received but a hazy appreciation of the fire situation. They rode through streets converted by incendiary bombs into passages with flaming walls and picked themselves up after being blasted from their machines by a near miss. They skidded around unexploded bombs and heaps of rubble,

When discussing the Abbey Road disaster with Cyril he pulled out this photograph taken outside the School in September 1939. 'It's getting close to fifty years since this picture was taken so it's hardly surprising that I cannot recall all their names. Derek Godfrey is third from the left and was a pre-war journalist on the *Evening News*. Derek saw service in the East End during the Blitz and later became PRO to No. 36 Fire Force Area when the National Fire Service was formed. I can also recognise Tom Soar (the tall chap fifth from the right) who was formerly musical director at the Carlton Cinema in Green Street. Poor Tom was so despondent when he came to us in 1939. He had seen his world crash about him when the cinemas were closed on the outbreak of hostilities after his prospects had seemed so bright. These two chaps exemplify the wide range of professions serving in the Auxiliary Fire Service. They are wearing their one and only uniform. A year later many of those in this group attended the fires at Thameshaven and Shellhaven, soaked waist-high in a mixture of oil, water and stinking foam, returning to London to fight the fires the following day. We regulars helped out with the loan of the odd tunic or trousers but there was much hardship until the Minister was bullied into increasing the scale of issue. Incidentally, commented Cyril closely inspecting the photograph, 'the sandbags in the background form the blast wall of the brick surface shelter featured in the story of the shell-shocked RAF airman I wrote for Volume 1'.

The blaze in the riverside warehouses being tackled by firemen manning special shallow-draft fire boats, fitted with coffer dams which could suck up water within themselves, and deck-mounted water cannons.

frequently arriving at the Control Rooms to deliver their messages covered in dust or mud and often with grazed knuckles, eager to get back to the fireground and accepting the conditions as all part of the job.

People living in the streets adjoining the southern boundary of King George V Dock found themselves sandwiched between serious dock fires and a line of great factories ablaze along the length of Factory Road, opposite. Conditions in North Woolwich were unimaginable. Demolished buildings, large and small, spilled debris over the roadway, blocking the passage of fire and rescue vehicles. Terrified families scurried back and forth, seeking shelter from the awesome fires and the explosions that rocked the area as delayed action bombs exploded and others were dropped by fresh flights of bombers. Some refugees found their way to a public shelter at the baths in Oriental Road, only to become the target for a random bomb. The situation in the area became out of hand and it was decided to evacuate the entire civil population from North Woolwich. The only road giving access in or out of the area was blocked to traffic and refugees, young and old, active and infirm, were conducted to North Woolwich Pier where they embarked on small craft and were rowed to safety via the River Thames.

And so it continued throughout the night. Bombers delivered their quota of HE and fire bombs on the eastern suburbs on both banks of the river, then returned to their bases in northern France to refuel and bomb up for a return trip. Fire pumps were mobilised from as far distant as Yarmouth and Brighton, Rugby and Swindon, bringing crews of auxiliary firemen with a sprinkling of regular fire officers to face up to the fury of the Blitz. Soon, it would be the turn of their home towns, when London firemen would return the compliment.

'When the real dawn came about five, the Germans eased off their blitz. The All Clear raised a weary cheer. At seven o'clock I was hunched half-asleep across the branch holder. At last the relief crews arrived. Knowing that we were returning home gave us that extra ounce of strength without which we could hardly have hoisted the rolled-up lengths on our shoulders.' An Auxiliary fireman recalling September 7 in Dockland.

The first glimpse of dawn tinged the eastern sky at about five o'clock when the Luftwaffe decided to call it a day. The All Clear sirens announced their departure leaving firemen in action at nine conflagrations (large areas of fire involving blocks of buildings, spreading and not yet under control); nineteen serious fires each requiring the attendance of at least thirty pumps and many, many more ten-pumpers.

Londoners emerged from their shelters to scenes of devastation. Many came face to face with great fires; others faced the dismal sight of burned out buildings, with wisps of smoke and steam rising from the charred embers of the homes of friends and neighbours. The first thought of many was for a cup of tea, but they were to be disappointed, for there was no water, gas or electricity available. They were faced for the first time with the problems that would confront them for fifty-seven mornings in succession.

During the first day and night of the attack, 436 men, women and children were killed and some 1,600 severely injured. It was a night that none who lived through it will ever forget.

CYRIL DEMARNE, 1986

While the men at the sharp end were fighting the battle on the ground and in the air, at the highest level momentous decisions were being made. Since the beginning of September RAF photographic reconnaissance had detected an alarming build up of barges in Belgian and French channel ports. At Ostend the number increased from 18 on August 31 to 270 on September 7, with substantial numbers at Flushing, Dunkirk and Calais. Enigma decrypts had revealed that the planned transfer of bombers from Norway to France had been completed by September 6 and the Joint Intelligence Committee advised that between September 8 and 10 the conditions of moon and tide would be particularly favourable for landing on the British coast. Interrogation of the spies who had landed earlier in the week *(see Volume 1 page 317)* also disclosed that their purpose was to report on conditions in the invasion zone. Putting all these facts together, an emergency meeting of the Chiefs of Staff was called for 5.30 p.m. on Saturday. No sooner had they sat down in the underground war room in Whitehall *(Volume 1 page 301)* than the thud of bombs was heard drawing closer. Deeming it to reflect the beginning of the pre-invasion softening up process, the Chiefs decided to order all defence forces in the United Kingdom to 'standby at immediate notice'. Two hours later, just as the bombers returned to help stoke up the conflagration raging along the Thames, the codeword 'Cromwell' was issued, bringing all forces to 'immediate action'. ***Above:*** **A typical scene that Sunday morning: the corner of Selsey Road and St Paul's Way, Bow Common.**

So complete was the damage by the end of the war that the whole area was designated for redevelopment with nothing now to be seen of the former buildings.

3/ZG2 Messerschmitt Bf 110C-4 (2216). Engine damaged in attack by Squadron Leader M. W. S. Robinson and Pilot Officer N. C. Langham-Hobart of No. 73 Squadron during escort sortie to London. Crashed and burned out at Old Tree Farm, Hoath, near Herne Bay 5.20 p.m. Lt. F. Kislinger killed. Uffz. R. Dahnke baled out and captured unhurt. Aircraft 3M+LL a write-off.

Site excavated in November 1979 by the Historic Aircraft Archaeological Group. Quantities of shattered airframe and several interesting components recovered. Pieces also in the Vizard collection.

3/ZG2 Messerschmitt Bf 110C-4 (3117). Believed both engines damaged in attack by Sergeant G. W. Garton of No. 73 Squadron during escort sortie to London. Broke up over a housing estate at Eythorne, near Deal 5.20 p.m. Hauptfw. F. Oligschläger and Oberfw. E. Otterbach both baled out but killed. Aircraft 3M+FL a write-off.

Stab II/ZG2 Messerschmitt Bf 110D/0 (3334). Shot down by Flying Officer J. B. Holderness of No. 1 Squadron and Pilot Officer S. Janough of No. 310 Squadron during escort sortie to London. Also attacked by Flight Lieutenant B. J. E. Lane of No. 19 Squadron. Crashed at Park Corner Farm, Hacton Lane, Hornchurch 5.10 p.m. Lt. K. Schünemann (Gruppe TO) baled out too low and killed. Uffz. H. Mescheder also baled out too low but parachute failed and fell to his death at Franks Cottages, St. Mary's Lane, Cranham. Aircraft A2+NH a write-off.

Both these airmen are now buried in the Soldatenfriedhof, Cannock Chase where their dates of death are incorrectly recorded as September 9.

Major recovery by Essex Historical Aircraft Society in September 1984 yielded Daimler-Benz DB 601 engine and undercarriage leg together with numerous other relics including proof of identity.

4/ZG2 Messerschmitt Bf 110D/0 (3185). Shot down by Squadron Leader D. R. S. Bader and Sub Lt. R. J. Cork of No. 242 Squadron during escort sortie over London. Crashed and burned out at Swan Lane, Downham Hall, Wickford 5.15 p.m. Lt. H-D. Abert and Uffz. K. Scharf killed. Aircraft A2+BH a write-off.

The first name of the gunner from this aircraft is subject of some confusion. His headstone in the Soldatenfriedhof at Cannock Chase names him as 'Karl', whereas contemporary Luftwaffe casualty returns and the independently compiled RAF Intelligence report on the incident both describe him as 'Hans'.

Site investigated by the Essex Historical Aircraft Society and surviving remains unearthed.

4/ZG2 Messerschmitt Bf 110D/0 (3328). Engaged by Hurricanes of No. 242 Squadron during escort sortie over London. Attacked by Pilot Officer D. W. Crowley-Milling and then port engine set alight by Sub Lt. R. E. Gardner. Crashed and burned out at Bullers Farm, Little Burstead 5.30 p.m. Lt. K. Stix baled out wounded and captured. Gefr. H. Hetz killed. Aircraft A2+JH a write-off.

The surname of the gunner from this aircraft, recorded as 'Heinrich Hetz' in the Soldatenfriedhof at Cannock Chase, has been variously interpreted. He is described in some contemporary German records as 'Fiez' or 'Pietz (amended to) Fietz'.

6/ZG2 Messerschmitt Bf 110C-4 (3570). Sortied as escort for bombers attacking London and engaged by Hurricanes of No. 310 Squadron. Engines disabled in attack by Sergeant B. Furst. Ditched in the sea 5 miles off Birchington 5.20 p.m. Oberlt. W. Brede rescued by motor lifeboat *J. B. Proudfoot* and captured slightly injured — landing at Margate. Uffz. A. Galla killed. Aircraft A2+ML lost.

3(F)/123 Junkers Ju 88A. Sortied on armed reconnaissance over Bristol and Liverpool and intercepted by Sergeant L. S. Pilkington of No. 7 OTU. One engine severely damaged so forced-landed at Hafotty-y-Bulch, Mallwyd, Machynlleth 12.30 p.m. Oberlt. H. Kauter, Lt. E. Böhle, Fw. W. Kobold and Uffz. G. Leisner captured wounded. Aircraft 4U+BL a write-off.

Discarded radio panel found at this location by the Warplane Wreck Investigation Group.

Due to its pacifist background and its reluctance to budget for ARP measures, when West Ham became the victim of the first full-scale air attack on this country there was no satisfactory system in being for co-ordinating the various relief services. There was a shortage of wardens and the lack of support from the local authority caused one particular district to be labelled the 'Land of Forgotten Men'. One effect of Black Saturday was a disorganised evacuation of the worse hit areas, Epping Forest becoming a home from home for many. Another bone of contention was to be the choice of the ARP controller, the Regional Commissioner preferring the experience of the Town Clerk whereas the Council wanted to appoint the Mayor-elect for prestige reasons. The main ARP control centre for West Ham was here in this shored-up, bricked up building in Stratford High Street. This picture dates from 1941 following the demolition of the Times Furnishing store which originally stood next door on the corner of Chapel Street.

GILLMAN'S DAREDEVILS

At about the time when the great German Offensive in the spring of 1918 had sent the Allied armies reeling back almost to the gates of Paris, Bill Gillman, then 18 years of age, was fighting in the trenches. He had joined up a year earlier having given a false age, and had become a veteran under intensive action. With the Allies in grave danger of defeat, the British Commander-in-Chief, Field-Marshal Sir Douglas Haig, issued his famous appeal to the troops 'To fight with your backs to the wall'.

Bill Gillman has many vivid memories of those desperate days, not least of which was the vital importance of secure lines of communication. Twenty-one years later, with Britain again at war with Germany, Bill, then a West Ham County Borough Councillor, joined the Corps of Civil Defence. He was appointed Assistant Controller, Operations, and gave priority to a critical examination of the Civil Defence communications network in West Ham. His World War I experience was confirmed by reports of the bombing of Warsaw and Rotterdam and he realised that with telephone links so vulnerable to aerial bombardment, a secondary system must be organised and maintained.

'I had the idea of a band of cyclists,' he told me, 'to carry messages between the various Controls and street posts, etc. Men were being called up for the Forces and we had to rely on these volunteers. We set a minimum age of sixteen and had to turn away many who, obviously, were no more than fourteen or so. We required them to provide their own cycles, which we arranged to be painted yellow, and provided each lad with a tin hat and an arm-band with a large number for identification. They were great kids, brimming with native cockney wit and they performed their duties with great bravery.'

They were referred to in Civil Defence circles as 'Gillman's Daredevils' and fully justified their designation. Here is one lad's modest account of events on September 7, 1940, the first night of the London Blitz:

'I was ordered to Headquarters at Stratford with a message and had to ride through a patch of burning paint on the roadway in Camel Road, Silvertown, from the blazing paint works on the corner. The paint stuck to my tyres and set them alight but I rode on the pavement until the flames were out. All the time there were explosions and incendiary bombs coming down and I had to keep flinging myself off the bike to take cover. It was quite an adventure.'

Devotion to duty appeared to be an ingrained quality possessed by most Civil Defence volunteers. Gillman tells of an incident following the demolition by HE of the Times Furniture showrooms in Stratford High Street. Flames from the burning furniture store spread to Civil Defence HQ next door and, gradually, the Control Room in the basement filled with smoke and became untenable. The Assistant Controller decided to evacuate the building, transferring staff to the Secondary Control which had been set up in The Borough Theatre, a hundred yards or so along Stratford High Street.

Gillman: 'I said to the women switchboard operators: "All right girls, time to get out" but none of them moved although they were all suffering from the effects of the smoke, coughing and spluttering and wiping their eyes. "Did you hear what I said? It's time to go."

'"But we've still got calls coming in", one said and I had to pull the plugs before they would leave their seats.

'If they lacked anything at all, it most certainly was not spirit.'

CYRIL DEMARNE, 1986

The London Borough of Newham, created following the amalgamation of East and West Ham Municipal Borough Councils in 1965, still operates a department from the repaired and refurbished Civil Defence HQ (originally the old Alexander Hotel), but the corner was still what one would class as a bomb site when Andrew Hyde photographed it in August 1985.

SUNDAY, SEPTEMBER 8

Sunday morning down Stepney way. With roads leading to the docks sealed against sightseers, neighbours stand in small groups in stunned silence as they survey what the night has wrought. Perhaps amongst those here on Stepney Way are 80-year old Martha Dempsey from No. 183 or David and Lotte Ehrlich and their 17-year-old daughter Ruth from 185 — little could they know that their turn was to come just ten days later. Right now Stepney's night of trial was just around the corner: no sooner had battle commenced than 78 people lost their lives when Peabody Buildings was struck in John Fisher Street in the shadow of the Tower of London.

During the day, between 1100 and 1300, a raid of about 100 aircraft attacked objectives in Kent, penetrating northwards as far as Sheppey and the Thames Estuary. Little damage and few casualties were caused. Some reconnaissance flights were plotted between Beachy Head and Start Point, off the East Coast between Sunderland and the Wash. No bombs were dropped.

By night, commencing at 1930, a raid of 30 aircraft directed on London crossed the coast between Beachy Head and Shoreham. Bombing began at about 2000 and continued throughout the night until 0500 the next morning. Considerable damage was done to railway and road communications. Many serious fires were started. The heaviest bombing occurred in riverside districts but bombing was widespread and involved every Metropolitan Borough.

No. of bombs dropped: no accurate estimate is available. Enemy aircraft destroyed: 7 certain, 3 probable, 8 damaged. (Air Ministry reports show that the total enemy aircraft destroyed during the 24 hours ending 0600 8th September is now confirmed as 95, 21 of which were destroyed by A.A. fire.)

After the efforts of the previous day activity was inevitably reduced, resulting in something of a lull equally welcomed on both sides of the Channel. However, London remained the main target and German bombers returned in strength at night adding fresh fires to those still raging out of control from the previous day's raids. The Luftwaffe lost another 12 aircraft and 3 more damaged on operations; 4 more being destroyed and 5 damaged in accidents.

3/JG53 Messerschmitt Bf 109E-4 (867). Shot down in combat with Hurricanes of Nos. 46 and 605 Squadrons during escort sortie for KG2 Dorniers attacking London Docks. Probably that claimed by Pilot Officer C. F. Ambrose and Sergeant W. A. Peacock of No. 46 Squadron. Crashed at Seal, near Sevenoaks 12.40 p.m. Uffz. B. Adelwart killed. Aircraft a write-off.

Site excavated by the Halstead War Museum and remains of shattered airframe recovered together with one complete 20mm cannon. Other items held by the Hawkinge Aeronautical Trust.

Hitler came this way . . . but is the legacy any the better than what went before?

5/KG2 Dornier Do 17Z-3 (2668). Severely damaged by AA fire during sortie to bomb London Docks. Abandoned by crew and crashed near Farningham Road railway station 12.45 p.m. Oberlt. J. Schneider, Uffz. J. Schumacher, Obergefr. H. Hoffmann and Flgr. W. Kohl all baled out and captured wounded — believed admitted to Royal Herbert Hospital at Woolwich. Aircraft U5+BN a write-off.

Surface fragments from this aircraft or that below recovered from general area of crash site by the Kent Battle of Britain Museum and now in the Hawkinge Aeronautical Trust collection.

5/KG2 Dornier Do 17Z-2 (1130). Suffered direct hit by AA fire during sortie to bomb London Docks. Exploded over Farningham Road railway station 12.40 p.m. Lt. O. Landenberger, Obergefr. F. Lotter and Gefr. P. Schütze killed. Oberfw. M. Strobel captured wounded. Aircraft U5+FN a write-off.

5/KG2 Dornier Do 17Z (3415). Engaged by Hurricanes of Nos. 46 and 605 Squadrons during bombing sortie to London Docks. Believed that sent into a spin following attack by Sergeant S. Andrew of No. 46 Squadron. Exploded in mid-air over Leeds, near Maidstone 12.40 p.m. Oberlt. M. Ziems killed. Uffz. H. Flick, Uffz. W. Trost and Uffz. W. Selter missing believed killed. Aircraft U5+LN a write-off.

Due to the severity of this crash and the wide area over which wreckage was strewn, the authorities were only able to identify the remains of Martin Ziems who was buried in Maidstone Cemetery. What little was found of the rest of the crew defied proper identification and was

buried in two 'Unknown German Airman' plots in St Margaret's churchyard at Broomfield — close to where they fell. None has been reinterred since and they remain there to this day.

Surface fragments collected from strawberry plantation at Hollingbourne by the London Air Museum said to be from this aircraft.

That afternoon a grim-faced Churchill went down to the East End to see the effects of the night's raid for himself. His route was kept secret and the photographs taken were gone over by the Press and Censorship Bureau of the Ministry of Information at the University of London to ensure no clues appeared as to the locations visited. Normally street names were obliterated in red ink on a print; in this case *(above left)* the actual negative has had the name scratched out, making the establishment of his route rather difficult. When in 1946 Churchill came to prepare the manuscript for his *History of the Second World War* he, too, could not remember where he had gone and he wrote to his old Chief-of-Staff, Major General Sir Hastings Ismay, to see if he knew.

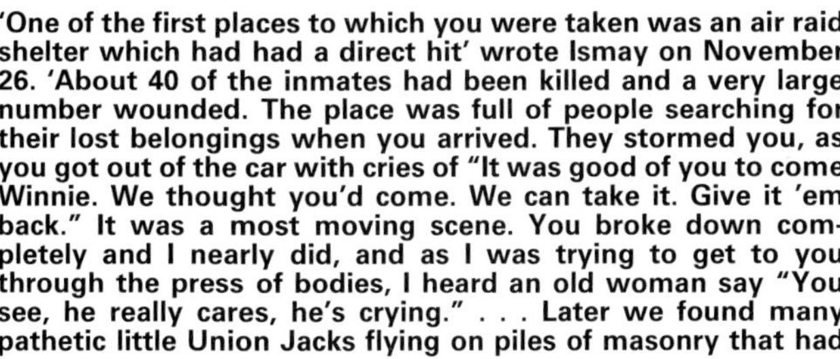

'One of the first places to which you were taken was an air raid shelter which had had a direct hit' wrote Ismay on November 26. 'About 40 of the inmates had been killed and a very large number wounded. The place was full of people searching for their lost belongings when you arrived. They stormed you, as you got out of the car with cries of "It was good of you to come Winnie. We thought you'd come. We can take it. Give it 'em back." It was a most moving scene. You broke down completely and I nearly did, and as I was trying to get to you through the press of bodies, I heard an old woman say "You see, he really cares, he's crying." . . . Later we found many pathetic little Union Jacks flying on piles of masonry that had once been the homes of these poor people.' The visit lasted all afternoon and into the hours of darkness. Fires were still burning in many of the stricken buildings, and, Ismay recalled that, 'the Luftwaffe returned to this blaze of light before you left the docks. The car had a long job getting out through narrow streets, many of which were blocked by houses having been blown across them'. *Top:* The PM is seen here with West Ham Town Clerk, Charles E. Cranfield, on the corner of Winchester Street and Factory Road inspecting the smouldering ruin of the Silvertown Rubber Company. *Above:* There were 53 branches of the Temperance Billiard Halls in London: this is the one in Mare Street, Hackney.

VERY COMMANDING OFFICER

On October 25, 1939, when I left the full-time Auxiliary Fire Service I thought I should have nothing further worth writing about. But I was mistaken. I hadn't even started.

Sunday, September 8, 1940. A bright morning, and I was working in the garden digging for victory, when my wife came and told me that I was urgently wanted on the phone by Station No. 1. Our part-time Station Officer was on the other end when I answered and he asked me if I could get round to the station within five minutes for an urgent job. Of course, I said I could, so jumped into my kit, on to my bike and was round there in four minutes.

I had no notion of what was in store, but there were rumours of Stratford. Four other fellows turned up at intervals, Dick Reynolds, part-time Patrol Officer, Gordon Hunter, Dennis Cooper with his car, and Phil Evans.

We waited and waited — must have been an hour at least I should say — when word came that we were to proceed to the Gaumont Cinema at Rose Hill. Off we went, and on arriving found another car with four firemen standing by it. We have to wait here for some others and form a convoy. More waiting for the rest (please bear in mind that we were all round to the Station in under ten minutes) and presently the VERY COMMANDING OFFICER arrives.

He had us all out of the cars (you do not dismount until told), lines us up and harangues us. We are to keep together,

Jim Barker's tongue-in-cheek account of his unit *(above)* on their first day of action must be seen against the confusion caused by the unprecedented weight of that first mass attack. In peacetime a fire requiring 30 pumps is a big fire but that first night there were six 100-pumpers in the docks and Bishopsgate Goods Yard; a 130-pumper in the Surrey Docks *(below)*, 200 pumps at the Woolwich Arsenal — London No. 1 military target — with another 300-pump monster conflagration in Quebec Yard. The latter even set alight wooden blocks in the road and solid embers a foot long from the stacked timber were showered down to start fresh fires. The heat was so intense that it blistered paint on fireboats 300 yards away. In 1942 the Ministry of Information admitted that 'the early nights confronted the brigades with unheard of problems of mobilisation — the task of having the right number of pumps turned out from the right stations and present at the right fires — and of transport along roads pitted with craters and littered with debris.'

fall in for roll call on arrival at destination, keep with him all the time, fall in again and roll call when relieved, we are expected to do six hours duty, etc: and HE IS IN CHARGE.

Hurrah, at last we are off. Still do not know where, but we are going. We now try to make up for all the wasted time and tear through traffic lights and law abiding traffic, horns blaring all the time — chap behind us has a very expensive pair of twin horns and, my, isn't he proud of them.

Mitcham, Streatham, Brixton, Elephant, just like that. Hold up a little at the Elephant, then on again. Borough, London Bridge, Aldgate, and then the fun starts — VERY COMMANDING OFFICER doesn't know where he is going. Inquire at Gardiner's Corner, go along left fork road and find a sub-station around Canning Town way, and here we all stop. We get out to stretch our legs while inquiries are made. I have been wedged between Reynolds and Hunter and am glad of the change.

During the time of waiting here the air raid warning sounded and we were amazed at the way the people RAN for shelter. We didn't know then. Five minutes later we were bundled back into the car, bound for Abbey Road. This was located fairly quickly in comparison with our later travels.

More inquiries by our VERY C.O. who later comes back and tells us that we have to go somewhere else. Also tells us that the Chief Officer at the station pointed out that there was a warning on and would we like to take cover with his chaps? VERY C.O. says 'No, you've had your share, WE'LL carry on.' Said it just like that too. (Blimey, can't this fellow talk). All right, off we go again to find a certain station. Up one road, down another, get on the Southend Road nearly to Dagenham, turn back again, find the crossroads we left ten minutes before, and try another tack. Off again, still following VERY C.O. Drive three minutes and all reverse (six cars).

Try another way. Seems we have to go over a viaduct where there is a police barrier across the road with a warning of unexploded bomb.

Out of car, take down notice, hold down ropes until cars have gone over, put back notice and get in car. Past bomb crater (funny feeling) and two hundred yards further up the road find a policeman. What did you expect? We've come the wrong way. All reverse (six cars) past bomb crater (more funny feeling), take down police barrier, cars go over, replace barrier and stop.

What will VERY C.O. do now? We don't know. He makes a decision and we go in another direction. By the way, Dennis Cooper swears that we went over that bridge at least a dozen times. So you will have to take your choice. I suggest you split the difference. To get back — along by railway this time, all reverse after about a mile, and back to the police barrier. All reverse here once more (six cars) and go back to the crossing. Turn right when over crossing, but it does not seem to lead anywhere,

South of the river: bombed out in Arnott Street. What Hitler failed to achieve in 1940 post-war redevelopment has completed as Arnott Street has now been expunged from the map — only this small section *(below)* of Theobald Street (at the far end) remaining as the approach road to the school, just off the New Kent Road.

so we reverse (six cars) and go back the way we've just come, but this time branch off over a level crossing. Turn right when over crossing, but it does not seem to lead anywhere, so we reverse (six cars) and go back over that crossing. That's that. Carry on along the same road for a bit and find another level crossing, go over this, up and down the road for a bit, back over the first crossing, turn left, right, left, right, etc., and find ourselves — where do you think?

All get out for general confab (we have been running round for an hour). One chap says 'Where do you want to get?' VERY C.O. says 'Silvertown, and if you think you know where it is you had better lead.' Chap says 'O.K.' We are there in five minutes.

At Silvertown there are dozens of buses and scores of cars, and here we all wait again.

By now we are all pretty hungry and wonder what is happening regarding grub. Someone tells us that there is a mobile canteen a little further up the road, so we go along to see what we can get. All we can get is chewing gum and a packet of chocolate. A little later we hear that there is some grub going at the fire station, so two of the chaps go along to see what they can get. They came back with an unopened tin of bully beef and a hatful of biscuits, and what biscuits they were. Hard tack. Another chap and myself go back to see if *we* can get anything and we also are fortunate. So far we had had nothing to drink, but remembered passing a pub a little way back along the road, so Hunter, Cooper and myself go along to try and get some drink. Hell of a crowd in the pub, so Cooper and me tell Hunter it is no good us all going in, so we leave him to get beer and cider. I had seen a notice

In August 1941 the London County Council paid tribute to a force which had, during the past year, 'grappled with the greatest emergency in the history of fire-fighting. . . . When the fire bombs were dropped 25,000 firemen of the Auxiliary Fire Service followed the London Fire Brigade into their first major action . . . For the great majority it was their first fire-fighting job . . . far beyond the experience of even the tired firemen of the regular Brigade.' ***Above:*** **Although lacking a precise date, this picture shows a typical London scene early in September. It is, in fact, Little Portland Street in the West End.**

indicating where a crashed German bomber was to be found, so I made my way towards it. I found no bomber but I *did* find Cooper, who had taken advantage of poor Hunter and left him fighting in the pub.

We could not find the bombers, so we went back and waited for Hunter. When he came out (sweating and cursing) we went to the car and had our refreshments. Still no sign of any movement on our part. Another long wait and at last we get news. We are relieving at the docks.

Cars get together, we get in and off we go through dock gates. Various bits roped off owing to time bombs. More starting and stopping, find out where we have to go, park cars, and VERY C.O. gives Evans and me a job. There is a little thing that Phil Evans reminded me about, and that is, our axes. These axes have been our pride and joy ever since we have had them. Bright and always shining, the least speck religiously removed. Getting a few spots of water on them while training at the sewage farm meant hours of polishing to get them back to their former glory. Phil and I don't know where the other chaps went, so when we had finished our job we tacked ourselves on to some men from No. 3 Station. On this job it is necessary to get help as we cannot get enough water, and the leading fireman sends me back to the VERY C.O. to see if he can let him have another line of hose. I find the VERY C.O. and explain the position to him and he says that he has lost a heavy pump, hasn't seen it all day. Will I go and find it. I said 'O.K.' and wander off to try to find this particular pump. Talk about needles in haystacks. I found hundreds of others, light, medium and heavy, but nowhere could I see the one I was looking for. Went down a road running with molten rubber and tar. Slippery as the road to hell. Made inquiries, fruitless, and went back to report failure to VERY C.O.

Found him at work on a job which I had left half an hour before and told him I could not find it. (It was not located until that night).

He lost interest in us again now and we had to find a job for ourselves. A little way up the river we saw some barges and a ship burning like billy-ho, and we wished we could get to them. It seemed like an answer to prayer, for a Port of London Authority boat came in and our Patrol Officer got permission to go in it over to the barges.

We wondered how we were going to get a pump on board and where we were going to get one, when the Captain told us that he had a couple of deliveries on board with hoses already coupled. Good enough. We all trooped on board hoping not to be sea sick. On getting over to the barges we ask for water on and get a surprise. Our pumps are rotary pumps and the water comes through with a steady flow if you have a reasonable motor-man, but this came through with a THUMP, THUMP, THUMP, that nearly had us off our feet at first.

We cooled down the nearest barge so that we could board it and put out the fire inside it. We kicked up clouds of smoke and nearly asphyxiated Reynolds and Hunter who were down wind from us.

Having got this one out we started playing on a barge alongside so as to cool that one enough to board and to get that much nearer to the burning steamer. When we considered we had got it cool enough, we called for water off and jumped across. When we got water on again we found that we wanted more hose so that we could play into the hold of the vessel which was immediately below us, so Den Cooper left me holding the branch (the brass bit that squirts, to non firemen) to haul forward some more slack. With Cooper hauling and the thump thump of the pump I sat down on the iron deck of the barge. And did I say it was cool? I dare not let go of the branch and had to stick it out until Cooper could come to my help. Glad to say that the deck was not hot enough to scar but it was mighty uncomfortable. In any event, what's the use of having scars where you cannot show them. We spent some time in getting this barge out and we were all surprised at the amount of water we shoved into it before getting it out. After we had got it out we turned our attention to the steamer, but found that our jet would not reach high enough to do any good, so as the crew of the PLA boat finished at six o'clock we got on board and went back to our dock. We had some tea on the boat. You should have seen it. I

On September 8, as the weary men returned to their stations to snatch a few hours' sleep, an internal official communiqué from Fire Service Headquarters read: 'The way in which the situation was dealt with gave rise to real confidence in the organisation and mobilising arrangements — and in the morale and efficiency of the auxiliaries.' This second picture shows the opposite view with a close up of the Dennis trailer pump. Water is being taken from the street mains, the pump being used to increase the pressure to 75 pounds per square inch, sufficient to throw the jets 70 feet high. The branch on the left has been dropped damaging the nozzle and causing the jet to feather (break up).

thought firemen could make tea, but this stuff was so strong that one pot would make tea at a sub-station for twelve months. We ourselves were supposed to be relieved at six o'clock (18 hours AFS time) so tried to find VERY C.O. to see what about it. We could not find him so went back to the car for some grub.

It was during this time that we really had time to look around. The mind boggled at what we saw. Simply couldn't grasp at the time. Buildings just shells. Four steamers sunk. One Russian, one Estonian, and two British. Sacks of grain floating in the water. Blazing oil tanks, jute or hemp stores. Burnt out wood yard, yet a lorry laden with timber standing no more than six yards away not even scorched. In another shed which was burnt out was a cupboard made from soap boxes which contained workmen's overalls, absolutely untouched. Saw all kinds of inexplicable things like that. Twisted girders. Bulging walls. Holes torn in railway tracks. Broken glass. Molten rubber. Roads running with oil and tar. Den Cooper and I went back to the lavatories at the fire station and saw a thing which struck us as most eloquent, but I fear I shall not be able to put on paper. The floors were running with water and in the middle of the floor were a pair of Wellingtons with waterproof leggings welded into a solid lump with rubber and tar. We could imagine the poor blighter coming in dead tired, kicking off those boots with a curse, abandoning them, and paddling through water in his socks, flinging himself down in a dry spot somewhere and going to sleep.

It was not until some time after that I was able to think SO WHAT? Boats could still draw into the docks. The cranes were apparently O.K. At least one building that we went into wanted little more than glass to make it all right. One of the steamers was only down by the bows, and two others were foreigners. Do not think I am trying to belittle the damage, I'm not. It was colossal, but certainly not crippling.

On our way to the car we met a Patrol Officer who asked us if we would like a drink. We said 'No thanks', thinking that he meant he would buy us one, but he said 'Only I know where there is some going free.' We said 'where?' 'Follow those two men' said he. We did, and found the beer. (I cannot be more explicit about this little episode.)

Now that we were refreshed we once more set about finding the VERY C.O. We found him down by the water's edge where some barges were burning feebly. He said 'we'll just put these out and then call it a day'. We soon fixed these but saw no more of the VERY C.O. So as there were no more fires on our ground, we poked around a bit to see if we could find any souvenirs.

One chap found a bullet and two of the other chaps had a pail each. We put the pails in the back of the car and hung around.

Time was getting on now and we wanted a proper meal. It was also essential for one chap and myself to be back in Sutton first thing in the morning, so we made a determined effort and hunted down the VERY C.O. Told him we were sorry but if we were not relieved very soon we should have to dismiss ourselves, having done considerably more than six hours. More palaver. VERY C.O. telephones and tells us relief is on the way.

He had us all lined up in the street to tell us this. The air raid warning had sounded but we ignored it as usual. Suppose we thought it was going to be like Sutton, when suddenly SWISH — CRUMP. VERY C.O. yelled 'take cover' and streaked for it. Ran nearly as well as he talked. We broke ranks and rushed for shelter but did not have time. Swish. I dived down behind a heap of sandbags, and as soon as the bomb landed, jumped up and made for shelter. Half way there when I heard another one coming, so got under a pump or lorry or something. This one fell to the right. Up again and on to shelter. I was just about to enter the shelter when we heard yet another coming. I tried to fling myself down again but got washed into the shelter on all fours by rush of chaps behind me. I found afterwards that Gordon Hunter had congratulated himself on finding

It is remarkable how — except for this incident — the street came through the war virtually unscathed . . . and how it has even survived another forty years without experiencing the grasping hand of the property developer.

Great Scotland Yard near the corner of Northumberland Avenue. Apart from the branch on the turntable ladder, other jets are being brought to bear from across the street.

good cover after the first bomb but on looking up found that he was standing under an open girder tower. He didn't stop there. Phil Evans and I were together but what happened to the other chaps I don't know.

We stuck in this shelter waiting for relief for I don't know how long. This struck us as rather senseless as we were doing nothing and didn't need any relief to do that. Found later that other chaps had got into the shelter by another entrance, and wended my way along to them.

All the chaps in the other half of the shelter were in an attitude of prayer. Heads bowed on hands. Asked one of them what they thought they were doing, and was told 'taking sensible precautions'.

Tried it and found it a good idea. Sit away from walls, put head on hands, elbows on knees, tip tin hat on to back of head. Didn't feel half so bad when shelter jumped.

After what seemed a week of this we heard our VERY C.O. calling Sutton and Carshalton men.

We gathered round him and he told us that we were to get to Abbey Road and form a convoy there. We came out and found it as bright as day, fires all round, absolutely indescribable, and even if I could adequately describe it you would not believe it. When we were in the shelter we had heard chaps cursing others for lighting matches in the doorway and so showing a light, but it must have been as noticeable as striking one in front of a car headlamp.

Got into the car in the same order in which we came down, between Reynolds and Hunter. Hit my shin on the pails and cursed. All O.K. and we start for home. No lights. Not necessary.

Where's Abbey Road? What's the good of asking us, we having come all round the moon between there and Silvertown. Get to the viaduct where the unexploded bomb is. We don't go up there we know. Stop. Don't think we turn right so go straight on. Another discussion at the next main road as to whether Abbey Road is likely to be up there. Not a soul about to ask, so carry on in what we hope is the right direction. We've got the sun roof of the car open so that we can see what's happening overhead. Plenty.

Come out at Canning Town Station so we reckon we'll abandon Abbey Road and make for home. Every bump scraped my sore leg on the pails. For a change ride with one foot in them. Get cramped worse so go back to my original position.

Aldgate, Gardiner's Corner. Huge fire raging. More diversions. Broken glass, hoses, pumps and AFS men.

Thinks it will be better to go Vauxhall rather than London Bridge way, so go along King William Street, Queen Victoria Street, and along embankment to Lambeth Bridge. Darker here. Somewhere about here Dennis runs us neatly over what looks like an unexploded bomb crater, even if it wasn't I got that same funny feeling. Going past Doulton's or somewhere near there the barrage suddenly intensifies (I hope that's the right word, for it's been going like blazes nearly all the time) and we think we ought to take cover. Scramble out of car to find it. Nothing doing. We try to squeeze between some iron railings that are only about five inches apart, to get under a porch. Hopeless of course. Hobson's choice is that we carry on. All get in again. Blast those pails. Try again. Vauxhall, Stockwell, Clapham and then branch off along Bedford Road. Over Acre Lane and along King's Avenue.

Now pitch dark. Side lights on but almost useless. We are stopped at the next cross roads by a policeman who tells us there are some time bombs somewhere along the road. Doesn't know where and advises diversion. Turn left and take first right which brings us back to King's Avenue about half a mile further on. At the junction another policeman stopped us and told us to mind the bomb crater. We thanked him and Den Cooper said 'Which way shall we go then?' Cop said 'straight on.' So Cooper went on and down the bomb crater we went. Cop said 'Didn't you see the red lamps?' Of course we had seen the lamps and Cooper had driven between them thinking, as we all did, that they marked the passage. There was a bar across the road but we couldn't see it.

All get out. Haul the car out. Put the bar up again and get in, minding the pails. (Seems to me I've spoken somewhere else about putting bars up.) Down a road half of which is up for repairs to the sewer. Was it dark? Cooper must be driving by smell. Hunter and I are pilots through this part of the country, and work our way round to Tooting Bec Common. All this time the Blitz was going fine. Took a wrong road somewhere about here but sorted ourselves out again. (I shudder to think what the VERY C.O. could have done.) Down to Amen Corner and feel we are in home country once more. Straight ahead and in no time we see the

With its negative deteriorating with age, this photograph shows the morning scene in Kingsway, the original caption stating that 'firemen are playing on the flames of a gas explosion to keep the flames in check after the air raid on Central London last night'. However, even with this vague caption, the censor stopped its publication.

traffic lights at The Grapes like welcoming beacons. Back at Station 1 at 1.30 a.m. Monday morning and are we glad. Nearly two hours on the road. Have a cup of tea. See myself in a mirror. Filthy dirty.

Outstanding events, or rather, perhaps, things that have stuck in my mind: The drive there; of course, the fire; the Ship's tea; Cooper's driving; those London Firemen — have they got guts, or have they? And those bloody pails!

JIM BARKER, 1940

Holborn Tramway Station was opened in 1906 and the route ran from the Embankment to just below Waterloo Bridge, then via a tunnel under the Aldwych and Kingsway to the junction of Southampton Row and Theobalds Road. The station was closed in 1952, a few months before the last trams were withdrawn in London. Part of the southern section of the subway is now used as a traffic underpass and the northern section, including the site of the tramway station, was, at the time of our visit in 1983, used as the London flood control centre.

DAILY EXPRESS, Monday, September 9, 1940.

No. 12,573 — Monday, September 9, 1940 — One Penny

Goering gloats as his bombers take off to restart the Battle of London

MASS BOMBING OF LONDON RESTARTS AT BLACK-OUT

Two buses hit: Hospital ringed by explosions

EAST END ATTACKED AGAIN

GOERING RESTARTED HIS GREAT BLITZKRIEG ON LONDON PROMPTLY AT BLACK-OUT TIME—7.59—LAST NIGHT. HALF AN HOUR BEFORE THAT TIME HE MADE A GLOATING, BOASTING BROADCAST TO THE GERMAN PEOPLE.

"A terrific attack is going on against London," he said. "Adolf Hitler has entrusted me with the task of attacking the heart of the British Empire.

"From where I stand [presumably his headquarters] I can see waves of planes headed for England."

Six minutes after the news of his broadcast reached the Daily Express office the sirens howled the Alert.

Bombs began to fall almost immediately. High explosives. Screamers. Incendiaries.

German airmen, evidently using the smouldering fires of Saturday night's raids to guide them, made for the same targets—London's dockland.

While the work of succour went on among the wreckage of the little houses of the East End, while the people still searched the ruins of their homes, the Germans droned overhead, dropping more bombs, adding to the destruction.

The outer defences, blazing away at the raiders, were joined by the guns in inner London.

The noise was deafening. Bomb flashes and bursting shells made a pattern in the darkening sky.

Three-quarters of an hour after the alert a second wave of bombers circled the east London area. But they were fewer than came over on Saturday. The continuous barrage, from the coast to London, had held off the main forces.

FIERCEST FIRE

For ten minutes there was silence. Not even the sound of an engine.

Then, as one, London's guns roared again into the heaviest A.A. bombardment of the war. The raiders were back. The screaming of the bombs as they fell, the dull crumps as they exploded, proved that.

A raider caught in a frame of bursting shells at the intersection of a score of searchlights unloaded his bombs on a London suburb.

One fell in a road of big houses where a King's Bench judge lives. Others fell near by.

Five screaming bombs dropped around a London hospital. Sticks

→ BACK PAGE, COL. FIVE

INSIDE A BOMBED HOSPITAL

Doctors run out to see the damage

Daily Express Staff Reporter

FOUR high-explosive bombs were dropped in the grounds of a London hospital during the first three hours of last night's raid.

One demolished the laundry; the second wrecked the old nurses' quarters; another damaged part of a nurses' home; the fourth fell on open ground.

A fifth bomb pitched in the road right outside the hospital, making a big crater, blew in the sides of two trolley buses and shattered the windows of the building.

The medical staff was just finishing an emergency operation when this bomb fell near a public shelter.

FELL TO FLOOR

I was at the hospital inquiring about the effect of the first two bombs when the other three fell. In the dimly lit hall, with doctors, porters and members of the A.R.P. squad, I flung myself on the stone floor as they screamed down.

The building shook with the concussion; fragments of glass from shattered windows tinkled down. Then doctors and nurses ran through a back exit into the grounds to see what damage had been done.

At midnight it was believed nobody in the hospital had been injured. Many of the patients, and those of the nursing staff not on duty, were in secure shelters.

Fire in U.S. destroyer intended for Britain

BOSTON, Sunday.—Fire broke out today on the destroyer Mackenzie, one of the American vessels presumably intended for Britain. It was soon put out. Damage was small.

Cause of the outbreak is not known.—A.P.

"We'll stand any attack" —R.A.F. leaders say

Daily Express Air Reporter

NO matter how intensified the German air attack on Britain may become, R.A.F. executives are confident that our reserves of machines and men are sufficient to stand up to it.

London's Saturday night raid was a reprisal for the R.A.F. bombing of Berlin. It meant a diversion from the avowed German plan of destroying our Fighter Command as a prelude to invasion.

But it was not the biggest concentrated attack made on this country. In the night raids not more than 350 bombers and fighters were used; in all the day's attacks probably not more than 600 planes. Germany lost one in six of her machines.

Heavier raids on London must be expected, but they are limited by the extent that the enemy can knock out our fighters so as to give his bombers greater freedom of action.

Will get through

At night time many Germans will continue to get through. Civilians must be prepared for that, though our strength is increasing daily.

A.A. guns shot with great accuracy on Saturday night. They shot down twenty-one Germans and put up a big barrage—a satisfactory result.

This may be the most critical week in our history. The fact that Goering has gone to Northern France to direct operations personally is taken in London as an indication of the importance the Germans attach to their present operations.

If the Germans can satisfy themselves they have done sufficient damage to our fighter defences, they may attempt invasion.

Lady Borden dead

OTTAWA, Sunday.—Lady Borden, widow of Canada's Great War Premier, has died in Ottawa, it was announced today. She was seventy-six.—Reuter.

COCKNEYS IN THE FIGHT

Homes shattered—but not their hearts

Daily Express Staff Reporter HILDE MARCHANT

THE civilian population is taking its Dunkirk. Through the East End yesterday there trekked a ragged, sleepless army whose homes had been smashed through the night.

They pushed perambulators, carts, or took the best of their homes on their backs, climbing through streets that had once been two neat rows of houses and were yesterday like a ploughed field.

The very soil under their houses had been ripped open, scattered with brick and tile across their path.

Little houses, four rooms and a bath tub, eight shillings a week, had taken the attack.

All through the night they waited in their shelters while bombs slapped into the houses and streets around them. At daylight they came up and many saw the roots of their homes turned to the sky.

★

They dusted and shook what was left, then began trekking through the streets with one plan in their minds—another home, another room where this child, this mattress, this set of plates shall be put down again.

For this is not the end. These labourers, these people who have put their lives together round three pounds a week, and seen everything they loved and liked and worked for disappear to the earth, are eternal.

Hitler promised 300 tons of bombs, he promised he would raze our

BACK PAGE, COLUMN ONE

The docks carry on

STATEMENT last night by an official of the Port of London Authority:—

"While damage by fire at the docks is considerable, discharging and loading berths are intact, and all services of the port will be maintained.

"Though some warehouses have been damaged, the losses of foodstuffs are relatively small."

A Daily Express staff reporter who made a tour of the docks yesterday writes:—

"I found little damage of military importance.

"There was some timber ablaze, but as one of the dockworkers said: 'Canada is full of timber, and the docks are still open to unload a hundred times as much as has been lost.'"

Get-you-there services

MARKED improvement in transport services affected by the week-end raids was reported by the Ministry of Transport last night.

The statement added that "some interruption must still be expected, but everything would be done at railway stations to help people to get to work.

"Every assistance will be given, and no unnecessary formality will be allowed to stand in the way of travellers in journeying between their homes and places of work."

The eastern portion of the District Line and the East London Line were affected, and so were tram and trolley bus services in east and south-east London.

Bomb damage on lines and other property of the Southern Railway inconvenienced travellers yesterday, but services to most towns were maintained. Bus services in the Victoria Station district were diverted owing to damage done by bombs.

STOP PRESS

LONDON BOMBED FOR 8½ HOURS

Bombs were still dropping on London eight and a half hours after Alert sounded.

Raid was of even greater intensity than that of Saturday night.

Several new fires were caused. At times raiders appeared to fly very low. Spasmodic gunfire greeted them. Several salvos from A.A. batteries were followed immediately by explosion of bombs.

It was the longest London had experienced.

A soldier on leave joins unhappy trek

ON Saturday afternoon they were all safely in their London homes.

Then came the biggest enemy air raid of the war. . . .

. . . A pathetic little procession sets out, carrying bundled household treasures, in search of a new place to sleep.

A small boy steps sturdily along beside a soldier on leave.—

Other pictures, Pages Three, Five and Six.

Gunner of 22 gets three Dorniers in a minute

LONDON'S sirens sounded the Alert again at 12.29 p.m. yesterday—but a twenty-two-year-old gunner in the south-east stopped three of the raiders reaching the City. He shot them down within a minute.

The leader of the formation was blown to pieces with the gunner's first shot.

Wreckage of the bombers was scattered over many fields. The crews of two were killed. Those in the third were captured.

Bombs from the wrecked planes damaged shops and cottages, but no one was injured.

People reported seeing leaflets dropping from the raiders, but most of them apparently fell in the Thames and were carried away.

A communiqué from the Air Ministry and Ministry of Home Security said: Since dawn this morning enemy activty was negligible until shortly before midday when a large force of enemy aircraft approached the coast north of Dover.

They were promptly engaged by our fighters and anti-aircraft guns, and only small formations were able to penetrate inland. These flew north to the Thames estuary where they were dispersed and driven off.

Reports so far received show that though bombs were dropped they fell mostly in rural areas and did little damage. In Kent some houses and a railway station were hit and a road temporarily blocked. There wa a small number of casualties but only one person was killed.

London got the all-clear at 1.24 p.m.

Took pilot's place

CAIRO, Sunday.—Acting-Sergeant Ian Blair, aged twenty-two, of Glasgow, serving with the R.A.F. Middle East Command, has been awarded the D.F.M. for saving his aircraft after the pilot had been killed.

The bomber in which Blair was acting as navigator was attacked by two Italian fighters. After the pilot had been hit the plane went into a dive.

With the help of the air gunner Blair carried the pilot from his seat and took his place at the controls.

He flew back to the base 250 miles away and made a fair landing.—B.U.P.

Paraguay: New leader

BUENOS AIRES, Sunday.—General Morinigo has been appointed President of Paraguay in place of General José Estigarribia, who was killed in an air crash yesterday, says message from Asuncion.—Reuter.

86 French planes join British at Gibraltar

A message from Algeciras received in New York last night said that eighty-six French airplanes have landed at Gibraltar to join the British forces.

Japanese hold Briton

PEKING, Sunday.—The British Embassy today lodged a protest with the Japanese authorities in Peking about the detention at Kalgan, North China, of a British missionary, Mr. Benson. The Japanese authorities were asked to hand him over immediately.—Reuter.

Dublin security (2,000)

Mr. De Valera, with Mr. Oscar Traynor, Eireann Defence Minister, took the salute in Dublin yesterday at a march-past of 2,000 members of Dublin Security Corps.

Who gave order to ring the bells?

Daily Express Military Reporter

CHURCH bells—signal of attempted invasion—were rung on Saturday night in south-west and north-east England, in Wales and in Scotland. Yesterday officials were finding out why.

In the south-west the signal spread from Somedset through Devon and Cornwall.

Troops were recalled to barracks and camps in some districts, and naval men were sent for.

Orders to return to camp were flashed on cinema screens, and mobile police rounded up soldiers at public houses and dance halls.

The Home Guard was ordered to double its strength at a number of points. Loud-speaker vans and messengers were used to mobilise them.

Roads were cleared of all civilian traffic, and people in the streets were stopped and questioned.

Points manned

Strong points throughout the west were manned. Home Guards who had been specially called out stayed on duty until morning.

It is thought the alarm in the south-west may have been caused by boats seen unexpectedly in mist off the coast. They were part of a fishing fleet returning early to harbour after a lucky catch

No orders for bells to be rung in any district were given by the War Office. I was told last night: 'There was no evidence to suggest that an invasion might be attempted."

Britons fake Nazi communiqué

They sank Ark Royal again

ISTANBUL, Sunday.—How British residents hoaxed German propaganda officials at the Rumanian port of Constanza was told in Istanbul today.

Agents of Dr. Goebbels some time ago put up a bulletin board in the centre of Constanza on which announcements of German "victories" were posted daily. A group of Britons recently prepared a parody of a typical Nazi communiqué, and, at night, put the parody in place of the genuine communiqué.

This is what it said: "The Ark Royal was sunk for the fourth time yesterday—this time by Italians. The Fuehrer has postponed the visit which he was to have made to London in September. It is hoped however, that Mr. Churchill and members of the British Army will pay a visit to Herr Hitler in Germany shortly."

German officials next morning found a smiling crowd copying the parody to show their friends.—Reuter.

Monday morning and a shocked businessman, perhaps surveying his own office, stands amid the rubble and glass littering King William Street. This was caused by a large bomb which had been dropped at 3.27 a.m., the blast being felt 400 yards away. The modern, steel-framed buildings like the Guardian Royal Exchange in the background have stood up remarkably well but Lloyds Bank had to be subsequently pulled down. On the right a gas main has been fractured in the bomb crater.

MONDAY, SEPTEMBER 9

By day, one main attack took place at 1635 by some 300 aircraft. These crossed the coast between North Foreland and Dover. Up to 1730 the main trend was towards the Estuary and South London though one raid of about 35 aircraft penetrated to Central London. A drift westward then developed and small raids were plotted as far west as Salisbury.

Commencing at 2000, raids by night from the French coast came in between the Isle of Wight and Dungeness, and all proceeded to the London area. From 0230 activity increased and a larger series of raids came from the Dutch islands via Thames Estuary into the London area, homing over Dungeness. A few raids occurred before midnight in South Wales, Midlands, over to Liverpool, but except for Canterbury practically no damage was done from these.

No. of bombs dropped: no accurate estimate is available. Enemy aircraft casualties: 52 destroyed, 11 probable, 13 damaged.

London again featured most prominently on Luftwaffe target maps although another large raid was also launched against Farnborough during the afternoon. Both raids were largely thwarted and broken up by determined fighter opposition. As evening fell, sirens again began wailing over London which was about to receive its third consecutive night attack. The Germans lost 27 aircraft and another 12 damaged on operations on this day; 2 more of their machines being destroyed and 4 damaged in accidents.

4/JG3 Messerschmitt Bf 109E-1 (6138). Engine damaged in combat with fighters during escort sortie and possibly that attacked by Squadron Leader E. A. McNab of No. 1 (RCAF) Squadron. Ditched in the Channel 6 miles off Newhaven 5.55 p.m. Fw. A-W. Müller captured unhurt. Aircraft lost.

7/JG3 Messerschmitt Bf 109E-1 (6316). 'Bounced' by Spitfires during free-lance sortie and engine damaged. Forced-landed at Cooper's Field, Flimwell, near Hawkhurst 5.35 p.m. Uffz. M. Massmann captured unhurt. Aircraft 6+I a write-off.

Relics held by Malcom Pettit. Aircraft taken to RAE Farnborough for evaluation.

Stab I/JG27 Messerschmitt Bf 109E-4 (1394). Radiator damaged in fighter attack and engine over-heated trying to reach the coast. Forced-landed at Knowle Farm, Mayfield 5.45 p.m. Oberlt. G. Bode (Gruppe Adjutant) captured unhurt. Aircraft <+ a write-off.

5/JG27 Messerschmitt Bf 109E-1 (3488). Fuel tank and cooling system damaged in fighter attack during bomber escort sortie to London. Forced-landed on Charity Farm, Cootham, near Storrington 5.50 p.m. Oberlt E. Daig captured unhurt. Aircraft 13+— a write-off.

6/JG27 Messerschmitt Bf 109E-1 (6280). Believed shot down by Pilot Officer H. L. Whitbread of No. 222 Squadron during escort sortie to London. Crashed at Mounts Farm, Benenden 6.15 p.m. Uffz. G. Rauwolf baled out and captured unhurt. Aircraft 7+— a write-off.

Major recovery by the Lashenden Air Warfare Museum which unearthed the Daimler-Benz DB 601 engine, fuel injection pump, radiator, main spar, undercarriage leg, complete cockpit armour, instruments, gunsight, control column, first-aid kit, pilot's maps and cap.

With London hammered for a second night running, one of the main fears of the Government was that morale would crack, leading to panic and mass hysteria. Already hundreds were leaving the East End and not only those who had been bombed out. Although each borough had been expected only to look after its own homeless, in the event it was the surrounding areas which were presented with the problem of what to do with the unwanted refugees. For three hours on Monday the King toured east and south-east London. In Southwark he came to Arnott Street (see page 67) where a pathway had now been cleared through the rubble.

7/JG27 Messerschmitt Bf 109E-4 (1617). Engine set alight in attack by Sergeant J. Frantisek of No. 303 Squadron. Crashed in flames and burned out at Romans Gate Cottage, Rudgwick 6.00 p.m. after second attack. Uffz. K. Born tried to bale out but killed. Aircraft a write-off.

Crash site now under a main road. Visited by the Air Historical Group which acquired the radio from this aircraft from a local resident.

1/JG53 Messerschmitt Bf 109E-4 (1508). Caught fire under attack by fighters during escort sortie for bombers over London. Crashed on Cherry Tree Farm near the Old Jail Inn, Jail Lane, Biggin Hill 6.00 p.m. Fw. H. Hönisch baled out and captured unhurt landing on Pilgrims Farm, Titsey. Aircraft 5+ a write-off.

Relics donated to the Kent Battle of Britain Museum by an ex-airframe fitter based at Biggin Hill in 1940 now held by the Hawkinge Aeronautical Trust.

8/JG53 Messerschmitt Bf 109E (6139). Crashed and burned out at Sundown Farm, Ditcham following combat with fighters 6.15 p.m. Gefr. P. Becker killed. Aircraft a write-off.

3/KG1 Heinkel He 111H-3 (5713). Severely damaged in attack by Sergeant P. A. Burnell-Phillips of No. 607 Squadron following bombing sortie to London. Believed also attacked by Pilot Officer S. Zimprich of No. 310 Squadron. With cooling system damaged and one engine disabled, forced-landed at Sundridge, near Sevenoaks 6.00 p.m. Crew tried to set fire to the aircraft. Oberlt. E. Kiunka and Uffz. A. Stumbaum captured unhurt. Uffz. E. Marck and Gefr. H. Reinecke captured wounded. Oberfw. A. Heidrich baled out and captured unhurt. Aircraft V4+BL a write-off.

Parts taken at the time held by Steve Vizard.

The exact spot where the King once trod now occupied by Geoffrey Chaucer School, rebuilt since amalgamation with Trinity Girls' School.

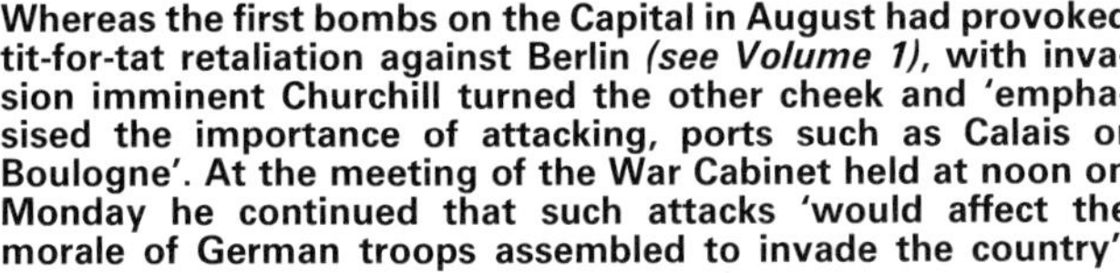

Whereas the first bombs on the Capital in August had provoked tit-for-tat retaliation against Berlin *(see Volume 1)*, with invasion imminent Churchill turned the other cheek and 'emphasised the importance of attacking, ports such as Calais or Boulogne'. At the meeting of the War Cabinet held at noon on Monday he continued that such attacks 'would affect the morale of German troops assembled to invade the country'. Later he wrote that the 400 German aircraft which had crossed the coast that evening had been 'met by at least 200 of our fighters who broke them up into small parties which fled after pursuit'. In all, only five of the bombers were prevented from leaving these shores — this is the Ju 88 from Stab II of KG30 which crash-landed on Bannisters Farm, Toulver Lane, at Barcombe in Sussex.

Stab/KG30 Junkers Ju 88A-1 (274). Believed shot down by No. 66 Squadron Spitfires during sortie to bomb London Docks. Forced-landed at Church Field, Newells Farm, Nuthurst, near Horsham 6.00 p.m. Oberlt. R. Heim (Geschwader Ia), Fw. A. Fuhs, Uffz. J. Beck and Uffz. W. Baustian captured unhurt. Aircraft 4D+AA a write-off.

Stab II/KG30 Junkers Ju 88A-2 (5074). Both engines disabled in attack by Squadron Leader R. H. A. Leigh of No. 66 Squadron during sortie to bomb London Docks. Possibly also attacked by Pilot Officer R. Deacon-Elliott of No. 72 Squadron. Harried by Pilot Officer H. R. Allen and Pilot Officer I. J. A. Cruickshanks of No. 66 Squadron prior to forced-landing at Bannisters Farm, Toulver Lane, Barcombe, near Lewes 5.40 p.m. Aircraft later caught fire and burned out. Oberlt. H-G. Gollnisch, Uffz. W. Rolf and Uffz. W. Hamerla captured unhurt. Uffz. E. Deibler killed. Aircraft 4D+KK a write-off.

Stab III/KG30 Junkers Ju 88A (333). Sortied to attack London but engaged by Spitfires of No. 602 Squadron and both engines disabled. Believed that attacked by Squadron Leader A. V. R. Johnstone and Pilot Officer A. Lyall. Then attacked by Flying Officer P. C. Webb and ditched in the sea off Pagham 5.50 p.m. Major J. Hackbarth (Gruppenkommandeur) and Oberfw. H. Manger captured unhurt. Uffz. W. Sawallisch and Gefr. F. Petermann killed. Aircraft 4D+AD a write-off.

Stab III/KG53 Heinkel He 111H-2 (2630). Engaged in bombing sortie to London and lost a wing in collision with crippled Hurricane flown by Pilot Officer G. M. Forrester of No. 605 Squadron. Crashed and exploded on Southfield Farm, Chawton, near Alton 5.50 p.m. Oberlt. K. Meinecke baled out slightly wounded and captured. Fw. O. Broderix baled out and captured unhurt. Fw. W. Wenninger, Fw. W. Döring and Fw. E. Wendorff killed. Aircraft A1+ZD a write-off.

The date of death of Wilhelm Wenninger, Bordmechaniker in this aircraft, is shown as October 4 in the records of the Soldatenfriedhof, Cannock Chase. The reason for this is unknown as he is not believed to have survived the crash of the aircraft.

Site excavated by the Southern Area Wartime Aircraft Preservation Society who recovered minor fragments from the airframe plus some shattered perspex and exploded 7.92mm machine gun ammunition.

15/LG1 Messerschmitt Bf 110C-4 (3298). Shot down by Pilot Officer H. N. Tamblyn of No. 242 Squadron during escort sortie over London. Believed also attacked by Flying Officer S. Fejfar and Pilot Officer V. Bergman of No. 310 Squadron. Crashed and exploded at the Maori Sports Club, Old Malden Lane, Worcester Park 6.00 p.m. Uffz. A. Pfaffelhuber and Uffz. O. Kramp killed. Aircraft L1+DL a write-off.

Major recovery from under a cricket pitch by the London Air Museum. Remains of both Daimler-Benz DB 601 engines excavated together with both undercarriage legs, oxygen bottles, remains of a rubber dinghy, first-aid kit, a parachute and masses of compressed airframe including one tail fin still bearing traces of painted Swastika. Tail fin now in the Tangmere Military Aviation Museum.

7/ZG76 Messerschmitt Bf 110C-4 (2137). Hit by AA fire following escort sortie over London and crashed at Munns Gore, Borden, near Sittingbourne 6.00 p.m. Uffz. G. Bierling and Uffz. F. Kurella baled out too low and killed. Aircraft 2N+FM a write-off.

Site excavated by Kent Battle of Britain Museum and remains of shattered Daimler-Benz DB 601 engines recovered together with large sections of compressed airframe, various components, propeller blade, oxygen bottles and aircrew forage cap and oxygen mask. Items now held by the Hawkinge Aeronautical Trust. Fragments recovered subsequently by Steve Vizard from a depth of eight feet included an engine badge.

9/ZG76 Messerschmitt Bf 110C (3108). Damaged in fighter attack during escort sortie over London and retired south. Attacked again over the coast and forced to ditch in the Channel 5 miles off Newhaven 6.00 p.m. Fw. H. Koops captured unhurt. Uffz. C. Weiher (of 7/ZG76) already wounded and drowned. Aircraft 2N+EP lost.

The body of the gunner, Christian Weiher, was subsequently recovered one mile west of Galloways, Lydd on October 20.

9/ZG76 Messerschmitt Bf 110C (3207). Rammed by crippled Hurricane flown by Flying Officer J. E. Boulton of No. 310 Squadron during escort sortie over London. Crashed in Woodcote Park Avenue, Woodmanstern 6.15 p.m. Lt. E. Ostermüncher and Gefr. W. Zimmermann both killed. Aircraft 2N+EP a write-off.

Few remaining fragments recovered by the Air Historical Group.

TUESDAY, SEPTEMBER 10

There was no major attack on the British Isles in daylight. Minor raids took place on Yarmouth, Newhaven, and a few other places in Kent and Sussex and there was coastal reconnaissance in the east and south. Some small raids approached London at 1715 but were intercepted and turned back.

Bombing was on a small scale and the civilian casualties reported are: 11 killed, 56 injured. Enemy aircraft destroyed: 2 certain, 1 probable.

British propaganda was quick to capitalise on what was headlined as 'Göring's triumphs', and pictures of bombed schools, churches and hospitals were held up as examples of the 'military and economic' objectives bombed under his personal direction. The first London hospital hit was, as we have seen, Queen Mary's (page 58); then came the turn of St Thomas's, which suffered a direct hit on Block 1 on September 9, followed by the London *(above)*, the premier East End hospital (although the picture is actually of one of the nurses' homes). *Below:* The first of many symbolic pictures of St Paul's — seen from Watling Street on the morning of the 10th. When the War Cabinet were informed at their meeting on Tuesday that the bombing of London was 'quite indiscriminate', it was agreed that, as an act of retaliation, British bombers over Germany should be instructed 'not to return home with their bombs if they failed to locate the targets which they were detailed to attack'. Now there were no holds barred; it was war in its totality.

Meanwhile down in the East End the night had brought a catastrophe which was to have long-lasting repercussions — a controversy lasting even to this day. Many hundreds of those who had fled from the Silvertown and Tidal Basin area of West Ham two days before had been concentrated in a school in Agate Street in Canning Town, still well within the danger area. Corridors, classrooms and halls were crowded, everyone awaiting the coaches promised for 'three o'clock'. And that was Sunday. That night more homeless arrived . . . but still no coaches . . . which had still not appeared as darkness fell on Monday. By now it was too late. In the early hours — at 3.45 a.m. to be precise — a heavy bomb scored a direct hit on South Hallsville School demolishing half the building and bringing down hundreds of tons of masonry. As rescue workers attempted to release the injured, a news blackout was imposed and a security cordon placed around the scene of the disaster to prevent already frightened onlookers from taking in the full implications of what had occurred.

After dark, most of England and Wales was under purple warning at some time and 37 red warnings were given, but outside London the only attempt at destructive bombing of important places was at Cardiff and Sheffield. Elsewhere there were a number of minor incidents chiefly in the area: Birkenhead-Liverpool, Berkshire and south-east England. London area was again bombed by single aircraft in succession, but probably rather fewer were employed than on previous nights and the casualties were far smaller.

The important incidents were major fires at St Katherine Docks and London Dock and some damage to railways. Most Boroughs received bombs, but in some cases only very few. Civilian casualties reported to date: 19 killed, 290 injured. Enemy aircraft destroyed — nil.

Air activity over the UK was slight due to dull weather which blanketed the whole of northern Europe. Widespread nuisance raids by small formations of German aircraft resulted in the loss of 4 machines and another 2 damaged. Another was destroyed and 3 damaged in accidents. In addition, 8 Heinkels of II/KG4 were destroyed and 2 damaged in an RAF bombing raid on Eindhoven airfield.

9/KG76 Dornier Do 17Z-3 (2778). Badly damaged by Spitfires of No. 72 Squadron during armed reconnaissance sortie to London and dumped bombs to escape. Then attacked by Pilot Officer T. S. Wade of No. 92 Squadron and pursued over Gatwick aerodrome where also hit by AA fire. Further attacked by Sergeant R. H. Fokes of No. 92 Squadron and crashed at Lower Sheriffs Cottages, West Hoathley 6.20 p.m. Oberlt. W. Domenig and Uffz. H. Strahlendorf killed. Uffz. E. Nürnberg captured badly wounded and admitted to Memorial Hospital, East Grinstead. Gefr. A. Greza captured slightly injured. Aircraft F1+ET a write-off.

Various reasons came out about as to why the coaches failed to arrive, and it seems certain that they were misdirected, either to Camden Town instead of Canning Town, or the leader of the convoy, ordered to rendezvous at the George, the well-known landmark at Wanstead, went to a pub of the same name in another borough. Be that as it may, it was the needlessness of the deaths, as a direct result of the poor organisation in West Ham, that made the tragedy all the more tragic. It is not known precisely how many died. Richie Calder, who visited the school on Tuesday morning and later wrote of the disaster in *The Lesson of London* put it at 450. The Council's official figure was 73.

Rumours are difficult to lay to rest and, in spite of official denials, locals still swear that many of the dead were buried where they lay in the crater. Cyril, whose men helped in the rescue, believes otherwise. Those that were recovered were buried in a mass grave in East London Cemetery.

Today a new South Hallsville School has arisen from the ashes of the old, and in 1982 Mayor Julie Garfield, a dispatch rider during the war, instituted an annual wreath-laying ceremony at the school that those who died in vain should no longer be forgotten.

WEDNESDAY, SEPTEMBER 11

Enemy activity by day consisted of one major attack between 1545 and 1645 by 250 aircraft on the Kent Coast. Of these about 30 penetrated to London. Bombing and shelling of Dover and Deal and bombing of Eastleigh were carried out simultaneously.

In the attack on London small numbers of the enemy reached their objectives. Unexploded bombs were dropped at Paddington, King's Cross, South Bromley, between Charlton and Charlton Lane. Five railway tracks at London Bridge were damaged by H.E.; bombs were also dropped at Woolwich, Greenwich, Deptford, Surrey Commercial and Victoria Docks, and Lewisham, causing major damage. Casualties were slight except at Lewisham where a public shelter was hit.

At Dover there was considerable damage to houses, shops and Priory Railway Station, and at Southampton some damage was done at Cunliffe Owen Aircraft Works, and a public shelter was hit, causing severe casualties.

Casualties: Dover: 7 killed, 122 seriously injured, 36 slightly injured. Southampton: 41 killed, 48 seriously injured, 43 slightly injured. During the day's operations, casualties to enemy aircraft were as follows: 60 destroyed by fighters, together with 34 probably destroyed and 44 damaged. Nine were destroyed by A.A. fire and nine were damaged.

Night bombing of London covered a large area and continued from 2020 to 0530 the following morning. Visibility was good and the enemy met an intense A.A. barrage

By now the boroughs of east London had to cope with another problem — the disposal of the dead — especially so when whole families were wiped out at a stroke . . . like the Chandler family at South Hallsville: father James, mother Eva and daughters Hazel, aged 4 and Edna, 6 months . . . or the Glitz's . . . or the Glovers . . . . Communal graves were an expedient, if impersonal, solution and suitable plots were opened. The Metropolitan Borough of Poplar chose this corner of what is now Tower Hamlets Cemetery at Bow: the prominent white cross is that of Auxiliary Fireman Jim Fletcher killed in West India Dock Road on September 10. In 1952, when this picture was taken, a suitably-inscribed memorial plaque was added. Sadly, those with no respect for the past have since added graffiti. The graves lie trodden underfoot.

Hackney's mass burial site can be found just inside the entrance to the East London Cemetery in Grange Road, Plaistow. Nicely maintained, the memorial plaque lists the casualties by name in date order beginning with Mary Hallett killed at St Scolastica's Retreat, Kenninghall Road, on September 8.

which was most effective. There was less damage and fewer casualties than on the previous nights. The excellent morale effect is evident everywhere today. Hits were made on recognisable targets such as Surrey Commercial Docks and Woolwich Arsenal, and important road and rail blocks were caused. There were five major fires. Two more hospitals were hit.

Night bombing on industry and communications was reported from Hull, St Helens, Warrington, Cardiff, Plymouth and Marlow. The main L.M.S. line Crewe-Lime Street, Liverpool was blocked near Sutton Weaver, and Vyrnwy pipe line supplying Liverpool was damaged. There was some damage to timber yards at Cardiff, casualties at Marine Barracks, Stonehouse, Plymouth, and minor fires at Hull and St Helens.

No large scale raids were launched against Britain until mid-afternoon when the weather improved prompting a major assault on London. Employing their now familiar tactic of sending over large formations of bombers in carefully timed waves, the Luftwaffe attempted to swamp the defences but found themselves countered by RAF squadrons now operating in pairs. A simultaneous attack on Portsmouth and Southampton succeeded in penetrating the fighter defences but caused relatively little damage. During the evening, RAF Bomber and Coastal Commands delivered attacks on French channel ports where invasion barges were assembled in growing numbers. London and Merseyside again provided the main targets for German night raiders at the end of a day on which the Luftwaffe lost 23 aircraft and 17 more damaged on operations; another 6 of their machines being destroyed and 2 damaged in accidents. With 10 days notice required by the Wehrmacht to complete their final preparations for the invasion of Britain, Hitler deferred a decision on the actual launch-date of 'Operation Sealion' for 3 days in order to continue the seemingly inexorable reduction of British resistance.

2/JG51 Messerschmitt Bf 109E-4 (1641). Shot down in flames by Sergeant W. B. Higgins of No. 253 Squadron. Crashed and burned out at Houndean Bottom, Lewes 4.00 p.m. Hptmn. E. Wiggers (Staffelkapitän) killed. Aircraft a write-off.

Site investigated by the Wealden Aviation Archaeological Group 1978. Little evidence remains of crash but tail panel bearing Swastika marking acquired from local resident, now on display in the Tangmere Military Aviation Museum.

8/JG51 Messerschmitt Bf 109E-1 (6293). Shot down by Flight Lieutenant G. R. Edge of No. 253 Squadron. Crashed and burned out at Foxhole Farm, Wadhurst 4.30 p.m. Fw. H. Siemer killed. Aircraft 9+I a write-off.

Spent rounds of 7.92mm ammunition and several fragments and minor components discovered by Steve Vizard.

Stab KG1 Heinkel He 111H-3 (5606). One engine disabled by AA fire over London during sortie to bomb Commercial Docks, other engine disabled by fighter attack over the coast. Believed that shot down by Pilot Officer A. B. Watkinson and Pilot Officer C. A. W. Bodie of No. 66 Squadron. Probably also that attacked by Flight Lieutenant J. C. Freeborn of No. 74 Squadron. Forced-landed on Broomhill Farm, Camber 4.30 p.m. and set alight by crew. Lt. O. Behn and Fw. J. Sommer captured unhurt. Uffz. P. Moeck, Uffz. G. Arndt and Gefr. M. Männich captured wounded. Aircraft V4+FA a write-off.

3/KG1 Heinkel He 111H-3 (3233). One engine hit by AA fire over London during sortie to bomb West India Docks. Lost formation then attacked and severely damaged by Flight Lieutenant D. G. Parnall, Pilot Officer T. F. Neil and Pilot Officer W. B. Pattullo of No. 249 Squadron. Forced-landed at Hildenborough 4.33 p.m. where crew attempted to set fire to the aircraft. Uffz. H. Steinecke and Uffz. W. Hirsch captured unhurt. Uffz. E.

At the rear of the same cemetery can be found West Ham's communal grave containing many of the unclaimed victims from South Hallsville. This picture was taken in September 1940.

Kramer, Gefr. W. Pfeiffer and Gefr. H. Pümpel captured wounded. Aircraft V4+KL a write-off.

Complete radio and other items in the Halstead War Museum.

During Wednesday, pilots of Fighter Command managed to bring down ten of the London-bound Heinkels, three force-landing within ten miles of each other just behind the coast. ***Above:*** **Two of KG1 even landed on the same farm at Camber where they were fired by their crews.** ***Below:*** **Feldwebel Friedrich managed to land at Burmarsh amid a forest of anti-invasion poles. Overhead the victor circles the vanquished.**

6/KG1 Heinkel He 111H-2 (5364). Both engines disabled by fighter attacks during sortie to bomb London Docks. Believed that shot down by Squadron Leader R. H. A. Leigh, Flying Officer R. W. Oxspring and Sergeant D. A. C. Hunt of No. 66 Squadron. Also attacked by Flight Lieutenant A. R. Wright of No. 92 Squadron. Dumped bombs and forced-landed at Broomhill Farm, Camber 4.40 p.m. where crew set fire to the aircraft. Uffz. B. Hansen, Uffz. K. Markert, Uffz. J. Krall and Gefr. G. Wilhelm captured unhurt. Uffz. H. Wildehopf captured wounded. Aircraft V4+RW a write-off.

1/KG26 Heinkel He 111H-3 (5680). Damaged by AA fire and then attacked by fighters, including Pilot Officer T. S. Wade and Pilot Officer D. G. Williams of No. 92 Squadron, during sortie to bomb London Docks. Dumped bombs and forced-landed at Burmarsh 4.00 p.m. Set alight by crew and burned out. Fw. H. George captured wounded. Fw. H. Friedrich, Uffz. K. Hofmann, Uffz. A. Dreyer and Uffz. H. Stirnemann captured unhurt. Aircraft 1H+CB a write-off.

Direction-finding loop aerial, removed at the time of the crash, now in the Hawkinge Aeronautical Trust collection.

1/KG26 Heinkel He 111H-4 (6962). Believed shot down by Pilot Officer E. S. Lock of No. 41 Squadron during sortie to bomb Woolwich Arsenal. Crashed at Cripps Corner, near Sedlescombe 4.30 p.m. and bomb load exploded. Hptmn. W. Künstler (Staffelkapitän), Fw. E. Büttner and Uffz. E. Schmidt captured unhurt. Fw. J. Schäfer and Uffz. W. Schang killed. Aircraft 1H+AH a write-off.

Representative items on display in the Robertsbridge Aviation Society Museum.

1/KG26 Heinkel He 111H-4 (6981). One engine disabled in attacks by Flight Lieutenant A. A. McKellar and Pilot Officer R. E. Jones of No. 605 Squadron during sortie to bomb London. Bombs dumped blind in an effort to escape. Severely damaged in further attacks and abandoned by pilot over Crowborough 4.10 p.m. Fw. W. Jabusch baled out wounded and captured on landing at Ketches Farm, Jarvis Brook, Uckfield. Aircraft brought under control by the observer, Lt. F. Zimmermann, and eventually forced-landed near Dieppe. One of the remaining crew, Fw. G. Schilling or Oberfw. W. Hasebrink believed wounded. Aircraft 1H+KH a write-off.

3/KG26 Heinkel He 111H-3 (3157). Hit in one wing by AA fire during bombing sortie over London. Lost formation and then both engines disabled in attacks by Flight Lieutenant G. R. McGregor, Flying Officer H. de M. Molson and Flying Officer A. Yuile of No. 1 (RCAF) Squadron; Squadron Leader M. V. Blake and Pilot Officer W. Rozycki of No. 238 Squadron; Pilot Officer J. F. J. MacPhail of No. 603 Squadron; Pilot Officer C. F. Currant and Pilot Officer W. J. Glowacki of No. 605 Squadron and Sergeant S. A. Levenson of No. 611 Squadron. Crashed and exploded at Hoopers Farm, Eden Road, Dormansland, near Lingfield 3.45 p.m. Oberlt. W. Abendhausen baled out and captured unhurt. Uffz. H. Hauswald baled out and captured wounded. Fw. H. Westphalen, Uffz. B. Herms and Gefr. F. Zähle killed. Aircraft 1H+ML a write-off.

5/KG26 Heinkel He 111H-3 (6903). Badly damaged in fighter attacks during sortie to bomb London and ditched in the Channel off Hastings 5.00 p.m. following further attack by Flying Officer B. Van Mentz of No. 222 Squadron. Oberlt. G-O. Bertram, Gefr. G. Schröder and Gefr. R. Endrich rescued by fishing boat and captured unhurt. Lt. F. Kramer killed. Aircraft 1H+JN lost.

3/LG2 Messerschmitt Bf 109E-7 (2029). Believed shot down in combat with Sergeant S. Wojtowicz of No. 303 Squadron but possibly that claimed by Sergeant J. Budzinski of 605 Squadron. Crashed in flames and burned out alongside the Pilgrim's Way at Wrotham Hill 4.15 p.m. Uffz. A. Hechmaier killed. Aircraft a write-off.

This pilot was buried locally in Wrotham Cemetery and has not been reinterred in the Soldatenfriedhof, Cannock Chase.

Excavated by the London Air Museum

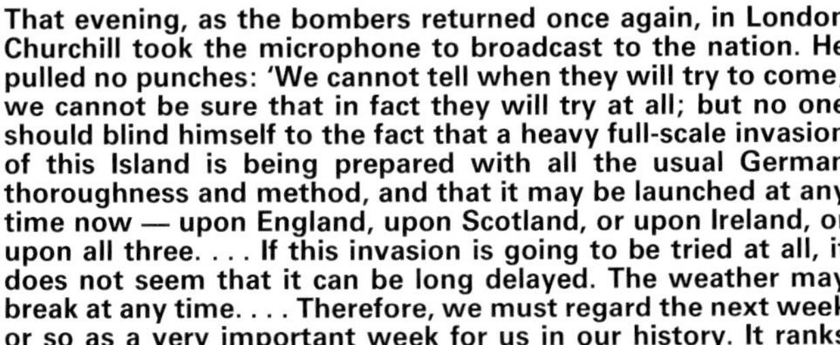

That evening, as the bombers returned once again, in London Churchill took the microphone to broadcast to the nation. He pulled no punches: 'We cannot tell when they will try to come; we cannot be sure that in fact they will try at all; but no one should blind himself to the fact that a heavy full-scale invasion of this Island is being prepared with all the usual German thoroughness and method, and that it may be launched at any time now — upon England, upon Scotland, or upon Ireland, or upon all three. . . . If this invasion is going to be tried at all, it does not seem that it can be long delayed. The weather may break at any time. . . . Therefore, we must regard the next week or so as a very important week for us in our history. It ranks with the days when the Spanish Armada was approaching the Channel, and Drake was finishing his game of bowls; or when Nelson stood between us and Napoleon's Grand Army at Boulogne. We have read all about this in the history books; but what is happening now is on a far greater scale and of far more consequence to the life and future of the world and its civilisation than these brave old days of the past.' ***Left:*** **That night St Katherine Docks was once again a focus of attention but who would have thought that one of the same warehouses, after standing derelict for nearly thirty years, would once again be 'blitzed': this time in 1968 for a scene in the film *Battle of Britain*** *(right).*

which unearthed masses of shattered airframe components including the top of the control column and pieces bearing the legend '2029'. Relics also in the Steve Vizard collection.

2/ZG26 Messerschmitt Bf 110C-3 (1372). Suffered engine failure during escort sortie for bombers attacking London and lost formation. Attacked by fighters and remaining engine disabled. Again attacked and severely damaged during forced-landing at Cobham Farm, Charing 5.00 p.m. Fw. H. Brinkmann captured unhurt. Uffz. E. Grüschow captured wounded. Aircraft U8+HL a write-off.

Stab II/ZG26 Messerschmitt Bf 110C-4 (3625). Sortied as escort for bombers and shot down in combat with fighters over Thanet. Probably that claimed by Flight Lieutenant A. W. A. Bayne and Flying Officer Count M. B. Czernin of No. 17 Squadron. Believed crashed in the sea 3 miles off Margate 4.24 p.m. Oberlt. W. Henken missing. Fw. J. Radlmair killed. Aircraft 3U+HM lost.

The body of the gunner in this aircraft, Josef Radlmair, was washed ashore at Broadstairs Jetty on October 23. He was buried in Manston Road Cemetery, Margate, where he remains to this day.

9/ZG26 Messerschmitt Bf 110C-4 (3231). Believed shot down by Sergeant B. J. Jennings of No. 19 Squadron during escort sortie to London. Possibly also that attacked by Pilot Officer W. J. Glowacki of No. 605 Squadron. Crashed at Barnes Cote, Harvel 4.00 p.m. Oberlt. J. Junghans killed. Gefr. P. Eckert missing. Aircraft 3U+LT a write-off.

The death of the pilot, Joachim Junghans, was subsequently confirmed by German authorities but no trace of his recovery or burial has been found in appropriate British records. His gunner, Paul Eckert, remains missing to this day and has no recognised grave.

Site excavated by the Kent Battle of Britain Museum. Daimler-Benz DB601 engine salvaged together with undercarriage leg complete with wheel and tyre. 20mm MGFF cannon and firing mechanism, ammunition drums, parachute buckles, crewman's pistol, cigarette case and Luftwaffe identity disc '60043/21' belonging to Gefr. Paul Eckert. Items now in the Hawkinge Aeronautical Trust collection. Relics also in Headcorn Museum from this aircraft but wrongly identified. Wound badge recovered on the surface in the Vizard collection.

These cruel, wanton, indiscriminate bombings of London are, of course, a part of Hitler's invasion plan. He hopes, by killing large numbers of civilians, and women and children, that he will terrorise and cow the people of this mighty Imperial city and make them a burden and anxiety for the Government, and thus distract our attention unduly from the ferocious onslaught he is preparing. Little does he know the spirit of the British nation, or the tough fibre of the Londoners whose forbears played a leading part in the establishment of Parliamentary institutions and who have been bred to value freedom far above their lives.

This wicked man, the repository and embodiment of many forms of soul-destroying hatred, this monstrous product of former wrongs and shames, has now resolved to try to break our famous island race by a process of indiscriminate slaughter and destruction. What he has done is to kindle a fire in British hearts, here and all over the world, which will glow long after all traces of the conflagrations he has caused in London have been removed. He has lighted a fire which will burn with a steady and consuming flame until the last vestiges of Nazi tyranny have been burnt out of Europe, and until the Old World and the New can join hands to rebuild the temples of man's freedom and man's honour on foundations which will not soon or easily be overthrown.

This is the time for everyone to stand together and hold firm, as they are doing. I express my admiration for the exemplary manner in which the air raid precaution services in London are being discharged, especially the fire brigades, whose work has been so heavy and also dangerous.

All the world that is still free marvels at the composure and fortitude with which the citizens of London are facing and surmounting the great ordeal to which they are subjected, the end of which, or the severity of which, cannot yet be foreseen. It is a message of good cheer to our fighting forces, on the seas, in the air and in our waiting armies, in all their posts and stations, that we send them from this capital city. They know that they have behind them a people who will not flinch or weary of the struggle, hard and protracted though it will be, but that we shall rather draw from the heart of suffering the means of inspiration and survival, and of a victory won not only for ourselves, but for all — a victory won not only for our own times, but for the long and better days that are to come.

WINSTON CHURCHILL, SEPTEMBER 11, 1940

DAILY EXPRESS Thursday, Sept. 12, 1940.

BLACK-OUT
ZERO HOUR
TO-NIGHT
UNTIL 6.3 A.M.
MOON RISES
MOON SETS

Daily Express

No. 12,576 — Thursday, September 12, 1940 — One Penny

Mr. Churchill (in a broadcast last night reported on Page Five) gave warning that invasion may be attempted soon and made this call to the nation:

Every man—and woman—will therefore prepare himself to do his duty, whatever it may be, with special pride and care . . . With devout but sure confidence I say that God defends the right.

TERRIFIC LONDON BARRAGE MEETS GREATEST RAID

While Navy and RAF pound massed Nazi invasion fleet

SUPER-BLITZ GETS A SHOCK

HITLER'S PLANS FOR INVADING BRITAIN ARE NEARING COMPLETION.

Mr. Churchill last night said the invasion may be launched at any time.

Next week must be regarded as "very important."

Germany, he said, is massing barges and ships in ports from Hamburg down to the Bay of Biscay. Preparations have also been made to carry a force from Norway.

While the Army stands confident and ready for the assault, the Navy and R.A.F. are shelling and bombing every one of Hitler's invasion ports. Barges and harbours are being continuously and heavily bombarded. This has been going on since Tuesday night.

LONDON BLITZ NIGHT No. 5 WAS A SENSATION.

It began at 8.34 after three daylight raids. Goering intended it to be a Super-Blitz night.

He sent over bigger-than-ever formations of bombers, and sent fighters to protect them.

AND WHAT A SURPRISE THEY HAD!

All round them broke the biggest anti-aircraft barrage London has ever seen.

From every part of London A.A. guns flashed and roared. Only a few raiders got through to drop bombs on inner London. Most had to drop their bombs haphazard on the outskirts. And all the time the intense gunfire drowned the noise of the bombs.

The indiscriminate bombing of London now stands revealed by the Premier as part of the invasion plan.

CHANNEL BASES SHELLED

HERE is the full story, told last night in Admiralty, R.A.F. and German communiqués, of the terrific massed attacks made against Hitler's invasion bases.

Navy is there

"Strong and repeated offensive actions are being taken by our naval light forces against German shipping movements, ports and concentrations of shipping," said the Admiralty.

"These operations have inflicted losses upon the enemy, as well as damage to port facilities which would be vital to him in the event of an attempt to invade England.

"Further details cannot be given without disclosing information which would be useful to the enemy."

R.A.F. blast docks

EARLIER it was announced by the Air Ministry that for hours, up to dawn yesterday, R.A.F. bombers unloaded high explosive and fire bombs on Hitler's invasion harbours, causing heavy damage.

A large part of the dock area round the Carnot Basin at Calais Harbour was left in flames. One fire alone blazed along 200 yards of the water front.

Bombs were dropped clean on to barges tightly packed along the whole east side of the basin, and the explosions threw debris high into the air.

Barges in another basin were hit, and then a large merchant ship suddenly burst into flames.

For three hours the pounding of the dock area went on. A railway was hit and fires were started round lock gates.

Our pilots dived low through thick cloud to pick out their targets, braving fierce shelling from the ground.

Six E-boats—fast motor torpedo-boats—at Dieppe were bombed, despite heavy fire from the ground and a patrol of Messerschmitt fighters.

After the bomb explosions, two of the E-boats had disappeared.

Ostend harbour was continually bombed for eight hours. Heavy loads of high explosive straddled barges in the port, and direct hits were made on a number of ships.

German ships in Boulogne harbour were attacked, and other bomber squadrons unloaded on to the docks at Flushing.

Enemy fighters tried to find the raiders, but the R.A.F. pilots gave them the slip in the clouds.

From all these raids, and an attack on Berlin (reported on Page Three), four of our planes did not return.

The Nazi story

A GERMAN communiqué last night admitted the naval attack.

"Shortly after midnight last night," it said, "British warships approached the French Channel coast and opened fire.

"German coast artillery fired on the British warships, and several German motor speedboats, which were patrolling in the neighbourhood, joined in the action.

"A fire on one of the six enemy destroyers was noticed. Soon afterwards, the British ships ceased firing and disappeared into the darkness."

Gunfire louder than the bombs

FEWER searchlights—but MANY more guns—greeted the German raiders when they approached London last night within a few minutes of the sirens at 8.34.

It was the fiercest anti-aircraft barrage ever heard in London.

Chains of shells burst high in the sky, a curtain of steel. The sky must have been full of flying shrapnel.

It spattered on the rooftops at times like machine-gun fire.

The bombers and their escorting fighters were seen plainly in the moonlight, but when they disappeared their course was easily followed—not by their bomb flashes but by the red pin points of bursting shells.

With every minute the barrage increased, the gun flashes making an almost constant glow, the thunder of the guns shaking houses, even drowning the bomb explosions.

SOME OF THE GUNS SEEMED HEAVIER THAN ANY HEARD BEFORE. IT APPEARED TO BE A NEW SUPER-BARRAGE.

INCENDIARIES

The bombers could not face it and swung away east. Incendiaries whizzed down, but so far the raiders did not appear to have dropped high explosives.

One later raider, following the same route, was forced off his course too. He turned—straight into another barrage, and turned back again.

But as the first waves of the Germans, driven from London, made for home, the whistle of bigger bombs was heard.

They fell in south-east, south-west and west.

Then, mingling with the fireworks of the guns, watchers saw "Molotov breadbaskets" bursting to the south-east. Within a few minutes at least twelve were seen.

Bombs, including incendiaries, were dropped in three South London districts and in one area in West London.

And many of the bombs dropped in and out of London seemed to be a new type. They exploded with a vivid white flash followed by a very sharp crack after which, in every case, there was a succession of staccato reports like machine-gun fire.

There was no lull in the battle for more than an hour. Wave after wave of Germans met the barrage and were beaten back. Only an odd plane got through to drop his bombs, climb out of sight, and make off for home.

The lull lasted only five minutes. Flashing anti-aircraft guns down the Thames Estuary heralded yet another wave of attackers on their way to London.

Before they arrived the super-barrage was in full swing again, lashing hundreds of shells into the raiders' path.

"No aerial barrage of the last war compares with this," was the verdict of all who saw the red pin points peppering the skies.

In every part of London, in the suburbs and on the outskirts as far as the eye could see, A.A. guns were flashing. North, south-east and west their shells burst.

Reflections of the gun flashes danced off window panes. Great purple flashes ran along the horizon.

At the height of the battle another heartening note was added to the gun thunder—the whine of a plane diving steeply. If it crashed the noise was drowned by a new burst of gunfire.

Large formations or stragglers, they all got the same treatment, a withering "creeping barrage" right up the course of the Thames.

Soon after midnight the great barrage died down. It had become clear that the waves of the raiders were being forced to drop their bombs outside the London area.

MORE VIOLENT

Soon, however, the barrage opened up again, more violent than ever. A German plane flying comparatively low appeared over the Central London area.

Its course was marked by a continuous line of bursting shells. Flashes from the guns grew so great as the raider flew over the central area that the whole district was almost continually lit up. And the raider, harassed by the barrage, sheered away, followed by the bursting shells.

London had three alerts before the Great Night Battle began.

In the second Marshal Goering's "Yellow Nosed" Squadron—famed in Germany as the most daring fighting unit he possesses—were beaten by British Spitfires and Hurricanes when they led an attempt to penetrate the London defences.

The first warning, at 11.54 a.m., lasted sixteen minutes, the second was from 3.20 to 4.42, the third from 5.04 to 5.15.

Newspaper office bombed

A LONDON newspaper office was slightly damaged by a high explosive bomb early this morning. Windows were shattered and a water tank on the roof was burst.

No one was hurt.

Other bombs hit an A.F.S. station and a hall in the London area.

It was revealed last night, too, that Bond-street and the Burlington Arcade were damaged in Tuesday night's raid on London.

MORE GUNS—AND WHY

Daily Express Air Reporter

AN intensely powerful barrage of gunfire such as London heard last night not only keeps raiders at a great height but it makes districts where they are concentrated too hot for the enemy to linger.

It does NOT mean that attackers are prevented from dropping bombs, but at the heights they are forced to fly bombing becomes more difficult as the pilots are continually harassed.

It also becomes far less accurate, *—though this does not count for much when bombing is intended to be inaccurate.*

Wardens in some districts last night are reported to have warned people to stay indoors and not to be alarmed by the noise of the gunfire.

The sound of the guns shuld be reassuring. It is certainly a wise precaution for people to stay under cover when the air is full of falling shrapnel. Many casualties have been caused in raids by people forgetting that their own guns can be a danger to them.

And what of the lack of searchlights last night?

Searchlights have distinct disadvantages as well as advantages. If raiders keep above their range they can be a positive aid to the enemy by lighting up his target, as well as giving him directional aid for flying over a city.

90 DOWN

400 people killed on Monday night

NAZI squadrons tried twice yesterday afternoon and evening to thrust home attacks on airfields and on the London docks.

They paid with the loss of at least ninety aircraft—one of the most smashing defeats of the war.

As many of the planes brought down were bombers, Goering lost well over 200 airmen.

The two raids lasted altogether about two hours, so that the "death rate" was 45 an hour.

This news was issued after midnight. Earlier, it was stated that our losses were seventeen fighters, with three pilots safe. Here is the communiqué issued by the Air Ministry and Ministry of Home Security:—

Fuller reports are now available of last night's [Tuesday] enemy activity over the London area. Although much damage was done to private property, it was less than on previous nights and the casualties were fortunately very much less severe.

Incendiary bombs started many fires, but only one major fire was caused and all are under control. The work of the fire services has again been beyond praise, and their arrangements for mutual assistance are working smoothly.

Full reports of casualties are not yet available, but eighteen persons are known to have been killed and 280 injured in the London area.

School falls on families

Total casualties on Monday night are now reported to be in the neighbourhood of 400 killed and 1,400 injured—the majority of the fatalities occurring when an elementary school in the East End of London, which was affording temporary shelter to families whose homes had been destroyed, was hit and collapsed.

There was little enemy activity over this country today (Wednesday) until about 3 p.m., when a large number of enemy aircraft approached the London area. The enemy was driven off, but reports so far received show that some damage was done, mainly in three districts south of the river.

Particulars of casualties are not yet available.

Fighters have a grand day

Bombs were also dropped in another attack on a town on the south coast, where some casualties are reported, a number of which were fatal.

Reports up to 7.30 p.m. showed that of seventy-three enemy aircraft then known to have been destroyed by our fighters, forty-three were bombers, nineteen fighter-bombers, and eleven fighters.

A.A. batteries along the Thames are also believed to have shot down several.

Berlin has guest

Serrano Suner, Spanish Minister of the Interior, and brother-in-law of General Franco, has arrived in Berlin for a visit of several days, Berlin announced last night.

ENGLAND
Harwich
LONDON
Dover
Dunkirk
Calais
Boulogne
Ostend
Flushing
Brussels
BELGIUM
Aachen
Hague
HOLLAND
Texel
Helder

Invasion ports—bombarded

DOVER SHELLED: WE SHELL CONVOY

Daily Express Staff Reporter FRANK BUTLER

DOVER, Wednesday.

GERMAN long-range guns and dive-bombers opened a fierce attack on Dover this afternoon, apparently to cover the movement of at least twelve Nazi ships which were seen sneaking along the coast towards Boulogne harbour.

Big guns on the British shore answered the German shelling, and at once a smoke screen was flung out by the Nazi ships.

Later, large forces of R.A.F. bombers headed towards the French coast, and it appeared that many bombs were dropped east of Calais.

Salvos of six shells at a time were hurled at Dover by the Nazis; and a dozen German heavy bombers flew high over the town while the shelling was going on.

Bombs were dropped at random. Shops and houses were hit, and fires started.

The combined attack was the severest Dover has known since the war began. A few people are reported killed and some injured.

More guns barked — anti-aircraft guns on the English coast—and one shell burst clear on a bomber and blew it to bits.

The rest of the raiders droned away, but the German shelling continued for three-quarters of an hour.

The people of Dover were grand.

With shells bursting all round, A.R.P. workers, firemen and police went about

→ BACK PAGE, COL. FIVE

PALACE BOMB

Explodes near the King's sitting-room

Daily Express Staff Reporter HILDE MARCHANT

BUCKINGHAM PALACE has been bombed. A time bomb dropped into the Terrace on the North Wing just outside the King's sitting room. The King and Queen, who have used the Palace regularly throughout the raids, were away for the night.

It exploded at 1.30 on Tuesday morning. Both the King and Queen spent the night in the country, and members of the Palace staff were sleeping safely in shelters well away from the spot. No one was injured.

The swimming pool and corner of the terrace were wrecked. There is practically no glass left in the back of the Palace, and the explosion broke windows on the Park side.

The Germans seem to have made two attempts to bomb the Palace for there is another huge crater fifty yards outside the Palace grounds.

I went to the Palace yesterday morning to see the damage. There is a crater eighteen feet deep and forty feet wide.

WALLS TORN

It must have been a large bomb—probably 250 pounds—for thick pillars ten feet high and the heavy stone balustrade of the terrace had collapsed into the crater.

The wall of the swimming pool was torn wide open and the green painted steel diving steps were twisted like sticks of liquorice.

Walls were charred with black smoke and one heavy piece of stone had been blown over the Palace and had landed eighty yards away.

The King and Queen came back to the Palace the following day to look at the wreckage. The day before the King had been round the East End to look at the wrecked homes of the working-class people there.

Now they looked at their own home, with one wall wrecked, the windows of their rooms blown wide open to the sky and the wreckage all round the garden.

The furniture did not suffer much damage, but in the Chinese room I saw the frame of one of the tapestries had been broken.

Wire netting over the windows had prevented the glass blowing inwards, but a glass porch over the

☛ BACK PAGE, COL. THREE

STOP PRESS

Raider's crew caught in North London

Enemy plane was brought down in North London early this morning. Its crew were captured.

Relays of single raiders were flying at about ten-minute intervals over central London area. Germans appeared to be using very fast machines which sped back and forwards.

Hardly had drone of one machine died away before it was followed by another. Some of planes had steadier and faster engine beat than usually associated with night raiders. Terrific gunfire still in progress in late morning.

Fire bomb falls in Goebbels's garden

BERLIN, Wednesday.—The official German News Agency says tonight:—

"During the British raid on Berlin last night a 15lb. incendiary bomb fell ten feet from Dr. Goebbels' residence and tore a deep hole in the garden."—B.U.P.

What we did to Berlin—*See pages 3 & 5*

For three nights the Luftwaffe had ranged over London unopposed with only occasional opposition from the anti-aircraft guns: largely due to failure in communications and the inadequacy of the sound detection system which was deployed on the assumption of an approach up the Estuary. By Wednesday General Pile had increased the number of guns from 92 to 203 and given instructions that those which could not fire on the Fixed Azimuth System could fire at will. The result described by the GOC was 'wild and uncontrolled shooting' but Londoners loved it! (The Stop Press report referring to the capture of a German crew cannot be reconciled with any known loss.)

Of all Sir Christopher Wren's City churches, the most special to Londoners, particularly those born within the sound of its bells who can then claim to be true Cockneys, is St Mary-le-Bow in Cheapside. When Wren designed his ring of churches around the cathedral they were the gems in a coronet which, by virtue of their graceful spires, in turn inspired the jewel at the centre. *Left:* **In this pre-war view its steeple, ascending in stages, draws the eye towards its weathervane — a dragon — symbol of the City of London.** *Right:* **On September 11 this is how it appeared: wreathed in smoke as the fire crews deal with the aftermath of the night's raid. Later when the nave was destroyed the historic Bow Bells crashed to the ground and were smashed but were recast after the war from the original metal which had been carefully saved.**

THURSDAY, SEPTEMBER 12

By day, there was a marked increase in the number of hostile reconnaissances especially in south-eastern and southern areas. Otherwise enemy activity was on a much reduced scale.

Enemy activity by night was also on a much reduced scale compared with recent nights. The majority of the raids were plotted as single aircraft. Raids penetrated to South Wales, West Midlands and Liverpool areas. A series of raids flying from Dieppe to London appeared for the most part to use identical tracks and several were plotted as turning at Whitehall whence they flew back on reciprocal tracks.

Enemy aircraft: 3 destroyed, 4 damaged. Casualties (approx.): 57 killed, 128 injured, 84 of these seriously. It is reported that the approximate casualties in London region in raids on 11/12th September are: 110 killed, 260 seriously injured, 230 slightly injured. Casualties for the Metropolitan Police area for 24 hours ending 1830, 9th September, are reported to be: 412 killed, 747 seriously injured.

Another day of reduced activity with isolated reconnaissance and nuisance raids continuing to frustrate the British defences. Single aircraft operated over London again during the night. The Luftwaffe lost 4 aircraft and 4 more damaged on operations; another 3 of their machines being destroyed and 3 damaged in accidents. None fell in Britain.

None of Wren's masterpieces survived the war unscathed, St Mary's having since been skilfully rebuilt by the modern architect Laurence King.

The Adjutant R.A.S.C.
Woolwich

Waves of enemy aircraft, flying at a height of approximately 25,000 feet passed over Woolwich during the night and early hours of the morning. The sky was cloudless and bathed in brilliant moonlight . . . an occasional searchlight clawed feebly with ghostly fingers as though to clear the heavens of human-carrion. The dull rumble of A.A. batteries could be heard faintly in the distance, suggestive of the forerunner of some horrible catastrophy that was about to occur. The noise of gunfire increased in volume, the crump of crashing bombs was conspicuous by its absence . . . the drone of hostile machines could now be heard approaching Woolwich . . . the sky became heavily pregnant with Nazis . . . A roar from A.A. batteries of various calibre greeted these 'gate-crashers' . . . a roar symbolic of the might of Britain . . . flashes from bursting shell illuminated the sky . . . shrapnel whined and moaned like a tortured soul in a tropical storm . . . surely even Fiends Incarnate would not defy such withering fire? The Nazi pilots, harassed by flying steel, wavered, then changed direction in an effort to escape the punishment being meted out to them. Their course was marked by a milky way of smoke from exploding shells. The 'All Clear' sounded a few minutes after 5 a.m. . . . Dawn broke; the sun rising majestically over the horizon, purifying the polluted atmosphere left in the wake of the departed raiders.

LIEUTENANT E. B. TAPSELL
WOOLWICH DEFENCE OFFICER
WAR DIARY, SEPTEMBER 11/12, 1940

UXB

The morning of the 12th highlighted a new form of attack — not novel and quite often not physically damaging but nevertheless one more potently disruptive: the bomb which failed to explode. Were they delayed-action or duds? Churchill wrote that 'there is no doubt that it is a most effective agent in warfare on account of the prolonged uncertainty which it creates . . . I had urged its use by us both in Norway and in the Kiel Canal . . . We were now to taste it ourselves.' What brought the menace home to the public more than anything else was the news (released on Sunday the 15th) that for three days St Paul's had been under the threat from 'the biggest bomb ever dropped on London'.

The St Paul's bomb — actually an ordinary SC 1000 — had been dropped at 2.25 a.m. on Thursday morning. Hitting the pavement at the south-west corner of the cathedral, it had penetrated on a curving path and had ended up almost underneath the clock tower. The whole area was cordoned off yet little could be done the first day as a gas main had been severed but when the fire had been put out and the gas turned off excavations began. This picture was taken at five to one on Thursday afternoon.

Prior to 1939, no real steps had been taken to establish some sort of organisation to deal with unexploded enemy aircraft bombs, though this problem had been recognised from information received from Spain during the civil war in 1938. Again, when Germany invaded Poland in September 1939, details were obtained on the massive air attacks on Polish airfields and towns, and of the disorganising effects of the bombs that failed to explode. It had now become clear that unexploded bombs, if not tackled with some degree of urgency, could affect the war effort considerably. To meet this situation, if it should occur, it was proposed that personnel of the Civil Defence should deal with any unexploded bomb situation that should arise. (It was then thought that any unexploded bombs would be lying on the surface or just below.) As this meant that Civil Defence personnel would have to be trained in the handling of explosives, it was decided that the War Office would undertake the responsibility until the Civil Defence people could be trained. Subsequently, in November 1939, a number of personnel from Royal Engineers' Field Companies were formed into Bomb Disposal Parties, RE. These parties consisted of a corporal, two sappers, equipped with two picks and two shovels, one vehicle, 75lb of explosive and 500 sandbags. When trained, these parties were sent to areas that were likely to become targets for enemy bombers. Though these parties were small, all that was required of them was the sand-bagging and exploding of the bomb in situ, this again being based on the theory that the missiles would be found above the ground or just under the surface. By this time the Royal Navy and the Royal Air Force had also decided to establish demolition parties to deal with unexploded bombs on their establishments.

In December 1939, following a German raid on the Shetland Islands, several unexploded SC 50 bombs were recovered with impact fuzes. On examination of the fuzes, it was realised that more sophisticated fuzes could be expected and the recovery and disposal of German unexploded bombs would be a highly dangerous operation.

By February 1940 the Home Office had declared its inability to find civilians to form the bomb clearance personnel but, as it had now been realised that this work would have to be done by highly trained troops, it was decided that the War Office should take over the responsibility for bomb disposal in the United Kingdom. In May 1940 the first Formation Order for Bomb Disposal authorised an establishment of 24 Bomb

Disposal Sections, later increased to 109, which by the end of June had risen to 120. Each section consisted of an officer, sergeant and 14 other ranks, equipped with picks, shovels, hammer and cold chisel, block and tackle, cordage, sandbags and explosives. The original Bomb Disposal Parties were now absorbed into these new sections. For a period, these units were attached to Home Defence Battalions for accommodation, rations and discipline and placed under the operational command of the various area commanders but, with the increased enemy air attacks, it soon emerged that this system was unsatisfactory and a more fully co-ordinated organisation was required. It was now decided that the complete Bomb Disposal system should be placed under the command of one officer, and Major G. B. O. Taylor was appointed Director of Bomb Disposal, later succeeded in 1942 by Brigadier H. H. Bateman.

The Bomb Disposal Sections were now removed from the area commanders' control and detached from the Home Defence Battalions, the completion of this re-organisation coming just in time to meet the increased bombing which began in July 1940. During this initial phase the organisation proved inadequate and was soon overwhelmed and by August 2,500 unexploded bombs remained to be dealt with. (In August, mobile RAF Bomb Disposal Squads were formed to replace the RAF demolition parties, each mobile squad was responsible for the airfields within its own regional area.)

By September the number of UXBs had reached 3,759 and to combat this

The operation was tackled by 16/17 Section of No. 5 Bomb Disposal Company under Lieutenant Robert Davies and, although 'Hermann' was first uncovered 15 feet down, as the men dug around it the bomb slipped another 12½ feet before it was finally arrested. It was seen to be fitted with a Type 17 series long-delay fuze which by this date were known to be protected by a ZusZ 40 anti-withdrawal device, a successful defuzing in Swansea just ten days before having led to its discovery. However no remedy had yet been developed to counter the new threat and instructions were issued to explode all Type 17's in situ. Because of the large number of reported unexploded bombs waiting to be tackled by the hard-pressed, understrength units, on September 8 it was announced that henceforth UXBs were to be classified according to risk: (*a*) Bombs in fields and localities where little danger existed; (*b*) Bombs in localities where explosion would cause damage which could, if need be, be tolerated); (*c*) Bombs which would seriously interfere with the war effort and must be removed at once if the Regional Commissioner so directed.

There was little doubt that if the St Paul's bomb exploded, the cathedral would be very badly damaged and therefore the decision was taken to take a chance and remove the bomb complete. Two lorries were drawn up linked in tandem and the bomb was bodily pulled from the ground and quickly loaded aboard. Lieutenant Davies then took the wheel in order to shield his men from any further danger and quickly drove off out of the City.

Bomb 'cemeteries' had already been established round London, where fuzes could be destroyed, casings disposed of or, in extreme cases, live bombs exploded. There were cemeteries at White City and Richmond but the nearest to St Paul's was on Hackney Marshes and police quickly cleared a route through the East End. Reaching Marshgate Bridge *(left)* a track led along the side of the canal and then across to the centre of the marsh. The resulting explosion blew a crater 100 feet across *(right).*

Bill Kerr, long standing reader of *After the Battle*, lived close by at the time and remembered the explosion — and many others. 'Police cars used to drive around warning residents to open their windows to reduce the breakages', writes Bill. 'During the Blitz and after, debris from bombed buildings was dumped fifteen feet deep across the low marshes covering a large crater full of defuzed and steamed out bomb casings. I know because I took home an AA shell from it!'

threat, the size and number of the Bomb Disposal Sections were doubled to the authorised strength of 220 sections. High priority was also given to the research, development and production of special Bomb Disposal equipment. To handle the increased sections, company headquarters, each to control 12 Sections, were set up and senior officers made available to liaise with the various Civil Defence headquarters. To find the personnel for this expansion, seven General Construction and four Tunnelling Companies of the Royal Engineers were converted to Bomb Disposal duties as an emergency measure. Meanwhile, additional companies were being formed at Halifax with a nucleus of trained men, to which were added in each unit 200 men from RE training battalions. In January 1941 these units relieved the Tunnelling and Construction Companies, absorbing from the latter experienced men surplus to their normal establishment. To enable the Bomb Disposal organisation to deal with the large number of UXBs that had built up, a new method of reporting and dealing with unexploded bombs was introduced. Selected individuals from the police and the ARP were trained as bomb reconnaissance officers (BRO) whose duties were to

Congratulations for saving the cathedral poured in from as far away as South Africa, and the Ministry of Home Security recorded that 'only the courage and tenacity of the officer, his NCOs, and the men prevented St Paul's being levelled to the ground.' As a result of this and the many other outstanding acts of gallantry which had already marked the impact of war on civilian life, later that month the King approved the introduction of a new award to bear his name. The first servicemen to be awarded the George Cross when it was introduced on September 30 were Lieutenant Robert Davies and Sapper George Wylie, and British Empire Medals were awarded to Sergeant Jim Wilson and Lance Corporal Bert Leigh. *Left:* Unfortunately two years later Captain Davies, as he was by then, blotted his copybook and was caught stealing government property, and was had up for fraud and obtaining money by false pretences. Court-martialled and cashiered from the Army, he faded into obscurity. After the war he went to Australia and was all but forgotten when his GC came up for sale in 1970. It made £2,100 at auction, a then world record. Five years later Davies died. In 1983 the medal again came up for sale, making £16,000. A year later George Wylie, photographed *(right)* in front of the cathedral, in a spirit of some disillusionment in that he no longer felt a hero in a country where women and pensioners were mugged, offered his George Cross for sale. However following the generous intervention of Charterhouse Japhet, a merchant bank whose offices overlooked the cathedral, the medal was purchased by them for £12,000 and donated to St Paul's. Two years later George Wylie died in Bow.

investigate reports of UXBs in their districts. All unexploded bombs were allocated priorities, these categories being entered into Part Two of the new UXB Report Form and consisting of the following classifications:

Category 'A'

A.I Immediate disposal essential to the war effort, but deliberate demolition of the bomb cannot be accepted. (UXBs in munition factories, etc.)

A.II Immediate disposal essential to the war effort, demolition of the bomb can be accepted.

Category 'B'

Disposal important to war effort and to public morale, but not at the risk of BD personnel which immediate action would entail.

Category 'C'

Disposal necessary but not urgent.

Category 'D'

To be dealt with when convenient. (UXBs in fields or open spaces.)

Responsibility for allocating these classifications rested on the Regional Commissioners of the Civil Defence regions who were in close liaison with the Bomb Disposal organisation. Reporting was now based upon the passing of a UXB report (known as the Buff Form) through the appropriate authorities concerned. The Buff Form consisted of four parts:

Part I This part was completed by the Police or Civil Defence bomb reconnaissance officer.

Part II This was filled in at the Civil Defence Headquarters by the CD area or regional commander, who allotted the incident a priority category.

Part III This part was completed by the Bomb Disposal officer who was in charge of disposal and it formed a permanent record of the work done.

Part IV This was a tear-off slip which, on being signed by the Bomb Disposal officer, became a clearance certificate and formed the authority for the police to permit the public to resume normal activities in the area.

Once the Bomb Disposal unit received the 'Buff Form' with the priority category allotted, it was free to proceed. All low categories then being worked on could thereupon be dropped in favour of any 'A' incident, so squads were liable to be moved from one area to another with incidents of a higher priority.

Responsibility for the clearing and disposal of unexploded bombs and other missiles that fell on the United Kingdom was divided between the three services, with each service being responsible for certain areas. The Royal Navy was responsible for dealing with those found on Admiralty property or on areas occupied by the Navy. They were also responsible for buoyant mines and other marine weapons that were washed ashore, and for parachute mines

For Official Use.

U N E X P L O D E D   B O M B   R E P O R T.

T O   R E G I O N A L   H E A D Q U A R T E R S.   SERIAL NO...........

PART I.

1. EXACT LOCATION.

Time of falling.   Date

2. PHASE AFFECTED. (a) Industrial War Effort.
(b) Communications or P.U. Services.
(c) General Industry.
(d) Civil Population.

3. STATE (a) Diameter of Hole of entry.   (b) Estimated Size & Depth.
(c) Type of ground.   (d) Reasons for suspecting U.X.
(e) Proximity of (i) Buildings   (ii) Gas Mains
(iii) Water Mains   (iv) Electricity Mains
(v) Telephone Mains   (vi) Sewers.

4. IF ON RAILWAYS STATE PROXIMITY OF (a) Running Tracks   (b) Cuttings
(c) Embankments   (d) Rail over Road Bridges   (e) Road over Rly Bridges

5. DESCRIBE (a) Any Part of Bomb if exposed
(b) Any portion of Bomb found anywhere
(c) Colour and Markings found on any part

6. STATE where portions of Bomb have been deposited.

7. ANY SPECIAL REMARKS. (Restrictions imposed, rough dimension sketch plan etc.)

SIGNED
RANK
SERVICE

SUGGESTED BOMB CATEGORY.   SIGNED
DESIGNATION.
FOR GROUP OR COUNTY CONTROLLER.

PART II.

BOMB CATEGORY ALLOCATED.
PASSED FOR ACTION TO   B.D.GROUP/COY.R.E.   SIGNED
TIME.   DATE.   FOR REGIONAL COMMISSIONER.

PART III.

TO O.C.   B.D.COY.R.E.   Date   TO O.C.   B.D.SECTION.R.E.   Date

1. REPORT VERIFIED. Time   Date.   8. HOW FUZES DEALT WITH
2. OPERATIONS COMMENCED Time   Date   9. HOW BOMB DISPOSED OF
3. OPERATIONS CARRIED OUT BY   SECN. R.E.   10. OPERATIONS COMPLETED   Time   Date
4. OPERATIONS CARRIED OUT BY   AUX.B.D.UNIT.   11. CLEARANCE CERTIFICATE HANDED TO
5. SIZE AND TYPE OF BOMB.
6. FUZE OR FUZES FITTED   Time.   Date.
7. PENETRATION   OFFSET

SPECIAL OBSERVATIONS (Sketches of Works on reverse)

SIGNED
RANK
UNIT

RETURNED
TO O.C.   B.D.GROUP   Date   TO O.C.   B.D.COY.R.E.   Date

PART IV.

CLEARANCE CERTIFICATE.   SERIAL NO.............

1. THE UNEXPLODED BOMB/S AT
HAS (HAVE) NOW BEEN (a) Disposed of
(b) Discredited
(c) Abandoned

2. TIME   DATE.

SIGNED
RANK
UNIT

The four-part Unexploded Bomb Report form

that were dropped on land. In the event of a parachute mine burying itself in the ground, Army Bomb Disposal personnel excavated the mine which was then defused by officers of the Land Incident Section, Royal Navy.

The Army had full responsibility for all unexploded missiles (other than parachute mines) dropped on the mainland, not including Royal Navy or Royal Air Force establishments. This included a variety of explosive objects that ranged from unexploded bombs, 40mm to 4.5-inch anti-aircraft shells, 2-inch and 3-inch 'Z' Battery anti-aircraft rockets, 13mm to 30mm German cannon shells, British trench mortar bombs and other similar items. From 1943, Bomb Disposal units were engaged in clearing certain beaches of British mines. The total number of major explosive items dealt with in the United Kingdom up to the end of hostilities amounted to more than 50,000 high explosive bombs of 50kg and over, 6,983 anti-aircraft shells and nearly 300,000 beach mines. Casualties were 55 officers and 339 other ranks killed, and 37 officers and 172 other ranks wounded.

The Royal Air Force was responsible for dealing with unexploded bombs and other missiles (other than parachute mines) that fell on Air Ministry property, found in grounded aircraft and in crashed enemy aircraft.

The closest collaboration was maintained between the three services. Associated with the Army Bomb Disposal was the Voluntary Auxiliary Bomb Service. This formation had been sponsored by the Ministry of Production in 1940 and consisted of employees from industrial plants who had volunteered to be trained to assist the regular Bomb Disposal squads with unexploded bombs that fell within the factory area. When trained by Bomb Disposal officers, some of these auxiliary squads proved that they were capable of operating on their own, and on some occasions did so. The Voluntary Auxiliary Bomb Disposal Services were later affiliated to the Home Guard and wore a uniform with the Bomb Disposal arm badge, and 132 such auxiliary squads were formed during the war.

Another group that became involved with bomb disposal was the Non-Combatant Corps (NCC). This was a non-combatant unit composed of conscientious objectors that had been raised on July 12, 1939 as the Non-Combatant Labour Corps, the title being changed in April 1940 to Non-Combatant Corps. In November 1940 the Director of Bomb Disposal agreed to accept volunteers from the Corps, and by March 1941, 250 men had volunteered for bomb disposal and, after a modified RE training, were sent to various Bomb Disposal units.

PETER CHAMBERLAIN, 1986

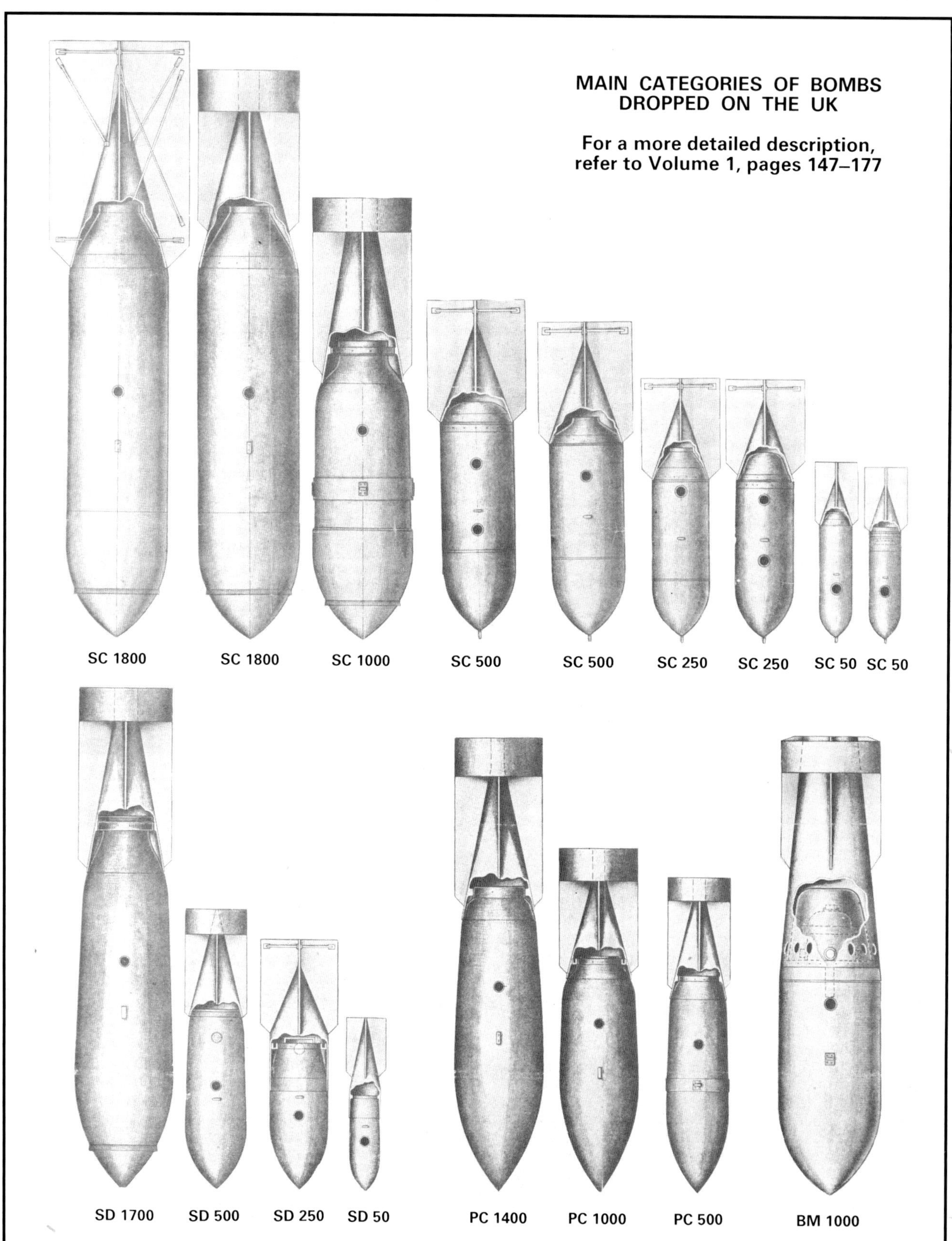

These illustrations with bomb disposal personnel on the job give, perhaps, a better idea of the comparative size of the weaponry which had to be tackled. *Left:* This is the SC 250 which could be carried by all the aircraft employed in bombing Britain. Usually the tail fins stripped from the casing when the bomb penetrated the ground, this particular specimen being recovered after the big raid on the Vauxhall factory at Luton on August 30 *(see Volume 1 page 272-273)*. It took six weeks to clear all the unexploded bombs from the factory. This picture, not released until the war was over, unfortunately does not identify the REs concerned but it is recorded that one George Medal was awarded for the work. *Right:* Drama of another kind near Norwich Theatre: this peformance being on September 19 starring an SC 500.

Above: Peter Chamberlain, far right, a member of No. 11 Section, 20th Bomb Disposal Squadron (OC Lieutenant R. Howard), with an SC 1000 — the same type as recovered from St Paul's. *Right:* An SC 1800 Satan is hoisted from its lair.

Final performance under the arcs — this is White City, the London District Central Salvage Depot, in March 1942.

Referring back to the *Daily Express* of September 12, one of the front page stories concerned the bombing of Buckingham Palace. Following the royal visit to the East End on Monday (September 9), the King and Queen had travelled to Windsor Castle, 20 miles to the west of London. Early Tuesday morning a bomb which had been dropped on the terrace outside the north wing exploded, blowing in the windows in the King's sitting room. *Above:* Their Majesties inspect the damage.

FRIDAY, SEPTEMBER 13

By day, Northern Ireland experienced its first air raid when a single aircraft dropped I.B.s at Bangor (Co. Down), causing several small fires. Except for the above incident, bombing was confined to the London area, Essex, Kent, Surrey and Sussex. The raids on London caused the longest daylight warning in London yet experienced (0945-1355). About 90 enemy aircraft took part in these raids. Damage was on a minor scale.

By night, raiding was mainly confined to London and the South-East. There was less major damage than on previous occasions. Elsewhere major damage was caused at Cardiff and minor damage at three other towns in South Wales and at Weymouth and Ventnor (Isle of Wight).

Enemy aircraft destroyed: 3 certain and 3 damaged. Bad visibility hindered interception by our aircraft. Approximate civilian casualties: London: 31 killed, 224 injured; other regions: 6 killed, 46 injured.

We went to London [from Windsor] and found an air raid in progress. The day was very cloudy and it was raining hard. The Queen and I went upstairs to a small sitting-room overlooking the Quadrangle (I could not use my usual sitting-room owing to the broken windows by former bomb damage). All of a sudden we heard the zooming noise of a diving aircraft getting louder and louder, and then saw two bombs falling past the opposite side of Buckingham Palace into the Quadrangle. We saw the flashes and heard the detonations as they burst about eighty yards away. The blast blew in the windows opposite to us, and two great craters had appeared in the Quadrangle. From one of these craters water from a burst main was pouring out and flowing into the passage through the broken windows. The whole thing happened in a matter of seconds, and we were very quickly out into the passage.

HM KING GEORGE VI, SEPTEMBER 13, 1940

In all six bombs were dropped: the two which exploded in the quadrangle, two outside the front of the Palace, one in the garden and one in the chapel. This is the Palace Chapel — before and after.

'A magnificent piece of bombing, ma'am, if you'll pardon my saying so.', a policeman on duty is reputed to have remarked to the Queen after the attack. This is the view from both sides of the fence, the comparison being reproduced by the gracious permission of Her Majesty Queen Elizabeth II.

Buckingham Palace was bombed at 1110. H.E. fell on the quadrangle, on the Chapel and in the forecourt. Three of the staff and one warden were slightly injured. Damage was slight. A German broadcast from Zeszen in English, timed 0324 14th September, stated: 'Several German bombers of Do 17 type bombed a large oil depot situated in the vicinity of Buckingham Palace this afternoon.' Although bombing incidents were widespread there was little major damage anywhere. Ravenhill School, West Ham, which was housing persons previously rendered homeless, was demolished. There were 50 casualties.

Operating in poor weather conditions, single aircraft penetrated the defences to bomb London during the morning. Larger formations of German aircraft aimed for the airfields at Biggin Hill and Tangmere during the early afternoon. At night their attacks continued relentlessly — over 100 aircraft being dispatched against London during the night and early morning. Six German aircraft were lost on operations, another being destroyed and 2 more damaged in accidents. One fell in Britain.

8/KG27 Heinkel He 111P (2670). Collided with balloon cable over South Wales following bombing attack on Ellesmere Port. Crashed and burned out at 32 Stow Park Avenue, Newport 3.15 a.m. Oberlt. H. Wappler baled out and captured injured. Oberfw. J. Elster, Uffz. F. Berndt and Uffz. H. Okuneck failed to bale out and killed. Aircraft 1G+DS a write-off.

During his visit to the badly hit areas (page 74) of the Capital on Monday it had been rumoured that the King had been booed; now the Queen remarked thankfully: 'I'm glad we've been bombed. It makes me feel I can look the East End in the face.'

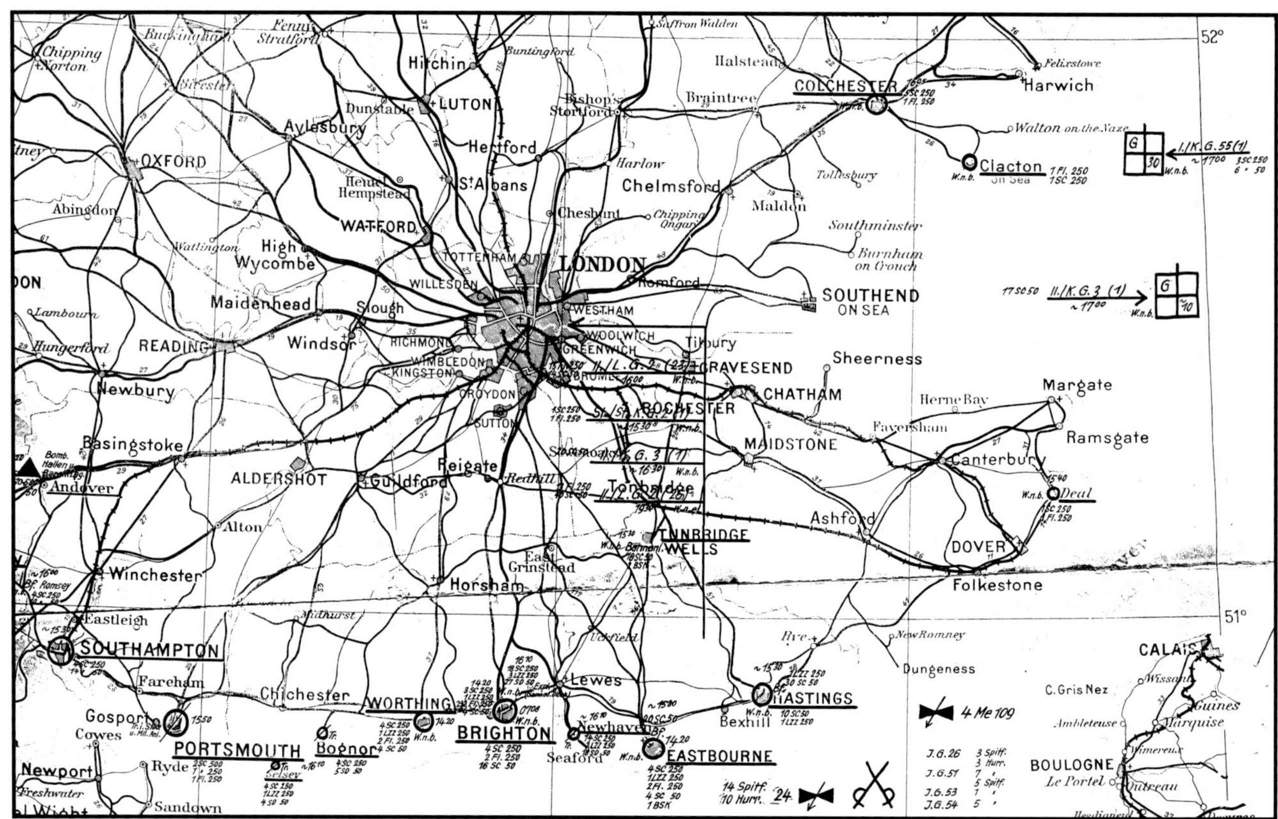

The Luftwaffe operations map for September 14, German claims being 14 Spitfires and 10 Hurricanes at the cost of 4 Bf 109s. Their losses are accurately stated as a fourth fighter, not listed here for reasons explained earlier, crashed in France. (The Air Ministry claimed 18 German aircraft brought down.) However only 6 Spitfires were shot down although 5 RAF machines came back badly damaged which, understandably, may well have been claimed as kills by German pilots.

SATURDAY, SEPTEMBER 14

Two attacks by day were directed against London through Kent and Thames Estuary. In each raid about 100 and 150 aircraft were employed. Certain elements succeeded in penetrating the Inner Defence Zone. Successful interception by fighter squadrons was made, and casualties were inflicted. Damage was on a small scale.

Bombs were dropped at the following coastal towns: Clacton, Great Yarmouth, Ipswich, Southampton, Bournemouth, Hastings, Selsey, Brighton, Littlehampton and Worthing. There were casualties at Brighton where a cinema was hit (35 killed, 82 seriously injured, 75 slightly injured), but only minor damage elsewhere.

A low-flying aircraft dropped two H.E. on a works canteen at Warrington during a Gala, burying 150 people. Casualties amounted to 14 killed, 21 seriously injured, 22 slightly injured.

Large numbers of bombs, H.E., I.B. and oil, fell in Chelsea, Fulham and Westminster between 1818 and 0329, causing considerable damage to residential property. Casualties: 19 killed, 12 seriously injured, 19 slightly injured.

By night, there were fewer incidents in the London area, although weather conditions were favourable. Raiding occurred between 2131 and 2150, and 0116 and 0325. Areas mainly affected were Chelsea, Fulham, Finsbury, Leyton and Lewisham. Minor bombing was reported between 2100 and 2200 from Preston (Lancs.), Bootle, Leicester, Desborough and Ipswich.

Enemy aircraft destroyed: 16 certain, 3 probable, 12 damaged. Civilian casualties (approx.): London: 27 killed, 108 injured; other regions: 67 killed, 318 injured. Fires: 1 major, 6 medium, 35 small.

South-east and south-west areas have been raided consistently. Bombs dropped, near misses and UXBs suggest that the enemy

September 14, 1940

Our leaders announce: 'Der Tommy ist am Ende!' [Tommy is at his last gasp].

In the first place they are said to have no more pilots left over there but also to have a grave shortage of aircraft. Our fighters are said to have virtually wiped out their numerically inferior opponents.

We in fact know something different. But that news is too good not to be believed. And our officers will already know what they are saying. But how can it be that there are supposedly no more reinforcements to be thrown in? We can't in fact fly very far into England, and aren't they undisturbed further in?

At all events, as an example an individual attack on the London docks in broad daylight has been ordered. We wait tensely to see how it will work out.

Take-off 11.20 hours . . . Splendid seas of cloud, in fantastic shapes, which we fly over at a height of 5000 metres; as a precaution, that is to say, 3000 metres higher than the usual altitude. But as we approach the enemy coast, the clouds become fewer and fewer . . . Suddenly, I hear: 'Fighter above us in the rear.' So they still have one at least which is attacking us.

As our lone, unwieldy cargo-ship had no chance of surviving, we put the nose down before we had yet released the bombs. It's a good thing that we are flying high. The trusty Heinkel whistles as it dives . . .

The fighter, which, as one of us says, 'Must surely be one of the reserves', sticks closely to our tail and dives with us, so that the radio operator can't fire without shooting away our own tail unit. And from inside the turret I can't see him. The gun in the cockpit above me had jammed, and its operator cursed as he tugged at it. The fighter, probably a Hurricane, dived leaving a trail of smoke behind it; then tried to catch us up again, but didn't quite succeed. At last there was a cloudbank, and in we went. Our pursuer has disappeared and we are safe — as safe as in a bunker. Repulsed and irritated, we fly off low over the sea towards France. Beneath us is a heavy swell, with only white crests everywhere. What a good thing that we didn't have to go down into that.

We later found that the 'reservist' had nevertheless chalked up a hit — there was a single small hole in the left wing.

Not one of our bombers flying singly had succeeded in reaching London. All of them had already been repulsed on the coast. One crew even claims to have seen six fighters. So just as before, single flights are still impossible. Tommy is still pulling himself together. The optimism was premature.

ROBERT GÖTZ

The widespread, highly-organised German night attacks found Fighter Command desperately looking for effective counter-measures. There was little chance of intercepting unilluminated bombers and not until suitable aircraft entered service in sufficient numbers, equipped with effective airborne interception radar, would the problem be resolved but that was months away. The destruction of the Heinkel on the night of the 14/15th was due to it being caught in searchlights north of North Weald and spotted by the crew of a Blenheim of No. 25 Squadron on patrol over London at 10,000 feet. Climbing to the attack, as the Blenheim closed from astern to within 50 yards, the Heinkel jettisoned its bombs before crashing in the grounds of Down Hall east of Harlow. ***Right:*** **Cliff Canning, a youngster of 12 living nearby at Matching Green, couldn't believe his luck — a German aircraft down on his doorstep and no school as it was a Saturday — and he quickly cycled over with some friends eager to get some souvenirs. Cliff took us back to the spot and pointed out exactly where the tail section had lain.**

attaches considerable importance to the dislocation of road and rail communications and the destruction of power houses. Unexploded and delayed action bombs are causing many diversions of traffic and considerable temporary evacuation of houses. The estimated scale of enemy effort by night was almost three times as great as by day. Fighter escorts have not escorted enemy bombers during the last two days. The absence of fighter escorts and the employment of few long-range bombers during the last two days suggest that they are being rested, or re-organised for some other purpose.

Despite decent weather conditions, a day of desultory attacks followed by reduced activity during the night. In Britain, astute observers claimed this to herald a day of intensive action on the morrow — a prediction soon to be fulfilled beyond their worst expectations. With little change to the overall situation, Hitler again deferred a decision on the launch of 'Seelöwe' for a further 3 days, pending the final and inevitable disintegration of RAF Fighter Command. Operations on the day cost the Luftwaffe 12 aircraft and another 7 damaged; another of their machines being destroyed and 1 more damaged in accidents.

3/KG4 Heinkel He 111H-4 (3294). Held in searchlights during bombing sortie over London and attacked by Blenheim night-fighter crewed by Pilot Officers M. J. Herrick and A. W. Brown of No. 25 Squadron. Bombs dumped during attack which set both engines on fire. Crashed and burned out at Down Hall, Newmans End, near Sheering 1.55 a.m. Oberlt. H. Kell (Staffelkapitän) and Fw. W. Hobe both baled out and captured unhurt. Uffz. W. Müller-Wernscheid and Uffz. H. Töpfer killed. Aircraft 5J+BL a write-off.
Site investigated by the Essex Aviation Group 1980 and several interesting items including instruments recovered. Relics taken by a local resident at the time of the crash, including access panel and ammunition, now in the After the Battle collection.

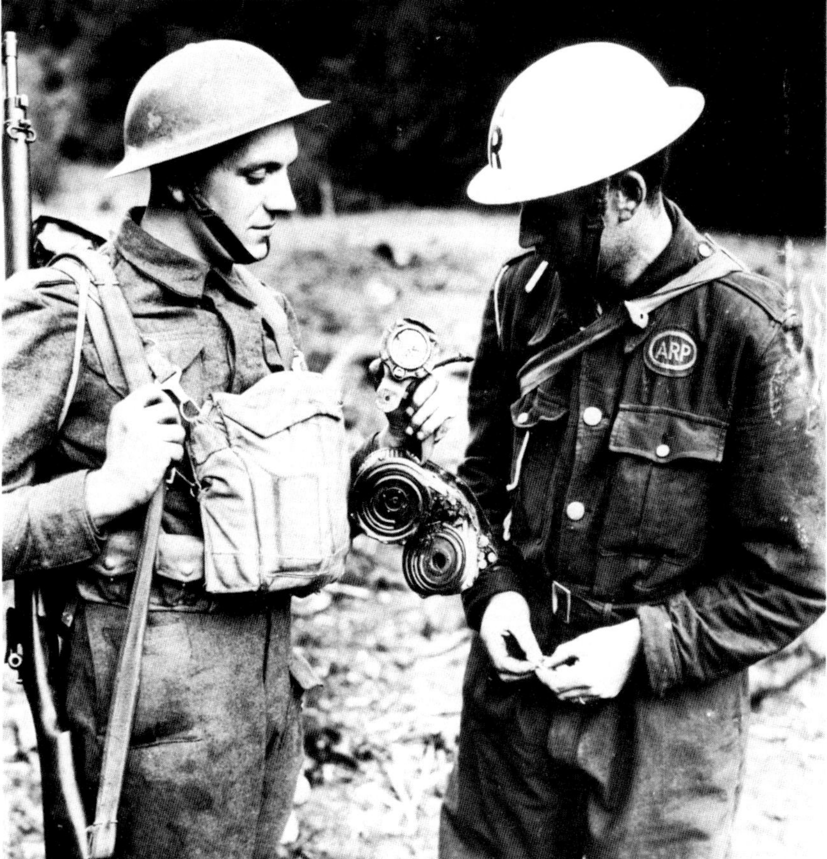

One souvenir Cliff and his mates didn't get their hands on: the clock from the Heinkel's control column (see picture page 27) and a saddle drum magazine from its MG15. This chap is armed with one of the half-million ex-WWI .30 rifles recently obtained from the United States government to replace weapons lost at Dunkirk. To avoid an ammunition problem, the American rifles were issued to the Home Guard which freed 300,000 SMLEs, chambered for the traditional British calibre of .303, for reissue to the Army. Meanwhile the ARP Rescue Officer rolls a second cigarette.

On September 14 Home Security made particular mention of the increasing disruption caused by delayed-action bombs. The previous day the Prime Minister had memoed to the Secretary of State for War, Anthony Eden, that 'it appears to be of high importance to cope with the UXB in London and especially on the railways. The congestion in the marshalling yards is becoming acute . . .' *Above left:* Burning railway trucks smoulder alongside the gutted and demolished shell of the London and North Eastern Railway's warehouses at Fenchurch Street Station. Destroyed on September 10, 1940, the site *(right)* now provides part of the new Docklands Light Railway built to link the City to the new Docklands development area.

Stab I/JG26 Messerschmitt Bf 109E-1 (5813). Exploded under attack by Sergeant A. S. Dredge of No. 253 Squadron in combat over Teynham. Main wreckage fell at Beacon Hill, Stone 4.00 p.m. Oberlt. K. Dähne killed. Aircraft a write-off.

Wing, believed to be from this aircraft, now in the Hawkinge Aeronautical Trust collection.

1/JG77 Messerschmitt Bf 109E-1 (3854). Engine badly damaged in attack by Flying Officer B. R. MacNamara of No. 603 Squadron during free-lance sortie over London. Possibly also that attacked by Sergeant I. Hutchinson of No. 222 Squadron. Forced-landed at Long Barn Farm, Boxley Hill, near Detling 4.30 p.m. and set alight by pilot. Fw. H. Ettler captured unhurt. Aircraft 4+ a write-off.

Part from fuselage in the Vizard collection.

6/LG2 Messerschmitt Bf 109E-7 (2014). Shot down by Pilot Officer J. P. Lloyd and Sergeant W. T. E. Rolls of No. 72 Squadron in combat over Ashford following escort sortie to London. Possibly also that attacked by Pilot Officer E. S. Lock of No. 41 Squadron. Crashed at Tennant Wood, New Street Farm, Great Chart 6.35 p.m. Uffz. V. Blazejewski baled out and captured unhurt. Aircraft ▲+I a write-off.

Site excavated September 1981 by Brenzett Aeronautical Museum and Kent Battle of Britain Museum. Few remaining fragments recovered now in the Hawkinge Aeronautical Trust collection.

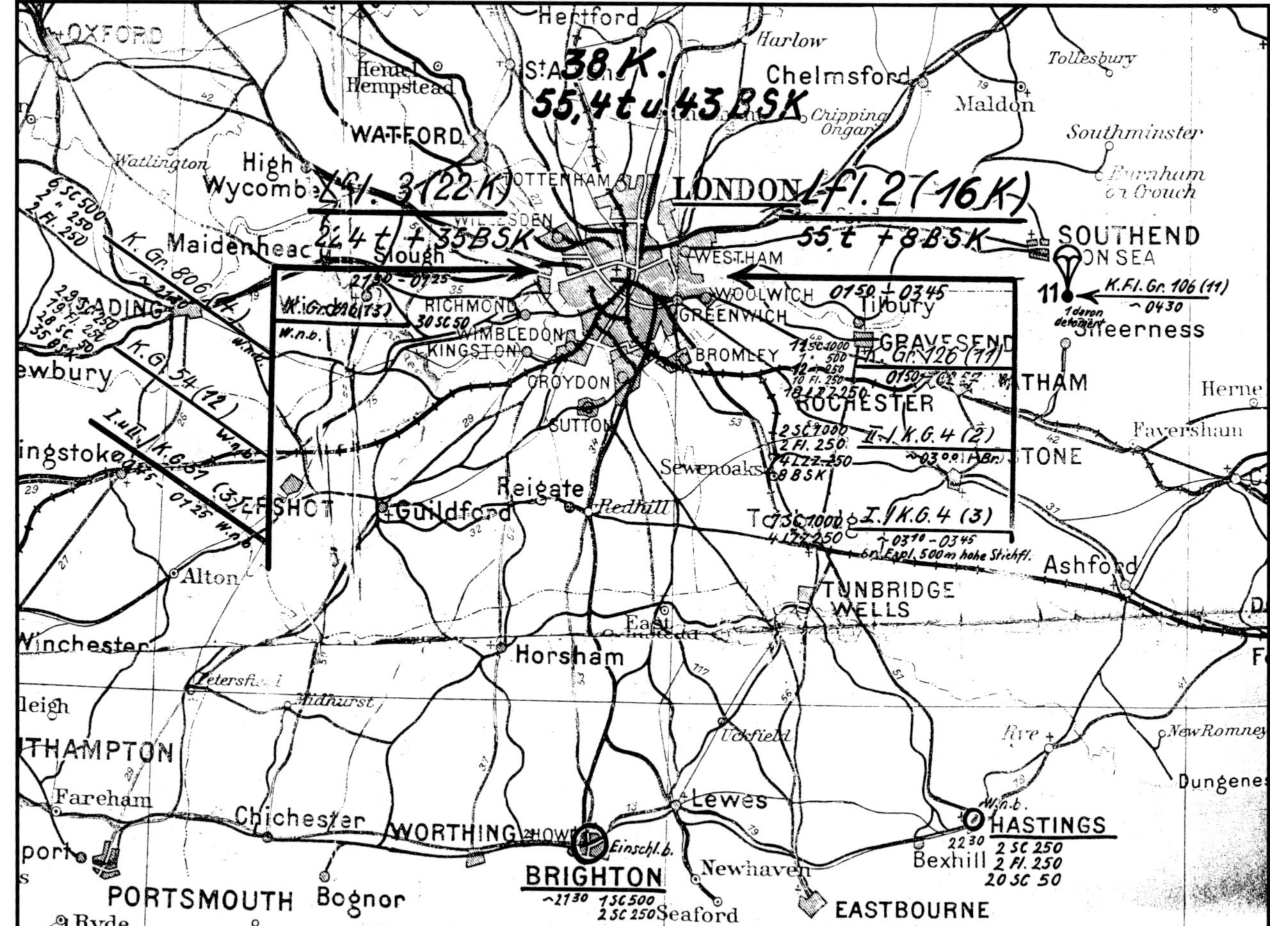

Night operations over the Capital on September 14-15. The number of each aircraft from each unit are given as well as the bomb load carried. 'LZZ' refers to the fuzing of the bombs, i.e. long-delay and 'BSK' a container holding incendiary bombs. Note the 11 parachute mines sown in the Thames Estuary — one of which was seen to explode on landing.

SUNDAY, SEPTEMBER 15

There were two main raids on London and the South-East during daylight in each of which between 80 and 100 aircraft penetrated the inner defences. During the first raid few casualties were caused and little material damage was done. In the late afternoon an attack was made on Southampton. Portland was also visited during the afternoon. There was little activity over the rest of the country. Approximately 600 enemy aircraft were over this country during the day.

No enemy activity by night is reported from the following Regions: 1, 2, 3 (except for one minor incident in Nottinghamshire and one in Lincolnshire), 9 (except for a few minor incidents in Warwickshire and Shropshire) or in Scotland. After 2000 raiding became general over the rest of the country. London was again subjected to a continuous series of attacks until 0500 the following morning.

Enemy aircraft destroyed: 188 certain, 45 probable, 78 damaged. Approximate civilian casualties: By day: London 52 killed, 87 seriously injured, 66 slightly injured. Elsewhere 10 killed, 32 seriously injured, 31 slightly injured. By night: London (not yet available). Elsewhere 4 killed, 17 slightly injured. The final figures for London may be found to exceed those for the last few days since a number of persons are reported trapped whose fate is not yet known.

'Last briefing before starting.' A snap from the album of Robert Götz.

September 15, 1940

'The second and first Staffels belong to No. III Gruppe, which will fly over the airfield at 14.45 hours.' Another attack on the South Coast, on the Portland naval base.

We boarded the plane in good time, and sat waiting. It was clear to us that we were facing a somewhat tricky situation, as this time we would be the ones to fly in the extreme rear, as the butt for the bullets, which usually got chopped up.

No. III Gruppe appeared over the airfield in rather ragged formation, which even at the take-off drew mighty curses from the pilot, Feldwebel Peters. So we took off and attached ourselves. But the formation flying didn't improve. If the Gruppe was going to remain so strung out over England, it would be quite a party!

Our own captain has a tighter grip for this sort of thing. And absolutely no fighter protection has been assigned to us . . . While we are still over France, I fitted the drums on my MG, and put reserves within easy reach, since things were likely to hot up soon and mainly involve us, the last planes.

In bright sunshine, the formation flew above magnificent banks of cloud with gaps in them, along the French coast. Even at our height, the white heads of the breakers in the Channel could be recognised; looking like a pond with patches of white water-lilies. I couldn't see enough of these continually changing, overpowering, undreamed-of pictures. Am I once more on 'a long trip' — as during the years of the Catholic Youth Movement? Yes — I'm on a long trip again. But accompanied by the seriousness of its unknown outcome.

We are part of a minute but clearly defined point in the sunlight, as we move towards our encounter — perhaps the last of these — through all the tremendous, inconceivable brightness. Inescapably enclosed by our determination and duty, and the destiny rushing towards us, we calmly wait to see what our rôle will be; entirely ready to accept whatever may be meted out to us in forty minutes time. Lord God, how can I thank thee for showing me all this, for allowing me actually to experience it, and at the same time letting me serve my native land?

We fly over Cherbourg and set our course for Portland. Closely aligned, sometimes above us and sometimes below, are our two watchdogs. It nevertheless feels good not to be flying around in this ocean of sunlight entirely alone. All the time I am looking in the direction of the sun, as it is from there that 'the others' like to come hurtling down. Portland comes in sight, and with it the fighters with their roundels, who now no longer look as petrifying as they had done. Three or four of them are approaching our last two planes from above, without visible success. I drop down into the turret. Now they are already coming down. Two, then three pull out, climb steeply from beneath us, cross our tracer streaks, and pull down again.

Meanwhile, the bombs are falling thickly onto the oil containers and industrial installations on the triangular headland; close together, like patterns on a drawing-board. Only one stick of bombs ends up in the water. Our heavy bombs also roll out. There are flashes all over this scrap of land, and we seem to see the earth trembling. The oil-bombs explode like gigantic, blood-red slabs. Smoke is covering everything. But the fighters are spoiling our picture.

There now, the Heinkel from No. III Gruppe, which had hung back from the beginning — hardly reassuring for the others — and which was probably a newcomer not good at formation flying, is still hanging back alone above the coast while the Gruppe is already above the water again. There is a stream of smoke coming out behind the He 111, and it continues to pour out. The crew are fighting for their lives in a way that had to be admired. Then a Hurricane turns away with smoke coming from it, and after further approaches the second one also gives up. To the great joy of all of us, I caught sight of the valiant plane again above white clouds in the middle of the Channel. One engine still seems to be working.

The Wehrmacht communiqué on the following day reported large-scale fighter combats over London and big losses on both sides. So now we know why we had no fighter protection. Our task had merely been to relieve the intensity on a main thrust in the direction of London. But the idea of us having an outing over England alone and in daylight was indeed an illusion. And if things stay that way, and we can only fly as far in as our short-range fighters can accompany us, how are we supposed to overcome the island? Will the 'morale effect' of our appearance over the South Coast alone be sufficient? Will the potential threat of the destruction of individual cities, and above all London, bring the English to the point of giving up?

Our leaders proclaim their belief in this, and our officers show no doubts about it. They are all convinced that we have as good as won the war and that our leadership holds unbeatable cards.

ROBERT GÖTZ

True or false? According to the German News Agency, Reichsfeldmarschall Göring flew over London on the night of Sunday, September 15. The report stated that he left his headquarters in Normandy, 'a small village which is extremely well camoflauged, in Germany's latest bomber, the Junkers 88. The Reichsfeldmarschall was himself at the controls. He rejected any kind of special protection or escort though he was accompanied by two fighter bombers which flew right and left of him at his rear.' British newspapers were sceptical: 'He has the reputation of being brave — but never foolhardy', said the *Evening News*. This photograph has also had its authenticity queried in the past because the roundels on the Spitfire appear to be too far inboard from the designated distance from the wingtip. Compare with the machine opposite.

The morning Sunday, September 15 — now celebrated as 'Battle of Britain Day' — started quietly enough with desultory early reconnaissance flights.

The first main attack eventually formed up over the French coast in clear view of British RDF and crossed inland at Dungeness about 11.30 a.m. — a solid phalanx bound for London. As the German bombers fought their way inland toward the capital in the teeth of determined fighter opposition, many of their crews were already harbouring serious doubts as to the sanity of continuing these heavy attacks by day. Countered by 22 RAF squadrons, the bombers reached their target around noon and after shedding their bombs dived away south harried by fighters.

A two hour respite followed until at 2.00 p.m. another massive raid was mounted against London. Again, RDF provided precious early-warning of German intentions and British fighters clashed with three successive waves of enemy aircraft as they forged inland across Kent and Surrey. The first two waves of the attack were largely turned away and dispersed, but the third reached its target only to meet 300 British fighters who slammed into its flanks as bombs rained down on the suburbs of London. No less than 31 British squadrons sortied to meet this raid and their impact on the German bomber crews, many of them exhausted after nearly two months of continual operations, must have been devastating. German efforts at destroying the very fabric of RAF Fighter Command and its capacity to resist were vividly shown to have been in vain. Their leaders' confident exhortations that the British were finally reduced to their 'last 50 Spitfires' would no longer provoke even hollow laughter amongst the survivors of these tired crews.

Even as the remnants of this attack retired south, a small force of Heinkels from III/KG55 sucessfully penetrated the defences and bombed Portland causing slight damage. Three hours later, an attack on the Supermarine Works at Woolston by Bf110s of the specialist precision-attack unit ErproGr210, thwarted by the AA defences at Southampton. Hampered in their aim by intense AA fire, the dive-bombers failed to hit their target but escaped detection by British fighters vectored to meet them. This was the last raid of any significance during the day but upwards of 180 German bombers ranged across Britain at night, most of them aiming at London where large fires resulted.

As the day drew to a close, it became apparent that far from the final coup-de-grace expected by the Luftwaffe High Command, they had suffered their highest losses of the battle since August 18. Far from consolidating their successes of September 12 the unequivocal and crushing defeat of the German bomber force could not be denied and would soon spark off loud recriminations against the fighters who, it would be claimed, had so patently failed to protect them.

From the British standpoint, the day had witnessed a great victory — already momentous to all those directly involved. The ecstatic claim that 185 German aircraft had been destroyed being indicative of the euphoria at large. In the event, the Luftwaffe lost a total of 58 aircraft on operations this day, another 23 returning with wounded crews and combat damage. One other machine was damaged in an accident. The following fell over Britain:

Stab JG3 Messerschmitt Bf 109E-4 (5205). Engaged by fighters during free-lance sortie and radiator severely damaged in combat. Possibly that attacked by Pilot Officer R. H. Holland of No. 92 Squadron. Engine overheated so attempted a forced-landing but crashed into outbuildings at Tarpots Farm, Bilsington 12.15 p.m. Oberstlt. H. von Wedel captured unhurt. Aircraft —+— a write-off.

Petrol injection unit from this aircraft held by the Hawkinge Aeronautical Trust.

1/JG3 Messerschmitt Bf 109E-1 (2685). Shot down during free-lance fighter sweep over Kent. Possibly that attacked by Pilot Officer D. W. Crowley-Milling of No. 242 Squadron. Crashed and burned out at St Michael's, near Tenterden 3.00 p.m. Oberfw. F. Hessel baled out and captured unhurt. Aircraft a write-off.

Site excavated by Andy Cresswell in 1983. Daimler-Benz DB601 engine, propeller blade, undercarriage leg, armament and oxygen bottles recovered. Undercarriage leg and oxygen bottle in the Vizard collection.

3/JG3 Messerschmitt Bf 109E-4 (1606). Shot down in combat with RAF fighters, crashed and burned out at Thorn Farm, near Pluckley Brickworks 3.30 p.m. Oberlt. H. Reumschüssel (Staffelkapitän) baled out and captured unhurt. Aircraft a write-off.

Major recovery by the Brenzett Aeronautical Museum. Most interesting items excavated included remains of pilot's flying helmet and oxygen mask and manufacturer's labels confirming identity as '1606'. Relics now held by the Hawkinge Aeronautical Trust.

2/JG27 Messerschmitt Bf 109E-1 (6147). Engaged by Spitfires, believed No. 19 Squadron, during escort sortie for KG76 attack on London and suffered damage to radiator causing engine fire. Possibly that claimed by Sergeant D. G. S. R. Cox. Forced-landed near Lodge Wood, Homestead, Isfield, near Uckfield 12.30 p.m. Uffz. A. Walburger captured unhurt. Aircraft 5+ a write-off.

7/JG51 Messerschmitt Bf 109E-4 (3266). Engaged on escort sortie and engine caught fire under attack by fighters. Believed that claimed by Pilot Officer W. Cunningham of No. 19 Squadron. Crashed and burned out at Nelson Park, St Margaret's-at-Cliffe, near Dover 2.50 p.m. Lt. K. Bildau baled out and captured unhurt. Aircraft a write-off.

Site excavated by the Brenzett Aeronautical Museum and some minor components and fragments recovered, now in the Hawkinge Aeronautical Trust collection.

9/JG51 Messerschmitt Bf 109E-4 (2803). Shot down in combat with fighters. Crashed at Skinners Corner, Mascalls, near Paddock Wood 2.20 p.m. and later exploded. Lt. F. Klotz killed. Aircraft a write-off.

Site excavated by local enthusiast Malcolm Pettit of Tonbridge and also investigated by Steve Vizard who recovered some fragments from a depth of six feet.

Stab I/JG52 Messerschmitt Bf 109E-4 (3182). Reputedly collided with another 109 during free-lance sortie over Ashford but actually subject of RAF fighter attack. Shot down by Pilot Officer G. H. Bennions of No. 41 Squadron but possibly that also attacked by Pilot Officer C. A. McGaw of No. 73 Squadron. Crashed and burned out near Dering Wood, opposite Berry Court, Biddenden Green 12.00 p.m. Lt. H. Bertel baled out and captured unhurt on landing at Bounds End Farm, Staplehurst. Aircraft ◁+ a write-off.

Surviving remains unearthed by Andy Cresswell in 1985.

1/JG53 Messerschmitt Bf 109E-4 (5197). Petrol tank set alight in fighter attack during free-lance sortie over Canterbury. Believed shot down by Flying Officer A. D. J. Lovell of No. 41 Squadron but possibly also attacked by Pilot Officer J. D. Smith of No. 73 Squadron. Abandoned aircraft crashed and burned out at Adisham Court, near Bekesbourne 12.09 p.m. Fw. H. Tschoppe baled out and captured severely burned. Aircraft a write-off.

2/JG53 Messerschmitt Bf 109E. Shot down by Pilot Officer J. F. J. Macphail of No. 603 Squadron during combat over Maidstone. Crashed in flames in Gore Wood, Aldington Court Farm, Bearstead 12.45 p.m. Oberlt. R. Schmidt killed. Aircraft a write-off.

Rudolf Schmidt was buried in nearby St Mary's Churchyard, Thurnham, where he remains to this day.

Site investigated by Ron Gamage and later by the London Air Museum which salvaged the shattered remains of the Daimler-Benz DB601 engine and a propeller boss together with remnants of airframe. Some items now held by the Tangmere Military Aviation Museum.

3/JG53 Messerschmitt Bf 109E-4 (1590). Shot down during escort sortie for KG76 attack on London and combat with fighters over the target area. Believed that claimed by Flight Sergeant G. C. Unwin of No. 19 Squadron but possibly also attacked by Flying Officer A. D. Nesbitt of No. 1 (RCAF) Squadron. Abandoned aircraft crashed and burned out in Mullard Wood, Norheads Farm, Biggin Hill 12.50 p.m. Oberlt. J. Haase (Staffelkapitän) baled out but killed due to parachute failure. Aircraft a write-off.

Major recovery by local enthusiasts in 1969. Complete Daimler-Benz DB601 engine excavated from beneath 15 feet of clay together with other relics now in the Halstead War Museum. Also represented in the Vizard collection and the After the Battle collection.

3/JG53 Messerschmitt Bf 109E-1 (3619). Sortied as escort for KG76 raid on London and engine damaged in combat with Spitfires south of the target area. Possibly that attacked by Flight Sergeant C. Sydney of No. 92 Squadron. Eventually crashed during forced-landing at Grand Redoubt, between Hythe and Dymchurch 12.42 p.m. Uffz. K-H. Feldmann captured unhurt. Aircraft 2+ a write-off.

Stab I/JG77 Messerschmitt Bf 109E-4 (3759). Shot down in combat with RAF fighters and crashed into a dyke near Stuttfall Castle, Lympne 3.30 p.m. Oberlt. H. Kunze (Gruppe Adjutant) killed. Aircraft a write-off.

Representative pieces recovered by the Brenzett Aeronautical Museum and now held by the Hawkinge Aeronautical Trust.

5/KG2 Dornier Do 17Z-3 (2678). Sortied to bomb Victoria Docks in London and initially engaged by Spitfires of No. 602 Squadron, including Pilot Officer A. Lyall, during return flight. Then pursued over the Sussex coast, attacked and severely damaged by Spitfires of No. 609 Squadron including Squadron Leader H. S. Darley, Flying Officer J. C. Dundas and Pilot Officer M. E. Staples. Turned back for land and forced-landed, both engines dead, on Eighteen Pounder Farm, Westfield, near Hastings 3.15 p.m. Possibly that also attacked by Flight Lieutenant G. ff. Powell-Shedden of No. 242 Squadron. Uffz. F. Reinisch captured unhurt. Oberlt. U. Latz and Fw. K. Haase both captured wounded. Oberfw. W. Hafner baled out over the Channel and missing believed drowned. Aircraft U5+CN a write-off.

Incident investigated by the Wealden Aviation Archaeological Group 1977 and control column liberated in 1940 donated by a local resident now on loan to the Tangmere Military Aviation Museum. Label held by Andy Saunders.

8/KG2 Dornier Do 17Z (3440). Sortied to bomb London Docks but port engine damaged in attack by Sergeant R. A. Innes of No. 253 Squadron prior to reaching target area. Bombs dumped blind over Walderslade and tried to escape into clouds but came under further attack from Flying Officer R. W. Oxspring of No. 66 Squadron. Also engaged by AA fire so abandoned by crew and crashed into The Chase, City Way, Chatham 3.05 p.m. Possibly also attacked by Pilot Officer H. P. Hill of No. 92 Squadron. Oberlt. W. Kittmann, Uffz. P. Langer, Uffz. J. Stampfer and Flgr. W. Köhler (Kr.Ber.) baled out and captured unhurt. Aircraft U5+PS a write-off.

9/KG2 Dornier Do 17Z (3405). Starboard engine severely damaged in attack by Pilot Officer W. B. Pattullo of No. 46 Squadron during sortie to bomb St Katherine Docks in London. Bombs dumped prior to crashing in the sea off Herne Bay 3.15 p.m. Probably that also attacked by Pilot Officer B. G. Stapleton of No. 603 Squadron. Uffz. H. Hoppe and Oberfhr. K-O. Staib believed baled out but killed. Gefr. A. Hoffmann and Gefr. J. Zierer picked up by RN vessel and captured unhurt. Aircraft U5+FT lost.

The wireless operator, Hans Hoppe, was washed ashore on the Isle of Sheppey on September 18, and the body of the pilot, Karl-Oskar Staib, was washed up on Graveney Marsh on September 30. Both these dates are now incorrectly recorded as their actual dates of death in the records of the Soldatenfriedhof, Cannock Chase.

On September 15 we were called out to Roman Road, just off Ilford Lane, on the southern edge of our boundary with Barking. It appeared that on this Sunday lunchtime enemy bombers had swooped low over Barking, each carrying two 500lb bombs, one under each wing. It was thought at the time that the target may have been the gun battery in Barking Park or the chemical factory (Howards) in Uphall Road.

When we got there several people had cuts and other minor injuries, and of course shock. Many were taken to hospital for treatment. However, there was one terrible incident, one of the bombs had made a direct hit on an Anderson shelter situated at the end of a short garden belonging to one of the small terraced houses. A warden said that a family of six had been in the shelter, now blown to pieces with its occupants, parts of bodies were scattered over a large area, one large piece was on a slated roof. A ladies arm was brought to me, on one of the fingers was an engagement ring, we heard that the girl had been about twenty and that she was due to be married on the following Sunday.

There was a great problem here, as our Rescue vehicle only carried one shroud; and as our chaps were collecting the remains I realised that we had nothing to hold all these gruesome objects, and I sent a man to the greengrocer's shop to obtain a dozen potato sacks. Each sack was filled and labelled.

I had sent for the mortuary van, but when it arrived there was an instant outcry from local residents, they were incensed at the thought that a Council dustcart was being used, even though it had been thoroughly cleaned and painted black. We explained our difficulties to these shocked people and promised to report their feelings to the Town Hall. As a result the Council acted very quickly: they obtained a removal van from Harrison and Gibsons, a large store in Ilford. This vehicle was suitably fitted out to carry six bodies on stretchers.

To conclude about this incident, the dinner was still on the table in the back room, the family having left it to go down the garden into their shelter.

The family in the next door house had survived the explosion, all suffered from shock, but their Anderson shelter had protected them from injury.

ALF TYLER, 1985

Unfortunately the picture has no original caption or date so cannot be tied in with any particular claim. On September 15 the Air Ministry announced the loss of 30 fighters — a reasonably accurate figure — but vastly over-claimed German losses. Instead of the much vaunted '185 shot down' the total shrunk with post-war research to 61.

If 'Practice makes perfect', Woolwich-ites have every reason, in the immediate future, to feel more 'at home' in proceeding to their respective shelters, than dangling tea-cups between finger and thumb and discussing politics . . . or the price of chickens.

Yesterday, the siren sounded four 'Alerts' between dawn and dusk, followed by the drone of aircraft above the clouds. At about 1435 hours, a group of 14 Bosch planes became clearly visible flying at a great height as they emerged from a heavy cloud-bank into a patch of rain-washed rich-blue sky . . . well timed 'bouquets' hurled at them by A.A. batteries immediately broke up this formation, and two bombers were seen hurtling earthwards; spasmodic bursts of machine gun fire above the clouds indicated the presence of our fighters, and within a few minutes a Heinkel twin-engine bomber glided into view, losing height in a graceful spiral, and rather resembling the movements of a prehistoric spider binding its intended victim — Woolwich — with coils of death. This machine crashed in the Arsenal.

LIEUTENANT E. B. TAPSELL
WOOLWICH DEFENCE OFFICER
WAR DIARY, SEPTEMBER 15/16, 1940

9/KG2 Dornier Do 17Z-2 (3230). Believed shot down by No. 611 Squadron Spitfires during sortie to bomb London Docks. Probably that attacked by Squadron Leader J. E. McComb, Flying Officer M. P. Brown, Flying Officer T. D. Williams and Pilot Officer J. W. Lund. Crashed, port engine in flames, and burned out near Cranbrook 2.45 p.m. Uffz. R. Lenz, Uffz. O. Krummheuer and Fw. H. Glaser killed. Uffz. J. Sehrt believed baled out and captured slightly wounded, landing near Hawkhurst Golf Club. Aircraft U5+ET a write-off.

4/KG3 Dornier Do 17Z-2 (3294). Intercepted by fighters during sortie to bomb rail targets in London. Attacked by Pilot Officer A. E. Johnson of No. 46 Squadron, Pilot Officers H. P. Hill and D. G. Williams of No. 92 Squadron and Pilot Officer R. G. A. Barclay of No. 249 Squadron. Probably that also attacked by Flying Officer B. Van Mentz of No. 222 Squadron, Flying Officer P. S. Turner of No. 242 Squadron and Flying Officer J. R. Hardacre of No. 504 Squadron. Crashed, petrol tanks on fire, and exploded in Gladstone Road, Laindon Hills, Billericay 2.33 p.m. Lt. K. Dümler, Uffz. H. Maskolus and Fw. A. Vogel believed to have attempted to bale out but killed. Uffz. G. Friebe baled out and captured unhurt. Aircraft 5K+DM a write-off.

Site excavated by No. 2243 (Basildon) Squadron ATC. Intact Bramo 323 engine complete with reduction gear and propeller boss donated to the Essex Aviation Group.

4/KG3 Dornier Do 17Z-2 (3457). Engine hit by AA fire during sortie to bomb London Docks and tried to reach cloud cover. Intercepted and shot down by Squadron Leader J. Sample of No. 504 Squadron and abandoned by crew. Crashed through trees into houses at Perry Street, adjoining Barnehurst Golf Course, near Dartford 2.45 p.m. and later exploded. Uffz. K. Hausburg baled out during fighter attack and killed — believed due to parachute failure. Lt. H. Michaelis and Flgr. H. Börmann baled out and captured wounded. Uffz. W. Burbulla baled out and captured severely wounded — died 2 days later in Dartford Hospital. Aircraft 5K+JM a write-off.

Wireless operator's code books and log book donated to the Kent Battle of Britain Museum together with manufacturer's plate from engine. MG15 ammunition drum and other items removed from the crash in 1940 now held by the Shoreham Aircraft Preservation Society.

4/KG3 Dornier Do 17Z-3 (2881). Damaged by AA fire and engaged by fighters during sortie to bomb railway targets along the Thames. Both engines disabled in attacks by Flight Lieutenant E. N. Ryder and Flying Officer J. G. Boyle of No. 41 Squadron, Flying Officer S. Fejfar of No. 310 Squadron and Pilot Officer R. Berry of No. 603 Squadron. Forced-landed and burned out at Lower Stoke, Isle of Grain 2.45 p.m. Gefr. E. Schild captured unhurt. Uffz. G. Wien, Fw. M. von Görtz and Gefr. H. Weymar captured wounded. Aircraft 5K+CM a write-off.

5/KG3 Dornier Do 17Z-2 (1176). Attacked by fighters and port engine set alight during bombing sortie to London. Crashed in the Thames Estuary 3.00 p.m. Fw. K. Falke baled out and captured unhurt landing at Fawkham, near Greenhithe. Fw. W. Franke killed. Hptmn. E. Püttmann (Staffelkapitän) and Oberlt. A. Langenheim both missing believed killed. Aircraft 5K+DN lost.

The body of the Bordmechaniker, Willy Franke, was washed ashore at Sheerness on September 30, which is incorrectly recorded as his date of death in the Soldatenfriedhof, Cannock Chase.

5/KG3 Dornier Do 17Z-3 (3458). Engaged by fighters during sortie to bomb installations along the Thames. Believed that which collided with a Hurricane flown by Pilot Officer P. J. T. Stephenson of No. 607 Squadron and crashed in Combwell Wood, Kilndown, near Goudhurst 3.15 p.m. Oberlt. H. Becker-Ross, Oberfw. G. Brückner, Fw. A. Hansen and Fw. W. Brinkmann all missing believed killed. Aircraft 5K+GN a write-off.

The bombload of this aircraft later exploded with great violence and what little was found of the crew defied proper identification and was buried as 3 'Unknown German Airmen' in All Saints Churchyard, Staplehurst, where they remain to this day.

Site excavated by the Wealden Aviation Archaeological Group 1972 and several interesting relics recovered. Nose portion of one of the exploded high-explosive bombs now in the Tangmere Military Aviation Museum. Engine maker's label held by the Hawkinge Aeronautical Trust. Items also displayed in Robertsbridge Aviation Society Museum.

5/KG3 Dornier Do 17Z-2 (4200). Sortied to bomb installations along the Thames and engaged by Hurricanes of No. 605 Squadron. Inadvertently rammed by Pilot Officer T. P. M. Cooper-Slipper during his attack. Abandoned by crew and crashed and exploded in Widehurst Woods, Marden 2.30 p.m. Oberfw. E. Rilling baled out too low and killed. Oberfw. H. Howind baled out and captured unhurt landing at Widehurst. Oberfw. H. Höbel and Fw. E. Zimmermann baled out and captured unhurt landing at Cannon Farm, Marden. Aircraft 5K+JN a write-off.

Site investigated by Lashenden Air Warfare Museum which collected a Luftwaffe pay book, Iron Cross and many small parts. Also represented in the Vizard Collection. Belgian and German money, removed from the body of Oberfw. Rilling in 1940 by a local resident, now in the After the Battle collection.

Two of the bombers crashed in the London area, one directly on the Woolwich Arsenal. According to a Local Defence Volunteer, it appears that the crippled Heinkel was attempting to land in the isolated area near the river allocated for the hazardous task of shell-filling. Each building was built partly underground surrounded by a water-filled moat (visible on the picture bottom left on page 51 beneath the centre aircraft) and the aircraft hit one with its wing. Ending up in the moat, the bomber exploded. In 1986 redevelopment of the Arsenal site led to some wreckage being uncovered: this section now with the Hawkinge Aeronautical Trust.

1/KG26 Heinkel He 111H-4 (6985). Starboard engine damaged by fighters during bombing attack on London. Bombs dumped in the Thames during further attacks from Squadron Leader E. A. McNab of No. 1 (RCAF) Squadron, Sub-Lt. A. G. Blake of No. 19 Squadron, Pilot Officer H. C. Baker of No. 41 Squadron, Pilot Officers A. C. Cochrane and P. A. Mortimer of No. 257 Squadron and Sergeant E. M. C. Prchal of No. 310 Squadron. Forced-landed below high-water mark at Asplens Head, Foulness 3.00 p.m. Lt. H. Streubel and Fw. H. Schwarz captured unhurt. Fw. W. Marenbach, Fw. K. Potenberg and Gefr. E. Domes captured wounded. Aircraft 1H+IH a write-off.

Site within a restricted MoD area visited by the Essex Aviation Group 1971 when surface wreckage was still visible. Undercarriage leg and tyre and propeller assembly donated to the Kent Battle of Britain Museum and now held by the Hawkinge Aeronautical Trust.

Stab KG53 Heinkel He 111H-2 (3140). Shot down by fighters during bombing sortie over London and attack on Becton Gasworks. Possibly that claimed by Sergeant B. Furst of No. 310 Squadron but possibly also attacked by Flying Officer B. D. Russel of No. 1 (RCAF) Squadron. Believed to have attempted a forced-landing but crashed and exploded in the shell-filling area of Woolwich Arsenal 2.50 p.m. Fw. A. Benz, Fw. A. Schweiger, Uffz. H. Meyer and Uffz. G. Geiger killed. Fw. M. Cionber believed baled out, captured badly wounded and admitted to the Royal Herbert Hospital. Aircraft A1+DA a write-off.

Undercarriage leg and tyre, together with large section of fuselage incorporating ventral gondola, plus oxygen bottles and MG15, unearthed during development work, donated to the Hawkinge Aeronautical Trust in 1986.

3/KG53 Heinkel He 111H-2 (5120). Port engine damaged in fighter attacks following bombing sortie to London Docks, further attacks setting starboard engine on fire. One wing torn off in forced-landing near Horstead Hall, Botany Farm, Orsett Fen 2.55 p.m. where aircraft set alight by crew. Fw. F. Grotzki killed. Uffz. A. Gerding captured unhurt. Lt. H. Boeckh, Uffz. K. Altmann and Obergefr. R. Kurzawski captured wounded. Aircraft A1+EL a write-off.

3/KG53 Heinkel He 111H-2 (5481). Pilot severely wounded in fighter attack during sortie to bomb London. Abandoned by crew during further attacks and crashed on Bourne Farm, Sandhurst 3.30 p.m. Possibly that engaged by various Spitfires of No. 92 Squadron including Pilot Officer H. P. Hill. Uffz. A. Lehner and Fw. K. Röthig killed. Oberlt. G. Büchner baled out and captured unhurt. Gefr. H. Stamminger and Gefr. H. Richter baled out and captured wounded. Aircraft A1+GL a write-off.

Propeller blade from this aircraft in the Hawkinge Aeronautical Trust collection. Some items in Robertsbridge Aviation Museum also accredited to this machine including navigator's maps.

Stab II/KG53 Heinkel He 111H-3 (6843). Port engine hit by AA fire during sortie to bomb Victoria Docks in London. Bombs dumped blind and attempted to reach cloud cover but engaged by fighters. Believed that engaged by various Spitfires of No. 92 Squadron including Pilot Officer D. G. Williams. Abandoned by crew, crashed and broke up on Peasridge Farm, Frittenden, near Staplehurst 4.00 p.m. Major M. Gruber (Gruppenkommandeur), Oberlt. H-P. Schierning and Oberfw. G. Schmidt baled out and captured unhurt. Uffz. E. Schilling and Fw. M. Nagl baled out and captured wounded. Fw. A. Grassl killed. Aircraft A1+GM a write-off.

Andreas Grassl, the gunner in this machine, was killed during the fighter attacks and crashed with the aircraft. Originally buried at Frittenden, he is now reinterred in the Soldatenfriedhof, Cannock Chase, whose records incorrectly show his date of death as 15.9.1942.

Propeller blade recovered at the time donated to the Lashenden Air Warfare Museum.

5/KG53 Heinkel He 111H-2 (5718). Sortied on forward weather reconnaissance mission for attack on London and engaged by fighters after joining the main formation to observe results of bombing. Possibly that attacked by various No. 92 Squadron Spitfires including Pilot Officer R. Mottram. Both radiators badly damaged and forced-landed on Trafford Farm, Benenden 2.30 p.m. Fw. O. Maier and Gefr. A. Hoffmann killed. Lt. H. Bänsch and Uffz. S. Bauer captured unhurt. Uffz. E. Buttler captured wounded. Aircraft A1+LN a write-off.

A Messerschmitt 110 'uber dem Kanal 1940' — the type attacked by Squadron Leader Stanford Tuck over the London area and described by him in a BBC broadcast in 1941: 'September 11th of last year is a day I shall always remember, for it was then I was promoted and given command of the Burma Squadron [No. 257] of Hurricanes. The first day I took them into action was a Sunday four days after my arrival [at Martlesham Heath]. We found a big bunch of mixed bombers, flying in formations of anything from thirty to sixty, with escorting fighters above them. As I led my new squadron in, I saw three of these parties nearing London. As the boys waded into the bombers, I went for some of the fighters. I picked off an Me 110 which I shot down over Barking, and one of his pals nearly got his own back when he put a bullet through my windscreen . . . ***Below:*** **This is the matching entry in his log book although it is difficult to pinpoint the aircraft concerned, the only Bf 110 coming down on land being 50 miles south-east of Barking near Ashford.**

15-9-40	Hurricane	Self	Solo	20	2000	To Debden.	Conference.
11.25	V6555						
15-9-40	Hurricane	Self	Solo	20	2000	To Martlesham.	Return trip.
13.30	V6555						
15-9-40	Hurricane	Self	Solo	1.45	22000	Over S.E.	Big bunch of bombers:- HE.111. JU.88.
14.45	V6555					London.	DO.17. & 215's with fighter escort.
							Shot down one ME.110 & a probable
							ME-109. received one bullet through
							windscreen. Squadron bagged
							fine with no losses.
16-9-40	Hurricane	Self	Solo	1.40	23000	Over London.	Fighter patrol.

5/KG53 Heinkel He 111H-1 (2771). Shot down by fighters during sortie to bomb London Docks. Attacked by various pilots including: Flying Officer R. W. Oxspring, Sergeants C. A. Parsons and D. A. C. Hunt of No. 66 Squadron, Pilot Officer H. P. Hill of No. 92 Squadron, Flight Lieutenant R. F. Rimmer, Flying Officers V. M. Bright and G. M. Simpson of No. 229 Squadron, Squadron Leader M. V. Blake of No. 238 Squadron, Flying Officer N. K. Stansfeld of No. 242 Squadron, Pilot Officer K. T. Lofts of No. 249 Squadron, Squadron Leader J. Sample and Flying Officer P. T. Parsons of No. 504 Squadron and probably also Flying Officer P. W. Lochnan of No. 1 (RCAF) Squadron. Harried by repeated fighter attacks so dumped bombs and forced-landed, one engine disabled, at West Malling airfield 3.00 p.m. Obergefr. E. Sailler and Gefr. H. Lange killed. Uffz. O. Zilling captured badly wounded. Fw. R. Lichtenhagen captured wounded. Fw. K. Behrendt captured unhurt. Aircraft A1+AN a write-off.

1/KG76 Dornier Do 17Z (2361). Set alight in repeated fighter attacks during sortie over central London and abandoned by crew. Engaged by various fighters including: Flight Lieutenant J. Jefferies, Sergeants J. Hubacek, R. Puda and J. Kaucky of No. 310 (Czech) Squadron, Pilot Officers J. Curchin and A. K. Ogilvie of No. 609 Squadron, Flying Officer P. T. Parsons of No. 504 Squadron and possibly that also attacked by Pilot Officer A. C. Cochrane of No. 257 Squadron. Finally struck by Hurricane flown by Sergeant R. T. Holmes of No. 504 Squadron during further attack and broke up over Vauxhall and Fulham, main wreckage falling into the forecourt of Victoria railway station at Wilton Road 11.50 a.m. Uffz. H. Goschenhofer and Uffz. G. Hubel killed. Oberlt. R. Zehbe badly wounded baled out and fiercely attacked by civilian mob on landing at Kennington — died of injuries the following day. Obergefr. L. Armbruster baled out and captured unhurt on landing in Wells Park Road, Sydenham. Uffz. L. Hammermeister baled out wounded and captured on landing in Dulwich. Aircraft F1+FH a write-off.

The unfortunate pilot of this aircraft, Robert Zehbe, was buried in Brookwood Military Cemetery where he remains to this day. His comrades on that last mission, Hans Goschenhofer and Gustav Hubel, are both interred in the Soldatenfriedhof at Cannock Chase.

Werk plates bearing '2361' taken at the time of the crash held by Simon Parry and the Shoreham Aircraft Preservation Society.

The most spectacular crash that day as far as Londoners were concerned occurred right in the centre of the West End. Three of the crew managed to bale out before the wingless, tail-less bomber smashed down on the corner of Wilton Road and Terminus Place, partially wrecking James Walker's shop on the right and scarring the facade to Victoria Station.

Up to 1980 the damage could still be seen but refurbishment has now destroyed a unique piece of London's wartime battle damage.

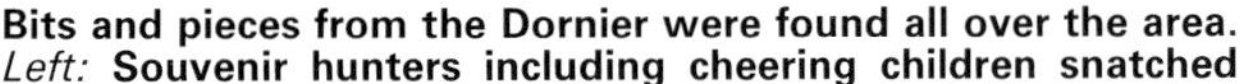

Bits and pieces from the Dornier were found all over the area. *Left:* **Souvenir hunters including cheering children snatched pieces as one of the wings was brought in.** *Above:* **The tail unit landed on this rooftop in Vauxhall Bridge Road.**

3/KG76 Dornier Do 17Z-3 (2651). Sortied to bomb London but intercepted by fighters before reaching the target area. Attacked by Pilot Officer J. R. B. Meaker of No. 249 Squadron then further damaged in attacks by Flight Lieutenant W. J. Leather, Flying Officer T. D. Williams and Pilot Officer P. S. C. Pollard of No. 611 Squadron. Also engaged by Flight Lieutenant K. McL. Gillies and Pilot Officer C. A. W. Bodie of No. 66 Squadron and possibly also that claimed by Flight Lieutenant J. W. Villa of No. 92 Squadron. Crashed in flames and exploded in trees on Alcrofts Farm, Sturry 12.40 p.m. Oberfw. K. Niebler, Fw. K. Wissmann and Uffz. J-F. Schatz killed. Oberlt. K-E. Wilke baled out and captured severely wounded. Uffz. H. Zrenner baled out and captured slightly wounded. Aircraft F1+FL a write-off.

Site established by Steve Vizard and surface fragments unearthed.

8/KG76 Dornier Do 17Z (2578). Sortied to bomb London docks and intercepted by fighters. Believed that shot down into the sea 4 miles NW of Herne Bay by Pilot Officer A. R. H. Barton of No. 253 Squadron 12.20 p.m. Fw. L. Keck and Uffz. G. Rosenow killed. Uffz. O. Zahn and Uffz. H. Heitmann missing believed killed. Aircraft F1+BS lost.

The body of the pilot, Lorenz Keck, was washed ashore at Herne Bay on September 29. That of the radio operator, Günter Rosenow, came ashore at Southwold on October 15, which is incorrectly recorded as his date of death in the Soldatenfriedhof, Cannock Chase.

In 1984 Colin Prately was exploring Kenley aerodrome when he came across thousands of aircraft serial plates on the site of the old AI1(g) block — apparently all the evidence gathered from their wartime investigations of crashed German aircraft and possibly later buried on the site. Then our author Simon Parry, scavenging the spot some time later, found this one with the Werke Nr. 2361 — the constructors' number of the Victoria Station Dornier.

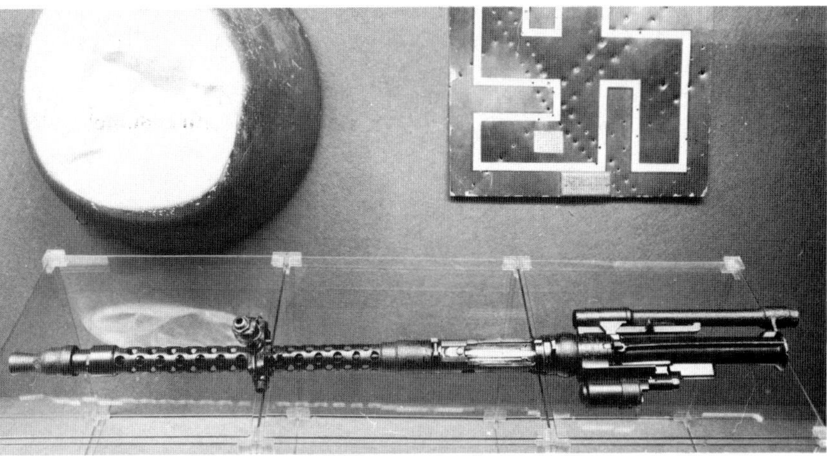

For more than 20 years one of the spinners, left, and an MG17, both reputed to have been part of the aircraft, were kept at Rochester Row Police station. Now they are on display at the Royal Air Force Museum at Hendon. (The swastika panel comes from another Dornier shot down at Leaves Green on August 18 — ***see Volume 1, page 213*****).**

By now the number of deaths from bombing in the built-up areas was such that if a German airman fell into civilian hands, he stood a grave risk of being ill-treated if not bodily injured. The pilot, Oberleutnant Robert Zehbe, was set about by a mob when he landed in Kennington and was so badly beaten that he subsequently died. He was buried at Brookwood in Plot 6, Row L, Grave 4 and this close-up of the mis-spelt Imperial War Graves Commission marker featured prominently in the fourth American wartime documentary in the 'Why We Fight' series entitled ***Battle of Britain*** **— without any mention of Zehbe's violent end. When the cemetery was redesigned after the war the location reference became Plot 15, Row A, Grave 2.**

8/KG76 Dornier Do 17Z (2555). Severely damaged by fighters and AA fire during sortie to bomb London docks. Finally attacked by Flying Officer J. C. Dundas and Pilot Officer E. Q. Tobin of No. 609 Squadron and bombs dumped prior to forced-landing, starboard engine dead, at Castle Farm, Shoreham 12.10 p.m. Fw. S. Schmid captured severely wounded — died later the same day. Fw. H. Pfeiffer and Fw. M. Sauter captured wounded. Fw. R. Heitsch captured unhurt. Aircraft F1+FS a write-off.

Relics believed to be from this aircraft held by local enthusiast Murray Barber. Forage cap, once the property of Fw. Martin Sauter, together with undercarriage position indicator gauge donated to the Shoreham Aircraft Preservation Society.

9/KG76 Dornier Do 17Z (2814). Port engine set alight in attack by Flight Sergeant J. Kominek of No. 310 (Czech) Squadron during bombing sortie to London. Further engaged by Sergeants C. A. L. Hurry and G. W. Jefferys of No. 46 Squadron and bombs dumped blind. Probably that also attacked by Pilot Officer V. M. M. Ortmans and Sergeant R. J. Ommaney of No. 229 Squadron. Crashed and burned out at Argos Hill Lodge, Red Lane Farm, Rotherfield 12.20 p.m. Obergefr. K. Böhme, Gefr. J. Kotonc and Lt. A.

This bullet-holed Dornier from the 8th Staffel of KG76 managed to make a wheels up landing on Castle Farm at Shoreham. ***Below:*** **Two of the crewmen are carried from the field of battle.**

From a battlefield to a field of nectar. Nearly half a century later the fields of Kent held out the hand of peace as Martina, the daughter of one of the wounded crewmen, Feldwebel Martin Sauter, was taken back by members of the Shoreham Aircraft Preservation Society to see the spot where her father ended his war.

Official caption passed by the Censor on September 18: 'ROAD UP — WARTIME STYLE. A main road in a London suburb wrecked by a bomb.' It is in fact Leytonstone High Road near Rivett's famous motor-cycle shop.

Wagner killed. Gefr. P. Holdenried attempted to bale out but killed due to parachute fouling the tailplane. Aircraft F1+AT a write-off.

Site investigated by the London Air Museum. Many surface fragments recovered including parachute buckles, uniform buttons and chunks of melted alloy, now held by the Tangmere Military Aviation Museum. Steel helmet donated to Robertsbridge Aviation Society said to have originated from this aircraft.

9/KG76 Dornier Do 17Z-2 (3322). Shot down by fighters during sortie to bomb London. Attacked by various aircraft including: Sergeant E. Tyrer of No. 46 Squadron, Flight Lieutenant R. F. Rimmer of No. 229 Squadron, Flight Lieutenant P. M. Brothers and Pilot Officer P. A. Mortimer of No. 257 Squadron and Sergeant E. W. Wright of No. 605 Squadron. Believed also that attacked by Pilot Officer H. N. Tamblyn of No. 242 Squadron. Crashed in flames and exploded at Underriver, near Sevenoaks 12.30 p.m. Oberfw. H. Streit and Fw. W. Seuffert baled out and captured wounded. Fw. W. Raab baled out and captured unhurt. Uffz. E. Malter believed attempted to bale out but killed due to parachute fouling the aircraft. Aircraft F1+DT a write-off.

Bullet-holed prop blade recovered at the time now owned by Steve Vizard together with other relics. Display board presented to Wilhelm Raab on his visit to the crash site in August 1979.

13/LG1 Messerschmitt Bf 110C-3 (3802). Shot down by fighters during escort sortie to London. Crashed at Rippers Cross, Hothfield Farm, Hothfield, near Ashford 3.15 p.m. Oberlt. H. Müller (Staffelkapitän) killed. Fw. A. Hoffmann mortally wounded — died the same day. Aircraft L1+IH a write-off.

MGFF 20mm cannon found in nearby ditch 1974.

1/LG2 Messerschmitt Bf 109E-7 (2061). Sortied as escort for Dorniers attacking London and engaged by fighters. Believed that shot down by Sergeant M. Wojciechowski of No. 303 Squadron but possibly also that claimed by Sergeant G. J. Bailey of No. 603 Squadron. Crashed in flames in Hartlip Churchyard, near Rainham 3.00 p.m. Uffz. H. Streibing baled out and captured unhurt. Aircraft a write-off.

Pieces taken at the time of the crash owned by Steve Vizard and the Hawkinge Aeronautical Trust.

3/LG2 Messerschmitt Bf 109E-7 (2058). Radiator damaged in fighter attack during escort sortie to London. Possibly that engaged by Flying Officer L. A. Haines of No. 19 Squadron. Turned for home but engine seized so crash-landed at Shellness 2.45 p.m. Uffz. A. Klick captured unhurt. Aircraft 2+ a write-off.

Now in the Shoreham Aircraft Preservation Society collection — the forage cap once worn by Feldwebel Sauter.

This one, taken about a mile to the north, states: 'A Savings Bank was damaged when a gas main exploded in a suburban street.' Probably true, for fires and accidents happened equally in war as well as during peacetime.

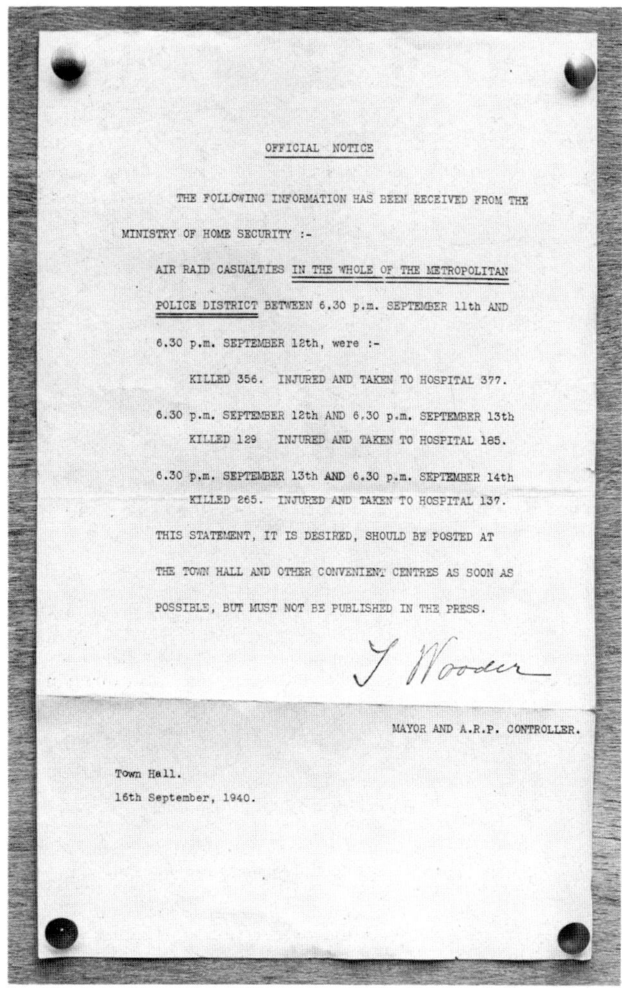

OFFICIAL NOTICE

THE FOLLOWING INFORMATION HAS BEEN RECEIVED FROM THE MINISTRY OF HOME SECURITY :-

AIR RAID CASUALTIES IN THE WHOLE OF THE METROPOLITAN POLICE DISTRICT BETWEEN 6.30 p.m. SEPTEMBER 11th AND 6.30 p.m. SEPTEMBER 12th, were :-

KILLED 356. INJURED AND TAKEN TO HOSPITAL 377.

6.30 p.m. SEPTEMBER 12th AND 6.30 p.m. SEPTEMBER 13th

KILLED 129 INJURED AND TAKEN TO HOSPITAL 185.

6.30 p.m. SEPTEMBER 13th AND 6.30 p.m. SEPTEMBER 14th

KILLED 265. INJURED AND TAKEN TO HOSPITAL 137.

THIS STATEMENT, IT IS DESIRED, SHOULD BE POSTED AT THE TOWN HALL AND OTHER CONVENIENT CENTRES AS SOON AS POSSIBLE, BUT MUST NOT BE PUBLISHED IN THE PRESS.

T. Wooder

MAYOR AND A.R.P. CONTROLLER.

Town Hall.

16th September, 1940.

How the news of casualties was broken to the public. Back in July the War Cabinet had decided not to release casualty totals in official communiqués. On September 15 Churchill inquired how many service personnel had been killed to date, and was told that 79 were included in the total of 1,286 dead. Now that the public was well aware of the scale of the deaths, it was considered that there would be more to be gained by releasing the information rather than to endanger morale and increase rumours by witholding it. Notices were posted outside local Town Halls which informed the populace without the risk of the news reaching a listening enemy via the wireless.

Kent

The conduct of the public is best described as being very satisfactory . . . In some districts where the sounding of sirens alone fails to galvanise some sections of the public into taking cover quickly, gun-fire in the vicinity induces such people to seek shelter at once . . . The solitary night-bombing aeroplane seems to cause more apprehension among the public than do the larger formations by day.

Buckinghamshire

Bombing of London and the sight of refugees have aroused considerable indignation and pity, but there is no sign of weakening morale.

Isle of Wight

The conduct of the public is becoming more callous . . . we cannot get the public to take cover. They will stand about in doorways and gossip at corners.

Cardiff

The public of this city have taken severe bombing in residential areas and a shopping centre with splendid calmness. It was necessary to evacuate a large number (approximately 400 persons) on account of unexploded H.E. bombs . . . in less than two hours accommodation was found. The spirit of such evacuees was really a tonic to workers and highly commendable considering that some workers had lost most of their worldly possessions and not a few had sustained casualties and family bereavements.

Coventry

Public Warning was sounded . . . during the progress of a football match, there being 3,000 people present . . . a few persons left but the others pressed for the game to go on, which it did.

Clitheroe

Enquiries show that during the evenings when the cinemas are giving shows and the receipt of the "ACTION WARNING" has been announced from the stage, practically no one has left, everybody being content to remain and see the show through.

Northumberland

When a German bomber was shot down by A.A. Batteries on Tyneside crowds of people all over the south-eastern part of the county watched the action and cheered wildly when the bomber was finally seen to be destroyed. There have been no signs of panic.

CONFIDENTIAL POLICE REPORTS
SEPTEMBER 15, 1940

SUNDAY, SEPTEMBER 16

At about 0800 some 350 enemy aircraft crossed the South-East Coast, but they were turned back before they reached the London area. Apart from this abortive attack there were sporadic, scattered raids during the day; some 150 single enemy aircraft being engaged at one time or another. There was minor bombing in several London areas. Only slight damage and few casualties were caused.

By night, enemy aircraft were active over most parts of England and Wales, and the total number of aircraft engaged is estimated at about 170, of which about 130 were over the London area. London was the chief object of the attack and bombs were dropped in 65 local authorities' districts in the London Region. Many fires were started, but the damage and casualties were not heavy.

Enemy aircraft destroyed amounted to 2 certain and 1 damaged. Approximate civilian casualties in London during daylight were 45 killed and 110 seriously injured. Elsewhere by day, 6 people were killed and 22 were injured, 8 of them seriously. By night approximately 20-30 people in London were killed and 250-350 seriously injured. Elsewhere during the night, 17 were killed and 68 injured, 39 of them seriously.

With the Government at pains to portray a London carrying on as normal, detailed descriptions and photographs were permitted in the Press of revelling and banqueting still in full swing in the West End. It was an insensitive move which failed to consider the effect on those members of the population reeling from concentrated bombing. Communist agitators made the most of the opportunity to fuel the long-running Deep Shelter controversy: the Left-wing line being that the Government was deliberately leaving the poor without sufficient air raid shelters while the rich were able to take advantage of their country retreats. On the evening of September 15 about a hundred people, including one very pregnant lady in the van, surged into the Savoy Hotel on the Embankment demanding shelter. As the Alert had sounded, the manager felt he could hardly eject the intruders and he called the police for advice. Fortunately the All Clear sounded in time to defuse the situation and avoid an ugly incident. Although the Censor managed to suppress details in Britain, American journalists in the hotel flashed the news to the United States from where it reached Germany. Dr Goebbels made capital out of the incident as he released lurid details of infuriated mobs of East Enders storming luxury hotels and being shot by police. ***Above:*** **Pillbox located along from the Savoy on the Embankment positioned to guard the approach to the seat of Government in Whitehall.**

Prize catch on a Northumberland beach. This Heinkel captured some miles offshore was towed seven miles upside down by fishermen and brought ashore at Eyemouth harbour. Expecting a reward, they got nothing — except the petrol in the tanks, and parachute silk for their ladies. Twenty years later, after a visit to the port, aircraft historian extraordinaire Christopher Elliott came away with these instruments ***(opposite)*** **to add to his large collection of aviation memorabilia.**

Dull weather blanketed northern Europe precluding any major attacks as both sides reflected on the previous day's events. The Luftwaffe High Command decided to return to a strategy of direct attacks on RAF Fighter Command. Future attacks on London would now take place only in favourable weather conditions and then by smaller formations of bombers closely protected by heavy fighter escort. The Luftwaffe lost 11 aircraft on operations, 3 more suffering damage. Four more were damaged and another destroyed in accidents. Two hundred tons of bombs fell on London during the night.

3/506 Heinkel He 115C (3261). Severely damaged by AA fire during torpedo attack on convoy and forced-landed on the sea 7 miles NE of Alnmouth 3.00 p.m. Crew took to their dinghy and attempted to sink the aircraft by shooting into its floats but only partly successful. Capsized aircraft eventually towed into Eyemouth harbour and beached. Hptmn. E-W. Bergmann (Staffelkapitän), Oberlt. C. Lucas, Fw. E. Kalinowski and Hptmn. H. Kriependorf (Staffelkapitän 1/506) all rescued by fishing boat and captured unhurt. Aircraft S4+CL a write-off.

1/906 Heinkel He 115C (2754). Crew lost their bearings in deteriorating weather conditions during sortie to Kinnairds Head. Eventually hit the ground in mist and crashed near Aberdour 10.00 p.m. Hptmn. H. Kothe and Uffz. H. Meissner captured unhurt. Lt. zur See H-O. Aldus captured injured. Aircraft 8L+GH a write-off.

1/KG54 Junkers Ju 88A-1 (7087). Crew lost their bearings during bombing sortie to Banbury. Collided with a balloon cable near Coventry shortly after dumping their bombs and both engines caught fire. Crashed and burned out at Withybrook 11.06 p.m. Fw. H. Baur and Fw. K. Perleberg baled out and both captured injured. Hptmn. W. Henke (Staffelkapitän) and Uffz. H. Rattay killed. Aircraft B3+HH a write-off.

Both the pilot of this aircraft, Willi Henke, and his Bordmechaniker, Heinrich Rattay, are buried in Oaston Road Cemetery, Nuneaton. They were not reinterred in the Soldatenfriedhof, Cannock Chase postwar.

Yesterday eclipses all previous records of the Fighter Command. Aided by squadrons of their Czech and Polish comrades, using only a small proportion of their total strength, and under cloud conditions of some difficulty, they cut to rags and tatters three separate waves of murderous assault upon the civil population of their native land, inflicting a certain loss of 125 bombers and 53 fighters upon the enemy, to say nothing of probables and damaged, while themselves sustaining only a loss of 12 pilots and 25 machines. These results exceed all expectations and give just and sober confidence in the approaching struggle.

WINSTON CHURCHILL, SEPTEMBER 16, 1940

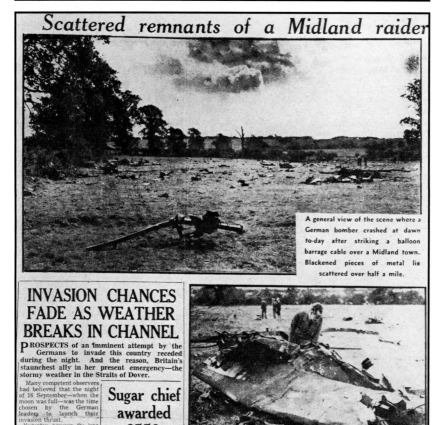

Scattered remnants of a Midland raider

A general view of the scene where a German bomber crashed at dawn to-day after striking a balloon barrage cable over a Midland town. Blackened pieces of metal lie scattered over half a mile.

INVASION CHANCES FADE AS WEATHER BREAKS IN CHANNEL

PROSPECTS of an imminent attempt by the Germans to invade this country receded during the night. And the reason, Britain's staunchest ally in her present emergency—the stormy weather in the Straits of Dover.

Many competent observers had believed that the night of 16 September—when the moon was full—was the time chosen by the German leaders to launch their invasion thrust.

Yesterday, however, the long spell of fine weather and calm seas broke—and rain, fog, and gales took their place.

All night long a wild south-westerly gale howled through the Straits of Dover, whipping

Sugar chief awarded £550 damages

One of the larger pieces of

After taking off from its base at Evreux, a Junkers 88 from the 1st Staffel of KG54 came a cropper when it fouled a balloon cable over Nuneaton, Warwickshire. The aircraft exploded over Hopsford Old Hall Farm, scattering itself across land now farmed by Mobbs Wood Farm. We are grateful to Delwyn Griffiths for the newspaper cutting ***above*** **and the comparison** ***below*.**

TUESDAY, SEPTEMBER 17

By day, reconnaissance activity was on a reduced scale but a big attack was launched in the East Kent area at about 1530 by a raid of some 300 aircraft. These crossed the coast at Lympne, Dover and Deal, but were intercepted and did not penetrate the Inner Artillery Zone.

By night, activity was again concentrated mainly on the London area and the south-eastern counties, with a few raids penetrating to Wales and the Liverpool area. First hostile raids crossed the coast between Selsey Bill and Dungeness at about 2000. The majority flew towards London, but many turned south without penetrating the A.A. barrage.

Between 2100 and 0030 raids flew to South Wales and Liverpool. Raids were also plotted over East Anglia and in the Digby, Middlesbrough and Glasgow areas.

After 0100 activity was almost entirely confined to London area, East Anglia and south-eastern counties.

Minelaying suspected in the Thames Estuary, and off Southwold and Foreness.

Enemy casualties by day amounted to 7 destroyed, 4 probable and 2 damaged. By night, 3 aircraft were destroyed. Own casualties (approx.): London: 108 killed, 385 injured. Elsewhere: 63 killed, 185 injured.

The dropping of parachute mines, the feature of which is their terrific blast effect extending over a distance of as much as two miles, is a new departure.

It is possible from the last two nights' bombing in Marylebone that the B.B.C. is the objective.

Another day of reduced activity apart from German fighter sweeps over Kent mid-afternoon which provoked some combat. Hitler decided to postpone 'Seelowe' until further notice, though a high state of readiness was to be maintained. Göring still clung to the vainglorious hope that his Luftwaffe would yet bomb the British into submission and render any invasion unneccessary. Eight German aircraft were lost and 4 damaged on operations — while 5 more suffered accidental damage.

7/JG26 Messerschmitt Bf 109E-1 (6294). Experienced engine trouble during free-lance sortie over London and turned for home. Engine eventually failed completely so forced-landed at Broomhill Farm, Camber, near Rye 3.45 p.m. Uffz. K-H. Bock captured unhurt. Aircraft 2+I a write-off.

9/JG53 Messerschmitt Bf 109E-1 (3177). Shot down by Pilot Officer G. H. Bennions of No. 41 Squadron during combat over Faversham. Crashed and burned out in Bishopden Wood, Dunkirk 3.40 p.m. Uffz. M. Langer killed. Aircraft a write-off.

Wreckage excavated by amateur enthusiasts and left scattered throughout woodland to the consternation of local authorities. Site 'cleared up' by members of the Kent Battle of Britain Museum who collected parachute release buckle, exploded 7.92mm ammunition and metal plate bearing legend '3177' — items now held by the Hawkinge Aeronautical Trust. Subsequently re-excavated by the Wealden Aviation Archaeological Group which removed the Daimler-Benz DB 601 engine in February 1979; subsequently donated to the Warplane Wreck Investigation Group. Site also investigated by the London Air Museum which recovered the propeller boss, an MG17 machine gun and various fragments and minor components. Some relics held by Halstead War Museum. Pilot's wrist watch and pieces of uniform reputed to be in Warplane Wreck Investigation Group collection.

The scene in the Strand on the morning of the 17th. In the background St Mary-le-Strand built in 1714–17 by James Gibbs, seen here *(right)* undergoing restoration after many post-war years of neglect due to the absence of a viable congregation.

3/KG54 Junkers Ju 88A-1 (2152). Sortied to bomb London Docks but intercepted and shot down by Sergeants G. Laurence and W. T. Chard in Defiant night-fighter of No. 141 Squadron. Broke up over Maidstone, main wreckage falling on St Andrews Close and Tonbridge Road 11.45 p.m. Lt. R. Ganzlmayr, Oberfw. W. Fachinger, Uffz. E. Bauer and Uffz. K. Schlössler killed. Aircraft B3+OL a write-off.

This crew was buried in Maidstone Cemetery where they remain to this day.

Pistol and leather spent ammunition pouch from 7.92mm MG15 machine gun donated to the Kent Battle of Britain Museum. Pilot's badge together with documents and photographs also presented to them by the family of the late Rudolf Ganzlmayr. These items now in the Hawkinge Aeronautical Trust collection. A

> *Sunday's action was the most brilliant and fruitful of any fought upon a large scale up to that date by the fighters of the Royal Air Force. The figures have already been made public. To the best of my belief — and I have made searching inquiries and taken several cross checks — those figures are not in any way exaggerated. . . .*
>
> *The German attacks upon the civil population have been concentrated mainly upon London, in the hopes of terrorising its citizens into submission, or to throw them into confusion, and also in the silly idea that they will put pressure upon the Government to make peace. The deliberate and repeated attacks upon Buckingham Palace and upon the persons of our beloved King and Queen are also intended, apart from their general barbarity, to have an unsettling effect upon public opinion. They have, of course, the opposite effect. They unite the King and Queen to their people by new and sacred bonds of common danger, and they steel the hearts of all to the stern and unrelenting prosecution of the war against so foul a foe.*
>
> WINSTON CHURCHILL, SEPTEMBER 17, 1940

Another road reported blocked in the Ministry of Home Security appreciation for the 17th–18th was that leading to the Blackwall Tunnel — one of the two underwater crossings of the Thames in London. With so many bombs having dropped in the area during five years of war, it is difficult to identify precisely which caused this damage — arguably some of the most dramatic left in London — which could be seen on the approach to both ends for many years after the war. When the second tunnel was built alongside the old one, the walls were reclad in cement and the blast marks removed.

7.92mm MG15 machine gun 'liberated' by local fireman now held by Lashenden Air Warfare Museum. Flying boot and access panel, both removed at the time of the crash, in the Vizard collection.

A night fighter kill in the streets of Maidstone. This particular piece from Ju 88 B3+OL lies behind Tonbridge Road in what is now St Andrew's Close.

Stab II/LG1 Junkers Ju 88A-1 (3188). Engaged by Spitfires of Blue Section No. 152 Squadron (Flying Officer P. G. St G. O'Brian, Pilot Officer E. S. Marrs and Sergeant K. C. Holland) during sortie to bomb aircraft factory at Speke. Hit in one engine and crashed attempting a landing at Ladywell Barn, near Warminster 2.00 p.m. Major H. Cramer (Gruppenkommandeur) captured unhurt. Oberfw. P. Stützel and Fw. F. Schultz captured wounded. Lt. O. Heinrich killed. Aircraft L1+XC a write-off.

WEDNESDAY, SEPTEMBER 18

The main enemy activity by day was centred on the London area, on which the enemy made three major attacks at approximately 0900, 1230 and 1630. It is noticeable that in the first attack the enemy aircraft were all fighters. Up to 1955 London Central was under red warning eight times. Five of these were caused by single aircraft which did not in every case reach the London district. During the day a total of about 800 enemy aircraft were involved, but no damage was caused in the London area, and the only material damage elsewhere was at one or two places on the Thames Estuary.

London was persistently and widely bombed by night between 2100 and 0500 the following morning, and it is estimated that altogether 230 aircraft were in operation over this area during the night. Aircraft in smaller numbers were over many other parts of the country during the night, but apart from substantial raids in the Liverpool Region and in towns on the north-east coast, bombing was on a minor scale outside London.

Enemy aircraft casualties amounted to 46 destroyed, 15 probable and 19 damaged. Civilian casualties (approx.): London: 200 killed, 550 injured. Elsewhere: 39 killed, 160 injured.

The repeated heavy attacks by day with large numbers of fighters appears to have been directed primarily to wearing down our fighter defences. The indiscriminate bombing of London by night was continued on an increasing scale, and a larger use was made of mines for this purpose.

Employing their new tactics, smaller formations of German bombers with close fighter escort were a feature of the day's action. One raid by III/KG77 in the late afternoon was met by 14 British squadrons, including the Duxford Wing, and suffered appalling casualties. In all 18 German aircraft were lost on operations this day, another 7 returning with damage and wounded crews. Two more of their machines were destroyed and another damaged in accidents. The following fell in Britain:

4/AufklärungsGruppe Ob.d.L. Dornier Do 215 (0038). Intercepted by Hurricanes of No. 303 Squadron during photo reconnaissance of British airfields and weather reconnaissance sortie over Kent. Suffered repeated attacks, abandoned by crew and crashed at Collier Street, near Yalding 1.15 p.m. Lt. H. Poser and Uffz. A. Linsner baled out and captured unhurt. Uffz. A. Wiesen baled out and captured wounded. Fw. H. Schütz killed. Aircraft G2+KH a write-off.

Site excavated by local enthusiast Alfred Batt. Surface fragments in the Steve Vizard collection.

1/JG27 Messerschmitt Bf 109E-4 (5388). Shot down in combat with fighters over Sittingbourne and crashed in Squirrels Wood, Stockbury 12.30 p.m. Believed that claimed by Pilot Officer A. G. Lewis of No. 249 Squadron but possibly also attacked by Pilot Officer R. Reid of No. 46 Squadron. Oberlt. R. Krafftschick missing believed killed. Aircraft a write-off.

No trace of Rudolf Krafftschick was ever reported found and he remains listed as 'missing'. However, a postwar unit history of JG27 records him 'captured' though no evidence for this has yet been found.

Site excavated by London Air Museum which recovered DB 601 engine, remains of cockpit including many instruments and controls, control column, maps, pilot's watch together with various French and Belgian coins. Manufacturer's plate con-

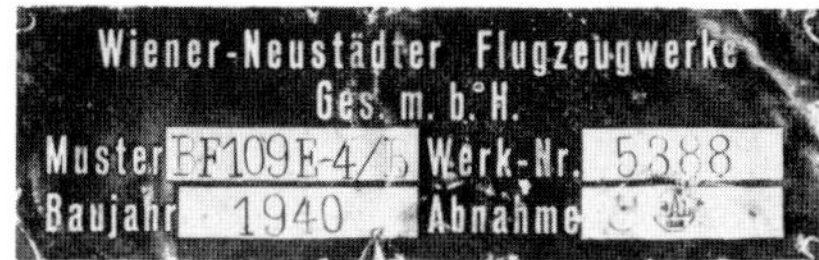

firming identity as '5388' subsequently recovered from site by Steve Vizard who now also holds the control column and parachute release buckle. Engine, bomb arming panel, coins and watch now in the Tangmere Military Aviation Museum.

9/JG27 Messerschmitt Bf 109E-1 (6327). Pilot wounded in combat with No. 603 Squadron Spitfires over Canterbury and forced-landed near Harringe Court, Sellindge 1.15 p.m. Possibly that attacked by Pilot Officer J. S. Morton. Fw. E. Schulz captured severely wounded and admitted to hospital. Aircraft 7+ a write-off.

Ernst Schulz was later transferred to the high-security 'Luftwaffe Ward' of the Royal Herbert Hospital, Woolwich where he died of his wounds on September 26.

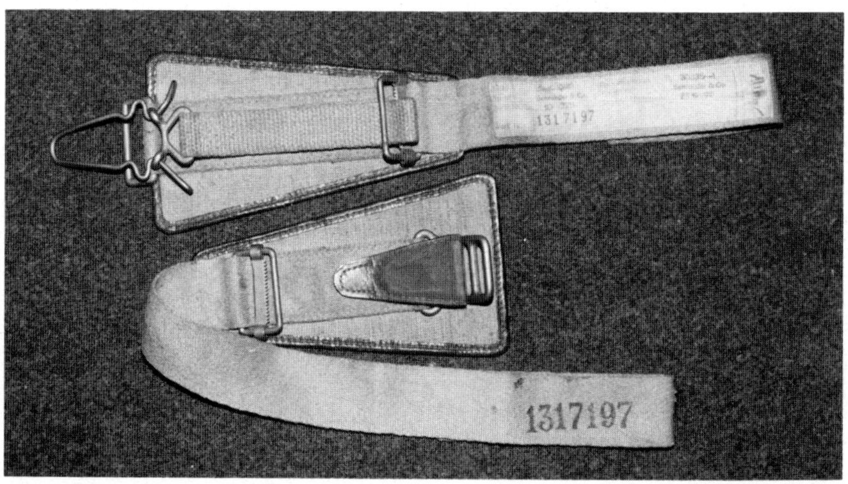

A nice souvenir now in the possession of the Severnside Aviation Society: a seat harness from the Ju 88 of Stab II/LG1 down near Warminster on September 17.

The famous John Lewis store in Oxford Street was gutted during the early hours of September 18. An eyewitness described the building as a 'charred skeleton with its blackened walls and gaping windows and rust orange girders and its wax models lying like corpses on the pavement'.

9/JG27 Messerschmitt Bf 109E-1 (2674). Petrol feed severely damaged in combat with No. 603 Squadron Spitfires over Canterbury 1.10 p.m. Possibly that attacked by Flying Officer W. A. A. Read. Forced-landed on the Royal St George's Golf Links at Willow Farm, Sandwich and set alight by pilot. Gefr. W. Glöckner captured unhurt. Aircraft 1+ a write-off.

First aid access panel marked '2674' in private collection.

4/JG53 Messerschmitt Bf 109E-1 (4842). Engaged on a free-lance sortie over Canterbury and intercepted by Spitfires of No. 66 Squadron. Caught fire under attack by Flying Officer R. W. Oxspring. Abandoned aircraft crashed in flames and burned out at Guilton, Ash, near Sandwich 5.05 p.m. Lt. E. Bodendiek baled out and captured seriously wounded. Aircraft 10+— a write-off.

Site excavated by the Kent Battle of Britain Museum which recovered remains of shattered Daimler-Benz DB 601 engine, complete tail wheel, cockpit instruments and controls including control column, flap and trim controls and the aircraft main identity plate confirming '4842'.

Stab III/KG77 Junkers Ju 88A-1 (3173). Attacked by Spitfires of Red Section of No. 19 Squadron (Flight Lieutenant W. G. Clouston, Pilot Officer W. J. Lawson, Pilot Officer W. Cunningham and Sergeant D. E. Lloyd) following bombing attack on Tilbury Docks. Crashed and burned out at Eastry Mill, near Sandwich 6.30 p.m. Major M. Klehs (Gruppenkommandeur) and Oberlt. F. Lauth (Gruppe Ia) killed. Fw. F. Himsel baled out and captured wounded. Fw. F. Pröbst baled out and captured unhurt. Aircraft 3Z+ED a write- off.

The date of death of Fritz Lauth, the observer in this aircraft, is recorded as September 19 in the Soldatenfriedhof at Cannock Chase. No reason for this can be given as he is not known to have survived the crash of the aircraft.

Site investigated by Steve Vizard who recovered remains of shattered engine, airframe components and several manufacturer's labels.

7/KG77 Junkers Ju 88A-1 (5098). Severely damaged by fighters during sortie to bomb Tilbury Docks, dumped bombs and ditched in the sea 25 miles off Shoeburyness 5.30 p.m. Believed that attacked by Pilot Officer C. A. W. Bodie of No. 66 Squadron prior to ditching. Fw. E. Wurche, Fw. J. Nolte, Fw. E. Friedel and Uffz. G. Stammnitz all believed vacated the aircraft safely but subsequently drowned. Aircraft 3Z+KR lost.

The bodies of three of this crew were later recovered from the sea; Erich Wurche and Johannes Nolte being washed ashore at Southend on October 4 and Erhard Friedel at Caister on October 25. Today they are all buried in the Soldatenfriedhof at Cannock Chase where the date of death of Fw. Wurche is incorrectly recorded as October 4.

8/KG77 Junkers Ju 88A-1 (3147). Attacked and severely damaged by No. 92 Squadron Spitfires during sortie to bomb Tilbury

Left: **Cleared by the time this picture was released in 1942, the store was rebuilt between 1958–60** *right.*

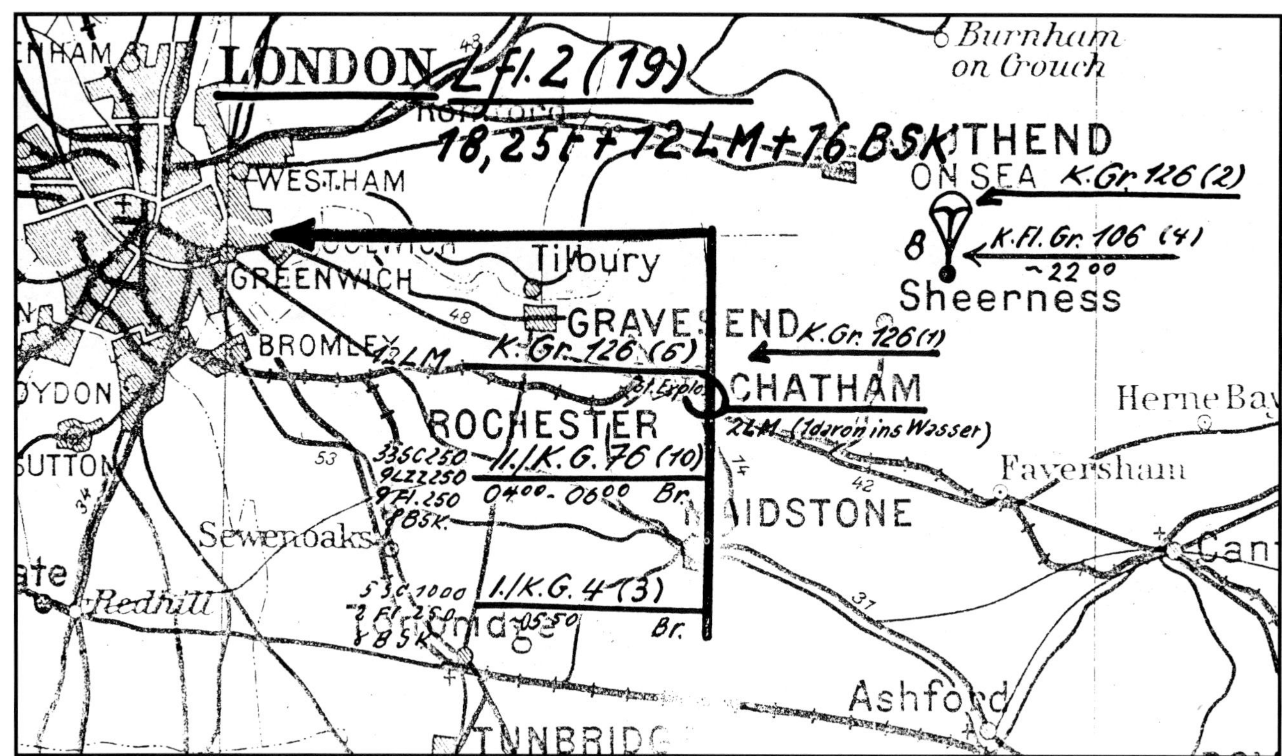

The date that the first Luftmine was dropped on London would appear from Home Security reports to be the night of September 16/17 (see page 106). This is substantiated by the appropriate Luftwaffe ops map for the period which indicates that '12 LM' were dropped on south-east London by six aircraft of KGr126. Home Security lists parachute mines down at Bethnal Green, Stepney, Dagenham, Woolwich, Orpington, Rochester, Swanley, Bellingham, Swanscombe, St Mary Cray, Bromley, Chislehurst, Chelsfield, Chipstead and Beckenham, a total of 15 incidents so at least three were probably caused by SC 1000s from the bomb loads of KG4. It was an escalation which Churchill could not let pass by.

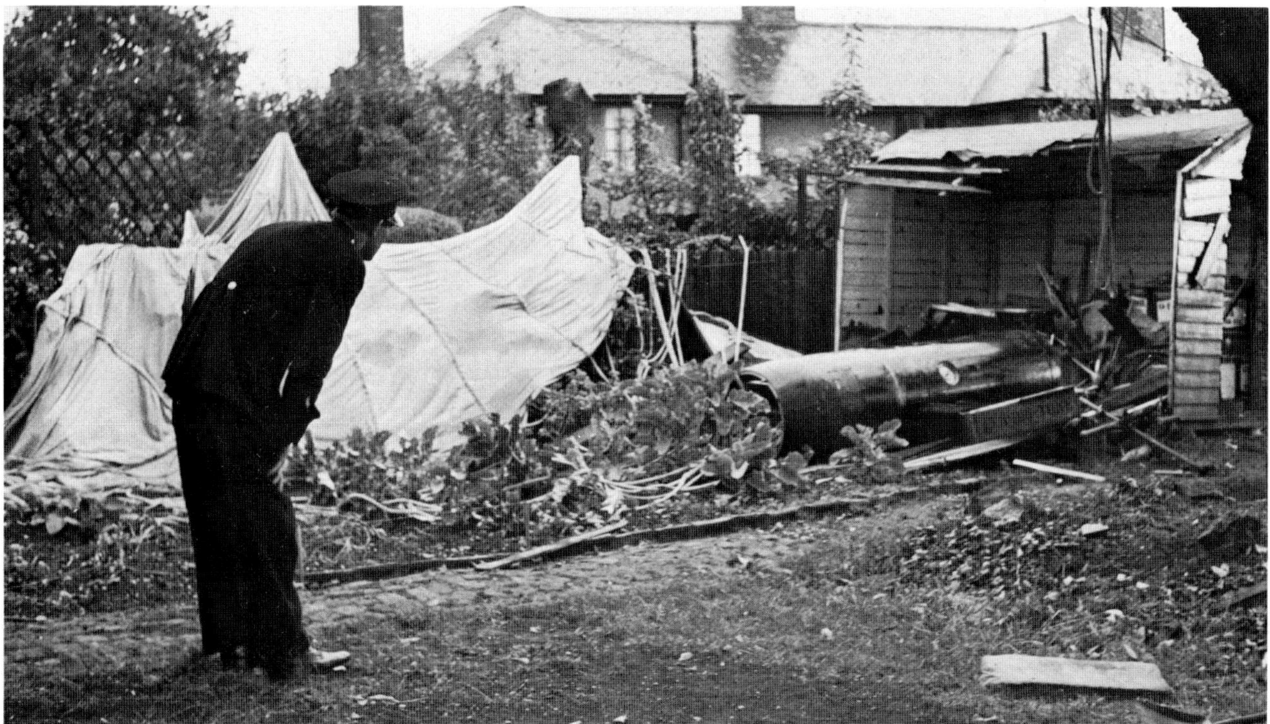

When early on September 19 another 36 mine explosions were reported, the PM lost no time in making his feelings known: 'We must drop two for every one of theirs.' That morning he sent a minute to the Chiefs of Staff: 'It was not solely on moral grounds that we decided against retaliation upon Germany. It pays us better to concentrate upon limited high-class military objectives. Moreover in the indiscriminate warfare the enemy's lack of skill in navigation, etc., does not tell against him so much. However, the dropping of large mines by parachute proclaims the enemy's entire abandonment of all pretence of aiming at military objectives. At five thousand feet he cannot have the slightest idea what he is going to hit. This therefore proves the "act of terror" against the civil population. We must consider whether his morale would stand up to this as well as ours. Here is a simple war thought. My inclination is to say that we will drop a heavy parachute mine on German cities for every one he drops on ours; and it might be an intriguing idea to mention a list of cities that would be black-listed for this purpose. I do not think they would like it, and there is no reason why they should not have a period of suspense . . .' This picture, unfortunately only identified as a 'SE London suburb', shows one of the 36 *(sic)* 'weapons of hate' which failed to explode. It is a Luftmine B but called by the Admiralty, who had the job of defuzing them, a Type C *(see Volume 1, page 157)*.

A typical 'dig' by UK wreckologists, in this case members of the Battle of Britain Museum in Kent. Originally located at picturesque Chilham Castle, the museum joined forces with the Brenzett group and a new museum was opened in 1982 on the forward aerodrome at Hawkinge. ***Left:*** **This is the crash site of Leutnant Bodendiek at Guilton.** ***Right:*** **The Daimler-Benz engine is lifted from its forty-year tomb.**

Docks. Believed that also attacked by Pilot Officer H. M. T. Heron of No. 66 Squadron and Pilot Officer S. Wapniarek of No. 302 Squadron. Crashed into the Thames Estuary off Southend 5.50 p.m. Uffz. P. Wiedemüller baled out too low for parachute to deploy and plunged into the sea off Southend where he was picked up and captured badly injured. Uffz. A. Smorlarczyk (Lw.Kr.Ber.Komp.4) also baled out too low and killed. Uffz. K. Künkler and Oberfw. W. Brendel missing believed killed. Aircraft 3Z+AS lost.

Front canopy frame recovered from Southend beach and now held by the Hawkinge Aeronautical Trust probably originated from this machine.

8/KG77 Junkers Ju 88A-1 (5100). Sortied to bomb Tilbury Docks, intercepted by Spitfires of No. 92 Squadron and port engine set alight. Further damaged in fighter attacks, possibly by Squadron Leader D. R. S. Bader of No. 242 Squadron, Flight Lieutenant K. McL. Gillies of No. 66 Squadron and Pilot Officer R. G. A. Barclay of No. 249 Squadron, and forced down to sea level. Believed also attacked by Pilot Officers E. Pilch and W. E. Karwowski of No. 302 Squadron. Finally crashed into the Thames Estuary off Sheerness 5.30 p.m. Fw. W. Häret baled out and captured badly wounded. Oberlt. H-L. Weber and Fw. A. Krimpmann killed. Gefr. M. Neuweg missing believed killed. Aircraft 3Z+HS lost.

8/KG77 Junkers Ju 88A-1 (5097). Shot down by fighters during sortie to bomb Tilbury Docks. Believed that attacked by Flying Officer L. A. Haines, Flight Sergeants G. C. Unwin and H. Steere of No. 19 Squadron. Crashed, both engines on fire, at Mocketts Farm, Harty, Isle of Sheppey 5.00 p.m. Fw. H. Damschen killed. Oberfw. W. Semerau and Uffz. H. Treutmann missing believed killed. Uffz. K. Eggert baled out and captured badly wounded — died in the RN Hospital, Chatham on September 24. Aircraft 3Z+ES a write-off.

Site excavated by the Kent Battle of Britain Museum and propeller boss unearthed together with quantities of minor components, parachute clips and buckles and Luftwaffe identity disc '65108/51' belonging to Uffz. Hans Treutmann. Items now in the Hawkinge Aeronautical Trust collection.

8/KG77 Junkers Ju 88A-1 (3162). One engine damaged by AA fire during sortie to bomb Tilbury Docks and then attacked by fighters. Probably that attacked by Pilot Officer H. P. Hill of No. 92 Squadron and also possibly that engaged by Squadron Leader D. R. S. Bader of No. 242 Squadron and Flying Officer J. Kowalski and Sergeant S. Paterek of No. 302 Squadron. Crashed in the sea off the Nore, Sheerness 5.30 p.m. Oberlt. G. Fuchs believed baled out but parachute fouled the tailplane and killed. Fw. H. Stier baled out into the sea, picked up by MTB and captured badly wounded. Obergefr. P. Baumann also baled out into the sea, picked up by MTB and captured suffering shock. Gefr. J. Föhlinger missing believed killed. Aircraft 3Z+FS lost.

Complete bomb sight, exhausts, clock, Walther signal pistol and other items including compass bearing '3162' recovered by local enthusiast Dick Walker and other divers from Southend.

9/KG77 Junkers Ju 88A-1 (5104). Port engine set alight in fighter attacks during sortie to bomb Tilbury Docks. Finally shot down by Sergeant S. Plzak of No. 19 Squadron. Crashed both engines alight, broke up on impact and burned out at Cooling Court, Cooling 5.00 p.m. Uffz. A. Kurz and Gefr. R. Kuhn killed. Uffz. K. Burkant and Uffz. H. Glaeseker both baled out and captured unhurt. Aircraft 3Z+DT a write-off.

Site investigated by the Wealden Aviation Archaeological Group in 1979 and elevator trim tab collected from a local farmer, now in the Tangmere Military Aviation Museum.

9/KG77 Junkers Ju 88A-1 (3168). Engaged by Hurricanes of No. 310 Squadron following bombing attack on London railway targets. Attacked by various pilots including Flying Officer S. Fejfar, Flight Sergeant M. Jiroudek, Sergeant E. M. C. Prchal, Sergeant R. Puda and possibly also Pilot Officer V. Bergman, and starboard engine set on fire. Crashed and burned out near Vange Creek, Pitsea Marshes, near Basildon 5.40 p.m. Fw. O. Wahl, Gefr. H. Buschbeck and Gefr. P. Lesker killed. Fw. O. Graf baled out and captured wounded. Aircraft 3Z+FT a write-off.

Major recovery by the Essex Aviation Group, October 1979. Main wing spars, tail wheel, oxygen cylinders, propeller blades and assorted wreckage excavated. Bomb disposal team called in due to suspected presence of explosives.

From below the ground . . . to on the ground . . . to beneath the waves. ***Left:*** **This canopy from the KG77 Junkers 3Z+AS was found on Southend beach by Bill Gent.** ***Right:*** **Nice Walther signal pistol, also recovered in the Southend area, from 3Z+FS shot down on the same mission to Tilbury.**

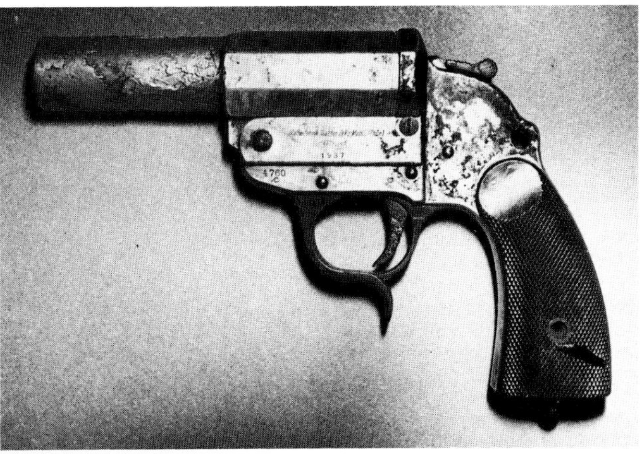

May 1939 — Britain prepares for war. Natural features formed ready made shelters and 12–15,000 people were able to use the 22 miles of Chislehurst Caves during the raids in the autumn of 1940. Formerly used for the cultivation of mushrooms, electric light and a water supply were installed (by two private citizens) and, following a campaign in Parliament and the Press, the Government put up the money to add bunks and install a medical post. Later it was taken over by the local authority.

LIFE IN THE SHELTERS

The watchword of the official policy concerning shelter from bombing (or lack of policy as its critics maintained) was 'dispersal' — the prevention of large numbers of people seeking shelter in one place. The first and obvious official concern was to reduce the risk of 'incidents' in which vast numbers of people might be killed at a stroke, but underlying the desire to prevent mass casualties was also the fear of what effect large-scale tragedies might have on morale. To a certain extent the policy was a legacy of the First World War, for the daylight air attacks over London in the summer of 1917 had caused large crowds to seek shelter in the Tubes, and the moonlight attacks of September of that year brought about a tendency to panic among the large numbers of people in the East End who knew only too well just how flimsily built their homes were. Trekking to the safer parts of London 'up West' had become commonplace.

In 1929 the idea of constructing a full-scale system of bomb-proof shelters below ground had been judged by the Ministry of Works as being too costly to contemplate as a practical proposition, although it was conceded that it would not be possible to provide adequate protection for London's population in existing buildings. The Underground system, though able to offer adequate if limited protection, would probably be needed more than ever in time of war for essential transport. All three considerations remained valid in the formulation of ARP policy during the 1930s, and the question of morale — not merely as it might be affected by mass casualties, but the imponderable of a rabbit-like 'shelter mentality' developing — was never far from the Whitehall mind.

In the legislation framed for the Air Raid Precautions Act of 1937, among the major items which local authorities were made responsible for providing, and for which Government grant aid was to apply, were 'structural precautions in public buildings [and] public refuges'. Follow-up regulations in March 1938 required local authorities to conduct surveys of buildings, especially in shopping areas, for possible use as public shelters, and also to make plans for the construction of an organised system of trenches in parks and open spaces.

The policy of 'dispersal' assumed that people would generally do what they could to 'increase the natural protection of their homes', and that employers would take steps to protect their premises and introduce air raid drill. The provision of public shelters (which were to be proof against blast, splinters and gas: not 'bomb-proof') was intended for those caught during a raid in the streets. In April 1939 the intention was to provide outdoor protection for about ten per cent of the population of mainly residential areas, and about fifteen per cent of the full-time population of business districts.

Public air raid shelters began to replace the early crude trenches which had been quickly dug after Munich. ***Left:*** **This 400-seater lay in Parliament Square, the picture showing the occupants leaving after the morning raid at 11.32 a.m. Unfortunately the caption writer in 1940 forgot to add one essential piece of information: the date!** ***Right:*** **The Fowell-Buxton memorial on the right commemorating the abolition of slavery within the British Empire in 1834 is now in the Victoria Gardens, Millbank.**

Left: **Substantial buildings with basements were requisitioned, this one — No. 14 Waterloo Place — sporting a profusion of shelter signs which soon became part of the everyday scene in Britain.** *Right:* **Pristine stonework gives little clue forty years later to its wartime rôle . . .**

It was to tell people how to implement the advice they were given — namely, to stay indoors during an air raid in a gas-proof room or refuge — that fourteen million copies of a Government booklet, *The Protection of Your Home against Air Raids*, were rushed out by His Majesty's Stationery Office in the autumn of 1938 for distribution to every householder in the country. By the same token, the announcement in December of that year of a new domestic shelter — the 'Anderson' — to be supplied free to some two and a half million families on low incomes living in the main target areas, stemmed from the urgent implementation of practical research into ways of improving household protection — for the Anderson had in fact originally been conceived as a shelter to be erected indoors.

Steel fittings to strengthen basements were supplied free on the same basis as the Anderson, and once free distribution of the shelter was completed it was to be offered to the public for sale. A brick and concrete alternative to the Anderson was devised (though few were built), and in March 1940 a larger version to accommodate forty-eight people — the communal domestic surface shelter — was introduced for the occupants of adjoining houses or flats without gardens in which to erect Andersons or basements to strengthen.

After Munich, it had been decided to make the majority of the trenches dug during the crisis permanent by lining and covering them with concrete or steel. After a slow start, as war approached, some three-quarters of London's Munich trenches had been thus reconstructed. By that time, the designation of buildings for use as public shelters was well in hand, but although notices stating 'Public Shelter' rapidly appeared outside town halls and other civic buildings, railway stations, offices, shops, and at the entrances to vaults, basements and cellars, progress in structural adaptation was in many ways negligible.

In May 1940 a new booklet, *Your Home as an Air Raid Shelter*, distributed to all householders, gave fresh and more detailed advice on how to obtain substantial protection from an ordinary soundly-built house, placing less emphasis on gas-proof refuge rooms, since all adults and children now possessed gas masks.

During the respite of the Phoney War, the Government's aim of providing protection against blast and splinters for twenty million people had been attained, and at 12,000 factories shelter schemes had been implemented — but sights had since been set higher, and efforts to improve shelter provision continued apace. Only in August 1938, however, when it had become obvious that trenches and reinforced buildings would not be enough to provide protection for people caught outdoors, had a brick and concrete surface structure specifically designed as a public shelter been introduced. Similar in design to (but not to be confused with) the communal or 'multiple unit domestic shelter', it was envisaged as being capable of being erected 'at considerable speed' — as indeed both types were in the summer of 1940. (Indicative perhaps of the policy of dispersal, the full cost of constructing communal shelters was borne by the Government;

. . . but occasionally the observant traveller can strike gold. *Left:* **A fading piece of history on the wall of the former headquarters in Upper Grosvenor Street of General Wladyslaw Sikorski, leader of the Polish Government in Exile.** *Right:* **Although repainted, another striking inscription can be seen in the playground of Staples Road School in Loughton, Essex.**

The Anderson — cold, wet and cramped. Originally envisaged as an indoor shelter, although 1,500,000 had been delivered by the outbreak of war, many had been badly sited or incorrectly installed in gardens where they quickly became waterlogged. To leave the house on a cold, dark night and try to keep warm around a candle burning in an inverted flower pot caused many people to forsake them for a makeshift shelter beneath the stairs. Pictures like these were released to show how much fun it all was — draughts and all!

public surface shelters being only grant-aided.)

Dissatisfaction with shelter arrangements found most fertile expression in a demand for some system of 'deep' or 'strong' shelters. For some time before the war various planning proposals were put forward to incorporate shelters in buildings with a peacetime use, such as underground garages, warehouses, shops and cinemas; then in August 1938 a full-blown scheme for deep shelters was presented by a pressure group calling itself 'The ARP Co-ordinating Committee'. Already the example of Barcelona and other bombed cities, where tunnels beneath the streets had provided good protection during air raids, seemed to reinforce the arguments of a few Members of Parliament with first-hand knowledge of events in Spain, and by the end of 1938 both the Labour and Liberal parties favoured a long-term policy of some form of deep shelters. Well into the Blitz the deep shelter campaign orchestrated by the Communists and Far Left was to prove a thorn in the Government's flesh, but it was because of public unease that in early 1939 Ministers decided to appoint an independent inquiry to look at the entire issue.

Throughout the deep shelter controversy the Government held to the view that, apart from the cost, the stupendous drain on the war effort which a deep shelter programme would involve made it prohibitive. The independent inquiry (the Hailey Conference) came to a similar conclusion and, as it pointed out, 'time was now also of the essence'. One of the factors to which its long, detailed assessment drew attention was that of access. With a maximum of seven minutes warning of an impending raid, the inquiry calculated that this would mean that only people living within 300 yards of a deep shelter would stand a chance of reaching safety (or within 150 yards at night). Such shelters would need long ramps or stairs, thus adding a serious danger of confusion or panic. If a bomb should happen to penetrate one, mass casualties would occur, which applied also to schemes for premises below ground combining shelter provision with peacetime use. London's Underground system, the inquiry assumed, would continue to be used in war for traffic, and for the movement of troops and essential services, and could in any case make only a small contribution to the problem.

The inquiry expressed concern too that a deep shelter system might create a 'shelter mentality' which would interfere with war production. Here lurked Whitehall's deep-seated fear, that of hordes of people who might descend to the bowels of the earth and decide not to come up again, effectively contracting themselves out of the war effort. In this sort of nightmare, the feeding, medical and sanitary problems loomed insuperable, and official imagination conceived subterranean dwellers breeding anything from mass hysteria to defeatism.

Typifying the whole concept of dispersal, with its corollary that the chief protection available to most people would be that afforded by their homes, the Anderson consisted of two curved walls of corrugated steel sheets meeting at a ridge at the top and then bolted to stout rails, weighing altogether about eight hundredweight. In the garden or backyard where it was erected, and where many lie mouldering today or survive as garden sheds, the Anderson could accommodate four to six people. To increase its resistance to blast, the structure was sunk three feet into the ground, with additional protection being obtained by covering the curved corrugated iron shell with the excavated soil.

The greatest problem with the below-ground Anderson was its susceptibility to flooding. Being wet, damp and cold inside, for those who trudged out into the garden or backyard in rotten weather to trust their salvation to the Anderson, it was not really an attractive proposition, though with the addition of 'home comforts' many were made more habitable.

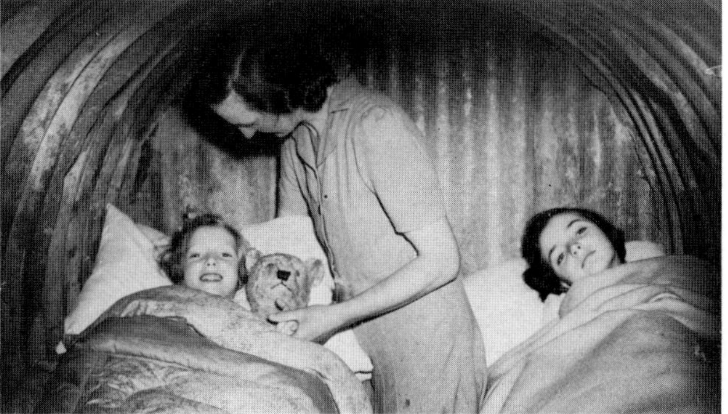

Attempts were made to overcome its failings — one borough in Kent devising the idea of not sinking them so far in the ground and shielding them with concrete with a waterproof rendering rather than earth.

It had been load tested to support the weight of a house collapsing on it, but not until some time later was it subjected to explosion tests out in the open, when it was established that it would withstand the blast of a 250kg bomb falling 50 feet away. Many people owed their salvation to the structure which withstood many a dramatic incident. ***Left:*** **On August 17, 1940 and** ***right*** **December 2, 1944, but where? Blitz captions are frustrating!**

A rather more comfortable means of getting through a raid was the Morrison shelter for use indoors. Introduced in the autumn of 1941, it was named after Herbert Morrison, the Home Secretary and Minister of Home Security who replaced Sir John Anderson, and was tested at Downing Street by Churchill himself before a firm order for half a million was placed. It was a solid rectangular steel frame 6 feet 6 inches in length by 4 feet 2 inches high with wire mesh sides. It was claimed that it was strong enough to hold up under the weight of a typical house should it collapse, and the inhabitants of the property could easily slip underneath it whenever a raid began. Its effectiveness was proven time and again in photographs during the Blitz showing survivors crawling out from the ruins of their homes usually because they made use of their Morrison. It was far better than spending an uncomfortable night in the Anderson, and at least a fair amount of warmth and comfort could be gained by remaining indoors. The one big setback was that if the house was hit the people inside would face a bigger chance of being trapped, perhaps with fatal consequences.

The Morrison. Since many people were determined to remain in their homes, the Government instructed the Research and Experimental Department of the Home Office to come up with designs for an alternative indoor shelter — and quickly. By the end of 1940 a steel 'table' an eighth of an inch thick had been produced, being personally tested by Winston Churchill. ***Above:*** **If a little claustrophobic, it could withstand the weight of a whole house — or two — according to the details supplied with this 1943 picture.**

The public shelter. Lacking toilet facilities — purpose-built ones that is — and poorly ventilated, they became foul, dank places of necessity only. It is surprising how soon one forgets detail — like the 'St Andrew's cross' permanent obstruction lamps and even the bright steel studded road markings. This is the junction of Charles II Street and Regent Street.

In pressing ahead in an effort to build more shelters in the summer of 1940, such time-consuming regulations as those which applied to their erection on the roadway were soon disregarded. As it transpired, however, the rate at which public and communal shelters (as well as their factory equivalents) had increased since the spring was to some extent at the expense of sound construction, and a scandal was to erupt in which the blame for their structural weakness was laid on Government specifications issued in April 1940 designed to alleviate a national shortage of cement and reduce the demands of the shelter programme on transport. The specifications were for lime to be used as much as possible for mortar used in the masonry of surface shelters, but the way in which they were worded caused them to be interpreted by certain borough engineers and local builders as permitting shelters to be put up without any cement in the mortar at all, making them completely useless against shock waves from bombs. When the error was discovered and remedial measures taken to strengthen or, after experience of bombing in 1940-41, to demolish and rebuild them, the full extent of the problem was finally revealed: over 5,000 faulty shelters in the London region alone!

How long could a raid be expected to last? Three or four hours at the most was a pre-war estimate many experts agreed upon ai being most likely, but it soon turned out that heavy, concentrated and determined attacks by the Luftwaffe could continue for up to fourteen hours at a stretch. During that time, people seeking refuge in a public shelter would of course begin to sweat, or feel the need to relieve themselves — only finding that no sanitary arrangements existed. Four hours — let alone fourteen — was too long to expect people to stand during a raid, yet there were few public shelters fitted with benches. Being in the dark under fire was enough to test most people's nerves, but lighting had not been envisaged as a vital component of a shelter that it was assumed would be occupied for only a short time. The dark, cramped, cold and damp conditions made such places completely unsuitable during a lengthy raid, and many soon resembled a 20th century version of the Black Hole of Calcutta. Since most lacked adequate ventilation, within a couple of hours the air turned foul, rancid, smelly and a definite health risk, so that their occupants were faced with the choice of either sticking it out or taking a chance outside.

As time passed, improvements and changes in the original layout and design of the shelters took place, and they eventually became reasonably decent places in which to spend long and arduous hours during a raid. In typically British fashion, community spirit grew out of hard times and dangers shared. The sound of a banjo or an accordion might be heard, drowning the whistle and crump of bombs; sing-songs developed, card schools started, flasks of tea and sandwiches would be handed round. Slowly the spirits of the courageous would pass into those of the frightened, and a strange, perhaps eerie new way of life would evolve.

Every so often a warden would pick his way through the ever-growing piles of rubble and poke his head round the

'Surface shelters can take it' says the message on one in Waterloo Place . . . or can they?

shelter door to see if everything was all right. He would more often than not be invited in for some tea or a sandwich, and might spend a few minutes in the shelter telling those inside that everything was OK out there. Inside, he would experience every possible emotion . . . near panic from some . . . self-disciplined restraint from others . . . or stoicism from people who really wanted to burst out crying but who knew that their fortitude strengthened that of others. There would always be the character who knew exactly what Jerry was up to and what street he was going to bomb tonight; perhaps another who would be doing his best to tell jokes and cheer everyone up, but for the most part the shelters would be occupied by quiet, contemplative and calm people just waiting for the raid to end and hoping to God that their home was still going to be there when they went back to it.

On some occasions a shelter might receive the attention of what became known as the 'Shelter Crawlers', bands of merrymakers who would travel from one to the other and taste what the various shelterers had to offer.

Gradually, newer and better shelters, designed by men like Sir Giles Scott, began to appear. They included among others, the Pillbox, Dormitory, Metaform, Arch and Hollow Block; likewise the 'Raidsafe', which was intended for use in factories.

Meanwhile, among those who sought shelter as the bombing of London intensified, the Tube stations increasingly came to be regarded as a safer and more certain place to spend the night. The fear of the 'deep-shelter mentality' still prevented the Government officially sanctioning their use as shelters, but individuals were beginning to use them anyway, sometimes buying a ticket and not coming up again until the raid was over. More people were beginning to insist openly that it was stupid not to permit this obviously sensible use of the Underground, it being the safest possible place to be during an air raid.

One Government regulation issued soon after the war started, designed to conserve cement and demands on transport, was that the mortar mix used in the masonry of all surface shelters was to be one part cement to two parts lime. In April 1940 an ambiguous instruction was misinterpreted to mean that a lime-sand mix was permissible. Before the mistake was realised in July, thousands of shelters had been built with ungauged lime mortar, producing a fatally dangerous structure to be in during a bombing attack. After some tragic incidents had brought the error to light, in December 1940 authorities were given detailed instructions for inspecting all shelters on their patch; to close those that were obviously unsafe and to strengthen others. This picture was passed for publication in August 1941 stating: 'Surface shelters are now being reinforced with an added brick wall and roof being built around them.'

Gradually the approach to shelter building became more scientific with structures like this one designed by Sir Giles Scott and seen being erected *right* in Page Street and *below* on a site between Strutton Ground and Matthew Street, Westminster.

Oddball Specials 1. The Raidsafe moveable shelter specifically designed for use inside factories to provide last-minute protection where production had to be maintained even during air raids. Constructed of 12-inch reinforced concrete, the small square openings were for use when the shelter was occupied by fire-watchers.

Government resistance to the use of the Underground in this way continued until 79 stations were 'occupied', and the shelterers made it clear that they intended making these new sanctuaries their homes during raids from then on. After bowing to the inevitable, the Government was agreeably surprised to discover that no deep-shelter mentality was going to take hold of those who used them, and in fact only a few hundred of the average 60,000 Tube shelterers remained down there for weeks on end. Most of these only did so not out of any great fear but simply because their homes had been destroyed and overcrowding of rest centres and so forth gave them very little alternative than to use the Underground until they could find somewhere else to stay during the raids.

People usually arrived at the shelter entrances at about 10.30 a.m., up to a quarter being children who were told by their parents to go along and save a place for them when they returned from their day's work. Many others were women who left their prams outside and joined the long spiralling queues which waited for the stations to open at about 3.30 p.m. and within half and hour every inch of space had been taken. A mother might start to feed her baby while the rest of the children played on the platform, dashing back to their mum if the trains were still running whenever one whooshed into the station to disgorge people in search of their spot or making their way home.

Spivs, those profiteers who traded in every scarce commodity and who used their business acumen to gain from the war situation, had early on appreciated that a lucrative means of making a fast buck was to go down with the shelterers and stake out a number of patches with bundles of rags, proceeding to sell the spaces later on for as much as half a crown. Once the authorities caught on to this racket they foiled it by issuing tickets to the shelterers.

Just as with the surface shelters, the Underground, never built for the purpose for which it was now being put, with few toilet facilities or other sanitary arrangements, soon became unsavoury. However, things improved as organisation took charge and the Salvation Army and the Women's Voluntary Service applied themselves to supplying food in a sort of 'meals-on-wheels' service, amounting on one night to a total of seven tons of food and 2,400 gallons of coffee, tea and cocoa being consumed. Because of the possible inci-

Oddball Specials 2. When we came across a Consul fire-watchers shelter in a front garden in Bisterne Avenue, Walthamstow (F District, most probably something to do with E Post), we very soon had it away for the *After the Battle* collection — with the owner's permission of course! When we ordered up a crane lorry the only thing we didn't realise (as the advert doesn't show it) is that Consuls were bolted to a huge 4-foot block of buried concrete and when we first tried to lift it, the lorry itself came off the road! After that we dug it out, undid the nuts and did it properly.

dence of disease, about 30 doctors and 200 nurses kept an eye open for such things as dysentry and other related ailments. No outbreaks of disease materialised, though there were lice and mosquitoes to be dealt with and some cases of impetigo and scabies.

Thus it was that the shelterers settled themselves down at last along the fifteen miles of Tube stations set aside for this purpose. On bunk beds, or on the floor, they made themselves as comfortable as possible, keeping well to their side of the white line that divided the platform so they would not hamper those using the trains. Six feet of platform was assigned to six people, three in bunks and three side by side on the floor, making what use they could of the blankets they had and their coats or whatever else they decided to take down with them. Many found it difficult to sleep in such surroundings and, on average, men got four and a half hours sleep a night and women three and a half; most spent their time chatting, watching any entertainments that might have been organised, listening to records or the wireless. Others read books, and fifty-two libraries kept the Underground supplied to help while

A quarter to four and all's well. The tangled mass of humanity at the Elephant and Castle surreptitiously photographed in November 1940. The take-over of the Underground system by the public began quite unofficially in September and the Civil Defence historian, Terence O'Brien, states quite clearly that 'it is doubtful whether any serious attempt could have been made to dislodge the shelterers'. Because the authorities were very concerned that the presence of so many people on the platforms might seriously disrupt the Tubes, in November the London Passenger Transport Board appointed a manager to be specifically responsible for the use of the Tubes as shelters. One amenity which had to be provided quickly was chemical toilets although, because the platforms were well below the level of the sewers, these had to be emptied laboriously by the local authority. Later compressed air was used to force the sewage up to where it could be discharged directly into the sewers.

In October it was agreed that bunks could be installed and these were assembled by Home Security at Ealing. By February 1941 all but three stations had been so equipped with standard three-tier steel bunks and a system of place reservation devised which ended the daytime queues outside stations. We took our Underground comparison just before London Transport embarked on its massive refurbishment scheme which has since dramatically transformed the atmosphere below ground.

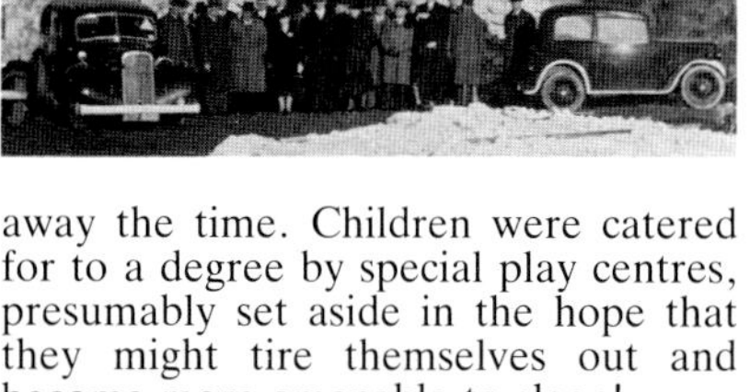

By the beginning of 1941 the Government had decided against attempting to build 'bomb proof' surface shelters (unlike the massive above-ground air raid bunkers which were provided for civilians in many German cities), and instead a programme of deep bored shelters was begun, linked to the Underground system. However, as these were not completed until long after the Night Blitz ended, they rightfully come much later in our story. *Above:* **At Portsmouth an official inspection in December 1941 by the mayor.** *Below:* **Work proceeding apace the following month at another deep shelter in Birkenhead.**

away the time. Children were catered for to a degree by special play centres, presumably set aside in the hope that they might tire themselves out and become more amenable to sleep!

Yet the sense of security — and of 'togetherness' as it might be termed today — that was engendered to some extent by being beyond the actual noise of the Blitz did not necessarily mean that shelterers in the Underground were beyond the reach of the bombs, and tragedies did occur. In the worst of them, at Balham Tube Station on October 14, 68 people died (17 having been killed the previous evening at Bounds Green; 7 the evening before that at Trafalgar Square), and in another bad incident in January 1941, at Bank, a bomb which crashed through the booking hall area accounted for 56 dead.

Railway arches were ready-made refuges, just as they were during the German air raids of the First World War. One arch in Stepney in London's East End was 'Mickey's Shelter', named after Mickey Davies, a local optician who was a hunchback and stood only just over three feet tall. It was run by an elected committee and became very popular, with Mickey inspiring many people with a great deal of faith and confidence. Even Marks and Spencer were impressed enough to donate a canteen which was run so well that the children were able to be supplied free milk out of the profits.

The provision of shelters in places such as Merseyside and Portsmouth included constructing huge bunkers in their hillsides, and in Kent the existence of numerous caves in the chalk of the coastal cliffs and The Downs led to their being adapted and utilised.

However, by no means everyone forsook their beds for either a public or domestic shelter. In November 1940 inner London contained some 3,200,000 people, but not more than 300,000 of them used public shelters. Also it is believed that no more than 1,150,000 people used domestic shelters. Thus, that month, out of every hundred Londoners living in the central urban areas, 9 were in public shelters, of whom perhaps 4 were in communal shelters; 27 were in domestic shelters, and 64 in their own beds or else doing their bit on duty or at work as part of the war effort. At the same time, in outer London, with a population of over 4,500,000, only 4 per cent used the public shelters.

The highest single number ever con-

What now remains? Although declining year by year — several nice specimens being demolished since we began this project — it is still possible to find examples of wartime shelters. In back gardens, as well as the ubiquitous Anderson still performing a useful rôle as a shed or children's den, one can find more substantial brick edifices. *Above left:* **This one at Hackney now used as a kennel for two particularly ferocious Dobermanns.** *Above right:* **At Mitcham the family who now own the house would dearly like this elaborate construction removed — except that it will cost £1,000 to demolish it.**

centrated into shelters was on September 27, 1940, when there were 177,000 or more using them — more than the total population of Southampton, but even at the very peak of the Blitz, not more than 15 out of 100 metropolitan Londoners would have used public shelter, 6 or 7 of these the Tubes.

The work of the authorities was not of course made any easier by people choosing to remain in their homes. Wardens and police were expected to be able to account for everyone on their 'patch', and the best way for them to be able to do so was by people always going straight to their assigned shelters. Then their whereabouts were certain; otherwise the authorities could never be sure if they were lying amongst the rubble or perhaps out visiting friends or relatives.

So there can be very little doubt that the vast majority of the population decided that Hitler was not going to send them scurrying for cover like scared rabbits. Not for them a communal shelter or Tube station; they stuck it out where they felt best able to, and died or survived as they had lived. Certainly it can be said that the spirit of the Blitz owed as much to the majority who tossed and turned in their own beds through the nightly din of the ack-ack as it did to those who made the best of it in the shelters and Tubes.

ANDREW HYDE, 1986

Sunken shelter for the residents of flats in Amhurst Road, Hackney.

A turf covered concrete shelter in the grounds of Rush Green Hospital, Hornchurch.

Left: **An unusual shelter built with corrugated iron shuttering at Gravesend.** *Right:* **Playground shelter still standing in Romford.**

A scene so reminiscent of those magnificently recreated in John Boorman's 1987 film *Hope and Glory* — only this is for real! Taken somewhere in the Walthamstow–Leyton area, according to the caption the boys were 'very soon spotted by the eye of the law and told to seek playing fields elsewhere. The moral is that all Hitler's bombers will never, never break the spirit of Britain's youth.'

THURSDAY, SEPTEMBER 19

Raiding by day was on a much reduced scale. There were no major attacks but a considerable number of single enemy aircraft reconnaissances were made over south-east England, South Wales and Liverpool areas. About 70 enemy aircraft were over this country during daylight. Some bombs were dropped in the London area and in Essex, Sussex, Wiltshire and Dorset. Little material damage was done, though some casualties were caused, chiefly at Tilbury, Stepney and West Ham.

At night, between 2100 and 2200, there were six raids operating over London, a similar number in the Isle of Wight area, in Kent and in Wales. Liverpool was also visited during this period. Thereafter raiding was almost entirely confined to London, Kent, and the Thames Estuary and off the Suffolk coast. No incidents were reported from Nos. 1, 2, 3 (with the exception of two minor incidents in Lincolnshire), 8, 9 or 11 Regions. In the London area incidents were widespread, causing a considerable number of casualties. Material damage, however, was slight.

Enemy aircraft destroyed amounted to 6 certain and 1 probable. Approximate civilian casualties were: By day in London: 13 killed, 88 injured. Elsewhere: 4 killed, 8 injured. Of the above London casualties, all except two occurred at incidents in Stepney and Plaistow (West Ham) when no air raid warning had been given. By night in London: 46 killed, 8 injured. Elsewhere: 5 killed, 18 injured. London Region reports that the above figures are subject to increase. There were also several casualties (unspecified) in Liverpool during the night raiding.

> *Sirens announced the arrival of our uninvited guests at approximately 1955 hours, and lest we forget, our A.A. batteries resorted to heavy gun-fire until the 'All Clear' sounded at about 0525 hours this morning. Bomb explosions were heard at a distance. The sound of a few nearby 'whistling bombs' that was not followed up by the expected explosion during the early hours of this morning, is apt to be mistaken for delayed-action bombs. It is comforting to know, that, all is not H.E. that whistles; as I have, with great pleasure, personally dealt with two of this type of small incendiaries which had caused me several seconds of anguish. It would be wise, however, to err on the right side by connecting this whistling sound as part and parcel of the H.E.*
>
> LIEUTENANT E. B. TAPSELL
> WOOLWICH DEFENCE OFFICER
> WAR DIARY, SEPTEMBER 18/19, 1940

Rain over Britain reduced activity apart from isolated raids often by solitary aircraft. Nine German aircraft were lost and 7 damaged in operations, 2 more being damaged and another destroyed in accidents. In Germany, Hitler finally abandoned plans for any

Except that sometimes Britain's youth breaks up Hitler's bombers! This was a Junkers 88 before it smashed to pieces on Pitsea Marshes on September 18 — a gold mine of rich pickings for these local boys.

invasion of Britain in 1940 and ordered a halt to the assembly of the invasion fleet. Whatever his reasons, the continuing implacable resistance of RAF Fighter Command and the serious damage inflicted on the invasion ports by RAF Bomber Command over previous weeks certainly contributed to his decision. If, as many believe, the Battle of Britain was being fought to prevent an invasion of England, then the battle was truly won on this day. And although that truth was already hesitantly dawning across Britain, it was to be some time yet before tired British aircrews could relax their vigilance.

4(F)/121 Junkers Ju 88A-1 (362). Port engine developed a fault during photo and weather reconnaissance mission over Britain. Forced-landed at Oakington airfield 3.00 p.m. to avoid fighters. Lt. H. Knab, Uffz. H-J. Zscheket, Uffz. J. Thöring and Obergefr. E. Bresch captured unhurt. Aircraft 7A+FM a write-off.

3/KG51 Junkers Ju 88A-1 (7058). Sortied on daylight bombing attack to Gloucester but crashed into the Channel off the Sussex coast, exact cause unknown. Uffz. W. Henker and Oberfw. H. Luckhardt killed. Fw. W. Walter and Gefr. R. Röder missing believed killed. Aircraft 9K+DL lost.

The body of the Observer, Heinrich Luckhardt, was washed ashore at Seaford on October 14 — now incorrectly shown as his date of death in the records of the Soldatenfriedhof, Cannock Chase. The Bordfunker, Waldemar Henker, came ashore further along the coast at Brighton on November 4 and he remains buried there to this day.

3/KG55 Heinkel He 111P-2 (2146). Suffered direct hit by AA fire during sortie to bomb London and crashed at Thorley Wash, Spellbrook, near Bishop's Stortford 11.40 p.m. Uffz. H. Pohl, Uffz. W. Goliath and Fw. T. Alpers killed. Uffz. W. Gertz baled out and captured badly wounded. Aircraft G1+GL a write-off.

The three dead crewmen from this aircraft were buried in Saffron Walden Cemetery where they still remain to this day.

Site investigated by several individuals but no relics discovered due to nearby river improvement operations.

1/KG77 Junkers Ju 88A-1 (2151). Engaged by Hurricanes of 'B' Flight, No. 302 Squadron during bombing sortie to London. Attacked by many pilots including Flying Officer J. Kowalski and crashed in flames and burned out at Culford School, Bury St Edmunds 11.30 a.m. Uffz. P. Dorawa, Obergefr. E. Schulz and Gefr. H. Scholz killed. Uffz. E. Etzold captured wounded. Aircraft 3Z+GH a write-off.

Down on the morning of September 19 — the Ju 88 at Culford School, Bury St Edmunds.

FRIDAY, SEPTEMBER 20

By day, raiding was on a very small scale. One large force of about 100 aircraft, mainly fighters, was met over the south-east coast, only one or two penetrated to the London area, a few bombs being dropped in the south-east area. There were few casualties and little material damage. During this raid bombs were also dropped at Brighton, near the viaduct; 11 persons were killed, and the water supply will be affected for a short time.

Raiding by night was confined to the London area and eastern counties, bombs being dropped throughout the London Region, and at Ipswich, Colchester, Chelmsford, Romford and North Weald. Major fires were started in Southwark and Bermondsey. There was moderate damage to industrial premises at West Ham, Bethnal Green, Enfield and Greenwich. The gas works at Stepney sustained some damage and there was some interference with communications. Holborn Viaduct and St Paul's stations have been closed down owing to the railway bridge at Southwark, carrying lines to these stations, being severely damaged. On L.M.S., interference with railway traffic from St Pancras at Hendon was caused through UXB, and Broad Street–Poplar Line was blocked at Old Ford.

Parachute mines were dropped in London area and in rural districts of Kent and Essex. The number of fires reported during the period are far fewer than on previous nights.

Four enemy aircraft were destroyed, 1 was probably destroyed and 2 were damaged. Approximate civilian casualties for London are 70 killed and 250 injured. Outside London, 13 people were killed and 13 injured (10 seriously) by day, and 1 person killed and 9 seriously wounded plus 8 slightly hurt at night.

There has been an increased use of parachute mines. This most indiscriminate form of aerial attack has comparatively little destructive effect but may be aimed at the morale of the people, which nevertheless remains as high as ever after the intensive bombing during the last fortnight.

Towards midday a German fighter sweep over Kent resulted in combats in which RAF fighter pilots were again reminded of the deadly competence of their adversaries when unencumbered by their close escort duties. The Luftwaffe lost 8 aircraft on operations on this day, another 6 returning damaged.

9/JG27 Messerschmitt Bf 109E-4 (2789). Crashed and burned out at Ospringe 11.50 a.m. during free-lance sortie over Kent and combat with fighters. Uffz. E. Clauser killed. Aircraft a write-off.

The remains of Erich Clauser recovered from the wreckage of his aircraft defied any proper identification. He was buried in the local churchyard of St Peter and Paul, Ospringe as an 'Unknown German Airman' and remains there to this day.

Site investigated by Brenzett Aeronautical Museum and some minor fragments and components recovered. Reflector gunsight removed from the wreck in 1940 donated to them by a local resident. These relics now held by the Hawkinge Aeronautical Trust. Signal pistol and other components at one time in the London Air Museum. Site excavated by Steve Vizard in 1985 and a bullet-holed propeller blade recovered.

4/KG54 Junkers Ju 88A-1 (4148). Suffered serious loss of control during bombing sortie over London and crew ordered to bale out. Crashed onto Nos. 2 and 4 Richmond Avenue, Merton and exploded 00.20 a.m. Fw. W. Schlake baled out and captured slightly wounded. Oberfw. M. Röhrig, Fw. H. Fischer and Gefr. K. Neumann missing believed killed. Aircraft B3+HM a write-off.

This aircraft blew up with such violence that the crew who remained aboard were blown to pieces. No appreciable trace of any of them was ever reported found by the emergency services and as a result they have no known graves. However, their deaths were noted in contemporary German records — probably on the testimony of the gunner, Wilhelm Schlake.

Richmond Avenue, Merton, Surrey, September 20, 1940. It was not a bomb but a crashing German bomber which brought the grim reaper to this quiet suburban street. The smashed Anderson tells its own story: Mrs Mary Butcher, aged 25, died of her injuries six days later in Nelson Hospital. Of the German crew nothing was ever found, only Feldwebel Schlake surviving, having escaped by parachute.

SATURDAY, SEPTEMBER 21

Enemy reconnaissances were active along the East, South and South-West Coasts during the day. In the evening a strong formation, consisting mostly of fighters, made a sweep over Kent and the Estuary, some penetrating the eastern boundary of Central London.

By night, from 2009 a steady stream of enemy aircraft crossed the coast from Holland and Le Havre. Later raids came from the direction of the Belgian coast and later still from Le Havre and Dieppe. East Anglia received a good deal of attention and some of the raiders flew down to the London area. Many aircraft flew to Liverpool via the Bristol Channel and Wales.

Raiders also visited the Lancashire coast, north of the Tyne and the Midlands near Derby and Sheffield. Two raids were plotted off the Scottish coast south of Aberdeen.

Enemy aircraft casualties consisted of 2 destroyed, 1 probably destroyed and 6 damaged. Approximate civilian casualties are 6 killed and 17 injured in London by day and 7 injured elsewhere. At night 23 were killed and 240 injured in London and 13 were killed and 126 injured elsewhere.

The silken thread reported is probably cobwebs. At this time of the year the country in the early morning is smothered with them. A report of cobwebs having been seen to fall from the sky is contained in White's Natural History of Selborne, Letter No. 23 addressed to the Honourable Daines Barrington. It is a remarkable coincidence that the occurrence reported above was on the 21st September, 1741.

Another day of reduced activity apart from isolated nuisance raids and reconnaissance sorties, mainly of British coastal areas. A total of 9 German aircraft were lost and another damaged on operations, whilst 2 more were damaged in accidents. At Trondheim a Heinkel floatplane was destroyed in storm conditions.

An emergency water tank was built later on the cleared site. Nos. 2 and 4 were rebuilt in the early 1950s.

3/LG1 Junkers Ju 88A-1 (2088). Sortied on armed reconnaissance mission of RAF airfields and attacked over the south coast by Flying Officer C. T. Davis and Sergeant S. E. Bann of No. 238 Squadron and engine severely damaged. Then engaged by AA and further attacked by Pilot Officer A. Lyall and Pilot Officer O. V. Hanbury of No. 602 Squadron. Forced-landed near Old Fishbourne, Bosham 3.12 p.m. Oberlt. K. Sodemann (Staffelkapitän) captured slightly wounded. Fw. O. Bergsträsser, Fw. W. Lorenz and Gefr. E. Bossert captured unhurt. Aircraft L1+AL a write-off.

2(F)/121 Dornier Do 215 (0023). Intercepted by Pilot Officer D. A. Adams of No. 611 Squadron during return from photo-reconnaissance sortie over Liverpool. Pursued over North Wales, both engines damaged and crew wounded in attacks so crash-landed at Trawsfynydd, Merioneth 4.55 p.m. Uffz. G. Pelzer killed during fighter attacks. Lt. W. Book, Fw. K. Jensen and Fw. H. Kühl captured wounded. Aircraft VB+KK a write-off.

SUNDAY, SEPTEMBER 22

Enemy activity by day was on a comparatively small scale with no mass raids or important engagements. Only 60 enemy aircraft were over this country. Bombing was entirely confined to Regions 4, 6, 12 and London. Little material damage was caused other than the blocking of the S.R. main line near Basingstoke.

By night, enemy activity started earlier than usual, the first raids having been plotted arriving over this country before dark. Bombing was again confined to Regions 4, 12 and the London area, with a few minor incidents in No. 6 Region before midnight, involving neither casualties nor damage. London was again the chief objective, though some damage was done and casualties caused at Luton at 2114 where a transport depot was extensively damaged and many houses wrecked, it is believed by a parachute mine.

Enemy aircraft destroyed: 1 certain and 1 damaged. Approximate civilian casualties in London were 72 killed, 224 injured. Elsewhere there were 6 killed, 14 seriously injured and 52 slightly injured.

German daytime activity being slight, Fighter Command flew less sorties on this day than on any other since the Battle began. Four Luftwaffe aircraft were lost and 3 damaged in operations, 2 more being destroyed and another damaged in accidents. At Trondheim, 2 more He115s were written-off by storm.

4(F)/121 Junkers Ju 88A-1 (0352). Sortied on weather-reconnaissance mission over the Channel and attacked by Pilot Officer T. M. Kane and Sergeant A. S. Harker of No. 234 Squadron. Starboard engine hit and forced to ditch in the Channel 50 miles SE of Start Point 4.54 p.m. Crew took to their dinghy and picked up by trawler after ten hours at sea. Lt. H. Böttcher, Fw. T. Vater and Uffz. W. Müller captured wounded. Uffz. P. Rabe captured unhurt. Aircraft 7A+AM lost.

The peace and quiet which reigned through the day, only broken by the howl of two short lived 'Alerts', were symbolic of the dullness of a Sabbath in pre-war times. The Nazis, however, by way of confirming the warning sound by the siren at 2010 hours, dropped three H.E. bombs in the south-west a few minutes later. The raiders gave me the impression of working singly and in ever widening circles, embracing Woolwich and the outlying districts . . . an extra loud explosion was heard in a northerly direction at 0055 hours this morning, causing a large fire, the flames of which appeared to be difficult to extinguish; a bright glow showing clearly on the horizon for a considerable time . . . a large number of H.Es. were dropped. Searchlights operated in force throughout the night, but no aircraft could be observed with the naked eye . . . bursting shells followed in the path of searchlights which appeared to touch on every point of the compass . . . as the morning wore on, enemy action diminished until the last of the raiders vanished like night-birds of bad omen . . . German eagles soaring their way home to nests built from their ill-begotten gains . . . the life-blood of women and children.

LIEUTENANT E. B. TAPSELL
WOOLWICH DEFENCE OFFICER
WAR DIARY, SEPTEMBER 21/22, 1940

MONDAY, SEPTEMBER 23

By day, about 200 enemy aircraft, composed mainly of fighters, attempted to attack London by several routes between 0930 and 1045. They were driven back before reaching the outer defences. Raids by single aircraft were made on south-east coast towns (and one aircraft dropped a few bombs on London) between 1300 and 1400). Hastings, Bexhill, Eastbourne and Seaford were under yellow warning at the time of the incidents but the damage was slight, and casualties were few. During the late afternoon, a raid by 40 aircraft failed to reach London.

By night, London was under red warning from 1941 to 0555. A considerable increase in the number of raids is reported, over 60 local authorities' areas being attacked. There was no outstanding incident, but considerable material damage was caused. Many fires are reported, and all are extinguished or under control. Railway communications were interfered with considerably, several important roads blocked, and two main sewers penetrated. Casualties are heavier than during the past few nights, mainly as a result of direct hits on a public shelter in East Ham, and on a shelter at Clarnico's factory, Poplar. Electric light failed over a wide area for about half an hour, due to breakage of Wimbledon-Battersea cable. All generating stations except Fulham are now in commission.

Night raiding in the provinces was mainly confined to Liverpool, East Anglia, and south-eastern counties. Sixty-three incidents are reported by No. 4 Region and 23 by No. 12 Region. Roads are blocked at Redhill; railway communications interfered with at Chadwell Heath. Damage was confined elsewhere to house property. Nearly 100 houses at Bury St Edmunds were affected — casualties were slight.

Enemy aircraft casualties: 12 destroyed, 7 probable, 7 damaged. Civilian casualties: London: 90-110 killed, 300-350 injured. Elsewhere by day, 3 were killed, 5 seriously injured, together with 28 slightly injured; by night, 12 people were killed, 23 seriously injured, and 2 slightly hurt.

At Hucknall, a British plane crashed on houses. Casualties, including the pilot who was killed, amounted to 5 killed and 6 seriously wounded.

As dawn broke, the nightly 'Blitz', mainly on London, continued to dominate events — daylight activity largely being confined to elusive high-level fighter sweeps. In retaliation, Berlin was the target for 119 British bombers this night while more than double their number attacked London. Fourteen German aircraft were lost and 3 damaged in operations, 3 more being destroyed and another damaged in accidents.

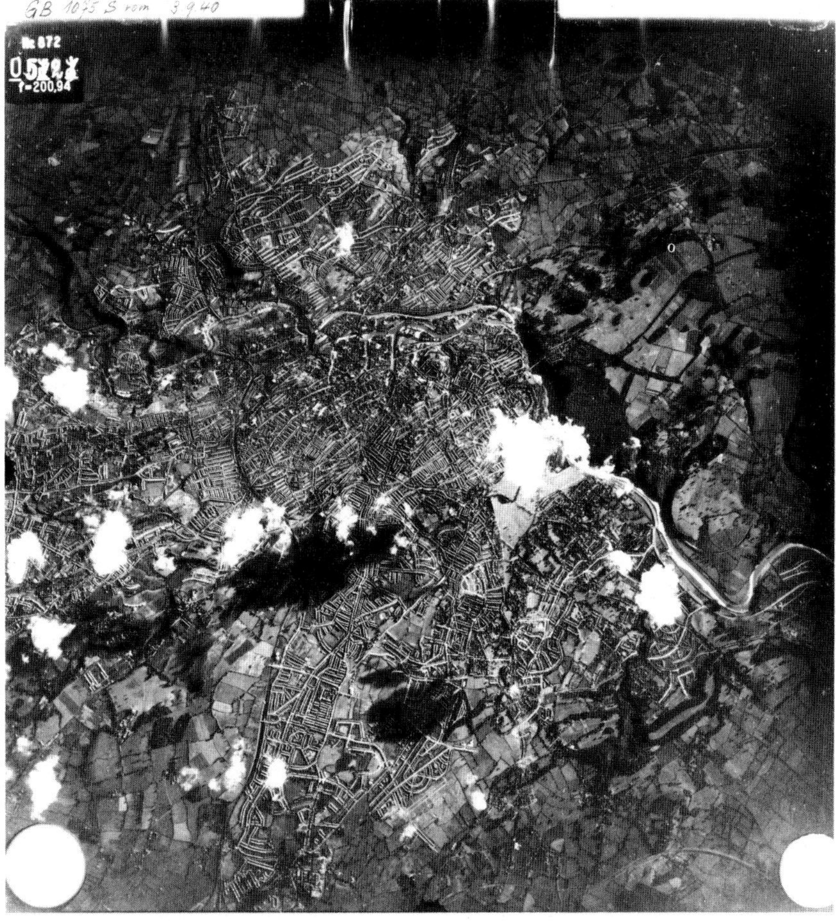

Although Target Loge (London) had been the main focus of Luftwaffe attention, as the Home Security reports show there were at the same time widespread attacks on other provincial targets. This picture was taken on September 23 — a slightly oblique view of Bristol where the camouflaged aircraft factory at Filton (bottom centre) had been singled out for a heavy attack. We are looking almost directly due south — the river is of course the Severn.

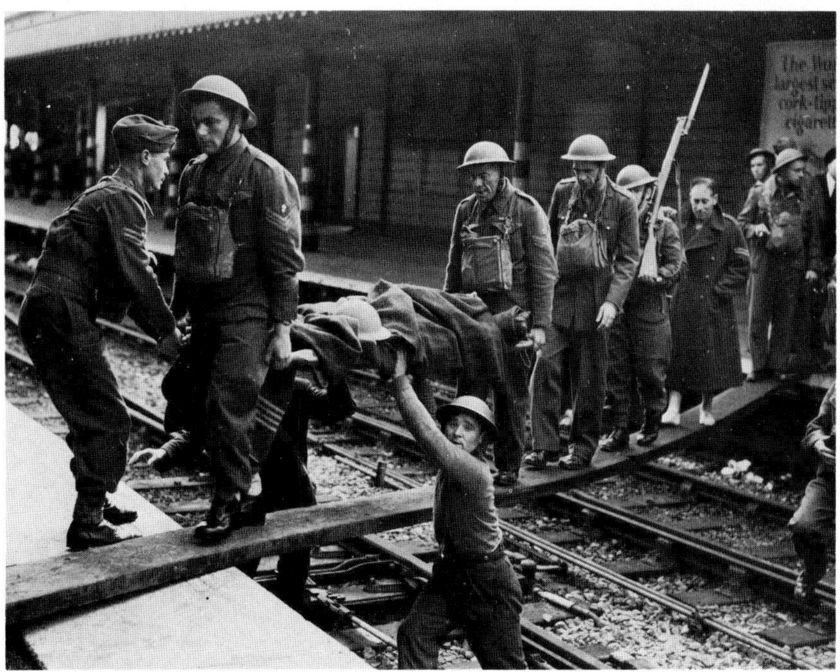

Wearing their gas mask haversacks in the 'Alert' position on the chest, a rather precarious procession crosses the tracks at Folkestone on Monday morning carrying Unteroffizier Dilthey who had just been rescued from the sea by 2nd Lieutenant Jacobs (with bare feet in corporal's greatcoat).

3(F)/123 Junkers Ju 88A-1 (0130). Crashed in the Channel during photo-reconnaissance sortie to London — exact circumstances unknown. Lt. E. Hauber, Lt. K. Keller and Obergefr. E. Euler missing believed killed. Oberfw. E. Götz killed. Aircraft 4U+CL lost.

The body of the Bordfunker, Engelbert Götz, was recovered from Stokes Bay on October 15 and was buried at Ann's Hill Cemetery, Gosport where he remains to this day.

4/JG2 Messerschmitt Bf 109E-4 (1969). Sortied to cover withdrawal of bombers returning from an attack on England and intercepted by No. 72 Squadron Spitfires. Severely damaged in attacks by Flight Lieutenant I. H. Cosby and Sergeant N. V. Glew and ditched in the Channel between Folkestone Railway Pier and Copt Point 10.00 a.m. Uffz. F. Dilthey wounded in the shoulder also suffered a broken leg but supported in the water by a soldier who swam out to him and helped him into a fishing boat. Aircraft 2+— lost.

Stab JG3 Messerschmitt Bf 109E-1. Shot down in combat with RAF fighters and crashed in the sea. Possibly that claimed by Squadron Leader R. R. S. Tuck of No. 257 Squadron 10 miles North of Cap Gris Nez 9.45 p.m. Oberlt. W. Hopp killed. Aircraft lost.

The body of Willi Hopp was washed ashore and buried at Ipswich on October 25. Promoted subsequent to his death, the records of the Soldatenfriedhof, Cannock Chase shows his rank as Hauptmann.

7/JG3 Messerschmitt Bf 109E-1 (6304). Engaged by Spitfires during free-lance sortie over Deal and rudder shot away. Believed that attacked by Pilot Officer G. H. Bennions of No. 41 Squadron. Crashed into the Channel off Kingsdown 10.22 a.m. Uffz. K. Elbing baled out and captured unhurt. Aircraft 3+I lost.

8/JG26 Messerschmitt Bf 109E-4 (5817). Intercepted by Spitfires of No. 92 Squadron during free-lance fighter sortie. Pursued south towards Hythe and eventually shot down by Flight Lieutenant C. B. F. Kingcombe. Crashed and burned out at Biddenden, near Tenterden 10.00 a.m. Oberfw. G. Grzymalla baled out and captured unhurt. Aircraft 9+I a write-off.

8/JG26 Messerschmitt Bf 109E-4 (3735). Engaged by Spitfires of No. 92 Squadron during free-lance fighter sortie over Maidstone. Radiator badly damaged in attack by Flying Officer J. F. Drummond so forced-landed and nosed into a dyke near Yantlett Battery, Grain Fort on the Isle of Grain 9.55 a.m. Fw. A. Küpper captured unhurt. Aircraft 4+I a write-off.

Pristine control column removed from cockpit by a local resident in 1940 as a souvenir donated to the Kent Battle of Britain Museum during local enquiries, now in the Hawkinge Aeronautical Trust collection.

3/JG54 Messerschmitt Bf 109E-4 (1516). Shot down in combat with Spitfires of No. 603 Squadron during free-lance sortie over Thanet. Believed that claimed by Flying Officer J. C. Boulter but possibly also attacked by Flight Lieutenant H. K. MacDonald. Exploded over Barham, bulk of wreckage falling at Broome Park 10.25 a.m. Oberfw. H. Knippscheer baled out, landed in the Channel off Dover but died. Aircraft 5+ a write-off.

The body of Helmut Knippscheer was eventually washed ashore at Reculver on October 27, which is incorrectly shown as his date of death in St John's Cemetery, Manston Road, Margate where he remains to this day.

TUESDAY, SEPTEMBER 24

At 0830 raids totalling some 200 aircraft crossed the coast by day and flew across Kent. They were dispersed within an hour but some bombs were dropped in the Thames Estuary area. A second large-scale attack was made about 1130 by about 180 aircraft. Objectives were towns on the Kent coast but little damage was done. The proportion of enemy fighters to bombers in each of these raids was approximately two to one. Twice during the afternoon raids of about 50 aircraft (half fighters, half bombers) approached via the Isle of Wight. Some damage was caused at Southampton and in Sussex coastal towns.

The enemy's attack on London by night was on a more extensive scale than recently. Bombs were dropped in almost every part of the London Region, the attacks being heaviest in Groups 1, 2 and 3 (Inner London North of the Thames). A large number of I.B. were dropped, causing many fires. Some damage was done to railways, but otherwise no material damage was caused to any military objective. It is estimated that about 110 enemy aircraft were engaged.

Activity outside London in the provinces by night was on a minor scale, and about 80 aircraft took part in scattered raiding. Damage was caused by fire at Liverpool, and slight damage was caused at a few places in Wales and in south-eastern England.

Enemy aircraft casualties: 7 destroyed, 8 probable, 13 damaged. Civilian casualties (approx.): In London, 70 people killed, 200 seriously injured, and 150 slightly injured. Elsewhere, by day, 39 killed, 118 seriously injured, and 67 slightly injured; by night, 4

The Brightling bomb. One of the newly formed bomb disposal sections of the Royal Engineers stationed at Brighton tackled this Hermann which they recovered from the little East Sussex village of Brightling. The broken cast alloy tail unit has been replaced for this picture taken for the records — a nice one to show the grandchildren.

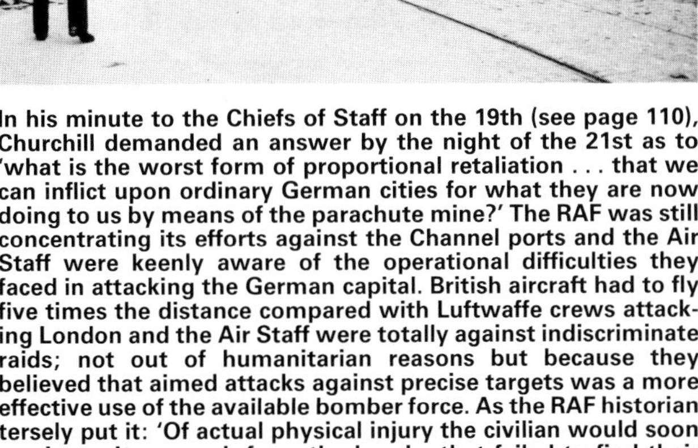

In his minute to the Chiefs of Staff on the 19th (see page 110), Churchill demanded an answer by the night of the 21st as to 'what is the worst form of proportional retaliation . . . that we can inflict upon ordinary German cities for what they are now doing to us by means of the parachute mine?' The RAF was still concentrating its efforts against the Channel ports and the Air Staff were keenly aware of the operational difficulties they faced in attacking the German capital. British aircraft had to fly five times the distance compared with Luftwaffe crews attacking London and the Air Staff were totally against indiscriminate raids; not out of humanitarian reasons but because they believed that aimed attacks against precise targets was a more effective use of the available bomber force. As the RAF historian tersely put it: 'Of actual physical injury the civilian would soon receive quite enough from the bombs that failed to find their mark on the factories.' Nevertheless the Air Chiefs realised they had to offer something to answer the popular request to 'give it 'em back', and agreed on the evening of the 21st to mount a raid on Berlin. It was, however, to be directed against the city's gas works and power stations and 129 aircraft were despatched on the night of the 23rd/24th. Weather conditions were severe, but 112 aircraft claimed to have found Berlin. Although the city's air raid records for this particular night are missing, it is believed that many of the bombs failed to explode, including one in Hitler's Chancellery garden, and only at Charlottenburg was a gasometer successfully set on fire. For the loss of 12 crew, 22 civilians had been killed. ***Above:*** **Meanwhile the Luftwaffe was continuing its programme over London. Tuesday was the day the lights went out permanently at the Vogue Cinema in the Mile End Road. Even today, nearly half a century later, many of the gaps blasted in East End streets still remain undeveloped — advertising hoardings being a tell-tale sign of many former bomb sites in an area still predominantly the home of the rag trade.**

people were killed, 11 seriously injured, and 9 slightly hurt.

The Supermarine Aviation Works at Southampton were attacked by 17 aircraft at 1350 and again by 3 aircraft at 1615. A shelter was hit (24 killed, 75 injured) but the works were only slightly damaged, and the effect on production will be small. Some damage to railway lines and private property, and numerous small fires were caused. Total casualties in the two raids — 33 dead, 69 seriously injured and 120 slightly.

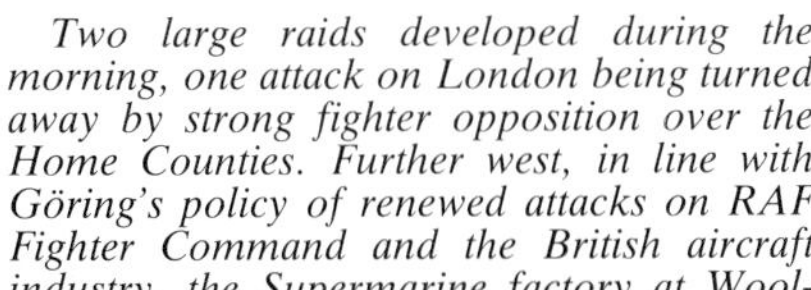

Two large raids developed during the morning, one attack on London being turned away by strong fighter opposition over the Home Counties. Further west, in line with Göring's policy of renewed attacks on RAF Fighter Command and the British aircraft industry, the Supermarine factory at Woolston was damaged in a characteristically well-executed dive-bombing attack by aircraft of ErproGr210. In total, 10 German aircraft were lost and 12 more damaged in operations on this day, another being destroyed and one damaged in accidents.

6/KG26 Heinkel He 111H-3 (3322). Sortied to bomb Beckton Gas Works but crew lost their bearings and dumped the bombs over Surrey. Caught and held by 460 Searchlight Battery and tail shot off by direct hit from AA. Abandoned aircraft broke up, crashed in flames and burned out near Gordon Boys Home, West End, Chobham 1.37 a.m. Uffz. K. Niemeyer, Gefr. H. Leibnitz, Gefr. S. Wenlich and Gefr. W. Jenreck baled out and captured unhurt. Aircraft 1H+GP a write-off.

Surface fragments collected by the Air Historical Group.

WEDNESDAY, SEPTEMBER 25

With the exception of attacks on Filton and Portland during the morning and Plymouth in the afternoon, daylight enemy activity was confined to small raids chiefly in the south-eastern area. In the main attacks the proportion of fighters to bombers was about equal.

At 1148 about 60 aircraft consisting of 27 bombers with fighter escort crossed the coast at Weymouth and successfully attacked the Bristol Aeroplane Co's Works at Filton. The attack was made at 11,000 feet and all bombs were dropped simultaneously. Seven bombers broke away from this formation and made an unsuccessful dive-bombing attack down to 500 feet on the oil tanks at Portland.

At 1647 approximately 24 bombers with an escort of 12 Me 110s crossed the coast at Start Point and attacked Plymouth.

At least one of that night's performers was brought down: a Heinkel from KG26 which lost its way to the Beckton gas works and ended up 30 miles away on a recreation ground at Chobham.

Left: **The King and Queen visit badly damaged St Thomas's Hospital.** *Right:* **The same entrance somewhat changed forty years on.**

In this battle for Britain, London, the mighty capital of the Empire, occupies the forefront. Other of our cities are being subjected to the barbarous attacks of the enemy. Our sympathy goes out to them all. But it is London that is for the time being bearing the brunt of the enemy's spite. I am speaking to you now from Buckingham Palace, with its honourable scars, to Londoners first of all, though of course my words apply equally to all the British cities, towns and hamlets who are enduring the same dangers. The Queen and I have seen many of the places here which have been most heavily bombed and many of the people who have suffered and are suffering most. Our hearts are with them tonight. Their courage and cheerfulness, their faith in their country's cause and final victory, are an inspiration to the rest of us.

To the men and women who carry on the work of the A.R.P. services I should like to say a special word of gratitude. The devotion of these civilian workers, firemen, salvage men, and many others in the face of grave and constant danger has won a new renown for the British name. These men and women are worthy partners of our armed forces and our police — of the Navy, once more as so often before our sure shield, and the Merchant Navy, of the Army and the Home Guard, alert and eager to repel any invader, and of the Air Force, whose exploits are the wonder of the world.

Tonight, indeed, we are a nation on guard and in the line. Each task, each bit of duty done, however simple and domestic it may be, is part of our war work. It takes rank with the sailor's, the soldier's, and the airman's duty. The men and women in the factories or on the railways who work on regardless of danger, though the sirens have sounded, maintaining all the services and necessitites of our common life and keeping the fighting line well supplied with weapons, earn their place among the heroes of this war. No less honour is due to all those who night after night uncomplainingly endure discomfort, hardship and peril in their homes.

Many and glorious are the deeds of gallantry done during these perilous but famous days. In order that they should be worthily and promptly recognised I have decided to create at once a new mark of honour for men and women in all walks of civilian life. I propose to give my name to this new distinction, which will consist of the George Cross, which will rank next to the Victoria Cross, and the George Medal for wider distribution.

As we look around us we see on every side that in the hour of her trial the Mother City of the British Commonwealth is proving herself to be built as a city that is at unity in itself. It is not the walls that make the city but the people that live within them. The walls of London may be battered, but the spirit of the Londoner stands resolute and undismayed. As in London, so throughout Great Britain, buildings rich in beauty and historic interests may be wantonly attacked, humbler houses, no less dear and familiar, may be destroyed. But "there'll always be an England" to stand before the world as the symbol and citadel of freedom, and to be our own dear home.

KING GEORGE VI, SEPTEMBER 24, 1940

The first picture to be taken of an AA battery in the Central London area is dated September 24 — the photographer exposing the plate by the light of the gun flashes. Unfortunately no location given.

In the London area, night activity was widespread and maintained throughout the night.

1930-2100: At about 1930 raiders flew to London from Le Havre via Portsmouth. These were followed by others from Cherbourg, which crossed the coast west of Beachy Head. Other raiders came from Holland over the Norfolk coast and the Wash. Some of the latter made a wide sweep and approached London from the north-west. Some raiders flew to South Wales and one to Derby.

2100-0100: About 100 enemy aircraft came inland, 19 of which proceeded to the Midlands, the West Country and South Wales. At 0115 a series of about 20 raids approached from Holland and made for the London area. In addition to the above there were a few raids in Lincolnshire, the Humber area and in the South-West.

Enemy aircraft casualties: 26 destroyed, 8 probable, 12 damaged. Civilian casualties (approx.): In London, 70 people were killed, 220 seriously injured, 150 slightly injured. Elsewhere, there were 74 killed, 191 seriously injured, 51 slightly hurt.

Even as the King was speaking to the nation, the Luftwaffe was ranging over the Capital. ***Above:*** **Tottenham Court Road suffered badly, the morning crowds of sightseers being kept back behind the barriers.** ***Below:*** **This end of the road still houses the makeshift shops built on the site . . .**

. . . but the opposite view northwards is now dominated by the massive bulk of Amoco-Central Cross House.

The Filton raid. Following the pre-strike reconnaissance (see page 125), a successful attack was mounted against the aero engine works of the Bristol Aeroplane Company by KG55. ***Above:*** **This is one of the He 111s of II/KG55 (G1+NP of the 6th Staffel) based at Chartres. Night flying camouflage: the fuselage markings have been blackened out rather crudely — some units applied the matt black night flying paint with some care but more usually it was slapped on with little regard for appearance.** ***Right:*** **A machine belonging to the 4th Staffel. (Robert Götz, who took part in the attack, was serving with the I Gruppe at Dreux — III Gruppe being stationed at Villacoublay.)**

September 25, 1940
7th Operational Flight

Attack on an aircraft factory at Filton. And three Me 110 fighter groups have been announced as heavy fighter protection. Over Cherbourg, they in fact suddenly appear above us. It is a very reassuring feeling to see so many big two-engine fighters up there, with their shark's teeth and similar symbols painted on them. And these can accompany us much further inland than the single-engined Me 109, and are supposed to have terrifying fire-power. But there have been rumours that they are by no means all that fast, as the circumstances would urgently require. However that may be, there they were as guardian angels and would soon show their teeth. Up there above Portsmouth the Spitfires are already appearing again, and attacking savagely. And no counter-action by our fighters is to be seen. This time the Flak is too dense.

Now we have already been flying over the island for a long while — over mazes of streets, fields, villages and small towns — and I am far calmer than during the first flights. In front of the target, there is now well-aimed Flak again. The puffs from the explosions are covering a wide area, and exactly at the height at which we are flying.

A second wave of fighters . . . quite a lot this time. With fantastic audacity and aeronautical skill of the highest quality, they dive between the fighters and ourselves: steep-banking, flying upside down, steep turns; firing from all positions and in all directions. There is a Heinkel already entering the clouds with a Spitfire behind it. With consternation I see an Me 110 flying quite low and slowly over a clear area, where it pulls up sharply. And equally slow, behind it, is a Spitfire which one can almost see being shaken by the bursts of fire that it is pouring into the body of the battered Zerstörer. And above us is flying the main body of our vaunted guardian angels, still in unbroken formation. But I hadn't seen them in action, whatever others had done. Perhaps, because of their alleged limited capacities, they had been ordered only to give us some degree of protection. They obviously had to look after themselves as well. But in that case, goodbye to daytime attacks on England.

As far as I can see, our bombs have covered the whole target. So our orders have been carried out. On the return flight, the Tommy fighters are still around us, and we are as usual accompanied by the Flak.

Behind us, and already far below, there is a smoking Heinkel accompanied by an evidently very courageous companion. The latter is still intact, but without regard to its own danger is covering it from behind. A nasty business, which takes some doing. The poor devils are being attacked continuously — a certain prey for the Tommys if they go at it all out.

'Has anyone seen our "Bruno"?', the captain kept calling out. Our watchdog was missing; where was he? In all the turmoil nobody has seen when and how he had fallen back. He was still not to be seen, and no news had come from him. On board were Jürges, the young Feldwebel who took a friendly interest in young whippersnappers like me, Hauptmann Köthke, Altrichter, and Müller, an only son, not to mention my friend Weisbach. Then we heard that the plane was said to have been seen again over the Channel. We took off again at once. The Staffelkapitän, our Kiel, wanted at all costs to find his lost watchdog by hook or by crook — but had no success. There is a heavy swell in the Channel. As we land again and clear out the masses of spent drums and cartridge cases, there are planes standing near to us with holes as big as a man's head — and even larger. We haven't a single scratch this time.

On the next day the Oberkommando der Wehrmacht (OKW) gives its report and acknowlegement. Our comrades' places, though, are empty.

ROBERT GÖTZ

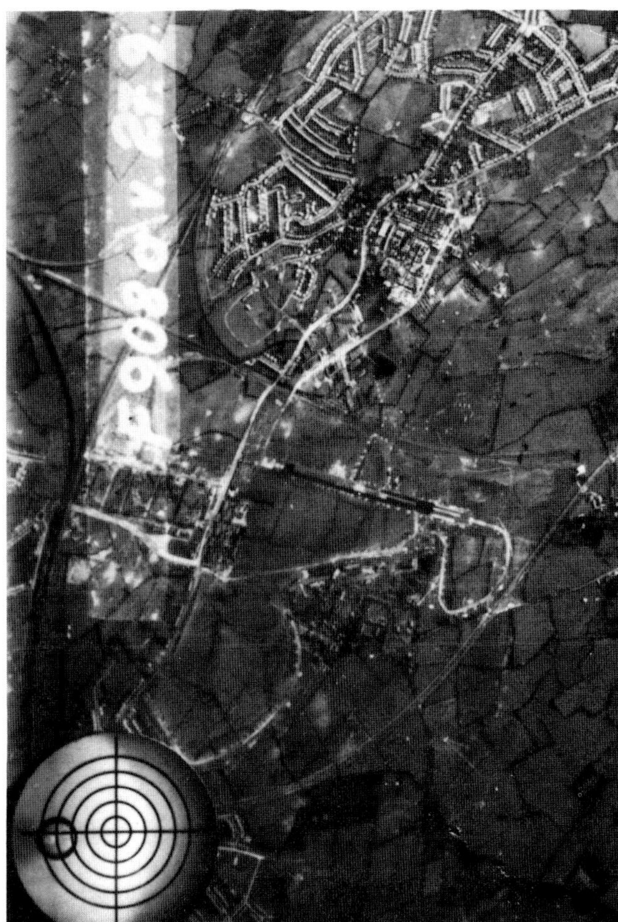

In this instance the attack on the factory was carried out in daylight. Major Friedrich Kless *(left)* was the Gruppenkommandeur of II/KG55, being awarded the Ritterkreuz for his leadership on the Filton operation. His unit had the task of dropping illuminating parachute flares and heavy calibre HE bombs to open many of the major attacks on British cities. From the end of 1940 Major Kless held a staff appointment with V Fliegerkorps, which controlled nine bomber Gruppen involved in the Blitz, and later served in Russia as an officer on the General Staff. At the end of the war he was a Generalmajor and Chief of Staff to Ritter von Greim, Göring's successor as Commander-in-Chief of the Luftwaffe. This signed photograph was given by him to our author Ken Wakefield. *Right:* An enlarged section from a semi-oblique taken by German reconnaissance two days after the raid, with the airfield at the bottom and badly damaged factory top right.

The damage to the Bristol Aeroplane works at Filton was serious enough to warrant an additional report by Home Security detailing the setbacks caused by the raid:

Estimated 60 dead, 150 injured. Rodney Works damage severe. Aero engines damage severe. Flight sheds damage severe. Water mains damaged, also electric power cables. Some UXBs not yet located but several dropped during raid are exploding at intervals. Impossible at present estimate damage or effect on production. Mr. George White has spoken Lord Beaverbrook personally and explained whole position at Works. At request of B.A.C. 300 navvies and 30 lorries for clearance of debris on roads and entrance to sheds has been arranged immediately. Nearly all casualties occurred in trench shelters hit by H.E.

A day of increased activity due in part to the redeployment of Luftwaffe forces along the northern coast of France. Mid-morning, with diversionary attacks on Falmouth, Plymouth, Southampton and Swanage, a heavy raid was mounted against the Bristol Aeroplane Works at Filton by the heavily escorted Heinkel bombers of KG55. The defences were caught off-balance, Yeovil thought to be the main target of the attack, and serious damage to the factory and adjoining area resulted. Pressure on No. 10 Group continued throughout the day, with further attacks on Portland and Plymouth. Operational sorties cost the Luftwaffe 15 aircraft and 5 more damaged, two more being destroyed and another damaged in accidents.

1/KG55 Heinkel He 111H (6305). Engaged by fighters following bombing attack on Bristol Aero Engine Works and severely damaged in attacks by Pilot Officer J. S. Wigglesworth of No. 238 Squadron and Pilot Officer J. Curchin of No. 609 Squadron. Lowered undercarriage prior to forced-landing at Westfield Farm, Studland, near Swanage 12.00 p.m. Hptmn. K. Köthke and Gefr. R. Weissbach captured unhurt; Fw. F. Jürges and Flgr. O. Müller slightly wounded. Uffz. J. Altrichter captured badly wounded and died the same day. Aircraft G1+BH a write-off.

The operation was not, however, carried out without loss and, as Robert Götz's diary entry records, there were empty places in the messes of KG55 that night. *Above:* Although not positively identified, we think this is part of G1+BH of the 1st Staffel which lowered its undercart before force-landing at Studland.

'One by one they shall fall as brother follows brother . . .' Another Heinkel spreads itself across three fields at Racecourse Farm, Portbury . . .

5/KG55 Heinkel He 111P (2126). Hit in the tail by AA fire during bombing sortie to Bristol Aero Works and controls damaged. Aircraft abandoned by crew, crashed and disintegrated across Racecourse Farm, Portbury 11.50 a.m. Oberlt. G. Weigel, Oberfw. A. Narres and Gefr. K. Geib captured unhurt. Fw. K. Gersmeier injured knee in heavy landing. Fw. G. Engel broke a leg. Aircraft G1+DN a write-off.

A surface crash investigated by the South West Aircraft Recovery Group. Bomb winch handle recovered at the time of the crash by local landowner presented to their museum.

6/KG55 Heinkel He 111P (1525). Attacked by fighters following bombing attack on the Bristol Works at Filton. Starboard engine hit and aircraft severely damaged in attacks by Flying Officer I. N. Bayles and Sergeant K. C. Holland of No. 152 Squadron, and Pilot Officer J. R. Urwin-Mann and Sergeant R. Little of No. 238 Squadron. Abandoned by crew and exploded on impact at Church Farm, Woolverton, near Frome 12.02 p.m. Oberfw. G. Wittkamp, Oberfw. R. Kirchhoff, Uffz. H. Merz and Gefr. R. Beck killed. Hptmn. H. Brandt (Staffelkapitän) baled out and captured wounded. Aircraft G1+EP a write-off.

Surface fragments recovered by Perry Adams.

7/KG55 Heinkel He 111H (2803). Port engine hit by fighters during bombing sortie to Bristol Aero Works, Filton. Harried south by Pilot Officers N. leC. Agazarian of No. 609 Squadron and J. R. Urwin-Mann of No. 238 Squadron. Also engaged by Pilot Officer R. F. G. Miller of No. 609 Squadron. Pursued at low level over Poole, abandoned by crew and crashed and burned out on 'Chatsworth', Westminster Road, Branksome Park 12.08 p.m. Uffz. K. Schraps baled out landing in the sea off Branksome Chine and captured unhurt. Oberlt. H-H. Scholz also baled out but landed dead. Uffz J. Hanft baled out into Poole Harbour and picked up dead. Uffz. G. Weidner fell dead due to parachute failure. Oberlt. H. Bröcker (Staffelkapitän) remained in the aircraft and killed. Aircraft G1+LR a write-off.

2/106 Dornier Do 18 (393). Shot down by Blenheim of No. 236 Squadron (Pilot Officer G. H. Russell, Sergeant D. E. Pearson and Sergeant J. E. Goldsmith) during reconnaissance sortie over St George's Channel. Ditched in the sea off Ushant 4.15 p.m. Crew took to their dinghy but subsequently lost at sea. Oberlt. J. Heuveldop, Fw. E. Brasch and Uffz. W. Kahlfeld missing believed killed. Oberlt. zur See H-D. Stelle killed. Aircraft M2+EK lost.

The body of Hans-Dietrich Stelle was washed ashore at Church Cove, east of Lizard Rock on October 26.

7(F)/LG2 Messerschmitt Bf 110C (2185). Intercepted by Pilot Officer J. M. F. Dewar of No. 229 Squadron during photo-reconnaissance sortie to London and one engine put out of action. Pursued at low level and eventually crashed attempting a forced-landing at Beeneys Lane, Beaulieu Farm, Baldslow, near Hastings 11.40 a.m. Caught fire and burned out. Oberlt. E. Weyergang killed. Fw. G. Nelson thrown clear and captured severely injured but died later the same day. Aircraft L2+ER a write-off.

Both these airmen were buried locally in Hastings Cemetery and have not since been reinterred in the Soldatenfriedhof, Cannock Chase.

Site investigated by the Wealden Aviation Archaeological Group in 1974 and surface fragments discovered. Relics also displayed in Robertsbridge Aviation Society Museum.

8/ZG26 Messerschmitt Bf 110C-4 (3591). Port engine set on fire in attacks by Pilot Officers W. D. Williams of No. 152 Squadron and H. C. Mayers of No. 601 Squadron during escort sortie for KG55 attack on Filton. Crash-landed at Well Bottom, near Boyton 12.15 a.m. Fw. W. Scherer captured seriously wounded, admitted to Warminster Hospital. Gefr. H. Schumacher killed. Aircraft 3U+GS a write-off.

. . . while a third crashes onto a house in Bournemouth. 'Chatsworth' in Westminster Road was so badly damaged it was never repaired and it stood derelict right up to the 1950s. Now a block of luxury flats occupies the spot in the Branksome Park estate.

With KG55 crashes scattered from Bristol to Bournemouth, the fourth came down midway along the route on Church Farm, Woolverton.

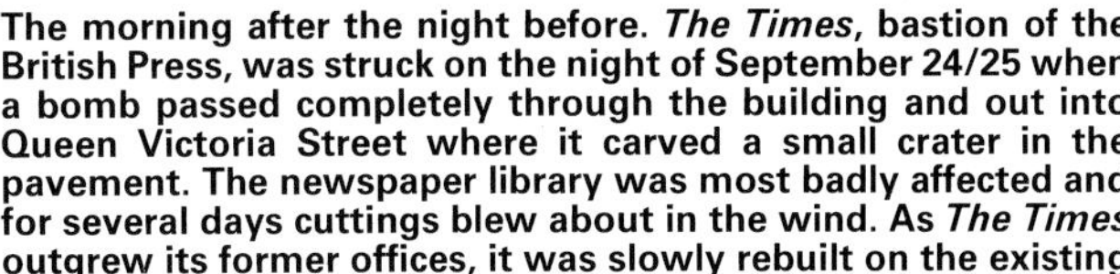

The morning after the night before. *The Times*, bastion of the British Press, was struck on the night of September 24/25 when a bomb passed completely through the building and out into Queen Victoria Street where it carved a small crater in the pavement. The newspaper library was most badly affected and for several days cuttings blew about in the wind. As *The Times* outgrew its former offices, it was slowly rebuilt on the existing site and finally demolished completely in 1962. In 1967 the newspaper was bought by the Thomson Organisation, and in 1974 moved to Grays Inn Road next door to *The Sunday Times*. Now a third move has taken place to Pennington Street, Wapping under new management. *Right:* The replacement building was occupied by *The Observer* when our comparison was taken in April 1984.

THURSDAY, SEPTEMBER 26

The main feature of the day's raiding was increased activity in the Provinces. London was under red warning twice but no major attack developed. During the morning bombs were dropped on Skinningrove Ironworks and Whitby; production is affected at the former, and considerable damage was done to property at the latter town. During the afternoon, raids were made on Henlow Camp, Coventry, and on many coastal towns between Folkestone and Southampton. At Coventry production is not affected, where a fire at Standard Motor Works was got under control quickly. The attack on Southampton was of major importance — enemy formations totalled about 100 aircraft and the main objectives were Supermarine Aviation Works and Vickers Armstrong, where severe damage was done. Production is suspended at both works. Casualties (approx.): Southampton: 36 killed; 60 seriously injured. Fighter squadrons intercepted and the enemy lost 31 aircraft in this action.

Damage to railway communications and house property, etc., is reported at Eastbourne, Hastings and Bexhill, and main services are affected.

Dover was shelled and 50 houses and shops in the centre of the town were seriously damaged.

Enemy activity in the provinces at night was at first widespread over the whole country south of a line Liverpool to Humber. Bombs were again dropped in the Liverpool area, where serious damage was done to shipping, docks and communications. At Liverpool, Birkenhead and Wallasey, many fires were started. Approximate casualties amounted to: 9 killed, 12 seriously injured, 12 slightly injured.

Other places bombed include Nantwich, Slough, Guildford and Bournemouth, but no major damage or serious casualties are reported.

Raids in London commenced at 2030 and continued until 0300. There was a lull

Coming hard on the heels of the UXB, which the Key Points Intelligence Branch described as 'an attempt at a dislocation of all forms of transport within the London region [which] had the result of severe congestion in all the marshalling and goods yards', the parachute mine was a devastating weapon of destruction. *Left:* Colindale Tube station virtually wiped off the map. *The Times* didn't even bother to submit this picture to the censor as they knew it would not get passed for publication. In the end they requested clearance in February 1944 but permission was still denied. *Right:* It is rather a difficult shot to match as the station lies right alongside the new Colindale Hospital.

between 0300 and 0500, and raiding finished at 0450. Enemy activity was again mainly confined to west, north-west and south-west districts. Extensive damage has been done to the Houses of Parliament. A UXB fell through the staircase leading to St Stephen's Hall, and the roof of the India Office was damaged by blast.

Railway communications have again suffered severely, the Southern Railway being most affected. L.M.S. lines from St Pancras are blocked.

Other damage in the West is not serious, and it is significant that casualties are small, which may be due to the large scale evacuation which has taken place.

Royal Small Arms Factory, Enfield, was again bombed and several fires were started, but quickly got under control. No serious damage resulted. In the East several fires are reported at Purfleet, Milwall Dock and West India Docks, but major damage is slight.

Careful analysis of reconnaissance photographs indicated to the Luftwaffe Command that the Supermarine Works at Woolston, still principal centre of Spitfire production, had escaped serious damage in all their previous attacks. Consequently, a heavy raid by Heinkel bombers of KG55, preceded by a strong fighter sweep of the area by Bf 110s of ZG26, laid a carpet of bombs across the target late in the afternoon causing severe damage and bringing production at the factory to a complete halt. This caused a distinct slowing of Spitfire deliveries in the weeks which followed but in isolation, and at this late stage in the battle, would not seriously threaten the capacity of Fighter Command to continue the fight. Seven German aircraft were lost and 4 more damaged on operations, two more being destroyed and two damaged in accidents.

September 26, 1940

Attack on aircraft industry in Southampton. So once again it's only the South Coast. We have received a new armoured plane. But won't the armour slow us up too much? And will the heavy casing still fly if an engine stops working?

Over Cherbourg some Me 109s — not very many — join up with us. And the enemy coast slowly comes into view. We climb . . . over the land now and not far from the target. Today the Flak is surprisingly heavy and accurate. Lying in the turret and looking out sideways, I see that we are ploughing through a large brown area, with small clouds becoming denser and denser. It will be almost a miracle if everything clears. But that is our business.

We must keep together, fly stubbornly straight ahead, and drop our bombs right on the target despite Flak or fighters; otherwise everything will be pointless. Up there, you feel particularly in the hands of the Creator, and know that one cannot be separated from his keeping and the comfort this gives. You remain surprisingly calm and cool, and on first sighting the enemy act correctly, promptly and without overmuch thought.

The bombs drop out, and disappear in a row into the slight mist. I photograph the target with my mother's old camera; those huge, systematically laid out industrial installations from which the smoke mushrooms up again over the whole area.

The picture Robert Gotz took with his mother's camera — the Spitfire works lie out of the picture to the left. One KG55 Heinkel failed to return — G1+GK of the 2nd Staffel — not listed here because it came down in the sea off the Isle of Wight and another from the 3rd Staffel arrived home badly damaged.

What is really happening down there in this area looking like a drawing-board? Clouds of smoke are throwing a veil over the picture, and above these clouds there are many barrage balloons sticking up undisturbed, like small Zeppelins. We can all imagine what could happen if a low-level attack tried to penetrate the wire cables hanging down from these balloons. Suddenly there was another gigantic burst of flame, with a huge column of smoke following it — from an oil or gas storage tank. Time to go, and set our course for home.

Attacks by fighters followed continuously — mostly from the direction of the sun. They attacked without paying any attention to their own Flak. What a good thing, I think, that we are armoured now. But thank God that I am very cool; only waiting for our 'friends' and bursting to see what will happen if I can get at one of them. I have one in line with my tracer bullets for a long time, and hope fervently that he has caught some share of them.

Suddenly there is a quite loud, heavy hammer-blow beneath my newly armoured turret. It is from Flak directly below us, and we'll be taking the splinters home with us. And the fighters are still there. Today they even outnumber our Me 109s, though these are bravely covering our withdrawal. As we are finally over the sea again, I see an Me 109 reel and disappear far below us. Let's hope he will still manage to come through — all alone where no one can help him.

Quite a long way below are three He 111s, with smoke starting to come from the middle of one of them. Suddenly, there are only two still there . . . We can only explain our situation by imagining that the English now have American or some other pilots, as they don't get any fewer. And why shouldn't pilots come to England from all the world-wide Anglo-Saxon countries, if things get hot there? But our leadership must no doubt know best. Eggs are anyway still being broken, that much is sure.

This time the fighters have scored seven hits; there are also Flak hits in the tank, and the petrol is leaking out again. But thanks to our splendid self-sealing fuel tanks, it will be all right till we reach home.

Still no news of our missing comrades. Have they had it? We all know that this can happen to any of us, any day. This would be very painful for me, only because of my mother and my little brother.

ROBERT GÖTZ

4(F)/14 Messerschmitt Bf 110C-5 (2187). Shot down during reconnaissance mission to Portland and crashed into the sea at Salt Mead Ledge, off Cowes, Isle of Wight 5.40 p.m. Possibly that claimed by Flight Lieutenant W. F. Blackadder of No. 607 Squadron. Lt. W. Pannek and Uffz. W. Schmidt killed. Aircraft 5F+CM lost.

The body of the pilot, Wilhelm Pannek, was recovered from the sea almost immediately — that of his gunner, Walter Schmidt, being washed ashore at Fawley, Southampton Water, on October 11.

Spinner raised from sea bed in the Vizard collection believed to be from this aircraft.

1/ZG26 Messerschmitt Bf 110C-4 (3028). Hit by AA fire during bomber escort sortie over Southampton and port engine stopped. Then attacked and further damaged by Pilot Officer J. R. Urwin-Mann of No. 238 Squadron and starboard engine hit. Made a high-speed forced-landing on Bleak Down Hill, Newport, Isle of Wight 4.30 p.m. Fw. H. Rohde captured wounded. Fw. E. Feder captured unhurt. Aircraft U8+HH a write-off.

'We must expect that the Whitehall-Westminster area will be the subject of intensive air attack any time now. The German method is to make the disruption of the Central Government a vital prelude to any major assault upon the country. They have done this everywhere. They will certainly do it here, where the landscape can be so easily recognised, and the river and its high buildings afford a sure guide, both by day and night.' Churchill, September 14.

7/ZG26 Messerschmitt Bf 110C-4 (3094). Shot down by Pilot Officer J. S. Wigglesworth of No. 238 Squadron during escort sortie over Southampton. Dived vertically into the ground at Tapnall Farm, near Freshwater, Isle of Wight 4.30 p.m. Lt. K-A. Konopka and Uffz. R. Eiberg killed. Aircraft 3U+AR a write-off.

The rank of the gunner in this aircraft, Rudolf Eiberg, is shown as 'Leutnant' in the records of the Soldatenfriedhof, Cannock Chase. Presumably he was promoted subsequent to his death.

Major recovery by Steve Vizard, John Ellis and Simon Parry in 1982. Both Daimler-Benz DB 601 engines and engine badges recovered, together with undercarriage, 20mm cannon and parachute. Propeller blade presented to the landowner.

FRIDAY, SEPTEMBER 27

During the day there were three major attacks on London and south-east England and one smaller attack on Filton. Balloons were attacked at Dover.

About 0900 some 180 enemy aircraft (100 fighters and 80 bombers) approached between Folkestone and Dover in six formations at heights between 15,000 and 20,000 feet. The attack was halted in the Maidstone and Tunbridge area but some enemy aircraft penetrated to London.

About 1200 six formations totalling 300 enemy aircraft approached between Dover and Lympne and headed towards Chatham. After engagement over Kent and East Sussex the attack was driven off. The enemy formations encountered were principally fighters.

The seat of Government was every bit as much a legitimate target as was the Chancellery in Berlin. ***Top:*** **September 27 — A famous symbol of the Blitz: Richard the Lionheart defending Parliament with his buckled sword.** ***Above:*** **Victoria Tower.**

It is not that often that one can come up with a positively identified picture of an aircraft taken in France before its loss over Britain. This picture from French Army archives shows 3Z+HN of 5/KG77 at Laon — the same code worn by the Junkers shot down in the Channel during the afternoon battles on the 27th. Code letters could be switched from aircraft to aircraft so one cannot be certain but one can speculate: are four of these crewmen about to die?

About 1500 nine formations totalling about 160 enemy aircraft (about half bombers) crossed between Dover and Brighton at about 22,000 feet and flew towards South London. They were intercepted and driven off but about 20 aircraft reached the London area.

In the morning about 1100 25 bombers escorted by about 50 fighters crossed near Swanage and flew towards Filton. They were driven off before they reached the Bristol Aeroplane Works.

At 1145 Dover balloons were unsuccessfully attacked by three enemy aircraft.

During the day it is estimated that altogether about 850 enemy aircraft took part in operations against this country.

Apart from some damage to the Southern Railway and a serious incident at Lambeth only minor damage was done in London.

At Maidstone extensive damage was done to house property and municipal buildings, and the railway station and sidings were hit. Eighteen people were killed and 80 injured. Elsewhere minor damage was caused in one or two areas.

Enemy activity by night was chiefly directed towards London from the French coast and lasted from 1940 to 0600, with a brief lull between 0215 and 0315. Damage to London was not severe though bombs were dropped in most parts of the Region. There were a few major fires. Heavy casualties occurred only in the St Pancras area.

There was minor bombing in Edinburgh just after dusk, and there were scattered raids in the Liverpool district, Birmingham and Nottingham, mostly up to midnight. The damage was not great and was confined almost entirely to houses. Elsewhere bombs were scattered in rural areas, causing little damage and few casualties.

Some 200 enemy aircraft took part in night raids. It is estimated that 120 penetrated to the London area.

Casualties to enemy aircraft: 133 destroyed, 35 probable, and 52 damaged. Civilian casualties (approx.): in London by day, 50 people were killed and 120 injured; by night there were 100 people killed and 170 injured; elsewhere 36+ people were killed, 100 seriously injured and 21 slightly injured.

Bombs were scattered indiscriminately over the Home Counties and suburbs during morning raids on London by Bf 110s escorted by Bf 109s, many of which also carried bombs. Some were repulsed over the Surrey/Sussex border by strong fighter opposition, V(Z)/LG1 suffering particularly heavy casualties. Those German fighters that penetrated as far as London remained as long as their fuel permitted, attempting to sweep the skies clear of British fighters in readiness for two waves of bombers which followed. These were in fact broken up over the south coast by strong fighter opposition, elements of KG77 suffering appalling losses. Many of the determined Messerschmitt pilots were also badly mauled during their eventual withdrawal from London. Later in the morning two simultaneous raids were mounted in an attempt to split British defences. Whilst bomb-carrying Bf 110s of ErproGr210, closely escorted by Bf 110s of ZG26, penetrated No. 10 Group's defences and fought their way inland towards Bristol, a phalanx of German aircraft crossed the south coast between Brighton and Dover aiming for London. The London raid was broken up half way to their target and scattered under determined fighter attacks. The Bristol raiders also suffered heavy losses as they retired south across Dorset harried by the five British squadrons which countered

Three 'Alerts' were sounded, viz: 1146 hours, 1618 hours, and 2332 hours. A false 'Alert' was sounded by a single siren at 1745 hours. Successive waves of enemy aircraft flying in small forces and singly, passed over Woolwich at a great height during the night and early hours of this morning . . . Most of these aircraft were travelling in a S.E. direction. During the early part of the night a fire was aglow in the direction of the Arsenal although no explosion was heard at that time. . . . This was put out in a very short space of time. The night was fairly quiet . . . A.A. batteries became moderately active at 0145 hours and again shortly after 0400 hours. . . . At approximately 0450 hours two H.E. bomb explosions were distinctly heard in a S.W. direction. 'Alert' sounded 0910 hours. Two formations of enemy bombers approached Woolwich from the east passing in a westerly direction. . . . 0925 hours first formation consisted of sixteen bombers which appeared to be unescorted by fighters, unless these were flying at a highter altitude and were invisible to the naked eye. Five minutes later a second flight of thirty bombers with an equivalent number of fighters approached from the east, passed over Woolwich and turned south. . . . Both these waves of aircraft met with a heavy reception from our A.A. batteries. 'All Clear' at 0952 hours. . . . British fighters passed at 0940 hours travelling in a S.E. direction; these returned travelling N.E. at 0955 hours. Twenty-five Hurricanes (?) in three formations were observed flying east at 1035 hours. A.A. batteries opened fire on a solitary Bosch at 1055 hours. . . . This machine was flying at approximately 20,000 feet and at a terrific speed, passing over Woolwich from east to west, and breaking back on its tracks and returning from whence it came, whilst still visible from No. 2 L.M.G. Post . . . No siren was sounded. 'Alert' 1145 hours (invisible). No bombs have been heard to drop near Woolwich since daylight. A.A. fire in the west . . . 1210 hours, two formations of twenty-one British aircraft observed moving east. 'All Clear' sounded 1230 hours.

LIEUTENANT E. B. TAPSELL
WOOLWICH DEFENCE OFFICER
WAR DIARY, SEPTEMBER 26/27, 1940

Little could Mrs Angas have known when she unveiled this plaque in 1918 that within a few short years the nation would once again be at war; and that the grounds of the building would have the remains of an enemy raider strewn across them. Today her Home for Aged Seamen is used by Bromley Health Authority to care for mentally handicapped patients.

them. In the heaviest day's fighting for some time, the Luftwaffe lost a total of 56 aircraft and 10 damaged in operations. Two more of their machines being damaged in accidents — one of them beyond repair. In addition, two Fiat BR20M bombers of the Corpo Aereo Italiano were also damaged in accidents as they deployed at bases in Belgium in readiness for operations against Britain under Luftflotte 2 command. The following German aircraft fell in Britain:

3(F)/123 Junkers Ju 88A-5 (393). Engaged on photo-reconnaissance sortie over Bristol and intercepted by Pilot Officer E. S. Marrs of No. 152 Squadron. Both engines put out of action in attacks so ditched in the sea just offshore at Porlock Bay 9.40 a.m. Oberlt. W. Rude, Fw. H. Ackenhausen and Fw. E. Riehle captured unhurt. Flgr. W. Reuhl drowned in the aircraft. Aircraft 4U+RL lost.

The body of the gunner, Wilhelm Reuhl, was recovered and buried in nearby Porlock Churchyard where his rank is shown as Obergefreiter. He remains buried there to this day.

Stab ErproGr210 Messerschmitt Bf 110D-3 (3378). Intercepted by Hurricanes of No. 504 Squadron during dive-bombing sortie to the Parnall Aircraft Works at Yate, Bristol. Attacked and badly damaged by a number of pilots and chased south. Believed finally brought down following attack by Flight Lieutenant A. Rook. Crashed into trees and burned out at Busseys Stool Farm, Cranbourne Chase 12.00 p.m. Hptmn. M. Lutz (Gruppenkommandeur) and Uffz. A. Schön killed. Aircraft S9+DA a write-off.

1/ErproGr210 Messerschmitt Bf 110D-3 (3888). Engaged by Hurricanes of No. 504 Squadron during sortie to attack the Parnall Works at Yate and pursued south. Shot down by Pilot Officer B. E. G. White. Dived vertically into the ground and burned out at Bradle Row, Kimmeridge, near Wareham 11.45 a.m. Lt. G. Schmidt and Fw. G. Richter killed. Aircraft S9+JH a write-off.

The remains of both these airmen were taken to Brookwood Military Cemetery for burial where they remain to this day.

Surface fragments discovered by Perry Adams.

2/ErproGr210 Messerschmitt Bf 110D/0 (4270). Intercepted by Hurricanes during dive-bombing attack on Parnall Works at Yate. Port engine disabled in attacks by Flight Lieutenant A. Rook of No. 504 Squadron, and starboard engine damaged in attacks by Pilot Officer M. H. Constable-Maxwell of No. 56 Squadron. Forced-landed at The Beeches, Preston Hill, Iwerne Minster 12.00 p.m. Fw. F. Ebner captured slightly wounded. Gefr. W. Zwick captured severely wounded. Aircraft S9+DK a write-off.

9/JG3 Messerschmitt Bf 109E-1 (3217). Shot down in combat with fighters during free-lance sortie over Canterbury — possibly that claimed by Pilot Officer R. Berry of No. 603 Squadron. Believed crashed in flames and burned out at Owens Court Farm, near Gushmore, Selling 3.40 p.m. Uffz. H. Struwe baled out and captured unhurt. Aircraft a write-off.

Site investigated by Steve Vizard but no relics discovered.

5/JG27 Messerschmitt Bf 109E-1 (3369). Sortied on bomber escort mission but radiator damaged and engine caught fire over Lewes — possibly due to AA fire. Abandoned aircraft crashed and burned out at Lower Mays Farm, Selmeston 9.25 a.m. Gefr. H-D. John baled out and captured unhurt. Aircraft 11+— a write-off.

Site excavated by the Wealden Aviation Archaeological Group in 1976. Only minor components and few fragments of shattered airframe recovered.

6/JG27 Messerschmitt Bf 109E-4 (1447). Lost a wing under attack by Sergeant J. H. Lacey of No. 501 Squadron during combat over Maidstone. Exploded and scattered debris over Hale Farm, Eccles, near Aylesford 12.40 p.m. Uffz. J. Scheidt killed. Aircraft 5+— a write-off.

Stab II/JG52 Messerschmitt Bf 109E-1 (3907). Severely damaged and wounded in surprise attack by Pilot Officer W. B. Pattullo and Sergeant E. Tyrer of No. 46 Squadron during free-lance sortie over Maidstone. Aircraft crashed and broke its

back in heavy forced-landing at Broad Street, Hollingbourne 1.00 p.m. Oberlt. C. Treiber captured wounded. Aircraft 8+— a write-off.

4/JG52 Messerschmitt Bf 109E-4 (5181). Attacked by No. 603 Squadron Spitfires and hit in petrol tank during free-lance sortie over Canterbury. Probably that damaged by Squadron Leader G. L. Denholm and Pilot Officer R. Berry. Further attacked by Flying Officer D. J. C. Pinckney prior to forced-landing. Crashed into landing obstacles tearing off one wing and rudder at Morrison House Farm, St Nicholas-at-Wade 3.40 p.m. Fw. F. Bogasch captured slightly injured. Aircraft 5+— a write-off.

4/JG52 Messerschmitt Bf 109E-1 (3442). Severely damaged and pilot wounded in combat with fighters during free-lance sortie over Thanet. Believed one of those claimed by Squadron Leader G. L. Denholm and Pilot Officer R. Berry of No. 603 Squadron. Crashed through HT cables in forced-landing at Northbourne Park, near Sandwich 3.50 p.m. Gefr. E. Bosch captured wounded. Aircraft 12+— a write-off.

4/JG52 Messerschmitt Bf 109E-1 (6245). Set alight in combat with Spitfires of No. 603 Squadron during free-lance sortie over Canterbury. Crashed in flames at Petham 3.45 p.m. Lt. H. Geist believed baled out and captured unhurt. Aircraft 4+— a write-off.

5/JG52 Messerschmitt Bf 109E-1 (3431). Attacked and pilot severely wounded by Pilot Officer R. G. A. Barclay of No. 249 Squadron during forward sweep over Kent. Pilot lost consciousness and came to still under attack but out of control, so abandoned aircraft. Crashed at Brick House Farm, High Halden, near Tenterden 12.50 p.m. Fw. H. Hoffmann baled out and captured wounded. Aircraft 3+— a write-off.

Exact point of impact partly under a road and investigated by the Brenzett Aeronautical Museum without result. Pilot's

On September 27 the Luftwaffe suffered some of its most grievous losses: it was the fourth highest total recorded on any day during the summer battle, being only exceeded on August 15, August 18 and September 15. Prominent amongst the losses on that Friday was the Messerschmitt 110 — the twin- engined machine not really cut out for its fighter rôle. *Above:* **Zerstörergeschwader 26 — the 'Horst Wessel' Geschwader — had aircraft based at Abbeville, Saint-Omer and Crécy. These three are identified as U8+HK, U8+BK and U8+AK of the 2nd Staffel.**

So many Bf 110s were lost by the V(Zerstörer) Gruppe that day that within 48 hours the whole unit, led by a 31-year-old Austrian, Hauptmann Horst Liensberger, had to be disbanded. Liensberger had been in action from the early days of the war, seeing action during the Battle of France and over Dunkirk. On August 13 he had led his unit in an ill-fated mission to draw off British fighters; a tactic which was intended to allow a later bombing raid to go unhindered whilst RAF fighters were on the ground being refuelled and rearmed after Liensberger's sortie. The Luftwaffe's plans misfired and the bombers were eventually sent much later, enabling RAF Fighter Command to intercept them. It was a tactical blunder which cost V(Z)LG1 five experienced crews, ten men in all. Göring was furious, and in his daily orders issued on August 15, ***(see Volume 1, page 197)*** **he berated those commanders who failed to obey his orders, citing the particular case of V(Z)LG1. At first sight it appeared to imply criticism of Liensberger himself although in reality the recipients of Göring's wrath were probably the senior commanders who had allowed the tactical errors of that day, for Göring saw fit to award the Goblet of Honour (Ehrenpokal) on August 28 for his outstanding achievements in the air war. His further exploits, however, were to be short lived and on September 27 the annihilation of V(Z)LG1 which had begun on August 13 was completed. Amongst the victims was Liensberger himself, struck down in a furious dogfight over Sussex when his opponent, Pilot Officer Percy Burton, in a Hurricane of No. 249 Squadron, apparently out of ammunition, rammed his Messerschmitt from the sky, for it to**

gravity knife now in the Hawkinge Aeronautical Trust.

8/JG54 Messerschmitt Bf 109E-4 (1538). Severely damaged in fighter combat during sortie over Tilbury. Believed that shot down by Sergeant J. K. Norwell of No. 41 Squadron but possibly that claimed by Pilot Officer A. G. Lewis of No. 249 Squadron. Attempted a forced-landing but hit a fence, somersaulted over the main road, crashed and burst into flames at Brenley House, Boughton, near Canterbury 12.05 p.m. Oberlt. A. Schön killed. Aircraft a write-off.

1/KG77 Junkers Ju 88A-1 (8090). Engaged on bombing sortie to London and hit by AA fire during approach to target. Abandoned by crew and broke up over Cudham, main wreckage falling in the grounds of the Angas Home for Aged Seamen 11.05 a.m. Oberfw. H. Müller baled out and captured unhurt. Oberfw. R. Müller and Uffz. M. Kollmannsberger baled out and captured wounded. Gefr. G. Zabel baled out but killed due to parachute failure. Aircraft 3Z+DH a write-off.

2/KG77 Junkers Ju 88A-1 (8095). Starboard engine set on fire in fighter attacks during sortie to bomb London. Dumped bombs blind when port engine set alight in further attacks and abandoned by crew. Possibly that claimed by Pilot Officer M. Feric of No. 303 Squadron. Crashed and burned out at Folly Farm, South Holmwood, near Dorking 9.30 a.m. Uffz. R. Schumann and Uffz. H-J. Tenholt baled out and captured unhurt. Uffz. A. Ackermann baled out and captured wounded. Uffz. W. Menningmann killed. Aircraft 3Z+HK a write-off.

The Bordfunker, Wilhelm Menningmann, was buried in Leatherhead Cemetery and has not been reinterred in the Soldatenfriedhof at Cannock Chase.

Site excavated by the Air Historical Group and Southern Area Wartime Aircraft Preservation Society 1976. One engine and undercarriage leg together with forage cap and first-aid kit held by the Surrey and Sussex Aviation Society.

2/KG77 Junkers Ju 88A-1 (2164). Severely damaged in fighter attacks during bombing sortie to London. Finally both engines hit in attacks by fighters including Sergeant C. F. Babbage of No. 602 Squadron. Ditched in the Channel just offshore at Lydd 9.40 a.m. Uffz. G. Schmidt and Uffz. H. Sergocki picked up and captured unhurt. Flgr. W. Krebs and Uffz. W. Hertlein believed drowned in the aircraft and both missing. Aircraft 3Z+IK lost.

3/KG77 Junkers Ju 88A-1 (8109). Starboard engine developed a fault during sortie to bomb London and aircraft lost formation. Cockpit destroyed in attacks by Blue Section of No. 1 (RCAF) Squadron (Squadron Leader E. A. McNab, Flying Officer D. de P. Brown and Pilot Officer B. E. Christmas) and Pilot Officer J. E. L. Zumbach of No. 303 Squadron. Abandoned by crew and crashed onto North End Lodge, East Grinstead 9.20 a.m. Fw. A. Bräutigam baled out landing in a tree at Tye Farm, Hartfield with a broken leg — admitted to Queen Victoria Hospital, East Grinstead. Uffz. H. Winkelmann baled out landing at Broxhill Farm, Hartfield with severe head injuries — admitted to Queen Victoria Hospital but died the same day. Fw. R. Precht baled out but fell dead in Scarlets Wood, Hartfield due to parachute failure. Uffz. H. Kasing stayed in the aircraft and killed. Aircraft 3Z+BL a write-off.

Dinghy inflation bottle since donated to the Robertsbridge Aviation Society Museum.

3/KG77 Junkers Ju 88A-1 (5103). Shot down by Flying Officer D. de P. Brown of No. 1 (RCAF) Squadron during bombing sortie to London. Crashed and burned out at Hononton Park, near Horsmonden 3.30 p.m. Uffz. H. Damerius, Uffz. F. Hastrich and Uffz. M. Merschen killed. Uffz. R. Ludwig captured seriously wounded. Aircraft 3Z+CL a write-off.

The bodies of Helmut Damerius and Franz Hastrich were recovered from their aircraft and buried in nearby All Saints Churchyard, Brenchley. Apparently, no trace of Matthias Merschen was ever found and he has no known grave.

3/KG77 Junkers Ju 88A-1 (8099). Damaged by AA fire during bombing sortie to London and then attacked by Spitfires. Both engines disabled in attacks by Sergeants C. A. Parsons of No. 66 Squadron and H. Bowen-Morris of No. 92 Squadron so forced-landed on Graveney Marshes, near Faversham 3.40 p.m. Crew attempted to destroy the aircraft and reputedly opened fire on those coming to arrest them. Uffz. F. Ruhlandt, Uffz. E. Richter and Gefr. J. Reiner captured wounded. Uffz. G. Richter captured unhurt. Aircraft 3Z+EL a write-off.

Constructor's plates held by both Steve Vizard and Colin Pratley.

Stab II/KG77 Junkers Ju 88A-5 (293). Believed hit by AA fire during bombing sortie to London and starboard engine damaged. Then caught fire under attack by fighters and abandoned by crew. Probably that claimed by Sergeant H. J. Davidson of No. 249 Squadron but possibly also attacked by Pilot Officer D. B. H. McHardy of No. 229 Squadron. Crashed in flames at Vexour Farm, Penshurst, near Tonbridge 3.30 p.m. Fw. A. Zeller and Uffz. E. Brodbeck baled out and captured wounded. Fw. H. Adler killed. Oberlt.

fall in Simmons Field between Mill Road and Station Road, Hailsham, while the Hurricane crashed nearby. Liensberger and his gunner, Albert Köpge, and Burton, all perished. Seven aircraft out of thirteen failed to return and the unit was stood-down and remustered in Bavaria as the 1st Gruppe of a new night fighter unit, NJG3. The intolerable losses of the 27th had resulted in all of the units original members and 'old sweats' remaining on British soil as casualties or prisoners, save for the adjutant, Oberleutnant Ernst Zobel. He later helped to form the new unit in Germany although bad luck caught up with him on October 16 when he was injured in a crash. Writing of Liensberger's loss at the time, Hauptmann 'Papa' Haarman, a staff officer on the unit, said: 'The 27th September was a black day for the outfit. I regarded Horst Liensberger highly as my commander and as a human being and, despite the age difference, I venerated him. I am sure he will come back after the war. Over the radio we heard his last message: "Both engines are hit . . . am trying to turn . . . it's impossible . . . I will try to land." Then, nothing more. He will return I am sure.' Even as those very words were being written on October 2, Liensberger was being laid to rest in Hailsham Cemetery, *right*, close to the boundary fence between the two fir trees, although Liensberger's comrades-in-arms on V(Z)LG1 shared Haarman's optimism. Indeed Horst was to return home . . . but not until long after the war. In a departure from normal custom and practice, instead of being transferred to Cannock Chase in 1962 his remains were repatriated to his native Innsbruck for burial in the family grave.

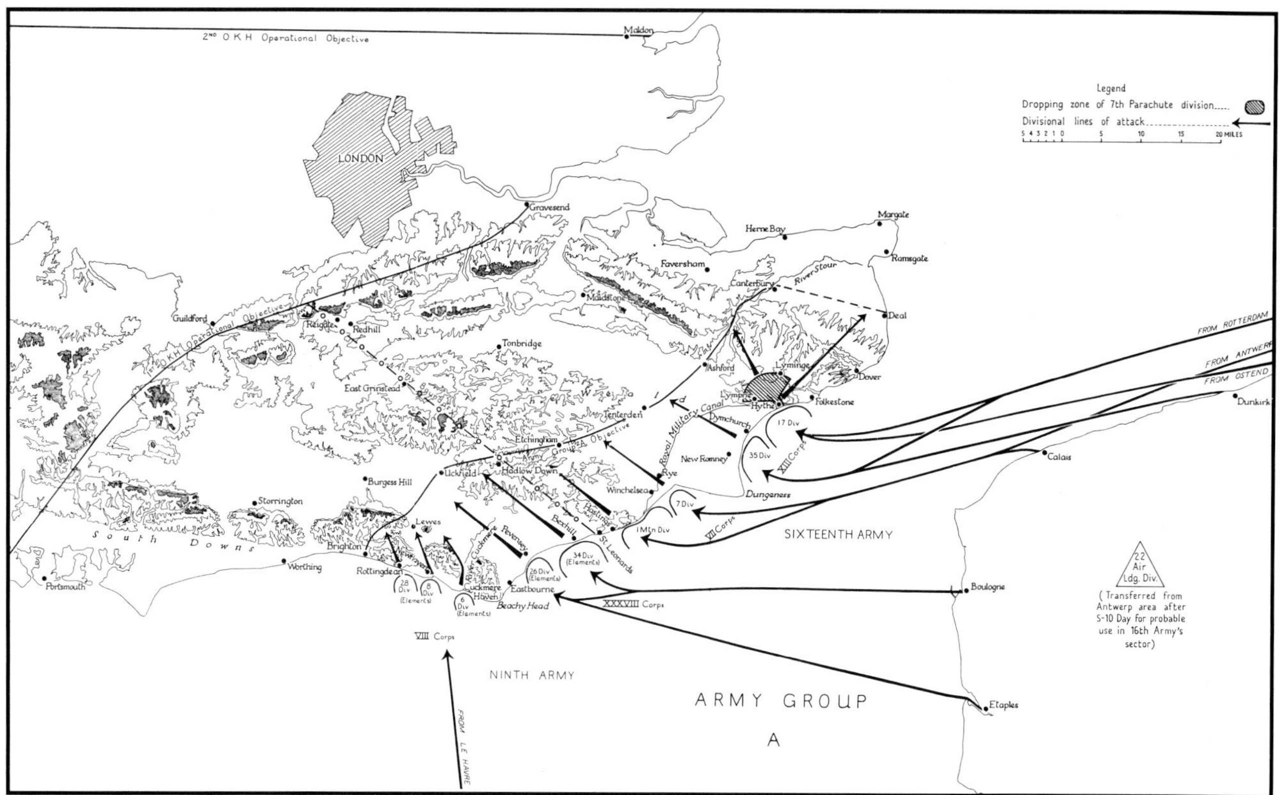

The mid-September invasion plan showing the initial landing stages as planned by OKH, reproduced with acknowledgement to Ronald Wheatley from *Operation Sealion. (See also Volume 1, pages 294-295.)* Following the change of tactics (albeit for emotional reasons) on September 7, after a week of intensive bombing the Luftwaffe High Command was able to claim in their intelligence reports that the RAF was all but destroyed. However to the crews at the sharp end (like Robert Götz — see page 92), who found themselves being attacked by units they had been told no longer existed, it was a rude awakening. For the Führer, isolated from the actual battlefield, possibly lulled into a false sense of reality by the rosy reports from France (or perhaps believing only that which he wished to believe), it was a clear indication that Göring had not achieved the air superiority necessary to launch Sealion. Hitler admitted that bombing alone would probably not cause Britain to give in and was nervous about the losses he might sustain on an invasion. 'We conquered France at a cost of 30,000 men', Hitler remarked to his adjutant Karl-Jesko von Puttkamer. 'During one night of crossing the Channel we could lose many times that — and success is not certain.' On September 17 Hitler announced that Operation Sealion was to be postponed until further notice. We now know of course that the postponement was to be permanent — that Hitler was soon to turn his attention towards the East — but to the British War Cabinet, in spite of conflicting decoded signals intercepted by the Bletchley decryption organisation *(see Volume 1, page 283)*, the invasion was still a very real threat. On the 27th, while his airmen were fighting and dying over the skies of England, the high spot in Hitler's day was the creation of the Berlin–Rome–Tokyo Axis with the signing of the Tripartite Pact recognising a 'New Order' in Europe and the Far East.

K-H. Lutze missing believed killed. Aircraft 3Z+DC a write-off.

No trace of the pilot, Karl-Heinz Lutze, was ever reported found and he has no known grave.

Site excavated by the Halstead War Museum which recovered various components including both propeller bosses. Various relics also in the Steve Vizard collection.

5/KG77 Junkers Ju 88A-1 (4117). Heavily damaged in repeated fighter attacks during sortie to bomb London. Crashed in the Channel SW of St Leonards 4.00 p.m. Possibly that claimed by Flying Officer W. Urbanowicz of No. 303 Squadron. Oberlt. F. Ziel and Fw. F. Niederer managed to vacate the aircraft but drowned. Gefr. J. Feichtmayer rescued by the Hastings lifeboat *Cyril and Lilian Bishop* after two hours in the water and captured wounded. Uffz. H. Isensee believed killed in the aircraft and missing. Aircraft 3Z+DN lost.

The body of the observer from this aircraft, Franz Niederer, was washed ashore near Battle on October 21. That of the pilot, Friedrich Ziel, came ashore at Hastings the next day, which is incorrectly recorded as his date of death in Hastings Cemetery where he remains to this day.

5/KG77 Junkers Ju 88A-1 (7109). Shot down by fighters during sortie to bomb London. Believed crashed in the Channel 6 miles off Beachy Head 4.00 p.m. Possibly that claimed by Flight Lieutenant J. A. Kent of No. 303 Squadron and also attacked by Pilot Officers W. H. Millington and T. F. Neil of No. 249 Squadron. Lt. W. Pflüger, Uffz. O. Grönke and Gefr. F. Reinhardt missing believed killed. Gefr. M. Zott killed. Aircraft 3Z+GN lost.

The body of Max Zott was washed ashore at Crow Link Gap, west of Beachy Head on November 1.

5/KG77 Junkers Ju 88A-1 (7112). Shot down by fighters during bombing sortie to London. Believed crashed in the Channel 15 miles off Bexhill 4.00 p.m. following attack by Flying Officer V. M. Bright of No. 229 Squadron. Hptmn. G. Zetsche (Staffelkapitän), Fw. W. Mahl and Gefr. A. Burkhardt missing believed killed. Obergefr. A. Kuhn killed. Aircraft 3Z+HN lost.

The body of Alfred Kuhn came ashore near Walton-on-the-Naze on October 30 which is incorrectly recorded as his date of death in the Soldatenfriedhof, Cannock Chase.

6/KG77 Junkers Ju 88A-1 (4118). Attacked by fighters following bombing mission to London. Burst into flames under attack by Sergeant H. J. Davidson of No. 249 Squadron and broke up over Sevenoaks, main wreckage falling near Chiddingstone 3.30 p.m. Oberlt. E. Seif, Fw. A. Eichinger and Uffz. S. Gebhardt killed. Fw. H. Zinsmeister baled out and captured wounded. Aircraft 3Z+DP a write-off.

Werk plates taken at the time of the crash now held by Steve Vizard.

7/LG1 Junkers Ju 88A-5 (3197). Shot down over St George's Channel by Red Section of No. 79 Squadron (Squadron Leader J. H. Heyworth, Pilot Officer R. W. Clarke and Pilot Officer G. H. Nelson-Edwards). Crashed 50 miles NW of St David's Head 6.45 p.m. Uffz. R. Wächtler killed. Fw. J. Krings, Uffz. F. Wurm and Oberfhr. H-G. Vanselow missing believed killed. Aircraft L1+DR lost.

The body of Bordfunker Rudi Wächtler was washed ashore at Cronellard, Courtown Harbour, County Wexford on October 20 which was incorrectly recorded as his date of death on his burial in Ireland.

7/LG1 Junkers Ju 88A-5 (4153). Shot down over St George's Channel by Red Section of No. 79 Squadron (Squadron Leader J. H. Heyworth, Pilot Officer R. W. Clarke and Pilot Officer G. H. Nelson-Edwards). Crashed 50 miles NW of St David's Head 6.45 p.m. Oberlt. R. Strasser, Fw. R. Söchtig and Uffz. W. Forster missing believed killed. Gefr. W. Lorenz killed. Aircraft L1+BR lost.

The body of the gunner, Wilhelm Lorenz, was washed up at Ardcavan, County Wexford on October 20 which was incorrectly recorded as his date of death on his burial in Ireland.

Stab V/LG1 Messerschmitt Bf 110C-2 (3560). Intercepted by fighters during sortie over Redhill and chased south by Flying Officer P. R-F. Burton of No. 249 Squadron. Pursued at very low level and eventually deliberately rammed losing its tailplane over Hailsham. Crashed and broke up at Simmons Field, near Hamlins Mill, Hailsham 9.50 a.m. Hptmn. H. Liensberger (Gruppenkommandeur) and Uffz. A. Köpge killed. Aircraft L1+XB a write-off.

Both originally buried at Hailsham Cemetery, only Albert Köpge is now reinterred in the Soldatenfriedhof at Cannock Chase, his pilot, Horst Liensberger, being repatriated to Innsbruck, Austria for reburial postwar.

Engine revolution counter and 7.92mm ammunition belt removed at the time of the crash held by Andy Saunders and currently on display in the Tangmere Military Aviation Museum. Engine maker's plate held by the Hailsham Historical Society.

13/LG1 Messerschmitt Bf 110D/0 (3333). Intercepted by fighters during sortie over the Redhill area and pursued south. Believed that chased over Folkestone at low level and left both engines disabled following attacks by Sergeant E. W. Wright of No. 605 Squadron. Crashed in the Channel 9.40 a.m. Gefr. H. Swietlik missing believed killed. Gefr. H. Welz killed. Aircraft L1+BH lost.

The body of the gunner from this aircraft, Heinz Welz, was washed ashore near Princes Golf Club, Sandwich on October 25. This date is recorded as his date of death in Manston Road Cemetery at Margate where he remains to this day.

13/LG1 Messerschmitt Bf 110D/0 (3304). Engaged by fighters over Redhill during sortie to London and shot down in repeated attacks by Squadron Leader E. A. McNab and Flying Officer B. D. Russell of No. 1 (RCAF) Squadron, and Pilot Officer C. F. Currant of No. 605 Squadron. Probably that also attacked by Flight Lieutenants J. M. Strickland and J. E. J. Sing of No. 213 Squadron. Dived into the ground behind 'The Gale', Chelwood Gate in Ashdown Forest 9.40 a.m. Fw. A. Bruns and Gefr. F. Gröbl killed. Aircraft L1+CH a write-off.

Both originally buried at Danehill Cemetery, only the gunner, Franz Gröbl, has since been reinterred in the Soldatenfriedhof, Cannock Chase.

Site excavated by the Wealden Aviation Archaeological Group in 1973. Remains of Daimler-Benz DB 601 engine recovered with manufacturer's badge. Bullet-scarred propeller blade recovered in 1940 also donated by a local resident. Site investigated by the London Air Museum which excavated a propeller boss with one blade and a map box containing remains of four charred maps. Propeller blade and map box now in the Tangmere Military Aviation Museum. Engine badge held by Andy Saunders.

14/LG1 Messerschmitt Bf 110C-2 (3548). Engaged by fighters over Redhill area during sortie to London and chased away south. Believed that which exploded under attack by Flying Officer A. F. Eckford of No. 253 Squadron but possibly also that claimed by Pilot Officer A. G. Lewis of No. 249 Squadron. Crashed at Coppice Farm, Three Cups, Dallington, near Heathfield 9.50 a.m. Obergefr. A. Hübner and Fw. F. Lindemann killed. Aircraft L1+CK a write-off.

Site investigated by the Wealden Aviation Archaeological Group in 1975 and surface fragments collected. Complete mainspar recovered from nearby ditch.

15/LG1 Messerschmitt Bf 110D/0 (3147). Intercepted by fighters during free-lance sortie over Redhill and chased south. Attacked by many pilots including Flying Officer P. W. Lochnan of No. 1 (RCAF) Squadron, Sergeant R. D. Hogg of No. 17 Squadron, Sergeant H. J. R. Barrow of No. 213 Squadron and Pilot Officer W. P. Hopkin of No. 602 Squadron. Pursued at low level over Gatwick aerodrome and also engaged by ground defences. Crashed in flames and exploded 10.00 a.m. Oberlt. U. Fr. von Grafenreuth (Staffelkapitän) and Fw. O. Reinhold killed. Aircraft L1+BL a write-off.

15/LG1 Messerschmitt Bf 110C-2 (3849). Engaged by fighters during free-lance sortie over the Redhill area. Starboard engine set alight and gunner killed in attacks by Pilot Officer D. C. Leary of No. 17 Squadron, Flying Officer W. Urbanowicz of No. 303 Squadron, Squadron Leader H. A. V. Hogan of No. 501 Squadron and Flying Officer P. P. C. Barthropp of No. 602 Squadron. Believed that also attacked by Pilot Officer W. B. Pattullo of No. 46 Squadron. Abandoned aircraft crashed and burned out at Horham Manor Farm, near Horam 9.50 a.m. Uffz. H. Bechthold baled out and captured unhurt. Uffz. H. Koch killed. Aircraft L1+GL a write-off.

Few small fragments excavated by the Wealden Aviation Archaeological Group, August 1979.

15/LG1 Messerschmitt Bf 110C-2 (3533). Intercepted by fighters during free-lance sortie and both engines hit in attacks by many pilots including Sergeant G. A. Steward of No. 17 Squadron, Pilot Officer A. E. Johnson and Sergeant R. F. Sellers of No. 46 Squadron, Flying Officer J. F. Drummond of No. 92 Squadron, Pilot Officers K. T. Lofts and J. R. B. Meaker and Sergeant H. J. Davidson of No. 249 Squadron and Sergeant J. Budzinski of No. 605 Squadron. Forced-landed near Socketts Manor, Oxted 9.45 a.m. Oberlt. O. Weckeiser captured unhurt. Gefr. H. Brüsgow captured wounded. Aircraft L1+LL a write-off.

Rate of climb indicator, removed at the time of the crash, now held by Steve Vizard.

2/ZG26 Messerschmitt Bf 110C-4 (2162). Both engines set alight in attacks by Flying Officer M. E. A. Royce of No. 504 Squadron during escort sortie over Bristol. Exploded over the Stapleton Institution, Fishponds 11.45 a.m. Oberfw. H. Tiepelt and Uffz. H. Brosig killed. Aircraft U8+FK a write-off.

Hans Tiepelt and Herbert Brosig were buried in Bristol's Greenbank Cemetery, Tiepelt's date of death incorrectly recorded. They have not been reinterred since in the Soldatenfriedhof at Cannock Chase.

Propeller blade from this aircraft in Bristol Police Museum.

3/ZG26 Messerschmitt Bf 110C-4 (3352). Engaged head-on and petrol tank set on fire during escort sortie for ErproGr210 raid on Yate. Probably that attacked by Sergeant H. D. B. Jones of No. 504 Squadron but possibly that claimed by Flying Officer T. H. T. Forshaw of No. 609 Squadron. Abandoned aircraft crashed and burned out at Haydon Farm, near Radstock 11.45 a.m. Lt. J. Köpsell baled out and captured unhurt, landing at Terry Hill, near Mells. Uffz. J. Schmidt fell dead near Kilmersdon Colliery railway with an unopened parachute. Aircraft U8+GL a write-off.

Portion of starboard tail fin bearing part of Swastika marking and '3352' recovered at the time now owned by Ken Wakefield.

The airfields in the coastal area are excellently constructed and camouflaged [reported Generalmajor Warlimont after his inspection tour of the invasion front on September 18–21]. The C-in-C of Luftflotte 2 [Kesselring] and his Chief of Staff [Speidel] had complained about the weather which is as unfavourable as ever and has made it necessary again and again to postpone the employment of strong formations. Even now co-operation between fighter and bomber formations still seems to cause difficulties.

The Chief of Staff, Generalleutnant Speidel, gave the following account of the course of the air war to date. The first phase was characterised by the successful struggle against the enemy fighters, who increasingly lost in numbers and attacking power. When the Luftflotte then wanted to proceed to the major attack on London, this operation was not approved at first, and permission was only granted after much pressure. By then however, only one day of good weather was still available, so that the attack could not be carried out in the form planned. This breathing space allowed the English to draw on personnel and equipment from all their schools and to use fighter aircraft from the factories which had not even been painted. In consequence the enemy's fighter defence gradually increased again in the following days. During this phase, the English had also allowed fighter squadrons, which were less well trained, to fly, undaunted, against the German bomber formations; and in many cases, it was observed that they rammed their opponents as a last resort. On the other hand, German fighter aircraft were for the most part only attacked by more experienced English fighters.

This development led a few days ago to the need to renew the battle against the enemy fighters. Now, in the third stage of the air war, strong bomber formations and strong fighter forces are employed simultaneously, although the bombers are mainly used at night. Our forces feel greatly superior to the enemy as before, and there reigns complete confidence in the successful continuation of the air war.

OKW OPERATIONS STAFF WAR DIARY
SEPTEMBER 23, 1940

An interesting account by Generalleutnant Spiedel concerns the *'many'* cases of British fighters ramming German bombers. One such incident was described on page 52-53; undoubtedly there were others like that of Percy Burton on this Friday.

Above left: **Another 110 scattered itself over the grounds of the Stapleton Institute at Fishponds, Bristol.** *Right:* **Now the building is Manor Park Hospital and Ian Macrae, left, of the Severnside Aviation Society took back one of the prop blades recovered at the time to have it photographed on the crash site. With Ian is the general manager of the hospital, Kevin Hogarty. The propeller is now in the Bristol Police Museum.** *Below:* **The two crewmen were buried in the city's Greenbank Cemetery, Tiepelt's death incorrectly recorded giving the impression that he died three days later.**

4/ZG26 Messerschmitt Bf 110C-4 (3629). Both engines disabled in attacks by Pilot Officer M. E. Staples of No. 609 Squadron during escort sortie over Warmwell. Retired east probably seeking a forced-landing but exploded over Salters Wood, Middle Bere Farm, near Arne 11.45 a.m. following further attack by Pilot Officer A. R. Watson of No. 152 Squadron. Possibly also hit by AA fire. Oberlt. A. Niebuhr (Staffelkapitän) and Uffz. K. Theisen killed. Aircraft 3U+IM a write-off.

Artur Niebuhr and Klaus Theisen were both buried in St Mary's Churchyard at Wareham. They have not been reinterred since at Cannock Chase.

8/ZG26 Messerschmitt Bf 110C-4 (3290). Sortied as escort for bombing attack on Bristol and engaged by Spitfires of No. 152 Squadron east of Portland. One engine disabled and set alight in attacks by Pilot Officer A. R. Watson. Forced-landed at Kimmeridge, near Wareham 11.45 a.m. Uffz. F. Schupp and Gefr. K. Nechwatal captured wounded. Aircraft 3U+DS a write-off.

9/ZG26 Messerschmitt Bf 110C-4 (3297). Engaged on escort sortie and collided head-on with Pilot Officer R. F. G. Miller of No. 609 Squadron during combat over Warmwell. Exploded over Doles Ash and Bellamy's Farms, Piddletrenthide 11.45 a.m. Gefr. E. Liedtke killed. Gefr. G. Jackstadt baled out and captured wounded. Aircraft 3U+FT a write-off.

The gunner from this aircraft, Emil Liedtke, was buried in Brookwood Military Cemetery where he remains to this day.

Stab ZG76 Messerschmitt Bf 110D-3 (4215). Radiators severely damaged by fighters during bomber escort over London. Made for home pursued by fighters and probably that chased over Seaford by Pilot Officer P. A. Worrall and Sergeant G. C. C. Palliser of No. 249 Squadron but possibly that claimed by Flight Lieutenant A. C. Rabagliati of No. 46 Squadron. Aircraft caught fire and eventually ditched in the Channel off Hastings 10.00 a.m. Oberlt. W. von Eichborn (Geschwader Adjutant) rescued by fishing boat after two hours in the water and captured face badly burned. Uffz. E. Bartmuss probably wounded and missing believed drowned. Aircraft M8+XE lost.

THE BATTLE OF GRAVENEY MARSHES

Was this remote marshland less than 50 miles from London the field of battle for the one and only occasion of armed conflict between British and German forces on land within the UK during the war? Andy Saunders sets out to examine the evidence.

Officially the last battle on land within the British Isles between servicemen of a foreign power and the defending British forces was at the Battle of Fishguard on February 23, 1797, when 1,200 French troops were routed by the Pembrokeshire Yeomanry following an ill-fated raiding mission. Rumour has persisted that there was a skirmish between the crew of a German bomber and British soldiers after a Junkers 88 had been shot down at Graveney, Kent, on September 27, 1940. Uncovering the facts and extricating them from the fiction and myth which understandably surrounds such an incident has proved difficult, but we are able to tell now for the first time the facts of the episode so far as they are known, and it seems possible that there may be some substance in claims that the last shots in anger on British soil between a foreign enemy and the English were fired in 1940 and not 1797. However, readers must draw their own conclusions!

Friday, September 27 saw a heavy daylight raid against South London during the afternoon when 55 Junkers 88s of I and II Gruppen of KG77 took part. Unfortunately for the German airmen they missed their rendezvous with the fighter escort and pressed on unprotected; a tactic which was to cost KG77 twelve aircraft and crews. One of them, 3Z+EL, W.Nr. 8099, was hit by AA fire over the target and damaged, thus becoming easy prey for the waiting Spitfires and Hurricanes eager to pounce on stragglers or lame ducks. Over Faversham its fate was sealed as three Spitfires closed for the kill, raking the bomber with gunfire and stopping its remaining good engine.

Farm labourer Eddy Goodwin, working at Monks Hill Farm, Graveney, heard the sound of gunfire and saw the Junkers losing height above the village, travelling south to north and heading for Whitstable Bay. When overflying Goodnestone a twin-Lewis gun emplacement at a searchlight battery opened fire on the German, though it is not known if any hits were secured. As it passed near to Graveney church the German crew released the cockpit canopy in preparation for a forced landing, the jettisoned 'greenhouse', complete with MG15 machine guns, crashed to earth at Odding Path, narrowly missing farm worker Jack Gurr.

Meanwhile, the Junkers 88 skimmed above Graveney Hill and touched down on the billiard-table flat green meadows of Graveney Marshes. As it landed the gently windmilling propellers struck the banks of a ditch, shearing off both assemblies. As they tumbled underneath and past the skidding bomber, the propellers all but sheared both tailplanes and elevators, leaving the aeroplane to come to rest, otherwise intact, a few hundred yards WSW of The Sportsman Inn on the South Oaze sea wall between Graveney and Seasalter. As it stopped, troops of the 1st London Irish Rifles rushed from the Sportsman Pub where they were billeted and prepared to take the crew. Leading them was Lieutenant-Colonel J. R. J. Macnamara. Captain of the aircraft and its pilot was Unteroffizier Fritz Ruhlandt. With Ruhlandt in the Junkers 88 were the Observer, Uffz. Gotthardt Richter, the Wireless Operator, Uffz. Erwin Richter, and the Gunner, Gefr. Jakob Reiner. Writing in December 1987, Fritz Ruhlandt avoided any mention of the exact circumstances of his capture, merely commenting that: 'This was the first mission I had flown with this crew, apart from Erwin Richter. Personally I had already flown missions in Poland, France and some reconnaissance flights over England. My captivity was spent with my comrades in Canada where I was eventually released on 6th December, 1946. The treatment throughout was good.'

His comrade, Erwin Richter, was, however, rather more forthcoming. Also writing in 1987, he said: 'During an anti-aircraft engagement over London one engine failed. As a result we were separated from our unit and immediately attacked by three fighters. Ruhlandt dived at once, and as he

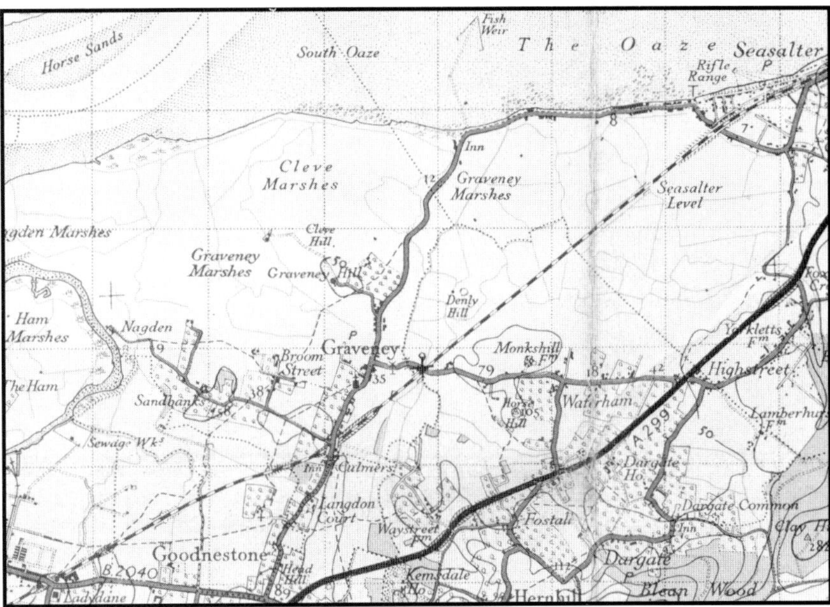

Graveney Marshes lie near the point where the Swale meets the Thames.

'Tough in the gangster manner' according to Squadron Leader Laurence Irving who saw the prisoners the following day. *Above left:* **Unteroffizier Erwin Richter, seen at his wedding in June 1940, and** *right* **Unteroffizier Fritz Ruhlandt.**

neared the ground he found that the second engine had failed as the result of fighter fire. There was no longer any opportunity to get out, as we were so near the ground, so we had to make an emergency landing. During the fighter attack I was wounded in both eyes by glass splinters. Uffz. Ruhlandt was wounded by a shot through the ankle on the ground. The other crew members remained unwounded. A detachment arrested us and took us into custody and we were very well treated. After interrogation I was taken to a hospital and operated on in both eyes.'

On September 27, Squadron Leader Laurence Irving, an RAF Intelligence Officer attached to the Army with No. 13 Group, noted a message from the London Irish Rifles in his diary to the effect that a 'Ju 88 A.1 No. 088 8099 landed fairly intact near Sportsman Inn (Map Ref. 500829) Crew of 4 (3 wounded) at Mount Ephraim, London Irish (Map Ref. 505782) Reported to A.I.I.(G) and A.I.I.(K) at Barnet.'

The following day's entry, however, is rather more interesting, giving as it does written evidence that shots were indeed fired during the capture of this Luftwaffe crew. It reads as follows:

'September 28th. Went off early to see the above Ju 88. At scene of crash met Col. Macnamara and Divisional Commander. The former told me that he happened to be near the platoon quartered at the Sportsman Inn. The crew of E/A got out and opened fire with two machine guns and a sub-machine gun on this platoon, who were preparing to take charge of the aircraft. Colonel Macnamara deployed his men and advanced across 300 yards of absolutely flat country, cut up with dykes. When they got within 100 yards of the E/A the crew waved a white rag. As the troops approached, however, one of the Germans made a dart for the aircraft whereupon the Sergeant dashed in, loosing off his revolver. In this melée three of the crew were slightly wounded but the aircraft was not fired. It appears to have left the factory in July 1940 and contains a bomb sight which looks very new to me. I lunched with the London Irish and later saw the German prisoners. All except one, a very poor type, were tough enough in the gangster manner.'

Without doubt, this account, written as it was on the day by a trained Intelligence Officer expert in sifting fact from fiction and recording the details, can be looked on as reasonably reliable, but unfortunately for the historian, however, there are conflicting reports held in Air Intelligence files by the Air Historical Branch which do not seem to concur exactly with Squadron Leader Irving's report, quite apart from the accounts of Ruhlandt and Richter! The original AI1(K) report includes the following: 'The crew are also said to have fired at people trying to prevent them destroying their aircraft and coming to arrest them; this, however, cannot be confirmed, and is completely denied by the crew,' and 'During this engagement 3 of the crew were wounded.'

The apparent contradiction in these two sentences can possibly be explained by the fact that the report earlier makes mention of AA fire and an attack by Spitfires, so the sense of this statement could well be that the crew were wounded in this way rather than by gunfire on the ground which RAF Air Intelligence officially refused to acknowledge had taken place. Laurence Irving, however, certainly reported that the men were wounded as a result of shots fired by the Army.

Eddy Goodwin, like many residents of Graveney and Seasalter, heard rumours of a battle between the Germans and soldiers, but he recalled in 1986 that he never knew exactly what went on. Certainly he recalled the sound of gunfire, but the rather more colourful stories of the action which proliferate in this district can be taken as no more than a fanciful myth. Stories of the Germans 'holding out for hours' and taking over a sanbagged emplace-

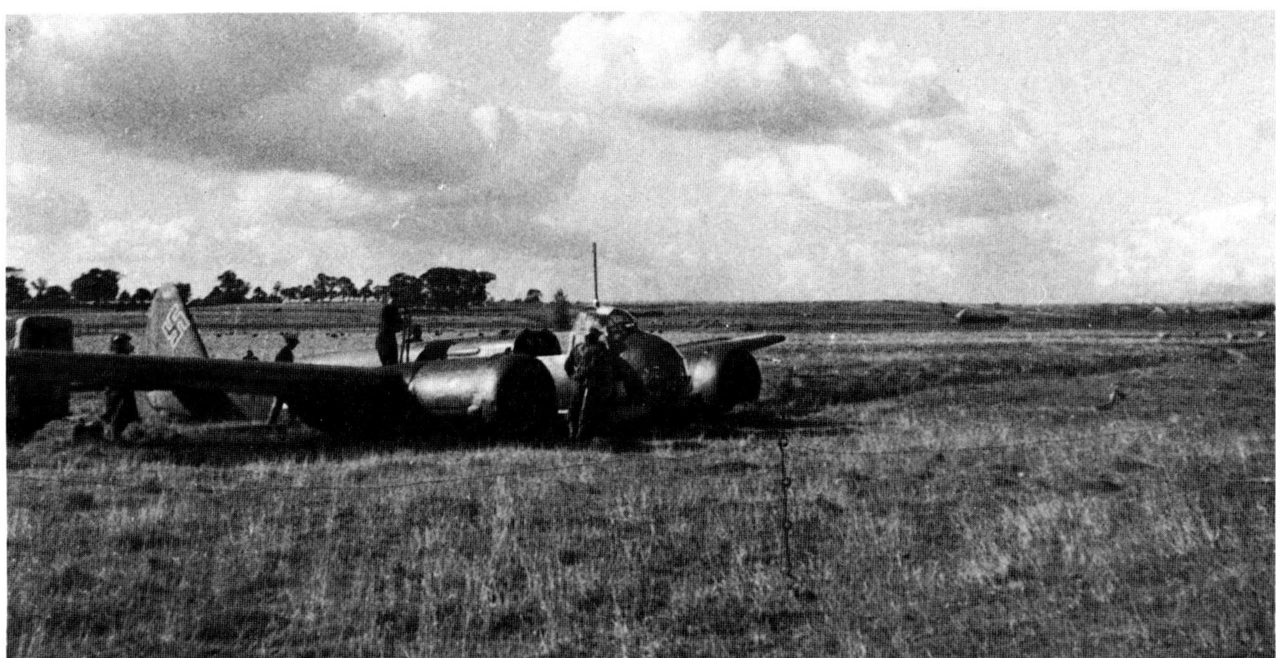

ment are certainly untrue, although a common thread which runs through all these tales is that the airmen had orders to avoid capture and prevent their aircraft falling into enemy hands.

Therefore, no absolutely clear picture emerges as to what happened on Graveney Marshes. Perhaps the most plausible explanation is that the Germans did fire at their aircraft in an attempt to destroy it and that the London Irish mistook the shots as being directed at them as they advanced from the Sportsman Inn. Consequently, the soldiers would have been very wary as they neared the bomber, the sudden movement of one of the crew being enough to provoke the Sergeant's revolver shots. If this scenario is what actually happened, then it can be seen how easily the facts could be embroidered over the years to create the legend of a full-scale battle.

Of the aircraft itself another report exists in the files of Air Intelligence but it throws no light on the controversy. It reads: 'Ju 88 A1. Crashed on 27.9.40 at 17.45 hours at Graveney Marshes near Faversham. Map Reference R5082. Markings 3Z+EL (E in yellow). Airframe built by Siebel Flugzeugwerke Halle. Acceptance date 28.7.40. Tail and elevators made by Allgemeine Transportanlage GmbH, Leipzig. Engines two Jumo 211. Plates not found. Aircraft made forced landing following fighter action. Several .303 strikes through starboard oil cooler and port wing fuel tank. Crew four, all prisoners, one wounded. *[This differs from the other reports of three wounded.]* Armament cannot be ascertained as all guns removed before the arrival of Intelligence Officer. Armour: pilot's seat armour standard but headpiece increased in size to 17 inches deep, thus reaching roof of cockpit. Seven five-inch strips, 5mm thick, running fore and aft fitted to the full length of the under door of the cockpit. Usual external bomb racks under the wings, two each side of the fuselage. Kuvi bomb sight fitted. Pilot has Revi sight for dive bomb aiming with bomb release handle on control column. Second bomb release handle near Kuvi sight in front position.'

Today there are but few surviving relics of Werke Nr. 8099, although the tail wheel survived for many years at the Sportsman Inn, now Ye Olde Sportsman Public House. Whatever the truth of the incident, the fact remains that locally the story of the 'Battle of Graveney Marshes' will doubtless live on, even if the available evidence implies that it was perhaps more legendary than factual!

ANDY SAUNDERS, 1987

SATURDAY, SEPTEMBER 28

Two formations of 120 to 150 aircraft attempted to reach London during the day. About 25 aircraft penetrated to the Thames Estuary during the morning, and bombs were dropped at Poplar, Deptford and Woolwich. There were few casualties and damage was slight.

The second attack was launched about 1330, but the raiders were intercepted over the Channel, and only a few succeeded in dropping bombs at Hastings. There were no casualties, and only minor damage to property is reported.

At 1420, a third formation attacked the Portsmouth and Southampton area, but were prevented from reaching their objectives. No incidents have been reported. The enemy are reported to have jettisoned their bombs over the sea.

At 1800 a few bombs were dropped at Ramsgate, Folkestone and Eastbourne. There are several UXBs at Folkestone Harbour Station, and a local diversion in Folkestone-Dover road is being used owing to road blocked. A few houses and shops were demolished at Eastbourne.

During the night, enemy activity was widespread. Excluding London, most incidents occurred in Regions 6 and 12. Little damage has been reported from the provinces and there is none of military or industrial importance. Casualties are very small. A large number of bombs fell around Vickers Armstrong and Hawkers Aircraft Works at Weybridge. There was no damage except the blockage of a road opposite the former works. A few houses were slightly damaged.

In the London area a major fire occurred at Green School, Isleworth. Heavy bombing is reported from Ealing, Willesden, Acton, Chiswick, Southall, Croydon, Stepney and Poplar. Light bombing was also reported by 45 Boroughs. Croydon, Acton, Brentford, Ealing, Southall and Heston suffered severely from fires.

Several factories were hit in the Acton and Ealing district and 8 hospitals received damage. At New Southgate in the Friern Hospital casualties reported amount to 24 killed, 7 injured — 14 people are believed to be trapped. Sixty casualties have been reported at Wandsworth. Some H.E. bombs fell on Selfridges Stores, Oxford Street, and a timber yard, police station and cinema were damaged by fire at Southall. Incendiary bombs appear to have been used on a very extensive scale both in London and the provinces.

Six enemy aircraft were shot down, together with 4 probable and 1 damaged. Civilian casualties in London during the day amounted to 10 injured, by night, to 72 people killed and 160 injured. Elsewhere 5 people were seriously injured and 6 slightly hurt.

Another day of bitter fighter clashes over the southern counties of England as tired British pilots rose to meet raids of fast bomb-carrying Bf 110s and Ju 88s escorted by literally hundreds of high-flying Bf 109s which threatened to overwhelm the Hurricanes and Spitfires sent to meet them. In all, 10 Luftwaffe aircraft were lost and one damaged in operations, 2 more being destroyed in accidents.

3/JG26 Messerschmitt Bf 109E-1 (6273). Believed severely damaged in combat with Pilot Officer J. S. Morton of No. 603 Squadron and prepared to ditch in the Channel off Hythe. Believed then further attacked by Pilot Officer C. F. Currant of No. 605 Squadron and crashed in the sea 10 miles SE of Dover 10.45 a.m. Fw. F. Schür killed. Aircraft lost.

The body of Fritz Schür was eventually found washed ashore at Sheerness on October 27.

8/KG4 Junkers Ju 88A-1 (4071). One engine disabled by AA fire over the English coast during sortie to bomb London. Turned for home but second engine failed and aircraft crashed in the sea off Beachy Head 10.00 p.m. Gefr. F. Marschardt baled out, rescued after two hours in the water and captured unhurt. Oberfw. H. Camp killed. Lt. F. Lange and Obergefr. A. Kieg missing believed killed. Aircraft 5J+GS lost.

The body of Hermann Camp, the observer in this aircraft, was recovered from the sea and buried in Felixstowe New Cemetery on October 25.

Holland House, Kensington, completed in 1606 for Sir Walter Cope, James I's Chancellor of the Exchequer. During the raid on September 27/28 some 22 incendiaries landed on or near the house, unobserved by firewatchers occupied at the time with a fire in a cottage on the estate. By the time the blaze was finally reported at 3.55 a.m. it was too late. The owner, Lord Ilchester, was informed and he arrived just in time to witness the final death throes of his house.

The Jacobean mansion stood derelict until 1952 when it was purchased by the London County Council and since 1959 the east wing has housed the King George Memorial Youth Hostel Association. The house and grounds are open to the public.

SUNDAY, SEPTEMBER 29

There were no large-scale attacks during daylight hours. Shortly after 1610 three or four small raids crossed the Kent coast and flew west and south of London. The aircraft appeared to be fighters flying at a great height. Otherwise enemy activity was concentrated on attacks on convoys and reconnaissances over the East, South and West coasts. Wolverhampton was slightly bombed at 1845, and Sittingbourne more severely at 1800. Lowestoft and places in Kent and Sussex were bombed during the morning.

Civilian casualties (approx.): London, 1 killed, 2 injured. Elsewhere, 9 killed, 28 injured. Enemy aircraft casualties: 4 certain, 3 probable.

Raiding was continued after dark by single aircraft, the principal objectives being London, Liverpool and Birkenhead. The counties of Surrey and Sussex were also bombed but without great damage. Aberdeen and Edinburgh were bombed in the early hours of darkness, but damage was mostly confined to private property.

Civilian casualties (approx.): London, 44 killed, 157 injured. Elsewhere, 5 killed, 74 injured. Enemy aircraft casualties: 1 (by A.A. fire).

A day of reduced activity on which many of Dowding's pilots drew welcome respite from the heavy demands again made of them over previous days. Operational sorties cost the Luftwaffe the loss of 8 aircraft with another 7 of their machines returning damaged. One more was destroyed and 2 damaged in accidents. None fell in Britain.

Unusual humming sound noted during the past three nights when enemy aircraft were either overhead or in the vicinity of Woolwich. This sound resembles the hum produced by telegraph wires in the wind, but in a much deeper key . . . barrage balloon wires might, by coincidence, be the cause of this noise. Is a new type of Bosch engine now in vogue? Or are wireless waves to jam inter-communication between enemy aircraft being used? Characteristics: low, continuous, distinct, even hum, all-pervading . . . this was again noted during the early hours of this morning when no breeze was present.

LIEUTENANT E. B. TAPSELL
WOOLWICH DEFENCE OFFICER
WAR DIARY, SEPTEMBER 29/30, 1940

2/JG77 Messerschmitt Bf 109E-4 (3746). Believed shot down in combat with fighters over the Thames Estuary and possibly that claimed by Pilot Officer R. Berry of No. 603 Squadron 5.00 p.m. Crashed in the sea. Oberlt. W. Leyerer killed. Aircraft lost.

The body of Walter Leyerer was washed ashore on the Suffolk coast on October 25 and was originally buried at Ipswich.

MONDAY, SEPTEMBER 30

By day, there were four major attacks in East Kent and two others in the Portland area.

Kent: 1st Attack: At 0900 some 80 aircraft consisting mostly of fighters crossed the coast at Dungeness and penetrated to Biggin Hill and Kenley.

2nd Attack: At 1010 a further raid of 75 aircraft crossed the coast at Dungeness and again flew to Biggin Hill and Kenley area where the formations were broken up.

3rd Attack: At 1310 180 aircraft flew inland at Lympne and made for London. This raid was principally held up 20 miles from Central London but a few aircraft penetrated and bombs were dropped at Ealing.

4th Attack: At 1608 four raids totalling some 200 aircraft flew over Dungeness to Biggin Hill and then scattered over East Kent from Kenley to Hornchurch. Some flew west as far as Reading and Middle Wallop.

Portland: 1st Attack: At 1055 some 100 aircraft crossed the coast at St Alban's Head. Some 25 split and flew over Dorset and Devon to Somerset border. The remainder only penetrated about 15 miles inland.

2nd Attack: At 1635 some 100 aircraft flew inland about 20 miles. Bombs were dropped at Weymouth and Sherborne.

There was considerable activity at night

September 30, 1940
9th Operational Flight

Attack on Yeovil aerodrome — take-off 15.24 hours. Once again we went up in two wings of 30 to 40 Heinkel 111s from Cherbourg, where strong fighter protection was assigned to us.

While we were still over the Channel, the Tommys were already there — earlier than before. A Hurricane came close to us, as if he was keeping his distance in a formation flight; trying to have a look at us, as if we were quite harmless. Truly a crazy devil, perhaps a senior officer, who wanted for once to have a really close look at German bombers? The coloured circle on the upper fuselage flying alongside us took my breath away. Everything then took its natural course, with our small machine guns banging away as hard as they could. And suddenly — to our great surprise — there were actually flames and smoke streaming out from the unwary intruder. He staggered into a dive . . . and disappeared. So our small, single machine guns, which give the depressing feeling that they hardly worry the attacking fighters, let alone do any serious damage to them, are after all not altogether useless.

Our squadron commander, who had obviously been impressed by the bold behaviour of this Hurricane pilot, was then heard yelling through the intercom: 'Did he get away? Has he baled out? Give your position on the air-sea rescue frequency . . . ' I wondered if it did the fellow any good. But once again there are enemy fighters in front, behind, and beside us. And our own fighters all seem to be flying over one spot again. They really seem to be hopelessly inferior in individual combat, as had been rumoured, and only able to save themselves when in formation. This does not help us much as far as the fighter cover for our flights over England is concerned.

A Heinkel has been forced down into the clouds. A Spitfire came so close to us from in front that I could hear it firing as it flew by. Or was it firing at the plane next to us? It turned away and kept its distance. Then I saw one of our own fighters approaching it quite gradually from behind, but apparently at full throttle. So they are in fact fighting each other. Our fighter got closer and closer, with difficulty. Suddenly, when they were as near each other as they could get, the Englishman must have seen him in his rear mirror. He tore into him, and badly scared, he plummeted vertically like a Stuka. I really wouldn't like to be flying one of those fighters. You feel quite sorry for them. Their painted shark's teeth also don't seem to help. Ground visibility is nil in all directions, let alone being able to see the Yeovil fighter aerodrome and all that, in order to try and find a break in the sea of clouds . . . It's a dull and depressing feeling.

ROBERT GÖTZ

The pilot in the Hurricane mentioned by Robert Götz could well have been Flying Officer John Hardacre of No. 504 'City of Nottingham' Squadron based at Filton. His body was washed ashore at Yarmouth on October 10 and buried in All Saints' Churchyard, Fawley, Hampshire.

Chariot of War. September 30 saw another major daylight effort — a day on which the Luftwaffe were to lose 46 aircraft — this Messerschmitt Bf 109 being one of them: Leutnant Herbert Schmidt's machine, Yellow 3, at Crépon airfield.

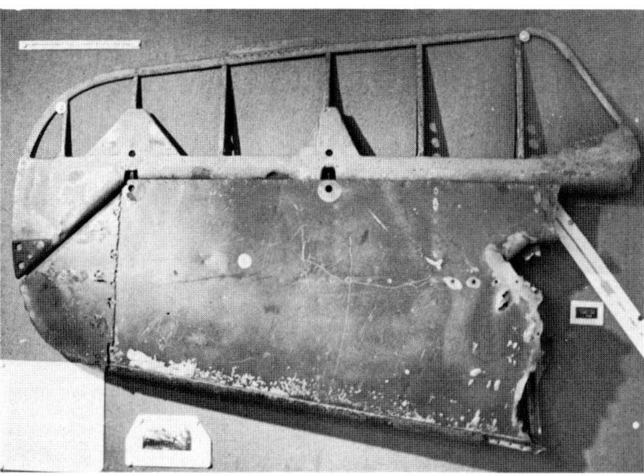

Trophy of War. Four decades later part of the tailplane, taken as a souvenir at the time the aircraft crashed near Haslemere, now hangs as one of the exhibits in the museum on Tangmere aerodrome.

over a widespread area up to 2330 after which raids were less in number, and from 0100 raids were confined almost entirely to an area south of a line from the Wash to St David's Head. At dusk the first night raiders headed for London from the south and also from the north via Harwich. From 2100 raids flew from Cherbourg and Havre to Bristol Channel, South Wales and the Midlands, up to Liverpool and Mersey area.

From 2200 raids approached from the east, crossing the coast between the Wash and the Thames Estuary, some headed for London whilst others flew through Lincolnshire and the Nottingham area. It was estimated that some 275 enemy aircraft operated over the country and that 175 penetrated to Central London. Minelaying was suspected in the Firth of Forth, Thames Estuary and off Harwich.

Casualties to enemy aircraft: Destroyed 46, probable 32, damaged 29. In London during the day, 1 civilian was killed and 23 injured, 11 of them seriously. At night 35 were killed, 139 seriously injured and 174 slightly hurt. Elsewhere by day, 22 were killed and 77 injured, 41 of these seriously. After dark, 5 civilians were killed, 5 seriously injured and 14 slightly hurt.

Following the customary early morning reconnaissance flights, the first major raid of the day developed around 9.00 a.m. when some 200 German aircraft in two waves crossed the coast at Dover heading for London. They were met over Maidstone by 12 British squadrons and turned away prior to reaching their target. Later mid-morning, a formation of German fighters clashed over Weymouth Bay with almost 80 British fighters and were forced to retire before reaching the coast. Early in the afternoon, another heavy raid comprising of some 100 bombers escorted by 200 fighters crossed the Sussex coast and fought its way inland towards London in the teeth of determined fighter opposition. Fighter combats reminiscent of the hectic days of August fanned-out and spilled across the southern counties. Later in the afternoon, a smaller raid comprising elements of I and II Gruppen of KG55 penetrated No. 10 Group's defences and, escorted by Bf 110s of II/ZG26, forged inland bound for the Westland factory at Yeovil. Thwarted by fighters and finding scattered cloud over the target area, they retired south suffering several casualties despite sterling efforts on the part of their escorts. The Luftwaffe lost 46 aircraft and another 12 damaged in operations, 2 more of their machines being damaged in accidents — one of them beyond repair. Though none could suspect it at the time, the last of the great daylight battles over Britain had been fought.

Above: **An even larger trophy — Unteroffizier Horst Perez's Messerschmitt virtually intact on a hillside at Eastdean. The whole aircraft was shipped to Canada early in 1941 to help raise money for the 'Bundles for Britain' campaign and then moved south for exhibition in the United States.** *Below left:* **This picture shows it being unloaded in New York in June 1941. It returned to Canada at the end of the war and was finally rescued from the scrap heap by a consortium of British enthusiasts. Wrangles as to its ownership have kept it under wraps for more than 10 years while it undergoes a complete rebuild** *below right.*

Before . . . then . . . and now. Built in 1708, this three storey house in Park Lane, Croydon, became the Society of Friends school from the 1820s until 1879. When the Luftwaffe visited it on September 30, 1940 it housed St Anselm's, a small prep school; their calling card — a parachute mine.

1(F)/123 Junkers Ju 88A-1 (385). Engaged on reconnaissance sortie to Yeovil but crashed into the Channel off the Isle of Wight — exact circumstances not known. Possibly that engaged over Dorchester and starboard engine set alight by No. 87 Squadron Hurricanes 4.30 p.m. Fw. F-K. Waack, Uffz. H. Essmann and Uffz. J. Obermayer killed. Lt. W. Frenzel missing believed killed. Aircraft 4U+MH lost.

The bodies of Heinrich Essmann and Johann Obermayer were washed ashore at Ventnor on October 11. That of Friedrich-Karl Waack at Brook three days later. All were originally buried at Parkhurst Military Cemetery but only Uffz. Obermayer and Fw. Waack have since been reinterred in the Soldatenfriedhof at Cannock Chase where their dates of death are incorrectly recorded as October 11 and 14 respectively.

5/JG2 Messerschmitt Bf 109E-4 (4861). Shot down by Flying Officer T. Nowierski of No. 609 Squadron in combat over Warmwell. Crashed and burned out at Sprakefield, Hundred Acres Farm, Sydling St Nicholas 4.50 p.m. Uffz. A. Dollinger baled out but killed due to parachute failure. Aircraft a write-off.

Site excavated by Peter Foote and Philippa Hodgkiss and surviving remains recovered.

Stab JG26 Messerschmitt Bf 109E-4 (5818). Shot down in combat with fighters and crashed in flames at Hides Farm, Roundhurst, North Chapel, near Haslemere 4.40 p.m. Possibly that attacked by Flying Officer W. Urbanowicz of No. 303 Squadron. Major W. Kienzle baled out and captured seriously wounded. Aircraft a write-off.

Minor components and fragments of airframe, exhaust stub and 20mm MGFF magazine recovered by the Southern Area Wartime Aircraft Preservation Society. Also excavated by the Wealden Aviation Archaeological Group in 1976. Relics from this aircraft including radio mast held by the Kent Battle of Britain Museum, now in the Hawkinge Aeronautical Trust collection.

4/JG26 Messerschmitt Bf 109E-4 (1190). Severely damaged in combat with Spitfires during escort sortie over Beachy Head. Believed that attacked by Sergeant D. E. Kingaby of No. 92 Squadron. Forced-landed on dead engine at Eastdean, near Eastbourne 5.30 p.m. Uffz. H. Perez captured badly injured — reputedly shot and wounded by troops after landing. Aircraft 4+— a write-off.

Complete airframe shipped to Canada for use in connection with 'Bundles for Britain' drive 1941. After touring Canada and the USA, it was eventually delivered to Arnprior Research Station, Ontario, in 1945. Sold as scrap in 1957, it was eventually discovered in a junk yard in 1961 and acquired by three British enthusiasts. Returned to the UK, this aircraft is currently under restoration at Hurn airport.

7/JG26 Messerschmitt Bf 109E-4 (3645). Shot down in combat with fighters during escort sortie for KG77 attack on London. Crashed in the sea 4.50 p.m. Gefr. H. Ziemens killed. Aircraft lost.

The body of Helmut Ziemens came ashore at Southwold on October 18. Today he is reinterred at Cannock Chase where his date of death is incorrectly recorded as September 24. No reason for this curious anomaly has been found.

9/JG26 Messerschmitt Bf 109E-1 (4820). Believed exploded under attack by fighters over Canterbury during escort sortie for KG77 attack on London. Wreckage scattered over a wide area, debris falling at Canterbury Artillery Barracks, Honey Wood and Old Park Farm, near Tyler Hill. Gefr. H. Hornatschek killed. Aircraft lost.

Today the spot has been lost under the post-war Croydon flyover.

The King's prize. This Messerschmitt overturned attempting to land in His Majesty's own park at Windsor. Later it was put on show outside the Castle to help raise funds for the local Spitfire fund. As more German aircraft became available from force-landings, many such displays were held throughout Britain for various fund-raising causes. Naturally they were popular with small boys eager for souvenirs and all loose parts soon disappeared. One of the windscreen panels removed at the time turned up years later and now reposes in Nigel Parker's collection.

Stab I/JG27 Messerschmitt Bf 109E-4 (3763). Shot down in combat with Hurricanes over East Grinstead. Crashed and burned out at Nettlefold Field, Bell Lane, Nutley, near Haywards Heath 9.45 a.m. Oberlt. H. Bertram (Gruppe Adjutant) killed. Aircraft a write-off.

Small fragments of airframe excavated by the Wealden Aviation Archaeological Group in 1974. Surface fragments recovered by the Kent Battle of Britain Museum (now held by the Hawkinge Aeronautical Trust) and also by the London Air Museum. Site excavated by Malcolm Pettit in 1981 and cockpit components and assorted wreckage recovered. Piece of gold neck chain and parachute fragments picked up at the time of the crash held by Andy Saunders.

3/JG27 Messerschmitt Bf 109E-4 (3630). Shot down in combat with Hurricanes over East Grinstead. Crashed in flames into a pond on Cinderhill Farm, Horsted Keynes, near Haywards Heath 9.45 a.m. Uffz. A. Sander killed. Aircraft a write-off.

Site investigated by the London Air Museum and components recovered at time of crash donated by local landowner.

4/JG27 Messerschmitt Bf 109E-1 (6306). Radiator damaged in combat during escort sortie. Turned for home but engine temperature rose so forced-landed near the cricket pavilion at Pelsham House, Peasmarsh 1.30 p.m. Possibly that attacked by Sergeant R. H. Fokes of No. 92 Squadron. Uffz. R. Hammer captured slightly injured and admitted to Benenden Military Hospital. Aircraft 7+— a write-off.

6/JG27 Messerschmitt Bf 109E-1 (3895). Engine set alight in surprise fighter attack during bomber escort sortie to London. Possibly one of those claimed by Sergeant J. Frantisek of No. 303 Squadron. Abandoned aircraft crashed and burned out at Holmans Grove, Grayswood, near Haslemere 4.40 p.m. Lt. H. Schmidt baled out and captured unhurt. Aircraft 3+— a write-off.

Site investigated by the Wealden Aviation Archaeological Group in 1977 and piece of wing recovered from surface now in the Tangmere collection. Few small pieces salvaged. Relics also held by the Southern Area Wartime Aircraft Preservation Society. Complete starboard tailplane donated to the Tangmere Military Aviation Museum.

7/JG27 Messerschmitt Bf 109E-1 (4851). Engaged on bomber escort sortie to London and hit in radiator and petrol tank during combat with fighters. Possibly that claimed as damaged by Pilot Officer P. G. Dexter of No. 603 Squadron. Overturned in forced-landing near Queen Anne's Gate, Windsor Great Park 5.00 p.m. Oberlt. K. Fischer captured unhurt. Aircraft 9+ a write-off.

Front cockpit canopy panel taken at the time of the crash held by Nigel Parker.

7/JG51 Messerschmitt Bf 109E-1 (3391). Shot down in combat with Spitfires over Tonbridge. Crashed and burned out at Kennard's Farm, Leigh 1.45 p.m. Possibly attacked and port wing set alight by Pilot Officer R. Berry of No. 603 Squadron. Fw. K. Hübel killed. Aircraft a write-off.

Site excavated by the Halstead War Museum which recovered pilot's pullover, wallet, watch strap and fountain-pen. Relics also held by the Hawkinge Aeronautical Trust and Steve Vizard.

7/JG51 Messerschmitt Bf 109E-1 (4856). Shot down in combat with fighters. Crashed and burned out at Kentwyns, Nutfield, near Redhill 1.45 p.m. Possibly that claimed by Pilot Officer R. B. Dewey of No. 603 Squadron. Uffz. P. Limpert killed. Aircraft a write-off.

Stab I/JG52 Messerschmitt Bf 109E-1 (1391). Radiator badly damaged in attack by Spitfire during free-lance sortie over the Channel. Possibly that claimed by Flight Lieutenant A. R. Wright of No. 92 Squadron. Forced to ditch in the Channel off Newhaven 4.00 p.m. Lt. K. Kirchner captured unhurt. Aircraft lost.

3/JG52 Messerschmitt Bf 109E-4 (1262). Intercepted by fighters during free-lance sortie to London and lost control during violent evasive manoeuvres. Engine cut and aircraft abandoned. Crashed at Clayton Farm, Peasmarsh 2.00 p.m. Uffz. K. Wolff baled out wounded in the leg and landed at House Field, Hammonds, Udimore — admitted to Benenden Military Hospital. Aircraft 14+ a write-off.

Site excavated by the Wealden Aviation Archaeological Group 1975. Rusty propeller boss and remains of shattered Daimler-Benz DB 601 engine unearthed from a depth of 4–5 feet.

4/JG52 Messerschmitt Bf 109E-4 (3417). Engaged by fighters during bomber escort sortie to London. Reported radiator damaged in attack by another 109 but believed actually that claimed as damaged by Flight Lieutenant E. Holden of No. 501 Squadron. Overshot attempting to land at Detling and forced-landed near the airfield boundary 2.00 p.m. Gefr. E. Mummert captured unhurt. Aircraft 2+— a write-off.

First-aid kit and wing leading edge panel 'liberated' from this aircraft in 1940 donated to the Kent Battle of Britain Museum and now in the Hawkinge Aeronautical Trust collection.

6/JG52 Messerschmitt Bf 109E-1 (3192). Exploded and lost one wing under attack by fighters during escort sortie to London. Abandoned aircraft crashed and burned out near Kingswood Church, Dorking 2.00 p.m. Possibly that attacked by Pilot Officer J. S. Morton of No. 603 Squadron. Gefr. G. Strasser baled out and captured seriously wounded. Aircraft a write-off.

Surviving fragments held by Simon Parry.

3/JG53 Messerschmitt Bf 109E-4 (1325). Forced-landed out of fuel at Langley, near Eastbourne 2.05 p.m. following bomber escort sortie to London and combat with fighters. Fw. W. Scholz captured unhurt. Aircraft 13+ a write-off.

6/JG53 Messerschmitt Bf 109E-1 (6384). Intercepted by fighters over Tunbridge Wells during bomber escort sortie to London. Engine failed so turned for home but attacked over the coast and crashed in the Channel off Beachy Head 1.50 p.m. Possibly that attacked by Sergeant S. Karubin of No. 303 Squadron. Uffz. K-M. Vogel captured unhurt. Aircraft 3+— lost.

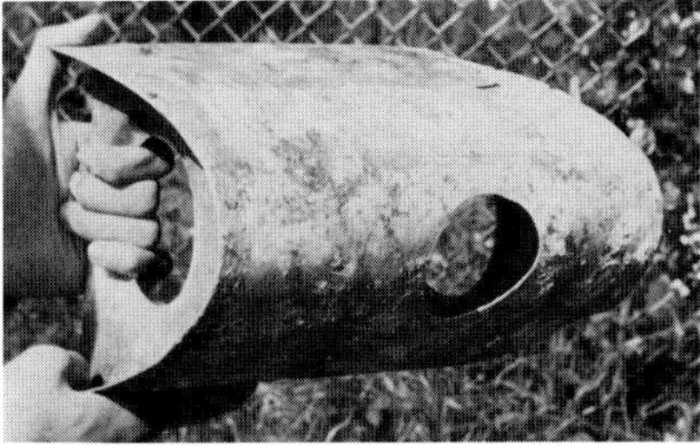

Nice discovery by the Shoreham Aviation Preservation Society at Strood near Rochester — a section of wing with the gun port. Its position on the leading edge of a 109 can be seen in the Windsor Castle machine opposite.

7/JG53 Messerschmitt Bf 109E-1 (5175). Engine and radiator badly damaged by fighters during bomber escort sortie to London. Possibly that attacked by Sergeant K. B. Parker of No. 92 Squadron. Aircraft broke its back in heavy forced-landing at Strood, near Rochester 2.00 p.m. Uffz. E. Poschenrieder captured severely injured. Aircraft 12+I a write-off.

7/JG54 Messerschmitt Bf 109E-1 (6050). Radiator damaged in combat with fighters during bomber escort sortie to London. Possibly that attacked by Flight Lieutenant A. R. Wright of No. 92 Squadron. Attempted to reach the coast but engine overheated so forced-landed and caught fire at Rock House Banks, near Normans Bay, Pevensey 1.56 p.m. Uffz. F. Marcks captured unhurt. Aircraft 4+ a write-off.

9/JG54 Messerschmitt Bf 109E-4 (5116). Believed shot down in combat with No. 603 Squadron Spitfires during bomber escort sortie to London. Crashed and burned out on Dairy Farm, Golden Green, near Tonbridge 1.45 p.m. Probably that first attacked by Pilot Officer J. S. Morton and further attacked by Pilot Officer R. Berry. Uffz. W. Braatz killed. Aircraft 6+ a write-off.

Originally buried at Hadlow Cemetery, Wilhelm Braatz is now reinterred in the Soldatenfriedhof at Cannock Chase where his date of death is incorrectly recorded as October 3. No reason for this has been found but it is possibly the date of his actual recovery from the wreckage of his aircraft.

Surface fragments in the Vizard collection.

1/KG51 Junkers Ju 88A-1 (2063). Intercepted and shot down by No. 602 Squadron Spitfires during sortie to bomb Portsmouth. Dived through cloud and crashed into the Channel 3 miles SW of Selsey Bill 4.15 p.m. Gefr. R. Penka and Gefr. M. Hoppert killed. Fw. F. Paczinski and Gefr. E. Dürrschmidt missing believed killed. Aircraft 9K+DH lost.

The body of the Bordfunker, Rudolf Penka, was recovered from the sea that afternoon by the Selsey lifeboat *Canadian Pacific*. That of the gunner, Max Hoppert, being found on October 15. Both were buried in St Nicholas's Churchyard at West Thorney where they remain to this day.

4/KG55 Heinkel He 111P-2 (2643). Attacked by Hurricanes of Nos. 238 and 504 Squadrons during bombing sortie to Yeovil. Shot down into the Channel off Portland 4.40 p.m. Obergefr. W. Schocke killed. Oberfw. H. Güttler, Uffz. E. Rudeck, Gefr. K. Bauer and Gefr. F. Strauss missing believed killed. Aircraft G1+CM lost.

The gunner from this aircraft, Willi Schocke, was washed up at Horsesand Fort on October 14 which is incorrectly recorded as his date of death in Ann's Hill Cemetery, Gosport where he remains to this day.

2/KG77 Junkers Ju 88A-1 (2142). Hit by AA fire and pilot wounded during sortie to bomb London. Turned for home but then attacked by Sergeant P. C. P. Farnes of No. 501 Squadron and both engines badly damaged. Forced-landed at Gatwick Race Course 4.45 p.m. Oberlt. F. Oeser, Oberfw. G. Goerke and Gefr. R. Hülsmann captured wounded. Uffz. G. Klasing killed. Aircraft 3Z+DK a write-off.

Prize of the month in 1940 went to Mrs Kate Whitcombe of Kilmersdon. When the Bf 110 of ZG26 crashed on September 27 on Haydon Farm (see page 141), Johann Schmidt's forage cap was picked up and raffled by the people of Radstock in the village hall to raise money for the Forces Comfort Fund. Mrs Whitcombe was the lucky lady and she still has her prize today.

Educating the public to the sounds of the Blitz. Harry Gregson, writing for *The War* in September 1940, explained to readers 'How to tell the night guns by their sound.' 'An incredible variety of guns, some designed for AA work and others adapted to this purpose, are now putting up a barrage against the invaders. Among them we may distinguish the AA guns proper. These, firing high-velocity shells, utter a short, sharp bark, when heard from about a mile away. It is seldom that the bark of a 3.7 gun will be heard alone. Usually the guns operate in batteries, so a succession of sharp barks almost always indicates the 3.7 gun. The 3.7 gun is like an elongated 18-pounder and is mobile. For this reason it is sometimes heard outside your back door. When that happens the report is no longer like a bark, but becomes an ear-splitting roar and the barrel emits a 30-foot sheet of flame.'

PUT THAT LIGHT OUT!

Life after dark was very strange during the war: every house had to put up shutters over the windows, or draw lightproof curtains across them, all through the hours of darkness. There were no street lights, and the few cars that were on the streets had special masks over their lights so that only a small amount of light showed in a horizontal direction. Buses and trains had the same restriction on lighting, and the whole situation was summed up by calling it 'The Black-out', a fitting enough description. On a moonless night it was really pitch black, many accidents resulted, but the German bombers were denied the chance to navigate with the assistance of the lights that would have been displayed in peacetime. Cries of 'Put that light out!' were commonplace, and persistent offenders were liable to prosecution. Moonlight nights were not welcomed, the term 'Bomber's Moon' developed, and it was on such nights that we could expect visits from the Luftwaffe, now only a half hour's flight away. There is no doubt that courting couples found considerable advantages in the 'Black-out', there was privacy almost everywhere outdoors, and I have no doubt that many romances blossomed as a direct result — well there have to be compensations to make up for all the other hardships!

As the war progressed, the strength of the anti-aircraft defences increased by leaps and bounds and, as a result, the tactics of the attacking planes changed. In the early days, even in broad daylight, the German bombers flew across London at medium height, in some semblance of formation, without much risk of being shot down. What few guns that were firing were not particularly accurate, and probably did more good in terms of boosting the morale of the population than in numbers of planes hit. By the middle of the six years the conflict lasted, and more so towards the last year or so, the fire-power over London was devastating. Nearly every park and recreation ground was the home of a gun site or a barrage balloon. The guns were most commonly 4.5-inch in batteries of eight, each gun being mounted in a thick concrete emplacement, and all the associated range and height finding equipment being protected in the same way. The whole site would be surrounded by barbed wire and was guarded by sentries. Gunners quarters would be sited nearby so that in the event of enemy aircraft approaching the guns were manned in double quick time. Some of the personnel were women, the ATS they were called, and later in the war the Home Guard did their share of the duties.

It is very difficult to describe the noise that a gun of this type makes; it is a sharp crack not unlike an empty cupboard banging shut, but of course magnified many times over. The flashes from the group of eight guns sited in Barking Park, about half a mile from Grange Road, Ilford, would penetrate our black-out shutters and light up the rooms with lightning-like brilliance. Following the firing came a train-like roaring, loud at first, then fading as the shells climbed up towards their target. The sound and sight of the shellburst in the night sky was not very spectacular, just a pin-prick of orange light for a fraction of a second, and later the 'bok-bok' sound of the explosion.

I believe that the geography of London had a lot to do with the sounds of an air raid as the Thames Valley made the acoustics rather like that of a large empty room, the sound waves echoing back and forth across the river between the terraces of the suburbs on either side.

There were other types of guns apart from the 'heavies' as the 4.5s were known. There was the 3.7-inch type, not usually on a permanent site, which were intended to be mobile to provide fire-power where it was required at any particular time. The 4.5-inch gun was capable of propelling a shell weighing about 50 pounds to a height of eight miles in approximately fifty seconds. The height could be set by adjusting a cap on the nose of the shell, so that the detonation would be at the same height as the attacking aircraft. Of course each shell that was fired meant that a shower of jagged pieces of shrapnel would be falling to the ground if they did not become embedded in their target, and the hazards of walking out in the open during a raid are obvious, particularly as some shells did not explode until they

'The other standard AA gun is the 4.5, distinguishable from the 3.7 because the report is deeper. Heard from a distance, the 3.7 gun's report may be compared to the yapping of a small dog, while the 4.5 may be likened to the bark of a sheep dog. The 4.5 is not mobile and will not, therefore, be heard in streets.'

had returned to the ground all in one piece. The 3.7-inch shell was lighter, of course, but the rate of fire was higher which was an advantage if planes were flying at medium altitude, passing from horizon to horizon quite quickly.

The Bofors gun was a light, mobile, quick-firing weapon firing up to 120 two-pound shells a minute to a height of six thousand feet. Sometimes these light guns were towed to a particular area of London where an attack was taking place and quickly set up to add to the local permanent fire-power.

Apart from guns the defences included balloons and searchlights. The barrage balloons were 63 feet long, silver in colour, and each one trailed a steel cable, the idea being to deter the enemy from making low-level raids. The balloon crews were often WAAFS, that is, members of the Women's Auxiliary Air Force, and the site would often be in a small park or piece of open ground, the winding gear for the cable being mounted on the back of a lorry. On most days the balloons were up at fairly low level, and then, if any German planes approached the coast, they would be flown much higher, often in or above the clouds. I recall one Saturday afternoon — a grey day with thick clouds only a couple of thousands of feet above the ground. We heard an aircraft, but took little notice since the sirens had not sounded, so we assumed it was 'one of ours' until we heard several bursts of machine gun fire. When Dad arrived home he told us that a Jerry had shot down the balloon that was sited in Valentines Park, a couple of miles away. It was unusual for the Germans to sneak through the defences like that, but it did happen. Now and again a balloon would break away from its moorings in a high wind, and the cable would be trailed across the roofs of houses, power lines and factories, often causing considerable damage. Lightning brought down many balloons in flames, in fact 80 were lost during one autumn afternoon in 1939 after they were struck. Needless to say that orders went out to stop them being flown during storms. Although balloons were basically a deterrent, there were cases of enemy aircraft actually hitting the cables and crashing, so they were well worth flying. Our own pilots testified that the German balloons certainly put the wind up them, as the saying goes.

Searchlights were another deterrent, and quite often we saw bombers caught in a cone of their beams, looking like a moth attracted to the light of a candle. They must have been a considerable nuisance to the enemy bomb-aimers as they tried to sight their targets. Very often the lights were used to guide our planes across the night sky.

JACK DYER, 1986

Not explained by Mr Gregson was the fact that Britain had to retain many of the old 3in 20cwt anti-aircraft guns which had first entered service in 1914. By 1939 various marks of fhe weapon on a variety of mountings were to be seen reinforcing the more modern 3.7in batteries.

Harry Gregson: 'Of the lighter guns, the Bofors AA gun is unmistakeable. It sounds like an outsize machine gun — a heavy rat-tat-tat. Another method of identification of the Bofors is its speed of fire. It sends a continuous stream of 40mm two-pounder shells into the air, and when it is in action it usually means that the hostile aircraft are flying low. The Bofors is primarily designed for dealing with low-flying and dive-bombing aircraft. When tracer shells are used with this gun the effect is that of a rocket. The pom-pom gun, also used against low-flying aircraft, has a higher note than the Bofors. "Pom-pom-pom" describes its tone fairly accurately. The Bofors and Pom-Pom guns fire high-explosive shells, and are therefore easily to be distinguished from the Bren gun or the ordinary machine gun, the firing of which is more staccato and without the dual explosion — that is, the explosion in the gun chamber and the explosion in the air.'

Before and after. The Supermarine plant at Woolston, Southampton. We believe the picture on the right was taken on October 1, five days after the raid, although not published in the Luftwaffe's own magazine *Der Adler* until October 29.

TUESDAY, OCTOBER 1

One attack was made by day towards Poole and the Isle of Wight and three attacks in the Kent area. In each case the number of aircraft employed was fewer than of late. Reconnaissance flights and patrols were less active.

1st Attack: During the morning 30 enemy aircraft penetrated 10 to 15 miles inland in Poole-Swanage area, and a raid of 50 aircraft was turned back off Isle of Wight. A single aircraft flew over North Wales, Bristol Channel, Exeter, to St Malo.

2nd Attack: At 1312, 50 aircraft crossed the coast at Dover. Of these, 30 flew to Maidstone and Biggin Hill. No bombs were dropped.

3rd Attack: About 1405, 50 aircraft appeared flying north-west to Biggin Hill, followed by a similar number which quickly turned back. Bombs were dropped at Lyminge and New Romney.

4th Attack: At 1610, 70 enemy aircraft in three waves flew towards Kenley. None penetrated to Central London.

In addition, between 0600 and 1300 some 16 raids by single aircraft and one by 6 aircraft were made in the Thames Estuary and round the coast to Beachy Head. At 0613 one of these flew inland to Croydon and bombed and machine-gunned the town. Some bombs also fell in coastal areas.

Three reconnaissances were made off the Aberdeenshire coast and three over the Moray Firth. One reconnaissance off the Norfolk coast and of a convoy were reported in the afternoon.

Enemy activity by night was of a reduced intensity though bombing was widespread during the earlier part of the night. Later, apart from one raid plotted in the Glasgow area, enemy activity was almost entirely confined to London and the south-eastern counties. Little material damage was done and casualties appear to have been as light as for the last 48 hours.

Widespread damage was done at Manchester between 2130 and 2250, where 40 fires (all extinguished) were started. A surface shelter was hit, 8 of the 9 occupants being killed. In all some 50 casualties were caused, 12 being fatal.

At Birkenhead at 1937, little material damage was done. A shelter was hit and bombs were dropped near the entrance to Mersey Tunnel and near Cammell Lairds, No. 3 Graving Dock. Sixty-two casualties resulted, six of them fatal. Otherwise bombing was almost entirely confined to London, No. 6 Region, chiefly in Surrey, Nos. 4 and 12 Regions.

Approximate casualties in London during daylight amounted to 8 killed and 41 injured, and by night 30 civilians killed and 164 injured. Elsewhere during the day 2 people were slightly injured. At night, however, 29 were killed, together with 114 injured, 99 of them seriously. Enemy aircraft destroyed: 4 certain, 1 probable, 5 damaged.

A heavy raid on Portsmouth and Southampton mid-morning gave prelude to a day of fairly regular attacks by formations of German fighter-bombers. Late in the afternoon, bombs were dropped on South London by high-flying Messerschmitt 109s but caused negligible damage. The Luftwaffe lost 6 aircraft and 2 more damaged on operations, whilst 6 were destroyed in accidents.

4/JG26 Messerschmitt Bf 109E-1. Shot down by Squadron Leader D. O. Finlay and Pilot Officer D. A. Adams of No. 41 Squadron in combat over Sussex 2.30 p.m. Dived vertically from 28,000 feet and exploded on Balmer Down, Falmer. Uffz. H. Bluder killed. Aircraft a write-off.

This aircraft exploded with such violence that little remains of the hapless pilot were ever recovered. He has no known grave.

Site investigated by the Wealden Aviation Archaeological Group in 1973 and surface fragments discovered. Elevator mass balance weight in private hands locally.

1/JG51 Messerschmitt Bf 109E-4 (5814). Shot down by Flying Officer A. D. J. Lovell of No. 41 Squadron during escort sortie over Ashford. Crashed at 'Chequers', Shadoxhurst 4.50 p.m. Uffz. E. Garnith baled out and captured unhurt. Aircraft 9+ a write-off.

Shattered Daimler-Benz DB 601 engine recovered by the Lashenden Air Warfare Museum which presented part to the pilot's widow. Site subsequently investigated by members of the Wealden Aviation Archaeological Group who discovered engine badge, now held by Andy Saunders.

Eager to get a piece for themselves, locals at Limpsfield Common (near Oxted, on the edge of the North Downs) crowd round to pick over the carcase of Oberleutnant Radlick's machine which came down on Wednesday morning. The pilot of the fighter baled out but his parachute failed to open and he smashed into the ground in Hookwood Park.

WEDNESDAY, OCTOBER 2

By day, the enemy made six attacks through Kent towards London using mainly fighters, for although bombing occurred in several of these raids, on only one were bombers (six) identified as taking part.

During the morning three attacks occurred — formations totalling from 20-50 aircraft, and on each occasion the enemy penetrated to the Inner Artillery Zone, but quickly made for home. Bombs were dropped at Woolwich, Camberwell, Beckenham and Lewisham, and on the return journey at Hastings, Margate and Lympne.

During the afternoon attacks about 50 aircraft were used in each attack and a few penetrated to London, bombs being dropped at Camberwell and Aylesford, but it was the south-east coastal towns which received most attention. At Margate, Dover, Hastings, Eastbourne and Worthing damage was confined to house property, and there were only a few casualties.

In each raid our fighter squadrons were sent up to intercept and casualties were inflicted on the enemy with the loss of only one of our own aircraft, of which the pilot is saved.

A single aircraft machine-gunned motor vehicles at Colchester and Nayland, but only slight damage and few casualties resulted.

At Penzance at about 0655 bombs were dropped. The railway station and offices and about 17 houses were damaged. There were few casualties.

Enemy aircraft night activity over Great Britain was on a reduced scale. Bombing was again mainly confined to western districts.

There were two periods of inactivity over London between 2045-2145 and between 0200-0300. It was the quietest since September 7th, the only serious incident being a thirty-pump fire at St Quintins Park, Hammersmith. Railway communications were interfered with on the L.N.E.R. main line near Enfield and at Wembley.

Provincial raids were made on Manchester and on neighbouring towns, but apart from a serious fire at the rubber works, Audenshaw, there was little material damage and few casualties were reported. In Stockport 300 people were evacuated owing to the presence of an unexploded bomb. Minor incidents on a much reduced scale, and mainly confined to the southern and south-eastern counties. A number of heath fires were reported in Hertfordshire and Aldershot districts.

Approximate civilian casualties in London during the day consisted of 15 killed, 31 seriously injured and 46 slightly hurt. At night 7 Londoners were killed and 77 injured, 35 of them seriously. Elsewhere during the day, 2 people were killed, 14 seriously injured and 24 slightly hurt. After dark, there were 11 killed and 35 injured, 9 of these seriously. Ten enemy aircraft were destroyed, together with 1 probable and 2 damaged.

Formations of Messerschmitt 109s, many now carrying 250kg bombs in a Jagdbomber role, sortied over the southern counties at great height throughout the morning and some bitter combats ensued. Attacks on London continued throughout the night. Fourteen German aircraft were lost and 3 damaged on operational sorties, another 4 being damaged accidentally.

1/506 Heinkel He 115C (3266). Sortied to attack merchant shipping in the Firth of Forth but engaged by Hurricanes of No. 145 Squadron. Shot down by Pilot Officer B. M. G. de Hemptinne and forced-landed on the sea 5 miles south-east of Kinnairds Head 7.20 p.m. Oblt. G. Lenz, Uffz. R. Schweetke and Obergefr. H. Neuburg took to their dinghy and picked up unhurt by RN destroyer. Aircraft S4+AH lost.

8/JG53 Messerschmitt Bf 109E-4 (5901). Radiator damaged in attack by Sergeant G. J. Bailey of No. 603 Squadron during bomber escort sortie over north Kent. Crash-landed at Addelsted Farm, East Peckham 10.15 a.m. Oberlt. W. Fiel captured unhurt. Aircraft 7+I a write-off.

8/JG53 Messerschmitt Bf 109E-4 (5374). Shot down by Pilot Officer P. G. Dexter of No. 603 Squadron during combat over southern outskirts of London. Crashed into a house in Sutherland Avenue, Biggin Hill 10.00 a.m. Oberlt. S. Stronk killed. Aircraft 4+I a write-off.

This officer's date of death is incorrectly shown as October 5 in the Soldatenfriedhof, Cannock Chase. No reason for this can be found as Siegfried Stronk died in the crash of his aircraft and his date of death was correctly recorded on his original burial in St Paul's Cray Cemetery.

Radiator held by the Hawkinge Aeronautical Trust. Piece of perspex in the Vizard collection.

8/JG53 Messerschmitt Bf 109E-1 (6370). Badly damaged in combat with No. 603 Squadron Spitfires during bomber escort sortie over South London 10.00 a.m. Forced-landed at Forge Farm, near Goudhurst, Kent. Gefr. H. Zag captured severely wounded. Aircraft 3+I a write-off.

9/JG53 Messerschmitt Bf 109E-1 (6291). Shot down by Pilot Officer J. B. Kendal of No. 66 Squadron and crashed near 'Swallowfields', Limpsfield Common 10.00 a.m. Oberlt. W. Radlick (Staffelkapitän) baled out but fell dead into Hookwood Park due to parachute failure. Aircraft a write-off.

Top of control column found at the crash site by Steve Vizard.

Stab KG2 Dornier Do 17Z (3423). Shot down by Hurricanes of No. 17 Squadron (Flight Lieutenant A. W. A. Bayne, Flying Officer H. P. Blatchford, Pilot Officer J. K. Ross and Pilot Officer L. W. Stevens) following bombing and strafing attack on Colchester, Essex. Forced-landed and burned out at Rookery Farm, Cretingham 10.28 a.m. Oberlt. H. Langer (Staffelkapitän), Oberlt. E. Eitze, Uffz. H. Bellmann and Uffz. R. Seidel captured unhurt. Aircraft U5+FA a write-off.

8/KG4 Junkers Ju 88A-5 (8128). Sortied for a night attack on London but lost bearings due to failure of navigational equipment. Forced to land at West Marsh Point, near Brightlingsea 6.10 a.m. when fuel exhausted. Uffz. H. Maierhofer, Obergefr. G. Hansmeier, Obergefr. R. Preughaus and Obergefr. W. Scholz captured unhurt. Aircraft 5J+US a write-off.

1/KG53 Heinkel He 111H-5 (3554). Port engine disabled by Pilot Officer I. S. Smith of No. 151 Squadron during reconnaissance sortie and forced to ditch in the sea off Chapel St Leonards 6.20 p.m. Oberlt. H. Seidel, Oberfw. V. Weidner, Oberfw. W. Zickler, Oberfw. K. Zinner and Uffz. A. Kreuzer swam ashore and all captured unhurt. Aircraft A1+CH lost.

Both engines recovered September 1967 by the Lincolnshire Aviation Society. One currently held by the Lincolnshire Museum, Tattershall, the other being displayed by Newark Air Museum. Remains of this wreck subsequently blown up by Royal Navy, March 1973.

On Thursday morning Oberleutnant Siegward Fiebig and his crew were detailed to bomb 'Reading' aerodrome — one assumes Woodley, home of the Phillips and Powis (Miles) Company aircraft factory. The Bordfunker, on his first flight over England, was Oberfeldwebel Erich Goebel. They failed to find the target due to bad visibility and, turning eastwards seeking an alternative objective, came upon the de Havilland works adjoining Hatfield aerodrome near St Albans. However the defences were alert and the Junkers was met by machine gun and Bofors fire. Both engines were hit and the aircraft caught fire. The crew managed to leave the burning machine before it was engulfed in flames on Eastend Green Farm at Hertingfordbury in a field used by Jack Barker, left, the racehorse owner/trainer.

THURSDAY, OCTOBER 3

There were no attacks in daylight by formations of enemy aircraft, probably owing to adverse weather conditions, but, especially after midday, there was a fairly continuous succession of raids by single aircraft in various parts of the country. Bombs were dropped in many places, particularly in London and the Midlands. In London damage was confined for the most part to house property and casualties were small. In the Midlands considerable damage was done to the de Havilland Aircraft Factory at Hatfield. Casualties and some damage were caused at Worcester, Banbury and Rushden. No enemy aircraft were brought down by fighters but one was shot down by a light A.A. gun.

Enemy activity by night was on a much reduced scale compared with previous nights. Up to 2100 only eleven raids of single aircraft had entered the country. Between 2130 and 2300, seven aircraft crossed most parts of south-east England and penetrated to London. Between 2300 and 0100 a further 18 aircraft flew to the London area and later three more aircraft visited London and Northolt.

Between 0200 and 0530 no enemy aircraft were over this country, but at 0530 a single aeroplane flew towards Biggin Hill and then turned back, and by 0650 the country was free of raiders.

The only incidents reported from London, apart from minor bombing in a number of boroughs, were at Feltham, where the main hangar of the General Aircraft Works was hit, and at Dagenham, where two factories received minor damage. Casualties were slight. Elsewhere no important damage and only slight casualties were caused.

Civilian casualties in London by day and night amounted to 24 people killed and 74 injured. Elsewhere by day there were 46 killed, 65 seriously injured and 99 people slightly hurt. One enemy aircraft was shot down by A.A. fire.

Bad weather severely limited the scale of activities on this day and sporadic raids over the country featured aircraft operating singly or in pairs. The Luftwaffe in the West lost 9 aircraft and 2 damaged in operations, 2 more being damaged in accidents or routine domestic flights.

3/606 Dornier Do 17Z (3491). Crashed into the sea off Cornwall during sortie to attack St Eval airfield — cause unknown. Lt.zur See M-D. Schmid and Hauptgefr. J. Dorfschmid both killed. Fw. J. Wilms and Uffz. R. Seidenzahl both missing believed killed. Aircraft 7T+EL lost.

The body of the flight-engineer from this aircraft, Josef Dorfschmid, was washed up at Constantine Bay, west of Padstow 2 days later. The body of the observer, Max-Dieter Schmid, came ashore on November 2 and this is incorrectly shown as his date of death in the records at Cannock Chase.

Stab I/KG77 Junkers Ju 88A-1 (4136). Hit by ground-fire during bombing attack on the de Havilland works adjoining Hatfield aerodrome. Crash-landed in flames and burned out on Eastend Green Farm, north of Hertingfordbury 11.40 a.m. Oberlt. S. Fiebig, Oberfw. E. Goebel, Fw. H. Ruthof and Uffz. K. Seifert all captured unhurt. Aircraft 3Z+BB a write-off.

In November 1979 we sought out the crash site. John Mousley (left), during the war a Special Constable in the Hertford Constabulary, took Wilf Nicoll, a post-war Police Constable with the Met., back to the exact spot where he had guarded the aircraft in 1940 before the Army took over. (Since then both John and Wilf have died.)

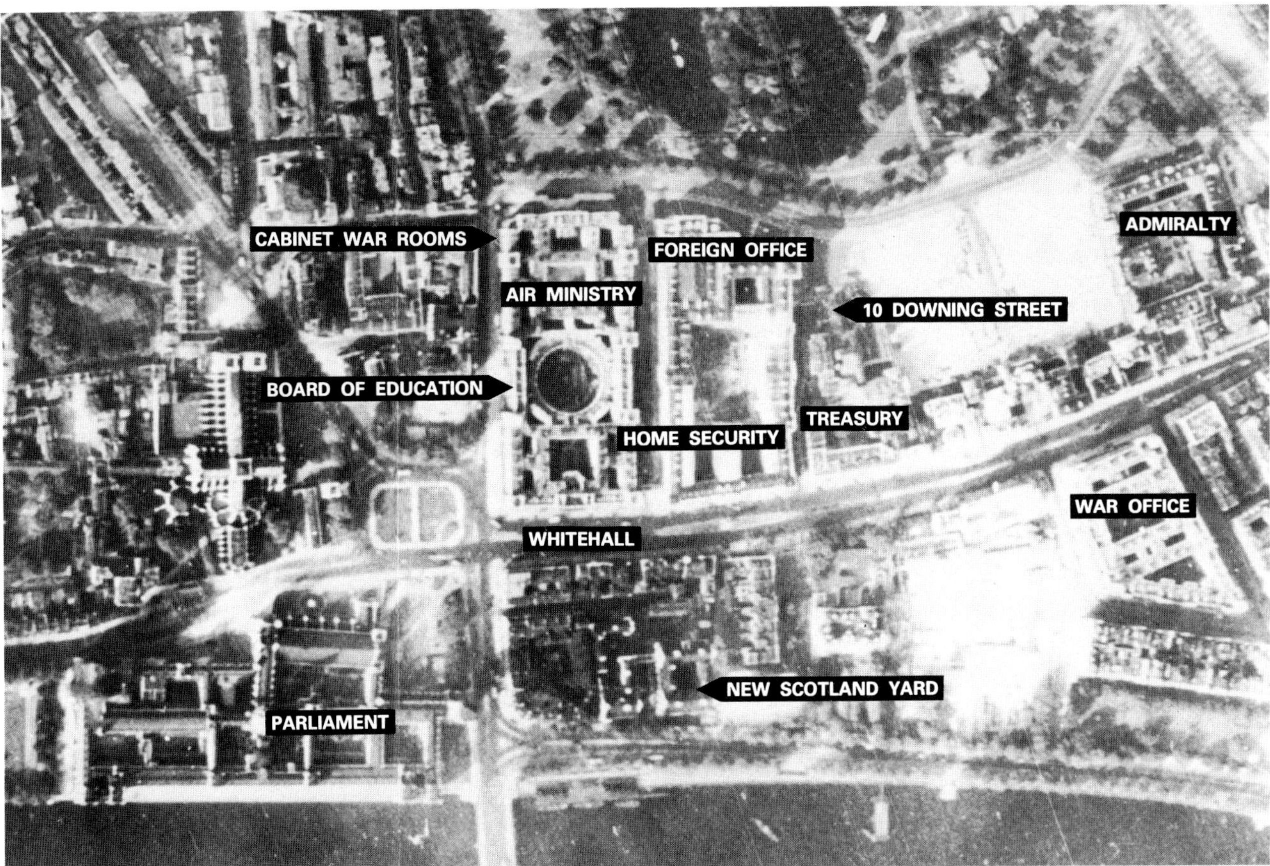

Bombs had already scarred the Houses of Parliament and soon it was to be the turn of No. 10 itself. Long-term plans had already been prepared for the protection of Government departments, the War Cabinet having its own improvised headquarters at Westminster. ***(See Volume 1, page 301.)*** **Although one assumes its position was unknown to German intelligence, nevertheless Whitehall was vulnerable to attack. This picture is dated September 27, 1940 but unfortunately the quality is poor, making it difficult to identify the damage of the previous night's raid. (The annotation is ours.)**

PADDOCK

'Paddock' was the name given to the alternative underground emergency accommodation for the War Cabinet at the pre-war Post Office Research and Development Station at Dollis Hill in north-west London. The area on which the research station was built had been a farm, and the underground centre was situated in a former paddock.

Detailed plans had been drawn up before the war in anticipation of the entire headquarters machinery of Government being moved out of London. These were categorised into 'Black' and 'Yellow' moves: Black for the evacuation of the seat of Government — Cabinet, Parliament, essential staffs, numbering about 16,000 — and Yellow for the less essential staffs of various departments, about 44,000. Instructions for the Yellow move to be put into operation were issued within a few days of the outbreak of war, and the requisitioning of accommodation for the Black move was also carried out — the move itself only to be made when bombing rendered the higher reaches of the Administration unable to function effectively. Under the Yellow move, upwards of 25,000 civil servants, with all their records, belonging to the branches of departments which included the Admiralty (destined for Bath) and the Air Ministry (Harrogate) were sent out of London to the provinces. Private firms were advised to move their premises from London too.

In London and the danger zones the degree of shelter provided for Government offices was at the same level as that recommended for private industry, and took the form of basements recently or in the process of being strengthened, gas-proof refuges and surface shelters. In the Yellow areas it was at a similar level to that already in being, in order both to save resources and avoid creating an acute sense of air raid consciousness in towns where people already felt vulnerable because of the arrival of Government establishments.

During the respite of the Phoney War, in the Black areas work proceeded unobtrusively with the bricking up of buildings and other preventive measures. If the Black move became necessary, the plans drawn up in the late 1930s envisaged it in two stages: first to the London suburbs, where a number of strongholds such as Paddock were built, and then, if necessary, to the West Country. However in January 1939 it was recommended that the move be made in one step — straight to the West Country.

By the outbreak of war, strong though not 'bomb-proof' accommodation had been provided in London for the Central and Air Ministry War Rooms in the New Public Offices and for the Home Security headquarters in the basement of the Home Office. A scheme for a system of underground chambers in Whitehall was turned down by the Government in October 1939 as it would not only have required an enormous amount of steel and cement but might well have taken some two years to complete.

After the fall of France, the Black element of the dispersal plan was abandoned. The consequences for France — for the country's morale and administration — of the French Government's move from Paris to Tours and thence to Bordeaux had been only too clear; also, with the Luftwaffe establishing bases on the Channel coast, the West Country had become equally vulnerable to air attack. If the Government should be driven out of Whitehall by bombing, it would therefore move to its alternative accommodation within the defended area of London. The accommodation earmarked in the West Country henceforth was to be used by military and other staffs not required in London. Official policy regarding private firms was by then to discourage all unnecessary movement.

Under the impact of the bombs, 'the desire and resolve of the Government and of Parliament to remain in London was unmistakable', Churchill wrote in his memoirs, adding, 'and I shared this feeling to the full'. At the onset of the Blitz in September, he made clear in a minute to the Secretary to the Cabinet and his private staff his refusal to contemplate any 'wholesale movement' of civil servants from the capital.

'Anything of this nature', he wrote 'is so detrimental that it could only be forced upon us by Central London becoming practically uninhabitable. Moreover, new resorts of Civil Servants would soon be identified and harassed, and there is more shelter in London than anywhere else. . . . The movement of the high control from the Whitehall area to "Paddock" or other citadels stands on a different footing. We must make sure that the centre of Government functions harmoniously and vigorously. This would not be possible under conditions of almost continuous air raids. A movement to "Paddock" of echelons of the War Cabinet, War Cabinet Secretariat, Chiefs of Staff Committee, and Home Forces GHQ must now be planned, and may even begin in some minor respects. War Cabinet Ministers should visit their quarters in "Paddock" and be ready to move there at short notice. They should be encouraged to sleep there if they want quiet nights. Secrecy cannot be expected, but publicity must be forbidden.'

This minute was dated September 14, and ended with a request for complete 'step by step' proposals to be presented to him by the following evening — Sunday — detailing 'all the necessary measures for moving not more than two or three hundred principal persons and their immediate assistants to the new quarters', in order that he might put them before the Cabinet on Monday.

On Friday, September 20, the Prime Minister paid a brief visit to the site on his way to Chequers, inspecting the underground complex and the quarters assigned to him which he was to use should the need finally arise, and on September 29 he prescribed a dress rehearsal: 'I think it important that "Paddock" be broken in. Thursday next therefore the Cabinet will meet there. At the same time, other departments should be encouraged to try a preliminary move of a skeleton staff. If possible, lunch should be provided for the Cabinet and those attending it.' In his memoirs Churchill described how, that day, 'We held a Cabinet meeting at

In his memoirs published in 1949, Churchill referred to an alternative 'citadel' which had been constructed 'near Hampstead' but gave no further enlightenment as to its precise location. Historians were greatly intrigued but no further information as to its whereabouts was forthcoming from official sources, one presuming it was still earmaked for future use. When in 1970 Peter Laurie brought out his exposé of Regional Seats of Government and the Government's preparations for a nuclear war under the title *Beneath the City Streets*, he speculated that Paddock was on part of the Northern Line Underground at the unfinished North End Station, begun 230 feet below the surface in 1906 but never completed. However, it was Nigel West who stumbled on the truth in 1980 when he found a restricted Cabinet file at the Public Record Office devoted to Cabinet War Rooms 1 and 2. Nigel kept the secret to himself and released it in a television interview publicising his new book *MI5* in October 1981. Its location turned out to be beneath Building 11 on the Post Office Research Station at Dollis Hill in Willesden, Churchill's 'Hampstead', two miles to the east, being somewhat of a red herring.

Fortunately we did not have to face the problem of getting official permission to visit a secret bunker to take photographs as the whole site had been evacuated by the Post Office in September 1976 and was in the hands of a property company, Evans of Leeds Ltd. When we approached them they readily granted us access as the Cabinet War Rooms 2 had not yet been let. *Above:* At ground level just a typical public service-type of building backing onto Brook Road, still with faint traces of wartime camouflage paint remaining on the brickwork of the ventilation shaft.

Left: **It was obvious that the ground floor had been in use by the Post Office right up to 1976. From this level a door opened onto a staircase leading down to the basement and sub-basement which covered a total floor area of over 15,000 square feet.** *Right:* **The corridor at the lowest level was flooded with an inch or two of water.**

"Paddock" far from the light of day, and each Minister was requested to inspect and satisfy himself about his sleeping and working apartments. We celebrated this occasion by a vivacious luncheon, and then returned to Whitehall.'

The Prime Minister's verdict on Paddock was pronounced in a minute to the Secretary to the Cabinet on October 22 in which he raised the subject of the long-term plans to be made for safely housing the Central Government machine. 'The accommodation at "Paddock" is quite unsuited to the conditions which have arisen', Churchill minuted Sir Edward Bridges. 'The War Cabinet cannot live and work there for weeks on end, while leaving the great part of their staffs less well provided for than they are now in Whitehall. Apart from the citadel of "Paddock", there is no adequate accommodation or shelter, and anyone living in Neville Court [part of the Dollis Hill complex] would have to be running to and fro on every Jim Crow warning. "Paddock" should be treated as a last resort, and in the meantime should be used by some department not needed in the very centre of London.'

Churchill thought it likely that 'the bombing of Whitehall and the centre of Government will be continuous until all old or insecure buildings have been demolished', and he therefore urged that accommodation be provided as soon as possible for large nucleus staffs and Ministers in the strongest buildings

The nerve centre. With observation panels from what we assumed was Churchill's own office at the far end and that of the controllers on the left, this would have been the room from where the final last ditch defence of England would have been conducted should the invasion have taken place. Here the War Cabinet met for the first and only time on October 3.

The bunker was virtually gutted of any original wartime fittings, save for the rusting air ducting . . . and this directional indicator which could be illuminated, one presumes, to show the direction of an attack.

in existence or that were capable of being fortified. He quoted the example of the Treasury in Whitehall as one of the older Government buildings, nearly all of which were 'either wholly unsafe or incapable of resisting a direct hit'. 'We must press on', he said, with the work he had authorised for strengthening overhead cover at the War Room [Great George Street] and Central War Room offices, and that of the Home Forces located in the Board of Trade Building. Strong modern buildings ought to be taken over for the War Cabinet and its secretariat, and he proposed to ask on the 24th for an adjournment of the House of Commons for two weeks, during which time plans could be made to meet elsewhere.

To supervise matters on the Cabinet's behalf Churchill appointed Lord Beaverbrook, and work began on the construction of a number of 'bomb-proof' strongholds to serve as the offices of essential staffs of several Government departments. Examples survive today, in New Oxford Street and on the Embankment, their drab, bleak, utilitarian designs erected with little time to worry about how they might look after the war.

In 1982 I paid a visit to the site in north-east London, now in the Dollis Hill Industrial Estate. Paddock itself sits rather close to the boundary of the old research centre, on the western side parallel to Brook Road. From the exterior the building above ground appears as a typical wartime structure (although built before the war), with part of it used today as a gatehouse, partially demolished so that a second entrance to the estate could be constructed. The actual underground complex, being so deep below ground, has not been altered structurally. It covers an area of some 15,200 feet spread over two levels. Because signs or any form of notices were few and far between, it proved difficult to find one's way around, and the whole place presented itself simply as a maze of corridors and rooms, large and small, giving no clue as to their wartime function. One room, however, on the very lowest level, appeared to be the main operations room and nerve centre. On one wall was fixed a vertical, prism-shaped, lighted panel which, when illuminated, indicated from which direction the enemy bombers were approaching. Churchill, from his bedroom, adjacent, could see via a glass window this panel and everything taking place in the room at any time he wished without leaving his study.

One long, unbroken corridor passes the room, and many others which were more than likely the Ministerial quarters mentioned by Churchill. At either end are emergency staircases, and at the far end a large generator room whose machinery would have provided an independent power source for the entire complex. It is still in working order.

An empty and mysterious place to visit, it nonetheless takes little imagination to visualise how as a Whitehall nerve centre it might have hummed into life if the conduct of Government had been forced underground by a combination of wholesale bombing and/or invasion.

ANDREW P. HYDE, 1986

The fifty rooms at Paddock could only accommodate the nucleus of the War Cabinet and its Secretariat; the Chiefs of Staff and the GHQ of Home Forces. Alternative arrangements had been made for the War Office to go to Kneller Hall at Twickenham; the Air Ministry to the Stationery Office Annexe at Harrow, and the Admiralty to Cricklewood — all in the north-west London area. Home Security would remain in the centre but transfer to Cornwall House in Stamford Street. Other parts of Dollis Hill had equally historic rôles. This is the building which housed the so-called windowless room where the 'Colossus' computer was constructed which played such an important part later in the war in assisting in the decoding of German Enigma-coded messages: the whole operation — the Ultra secret — only being revealed in 1974.

FRIDAY, OCTOBER 4

Throughout the day activity was confined to raids by single aircraft or very small formations, the areas concerned being south-eastern England and London.

Between 1000-1100 two raids flew to the Bristol Channel area and to Liverpool respectively, but no bombing is reported as a result. Otherwise activity by day was confined to reconnaissances of shipping and of convoys and to minor bombing in East Anglia, Kent and Sussex.

The weather over England was overcast and at times a stream of single aircraft were employing the same tactics as at night, namely flying behind the clouds and dropping occasional bombs. London was under red warning for five hours by day, but very little material damage was done except to house property.

The enemy attacked, but failed to hit, the petroleum refineries at Shellhaven and Corringham — otherwise there is nothing to indicate that he was attacking targets of national importance.

By night, from 1940 onwards the enemy directed single aircraft on London — they came in at very short intervals and it is estimated that by 0130 about 270 aircraft had been employed, of which approximately 175 reached London. There was a lull between 0120 and 0210, and thereafter about 20 aircraft flew over London.

Bombing was widespread but mainly in the outer suburbs and serious damage was done at Willesden Power Station — otherwise damage was mainly confined to private property.

Elsewhere there was scarcely any activity outside Essex, Kent, Surrey and Sussex, and the only damage of note was to the L.N.E.R. railway station at Brentwood where the main line was blocked.

Civilian casualties (approx.). London: By day and night: 60 killed and 200 injured. Elsewhere during the day 9 people were killed, 45 seriously injured, and 41 slightly injured. Enemy aircraft casualties: destroyed 3, probable 3.

Approximate civilian casualties outside London: 7 killed, 13 seriously injured, and 15 slightly injured.

Indifferent weather conditions continued to hamper German attacks throughout the day. British efforts to counter the new German tactic of high-flying formations of Messerschmitt Jabos included fresh instructions to Squadron Commanders and Sector Controllers and the deployment of special 'spotter' flights to report the 'make-up' of incoming raids. The Luftwaffe lost 15 aircraft on operations whilst 5 more returned damaged. Two more were damaged and another lost in accidents.

II/KG1 Heinkel He 111H-2 (5586). Believed hit by AA fire during sortie to bomb rail junctions at Camden Town, London. Crashed at Mountfield, near Battle, Sussex 10.00 p.m. Uffz. E. Hildebrandt, Uffz. H. Bauer and Gefr. W. Tschöp killed. Gefr. F. Zuckriegel baled out and captured unhurt. Aircraft V4+FW a write-off.

Relics from this machine held by the Robertsbridge Aviation Society Museum.

3/KG26 Heinkel He 111H-3 (5609).Crashed into the North Sea during sortie over the east coast of England. Cause unknown. Lt. H-H. Zingel, Uffz. F. Winter, Uffz. W. Reinelt and Uffz. K. Blasius killed. Aircraft 1H+EL lost.

The bodies of Kurt Blasius, Fritz Winter and Hans-Hugo Zingel were recovered from the sea off Hollesley Bay on October 30, the crew's original burial at Ipswich cemetery incorrectly recording this as their dates of death. Now reinterred in the Soldatenfriedhof at Cannock Chase, only Lt. Zingel's grave shows the correct date of death — October 4.

6/KG76 Junkers Ju 88A-1 (6156). Hit by AA fire and set alight during bombing sortie over London. Dived vertically into the ground and exploded at Meesons Lane, Belmont Castle, Grays, Essex 4.50 p.m. Oberlt. J. Holzer, Fw. R. Kolb, Uffz. H. Deiseroth and Gefr. J. Graf killed. Aircraft F1+LP a write-off.

The dates of death of both the pilot of this aircraft, Johann Holzer, and the observer, Rudolf Kolb, are incorrectly

Of all the battle scars received by the Tower down the centuries, those in the Battle of London had the most lasting effect. Several times during the war bombs came close but on October 5 a direct hit on the North Bastion killed Yeoman Warder Sam Reeves.

The destruction of the Victorian stonework uncovered the much older line of the curtain wall which was subsequently rebuilt instead of the bastion, completely altering the aspect on the northern side. Behind the Tower can be seen the Tower Hotel constructed in the same style as the warehouses of St Katherine Docks (see pages 61 and 81) on which it stands.

Fritz von Herwarth-Bittenfeld of 1/JG3 wheels over the Channel in his 109E homeward bound. His war ended just after midday on Saturday when his aircraft was set alight near Ashford.

recorded in the records of the Soldatenfriedhof Cannock Chase as October 5. The reason for this is not known as none of the crew are believed to have survived the crash of the aircraft.

Site investigated by the Essex Historical Aircraft Society who recovered remains of shattered airframe, engine plate and a small pen knife.

3/KG77 Junkers Ju 88A-1 (3160). Shot down into the sea off Southwold 10.10 a.m. by Squadron Leader R. R. S. Tuck of No. 257 Squadron during operational sortie to London. Uffz. W. Herold reported killed. Stabfw. E. Hartmann, Obergefr. H. Hackmann and Gefr. A. Simbrick missing believed killed. Aircraft 3Z+HL lost.

Complete starboard undercarriage assembly and fully inflated tyre recovered from the beach at Easton Bavents just north of Southwold by the Norfolk and Suffolk Aviation Museum.

6/LG1 Junkers Ju 88A-1 (6116). Believed shot down into the Channel off Dungeness 12.15 p.m. by Pilot Officer C. F. Currant and Pilot Officer J. A. Milne of No. 605 Squadron. Gefr. P. Schöffmann killed. Uffz H. Kirchenbaur, Uffz E. Kroos and Gefr. W. Jahn all missing believed killed. Aircraft L1+EP lost.

The body of the gunner from this aircraft, Peter Schöffmann, was washed ashore at Dover on November 18.

SATURDAY, OCTOBER 5

There were four attacks by day in the South-East and two in the Portsmouth, Southampton area.

East Kent:

First attack. At 0930, a small-scale attack by 30 Me 109s was made on Dover, interception was effected at Maidstone.

Second attack. At 1045, 150 enemy aircraft crossed the coast at Lympne and spread fanwise through Kent — a formation of 100 enemy fighters flew towards London, but only some 10 penetrated the Inner Artillery Zone.

Third attack. At 1345, 120 enemy aircraft flew inland between Eastbourne and Folkestone. Of these, 70 aircraft continued towards London, 50 penetrated the Inner Artillery Zone; the remaining 20 got no further than South London.

Fourth attack. At 1545, 20 aircraft crossed the coast at Hastings and flew towards Kenley. At the same time 20 more enemy aircraft crossed at Dungeness flying towards Biggin Hill.

Until 1630 hours strong patrols were maintained in the Straits.

Portsmouth and Southampton:

First attack. At 1345 a raid of 30 enemy aircraft flew to Southampton via the Needles. This raid penetrated some 25 miles inland. At the same time about 50 enemy aircraft crossed the coast at Swanage and flew over Poole and Weymouth, some of them penetrated 30 miles inland before they returned.

Second attack. At 1715, 50 enemy aircraft crossed the Isle of Wight and flew inland covering Portsmouth, Southampton and Tangmere; these had turned south by 1730 hours.

By night, enemy activity was considerable and was concentrated mainly on London.

Between 1900 and 2100, some 40 enemy aircraft crossed our coast. During this period practically all concentrated on London.

Between 2100 and 2300, 48 enemy aircraft were plotted — some 17 from the Dutch coast and the remainder from France, the main objective being London — but raids were also widespread in Essex and Cambridgeshire. Two aircraft were plotted over Liverpool, and minelaying was suspected in the Thames Estuary, the Humber and off Flamborough Head.

Between 2300 and 0100, 36 additional aircraft crossed the coast, the majority headed for London, although Cambridge and Norfolk were also widely covered. Seventeen of these raids came from the Dutch coast and the remainder from the usual French sources.

Between 0100 and 0600, activity continued on a similar scale to 0130, but had lessened by 0200, only 6 enemy aircraft then being plotted over England. At 0245, about 20 enemy aircraft were operating almost entirely in the London area; single raiders, however, visited Oxford, Northampton, and Leicester areas. Activity then ceased, but resumed at 0350 on a small scale in south-east England. At 0555 the last enemy aircraft was reported going south of London and no fresh raids were approaching. The whole country was clear at 0602.

Civilian casualties in London by day amounted to 20 people killed and 134 injured, 57 of them seriously. By night the casualties amounted to 25 killed and 85 seriously injured, together with 110 minor casualties. Elsewhere by day, 20 people were killed and 64 injured, 22 of these seriously. By night, one person was killed, 9 seriously injured and 7 slightly hurt. Enemy aircraft casualties amounted to 23 destroyed, 5 probably destroyed and 16 damaged.

A slight improvement in the weather gave the Luftwaffe an opportunity to launch strong attacks on a variety of targets during the day. London and the airfields guarding its southern approaches were raided in the morning, whilst Southampton drew a sharp attack during the afternoon. Thirteen German aircraft were lost and 9 damaged on operations, 2 more being destroyed and another damaged as a result of accidents.

October 5, 1940
10th Operational Flight
18.33 hours

Five planes were taking part in a sundown attack. Naturally without fighter cover, and once again on Yeovil — that nest of enemy fighters. When we were above the cloudless coast of England, our Hauptmann told us that we would reach our target while it was still light and that we might find things correspondingly tricky. 'If fighters come', he said, 'keep firing hard at them . . . Any questions?' None of us had any, so that was it. If the Tommys were on their toes, woe betide us. But in fact they weren't. It then turned misty. We were still flying in close formation, and glided steeply down to 2800 metres as at 2500 metres there were the barrage balloons. We circled around above the countryside but couldn't find our target, although to our despair we could still identify everything else. In the gathering darkness we went on circling round for a long time without being able to locate the airfield of our persistent enemy.

So we flew on to Portland and dropped our bombs on the harbour, which was clearly visible. Searchlights and Flak were looking for us much higher up, so we were able to return home without any problems.

In the west we saw a huge arc of fire, although it was already night. It was the sun which had just set. Somebody began to sing:

'Wild geese are rushing through the night
with shrill cries they fly northwards.
Their journey is unsteady, take care,
Take care . . . '

ROBERT GÖTZ

In death all men — and women — are equal. At Folkestone New Cemetery, on the edge of Hawkinge aerodrome, former adversaries lie side by side where they were buried in 1940. Here Duensing and Krappatsch were taken, killed on October 5 . . .

1/ErproGr210 Messerschmitt Bf 110D-3 (3383). Shot down in combat by Sergeant A. Siudak of No. 303 Squadron during sortie to attack Beckton gasworks. Probably also attacked by Squadron Leader H. A. V. Hogan of No. 501 Squadron. Dived vertically into the ground and exploded at the Industrial School, Millbank Place, south of Ashford 11.30 a.m. Fw. F. Duensing and Fw. H. Krappatsch both killed. Aircraft S9+GH a write-off.

This crew was buried at Folkestone New Cemetery, Hawkinge and have not been reinterred at Cannock Chase.

1/JG3 Messerschmitt Bf 109E-1 (4865). Abandoned when petrol tank set alight in combat over Ashford 12.30 p.m. Crashed and burned out at Runsell Farm, Bethersden. Probably that attacked by Sergeant S. Karubin of No. 303 Squadron. Fw. F. von Herwarth-Bittenfeld wounded, baled out and captured badly burned. Aircraft 2+ a write-off.

Tailwheel, taken at the time of the crash, now in the Vizard Collection.

1/JG53 Messerschmitt Bf 109E-4 (1564). Crashed and burned out at Sheerlands Farm, Pluckley following combat with fighters 11.40 a.m. Possibly that attacked by Flight Lieutenant G. R. McGregor of No. 1 (RCAF) Squadron. Lt. A. Zeis baled out and captured unhurt. Aircraft 3+ a write-off.

1/JG53 Messerschmitt Bf 109E-4 (1804). Shot down by Sergeant J. Palak of No. 303 Squadron during free-lance fighter sweep over Kent 11.45 a.m. Forced-landed close to Frith Farm, near Aldington. Uffz. W. Gehsla captured unhurt. Aircraft 10+ a write-off.

6/LG2 Messerschmitt Bf 109E-4 (3726). Engine damaged by fighter attack during a free-lance sortie over southern England. Possibly that engaged by Flying Officer B. J. G. Carbury and Sergeant A. S. Darling of No. 603 Squadron. Forced-landed near Pelsham Farm, Peasmarsh, Sussex 11.30 a.m. Fw. E. Pankratz captured wounded. Aircraft I▲+M a write-off.

ESSEX Dagenham M.B.

HOPKINS, Harry, age 26; of 145 Grafton Road. Husband of Rosina Marjorie Hopkins. 29 September 1940, at 145 Grafton Road.

HOPKINS, Rosina Marjorie, age 24; of 145 Grafton Road. Daughter of James Frederick Shipp, of 73 Marvels Lane, Grove Park, London, and of the late Julia Sarah Shipp; wife of Harry Hopkins. 29 September 1940, at 145 Grafton Road.

HORWILL, Allen Keith, age 2 months; of 30 Stockdale Gardens. Son of P.O. Sidney Ernest Horwill, R.N., and Annie M. Horwill. 1 August 1944, at 30 Stockdale Gardens.

HOY, Catherine Margaret, age 23; of 7 Cartwright Road. Daughter of Harry and Kathleen Hoy. Injured 19 September 1940, at 7 Cartwright Road; died 22 September 1940, at Isolation Hospital.

HUDSON-PARKER, George Leonard, age 24; of 183 Osborne Square. Husband of Kathleen Florence Hudson-Parker. 11 November 1944, at 183 Osborn Square.

HUDSON-PARKER, Kathleen Florence, age 23; of 183 Osborne Square. Daughter of Louisa Inwood; wife of George Leonard Hudson-Parker. 11 November 1944, at 183 Osborne Square.

HUDSON - PARKER, Patricia Jean Margaret, age 20 months; of 183 Osborne Square. Daughter of George Leonard and Kathleen Florence Hudson-Parker. 11 November 1944, at 183 Osborne Square.

JACKS, Elizabeth, age 46; of 96 Auriel Avenue. Wife of John Joseph Jacks. Injured 12 November 1940, at 96 Auriel Avenue; died 13 November 1940, at Isolation Hospital.

JACKS, John Joseph, age 46; of 96 Auriel Avenue. Husband of Elizabeth Jacks. 12 November 1940, at 96 Auriel Avenue.

JOHNSON, Edward, age 44; of Margaret, South Street, Rainham. 16 October 1940, at Ford Works.

JONES, Elizabeth Ann, age 3; of 5 Woodlands Avenue. Daughter of Patience Mary Jones, and of the late L/Cpl. Charles Thomas Jones, Royal Corps of Signals. 7 January 1945, at 5 Woodlands Avenue.

JONES, Patience Mary, age 31; of 5 Woodlands Avenue. Daughter of John Owen George and of the late E. E. George; widow of L/Cpl. Charles Thomas Jones, Royal Corps of Signals. 7 January 1945, at 5 Woodlands Avenue.

KELLY, Denis George, age 35; of 85 Sisley Road, Barking. Husband of Charlotte E. Kelly. 15 October 1940, at Vicarage Road.

KIFF, Frederick William, age 38; Air Raid Warden; of 6 Margery Road. Husband of Lily Kiff. 28 December 1939, at Warden's Post, Junction of Neville Road and Seabrook Road.

LAMB, Alice Louisa, age 69; of 62 Loddiges Road, Mare Street, Hackney, London. Daughter of Louis William and Jane Briault, of 29 Northampton Street, Islington, London; wife of William Lamb. 5 October 1940, at 46 Windsor Road.

LAMB, William, age 71; of 62 Loddiges Road, Mare Street, Hackney, London. Son of James and Elizabeth Lamb, of 9 Queen Street, Bethnal Green, London; husband of Alice Louisa Lamb. 5 October 1940, at 46 Windsor Road.

LEADER, Beatrice May, age 51; of 3 Woodlands Avenue. Wife of George Alfred Leader. 7 January 1945, at 3 Woodlands Avenue.

LEADER, George Alfred, age 50; of 3 Woodlands Avenue. Husband of Beatrice May Leader. 7 January 1945, at 3 Woodlands Avenue.

LEGON, William Frederick, age 48; Firewatcher. Husband of E. M. Legon, of 58 Halbutt Street. Injured 20 February 1944, at Halbutt Street; died 19 March 1944, at Rush Green Emergency Hospital.

LENNOX, Elizabeth Grace, age 35; of 31 Gordon Road. Daughter of Harry Samuel Freestone, of 22 Studley Road, Forest Gate; wife of Sidney Albert Lennox. 22 September 1940, at 31 Gordon Road.

LENNOX, Kenneth Arthur, age 9; of 31 Gordon Road. Son of Sidney Albert and Elizabeth Grace Lennox. 22 September 1940, at 31 Gordon Road.

LENNOX, Sidney Albert, age 45; of 31 Gordon Road. Son of Margaret Lennox, of 24 Studley Road, Forest Gate; husband of Elizabeth Grace Lennox. 22 September 1940, at 31 Gordon Road.

LODGE, Louise, age 55; of 12 Vicarage Road. Widow of T. Lodge. 15 October 1940, at 12 Vicarage Road.

MACEY, John Henry, age 26. Son of John Henry and Margaret Macey, of 73 Giraud Street, Poplar, London. 5 October 1940, at 3 Halbutt Gardens.

MANN, Annie, age 32; of 38 Godbold Road, West Ham. Daughter of John and Elizabeth Mann. 5 October 1940, at 232 Halbutt Street.

MANN, Charles, age 6; of 232 Halbutt Street. Son of Manfred John and Elizabeth Mann. 5 October 1940, at 232 Halbutt Street.

MANN, Elizabeth, age 54; of 38 Godbold Road, West Ham. Wife of John Mann. 5 October 1940, at 232 Halbutt Street.

MANN, Elizabeth, age 34; of 232 Halbutt Street. Daughter of William Bradley, of St. Angus Road, Barking; wife of Manfred John Mann. 5 October 1940, at 232 Halbutt Street.

MANN, Florence, age 29; of 38 Godbold Road, West Ham. Wife of George Mann. 5 October 1940, at 232 Halbutt Street.

MANN, George, age 28; of 38 Godbold Road, West Ham. Son of John and Elizabeth Mann; husband of Florence Mann. 5 October 1940, at 232 Halbutt Street.

MANN, Iris, age 4; of 38 Godbold Road, West Ham. Daughter of George and Florence Mann. 5 October 1940, at 232 Halbutt Street.

MANN, John, age 58; of 38 Godbold Road, West Ham. Husband of Elizabeth Mann. 5 October 1940, at 232 Halbutt Street.

MANN, Joyce, age 18 months; of 232 Halbutt Street. Daughter of Manfred John and Elizabeth Mann. 5 October 1940, at 232 Halbutt Street.

MANN, Manfred John, age 34; of 232 Halbutt Street. Son of John and Elizabeth Mann; husband of Elizabeth Mann. 5 October 1940, at 232 Halbutt Street.

MARTIN, Alfred James, age 52; of 2 Victoria Cottages, New Road. Son of Susan Martin, of 18 New Road; husband of A. E. Martin. 23 January 1945, at 2 Victoria Cottages, New Road.

MARTIN, Arthur Harold, age 42; of 402 Whalebone Lane. Son of Albert Henry and Hannah Martin. 3 August 1944, at 402 Whalebone Lane.

MARTIN, Elizabeth Alice, age 24; of 52 Windsor Road. Wife of Henry Charles Martin. 5 October 1940, at 52 Windsor Road.

MARTIN, Henry Charles, age 35; of 52 Windsor Road. Husband of Elizabeth Alice Martin. 5 October 1940, at 52 Windsor Road.

MARTIN, Ronald, age 3 months; of 52 Windsor Road. Son of Henry Charles and Elizabeth Alice Martin. 5 October 1940, at 52 Windsor Road.

MARTIN, Sylvia, age 3; of 52 Windsor Road. Daughter of Henry Charles and Elizabeth Alice Martin. 5 October 1940, at 52 Windsor Road.

MATHER, Jeanette, age 7. 23 January 1945, at 7 Victoria Cottages, New Road.

MITCHELL, Lily Dorothy, age 19; of 111 Crescent Road. Daughter of Mr. F. R. Plummer, of 10 Wells Gardens; wife of Horace Mitchell. 27 December 1940, at 111 Crescent Road.

MOLLENHOFF, Ernest, age 29; of 219 Hunters Square. Son of Mr. and Mrs. A. Mollenhoff, of 165 Litchfield Road; husband of Ethel Emily Mollenhoff. 29 September 1940, at 145 Grafton Road.

MOLLENHOFF, Ethel Emily, age 28; of 219 Hunters Square. Daughter of James Frederick and Julia Sarah Shipp, of 73 Marvels Lane, Grove Park, London; wife of Ernest Mollenhoff. 29 September 1940, at 145 Grafton Road.

MORGAN, Margaret Rosina, age 27; of 45 Adelaide Gardens. Daughter of Mrs. M. Gondge, of 68 Belle Vue Road, Southchurch, Southend-on-Sea; wife of Edward George Ernest Morgan. 27 December 1940, at 45 Adelaide Gardens.

MOY, Alfred, age 40; of 83 East Road. Son of Mr. G. Moy, of 3 Lynne Road, Swaffham, Norfolk, and of the late P. Moy; husband of M. E. Moy. 31 August 1944, at 83 East Road.

MURPHY, Walter Francis, age 42; of 13 Aldborough Road. 9 December 1940, at 13 Aldborough Road.

NEALL, Carlotta, age 33; of 59 Oglethorpe Road. Daughter of Mrs. H. S. Blackman, of 65 Sherwood Gardens, Orpington, Kent; wife of James Alexander Neall. 2 October 1940, at 117 Connor Road.

NEALL, James Alexander, age 36; A.R.P. Rescue Service; of 59 Oglethorpe Road. Son of Mr. J. Neall, of 6 Stanhope Gardens; husband of Carlotta Neall. 2 October 1940, at 117 Connor Road.

NEWTON, Lilian Florence Mary, age 32; of 133 Valence Wood Road. Widow of George Richard Newton. Injured 29 January 1944, at 133 Valence Wood Road; died 2 February 1944, at Rush Green Emergency Hospital.

NEWTON, Peter James, age 3; of 133 Valence Wood Road. Son of Lilian Florence Mary and of the late George Richard Newton. Injured 29 January 1944, at 133 Valence Wood Road; died 30 January 1944, at Rush Green Emergency Hospital.

NICHOLSON, Edwin Charles, age 43; of 531 Becontree Avenue. Husband of Florence W. E. Nicholson. 19 April 1941, at 531 Becontree Avenue.

NICHOLSON, Edwin George, age 6; of 531 Becontree Avenue. Son of Florence W. E. Nicholson, and of Edwin Charles Nicholson. 19 April 1941, at 531 Becontree Avenue.

NICHOLSON, Nellie Shirley Rita, age 4; of 531 Becontree Avenue. Daughter of Florence W. E. Nicholson, and of Edwin Charles Nicholson. 19 April 1941, at 531 Becontree Avenue.

ONSLOW, Henry Edward William Bosanquet, age 34; of 122 Chittys Lane. 15 September 1940, at Isolation Hospital.

PURKISS, Eliza Catherine, age 77; of 112 Auriel Avenue. Wife of William Henry Purkiss. 20 March 1941, at 112 Auriel Avenue.

ESSEX Dagenham M.B.

. . . the same day that the Mann family was wiped out at Dagenham. The pages of the Civilian War Dead Roll tell an unending story of pain and suffering, as wives were parted from husbands, parents from their children: John and Elizabeth Mann from West Ham with their daughter Annie, son George and his wife Florence killed while at Manfred's — their other son's house in Halbutt Street, Dagenham — together with their daughter-in-law Elizabeth, and their grandchildren Charlie, aged 6, Iris, 4, and little Joyce just 18 months. Just one family . . .in one street . . . in one town . . . on one day . . .

'Our fighter boys.' ***Above:*** **This is Northolt in October 1940 with the Hurricanes of No. 615 Squadron at dispersal. The Battle of Britain has nearly reached its victorious finale — thanks to the untiring efforts of the 3,000 men who were to go down in history as 'The Few'. Of their number over 500 were to lose their lives by the battle's end.**

SUNDAY, OCTOBER 6

Generally, operations by day and night have been on a small scale and generally carried out by single aircraft. The outstanding feature of the period is that the total number of fires reported within the London Region amount to seven small fires, all of which are extinguished.

Three threatened daylight attacks in force over the Channel did not materialise. There were two raids over a convoy off the East Coast between 1330-1430, and enemy aircraft which flew inland dropped bombs at Framlingham, where the damage was not serious, but a number of houses were damaged. There was slight damage to property at Felixstowe, Wickham Market and Harwich from machine-gunning. Dive-bombing is reported at Northolt aerodrome where hangars and three aeroplanes were damaged. There were some casualties.

The raids during the morning were directed particularly against the Dover-Deal area, and bombs were dropped at Folkestone, Hythe, Bexhill, Eastbourne, Deal and Ashford. In addition, incidents are reported from Southampton, Fareham, Middle Wallop and Woodley. There was little major damage. Several houses were demolished at Folkestone and the casualties amounted to 5 killed, 6 seriously wounded and 21 slightly

And there were the indispensable ground crews. Looking at this picture (taken at Northolt just before the war) it's no wonder airmen were dubbed Brylcreem boys! One is intrigued to know just what the confident type is trying on the blonde job with that ingratiating smile — or is it a leer?

Not much to laugh about at Northolt on October 6 when a lone Ju 88 did this with two bombs from 200 feet. Sergeant Siudak, who was taxying the Hurricane, and AC2 Stennett, acting as lookout on the hangar roof, were both killed.

hurt. Unexploded bombs are reported at Phillips and Powis Aircraft Ltd, Woodley; Vauxhall Motor Works, Luton, and R.A.F. aerodrome, Middle Wallop.

In the afternoon there was slight damage to Hawker Works, Langley, Friern Hospital, Friern Barnet, and up line traffic was suspended between Hinchley Wood and Surbiton.

Both London and the provinces had a very quiet night and there was no major damage. Between Hatfield and Welwyn Garden City four lines of the main line to York were blocked by debris caused by H.E. on the embankment. This blockage will be quickly cleared. At 0515 raids in the direction of Debden, Blackwater and Brighton were reported and these were still in progress at 0600 hours.

Civilian casualties in London by day amounted to 13 killed and 38 injured. Elsewhere during the day, 10 people were killed, 33 seriously injured and 25 slightly hurt. There were no casualties at night. Enemy aircraft casualties are 1 destroyed and 1 damaged.

Dismal weather throughout the day prevented any significant attacks from developing. Single aircraft sortied to raid airfields with some success. Seven German aircraft were lost and 4 more damaged on operations, another 2 being lost and 1 more damaged in accidents.

4/KG30 Junkers Ju 88A-5 (8045). Crashed in flames and exploded at Netherstead, near Colmworth 0.55 a.m. during night sortie over England. Exact cause unknown. Oberfw. G. Wilkening, Fw. G. Koschella, Uffz. H. Thal and Uffz. A. Bednarek killed. Aircraft 4D+HM a write-off.

Major recovery by the London Air Museum. Both Junkers Jumo engines excavated together with undercarriage legs and tyres, large section of compressed airframe, eight oxygen bottles, one parachute and a first-aid kit. Bulk of remains now in the Tangmere Military Aviation Museum. First-aid kit now in the After the Battle collection. Site re-excavated by Brian Sadler, September 1986. Several interesting relics including maker's labels and parachute 'D' ring discovered.

7/KG76 Dornier Do 17Z-3 (4221). Shot down by Red Section of No. 253 Squadron (Flight Lieutenant R. M. B. D. Duke-Woolley and Flying Officer L. C. Murch) during armed reconnaissance sortie over southern England. Collided with a tree during crash-landing at Snape Wood Reservoir, near Wadhurst, Sussex 11.05 a.m. and later exploded. Uffz. H. Wagner killed. Lt. F. Morr, Fw. R. Pohl and Uffz. F. Mroszinsky all captured wounded. Aircraft F1+FR a write-off.

Fragments in Robertsbridge Aviation Society Museum.

MONDAY, OCTOBER 7

The improvement in weather conditions by day led, as was to be expected, to greatly increased enemy activity, in spite of which comparatively few bombs were dropped. There were five main raids during daylight:

0920 — Ten enemy raids totalling 120 aircraft crossed the south-east coast and penetrated to Gravesend and East London. The proportion of fighters to bombers is reported to have been 3:1.

1250 — 130+ enemy aircraft crossed the coast between North Foreland and Beachy Head, penetrating to Biggin Hill, South and South-East London.

1520 — 50+ crossed the coast at St Alban's Head, penetrating to Yeovil.

1530 — 50+ crossing at Romney penetrated again to Biggin Hill and East London.

The obscene violence of death in battle. This is all that was left after a 10-ton German bomber smashed into the ground and exploded at Netherstead Farm, Colmworth, Bedfordshire, on the night of October 5-6. Its entire crew of four perished and an elderly villager, then in the Home Guard, told us that most of what remained of the crewmen was hanging in shreds from the surrounding trees.

The decades rolled by and all became a distant memory until young men, many of whom were not even born in 1940, yet filled with a passion for the history of the period, came to discover what still remained.

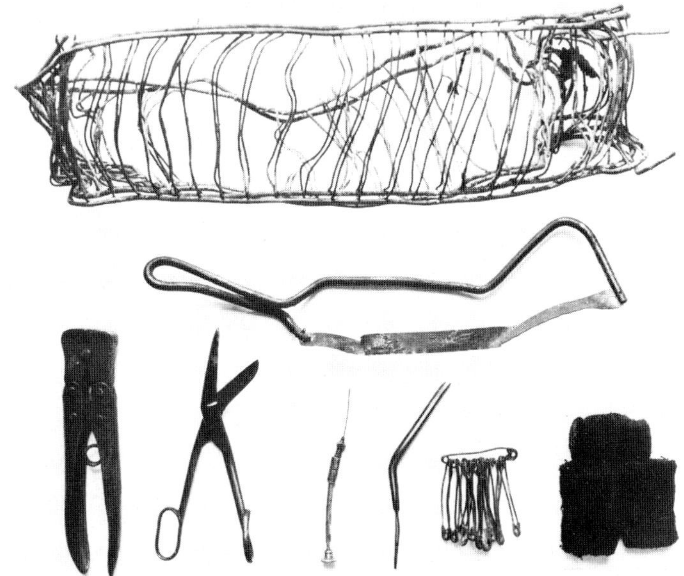

Not for the squeamish. Recovered on the first examination of the site, the twisted instruments from the on board first aid kit.

Just as the First World War had its Immelmann, Boelke and Richthofen, the air war of 1940 produced a similar crop of aces: Galland, Wick, and the Mölders brothers, the younger Victor (right) being rather overshadowed by his brother Werner, left, commander of Jagdgeschwader 51. September had brought a new rôle for the Messerschmitt 109 — that of a 'Jabo' dive-bomber carrying a single 250kg bomb beneath the fuselage *(see Volume 1, page 177)* and on October 7 Victor, commanding the 2nd Staffel of JG51, was to attack 'targets of opportunity' on the banks of the Thames, top cover being provided by the 1st and 3rd Staffels led by his brother.

1630 — 30+ crossing at Dungeness penetrated to Central and North-East London.

In addition, there were numerous reconnaissance flights both in the morning and early evening.

Enemy activity at night was on a large scale. A continuous attack was directed against London. Manchester and Liverpool were raided for about three hours. Minelaying is suspected in the Thames Estuary, Firth of Forth, off Flamborough Head, in the Tyne and Merseyside.

Between 1900 and 2100: As many as 80 enemy aircraft visited Midlands and Lancashire, Newcastle and East Anglia, the bulk operating in the London area. During this period aircraft from Denmark visited Edinburgh and Arbroath.

Between 2100 and 2300: Forty enemy aircraft were over this country, of which 15 operated in south-east England and the London area, the remainder over South Wales and the Bristol Channel, Midlands and Lancashire, Sunderland, East Anglia and Firth of Forth.

Between 2300 and 0100: Only 10 enemy aircraft were plotted, mostly over Kent, Sussex and London, whilst single aircraft again visited Wales, Merseyside and the Potteries.

From 0300 to 0600: Enemy activity was confined to the East Coast and London with a single aircraft operating as far north as Kinnairds Head.

Considerable damage, chiefly to private

'We flew extremely low on the bomb run, almost between the rooftops of the city,' recalled Victor in 1986. 'Suddenly we saw behind us, and at a considerable altitude, some 30 Spitfires which came screaming down upon us. There took place an intense air battle wherein the Spitfires were at a great advantage.' According to others involved that day, Victor then made a fatal tactical error. For a critical 15 or 20 seconds he kept his Staffel on course before ordering 'Release Bombs!' While the rest of the Staffel banked for home, Victor went into a wide climbing turn with his wingman Leutnant Meyer to observe the impact of the bombs. At this point the two Bf 109s were caught by the Spitfires, raking both with fire. 'My aircraft received some 32 hits,' remembered Victor, 'and the cooling system was damaged. Soon the propeller turned no more. As I was too low to bale out I headed for open country and made a belly landing in a large, flat field between many artificial obstacles.'

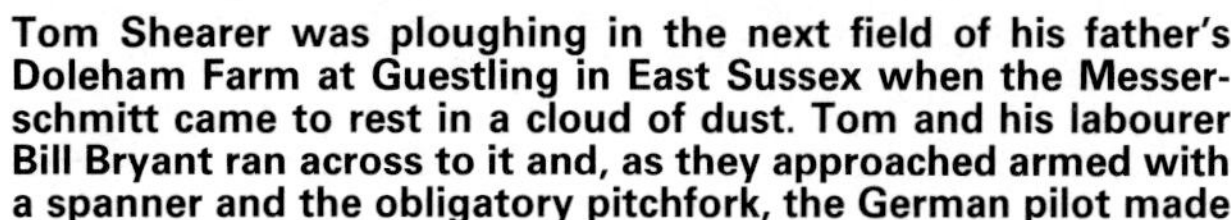

Tom Shearer was ploughing in the next field of his father's Doleham Farm at Guestling in East Sussex when the Messerschmitt came to rest in a cloud of dust. Tom and his labourer Bill Bryant ran across to it and, as they approached armed with a spanner and the obligatory pitchfork, the German pilot made clear his intention to surrender. Tom's father soon arrived by car armed with his Home Guard rifle and when they reached the farmhouse the police were called. Later in captivity Victor made this interesting series of drawings to illustrate the events which followed his capture.

property, was caused in the Manchester area during raids lasting for over three hours; at Rochester where the gasworks were partially demolished, and at Liverpool where a cinema and school were hit. Elsewhere, outside London, few bombs were dropped and damage was practically confined to private property.

During the day approximately 11 people in London were killed and 70 injured. Elsewhere 9 were killed and 42 injured, 22 of them seriously. By night, 65 people in London were killed and 215 injured. Elsewhere 11 were killed, 28 seriously injured and 60 were slightly injured. Twenty-seven enemy aircraft were destroyed, together with 5 probables and 14 were damaged.

Better weather resulted in a steady progression of Bf 109 formations across the southern counties throughout the day and sorely tested the defences. Mid-afternoon a heavy raid launched against the Westland factory at Yeovil met with stiff opposition. Increased activity resulted in higher losses, the Luftwaffe losing 19 aircraft on operations plus 3 more damaged. Four machines were damaged and another destroyed in accidents on the Continent.

5/JG27 Messerschmitt Bf 109E-1 (3665). Radiator damaged in attacks by Flying Officer C. W. Passy, Sergeant S. Duszynski and Sergeant E. W. Wright of No. 605 Squadron during escort sortie for Bf 109 Jabos of II/LG2. Forced-landed at Bedgebury Wood, near Cranbrook 4.40 p.m. Uffz. P. Lederer captured slightly wounded. Aircraft 10+— a write-off.

5/JG27 Messerschmitt Bf 109E-1 (3881). Shot down by Flight Lieutenant A. A. McKellar of No. 605 Squadron during combat over Sussex. Crashed and burned out at Mayfield Flats, Hadlow Down, near Heathfield 4.45 p.m. Uffz. P. Lege killed. Aircraft a write-off.

Site investigated by the Wealden Aviation Archaeological Group in 1972 and some minor components excavated, items now held by Pat Burgess. Dubious panel in Robertsbridge Aviation Museum also attributed to this aircraft.

In the farmhouse kitchen Mrs Shearer provided tea and cakes *(left)* but the hospitality of the Shearer family in treating their prisoner with courtesy was not shared by their mongrel Mussolini who showed his displeasure by cocking his leg up the airman's flying boots! *Right:* Eventually PC 169 Bill Watts arrived and, after allowing young Victor to finish his cigarette, escorted him to Battle Police Station.

9/JG27 Messerschmitt Bf 109E-4 (751). Set alight in attacks by Flight Lieutenant A. A. McKellar and Pilot Officer R. W. Foster of No. 605 Squadron during free-lance fighter sweep over London. Broke up, crashed and burned out at Oak Farm, Headcorn 2.00 p.m. Uffz. L. Bartsch baled out and captured unhurt. Aircraft 13+ a write-off.

Site excavated by Steve Vizard in 1975 and remains of shattered airframe and many minor components found at a depth of 5-6 feet.

2/JG51 Messerschmitt Bf 109E-4 (4853). Radiator damaged in attacks by Squadron Leader H. A. V. Hogan and Pilot Officer K. W. MacKenzie of No. 501 Squadron during return flight from escort sortie for Bf 109 Jabos attacking London Docks. Ditched in the Channel south of Sandgate 1.58 p.m. Lt. E. Meyer took to his dinghy, rescued by coastal patrol vessel and landed at Dover unhurt. Aircraft lost.

Epic recovery by the Brenzett Aeronautical Museum in 1976. Complete aircraft minus tail section recovered from the seabed and subject to restoration work.

2/JG51 Messerschmitt Bf 109E-4 (4103). Severely damaged by fighters following fighter-bomber attack on London. Probably that attacked by Sergeant E. W. Wright of No. 605 Squadron. Forced-landed at Doleham Farm, Guestling 11.00 a.m. Oberlt. V. Mölders (Staffelkapitän) captured unhurt. Aircraft 1+ a write-off.

5/KG51 Junkers Ju 88A-1 (8064). Shot down by Pilot Officer R. F. T. Doe of No. 238 Squadron and abandoned during sortie to bomb Yeovil. Also attacked by Sergeant E. E. Shepperd of No. 152 Squadron. Crashed and burned out at Sidling St Nicholas, Dorset 4.20 p.m. Oberlt. S. Hey, Lt. F. Bein, Oberfw. C. König and Oberfw. J. Troll all baled out and captured unhurt. Aircraft 9K+SN a write-off.

Site investigated by Perry Adams, Peter Foote and Philippa Hodgkiss and several items including dive brake bearing Balkenkreuz unearthed.

'The next day I was taken by truck *(left)* to an interrogation camp' *(right)*. *[Cockfosters — see Volume 1, page 114].* There they felt sure they had captured my brother Werner. When they found out it was only me, they were, I think, very disappointed.' Two weeks later RAF Intelligence again thought they had captured Werner Mölders himself when Hans Asmus was shot down in the ace's own Messerschmitt who was flying in the first of the new 109Fs (see page 200).

Peter Foote with a Ju 88 dive brake which had lain undiscovered in undergrowth at Sidling St Nicholas, Dorset, since it was 'lost' there on October 7, 1940.

4/LG2 Messerschmitt Bf 109E-4 (5391). Crashed in the Channel 2 miles off Greatstone following attack by fighters during fighter-bomber sortie over London 2.00 p.m. Possibly that claimed by Flying Officer M. Pisarek of No. 303 Squadron. Uffz. H. Bley rescued by the Dungeness life-boat *Charles Cooper Henderson* and captured with slight head injuries. Aircraft ▲+A lost.

Aircraft located on the seabed by the Brenzett Aeronautical Museum and exact position plotted for possible future recovery venture.

4/LG2 Messerschmitt Bf 109E-4 (5566). Seriously damaged by fighters during fighter-bomber sortie over London. Believed that attacked by Flying Officer P. W. Lochnan of No. 1 (RCAF) Squadron. Crashed at Spa Golf Club, Tunbridge Wells 1.50 p.m. Uffz. G. Mörschel captured wounded. Aircraft ▲+F a write-off.

4/ZG26 Messerschmitt Bf 110E-1 (3427). Believed shot down by Pilot Officer E. S. Marrs of No. 152 Squadron during escort sortie for attack on Yeovil by Ju 88s of II/KG51. Crashed in the sea at Ringstead Bay, Dorset 4.00 p.m. Oberfw E. Gensler baled out and captured unhurt. Uffz. F. Häfner baled out and captured slightly wounded. Aircraft 3U+FM lost.

6/ZG26 Messerschmitt Bf 110C-7 (3418). Shot down by Flight Lieutenant M. L. Robinson of No. 609 Squadron during escort sortie for II/KG51 attack on Yeovil. Possibly also that attacked by Flight Lieutenant F. J. Howell. Crashed and exploded at Kingston Russell Dairy Farm, Long Bredy, near Dorchester 4.00 p.m. Oberfw. K. Herzog and Obergefr. H. Schilling killed. Aircraft 3U+JP a write-off.

This site was originally disturbed by unidentified enthusiasts and partial human remains recovered which were buried as 'unknown airmen' at Cannock Chase. In August 1976, Peter Foote and the Wealden Group carried out a major recovery, identifying further remains of both crewmen who were buried at Cannock with full military honours. Tail wheel oleo, flare pistol and MG17 now in the Tangmere Military Aviation Museum.

Stab III/ZG26 Messerschmitt Bf 110E-1 (3421). Shot down by fighters during escort sortie for II/KG51 bombers attacking Yeovil. Ditched in the sea at Weymouth Bay 4.15 p.m. Lt. B. Sommer captured unhurt, Uffz P. Preuler wounded. Aircraft 3U+DD lost.

9/ZG26 Messerschmitt Bf 110C-4 (3283). Shot down by fighters during escort sortie for II/KG51 bombers attacking Yeovil. Possibly that claimed by Flying Officer J. C. Dundas of No. 609 Squadron. Crashed and exploded at Hart Hill, Stoborough near Wareham 4.20 p.m. Lt. K. Sidow and Gefr. J. Repik killed. Aircraft 3U+BT a write-off.

This crew was buried at Brookwood Military Cemetery and not reinterred in the Soldatenfriedhof, Cannock Chase post-war.

Site excavated by David Summersby and DB 601 engine recovered. Site re-excavated by Perry Adams in 1984.

9/ZG26 Messerschmitt Bf 110C-4 (3640). Severely damaged in attack by fighters during escort sortie to Yeovil. Eventually forced to ditch in the sea off Weymouth 4.15 p.m. Oberlt. H. Grisslich rescued and captured unhurt. Uffz. L. Obermeier believed baled out over land and captured seriously wounded. Aircraft 3U+GT lost.

9/ZG26 Messerschmitt Bf 110C-4 (3564). Shot down by fighters during escort sortie for II/KG51 attack on Yeovil. Probably that claimed by Flight Lieutenant M. L. Robinson of No. 609 Squadron and also attacked by Flying Officer R. E. P. Brooker of No. 56 Squadron. Crash-landed near Corfe Castle 4.00 p.m. Obergefr. J. Bachmann (of 8/ZG26) killed. Gefr. B. Demmig (also of 8/ZG26) captured unhurt. Aircraft 3U+JT a write-off.

Fragments discovered at the site by Peter Foote and Perry Adams.

TUESDAY, OCTOBER 8

There were four main attacks during the morning. Two penetrated to London and two operated in Kent. In the afternoon small raids by single aircraft attacked towns on the East Sussex coast. It is believed that all the attacks in force were made by Me 109s.

Main attacks by day:

At 0833, 50+ enemy aircraft crossed the coast near Dungeness and attacked London. At 0850 they then split into small sections and flew out, being met by a raid of 100+ which reached the south of London, Biggin Hill, Kenley area by 0915.

At 1025, 30+ aircraft crossed the coast at Lympne, and after reaching the Hornchurch area left by Folkestone at 1058.

At 1115, a further raid of 30+ enemy aircraft also came in over Lympne and penetrated to South and East London.

At 1225, two raids of 20+ each flew inland over Folkestone to the Kenley, Biggin Hill area and out at Kent.

Isolated attacks were reported at Bexhill, Eastbourne (2), Hastings and Fairlight during the afternoon.

During the day reconnaissances were made in Sussex, Kent, Dorset, Somerset and East Anglia.

By night:

Between 1900 and 2100 hostile activity commenced from Cherbourg. This took the

The former residence of HM the King and Queen when they were the Duke and Duchess of York was hit on the night of October 7/8. No. 145 Piccadilly was unoccupied at the time; now it is the site of the Inter-Continental Hotel.

October 8, 1940
18.45 hours

We are bound for a fighter airfield; this time it is Dorchester [Warmwell]. Again there are only three planes in our flight, in the clear twilight over the British coast. Again we do not meet any fighters. Were the night fighters off duty till 20.00 hours?

There is a cloudless sky over the island and the atmosphere is uneasy. But Hauptmann Kiel continues to lead us imperturbably. Searchlights accompany us on our way. All our machine guns are sputtering at those ghastly lights. Our planes are spitting out red strings of pearls. We are flying over England at a speed of 320 kilometres an hour, with both sides firing at each other. Following all the firing instructions which I have memorised, I took particular aim at one of the searchlights and saw it snuff out. Not much Flak, but pretty accurate. I hope we have also hit the airfield, but from where I sit in the turret I'm rather doubtful.

We shook ourselves loose and disappeared one by one into the mist and darkness, in the direction of France.

In the distance, over Cherbourg, we could see an infernal, richly coloured witch's cauldron consisting of flashes, countless tracer bullets, searchlights, and explosions. It was very instructive to see what our British colleagues were doing there and the reception they were getting.

After we landed we were treated to a concert by the Wehrbetreuungs-vorstellung [Forces' Welfare Services]: Schubert, Brahms and Mozart.

I am happy that our country sends us entertainment of such quality instead of some sort of rubbish.

ROBERT GÖTZ

rather unusual form of a concentration of about 20 aircraft on a wide front between Portland and Southampton area. Other raids entered the country from France and the Dutch islands, the majority having the London area as their objective, whilst a few were operating in East Anglia and Liverpool. It is suggested that 100 enemy raids entered during this period.

Between 2100 and 2300 activity was maintained during the early portion of this period, but slackened during the latter. The areas covered were practically identical with the earlier ones.

Between 2300 and 0100 activity was somewhat reduced and London was the objective.

Between 0100 and 0300 activity was intensified and still confined to the London area. A few raids were directed as far north as Peterborough via London and returned on the same tracks, while a single enemy aircraft reached the Church Fenton area from the Wash.

Between 0300 and 0600 London continued to be the main objective, but a succession of raiders entered over the Kent coast from the Dutch isles and penetrated to East Anglia and the east Midlands. This influx was maintained and increased in strength, while the rest of the country including London was clear.

Enemy aircraft casualties: destroyed 6; probable 2; damaged 3. Civilian casualties (approx.) in London by day, 63 killed and 197 injured; by night, 138 killed and 178 injured. Elsewhere by day, 5 were killed, 12 seriously injured and 18 slightly injured; by night 19 people were killed, 28 seriously injured and 22 slightly injured.

The following fires have been reported in London Region: Conflagrations 1, Major 1, Serious 5, Medium 50, Small 320. The conflagration was at L.E.P. Transport Ltd, Corney Road, Chiswick. The major fire was at Hays Wharf, Tooley Street, S.E.1. Serious fires were at Hammersmith No. 6 Warehouse, London Docks, Skin Shed, London, Battersea and Shoreditch. In the regions outside London fires were reported from Nos. 4, 6, 7, 10 and 12. All fires mentioned above are either extinguished or under control.

London again proved to be the main target for regular Jabo attacks which penetrated the defences by operating at increasingly greater height. Thirteen German aircraft were lost and 11 more damaged on operations, whilst 3 more were destroyed and 4 damaged on routine domestic flights.

2(F)/22 Dornier Do 17P (3576). Forced to land on the sea off Rattray Head, Aberdeen 3.00 p.m. due to engine failure during reconnaissance sortie over Peterhead and Fraserburgh. Hptmn. K. Hardt (of Stab Gen.Kdo.X Fl.Korps), Oberlt. E. von Eickstedt and Oberfw. H. Freund rescued from their dinghy and captured unhurt. Aircraft 4N+GK lost.

4/JG3 Messerschmitt Bf 109E-4 (1656). Engine severely damaged in attack by Sergeant H. Cook of No. 66 Squadron during sortie over London and forced to ditch on the foreshore at Abbotts Cliff, Folkestone 12.12 p.m. Oberlt. W. Voigt (Staffelkapitän) captured unhurt. Aircraft lost.

4/JG52 Messerschmitt Bf 109E-1 (3465). Radiator damaged in attack by Pilot Officer R. Berry of No. 603 Squadron during free-lance sortie over the Thames Estuary. Forced-landed and careered into a haystack on Little Grange Farm, Woodham Mortimer, Essex 9.25 a.m. Fw. P. Boche captured wounded. Aircraft 2+a write-off.

4/KG51 Junkers Ju 88A-1 (6115). Attacked by Pilot Officer E. F. Edsall and Pilot Officer T. A. Vigors of No. 222 Squadron during bombing sortie to London. Then intercepted and shot down in flames by four Hurricanes of 'A' Flight No. 605 Squadron led by Pilot Officer C. F. Currant. Exploded and crashed onto Toovies Farm, near Three Bridges, Sussex 11.20 a.m. Lt. G. Döttlinger, Uffz. G. Semper, Gefr. S. Kühne and Uffz. J. Büttner all killed. Aircraft 9K+DM a write-off.

8/KG55 Heinkel He 111P-2 (1715). Hit by ground fire from a searchlight post at Lee during armed incursion over Thorney Island and exploded in mid-air over Stansted House, near Rowlands Castle 7.30 p.m. Fw. E. Ens killed. Lt. U. Flügge, Uffz. J. Ehrensberger, Uffz. E. Herber and Gefr. H. Pawlik all missing believed killed. Aircraft G1+MS a write-off.

This aircraft exploded with such violence that only the remains of the pilot, Ernst Ens, were ever identified. He was buried at St Nicholas Churchyard, West Thorney and not reinterred in the Soldatenfriedhof, Cannock Chase postwar. His comrades have no known graves.

Many large pieces of airframe found scattered throughout woodland here by Wealden Aviation Archaeological Group in 1976. Ernst Ens' belt buckle, removed at the time of the crash, held by Andy Saunders.

2/KGr806 Junkers Ju 88A-1 (4068). Shot down by Yellow Section of No. 312 Squadron (Flight Lieutenant D. E. Gillam, Pilot Officer A. Vasatko and Sergeant J. Stehlik) during bombing sortie to Liverpool. Forced-landed at Bromborough Dock, Port Sunlight, near Birkenhead 4.15 p.m. Oberlt. H. Brückmann captured unhurt, Uffz. H. Weth slightly injured and Sonderfhr. H. Lehmann (of Lw.Kr.Ber.Komp.2) wounded. Lt. zur See H. Schlegel killed. Aircraft M7+DK a write-off.

Site investigated by the Warplane Wreck Investigation Group.

Still with its warlike stores aboard, this Ju 88 of 2/KGr806 was forced down during the afternoon attack on Liverpool.

TIEF-ANGRIFF AM ENGLAND

October 8, 1940, saw a series of bombing and machine-gunning incidents along the Sussex coastline which would probably have been described by the British authorities and news media of the period as 'nuisance raids'. The description, however, belies the widespread nature of the damage and destruction caused by this low level incursion by three Heinkel He 111 bombers of the 8th Staffel, Kampfgeschwader 55. Despite the substantial material damage, civilian fatalities, and some hits on military targets, the raid was not without cost to the Luftwaffe: one of the bombers being lost to ground fire and its entire crew killed.

The early hours of the morning saw the home base of 8/KG55 at Villacoublay coming alive with preparations for the days operations. It was also the birthday of one of the Staffel's stalwart wireless operator/air gunners, Oberfeldwebel Fritz Pons; a fact not lost on the Staffelkapitän, Oberleutnant Jurgen Bartens, who announced: 'Fritz, today it's your birthday so you will go on a raid over England to celebrate!' It was not the sort of celebration Fritz needed after active service since the outbreak of war, participating in the Battle of France and throughout the Battle of Britain, but clearly the Staffelkapitän felt this was the way that Pons would be spending his day! Three aircraft were detailed — the target was to be RAF Thorney Island.

During the afternoon the aircraft were readied. Bomb loads were put aboard, made up of a full complement of 50kg HEs, and the aircraft were fuelled-up once final checks and air tests had been made. The flight mechanics checked the engines in ground runs and the oil, hydraulic and cooling systems, whilst the observers checked flight plan details and the bomb loads, leaving the pilots to carry out overall pre-flight checks of the airframes, controls and instruments.

The wireless operators and air gunners, too, were busy. There were frequencies to check, and equipment to test to see that it was transmitting and receiving properly. Meanwhile, gunners checked that the full quota of MG15 saddle drums were stowed and ready before stripping, cleaning, checking and testing their weapons.

Fritz Pons had duties as both wireless operator and air gunner, but his tasks in the latter category were double that of his contemporaries. Dissatisfied with the standard solitary MG15 defensive armament installed in his mid-upper position, Fritz had fashioned his own addition to the gun mounting rail which allowed a second MG15 to be added. The 'doppel MG15' fitted to G1+LS became quite famous on the Geschwader, but, so far as is known, it remained unique throughout KG55 and other operational He 111s of the period.

During the afternoon, Fritz recalled in an interview in 1976, his friend, Gefreiter Hans Pawlik, confided in him that he did not want to go on this raid. Pawlik, a young village greengrocer's barrow-boy turned Luftwaffe air gunner, did not normally fly with Pons but was, nevertheless, very friendly with him. 'He was', recalled Fritz, 'very gloomy. He didn't want to go. It wasn't that he was a coward or losing his nerve. Nothing like that. He just had a bad feeling, some kind of premonition about the mission to be flown. I tried to reassure him. I told him: "Well, it's my birthday, I don't want to go either", but it was no use. He just wouldn't be consoled. He stayed with me right up until it was time to board our aircraft. As it turned out, his premonition came true. I was never to see Hans Pawlik again.'

During the early evening, the three Heinkels took off from Villacoublay and headed out over the northern French coast and across the English

Franz Vornier (left), the pilot of G1+LS and Fritz Pons, the wireless operator. Their luck finally ran out when they were shot down during a night raid over London on April 8/9, 1941: Fritz Pons and the flight mechanic Hermann Kübler both survived although injured; Franz Vornier and Jürgen Bartens died when their Heinkel crashed in Windsor Great Park.

Gefeiter Hans Pawlik.

The famous 'Doppel MG15' of 8/KG55 designed by Fritz Pons.

Observer of G1+MS, Leutnant Flügge.

Channel, keeping at low level to avoid radar detection. The aircraft took up a loose 'V' formation, with the lead taken by the Staffelkapitän's aircraft (G1+LS), flown by Oberfeldwebel Franz Vornier, with Oberleutnant Bartens (St. Kap.) acting as observer and captain of the aircraft, Oberfeldwebel Fritz Pons as wireless operator, Feldwebel Hermann Kübler the flight mechanic, and Unteroffizier George Maier the air gunner operating the ventral gondola weapon, lying on his padded couch known as 'das Sterbebett' (the deathbed) and armed with a single MG15.

On the starboard wing of G1+LS flew G1+BS, Werk Nr. 2909, piloted by Brauckman with Sudel as the wireless operator and Wochner the flight mechanic. Unfortunately, the Christian names and ranks of these men are unknown, but the observer was Unteroffizier Herbert Heinzl and the gunner Unteroffizier Josef Bogner. On the port side flew Feldwebel Ernst Ens in G1+MS, Werk Nr. 1715, with Leutnant Ulrich Flügge as observer, Unteroffizier Johann Ehrensberger on the radio, Unteroffizier Ernst Herber as flight mechanic and Gefreiter Hans Pawlik the gunner.

Shortly before seven o'clock, local time, the three aircraft crossed the Sussex coast just west of Brighton, turning to port and following the coast towards Worthing. They were flying at a height of 200 metres — about 650 feet.

'I recall,' said Fritz, 'that I was looking down onto a long straight road. I could clearly see the surprised faces of people looking up at me.' From this point the exact course of events have been unravelled from sketchy police reports, the Operations Record Books of RAF Ford and Thorney Island and the memories of Fritz Pons. Unfortunately, some of the times of incidents reported by the West Sussex Constabulary do not follow in chronological pattern but it may be assumed that this was largely due to a delay of some minutes in reporting incidents, or, in some cases, the times given for incidents were in actual fact the times the events were logged, rather than when they actually happened. Be that as it may, at around 1903 the first bombs were released from the three Heinkels; a few minutes earlier a machine-gunning incident was reported at Lower Beeding.

The first bombs, twenty-four in all, exploded in a residential area of Southwick, although three failed to explode. Those that did caused extensive damage, demolishing one bungalow and resulting in another building (described in police records as a 'Store') being burnt out. The human toll was also high, with one fatality and eight injuries; but this was just the start of a long trail of death and destruction along the South Coast. Next to be hit was Worthing. Fifteen 50kg HEs fell in the vicinity of Worthing gasworks, and, although two failed to explode, considerable damage and carnage resulted. The engine house at the gasworks was badly damaged and a main electric cable supplying Worthing was severed. Five civilians suffered fatal injuries as many of the bombs fell wide and into a residential area. Mrs Hansell and her 20-year-old daughter died as their home received a direct hit, whilst a young woman visiting neighbours of the Hansell's was fatally injured. Another bomb exploded five yards away from the forecourt of a petrol-filling station, mortally wounding a lorry driver, Percy Reed, as he refuelled his builders merchants' lorry. A small shop was hit, just as Robin Kennard of the Home Guard was purchasing a packet of cigarettes. The 47-year-old member of 5th Sussex (Worthing) Battalion Home Guard was killed outright.

A further twelve people were injured and as the three Heinkels sped westwards they left behind a scene of destruction. Apart from the human toll, five properties had been demolished and a further 120 were damaged. The gasworks, badly hit by bombs, also had a gasometer set on fire by incendiary bullets. Exactly why the bombs were released at this point, or by which aircraft, when the officially stated target was RAF Thorney Island remains unclear.

Fritz Pons recollection of where, when and by whom the bombs were released is uncertain, but the course now took the aircraft towards Littlehampton, following the Southern Railway South Coast Line towards RAF Ford. Here, the first military target came under attack with several more bombs being released and machine gun bullets raking across the airfield causing superficial damage to buildings and ancilliary equipment. More serious, however, was the loss of one of the RAF's newest aircraft, a Boston I of No. 23 Squadron, AX850, which was totally destroyed. Fortunately, there were no personnel casualties, although a number of cases of shock were reported. Further incidents of machine-gunning were experienced at Bognor Regis, then Bersted as the formation turned northwards and released five more bombs at Elbridge House but causing no damage.

Passing close to Tangmere the airfield defences were alerted and Bofors guns opened fire on the Heinkel formation. Walking in the fields between Tangmere and Westhampnett, Frank Stenning of Chichester was caught up in what he noted in his diary for October 8, as 'another frightening experience'. He went on: 'It was a very quiet evening, no air raid warnings. I heard the sound of gunfire and observed Bofors shells rising from Tangmere and the sound of heavy aircraft. Coming out of the haze directly towards me was an He 111 with its front turret gun firing. It was only a few hundred feet up and continued firing; I saw the spurts of the bullets coming towards me so flung myself into a ditch. I watched this aircraft pass over me then fly over Chichester before turning south towards the sea.' Frank Stenning makes no mention of the other two aircraft, but the 'V' formation at this stage had spread quite wide and, in any event, the other two could easily have been lost to his view because of their low altitude or

Rare shot of the Staffel insignia of 8/KG55, seen here on 2808 — a sister aircraft of G1+BS (2809).

Pilot of G1+MS, Feldwebel Ernst Ens.

A piece of wing from G1+MS under guard at Stansted Park. An RAF officer, Pilot Officer Gilbert Elliot of No. 5 RMU, billeted at Stansted House, was fatally injured by exploding ammunition as he approached the wreckage, dying in the Royal West Sussex Hospital at Chichester two days later.

the hazy conditions. However, before the final turn due south towards Thorney Island, one of the aircraft had swung much further inland to release three bombs at Redlands Piggeries in Elsted. The explosions caused no damage, but a fire was started by incendiary bullets in which the piggeries were burnt out. (West Sussex Constabulary records do not relate the fate of the pigs!) Further bombs were released by the aircraft seen by Frank Stenning, four exploding on Westhampnett aerodrome but causing no damage.

Whilst Fritz Pons could not recall details regarding the bombs he was clear in his memory about the machine-gunning. 'Maier, the gunner, was on his first low-level raid. I think he was nervous, or over-excited, and he opened fire with his MG15 at random. I thought this would only attract British defences to our presence and tried to tell him to stop. I could not attract his attention so, in desperation, I flung my steel helmet at him to try to get him to stop.' Fritz Pons belief that the machine-gunning would attract ground fire was, in his view, confirmed by anti-aircraft guns opening up on them from trees to starboard, although in reality they had probably been alerted by the bomb explosions if not through reports from the Observer Corps.

As soon as the AA fire began Fritz Pons fired his 'doppel MG' towards the gun positions, whereupon the firing stopped. Suddenly, he was aware of a huge explosion to port. Swinging round in his seat he saw a huge mushroom cloud of smoke and fire coming up from the trees below. Only one aircraft was now following G1+LS. 'Fritz! Fritz! Look behind! What was that? What is it?' shouted Vornier over the radio. Sadly, and realising that Pawlik's premonition had come true, he replied: 'It must be Ens. There can't be any survivors.'

Leaving behind them a billowing black cloud, the two Heinkels approached Thorney Island, where, the Operations Record Book states: 'Enemy aircraft machine-gunned aerodrome from 100ft. Defence posts opened fire. It is believed one hit was secured.' The record book does not make it clear if the 'defence posts' were Thorney Island's immediate anti-aircraft defences or guns further afield. If the latter were the case then the hit reported may well have been that secured on G1+MS, bringing about its demise. Alternatively, it may well have been fired directly from the RAF station, possibly causing the hits on G1+BS which wounded Heinzl and Bogner.

Ironically, no damage was reported at Thorney Island, only some desultory machine-gunning at West Wittering as the Heinkels re-crossed the Sussex coast. Meanwhile, an RAF Anson had taken off from Thorney Island and passed 150 feet above G1+LS — apparently unaware of the drama going on around it at that moment! 'There was nobody in the mid upper turret; I remember that clearly!' said Fritz. The Anson, however, was left to its own devices.

Ernst Ens's Heinkel had crashed into the wooded Stansted Park at Stoughton, exploding amongst the beech trees and scattering wreckage far and wide. First on the scene was PC Sid Reynolds, who shared the assessment of Fritz Pons that there could be no survivors. This was confirmed when he came across a grisly discovery. One charred torso was the only trace that could be found of the crew. All its clothes had been burnt off, only a blackened remnant of a leather belt remained — its aluminium buckle still in place. Without any further thought for its unfortunate owner, PC Reynolds removed the buckle and slipped it in his pocket as a souvenir. 'After all, this was a war; I'm ashamed now to say that I had little fellow-feeling at that time for the poor man', said Mr Reynolds when he handed me the buckle forty years later. Its owner had been the Heinkel's pilot, Ernst Ens. He was the only one of the crew to be buried and, by grim irony, his grave was to be in the churchyard of St Nicholas on Thorney Island — Ens's intended target.

RAF investigators reported that 'the aircraft had red spinners. On rudder is a yellow shield with three red fishes. Engines DB.601. Cause of crash is uncertain. Aircraft came down in flames with crew on board and exploded on impact. Wreckage scattered over several acres. Traces of 3 MG's found. One 50 kilo bomb unexploded near wreckage. Crew presumed five, all killed. Owing to condition of crash no further details possible.'

In the 1970s parts from the He 111 were still to be found in the parkland, a large section of tailplane being retrieved from a treetop by Chichester Squadron Air Training Corps, although this has since been scrapped leaving only Ens's grave and his belt buckle as reminders of a grim incident on an October day in 1940 which claimed twelve lives, injured fourteen, and left a trail of damage and destruction across some thirty-five miles of Sussex countryside.

ANDY SAUNDERS, 1986

Ernst Ens's belt buckle, removed by Police Constable Sid Reynolds who was the first person on the scene.

A month has passed since Herr Hitler turned his rage and malice on to the civil population of our great cities, and particularly on London. He declared in his speech of September 4 that he would raze our cities to the ground, and since then he has been trying to carry out his fell purpose.

Naturally the first question we should ask is to what extent the full strength of the German bombing force has been deployed. I will give the House the best opinion I have been able to form on what is necessarily to some extent a matter of speculation. After their very severe mauling on August 15, the German short-range dive-bombers, of which there are several hundreds, have been kept carefully out of the air fighting. This may be, of course, because they are being held in reserve so that they may play their part in a general plan of invasion or reappear in another theatre of war. We have therefore had to deal with the long-range German bombers alone.

It would seem that, taking day and night together, nearly 400 of these machines have on the average visited our shores every 24 hours. We are doubtful whether this rate of sustained attack could be greatly exceeded; no doubt a concentrated effort could be made for a few days at a time, but this would not sensibly affect the monthly average. Certainly there has been a considerable tailing off in the last ten days, and all through the month that has passed since the heavy raids began on September 7 we have had a steady decline in casualties and damage. . . .

What is the explanation? There can only be one explanation — namely, the vastly improved methods of shelter which have been adopted. In the last war there were hardly any air raid shelters, and very few basements had been strengthened. Now we have this ever-growing system of shelters, among which the Anderson shelter justly deserves its fame, and the mortality has been reduced to one-thirteenth, or say, at least one-tenth. This appears, as I say, not only to be remarkable, but also reassuring. It has altered, of course, the whole of the estimates we had made of the severity of the attacks to which we should be exposed.

Whereas when we entered the war at the call of duty and honour we expected to sustain losses which might amount to 3,000 killed in a single night and 12,000 wounded night after night, and we had made hospital arrangements on the basis of 250,000 casualties merely as a first provision, we have actually had, since it began, up to last Saturday, as a result of air bombing, about 8,500 killed and 13,000 wounded. This shows that things do not always turn out as badly as one expects. Also it shows that one should never hesitate, as a nation or as an individual, to face dangers because they appear to the imagination to be so very formidable.

Since the heavy raiding began on September 7 the figures of killed and seriously wounded have declined steadily week by week from over 6,000 in the first week to just under 5,000 in the second week, to about 4,000 in the third week, and to under 3,000 in the last of the four weeks. These are casualties — dead and seriously wounded.

Smiles amid the destruction in Liverpool — the image Churchill and the Press went to great lengths to portray.

Let us now proceed to examine the effect of this ruthless and indiscriminate attack upon the easiest of all targets — namely, the great built-up areas of this land. The Germans have recently volunteered some statements of a boastful nature about the weight of explosives which they have discharged upon us during the whole war and also upon some particular occasions. These statements are not necessarily untrue and they do not appear unreasonable to us.

We were told on September 23 that 22,000 tons of explosives had been discharged upon Great Britain since the beginning of the war. No doubt this included the mines on the coast. We were told also that on last Thursday week 251 tons were thrown upon London in a single night; that is to say, only a few tons less than the total dropped on the whole country throughout the last war.

Now we know exactly what our casulaties have been. On that particular Thursday night 180 persons were killed in London as a result of 251 tons of bombs; that is to say, it took one ton of bombs to kill three-quarters of a person. We know, of course, exactly the ratio of loss in the last war, because all the facts were ascertained after it was over. In that war small bombs of earlier patterns which were used killed ten persons for every ton discharged in the built-up areas. Therefore, the deadliness of the attack in this war appears to be only one-thirteenth of that of 1914-1918, or let us say, so as to be on the safe side, that it is less than one-tenth of the mortality attaching to the Germans' bombing attack in the last war.

The destruction of property has, however, been very considerable. Most painful is the number of small houses inhabited by working folk which have been destroyed, but the loss has also fallen heavily upon the West End, and all classes have suffered evenly, as they would desire to do. I do not propose to give exact figures of the houses which have been destroyed or seriously damaged. That is our affair. We will rebuild them more to our credit than some of them were before. London, Liverpool, Manchester, Birmingham, may have much more to suffer, but they will rise from their ruins more healthy and, I hope, more beautiful.

Statisticians may amuse themselves by calculating that, after making allowance for the working of the law of diminishing returns through the same house being struck twice or three times over, it would take ten years at the present rate for half the houses of London to be demolished. After that, of course, progress would be much slower. Quite a lot of things are going to happen to Herr Hitler and the Nazi regime before even ten years are up, and even Signor Mussolini has some experiences ahead of him which he had not foreseen at the time when he thought it safe and profitable to stab the stricken and prostrate French Republic in the back. Neither by material damage nor by slaughter will the British people be turned from their solemn and inexorable purpose.

WINSTON CHURCHILL, OCTOBER 8, 1940

'Oranges and lemons, say the bells of St Clements . . . ' On the night of October 8/9 bombs straddled St Clement Danes in the Strand, some of the spang marks still remaining to be seen today. By now most other London buildings had lost their railings in the massive scrap metal drive which was to denude the Capital of its architectural ironmongery. The Duke of Bedford put up a vehement protest, much argued in the Press, which did little to stop the removal of those in Bedford Square.

WEDNESDAY, OCTOBER 9

Enemy formations by day numbering between 30 and 170 aircraft made three attempts during the day to penetrate to London. In the afternoon raid about 60 enemy aircraft reached the capital and bombs were dropped in several boroughs, mainly in the Thames Estuary. There were casualties at Finsbury, Shoreditch and West Ham, and some damage was caused to docks and factories, which was not of a major character. Several persons were trapped and some are still buried at Shoreditch. East Ham Memorial Hospital was hit and the L.M.S. electric railway at Stevenage Road was blocked.

In the provinces during the morning considerable damage to property is reported from Maidstone, Hastings and Canterbury. At Stafford the English Electric Co., Ltd was hit and some casualties occurred, but the effect on production is only very slight. Bombs were dropped at Shrewsbury at 1903 whilst under yellow warning. The railway line between Shrewsbury and Crewe received a direct hit and railway telephonic communications with Crewe were cut off. Both lines were blocked, but single line traffic is now being operated.

Between 1810 and 1850, 30 bombs were dropped at Penrhos aerodrome, but little damage was done and there were no casualties.

Bombing of London by night commenced at 1850 and London remained under red warning until after 0600. Incidents occurred throughout the night mainly between the hours of 1900-2100 and 0300-0600. Military damage was slight, but there was damage to house property and casualties will probably be on a higher scale than on recent nights. Bombs fell in all nine groups and in the areas of 50 local authorities, chiefly north of the river.

At 0600 a bomb fell on St Paul's Cathedral, exploding inside the East Roof and making a hole 25 feet by 12 feet in the roof. The High Altar is extensively damaged by

If we glimpse ahead in time this is the aspect we would see after the war, following St Clements's ordeal by fire on May 10, 1941 which left it a charred ruin. All the bells crashed down, save one, and only the pulpit and six carved wooden cherubs were spared the flames.

Being the nearest church to Adastral House on the corner of Kingsway and Aldwych, the Royal Air Force 'adopted' the ruin and St Clements was restored at a cost of £234,144 and rededicated in October 1958 to the memory of crews of the RAF, Commonwealth and Allied Air Forces.

KG51 lost Ju 88s on both the 8th and 10th. Here a barely discernable fuselage code 9K+?, with possibly Werke Nr 6145 on the fin, takes off on another sortie to England.

falling masonry, but damage to windows is slight. There were no casualties. The Royal Courts of Justice have been hit, and the Strand blocked in the same vicinity. The Southern Railway has been cut in two places near Surbiton.

At 1912 Falmouth was bombed whilst under yellow warning and there was some damage to buildings and services. Casualties amounted to 3 killed, 12 seriously injured and 3 slightly injured. Red warning was not received until 1954.

In Manchester some H.E. and a large number of I.B.s were dropped and incidents were also reported at Trafford Park and other places in Lancashire, South Wales (Newport), Cornwall (St Eval aerodrome) and a large number in Regions 4 and 6.

Enemy aircraft casualties: 4 destroyed; 4 probable and 5 damaged. Civilian casualties (approx.): In London, by day 77 killed and 295 injured. Elsewhere, by day 4 people were killed, 4 seriously and 34 slightly injured; by night, 19 were killed, 60 seriously injured, and 14 slightly hurt.

Heavy squalls provided ideal conditions for small formations of German Jabos to slip through the defences and hit 11 Group airfields causing some heavy damage. Night attacks, across the whole country, reached a new peak of intensity. Ten German aircraft were destroyed and a similar number damaged on operations, another 3 being damaged in accidents.

7/JG54 Messerschmitt Bf 109E-4 (5327). Engaged by fighters during an attack on No. 41 Squadron Spitfires over Chatham and damaged by Flying Officer E. H. Thomas of No. 222 Squadron. Forced-landed on Meridan Hunt Farm, west of Hawkinge 4.00 p.m. and set alight by pilot. Fw. F. Schweser captured unhurt. Aircraft 6+ a write-off.

Left: **Having narrowly escaped the threat of destruction from the earlier UXB, St Paul's Victorian High Altar was reduced to a pile of rubble by a bomb which penetrated the roof on the morning of October 10.** *Right:* **The new High Altar was consecrated in 1958 and honours the British Commonwealth dead of both world wars. Behind the High Altar stands the former Jesus Chapel, which also suffered damage in 1940, and upon its restoration was dedicated to the 28,000 Americans who were killed during the war whilst based in the United Kingdom.**

Services uprooted in Cornhill undergoing inspection by workmen of the Gas, Light & Coke Co Ltd, which disappeared upon the nationalisation of the utilities soon after the war.

9/JG54 Messerschmitt Bf 109E-4 (1573). Shot down in combat with No. 41 Squadron Spitfires during free-lance sortie over Canterbury. Probably that claimed by Pilot Officer E. S. Lock and Pilot Officer J. R. Walker. Ditched in the sea 10 miles off Dover 4.10 p.m. Lt. J. Eberle (Gruppe NO) killed. Aircraft lost.

The body of Josef Eberle was washed ashore near Harwich on October 26.

1/JG77 Messerschmitt Bf 109E-4 (966). Lost control when dinghy accidentally inflated in the cockpit during free-lance sortie over southern England. Forced-landed near Vensons Farm, Eastry 7.45 a.m. Lt. H. Escherhaus captured unhurt. Aircraft 10+ a write-off.

THURSDAY, OCTOBER 10

Home Office instruct that Daily Appreciation for the above period was not issued.

Almost constant raids by often small formations of aircraft continued to pose problems for the British defences and were proving exceedingly difficult to counter. The Luftwaffe lost 5 aircraft plus 6 more damaged on operations, with 7 aircraft lost and 5 more damaged in accidents.

8/KG51 Junkers Ju 88A-1 (299). Hit by AA fire and abandoned by crew over Stanford-le-Hope during sortie to bomb West India Docks. Crashed into the River Roach at Horseshoe Corner 4.30 a.m. Uffz. R. Metschuldt, Uffz. K. Kafka, Uffz. A. Schragl and Fw. H. Wolff baled out and all captured unhurt. Aircraft 9K+HS a write-off.

FRIDAY, OCTOBER 11

There were seven main attacks and several small raids during the day. Only one of these raids penetrated to Central London. Two of the main attacks consisted entirely of fighters, the remainder being composed of 75 per cent fighters and 25 per cent bombers. There was a lot of reconnaissance activity, mainly in the south-east, south and south-west areas, though the coast of Aberdeen, the Firth of Forth and East Anglia were reconnoitred.

By night: 1900-2100. Night raiding commenced at 1835. London was again the main objective, but other raids were made over Liverpool and attacks on this area were maintained. Enemy aircraft were also plotted over Aberdeen and the Firth of Forth. Minelaying is suspected between Flamborough Head and Berwick. During this period there were approximately 55 raids.

2100-2300. Little alteration in scale of operations, but a slackening in the London area was indicated at 2245. Aircraft were plotted over Liverpool, Manchester and Bristol areas.

2300-0100. Activity in London was confined to isolated raids. There was continued operation towards Liverpool up to 2330, after which time the country was clear except in the London area, which was finally clear by 0220. Operations were doubtless curtailed on account of fog.

Civilian casualties in London by day amounted to 1 killed and 8 injured. Elsewhere 7 were killed and 49 injured, 17

92 10 OCT 1940

X123.

D'SENDER IN GERMAN FOR GERMANY 14.00 10.10.40

GERMAN HIGH COMMAND COMMUNIQUE (OUR TRANSLATION)

FROM EARLY MORNING UNTIL DUSK WAVES OF REPRISAL ATTACKS BY LIGHT AND HEAVY BOMBERS CONTINUED UNINTERRUPTEDLY AGAINST THE BRITISH CAPITAL. IMMEDIATELY FOLLOWING THESE RAIDS, NIGHT ATTACKS OF HEAVY BOMBERS STARTED, LASTING TILL THE EARLY HOURS OF THE 10TH OCTOBER.

VERY HEAVY DAMAGE WAS CAUSED IN THE DOCKS IN THE BEND OF THE THAMES. BOMB EXPLOSIONS ALSO CAUSED EXTENSIVE DESTRUCTION TO RAILWAY INSTALLATIONS AND RAILWAY TRACKS IN THE CENTRE OF THE TOWN. DURING THE NIGHT, NUMEROUS EXTENSIVE CONFLAGRATIONS WERE OBSERVED.

SINGLE BOMBERS SUCCESSFULLY ATTACKED PORT INSTALLATIONS TROOP ENCAMPMENTS RAILWAY TRACKS (BAHNKOERPER) AND ARMAMENT FACTORIES IN THE SOUTH OF ENGLAND WITH BOMBS OF HEAVY AND HEAVIEST TYPES. THEY BOMBED SEVERAL AERODROMES IN THE SOUTH OF ENGLAND AND THE ENGLISH MIDLANDS. AT ~~SEVERALXXXX~~X ST. EVAL PENROSE AND ST. MERRYN WE SUCCEEDED IN DESTROYING HANGARS AND LIVING QUARTERS BY DIRECT HITS AND ALSO AIRCRAFT ON THE GROUND.

BOMB HITS IN THE HARBOUR BASIN AT CARDIFF CAUSED VIOLENT EXPLOSIONS WHICH WERE FOLLOWED BY A HUGE FIRE. AN ENEMY MERCHANT VESSEL OF ABOUT FOUR THOUSAND GROSS REGISTERED TONS WAS HIT AMIDSHIPS BY SEVERAL BOMBS. IT LAY ~~BURJNXX~~ BURNING WITH A STRONG LIST.

A U. BOAT SANK TWO ARMED ENEMY MERCHANT VESSELS TOTALLING SEVEN THOUSAND GROSS REGISTERED TONS.

THE MATERIAL DAMAGE CAUSED IN WESTERN GERMANY AND IN THE OCCUPIED TERRITORIES BY ENEMY NIGHT BOMBING COULD BE SPEEDILY REPAIRED. SOME DWELLING HOUSES WERE DESTROYED A FARM HOUSE WAS COMPLETELY BURNED DOWN.

THE ENEMY LOST TEN PLANES YESTERDAY ONE OF WHICH WAS BROUGHT DOWN BY A.A. ARTILLERY. FOUR GERMAN PLANES ARE MISSING.

14.45 10.10.40

For some reason which we have been unable to determine, the Ministry of Home Security instructed that the Daily Appreciation of events for Thursday, October 10 was not issued. By way of a contrast, we have therefore turned to German sources — to the OKW bulletin put out by Deutschlandsender radio at 14.00 hours Central European Time. This is the translation of the intercepted broadcast.

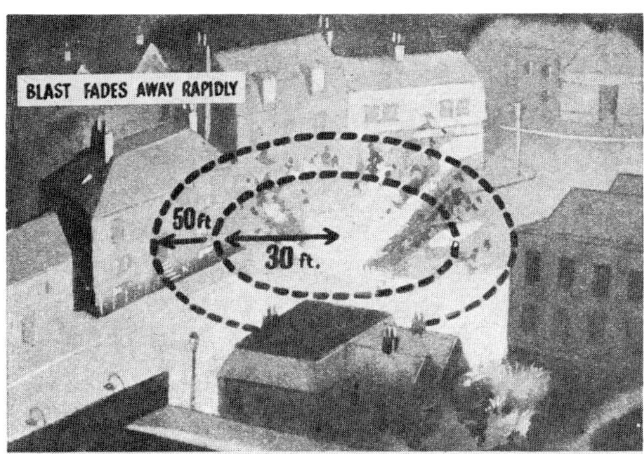

(1) When a 500-lb. bomb bursts, it creates a wind of 3,000 miles an hour—six times as violent as a tornado. That is what we call "blast." But this terrific wind is so strong only within a radius of 30 feet. Outside that its strength falls rapidly. At 50 feet it is almost innocuous. Blast alone is not believed to be lethal, except within the "direct hit" area, though it may kill by damaging the lungs of a person who keeps his mouth shut, or by shock to the heart. The picture-diagram above shows that when a bomb falls, houses only 50 feet away may have no more damage than one or two broken windows.

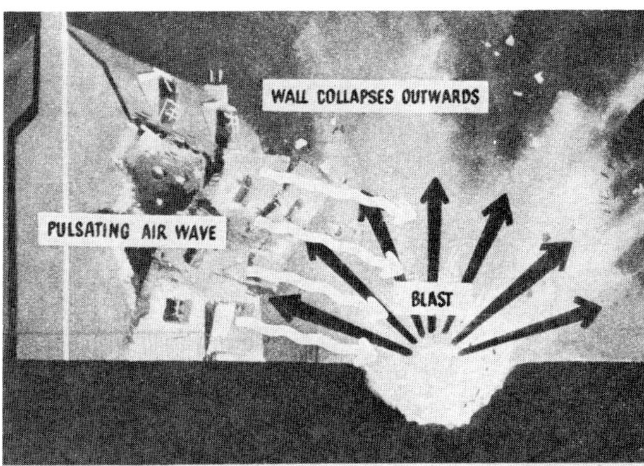

(2) Immediately following the blast comes a pulsating air wave and the first pulsation seems always to be inwards towards the bursting point. Thus, as shown above, a house-front on the edge of a bomb crater is liable to be pulled outwards—not pushed in as you might expect. The theory that up to a certain distance blast blew windows in and beyond that distance sucked them out is now found to be incorrect. Actually there is a violent to-and-fro wave, which accounts for the freak effects so often seen.

seriously. By night 61 Londoners were killed and 245 were injured; elsewhere 8 people were killed, 20 seriously injured and 29 slightly hurt. Eight enemy aircraft were destroyed, together with 4 probable and 1 damaged.

Large formations of bomb-carrying Bf 109s operating at heights up to 30,000 feet penetrated the British defences throughout the day. Various towns in the south-east were attacked and many casualties resulted. The Luftwaffe lost 7 aircraft and 4 more damaged in operations, whilst 3 machines were destroyed and 3 damaged in accidents.

1/606 Dornier Do 17Z-3 (2772). Shot down by Red Section of No. 611 Squadron (Flight Lieutenant W. J. Leather, Pilot Officer P. S. C. Pollard and Pilot Officer J. R. G. Sutton) during sortie to bomb Speke aerodrome, Liverpool. Forced to ditch in Caernarvon Bay 16 miles off Bardsey Island, 6.30 p.m. Lt. zur See J. von Krause, Fw. H. Arpert and Gefr. H. Sudermann picked up by a trawler off Holyhead, Anglesey and captured unhurt. Fw. J. Vetterl missing believed killed. Aircraft 7T+EH lost.

1/606 Dornier Do 17Z-3 (2787). Attacked by Red Section of No. 611 Squadron (Flight Lieutenant W. J. Leather, Pilot Officer P. S. C. Pollard and Pilot Officer J. R. G. Sutton) during sortie to attack Speke 6.30 p.m. Set alight but returned to Brest badly damaged. Uffz. H. Johannsen baled out over Capel Curig but fell dead due to parachute failure. Fw. H. Staas baled out landing at Marthalyn and captured unhurt. Aircraft 7T+HH 45% damaged.

2/606 Dornier Do 17Z-3 (3475). Shot down by Flying Officer D. K. Watkins and Flying Officer T. D. Williams of No. 611 Squadron during sortie to bomb Liverpool. Crashed in the Irish Sea, 50 miles west of Holyhead 6.35 p.m. Oberlt. F-W. Richter, Lt. zur See H. Felber and Gefr. W. Hoppmann killed. Uffz. E. Weber missing believed killed. Aircraft 7T+EK lost.

The bodies of the observer and wireless operator from this aircraft were both washed ashore in Ireland on October 26; Horst Felber at Laytown, County Meath and Walter Hoppmann at Clogher Head, County Louth. The latter was buried in Dublin War Cemetery. The pilot, Friedrich-Wilhelm Richter, was washed up at Bull Bay, Amlwch, Anglesey on November 7. He was promoted Hauptmann subsequently and this rank now appears in the records of the Soldatenfriedhof at Cannock Chase.

The Editor of the George Newnes weekly, *The War*, complained in October about the lack of photographs being released showing 'the havoc the RAF is creating on the enemy's military targets'. Such material, wrote Mr R. J. Minney, 'would be welcomed by the public, both here and in the USA. So what about it Sir Archibald Sinclair and Mr Duff Cooper?' In the meantime readers had to make do with graphic illustrations — these are reproduced with original captions.

ORDERS TAKEN
HERE FOR THE
DESPATCH OF
NEWSPAPERS
BOOKS AND
THE WORLD
THIS BUILDING WAS
THE HEAD OFFICE OF
W. H. SMITH & SON
FROM 1920 TO 1976.
THE ABOVE SIGN WAS
DAMAGED BY SHRAPNEL
FROM A GERMAN BOMB
DURING AN AIR RAID
ON THE NIGHT OF
10TH OCTOBER 1940

The premises of one of the foremost distributors of the Press — W. H. Smith & Son — were struck on October 10. With a nice sense of history this relic has been preserved and remains to be seen in Portugal Street.

SATURDAY, OCTOBER 12

There were seven main attacks during the day, of which 5 penetrated via Kent to London. The first raid consisted entirely of fighters, and the others employed about 75 per cent fighters. A total of some 400 enemy aircraft were involved. There was some reconnaissance in the Channel and Thames Estuary between 0650 and 0900.

By night: 1900-2100. At 1840 raids directed on London left the Dutch islands and the Dieppe area. No raids on London came from the Cherbourg area, but a strong force (15 tracks) from there appeared at 2030 and made for Birmingham and Coventry via Bristol. Minelaying between the Humber and Farne Islands was apparent.

2100-2300. Raids from the Dutch islands and Le Havre/Dieppe continued with the same intensity against London until 2130, and activity in the Midlands continued until 2245, when the country was almost clear again.

2300-0300. There was slight activity in the London area until 0130 and minelaying was reported off the South Coast and from the North Foreland to Southwold. The country was clear by 0222.

Approximate civilian casualties in London by day amounted to 23 killed and 149 injured. Elsewhere 5 people were killed and 8 were injured, 5 seriously. By night 47 Londoners were killed and 186 were injured. Elsewhere 24 were killed and 96 injured. Of these, 19 were killed and 69 were injured in Coventry alone. Eleven enemy aircraft were destroyed. Another 11 were probably destroyed and 7 were damaged.

Pressure on the British defences was maintained throughout the day despite poor weather conditions. Since late September it had become increasingly evident to the German High Command that Operation Seelöwe would not now be accomplished before the end of the year. Hitler was therefore forced to shelve plans for the invasion of England for reconsideration the following spring. This decision was communicated to German forces on this day. Thirteen German aircraft were lost on operations and one was damaged. Another machine was destroyed in an accident.

1/JG52 Messerschmitt Bf 109E-3 (1966). Radiator damaged in combat with Spitfires during free-lance sortie over London. Possibly that attacked by Pilot Officer F. D. S. Scott-Malden of No. 603 Squadron. Abandoned aircraft crashed at Deans Hill, Harrietsham 4.30 p.m. Oberlt. G. Büsgen (Staffelführer) baled out and captured wounded. Aircraft 11+ a write-off.

Surface fragments in the Vizard Collection. Some items, including gunsight, held by the Hawkinge Aeronautical Trust.

2/JG52 Messerschmitt Bf 109E-7 (4132). Shot down by Spitfires during escort sortie for Bf 109 Jabos attacking London. Probably that claimed by Pilot Officer T. S. Wade and Sergeant D. E. Kingaby of No. 92 Squadron. Crashed at Chantry Farm, Hollingbourne 4.30 p.m. Oberlt. K. Sauer baled out and captured slightly wounded. Aircraft <|+ a write-off.

3/JG52 Messerschmitt Bf 109E-4 (5283). Shot down by Spitfires of No. 92 Squadron during Jabo attack on Biggin Hill and London. Crashed at The Limes, Brabourne Down, near Ashford 4.30 p.m. Fw. S. Voss baled out and captured unhurt. Aircraft 3+ a write-off.

Sundry items excavated by the Brenzett Aeronautical Museum and now held by the Hawkinge Aeronautical Trust. Subsequently re-excavated by Andy Saunders in 1986 when ammunition and other items recovered.

4/JG52 Messerschmitt Bf 109E-4 (5256). Shot down in combat with fighters and crashed in the sea off Sheerness. Fw. W. Reichenbach baled out into the sea and drowned. Aircraft 1+ lost.

The body of Willi Reichenbach was washed ashore at Sheerness two days later and his date of death is therefore incorrectly recorded as October 14 in the Soldatenfriedhof, Cannock Chase.

Stab II/JG54 Messerschmitt Bf 109E-4 (4869). Shot down by Squadron Leader R. R. S. Tuck of No. 257 Squadron (flying a No. 92 Squadron Spitfire) during combat over Ashford. Forced-landed near Chapel Holding, Small Hythe, Tenterden 10.20 a.m. Lt. B. Malischewski (Gruppe NO) captured unhurt. Aircraft <|+ a write-off.

October 13 and 14-year-old Princess Elizabeth gives her first broadcast to British children everywhere; at home, in the Dominions, and those evacuated to North America: 'My sister, Margaret Rose, and I feel so much for you, as we know from experience what it means to be away from those we love most of all. To you, living in new surroundings, we send a message of true sympathy, and at the same time we would like to thank the kind people who have welcomed you to their homes in the country. I want, on behalf of all the children at home, to send you our love and best wishes — to you and to your kind hosts as well. Before I finish, I can truthfully say to you all that we children at home are full of cheerfulness and courage. We are trying to do all we can to help our gallant sailors, soldiers and airmen, and we are trying, too, to bear our own share of the danger and sadness of war. We know, every one of us, that in the end all will be well, for God will care for us and give us victory and peace. And when peace comes, remember it will be for us, the children of today, to make the world of tomorrow a better and happier place.'

That Sunday evening was to be the last one for many of the children to whom the Princess spoke — and their parents — in what Miss Hilda Marchant of the *Daily Express* called 'the greatest bombing tragedy of the whole of London'. Where the Great Cambridge Road enters north London it changes its name: at Tottenham it is plain High Road; a couple of miles to the south it is Stamford Hill, soon becoming Stoke Newington High Street. Fifty yards further on, facing Amhurst Road, the Industrial Dwellings Society had erected several blocks of flats in the last century with the rather misleading title of Coronation Avenue. To the casual passer by in 1988 the fact that some of the brickwork appears to be of recent origin is probably of little consequence for there is no plaque or marker to tell the story: that here, on one night in 1940, more than 150 people were killed in the most horrific conditions —drowned while trapped in a basement shelter.

Monday morning — rescue workers stand in stunned groups, helpless at the mountain of rubble covering the shelter entrances. *Right:* On the opposite side heavy plant is brought up . . . but there is really little that can be done to save those trapped.

DISASTER AT CORONATION AVENUE STOKE NEWINGTON

On the night of Sunday, October 13 about 210 bombers attacked the capital. One or more flew over Stoke Newington, and dropped an indefinite number of bombs, one hitting a block of flats called Coronation Avenue.

Alerted by the sirens, many of the inhabitants of the flats, augmented by passers-by, had crammed into the public shelter in the basement of the block, officially designated 'Public Shelter No. 5', and here they prepared to sit out the raid. As they sat huddled together in the basement shelter, no doubt keeping themselves cheerful with songs and party pieces, the bomb suddenly brought everything to an end, piercing the flats approximately half way along the length of the building.

It must have been a very heavy one as it was able to penetrate through the five floors above the basement shelter before it detonated. An ear-shattering explosion combined with choking smoke, dust and blinding brick dust, filled the shelter. The complete weight of the floors above bore down on the people below, those who survived the initial impact finding themselves trapped, with every exit blocked by rubble, furniture, stonework and various other forms of debris. The power of the explosion which ripped apart the five floors of the building also ruptured water mains, gas mains and sewage pipes, and water and effluent poured into the shelter, rising steadily.

By this time the rescue parties had been alerted of the incident, and all available manpower was rushed to the

Apart from some subtle changes to minor architectural details, there is little to distinguish the new from the old. When first rebuilt after the war the rooms in the new section were back to front, i.e. the bedrooms overlooked Stoke Newington Road. Some time later this was corrected in keeping with the other flats to enable residents to get a peaceful night's sleep.

As work proceeds, carpenters begin to erect a hoarding to hide the tragedy from inquisitive eyes. In fact our author Denis Bateman, then a 12-year-old schoolboy, lived just down the road and recalls 'the sickening smell permeating the air; two weeks later I saw bodies — just flat sacks containing the remains — still being carried out. I was on the other side of Victorian Road — just about opposite the right-hand car in this picture.'

scene. Yet even as they pitched into action in the darkness, stretched to the limit in their efforts to dislodge the masonry which blocked the exits and to force their way into the smashed shelter to extricate those entombed below, the survivors were being drowned and suffocated as the water rose and the air ran out.

Though assisted by back-up squads from outside the borough, finally the Civil Defence services had to concede that there was nothing further they could do to rescue those trapped. So compacted were the layers of rubble that it was to take over a week before the last victims were retrieved. Twenty-six were recovered on the 13th, 2 on the 16th, 9 on the 17th, 7 on the 18th, 10 on the 19th, 5 on the 20th, 7 on the 21st, 44 on the 22nd, and 45 on the 23rd. The bodies were transported to the soon-overcrowded St Olave's mortuary and, by the time the final corpses were removed, many were in such an advanced state of decomposition that gas masks had to be worn.

No 26

FORM C.W.D.

DEATH DUE TO WAR OPERATIONS.

Name and Address of Mortuary St Olaves

A.—TO BE ENTERED IMMEDIATELY UPON RECEPTION OF THE BODY AT MORTUARY.

Date 14.10.40 Hour 11.0 AM of Reception.

1. Place {of Death* / of Finding the Body*} — Public Shelter 157/161 Stoke Newington Rd. N16 — Full postal particulars of house or street.
* Cross out whichever is inapplicable.

2. Date and hour {of Death* / of Finding the Body*} 13.10.40 2100 — 3. Sex. Female — 4. Probable Age.
* Cross out whichever is inapplicable.

5. Cause of Death [see Note 1]. Blown to pieces

Signature H Soulsby Official Description C.D. Squad
Date 14.10.40

B.—BODY CLAIMED AND REMOVED FOR BURIAL BY RELATIVES OR FRIENDS.

1. Signature of Relative or Friend
2. Address
3. Deceased identified by Relative or Friend as
4. Serial Identification Number (if any) [See Note 2.]

C.—BODY NOT CLAIMED FOR BURIAL.
(Enter following identification particulars so far as ascertainable.)

1. Name, in Block Letters (Surname first) ... ...
2. Residence (Full Postal Address) ... ...
3. Occupation or Description ... ...
4. Whether Single, Married or Widowed 5. Age 6. Sex
7. Cause of Death (based upon A.5 above and any further inspection and examination) [see Note 3].
8. If Identified on Inspection of the Body by a Relative or Friend. — Signature of Person Identifying / Relationship to Deceased
9. If Identified by personal effects only (including Identity Card, if any). — Nature of Evidence / Serial Identification Number (if any) [See Note 2.]

Signature Official Description
Date

NOTES.—1. The entry should state the apparent cause of death, e.g., whether due to bomb-splinter, falling masonry, fire, etc.
2. If National Registration is in force and an Identity Card is found on the body, the Serial Identification Number must be entered, as directed, either in Part B or Part C. The Identity Card itself should be marked "Dead: War Operations" and forwarded with this form to the Clerk of the Council, for transmission to the Registrar-General.
3. This entry should confirm (or modify as required as a result of any further examination), the entry made in A.5. It is not intended that any attempt should be made to give medical details (e.g., the precise location of wounds, or vital organs affected), but the particulars furnished should relate to the nature of the violence which caused the wounds rather than to the medical nature of the wounds themselves.

51-3462.

D.—TO BE ENTERED PENDING IDENTIFICATION [See Note 4.]

Height 5 ft 3 ins. Build Slim
Dress Blue Slip Remainder of Clothes blown to bits
Hair Dark Moustache — Beard
Complexion Unrecognisable Eyes do.
Shape of Nose do. Shape of Face do.
Physical Marks or Peculiarities
Names or Identification Marks upon Effects 1 Silver Bangle (Ebony Black Cat)

Signature J Walker Official Description Supt
Date 14.10.40

INVENTORY OF CLOTHING AND EFFECTS.
(For entry in accordance with such instructions as may be given by the Local Authority.)

Signature Official Description
Date

To the
REGISTRAR OF BIRTHS AND DEATHS for the STOKE NEWINGTON Sub-district.
(NOTE.—The space below should *not* be signed if the form is sent to the Registrar in connection with Section B only.)

The Particulars overleaf with respect to a death, which I hereby certify to be due to war operations, are sent to you for Registration.

Signature E J Pitt
Deputy Clerk to the
STOKE NEWINGTON Council.

NOTE 4.—Unless the body has been identified, in which case either Part B or Part C of the form must be filled up, Part D should be filled up before the body is removed from the Mortuary.

The awful task of identification of the dead at St Olave's Mortuary is illustrated by this representative set of documents for a 'female blown to pieces', subsequently named as Mrs Iris Romer. Her name, together with 86 of the other casualties, is inscribed on the Stoke Newington Borough memorial on the mass grave at Abney Park Cemetery.

By the tenth day, it was decided that identification would take place behind screens at the scene of the incident, the identified being taken to the mortuary and the unidentified direct to Abney Park Cemetery.

In all, 128 of the 154 who died were named. Identification was by no means easy. Many identity cards and other papers had been ruined by the water, and there were so many sodden papers from which the ink had run that the water that filled the basement had an eerie inky tinge to it. A particularly unpleasant task was that of separating the papers and personal effects from a corpse in which they had become embedded before they could be put into a 'Dorothy Bag', which was labelled with a metal disc for future reference.

In deference to the Jewish faith, as far as possible all Jewish dead were kept apart from Gentile, before being buried by arrangement with the United Synagogue Society in Rainham Cemetery. A memorial service was held for them on November 11, at 11.00 a.m., led by the Jewish Rabbi, Doctor Rabinowitz.

Eighty-six of the victims were finally laid to rest at Abney Park Cemetery, and 24 by the Jewish Burial Society. Eighteen Gentiles and 26 Jews received private burials.

The incident provoked such a sense of outrage that the King and Queen visited the site to see for themselves the circumstances of the deaths. They were accompanied by Ernest Gowers, Senior Regional Commissioner for London, and Admiral Sir Edward Evans.

ANDREW P. HYDE, 1986

FORM CWD/P/13.

Address of Mortuary.
St Olaves N4

To the Town Clerk,
Stoke Newington Town Hall,
Stoke Newington Church Street,
N. 16.

Dear Sir,

I have to inform you that the body numbered 26 has been identified, and the following information is given in connection therewith:-

Name Iris Elsie Romer
Address 38 Shakespeare Walk N16
Occupation or Description Domestic help Dtr of Mr Henry Romer a Master Builder (Decd).
Whether single, married or widowed Single
Age 27 Sex Female
Cause of Death Multiple Injuries
Identified by G. D. Jones
Relationship Brother in law

Yours faithfully,

[signature]

Mortuary Superintendent.

FORM CWD/P/12.

Name (if known) I. E. Romer No. 26

INVENTORY OF CLOTHING & PERSONAL EFFECTS.

Inventory of Clothing (Males).

Article	No.
Coats	
Waistcoats	
Trousers	
Shirt	
Vests	
Pants	
Socks (prs)	
Boots or Shoes (prs)	
Collars	
Ties	
Braces	
Hat	
Sundries	
Surgical Belts etc.,	
Trusses etc.,	
Handkerchiefs	

Inventory of Clothing (Females).

Article	No.
Aprons	
Blouses	
Skirts	
Petticoats Blue Slip	1
Corsets	
Vests	
Knickers	
Stockings (prs)	
Shoes (prs)	
Costumes (Coat and Skirt)	
Hat	
Sundries	
Shawls etc.,	
Handkerchiefs	

Money and Personal Effects	
Notes (£)	
" (10/-)	
Silver	
Copper	
Total £	
Wallet	
Pocket Book	
Watch	
Chain	
Rings	
Cigarette Lighter	
Cigarette Case	
Pocket Knife	
Keys	
Pencils	
Fountain Pen	

Money and Personal Effects	
Notes (£)	
" (10/-)	
Silver	
Copper	
Total £	
Handbag	
Watch (Wrist)	
Rings	
Necklace	
Brooches	
1 Silver Bangle Ebony Black Cat	1

I certify that the above is a complete list of clothing and personal effects removed by me from Body No. 26
Name (if known) I. E. Romer
Date 14.10.40 Signed [signature]

RECEIPT FOR CLOTHING AND PERSONAL EFFECTS.

I, the undersigned, being the Brother in law of the late I. E. Romer of 38 Shakespeare Rd N16 hereby acknowledge receipt of the articles of clothing, free from any unnecessary damage, and personal effects detailed above.

Signed George D Jones
Address 4 Beatty Road N.16
Date 26.10.40

This form to be completed in triplicate.

SUNDAY, OCTOBER 13

There was little damage caused either in London Region or elsewhere by day. Railways in East and South-East London received most attention. The Waterson Street L.M.S. railway bridge at Shoreditch was demolished and lines were damaged in six other places. Serious fires were caused at the Abbey Lane gasworks, West Ham, as a result of H.E., and at the Gas Light and Coke Co's Stratford works. Mile End and Shoreditch districts suffered most heavily, 20 persons being killed and 57 injured.

Some 180 aircraft were over this country during the day. There were four main attacks all in the afternoon. Portions of all but the first attack penetrated to Central London. The first attack and the remaining portions of the other three attacks confined their operations to Kent. Very few of the enemy aircraft employed were bombers.

A few reconnaissances were also made in the South-East and off the South Coast from the early morning onwards. There were considerable reconnaissances off the North-East and East Coasts in the afternoon.

1248. Twenty-five+ enemy aircraft came inland at Hythe to Lympne and left at 1300.

1335. Two waves of 30+ flew up the Medway. The first wave penetrated to Central London. The second did not proceed beyond Dartford.

1406. Three waves of 30+ crossed the coast near Dungeness, flying north-west. The first wave penetrated to Central London, the second as far as Dartford, and the third wave concentrated on the Biggin Hill and Kenley area.

1535. A raid of 50+ flew over Maidstone and split, one part towards Hornchurch and the other via Dartford to Central London. All these aircraft had left this country by 1610.

Raiding by night was of longer duration and more widespread than of late. In all some 300 enemy aircraft flew over this country, 80 of which operated over London.

Several communal shelters in London and Middlesbrough were demolished and a block of flats in Stoke Newington collapsed, burying some 250 persons who were sheltering in the basement. In addition, 1 tube station and 1 Metropolitan Underground station were hit. Casualties were, therefore, considerably greater than for some time past.

The scale of attack was heaviest between 1900 and 2300, after which it decreased, finally ceasing at 0600. The main concentration was on London, but the Liverpool area received considerable attention. Raids were also plotted in the Bristol area, Wales, the Midlands, East Anglia, Lincolnshire and over the North-East Coast as far north as Newcastle.

Minelaying is suspected between Flamborough Head and the Wash, off Harwich and between Liverpool and Blackpool.

Approximate civilian casualties in London during daylight amounted to 25 killed and 108 injured. Elsewhere 1 person was seriously injured. At night in London 175 people were killed and 458 were injured. These figures do not include the persons (feared 200) trapped in the shelter in Stoke Newington. Elsewhere during the night, 33 were killed and 68 were seriously injured, together with 83 people who were slightly hurt. Two enemy aircraft were destroyed and 5 were probably destroyed.

German Jabo formations continued to press home their attacks on London during the day despite strong opposition from the British defences. The Luftwaffe lost a total of 6 aircraft, 2 in accidents, whilst four more returned from combat sorties damaged. Another 2 German machines were damaged during non-operational sorties. Only one came down in the UK:

That same night rescue services were faced with another bad incident three miles away at Bounds Green, when at 8.55 p.m. a bomb blew a wide crater penetrating into the underground railway tunnel 55 feet below ground. Preliminary reports indicated 14 killed, 51 injured, with 15–20 still to be extricated. The final death toll was 19, all except three being Belgians from a local colony of refugees. (See also pages 244–249.) The following night another bomb hit Balham High Street, breaking through into the Northern Line tunnel about a hundred yards from the station entrance. George Hitchin was driving his omnibus north towards Vauxhall when the bomb struck 25 yards ahead of him. The bomb exploded and when he came to George found himself lying where he had been blown in a shop doorway. After having been treated at the first aid post in Ducane Road, he thought he ought to go back to his vehicle but as he approached the spot there was no sign of it. 'It's OK,' he thought to himself, 'someone's moved it.' It was only when he came nearer that he saw to his horror that only the roof was protruding from the crater.

7/JG3 Messerschmitt Bf 109E-4 (860). Severely damaged by Flight Lieutenant C. B. F. Kingcombe of No. 92 Squadron during escort sortie for Bf 109 fighter-bombers attacking London. Forced-landed at Cuckold Coombe, Hastingleigh, near Ashford 2.10 p.m. Gefr. H. Rungen captured unhurt. Aircraft 7+I a write-off.

MONDAY, OCTOBER 14

Enemy activity by day was on a small scale and consisted of scattered raids by individual aircraft, except at 1635 when 35 enemy aircraft, identified as Dorniers, flying at 20,000 feet, flew to Selsey Bill where they split, one formation to the Portsmouth area and the remainder over an area about 12 miles inland. By 1645 these raids had turned back towards France. Hostile patrols and reconnaissances were maintained in the Channel and the Straits of Dover.

Enemy activity by night was concentrated chiefly on London and Coventry.

Between 1900 and 2100 some 70 raids crossed the coast; 27 between Shoeburyness and Orfordness, and some 40 between Shoreham and Dungeness. The majority of these raids flew to the London area, but a few appeared to be active over East Anglia.

About 600 people were sheltering in the station when the bomb hit. The lights went out and immediately water began to trickle in, soon becoming a torrent washing down tons of sand and gravel. There was also a fearful smell of gas.

A few raids also crossed the coast between Poole and Portland and flew to the Birmingham and Coventry area. Isolated raids were over the Liverpool, Blackburn and Preston areas.

Between 2100 and 2300 a few raids came in from the Dutch islands and about 30 from the French coast. London was still the main target, but raids continued to cross between Poole and Portland and fly to Birmingham and Coventry.

Between 2300 and 0100 activity from the French coast continued towards London, and a few raids were still plotted towards Birmingham. Elsewhere raids appeared over Peterborough, Wittering, and East Anglia.

Between 0100 and 0600, all raids concentrated on London during this period and the country was finally clear by 0533.

Civilian casualties (approx.): By day in London, 2 people were killed, 5 seriously injured, and 76 were slightly injured; elsewhere, 15 were killed and 26 seriously injured. By night in London, 170 people were killed and 632 seriously injured; elsewhere, 12 people were killed and 108 seriously injured. Enemy aircraft casualties: destroyed nil; probable nil; damaged 3.

One of the survivors recalled the scene: 'It was about 8.00 p.m. I was standing on the platform talking to people when there was a terrific explosion above the station and, at the same time one of the platform lamps "arced", and that put the station in darkness. When the station went into darkness panic started; it was bad panic. I said to them, "It will be all right; we will have a light on in a few moments." . . . I didn't realise that the tunnel had collapsed . . . I got my torch and I flashed it up and saw water was pouring down in torrents . . . I was up to my knees in water . . . soon it was like a waterfall. In about five minutes all the anti-suicide pits were full. The water went up to about the second stair of the escalator.' This picture of the long operation to clear the station was not released until 1944.

Many lives were saved by the action of two London Passenger Transport Board staff who opened flood gates but in all 68 people died, four being LPTB staff. Service on the line had to be suspended from Clapham Common to Tooting Broadway — a distance of about 2½ miles — while 7 million gallons of water, sewage and silt was cleared, and the line was not reopened until January 19, 1941.

The German strategy of maintaining constant pressure on the RAF was demonstrably achieving its purpose and aerial superiority once again swung in the Luftwaffe's favour. Continuing sorties by German bombers at night caused considerable damage to the capital with 500 Londoners being killed and thousands injured and rendered homeless in raids which presaged the onslaught of the London 'Blitz'. Three German aircraft failed to return from combat sorties and another was lost in an accident. In addition, 6 of their aircraft were damaged, 3 in accidents.

7/JG2 Messerschmitt Bf 109E-7 (720). Reputedly crashed from high altitude and burned out at Durns Town, Sway during sortie over the Channel. Exact cause unknown but possibly that attacked by Pilot Officer R. G. A. Barclay of No. 249 Squadron. Obergefr. J. Lux missing believed killed. Aircraft 12+~ lost.

TUESDAY, OCTOBER 15

During the day the enemy made 5 fighter attacks over Kent and Sussex employing about 550 enemy aircraft. One formation of fighters flew over the Portsmouth and Southampton area, and some aircraft penetrated to Hornchurch and Central London. Southern Railway lines were temporarily blocked at Waterloo Station and Vauxhall and there was interference with railway traffic between Richmond and Twickenham. Damage was done to factories in West Ham and to sheds in the King George V Dock. In Southwark casualties amounted to approximately 6 killed and 40 injured. In Kent and Essex damage and casualties were slight, only a few bombs being dropped.

There was intense enemy activity throughout the night in London and Birmingham and many incidents are also reported within the area south of the Wash — Birmingham — Bristol Channel. Flying conditions were good at full moon, and many I.B.s, reported to be a new type, were dropped during the early part of the night causing numerous large fires. Later raiders dropped large numbers of land mines and H.E. bombs causing considerable damage to public utilities, industry and private property, and high casualties resulted in the London area. Elsewhere, damage is not serious, and casualties are low. It is estimated that the enemy's effort consisted of 300 aircraft, with 200 concentrated on London.

The church of St James's, Piccadilly, built by Wren between 1676 and 1684, as part of the general redevelopment of the area being undertaken by Lord Alban. Damaged several times during the war, for the first time on October 14/15, 1940 and more than once afterwards, it was restored between 1947 and 1954, the spire being replaced in 1968. The churchyard was made into a garden and this plaque unveiled by Queen Mary, the Queen Mother, in 1946.

Although the invasion had been officially postponed, Enigma decrypts of German orders picked up in Britain on October 13 and 14 still indicated that the threat of an enemy landing was very real. The intensified bombing on the night of the 14th/15th seemed to bear this out; London came in for some heavy treatment and No. 10 was badly damaged from a near miss from bombs which plastered Whitehall. Churchill was dining in the basement at the time and escaped injury: 'My detective came into the room and said much damage had been done. The kitchen, the pantry, and the offices on the Treasury side were shattered. We went into the kitchen to view the scene. The devastation was complete. The bomb had fallen fifty yards away on the Treasury, and the blast had smitten the large, tidy kitchen, with all its bright saucepans and crockery, into a heap of black dust and rubble. The big plate-glass window had been hurled in fragments and splinters across the room, and would of course have cut its occupants, if there had been any, to pieces.'

The problem of just how much news, and to what degree the extent of the bombing, could be released to the public was a thorny problem. On October 15 Home Security commented on precisely this subject: 'In the 8 o'clock News Bulletin on Tuesday it was stated: "This morning's official account of last night's air raids says: 'London and a town in the Midlands were the principal objectives during last night's raids which were on a somewhat smaller scale than those of the previous night'." There has been a lot of discussion this morning on the subject because many people in the London area had a terrible night and found it very disheartening to hear this bulletin. Individuals in the following districts [there followed a list of 21 areas] believe that Monday night was definitely worse than Sunday night.' This is Austin Friars, EC2.

Very serious damage in London to New River Bridge, Edmonton, where a 24in culvert was broken, will deprive City and all areas served by it of water supply, which amounted to 46 million gallons per day. 15 millions can be restored in about 24 hours by diverting water through the old channel, now disused. An excavation of 2,000 cubic yards of soil must be carried out, and 2,000 men of A.M.P.C. have mobilised for this work. Areas affected are Hampstead, St Pancras, City, Finsbury, Islington, Stoke Newington, Hackney, Holborn, East Westminster, Shoreditch, Hornsey, Tottenham, Edmonton, Wood Green, Southgate, Enfield and Cheshunt. Water will probably not be available in the higher parts of these districts, and elsewhere supply will be severely restricted.

The most serious incidents, involving heavy casualties (killed and injured), occurred at: Morley College, Westminster Bridge Road, Waterloo, 250; Lady Owen's School, Finsbury (48 trapped), 110; Prospect Terrace, St Pancras, 100; Cumberland Place (Seymour Street) Marylebone, 100; Trench shelter, Kennington Park, Lambeth, 100 (trapped); Trench shelters, Cadogan Terrace, Poplar, 100; Two shelters, Southwark (many trapped); Warwick Way and Lupus Street, Pimlico (many). (As large numbers of casualties have been trapped, firm figures are not yet available, and it is probable that the total will have to be revised.)

Civilian casualties (approx.): By day in London, 48 killed, 222 injured; elsewhere, 9 seriously injured, 6 slightly injured. By night in London, 213 killed and 915 slightly injured; elsewhere, 27 killed, 145 people injured. Enemy aircraft casualties: destroyed 19; probable 5; damaged 10.

Several well executed Jabo attacks on London caused significant disruption to the rail services, whilst the capital again bore the brunt of heavy German attacks throughout the night, many thousands of homes in the eastern boroughs being reduced to rubble. Increased effort on this day cost the Luftwaffe the loss of 13 aircraft with another 7 returning from sorties with damage. Three more aircraft were destroyed and a similar number damaged in accidents.

3/JG2 Messerschmitt Bf 109E-4 (1588). Hit in the petrol tank by fighters during free-lance sortie over the Channel. Possibly that claimed by Pilot Officer N. le C. Agazarian of No. 609 Squadron. Believed also attacked by Pilot Officer B. Wlasnowolski of No. 213 Squadron. Forced-landed at Bowcombe Down, near Newport, Isle of Wight 12.45 p.m. Fw. H. Hellriegel captured unhurt. Aircraft 8+ a write-off.

Radio mast taken at the time donated to the Kent Battle of Britain Museum and now in the Hawkinge Aeronautical Trust.

4/JG2 Messerschmitt Bf 109E-1 (3279). Shot down by Flying Officer T. Nowierski of No. 609 Squadron during sortie over the Channel. Crashed and exploded at Everton, near Lymington, Hampshire 12.40 p.m. Gefr. A. Pollach baled out at very low level but survived and captured unhurt. Aircraft 10+— a write-off.

8/JG3 Messerschmitt Bf 109E-4 (1294). Radiator damaged in fighter attack during

Stationers' Hall, built in 1673 to replace the one destroyed in 1666 was itself badly damaged on October 15. It would have been entirely lost had it not been for the Hall Keeper, Mr Price, who dashed up to the roof and managed to deal with several incendiaries with the incendiary scoop *(see Volume 1, pages 60 and 61)*. The Hall was restored between 1951–56 by Godfrey Gurney.

I/KG51: Many fires seen after bombs away. Glare seen as far as mid-Channel.

II/KG51: Bombs on Clapham Junction Station. Near Regents Park 1 large and 8 smaller fires seen.

III/KG51: At least 14 fires seen.

I/KG54: One of our 1000kg bombs caused a new fire 2 km west of Fulham gasworks.

II/KG54: Many smaller fires seen in East End.

I/KG55: Many large fires in south of city.

II/KG55: As the first aircraft flew over the French coast we saw the glare of fires in London. We saw 5 large and 8 smaller fires start. A big fire NW of the Thames bend and in the City.

I/LG1: Bombs dropped near railway yards south and west of Kensington. Three fires started East End.

II/LG1: Eight of us dropped on north of Thames between London Bridge and Waterloo Bridge; 3 of us on East End, 1 south of Surrey Docks. Fires seen in King George and Royal Albert Docks.

III/LG1: Crews say that these fires are the biggest ever.

KG76: Good visibility, good hits. We saw a darting blue-green flame and a burning factory and 26 big fires with much smoke.

KG26: First attack. Many fires, especially to east of Battersea Park. Also huge explosion apparently a gasometer.
Second attack. Caused a big fire to south of Thames. With one of our SC 1800 we hit a factory and caused a fire.

CREW REPORTS, OCTOBER 16, 1940

free-lance sweep over London. Forced-landed on the beach adjacent to Princes Golf Course, Sandwich 9.17 a.m. Oberfw. W. Bauer captured unhurt. Aircraft 7+I a write-off.

8/JG27 Messerschmitt Bf 109E-4 (2790). Shot down by Sergeant R. H. Fokes of No. 92 Squadron during combat over Kent and crashed at Trimworth Manor, Olantigh 1.00 p.m. Possibly that also attacked by Pilot Officer R. H. Holland. Oberlt. G. Deicke (Staffelkapitän) baled out and captured unhurt. Aircraft a write-off.

Major recovery by the Kent Battle of Britain Museum. Remains of the Daimler-Benz DB 601 engine excavated together with both undercarriage legs, quantities of compressed airframe, some still bearing the original painted Gruppe badge, cockpit instruments and controls including the control column, reflector gunsight, complete seat harness, signal pistol, pilot's maps and aircraft identity plate confirming '2790', now in the Hawkinge Aeronautical Trust. Some items donated to the London Air Museum and now held by the Tangmere Military Aviation Museum.

4/JG51 Messerschmitt Bf 109E-1 (3535). Engine set alight in combat with fighters during free-lance sortie over Kent. Crashed at Owls Castle Farm, Lamberhurst 8.35 a.m. Uffz. E. Höhn baled out and captured unhurt. Aircraft 2+ a write-off.

Excavated by the Wealden Aviation Archaeological Group in 1974 and fragments of the shattered airframe recovered. Re-excavated by the same group in 1979 when remains of Daimler-Benz DB 601 engine were unearthed together with various pieces of airframe bearing number '3535' and propeller boss. Propeller boss and elevator mass balance weight now in the Tangmere Military Aviation Museum.

3/KG2 Dornier Do 17Z. Sortied to attack London at night and abandoned in error 10.40 p.m. Gefr. H. Fellmann baled out landing at Little Butts Farm, Cousley Wood, near Wadhurst and captured unhurt. Lt. H-J. Brudern, Uffz. R. Trinkner and Uffz. H. Fahrenbach returned safely to base. Aircraft undamaged.

Stab I/LG2 Messerschmitt Bf 109E-7 (3734). Exploded over Spruce Lawns, Elham 9.20 a.m. during fighter-bomber sortie over Kent. Exact cause uncertain, but probably detonation of bomb-load. Lt. L. Lenz fell with cockpit section at Olders Bank and died of his wounds. Aircraft <+ a write-off.

Ludwig Lenz was buried in Folkestone New Cemetery, Hawkinge and not reinterred at Cannock Chase.

Although the spotlight was on London, provincial towns were also being struck by the Luftwaffe. On Wednesday evening Dorniers from Küstenfliegergruppe 606 at the aerodrome of Lanvéoc-Poulmic near Brest took off to attack Liverpool. 7T+HK from the 2nd Staffel is believed to have got lost and, attempting a forced landing short of fuel, it came down here at Masbury Ring in Somerset — despite the attempt by wartime caption writers to credit its demise to 'RAF fighters near Shepton Mallet'! *Right:* Steve Casely found the crash site and adopts a characteristic pose with his counterpart of forty years ago.

July 1987 and Herr Konrad Faupel comes to Cannock Chase War Cemetery to seek out the grave of his brother Heinrich *(right)*, lost on operations over England.

Each 24-hour period covered by the Ministry of Home Security reports runs from 6.00 a.m. one morning to 6.00 a.m. the next day. Thus, for example, the October 16 appreciation covers daytime events on Wednesday and on through the night to 6 o'clock Thursday morning.

WEDNESDAY, OCTOBER 16

Enemy activity was on a very small scale during the day, and almost entirely confined to sporadic raids by single aircraft, mostly in the South-East. Only one raid penetrated to London. One raid was plotted near Arbroath and others in Liverpool, Swansea, Cardiff and Gloucester areas. Few bombs were dropped and damage was negligible. Forty enemy aircraft in all were plotted over this country.

Enemy activity after dark was on a heavy scale until midnight, after which only a few isolated raids entered the country. The main attack was directed against London and its suburbs, but a small number of early raids visited Wales and the Midlands. Damage and casualties in London Region were on a smaller scale than of late. Bombs were dropped in Liverpool and Birmingham areas between 2000 and 2130, but damage was slight though there were a few casualties in both areas, some of which were fatal.

No incidents are reported from Nos. 1 Region (except at Thirsk at 1950), 2, 3, 10 (except on Merseyside), 11 (except at Glenquaich, near Amulree). Elsewhere although bombs were dropped before midnight in several localities damage was slight and casualties relatively small.

Civilian casualties (approx.): Outside London by day, 3 people were seriously injured and 5 slightly injured. By night, in London 46 were killed and 209 injured; elsewhere, there were 24 people killed, 44 seriously injured, 46 slightly injured. Enemy aircraft destroyed: certain 3 (at night), damaged 1.

Enemy balloons with attachment containing leaflets have been reported from Eastern, South-Eastern and North Midland Regions. Balloons are believed to measure 10 to 20 feet and to carry a small explosive charge operated by clockwork and intended to scatter the leaflets. Care is therefore required in handling.

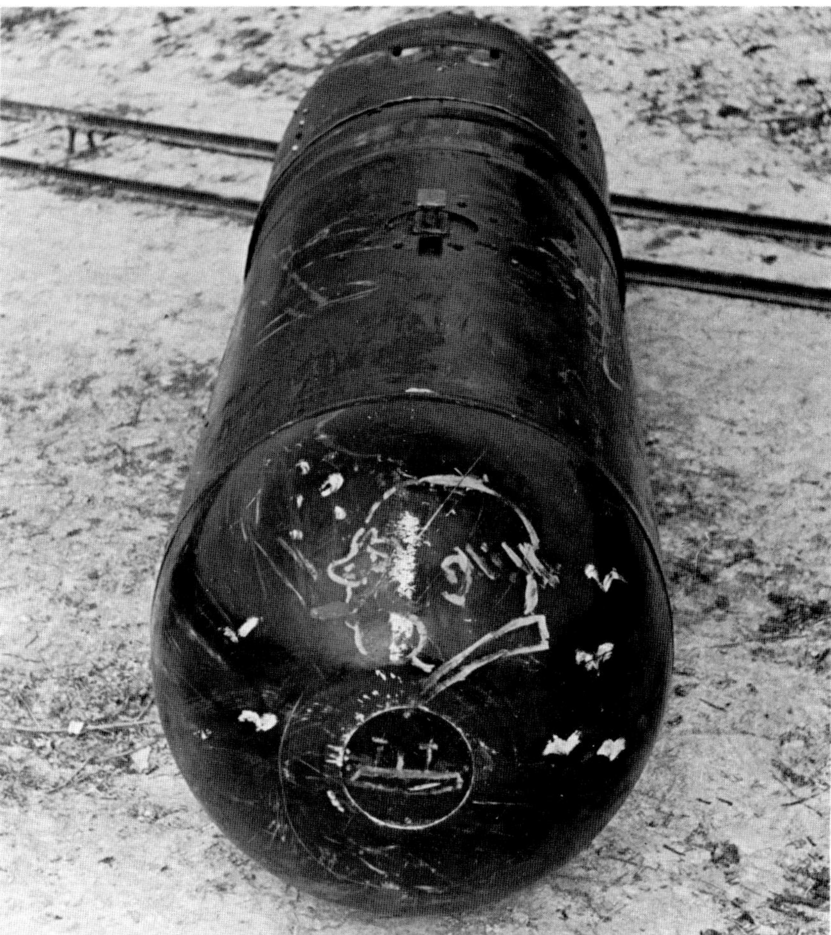

During the previous week, of the 1,500-odd casualties, nearly 1,400 had been killed in London and the War Cabinet had expressed fears that there was a general feeling that Britain was not 'hitting back hard enough at Germany'. When on the morning of the 16th Churchill learned that much of the previous night's damage had been caused by parachute mines, he rose to the bait: 'It is now about three weeks since I began pressing for similar treatment. . . . Who is responsible for paralysing action?' One wonders if the Prime Minister was goaded by the sight of this particularly cheeky piece of Teutonic artwork on a mine recovered on the railway embankment at Stonards Hill, Epping.

So worried was Churchill about the effect of the weapon on morale that on October 23 an official note was sent to the Air Ministry, War Office, Ministry of Home Security and Ministry of Information: 'No disclosure should be made of the severity of effect, in the public estimation, of these mines. From their size it would be apparent that they constituted a severe attack, but the added danger of their magnetic properties and the widespread destruction of house property they caused should not appear.' Meanwhile the Air Minister replied to the Prime Minister's demand for action saying that the use of British mines still awaited a War Cabinet decision and that Hampdens, the only aircraft capable of carrying the weapon to the heart of Germany, were fully engaged in attacking naval units at Kiel. *Above:* This is an example of the news black-out. The left-hand picture was submitted to the Press and Censorship Bureau by the Express & Independent newspaper at Leytonstone, in East London, but it was returned stamped 'Not to be published'. The one on the *right* of the same incident but with less visible damage, also submitted by the paper with the caption: 'Houses and business premises demolished by a land mine which dropped in a London suburb' was returned approved for publication with the word 'bomb' substituted for 'land mine'.

[Printed by authority of the Registrar General.]

CERTIFIED COPY of an ENTRY OF DEATH
Pursuant to the Births and Deaths Registration Act 1953

HC 105620

D. Cert.
S.R.

Registration District ROMFORD

1940. Death in the Sub-district of Dagenham. in the County of Essex.

Columns:—	1	2	3	4	5	6	7	8	9
No.	When and where died	Name and surname	Sex	Age	Occupation	Cause of death	Signature, description, and residence of informant	When registered	Signature of registrar
64	Twenty first September 1940 Oval Road North Dagenham U.D.	Reginald Vincent ELLINGWORTH	Male	42 years	of 362 Copnor Road Portsmouth Chief Petty Officer (Royal Navy)	"Due to War Operations"	Certificate received from F. W. Allen Clerk to Dagenham Borough Council	Seventh October 1940	Frank Bundy Registrar.

Clerical omission in columns 2 & 4 corrected on the 17th January 1941 by me, Frank Bundy Registrar, on the authority of the Registrar General

Certified to be a true copy of an entry in a register in my custody.

Audrey L. Poole Deputy Superintendent Registrar.

1st March 1988 Date.

CAUTION:—It is an offence to falsify a certificate or to make or knowingly use a false certificate or a copy of a false certificate intending it to be accepted as genuine to the prejudice of any person, or to possess a certificate knowing it to be false without lawful authority.

The inability of the Press to cover mine incidents in greater detail, restricted by the sort of subterfuge shown on the previous page, meant the deaths of two of the Royal Navy's leading mine warfare experts from HMS *Vernon* passing unnoticed, in spite of bravery which was to result in the award — posthumously — of the George Cross. Readers referring to Volume 1 (pages 79-83) will recall the exploit of Lieutenant Commander Richard Ryan and Chief Petty Officer Reginald Ellingworth in tackling the first magnetic mine found in a German aircraft at Clacton. Although the timer was normally set to explode 22 seconds after its fall, if it failed to operate the detonator there was no way of knowing just how much time was left to run. Even a footfall might set the clock running, leaving perhaps only a few seconds at most in which to escape. Since April Lieutenant Commander Ryan and his assistant, CPO Ellingworth, had worked on six mines before another dropped on Hornchurch aerodrome on September 20. The following day the pair arrived to deal with the mine which lay on the peri track in the south-western corner. After defuzing it successfully, Ryan and Ellingworth were entertained for lunch in the mess before going on to tackle two other mines which had fallen in Dagenham. One had come down in New Road outside the Princess Cinema, while the second had come to rest in the upstairs room of a house in Oval Road North *(below)*. What happened that day can only be conjecture. Was there a brief moment of truth as their eyes met as the clock dropped the final seconds before oblivion, both knowing that their time was finally up? Or did the end come swiftly without warning? We shall never know. Of the two nothing was ever found; for them there was no grave — not even the sailor's grave of the sea.

TWO LAND MINES IN LONDON

On October 1, 1969, the Kentish Town police reported the discovery of an object on a building site at Burghley Road in north-west London. The object turned out to be the first German parachute mine to be recovered in London since the end of the war.

These mines were designed to be dropped by parachute into busy but shallow shipping lanes and there to sit on the bottom until an unwary ship passed in their direction. They were fitted with magnetic and/or acoustic units which detonated the mine as the ship passed over the top of them. Because of their sophisticated fuzing they were also fitted with a self-destruct device, so that if they fell on land they destroyed themselves to protect the secrets of the mine. This device was a relatively simple bomb fuze. On impact, whether on land or water, a clock started to tick; if, within 22 seconds, pressure such as would be found in a given depth of water was not applied to the fuze, the mine exploded.

When they accidentally fell on land these mines were so efficient as blast bombs that large numbers were deliberately dropped on the cities of the UK. Many continued to have full magnetic and acoustic options and all contained the self-destruct bomb fuze. Thus if one failed to detonate on impact, the slightest movement was likely to start or restart the clock, with a maximum of 22 seconds to run before the mine exploded. During this time the mine clearance officer had the option of running too, or attempting to gag the fuze with specially designed tools.

RAF Hornchurch, Station Operations Record Book: 'At 4.30 p.m. we heard a loud explosion — and Ryan and his Petty Officer were killed'. Surely there can only be one name for this quiet suburban road today: Ryan-Ellingworth Avenue. Yet the courage of such men is not unique to the war period alone; as Major Hogben describes here, the menace of the mine is still with us today.

Such was the beast that faced Major G. R. Fletcher, MBE, RE, and Sergeant Major S. D. Hambrook, RE, when they responded to a call from the Kentish Town police that day in October 1969. After investigation they decided that since the mine was firmly embedded in London clay it would be easier and safer to remove the end filling plate and steam out the explosive without attempting to dig around the mine to find and immunize the bomb fuze, thus reducing the risk of disturbing the mine.

After an extremely exciting, hazardous and downright unpleasant night, all 1,620 lb of the hexamite explosive filling was removed and the fuze destroyed. As a result of their night's work Major Fletcher and Warrant Officer Hambrook were both subsequently awarded the George Medal.

Just four months later, on February 5, 1970, a similar mine was discovered at the reservoir at Coppermill Lane, Walthamstow, as it was emptied. This time in response to a call from the Walthamstow police Major M. J. V. Hoskins, GM, RE, and again Warrant Officer Hambrook deployed from the Royal Engineer Bomb Disposal Unit. In this incident the disposal was carried out as a Joint Service operation. A Royal Navy team under the command of Lieutenant C. Churcher, RN, rendered safe the various fuzes in the mine and the Royal Engineers removed its explosive. Again a very difficult and hazardous operation, not helped by appalling weather conditions.

MAJOR A. S. HOGBEN, 1987

Hundreds of people were evacuated from their homes as Major Fletcher and Sergeant Major Hambrook set about the mine, buried some three feet or so in solid clay.

Within four months a second Luftmine B (the Admiralty called them C-mines), was discovered in Warwick Reservoir at Walthamstow while it was being drained by the Metropolitan Water Board. There it had lain for thirty years just a few hundred yards from the heavily built-up area of South Tottenham. A thousand workers in nine factories were evacuated, and 500 households and a primary school in an area up to 800 yards radius were warned to leave their windows open. Here Sergeant MacAndrew supervises the building of a coffer dam preparatory to steaming out the explosive.

Fog disrupted aerial activity and resulted in few daylight combats. Night attacks continued unabated with London and Birmingham being the main targets. The Luftwaffe lost 13 aircraft and 5 more damaged on operations, whilst 2 were destroyed and 3 more damaged in routine domestic flights.

2/606 Dornier Do 17Z (2691). Crashed attempting a forced-landing at Masbury Ring, near Wells 11.55 p.m. during night sortie to bomb Liverpool. Exact cause unknown but believed to have lost their bearings and run out of fuel. Oberlt. zur See E. Blanck, Fw. H. Faupel, Fw. G. Steppat and Obergefr. W. Schnake all killed. Aircraft 7T+HK a write-off.

3/606 Dornier Do 17Z (2682). Sortied to attack Liverpool but crashed into a hillside in fog and exploded at Nantglyn, Denbighshire 7.25 p.m. Lt. zur See H. Havemann, Uffz. G. Löcknitz, Uffz. K. Hölscher and Gefr. R. Faehrmann all killed. Aircraft 7T+LL a write-off.

Site excavated by Philippa Hodgkiss. Many items including oxygen bottles, propeller boss, parachute release buckle and bomb load unearthed. Ordnance exploded by the authorities.

Stab II/KG30 Junkers Ju 88A-5 (317). Crashed with full bomb load and exploded near Bishop's Stortford Church 7.50 p.m. Exact cause unknown. Hptmn. E. Hass (Gruppenkommandeur), Fw. J. Kessels, Fw. G. Suhr and Kriegsberichter A. Doppelfeld (of Lw.Kr.Ber.Kp.1) all killed. Aircraft 4D+DM a write-off.

Surface fragments including oxygen mask clip discovered during the taking of comparison photographs in the After the Battle collection.

2/KGr126 Heinkel He 111H-4 (6955). Engaged on minelaying sortie over the Thames Estuary and shot down by No. 264 Squadron Defiant night-fighter (Pilot Officer F. D. Hughes and Sergeant F. Gash). Crashed and exploded at Creaseys Farm, Hutton near Brentwood 2.00 a.m. Lt. K. Newald and Gefr. H-J. Granetz baled out and both captured unhurt. Uffz. K. Gläser and Gefr. J. Twrdik killed. Aircraft 1T+BB a write-off.

Details of this aircraft quoted above are based on original contemporary Luftwaffe records. Documentary evidence and the excavation of the machine suggests actual Werk Nummer 5709 and codes 1T+LK.

Major recovery by the Essex Aviation Group July 1978 with assistance from the East Anglian Drainage Authority. Intact Junkers Jumo 211F engine excavated together with propeller boss and blades, seat armour, cockpit instruments and controls, magazines of 7.9mm MG15 ammunition and navigator's flight bag containing navigation aids and instruments.

2/KGr126 Heinkel He 111H-5 (3510). Engaged on minelaying sortie but blundered into the balloon barrage and crashed deep in mud on the foreshore at Shotley, Suffolk 10.20 p.m. Oberlt. zur See W. Stender, Fw. H. Günther, Uffz. H. Martin and Obergefr. E. Irrgang all killed. Aircraft 1T+JK lost.

This crew was originally buried in Ipswich cemetery. Today they are re-interred in the Soldatenfriedhof, Cannock Chase where the date of death of the Bordmechaniker, Heinz Günther, is incorrectly recorded as October 10.

Site originally investigated by the late John Fisher. Components from Junkers Jumo engine later recovered by the Essex Aviation Group. Propeller boss and blades together with exhaust manifolds recovered by Sean Tinley in December 1981.

The war — and its attendant nervous excitement — returns once again to a lonely field in the extreme north of Wales. On the spot where the second KüFlGr 606 machine crashed in a ball of flame in October 1940, a Royal Engineers Bomb Disposal team attends to deal with ten 50kg bombs discovered when the crash site was excavated in September 1983. Lieutenant Alan Miller led the sappers from Chattenden in Kent who successfully recovered and exploded all the bombs in a nearby quarry.

When the Ju 88 of Stab II/KG30 crashed alongside the old A119 to Much Hadham, the bomb-load exploded, scattering pieces of aircraft and crew far and wide. Even after the clear up in 1940 we found fragments on the surface in 1985.

A repair party from the Gas, Light & Coke Company Ltd in Leicester Square on the morning of October 17. In the background is the headquarters building of the Automobile Association, designed by Andrew Mather in 1923. The offices were extended between 1956-59. However, it would seem even the skills of this venerable organisation would have been insufficient to get these motorists back on the road!

THURSDAY, OCTOBER 17

During the day the enemy made four fighter raids over Kent, some of which reached the London district and the Thames Estuary. Approximately 300 fighter aircraft were employed, some of which carried bombs.

At 0820 some 15 aircraft reached Hornchurch where they turned south-east and were intercepted. At 0900 a second wave of 60 aircraft in two formations — one formation turned north to the Estuary and then home eastwards, the other penetrated Central London and then dispersed.

At 1305 two raids of 25 aircraft each passed over Gravesend and divided, some turned south-east and others reached Hornchurch before turning back.

At 1510 four raids totalling about 80 aircraft approached East London and the Kenley-Biggin Hill areas. Some of these aircraft penetrated to Central London.

At 1630, 60 aircraft in three waves approached Kenley and Biggin Hill areas and attacked Kenley aerodrome. In addition to the above, hostile aircraft were active in the Thames Estuary and the Channel during the day.

Raids were plotted by night leaving the Dutch islands and the Somme at 1825.

At 1825 London was the main objective, but some raids from Cherbourg flew to the Midlands, Birmingham in particular, and later to Liverpool which received considerable attention.

1900-2100. Raids flew to London via the Estuary, Hastings, Beachy Head and to Birmingham and the Midlands via Weymouth Bay and Bristol. A few raids were plotted over East Anglia, up to the Humber, and minelaying is suspected in the Thames Estuary and off South Wales.

Between 2000 and 2300 no raids appeared from Holland, but raids approached London from France. Raids to the Midlands continued north to Liverpool area where considerable hostile activity was plotted.

At 2300-0100, activity appeared to slacken, but a few fresh raids appeared from Holland. A few raids returned from the Midlands, but otherwise activity was confined to London and South-East.

0100-0300. A small number of raids continued to approach London from the Dutch islands and from France, but the rest of the country was clear.

Between 0300 and 0600, small raids continued in the London area.

Civilian casualties (approx.): By day in London, 7 killed, 78 seriously injured; elsewhere during the day, 1 killed, 5 slightly injured. By night in London, 97 people were killed and 365 injured; elsewhere, 28 killed, 50 seriously injured, 29 slightly injured. Enemy aircraft destroyed: certain 4; probable 6; damaged 5.

German tactics remained unchanged throughout the day which was signified by the issue of fresh instructions to RAF fighter controllers and unit commanders on the engagement of high-flying fighter raids which continued to pose considerable problems for the British defences. Twelve German aircraft were destroyed and 4 damaged in operational sorties, whilst 4 more were lost and 4 damaged in accidents.

Stab I/JG53 Messerschmitt Bf 109E-7 (4138). Shot down in combat with fighters over the Channel and crashed into the sea. Hptmn. H-C. Mayer (Gruppenkommandeur) killed. Aircraft lost.

The body of Hans-Carl Mayer was washed ashore at Littlestone 10 days later and buried in Folkestone New Cemetery, Hawkinge where, to this day, his date of death is incorrectly recorded as October 26.

3/JG53 Messerschmitt Bf 109E-4 (1106). Radiator severely damaged in attack by Pilot Officer B. V. Draper of No. 74 Squadron during combat off Gravesend. Engine temperature rose so forced-landed at Manston airfield 3.45 p.m. Oberlt. W. Rupp (Staffelkapitän) captured unhurt. Aircraft 1+ a write-off.

Left: **A City of London police photograph of detectives inspecting the results of an incident at Nos. 57-58 Gracechurch Street. According to the police caption, the damage was caused at 10.55 p.m. on October 19, another night of heavy bombing on London.** *Right:* **The Australia New Zealand Banking Group building now stands on the site with the Republic Bank of Dallas now occupying the one on the right.**

FRIDAY, OCTOBER 18

Enemy activity by day and night was on a very reduced scale, and consisted mainly of reconnaissance flights by single aircraft.

By day: At 0645, 0730 and 0900 single aircraft approached the Kent coast.

Between 1025 and 1030 one raid visited the Forth Estuary and several bombs were dropped at Crail, little damage being done, and two raids approached Harwich.

Between 1130 and 1300 ten shells were dropped in the Dover district but there was only slight damage.

Between 1300 and 1700, single aircraft were active over London and East Anglia and bombs were dropped at Harrow, Crayford, Ashford, Odiham and a naval camp at Fareham.

Between 1700 and 1900 there were raids plotted at Southwold, Kenley, Northolt and in the Bristol and Southampton districts. There was some damage to houses but very few casualties were reported.

By night: 1900-2000 approximately 80 raids were plotted, some penetrating to London and others to Bristol, Liverpool and Birmingham, where bombs were dropped. In Birmingham the first bombs were dropped at 2008 where the raid was moderately severe. Minor incidents occurred in Wednesbury, Dudley, Lichfield and Stafford. The Fire Services had to contend with over 200 fires, and it is reported that all incidents had been dealt with satisfactorily. Total casualties: 4 killed; 16 seriously injured; 16 slightly injured.

Between 2000-2100 reduced activity occurred with six raids on London and six in the Midlands.

2100-2300. A stream of raids was maintained, but confined almost entirely to London, Kent and Essex, with an occasional raid plotted in Buckinghamshire. At Wheatley (G.W.R.) Oxford-Wickham line was blocked, and Wheatley Bridge damaged.

2300-0100. Activity greatly declined, a few raids being plotted over London, but Liverpool, Midlands and the West Country were now completely clear.

0100-0600. By 0100 no raids were left over the country till 0355 when six raids were reported plotted over London. The country was clear by 0550.

In London the only incidents of any importance were the bombing of Beckton gasworks at East Ham at 0537 where a fire was started which was quickly got under control, and at Lambeth where a public house was demolished and about 40 persons were trapped, 2 killed and 6 seriously wounded.

Civilian casualties: By day in London, 5 seriously injured; elsewhere, 5 killed, 12 seriously injured, 11 slightly injured. By night in London there were 45 people killed and 134 seriously injured; elsewhere, 8 were killed, 32 seriously injured and 23 slightly injured. Enemy aircraft destroyed: nil.

Fog again considerably limited activity over Britain and few interceptions took place. An address by Göring to his airmen on this day exhorted them with the news that they had 'reduced the British plutocracy to fear and terror', a seriously misguided impression of the effects of their bombing campaign against England. A further 13 aircraft were lost and 9 more damaged on operations, many in landing accidents. Two more machines were destroyed and another damaged in accidents during domestic flights. None fell in the UK.

SATURDAY, OCTOBER 19

Enemy activity by day was on a reduced scale, being limited to one attack by fighters on London (at 1430), and reconnaissances mainly off the South and East Coasts, a few of which penetrated inland.

Coventry was visited by a single aircraft at midday, which dropped ten H.E. bombs damaging some 27 houses, and machine-gunned the Coventry bypass. There were no casualties or damage of military importance.

Margate was bombed about 1145, considerable damage being done to houses and a Mission Hall. Three persons were killed and 2 injured.

A few bombs were dropped at Strawberry Hill, Twickenham and Rotherhithe (the only incidents in the London Region), Southend, Maidstone, Weymouth and Shotley, causing only slight damage. In all, some 230 enemy aircraft operated off or over our coasts.

Enemy activity by night started at dusk and was abnormally heavy during the first four hours, thereafter continuing on a more usual scale. The main attacks were against the London area, while outside London, Coventry and Merseyside received considerable attention.

No incidents are reported from Scotland or No. 2 Region, and only minor incidents from Nos. 1, 3, 7, 8 and 9 (except at Coventry and Leamington).

After a short interval between 0200 and 0220 when no enemy aircraft were plotted over the country, activity was resumed, single aircraft alternating from the Somme and Belgium every 20 minutes. Those from Belgium flew by the Estuary over London to the Somme, those from the Somme reversed this procedure. This well-organised activity continued steadily until 0550 hours when the country was reported clear.

Railways and docks in the London area received more attention than of late, but the damage done was not of major importance.

At Coventry, though several factories were hit, little industrial damage was caused.

On Merseyside and in south-eastern districts damage was mostly confined to house property.

Armour House on St Martin's-le-Grand went up between the wars along with other buildings along the street. Built on the site of the old headquarters building of the General Post Office constructed here by Robert Smirke between 1824 and 1829, in 1903-10 the new GPO HQ was erected on the site of Christ's Hospital in King Edward Street, and Smirke's buildings were demolished in 1912. The Luftwaffe did their best to knock down the replacement in October 1940 but the imposing edifice came through — the repair now skilfully matched to the original stonework.

When seeking out illustrations for this book, we came across many, many uncaptioned pictures — either with no clue as to the location or any reference as to the date they were taken. This picture is a case in point. All that was scrawled on the back in pencil when we found it was 'London Blitz'. Well at least with this one Andrew Hyde, who took the majority of our comparisons, had a place to work on — even though the area covered was over 100 square miles! Nevertheless with Andrew's intimate knowledge of the area, something rang a bell as he recalled the serrated roof line of the building on the left . . . still remaining in St Leonard Street in Shoreditch. Well done; now all we need is a date!

Casualties in London were the heaviest recorded since the night of 15th/16th October. This was due more to the very widespread nature of the enemy bombing rather than to any individual incidents involving large numbers of casualties.

Approximate civilian casualties in London by day amounted to 3 killed and 4 injured; elsewhere 3 people were killed and 4 were slightly hurt. By night in London 174 people were killed and 538 were injured. Elsewhere 18 were killed and 87 were injured, 52 seriously. Two enemy aircraft were destroyed and 1 was damaged.

A quiet day overall, punctuated by sporadic engagements over south-east England. The Luftwaffe lost 2 aircraft on operations and 3 in accidents. Two more machines returned from sorties with damage and another was damaged in a taxying accident. None fell in the UK.

SUNDAY, OCTOBER 20

There were five main attacks during the day, all in south-east England, some of which penetrated to Central London where a few bombs were dropped but little damage done. The bulk if not all of the enemy aircraft engaged would appear to have been fighters and fighter-bombers.

Patrols were maintained in the Channel and Straits. Reconnaissance flights were made over Bristol, Sealand, Kendal, Shrewsbury, and over Lancashire. A single raider was plotted 100 miles east of the Firth of Forth and over the coast into west Perthshire. Reconnaissance was also active over East Anglia and Portland and the Dutch coast.

The main concentrations of enemy aircraft by night were on London and the Midlands, notably the Birmingham and Coventry areas. Activity was heavy and steadily maintained till about 0100 when the numbers engaged against London began to diminish rapidly. Minelaying was suspected off East Anglia and from the Humber to the Tees.

1900 to 2100: First raid from France crossed the coast at 1900 and those from Holland at 1918. During this period 45 enemy aircraft crossed the south coast and 11 flew to the Essex coast. The majority of raids from the south went to the London area, a few passing west of London to the Northampton-Bedford area. There were 7 raids which had Birmingham and Coventry as their objectives.

2100-0100: Approximately 30 raids flew from the south coast to the London area and northern environs. Another 30 flew to the Midlands with special concentration on Birmingham and Coventry. Twenty-five raids also crossed the Essex coast and appeared to go to North London.

0100 and 0300: Activity over London was heavy and by 0245 no new incoming tracks to the Inner Artillery Zone were showing. Raids to the Midlands, however, continued to fly in between Portland and Selsey Bill and appeared to concentrate on Birmingham and Coventry. Individual raids were also plotted in the Catterick, Peterborough, Manchester and Cambridge districts.

0300-0600: London area was practically clear during this period. Activity in the Midlands continued on a lessening scale till 0530 when the last raid left. In addition to Wolverhampton and Coventry, activity was also plotted over Manchester, Sheffield, Nottingham and Leicester.

Approximate civilian casualties in London during the day amounted to 13 people killed and 52 injured. Elsewhere 4 people were killed and 4 were seriously injured. Seven people were slightly hurt. By night in London, 76 were killed and 320 injured. Elsewhere during the night, 58 people lost their lives, 116 were seriously injured, together with 111 slightly hurt. Nine enemy aircraft were certainly destroyed, 7 probably. Six were damaged.

As if by contrast with the preceding day, strong formations of Bf 109E fighter-bombers again trailed their coats over the southern counties. London and Coventry both suffered heavy attacks during the night. Ten German aircraft were lost and 7 more damaged in operations. Another machine was destroyed and 4 more damaged in accidents. The following aircraft came down in Britain:

5/JG52 Messerschmitt Bf 109E-7 (5930). Shot down by Flying Officer M. P. Brown of No. 41 Squadron during escort mission for Bf 109 fighter-bomber attack on London. Crashed into Mereworth Wood, near West Malling 2.15 p.m. Fw. L. Bielmaier baled out unhurt and captured on landing at Wrotham. Aircraft 4+ a write-off.

Major recovery organised by the late Alan Fall of the Air-Britain Excavation Committee 1973. Intact Daimler-Benz DB 601N engine amongst the many items unearthed now displayed in the Lashenden Air Warfare Museum. Pieces in the Vizard collection.

6/JG52 Messerschmitt Bf 109E-4 (2780). Exploded under attack by Pilot Officer B. V. Draper of No. 74 Squadron during fighter combat over South London. Fell apart over Plumstead, Welling and Woolwich 1.45 p.m. Oberfw. A. Friedemann killed. Aircraft 1+ a write-off.

9/JG54 Messerschmitt Bf 109E-4 (1525). Shot down by Flight Lieutenant A. A. McKellar of No. 605 Squadron during free-lance fighter sortie over Maidstone. Forced-landed engine in flames at North Fording House, near New Romney 10.20 a.m. Fw. A. Iburg captured wounded and slightly burned. Aircraft 6+ a write-off.

Seventeen properties were completely destroyed in Tonbridge, Kent, during the war from the 142 high explosive bombs which hit the town, the majority of which were probably jettisoned loads from lost aircraft. In Dernier Road *above* Frances Couchman was killed at No. 12 and Alice Ford at No. 20 on October 21.

3/JG77 Messerschmitt Bf 109E-1 (4007). Shot down during free-lance fighter sortie and crashed at Foxhunt Green, Chervey Farm, Waldron near Uckfield 2.38 p.m. Possibly that claimed by Pilot Officer H. M. Stephen of No. 74 Squadron. Fw. K-H. Wilhelm baled out and captured unhurt. Aircraft 11+ a write-off.

Site partially excavated by the Halstead War Museum and later completely cleared by the Wealden Aviation Archaeological Group in 1973. Manufacturer's badge from the engine presented to the surviving pilot by London aviation artist Geoffrey Stevens.

3/LG2 Messerschmitt Bf 109E-7 (2059). Believed shot down by Flying Officer J. C. Mungo-Park of No. 74 Squadron during combat over London. Crashed in flames on Chapel Farm, Lenham Heath 2.00 p.m. Uffz. F. Maierl baled out but fell to his death with parachute on fire. Aircraft a write-off.

Franz Maierl was buried in Lenham cemetery, close to where he fell. He was not reinterred in the Soldatenfriedhof at Cannock Chase postwar.

Major recovery by the London Air Museum. Complete Daimler-Benz DB 601 engine excavated with propeller boss, two 20mm MGFF cannon and remains of shattered airframe.

7(F)/LG2 Messerschmitt Bf 110C-5 (2228). Intercepted and shot down by Flight Lieutenant J. W. Villa, Pilot Officer R. Mottram and Sergeant D. E. Kingaby of No. 92 Squadron during mission to photograph bomb damage along the Thames. Also attacked by Pilot Officer H. P. M. Edridge and Flying Officer D. A. P. McMullen of No. 222 Squadron. Forced-landed and caught fire at Bockingfold, Horsmonden 12.50 p.m. Oblt. R. Semmerich captured unhurt, Uffz. R. Ebeling killed. Aircraft L2+MR a write-off.

MONDAY, OCTOBER 21

Enemy activity by day was on a small scale. During the morning and afternoon, raids mostly by single aircraft approached the London area, the Midlands and Liverpool. Owing to bad weather conditions many aerodromes were unserviceable, the fighters were only able to take off after 1100 hours from four aerodromes.

Between 0700 and 1100 bombs were dropped at Liverpool. Westbury (Wilts.), Portland and Weymouth and several factories in the Willesden-Hampstead area received some damage.

Between 1100 and 1400 several raids flew towards London and a few continued to Bedford and Northampton areas, whilst one raid was plotted in the Bristol Channel area. Bombs were dropped at Brockworth aerodrome (Gloster Aircraft Company), Bedford, Watford, Thames Estuary and North London. Casualties were few and little damage was done.

During the afternoon activities decreased. A few raids were plotted in the west and towards London. Bombs were dropped at Bournemouth and some damage to residential property was caused, but elsewhere there was no damage. Dover was shelled between 1400 and 1530 resulting in slight damage to house property. Casualties were small.

Activity by night was considerable and concentrated on London, the Midlands, and Liverpool, but London had a quiet night. Irregularities of communications at some stations made it difficult to record accurate plottings over the South-East Coast after 2230.

1900-2100. Raids flew to London, Birmingham, Coventry and Wolverhampton and a few on Liverpool. The most serious incidents occurred at Coventry where several factories were hit and fires started. A number of casualties occurred but few are fatal.

At Southwark about 30 were trapped when there was a direct hit on a shelter and some damage to railway communications is reported in the St Pancras and Tottenham areas.

2100-0100. Twelve raids concentrated on the Midlands until 2300 when activity appeared to cease. Also about 40 raids approached London via the Thames Estuary.

Damage and casualties in London were small, but at Coventry a second attack caused severe damage to several factories and many houses were demolished. Casualties were not heavy. Between 400 and 500 persons have been rendered homeless. It is also reported that the damage and casualties would have been more serious but for the excellent work done by the Fire Services. Several small fires occurred at Birmingham, but little damage was caused.

0100-0300. There was restricted activity in the South-East — no raids were reported from the Midlands, but a few raids were plotted in the Thames Estuary, some of which were employed on minelaying. A single raider dropped parachute mines at Hull, causing extensive damage to private property.

0300-0600. All incoming raids ceased at 0300 and London was clear at 0400.

0410. Six raids flew over Devon, Cornwall and the Bristol Channel, a few bombs being dropped in the vicinity of Swansea, but no damage or casualties are reported.

Civilian casualties (approximately) by day amounted to 25 people in London killed, together with 91 injured. Elsewhere 14 people died, 57 were seriously injured and 109 were slightly hurt. After dark in London 22 were killed and 246 were injured. Elsewhere 15 people lost their lives, 94 were seriously injured and 143 slightly injured. Casualties at Coventry included in these totals amounted to 9 killed, 65 seriously injured and 68 slightly hurt. Two enemy aircraft were certainly destroyed, together with three damaged.

New life springs from the old. In all, Tonbridge mourns the deaths of nine of its townspeople, another 128 being seriously injured.

The Ministry of Information was still agonising over the release of details of incidents to the population; would too much information be counter-productive or would it reassure an increasingly sceptical public of the believability of official communiqués? At the Duty Conference of the MoI on October 20 it was agreed that consideration should be given as to whether it was possible 'to include some reference to repair work which is being done in order to offset the constant mention of damage.' This is 'a main line station in October 1940 following enemy action' — in reality St Pancras.

Individual raiders penetrated the British defences throughout the day taking full advantage of the low cloud and fog which prevailed. Six German machines were destroyed, including 1 by accident and 7 more damaged, 4 of them on operational sorties. Only one fell in Britain.

1/KG51 Junkers Ju 88A-5 (8116). Shot down, starboard engine in flames, by Flight Lieutenant F. J. Howell and Pilot Officer S. J. Hill of No. 609 Squadron during bombing sortie over England. Crashed and exploded at Manor Farm Field, Black Bush, Milford-on-Sea 1.47 p.m. Oberlt. M. Fabian, Uffz. E. Wilhelm, Uffz. M. Scholz and Gefr. F. Stadelbauer all killed. Aircraft 9K+BH a write-off.

TUESDAY, OCTOBER 22

Enemy activity in the morning was confined principally to coastal reconnaissances, bombs being dropped on south-east coastal towns only. Better weather conditions led to slightly increased activity in the afternoon. There were two main raids, one over Kent and the other towards South-East London and the Estuary. These were by fighters, few bombs being dropped — mostly in rural areas.

By night, raids were on a very much reduced scale. Bombs were dropped in London and the Home Counties, Midlands, Liverpool and South Wales.

1830-2100: Between 1830 and 1900 some forty raids were tracked coming in from France and Holland. Thereafter activity slackened. Several of these raiders turned back before reaching the coast. The majority concentrated on London and the Birmingham-Coventry area, though a few raids penetrated to Liverpool, Bristol and South Wales areas. One raider attacked a convoy in the Thames Estuary.

2100-2300: Eighteen raids were plotted to London and environs, one to Bristol and one to Amersham. Three raids visited Liverpool, three in South Wales and six were in the Birmingham area. At 2300 the country was clear of enemy aircraft.

2330-0600: At 0038 one enemy aircraft flew to the Thames Estuary in London leaving at 0215. There was no further activity till 0515 when two raids flew to South Wales and one was plotted off Devon at 0550.

Approximate civilian casualties by day outside London amounted to 7 killed and 38 injured, 6 of them seriously. There were no casualties in London during the day. At night, however, 25 Londoners were killed and 60 were injured. Elsewhere 3 people died and 43 were injured, 24 seriously. Three enemy aircraft were destroyed, together wth 1 probable and 1 damaged.

Birmingham reports that about 100 men and women and children left Coventry yesterday and were accommodated at Wolston. This after three nights heavy bombing speaks well for the public morale.

Fog over southern England restricted operations until the afternoon when coastal shipping came under attack, the convoy 'Fruit' off Dover attracting a heavy raid around 4.00 p.m. The Luftwaffe lost 12 aircraft in operations, 5 more returning damaged. Another machine was destroyed and 2 more damaged in accidents. The following aircraft came down in the United Kingdom:

Wing Commander Warburton was the person at the Ministry of Home Security Intelligence Branch responsible for issuing communiqués and was advised of two practical difficulties in the proposal. 'The first is the obvious and security one; if we inform the Germans, and publication in the Press does inform the Germans, that we have repaired a considerable area, for example in the docks, it is to be supposed that they will direct fresh attacks upon it. The second difficulty is that it is not possible, I think, from the information already in our possession to estimate what amount of repairs has, as a matter of fact, been done. I am not sure that we could obtain this information except by consulting London Region, who could either make reports or ask for returns from the Borough Surveyor. . . . What might be possible, and what was asked for in *The Times* leader of the 17th October, is to issue some form of periodical communiqué, which might state the buildings of importance during the preceding month or fortnight which had been destroyed or injured, and also give some possibly rough estimate of the reparations, which had in general been made. The propaganda value of reassuring the public and informing neutral countries can scarcely be over-estimated, but it has to be balanced all against the security aspect and the practical difficulty of supplying information.' This is the Naval Barracks in Edinburgh Road, Portsmouth.

1/606 Dornier Do 17Z-5 (2783). Briefed to attack Liverpool but flew into severe magnetic storms over England which disabled the W/T system and magnetic compass. Lost bearings and abandoned by crew over Salisbury Plain when fuel ran low. Aircraft flew on for 120 miles on automatic pilot and eventually came down intact on estuary mud at Ness Point, Erwarton, Suffolk 1.04 a.m. Lt. W. Stirnat, Lt. zur See H. Würdemann, Uffz. F. Schörnisch and Uffz. M. Küttner baled out landing at Chilmark, East Knoyle, Hindon and Wylye near Old Sarum and all captured unhurt. Aircraft 7T+AH a write-off.

They always say that truth is stranger than fiction and one of the strangest flights to occur during the Blitz concerned this aircraft — a Dornier 17Z from Küstenfliegergruppe 606, which landed in darkness on the mud flats near Erwarton in Suffolk on the morning of October 22. In spite of the aircraft having made an almost perfect force-landing, there was no sign of the crew; that is, not until police in Wiltshire reported the capture of four German airmen who apparently believed they were back in France! In fact they had run into bad weather en route to Liverpool and, turning back, were caught in a severe electrical storm which affected the compass so much that although they had reached France it indicated that they were flying north. Performing another about turn they then flew back to England, by which time they were running low on fuel. Unable to recognise any features, but believing themselves safely back over France, they decided to bale out rather than risk putting the aircraft down. Setting the autopilot, the four men jumped out and one can imagine their horror to find on landing a notice in English. Meanwhile the Dornier continued to fly east a further 130 miles before gently setting itself down on the bank of the River Stour.

2/JG26 Messerschmitt Bf 109E-4 (1124). Broke up under attack by Flying Officer The Hon. D. A. Coke of No. 257 Squadron during combat over the Channel off the Sussex coast 3.30 p.m. Main wreckage crashed into the sea off Littlestone golf links. Uffz. H. Arp killed. Aircraft 10+ lost.

The body of Heinrich Arp was washed ashore at Littlehampton 2 days later along with pieces of his aircraft. He was buried at Folkestone New Cemetery, Hawkinge and not reinterred in the Soldatenfriedhof, Cannock Chase after the war.

3/JG51 Messerschmitt Bf 109E-1 (4822). Severely damaged in attacks by Squadron Leader A. G. Malan and Flying Officer J. C. Mungo-Park of No. 74 Squadron during escort sortie for Bf 109 Jabos attacking London. Crashed into the Channel 4 miles east of Hastings 2.30 p.m. Fhr. K. Müller baled out unhurt and rescued from his dinghy by the Hastings lifeboat *Cyril and Lilian Bishop*. Aircraft 10+ lost.

3/KG40 Focke-Wulf FW 200C (0024). Crashed into the Irish Sea during a weather reconnaissance sortie. Oberlt. T. Schuldt and Meteorologe Dr. H. Sturm both killed. Fw. W. Berghaus, Fw. F. Gruber, Fw. F. Hoeger and Gefr. W. Grässle missing. Aircraft F8+OK lost.

The bodies of Oberlt. Schuldt and weather specialist Hans Sturm were both washed ashore and buried in Ireland.

Another five miles and it would have missed England altogether and disappeared for ever beneath the waters of the North Sea. In the background on the far bank the docks of Parkeston Quay at Harwich.

Birmingham, Bennetts Hill, where the menace of falling masonry has given way to the menace of parking meters. The City had suffered its first casualty on August 9 when Mr Vivian Fry was killed in Montague Road in the northern suburb of Erdington. Most citizens realised on the outbreak of war that, providing German bombers had the range, Birmingham with its many industrial targets, from vehicle factories to armaments plants, would become a prime objective. This is just one section from the German 9-sheet intelligence coverage of the city reprinted from the British 6-inch survey, with overprint information added from Luftwaffe aerial reconnaissance in September 1940. An associated key lists the targets as follows: 15 Saltley und Nettchell's Gaswerk; 16 Güterbahnhof Birmingham O, Courzon Street-Station und Lawley Street-Station; 17 Autofabrik Morris Commercial Cars Ltd.; 18 Rover Co. Ltd., Flugzeugmotorenbau; 19 Saltley Elsenbahn-, Last- und Güterwagen-Werke; 20 Midland Elsenbahn-, Last- und Güterwagen-Werke; 21 Windsorstreet Gaswerk; 22 Dunlop Rubber Works, Gummifabrik; 23 Climax Tube Works, Röhrenfabrik; 24 Umspannwerek; 25 Kasernen; 26 Standard Motor Co. Ltd., Flugzeugzellenbau; 79 Vermutlich Wolseley Works Ltd., Autofabrik; 92 British Timken Ltd., Elsengießerei, Kugellagerfabrikation; 104 Bordesley Viadukt, ungefähr 900 m lang; 105 British Optical Lens, Kamerabau, Linsenfabrikation, optische Geräte; 111 Electric & Ordenance Accessories Works, Elektrogerätebau; 112 Papierfabrik Welß- und Buntpapiere.

WEDNESDAY, OCTOBER 23

Enemy activity by day was on a small scale — no raids being reported between 0600 and 1200. All raids except one appear to have been made by single aircraft.

During the hours of darkness activity was slight. Ten tracks were plotted from the Dutch islands via the Estuary to London, and 17 from the Somme area towards the same objective.

2100-0100: There was only one raid inland. Slight activity was continued towards London mainly from eastern areas. Twelve enemy aircraft penetrated to the Yorkshire coast from the east. These were tracked to the western seaboard and a short distance out to sea off the Lancashire coast and minelaying was suspected.

0100-0600: Thirteeen raids approached Montrose at 0150, continuing west and returning on the same tracks. Southern England was clear by 0152, but new waves appeared from Dieppe at 0440 and from Holland at 0500, heading for London.

Civilian casualties in London during the day were approximately 4 killed and 16 injured. Elsewhere 2 people were seriously injured. By night, 14 people in London were killed and 17 were injured. Elsewhere 6 people were killed and 18 were injured, 11 seriously. One enemy aircraft was damaged.

Persistent low cloud and drizzle prevented any notable raids on this day. Night attacks on London and Glasgow continued to thwart the British defences. Four German aircraft were lost and another damaged, whilst 2 more machines were damaged in accidents. None fell in the UK.

THURSDAY, OCTOBER 24

There was little enemy activity by day in London, and raids were carried out mainly by single aircraft. Most of the incidents recorded occurred between 1400 and 1500. An H.E. caused a large fire at Fairey Aviation Company's factory at Hayes and involved the main store but there were few casualties, and elsewhere there was only minor damage to house property, gas and water mains.

The G.W.R. line was blocked at Yatton (Somerset), trains being diverted and bombing on a small scale was reported from Hythe and one or two inland villages of Kent. There was little material damage and a few casualties.

1900-2100: Enemy aircraft began to appear by night about 1900. The main objectives appeared to be London and Birmingham. The latter city was bombed severely for half an hour although they were under red warning between 1946 and 2313.

The effect on production is negligible. The Fire Services were heavily engaged, fires were quickly got under control, but it was necessary to call for assistance from neighbouring brigades. G.W.R. Snow Hill Station suffered slightly from fires in buildings and a signal box but the service is not affected. Considerable damage was done in the centre of the city involving the Council House, Town Hall, University, Bank of England, Midland Hotel, New Street Station and numerous large shops. Casualties reported are 7 killed, 79 injured, 14 trapped.

In London 21 areas were affected but

Birmingham was not only the centre of established munitions companies — amongst them Birmingham Small Arms and Kynoch's — but the location of the new 'shadow' factories constructed as a result of the Government's pre-war plans for the rapid expansion of the aircraft industry under the control of the existing motor car manufacturers in the city. To the south-east the Rover shadow factories were built at Acocks Green and Solihull; Austin's in the south-west at Crofton Hackett and the Nuffield Organisation's (Morris Motors) plant at Castle Bromwich. First deliveries from Castle Bromwich Aircraft Factory began in June 1940; this picture shows work proceeding early in 1941. *Below:* Where the mighty Merlin-engined fighters once rolled off the assembly line — now being refurbished to produce the Jaguar XJ40.

After a lull, the city suffered its first major raid when some fifty aircraft attacked Birmingham on the night of August 25/26, killing 25. The Luftwaffe returned the next night and sporadic attacks followed throughout September and October. A particularly heavy raid on October 15/16 killed 59. This is International House, on the corner of Church and Edmund Streets, hit on October 28.

there was very little damage and it was almost entirely confined to house property and small mains.

2100-0500: The moderate intensity of the raids on London diminished at the commencement of this period and there were few reports of bombing, which occurred mainly in eastern boroughs.

At 2330 single aircraft were plotted from the Yorkshire Coast to Liverpool Bay and towards the Clyde from a south-easterly direction. A parachute mine and several H.E. were dropped at Greenock but there was no material damage or casualties.

Minelaying appeared to be extensive in the Thames Estuary off the East Essex coast, between Scarborough and the Tyne and in the Firth of Forth.

Approximate civilian casualties in London during the day amounted to one killed and 36 injured. Elsewhere one person was killed, 14 seriously injured and one slightly hurt. By night, one person in London was killed and 31 were injured. Elsewhere, 9 died and 82 were injured. Between 10 and 14 people are reported trapped.

Two enemy aircraft were destroyed and one was damaged. It is also reported, but not confirmed, that an enemy aircraft was shot down near Oxford at about 2110.

One of the aircraft operating the Midlands photo-recce run was L2+KS despatched on the 24th by Messrs. Brown, Clowes and Kershaw over Bedfordshire. The bits and pieces, including three of the crew who baled out too low for their parachutes to open, scattered themselves across the field behind the Crown Inn at Eaton Socon.

Some improvement in weather conditions and better visibility resulted in more raiders and the occasional fighter sweep over southern England. The Luftwaffe lost a total of 12 aircraft, half of them in accidents, with 2 more machines being damaged on operational sorties and another 2 damaged accidentally.

3/Aufkl.Gr.Ob.d.L. Dornier Do 215B (0060). Shot down, both engines alight, by Flight Lieutenant M. H. Brown, Pilot Officer A. V. Clowes and Pilot Officer A. Kershaw of No. 1 Squadron during photo-reconnaissance sortie to Coventry and Birmingham. Hit ground in a shallow dive, broke up and burned out behind the Crown Inn, Eaton Socon 12.35 p.m. Gefr. M. Dorr baled out and captured badly injured. Lt. E. Meyer, Uffz. E. Hofmann and Uffz. H. Broening all baled out too low and killed when parachutes failed to deploy. Aircraft L2+KS a write-off.

FRIDAY, OCTOBER 25

Enemy activity by day was considerably greater than of late. Reconnaissances were made from Orkneys southwards to the Thames Estuary, then along the South Coast to Lands End. Four enemy fighter sweeps were made in Kent which developed towards London.

1st attack 0845: Fifty enemy aircraft, later increased by further raids of 52 and 90+, flew over Kent, some 70 aircraft penetrating to Central London between 0920 and 0955. By 1010 these attacks had spent themselves. During this period bombs were dropped in East Ham, Poplar, several places in South London, and in Kent and Surrey.

2nd attack 1154: One hundred enemy aircraft flew inland at Dover and flew over Maidstone. The formation split into many small sections and covered the South-East from Hornchurch to Hastings. Bombs were dropped at Erith and several places in Kent and Sussex including Maidstone.

3rd attack 1305: Fifty enemy aircraft followed by 20 others flew inland at Dungeness. The main body flew to Central London, splitting into small formations en route. Bombs were dropped in several localities in London north of the river. The country was clear by 1345.

4th attack 1505: Sixty enemy aircraft flew inland by the usual route, 30 penetrating to Central London. A further 40 aircraft crossed the coast at Beachy Head, turned near Kenley and spread out over an area between Tangmere and Maidstone. Enemy aircraft were returning to France in small sections by 1540. During this attack bombs were dropped at Twickenham, Poplar, Deptford and a few places in No. 12 Region including Eastbourne. In addition a convoy off the North Foreland was attacked at 1744.

The main attacks by night were on London and Birmingham; Liverpool and Bootle were also raided, chiefly by I.B., whilst minor incidents were widespread over the country. After 0100 enemy activity was largely concentrated on minelaying which appears to have extended from the North Foreland to Aberdeen.

In London bombing was heavy early in the evening. Sixty-four areas were affected, but of these only 24 reported incidents after 2100 and only 7 after midnight. London was, however, under red warning continuously from 1844 to 0657.

Birmingham was under warning from 1949 to 0012 and bombing was particularly severe. A large number of heavy calibre H.E.s, D.A.B.s and I.B.s fell in various districts. Fires did widespread damage to some 40 industrial undertakings in the centre of the city where the premises of a number of large concerns were gutted. A large number of commercial concerns were damaged in other parts of the city. Several Key Points were hit. Extensive damage was done to residential property and a number of streets and roads are blocked. Railways were not seriously affected.

Approximate civilian casualties in London by day amounted to 35 killed and 200 injured. Elsewhere 7 were killed, together with 8 seriously injured and 8 slightly hurt. By night, 99 people in London were killed, together with 200 injured. Elsewhere 70 were killed and 120 were seriously injured, plus 8 slightly injured. In Scotland one person was killed and 19 were seriously injured.

Fourteen enemy aircraft were certainly destroyed, 12 probably destroyed and 16 were damaged.

Continuing slight improvement in the weather brought a noticeable increase in daylight operations and once again fighters clashed high over Kent and Sussex. The first raid on England by the Regia Aeronautica, recently deployed to Belgian bases, was launched against Harwich at night. Twenty German aircraft were destroyed on operations, 13 more being damaged. Four more were lost and another damaged in accidents.

2(F)/122 Messerschmitt Bf 110C-5 (2257). Shot down by Pilot Officer N. R. Norfolk of No. 72 Squadron during a reconnaissance sortie to the Rolls Royce works at Derby. Ditched in the North Sea off Yarmouth 2.40 p.m. Lt. K. Wacker picked up by HMS *Widgeon* and landed at Harwich. Gefr. G. Gneist missing. Aircraft F6+MK lost.

5/JG26 Messerschmitt Bf 109E-4 (3724). Shot down by Pilot Officer J. B. Kendal of

'0952 hours. Southern Region. Charing Cross — London Bridge Railway. Bridge over Blackfriars Road damaged by HE, 5 trams in roadway destroyed. Casualties: Killed 2, Injured 48'. Home Security report, October 25, 1940.

No. 66 Squadron during combat over Hawkhurst. Broke up over Bardown and Church Street Farms, near Ticehurst Road railway station 9.50 a.m. Oberlt. K. Eichstädt baled out but fell dead at Shovers Green with unopened parachute. Aircraft 12+— a write-off.

Representative pieces dislayed in Robertsbridge Aviation Society Museum.

8/JG26 Messerschmitt Bf 109E-4 (5815). Shot down by Flying Officer E. H. Thomas of No. 222 Squadron during free-lance fighter operations over Kent. Crashed at Congelow Farm, Yalding 1.30 p.m. Fw. J. Gärtner baled out and captured slightly wounded. Aircraft 7+I a write-off.

Site excavated by local enthusiast, Alfred Batt. Elevator mass balance, 7.92mm MG17 ammunition and fabric from rudder bearing victory tabs in Kent Battle of Britain Museum. Several relics also in the Steve Vizard collection. Engine, control column and clock recovered by the Shoreham Aircraft Preservation Society.

8/JG26 Messerschmitt Bf 109E-4 (5795). Engaged on free-lance sortie over Kent and intercepted by Spitfires. Shot down by Pilot Officer T. B. A. Sherrington of No. 92 Squadron. Broke up over Riverhill House, south of Sevenoaks 1.40 p.m. Lt. H. Ripke fell dead 5 miles away with unopened parachute. Aircraft 2+I a write-off.

Tail wheel from this aircraft used for several years on a local resident's wheelbarrow until acquired by the Halstead War Museum in 1963. Site impossible to excavate but investigated by Steve Vizard and several fragments collected from hilltop. Fuel tank dipstick, taken in 1940, held by the Shoreham Aircraft Preservation Society.

Stab JG51 Messerschmitt Bf 109E-4 (3737). Exploded high over Milebush, Marden during combat with Hurricanes of No. 501 Squadron 12.05 p.m. Shot down by Flight Lieutenant E. Holden and Pilot Officer V. R. Snell, but also attacked by Pilot Officer K. W. MacKenzie. Hptmn. H. Asmus baled out and captured wounded. Aircraft <—+— a write-off.

Large fuselage panel marked '3737' in the Lashenden Air Warfare Museum. Reflector gunsight in the Hawkinge Aeronautical Trust collection attributed to this aircraft but equally possibly from a 7/JG26 machine lost on October 30. Cowling clip in the Vizard collection.

7/JG51 Messerschmitt Bf 109E-1 (3548). Radiator damaged in attack by Pilot Officer V. Zaoral of No. 501 Squadron during escort sortie for Bf 109 Jabos attacking London. Engine over-heated so forced-landed at Stonewall Farm, Hunton 12.00 p.m. Fw. L. Birg captured unhurt. Aircraft 4+I a write-off.

Fragments in Alfred Batt's collection.

7/JG51 Messerschmitt Bf 109E-1 (6281). Engine set alight in attacks by Flight Lieutenant E. Holden and Sergeant R. J. K. Gent of No. 501 Squadron during free-lance fighter operations over Sussex. Crashed into a drainage ditch on Lidham Hill Farm, Guestling 3.30 p.m. Fw. W. Koslowski baled out and captured severely burned. Aircraft a write-off.

Site excavated by the Brenzett Aeronautical Museum and the Wealden Aviation Achaeological Group in August 1975. Propeller boss recovered together with blades, undercarriage leg, reflector gunsight and cockpit clock. Bulk of this aircraft sunk over 35ft in mud at the bottom of a dyke.

5/JG54 Messerschmitt Bf 109E-4 (1988). Radiator damaged in attack by Spitfires of No. 41 Squadron during Jabo escort mission to London. Probably that attacked by Flying Officer H. P. Brown. Engine temperature rose so forced-landed at Broom Hill, near Lydd 9.30 a.m. Oberlt. J. Schypek captured unhurt. Aircraft 7+ a write-off.

5/JG54 Messerschmitt Bf 109E-4 (5178). Attacked by RAF fighters during Jabo escort sortie and evaded by flying into cloud over the coast. Became completely disorientated and forced-landed west of Galloways, near Dungeness 1.55 p.m. Lt. E. Wagner captured unhurt. Aircraft 2+ a write-off.

3/JG77 Messerschmitt Bf 109E-4 (5104). Engaged by RAF fighters during Jabo escort sortie over London and engine and radiator damaged during combat. Forced-landed at Harveys Cross, Telscombe, north of Saltdean 1.30 p.m. Gefr. K. Raisinger captured unhurt. Aircraft 13+ a write-off.

SATURDAY, OCTOBER 26

Enemy activity during the day consisted chiefly of raids by small formations of Me 109s on the south-eastern area. There was only one major attack and few enemy aircraft penetrated to Central London. There was some activity in the Straits of Dover and the Channel.

Some 80+ aircraft crossed the coast at Lympne. Some of these did not penetrate very far inland, whilst others flew to Tonbridge and some on to London. There was considerable reconnaissance activity in the south, south-east, south-west and the east.

The main attacks by night were directed against London and Birmingham. The attack was moderately heavy during the earlier part of the night, but later, only London was kept on the 'Alert' by a succession of single aircraft.

1800-2100: Ninety-five raids were plotted entering the country towards London, the majority reaching the capital. Others flew

'Birmingham nach dem deutschen Bombenangriff.' Unfortunately issued without a precise date — merely 1940 — the area covered is indicated on the 1:50,000 Ordnance Survey extract.

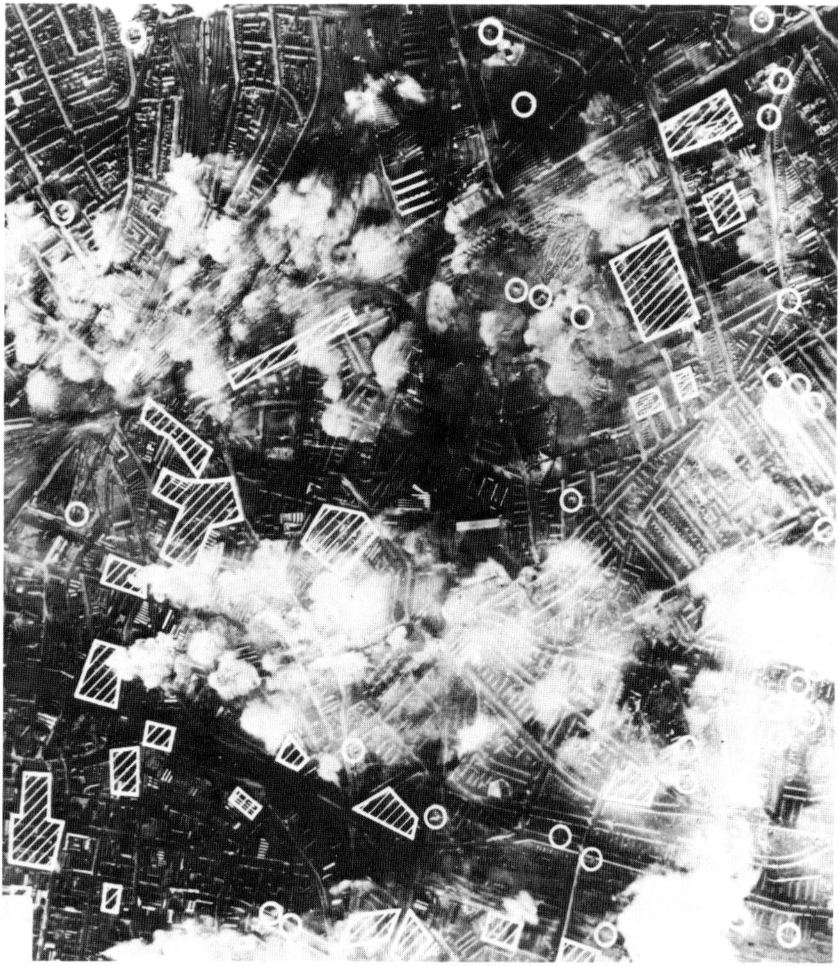

towards Bedford, Northampton and Chesterfield. Between 1800 and 1900 18 raids crossed the South Coast in the Swanage area and went to Bristol, the Midlands, Manchester and Liverpool. Minelaying was suspected off the Essex coast.

2100-0100: There was a gradual decrease of effort against London. The attack on the Midlands had ceased by 2330. There was considerable minelaying activity on the Lancashire coast from Flamborough Head to the Firth of Forth and in the Estuary.

0100-0600: The attack on London was maintained by a small number of aircraft in relays during this period. Minelaying was suspected in the Estuary.

Approximate civilian casualties in London by day amounted to 17 killed and 59 injured. Elsewhere 5 people were killed and 31 injured, 7 seriously. After dark, 57 people in London were killed and 160 were injured. Elsewhere, 88 people were killed and 236 were injured, 117 of them seriously.

Enemy aircraft casualties amounted to 6 certainly destroyed, 4 probably destroyed plus 8 damaged. A German barrage balloon was grounded at Plumstead.

High-flying daylight fighter-bomber raids plus the continuing night attacks against London by a steady stream of single aircraft, maintained a constant pressure on British defences still trying to find effective measures to counter German tactics. Ten German aircraft were lost and 10 damaged in operations, another 4 machines suffering accidental damage.

1/506 Heinkel He 115B (1889). Engines damaged in attack by RAF Hampden during patrol off the English East Coast and forced to land on the sea 9.00 a.m. Lt. zur See K-H. Kemper, Uffz. G. Grotefeld and Obergefr. K. Forster took to their dinghy and captured unhurt on landing at Yarmouth next day. Aircraft S4+AH lost.

1/JG52 Messerschmitt Bf 109E-7 (5929). Believed shot down into the Channel during combat with fighters. Oberfw. O. Strack missing believed killed. Aircraft 6+ lost.

The body of an unidentified German airman, washed ashore at Littlestone on this date, was taken for burial at Folkestone New Cemetery, Hawkinge where he remains to this day. Whilst it is possible that this was Oskar Strack there is no evidence to support such a contention — records do not offer any estimate as to how long the body had been in the water. It is equally likely that these were the remains of some other airman, lost maybe weeks before, which became subject to the vagaries of winds and tide.

6/JG53 Messerschmitt Bf 109E-1 (6391). Shot down by Sergeant R. H. Fokes of No. 92 Squadron during combat over Tunbridge Wells. Crashed at Chalket Farm, Pembury 10.30 a.m. Uffz. K. Geiswinkler killed. Aircraft 8+— a write-off.

Due to the severity of this crash, the body of Karl Geiswinkler defied proper identification and he was buried as an 'Unknown German Airman' in nearby Tunbridge Wells cemetery. His remains were not reinterred in the Soldatenfriedhof, Cannock Chase postwar.

Site excavated by the Halstead War Museum and complete Daimler-Benz DB 601 engine recovered together with many major components. Some minor components also held by the Hawkinge Aeronautical Trust.

A raid in the making. This Ju 88 of the Stab Geschwader of KG77 was most probably photographed at Laon-Athies. Ken Wakefield, our night Blitz expert whose massive contribution begins with the Coventry raid on November 14/15 comments on the fact that Dietrich Peltz (2nd from left) had a meteoric rise to fame; an Oberleutnant in 1940, he rose rapidly to reach Generalmajor rank in 1942 and in March 1943 was appointed Angriffsführer England, in charge of the renewed bombing offensive against Britain.

3/KG26 Heinkel He 111H-3 (6854). Hit by ground defences during low level bombing attack on Lossiemouth aerodrome and exploded in mid-air over the target 6.30 p.m. Oberlt. G. Imholz, Uffz. E. Radloff, Uffz. H. Weniger and Oberfw. W. Bastian all killed. Aircraft 1H+BL a write-off.

This crew were buried together at Lossiemouth Burial Ground and have not been reinterred at the Soldatenfriedhof, Cannock Chase. The date of death of the observer, Walter Bastian, is recorded as October 30 although none of the crew is believed to have survived the crash of their aircraft.

Site identified by the Scotland West Aircraft Investigation Group.

SUNDAY, OCTOBER 27

During the day the enemy made four attacks in south-east England and in the afternoon and evening two attacks, one in the Portsmouth/Southampton area and another on aerodromes in East Anglia, Lancashire and Yorkshire.

Between 0740 and 0900, about 10 enemy aircraft reached Central London and bombs were dropped in south-western and south-eastern districts. At Sutton, pumping mains, at Worcester Park, sewage works, were badly fractured.

At 1125, a second attack by 60 enemy aircraft was made but it failed to penetrate to London and during the third attack at 1320 about 20 aircraft reached the Central London area. A few bombs were dropped but little damage was done and casualties were few.

An attack by about 50 fighters and a few Ju 88s in the direction of Southampton-Portsmouth was turned back near the coast but a few managed to penetrate to Portsmouth. No military damage is reported and there were few casualties.

The raids on aerodromes occurred between 1630 and 1900, the first attack being made against Martlesham which was ineffective. Bombs were also dropped at Catfoss, Lindholme, Leconfield, Coltishall, Feltwell, Hawkinge, Caistor, Kirton, Hatfield, Newmarket, Massingham, Driffield, Dishforth, Linton-on-Ouse, Mildenhall and Honington. At Massingham there were a few casualties and two aircraft destroyed. At Honington, damage to a hangar, buildings and 3 aircraft was caused, and there was slight damage also at Lindholme and Feltwell. This attack is a reversion to the enemy's initial tactics of attacking R.A.F. aerodromes by daylight which were frequently carried out during the months of June and July.

Night raids were made by about 200 aircraft and were very widespread. In built-up areas attacks were mainly concentrated around Liverpool, Coventry and London but were not so heavy as on previous nights. Hits were reported on the following factories at Coventry but the damage caused is not serious: Armstrong Siddeley Ltd, Alfred Herbert Ltd, The Royal Naval Ordnance Stores, and Valves Ltd. Considerable damage was also done to the sorting office of the G.P.O. and the Central Market Hall.

In London 22 areas were affected. At the Fairey Aviation Works, Hayes, the tinsmith shop was damaged. Production is temporarily stopped owing to reported U.X.B.s in the grounds.

At Lostock Hall, near Preston (Lancs.), 13 fatal casualties resulted from several demolished houses, and 20 are reported missing — rescue work is proceeding.

The most interesting feature of the night's raiding is the scale of effort in the Home Counties. The number of minor regional incidents reported during the period amount to 223.

From the reports so far received, at least 450 H.E., 500 I.B., and 20 oil bombs were dropped. In addition, reports from 31 places do not include the number of bombs.

Approximate civilian casualties by day in London amount to 4 killed and 23 injured. Elsewhere by day 9 people were killed and 36 were injured seriously and 11 were slightly hurt. By night 25 Londoners were killed and 64 were injured. Elsewhere after dark, 23 people died and 15 were seriously injured (others are still missing), together with 13 slightly hurt. Eight people are reported trapped.

Enemy aircraft casualties amounted to 10 certain, 7 probable and 9 damaged.

Ipswich report that a new type of bomb is being used which releases shot, causing wounds resembling multiple gun-shot wounds.

Taking full advantage of the cloudy weather, mixed fighter and fighter-bomber sweeps and small formations of enemy bombers penetrated the British defences during the day. Targets were widespread and many nuisance raids were launched against RAF airfields. Operations cost the Germans the loss of 13 aircraft and 9 more damaged, 3 being lost and 5 damaged in accidents.

Stab I/JG3 Messerschmitt Bf 109E-7 (4124). Shot down by RAF fighters during free-lance fighter sortie over Kent. Crashed at Fisher Farm, West Wickham 12.00 p.m. Lt. E. Busch (Gruppe NO) baled out and captured slightly wounded at Addington. Aircraft <—+ a write-off.

The operations board for a night attack by II/KG77, with Oberleutnant Peltz scheduled to command a Ju 88 with the markings 3Z+AP. The crews for 'EP' and 'DP' are also visible.

Ken Wakefield: 'I like this one — good atmosphere shot of crews preparing for a raid. Pity we don't have the precise date. Board on right appears to give airfield information, possibly for diversion purposes; that on left lists code numbers to be used when reporting by radio various positions, etc., (40 French Coast, 41 Channel, 42 English Coast, 43 Something illegible followed by "Loge", the code-name for London, 54 Weather for attack unfavourable, 55 Weather for attack favourable). From fairly early in 1941 radio silence was normally the rule so thereafter presumably these code numbers were for use in an emergency or when operationally required.'

Site excavated by Chris Bennett, 1985 and surviving remains unearthed. Complete radio, taken at the time of the crash, donated to the Tangmere Military Aviation Museum.

8/JG27 Messerschmitt Bf 109E-4 (1603). Shot down in combat with RAF fighters during free-lance sortie over Kent. Probably that claimed by Pilot Officer H. M. Stephen of No. 74 Squadron. Crashed near Hooks Wood, Lenham 9.00 a.m. Oberlt. A. Pointer (Staffelkapitän) baled out and captured unhurt. Aircraft 10+ a write-off.

Site excavated by local enthusiasts, John Rawlings and Alf Batt, who recovered many components and fragments of airframe together with various manufacturer's labels, one confirming identity as '1603'. Some relics also in the Vizard collection.

2/JG52 Messerschmitt Bf 109E-4 (1268). Believed shot down by Flight Lieutenant A. A. McKellar of No. 605 Squadron during free-lance sortie to London. Crashed and burned out at East Park, near Newchapel, East Grinstead 8.30 a.m. Gefr. C. Bott baled out and captured unhurt. Aircraft 5+ a write-off.

Remains of shattered Daimler-Benz DB 601 engine, engine maker's plate and badge together with minor airframe components recovered from under a tarmac drive by the Air Historical Group.

3/JG52 Messerschmitt Bf 109E-4 (2798). Radiator damaged in combat with No. 74 Squadron Spitfires during escort mission for Bf 109 Jabos attacking London. Crashed at Upstreet, near Canterbury 9.40 a.m. Oberlt. U. Steinhilper baled out and captured slightly wounded. Aircraft 2+ a write-off.

Major recovery by the Kent Battle of Britain Museum 26.10.80. Intact Daimler-Benz DB 601 engine, control column, propeller boss and major components excavated. Pilot's wrist compass and piece of Swastika marking from the tail of this machine also donated by a local resident. Relics now in the Hawkinge Aeronautical Trust collection.

3/JG52 Messerschmitt Bf 109E-4 (3525). Severely damaged in combat by Pilot Officer P. Chesters of No. 74 Squadron and put down at Penshurst emergency landing-ground 9.15 a.m. Fw. L. Schieverhofer captured unhurt. Aircraft 4+ a write-off.

Radio frequencies card 'liberated' from the cockpit of this aircraft in 1940 donated to Brenzett Aeronautical Museum by a local resident and now held by the Hawkinge Aeronautical Trust.

7/JG54 Messerschmitt Bf 109E-1 (3576). Engine damaged in combat with No. 605 Squadron Hurricanes during free-lance fighter sweep over Tunbridge Wells. Possibly that attacked by Sergeant E. W. Wright. Belly-landed on beach near Lydd water tower 9.40 a.m. Uffz. A. Zimmermann captured slightly wounded. Aircraft 13+ a write-off.

I/KG1 Heinkel He 111H-2 (5541). Believed hit by ground defences during bombing attack on Horsham St Faith aerodrome and forced to ditch in the sea off Clacton 11.30 a.m. after starboard engine caught fire. Uffz. M. Behres, Uffz. R. Heinhold, Gefr. K. Rosenberg, Gefr. R. Hartleib and Fw. W. Saumsiegel all took to their dinghy and captured unhurt on drifting ashore at 3.00 a.m. the following day. Aircraft V4+HW lost.

7/KG4 Junkers Ju 88A-5 (6129). Hit by ground fire during low-level attack on Linton-upon-Ouse aerodrome 6.00 p.m. Belly-landed on Richmond Farm, Duggleby, Yorkshire. Oberlt. F-F. Podbielski (Staffelkapitän), Uffz. H. Heier and Uffz. K. von Kidrowski captured unhurt. Uffz. O. Piontek captured severely wounded and died of injuries November 15. Aircraft 5J+ER a write-off.

7/KG76 Dornier Do 17Z-2 (1150). Briefed to attack Stradishall aerodrome but hit by AA fire following bombing attack on Ipswich. Also believed that attacked by Pilot Officer J. K. Ross of No. 17 Squadron. Crashed in Holbrook Creek, River Stour 6.50 p.m. Uffz. F. Ebeling, Uffz. K. Fritz, Uffz. R. Carl and Obergefr. G. Wülpern killed. Uffz. E. Johannes missing. Aircraft F1+HR lost.

The body of the pilot, Friedhelm Ebeling, was washed ashore on the English coast some days later. That of the gunner, Gustav Wülpern, was recovered at Wrabness on December 11, which was incorrectly recorded as his date of death. The body of Richard Carl, the wireless operator, was not washed up until March 30, 1941, also incorrectly recorded as his date of death. These three are now interred in the Soldatenfriedhof at Cannock Chase. The observer, Karl Fritz, was washed ashore at Landguard Point on December 15 — incorrectly given as his date of death — and buried in the New Cemetery, Felixstowe where he remains.

On October 27, taking advantage of poor weather conditions, a new angle was introduced to the battle with surprise attacks launched against aerodromes in south-east England. I/KG77 (*above*) contributed three Ju 88s to attack the vital bomber station of Scampton, with four more from II/KG76 targeted on Great Massingham. They claimed hits from a height of 30-50 metres on 8-10 Bristol Blenheims and 20 Whitleys. KG4 lost a Ju 88 while attacking Linton-on-Ouse. Dornier 17s were sent by III/KG76 against Stradishall (although they failed to find the airfield in heavy rain and bombed Ipswich instead), Wattisham, and Woodbridge. Heinkels from I/KG1 sortied against West Raynham; from II/KG1 to Norwich (presumably Horsham St Faith), with KG26 sending three raiders to Waddington.

Following his decision concerning the unsuitability of Paddock as a long-term working environment, on October 22 Churchill authorised the provision of a 'substantial measure of overhead cover above the War Room' — referring to the complex currently being used for War Cabinet meetings below the New Public Offices in Great George Street. He realised also that No. 10, already badly damaged from the near miss on the 14th, was not a safe location for the normal day-to-day routine of his staff, or for his own accommodation, and a suite of rooms on the ground floor of the New Public Offices was adapted for his use as the 'No. 10 Annexe'. *Left:* Steel shutters protected the windows of the Annexe, the ground floor map room being behind the two windows to the left of the central entrance block and the Prime Minister's own quarters behind the first four windows on the right. The sub ground floor — actually level with the pavement — was filled with a reinforced concrete slab, three feet thick, and protected against bombs coming at an angle by a concrete apron wall outside the building. *Right:* Today the shutters have gone and the building is used by various departments of the Government and Cabinet Office.

Conversion work began on the Annexe in mid-October and, until his suite was ready, Churchill spent most nights in the war headquarters of the Railway Executive Committee which had been constructed deep underground below the disused Down Street Station. *Left:* The station on the Piccadilly Line had been closed in 1932 when it was replaced by Green Park. *Right:* Entry from the street was via the door in the bricked up entrance but it was also possible for officials to board the motorman's cab at Piccadilly and get off at a small platform which had been retained beside the line. As the rest of the train would be simply stopped in the tunnel, members of the public would have been completely unaware of the reason for the unscheduled halt.

Unfortunately no photographs appear to have been taken of Churchill in residence in 1940. *Left:* This is the Committee Room with the Executive in session. *Right:* We photographed the same room, mouldering and inches deep in dirt, in 1975.

As the autumn evenings began to give way to the lengthening hours of darkness, there was little the RAF could do to protect those now suffering nightly air raids of increasing severity. This is Liverpool, where the cathedral (still to be completed) had taken some 75 years to build. Now, demolition was threatened in a single night. The longest of Britain's cathedrals, she survived; her sandstone walls marked and chipped from countless near misses. The narrow surrounding streets did not.

MONDAY, OCTOBER 28

Two minor sweeps and one major attack were made in the south-east area during daylight, the latter in conjunction with a demonstration in the Portsmouth area. In none of these did enemy aircraft penetrate to Central London.

Reconnaissances were fairly active in the Estuary and the Bristol Channel during the period.

First attack 1300: 20 to 30 enemy aircraft crossed the coast to Dungeness and flew on a 5-mile front towards Biggin Hill but split into several sections and turned away before reaching it. They were recrossing the coast by 1315. The only incident reported was the dropping of 15 H.E. at Maidstone at 1308.

Second attack 1427: 18+ enemy aircraft flew in from Dover to Maidstone and the Biggin Hill area. As in the previous sweep, penetration was not made further north-westwards. The enemy were heading south-east by 1440. Four H.E. bombs were dropped at Eynesford (Kent) at 1430 hours.

Third attack 1605: While 65+ aircraft were circling off Calais, a raid of 30+ flew northwards from Le Havre towards the Isle of Wight. They were over Portsmouth at 1630 and remained there until 1650. Meanwhile, of the Calais formations which had increased, 20 made a landfall at Dungeness and flew to Maidstone, and 80 — crossing to Beachy Head — made for Biggin Hill. Neither raid penetrated further than the Biggin Hill-Kenley area, and they were recrossing the coast by 1635.

At 1642, fresh formations of 50, 30+ and 50 aircraft came inland between Beachy Head and Dungeness, one raid going to Hornchurch and the others to Biggin Hill. They were all retiring eastwards down the Estuary and across the south coast by 1710. Bombs are reported at various localities although only Me 109s appear to have been operating. Two squadrons were despatched to the Portsmouth feint and 9 squadrons to the Kentish attack. Little damage is reported from any Region.

Enemy activity by night was again on the reduced scale of recent nights. Early raids were widespread over most of the country and the main objectives were London and its suburbs, and the Midlands where Birmingham received most attention.

The first raids showed strengths of 1+ to 3+ aircraft, but later raids were plotted as single aircraft. The first raider reached Beachy Head at 1843 from the direction of Abbeville. One enemy aircraft was shot down by A.A. guns near Poole, and another was damaged by No. 85 Squadron near Binbrook.

1900-2100: Activity was fairly widespread over most of the country, but the majority of raids made London and its suburbs their objective, although many appeared to turn back without penetrating the I.A.Z. In the Midlands, Birmingham was the principal target but raids were also plotted over Liverpool, Manchester, Coventry and Reading. One or two raids appeared in the

The cathedral seen from its less salubrious surroundings in June 1981 with a war-torn building still standing alongside. Hitler having cleared the slums, the intention was to landscape the area and place the building in the setting it rightfully deserved.

In the last two months we have fought and won one of the decisive battles of history. It is this air battle over England to which Hitler and Göring looked to ensure the success of the invasion which was to have ended the war with our overwhelming and irretrievable defeat. That plan has miscarried, thanks to the heroism of a few thousand young men in our Air Force and to the steadiness of a great nation. Every attempt of the German Air Force to come over in strength was defeated by the sheer courage, nerve and gay gallantry of our airmen. It has been a remarkable victory of quality over numbers. . . .

The Battle of Britain may not be over, but its issue is, I believe, already decided. . . . It is still too early to say whether the much heralded invasion is still to be attempted or not. Two things can, however, already be said with confidence. One is that if attempted it will be a failure. The second is that if abandoned it will be no less a failure. In either case it will mark the definite turn of the tide of this war. Abandonment would be not only a terrible blow to Hitler's prestige, but all the gigantic effort put into getting where he wanted to be in order to launch his attack will have been largely wasted. I believe that this invasion by its failure, in whichever way it fails, will in large measure make Dead Sea fruit of all his previous victories.

LEOPOLD AMERY,
SECRETARY OF STATE FOR INDIA,
OCTOBER 27, 1940

After a lengthy post-war examination of the records of both sides, the official British end to the Battle of Britain was stated in 1960 by the Air Ministry as being Thursday, October 31. However, as far as Germany was concerned, the battle was nowhere near over and their airmen were still fighting and dying for their cause. At the end of the war an extensive organisation — the Missing Research and Enquiry Service — was set up to try to trace the thousands of RAF airmen still missing after raids over the Continent. By 1950 some 20,000 out of the 40,000 aircrew who failed to return from operations had been found — either buried by the Germans in cemeteries close to where they came down or else recovered from the crash sites themselves. However little effort was made to look for missing airmen in the UK; memories of the aerial battles of 1940 were already fading and it would seem that it was assumed that all crews coming down on home ground had surely been accounted for. Even less interest was paid to the likely whereabouts of missing enemy pilots and for thirty years no one had any idea of the number of airmen whose remains still lay buried where they had fallen. Thus the Press made a big thing of the discovery of a German pilot in 1973 — this extract is from the *Daily Mirror* of September 11. The finding of Werner Knittel at Burmarsh (and Pilot Officer George Drake the previous year — also by the Ashford and Tenterden Recovery Group) had astounded many and, contrary to the *Mirror*'s headline, it was the 'first of the many' as more and more groups were formed to pursue the new-found hobby of aircraft wreckology. Since those early days, up to the time of writing (March 1988), a total of 14 'Battle of Britain' airmen have been recovered by wreck groups in Britain: five British, one Canadian, one South African, one Polish and six German. Save when the remains are repatriated to their families, all the Luftwaffe crewmen are buried in Block 8 at Cannock Chase. Here the empty grave lies ready for Unteroffizier Fritz Buchner on May 8, 1987 *(see Volume 1)*. Knittel's grave is second from left together with Herzog and Schilling (see page 168).

THE LAST OF THE MANY

By ELLIS PLAICE
Air Correspondent

THE Luftwaffe has been asked to help guide home Germany's lost Battle of Britain pilot.

He went missing thirty-three years ago, as dogfights with RAF planes raged over South-eastern England.

His Messerschmitt was last seen falling towards the Kent marshes.

Now his body has been found entombed in the wreckage of his machine, 25ft. below ground at Burmarsh, near Hythe.

And an inquest has been ordered so that he can be sent home at last for burial.

Mission

The Luftwaffe has been asked to search its records in Berlin to confirm details of the mission on which the pilot died, at exactly ten minutes past noon on August 25, 1940.

The body has been sent to Folkestone's Royal Victoria Hospital.

The South Kent coroner, Mr. John Clarke, said: "We believe we can identify the pilot.

"But an inquest is necessary so that the proper documents can be issued if, as we expect, the Germans wish to take him back home."

Berlin has been asked for a formal declaration of the mission, and local people are expected to give evidence about the crash.

The remains were found by members of the Brenzett Aeronautical Museum, who search and excavate the sites of wartime crashes.

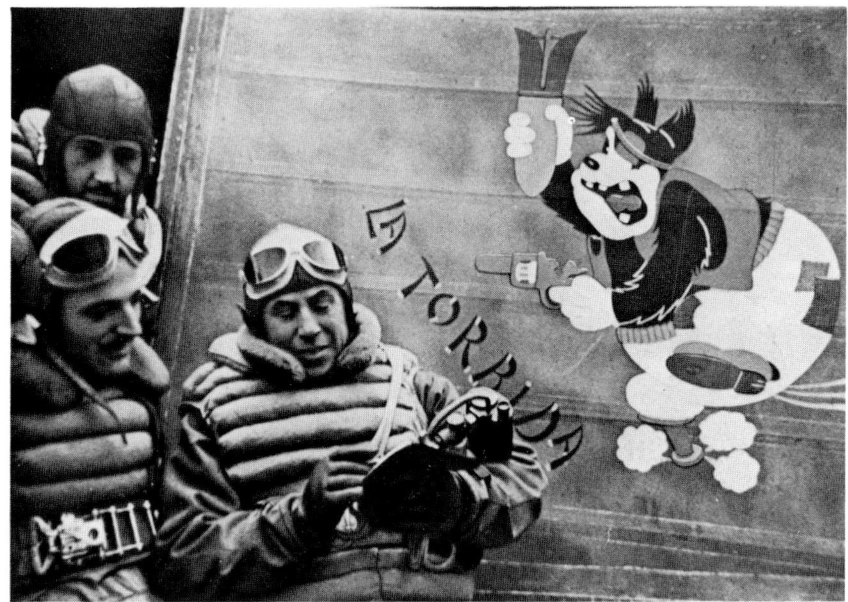

And to reinforce the depleted ranks came Mussolini's men. Far from their usual bases in sunny Italy and North Africa, the Regia Aeronautica had arrived in Belgium in mid-September, the Duce anxious to avenge the increasing air raids by the RAF on Italy. No doubt he also wanted to participate in what seemed a few weeks earlier would be another sweeping German victory. However his Airforce arrived too late to participate in the great daylight battles and the first Italian bombing raid took place on October 25 at night. No doubt Walt Disney would have been none too happy to find Peg-leg Pete personified as a figure of war.

Sunderland area while others were plotted near aerodromes in Lincolnshire and East Anglia. Minelaying was suspected by about 6 raids in the Estuary.

2100-0100: Forty-three incoming raids were plotted from the French coast, and about 12 from the direction of Holland. London and Birmingham continued to be the main objectives. Between 2100 and 2300, there was considerable activity along the coast between Newcastle and Aberdeen but no penetration inland of more than a few miles. Enemy activity lessened considerably towards the end of this period.

0100-0600: A few sporadic raids from the Dutch coast continued the attack on London via the Estuary. One raid penetrated towards Bedford before recrossing the coast at Southwold.

London was under red warning throughout the night as usual. Bombing until midnight was more intense than on the previous night but activity weakened thereafter. Little damage was caused, except at Southwark and Croydon where direct hits on public shelters caused a considerable number of casualties, and at Woolwich Arsenal where two buildings were seriously damaged by explosion and fire. Birmingham was again raided with considerable severity. The enemy employed mostly incendiary bombs, which caused some 200 fires with much resulting damage.

Civilian casualties (approx.) by day amounted to 3 killed, 5 seriously injured and 36 slightly injured outside London during the day. By night in London 60 people were killed and 250 were injured. Elsewhere after dark 10 were killed, 32 were seriously injured and 45 were slightly hurt.

Mist and fog again hampered daylight operations until the late afternoon when a large formation was prevented from reaching London. Night raids on the capital and the industrial midlands continued unabated. Ten German aircraft were lost and 4 more damaged on operations. Accidents accounted for another 4 machines destroyed and 2 more damaged.

1/KG3 Dornier Do 17Z-2 (2544). Suffered engine failure during night sortie to London and crash-landed at Boughton Malherbe, near Maidstone 1.00 a.m. Fw. K. Vosshagen and Fw. A. Schreiber both captured badly injured. Fw. R. Nitsch and Uffz. H. Hausdorf both baled out too low over Boughton Malherbe and killed. Aircraft 5K+CH a write-off.

The observer, Albin Schreiber, succumbed to his injuries the following day and was buried in Maidstone cemetery. He was not reinterred postwar.

5/JG27 Messerschmitt Bf 109E-8 (4906). Shot down by Pilot Officer G. K. Gilroy of No. 603 Squadron during free-lance fighter sweep over Gravesend. Crashed close to Pinewood Garage, London Road, Leybourne near Maidstone 2.30 p.m. Uffz. A. Gonschorrek baled out and captured slightly wounded. Aircraft 2+— a write-off.

Pieces picked up at the time now owned by Ron Gamage.

Stab II/JG51 Messerschmitt Bf 109E-4 (5095). Shot down in combat over the south coast and crashed at Fielding Land, Dymchurch 5.10 p.m. Probably that claimed by Sergeant A. S. Darling of No. 603 Squadron. Lt. W. Knittel (Gruppe Adjutant) killed. Aircraft <+ a write-off.

Major recovery by the Brenzett Aeronautical Museum in 1973. Excavations revealed all major components, cockpit controls and instruments and remains of the pilot who was buried with full military honours following statutory inquest. Relics now in the Hawkinge Aeronautical Trust collection.

4/JG53 Messerschmitt Bf 109E-4 (1531). Shot down in combat with RAF fighters and crashed and burned out at North Common, Chailey, near Haywards Heath 5.00 p.m. Probably one of those claimed by Squadron Leader R. R. S. Tuck of No. 257 Squadron. Fw. A. Berg baled out and captured unhurt. Aircraft 3+— a write-off.

Site excavated by the Wealden Aviation Archaeological Group in 1973. Remains of shattered Daimler-Benz DB 601 engine and propeller boss salvaged.

Fiat BR 20 bombers were based at Chièvres — here ground crews have to use a warm-air heater to get the engines started.

Up to their knees in muck and bullets, these young men said afterwards that they were enjoying themselves — ferreting about in the mire for the remains of the Heinkel of the 9th Staffel of KG53 which crashed in the River Stour on October 29. In this case no chance of finding dead crewmen as all baled out safely before she hit.

TUESDAY, OCTOBER 29

The most interesting feature of the raiding during daylight hours is the marked similarity between the bombing over the period and that of the 27th/28th October. Enemy activity consisted of five main attacks in the south-east, two attacks in the Portsmouth area and an attack at dusk on aerodromes in East Anglia, Lincolnshire and Yorkshire. Our fighters were very successful in destroying 27 enemy aircraft whilst our own losses were only 7, of which 5 pilots are safe.

First attack, 1025-1115: About 15 enemy aircraft flew towards London and some penetrated to the west and north-west, dropping bombs in Westminster, Kensington, Paddington and Lambeth. There were four fatal casualties but little damage was done.

Second, third and fourth attacks: At 1045 an attack by 9 enemy aircraft swept over Manston, flying out along the Estuary but there were no reports of bombing. At 1220 and 1253 two raids of approximately 25 aircraft flew to West London and then turned east. Bombs were dropped in the boroughs of Camberwell, Lewisham and Beckenham. The South Metropolitan Gas Company, Camberwell, was hit and there were four fatal casualties, but the damage is slight. A fire was also caused at an optical works at Lewisham.

Fifth attack: At 1630, raids totalling 50 aircraft entered the Thames Estuary and approached Hornchurch and North Weald. About 30 H.E. were dropped on the aerodrome at North Weald where damage was caused.

At 1430, 50 enemy aircraft approached the Isle of Wight, where they split up, one part approaching Portsmouth and the other part flew to Thorney Island area. There are no reports of bombing during this raid.

At about 1700, 30 enemy aircraft approached from the Selsey Bill direction, attacked Portsmouth and were quickly dispersed, but a few succeeded in dropping bombs on the city. Several shops were demolished and a considerable number of houses badly damaged, but there was no military damage. Casualties amounted to 3 killed, 12 seriously wounded, 21 slightly wounded.

Attack on aerodromes: Attacks on aerodromes commenced at 1740, and were carried out by formations of 1 to 6 aircraft. Bombs were dropped at Wattisham, Leeming, Newmarket, Honington, Matlask, Linton-on-Ouse and Lockington. Casualties were slight and damage small. During the period of these attacks about 40 other incidents are reported from towns and villages in East Anglia, and it is stated that explosive bombs have been dropped at several places.

Enemy activity by night was on a reduced scale, about 150 aeroplanes being used, but a larger proportion visited the Midlands, where the Birmingham-Coventry area was again the main objective. Bombing is also reported from Liverpool and out of 150 minor incidents about 75 per cent were in Regions 4, 6 and 12.

London had a comparatively quiet night during which there were no serious incidents and casualties were small.

The Birmingham raid commenced at 2250 and lasted for approximately 1¼ hours. There were three serious fires out of a total of 50, but the extent of the damage has not yet been reported. All fires were under control by 0200. There was some damage to railways, but no fatal casualties were reported.

Coventry: Two raids were carried out at 2000 and 2250. In the first raid bombs dropped were nearly all I.B.s and 51 fires, none of which were serious, were started. During the second raid nearly all bombs were H.E.s. Some damage is reported on the works of Humber Ltd, and the Royal Naval Ordnance Stores. The Coventry-Nuneaton road is blocked and the L.M.S. railway between the same towns has been diverted owing to U.X.B.s. Casualties amounted to 5 killed, 3 seriously wounded, 4 slightly wounded.

Liverpool: Some fires were started in the centre of the city but were quickly extinguished. The only major damage was to the Telephone Exchange which is temporarily out of action.

Approximate civilian casualties during the day were: In London, 10 people killed and 49 injured. Elsewhere, 7 killed, 16 seriously hurt and 31 slightly injured. By night in London, 12 people were killed and 25 injured. Elsewhere there were 6 fatalities, 20 people seriously injured and 20 slightly injured.

Twenty-seven enemy aircraft were certainly destroyed, 10 probably and 8 were damaged.

The tactics adopted by the enemy during the 27/28th and 29/30th October are similar to several periods between 21st/22nd June and 30th June/1st July. It was then considered that the enemy was concentrating on the training of large numbers of pilots. The enemy appears to be concentrating on R.A.F. establishments at dusk, and industry and railways by night.

The large number of minor incidents reported from the Home Counties suggest that enemy pilots have considerable respect for the defences of London. It is possible that the enemy are concentrating on the training of Italian pilots, the presence of their aircraft having been recently established in France.

Large formations of fighters and fighter-bombers clashed high above the southern approaches to London during the morning in combats reminiscent of the Summer battles. For the last time during the official period of the 'Battle of Britain' the ratio of losses swung heavily in the RAF's favour. Twenty-two Luftwaffe aircraft were destroyed on operations, another 2 being damaged. In addition, 6 machines were lost and 2 more damaged in accidents.

9/JG3 Messerschmitt Bf 109E-4 (5153). Forced-landed near Wootton Crossroads, Shepherdswell 5.15 p.m. with damage sustained in combat with No. 74 Squadron Spitfires. Oberlt. E. Troha (Staffelkapitän) captured unhurt. Aircraft 5+I a write-off.

8/JG26 Messerschmitt Bf 109E-4 (5794). Shot down by Pilot Officer T. L. Kumiega and Sergeant R. D. Hogg of No. 17 Squadron during free-lance sortie over England. Crashed at Marsh House Farm, Tillingham 5.00 p.m. Fw. C. Jäckel baled out and captured unhurt. Aircraft 1+I a write-off.

3/JG51 Messerschmitt Bf 109E-1 (4816). Shot down by Pilot Officer R. M. Trousdale of No. 266 Squadron during a free-lance sortie over Dover. Crashed and exploded at the Gate Inn, west of Elham 5.00 p.m. Fw. K. Bubenhofer baled out and captured at Rhodes Minnis. Aircraft 13+ a write-off.

4/JG51 Messerschmitt Bf 109E-4 (5370). Shot down by Flying Officer W. H. Nelson of No. 74 Squadron during combat over Tunbridge Wells. Lost height and ploughed into the ground at Dodds Farm, Langton Green possibly attempting a forced-landing 5.20 p.m. Lt. H. Tornow killed. Aircraft 9+ a write-off.

4/JG51 Messerschmitt Bf 109E-1 (4828). Shot down by Pilot Officer G. Marsland of No. 253 Squadron and hit obstructions attempting a forced-landing at Plummers Plain, Horsham. Crashed and burned out 5.15 p.m. Uffz. A. Lenz captured mortally wounded and died same day. Aircraft 5+ a write-off.

9/KG53 Heinkel He 111H-2 (5536). Lost bearings due to W/T failure during sortie to bomb Gravesend aerodrome. Abandoned by crew when thought to be over Holland. Crashed in the River Stour, near Parkeston Quay 1.07 a.m. Oberfw. K. Penzel baled out and captured unhurt. Oberfw. H. Metzger, Uffz. F. Sigger, Uffz. J. Klitscher and Uffz. H. Lüdecke all baled out and captured slightly injured. Aircraft A1+LT lost.

Epic recovery operations in 1984 and 1985 under difficult conditions, masterminded by Steve Vizard, revealed many interesting items including aircraft log book, oxygen masks, first-aid kit and many other documents and relics.

4/LG2 Messerschmitt Bf 109E-4 (5593). Severely damaged by No. 249 Squadron Hurricanes following low-level Jabo attack on North Weald aerodrome. Believed that attacked by Sergeant M. K. Macejowski. Forced-landed with seized engine at Langenhoe Wick 5.00 p.m. Oberfw. J. Harmeling captured slightly wounded. Aircraft ▲+N a write-off.

And its amazing what they found after forty years in the mud!

4/LG2 Messerschmitt Bf 109E-4 (5562). Shot down by Flight Lieutenant R. A. Barton of No. 249 Squadron following low-level Jabo attack on North Weald. Crashed alongside the Goldhanger Road at Maldon 4.53 p.m. Fw. H. Rank baled out wounded and badly burned and died of his injuries the same day in St Peter's Hospital. Aircraft ▲+B a write-off.

Site investigated by the Essex Aviation Research and Recovery Group 1974. Engine components in the Tangmere Military Aviation Museum.

5/LG2 Messerschmitt Bf 109E-4 (4145). Shot down by No. 249 Squadron Hurricanes following low-level Jabo attack on North Weald. Possibly that claimed by Sergeant G. A. Stroud. Believed crashed in the sea 12 miles east of the Blackwater Estuary 5.10 p.m. Oberlt. H-B. von Schenk (Staffelkapitän) killed. Aircraft ▲+S lost.

The body of Hans-Benno von Schenk is believed to have been recovered from the sea at Southend on November 3.

3/ErproGr210 Messerschmitt Bf 109E-4 (2024). Engaged by No. 222 Squadron Spitfires during Jabo sortie to London Docks. Attacked by Flying Officer E. H. Thomas but eventually shot down by Sergeant J. H. H. Burgess. Crashed at Sheerlands Farm, Pluckley 2.30 p.m. Oberlt. O. Hintze (Staffelkapitän) baled out and captured slightly wounded. Aircraft 6+ a write-off.

Joint recovery by the Kent Battle of Britain Museum and the London Air Museum, April 1976. Complete Daimler-Benz DB 601 engine and propeller boss recovered and retained by the latter. Armament, various fragments and components together with aircraft identity plate confirming '2024' in the Kent Battle of Britain Museum and now held by the Hawkinge Aeronautical Trust. Some items also in the Tangmere Military Aviation Museum. Pilot's map case, confiscated by the local police in 1940, now in the Vizard collection.

Above: **This dirty object (the MG not the man) was a rare prize, with** ***below*** **a gravity knife, fuel tank record and oxygen mask.**

Tankausweis für Flugzeug 550K Heimathafen: ...

Durchschrift

Der Unterzeichnete bescheinigt, im Auftrag und für Rechnung

für das obengenannte Flugzeug von der ...

folgende Flugbetriebsstoffmengen empfangen zu haben:

Menge in Liter	Flugbetriebsstoffart	Bemerkungen	Prüfungsvermerke
9 200	B IV	87	

Kontroll-Nummer:

den 22 ten ... 193 9

Empfänger

LE. Nr. 32

WEDNESDAY, OCTOBER 30

There were two main attacks by fighters during the day over south-east England. A few single reconnaissance aircraft were reported in other parts of the country.

First attack, 1130-1245: About 150 aircraft operated in three waves. The first wave of about 60 aircraft came in over the North Foreland to Shoeburyness and flew out over Kent. The second wave followed and turned south over the North Foreland and flew out over Hawkinge. A third wave crossed at Hastings but turned back at Ashford. Some bombs were dropped in Kent during these raids.

Second attack, 1540-1650: This attack was in two phases. In the first about 80 aircraft approached Maidstone, 40 of them reached south-east London where a few bombs were dropped. In the second phase about five small formations totalling about 50 aircraft crossed betweeen Dover and Beachy Head, one formation of 12 reached Harwich. Reconnaissances were reported in the Straits and the Channel in the morning, and off Exeter, Portland and the Firth of Forth in the afternoon.

During the early evening London and the south-east counties were the recipients of a major attack, with minor raids in the Midlands, in the latter part of the night activity was very slight, at times sinking to zero. The 'Raiders Passed' was sounded in Central London at 0337.

1830-2100: Approximately 60 raids converged on London but only a very small proportion penetrated to Central London. The main activity being in south-eastern counties. Four raids crossed the coast in the Portsmouth district and proceeded to the Nottingham-Sheffield area, returning via London. Minelaying was suspected off the North Foreland, the Estuary and Harwich.

2100-0100: Activity decreased considerably. The Midlands received some attention. Only odd raids penetrated to Central London. A few raids visited the Duxford-Debden area. After 0100 activity declined to practically nothing and by 0400 the country was clear of raids.

Civilian casualties outside London are 2 people killed, 14 seriously injured and 12 slightly injured. There were no casualties within London during the day. By night, 8 Londoners were killed and 131 were seriously injured, together with 39 slightly hurt. Elsewhere after dark, 5 people died, 16 were seriously injured and 8 were slightly hurt.

Enemy aircraft casualties amount to 9 certain, 8 probable and 7 damaged.

As if to herald the end of the 'Battle of Britain', comparatively few raids of any significance took place and activity was slight. Eight German aircraft were lost on operations, another 10 being damaged, 2 of them accidentally. Four fell in Britain as follows:

6/JG3 Messerschmitt Bf 109E-4 (6360). Shot down by Flying Officer R. C. Dafforn and Sergeant J. H. Lacey of No. 501 Squadron during combat over north Kent. Lost a wing and crashed in flames at Leylands, Meopham 4.15 p.m. Uffz. A. Fahrian baled out slightly wounded and circled by Flying Officer A. F. Eckford of No. 253 Squadron. Aircraft 9+— a write-off.

Site investigated and dug by several groups including Halstead War Museum but only small pieces recovered.

6/JG3 Messerschmitt Bf 109E-4 (1474). Crash-landed in hop field at Court Lodge Farm, East Farleigh 4.05 p.m. following combat with RAF fighters. Possibly that attacked by Sergeant G. Griffiths of No. 17 Squadron. Gefr. E. Schuller captured wounded. Aircraft 1+— a write-off.

The price of victory — won with the blood of these few men. This time Britain had been saved from invasion by knights riding mechanical beasts of war, fighting almost non-stop battle for four months.

As yet it was too soon to see the ultimate victory but we now know that the invasion would never come . . . and that Hitler's chance of the subjugation of Europe, and possibly world domination, ended here in October 1940.

7/JG26 Messerschmitt Bf 109E-4 (5242). Exploded under attack by Pilot Officer F. J. Aldridge of No. 41 Squadron 12.00 p.m. Wreckage falling on Brook Farm, Marden. Uffz. K. Töpfer killed. Aircraft 8+I a write-off.

Few fragments recovered by Lashenden Air Warfare Museum.

8/LG1 Junkers Ju 88A-1 (5008). Sortied on armed reconnaissance of the Metropolitan Vickers electrical works at Salford. Intercepted and shot down by Blue Section of No. 1 Squadron (Pilot Officer G. E. Goodman, Pilot Officer V. Jicha and Flying Officer R. G. Lewis). Crash-landed at Priggs Yard, Middle Fen, Stuntney, near Ely 2.50 p.m. Uffz. W. Arndt and Uffz. A. Brönner captured unhurt, Obergefr. P. Flieger and Gefr. W. Kellner baled out over Sutton Bridge and both captured slightly injured. Aircraft L1+GS a write-off.

THURSDAY, OCTOBER 31

Hostile activity by day was very slight in the morning. In the afternoon it was a little more marked and increased again in the late afternoon. This activity, which resembled night operations on a reduced scale, appeared to have as its objective the reconnaissance of aerodromes. The most remarkable feature was the number of instances of machine-gunning whether accompanied by bombing or not.

Enemy activity by night was divided into two phases; one in the early evening and the other in the early morning.

First phase, 1825-2100: At 1825 the first night raiders (approx. 30) left Dieppe on the usual north-west route. Strong westerly gales blew them off course so that they crossed the coast in the Hastings-Dungeness area. These raids were joined by two from Calais and all proceeded towards West and Central London, though only a few achieved their object. Aberdeen was also raided. By 2100 no enemy raiders were over the country.

Second phase, 0245-0600: Two attacks developed with London and the Midlands as objectives. Approx. 6 aircraft made landfall at Weymouth, the majority proceeding to Birmingham and one or two further north. Approximately 25 to 30 raiders were concerned in the attack on London.

Civilian casualties outside London during the day amounted to 6 people killed, 28 seriously injured and 78 slightly hurt. By night, 12 people in London were killed and 52 were injured. Elsewhere, 3 people were killed and 21 were injured, 20 of them seriously. No enemy aircraft were destroyed or damaged.

The 'Battle of Britain' came to a damp end on a dismal day of almost continual drizzle which reduced activity by day and by night. The Luftwaffe lost 3 aircraft — 1 of them accidentally, whilst another 3 were damaged — 1 on operations. None fell in the UK.

Since the battle started in earnest in July Germany had suffered the loss of over 2,600 crewmen killed with more than 950 made prisoners of war. Together with 1,800 aircraft destroyed, these totals can be set against the number of RAF lives lost: 541 alone if one counts only Fighter Command with just over 1,000 aircraft destroyed.

The outcome of this battle, on which so much depended, had been largely decided 19 days earlier with Hitler's declaration of October 12. Yet the Luftwaffe, which had expended so much during its four months struggle against England, remained a force in being and as yet undefeated — a force which would continue to harry and thwart British defences and the RAF throughout the months and years of war which lay ahead.

Der Adler — the Luftwaffe's fortnightly house magazine — was launched in 1939 by the Reichsluftfahrtministeriums in Berlin. Foreign language editions were published — this is the Spanish/German edition of October 29. The Editor was Hermann Schreiber, the cost 44 Reichspfennigs. The magazine relied heavily on artists' illustrations to make up for the lack of action photographs and many photographs were heavily retouched with diving aircraft or falling bombs added for greater effect. Pictures of actual bomb damage lagged several weeks after the actual event — possibly partly due to the extended lead time necessary to produce a multi-language magazine by the photogravure process.

FRIDAY, NOVEMBER 1

Enemy activity during the day was on a moderate scale. Some five raids larger than 20+ aircraft penetrated inland, only a few aircraft reaching the London area. An abortive attack was made on Portsmouth and Southampton. Convoys and trawlers off the Yorkshire coast and the Channel were attacked. Bombs were dropped on the East Coast, East Anglia and the East End of London. Damage and casualties were slight. A few reconnaissance flights were made in the morning and late afternoon in the south and east areas.

Activity by night was divided into two phases. The first and heavier attacks were directed chiefly against London, the Midlands, and southern Scotland; the second being the minor one and directed against South and East London.

From 1800-2100 thirty-two raids were plotted to London and the south-eastern counties; three to four raids visited the Norfolk area, and the same number to the Northumberland district. Raids were also plotted over the Bristol Channel district penetrating to Cardiff and Liverpool. Minelaying was suspected in the Thames Estuary.

From 2100-0100 approximately thirty single raiders were plotted to London. Six raids visited the Birmingham and Coventry districts and minelaying was reported in the Firth of Forth and the Firth of Tay.

From 0100-0500 there were no raids plotted inland, and at 0205 the 'Raiders Passed' was given. At 0245 about ten raids penetrated to the South and East London area. At 0422 the 'Raiders Passed' was again given. At 0540 slight activity was renewed, some raids were plotted to the South Wales area.

Fourteen enemy aircraft were destroyed, 7 were damaged, and 4 were probably destroyed. By day, civilian casualties in London consisted of 6 killed and 51 injured. Elsewhere 12 people were killed, 12 seriously injured and 45 slightly hurt. By night, 59 people in London were killed and 211 were injured. Elsewhere, 25 were killed and 55 seriously injured and 11 slightly injured.

The first day of November saw the brief re-emergence of the Ju 87 Stuka dive-bomber which had had to be withdrawn from the battle in August due to horrendous losses *(see Volume I, pages 214-216)*. The Ju 88 displays night camouflage (see pages 250–251) with carefully applied matt black temporary paint covering the side and undersurfaces but not the stark white outlines of the Hakenkreuz and Balkenkreuz.

On November 1, for the first time since August 18, Junkers Ju 87s operated in strength over England when they attacked shipping in the Thames Estuary. They were supported by fighters and an estimated 400 sorties were flown during this and other sweeps. The following aircraft came down over the United Kingdom:

1/JG2 Messerschmitt Bf 109E-4 (5159). Damaged by Pilot Officer J. H. M. Offenberg in a Hurricane of No. 145 Squadron. Pilot made a forced landing at Mapson's Farm, Sidlesham, Sussex 4.05 p.m. Oberlt. H. Reifferscheidt (Staffelkapitän) taken prisoner. Aircraft White 9+ captured damaged.

8/KG30 Junkers Ju 88A-1 (7089). Flew into a hill in conditions of bad visibility during a sortie to Church Fenton. Crashed at Glaisdale Head, near Whitby, Yorkshire at 5.45 p.m. Fw. W. Wowereit, Oberfw. H. Schulte-Mäter, Uffz. A. Rodermond, Uffz. G. Pohling all killed. Aircraft 4D+TS destroyed.

5/StG1 Junkers Ju 87B-1 (5227). Shot down by AA fire from a small ship it had attacked, engine set on fire and landed in the Thames Estuary east of the Nore 2.30 p.m. Gefr. W. Karrach killed. Gefr. M. Aulehner picked up by a motor torpedo boat and taken prisoner. Aircraft 6G+KS sank in sea.

The slapdash way the blacking out process was performed by some units is illustrated on the fin of this Ju 88 which was hit by AA fire while attacking Birmingham on the evening of November 1. It managed to get as far as Storrington in East Sussex before attempting an abortive forced landing in the grounds of Greyfriars.

The second raider brought down during the night, a Heinkel from KG55, had taken off at 7.00 p.m. bound for London. At the controls was Leutnant Hans-Adalbert Tüffers who was originally on the strength of the 9th Staffel before he transferred to the 8th on October 15 after a disagreement with his Staffelkapitän. He had already been shot down once before, over the Channel, but had been rescued by the Seenotdienst; now he was on his ninth war flight to England. London was crossed from west to east at 19,000 feet without the crew spotting their specific target and bombs were released blind. When passing over Romford, AA scored a direct hit on the tail of the aircraft which entered a steep dive. Leutnant Tüffers gave orders to bale out when passing 13,000 feet and he and his observer, Unteroffizier Josef Haverstreng, managed to get clear before the aircraft crashed onto the back gardens between Station Lane and Matlock Gardens ***(above)*** **in Hornchurch.**

The main feature of the night's activities were raids on London and Birmingham. Additionally a Junkers Ju 88C of 3/NJG2 went missing during an intruder sortie and a Ju 88 of III/KG77 crashed at Noyon in France, being destroyed. Three more bombers were damaged.

8/KG55 Heinkel He 111P-2 (1571). Hit by AA fire at high altitude while participating in a raid on London 9.45 p.m. Crashed on row of houses at Matlock Gardens, Hornchurch, Essex. Lt. H-A. Tüffers and Uffz. J. Haverstreng baled out and taken prisoner. Uffz. R. Bubel and Uffz. J. Juvan killed. Aircraft G1+JS destroyed.

StabI/LG1 Junkers Ju 88A-1 (4145). Damaged by ground defences during a raid on Birmingham. Pilot attempted a forced landing but hit trees at 'Greyfriars', Waterworks Lane, Storrington, Sussex 9.35 p.m. Fw. F. Püschel captured badly injured, died next day. Uffz. G. Reinsberg and Uffz. G. Büscher killed. Uffz. W. Knappe taken prisoner, injured. Aircraft L1+MB wrecked.

The spectacular crash brought the Press hot-foot to the scene and several agencies sent photographers. Planet News claimed that 'the entire crew perished'; that the crash took place on 'November 2', instead of the 1st, and that '5 bombers were brought down in the raid', instead of just one as the LG1 Junkers was raiding Birmingham.

Floating to earth some four miles to the east, Leutnant Tüffers landed slightly injured in Belhus Park and surrendered to the lodge keeper in Aveley Road the next morning. An ambulance picked him up there at 11.45 a.m., at which time he was in the custody of Acting Sergeant Northover of the local police, and he was sent to Oldchurch Hospital under police guard. Unteroffizier Haverstreng had landed unhurt and had sought refuge in the waiting room of South Ockenden railway station where he surrendered to staff at 6.00 a.m. the following morning. He was handed over to the RAF for interrogation. Planet News captioned this picture: 'Mr and Mrs Percy Sowter who came down to get some coal and found one of the propellers in their coal bin.' It is certainly a good picture but what about our comparison with the coal bunker still standing? (Incidentally, Tüffers was promoted to Oberleutnant in April 1942 'in absentia' a PoW in Canada.)

The mutiliated remains of the other two crewmen, Unteroffizier Richard Bubel and Josef Juvan were extricated from the wreckage and set to one side covered by their parachutes and linoleum. No mention was made by the media of any civilian casualties but when the Heinkel crashed, blazing fuel engulfed the area, where several families were sheltering in their Andersons. The Bird family at No. 12 Matlock Gardens — mother Margaret, father William and baby Joyce, all perished.

Firemen still at work on the Ramsgate gasworks struck late morning on Saturday.

SATURDAY, NOVEMBER 2

During the day, three attacks were delivered by enemy aircraft towards London from the south-east, in one of which a few succeeded in reaching the capital. Some activity over convoys in the Thames Estuary was also reported, and at dusk there were a few raids in East Anglia.

First attack, 0750-0900. Seventy aircraft, apparently all fighters, flew towards Maidstone and Biggin Hill and were engaged by our squadrons which inflicted severe damage on the enemy.

Second attack, 0950-1040. About 90 aircraft, mostly fighter-bombers, approached from the Dover direction making for London. About five reached Central London and then turned eastwards. Bombs were dropped at Bromley and Chislehurst. An A.F.S. station at the former was hit and there were two fatal casualties to personnel, otherwise there was no serious damage and no casualties.

Third attack, 1120-1145. A formation of 16 bombers escorted by 20 enemy fighters attacked Ramsgate. About 60+ H.E. were dropped and some damage to gas works and property is reported. The casualties amounted to 5 killed, 5 seriously wounded, 18 slightly, 3 missing (believed killed).

A single aircraft penetrated to Tilbury, two tugs were sunk, and there was some damage to the quay. Casualties were 5 killed, 2 seriously wounded, 5 missing.

Between 0700-1000 reconnaissance activities were reported by single aircraft in the Channel, Coventry, and off Lands End. A few bombs were dropped at Coventry, but the slight damage was confined to house property, and casualties were very few. (Killed 1; seriously injured 3; slightly hurt 1.)

In the London area, bombs were dropped at Bexley and Chislehurst, and Woolwich. No major damage has been reported.

By night in London, about 80 aircraft were plotted almost exclusively over the Greater London and Home Counties areas. Fourteen boroughs in London reported incidents and there are also 86 minor incidents from the remainder of the country. Of these, 23 occurred in Region 4, and 52 in Region 12.

A serious fire occurred at Messrs. John Barkers, Kensington High Street, and there are a few road blocks and slight damage to railways, but none of them are serious.

In the provinces at Warbleton (Sussex) an omnibus was blown off the road, 5 people being killed and 1 seriously wounded. There are no reports of military damage and casualties are few.

Enemy aircraft casualties amounted to 10 destroyed, 1 probable and 7 damaged. Our losses consisted of 1 aircraft (pilot safe). Civilian casualties (approx.) by day were: London, 5 killed and 24 injured. Elsewhere, 12 killed, 11 seriously injured and 21 slightly injured. Eight people are reported missing. By night, 10 people in London were killed and 38 were injured. Elsewhere 7 were killed, 3 seriously injured and 5 people were slightly hurt.

Action again centred around the Thames Estuary. Additional losses to those listed below were Messerschmitt Bf 109s of 7/JG53 and 4/JG54 and Dornier Do 17s of Stab/KG2 and 4/KG3 which went down into the sea, making a total of seven aircraft lost. A Bf 109 of 6/JG52 was destroyed in a forced landing at

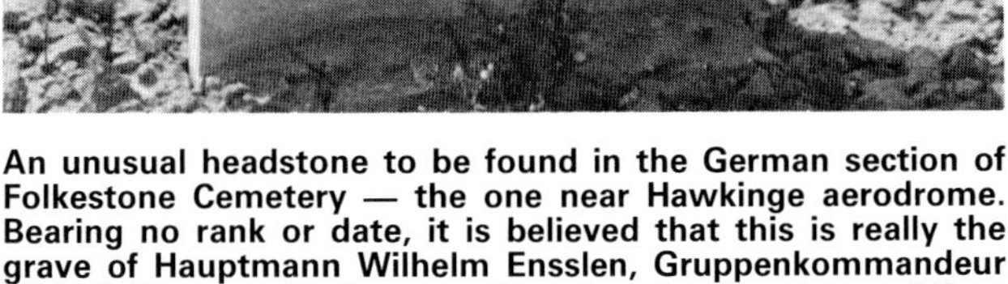

An unusual headstone to be found in the German section of Folkestone Cemetery — the one near Hawkinge aerodrome. Bearing no rank or date, it is believed that this is really the grave of Hauptmann Wilhelm Ensslen, Gruppenkommandeur with JG52, brought down by Squadron Leader 'Johnny' Kent who had joined the Poles of No. 303 Squadron early in August and had recently been promoted to CO of No. 92 Squadron. When the crash site was investigated in 1982 confirmation of the identity of the Messerschmitt came to light together with the top of the pilot's joystick.

Wissant, but its pilot was safe. An He 114B was damaged in a crash landing near Aalborg.

StabII/JG52 Messerschmitt Bf 109E-7 (3784). Shot down by Squadron Leader J. A. Kent in a Spitfire of No. 92 Squadron 8.55 a.m. Crashed at Burmarsh Halt, near Dymchurch, Kent. Hptmn. W. Ensslen (Gruppenkommandeur) baled out but was killed on landing. Aircraft +2 destroyed.

A major recovery by Steve Vizard in 1982 revealed the Daimler-Benz DB 601 engine, control column and large quantities of airframe. Aircraft work number plate found confirming its identity. The pilot remains buried at Folkestone New Cemetery (Hawkinge) in plot O, grave number 404, under the inscription 'A. Schenk'. The reason behind this is unknown, but the only identification found on the body were the Hauptmann's shoulder flashes and an identity disc 67005/1, confirming the identity of the body. In the light of post-war research there would seem to be no doubt that this is the grave of Hptmn. Ensslen.

StabII/JG52 Messerschmitt Bf 109E-7 (5933). Ditched into the sea 2 miles south-east of Dymchurch, Kent 8.50 a.m. following combat with Spitfires of No. 92 and No. 74 Squadrons. Fw. O. Junger taken prisoner. Aircraft Yellow 4+ lost.

8/JG53 Messerschmitt Bf 109E-1 (4034). Made a forced landing at Street End, Lower Hardres, Kent with engine failure after being in combat with Spitfires of No. 92 and No. 74 Squadrons, 9.00 a.m. Fw. X. Ray taken prisoner. Aircraft Black 6+I captured damaged.

A single aircraft from a small force attacking London during the evening was lost over Britain, but a Ju 88 of II/KG77 crashed near Reims killing its crew. An He 111 of 6/KG4 was damaged..

5/KG76 Junkers Ju 88A-1 (4159). Shot down by AA fire and crashed at New Barn Farm, Southfleet, Kent 7.30 p.m. Oberfw. O. Grünke, Oberfw. A. Vogl and Uffz. M. Biller killed. Uffz. E. Stumpp missing. Aircraft F1+DN destroyed.

Items recovered by the Kent Battle of Britain Museum included an identity disc and parachute release buckle.

Crewed by Leutnant Wolfgang Sonnenberg, pilot; Unteroffizier Ferdinand Zumbrock, wireless operator; and Gefreiter Willi Krohn and Feldwebel Johann Kleditzsch as observers, Dornier 5K+CS of the 8th Staffel of KG3 took off from its base at St Trond just after eleven o'clock for a solo attack on a target at Woolwich. While flying at 8,000 feet, the aircraft was violently shaken, probably damaged by AA fire. It was then attacked by two Hurricanes of No. 46 Squadron's Yellow Section flown by Flying Officer P. W. Le Fevre (Yellow 1) and Pilot Officer C. F. Ambrose (Yellow 2) who lost it in cloud over Gravesend at which stage it was smoking heavily. The aircraft crashed apparently attempting a forced landing and broke up in allotments alongside St Paul's Choir School in Wansunt Road, Bexley, after hitting an elm tree behind No. 39 and ploughing through a five-feet-high brick wall. Immediately prior to the crash, witnesses reported that the starboard engine was feathered and that the port engine was only idling, emitting clouds of black smoke. The aircraft hit the ground and the fuselage broke off level with the trailing edge of the wing. Both wings were torn off outside of the engine nacelles and the cockpit was completely smashed.

SUNDAY, NOVEMBER 3

Enemy activity by day was confined to reconnaissance work mostly in the afternoon and early evening, in the course of which a few bombs were dropped. Several instances were reported of machine-gunning from the air. Eight aerodromes were attacked, hangars being hit in three instances. The water works pumping station at Rugby was damaged and is temporarily out of action. Otherwise damage and casualties were small.

No enemy aircraft were plotted over England and Wales by night. Between 1800 and 0100 only one enemy aircraft was plotted. This crossed the Scottish coast at Aberdeen, thence south over Dundee and the Firth of Forth and away eastwards at 2100. It dropped some bombs in several places including Aberdeen without causing any damage.

Between 0100 and 0400: At 0135 six raids reported as ten aircraft approached Scotland from Norway, the leader crossing the coast at Aberdeen at 0150. All were inland by 0245 and by 0400 had left again on their way east. Bombs were dropped in several localities, but only in Aberdeen, where three tenement houses were demolished, were damage or casualties caused.

Civilian casualties in London by day amounted to 3 killed and 23 injured. Elsewhere 7 people were injured seriously and 5 were slightly hurt. After dark, 3 people were killed, 12 seriously injured and 32 slightly injured. All the night casualties occurred at Aberdeen — there were none elsewhere. Enemy aircraft casualties were: certain — 1; probable — nil; damaged — 1.

Bad weather severely curtailed operations, one aircraft being lost over Britain. The British were unaware of the losses suffered in Europe as a result of these missions, however. Those recorded were: two more Do 17s of KG3, a Ju 88 of Stab II/KG76, and two Ju 88s of II/KG76 which crash-landed at Amsterdam after being damaged by fighters or flak.

8/KG3 Dornier Do 17Z-2 (2573).Shot down by Flying Officer P. W. Le Fevre and Pilot Officer C. F. Ambrose in Hurricanes of No. 46 Squadron. Crashed at Wansunt Road, Old Bexley 12.30 p.m. Area evacuated due to unexploded bombs but little damage done to property. Lt. W. Sonnenberg captured badly wounded and died the next day; Fw. J. Kleditzsch two days later. Gefr. W. Krohn, Uffz. F. Zumbrock killed. Aircraft 5K+CS wrecked.

Propeller blade tip and Bramo Fafnir engine badge donated to the Tangmere Military Aviation Museum.

St Paul's School lays behind the photographer in the contemporary views but was demolished after the war and a new estate laid out on the site by an ex-master in the 1950s.

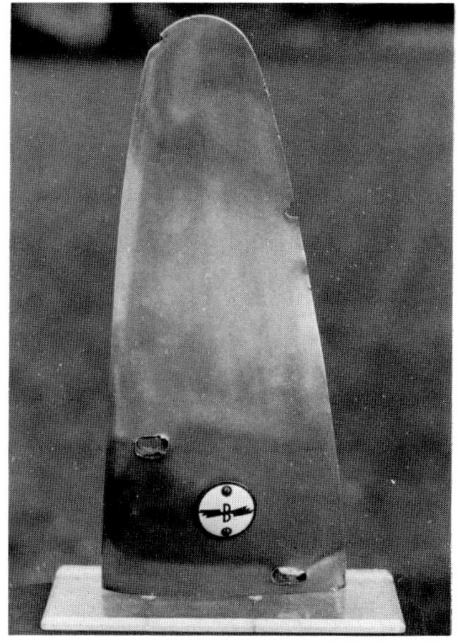

The body of Gefreiter Krohn was recovered from the wreckage and buried at Bexley Cemetery. Unteroffizier Zumbröck was taken to Dartford County Hospital where he succumbed to his wounds the same day. Leutnant Sonnenberg and Feldwebel Kleditzsch were also admitted to the hospital where they both died of injuries on November 4 and 5 respectively. They were all buried in the Borough Cemetery. The whole area was cleared while the bomb load of 20 SC 50s were defuzed and No. 49 Maintenance Unit from Faygate *(see Volume I, page 123)* cleared the wreckage. *Right:* **The tip of one of the blades, complete with bullet holes, cut off at the time, can now be seen in the museum at Tangmere.**

MONDAY, NOVEMBER 4

By day, enemy activity was on a small scale and consisted chiefly of single aircraft and coastal reconnaissance.

Activity by night commenced at dusk and during the first hours of darkness was considerable, especially in the London area and Scotland. Attacks in the North ceased early but those on London persisted. The Midland areas were also visited.

1830-2100: During this period some 35 raiders visited Scotland. Attacks were widespread with a main concentration on the Aberdeen-Perth and Dundee area, but central Scotland was also covered. Some raids penetrated to Glasgow. Some 40 tracks were plotted from Holland and France to Sussex, Kent, Essex and the London area.

2100-0100: Activity in Scotland ceased by 2300. It continued in the South-East in considerable strength. There were also regular plots to the Midlands throughout the period.

0100-0300: Activity in the South-East lessened although the steady stream to Birmingham and Coventry continued until 0200 when no incoming aircraft were reported. Attacks recommenced at 0245 from France and Holland.

0300-0600: Activity in London and the Home Counties was maintained throughout the period in moderate strength. At 0310, 14 tracks were plotted from Holland to East Anglia, some of these were suspected of minelaying off the coast, but the majority flew in over Norfolk and Suffolk. One penetrated to Bedford. This activity had subsided by 0500.

At 0600 there was still activity in the South-East and London, with new activity from Brittany to Milford Haven and Guernsey to Bristol.

Enemy aircraft casualties: nil. Civilian casualties in London during the day were 10 seriously injured. Elsewhere during daylight hours, 7 people were killed, 11 seriously injured and 8 slightly hurt. After dark, 30 Londoners were killed and 101 were injured. Elsewhere 5 people died, 15 were seriously injured and 30 were slightly injured. Note that these figures do not include 30 casualties reported from Finsbury about which further details are not available. It is also feared that some people are trapped in a shelter at Lambeth.

Although none of the raiders were brought down by the defences, a Dornier Do 17 of III/KG76 returned with flak damage. Two other machines, an He 111 of I/KG26 and a Junkers Ju 88 of 1(F)/120 were written off in crashes upon their return.

East Ham Hospital, then containing 20 beds, was opened by the Countess of Warwick in 1900. During the Great War it was used by the Army Council for the reception of British sick and wounded and was enlarged to take an additional 5 beds in 1915. In 1919 a general appeal was launched to raise funds for a General Hospital as a memorial to the men of East Ham who gave their lives in the war and the new 100-bed hospital, now known as the East Ham Memorial Hospital, was opened in 1929, the foundation stone having been laid by the Duchess of York accompanied by the Duke; the future King George VI. In 1939 an extension was begun for a Children's Ward and Maternity Ward and when opened in May 1940 the bed complement was increased to 131. Under the Emergency Health Service, from 1939 to 1945 the emergency beds were increased to 214. The hospital was damaged by enemy action on six occasions. In the first incident on October 9, 1940, a high explosive bomb struck the boiler house; two weeks later the new Children's Ward and Outpatients was hit: just after midnight on October 20. *Below left:* **In this picture released on November 4 the Hospital Committee are surveying the destruction with Shrewsbury Road in the background.** *Right:* **In May 1988 the hospital had closed but blast damage from the bomb was still visible on the wall beneath the railings.**

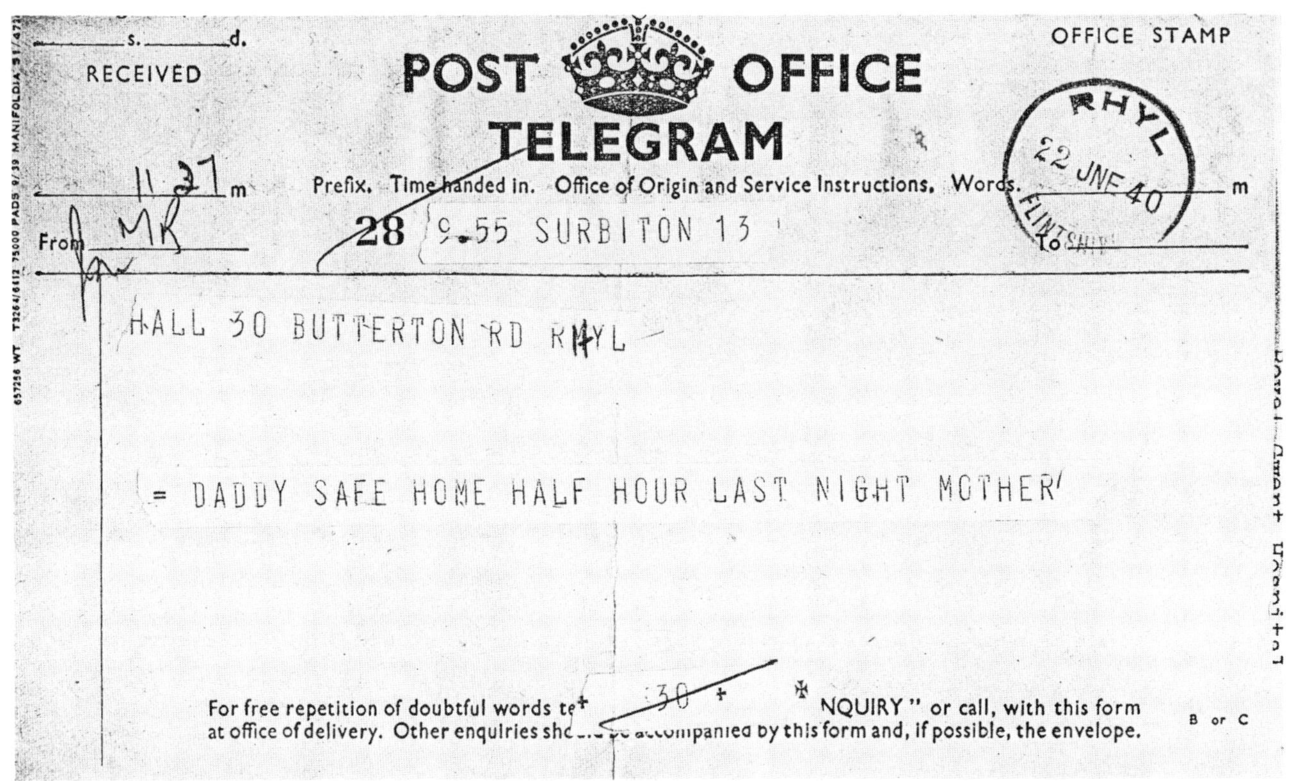

s. d.
RECEIVED

POST OFFICE
TELEGRAM

OFFICE STAMP

RHYL
22 JNE 40
FLINTSHIRE

11.27 m
Prefix. Time handed in. Office of Origin and Service Instructions. Words. m

From MK

28 9.55 SURBITON 13

To

HALL 30 BUTTERTON RD RHYL

= DADDY SAFE HOME HALF HOUR LAST NIGHT MOTHER

For free repetition of doubtful words te... NQUIRY" or call, with this form at office of delivery. Other enquiries sh... accompanied by this form and, if possible, the envelope.

B or C

A TELEGRAPH BOY REMEMBERS THE BLITZ

As far as Londoners were concerned the Blitz started in September 1940. Night after night the sirens would wail their warning of approaching enemy aircraft. Night after night whole families made their way into Anderson shelters in their gardens, Morrison shelters in their houses, public shelters in the streets, or into the nearest Tube station. A few brave souls stayed in their homes.

I lived with my parents and youngest sister in a ten-roomed Victorian terraced house in north London; also living there was a friend of my sister's and a lodger, a lady whose husband had been killed at the Battle of Loos in 1915. My eldest sister and her newly-born son, Geoffrey, soon joined us from the City of London Maternity Hospital, which was to suffer considerable damage in the coming air raids.

In September 1940 I was 12½ years old; my schooling had been interrupted by the mass evacuation to the country of London's teachers and children a year earlier, and when I returned to school after an enforced, but welcome, six months' holiday, it was for just half-a-day (mornings one week, afternoons the next).

In that lovely summer of 1940 I had watched contrails in the blue sky as Spitfire and Hurricane fought to the death with Messerschmitt 109 and 110. The aircraft had been flying too high for me to distinguish friend from foe; now however, in September, the foe was coming by night. The darkened sky, made darker by the black-out, was pierced with shafts of light as search-lights probed for the enemy we could hear but not see. As we sat or lay on our bunks in the confining space of our Anderson shelter; as hour after hour the air became even more stale (the black-out curtain over the narrow entrance restricted incoming fresh air); as discomfort succeeded discomfort; we heard, indistinctly at first, then growing louder and louder, the roar of aircraft engines, their uneven note heralding the nightly visit of the bomber force.

In June and July 1940 war had come very close to us; it had knocked on our door in the guise of a steel-helmetted policeman. In June we had to leave our home because an unexploded bomb had landed nearby, and the following month an aerial mine fell about half-a-mile away necessitating us to pack up again and evacuate. Each time we had thirty minutes to get out, so, loaded with as many clothes and personal things as

Although Britons were spared the dreaded midnight knock from the Gestapo experienced by those in the occupied countries, the arrival of the telegram boy was never a welcome sight in wartime Britain — not that we are implying in any way that 'our' Denis resembles the men in black. He was in fact reprimanded for not having his cap on straight in this picture taken for publicity purposes by the GPO! 'More often than not', says Denis, 'we were the harbingers of bad news.'

Charges to pay s. d. RECEIVED

POST OFFICE TELEGRAM

Prefix. Time handed in. Office of Origin and Service Instructions. Words.

From

No. OFFICE STAMP

Gifford Officer ... Squadron
Hearty congratulations from all at Sedbergh
Headmaster

For free repetition of doubtful words telephone "TELEGRAMS ENQUIRY" or call, with this form at office of delivery. Other enquiries should be accompanied by this form and, if possible, the envelope.

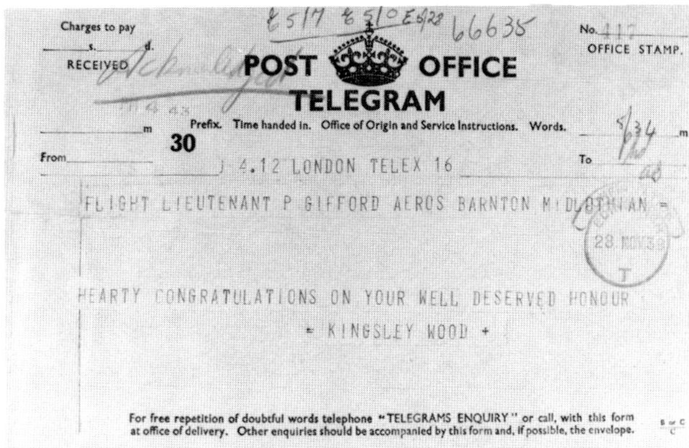
Charges to pay s. d. RECEIVED

POST OFFICE TELEGRAM

Prefix. Time handed in. Office of Origin and Service Instructions. Words.

30

From 4.12 LONDON TELEX 16 To

No. OFFICE STAMP.

FLIGHT LIEUTENANT P GIFFORD AEROS BARNTON MIDLOTHIAN =

HEARTY CONGRATULATIONS ON YOUR WELL DESERVED HONOUR

= KINGSLEY WOOD +

For free repetition of doubtful words telephone "TELEGRAMS ENQUIRY" or call, with this form at office of delivery. Other enquiries should be accompanied by this form and, if possible, the envelope.

Congratulations to Flight Lieutenant Patrick Gifford of No. 603 Squadron from his old headmaster and the Air Minister for bringing down the first enemy bomber on October 28, 1939 *(see Volume 1, pages 41-47)*.

possible, we joined scores of others, looking like the French refugees we had seen on the cinema screen a few weeks earlier. We left home not knowing if we would ever see it standing again and made our way to the house of a friend: the first time for just a day and a night, the second for a week. We must have looked rather funny. My eldest sister pushing a pram containing her two-month-old son was also balancing two bird cages on the pram: one — large, square and wooden, made by my father, contained eight budgerigars of various hues — the other, perched on top, a normal wire cage, housed our two canaries, Joey and Jackie. Walking alongside the pram was Paddy, our reddish-brown mongrel dog. My father carried two suitcases, and the rest of us anything we had managed to grab in the few minutes available to us.

The road had already been cordoned off with rope by the police so one end had to be opened to allow the residents to leave. The police hurried us along and about fifteen minutes later we arrived — unannounced — at the home of Mr and Mrs Baker who took us in. On the second occasion this happened the Royal Navy was brought in to defuze the mine and managed to neutralise two-thirds of it but had to explode the remainder. Although we were warned that an explosion would take place at a set time I managed to be outside our friend's house when the mine went up with a roar in a cloud of smoke and flame. Luckily, our house was not affected and we returned home that evening. A few days later, King George VI and Queen Elizabeth, together with Winston Churchill, visited the devastated site of the mine; I was able to stand quite close to them, there being only a few policemen around, and was much in awe of their presence. I remember that they were roundly cheered.

To return to the Blitz. Each night the family would go into the Anderson shelter in the back garden when the sirens began their banshee wail. Comments such as 'Here we go again' and 'They're early tonight' were made as we entered the small entrance and went down the three or four wooden steps to sit or lie in our usual places. I can still remember the earthy smell that pervaded everything, for the shelter was covered with earth for extra protection. By the light of a small oil or hurricane lamp we drank tea from thermos flasks, perhaps munched a sandwich and attempted to read or, in the case of the women, knit. Then to sleep, or at least to try to. I was often woken by the snores of our lodger, Mrs Fouldes, a very plump woman, who always seemed (to me) to take up more than her share of the limited available space. This caused tension and often bad feeling, probably helped by the worries and trials of our day-to-day living.

One night in October 1940 a section of a block of tall flats situated at one end of the road in which we lived was brought crashing to the ground by the impact of an aerial torpedo at the flats' base. Some 150 people were killed here and the disaster *[Coronation Avenue — see pages 179–181]* was made worse by the torpedo hitting the entrance to a public air raid shelter. The explosion fractured the gas and water mains, asphyxiating or drowning most of those not already killed by the blast. The whole area was covered with dust and a sickening smell permeated the air; two weeks later I saw bodies — just flat sacks containing the remains — still being carried out.

In the same month the docks were attacked and the sky was lit by the flames of the burning sugar refineries — a frightening sight to a 12-year-old boy. This decided my father to send my mother and me to the country, so we went to stay with my sister's in-laws at Caversham in Berkshire until my 14th birthday. Soon afterwards, I started work as a Boy Messenger, GPO (General Post Office), usually called telegraph boys, in the Western District (London's W1 area), which comprised shops, offices, hotels (among them the most select in the land) and residents. It included Mayfair and Soho and was a melting pot of races and creeds, wealth and poverty. We delivered telegrams to rich and poor, parsons and prostitutes, policemen and petty thieves. It was an education — I learnt more in six months than in years of schooling! With our distinctive uniform of dark blue piped with red and peaked pill-box cap we were part of the London scene as well as performing a vital service, and in so doing we carried on during air raids, only taking shelter if danger was imminent.

DENIS C. BATEMAN, 1985

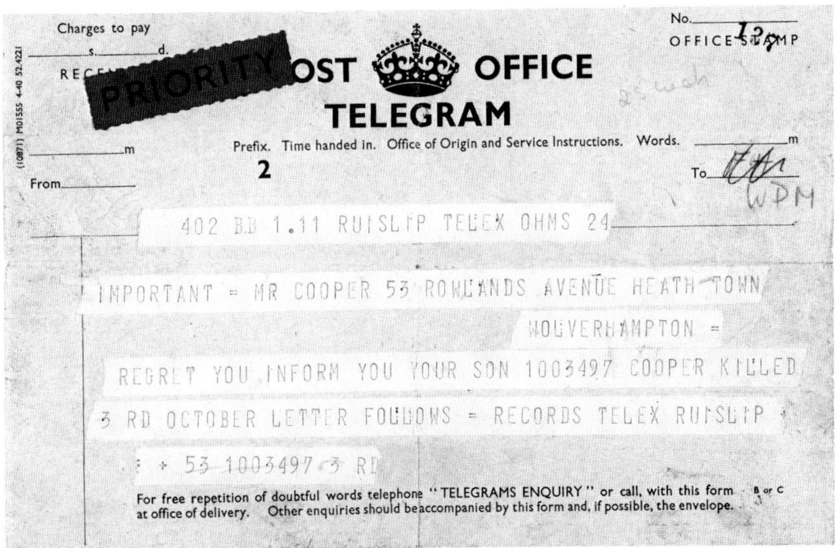
Charges to pay s. d. RECEIVED

PRIORITY

POST OFFICE TELEGRAM

Prefix. Time handed in. Office of Origin and Service Instructions. Words.

2

From To

No. OFFICE STAMP

402 BB 1.11 RUISLIP TELEX OHMS 24

IMPORTANT = MR COOPER 53 ROWLANDS AVENUE HEATH TOWN

WOLVERHAMPTON =

REGRET YOU INFORM YOU YOUR SON 1003497 COOPER KILLED

3 RD OCTOBER LETTER FOLLOWS = RECORDS TELEX RUISLIP +

+ 53 1003497 3 RD

For free repetition of doubtful words telephone "TELEGRAMS ENQUIRY" or call, with this form at office of delivery. Other enquiries should be accompanied by this form and, if possible, the envelope.

And the sadness. Leading Aircraftman Charles Cooper, a wireless operator with No. 600 Squadron, crashed in a rainstorm while on a routine patrol from Redhill on October 3, 1940.

A collision between two bomb-carrying Messerschmitt 109s at 13,000 feet led to both pilots of JG26 being taken prisoner. This is the remains of Walter Braun's machine at Wittersham Hall with the bomb shackle being displayed for the photographer.

TUESDAY, NOVEMBER 5

By day, there were three hostile fighter sweeps in South-East England and one in the Portland-Swanage area. Enemy aircraft were active over convoys off Deal and in the Thames Estuary. Isolated reconnaissances were made in East Anglia, Yorkshire and the Firth of Forth, with the usual activity in the Channel and Straits. Little material damage of importance was effected.

0934-1045: Fifty aircraft, probably all fighters, came in at Dungeness, part flying towards Sheppey and part to the Biggin Hill area, returning on similar courses. No reports of dropping of bombs was received.

1100-1200: Fifty aircraft, also probably fighters, came in between Dover and Dungeness, but only 12 continued into south-east Kent, flying between Rye and Ramsgate. Several minor incidents were reported, including a dive-bombing attack on Ramsgate.

1250-1345: Forty plus aircraft, probably all fighters, crossed the coast between Portland and Swanage, penetrating inland about 12 miles. Bombs were dropped in Portland Harbour without doing any damage.

1427-1620: Forty-two plus aircraft flew over a convoy at Deal, came in at Ramsgate and continued as far as Tilbury and Hornchurch where they split and turned back. Twelve aircraft also entered at Dungeness but did not penetrate beyond Tonbridge. two further waves followed of 12 plus and 15 plus which did not penetrate further than Sheppey-Maidstone area. Several incidents including an attack on Dover and a second raid on Ramsgate were reported.

By night, London was under red warning from 1816 to 0820. Numerous raids were plotted between 1730 and 1945, activity then declined rapidly although attacks on a reduced scale continued. Incidents were widespread but very little material damage of importance is reported.

1730-2100: Twenty raids were plotted from France to London, a few of which continued into Suffolk and west towards Reading and Newbury. Twenty-four raids, mostly engaged in minelaying, were plotted from Holland of which a few flew to London and some to Sussex and Suffolk. In addition, 12 raids from Norway were active between Kinnaird's Head and Aberdeen, one was plotted to Birmingham and Coventry, and three were minelaying in the Humber.

2100-0100: Activity continued on a very small scale. Three raids were in the Birmingham area, two over Cornwall and the Bristol Channel. Nuisance raids were maintained over London and the Home Counties.

0100-0400: Attacks were concentrated in the South-East, 26 raiders being plotted. The majority did not reach London but covered most of Sussex, Farnborough, Redhill, Gatwick, Guildford and coastal areas with no apparent objective. One track was plotted to South Wales and one to the Birmingham district.

0400-0600: Raids to the South-East continued active but again many stayed in Sussex and near the coast. Several raids from Brittany crossed Cornwall and continued north. Activity was still in progress at the end of the period under review.

Approximate civilian casualties outside London by day were: 5 killed, 10 seriously injured and 132 slightly hurt. There were no daylight casualties in London. By night in London, 25 people were killed and 80 were injured. Elsewhere 38 people were killed, 18 were injured and 53 were slightly hurt. (Note that the casualties occurring after dark do not include several that are still missing or trapped under debris.) Four enemy aircraft were destroyed, 2 probably destroyed and 2 damaged.

The crash position was near the village, which lies on the edge of the flat lands of the Rother Levels.

Improved weather conditions prompted a number of fighter sweeps over south-east England and Dorset. The only loss not listed below was the Messerschmitt Bf 109 of Oblt. F. Jäger from 5/JG51. Five Bf 109s were damaged during operations and another destroyed in a crash near Boulogne.

1/JG26 Messerschmitt Bf 109E-4 (1374). Shot down by Flying Officer W. L. McKnight of No. 242 Squadron and Flying Officer L. A. Haines of No. 19 Squadron, 4.45 p.m. Crashed in garden of house at Albion Road, Birchington. Fw. E. Scheidt baled out and was taken prisoner. Aircraft White 12+ destroyed.

Aerial insulator and other small parts found in the garden of a newly constructed bungalow by John Ellis now in the Steve Vizard Collection.

9/JG26 Messerschmitt Bf 109E-1 (3259). Involved in a mid-air collision with Lt. H. Ebeling. Crashed at Wittersham Hall, Kent 11.30 a.m. Uffz. W. Braun baled out and was taken prisoner. Aircraft Yellow 11+I wrecked.

Few remaining fragments recovered by Steve Vizard and Andy Saunders.

9/JG26 Messerschmitt Bf 109E-4 (3740). Involved in a mid-air collision with Uffz. W. Braun. Crashed at Smittings, Wittersham, Kent 11.30 a.m. Lt. H. Ebeling (Staffelkapitän) baled out and was taken prisoner. Aircraft Yellow 3+I destroyed.

Representative pieces found in a garden by Steve Vizard and Andy Saunders included the clock bezel and a propeller blade. The rudder marked with Ebeling's victory tally of eighteen kills was donated to the Brenzett Aeronautical Museum.

4/JG51 Messerschmitt Bf 109E-1 (4826). Shot down by Pilot Officer A. C. Bartley DFC in a Spitfire of No. 92 Squadron. Crashed at Manor Road, Laindon 3.05 p.m. Oberfw. J. H. Illner baled out and was taken prisoner, injured. Aircraft White 6+ destroyed.

During the night of November 5-6 London and the Midlands were the targets for the Luftwaffe's attentions. Apart from the following aircraft, a Junkers Ju 88 of 7/KG77 also failed to return, its crew were posted missing. Three other bombers were damaged.

4/KG53 Heinkel He 111H-2 (3144). Crashed into the Humber Estuary off Grimsby. Exact cause unknown but believed to have been a victim of ground defences. Oblt. H. Bannert and Uffz. W. Göhring killed. Bodies of Gefr. G. Werder, Uffz. E. Zahn and Gefr. H. Schmitz all found along the coast near Grimsby. Aircraft A1+KM lost.

WEDNESDAY, NOVEMBER 6

The only large scale attacks by day were a fighter sweep in East Kent, which synchronised with an attack on the southern area (Southampton) by a small bomber force escorted by fighters, but mainly activity consisted of reconnaissance around the coast and occasionally inland.

Hostile night-time activity commenced early and was chiefly directed to the south-east of England and the London areas. Considerable numbers were engaged until 2300 after which activity declined.

1800-2100: During this period about 60 enemy aircraft entered the country. The greater number of them flew over Kent, Sussex and the London area. A few went to the Midlands and south-west England. Aberdeen and Glasgow also received brief visits. Minelaying was suspected in the Thames Estuary.

2100-0100: Approximately 70 aircraft were over the country during this period, the majority between 2100 and 2300. Attacks were concentrated on Kent, Sussex, Hertfordshire, Berkshire, Surrey and the London area. A few raids were plotted in South Wales and the Midlands. Three raiders visited North Wales and Anglesey district. Minelaying was suspected in the Estuary, off the Kent coast, also off Cornwall and Milford Haven.

0100-0400: This period was quiet but a

Since I last addressed the House on general topics about a month ago, the course of events at home has not been unexpected, nor on the whole unsatisfactory. Herr Hitler declared on September 4 that as we would not bend to his will he would wipe out our cities. I have no doubt that when he gave the order he sincerely believed that it was in his power to carry his will into effect. However, the cities of Britain are still standing, they are quite distinctive objects in the landscape, and our people are going about their tasks with the utmost activity. Fourteen thousand civilians have been killed and 20,000 seriously wounded, nearly four-fifths of them in London. That has been the loss of life and limb. As against this, scarcely 300 soldiers have been killed and 500 wounded. So much for the attack on military objectives.

A great deal of house property has been destroyed or damaged, but nothing that cannot be covered by our insurance scheme. Very little damage has been done to our munitions and aircraft production, though a certain amount of time has been lost through frequent air raid warnings. This lost time will have to be made up as we get settled down to the new conditions.

None of the services upon which the life of our great cities depends — water, fuel, electricity, gas, sewerage — not one has broken down. On the contrary, although there must inevitably be local shortages, all the authorities concerned with these vital functions of a modern community feel that they are on top of their job, and are feeling it increasingly as each week is passed.

Transport has been a greater difficulty, as may well be imagined, when we think of the vast numbers who go in and out of our great cities every day. However, we are getting a good grip of that, and I say with some confidence that by one method or another, and probably by many methods at the same time, the problems connected with transport will be solved in a manner tolerable to the great numbers of people who are affected.

Shelters are being multiplied and improved, and preparations on an extensive scale are in progress for mitigating the inevitable severities of the winter to those who are using the shelters.

In these vicissitudes the bearing of our people, not only in London, but in Birmingham, Liverpool, Manchester and other places, has gained the unstinted admiration of all classes throughout the British Empire, throughout the United States and, so far as they have been allowed to hear about it, among the peoples of the captive countries. As I was going home the other night I asked a group of steel-helmeted men who stood about the door what was going on, and a deep voice in the background said: "It's a grand life if we do not weaken." There is the British watchword for the winter of 1940. We will think of something else by the winter of 1941. . . .

WINSTON CHURCHILL, NOVEMBER 5, 1940

Churchill pictured by Cecil Beaton in the Cabinet Room on the morning of November 20. Harold Nicolson, Parliamentary Secretary at the Ministry of Information, was at 10 Downing Street that day: 'He seems better in health than he has ever seemed. That pale and globular look about his cheeks has gone. He is more solid about the face and thinner. But there is something odd about his eyes. The lids are not in the least weary, nor are there any pouches or black lines. But the eyes themselves are glaucous, vigilant, angry, combative, visionary and tragic. In a way they are the eyes of a man who is much preoccupied and is unable to rivet his attention on minor things.'

steady stream of raids was plotted over Cornwall and North Wales; four raids from the Thames Estuary went into Wiltshire and one or two from France to South London.

0400-0600: One raid was reported in the Leeds area which also flew over Sheffield and Leicester. Activity in Central London was resumed.

Approximate civilian casualties were: During daylight hours in London, 3 people injured. Elsewhere, 29 killed and 58 injured, 36 of these seriously. By night in London, there were 88 fatalities and 257 injuries. Elsewhere 18 people were killed, 23 were injured and 14 slightly hurt. Enemy aircraft destroyed: 4 certain, 2 probable and 3 damaged.

During the day, two Bf 109s of II/JG51 were slightly damaged and a Breguet in service with Seenotflug Kommando 1 was shot down in flames near Jersey. In night operations a Junkers Ju 88 of II/KG77 crashed on take-off near Reims and was destroyed. A Ju 88 of 8/KG51 was lost on a sortie to London and a Dornier 17 of KüFlGr606 failed to return from a mission to Liverpool. Three more bombers were slightly damaged.

May I call your attention to a difficulty with which I am faced in my daily duty of telling the Information the Home Security history of the previous 12 hours, by reason of the fact that reports sent in by London Region and relating to London are so selective as to become inadequate.

I recognize that adjectives such as 'slightly', 'seriously' and so on, must be relative terms and therefore necessarily inexact; but surely the damage which I saw myself this morning at the Ministry of Information could scarcely be described as 'slight'. I admit, however, that my main complaint is against such reference as — and I quote from this morning's summary — 'reports have been received from nearly 60 London Boroughs', whereas the report itself only refers to less than two dozen. This is no help to anyone who wishes to make an appreciation or to import, or even receive, information to be told that bombs have been reported from 37 Boroughs (see yesterday's Situation Report) or 60 London Boroughs as it was said this morning, unless at all events the nominal roll is given.

I have felt this difficulty for some time, but it has been pressed on my notice particularly since undertaking my new duties vis-à-vis the Ministry of Information.

R. H. PARKEY
INTELLIGENCE BRANCH, NOVEMBER 8, 1940

5/JG2 Messerschmitt Bf 109E-4 (2751). Shot down by Sergeant A. McDowall DFM of No. 602 Squadron. Crashed into the sea off Monk's Bay, Bonchurch, near Ventnor, Isle of Wight 3.20 p.m. Bembridge lifeboat dispatched but failed to locate pilot. Oberfw. H. Klopp missing. Aircraft Black 1+ lost.

1/KGr100 Heinkel He 111H-2 (6811). Ditched in the sea at West Bay, Bridport, Dorset 4.49 a.m. Fw. O. Paul killed. Fw. H. Lehmann, Oberfw. L. Meyerhofer and Fw. H. Bitter waded ashore and were taken prisoner. Aircraft 6N+BH wrecked.

2.

BY DAY continued.

Chester	1342 - 1402
Cardiff	1448 θ 1530
Newport	1453 - 1521
Portsmouth	1844 - 2306

BY NIGHT

Norwich	2102 - 2229
	2311 - 0014
	0119 - 0258
	0451 - 0524
Grimsby	2112 - 2140
	2211 - 2348
	0143 - 0249
Birmingham	2002 - 2159
	2310 - 2339
Wolverhampton	2002 - 2159
	2256 - 2332
Newcastle	2113 - 2155
Stoke on Trent	2104 - 2146
	2302 - 2327
Manchester	2025 - 2146
Ipswich	0013 - 0239
	0407 - 0705

BY NIGHT

Weymouth	1859 - 1955
Bristol	1910 - 2214
	2329 - 2345
Newport	1929 - 1942
	2017 - 2110
London South	1920 - 0056
London Croydn.	1920 - 0457
London Centrl.	1920 -0637
London West	1927 - 0030
	0103 - 0336
London East	1923 - 0637
Cardiff	1929 - 1942
	2018 - 2110
Swansea	1929 - 1942
Hull	2116 - 2146
	2212 - 2348
	0108 - 0249
Rugby	2017 - 2200
	2317 - 2342
	0442 - 0505
Chester	2022 - 2145
Brecon	2019 - 2110
Liverpool	2022 - 2146

PART III - SPECIAL DAMAGE REPORT.

LONDON.

By Day:

Railways.

S. R. Charing Cross Station hit and out of commission. Bricklayers' Arms Loading Shed hit by H.E.
L.P.T.B: Charing Cross Underground Station out of commission.
L.N.E.R: Bethnal Green - H.E. in Bishop's Gate Goods Yard.

Roads.

Tower Bridge damaged by H.E. and out of Action.

Telecommunications.

UXB. in grounds of Buckhurst Automatic Exchange.

Government Buildings.

The following were damaged:-
Ministry of Agriculture.
Great Scotland Yard.
Paymaster General's Office.
War Office.
Somerset House.
King's College.
Air Ministry, Kingsway.
Horseguards Parade.
Metropole Hotel.

General.

Bushey and Hampstead Food Office suffered damage from H.E. & I.Bs.

By Night.

Hospitals.

SHOREDITCH. St Mathew's Hospital hit by H.E. Four wards demolished. 9 killed, 23 seriously injured and 60 unaccounted for or trapped.

Factories.

SOUTHGATE (North Circular Road), 2015. Metal Box Factory - H.E. in grounds. Extensive damage to factory shelters. No casualties.
CHISWICK: 2040. Fire at L.E.P. Transport Ltd. Depository Wharf - barge on fire. Production for Air Ministry ceased on account of failure of electricity supply.

/PUBLIC UTILITIES.

3.

PUBLIC UTILITIES.

SOUTHWARK, 2020. Fire at City of London Electric Light Co. Generating Station.
NORTHERN OUTFALL WORKS. Slight damage to electric cables and ironwater station.
BATTERSEA, 2108 Gas Holder on fire at Gas Light & Coke Co.
BATTERSEA, 2300. Fire at Transformer House; no damage.
BANKSIDE GENERATING STATION. Roof badly damaged and also 66,000 volt Switchgear.

DOCKS.

LONDON DOCK, 2200. Fire at Skin and Hide Warehouse.
SURREY COMMERCIAL DOCK, 2135. Suspected UXB in water near Island Yd.
HAY'S WHARF CO. Fire.
SOUTH THAMES WHARF and Tea Warehouse damaged by fire.
COTTON WHARF, BERMONDSEY, 2107. Fire.
WILSON'S WHARF, slightly damaged by fire.
FENNINGS WHARF - extensive damage. Expected to salvage most of goods (food stuff).
CHAMBERLAIN WHARF - slight damage.

ROADS.

High Road KILBURN blocked by Crater Oxford Road and Kilburn Park Rd.
ISLINGTON - 2044. Seven Sisters Road blocked by crater and debris.
King Street HAMMERSMITH blocked by H.E. 2226, at Junction with Macbeth Street.

RAILWAYS.

L. M. S.
KILBURN - Up and down, slow and fast lines blocked.
G. W. R. -
Goods Yard, BATTERSEA PARK ROAD. I.B's.
L. N. E. R -
FINSBURY PARK STATION, 2035. Damage to Station buildings and passenger train. Three down lines out of five blocked, but service being maintained in both directions.
Wagon Road Tunnel on main line North of HADLEY WOOD STATION has fractured roof due to H.E. - 0210.
All termini normal except the following:-
Restricted: Broad Street, London Bridge
Suspended: Marylebone, Blackfriars, Charing Cross, Euston (Steam Services only).

L. P. T. B.
Northern: Restricted service North of Golders Green, otherwise normal.
Bakerloo: Suspended Willesden Green - Wembley Park; otherwise normal.
District: Suspended Putney Bridge, Wimbledon; otherwise normal.
Metropolitan: Farringdon and Moorgate closed. East London closed to passenger traffic. Willesden Green - Wembley Park closed.
There are 19 U.X.Bs still awaiting disposal on the railways.

FIRES.

The following fires have been reported in London Region:-

Conflagrations	1
Major	1
Serious	5
Medium	50
Small	320

The conflagration was at L.E.P.TRANSPORT LTD. Corney Road, Chiswick.
The major fire was at Hays Wharf, Tooley Street, S.E.1.
Serious fires were at HAMMERSMITH No. 6 Warehouse, London Docks, Skin Shed, London, Battersea and Shoreditch.
In the regions outside London fires were reported from Nos. 4, 6, 7, 10, and 12. All fires mentioned above are either extinguished or under control.

/ ELSEWHERE

Seeing that the matter of the Ministry of Home Security's reports was raised on November 8 by the official designated to write them up, this would appear to be as good a time as any to illustrate the depth to which the daily War Room Report was prepared. In our daily extracts we can only give Part I — the summary — and even then at times of great activity, these have had to be edited. Following the summary, Part II listed the precise times that each area was under warning and Part III any special damage to services, buildings, roads, railways, etc. These two representative pages, reproduced in facsimile, are part of the Appreciation for 0600 on October 8 to 0600 on October 9. Space precludes us including such detail for each day but readers interested in consulting the originals can do so at the Public Record Office at Kew (files HO 202/1-10).

In a sortie to attack Birmingham, the aircraft became lost and eventually force-landed on the Dorset foreshore, the crew believing that they had reached France. The Army waited for the tide to recede before attempting to recover the aircraft. However, a Navy Captain who outranked the Army Officer claimed it but whilst towing 'the wreck' to a ship the ropes broke and the aircraft sank. The Navy then abandoned the recovery but it was later salvaged by the Army and X-Gerät beam navigation equipment recovered.

THURSDAY, NOVEMBER 7

Enemy activity by day consisted of three raids, one in the Thames Estuary and two in the Portsmouth-Isle of Wight area, which were probably intended as attacks on shipping.

Attack in the Thames Estuary: About 50 enemy aircraft penetrated into the country and attacked shipping near the Isle of Sheppey. The extent of the damage — if any — is unknown.

Attacks on Portsmouth-Isle of Wight: the first attack was at 1345 and two raids of about 100 aircraft approached from Le Havre direction, but were broken up by our formations before reaching Portsmouth. The second attack was at 1628. About 50 enemy aircraft from the Cherbourg direction flew towards the Isle of Wight and attacked a convoy near Ventnor.

Other activity: Convoys off Worthing, Shoreham, Wells-next-the-Sea and off the Naze were attacked by a few aircraft and calls for help were answered by our squadrons. Bombs were dropped at Dover, Deal and Folkestone and there was some damage to house property, but casualties are very few.

Enemy activity by night: London was again the main objective and attacks on a small scale were made in the Midlands and at Penzance. Minelaying was reported from various parts of the coast.

1900-0100: A considerable number of bombs were dropped in London during this period, incidents being reported from many boroughs. The chief targets seem to have been railways. At St Pancras the platform and booking hall were badly damaged and there were a few fatal casualties. The L.M.S. was also affected at Kensal Green tunnel where the up and down main lines were blocked. Eight incidents on the Southern Railway are reported, the most important being at the Bricklayers Arms depot and on the main line near Vauxhall. Extensive damage to a G.E.C. factory at Erith is reported and there are several roads blocked including Millbank, Warwick Road, Earls Court, and High Road, Finchley. At Richmond 100 flats and 6 houses were damaged and some casualties are reported. Forty casualties are reported from Southwark where a block of flats was hit and there is slight damage to the Ministry of Information building at Malet Street.

The only casualty during the day was a minor injury outside London. During the night, 76 Londoners were killed and 316 were injured. Elsewhere, 4 people were killed and 23 were injured — 17 seriously. Enemy aircraft destroyed amounted to 7 certain, 5 probable and 2 damaged.

Coastal shipping was indeed the target for the daylight raiders. No bombers were lost but a Messerschmitt Bf 109 of 3/JG26 acting as escort was reported shot down over the Thames Estuary. A Junkers Ju 87 of I/StG3 was damaged by flak over the Thames Estuary and a Bf 109 of 7/JG2 crashed on take-off from Theville and was damaged. No aircraft were brought down in the United Kingdom but the following came down within sight of land:

3(F)/11 Messerschmitt Bf 110 (2229). Shot down into the sea off Margate 3.00 p.m. by four Spitfires of No. 603 Squadron. Oblt. H. Kopetsch and Lt. H. Veil missing. Aircraft M1+ZC lost.

Part 2 - Detailed Summary.
No.1. Region (Northern).

At 2140 an H.E. fell near the R.A.F. Experimental Station at CRESSWELL near NEWBIGGIN in NORTHUMBERLAND blocking a road and causing one slight military casualty.

No.3 Region (North Midland).

At 2040 one petrol I.B. and one H.E. were dropped at OWSTON near OAKHAM. At the same time two cyclists were machine gunned with tracer bullets but not hit. At 0115 the Station and road at HABROUGH near GRIMSBY were machine gunned by a low flying aircraft.

No.4 Region (Eastern).

ESSEX. L.N.E.R. wagons were derailed between BISHOPS STORTFORD and TAKELY Station and the up and down lines blocked.

Bombs were dropped at STANFORD LE HOPE (1945), ORSETT(1945 gas mains damaged), FRYERNING (2005), ROMFORD (1955), MUCKING (2015) SOUTH OCKENDON (2030) ROYDON (2005) and GRAYS HILL (2040).

HERTS. H.E. fell at SANDRIDGE near ST. ALBANS.

CAMBS. Bombs fell at SOHAM (2005), MILTON (2035), WEST WICKHAM (2200 setting straw stacks on fire) and WEST WICK.

SUFFOLK 2 H.E. fell at FRECKENHAM at 2137 and about 100 I.B. between LANGHAM and HUNSTON at 2200.

No.5 Region (London).

FACTORIES. H.E. fell in the grounds of the Metal Box Factory at SOUTHGATE at 2015. Shelters were damaged but no casualties caused. I.B. fell at S.Smith & Sons' CRICKLEWOOD Works at 2045. No further information is yet available.

L.N.E.R.RAILWAYS. At 2035 station buildings at FINSBURY PARK Station and a passenger train which was standing at the station were damaged by H.E. and 7 casualties caused of which 3 were fatal. Three down lines are blocked.

L.M.S. At 2035 an H.E. fell on a freight train at KILBURN blocking all lines.

S.R. MOTSPUR PARK Station was put out of action but the lines have been cleared.

L.P.T.B. Traffic has been stopped north of HENDON CENTRAL owing to I.B at the rear of Colindale Hospital.

DOCKS. Between 2005 and 2030 I.B's were dropped at the LONDON DOCK causing several fires which were all extinguished, at the WEST INDIA DOCK without casuing damage, and at the SURREY COMMERCIAL DOCK where a UXB is believed to have fallen in the direction of Islan Yard.

A fire was caused in the Skin Shed at the LONDON DOCKS, SHAD but this was under control at 2400.

PUBLIC UTILITIES. At 2108 a gas holder at the Gas Light & Coke Co., BATTERSEA PARK Road, was set on fire and some casualties caused.

At 2330 I.B. fell on the Transformer House at BATTERSEA Power Station but the firest were at once extinguished.

At 2220 3 H.E. fell on the City of LONDON Electric Light Company's Generating Station, Sumner Street, causing a fire and some casualties including a number trapped.

OTHER INCIDENTS.

BATTERSEA. A fire was caused at the BATTERSEA Bus Garage in Hester Road.

BARNET URBAN. 8 casualties were caused by H.E. at 2055.

BERMONDSEY. Serious fires were caused at Cotton Wharf and Hayes Wharf.

-3-

BRENTFORD. A serious fire was caused at the Lep Depository Wharf, CHISWICK, a barge alongside the wharf was also set on fire.

HAMMERSMITH. Kings Street was blocked by H.E. at 2225 and a serious fire was caused at GAYFORD Road but subsequently brought under control.

HAMPSTEAD. Several large water mains were damaged and A.R.P. shelters and basements flooded. Pumping arrangements are being made.

ISLINGTON. Seven Sisters Road was blocked near Hornsey Road by H.E. at 2044.

MERTON. 8 casualties and some damage were caused by H.E. at 2223.

SHOREDITCH. At 2123 H.E. fell on St. Matthews Hospital, Shepherd's Walk. 26 casualties were treated at mobile units and another 90 were trapped. The structure was reported to be in a dangerous condition and rescue work could not be completed until daylight.

Minor bombing during the early part of the night is reported from a large number of Boroughs.

No.6 Region (Southern).

HANTS. At 1850 one H.E. demolished the canteen of General Electric Cables Ltd., at EASTLEIGH causing a few casualties. Nine UXB were also dropped in the Market and High Street.

Houses at HIGHCLIFFE were machine gunned at 1847 and electric cables at HINTON ADMIRAL were cut by machine gun fire at 1900.

10 H.E. were dropped at BURTON at 1858 and one man was seriously injured.

At 1840 machine gunning caused one casualty at LYNDHURST and at 1843 one person was seriously wounded at TOTTON and slight damage done to property.

At 1850 6 H.E. and one UXB were dropped on the aerodrome at LEE ON SOLENT which was also machine gunned. Machine gunning also occurred at SOUTHAMPTON at 1900 and one H.E. was dropped on a balloon barrage post at the Airport where 5 casualties, including 2 fatal, were caused amongst R.A.F. personnel. UXB were dropped on the Airport

One casualty also occurred at COBDEN BRIDGE.

Bombs were also dropped at SEAFIELD PARK, near STUBBINGTON (1910), DENVILLES near HAVANT(1910 damaging gas and water mains and causing a number of casualties). HAMBLEDON (2100), DENMEAD, where one slight casualty was caused by machine gunning from a low flying aircraft and BLENDWORTH (2100).

BERKS. Considerable damage was done to WELLINGTON College by H.E. and I.B. at 2015. The Headmaster was killed.

Bombs were also dropped at OLD WINDSOR where damage was done to windows at Beaumont College.

SURREY. Bombs were dropped at REDHILL (2000, causing fires and damaging gas and water mains), ASH, WATCHETTS, LEATHERHEAD (213[illegible] GUILDFORD (2027) where the main railway line was blocked, OUTWOOD. (2122) where a bungalow was demolished and 4 serious casualties cau[illegible] EARLSWOOD (2105) causing slight damage to property and two minor casualties, EAST HORSLEY (0002) NEWHAM (0010) and SHURLOCK ROW.

BUCKS. 2 H.E. and one oil bomb fell at ELLESBOROUGH (2055) da[illegible] was done to telephone wires only.

OXON. At 2035 6 H.E. fell near BRIZNORTON Aerodrome and BLAC[illegible] BOURTON railway bridge.

No.7 Region (South Western).

SOMERSET. At about 1900 H.E. fell on the residential parts o[illegible] YEOVIL. Some casualties were caused including 5 dead, no damage was done to the aircraft factory but there are UXB in the vicinity.

DEVON. Bombs fell on the G.W.R. BARNSTAPLE line at HELLINGS Tunnel but no damage appears to have been caused.

We have also made use in our research of another set of Home Security files (HO 203/1-16) which are the Daily Intelligence reports prepared 12 hourly and in even more detail covering not only air raid damage but other information of importance to Civil Defence and the liaison officers of Government departments. These two pages cover from 1800 to 0600 on the night of October 8/9. A further set of reports were prepared by the Key Points Intelligence Directorate and can be found in HO 201/1-23. These Key Points bulletins cover details of air raids to factories, public utilities, service establishments and other locations, and buildings of national importance with assessments and reviews of the effects of the enemy attack on key points and of various defence measures. (The Air Ministry also produced its own daily report.)

At a more informal level, another chronicler of daily events was Ethel Gabain (Mrs John Copley) who was appointed by the Ministry of Information to produce historical war pictures.

FRIDAY, NOVEMBER 8

Enemy activity by day was almost entirely concentrated in the South-East and in the morning consisted of fighter sweeps which penetrated less than usual — only one small wave reaching Central London. In the afternoon there were several attacks on convoys in the Thames Estuary, at Dover and off Spurn Head. Reconnaissance flights took place in Cornwall, Bristol Channel, Milford Haven, Liverpool, Birmingham/Coventry area, East Scotland and East Anglia.

0950: Fifty aircraft came in at Dungeness at 25,000 feet, flew to Maidstone and Biggin Hill and then fanned out north-east as far as Dartford. Bombs were dropped in a few places in Kent including Plaxtol, where 10 houses were seriously damaged and 30 slightly.

1030: Two waves, totalling 24 aircraft, came in at Dungeness, but only penetrated a few miles. They were followed by a further wave of 50 aircraft, which again did not reach further than 10 miles inland between Dungeness and Dover. The only incident reported was the causing of two slight casualties at Nonington by aeroplane cannon shell.

1110-1125: Two aircraft at 22,000 feet came in at Dover, flew to Sheppey and west to the edge of the I.A.Z. and then out eastwards via the Estuary. They did not drop any bombs.

1320-1350: Thirty aircraft came in at Hastings and flew to Biggin Hill, where the raid split. A part reached Central London, where it turned back immediately, and all sections of the raid were homing shortly afterwards. Bombs were dropped at West Ham at 1413 and at Hailsham at 1420.

1605-1708: Eighty aircraft, also from Calais area, passed just east of North Foreland at 15,000 feet and then split as if to attack two convoys in the Estuary, but appeared to miss their objective and were successfully intercepted by three squadrons and returned to Calais. Fifteen Ju 87s and 1 Me 109 were destroyed, plus 6 Ju 87s probable and 2 Ju 87s damaged.

1630-1650: Twenty aircraft from Calais at 18,000 feet flew over a convoy off Dover, passed over East Kent, reaching a convoy off Herne Bay, and returned, possibly attacking the Dover convoy en route.

1734: A raid was plotted near a convoy off Spurn Head, which reported that it was being attacked.

1700: Nine aircraft came in at Hastings, flew as far as Maidstone and went out at Dungeness. Throughout the day attacks were made on shipping off the East and South-East coasts.

Night operations showed no departure from the tactics usually adopted, although the scale on which they were conducted was not heavy. In the course of an attack on Honington Aerodrome a Ju 88 was destroyed by machine gun fire at about 1830. Bombing over London, though not heavy, was widespread and affected 56 districts. There was extensive damage to property and gas, electricity and water mains, but none of military importance. Incidents reported from the rest of the country were widespread, but in few cases was much damage done and casualties on the whole were light.

1800-2100: Activity commenced with a moderately heavy influx towards the London area, while there were rather widespread but not intense raids in other parts of the country. Tracks were plotted to Liverpool, the Midlands and South Wales, and raiders appeared to deviate from their direct tracks when going to and from their objectives. For the first time for several days the enemy approached the western coast of Lancashire via Flamborough Head and then crossed northern England. The purpose of these raids was probably minelaying, a process which appears to have been carried out along the north-east coast as far as the Firth of Forth, off East Anglia and possibly in the Bristol Channel. By 2100 activity had, however, appreciably lessened.

2100-0100: Activity steadily declined, such tracks as were plotted outside the south-east area being mainly those of possible mine layers, or of raiders returning from the Lancashire coast and from the Midlands. Although the attack on London temporarily ceased about 2030 it was resumed by 'nuisance' aircraft shortly afterwards, and this prevailed throughout the remainder of the period. No incidents are reported over the country outside London after 2300.

0100-0600: Apart from single raids, mainly intermittent, towards the capital, there was no hostile activity over the country. No raids were reported overland after 0400 and the 'All Clear' was signalled at 0540. Only two incidents are reported from London after 0100, these being in Southwark and in Kensington at 0425.

Approximate civilian casualties outside London (there were none inside London) were 2 people injured and 14 slightly hurt. By night, 43 people in London were killed and 228 were injured. Elsewhere 9 people were killed and 39 injured, 24 of these seriously. The following additional casualties in London are now available for the night of 7th-8th November: 8 killed and 3 injured. Enemy aircraft destroyed: 19 certain, 7 probable and 9 damaged. Our own losses were 6 aircraft, of which 3 pilots are reported safe.

It would appear that the enemy, having tried out his dive-bombers against land targets with disastrous results to himself, had decided to employ similar tactics against

On November 7 — a day of relative peace in London — she was out sketching in Camden Town.

shipping. The result can hardly have proved reassuring.

Junkers Ju 87s made two large attacks with forty aircraft on shipping targets near the Thames Estuary. Three were lost, two of 3/StG3 and one of 12/LG1, their fates being uncertain although no less than 15 were claimed destroyed by pilots of No. 17 Squadron. The following German aircraft returned with varying degrees of damage or were damaged in accidents: Bf 109s of 6/JG26 and 2/JG77; a Ju 87 of I/StG3; a Do 17 of 4(F)/14; and Ju 88s of 2(F)/123 and 5(F)/122. During night operations, a Do 17 of III/KG76 crashed and was destroyed near Amiens and two other bombers were damaged. The only German aircraft to come down on land was the following:

7/KG1 Junkers Ju 88A-5 (2186). Aircraft, believed at the time to be a Blenheim, circled RAF Honington, West Suffolk 6.00 p.m. Returned at 6.18 p.m. and dropped four or five bombs near the airfield. Station Lewis guns opened fire at between 50 and 100 yards range and the aircraft crashed near 'D' hanger 6.20 p.m. Uffz. A. Hilderbrandt, Gefr. W. Wille and Lt. P. Ungerer killed. Fw. B. Lahme baled out but killed. Aircraft V4+GR destroyed.

Small parts on display at the Norfolk and Suffolk Aviation Museum.

SATURDAY, NOVEMBER 9

Enemy daylight activity was on a small scale throughout the day, being confined to inland, coastal and shipping reconnaissances, and there were several reports of machine-gunning at coastal and Midland towns.

0700-0930: Patrols penetrated inland over Yorkshire and the Thames Estuary, and a few bombs were dropped at Whitby, Pocklington and Basingstoke. Trawlers in Scarborough harbour were machine-gunned. R.A.F. stations at Waddington, Catfoss and Pocklington were machine-gunned; little damage is reported and there were no casualties.

0930-1330: Raids by single aircraft were reported in South Wales, the Midlands and Hertfordshire. At Whitchurch (Salop) a petrol depot and observer post were machine-gunned, but there were no casualties. Bombs were dropped at St Albans which demolished two houses and damaged 70. Estimated casualties amounted to 4 killed, 3 seriously injured and 16 slightly injured.

In London at 1040 bombs were dropped at King's Cross Low Level and some damage to offices and a repair shop resulted. Casualties: 14 killed and 28 seriously injured.

Bombs were dropped at Elmdon R.A.F. Station at 1258 and 5 aircraft were damaged, of which 4 will be serviceable within 48 hours. There were no casualties.

1330-1800: During the afternoon incidents in London were reported at Hendon, Chelsea, Beckenham and Croydon. A bomb dropped at Golders Green Station caused suspension of services. There was much damage to windows from blast at Beckenham Hospital. There were few casualties.

Night operations commenced earlier than usual and were on a light scale. Incidents in London are reported from 12 boroughs but there is no major damage and casualties are few. At Bromley an enemy plane demolished 2 houses, where 2 people were trapped, and there were several casualties at Staines and Leyton, where a garage, stores and medical hutments were damaged. There were also a few incidents at Queens Club R.A.F. Depot, Fulham. All these incidents occurred before 2200. No activity is reported thereafter until 0345, when a few bombs were dropped at Harrow, Chislehurst and Warlingham, causing damage to house property. Thirteen people were reported trapped in Harrow.

In the provinces, there was no military damage, but there was slight damage to house property at Thame, Hanslope (Bucks.), Bournemouth and South Ascot. Several fires are reported at Bournemouth and a few roads are blocked. The approximate casualties amount to 2 killed and 4 seriously injured.

Approximate civilian casualties by day. In London: 16 killed and 26 injured. Elsewhere: 9 killed, 11 seriously injured and 24 slightly hurt. By night in London: 12 killed and 73 injured. Elsewhere there were 3 deaths and 17 injuries — 6 serious. Enemy aircraft destroyed amounted to 4 certain and 3 damaged.

The aircraft lost during daylight hours over the UK, and listed below, were the two Junkers Ju 88s of KG/77 which were engaged in what was described as a nuisance raid. A Bf 109 of III/JG2 was destroyed in an RAF bombing attack on Octeville.

1/KG77 Junkers Ju 88A-5 (2191). Shot down by Sergeant R. H. Fokes and Adjutant X. De Montbron in Spitfires of No. 92 Squadron during a raid on London. Crashed into the sea off Galloways Gap, Dungeness 10.55 a.m. Hastings and Dungeness lifeboats dispatched but could find no trace of the crew. Lt. K. Vaupel washed up at Dungeness. Obergefr. E. Schidlhauer, Uffz. H. Bergsch and Obergefr. H. Bartling missing. Aircraft 3Z+CH lost.

During the day she met Mrs Ada Merritt whose son Albert — a sergeant pilot in the RAF — was missing presumed killed following an operation in June. By the time this picture was taken, the Germans had already found his body washed up on the shore of Borkum, one of the East Frisian Islands off the northern shores of Germany in the North Sea on August 2 and buried it in Oldenburg Cemetery. Subsequently the Air Ministry presumed his date of death to be that of his last operation with a Blenheim — P8829 — of No. 82 Squadron on June 13.

Another kill for the good old ack-ack! Leutnant Max Probst, who claimed later that he had such a poor opinion of British anti-aircraft fire that he usually flew straight through it, had a rude awakening on the evening of November 9 when a shell completely blew off one of his wings. As a result his Heinkel flipped over on its back and Probst lost all control. Opening his roof hatch, he dropped out and pulled his ripcord. On landing he was quickly arrested and taken to Bromley Police Station but the rest of the crew were not so fortunate; one being trapped in the plane as it fell, the other two only getting clear when it was too late for their parachutes to fully deploy. All three were buried in St Luke's Churchyard, Southborough. The aircraft crashed onto No. 26 Johnson Road, Bromley, with its bombs still aboard, while the shot off wing fluttered down three miles away to land in the back garden of No. 45 Cranmore Road, West Chislehurst.

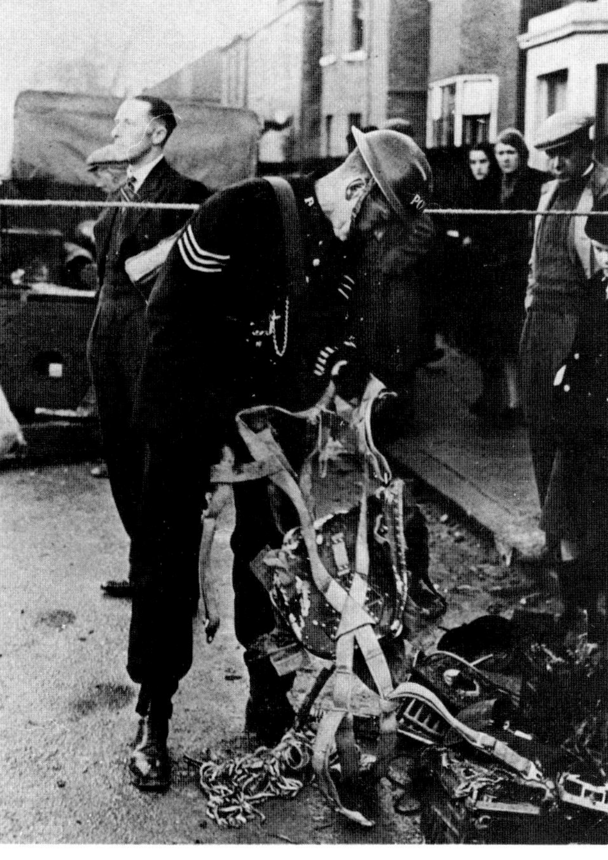

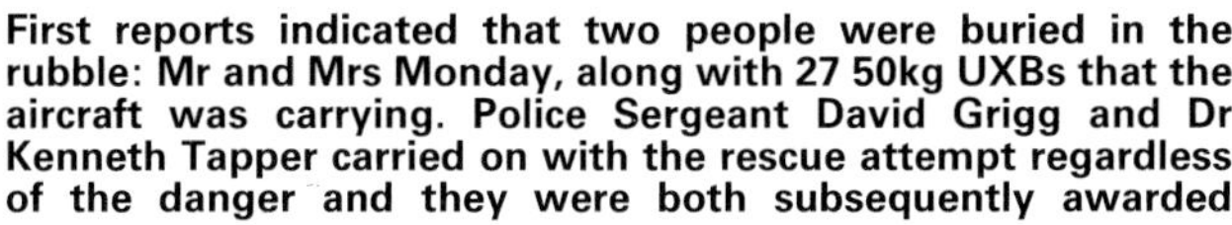

First reports indicated that two people were buried in the rubble: Mr and Mrs Monday, along with 27 50kg UXBs that the aircraft was carrying. Police Sergeant David Grigg and Dr Kenneth Tapper carried on with the rescue attempt regardless of the danger and they were both subsequently awarded George Medals. However, in spite of their gallant efforts, they were unable to save Mr Monday's wife Alice. ***Left:*** **After the bombs had been defuzed they were loaded aboard RAF transport.** ***Right:*** **Could this unidentified police sergeant examining one of the parachutes be David Grigg, we wonder?**

2/KG77 Junkers Ju 88A-5 (4184). Shot down by Flight Lieutenant R. M. B. D. Duke-Woolley and Pilot Officer G. Marsland of No. 253 Squadron 10.15 a.m. Force-landed at Elphick's Farm, Horsmonden, Kent. Lt. H. Wältermann, Uffz. H. Klaus, Gefr. W. Woito and Gefr. E. Leichsenring taken prisoner. Aircraft 3Z+BK destroyed.

Parts of the aircraft donated by a local resident in the Steve Vizard Collection.

During the night of the 9th-10th, widespread and scattered attacks led to the loss of three aircraft in or near Britain. A Ju 88 of 8/KG1 failed to return. Yet more machines were destroyed in Europe. An He 111 of 1/KGr126 crashed into the sea off German-occupied Europe; a Ju 88 of III/KG1 crashed near Ghent; a Do 17 of 5/KG3 crashed near Antwerp; two Ju 88s of II/KG51 collided on the ground at Orly. A Ju 88 of I/KG51 made a forced landing at Villaroche after engine failure.

2/KG1 Heinkel He 111H (3335). Hit by AA fire during a raid on London. Broke up in the air and fell on No. 26 Johnson Road, Bromley 7.28 p.m. killing Mrs Alice Monday and trapping six others. Lt. M. Probst baled out; taken prisoner after landing safely in the grounds of the Sundridge Park Hotel, Bromley. Gefr. R. Giesinger, Uffz. A. Krüger and Fw. R. Gey killed. Aircraft V4+JK destroyed.

Police Sergeant David Grigg and Dr. Kenneth Tapper received the George Medal for their rescue work among unexploded bombs from the aircraft.

4/KG2 Dornier Do 17Z (3495). Crashed into the sea off Kingsdown, near Deal 8.40 p.m. due to unknown causes. Lt. G. Mollenhauer, Oberfw. H. Fischer, Uffz. H. Reinsch and Uffz. L. Kaluza killed. Only 3 bodies subsequently washed up along the coast near Walmer. Aircraft U5+BM lost.

1/606 Dornier Do 17Z-3 (2683). Crashed at Boconnoc Woods, Liskeard, Cornwall due to unknown causes during a raid on Liverpool 8.15 p.m. Lt. zur See G. Seelhorst, Uffz. H. Winkler, Oberfw. W. Siefert and Obergefr. H. Haseloff killed. Aircraft 7T+KH wrecked.

Site investigated by noted aviation historian Alan Brown and later excavated by the Devon Aircraft Research and Recovery Team who unearthed three unexploded 50kg bombs which were exploded by an Army bomb disposal unit, February 1980.

The other bomber which came down on Saturday evening was heard circling the Bodmin area of Cornwall which it was crossing to reach Liverpool before it exploded on impact, scattering wreckage and the crew over woodland on the Boconnoc House estate. From the force of the explosion it was assumed the whole bomb load had exploded but in 1980 aircraft enthusiasts uncovered three UXBs which were detonated by the Royal Engineers. 'This caused a little excitement', recalls Mr B. H. Tweedale, the Estate Manager, 'but subsequently the crater has been levelled.'

SUNDAY, NOVEMBER 10

Sunday evening and nothing more pleasant than a friendly darts match at the local — in this case the Star in Church Road, Swanscombe (between Dartford and Gravesend) in Kent. With the pub packed and the competition in full swing, shortly after eight o'clock a chance bomb scored a direct hit, completely demolishing the building. From the initial report of 17 killed, the death toll slowly rose to 27 — Swanscombe's worst bombing incident.

The only enemy daylight activity on a large scale was an operation by 40 aircraft in the Poole area. Bombs are reported to have been dropped at Lulworth, but there was no damage. During the morning single aircraft were operating off the West, South-West and South-East Coasts, but very few penetrated inland. Bombs were dropped at Hastings on three occasions and also at Bexhill and Eastbourne. Damage was confined to house property and main services, but casualties were few.

Between 1300 and 1700 there were a few reconnaissance flights by single aircraft and bombs were dropped at Ramsgate, Great Yarmouth and Stowmarket, causing damage to house property. The L.N.E.R. line between Ipswich and Norwich was blocked, and there were no fatal casualties. Five aircraft are also believed to have laid mines in the outer Thames Estuary and off Harwich. London had a clear day.

Night operations assumed the normal characteristics, but were on a moderate scale. Aircraft are reported to have crossed the coast in formations of 3+, later splitting into single units.

London, 1800-2100: Activity was most intense during this period and bombs were dropped in many London boroughs. Factories were damaged in Brentford and Southgate and a 50 per cent loss of production is reported by the Metal Box Co. Ltd, owing to the failure of the gas supply. The Southern Railway track was blocked at Sutton, Beddington, Epsom and Penge and the L.P.T.B. at Bow Station received serious damage. Several road blocks are reported including Fulham Road, Cornwall Road (Lambeth), Tottenham Court Road and Vauxhall Bridge Road. Evalina Hospital, Southwark, was damaged, casualties being 1 missing and 10 injured.

2100-0100: At Fulham a UXB is reported on the premises of Rover Co. Ltd, and on the Southern Railway causing suspension between Waterloo and Clapham Junction. Railways were blocked between Clapham Junction and Wandsworth Common and damage was done to a bridge at Tulse Hill and to the Great Eastern Buildings near Bethnal Green. At Fulham there was a fire at the Central Electricity sub-station caused by an I.B. and at Acton a 36-inch gas main was broken by H.E. At Poplar a bomb fell on a stretcher party depot causing the following casualties: 1 killed, 14 seriously injured.

0100-0600: Activity was on a small scale and of the few incidents reported the most serious was a fire at Hackney on the premises of Horne Bros. factory. Provinces: A few aircraft are reported to have penetrated to the Birmingham Region, but apart from some damage to houses at West Bromwich there were no other incidents. At 1925, 8 H.E. were dropped on Portsmouth, causing damage to dwelling houses and to the railway track between Fratton and Green Lane. Casualties: 3 killed, 24 seriously injured, 15 slightly injured.

Between 2000 and 2030, bombs were dropped at Swanscombe and Stone (Kent) where a public house shelter and several houses were badly damaged. Casualties: 17 killed, 23 seriously injured, several trapped.

At 2055, bombs were dropped at Bournemouth causing some fires, but there was little damage and no casualties.

Daylight civilian casualties (approx.) in London amounted to 7 injured. Elsewhere 1 person was killed and 11 injured, 2 of them seriously. By night in London there were over 100 fatalities and between 200 and 300 injuries. Elsewhere 33 people died and 71 were injured, 59 seriously. Enemy aircraft destroyed: nil; damaged 1.

Although no aircraft fell near the British mainland, the following casualties were sustained by the Luftwaffe. Bf 109s of III/JG2 and 5/JG53 were damaged. Five bombers were destroyed: a Ju 88 of III/KG51 at Bapaume; an He 111 of II/KG53 at St Nikolaus; a Ju 88 of I/KG54 on the Fains/Mercy road; a Ju 88 of II/KG54 at St André. Finally, another Ju 88 of II/KG54 failed to return from its sortie to London.

MONDAY, NOVEMBER 11

After its début on October 29, on Armistice Day the Italian Air Force made its heaviest attack yet when around 50 machines from the 85th, 95th and 243rd Squadrons sallied forth to attack a merchant convoy off the East Coast. For the Regia Aeronautica the operation turned out to be a bloody defeat; to the men of No. 257 Squadron of the Royal Air Force it was a grand 'turkey shoot'.

Enemy daylight activity consisted of fighter sweeps in Kent towards London and attacks on convoys, one of which was carried out by Italian bombers and fighters. Strong enemy patrols were observed outside the Estuary, and in the Straits and there were isolated reconnaissances inland.

Between 0600 and 0800 single aircraft dropped bombs in several locations in No. 2 Region without causing damage or casualties and also at Maidstone, where damage was done to private property, to machinery in a stone quarry, and a water main.

0910-0950: Two raids totalling 60 aircraft crossed the coast in the Dungeness area and flew to Kenley and Biggin Hill, where they turned back, except for 4 aircraft which were tracked to the London area. At 0923 a second sweep of 20 aircraft came in at Hastings and flew to the same area. About 6 aircraft penetrated to London. During this raid bombs were dropped at Beckenham, Camberwell and New Romney. No damage and only a few slight casualties were reported.

1030-1105: About 50 aircraft entered via Dungeness and flew to Biggin Hill and South-East London, where they split, part returning by the Estuary and part over Maidstone. A few minor incidents were reported from No. 12 Region.

1140-1240: First attack on shipping. Two raids, totalling 100+, flew in from Gris Nez across the North Foreland to the Estuary, being plotted over the convoy area from 1215-1225. Three of our squadrons were waiting for them and a further 3½ squadrons went to assist. Nine German aircraft were certainly destroyed and 7 probably. In addition 5 were damaged.

1330: Second attack on shipping. After a raid of 18+ at 17,000 feet, which may have been a diversion, had penetrated a short distance inland from Dungeness, 2 raids from the Belgian coast approached convoys off Harwich. The raids apparently consisted of a formation of Italian bombers at 12,000 feet escorted by about 40 Fiat CR 42 fighters. The raid was intercepted by three squadrons which destroyed 8 bombers and 5 fighters, plus 1 bomber and 5 fighters damaged.

There were in addition numerous raids by single aircraft over shipping, chiefly in the Thames Estuary. Two raids attacked shipping off Southwold and Aberdeen at dusk.

Isolated raids proceeded to Bedford, Huntingdon, Leighton Buzzard, Gloucester and the Firth of Forth, and there were several to the southern outskirts of London. At 1620 one aircraft circled around from the north-west and dropped bombs in Westminster, causing one serious fire and several casualties. Rescue work is still in progress.

In the early part of the night an attempt was made to maintain activity at its usual intensity, but in less than three hours the effort had been abandoned, and all enemy aircraft had left the country.

1800-2100: The tracks of the first raiders reached the outskirts of London shortly before 1800, the great majority approaching from Holland up the Estuary. Twenty tracks were plotted in this area. Isolated aircraft also visited the Guildford and Tunbridge Wells areas, and others came inland at Southwold. The number of tracks gradually diminished until by 2100 the country was entirely clear of enemy aircraft.

Approximate civilian casualties in London by day amounted to 18 killed and 50 injured. Elsewhere 3 people died, 14 were seriously injured, 31 being slightly hurt. In addition, probably a further 8 to 10 killed, still trapped in London. By night, 3 people were killed in London and 11 injured. Elsewhere, 7 people

Their wizard CO was not flying that day otherwise no doubt Squadron Leader Tuck, right, would have added greatly to the score. (His personal Hurricane, with its Swastika score card under the cockpit, can be seen behind the pilots.)

The Romans return to Suffolk some fifteen centuries after they left. This is the Fiat BR 20 bomber which crashed in Tangham Forest. Note the national insignia crests have been cut from the fins — triumphantly displayed below by one of the pilots of 257 Squadron, appropriately decked out with an Italian 'elmetto' and bottle of Chianti.

were killed and several injured. The following casualties in London are additional to those previously reported for the period ended 0600 on November 11th: 5 killed, 4 injured.

Enemy aircraft destroyed were: German: certain 12, probable 9, damaged 5. Italian: certain 13, probable 1, damaged 6. Our losses amounted to 2 aircraft and their pilots.

It was on this day that the Corpo Aereo Italiano made a major appearance near Britain in force when an estimated 50 aircraft made to attack a convoy off Lowestoft. A total of three Fiat CR 42s and three Fiat BR 20s were lost and a further ten aircraft were found to be damaged on their return. The Luftwaffe in their attacks lost a Junkers Ju 88 from 8/LG1, five Messerschmitt Bf 109s, three from JG51 and two from JG53, along with two Junkers Ju 87s from 9/StG1. A Heinkel He 59 of Seenotflugkdo.3 and a Focke-Wulf FW 58 from StabIII/JG51 were lost on air-sea rescue sorties. In addition to these losses, the following were damaged: Bf 109s of 6/JG3 and 5/JG53; a Ju 88 of KGr806 which landed near Brest after sustaining combat damage. An He 115 from 2/Küstenfliegergruppe 506 was destroyed in a crash landing at Zwischenhahn. The night operations resulted in a Do 17 of 4/KG3 being abandoned when fuel ran out near Nijmegen. Two other bombers were damaged. Those down on or within sight of land were as follows:

1/JG51 Messerschmitt Bf 109E-1 (5635). Shot down over the Thames Estuary. Oblt. G. Claus (Staffelkapitän) taken prisoner. Aircraft lost.

9/JG53 Messerschmitt Bf 109E-8 (4888). Shot down by Flight Lieutenant A. Ingle in a Hurricane of No. 605 Squadron and crashed at Blackwall Bridge, Peasmarsh, East Sussex 9.30 a.m. Oblt. J. Volk baled out and taken prisoner. Aircraft Yellow 12+ destroyed.

First recovery by Ashford and Tenterden Recovery Group. Site later excavated by Andy Saunders when part of the engine and complete propeller hub were found.

Christopher Elliott, whose early post-war investigations of crashed aircraft sites have already been mentioned, visited Bromeswell in June 1953. There he found a clearing still covered with fallen trees sliced down when the Fiat crashed.

First of the CR 42 fighters to fall on land was 95-13 which ended up up-ended on the beach at Orfordness. Today you can see the very same aircraft on display in the Battle of Britain Museum at Hendon.

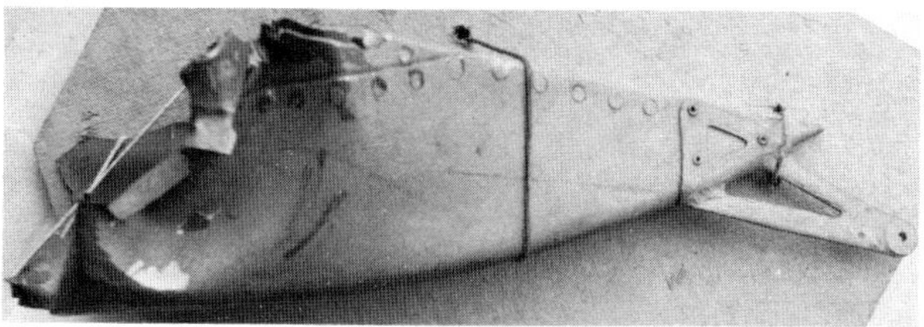

One other genuine relic we have traced as being from the Italian Armistice Day raid is this piece of BR 20 wing or tail, painted dark olive green, which was given to Chris Elliott by the local forester.

95 Squadriglia, 18 Gruppo, 56 Stormo Fiat CR 42 (MM5701). Damaged by Hurricanes of Nos. 46 and 257 Squadrons during a fighter escort sortie to Harwich and made a forced landing on the beach at Orfordness, Suffolk, 1.45 p.m. Sergente P. Salvadori captured. Aircraft 95–13 dispatched to Farnborough for evaluation.

Aircraft now preserved in the Battle of Britain Museum, Hendon.

85 Squadriglia, 18 Gruppo, 56 Stormo Fiat CR 42 (MM6976). Damaged by Hurricanes of Nos. 46 and 257 Squadrons during a fighter escort sortie to Harwich and made a forced landing near Corton Railway Station, Lowestoft, 2.30 p.m. Sergente A. Lazzari captured. Aircraft 85–16 dispatched to Farnborough for evaluation.

243 Squadriglia, 99 Gruppo, 43 Stormo Fiat BR 20 M (22621). Shot down by Hurricanes of Nos. 46 and 257 squadrons and crashed in Tangham Forest, Bromeswell, Suffolk, 2.00 p.m. Tenente P. Affriani, 1. Aviere Arm. E. Cerrosi, 1. Aviere E. de Gaspari and Aviere Scelto M. D. Pensa (Squadriglia photographer) taken prisoner. 1. Aviere A. Paolini and Sergente G. Ripolini killed. Aircraft 243-2 dispatched to Farnborough for evaluation.

Centre and left: **Forty-five minutes later a second CR 42 plopped down in the mire near Corton, in a field near the railway station.**

Right: **The same pasture abundant with crops when we visited the spot in the summer of 1986.**

TUESDAY, NOVEMBER 12

Hostile activity by day was on a very small scale and was confined to a few reconnaissances inland and round the coast. Minor bombing took place in Essex, Bucks, and South Coast towns.

By night, London was the main objective, with minor activity in the Liverpool area. After 2300 activity eased off and incoming raids concentrated on London and its suburbs.

1800-2100: The first raids approached the South Coast at 1820 and followed the usual routes to London. Six raids crossed the coast at Portland and were tracked to the Liverpool area. Bombs were dropped at Liverpool, Wallasey and Birkenhead.

2100-0100: Raids continued from France to London and the Home Counties. A few crossed in the Swanage area and penetrated to Wolverhampton, Birmingham, Stoke and Coventry. Bombs were dropped at Coventry and Cubbington. Towards the end of this period activity was considerably reduced and confined to the South-East. Minor bombing took place in No. 6 Region.

0100-0600: Isolated raids continued to approach the London area. Minor bombing took place in Nos. 4 and 12 Regions.

Sloane Square, booking office of Underground station demolished, two gas mains were set on fire. Train hit and buried under debris. Casualties 21 dead, 40 injured.

Approximate daylight civilian casualties were as follows: In London, 3 killed and 2 injured. Elsewhere, 1 killed and 3 slightly hurt. By night in London 108 people were killed and 242 were injured. Elsewhere 12 people were killed and 44 injured, 22 of them seriously. Enemy aircraft casualties were 1 certain and 1 damaged.

Although no aircraft were brought down, three bombers were written off after crashing in France: a Ju 88 of I/LG1 at Fécamp; an He 111 of III/KG26; a Ju 88 of II/KG76 at Sedan — two other bombers were seriously damaged.

The old District Line underground station of Sloane Square — complete with gas lamps, Victorian appointments and antique platform buffet — transformed in March 1940 when escalators were installed to replace the notorious 51 stairs which had been the cause of much grumbling from passengers for the past 70 years.

WEDNESDAY, NOVEMBER 13

During the day, there was one main attack over Kent and several raids by 1 to 3 aircraft in the South-East and in the vicinity of Birmingham and Gloucester. Our fighters were again successful in destroying and damaging a number of aircraft without sustaining losses to themselves.

Main attack over Kent: At 1118 formations of about 90 aircraft crossed the coast at Folkestone and split up over mid-Kent proceeding towards the Estuary. At Canterbury bombs were dropped and some damage to houses and the services is reported. There were no casualties.

Between 0600-0700 a number of I.B.s were dropped in the Heston-Isleworth districts causing several fires, including one serious one at Woolworths Limited, High Street, Hounslow.

H.E.s were dropped at Hunnington

On the evening of November 12 a direct hit caused massive damage, hurling a huge lump of concrete through a train which was just pulling away. Passengers standing on the platforms were cut down and many were trapped. Emergency repair gangs rushed to the scene, the flickering light of the acetylene cutters accentuating the scene of horror. Providentially the bomb missed the huge culvert, 15 feet above the platforms, which carries the piped River Westbourne from the Serpentine lake in Hyde Park to the Thames near Chelsea bridge.

Had the culvert been breached there would almost certainly been a disaster on the scale of Balham. As it was, casualties totalled 79 with three people being unaccounted for. The new escalators had been wrecked and ladders had to be used to get down to the track. Inner Circle trains were interrupted for a fortnight while repair work took place, the temporary wartime hoarding of corrugated iron remaining until the station was rebuilt in 1951.

Aerodrome, and at Kirton-in-Lindsey a Dornier dropped I.B.s from 100 feet. At both of these aerodromes there was no damage or casualties.

Between 1300 and 1700 miscellaneous raids penetrated to North-East London, Gloucester and Birmingham. Sixteen H.E.s were dropped at Upton St Leonards (Gloucester). There was no damage and no casualties.

In the Birmingham district some damage was caused to the Austin Motor Works at Longbridge. There is little interference with production. Casualties: 3 killed.

At Cofton Hacket the Austin Aero works was also bombed. The only damage sustained was to the water main. There were no fatal casualties.

During the early afternoon bombs on Dover damaged 80 shops, 100 houses, and the Salvation Army Citadel. Casualties: 5 killed, 2 seriously wounded, 11 slightly wounded.

At Heyford Aerodrome two machines were slightly damaged.

Enemy activity by night was on an extremely small scale and few incidents were reported. London was under red warning for only 3½ hours. Bombs were dropped on the Royal Small Arms Factory, Enfield, but caused no material damage, and there was slight damage to house property.

Elsewhere, at Romford an 18-inch gas main was set on fire.

In Scotland two enemy aircraft were destroyed at 2210 and an attack on Mephil docks (Fife) was made.

Parachute mines were dropped over Tynemouth but fell into the sea.

Over the rest of the country there were only 46 minor incidents involving little damage and very few casualties.

Approximate civilian casualties in London by day amounted to 1 person killed and 7 injured. Elsewhere 9 were killed and 27 injured, 13 of these seriously. At night 1 person in London died and 5 were injured. Elsewhere 7 people were slightly injured. Three enemy aircraft were destroyed and 8 were damaged.

Although only one aircraft fell in Great Britain, two Junkers Ju 88s of 2/KG30 and Stab II/KG76, and two Heinkel He 111s of 5/KG26 and 2(F)/22 were lost on various operations. Additionally, an He 111 of 1(F)/120 crashed in the sea and nine bombers were damaged to varying degrees either as a result of technical failure or combat damage.

8/LG1 Junkers Ju 88A-1 (6157). Engaged by Flight Lieutenant W. J. Leather and Pilot Officer Johnson in Spitfires of No. 611 Squadron during a reconnaissance of the Midlands. Aircraft made a good forced landing at Woodway Farm, Blewbury, Berkshire 2.45 p.m. Fw. W. Erwin, Uffz. H. Wermuth and Fw. E. Zins taken prisoner. Gefr. H. Bossdorf killed. Aircraft L1+LS captured damaged.

Aircraft was subsequently displayed in St Giles Street, Oxford for two weeks. A round of ammunition taken as a souvenir by a local resident now owned by Nigel Parker.

Springtime in Sloane Square, March 1986. Now one of the fashionable open spaces of the West End; the First World War memorial now having even more significance with the addition of those local people who died in the Second.

ON A MORTUARY VAN IN THE LONDON BLITZ

I have had some varied experiences since I ceased to paint landscapes at the beginning of the war and joined the No. 1 Ambulance Depot, at Wood Green, North London.

Of the months of training, and of the time when we had to act as combined policemen and nurse-maids to thousands of foreign refugees at the Alexandra Palace, after the collapse of France; and then as an attendant on the Hospital Mobile Unit, I could write a lot.

But the real horror of the war was not brought home to me until I finally became an attendant on the mortuary van.

There were three of us on this job, a driver, and two attendants. Davey, the other attendant, was a typical Cockney. Small and perky, like a London sparrow, his sharp curved nose and prim lips seemed to heighten the resemblance. He evidently thought our ARP overalls lacked the decorum necessary for his job, consequently he always wore a stiff white collar, black coat, and pin-striped trousers; this being the outfit he had worn at his wedding a few months previously. The only thing that spoilt the get-up was the steel helmet, perched precariously on his semi-bald head, its brim always seeming to endanger the pince-nez glasses he wore. It was he who provided the bit of black alpaca with which we curtained the small windows at the back of the van. Ironically, the mortuary van was a converted butcher's van, with the butcher's name still faintly discernible; so Davey and I set to work and painted it battleship grey lined out with black, thus making it more suitable for its melancholy function.

It was on October 2 that we had our first call. At about nine-thirty that night, I was in the big gymnasium attached to Bounds Green School which served as our living quarters, endeavouring to read, but finding it difficult, because some of our fellows were singing round the piano, trying to compete with the terrific barrage outside. After two months of the Blitz, I was getting quite used to it, but the present combination was too much for my powers of concentration.

The general din was punctuated at intervals by the dull explosions of bombs, and subconsciously I had been listening to them getting nearer, and to the sound of German planes, which formed a persistent throbbing background to the cacophony. Then, abruptly the singing stopped, and everyone listened. There was a roaring, vibrating sound against the background of gun-fire, as if an express train was descending on us from the skies.

Look out, it's ours!' someone shouted.

While some of us dived for shelter as might be afforded by billiard tables, etc., others stopped still, flung themselves flat or made for the door. It seemed an eternity before the bomb landed, and then, for a moment or so, the door swung wide open, and the windows cracked.

Then came the debris. As from the sack of some Olympian coal-heaver, it thundered, and crashed down on the flat roof above us; and isolated pieces continued to fall for several seconds after the avalanche had ceased. The big hall had become dim with the fine dust that hung about like a fog, and through it, we looked expressively at each other, and breathed again.

Most of the chaps rushed to get their kit; blankets, water bottles, first aid satchels, splints, etc., ready for the call they knew would come later, so I went out into the yard to see what had happened.

The yard was covered with debris, but otherwise I could see nothing wrong. So I went round the building into the playing fields belonging to the school adjoining our post, and was appalled at the scene I saw in the light of the gun-flashes which flickered like summer lightning over the sky.

On the field was an indescribable mess of debris, much of which seemed to be paper; every square inch of the big field appeared to be covered with leaves from books, photographs, etc. This incident was unique in that respect, I have never seen anything else quite like that.

Skirting the field on the far side, there stood a row of houses, and as these were silhouetted in the gun-flashes, I saw a huge gap had been made in them; about twenty-five yards from our depot were three houses, badly

In 1982 we first made contact with Alan Seymour as we had been told that he still had an unpublished manuscript which he had prepared on the Blitz while the war was still on. Descriptions written long after the event, perhaps many years later, are naturally coloured by the writer's subsequent experiences, so contemporary material is very valuable to give an insight as to how people felt at the time. After we agreed to include an extract, it had been our intention to take Alan back to the scenes he described, but alas he died in March 1985 before our photographic trip could take place. Our journey would have started here: the gymnasium attached to Bounds Green School which was his depot.

When we came to research the first incident described by Alan we hit a problem as there are no casualties listed in Durnsford Road — the road 'skirting the field on the far side' — on October 2. Edith Abbott, 18 years old, killed at No. 11 would appear to fit his description of the 'beautiful young girl about seventeen' but she was killed on September 26 so it would appear that Alan incorrectly recorded the date. This is the interior of the gym, which 'became dim with fine dust' when the bomb fell. Now it's a shrine to the prowess of athlete Daley Thompson.

When we asked Alan if he had any photographs of himself taken at the time he said he had none 'in the boiler suit and tin hat which passed for a uniform, nor do I seek any publicity of that nature. If there had been a group photo I would have been proud to agree, but a solo picture I feel would be presumptuous. I was only one of many thousands who had war jobs thrust upon them and had to put up with it without too much moaning, and just want to forget the whole mad business.' Photos to illustrate Alan's awful job on the mortuary van are virtually unknown as pictures of bombing incidents were always checked by the censor to make sure that the badly injured or the dead were never depicted. There are endless 'sanitised' photographs of wrecked buildings and one can easily forget that these are invariably taken some hours later after the casualties have been taken to the mortuary. This is an example. Here a mother was killed, her husband seeing the bomb fall from his spotter post some distance away. No date or location given, but we do know that the bomb struck six yards away; that their three children were brought out of the shelter alive. 'L' Police Division covers the Brixton area of south London.

damaged, but still standing, and they had, no doubt, screened us from the blast.

It seemed impossible that so much damage could be done in so little time. It is this terrible abruptness which impresses me more than anything, and is, in my opinion, the chief morale effect of bombing. To see the result of years of work swept away in a second leaves one with an awful feeling of instability.

I could hear screams, and shouts, and rushed across the field, but I found my way barred by a wire-netting fence, which, try as I might, I could not break through.

The screams had ceased, but I could hear a woman's shrill voice from the first floor of a half-demolished house, talking to someone; she was saying in a perfectly natural, though rather peeved voice, 'Where's my fur coat?' and kept monotonously repeating it. As in all these cases there was the steady swish of running water.

I realised I could do no good by remaining, and should be in the depot awaiting orders, so I started back. About fifty yards back I saw a garden roller, weighing about two hundredweight, that had been flung there by the explosion.

I got into the hall, just as the alarm bell rang. 'No. 1 Squad away!' was the first order, followed by 'No. 2 Squad!'; five minutes passed, then 'Mortuary Van!', and in less than two minutes we were on our way. As we had only to go around to the other side of the block, we arrived in a few minutes.

The first person we saw was the Incident Officer, and he directed us to a still form lying on the pavement, on the side of the road opposite the incident. 'There will be more to come, I expect', he said. We approached the figure, and I put down the stretcher I was carrying.

Now came the moment I had dreaded. My imagination, which I had nursed for years as my chief ally, now became my foe, and I had to fight hard to force myself to turn back that blanket; but I knew, the quicker I got hardened the better, so I bent quickly and turned it back.

I don't know what horror I expected to see, but all that was revealed was the calm, rather beautiful face of a young girl of about seventeen, unmarked as far as I could see. But she was lying on her side as if asleep.

We were not allowed to presume death, and always had to get the doctor's permission to remove a body, even when it was obvious life was extinct.

I took the shoulders to turn her on her back, and then realised she was beyond all aid, as when the torso turned, the leg remained in the same position as before. One of her hands touched mine, it was still quite warm. We decided the only way to lift the body was to roll it first in a blanket; this we did after a struggle, the lumbar region had a great hole in it, and there was a rush of blood as we moved it.

We finally got it onto a stretcher, and then, while Davey went to get particulars for the mortuary label, I went to see if I could help at the incident.

I saw several figures moving about in the gloom, and an occasional flash of a torch; and at times, the flashes from the guns, which were now spasmodic, lit up the whole scene, silhouetting the rescue party, and stretcher bearers, in dramatic relief on the huge heap of debris. I picked my way carefully towards them, slipping and sliding all over the place. One had to test every step of the way, as every now and then, a piece of debris would go crashing down into the crater beneath. In between the gun crashes, I could hear the shouts of the rescue party, directing each other.

From the use of a searchlight to light up the area, it is most likely that this is a late-war incident when more plentiful equipment and an easing of the black-out would have permitted its use.

The air was thick with dust, and the smell of escaping gas and cordite was very strong. The water rushing below me gave the impression of standing on a rickety bridge over a waterfall.

When I reached the centre of the operations, the rescue party had driven a pole into the centre of the pile, and were working beneath it, gradually clearing away the rubble.

There was a brief lull in the noise, and in that fraction of a second, I heard a kind of faint groan, deep down beneath my feet. I attracted the attention of a white-helmeted rescue leader, and he bade his men cease work and listen. They did so, and in this comparative silence, the sound was heard again, quite clearly, and operations were immediately directed to the spot.

I mucked in (it not being so important for me to keep my hands clean as it was for the stretcher bearers), and I worked like a dog, throwing bricks, etc., between my legs to behind me. There was plenty of glass about, and I cut my hands on it several times, but I didn't notice that until afterwards.

Curiously enough, I noticed very vividly the character of everything I handled; and pathetic indeed were some of the items. A case of spoons, a battered kettle, broken toys, a hat-box squashed flat with the ruins of the hat inside, etc. I sometimes think these relics more pitiably suggestive of life than the human remains.

Soon a hole was made, and in the light of the torch, an incredibly grimy face looked up at us. It was working spasmodically, and the first words that issued from that contorted mouth were, 'Take that damned light out of my eyes.' Then followed a good deal of abuse at our tardiness in coming to the rescue, which of course we ignored, knowing it was just shock. We gathered also that his wife was beneath him, he didn't know if she was still alive, and what about his daughter? She must be killed, she had been in the room upstairs.

The hole was enlarged sufficiently for the doctor to enter and make an examination, after which the stretcher party was able to lift the victim out. 'Come on Dad', said one of them encouragingly, 'We'll soon have you out of this'.

'Not so much of the Dad', retorted the old fellow.

The woman was then removed, alive, but with severe concussion and bruises. They owed their escape to two armchairs which had fallen over them, forming a protective arch.

I heard afterwards that they had been in the Anderson until just before the bomb fell, and had just come into the house for a cup of tea. Their daughter had gone upstairs for a book. The Anderson was intact.

I had little to do for a few days after this, although the stretcher party had been out every night; but in proportion to the damage done, and the number of bombs dropped, the deaths were remarkably few.

Then, on October 8, two heavy bombs were dropped at Lymington Avenue, and we were sent there. When we arrived we found two separate incidents. The bombs had landed about a hundred yards apart, each demolishing two large houses.

The corner of a street which bisected Lymington Avenue, and separated the incidents, was made the base for operations, and there we found two stretchers ready loaded. The burden on one looked very small under the blanket, and I thought it was a child, but one of the stretcher party who were standing by said he thought they were a man and woman. I found out the names and addresses from a police sergeant, and made out two mortuary labels.

I then went to the smaller figure, thinking it must be the woman doubled up a bit, and drew back the blanket. The flickering gun-flashes were not at that moment continuous enough for me to see distinctly, so I switched on my torch. A horrible sight was revealed in its light. The beam lit up first the head of a man, covered in dust and streaked with blood. The nose had gone, as in most of these cases. Then my light travelled downwards, over a filthy blood-stained shirt, which ended abruptly at the hips, in a ghastly mess of torn flesh and entrails. I tied a label to one of his fingers, and hastily replaced the blanket. As I got up from my task I noticed that a couple of people had been inquisitive, and judging from their expressions they wished they had not.

I turned to the other stretcher and removed the blanket. In this case the figure was that of a heavily built woman, according to the bust. The head and shoulders were crushed to pulp, and quite unrecognisable as anything human; the clothes and the rest of the

Photographs such as this one were seldom taken and, if they were, they were *never* published for fear of undermining public morale. It is only since the war that a few such pictures have seen the light of day. In this incident, 46 people were killed when a flying bomb struck the Aldwych on June 30, 1944.

Perhaps a little more acceptable: covered victims of the Sandhurst Road incident when the London school received a direct hit from FW 190 fighter-bombers in January 1943.

body were soaked in blood, and I didn't fancy touching it, I was still too new to the job, so I tied the label to the stretcher handle.

Davey, who had been along to one of the incidents getting information, returned and helped me to load the bodies into the van. He said there were more to come from the incident he had visited, so we walked along to see if they had been removed; but the sweating rescue men had not been able to reach the two people they believed to be beneath. Nor were there any for us at the further incident, although several were expected.

Part of the road was roped off; there was a delayed action bomb not twenty-five yards from the working party.

A policeman came along, calling out to be sitting there asleep when a bomb had fallen nearly opposite, and so he had made the discovery.

She was clean and unmarked, probably shock or heart failure had caused her death, and it was a relief to handle a body that bore some resemblance to humanity. She was wearing a red cardigan, and had a mass of pure white hair, and looked so pathetically frail. Somehow it seemed wrong to put her in the van with the others.

Mr. Brown, the mortuary attendant, was waiting for us when we arrived. He had been a mortuary attendant for about thirty years, and was very religious and sympathetic towards his poor charges. 'Poor soul', or 'Poor fellow', were his usual comments as we carried them in.

ity, and started to help the rescue squads as much as I could without hindering them. We worked until five o'clock, and had managed to penetrate to the bomb crater, but it was full of water and would have to be pumped out, so the Incident Officer decided as there was no chance of finding anyone alive, we could return to our depot, and directed that further operations should be suspended until daylight.

As we came away, we were hailed by an old man, who lived opposite. He offered us tea, which we gratefully accepted. I marvelled at the courage and fortitude of the old chap, whose wife was a permanent invalid, for whom he had to do everything; and who, although his house had not a pane of glass left, the walls were cracked, and

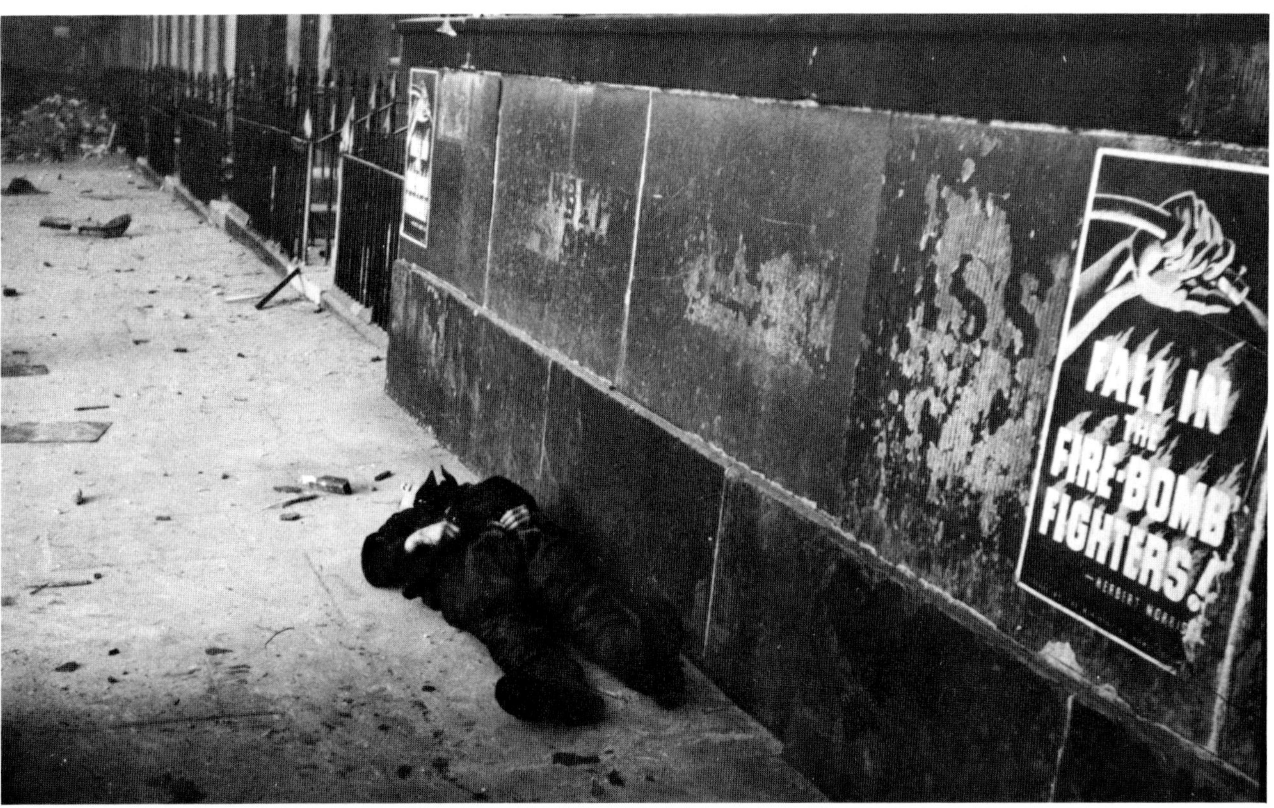

This picture, on the other hand, was cleared by the censor on May 8, 1941 with appropriate captioning: 'The great fire of London. He "fell in"! He did his duty! In fact he was doing his duty, when the Boche airman released his stick of bombs. This is not play-acting, it's WAR! This is a genuine, unposed study by the light of the fire, which only a few moments before he and brother firemen were fighting. Others were killed and injured — but the fire was still fought on — and for the moment he must lay — dead — between two posters grimly appropriate!' The 'great fire' had occurred four months previously and Cyril Demarne, our fire chief author, believes that this colleague was killed somewhere near the Elephant and Castle.

for the mortuary attendant. He told us to return to the van, as Doctor Malcolm Manson (the Medical Officer of Health for Wood Green) wished to examine the bodies; so back to the van, which we unlocked for the doctor to enter. When he had finished the examination, he told us there was another body for us to collect from the end of the road.

We were directed by a policeman to where an old lady was sitting in a doorway. It was hard to believe she was dead; it looked as though she had gone to sleep. As a matter of fact, that was why she had been unnoticed until now. She had looked so natural, sitting there, and then it had suddenly occurred to a warden that it was unusual for anyone

He was very concerned about the torso, and told us we must try to obtain as much of the body as possible. He took endless trouble with the fragments of bodies brought to him, trying to make them as human as he could, before relatives came to identify them.

After we had deposited the bodies at the mortuary, we returned to Lymington Avenue and removed two more; a man and a little girl about five years old; and then we hung about waiting for more.

Meanwhile the guns were banging away and shrapnel was falling heavily again; it seemed surprising that no one was hit by it.

Finally I got fed up with the inactiv-

the chimney missing, was calm and unaffected by an experience which might have prostrated many a person twenty years younger. Yet here he was, using their own ration of tea, sugar and milk, to provide us with drinks, and was much too proud to ask any sort of return. He told us that he had worked for years in Nigeria and China on big engineering jobs. Good luck to him. Some of those old people were simply wonderful.

There was an elderly warden quartered in the school adjoining our depot who had an uncanny instinct about time-bombs; he seemed to know exactly when they were going to explode, and saved many lives by that strange faculty.

DATE .... TIME ....

CRUSH INJURY **SYMBOL**

If MORPHINE has been given,
Time ....
Dose ....
If TOURNIQUET has been applied,
Time Applied ....
,, Released ....

LIMB COMPRESSED for ....
(period if known)
LIMB RELEASED at ....
(time)
BAKING SODA, etc. given .... teaspoonsful
TOTAL FLUID GIVEN
BEFORE RELEASE .... pints

SIGNED ________ Leader or Deputy ________ Party

All casualties, whether alive or dead, had to be labelled up before they were taken from the scene, a procedure which was the subject of an inquiry in 1943 to see if any undue risk was caused to the injured by the delay.

I wrote a short story a while back, using him as the central character, but the Editor thought him rather far-fetched. Well, there are many people in Wood Green who owe their lives to that 'far-fetched' person.

However, on our return to the depot, we were told that we must remain at the scene until relieved. So back we went. It was raining hard now, and as we had no great-coats then, we were thoroughly soaked through by seven o'clock when the coffee shop opened, and we decided we were entitled to a hot drink. But it was not until nine-thirty that we were relieved and I then returned to my own empty house (I had sent my wife home to Sussex to her people, as she was pregnant), and I didn't feel much in the mood for shopping or housework.

The mortuary van attendant on the other shift recovered five bodies that day, and on the following day we took six more along. There was one left, however, and we waited three days for that one; and yet another day while search was made for the remainder of the body we had first taken in. But we could only recover a foot.

By this time the rescue party had burrowed deep under the foundations, and now there was a muddy pool about sixteen feet down, and from this protruded, sticking straight up into the air, a pair of legs, youthful and bare, looking like white marble. Firemen were there with a pump, but this kept getting choked with rubble, and water continually seeped back into the hole.

Those of the men who could get hold of a utensil of any kind were assisting by bailing. One man picked up a small enamelled chamber pot (no doubt it belonged to the child we were trying to get out). It looked particularly ineffective in the hand of this huge fellow, but the expression on his tough weather-beaten face was that of a man, possibly with children of his own, who felt very strongly about the task upon which he was engaged. After pumping and bailing furiously for a time, and reducing the level of the water by about two feet, a member of the rescue party who was standing up to his waist in water would delve beneath the surface and attempt to loosen the body by breaking away pieces of clay with his hands; he was naturally loath to use a spade.

This went on for nearly four hours. I was standing on the edge of the crater, near the man in the water, when suddenly, after another tug beneath the surface, he turned to me with the pathetic dripping body and placed it in my arms. 'Ere you are mate', he said.

I won't attempt to analyse my feelings during that moment, except that they were a mixture in which overwhelming pity for the poor kid, and intense anger for those who caused his death, predominated.

Somebody came forward with a dirty tablecloth, salvaged from the debris, and we wrapped the body in it. The rescue party had erected a tarpaulin up above to screen us from the curious crowd, so when we emerged nothing could be seen except a small bundle on a stretcher, which we speedily put into the van and bore away.

One gets a peculiar insight into the psychology of individuals on these occasions. This sort of war seems to bring out the best and the worst in people. Generally speaking, the public have behaved wonderfully, far better than during the air raids of the last war, which I remember very well. I saw no signs of the panic we had been warned to expect; and the way my countrymen and women bore all this has quite cured me of my rather cynical pre-war attitude towards them.

Of course, there have been isolated instances of selfishness, but these have been extremely rare. One case however, stands out particularly in my memory. During the affair at Lymington Avenue, a man approached me as I had just put the body of a woman in the van. He asked: 'Is that Mrs — you've put in there?' I answered in the affirmative. Then he said, 'She was my mother. Where do I have to apply for her ring? And she has some gold teeth.' I answered briefly, 'At the mortuary.'

But against this I could give scores of instances of supreme heroism and unselfishness that may never be told. I have the greatest admiration for the rescue squads, who performed their arduous, dangerous, and often abhorrent tasks cheerfully and without complaint. They were nearly all men from the building trade, often rough and rather uncouth apparently, but who performed their job with dignity and a sense of unsurpassable delicacy, and it is a pity that those who have seen fit to make a public stir about one or two cases of looting by ARP men, none of them serious, by the way, could not have been with me, and seen how scrupulous these men were, working extra hours sometimes, in order to salvage some small cash for the owners. I have watched them, when they have been unconscious of my presence, picking money and small valuables out of the clay, things that could easily have been pocketed, and handing them over to their squad leader to be returned to their owners.

One thing that impressed me was the extraordinary lengths the authorities went to, to establish the number, sex, and if possible the identity of those killed. Everything was in such a state of chaos that at first one did not appreciate the amount of thought which had gone into preparations for this civilian war. I know my own impression at first was that they had been completely caught napping, but obviously there were some far-seeing types around, as my own experiences bore witness.

Soon afterwards we were sent to an incident involving a direct hit on an Anderson shelter, the first time I had seen such a thing, The curved corrugated iron roof was, by some explosive freak, quite near to the bomb crater, and the hole made by the bomb was so mechanically perfect, punched through like the hole in a bus ticket, that one

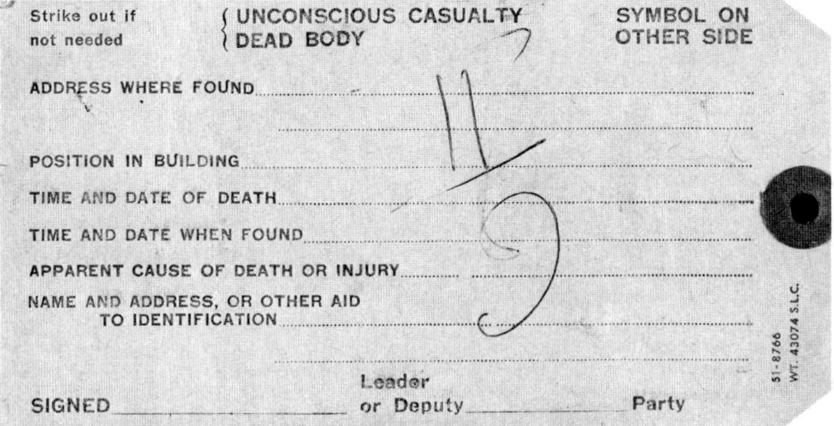

Strike out if not needed { UNCONSCIOUS CASUALTY / DEAD BODY

SYMBOL ON OTHER SIDE

ADDRESS WHERE FOUND ....

POSITION IN BUILDING ....

TIME AND DATE OF DEATH ....

TIME AND DATE WHEN FOUND ....

APPARENT CAUSE OF DEATH OR INJURY ....

NAME AND ADDRESS, OR OTHER AID TO IDENTIFICATION ....

SIGNED ________ Leader or Deputy ________ Party

51-8766 WT. 43074 S.L.C.

could tell the exact circumference of the bomb, and the terrific force of the impact. That it had been occupied was obvious by the huge stain on the inside, and we were told that it was believed to have sheltered two people. Our orders were to stay on the site until we had recovered enough to determine the number and sex of the victims.

Davey and I looked glumly at each other. We had had no sleep for two days and nights and we knew what to expect, having seen the results of similar explosions, but having been provided with shovels and a sieve, we got on with it.

We didn't expect to find anything, usually an explosion like this spread debris over a radius of several hundred yards, and the explosion is always upwards. But we found, after several hours of patient digging and sieving, that the weight of the bomb, having hardly any resistance, had probably driven the bodies deep into the clay before exploding, with the effect of decimating and driving the pieces of flesh even deeper. Finally we managed to accumulate several tiny pieces of flesh and bones, certainly not indentifiable as anything human.

The doctor visited us occasionally, and he would, after a perfunctory glance at the relics, mutter 'Keep on a bit longer, lads'.

Well, we did, and just as dawn was breaking we were rewarded; we found a part of a woman's suspender, and a bit of a man's braces, no more than about an inch apart, but it satisfied the doctor, and we were allowed to go.

We thankfully made our way back to the post. Jock and the van had long ago been conscripted for other duties while we were engaged on our grisly task, and it was only about half a mile away, but that was too far for us. But eventually we arrived, just in time for breakfast. We should have gone first to the mortuary, but to make sure there were enough bangers left for us we decided the morgue could wait.

We were covered from head to foot with dirt, most of it clay which clung lovingly to our ARP uniforms, and we were walking as if in a trance, with fatigue, but this was no uncommon sight at the post; we did not merit even a cursory glance.

We obtained our tea and bangers and found a place at the end of a table. I put the biscuit tin down at the end of the table, and got on with my meal. I then noticed that the man beside me was our driver, Jock. Jock never allowed anything to interfere with the important business of eating, so neither had he realised we were sitting there until he laid his knife and fork down, and drained his cup, which suited us; we were certainly not in the humour for conversation. At last, however, he favoured us with a glance.

'You get any out then?' he said.

I nodded.

'Want the van down there then', he went on.

'Not necessary', said Davey.

'What you done with them then, you'll want stretchers, won't you?' he demanded.

In 1938 a standard all-metal stretcher was introduced which could easily be decontaminated after use, and by the summer of 1939 fair quantities had been delivered to local authorities.

'Couldn't get 'em on stretchers', I said.

Jock began to think we were having him on.

'Where the hell are they, then?'

I pointed out the biscuit box.

'In there', I said.

There was a sudden silence at the table, and all eyes were on the box.

'Blimey', said Jock in a hushed voice. 'That all?'

Very soon we had the table to ourselves, and whether our sensibilities were blunted by our recent endeavours, or whether we were just too tired to care, I do not know, but our only reaction was to be thankful to be left alone to finish our meal.

I won't deny, however, that there were loopholes in the organisation, which I suppose was to be expected, but when they occurred, our overstrung nerves had little tolerance for them. One in particular brought us very near to mutiny.

Procreation goes on, indifferent to wars or other catastrophes, and there were many cases of childbirth in the shelters, and, as a large proportion of the populace were living in them, it was not surprising that many cases were premature because of shock and adverse conditions generally. This was anticipated and we were trained in emergency measures to deal with them. We were told that when the child was born we were not to worry about anything except getting mother and child to a hospital as soon as possible. The child was to be placed in the mother's lap and the cord left unsevered, and the whole bound around with a blanket. All very reasonable one would suppose; but like a great many of our first aid instructions we found to be impracticable, this too had a big drawback.

The first occasion in which I was involved was when we were waiting at an incident in case our services were required, and we were approached by a man whose wife was on the point of giving birth in a public shelter a few hundred yards along the road. We

Hospital and mortuary facilities had been established for 250,000 casualties by September 1939 but numbers never reached anywhere near this total, even at the height of the Blitz. Swimming baths were considered suitable locations for the reception of the dead — the one covering West Ham being established in the Romford Road baths.

A 724

Police Ilt.

MORTUARY RECORD

DEATH DUE TO WAR OPERATIONS

O. E. G. Prior T.C.

Name and Address of Mortuary: **MUNICIPAL BATHS, ROMFORD ROAD, E.15**

A.—TO BE ENTERED IMMEDIATELY UPON RECEPTION OF THE BODY AT MORTUARY.

Date 20/4/41 Hour 11-00. of Reception.

1. Place { of Death* / of Finding the Body* } 1 WOODGRANGE Rd / MR H. E. KAYE 5 Woodgrange Rd.
Full postal particulars of house or street.
* Cross out whichever is inapplicable.

2. Date and hour { of Death* / of Finding the Body* } 20.4.41, 10-00
* Cross out whichever is inapplicable.

3. Sex. MALE 4. Probable Age. 60

5. Cause of Death MULTIPLE INJURIES.

Signature R H Knight Official Description

Date 20/4/41

B.—TO BE ENTERED PENDING IDENTIFICATION (See Note 4).

Height 5 ft. 10 ins. Build HEAVY

Dress DARK GREY OVERCOAT DARK STRIPED SUIT WHITE SHIRT WOLLEN VEST & PANTS. NAVY BLUE SOCKS

Hair LIGHT BROWN Moustache NO Beard NO

Complexion FRESH Eyes

Shape of Nose STRAIGHT Shape of Face LONG

Physical Marks or Peculiarities

Kaye Herbert Emile

Names or Identification Marks upon Effects

Signature Official Description

Date

INVENTORY OF CLOTHING AND EFFECTS.
(For entry in accordance with such instructions as may be given by Local Authority)

3 PACKETS ANADIN TABLETS
GLASSES & CASE
BUNCH OF 8 KEYS

Married yes
Occupation Dentist (slip Son in law)
Ident. by F. D. Lunnon
Relationship 4 Elms Lane Wembley
Position or circumstances of casualty In street and blown into cellar

Signature R H Knight Official Description

Date 22/4/41

Plaistow Press, E.13.

hurried there, the baby was born and we followed instructions. We loaded her up in the van, hoping she didn't know the original purpose, and took her to the Cottage Hospital adjacent to our post.

To our consternation and fury, we were turned away. 'This is for casualties only', declared the matron. And argue as we might she was obdurate. We were informed after a 'phone message that the hospital dealing with 'this sort of thing' was in Central London, and we had to take the poor woman right across from North London in the middle of a raid when shrapnel was pelting down with no other protection than a canvas roof for the patient: to be met on arrival by an ambulance, into which the patient was transferred — and that was the last we saw of her.

On the way back we encountered a sight that brought home to me the extremely hazardous job the AFS and the professional firemen had. Normally we saw little of their activities in North London as the Germans concentrated their fire-raising mostly on Central London and the docks. We were approaching a hill, the top of which seemed entirely ablaze, like a volcano, but as we got nearer we saw that three houses were hopelessly ablaze, and two more, which the firemen were trying to control, looked not so badly affected. One fireman was in the act of dragging a hose up a tall ladder. My driver slowed and pulled to the side of the road.

'I'm not going through that lot', he said. 'Jerry will be chucking a load of HE into that presently.' (Only he didn't use the word HE.) 'An' I reckon those houses will be down any minute.'

I must say I wasn't anxious either to run the gauntlet of those blazing houses, apart from the bombs we expected Jerry to throw into it.

Jock had hardly finished speaking when we heard the 'planes overhead; the familiar intermittent throb we had come to recognise as Jerry's signature tune, and almost immediately he released his stick of bombs. It seemed to fill the sky, sweeping over our heads, curving away into the distance the long whining shriek that ended in the explosions.

He missed his mark, the nearest falling at the other end of the street. But after the flash of the explosion, I saw the fireman and his ladder were no longer there. I believe many firemen lost their lives in this manner, being swept away with their ladders like bits of straw in the wind.

We turned about and found another

We actually printed the record forms used there in our wartime factory (since demolished) at 19 Plaistow Road.

way round. We were very silent on our way back, both carrying with us, I am sure, the sight of that hellish blaze. Hardened as we were becoming to explosions, the blaze touched something more elemental, affecting us longer.

My wife had rejoined me, wishing to pay a pre-natal visit to her doctor, and as I had a little time off, I accompanied her. We lived quite a distance from the surgery, and we hadn't got very far when a raid started; my wife didn't want to miss the appointment, so we decided not to turn back. Soon we heard the sound of the German bombers. There seemed to be many of them, and they seemed to be directly overhead. The gun-fire grew intense and shrapnel started falling here and there on rooftops and pavements. I, of course, had my steel helmet, and naturally offered it to her, but she refused to put it on, and as I couldn't possibly wear it while she was unprotected, a couple of mad people continued to walk nonchalantly, one swinging a tin hat, through the thick of the falling lumps of iron, but our numbers apparently weren't on any of them.

My wife, incidentally, behaved magnificently all through the Blitz. I had great difficulty in persuading her to leave me for the comparative safety of Horsham, when she was pregnant, and I'm sure were it not for the child I would not have been successful.

The evening following this incident a lot of incendiaries fell in our street; we were first made aware of this by the sound of some hitting the pavement outside our front door. When I looked out I saw one blazing away but doing no harm where it was, but up and down the street were dozens more, not only on the pavements but on the roofs of houses, on cornices and window ledges; wherever they hit the street, the intense heat was melting the metal cases, and acting as a weld.

Everyone in the street turned out to help put out the flames. The most effective way I found was to bash at them with my tin hat when they were on the pavement but we were clambering about in each other's houses to reach those on roofs, etc. Sand had been recommended and stored for this purpose, but anyone who has attempted to run back and forth carrying buckets of sand will know how easy this is. But my wife, in spite of her condition, attempted to help in this way. Although so many of these little bombs fell they did little comparative damage by fire raising; the chief damage was the illuminations which could show Jerry where to drop his HE.

There was no let-up day and night for several months and everyone was feeling the strain. I think that the lack of sleep, and the depressing effect of the black-out affected us more than the actual bombing. One got a bit fatalistic about both. I think one builds up a resistance to fear eventually; it's too much of a strain being scared all the time. I often used to think that the authorities might have done a little more to boost morale; a bit of martial music perhaps, or lift the black-out when it wasn't strictly necessary. The perpetual gloom was so depressing, we don't realise how cheerful light is until we have to do without it. I know how much I longed to see the lights come on again in windows and the shops and streets. But although everyone must have felt the strain as much as we did, I saw little evidence on other people; as a matter of fact, a very powerful sustaining factor was this very real feeling of pride in my fellow countrymen and women. I saw no panic, and the very

To follow this particular incident through, Bert Kaye was taking his dog for a walk on April 20, 1941 when a land mine floated down and struck the Princess Alice, a pub on the corner of Woodgrange Road and Romford Road, not a quarter of a mile from the mortuary.

After the site had stood empty for twenty years . . .

. . . the present-day replacement was put up in 1962–63.

The bomb had struck Cranbrook and the Cedars, Bounds Green Road, completely demolishing them and penetrating right through to the station below.

few cases of hysteria I encountered were under conditions of extreme stress. The only evidence of strain I encountered, and this applies to myself as well, was on occasion exaggerated talk or behaviour which, I suppose, acted as a defence mechanism.

For instance, one day we, that is my driver and I, were going up a fairly long, steep hill. (The three of us very rarely travelled together, normally one remaining behind at the incident if it was a severe case to stand guard over any bodies that could not be accomodated in the van, taking it in turns to remain at the post in case of any calls.) About half-way up, my driver, who, as I have mentioned before, was not the most accomplished of drivers, decided to change gear. He must have put his foot on the brake by accident, because there was a terrific jerk, and we heard one of the laden stretchers slide along and hit the back of the vehicle; however, Jock managed to recover without stalling and we resumed our journey.

The barrage had started up again. Jerry sounded almost directly overhead, but as he passed over so the gun-fire followed, and it was then that we heard a banging sound at the back of the van. Jock and I looked at each other, and because the same thought must have occurred to us simultaneously, we both started a giggle that soon developed into a roar of laughter. It was fortunate for us that the road was deserted. The sight of two people in charge of a mortuary van, roaring with laughter, would, I'm sure, have invited a charge of inebriation to say the least. We both thought that the doors had opened at the back, and the picture of the stretchers with their loads sliding out and laying a trail behind us struck us as being very funny. Just a mild case of hysteria, I should think, but I suppose it relieved the tension.

Our next big job occurred about nine-thirty on October 13. We knew it was near, because we heard the bomb coming, and the explosion rocked our depot. Our yard was again sprinkled with the debris. Presently the warden came in escorting a man, in a very excited condition, who wanted to see the Superintendent. He said that Bounds Green Tube station had been penetrated by a bomb, and that hundreds of people were trapped and screaming for help. We heard this statement with reserve, knowing how shocked people tend to exaggerate.

However, very soon orders came from the MRC (Main Regional Control) to send all personnel to the incidents, one in the main road, the other down in the Tube station. The mortuary van was not included, but I begged to be allowed to go. I pointed out that I should be on the spot in any case, should I be needed in my official capacity. I received permission, and went along.

When I reached the station, a policeman told me the two incidents had been caused by the same bomb. It had demolished two houses further along the road, then penetrated the ground, exploded, and caused a section of the roof of the Tube to fall on people sheltering there. A continual stream of people were coming from the Tube entrance, escorted by stretcher bearers, some being borne on stretchers. They were being taken to the Cottage Hospital opposite, where formerly I had been stationed while on the mobile unit.

I decided to visit the surface incident first, and walked about fifty yards down the road to where a huge gap in the row of big Georgian houses, and a mountain of clay mixed with debris, indicated where two of the number had previously stood.

I was particularly moved by this incident because, when I used to patrol the grounds of the hospital, I often saw the people who lived in these houses. The men going off to business in the morning, and returning in the evening. The women going shopping, or gossiping with their neighbours, and the children running off to school, or playing in the front garden. And now their little universe, contained in the two strongly built houses, that looked as if they might have lasted a couple more centuries, was all swept away in a moment. Again I got that awful feeling of insecurity it always gives me to see how easily a house, and all its associations, can be suddenly blotted out.

I could see lights moving, and heard men's voices, and of course the usual sound of rushing water, and could smell coal gas. I picked my way gingerly over the rubble, and came upon two policemen tearing furiously at the debris. They looked far different from the usual immaculate London 'Bobby', being covered from head to foot with white dust and clay.

They were working at a tunnel they had made under a section of flooring which was holding up a great mass of debris. They stopped as I approached, thinking I belonged to the rescue party, but when I told them my job, one of them flashed his torch down the hole, saying, 'There's one down there for you'. I could see, in what was obviously the remains of a cellar, the torso of a woman in a yellow jumper, the rest of her body was buried in the debris.

The policeman told me he had attempted to wriggle down to her, but his bulk had not allowed him to do so, and they were trying to widen the passage. 'But', he added, 'I don't think it will stand much more pulling about, it's getting a bit shaky as it is.'

I am very slim, and decided to try. While the policeman held my legs, I wriggled down the hole. My progress was slow, as I had to extend my arms in front of me, there being no room to do otherwise, and I was afraid to wriggle too much for fear of precipitating a collapse of the tunnel. I got very hot, the perspiration trickled into my eyes. At last I managed to touch the woman's face, and tested for life by pinching the skin, although by the light of the torch I held, I had no doubt that she was beyond aid, apart from the fact that half her body was pinned down by a great mass of bricks.

I shouted to be pulled out, and at the expense of a bit of skin here and there was extricated. I was telling the policeman the conclusions I had reached, when the rescue men turned up and took charge.

I stayed and helped them for a while, and then decided that by now I might be needed at the Tube, and was about to leave, when a civilian came up to me from the roadway. He was very agitated, and wanted to know if I could give him any news of his wife and child. 'My wife was wearing a yellow jumper', he added.

I felt very sorry for the chap. He had just come home from work to find everything he loved and possessed, gone; and I didn't relish my task of dispelling what little hope he had. I had to tell him, however, that there was little hope for his wife, and advised him to keep away from the men who were working. He was docile enough, and looked so pathetic, hovering about miserably, picking at bits of his ruined

Where Alan Seymour tried to rescue Mrs Maud Page from the remains of the Cedars. Other casualties in the house were her 16-month-old daughter, Moya; Barbara Bowdich, aged 11, and Charles Norris, aged 63, in the Cranbrook. Today the tragic spot is occupied by Bounds Green Court, but next door Forrester House still survives.

home, in an aimless sort of way, that I sent him along to a warden's post, where I knew he would be taken care of; telling him that if there was any news of his child, he would be told.

By this time, although the barrage was at its height, and plenty of shrapnel falling, men from the gas and water companies were working on the roadway, in order to prevent more of these elements escaping into the debris.

I then started back to the Tube. I was just in time to be met by a warden, who was asking for the mortuary van attendant, and so I reported to the Incident Officer. I might mention at this point, that this official's main duty was to gather information and relay it to the proper quarters. He stands with a blue lamp at his feet, near an incident, and is thus easily found when required. Speaking from experience, I have found this an excellent idea, which saves a lot of needless running about after information, and the confusion that might result.

He told me that I was wanted down the Tube, and I made my way to where Davey was waiting for me with the van, and taking a stretcher, blankets and shrouds, we entered the station.

The entrance hall was comparatively clear of people, the police had seen to that, but on the way down the escalator we were passed by a continuous stream of people on the ascending stairway, most of them bandaged, and escorted by stretcher bearers. At the bottom of the stairs, a temporary dressing station had been fitted up, and the nurses of the mobile unit were on the job.

Everything up to now, except for the evidence I have mentioned, seemed fairly normal. There was no appearance of excitement or confusion. Then we turned onto the platform, and into an absolute bedlam.

Here was a scene of almost indescribable chaos. To the left of us the narrow platform was crowded with people; railway officials, police, stretcher and rescue parties and civilians. Over the heads of this crowd I could see a mountain of clay, reaching up and vanishing into a great hole in the roof, extending the whole width of the tunnel (which was completely blocked), and from that direction came an appalling mixture of screams and shouting, and the sound of clinking tools. These sounds were intensified in an eerie manner, echoing from the concave walls, and down the tunnel at the other end.

We placed our stretcher on a pile of others by the wall, and began to force our way through to the centre of operations. Arriving there, I realised why so many people were standing about doing nothing, there was simply no room for more to work there. I have never before seen people work so hard as those men did then. They tore and strained at the debris, utterly regardless of the damage to their persons. There were piteous cries from the people they were trying to free. Now and then I caught a glimpse, as the workers moved, of a portion of human anatomy protruding from the clay, a contorted face, a twitching limb, in one case a man buried from the waist downwards, with set face, patiently awaiting his turn.

'He told me that I was wanted down the Tube . . . and taking a stetcher, blankets and shrouds, we entered the station.'

Then suddenly, a man whom I recognised as our section leader, Bill, turned with a child about five years old in his arms. Her delicate little face was streaked with blood and grime and she was quietly clinging to his burly neck, her big eyes wide with shock. Bill, who prided himself on his toughness, and always affected to sneer at sentiment, was murmuring soft words of endearment that would not have been inappropriate from a mother.

I looked about for someone in authority, and saw an inspector of police standing by. I told him of my errand, and he showed me where five laden stretchers were ranged against the wall. The crowd had prevented me seeing them before. I asked if the doctor had passed them for removal; he did not know, but pointed out a grimy figure in blue dungarees, such as all ARP personnel wore, who was working vigorously with the other men at the pile of debris. 'There's Doctor Manson', he said.

I hardly recognised the grimy, perspiring face that was turned when I addressed the doctor, it was certainly not the well groomed head and face he was wont to present, but it was the face of a man, and had lost none of its noble characteristics through the addition of dirt. He nodded briefly. 'Be back as soon as possible', he said, 'There will be more to come'.

Davey, who had been escorting some wounded people to hospital, now returned, and we started to get the bodies upstairs.

When we lifted the first stretcher, we found that the body had been placed without regard to the problem of lifting it, or loading it into the van. The weight had not been evenly disposed, and the limbs were loose; this made our work very difficult, and by the time we reached the top of the stairs we both felt the strain. We decided to tidy things up a bit in the entrance hall, knowing we should never succeed in getting the stretcher into the van as it was.

We took the blanket off, and saw it was a woman, the features maltreated in the usual way, but the body was apparently undamaged. We rearranged it, and made out a label, as far as we could; because we had no other data, and no obvious way of getting it, we could only put the sex, name of incident, time and date.

After three journeys, we were feeling pretty well all in, but the fourth was the worst. The sturdy steel stretcher bent in a curve as we lifted it, and when we finally got upstairs after several rests on the way, we could hardly stand. The body was of a man, who must have weighed all of eighteen stone. I saw the

'On the way down the escalator we were passed by a continuous stream of people . . . most of them bandaged and escorted by stretcher bearers.'

'... Then we turned onto the platform and into an absolute bedlam ... A mountain of clay reaching up to and vanishing into a great hole in the roof ... and from that direction came an appalling mixture of screams and shouts ...'

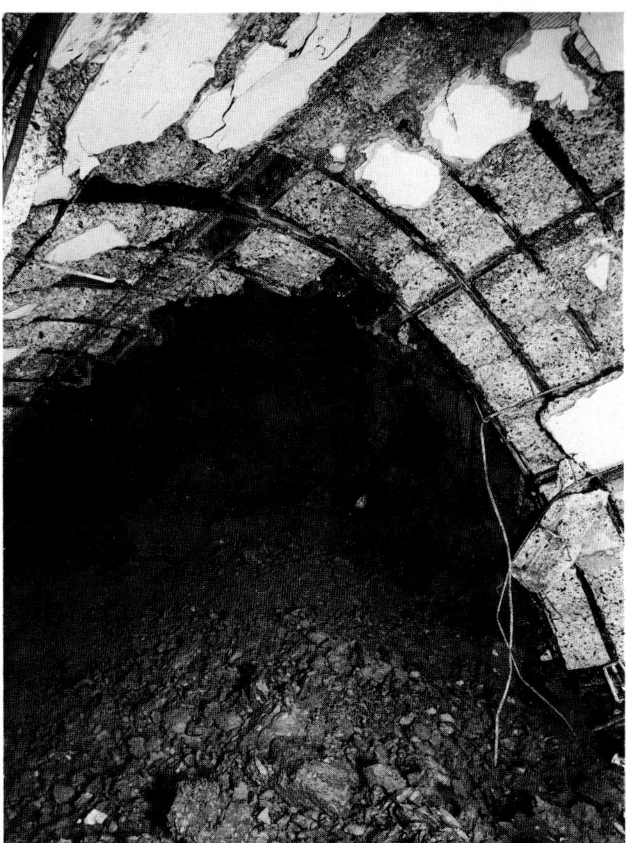

'Dr Manson was working hard . . . trying to free a man who was buried up to the waist in clay . . . '

unclothed body at the mortuary afterwards, and was then more able to admire, and feel sad at the magnificent physique displayed, but at the time we wondered if we would ever succeed in getting it loaded. To make matters worse, we had to lift it on to a top rack, the bottom one being filled, and we were reluctant to change them over in the street before the small crowd that had gathered, in spite of the gun-fire. However, we managed to get it on at last, and drove off at breakneck speed. Perhaps we would not have admired so much the way our driver took the corners at high speed if we had known at the time that this was the first time he had taken the van out without supervision; he had only passed his driving test the week previous. We found this out when he was involved in an accident a week later.

I have often wondered since, whether his being put on the mortuary van first was deliberate or not. There was certainly a grim humour in the situation, that I could appreciate afterwards.

We delivered our charges to Mr Brown, the mortuary attendant, who was waiting for us, with his son who assisted him, and then returned to the Tube. This time we found two bodies had been brought to the surface, and were ready for us in the entrance hall, then two men staggered along bearing another stretcher, which they placed alongside the others. They were very excited, and one of them began to abuse people standing about, demanding that they should 'muck in', and 'give a hand'.

Davey and I felt very annoyed, but appreciating the desire to help, pointed out gently that there were far too many people downstairs already, and that inexperienced people were more likely to hinder than help. He subsided, perhaps he was only relieving his feelings, he was young, and no doubt the scenes had rather unnerved him. But we privately cursed his zeal when we saw the way the stretcher had been loaded. The body was face downwards, and the limbs were hanging over the side, and so awkwardly placed that it would have been better to unload and rearrange it; but this we were unwilling to do, it was all too much of an exhibition already.

After a great deal of trouble, we finally managed to get it into the van, the difficulty being that there was only just enough room on the runners to take a stretcher, and the supporting bars in front were just wide enough to admit it.

We had the same difficulty with the other two stretchers, which had obviously been as hurriedly loaded. We decided we had to prevent a repetition of that sort of thing, and when we got below we were able to enlist the help of a police inspector to prevent any more of it.

I am not trying to deprecate the very valuable help the ARP had from the public, but it's not much use having a practical routine to work from, only to be prevented from carrying it out by persons unacquainted with it. In this case, for instance, apart from the inconvenience we experienced, we did not know if the doctor had seen the bodies and authorised their removal, although, as it happened, examination at the mortuary revealed mutilation that put any question of decease beyond doubt. But it might not have been so obvious, and it does not require much effort of the imagination to perceive other possibilities.

We made two more journeys, so that by now we had delivered twelve bodies to Mr Brown, and once again returned to the incident. This time I was sent for, from the first incident, where the body of the woman had been extricated, and also that of a child. As I put these two in the van, I thought again of the poor husband, and was glad he was not there. I particularly hated my job when I had to take the bodies of children, and don't think I should ever become hardened to the task.

I returned again to the Tube, and as no more had as yet been extricated, I was able to watch the rescue work. Doctor Manson was still working very hard with some rescue party men, trying to free a man who was buried up to the waist in clay. The imprisoned man seemed less concerned about himself than for his wife, who was near him and trapped by two metal girders. She was uninjured, physically, but kept up a monotonous, intermittent screaming. The doctor ignored it, however, and concentrated on freeing the man.

I tried in vain to quieten the wife by talking to her reassuringly. Her husband kept calling to her that he was all right but it was a long time before he was got out, and then he died almost immediately. Meanwhile the woman had been got at by another party, and had mercifully fainted.

The removal of the husband disclosed a hole beyond, in which was another

'It was two weeks before we were recalled . . . We took a couple of stretchers and started off downstairs . . . Before we had descended half way our nostrils were assailed by a fearful stench . . . I won't attempt to describe what we saw . . . '

person. The doctor crawled in and found he was still alive. Wooden props were brought, and attempts made to enlarge the hole.

Davey and I removed the body of the man who had just died, and returned just in time to see the doctor try to remove the injured person from the hole. He was well inside the hole, and struggling to release the man. His head reappeared and he brushed some dirt from his eyes and gasped for air but he had partially succeeded and the man's legs were now visible, where the doctor had drawn them to within about a foot from the entrance of the hole.

Mr Brice, a St John's man and our lecturer on first aid, went to the doctor's help, and both of them crouched for the final effort. Suddenly, there was a rushing noise from above. 'Look out', someone shouted, and the next moment the two men were blotted out by an avalanche of clay. They had heard the shout, and just before they were buried I saw the doctor look up, but neither of them made any attempt to escape, but made a last frantic effort to free the imprisoned man.

As soon as possible we rushed to the rescue, and after a period of frantic grubbing, we got the three of them out alive. Doctor Manson had both scapulae fractured, and Brice had a badly strained back. The rescued man had severe internal injuries. For this deed Doctor Manson was awarded the George Medal. In the opinion of most of us who had seen his bravery and zeal he had already earned it many times over.

The fall of the earth had closed down operations for the night. The extent of the fall made it obvious that further rescue attempts would be useless, nothing could live under the tons of clay that had fallen, and everyone was exhausted. It was necessary to rest, in case we had to go on another job; also most of us had been on duty for twenty-two hours.

It was, however, two weeks before we were recalled to the Tube. And if I imagined I was hardened by my experiences, I was soon disillusioned then. We had an inkling of what to expect when we entered the station, for we were met by some of the rescue men who, when we asked where the bodies were, glanced significantly at each other, and one said, 'Down there', gesticulating with his hand.

'Are they on stretchers?' I asked. He shook his head and grimaced. 'No, that's your job', he replied. 'And I wouldn't have it for a pension. Take my tip and put on your gas mask before you go down.'

We took a couple of stretchers and started off downstairs. Davey remarking as we descended that if the rescue men wouldn't touch them it must be pretty bad. I agreed, glumly. We had seen and admired the way these men had tackled some horrible jobs, and very soon we knew why they had jibbed at this one.

Before we had descended half way, our nostrils were assailed by a fearful stench which, as we drew nearer, became more powerful. We lit cigarettes, but even the smoke seemed impregnated with the odour, and it was as much as we could do to force ourselves to cover the remaining distance.

I won't attempt to describe what we saw, but we decided we must get some sort of protection before we tackled the job, and quickly escaped upstairs again. We asked our Superintendent if we could don our anti-gas clothes for the job and, receiving permission, put them on, together with our masks, and descended once again.

Even thus equipped, our task was most unpleasant, and although we were almost choked by the Dettol we had wiped round the inside of our masks, the nauseating odour still penetrated. We hurried over the job and removed the five bodies, placing the odd stretcher on the floor of the van to save us returning again. Finally our task was completed and, of all the jobs in the world, I think I envied that of Mr Brown the least.

When we returned to the depot, we had a hot shower in the decontamination chamber, and sprayed ourselves with Dettol, but even so the smell was persistent, and it was several days before we could get rid of it. We had no dinner that day.

In between our first and last visit to the Tube, our life was far from uneventful. The Blitz continued day and night, and there was seldom a night passed without some of us being sent for. There was no let-up, on or off duty, for at least three months, and we were all feeling the lack of sleep pretty badly.

But I think Jerry would have had to use far more planes, and kept it up longer, before he could have begun to have got us down. One gets used to it somehow.

As an experiment in breaking civilian morale, the Blitz has failed miserably in England. Now let us see how Jerry likes being the guinea-pig.

ALAN SEYMOUR, 1942

DOCTOR MALCOLM MANSON, MC, MB, Ch.B

A heavy HE bomb fell, causing a tunnel to collapse. A number of people were trapped under the debris and the clay which had fallen through the cavity.

Doctor Manson arrived on the scene within a few minutes of the occurrence, and immediately assumed the direction and leadership of the rescue work. For nearly three hours he worked without intermission, actively participating in the release of persons trapped in the debris heap, giving medical aid where it was needed and all the time keeping effective control. Throughout this period he was in grave personal danger from frequent falls of clay. It seemed likely that a further portion of the tunnel would collapse. At one period he was lying full length on the heap endeavouring to release a man partially buried when there was a shout from the lookout man of 'Run for it'. The Doctor ignored the warning and continued his efforts for the trapped man. There was a large fall of clay and the Doctor was struck by a large piece full in the back. He was partially buried and had to be dragged out feet foremost. He rested for a few minutes, and then, in spite of severe pain, carried on with the work.

Dr Manson's pertinacity, courage and disregard of personal safety set a wonderful example to the men and was no doubt responsible for the saving of a number of lives which otherwise would have been lost.

He sustained serious injuries during the rescue operations.

LONDON GAZETTE, FEBRUARY 7, 1941

With Swastika and fuselage markings blacked out for night operations, two Ju 88s of KG1 prepare to attack targets in Britain. Bombs can be seen slung beneath the aircraft which has left the ground while HE bombs of various sizes await loading on the second machine whose code appears to be V4+BS.

THE NIGHT OFFENSIVE

Mid-November 1940 saw the well-known attack on Coventry which heralded the change of tactics in the widening of the Night Blitz to take care of Britain as the German planning staffs got down to the business of eradicating 'the Russian menace'. London, of course, remained a primary target, with the crews of 1,539 night bombers having claimed to have bombed the capital in the 12 attacks of the first half of the month, a period in which there had been one night with no operations because of weather and one night with only 23 sorties.

The biggest attack was that against Coventry on the 14th, by 552 long-range bombers, and from then until the end of the month there were 13 major and two heavy attacks. Minelaying was carried out on seven nights in the same period. In total, for the period November 14-30, the Luftwaffe flew 4,203 long-range night bomber sorties over Britain together with 69 long-range night fighter sorties. Bombers of the CAI were active on four nights, completing 19 sorties with Harwich the main target. During the second half of the month major attacks were made on London (3), Southampton (3), Birmingham (3), Bristol, Plymouth and Liverpool/Birkenhead. In this same period 2,519 people were killed and 4,863 seriously injured: for the entire month the figures were 4,588 killed and 6,202 seriously injured. London, raided almost nightly in varying strength, suffered a particularly heavy assault on the night of the 15/16th when parachute mines caused extensive damage through their enormous blast effect. The German bomb load for the entire month comprised 6,205 tonnes of HE, 305 tonnes of incendiary bombs and 1,215 mines.

As was the case in October, the defences achieved little success against the raiders, claiming only three night fighter victories while the gunners of AA Command claimed 26.

An enormous amount of damage was done in the cities attacked, but mainly to residential and commercial premises. Industrial plants also suffered greatly, but quick remedial action proved possible and little lasting damage was reported. Even in Coventry, where much of the city's industrial output was temporarily halted, it did not take long to resume limited production and large scale production was re-introduced in many factories once public utilities were reinstated.

Although British claims of enemy aircraft destroyed at night (including dusk and dawn) during November totalled 29, the wrecks of only 14 were found on land in the British Isles. Actual German losses of long-range bombers during the month were 94, but this figure includes those lost on all types of flights by operational units and includes accidents and crashes due to mechanical failures, etc. Total aircrew losses for the month were 184 killed (including 31 officers), 108 wounded or injured (including 16 officers), and 334 missing (74 officers), a total of 626 casualties among

Summer turns into winter: the two different types of flying suit are shown in this shot of crew members of the same Kampfgruppe.

Groundcrew members applying temporary night-flying matt black paint to the fuselage of an He 111. The black paint — a form of distemper similar in appearance to lamp black — was intended to be washed off for daylight operations, but this was seldom done in practice as its removal was a messy and unpopular business.

flying personnel. These figures were recorded by the Luftwaffe's 6 Abteilung at the beginning of December when the November losses were tabulated, but the ratio of dead to missing (or PoW) was later changed as, for example, news was received through the International Red Cross of airmen killed or taken prisoner.

From these figures it is clear that only a very small proportion of German airmen listed as missing actually fell into British hands. Nevertheless, the consistency of attitudes displayed by PoWs convinced officers of AI1(k) Branch that they were typical and reflected general levels of morale, training and experience throughout the Luftwaffe. Further, despite the small numbers involved, the RAF was able to glean a tremendous amount of intelligence material by means of interrogation and other more cunning methods. Later on, however, there was a tightening up of security by the Luftwaffe and operational crews were given lectures on how to behave if taken prisoner, but this was not always sufficient. For instance, it was common British practice to put a newly captured airman into a room with a planted 'stool pigeon' acting the part of another prisoner. Usually these stool pigeons were fluent German-speaking immigrants, often refugees from Germany or Austria, and their task was to lead PoWs into revealing conversations which were monitored by means of carefully hidden microphones. After a period of time in solitary confinement, broken only by interrogation sessions, most PoWs were delighted to meet up again with a fellow 'prisoner' and many became quite garrulous.

Such a procedure was experienced by Leutnant Max Probst, an He 111 pilot shot down by AA fire over Bromley during an attack on London on the night of November 9. After capture he was taken to the AI1(k) Interrogation Centre at Cockfosters and, after a suitable period, found himself sharing a room with a fellow 'prisoner'. In the course of conversations which followed, Probst revealed to his new-found friend, who was, in fact, an 'SP' working for Air Intelligence, that a new form of large scale attack was to be launched in the coming full moon period, with major assaults directed at Coventry and Birmingham. This was of immense interest to Air Intelligence but was contrary, or so it appeared, to certain information already to hand.

Decrypts of German Enigma-coded W/T traffic intercepted by the 'Y' Service had revealed to Air Intelligence a forthcoming change in bombing policy by the Germans. This outlined plans for a major attack, or series of attacks, given the code-name 'Mondscheinserenade' (Moonlight Serenade), but exactly where the blow or blows would fall was not clear. The intercepted German messages included the word 'Korn' and mentioned certain target numbers and these were duly but erroneously related to numbers seen on a map recovered from a previously crashed German aircraft. These appeared to delineate certain areas of south-east England where, it was assumed, the attack or attacks would take place. The information obtained from the captured airman, however, did not agree with this supposition and Probst's version was rejected. Accordingly, a British counter-plan, code-named 'Operation Cold Water', took no account of the Midlands targets. Instead Fighter Command Operational Instruction No. 44, issued in the small hours of November 14, referred to probable target areas around London and in the South-East. Korn was the important word, however, for, unknown to the British, it was the German code-name for Coventry.

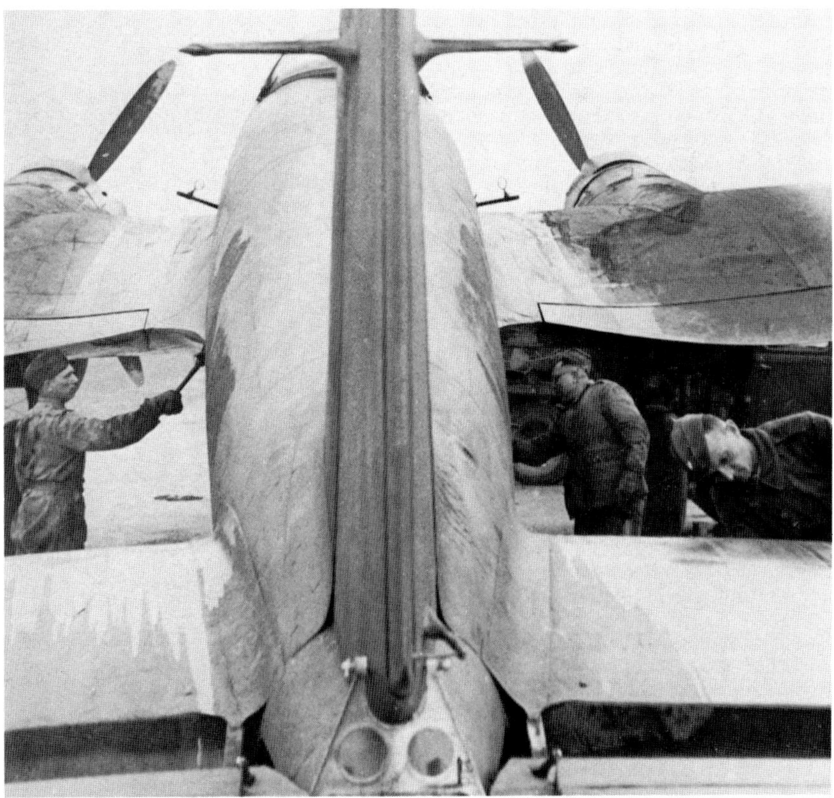

Standard Luftwaffe bomber camouflage, two shades of dark green (Schwarzgrün 70 and Dunkelgrün 71) for top and sides and light blue (Hellblau 65) for under-surfaces, was not intended for night operations. The application of non-reflective matt black appreciably helped to counter illumination by searchlights.

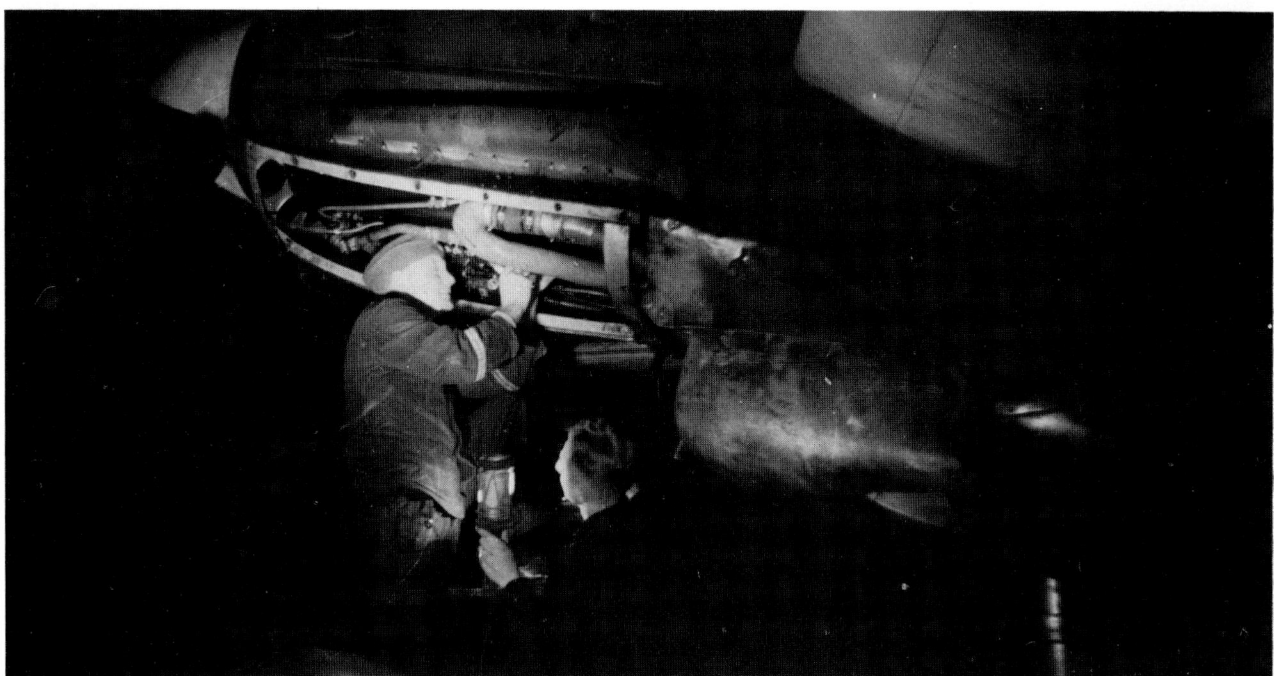

Unshielded, exhaust flames were readily visible to night fighter pilots and flame-dampening shrouds were fitted for night ops. Here mechanics, working with the aid of a lead-light, make adjustments to the left Junkers Jumo 211 engine of an He 111. The bottom cowling has been removed below the shroud covering the stub exhausts of this H-Series aircraft. Like the Daimler-Benz DB 601 installed in P-Series He 111s, the Jumo 211 was a supercharged 12-cylinder, inverted-Vee liquid cooled motor, fitted with a fuel injection system. Power varied from the 1,150 hp of the Jumo 211B to the 1,300 hp of the 211J2.

Cold Water called for a maximum effort by AA Command's guns and Fighter Command's night fighters, augmented by selected day fighters flown by pilots with night flying experience, while a retaliatory attack was to be made by Bomber Command on a German city. Just how a retaliatory attack was going to help matters is difficult to see; equally inappropriate, or so it would seem, was the decision to allow other RAF bombers to continue with an already established pattern of attacks on Italian targets. More appropriate was the requirement for other aircraft of both Bomber and Coastal Commands to attack German bomber airfields in France and the Low Countries. There was also to be a maximum effort by the RAF's Signals Branch to interfere with enemy radio navigation transmissions and a few aircraft of a special unit under the control of No. 80 Wing were to attack designated radio navigation transmitters in northern France. It was expected, the Operational Instruction stated, that the likely target would be known in the Air Ministry shortly after midday on the day of the proposed German attack and sure enough on the afternoon of November 14 the objective for the raid was known to be Coventry.

Flame dampeners fitted to the Jumo of a Ju 88 of KG1. Just what the officer (wearing winter flying overalls) is holding in his hands is not clear but, whatever it is, it appears to have made the mechanic, wearing the usual black overalls, and the armed guards somewhat apprehensive. The other crewman — the Beobachter — still wears his summer lightweight flying suit and has the standard issue navigation bag carrying the tools of his trade at his feet.

This information was obtained from two sources — an intercept of an Enigma-coded W/T message giving the VHF beam bearings for the forthcoming night's operations and the physical measurement of the beams' bearings as they were being set-up in advance of the attack.

In spite of this brilliant intelligence work, little could be done to alleviate or prevent the attack although a few additional barrage balloons were immediately dispatched to Coventry. There was insufficient time — or resources — to significantly improve the city's AA gun defences, nor was it practical to warn the population and organise a mass evacuation. Anything less than the latter would have led to widespread panic and there was, too, the certainty that forewarning the population would clearly indicate to the enemy that the British were able to deduce German plans in advance. This, of course, could only mean that the British were able to decode the Enigma messages and a loss of this very great advantage would have been a serious blow to British Intelligence.

The executive order to implement Cold Water went out during the afternoon of that fateful Thursday and that night RAF bombers were sent to Berlin, Hamburg, Ostend, Le Havre and Lorient. Most of the attacks, which were mainly directed against docks and shipping, followed Bomber Command's then current bombing policy and, with the exception of the 'reprisal' against Berlin, were outside the dictates of Cold Water. The Command did, however, send aircraft in a concerted attack with Coastal Command against 26 German-occupied airfields.

In a direct exchange of blows between the bomber arms of Britain and Germany in 1940, the British were certain to come off second best. Not only was Bomber Command much smaller than the enemy's bomber force, but it was faced with greater operating difficulties. Targets in the British Isles were but a short distance from the German bomber bases in France and the Low Countries; for the British to attack targets in the German homeland involved much greater distances. They were also more difficult to find at night, particularly those in the Ruhr, whereas many British targets were conveniently situated close to coasts, alongside estuaries or on easily recognisable rivers. As is now indisputably known, and should have been gravely suspected then, only a small percentage of bombs dispatched to Germany fell within even five miles of their intended targets.

To expect much, then, from Cold Water was wishful thinking on the part of the Air Staff so far as the offensive operations were concerned. And the events of the past two months had shown that Fighter Command and the guns of AA Command were next to useless at night. The subsequent events of that night can have come as no surprise, therefore, to those in charge of the nation's defence.

With hindsight it would appear that the best feature of Cold Water was the plan to attack German bomber bases, but this should have been appreciated at the time and pursued with all vigour, using the full and undivided resources, for a while at least, of Bomber Command supported by suitable aircraft of Coastal and Fighter Commands. British Air Intelligence was remarkably well informed on the German Order of Battle and knew the location of every German bomber unit in the West. Most German airfields were within easy striking distance, the 'Y' Service knew precisely which airfields were to operate on any particular night, and the frequencies and callsigns of their locator radio beacons (capable of use by both British and German bombers for 'homing') were known. It should have been possible, therefore, to send a constant stream of British aircraft to patrol the German bomber bases with the aim of attacking flare paths (necessarily lit to facilitate departures and arrivals) and any aircraft seen in the air or on the ground. Such harrassment could only have had a serious effect on German bomber operations.

Operations of this nature were not new to the RAF although previously they had been on a small scale. 'Security Patrols', as they had been called, had earlier been flown over German bomber bases, but they were abandoned in favour of what are now known to have been futile attacks on Germany. Had they been expanded and maintained throughout the winter of 1940-41, whenever weather conditions were suitable, it is possible that the Night Blitz shortly to be unleashed on Britain as a whole, for Coventry was only the beginning, would have been reduced in its effectiveness and perhaps, at times, averted. Instead Bomber Command continued, in the main, to pursue a policy which, at this stage of the war, proved wasteful and largely ineffective. And British cities and their inhabitants were to pay the price.

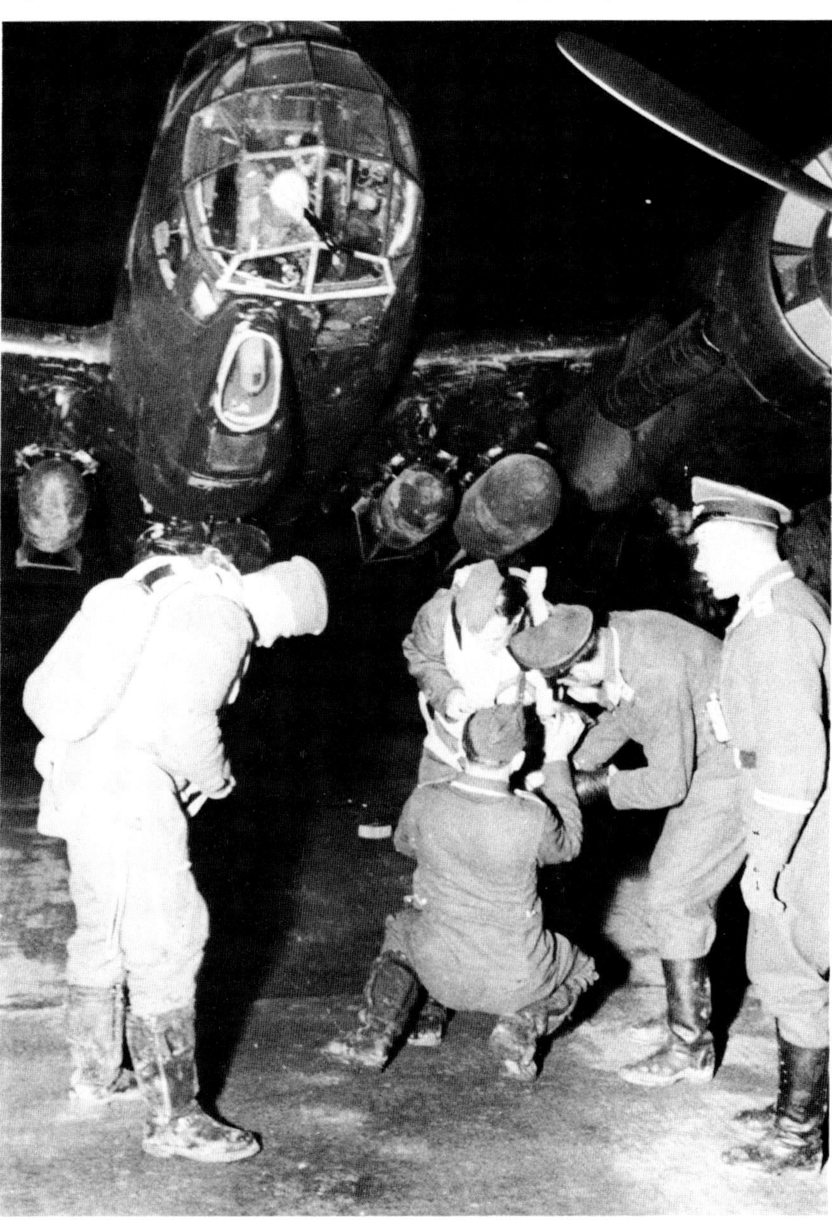

On German aircraft the navigator served in the dual rôle of bomb aimer. The Lotfe 7c periscope bombsight is visible through the Plexiglas front of the cupola beneath the nose. External bomb load consists of two SC 250s and two SC 500s.

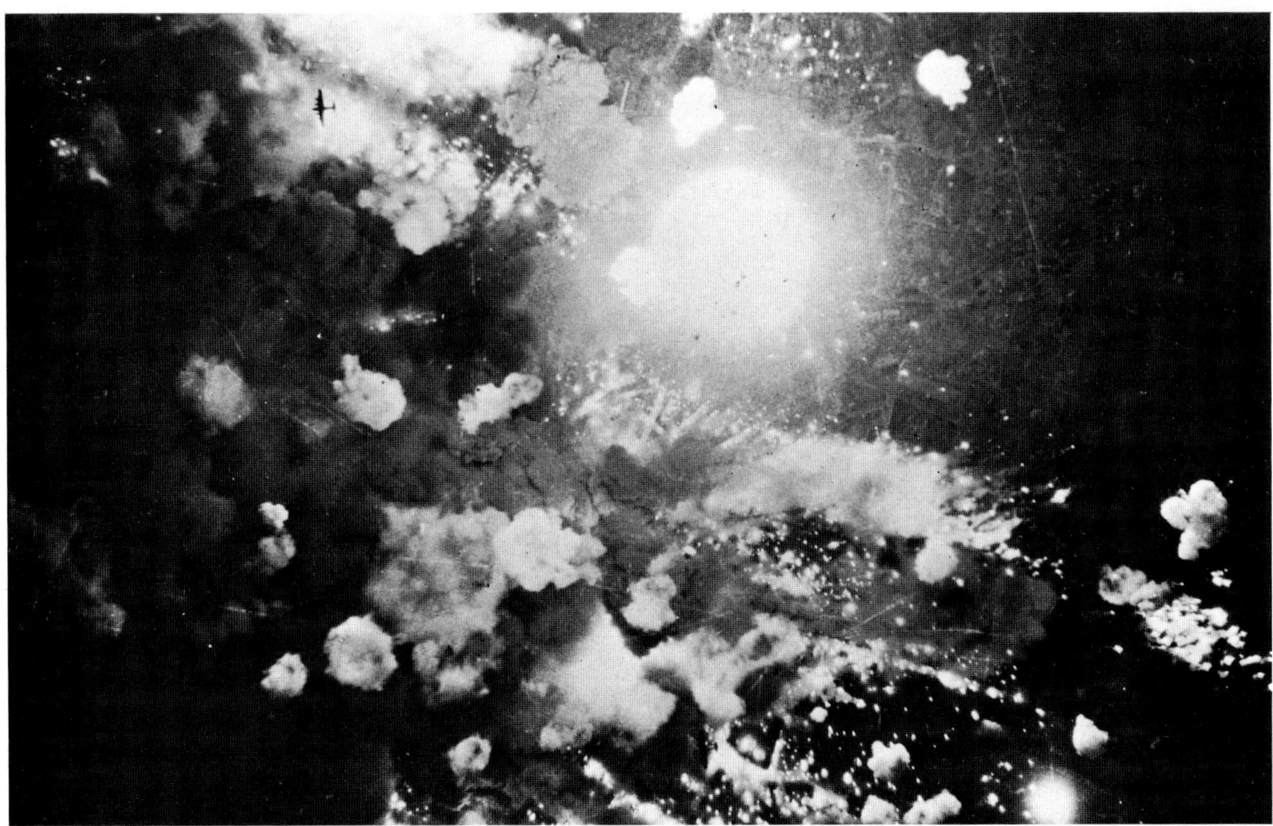

In the autumn of 1940 alterations in the top management of the RAF brought two significant changes to the leadership of the fighter and bomber arms. In came Air Marshal W. Sholto Douglas to replace Air Chief Marshal Hugh Dowding at the head of Fighter Command, while at Bomber Command Air Marshal Richard Peirse came to take over from Air Chief Marshal Charles Portal who became Chief of the Air Staff — the titular service chief of the RAF — on October 25. One of Portal's first directives was to set a 'winter priority' for targeting Germany, the main change being an implied, if not stated, acceptance of the inaccuracy of the RAF's night bombing. Facing reality, that it was just not possible to find and bomb accurately at night with the technology then available, henceforth the target — be it power station, oil refinery or gasworks — would be chosen because it was situated in a well-populated centre. As the RAF historian summed it up: 'While still intent on damaging individual factories, the Air Staff recognised that these were being hit less frequently than might appear from the crews' reports, and that at the same time some retaliation for the sufferings of British towns would not be amiss. Accordingly, they were now choosing, not merely profitable targets, but profitable targets in profitable surroundings. Likewise November saw an escalation of the concept of bombing areas rather than targets when Coventry became 'Coventrated' — a new word coined to express the apocalyptic obliteration of a city. When Bomber Command began to apply its increasing might to German cities, this led to the recording of scenes such as these when night photography by the bombers themselves was introduced in late 1941. Equivalent German night pictures of Britain, if they were taken, appear not to have survived.

On November 25 Air Chief Marshal Dowding was replaced as Air Officer Commanding-in-Chief, Fighter Command, by Air Marshal W. Sholto Douglas. Then, as now, this was seen as a controversial move, regarded by many as the shabby dismissal of the man who, above all others, had been responsible for the air defence system that had saved the country in the summer and autumn of 1940. But, be that as it may, the new air defence commander was a most capable officer and he immediately set about the task of continuing the battle against the night raider already set in train by his predecessor. Indeed, the very day after his appointment, the new AOC-in-C issued an Operational Instruction (No. 47) detailing a new experiment in night defensive operations.

The new directive called for the use of Handley Page Hampden bombers of No. 5 Group, Bomber Command, to maintain defensive patrols for the close protection of six nominated industrial centres (Coventry, Birmingham, Derby, Manchester, Sheffield and Bristol). The Hampdens reserved for this night fighting venture belonged to Nos. 44 and 49 Squadrons based at Scampton, Lincolnshire, but several other Hampden units were detailed for the rôle on a standby basis. When employed, the 'Hampden Patrol', as the operation was code-named, required the improvised night fighters to patrol for four hours within a radius of 10 miles of the centre of the target city. They were to fly with a vertical separation of 500 feet between each aircraft from 12,000 up to 20,000 feet; thus, 18 Hampdens were required for the operation and it was anticipated that they would reach their patrol area some 1½ hours after No. 5 Group received positive notification of the target for the night from Fighter Command. By arrangement with AA Command, guns were not to engage nor searchlights expose in the selected patrol area during the time that the Hampdens were in the area. However, time was to reveal the inadequacies of the plan. And no greater success was achieved by the Fairey Battle light bombers used by No. 29 Squadron to drop flares with the intention of illuminating enemy bombers so they could be picked off by the attendant night fighters. All the flares succeeded in doing, when they worked, was to give away the position of the Battle aircraft while lighting up the surrounding countryside for miles around.

Determined to explore all avenues Douglas, shortly to be promoted Air Marshal, called a Group Commanders' Conference on Friday, November 29. At this the AOC-in-C stated that at least 25 per cent of the total fighter force should be devoted to night fighting and it was unanimously agreed that the primary reason for the poor results obtained to date was the lack of night fighter facilities and the inadequate number of squadrons available. The Group Commanders expressed their views at length and, among other things, it was agreed that the bullet-proof windscreens of night-flying Hurricanes and Beaufighters should be replaced by clear vision screens to enhance visibility. It was also agreed to fit fishtail exhausts to Hurricanes and Defiants, together with exhaust shields, in an attempt to reduce glare.

At the same conference the GOC-in-C AA Command put forward a scheme to establish a number of GL stations in south-east England's Kenley Sector. Searchlights controlled by Elsie were to be used as visual pointers and with height information supplied by GL stations it was hoped to improve the interception rate on the approaches to London.

Various searchlight layouts were also discussed and it was finally agreed to adopt a 'carpet' system in Gun Defended Zones and 'clusters' of three or four lights in other areas. Douglas went on to outline the improvements planned for night fighter airfields and an improved disposition of night fighter squadrons.

Meanwhile, No. 80 Wing had been active in its attempts to unravel the mysteries of the various German radio navigational beams and to improve the effectiveness of its counter-measures. Several Aspirin anti-Knickebein transmitters were repositioned for ease of control and the first Bromide anti-X-Verfahren station at Hagley was joined by three more located at Kidsgrove, Kenilworth and Birdlip. The monitoring of German beam signals was further improved at this time by the take-over by No. 80 Wing of nineteen RAF and ten Royal Navy Watcher Stations, some of which were mobile units installed in RN vans. The control of the WIDU at Boscombe Down also passed to No. 80 Wing and on November 12 the first attempt was made by Whitley aircraft of this unit to bomb the source of the Cherbourg transmissions.

The capture of a crew from KGr100 on November 6 provided No. 80 Wing with some very useful information about the X-Verfahren. Interrogation by AI1(k) Branch, together with eavesdropping and the planting of a stool pigeon provided details of operating procedures and of the unit itself while documents found in the aircraft and the damaged X-Gerät, when recovered from the aircraft, enabled the counter-measures organisation to improve its jamming. Other captured documents enabled No. 80 Wing to publish a list of Knickebein stations with their code numbers and locations, and this also served to improve signals jamming. However, clearly the most effective radio counter-measure to date was the Meacon re-radiation of German radio beacons and to counter this interference the Luftwaffe started to change the frequency and call-signs of their beacons at irregular intervals, but all to no avail.

The 'Y' Service also continued to improve its monitoring of German W/T and R/T traffic and was able to pinpoint with uncanny accuracy the bases in use each night and the units operating from them. In this connection it is worth noting that Poix airfield, later to become of some importance as the main base of the Y-Verfahren equipped III/KG26, was first recorded in operation on the night of November 8/9.

During the month 54 German airmen fell into British hands as prisoners of war. The bodies of another 104 were recovered while 36 bodies from aircraft lost in October or earlier were washed ashore. These were lower figures than for some time past and were explained by the change from predominantly day to night operations and the subsequent reduction in losses that this occasioned.

The morale of German airmen captured during November remained high. One prisoner unhesitatingly declared his belief that 'England had no chance of winning the war'; he further claimed that the German Air Force had so far been restrained in its conduct of the air war against Britain and was capable of a much greater effort. Another PoW expressed the view that the eventual result of the war was a foregone conclusion, a view that was commonly shared and reflected the faith of German airmen in the invincibility of their armed forces and their Führer.

An analysis of about 20 PoWs showed that the ages of pilots were, in the main, between 21 and 24, but an Oberleutnant of 30, a Leutnant of 34 and a Feldwebel of 29 were shot down during the second half of the month. Many had served for four years or longer in the Luftwaffe.

KEN WAKEFIELD, 1986

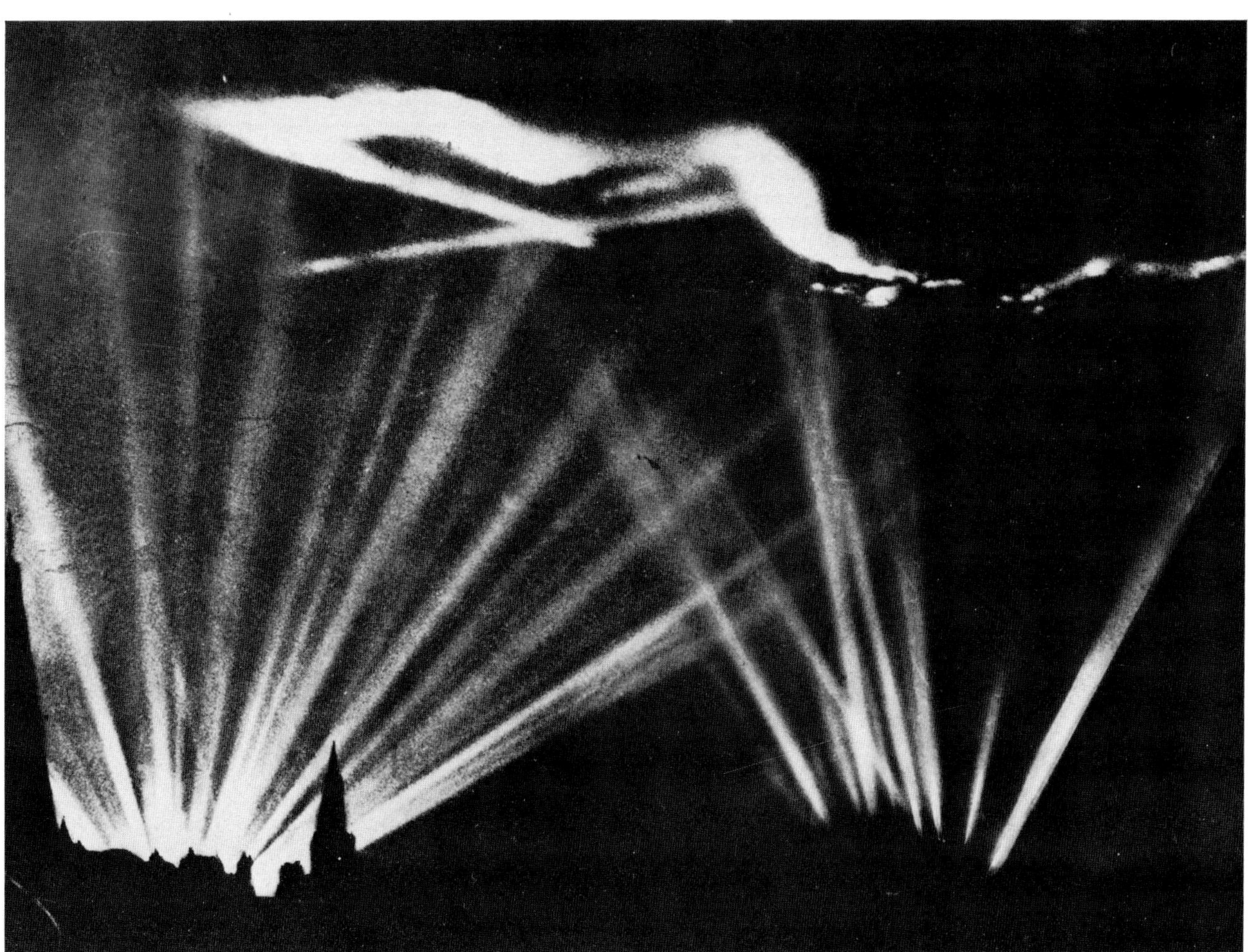

The night sky over London at the height of a raid, searchlights 'coned' for maximum effectiveness.

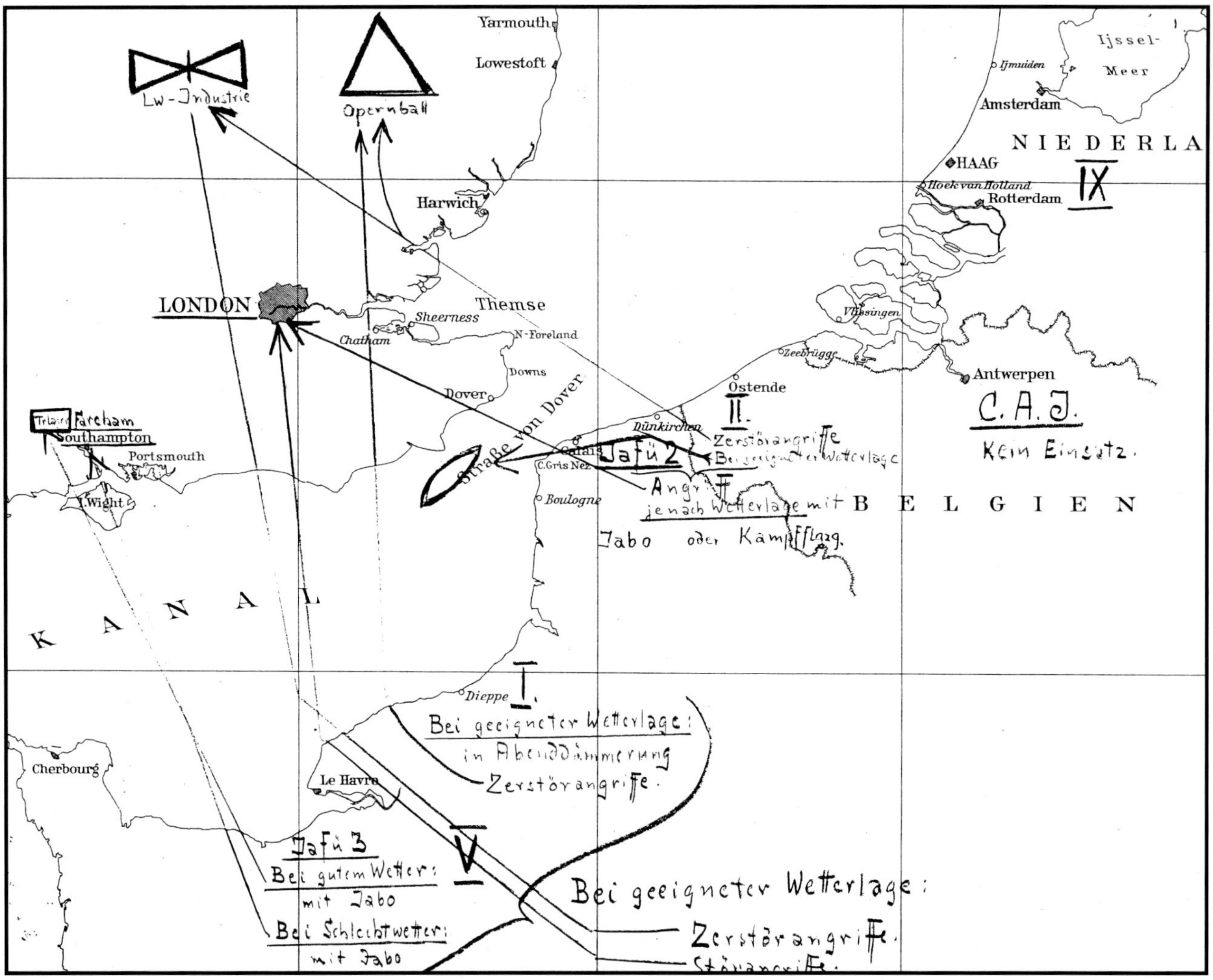

THURSDAY, NOVEMBER 14-15

Sunset: 1711 Sunrise: 0821
Moon: 1718-0817 (Full)

Major attack on Coventry. Minelaying on a small scale in the Thames Estuary and off the East Coast, Blyth and Dunbar.

UK — Mainly fair, becoming poor on the west coast of England and in Scotland. Little cloud with good visibility in the South and South-East. Mist and some fog patches towards dawn. Winds light westerly or calm.

The Continent — Mainly fair in all areas with small amounts of cloud and good visibility. Some mist later in the night.

The daylight hours were notable for three attacks on the South-East Coast, in the course of which 15 Ju 87 dive-bombers were claimed destroyed, with some 180 German aircraft reported over the country altogether.

The fourteenth of November — now synonymous with the destruction of Coventry — dawned fair over the Channel, paving the way for harrassing bombing attacks against London. The situation map shows fighter-bomber units of Luftflotte 2 and 3 so engaged, with a secondary operation 'Opera Dance', and fighters from Jagdfliegerführer 3 (i.e. JG2, JG27, JG53) attacking a troop camp at Farnham. Luftflotte 5 (off the map) were striking the Scottish east coast while the Italians (C.A.I.) had a day off.

An early morning loss was a Junkers of 3(F)/123 engaged on photo-reconnaissance over south-west England. Blue section of No. 152 Squadron from Warmwell both attacked the Ju 88 when west of Shaftesbury. Pilot Officer Marrs' attack set the port engine alight although his Spitfire was hit by accurate return fire. Oberfeldwebel Karl Hopf managed to turn southwards and had almost reached the coast when the aircraft plummeted into houses in Ringwood Road, Poole, setting several on fire and wrecking a garage containing a new car — much to the annoyance of the owner.

Meanwhile mechanics and fitters were making ready for the night's performance — given in German reports as being called both Moonlight Sonata and Moonlight Serenade. Whatever the music, it was scheduled to be played by some 500-odd bombers in the night sky over Coventry. KG51 *(above)* was one of the participants.

Night operations started at 1817 hours and although bombs fell at various points in the Midlands and elsewhere, the main concentration was on Coventry, where a considerable amount of damage was caused in what was the heaviest attack yet on a British target city. Bombing was almost continuous from 1920 to 0535 hours and the 449 aircraft which reached the Target Area dropped 503 tonnes of HE and 'Flambo', and 881 BSK (31,716 IBs). The Concentration Point encompassed the main aircraft and aircraft accessories factories and although 64 LC 50 flares were dropped, the full moon and especially favourable weather conditions rendered them almost superfluous. Most participating crews could make out their specific targets

SECRET COMMAND HEADQUARTERS DOCUMENT

Kampfgeschwader General Wever 4

Command Post – 13.11.40

Abt. Ia Nr.1334/40 g.K

4 Copies
Copy No. 2

Subject: Operational orders for: A) 'Mondscheinsonate'
B) 'Regenschirm'

I. *Enemy situation:*
See Enemy Information report KG4 No. 154 and 156, with sketch-plans, dispatched with KG4, Ic No. 3847/40, secret, dated 9.11.40.
Further enemy documentation, in particular regarding defence and searchlight installations, is currently to hand.

II. *Task:*
Subject to appropriate weather conditions, it is intended to carry out two operations similar to the London ones, in which all units of Luftflotten 2 and 3 will participate, against:
A) Coventry
B) Birmingham
These operations will constitute large scale attacks against an important part of the English war industry. It is my expectation that during these operations the crews will maintain their previous keenly aggressive spirit.

III. *Execution:*
1. *Actuation procedure:*
For the large A operation, the attack on Coventry, the code-word 'Mondscheinsonate' [Moonlight Sonata] will be used.
For the large B operation, the attack on Birmingham, the code-word 'Regenschirm' [Umbrella] will be used.
2. *Timing of attacks:*
Immediate implementation is to be expected.
Confirmation or cancellation of the operations will in each case take place up to 1200 hours before the night in question.
3. *Strength of formations:*
It is a question of committing as many planes as possible. Other assignments are to be postponed on the day of attack, and formations then at rest will likewise be drawn in.
4. *Targets:*
Care must be taken to see that there is appropriate dispersion of the formations when their attack begins, in accordance with the direction of the wind, in order that the entire target may be covered.
For attack A:
See moonlight chart 2.
Formations from IX Fliegerkorps will attack the respective entire target of Luftflotte . . . *
For attack B:
Entire target area, with concentrations on north-east, north-west and southerly sectors.
In addition to destruction of industrial targets, it is important to hinder the carrying out of reconstruction works and the resumption of manufacturing by wiping out the most densely populated workers' settlements.
Alternative target: Box
5. *Loading:* For each plane, two Luftmine, white.
6. *Attack times:*
KGr100 from 2030 hours to 2115 hours, in conjunction with Fl. Korps II and IX formations from 2115 hours to 2400 hours. Individual units are receiving further orders.
7. *Navigation:*
a) The crews with the best navigational qualifications will be committed first.
b) Flight routes, flight heights and attack heights will be itemised in further orders.
c) Navigational aids:
Long-distance radio beams 3 and 4 will provide target-aids as appropriate.
In addition, 'Elektra' and radio- and light-beacons will be available.
d) A new directional beam from the Helder area (detailed description follows) will likewise be operating as a target-aid.
8. Long-distance night fighters only in Anton area.
9. *Weather report:*
The KGr100 planes making the initial attack will report weather conditions from the target area.
Squadrons will listen to the weather reports from two ground-stations, and will pass on the weather conditions to the Groups by word of mouth.

IV. *Special instructions:*
During the preparatory period, crews will study the visual plans of the target with sufficient care to ensure that finding the target in entirely favourable weather conditions presents no difficulties.

Signed in draft
Rath
Correctness certified
[Signature]
Oberleutnant

* Apparent omission in German text

The reason for the raid stemmed from the fury with which Hitler had received an attack on Munich on the night of November 8 — the eve of the most important day in the Nazi calendar — der 'Neunte Elfte'. The 'ninth of the eleventh' was the day when all the old guard of the party would assemble with the Führer in the city to perform the annual memorial march in remembrance of the 16 of his followers killed in the putsch on November 9, 1923. The previous evening was always spent with beer and speeches in the Bürgerbräukeller, from where the marchers had set out, but a bomb planted in 1939 to kill Hitler at the November 8 meeting had wrecked the hall ***(left)*** **and killed seven of his supporters** ***(right)*****.**

In November 1940 the meeting had to be held at an alternative venue, the Löwenbräukeller. Coming exactly a year after the assassination attempt, it was a particularly emotional occasion, and one can imagine Hitler's wrath at the RAF's attack on that particular evening, no doubt assuming that it was a deliberate attempt to kill him — which it probably was! Anyway, since the British had started to bomb Germany at night, Hitler always began his speeches before it got dark, so the meeting was over before the bombers arrived. On the 8th he made his speech at 5.00 p.m., long before the RAF appeared, but the pounding Munich received that night aroused Hitler's ire. The choice of Coventry the following week was the result.

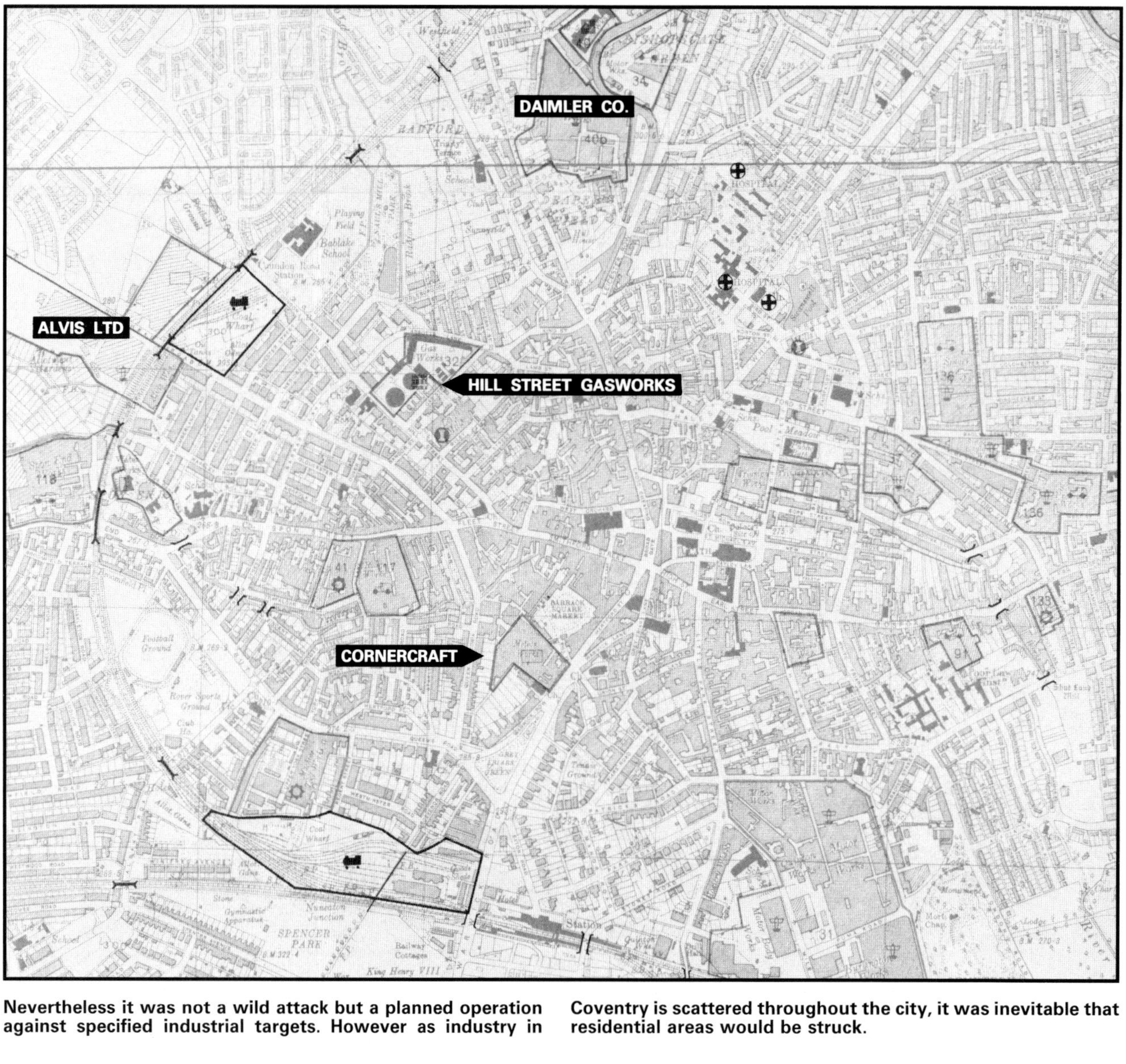

Nevertheless it was not a wild attack but a planned operation against specified industrial targets. However as industry in Coventry is scattered throughout the city, it was inevitable that residential areas would be struck.

Individual plants had the privilege of separate target maps, like the Cornercraft works which the Luftwaffe believed was producing aero engines. This was the target for Kampfgruppe 606.

without difficulty, enabling them to bomb visually and also check their results. Some 15 to 20 large and 40 to 50 smaller fires were soon reported and with the attack only one hour old crews reported that the entire inner part of the city was engulfed in a sea of flames. Crews with considerable operating experience over London stated that they had never previously seen results on this scale. Two night fighters were seen over the city and while the anti-aircraft guns put up a spirited resistance, the searchlights appeared weak and ineffective. Numerous decoy fires were also observed and on the approaches to the target crews reported various flashing light beacons, airfield flarepaths and other lights.

The attack — code-named 'Mondscheinserenade Korn' ('Moonlight Serenade Corn') was carried out by 145 aircraft of Luftflotte 2 and 304 of Luftflotte 3. Another 19 aircraft of Luftflotte 3 bombed alternative targets and the same number aborted for various reasons, mainly technical, while a total of 65 aircraft of Luftflotte 2 failed to reach the target. Altogether, then, the surprisingly high figure of 105 aircraft — or 18.6 per cent of the 552 bombers dispatched — failed to attack the assigned target. Participating units were as follows:

Luftflotte 3
I/LG1: 12 Ju 88, 0032-0050 (Standard Motor Co, and Coventry Radiator and Press Work Co. Ltd)
II/LG1: 12 Ju 88, 0103-0135 (western part of the town factory area)
III/LG1: 8 Ju 88, 0015-0145 (western part of the town)
I/KG27: 20 He 111, 2304-0028 (south-western area of the town)
II/KG27: 14 He 111, 2315-0105 (Alvis Ltd)
III/KG27: 13 He 111, 2307-0025
KGr100: 13 He 111, 1920-2005 (eastern part of town centre)
KGr606: 9 Do 17, 2250-2318 (5 aircraft to Cornercraft Ltd, 4 to the Hill Street Gasworks)
I/KG51: 16 Ju 88 0110-0200 (British Piston Ring Co.)
II/KG51: 10 Ju 88 0142-0235 (north-western area of the town)
III/KG51: 10 Ju 88 0215-0300
I/KG54: 11 Ju 88 0256-0400
II/KG54: 7 Ju 88 0352-0432
KGr806: 12 Ju 88 0352-0445
StSt/KG55: 2 He 111 2200-2230 (north-western part of the town)
I/KG55: 13 He 111 2300-0000
II/KG55: 16 He 111 2020-2055 (Maintenance Unit C)
III/KG55: 9 He 111 0005-0035 (Daimler Co.)
KG26: 28 He 111 2300-0242
KG76: 7 Ju 88, 13 Do 17 0135-0228
KG77: 25 Ju 88 0245-0510
KG1: 17 He 111, 7 Ju 88 0017-0235

Luftflotte 2
Units are not shown in German records but the following Gruppen were identified as operating by the RAF's 'Y' Service during the night of the 14-15th:
III/KG30, III/KG2, I/KG3, III/KG53

The leading German aircraft, first plotted by Fighter Command as they approached Lyme Bay, were 13 He 111s of KGr100 from Vannes. They arrived over the Target Area with intervals of three to four minutes between each aircraft and using X-Verfahren bombed the eastern part of the city centre with 48 SC 50s and 10,224 incendiary bombs. Units from Luftflotte 2 joined the initial phase of the attack and at 2020 hours the first

aircraft of II/KG55, Luftflotte 3's second Firelighter Gruppe, arrived over Coventry. After dropping parachute flares to illuminate the area, the He 111s of this unit then dropped some of the heaviest weapons in the Luftwaffe's armoury — five SC 1800s, eleven SC 1400s and five SC 500s, together with 64 50kg bombs of the SC and SD varieties and 2,412 incendiaries. More units of Luftflotte 2 continued the assault, with aircraft of Luftflotte 3 completing the final stages.

The last crews to leave the target were in no doubt of the unparalleled success of the attack on 'Korn'. Never before had an attack of such weight and intensity been unleashed against a centre of population and even the most experienced German airmen were staggered at the holocaust they produced. Willi Mahnke, the wireless operator in an He 111P-2 flown and commanded by Oberleutnant Klien of 6/KG27, had been engaged on operational flying since the first day of the war. He had taken part in the infamous attack on Warsaw and since then had completed many missions over Poland, France and Britain, including numerous attacks on London, but never had he seen anything like this. Nor was he to forget the sight and smell — from 10,000 feet it was possible to smell the burning city, and the fires could be seen for much of the return flight to Bourges.

The leading pathfinders from KGr100, navigating by X-Verfahren, arrived over the city at 7.20 p.m. Air Raid Message Red had reached the Coventry ARP Control Room just ten minutes earlier, the first marker bombs beginning to fall as the sirens died away.

Most participating crews had uneventful flights and when difficulties did arise they were mainly on account of weather conditions, natural hazards still proving more troublesome than the British night defences. This was discovered by Feldwebel Alfred Achtstelle, an observer with 5/KG53 making his first operational flight. At briefing that afternoon his Staffel was ordered to attack a water works on the west side of Coventry; taking off singly at one minute intervals they were to route from their base at Lille/Vendeville to the radio beacon on the French coast north of Dieppe and thence to intercept the beam of Knickebein III which would guide them to Coventry.

There was some mist in the Lille area and thin cloud in the lower levels, but the main cloud base over the Channel was at about 5,000 metres (17,000 feet). Achtstelle's pilot crossed the English coast at 4,500 metres (15,000 feet), tracking along the beam of Kn III until passing over South-West London when the signal faded. Circling around, in an attempt to pick up the beam signal again, the He 111 went into cloud and iced up rapidly. With ice accretion seriously affecting performance, the bomber lost height until, at about 4,000 metres (13,000 feet), it was decided to jettison the bombs in a bid to regain control. Level flight was then resumed and course set for Vendeville, where a safe landing was made without further incident.

The attack destroyed much of the heart of Coventry. There was considerable damage to industrial, commercial and residential premises, and electricity, gas and water supplies were seriously disrupted, as were road, rail and telephone communications.

Kampfgruppe 100 was backed up by Luftflotte 3's second Firelighter Group — II/KG55. KG55 aircraft, like these He 111Ps, had a unique night camouflage as the normal matt black distemper was applied in splotches over the side and upper surfaces as well.

COVENTRY

And now, comrades, you are acquainted with the nature and essentials of tonight's operation. Our task is, with other squadrons, to repay the attack on Munich by the English during the night of 8 November. We shall not repay it in the same manner by smashng up harmless dwelling houses, but we shall do it in such a way that those over there will be completely stunned. Even though the attack on Munich by the 'gentlemen' of the Royal Air Force was a complete failure, neither the Führer nor our Commander-in-Chief, Reichsmarschall Göring, is willing to let even the attempt at an attack on the capital of the movement to go unpunished, and we have therefore received orders to destroy the industries of Coventry tonight. You know what this means, comrades. This place is one of the chief armament centres of the enemy air force and has also factories which are important for the production of motor vehicles and armoured cars. Yes, it can be claimed to be the principal centre of the English automobile industry, and in particular, of the commercial vehicle industry. Quite a collection of factories for engines, engine parts and motor-cycles are also situated there. Amongst various other aircraft factories, the Rolls-Royce aero-engine works are specially noteworthy. If we can paralyse this armament centre tonight, we shall have dealt another heavy blow at Herr Churchill's war production. And that is not the least important purpose of the operation before us. We take off at 9.30. We shall not, of course, be the first squadron in order of flying, but there will still be enough left for us and the comrades who follow. But tomorrow morning the factories there must lie in smoke and ruins. We rest till 7.30. Then we get ready for the take-off. Well, comrades, 'good luck'!

PRE-FLIGHT BRIEFING 5.00 p.m. NOVEMBER 14, 1940

In January 1938 I moved from Romford and went to live in Coventry. I had secured a position in the Town Planning section of the City Engineer's Department and the increase in salary enabled me to get married. Life was pleasant in those days with good prospects of advancement and a steady career in Town Planning in a prosperous city but all that was to change with the coming of hostilities. My Town Planning work was suspended at short notice and, since I had been trained as a surveyor, my knowledge was put to use in assisting with the strengthening of basements of public buildings as protection against air raids and the construction of surface air raid shelters throughout the city. Both were regarded as a matter of urgency; Hitler had launched the Blitzkreig against his other enemies in Europe and it was expected he would not delay in taking action against this country.

We embarked on a programme of erecting surface shelters all over Coventry. These were of standard brick construction with a concrete slab roof. The bricks were bonded with sand and cement mortar. We were kept pretty busy in our permanent jobs but everyone was expected to take on war work of some kind and I joined a rescue party as a part timer, booking on duty at the Birley Road Depot every other night. We were given anti-gas instruction since it was thought that Hitler might employ gas warfare but we had no instruction in rescue work as such. We were expected to pick up what we could from watching the full-time teams mainly recruited from building workers, a sort of 'on the job' training except that there was nothing to do during those early days.

When the air raids started, many of the surface shelters split and collapsed because they were too rigidly constructed. Large chunks of masonry crashed down on the people inside and there were a number of fatal casualties. From then on, all new construction and repairs were carried out with the use of lime mortar which proved a safer method.

Then came the night of the major air raid on Coventry on November 14. I had been on duty with the rescue squad the previous night — this was my night off so I was at home. It was a bright, moonlit night and we just did not know what hit us. There was a roar of aircraft from about seven o'clock and then came the bombs, screaming down for hours on end. There was a terrace of four houses opposite our home hit by a bomb and demolished but, remarkably, no one was killed. All were sheltering in cupboards under the stairs; the party walls stood up and the staircases provided shelter from falling debris. How we got through that night I just don't know. It occurred to me that if the raid had been continued the next day we'd have to give up — we couldn't continue to carry on — it was nerve shattering. Most of the public utility services were cut off; those that had water had to boil it.

I went up to the city centre next morning to report to my rescue team and was given the job of searching through the debris of a demolished building. After a time I uncovered the body of a young woman and, nearby, that of a small child. It seemed the natural thing to place the infant in the arms of the woman and they were taken away to the mortuary together. Then we came across an old man — white hair and beard, lying pinned under a beam and obviously dead. When we moved the beam we saw that his body had been consumed by fire.

After we had finished there we went on to a place called Greyfriars Green, a four-storeyed terrace. It was all on fire and had partially collapsed. We were told that people were trapped in a basement shelter. Water from the firemen's hoses was coming down boiling hot through the fire as we made our way through the debris towards the shelter. Eventually, we came to a wall; the rescue leader banged on it, shouting 'Anybody there?' We got a reply.

'Yes, there's twelve of us here. Please come and get us out.'

Then a policeman apppeared.

'Come on, out you come. There's an unexploded bomb at the back and another at the front. Don't hang about.'

So we had no option but to abandon any further effort. Three days later, when the UXBs had been rendered safe, I heard that one old man had been brought out alive from that basement and I found that experience deeply depressing. We had been close enough to speak to them but could do nothing to help.

Another recollection I have is of a marvellous lady, Councillor Mrs Pearl Hyde, who was awarded the OBE for her services during the war. She was always in the thick of the action, helping in every way possible. This night I was working at an incident involving a bombed pub and had been handling a very messy body. Pearl Hyde came along and offered me a cup of tea which I was unwilling to accept because of the state of my hands, so I hid them and got her to hold the cup to my lips. We became rather callous — I think we had to be.

It was said in some quarters that the bombing was indiscriminate but our survey showed that the Germans had attacked targets with the object of doing damage to industrial installations. Of course, surrounding dwellings were demolished but, by and large, their aim was to destroy industries maintaining the war effort.

Then came a follow-up to the major Coventry raid in the following April. It was not so heavy or sustained but was a very sharp attack for all that and caused many casualties.

Some time later my call-up papers arrived and I became a member of the Airborne Forces.

REGINALD KING, 1986

The Unteroffizier and the Unterfeldwebel climb through the hatch into the body of the Ju 88: Oberleutnant Schmidfeder casts a glance over at the other aircraft, then follows his men.

The leading aircraft is airborne; soon the second follows. And now on to 'Bruno's' turn. The take-off is signalled and with engines roaring the Ju 88 shoots, bouncing and staggering over the aerodrome. Unterfeldwebel Handorf gently pulls the control column towards him, the bouncing ceases and the plane is in the air. Unteroffizier Bergengrun [the gunner] stands at his combat post at the rear, peering out into the dark night. Stars twinkle between jagged cumulus clouds floating across the sky only a little higher than the aircraft. Far away over the flat land the horizon can be picked out. Below everything is black-out. Now and then a faint shine sweeps over the land marking the straight ribbon of some road, ghostly visible to the airman's keen eye. Then everything is swallowed up again in the darkness. Oberleutnant Schmidfeder squats on his seat examining his map by the light of a small screen lamp. It is a street map of Coventry; all important objectives are marked with red circles. The light is switched off in the pilot's cabin; only the Oberleutnant's lamp and the blue light from the instrument board spread a faint gleam. The guttural tones of the R/T sound from time to time. Schmidfeder acknowledges in slow drawn-out sentences. Otherwise it is quiet except for the steady drone of the two powerful engines.

The enemy coast is not far away now; ahead the chalk wall of the steep cliffs shimmers indistinctly below. And now, in the distance, gleams the light of fires. The flight continues over enemy country, with course set for the Midlands. Now searchlight cones flit pointedly and hastily across the sky illuminating the cloud cover with a bluish tinge, stopping here and there, searching for minutes on end. From time to time they cling for a few seconds to one of the attacking aircraft, but the German aircrew bring them quickly and skilfully out of reach of the dazzling beams. A searchlight has caught Schmidfeder's aircraft and crew twice already. Each time Handorf pulls the rudder round with a quick jerk, works the ailerons putting the aircraft on its wing tips and dives away sharply into the darkness, 200 or 250 metres height are lost. Then, climbing again to over 2000 metres, weaving to and fro, but always getting right back on course: the aircraft roars unchecked towards its target. From time to time the Oberleutnant sees from port or starboard one of the other aircraft belonging to his Staffel flash suddenly in the cone of searchlights and dive away again just as quickly into the darkness. Irresistibly the aircraft press on towards their common objective — Coventry.

The aircraft are now over the edge of the city and far away stretch the plants of Coventry's engine and armament industry, a part of it already in bright flames. There lies the target: a large factory block. The giant chimneys stand dark and rigid in the bloody cloud of the neighbourhood; the plant down below stands out as bright as day in the light of the flares, muzzle-flashes show up on a few roofs, but the shells from the flak burst wide. Schmidfeder pulls the bomb lever. The Oberleutnant sees clearly in the last flicker of the dying flare the heavy bombs whistling down as Handorf banks the aircraft on its wing tips and makes a sharp curve. A few seconds later bright flames shoot up from the dark buildings; blazing columns of smoke and flame grow mushroom-like to cover the battered workshops and serpent up almost to the height of the Ju 88. A faint smell of burning penetrates through the cracks in the thick glass plating of the rear turret. Both bombs have found their mark. Handorf has brought the aircraft back over the target in a wide sweep; two heavy bombs still wait in the racks to complete their mission. This time there is no need for the Oberleutnant to drop a flare; the fires make the target area as light as day. The still undamaged buildings stand out dark against the red glare of the fire . . . two giant workshops still remain. A tug at the bomb lever, a sharp turn of the aircraft and the second bomb load whistles earthward. Once more a red fire glows steeply upward; here is another factory that will do no more war work for Herr Churchill.

Dense smoke clouds billowing higher and higher above the industrial quarter hide the view of destruction. The flat cloud cover which still lies at about 3000 metres above ground level has now assumed a red background, changing to a reddish colour here, to a greyish red there. Searchlights and the glowing path of tracers still flash almost invisible in the red reflection of the fires. Fresh hits flash in the distance as further waves of attacking aircraft arrive over their objectives. In front of 'Bruno', its nose set on course for the coast, the night sky lies dark under the cloud cover which still shimmers faintly red above the aircraft. Handorf sets his machine back on the old course, guiding himself by burning Coventry whose glimmer dies gradually away in the mist behind. Down below lies the dark English countryside only interrupted from time to time by some gleam of fire. Only rarely does the finger of some searchlight flit across the sky. The flak has died down too. The Channel coast must soon be in sight.

WAR BOOKS OF THE GERMAN YOUTH
CARL G. P. HENZE

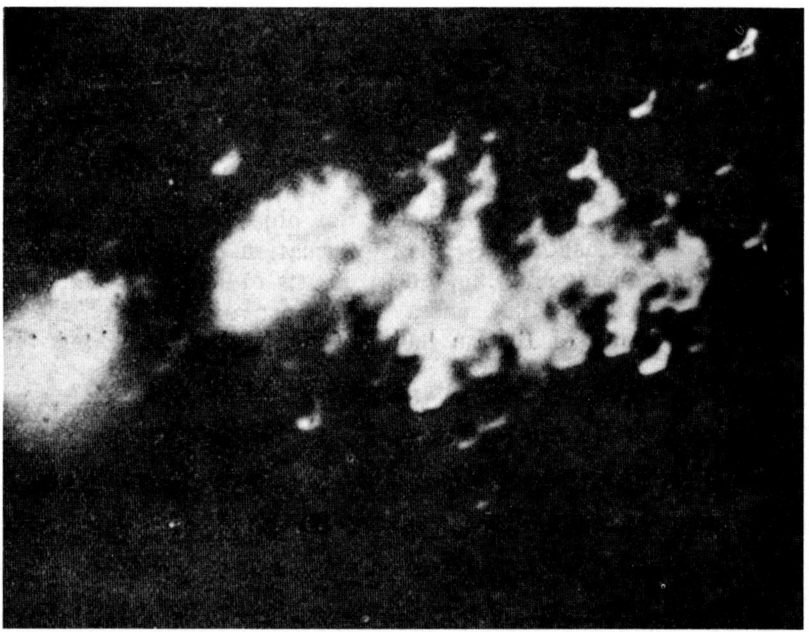

This picture, released in Germany, purports to show the fires soon after the raid began.

'The principal damage occurred in the medieval centre of the city. Of this at least one-third is completely destroyed, mainly by fire, and probably another third will require extensive rebuilding. The remainder of the city was extensively plastered with bombs of all types diminishing towards the outer suburbs. An inspection on foot was made of the commercial and shopping area round Broadgate. As far as I could judge, an area of about 600×400 feet had been completely destroyed. The principal buildings in the three street blocks in this area were Market Hall, Fish Market and cinema and Lion Iron Foundry. All these buildings were entirely destroyed. Lloyds Bank and the National Provincial Bank were extensively damaged by fire. Barclay's Bank had a direct hit with a 250kg bomb at the back of the banking hall, but were doing business on Saturday. In Hertford Street, the Empire Theatre, two hotels and the Central Post Office were either destroyed or seriously damaged. The department store of Messrs Owen and Owen, a new four-storey and basement steel-framed building, had received a direct hit from a large bomb and had also been gutted by fire.' Ministry of Home Security report, Saturday, November 16.

The same vista today. The old Market Hall with its characteristic tower has been replaced by Broadgate, and Owen and Owen's on the right — Coventry's most famous department store — replaced with a new £1 million building.

Those firemen ordered to the huge blaze at Owen Owen's, seen burned out here on the right, attended what became known as the second most 'famous' fire in the city that night — after that of the cathedral. George Kyrke was a member of the AFS: 'When we arrived the building was well alight. All doors were locked. An iron grille delayed action by us. By the time we gained entry we realised that it was impossible to save the place from the inside so we played on the fire from a hydrant outside. We had lost all notion of time but it must have been about midnight when we saw an object which appeared to be attached to a parachute falling in our direction. Four of my crew ran for shelter into Millets Stores' doorway, so Charles, my deputy, and I took over the hose and continued to damp down the raging fires. A terrific explosion threw us to the ground and when we recovered ourselves, very dazed but not seriously hurt, we found the rest of the crew had disappeared. Charles and I tore away bricks, stone and rubble and after what seemed an interminable time we managed to free one of the buried crew. He was still alive and asked for a cigarette but before we could light it, he died. We struggled with our pump but could not get it going; it was badly damaged. Then, climbing over the piles of rubble, we found a pump at the bottom of Cross Cheaping unmanned. Using the murky water of the River Sherbourne we managed to get the pump working, only to be foiled by leaking hose. There was nothing we could do so we decided to return to the Central Station — if it was still there.'

While bombing was well concentrated on the centre of the city, there was also damage in surrounding areas. In Coventry itself 525 incidents were reported and well over 200 fires were burning at one time. Casualties were heavy, with 554 people killed and 865 seriously injured. Many factories important to the war effort were damaged or destroyed and thousands were rendered homeless. In addition, the destruction of many retail shops subsequently made difficult the distribution of food and other essentials. And, of course, the interruption to gas and electricity supplies stopped production at a number of factories which had escaped serious damage, but this was a short term problem only for supplies were quickly reinstated. Outside of the Coventry area minor bomb damage was reported at Birmingham, Leicester, Chester, Wrexham, Bournemouth, Portsmouth, Leamington, Crewe, Stoke-on-Trent, Sheffield, Lincoln, Derby, and in various parts of London.

Mondscheinserenade Korn had gone much as forecast by British Air Intelligence, but despite foreknowledge and the implementation of Cold Water, the attackers achieved their aims with very little interference. By 1900 hours all AA guns in No. 11 Group, except those at Chatham and the Vange, were in action against unseen targets and

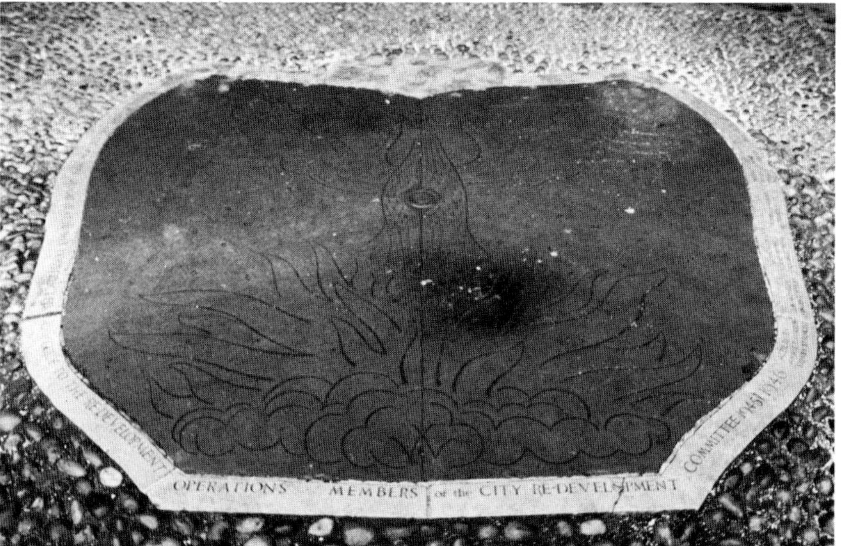

The reconstruction of the city began on Victory Day — June 8, 1946 — with the laying of this levelling stone in the city centre bearing the design of a phoenix rising symbolically from the ashes. The intention was that every level for the rebuilding work would be taken out from this central point.

BBC interviewee: 'There was a mist over the town as men and women began to crawl out of their shelters, look for their friends and survey the ruins of their city. They could hardly recognise it. Remnants of walls with their ragged brickwork stood up like drunken sentinels helplessly guarding a scene of chaos. Hardly a building remained intact. It was impossible to see where the central streets we knew so well had been. Fires were still raging in every direction and from time to time we heard the crash of a fallen roof or wall. Up to that night we were surprised if we heard that this or that building had been hit. That Friday morning we were surprised to hear that a building hadn't. And as we walked round the ruined streets we hardly knew what to do. It seemed so hopeless with our homes and shops and so much of our lovely old city in ruins. You might say we were dazed.' ***Left:*** **The troops arrive to give practical help and moral support to the shattered civil population.** ***Right:*** **A Ministry of Information loudspeaker van broadcasts instructions for obtaining food and shelter.**

eventually sites from Merseyside in the north to Portland in the south were in action. Approximately 16,000 rounds were fired by AA Command's heavy guns including some 7,000 by the 4th AA Division (covering north-west England and the Midlands) and 4,989 by London's Inner Artillery Zone (IAZ). The Coventry Gun Operations Room was hit and local communications were severed, but nevertheless the city's guns claimed one enemy aircraft destroyed. This proved to be a Do 17Z of 6/KG3 that crashed near Loughborough at 2200 hours after being illuminated by searchlights and hit by HAA gunfire as it approached the city, one engine being seen to stop. It was the only loss sustained during the night by the German Air Force.

In accordance with the dictates of Cold Water, aircraft of Bomber and Coastal Commands were dispatched to attack German-occupied airfields. Fires and explosions were reported at Vannes/Meucon, the base of KGr100, Melun, Chartres and elsewhere, but these operations did little to interfere with German operations. Greater concentration on the 20 or so main bomber bases by the entire British bomber force, spread throughout the night, would doubtless have achieved more disruption and, in some cases, perhaps the cancellation of operations. Instead, much of the British bomber force ranged far and wide over Germany and the occupied countries, achieving little success anywhere in attacks scattered from Berlin to Lorient and losing ten aircraft in the process.

The defensive operations of Fighter Command proved no more successful. Not one of the 124 night fighters sent up on patrol reported a successful encounter with the elusive enemy. A Blenheim of No. 12 Group fired on an enemy aircraft which it claimed 'damaged' and another aircraft of the same type from Wittering fired without apparent effect on an He 111 that passed beneath it, but altogether it was a most disappointing night for Fighter Command, illustrating yet again the almost total impotence of the night fighter force.

An apparently successful part of Cold Water, however, was the attack on the Cherbourg Knickebein transmitter by two Whitleys of the WIDU. Tracking in along the beam towards the station, bombs were released upon reaching the overhead 'cone of silence' position and shortly afterwards the German transmissions ceased for the remainder of the night.

No. 80 Wing was busily engaged on radio counter-measures throughout the attack and all possible action was taken to counter Knickebein, X-Verfahren and radio beacon transmissions. However, the bright moonlight and generally good visibility in the Target Area rendered radio aids to navigation superfluous.

1840 *Bramwell on duty.*
1850 *Entwhistle on duty.*
1905 *No. 5 Post reported (. . . Fry & Field).*
1912 *Red (Public Warning). Bright Moonlight (Full Moon and stars showing clearly.*
1920 *Incendiaries from NE to SE completing circle later from SE to NE all round city. Large fire developed 47°.*
1930 *Inner circle of incendiaries catching Cathedral, Palace Yard, Broadgate, Barclay's & Owen Owen, all round tower.*
1931 *HE's Corporation Street, Foleshill & Radford.*
1932 *No. 3 report fire Pool Meadow Area. Confirmed as Gasometer Fire (Gas Street).*
1940 *Cathedral blazing fiercely. HE's all over and around City Centre.*
1941 *No. 7 Post reported change of phone for the present.*
2030 *No. 6 report small red flashes from behind St Paul's Tower, Foleshill, about 100-200 ft. Light soon goes. Also seen by No. 1 Post (Entwhistle) in centre of town while explosive incendiaries were bursting around, coming from all directions. (Entwhistle) No. 1 Post sees Land Mine coming down by parachute.*
2056 *Phone out of order and tower vacated!*
2059 *(Entwhistle) No. 1 Post revisits Tower and reports huge fires, many HE's, Land Mines, etc., and vacates tower.*
2100 *Tower hit by HE?*
2130 *Building shook many times and fires are being allowed to burn and develop as Fire Brigades have insufficient water pressure, owing to mains being hit.*
0012 *Light failed! The city is now without electricity, gas, water and many roads are blocked.*
0015 *Fires developing, all over city centre and uncontrolled!*
0016 *Part of Cathedral roof falls in.*
0650 *Bramwell and Entwhistle signing off (after white).*
Note: *The night has been one of a very intensive raid of between 400 to 500 instances, 20 Land Mines, HE's and UB very large quantity, incendaries in huge numbers. (11 hours continuous intensive bombing.)*

The main feature has been lack of water for fire fighting. The Cathedral, Jordan Well, High Street, Broadgate, Palace Yard and Bayley Lane suffered mainly fire damage. (Could have been avoided and some of these buildings saved had an adequate water supply been available?)

Finally No. 1 Post Tower requires checking to ascertain whether now safe after tonight's hit.

Log book taken away for safety and will return later.

J. B. BRAMWELL, THURSDAY, NOVEMBER 14, 1940

Above: **The barren centre of the city after its clearance.** *Bottom:* **The design for its reconstruction was the brainchild of Donald Gibson, and in May 1948 Princess Elizabeth opened the new Broadgate — the first new city centre of its kind in Britain.**

Coventry is of course Lady Godiva country and it is fitting that her legendary naked ride through the streets — a dare against which her husband, the Earl of Mercia, promised to free the town from its heavy taxes — is commemorated right at the heart of the worst of the bombing. The church is Holy Trinity, which came through almost unscathed.

The Council House and Police Station, with coats still hanging unharmed on the back of the second floor door; a freakish event but not at all an uncommon sight during the Blitz. At the end of the street the most famous — or infamous — ruin of all those in Coventry — the cathedral. Its destruction has since made it one of the world's best known symbols of the Blitz . . . and its post-war replacement a renowned symbol of international reconciliation.

Without doubt the most successful branch of the defending forces was the RAF's 'Y' Service, which monitored German W/T traffic throughout the night and, indeed, during the preceding and following daylight hours. At about 1300 hours German W/T messages were intercepted, which, after Enigma decoding, gave details of VHF beam bearings. When plotted these gave a clear indication of the target for the forthcoming night and by 1500 hours, with River beams confirmed as centred on Coventry, all RAF Commands and the Ministry of Home Security were advised accordingly. Final confirmation was provided by 80 Wing's measurement of actual beam bearings as they were set up.

Daylight on Friday, November 15, revealed scenes of utter devastation, with much of the city centre little more than a mass of smouldering rubble. The population, shocked and dejected, were aided by emergency services and the army, and many who had lost their homes were evacuated. Others, whose homes were still intact, deserted the city in fear of a second, follow-up attack the next night, but there was a quick recovery of morale and by the 16th there was a general return to the stricken city.

The RAF crash examiners' investigation of the sole German loss of the Coventry raid — the Do 17Z that crashed near Loughborough — yielded some pertinent information. Despite the burnt out state of the aircraft, which had burst into flames upon crashing, careful sifting by the examiners produced a map and several documents including the navigation log. These revealed that the departure point was Antwerp, from where the route was to the radio beacon at Schouwen and thence to join the Knickebein II beam at a point off Orfordness for Coventry. A sketch map revealed that the target was a large group of buildings situated about 1,000 yards east of

Fires still burning, unchecked, all around the city centre, craters and rubble in the streets.
The devastation is indescribable.
Service personnel make their way slowly over the debris.
No one speaks.
My personal feeling is one of sadness.
Then, I recall the starling trilling a few notes of song as Entwhistle and I left the Council House this morning. Did the heat of the fires make the bird think it was spring, or could this be a message of hope for the future?

J. B. BRAMWELL, FRIDAY, NOVEMBER 15, 1940

For upwards of half a millenium St Michael's Cathedral had stood at the centre of the city; more a part of Coventry than Coventry itself. Of Britain's 59 cathedrals, St Michael's was the only one to suffer destruction on such a massive scale. This was the view from the doorway beneath the tower, the doors having been completely burned from the ironwork.

'Towards eight o'clock the first incendiaries struck the cathedral. One fell on the roof of the chancel towards the east end; another fell right through the floor beneath the pews at the head of the nave, near the lectern; another struck the roof of the south aisle, above the organ. The bomb on the chancel was smothered with sand and thrown over the battlements. The bomb on the pews was large and took two full buckets of sand before it could be shovelled into a container. The bomb above the organ had done what we most feared — it had fallen through the lead and was blazing on the oak ceiling below. It took a long time to deal with. The lead was hacked open and sand poured through the hole, but the fire had spread out of reach. We stirrup-pumped many buckets of water before the fire ceased blazing. Another shower of incendiaries now fell, penetrating the roof of the Cappers' Chapel on the south side and the Smiths' Chapel on the north side. These were ultimately subdued. Then another shower of incendiaries fell, four of them appearing to strike the roof of the Girdlers' or Children's Chapel above its east end. On the roof, smoke was pouring from three holes and a fire was blazing through. These were tackled by all four of us at once, but, with the failing of our supplies of sand, water and physical strength, we were unable to make an impression; the fire gained ground and finally we had to give in.' Provost Rev. R. T. Howard.

The day following the raid — even as fires were still burning in other parts of the city — a decision was made that a new cathedral should one day be built. When that might be no one could foresee; meanwhile the two underground chapels were repaired and refurbished — one as 'the cathedral', the other as a Chapel of Unity for all Christians — and a restoration fund opened. In the ruin itself two charred timbers — one of twelve feet, the other of eight — were erected at the east end: an epitome of 'the old rugged cross'. *Left:* This is the ceremony held on the sixth anniversary — November 14, 1946 — by which stage some £95,000 had been received towards the rebuilding fund. *Right:* Unfortunately fear of its theft led to the removal of the original cross in 1978 to the undercroft of the new cathedral, with a near replica put in its place.

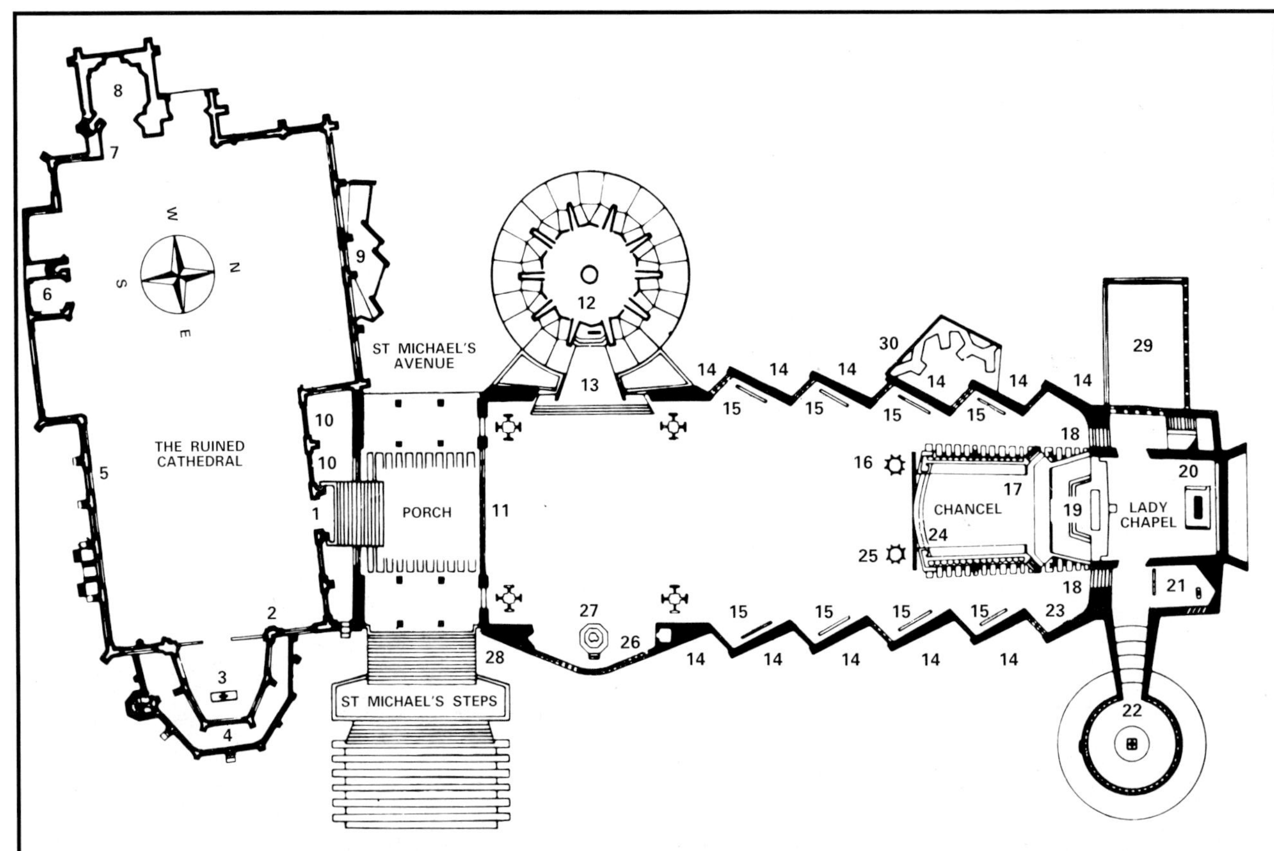

With St Michael's destruction having become a symbol of the wastefulness of war, the decision was taken to retain the empty shell alongside the new cathedral which was built — unusually — on a north-south axis. 1 The Queen's Steps; 2 Figure of Christ; 3 Charred cross; 4 International Centre; 5 'Ecce Homo'; 6 Haigh Chapel; 7 Gift shop; 8 Tower; 9 Gift shop; 10 Crypt Chapel entrances; 11 'West' window; 12 Chapel of Unity; 13 Head of Christ; 14 Nave windows; 15 Tablets of The Word; 16 Pulpit; 17 Bishop's Throne; 18 Organ; 19 High Altar; 20 Tapestry; 21 Chapel of Christ in Gethsemane; 22 Chapel of Christ the Servant (Chapel of Industry); 23 Plumbline and the City; 24 Provost's stall; 25 Lectern; 26 Baptistry window; 27 Bethlehem font; 28 St Michael and the Devil; 29 Restaurant; 30 Ruins of the church of St Mary's Benedictine monastery (1043).

At first Basil (later Sir Basil) Spence's design, selected from over 200 entries in 1951, was labelled as a 'concrete monstrosity', 'an aesthetic outrage', and 'the ugliest building in the Midlands'. Work on its construction had commenced as a priority in 1954 at the urging of the Minister of Works who declared that 'the cathedral is not a building which concerns Coventry and Coventry alone. The echo of the bombs which destroyed your city was heard round the world. We cannot tell how many people are waiting in this country and abroad for this church to rise and prove that English traditions live again after the Blitz.'

Humber Lane and just to the south of the main road to Binley. The height flown on the outward leg was 11,700ft and the attack height was to have been 6,500ft; the return flight was to be made at the same height, descending to 3,500ft after crossing the coast. The Kn II beam was aligned over Coventry from 1800 to 2200 hours with Kn V serving as the crossbeam. The aircraft was scheduled to be in the Target Area from 2120 to 2129 hours, but clearly was running late on this timing as it did not arrive over the Coventry area until nearly 2200 hours.

A paper, believed to belong to the pilot, gave the names of two Italian officers, and even this proved of value to AI1(k) — the interrogation of an Italian PoW revealed that both belonged to 243 Squadriglia of the CAI, flying Fiat BR 20 bombers based at Chiévres.

Eight 50kg bombs that did not explode in the crash were found near the wreckage.

Eight years later the building was completed and consecrated on May 25, 1962 in the presence of Queen Elizabeth and Princess Margaret whose father had stood in the ruined cathedral the day after it had been destroyed. Now the remains of the old were retained and incorporated as a vital adjunct to the whole concept of the new.

'In the background stood a mechanical trench-digger and groups of soldiers and labourers who had been working throughout the night at the grim task of carrying the coffins. When all was ready we moved in order towards the gate to meet the crowd of mourners, who were led up the road through the cemetery by a contingent of police, firemen and wardens. Then at the top of the rise the bishop and clergy, followed by the civic officials, took the lead to the graveside. It was a quiet and solemn procession. The soft beat of the rubber boots of the firemen, the measured tread of the police and wardens, marching in step across the gravel path seemed to accentuate the silence. At the graveside it was possible to turn and look back over the long line of mourners still approaching. It was a pathetic sight; women carrying wreaths; here and there a child with a bunch of flowers; the black suits and dresses relieved occasionally by a splash of colour of the uniform of a husband, a son or brother on compassionate leave. It seemed as if there were no end to this long dark line, which moved slowly across the grass. At last the great crowd was gathered around the graves. The Roman Catholic priest stepped forward and, hardly lifting his eyes from the book, read the service. Men and women in the crowd knelt on the grass or clay and crossed themselves. Then the Bishop stepped forward and a simple but dignified service followed. The Free Church ministers offered prayer expressing the thoughts and moods of those sorrowing folk. The service concluded with one or two beautifully phrased prayers of the English Prayer Book and the Blessing. The Mayor, carrying a wreath, led the mourners up and down the long gravesides, and as they followed they laid their wreaths and dropped their posies and sprays into the graves. Some peered anxiously at the bloodstained labels attached to the coffins to see if they could see the name of their relative or friend; most of the names were indecipherable. In the distance a Spitfire wheeled and twisted; the sound of its engine came fitfully to us down the wind.' Rev. Leslie E. Cooke.

The official death toll, not finalised until long after the raid, after much cross-checking, was 568 killed with another 863 seriously injured.

In 1951 a new garden layout was designed surrounded by a low stone wall to replace the mounds which had become overgrown and were difficult to maintain. The formal dedication ceremony of the memorial, to all the civilian war dead of Coventry, took place on the anniversary of the raid the following year.

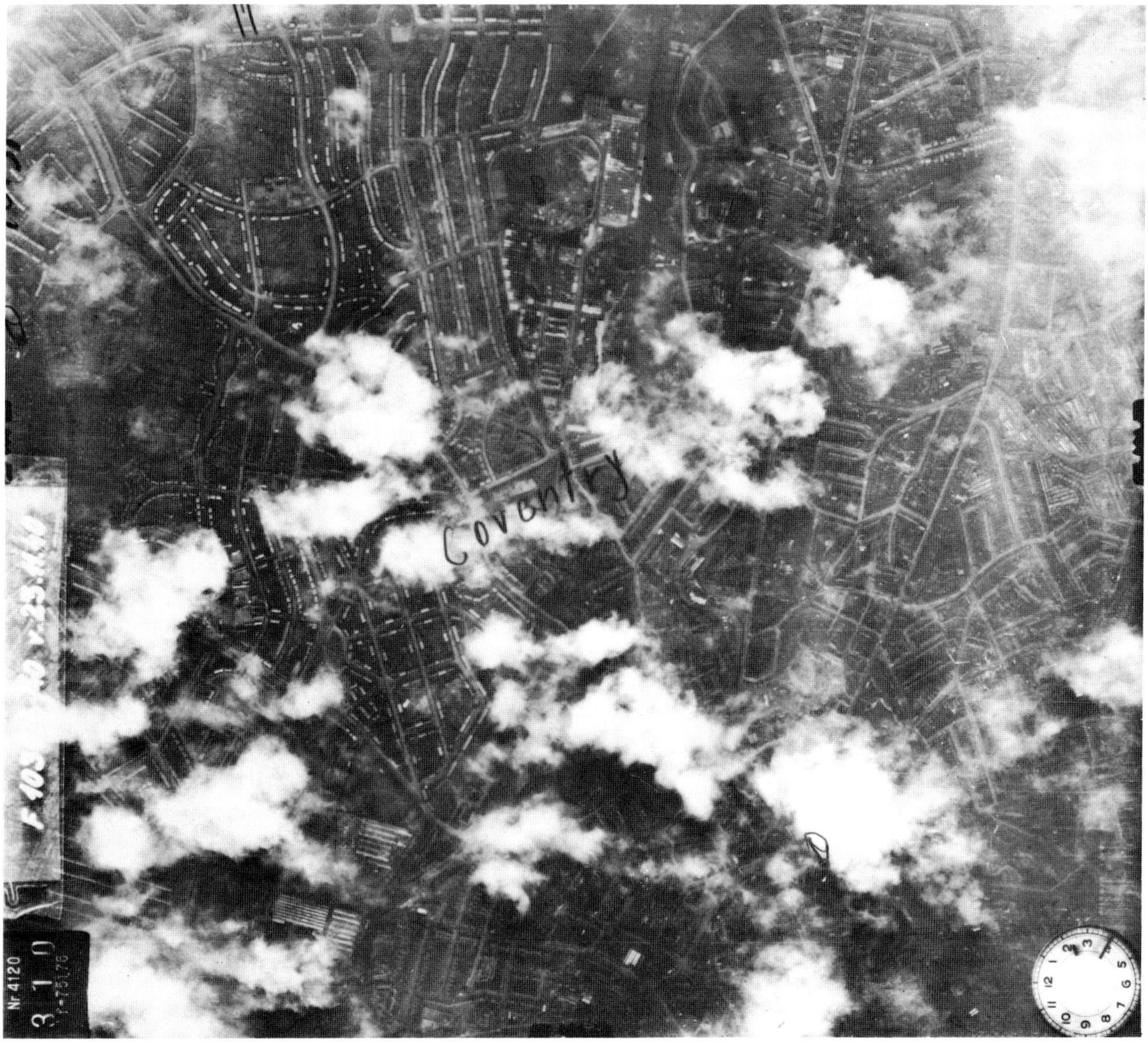

There were two mass burials, the first on Wednesday November 20 (illustrated *opposite*) for 172 of the dead, followed by an even larger ceremony for 250 on Saturday 23rd — the same day that Luftwaffe reconnaissance aircraft were over the city assessing the damage. *Above:* This picture shows the north-western part around Coundon with the Alvis factory in the bottom left-hand corner. *Below:* Before and after. This is what is now the famous Jaguar car factory at Browns Lane, Allesley.

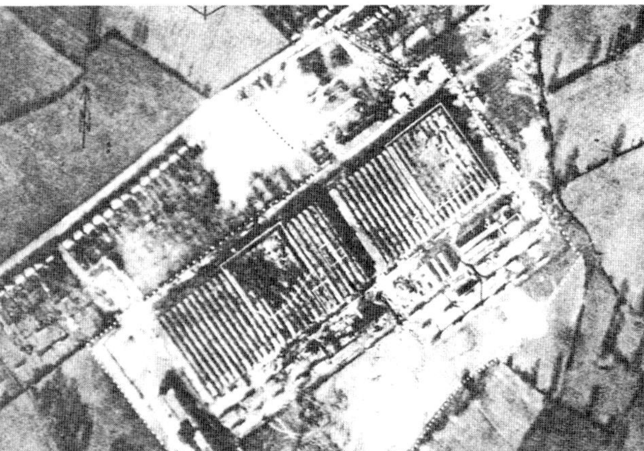

COVENTRATED. Well, who did invent the word which henceforth was to colour the language of total war? *The War Illustrated:* '"Coventrated" is what the Nazis called it. Gloating over the death and destruction wrought at Coventry by their aimless bombing, the Nazis invented a word for this perversion of aerial warfare. Historians of the future will point to the contrast presented by the work of RAF Bomber Command whose precise and effective attacks on military objectives are the marvel of military experts.'

COVENTRIERT. On November 15, 1940 the German High Command issued this communiqué: 'The non-stop attack of strong formations under the command of Feldmarschall Kesselring was particularly successful. Numerous factories making aircraft and other factories important to the war effort were bombed with bombs of every calibre. The utmost devastation was caused. After this large-scale attack which was an answer to the British bombing of Munich the English invented a new word, "to coventrate".

The four aircraft lost on daytime operations are all detailed below.

3(F)/123 Junkers Ju 88A-5 (0454). Crashed at the rear of Moore's Garage and numbers 465 and 467 Ringwood Road, Poole, Dorset, following action with the Spitfires of Pilot Officer E. S. Marrs and Sergeant A. W. Kearsey of No. 152 Squadron over Poole 9.40 a.m. Aircraft exploded and damaged Moore's garage and several houses. Oblt. A. von Kügelgen baled out but his parachute failed and his body went through the roof of the Kinson Pottery building. Fw. J. Duckgeischel, Fw. K. Löhn and Oberfw. K. Hopf killed in the crash. Aircraft 4U+FL destroyed.

1/JG51 Messerschmitt Bf 109E-4 (6266). Shot down by the Hurricanes of Flying Officer R. G. A. Barclay, No. 249 Squadron and Flight Lieutenant N. W. Burnett, No. 46 Squadron. Crashed in flames at Sacketts Hill Farm, St Peters, Broadstairs 2.45 p.m. Fhr. E. Vortbach, pilot, burnt to death in wreckage, shot in head and believed to lie buried at Cannock Chase as an unknown airman. Aircraft White 8+ destroyed.

9/StG1 Junkers Ju 87B (0436). Shot down during a battle over a convoy off North Foreland 2.19 p.m. Obergefr. H. Bietmeyer believed taken prisoner. Obergefr. J. Schmitt killed. Aircraft J9+ZL lost.

9/StG1 Junkers Ju 87B-2 (5641). Shot down two miles off South Foreland during a battle over convoy 'Booty', 2.30 p.m.. Oberlt. O. Blumers baled out, picked up by a motor torpedo boat and taken into captivity. Gefr. W. Koch killed. Aircraft J9+BL lost.

Lost during the night of the 14–15th:

6/KG3 Dornier Do 17Z-3 (2892). Shot down by AA fire and crashed at Prestwold Hall, Burton on the Wolds, Loughborough 10.00 p.m. Oberlt. O. Preiss, Fw. K. Dilthey, Uffz. G. Kuhne and Obergefr. W. Wellenbrock killed. Aircraft 5K+BP destroyed.

The four crew members remain buried in Loughborough Cemetery,

Site investigated by Peter Felix of the Derbyshire Historical Aviation Society, who recovered various surface fragments. Propellor blade taken at the time retained by the landowner.

In all, 449 aircraft reached and bombed Coventry; the 450th — the only one to be brought down that night — ended up here in the grounds of Prestwold Hall, Burton on the Wolds — 30 miles north of the city.

Ernest Parker, ex-Auxiliary Fire Service, was one of the crewmen on duty that night and when news of the crash reached his unit they rushed to the scene . . . only to find that they had been beaten to it by the Loughborough brigade, already busy putting out the fire. 'The plane had lost one wheel in one field,' remembered Ernest when he took us to the crash site, 'and it careered across into another, scattering bombs all over the place. An engine was blown into a clump of trees but we could not stop as we were sent on our way by the regular firemen.'

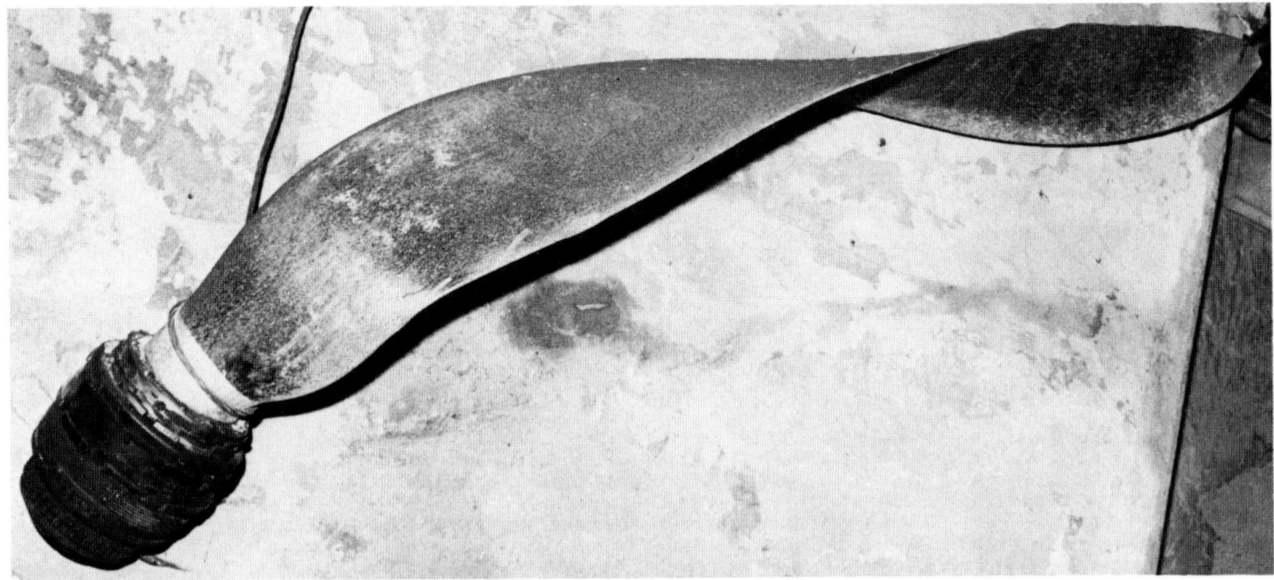

The only relic which has survived from a Coventry raider — a prop blade still hanging in one of the stables of the Hall.

FRIDAY, NOVEMBER 15-16

Sunset: 1709 Sunrise: 0821
Moon: 1752-Dawn (Full+1)

Major attack on London with a harassing attack on a very small scale against Coventry. Minelaying in the Thames Estuary, off Deal, Lowestoft and in the mouth of the Humber.

UK — A frontal belt of rain with low cloud (base 600ft) moved north-eastwards across Britain, followed by showery conditions with fair periods. Visibility moderate, poor locally becoming good generally after the passage of the front. Winds south-east to south-west, light to moderate but freshening, especially on coasts.

The Continent — Mainly fair but deteriorating as the belt of rain moved eastwards across northern areas.

Daylight activity included two attacks on the South-East, one on Southampton and another on the Isle of Wight, followed by an afternoon attack on London. Altogether 18 German aircraft were claimed destroyed for the loss of two RAF fighters.

Night activity was heavy and continuous from 1750 to 0400 hours and even persisted through a spell of bad weather which moved across Britain from 0200 hours onwards. A few aircraft penetrated to the Midlands while others, which crossed the Norfolk coast, attacked airfields in and around the Home Counties. London, however, was the centre of attention and suffered a very heavy attack by Luftflotten 2 and 3.

With unfavourable weather closing most Luftflotte 3 bomber bases in western France for much of the night, the attack was opened by aircraft of Luftflotte 2 from bases in Holland and Belgium, supported by some units of Luftflotte 3 based in central northern France. After midnight, with the weather clearing from the west, Luftflotte 3 joined in the attack in force, 238 of its aircraft reporting over the target compared with 120 bombers of Luftflotte 2. Kampfgruppe 100 did not operate, presumably because of weather conditions at Vannes, but II/KG55 was out in force.

The 358 bombers which reached London dropped 414 tonnes of HE and Flambo (including 18 bombs of the heaviest type) and 1,142 BSK (41,112 IBs). Nine LC 50 flare clusters were also dropped for target illumination. The Concentration Point for the bombing lay in Zielraum (Target Area) 'O' which covered the Government offices quarter between the City, Hyde Park and the Albert Bridge and included that part of London on the north side of the Thames from Fulham to the West India Docks.

A solid layer of cloud over London meant that many crews were forced to bomb by dead reckoning or radio navigation methods, but numerous fires could be discerned towards the end of the attack. Through occasional breaks in the cloud it was also possible for some crews to report certain incidents such as an SC 500 exploding in the vicinity of Paddington Station, a huge sheet of flame from a gas works in Kennington and a direct hit on the pumping station at the water works installations of the Northern Sewer Outfall between West Ham and Beckton. Waterloo Bridge was also claimed to have been hit and there were reports of some 20 expanding fires and ten large explosions.

Of the 261 aircraft dispatched by Luftflotte 3, 16 aborted, six bombed alternative targets and one was reported missing. The attackers comprised:

I/KG1: 4 He 111, 0447-0636
III/KG1: 13 He 111, 0000-0100
KG76: 12 Do 17, 2245-2336
KG77: 15 Ju 88, 1859-2047
KG26: 26 He 111, 0100-0343
LG1: 29 Ju 88, 0041-0220
I/KG27: 20 He 111, 2320-0048
II/KG27: 20 He 111, 2310-0110
I/KG51: 7 Ju 88, 0225-0330
II/KG51: 6 Ju 88, 0340-0420
III/KG51: 7 Ju 88, 0240-0310
Stab/KG51: 1 Ju 88, 0255
I/KG54: 11 Ju 88, 0457-0525
II/KG54: 5 Ju 88, 0535-0615
KGr806: 10 Ju 88, 0305-0410
Stab/KG55: 2 He 111, 2350-2355
I/KG55: 6 He 111, 2248-2310
II/KG55: 17 He 111, 2210-2240
III/KG55: 10 He 111, 0005-0035

Their bomb loads included six SC 1800s, 12 SC 1400s, 20 SC 1000s and 107 SC 500s, but no details of participating units of Luftflotte 2 and their bomb loads are available.

In view of the adverse conditions over the capital it is not surprising that bombing was widespread, with 40 London ARP districts reporting incidents. Most damage, however, occurred in the West End and the eastern suburbs. Parachute mines (presumably dropped by units of Luftflotte 2) were reported to have added significantly to the heavy damage, and casualties were heavy, with 142 persons killed and more than 430 injured. Seventy-six of the London Region's 95 boroughs were bombed and buildings damaged included Westminster Abbey and School, the National Portrait Gallery, Wellington Barracks and four hospitals. Nearly 30 incidents affected railway traffic and Euston Station was badly damaged, while at the Mount Pleasant GPO sorting office an unexploded SC 1800 — one of the first of these huge weapons to be encountered by the Bomb Disposal Squad — caused many problems.

Mondscheinserenade Loge, as it was codenamed, was the most intense raid yet experienced by London; a dozen or so factories were hit and commercial and residential premises suffered extensively at Laindon, Twickenham, Bushey, Hornchurch, Bagshot, Tunbridge Wells, Fareham, Dagenham, White Waltham, Finchley, Tottenham, Kensington, Malden, Willesden, Bethnal Green and Wandsworth. Elsewhere

No. 84 Cecil Avenue, Gidea Park, Hornchurch — bombed on November 15 killing Mr and Mrs Arthur Eke outright.

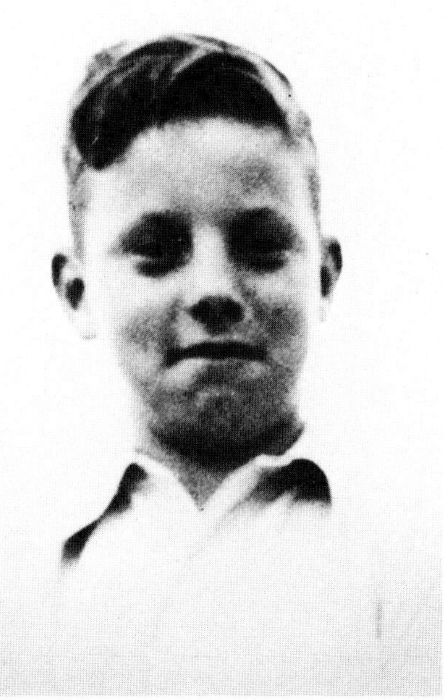

How proud mum and dad would have been to see their son Ron, 13 years old, receive the Boy Scouts' highest award for bravery 'in recognition of his heroic fortitude and thoughtfulness for others when he was fatally injured during an air raid on Hornchurch'. Ronald died the following day in Harold Wood Emergency Hospital; the posthumous award of the Bronze Cross being confirmed on January 1, 1941.

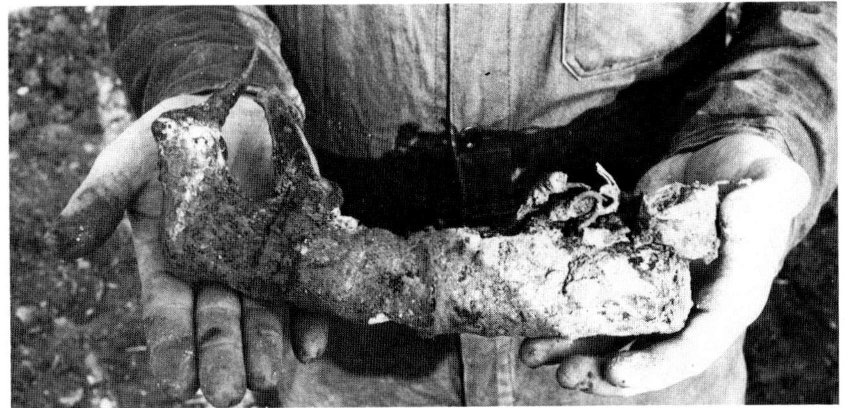

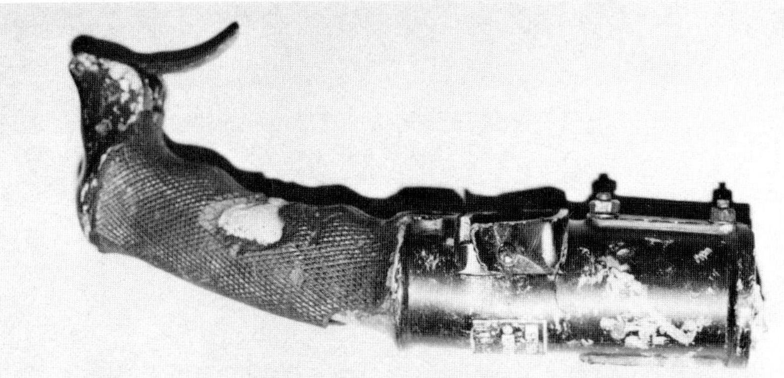

During the daylight battles over south-west Essex that Friday, a Messerschmitt 109 plunged into the ground near Horndon on the Hill. After an attempt to excavate and recover wreckage in 1973, the most highly prized trophy of all to aviation archaeologists — the joystick — came to light twelve years later. Here ex-Feldwebel Oswald Jaros examines items recovered by the Essex Historical Aviation Society.

bombs fell at Kettering, Derby, Royston, Bridgenorth, Mablethorpe, Swinderby, Kimbolton and Hawarden airfield, where an enemy aircraft made two bombing runs, dropping eight HEs and incendiaries from 5,000 feet and slightly damaging the water and heating systems in one hangar. Only slight damage was done at one or two other airfields, attacked, presumably, by some of the seven night fighters of the Nachtjagd-division which were roaming over the United Kingdom in search of British bombers and their airfields.

The attack on Coventry was carried out by only seven of the 16 aircraft dispatched. They bombed between 1940 and 2145 hours, dropping seven tonnes of HE and 32 BSK (1,152 IBs), but no results were observed by the German crews because of the adverse weather. In fact, little damage was done, but in the Birmingham area Great Barr railway station was hit and fires were started at Mosley and Edgbaston. Damage was also reported at Little Barford, near St Neots, with more fires at Leighton Buzzard and near Henlow airfield. Incendiaries and an HE also fell on Bournemouth.

To counter the German attack more than 10,000 rounds of HAA ammunition were expended nationwide, with 9,347 being fired within the IAZ. British aircraft raided enemy airfields at Stavanger in Norway and at Doullens, Cambrai, Saint-Malo and Rennes in northern France, but with most of Bomber Command's effort directed against Hamburg, Kiel, Ostend and Calais, German bomber bases suffered little harassment.

Night defensive patrols were flown by 28 fighters, comprising six Hurricanes, eight Defiants, three Beaufighters and three Blenheims of No. 11 Group, five Blenheims and a Hurricane of No. 12 Group and a Gladiator and Hurricane of No. 14 Group; because of unfavourable weather, night fighters of No. 10 Group did not operate. Two enemy aircraft were seen but only one was intercepted and this was lost in cloud. However, it was claimed as probably destroyed. AA guns were in action at Coventry, the Solent, Bramley, Birmingham, Farnborough and the London IAZ, with the latter claiming an enemy aircraft destroyed at 2342 hours. No night fighters were lost in action but Defiant N1569 of No. 264 Squadron was damaged when it taxiied into a bomb crater at Southend (Rochford) airfield, and Beaufighter R2084 of No. 219 Squadron was destroyed when it spun in on the approach to land at Kenley. Another Defiant (N1547) of No. 264 Squadron was destroyed when it struck some trees while approaching to land at Rochford after an operational patrol. One crew member was killed and the other injured.

An interesting incident occurred on the night of November 15-16 when He 111H-2, the A1+LN of 5/KG53, crashed near Bridgenorth. It was not, however, shot down, but crashed following a loss of control brought about by severe icing. Piloted by Leutnant Karl Svatha, the A1+LN departed Lille/Vendeville and was the second or third aircraft of twelve taking off from this base at two minute intervals. Initially flying at 10,500ft, the coast was crossed at Dover where the apparent proximity of barrage balloons caused the pilot to climb to 17,000ft. Although Kn III was aligned on Coventry, Svatha decided to disregard it and fly visually, for it was a clear night, but approaching the Target Area, where they were to bomb an aircraft factory, they ran into cloud and began to ice up. Nevertheless, the Coventry target was claimed bombed as planned, but just after turning on course for the return flight the aircraft became completely uncontrollable and was abandoned from 20,000ft. The aircraft broke up in the air at a considerable height and pieces were scattered over a wide area with some falling five or six miles from the main wreckage which came down at 0030 hours. Svatha and his observer, who was making only his second operational flight, landed safely and were taken prisoner but the other two crew members were killed.

Many attacks on south-east England during the day resulted in the loss of seven aircraft over Britain.

1(F)/22 Messerschmitt Bf 110 (2205). Crashed into the sea off Southend 10.39 a.m. Claimed by Southend AA battery and by Spitfires of No. 19 Squadron. Uffz. J. Boschen killed (originally buried at Southend). Lt. H. von Jakob baled out and captured. Aircraft 4N+BH lost.

1(F)/22 Messerschmitt Bf 110 (2242). Shot down by Spitfires of No. 19 Squadron and crashed into the Thames Estuary between 9.44 a.m. and 11.30 a.m. Fw. O. Kaiser and Gefr. H. v.d. Sande missing. Aircraft 4N+DH lost.

4/JG2 Messerschmitt Bf 109E-4 (5949). Shot down by Sergeant J. N. Glendinning in a Spitfire of No. 74 Squadron 4.15 p.m. Aircraft fell in shallow water at Felpham, near Bognor Regis, West Sussex. Uffz. R. Miese injured but baled out and was taken prisoner. Aircraft White 10+ destroyed.

3/JG26 Messerschmitt Bf 109E-4 (1250). Following fighter action aircraft made forced landing at RAF Eastchurch, Isle of Sheppey 1.45 p.m. Oberfw. R. Schiffbauer taken prisoner. Aircraft Yellow 2+ captured damaged.

3/JG26 Messerschmitt Bf 109E-4 (6353). Shot down by Sergeant E. W. Wright of No. 605 Squadron and crashed at Blackbush Corner, Horndon on the Hill, Essex 1.33 p.m. Fw. O. Jaros baled out and taken prisoner. Aircraft Yellow 9+ wrecked.

Excavated by Grays Thurrock enthusiast Dave Campbell in September 1973, when the engine, armour plate and a substantial amount of airframe were recovered. Re-excavated by the Essex Historical Aviation Society in September 1985, when the control column and main aircraft identity plate confirming identity '6353' were unearthed. Engine badge subsequently found on the surface by Brian Sadler.

4/JG54 Messerschmitt Bf 109E (1501). Believed that which crashed in the sea off Shoeburyness 11.00 a.m. Oberfw. P. Hier killed. Aircraft White 11+ lost.

5/KG3 Dornier Do 17Z-3 (2894). Crashed into the sea one and a half miles off Copt Point, Folkestone, Kent 9.30 a.m. Shot down by Sergeant D. A. S. McKay in a Spitfire of No. 421 Flight. Oblt. B. Buttker, Obergefr. H. Erwin killed. Fw. H. Lembke and Gefr. O. Fritz missing. Aircraft 5K+FN lost.

Almost like the landing spot of an extra-terrestial meteorite, the smoking crater on Latton Priory Farm signifies the Valkyrian end for one of the raiders of the night. All five crewmen perished when their Dornier smashed to pieces a couple of hundred yards from the ancient priory.

There were two losses over Britain during the night of the 15-16th:

5/KG53 Heinkel He 111H-2 (5509). Aircraft iced up at 20,000 feet and broke up in the air. Tail fell at Spoon Hill Wood, engines at Rutnoll and the fuselage at Derrington, near Brown Clee Hill, Shropshire 10.05 p.m. Lt. K. Svatha and Fw. A. Achstalle baled out and were taken prisoner. Uffz. J. Mutzl and Fw. H. Engelken killed. Aircraft A1+LN destroyed.

Site excavated by a local Vicar in the presence of a television crew. Parts of navigational instruments in the Warplane Wreck Investigation Group Museum. Items also featured in the Hodgkiss Collection.

9/KG76 Dornier Do 17Z (2798). Shot down by fighters and AA fire during a raid on London. Crashed at Latton Priory Farm, Rye Hill, Harlow 11.55 p.m. Lt. B. Wagner, Fw. R. Grömmer, Uffz. W. Hockendorf, Fw. A. Haas and Gefr. F. Heilig all killed. Aircraft F1+BT destroyed.

Although the bodies of four of the crew were removed to Cannock Chase in the mid 1960s, that of Fw. Grömmer does not appear in the burial register.

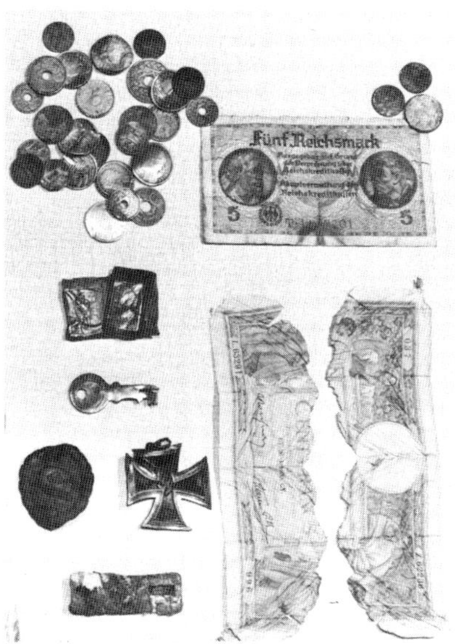

This site, like many other wartime crashes hurriedly dug up in the 1970s, has also been re-excavated at a more leisurely pace in later years. ***Left:*** **Relics from the first and** ***right*** **the second investigation.**

Site excavated by the London Air Museum. Some items, including personal effects, now on display at the Tangmere Military Aviation Museum. Re-excavated in 1984 by local enthusiasts, when further remains were unearthed.

Stanhope Row, Mayfair: before, after and now. Here 60-year-old Mrs Florence Hearn was grievously injured on November 16, succumbing to her wounds the same day in St George's Hospital.

SATURDAY, NOVEMBER 16-17

Sunset: 1708 Sunrise: 0823
Moon: 1832 — Dawn (Full+2)

Heavy attack on London. Minelaying on a small scale in the Thames Estuary, between Flamborough Head and the Tyne and in the mouth of the Humber. Slight activity over airfields in eastern England.

UK — Rain with low cloud and poor visibility in the South, improving towards dawn. In the North some mist or fog patches giving way to deteriorating weather, spreading from the South-West. Winds moderate to fresh, variable becoming westerly.

The Continent — Low cloud and strong winds, improving from the West.

During daylight hours only some 50 German aircraft were reported over Britain and most of this activity was concerned with reconnaissance and anti-shipping patrols.

Night operations were on a comparatively small scale with only 117 aircraft of Luftflotten 2 and 3 operating, and there was no activity at all between 0100 and 0400 hours. Low cloud, rain and poor visibility were no doubt contributing factors, but nevertheless London was attacked by 87 aircraft between the hours of 1745 and 0615. They dropped 104 tonnes of HE, including 28 very heavy bombs and a number of Flambo, and 68 BSK (2,448 incendiaries). As on the previous night, the Concentration Point lay on the north side of the Thames between Fulham and the West India Docks, with the principal target the City and Government buildings in the area bounded by Charing Cross, Hyde Park and the Thames. Despite the poor weather, crews reported seeing three large fires in the principal Target Area after the first stage of the attack and by the end of the second stage, at 0615 hours, four large and numerous small fires. By this time visual bombing was possible, but crews over the target in the first wave were forced to resort to radio and DR navigation. The following units took part, with bombing times as indicated:

Luftflotte 2
The crews of 35 aircraft reported over the target, but the units involved are not known.

Luftflotte 3
52 aircraft dispatched with seven aborts and one missing:
KG1: 10 He 111, 10 Ju 88, 1815-1910
KG1: 6 He 111, 0605-0628 (second sorties)
KG77: 13 Ju 88, 1755-1915
KG77: 5 Ju 88, 0528-0615 (second sorties)

From this it can be seen that crews of six He 111s and five Ju 88s flew double sorties. The missing aircraft, an He 111 of I/KG1, had sent a W/T message stating that it was flying over England on one engine; it subsequently crashed in Kent, claimed by the light AA machine gun of searchlight site DG43 which had illuminated the low flying raider.

Between 0100 and 0400 hours there was no activity at all over the UK, no doubt because of the low cloud and fog which prevailed over much of the country. Nevertheless, 22 fighters flew patrols during the hours of darkness. One Beaufighter was lost in a crash at Barkston, but without serious injuries to the crew. Another Beaufighter claimed the destruction of an He 111 near Colchester, but this cannot be substantiated.

AA guns were in action at Slough, Brooklands, Fareham, Bramley, Holton Heath and, in the London area, in the IAZ and at Thames and Medway North. Some 5,000 rounds were expended.

Damage was fairly widespread, despite the reduced scale of operations, and parachute mines were reported in several areas. Six fell on Southampton, causing 78 casualties and much damage to private houses, but London received comparatively little damage, with no reports of serious incidents affecting industrial plants. Bombs also fell at Uxbridge, Portsmouth, Thetford, Beaconsfield, Fordingbridge, Barton, Honington, Aylesbury and Market Harborough. More 'land mines' were reported at Rickmansworth, Beckenham and West Ham, and bombs fell in the vicinity of airfields at Eastleigh, Woodley, Tangmere, Ford, Croydon, Broxbourne, Odiham and Northolt, but only Brandon was actually hit.

Bad weather over most of Europe severely restricted the scale of effort, only one aircraft was lost from the 79 that attacked London.

1/KG1 Heinkel He 111H-3 (6897). Shot down by light AA fire and crashed at Palmtree Cross Roads, Woodnesborough, Kent 8.50 p.m. Lt. H. Pranesberger, Fw. E. Mikeska, Uffz. H. Wendtland and Uffz. L. Muegge killed. Aircraft V4+JH wrecked.

Few remaining pieces, propeller blade, spinner and other components recovered by Steve Vizard.

Yesterday and today. Monkhams Avenue, Woodford Green, struck by a parachute mine at eight minutes before midnight during the night's heavy attack on the Capital. Although blast from a mine could extend out to 650 yards — well over a quarter of a mile — in this instance, incredibly, only three people were slightly injured.

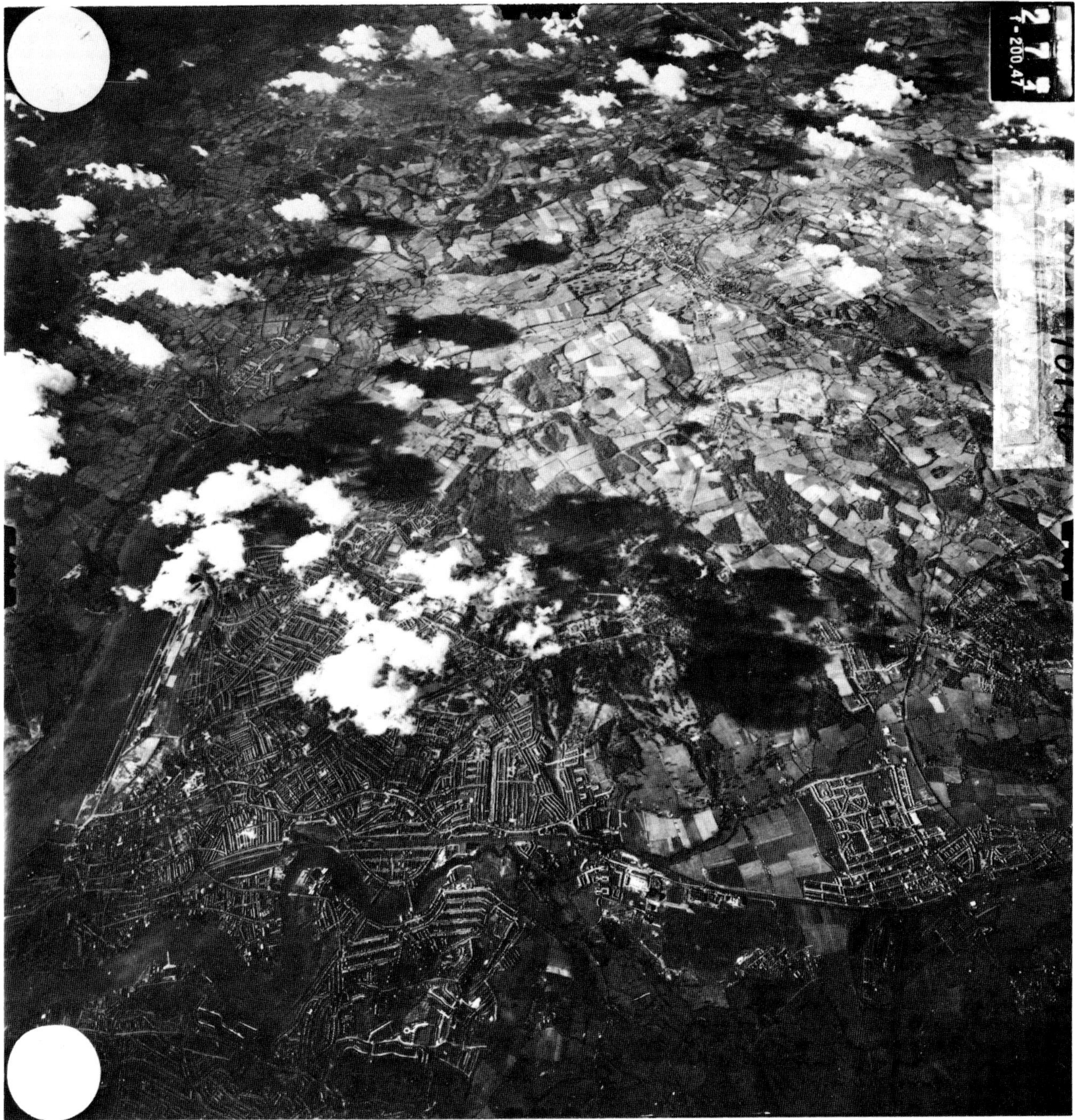

SUNDAY, NOVEMBER 17-18

Sunset: 1706 Sunrise: 0825
Moon: 1918 — Dawn (Full+3)

Major attack on Southampton; secondary attack on London. In addition a small force of Italian bombers attempted a raid on Harwich. Minelaying was carried out in coastal areas of the English Channel between the Isle of Wight and Hastings. Limited long-range night fighter-bomber patrols of airfields in eastern England.

Since September 7 London had borne the brunt of the attacks, but on the night of November 3/4 no air raid warning sounded or bomb fell in the Capital. It was a brief respite because the bombers returned the following night, but it heralded a change of tactics reinforced ten days later with the revenge raid on Coventry. Thereafter provincial cities suffered increasing attacks. With the new strategy for an intensified night Blitz, so we change the emphasis from daylight raids to Ken Wakefield's in-depth study of the night raids. Never before has such detail been extracted from surviving German records which has been set against the daily Home Security reports, from now on incorporated as a précis in narrative form. Next on the list after Coventry was Southampton — a 'major' attack to the Luftwaffe being signified as one on which more than 100 tonnes of high explosives were delivered. This oblique was taken on November 27, in the middle of the city's worst fortnight of the entire war, when nearly half of the overall total of 631 deaths in Southampton occurred.

UK — Depression centred over north-east England, moving south. Heavy rain clearing to showers and becoming fair. Visibility moderate, local fog patches developing before dawn behind the front. For most of the night southern England experienced rain with 10/10ths cloud at 600ft.

The Continent — Variable cloud. Visibility mainly good except in rain showers.

For the first time Southampton was selected for a major attack by night, with London the target for a smaller force of bombers. Preceding daylight activity consisted of an attack on shipping and a fighter sweep over East Kent during the morning and two afternoon raids on Kent and Sussex. In all some 270 German aircraft were involved on a day which was predominantly cloudy with poor visibility in rain.

The night attack on Southampton was planned to be carried out by 210 aircraft of Luftflotten 2 and 3, but in the event only 159 crews claimed to have reached and bombed their target. Extensive low cloud was the primary reason and only a few crews reported that they were able to bomb visually, the remainder relying on DR and radio navigation. In an attack lasting from 1845 to 0725 hours, the 159 attacking bombers dropped 198 tonnes of HE (including 39 bombs of the heaviest calibre) and Flambo, and 300 BSK (10,800 IBs), and in spite of the cloud many explosions and fires were observed. Searchlight activity was rendered useless on account of the weather; flak, according to participating crews, was variable in intensity and although accurate was without effect. Many night fighters were reported over and

This point in the campaign also obliges us to examine one facet which the official reports fail to cover — the visible cracks in morale. For obvious reasons, a defeatist attitude could not be allowed to be depicted during wartime, and pictures such as these, which appeared in the *News Chronicle* in December, were authorised for publication with positively-vetted captions: 'Southampton refugees on their way out of town to a new home. On the left are women and children waiting on the main road for a lift. Those made homeless in the heavy raids have been distributed over surrounding reception areas. In the streets of Southampton mobile canteens serve cups of tea and light meals. By last night provision had been made for nearly all the homeless people.'

on the approach to the target, with the crews of one unit claiming that about 16 biplanes (presumably Gladiators) were seen, but none attacked. In fact, only one Gladiator was flying that night.

Participating units, with bombing times, were:

Luftflotte 2
45 aircraft dispatched; 15 reported over the target, 21 bombed alternatives because of the weather conditions, five aborted and four were sent to other targets. The bomb load actually dropped on Southampton included 28 parachute mines (24 LMB and 4 LMA) and two SC 500s. The units involved belonged to IX Fliegerkorps, but details of specific units are lacking.

Luftflotte 3
165 aircraft were dispatched to Southampton, of which 144 reported over the target, four bombed alternatives and 17 aborted. No losses were sustained.

LG1: 16 Ju 88, 2055-2200
I/KG27: 15 He 111, 2130-2310
III/KG27: 9 He 111, 2215-2257
I/KG54: 7 Ju 88, 0156-0315
II/KG54: 7 Ju 88, 0129-0155
KGr806: 9 Ju 88, 0005-0120
I/KG55: 13 He 111, 2315-2355
II/KG55: 13 He 111, 1845-1940 (opened attack with illuminating flares)
III/KG55: 10 He 111, 2235-2320
Stab/KG55: 1 He 111, 2225
KG26: 22 He 111, 0425-0632
KG76: 16 Do 17, 6 Ju 88, 0540-0725

In addition two Do 17s of KGr606 were sent to Liverpool/Birkenhead and two more to Plymouth.

The attack on London was made by 49 aircraft (including 21 diversions from Southampton) of IX Fliegerkorps. Bombing lasted from 1755 to 0456 hours, in which time 60 tonnes of HE and Flambo and 64 BSK (2,304 IBs) were dropped. The IX Fliegerkorps aircraft which diverted from Southampton because of weather conditions — and which were normally used in sea mining operations — contributed to this bomb load with 23 LMB and nine LMA parachute mines.

Cloud cover over London was total and crews were compelled to bomb by radio and DR methods. Results were, therefore, difficult to assess, but after midnight breaks in the cloud enabled some crews to observe the detonations of their bombs to the south of the Thames and in and to the east of Southwark. The Concentration Point was again in what was termed Zielraum (Target Area) 'O', the City and Government offices districts situated between the Thames and Hyde Park. In addition, however, in a special mission three He 111s of III/KG26 attempted a precision Y-Verfahren guided attack on the Beckton gasworks (with three SC 500s, nine SC 250s and three Flam 250s), with the first aircraft bombing at 1802 hours and the last at 2320. The results could not be seen.

In the attack on Southampton the Fire Service was quick to bring fires under control and no doubt this saved the town from a worse fate. A large number of bombs fell on surrounding rural areas, but nevertheless extensive damage was caused in Southampton itself. Commercial premises, shops, public buildings, schools and private residences all suffered badly, but no lasting damage was done to the docks or other important war-connected factories.

Damage was also caused in London, particularly in Islington, West Ham, Lambeth, Woolwich, Wandsworth and at Surbiton and Hayes. Battersea Power Station was also hit and this raises a query about the Y-Verfahren attack by III/KG26; the German report states 'Beckton' Power Station, but it seems possible that, in fact, Battersea Power Station was the true target. The damage caused, however, was limited to an extension not in use.

Elsewhere in the country bombs were reported at Frome, Bath, Salisbury, Bristol, Weymouth, Honiton, Shaftesbury, Plymouth, Folkestone, Church Stretton, Liverpool, Birkenhead, Wallasey, Harleston, Thetford and Ely. Minelaying was carried out between the Isle of Wight and Hastings, but most of the IX Fliegerkorps aircraft operating were engaged in attacks on land targets.

To counter the German attacks, patrols were flown by 21 night fighters, including five by Beaufighters, but no interceptions were made. Some 5,000 rounds were fired by HAA guns which were in action at the Solent, Thames and Medway North, the IAZ, Holton Heath, Thames and Medway South, Portland and the Mersey.

In addition to the losses over Great Britain detailed below, Messerschmitt Bf 110s of 2/ Erprobungsgruppe 210 and 4(F)/14 together with three Messerschmitt Bf 109s were reported missing during the day.

1/Erprobungsgruppe 210 Messerschmitt Bf 110D-3 (3659). Aircraft fell into the sea at Aldeburgh, Suffolk 9.10 a.m. during an attack on Wattisham. Shot down by Flying Officer Count M. B. Czernin in Hurricane V7500 of No. 17 Squadron who was then shot down by Major Adolf Galland (Geschwader Kommodore JG26) to become his fifty-third victory. Uffz. W. Neumann and Obergefr. K. Stoff baled out and were taken prisoner. Aircraft S9+MH lost.

3(F)/122 Junkers Ju 88A-5 (0426). Believed crashed into the sea off Whitburn near Sunderland 8.45 a.m. Shot down in flames by HM paddle driven minesweeper *Southsea*. Lt. P. Thallmaier, Fw. A. Leise and Uffz. P. Hippenstiel missing. Uffz. H. Maisbaum killed. Aircraft F6+HL lost.

2/JG3 Messerschmitt Bf 109E-4 (4898). During fighter action aircraft dived on to a unit of Spitfires and failed to pull out of its dive for reasons unknown. Crashed at Melon Farm, Ivychurch, Kent 3.30 p.m. Gefr. R. Riedel killed. Aircraft Black 8+ destroyed.

Site excavated by Tony Graves and John Tickner of the London Air Museum October 1974 and later re-excavated by Brenzett Aeronautical Museum November 1974. Remains of pilot subsequently identified and interred at Cannock Chase with full military honours.

3/JG27 Messerschmitt Bf 109E-1 (4082). Crashed into the sea off Portsmouth after fighter combat 4.00 p.m. Uffz. W. Grotum made prisoner of war. Aircraft Yellow 6+ lost.

MONDAY, NOVEMBER 18-19

Sunset: 1705 Sunrise: 0826
Moon: 2012 — Dawn (Full+4)

No major attacks, but German activity was widespread with minor attacks on Liverpool, Birmingham, Coventry and Southampton. Long-range night fighter operations were flown against airfields and minelaying was carried out in coastal areas from the Tyne to the Thames Estuary.

UK — Poor in the East with extensive cloud, heavy rain and extensive fog. Cloudy elsewhere with generally good visibility.

The Continent — Showers with mainly good visibility except in rain, which was heavy at times. Fresh, blustery winds.

Owing to unfavourable weather conditions only a small number of German aircraft operated during daylight. Two raiders approached London and bombs fell here and on the Sussex, Kent and East Coasts, but the main activity was against shipping and Lowestoft. Night activity started soon after 1800 hours and lasted until 0300 when a short break preceded a second wave of attackers.

The attack on London lasted from 1805 to 0610 hours but involved only ten aircraft. They dropped five tonnes of HE and, as in previous attacks during the month, the attack was aimed at the City and Government quarter between the Thames and Hyde Park. However, thick cloud prevented visual bombing and recourse was made to DR and radio navigation; observation of the results was not possible. London's flak defence, according to participating crews, was of only medium strength but was apparently well directed.

Liverpool was the target for 14 aircraft of Luftflotte 3 (five He 111s of II/KG27, which bombed between 2135 and 2245 hours, preceded by nine He 111s of KGr100 which attacked between 1946 and 2035). They dropped five SC 250s, 15 SC 250mVs, three Flam 250s, 80 SC 50s, 48 SC 50mVs and 48 BSK (1,728 IBs). Only one crew bombed visually, the remainder relying on the inevitably inaccurate DR method. Nevertheless, fires were seen. Medium to strong flak was reported, but in the main was aimed too low to worry the German crews.

At Southampton, 19 crews claimed to have bombed their targets between 2038 and 0559 hours, dropping 14 SC 500s, two LZZ 500s, 12 SC 250s, four Flam 500s, six Flam 250s, 51 SC 50s, 16 SC 50mVs and 15 SD 50s. Participating units, with bombing times, were as follows:

I/KG54: 5 Ju 88s, 2136-2305
II/KG54: 5 Ju 88s, 2305-0040
KGr806: 7 Ju 88s, 0235-0559

In addition two aircraft engaged in the Liverpool attack bombed Southampton as an alternative target.

Five aircraft bombed Coventry between 0145 and 0445 hours with 14 SC 250s, 66 SD 50s and 22 BSK (792 IBs). Complete cloud cover made DR bombing necessary and it was not possible to observe the results. Both flak and searchlight activity were weak, according to the five crews of I/KG1 which made up the attacking force.

The attack on Birmingham was carried out by five He 111s of I/KG1, bombing by DR methods, and five He 111s of III/KG26 using the new Y-Verfahren precision bombing aid. Bombing was carried out between 0055 and 0350 hours and the bomb load comprised four SC 500s, 28 SC 250s, four Flam 250s, 66 SD 50s and 22 BSK (792 IBs). Cloud cover again prevented crews from assessing the results but they reported little interference by the slight, intermittent flak they experienced.

One aircraft aborted from the attack on Southampton, as did one engaged in the raid on Birmingham. Three aborted from the Liverpool operation and another three attacked alternative targets (two of them bombing Southampton). No losses were sustained by Luftflotte 3, which flew 54 sorties. The 33 aircraft of Luftflotte 2 were mainly engaged on minelaying operations and 20 long-range night fighters of the Nachtjadgdivision were engaged on offensive patrols over RAF Bomber Command airfields.

Damage and casualties were nowhere heavy and the war effort was little affected. Nineteen night fighters flew defensive patrols during the night but no interceptions were accomplished. AA Command had no more success for the expenditure of some 3,500 rounds of HAA ammunition.

On December 2 the Bishop of Winchester arrived in Southampton to find his people 'broken in spirit' with 'everyone who can do so leaving the town . . . struggling to get anywhere out of Southampton. For the time morale has collapsed. I went from parish to parish and everywhere there was fear.' Such accounts were only published long after the war was over and the exodus of the 'trekkers', as they were called, was really only acknowledged as a widespread problem by the Government later in 1941.

Back in 1937 a research project had been born to observe and record the reactions of everyday people to everyday life during a period in which Europe found itself increasingly dominated by Fascism. Today public opinion polls on a variety of topics are conducted regularly; then the experiment was unique, but the outbreak of war brought an abrupt halt to the dissemination of the vast flow of social information the Mass-Observation organisation had generated. The co-founder, and from September 1939 the overall director, was Tom Harrisson, later Professor at the University of Sussex. He realised that if his work was to continue during wartime, a totally free hand would not be possible, yet he deftly avoided signing the Official Secrets Act and managed to retain the right to full post-war use of the material. This was passed back to Professor Harrisson when he retired from the Colonial Civil Service in 1967 and deposited at Sussex University in a condition of some disorder. Although several authors writing on the Blitz have made use of the material, it was not until Professor Harrisson published his own detailed look at the Mass-Observation archive in 1976 under the title *Living through the Blitz* that the full richness of the material was widely publicised. Writing of Southampton in November–December 1940, he said: 'In so far as, clearly, government wished people to stay in habitable dwellings, trekking was a defect in leadership all the way down the line. It demonstrated an inability to understand the needs of ordinary people in extraordinary times. Moreover, by belatedly recognising trekking in May 1941 (when the needs were nearly satisfied), the truth was admitted. The policy had been wrong, in the highest judgement. Looked at from below, it seemed to be, to say the least, heartless. What then, really was the point of the King or the Prime Minister coming to look at the destruction afterwards? In a sense they were trekking, too. Imagine the effect if either one of them had decided to demonstrate official policy by staying the night in an average-sized home — or brick surface shelter — in the city's centre; or in the Civic Centre for that matter. Yet nothing less would have made the government's point: don't move unless you must.' Sadly, in January 1976 the Professor was killed with his wife in an accident in Bangkok just as the proofs of his book arrived for him to check.

TUESDAY, NOVEMBER 19-20

Sunset: 1704 Sunrise: 0828
Moon: 2112 — Dawn (Last Qtr-3)

Major attack on Birmingham, but incidents were also widely reported between Preston and the South Coast. Secondary attack on London.

UK — Clear sky with some fog at first, cloud and rain spreading from the West.

The Continent — Fair with moderate visibility at first, rain and low cloud spreading from the West.

In the course of a dull but dry day there was little air activity. Shipping reconnaissance and attacks on shipping constituted the major part of German daylight operations although a few bombs fell on Kent. However, the very low cloud which persisted for much of the day dissipated later on to permit large scale night activity which got under way from 1745 hours and continued until 2330 hours.

For the attack on Birmingham Luftflotten 2 and 3 dispatched 439 long-range bombers while another 51 were sent to London. However, of Luftflotte 2's 142 aircraft ordered to Birmingham, the crews of only 107 reported over the target; 22 bombed alternatives, 12 aborted and one was reported missing. Of Luftflotte 3's 297 aircraft, 249 reached Birmingham, 25 attacked alternatives, 19 aborted and nine were reported missing (one of which reported over the target before it was lost). In the secondary attack on London all nine of the Luftflotte 2 bombers reached the capital but two of Luftflotte 3's 21 aircraft aborted. Bombers assigned to the Birmingham raid which bombed London as an alternative brought the total number of crews which bombed the capital up to 37.

The work of Mass-Observation (the name continues to this day in the market research company, Mass-Observation (UK) Ltd) was carried out by panels of observer-interviewers, mostly volunteers, with a hard-core of full-timers. From early September 1940 until well into 1941 hundreds of observers were keeping diaries, and recording human reactions to being blitzed as the pattern of the attack unfolded throughout the British Isles. Anonymity was the keynote, enabling the observers to write honestly without the fear of later exposure. The frank reports have since been denounced in some quarters as 'unpatriotic', 'defeatist' and 'leftist'. Professor Harrisson's answer was brief and to the point: 'If any such charge is repeated in the fourth quarter of the twentieth century, it may only be because some Britons, especally responsible ones, cannot face the full facts about their "finest hours".' Mrs 'S', reacting to the third night of Birmingham's first big attacks which began on Tuesday night: 'We rushed down to the shelter, the gun-fire was hot and the effect of the fires in the triangle of windows facing us was terrifying because of the thought of all those houses on fire and we in the centre. We arranged ourselves as we could, Les bailed, the bombs were terrific, I covered G up as much as I could to save her ears, she could hardly breathe for bronchitis. The tension, the waves, good Lord I thought they would never stop, not 500 planes came over but a 1,000 I should think. G eventually dropped asleep from sheer exhaustion and stayed asleep till the All Clear, I was grateful for that. Mr Brown from next door came down during the gun-fire, he was afraid and he didn't mind admitting it, it didn't stop him from helping to put the fires out though, nor bringing us a cup of tea down. It was quite a relief having a chat to someone but he thought we had dozed off later, so he didn't come down after midnight. I dozed off, mind you.'

In Birmingham the principal targets included armaments works and factories associated with the aircraft and aero engine industry. The city, and its many important targets, were clearly visible to the bomber crews and only in a few cases were DR bombing techniques adopted. The 357 attacking bombers dropped 403 tonnes of HE (six SC 1800, nine SD 1400, 17 SC 1000, 32 LMB, 16 LMA, 105 SC 500, 22 Flam 500, three LZZ 500, 292 SC 250, nine LZZ 250, 45 Flam 250 and 2,139 SC 50) and 810 BSK (29,160 IBs). The result was an extremely serious and damaging attack, as was assessed by participating crews who were allocated three Concentration Points located in the north-west, north-east and south-west districts of the city. Fires were numerous and extensive and appeared to cover the entire city, rendering it visible to approaching crews from more than 75 kilometres away. Night fighters were seen over the target and both flak and searchlights were said to be lively. Minelaying aircraft of Luftflotte 2 were diverted from their normal task and, as can be deduced from the above bomb load details, dropped 48 parachute mines — weapons with great destructive power but having little capability of precision — on 'Regenschirm' (Umbrella), as Birmingham was codenamed. Participating units, with bombing times, were as follows:

Luftflotte 2
107 aircraft attacked Birmingham but units are not known.

Luftflotte 3
KG1: 10 Ju 88 and 12 He 111, 2145-2317
KG76: 14 Do 17 and 7 Ju 88, 2000-2110

Contrasts in Brum today. John Bright Street took many of the bombs most probably aimed at New Street Station. When we visited the city in 1983, some of the gaps blown in the street had been redeveloped *top*; others *above* had not.

KG77: 17 Ju 88, 2107-2344
KG26: 30 He 111, 1921-2330
LG1: 16 Ju 88, 2127-2208
I/KG27: 16 He 111, 2002-2202
II/KG27: 15 He 111, 2020-2135
III/KG27: 12 He 111, 2000-2138
KGr100: 13 He 111, 1935-2016
KGr606: 6 Do 17, 1950-2007
I/KG51: 8 Ju 88, 2130-2230
II/KG51: 10 Ju 88, 2100-2155
III/KG51: 9 Ju 88, 2210-2238
I/KG54: 5 Ju 88, 2325-0005
II/KG54: 5 Ju 88, 2344-0030
KGr806: 7 Ju 88, 2240-2318
Stab/KG55: 2 He 111, 2023-2025
I/KG55: 9 He 111, 1943-2050
II/KG55: 13 He 111, 1912-2010 (opened attack, illuminating target with flares)
III/KG55: 13 He 111, 2034-2111

Damage in Birmingham was much as the Luftwaffe had surmised. Railway installations, gas works, factories (including BSA, Lucas and GEC plants), shops, schools, churches and many thousands of houses were damaged or destroyed in what was the worst attack yet experienced by the city. More than 800 bomb incidents were reported and some 450 people were killed and 540 badly injured. On the whole, however, war production was not seriously affected.

Bombs also fell on Coventry, but damage was not extensive and although fires were started they were quickly brought under control. It was much the same story in London, where bombing was widely scattered, and reports of damage were also submitted by Leicester, Grantham and Northampton. Further incidents were reported in the counties of Lancashire, Norfolk, Suffolk, Gloucester, Buckinghamshire, Berkshire, Surrey, Essex, Somerset, Dorset, Hampshire, Kent, and in Ebbw Vale and Fife.

Night fighter patrols were flown by 19 aircraft, with six more at dusk, and one Ju 88 was claimed destroyed by a Beaufighter of No. 604 Squadon. The AA gun defences were active, too, and claimed four enemy aircraft destroyed while Balloon Command claimed one which impacted a balloon cable near Woolwich. The next morning the wrecks of three German bombers were confirmed at Barking, East Wittering and Wolvey, Warwickshire.

During the night AA Command's heavy guns used some 17,000 rounds of HAA ammunition, with batteries in action in the IAZ and at Chatham, Portland, Holton Heath, the Solent, Dover, Bristol, Bramley, Gloucester, Cardiff and Birmingham.

Anti-aircraft gun-fire claimed a German bomber on the night of November 19-20 when an He 111P-4, the G1+KL of I/KG55 from Dreux, crashed at Workshop Farm, Wolvey, Warwickshire. The pilot, Oberleutnant Hans Klawe, and a gunner were killed, but two crew members baled out safely.

There was little to be learned from the wreckage of the Heinkel, and the two survivors, whose morale was assessed as good by AI1(k) Branch, did not give away much information. It was known, however, that the observer belonged to 2/KG55 and that in May 1940 he regularly flew in the G1+HK. How this information was acquired by RAF Intelligence is not known, but it was recorded in AI1(k) Report No. 915/1940. Unit identification was confirmed, however, by the aircraft lettering, crew identity disc numbers and a Feldpostnummer (Field Post Office Number). Neither of the two survivors could give an explanation for the crash, but said they were in the midst of many AA bursts when the aircraft suddenly yawed violently. The W/T operator then saw the observer bale out and followed suit. Their two colleagues were still in the aircraft when it crashed.

AA Command was also partly responsible for the crash of another German aircraft that night. Apparently damaged by the HAA guns of the IAZ, the raider, an He 111H-5 (1H+AH) of I/KG26, then flew into two balloon cables which tore off its starboard wing before it crashed on the marshes at Barking, Essex. All five crew members were killed and their aircraft, which was bound for Birmingham, was totally destroyed in the explosion and fire which followed the crash. The crew was particularly noteworthy for it included three officers — Oberleutnant Albert von Schwerin (pilot), Oberleutnant Hunno Philipps (observer and Staffelkapitän), and a staff medical officer, Stabsarzt Dr Albert Leuchtenberg, who was on an air experience flight although shown on the crew list as a gunner.

All in all it was a bad night for KG26, for it lost two more aircraft in crashes near Beauvais airfield, killing nine crew members. One crash, which occurred on take off, killed the Geschwaderkommodore, Oberstleutnant Freiherr Karl von Wechmer, the Stabsstaffelkapitän, Oberleutnant Karl Streng, and three NCOs.

A Junkers Ju 88 of 6/KG30 was lost in addition to the losses incurred over the UK during the attack on Birmingham:

1/KG26 Heinkel He 111H-5 (3539). Aircraft hit a balloon cable at 2,800 feet and crashed near Jenkins Lane, Beckton Marshes, Essex 12.19 a.m. Oblt. A. von Schwerin, Oblt. H. Philipps (Staffelkapitän), Stabsarzt. Dr A. Leuchtenberg, Oberfw. H. Göhler and Oberfw. F. Gundlack all killed. Aircraft 1H+AH destroyed.

3/KG54 Junkers Ju 88A-5 (2189). Damaged by Flight Lieutenant J. Cunningham and Sergeant J. Phillipson in Beaufighter R2098 of No. 604 Squadron over the Midlands and flew on to crash at Stocks Lane, near East Wittering, Chichester 12.35 a.m. Recorded as the first 'kill' by an AI equipped Beaufighter. Uffz. K. Sondermeier and Gefr. G. Seuss baled out and taken prisoner. Uffz. H. Liebermann and Flieger P. May killed. Aircraft B3+YL destroyed.

Items recovered by the Wealden Aviation Archaeological Group in October 1977 included propeller blades now in the Tangmere Military Aviation Museum.

2/KG55 Heinkel He 111P-4 (2877). Hit by AA fire and crashed at Workshop Farm, Wolvey, Nuneaton 9.05 p.m. Oblt. H. Klawe and Gefr. X. Nirschel killed. Fw. W. Gutekunst and Uffz. R. Zeitz baled out and were taken prisoner. Aircraft G1+KL burnt out.

Site excavated September 1985 by Philippa Hodgkiss, when both engines and numerous other items were unearthed, including Werke plates confirming identity.

3/KGr100 Heinkel He 111H-2 (2768). One engine caught fire and a landing was attempted on Guernsey. Crashed and exploded on Crevichon Island west of Jethou, Guernsey 7.45 p.m. Lt. P. Dohr, Obergefr. H. Keylau, Uffz. K. Weidauer and Uffz. G. Seher all killed. Aircraft 6N+JJ destroyed.

The fiery end of one of the Birmingham raiders — 125 miles short of its target. Today the crash site has been lost under the expansion of the sewage plant on Beckton Marshes to the east of London *(see also Volume 1, page 93)*.

The failure of British night fighters to offer any solid defence to the massive night raids had provoked serious disquiet in the higher echelons of the Air Ministry and a special committee was convened under Sir John Salmond to look into the whole question of the production and use of night fighters by the RAF. On October 1, an eight-point plan was agreed and the recommendations implemented over the next few months. However, the success by John Cunningham on November 19 in bringing down a Ju 88 on the Birmingham raid did much to reassure the public when the news was released in January 1941 — especially when the magic ingredient was said by the Press to be carrots!

THE BIRTH OF A LEGEND

As Unteroffizier Kaspar Sondermeier taxied his Junkers 88 out onto the runway at Evreux at approximately 11.45 p.m. on the night of November 19, 1940 to raid Birmingham factory targets, one of the RAF's new Beaufighter aircraft of No. 604 Squadron was climbing out of Middle Wallop aerodrome far away across the Channel to begin a defensive patrol. At the controls sat a young, fresh-faced and unknown fighter pilot, Flight Lieutenant John Cunningham, and seated behind him in the fuselage his crewman, Sergeant J. R. Phillipson, huddled over the glowing cathode ray tube of the RAF's newest and most secret weapon — Airborne Interception Radar, or just simply AI. History was about to be made. A legend was soon to be born!

Sondermeier no doubt felt confident of the safe outcome of the mission as he set course across the channel in his Ju 88, W.Nr. 2189, B3+YL, with his NCO crew of Gefreiter George Seuss (Wireless Operator), Unteroffizier Heinrich Liebermann and Flieger Peter May (Gunner) of the 3rd Staffel of KG54, the 'Totenkopf' Geschwader. Flak could be a problem, but would probably not be too accurate and be more of a nuisance than a danger. As for fighters, there could be little or no chance of meeting them; unlike the daylight raids of a few months previously when the losses had been intolerably high. These night time raids, they no doubt thought, were at least free from the danger of fighters. Very soon all that was to change for the Luftwaffe crews.

Cunningham did not have long to wait as he flew around his patrol area (Slap B) and soon spotted a smoke trail going from south to north above him, and after climbing to investigate he encountered a number of twin-engined enemy aircraft, following and stalking them into and out of the clouds. After losing these contacts Cunningham returned to his patrol line and waited patiently for an AI contact. It was not long in coming, and under the guidance of Phillipson the Beaufighter was steered onto a single target somewhere in the vicinity of Brize Norton. Closing from astern to a range of two hundred yards Cunningham loosed off a salvo of 6 to 7 seconds and a death-dealing blow of 20mm cannon shells and ·303 bullets found their mark on Sondermeier's Ju 88.

Aboard the Junkers the panic and pandemonium can be imagined. Suddenly, and from nowhere, flashes of light lit up the aeroplane and its dazed and dazzled crew. One, Heinrich Liebermann, had been hit and lay dying across his Lotfe bombsight, and the young gunner, Peter May, jolted into action, returning the fire of his unseen adversary. As suddenly as the fusillade had started it had stopped, with just an eerie and a growing red glow appearing from around the starboard engine and flecks of red, white and orange phosphorescent sparks streaking back into the inky blackness as fire took hold. Somewhere out there in the dark lurked their attacker, unseen to a very shaken May who scanned the sky, finger poised on the trigger of his MG15 machine gun, waiting for another attack. Throttling back immediately, Sondermeier ordered the bomb load to be ditched, and the deadly cargo of 4×50kg HE bombs tumbled from the fuselage bays, followed by the two 250kg bombs slung from racks which nestled between the fuselage and wings. Turning for home Sondermeier feathered the starboard propeller but after a short duration the aircraft had dropped to 6,000 feet where the pilot attempted to re-start the dead engine which promptly burst into flames. At this point, over the Sussex Coast, he ordered the surviving crew to bale out, leaving the crumpled body of Liebermann in his blood-soaked overalls slumped in the cockpit. For Sondermeier and Gefreiter Seuss (the Wireless Operator) the parachute descent was to end in captivity as prisoners-of-war, but the hapless gunner, Peter May, drifted down on his parachute to perish in the icy English Channel. (His body was washed up on the foreshore some days later and buried in St Nicholas' churchyard, RAF Thorney Island, on December 12.)

The abandoned Junkers dived into open farmland near Stubcroft Farm, Stocks Lane, East Wittering, and buried itself on impact with the soft soil. Such was the total destruction and disintegration of the aircraft that the

Although not the first aircraft to have been brought down with the assistance of AI radar (that had taken place on July 22), a popular hero was just what was needed for civilian morale. Cunningham reluctantly went along with the 'cat's eyes' subterfuge to protect the secret of AI, but the seed sown by British propaganda was hard to live down within the Service, sickened by the glamour and the glory of the fighter boys. ***Above:*** **These are the digger boys of the Wealden Group prepared to do battle on the playing field at East Wittering in 1977.**

RAF Intelligence Officer Flight Lieutenant Michael Golovine, who visited the scene on the following day, was only able to report that: 'Markings were not decipherable, one plate found in wreckage showed airframe or component made by Henschel F.W. Licence Junkers. The cause of this crash said to have been night fighter action and a few ·303 strikes were found in a wing spar. Aircraft dived into ground and is completely wrecked. Crew presumably 4, 2 prisoners, one dead, one not yet traced. No further details possible.'

Although John Cunningham did not witness the actual demise of his victim it was later confirmed as destroyed as a result of Airborne Interception Radar. In order to more effectively cloak the secret of AI Radar a legend was created and eagerly swallowed by the Press that John Cunningham had such exceptional night vision that he could see in the dark — not unlike a cat! Hence the nickname 'Cats Eyes' was born, hated by Cunningham but nevertheless cheerfully tolerated to keep the closely guarded secret! It was also widely reported in the popular Press of the period that Cunningham ate a special diet of carrots to improve his night vision. 'Carrots D.F.C. is Night Blitz Hero' proclaimed one headline of March 1941!

The little remaining surface wreckage of the Junkers having been collected in 1940, the large water-filled crater was eventually filled in and the land continued in its former agricultural use until the 1960s when a new housing estate sprung up off Stocks Lane. With the increased post-war population of East Wittering the need for some form of recreation ground was recognised and thus a parcel of land was allocated behind the new housing estate for use as a public open space.

When the Wealden Aviation Archaeological Group began investigations of the site in 1976 it seemed likely that the new houses now covered the crash site. Original photographs of the wreckage gave no identifiable points of reference to locate the spot, apart from one shot of a wing section showing a number of houses and bungalows in the distance. However, this picture was not sufficient to locate the exact point of impact and in any case this section of wreckage could have fallen, or been carried some distance from the impact crater. Eventually, however, Mr Gentill of Stubcroft Farm provided the clue as to the exact location, which was later pin-pointed by the metal detector of professional treasure hunter Tony Hammond for the WAAG. During 1977 the group sought the permission of the parish council, which was granted, for the excavation of the site on October 15, 1977, subject to the reinstatement of the site to its original condition.

During the course of excavation both engines and propeller hubs were found, together with some propeller blades, an undercarriage leg and sundry other items down to a depth of twelve feet. Personal items belonging to Liebermann were also found, including a Mae West inflation bottle, parachute harness buckle, oxygen mask, part of a belt and a leather document case with fragments of maps and a pair of navigating dividers. Also found were a flying helmet headphone and a wallet containing seven coins. Amongst the cockpit wreckage was found a second oxygen mask — other than that which was presumed to be Liebermann's — probably discarded by one of the other crew members as he bailed out. Six loaded MG 15 saddle drums were also found.

Today, slight undulations on the surface of the playing fields are the only reminder of the traumatic incident in 1940, and the subsequent excavation in 1977, although relics of this aircraft are now held by the nearby Tangmere Military Aviation Museum.

ANDY SAUNDERS, 1986

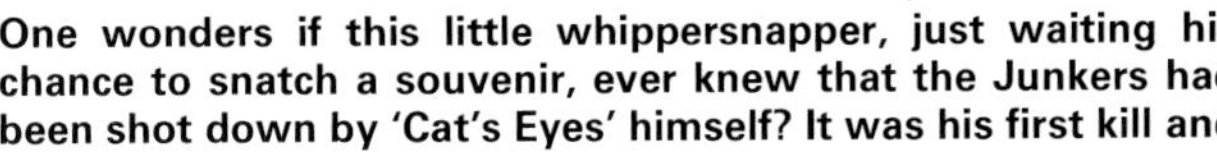

One wonders if this little whippersnapper, just waiting his chance to snatch a souvenir, ever knew that the Junkers had been shot down by 'Cat's Eyes' himself? It was his first kill and

John Cunningham ended the war a Group Captain with a score of 20 . . . and still a hero in small boys' eyes as de Havilland's chief test pilot.

When one reflects on the Blitz one tends to think that it was only civilians who were being killed by the bombing. Therefore we must remember that during the winter of 1940–41 hundreds of thousands of servicemen were on duty throughout the UK, the only fighting then going on overseas being in Greece and North Africa. The King's Own Scottish Borderers suffered the greatest number of casualties around this time when a billet in which they were quartered at Theydon Bois, Essex, received the full force of the blast from a mine on the night of Monday, November 18. Some 60 men of Nos. 7 and 8 Platoons and Company Headquarters were sleeping in Yates' Retreat *(left)*, a huge pre-war playground-cum-tea room on Coppice Row, when a sentry saw an object descending by parachute. Thinking it was an airman from a plane which had been heard circling the district, he withheld his fire. One mine brushed across the roof of the retreat and exploded on colliding with the helter skelter, while a second mine fell in a garden on Piercing Hill. The wooden billet was completely blown apart and from an initial count, 26 men had been killed, but this figure had risen to 30 by Wednesday morning. One soldier was never found.

WEDNESDAY, NOVEMBER 20-21

Sunset: 1703 Sunrise: 0830
Moon: 2217 — Dawn (Last Qtr-2)

A major attack on Birmingham with a minor raid on London. In addition small forces of Italian aircraft were dispatched to Ipswich and Harwich and night fighters attacked airfields in the east of England. Minelaying was carried out off Falmouth, Milford Haven, the Norfolk coast and in the Thames Estuary.

UK — Fair to fine in many areas with rain spreading from the West later in the night.
The Continent — Fair in Holland, but some low cloud in France and Belgium giving rain and moderate to poor visibility.

Activity during the day was on a small scale because of low cloud and poor visibility, and was largely confined to attacks on shipping and reconnaissance. Conditions improved, however, and permitted a continuation of the night offensive. Night activity started at 1810 hours but then slackened somewhat, only to be resumed with a new series of raids which came in with the rise of the moon after 2200 hours.

The repeat attack on Birmingham was made by 116 aircraft of Luftflotten 2 and 3 which bombed between 1935 and 0545 hours dropping 132.3 tonnes of HE and Flambo (including 39 of the 'heaviest' HEs) and 296 BSK (9,472 IBs). This time there was little or no cloud over the city before midnight, although conditions were misty, but thereafter cloud spread in from the West and by 0100 hours four cloud layers were in evidence, with the lowest at about 3,000ft. Only the earlier arrivals, therefore, were able to bomb visually and the majority used DR and radio methods. In general, however, good results were observed, with many fires.

Before the attack opened three small fires were seen, still burning from the attack of the previous night, and these were quickly joined by three more of large proportions in the north-east of the town. A linking of individual fires produced a 'fire area' of about 6 kilometres square with three more large conflagrations in the south-west districts of the city. Flak was encountered in variable strength but was mostly well directed; night fighters were seen on the approach to and over the city, but no combats were reported by returning crews.

ATKINS, Pvt. Richard. Liverpool (Anfield) Cemetery, Sec. 9. Nonconformist. Grave 639.
BOYD, Pvt. Thomas Gosnell. Age 23. Glasgow (Sandymount) Cemetery, Old Monkland, Compt. T. Grave 693.
CLARK, Pvt. William. Age 19. Edinburgh (Mount Vernon) Roman Catholic Cemetery, Sec. P. Grave 49.
COLTMAN, L/Cpl. William H. Age 20. Hawick (Wilton) Cemetery, Grave 1484.
CROZIER, Pvt. Allan. Age 22. Newcastle-upon-Tyne (Byker and Heaton) Cemetery, Sec. I. N. Cons. Grave 131.
DAVIDSON, Pvt. David Stewart McQuillin. Age 19. Ettleton Old Churchyard, Castleton, Row 2. Grave 56.
DICKSON, Pvt. John Brunton. Age 20. Jedburgh (St John) Churchyard.
DOBSON, Pvt. Allan Brown. Age 19. Jedburgh (Castlewood) Cemetery, 1st Extn. Grave 222.
DOUGLAS, Pvt. Godfrey Dalgety. Brookwood Memorial to the Missing, Panel 11, Column 1.
DOUGLAS, L/Cpl. John Turnbull. Age 21. Melrose (Wairds) Cemetery, Sec. B. Grave 274.
GAY, Pvt. Charles. Age 21. Tynemouth (Preston) Cemetery, Sec. F. Uncons. Grave 11669.
GIBB, L/Cpl. Alexander, Kelso Cemetery, Compt. B. Grave 238.
GLANCY, Pvt. Paul F. Age 23. Edinburgh (Mount Vernon) Roman Catholic Cemetery, Sec. O. Grave 25.
GOFF, Pvt. Esmond John. Age 23. Edinburgh (Comely Bank) Cemetery, Grave N. 1224.
HAY, Pvt Robert. Age 23. Edinburgh (Saughton) Cemetery, Sec. L. Grave 497.
HEWITT, Pvt. George Robert, Winlaton (St Paul) Churchyard Extension, Blaydon, Sec. E. South, Grave 59.
HUNTER, Pvt. John. Age 23. Melrose (Wairds) Cemetery, Sec. B. Grave 90.
JAMESON, Pvt. Thomas William. Age 25. Berwick-upon-Tweed Cemetery, Sec. C. A. Cons. Grave 1120.
KER, Pvt. James. Age 21. Kelso Cemetery, Compt. B. Grave 240.
LANNIGAN, Pvt. Michael, Liverpool (Ford) Roman Catholic Cemetery, Sec. S. B. Grave 547.
McCREADIE, Pvt. Samuel McClurg. Borgue Parish Churchyard, West Extn. Grave 122C.
McGUIRE, Pvt. James. Age 23. Edinburgh (Mount Vernon) Roman Catholic Cemetery, Sec. N. Grave 54.
MURRAY, Pvt. Robert Thomas. Age 21. Kelso Cemetery, Compt. B. Grave 239.
PROUDFOOT, Pvt. James Stevenson. Age 20. Castleton Churchyard, Grave 911
PURVIS, Pvt. Joseph. Age 21. Jarrow Cemetery, County Durham, Sec. 17, Grave 52.
REED, Pvt. Selby Douglas. Age 21. Newcastle-upon-Tyne (Byker and Heaton) Cemetery, Sec. 2. Grave 48.
ROGERS, Pvt. James. Age 23. Choppington (St Paul) Churchyard, Bedlingtonshire.
SHANKS, Pvt. David Wilson. Age 19. Bowden New Cemetery, Grave 268.
SHEARER, Pvt. Alan. Age 26. Portsoy Cemetery, Fordyce, Sec. B. Grave 24.
SKILTON, Pvt. Ronald Herbert. Age 29. Crystal Palace District Cemetery, Sec. V.11. Grave 17921.

According to the number of dead given in the KOSB war diary there would appear to be one further casualty although his name is not stated and his death is not recorded at Epping Registry Office. Army records also state 26 deaths as having occurred on the 18th whereas 28 were recorded at Epping for that date. Lance Corporal Coltman is recorded as having died of injuries on November 19 and Private Hunter on November 20.

'They shall not grow old, as we that are left grow old. At the going down of the sun and in the morning we will remember them.'

***Der Adler* did not publish their Birmingham 'before and after' pictures until January 1941. This is the Singer Works in Coventry Road.**

Participating units and bombing times (where known) were as follows:

Luftflotte 2
19 crews reported having bombed Birmingham. No further details available.

Luftflotte 3
144 aircraft dispatched to Birmingham of which 97 reached the target, as follows:

III/KG27: 5 He 111, 2145-0000
KGr100: 11 He 111, 1935-2052 (opened attack as Firelighters for main force)
KGr606: 6 Do 17, 2005-2025
II/KG51: 1 Ju 88, 2320
I/KG54: 4 Ju 88, 0108-0252
II/KG54: 3 Ju 88, 0030-0130
KGr806: 2 Ju 88, 0135-0252
I/KG55: 7 He 111, 2030-2130
KG1: 2 He 111 and 4 Ju 88, 0025-0040
III/KG76: 1 Do 17, 2218
I/KG77: 4 Ju 88, 2345-0050
II and III/KG77: 9 Ju 88, 0140-0218
KG26: 11 He 111, 2255-0040
III/KG26: 4 He 111, 2014-2203
I/KG27: 12 He 111, I/KG51: 5 Ju 88, III/KG51: 4 Ju 88, KGr606: 1 Do 17. These aircraft landed away from their normal bases and crew reports, bombing times, etc., are missing from Lfl 3 records in consequence.

A Ju 88 of KG77 crashed before landing at Reims, but no other losses were sustained by Luftflotte 3. Thirty aircraft bombed alternative targets (15 to London) and 17 aborted.

In a secondary attack on London by 45 aircraft of Luftflotten 2 and 3, 48 tonnes of HE and Flambo and 32 BSK (1,152 IBs) were dropped between 1857 and 0650 hours. The Concentration Point was the City area, but cloud conditions similar to that over Birmingham, together with thick mist, required crews to bomb by DR and radio methods and they were unable to check the results obtained. Strong flak was experienced, searchlights were very active and there were reports of night fighters over the target, but all without apparent success. Units involved were:

Luftflotte 2
No details available.

Luftflotte 3
KG27: 2 He 111
I/KG1: 1 He 111, 0120
III/KG76: 4 Do 17, 2150-2250
III/KG76: 6 Do 17, 2218-2345
I/KG77: 1 Ju 88, 0000
II and III/KG77: 3 Ju 88, 0140-0243
KG26: 2 He 111, 2315-0115

Twelve Fiat BR 20s of the CAI were sent to attack Harwich and Ipswich, their crews subsequently claiming to have dropped seven SC 250s and ten SC 50s on the former target and 36 SC 100s and 24 SC 50s on the latter. Explosions were claimed in both targets. One aircraft was reported overdue.

Elsewhere, aircraft of Luftflotte 3 attacked Bristol (two aircraft), Portsmouth (two aircraft), Southampton (one aircraft) and Portland (one aircraft). Various other towns and airfields were attacked as alternative targets. Eleven long-range night fighters were also operating over British bomber airfields, but no contacts were made with aircraft of Bomber Command.

The attack on Birmingham lacked concentration, because of existing weather conditions, and bombing was widespread over the Midlands. There were many incidents in Coventry and Leicester but, nevertheless, Birmingham experienced considerable damage to residential property. A bus depot and 40 buses were among the other properties damaged or destroyed and 20 people were killed and 84 seriously injured. Factory damage in Birmingham and the Black Country was not serious, but production at Wilmot, Breeden and Company's factory suffered because of the presence of an unexploded bomb. There was also a fire at the important Lucas factory. Two parachute mines were reported at Leicester, one of them causing extensive damage to the Steel Busks engineering works. Despite its double assault, Birmingham was quick to recover, mainly because its utility services — gas, water and electricity supplies — were not too badly affected and the damage that was caused was quickly repaired.

Bombs were also reported at Long Eaton (damaging the railway), Wellingborough, High Wycombe, Rustington, Yalding, Warehorn, All Hallows, Bethersden, Halling, Swingfield, Smeeth, Crayford, Southgate, Enfield, Acton, Hackney, Southall (where an HE damaged the gas works), Feltham, Coulsdon, Croydon, near Aylesbury, Henley, Scampton, Upper Heyford, Heston, Grantham, Stamford, St Neots, Sheffield and in various parts of Nottinghamshire and Derbyshire. In Wales incidents were reported at Llanmadoc (Glamorgan), and Llwynhendy (Carmarthenshire), and at several places in Monmouthshire.

No enemy aircraft were claimed destroyed by the defences although several raiders were seen (and two engaged) by night fighters, 64 of which were sent up. Countrywide some 6,500 rounds of HAA ammunition were fired, with guns in action at most sites south of the Midlands at some time during the night.

The only loss recorded during the day was of an aircraft performing a daylight reconnaissance of Birmingham.

3(F)/121 Junkers Ju 88A-5 (0458). On a daylight reconnaissance mission the aircraft was tracked over Coventry, Birmingham, Bromsgrove, Rochford, Filton, Hereford and the Welsh Mountains before being shot down by Flight Lieutenant G. D. L. Haysom in a Hurricane of No. 79 Squadron. Crashed into the sea off Strumble Head, Fishguard, Pembrokeshire 1.00 p.m. Lt. K. Lunnebach, Fw. G. Neurath and Gefr. K. von Heyden missing. Gefr. E. Brinkmann killed. Aircraft 7A+FL lost.

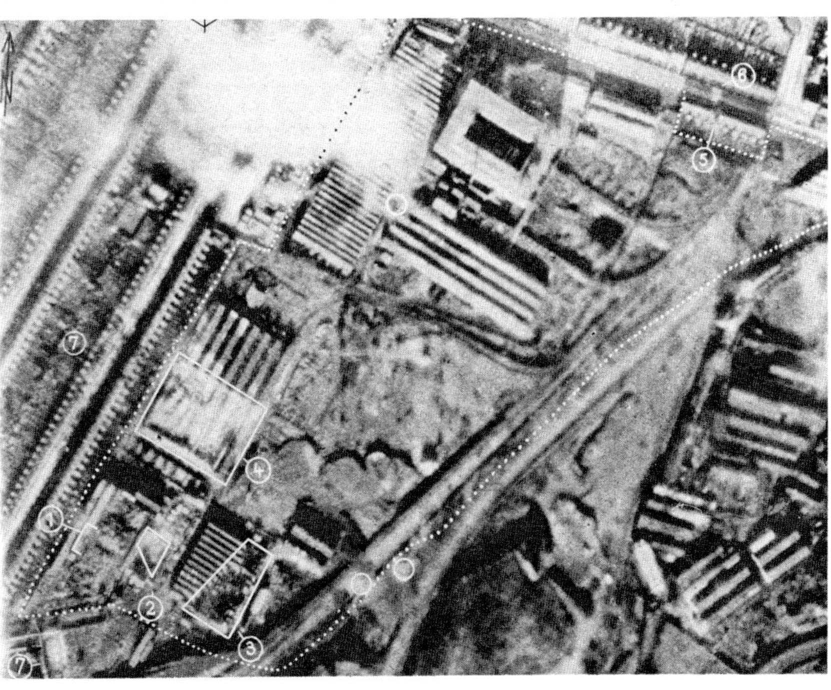

The sight of the horse in the midst of the destruction of T. S. Grieve's factory in Queen Street, Leicester, reminds us how important the animal was for local deliveries in the 1940s. This picture was taken by the Leicester Evening Mail on the morning of November 21 after the previous night's raid, yet it was not released for publication until January 1942.

THURSDAY, NOVEMBER 21-22

Sunset: 1702 Sunrise: 0831
Moon: 2327 — Dawn (Last Qtr-1)

No major attacks.

UK — Rain and low cloud in most areas.
The Continent — Cloudy in Holland and Belgium with moderate to poor visibility. Variable cloud in France with gale force westerly winds but conditions gradually improving.

During daylight small scale raids caused a few casualties and slight damage in East Anglia and elsewhere. Attacks were also made on a convoy off Harwich and the usual shipping reconnaissance missions were carried out.

Night activity, which was on a small scale, commenced at 1830 hours, but the country was clear of all enemy aircraft by 35 minutes after midnight, by which time continuous rain and low cloud covered most of Britain.

Despite the adverse conditions, Luftflotte 2 sent 40 aircraft to attack London, where the Concentration Point lay in the City and Government quarter, and 31 tonnes of HE and Flambo and 32 BSK (1,152 IBs) were claimed dropped between 1855 and 0618 hours. Bombing was carried out using radio aids and DR and during the first part of the attack explosions and fires were discerned. Later, the passage of a bad weather zone made ground observation impossible.

Thirty-eight aircraft of Luftflotte 3 were also operating, with 17 attacking Southampton, eight Bristol, five Birmingham and five going to Coventry. Three aircraft aborted, but none were lost. Few results were seen except that crews of six Ju 88s of I/KG51 engaged in the attack on Southampton reported bombs in the Target Area, accompanied by a large jet of flame.

Nowhere was any serious damage caused. Approximately 2,500 HAA rounds were fired during the night but no enemy aircraft were claimed destroyed. On the debit side a valuable Beaufighter was lost — the second by No. 219 Squadron in a week — when R2068 hit the sea in fog some five miles south of Brighton. Since starting to re-equip with the new fighter in September, No. 219 Squadron had now lost five Beaufighters and damaged four; it was involved in nine of the twelve incidents reported with this type between September 8 and November 21.

Two Heinkel He 111s of KG53 were lost during the day, the fate of the second going unrecorded other than that its crew were killed.

4/KG53 Heinkel He 111H-2 (3145). Collided with Spitfire Mk IIA P7387 of No. 603 Squadron, Sergeant R. E. Plant killed. Crashed in flames at Bucklands Cross, Teynham, Kent 12.30 p.m. A bomb exploded after the crash, killing two firemen who were fighting the blaze. Gefr. A. Hagsbiel, Gefr. W. Tieger and Obergefr. B. Volkmann missing. Gefr. R. Deutsch and Obergefr. H. Löffler killed. Aircraft A1+GM destroyed.

Site investigated by Steve Vizard. A good luck charm was donated to the London Air Museum by a local resident.

With a nice regard for history, the original archway dated 1902 has been retained alongside the new building.

With poor weather during the daylight hours for the second day running, Luftwaffe crews had time to relax in their messes after the big Midlands raids of Tuesday and Wednesday nights. The new edition of *Der Adler*, out on Tuesday, would have been read from cover to cover with such stimulating articles such as the Italian Air Force in France; Oberstleutnant Mölders and his exploits in the September battles; the latest awards of the Ritterkreuz; the nasty English who machine-gunned crews ditched at sea; and the signals troops linking Paris with the Channel coast. The lead story was of course the air war against England — the superimposed cover having a column of smoke added from 'einer abgechossen Hurricane'. *Right:* Even worse was to come inside where Propaganda Kriegsberichter Möller attempted to depict a night raid over London — only he got the U-bend of the Thames upside down! One wonders what wry remarks were bandied about by seasoned London veterans over this mistake! That evening they would be back again to Birmingham to try to achieve a knock-out blow as each provincial city was dealt in turn a quick double-punch.

FRIDAY, NOVEMBER 22-23

Sunset: 1701 Sunrise: 0833
Moon: 0040 — Dawn (Last Qtr)

Major attack on Birmingham. Extensive minelaying in the Bristol Channel, off the Isle of Wight, in the Thames Estuary and off the East Coast from Norfolk to the Firth of Forth. Minor, but lengthy, attack on London.

UK — Fine, becoming fair with increasing cloud.
The Continent — Fair in Holland and Belgium but some mist and local fog in places. Cloudy in France, improving to fair.

Daylight operations were again limited by poor weather conditions. After a morning of continuous rain, conditions over the UK improved during the afternoon but throughout the day the weather was poor over northern France. Accordingly, German operations consisted of raids by single aircraft, but not more than 12 crossed British coasts. By nightfall, however, a general improvement permitted another major attack on Birmingham, the third in four consecutive nights.

Night activity started at 1740 hours with six plots from the Dieppe area passing west of London's IAZ towards Birmingham where the first bombs fell at 1912. From then until 0512 the next morning, 209 aircraft of Luftflotte 3 bombarded the city with 227 tonnes of HE and Flambo and 457 BSK (16,452 IBs). Broken cloud permitted predominantly visual bombing and the results were a foregone conclusion. Almost at once some 45 fires were started, of which 15 were very large, and within 1½ hours fires were visible to approaching crews from more than 150 kilometres distant. An hour later and the conflagration was visible from the South Coast.

The attack was rated a great success by the Luftwaffe, but so large was the fire area and smoke that accurate detailing of the results was not possible. Flak was strong and, in part, well directed, but achieved little. Searchlights were described as 'lively' and although night fighters were seen over Birmingham and to the south of the city, no attacks were made. The attackers, all from Luftflotte 3, were:

KG1: 7 Ju 88, 0225-0410
KG76: 3 Ju 88 and 15 Do 17, 2100-2300
KG77: 25 Ju 88, 1912-2230
III/KG26: 5 He 111, 1912-2019 (bombing by means of Y-Verfahren)
I/LG1: 6 Ju 88, 0200-0246
II/LG1: 12 Ju 88, 0236-0326
III/LG1: 7 Ju 88, 0155-0327
I/KG27: 12 He 111, 2341-0140
II/KG27: 11 He 111, 2350-0130
III/KG27: 10 He 111, 2351-0120
KGr100: 9 He 111, 1914-1955 (bombing by X-Verfahren)
KGr606: 5 Do 17, 2032-2100
I/KG51: 4 Ju 88, 0206-0230
II/KG51: 10 Ju 88, 0235-0315
III/KG51: 5 Ju 88, 0400-0445
I/KG54: 7 Ju 88, 2058-2150
II/KG54: 8 Ju 88, 0435-0510
KGr806: 5 Ju 88, 2250-2325
I/KG55: 7 He 111, 0045-0145
II/KG55: 11 He 111, 1910-2010 (visual bombing after target illumination by flares)
III/KG55: 11 He 111, 2345-0020
Stab/KG55: 2 He 111, 2339 and 0130

Of the overall number of 336 bombers operating during the hours of darkness 243 were dispatched to Birmingham, with 209 reaching and bombing the target. Twenty-four aircraft attacked alternative targets, nine aborted and one was reported missing (a Ju 88 of KG76). Another aircraft, a Ju 88 of KG1, crash-landed near its base at Bapaume/Grevilliers.

In a subsidiary attack on London by 43 aircraft (seven from Luftflotte 3, unable to find their targets in Birmingham, and 36 from Luftflotte 2), thick ground mist hindered the early attackers but as the night wore on an improvement in visibility permitted visual bombing. The attack lasted from 1930 to 0706 hours and 34 tonnes of HE and Flambo and 20 BSK (720 IBs) were aimed at the City and Government offices area. A large fire was started (visible from the coast) and a large explosion with an enormous jet of flame was seen by some crews, emanating from the city centre. Bombs were seen to explode along the line Vauxhall Bridge/Charing Cross/St Pancras and along the railway from the docks (Poplar Station) northwards to Victoria Park Station. Night fighters were seen, but again no attacks were reported although both flak and searchlights were stated to be very active.

The practically simultaneous opening of the attack on Birmingham by aircraft of all three 'Pathfinder' or 'Firelighter' Gruppen — II/KG55 bombing visually in the light of

Houses . . . roads . . . industry . . . and shops: all hit in the eleven-hour attack which caused the highest death toll so far . . . and left the city without water. 'Over 600 fires were started, and Tyseley and Saltley were particularly badly hit. A BSA dispersal factory at Tyseley caught fire and their Small Heath works was again set alight. The neighbouring Warwick and Birmingham canal, from which water was being drawn for fire-fighting at many points in the city, reached a dangerously low level, but supplies held out long enough for the BSA fires to be brought under control. High-explosive bombs fractured three of the large gravitation mains feeding the general distribution system, and the situation was aggravated by the considerable local damage which had been done to the distribution system by the 19 November raid. Three-fifths of the city was deprived of mains water, forcing the fire services in many areas to rely even more heavily than usual on the canals, and to neglect fires in areas which were too far from such sources of water for temporary links to be set up. Some relief was afforded by the inter-connecting mains with neigbouring water authorities, which were immediately brought into operation. On the following day the Birmingham press, while admitting that the attack had been heavy, naturally made no reference to the water situation. The population were used to temporary local water cuts after raids, and could be allowed to remain unaware that most of the city was without supplies. It was estimated that Elan trunk main would take five days to repair, and Captain B. A. Westbrook, temporary chief of the Birmingham Fire Services, reported that another heavy raid on the following night would be disastrous. A company of Royal Engineers was detailed to blast fire breaks in rows of buildings in the city centre if an incendiary raid developed. Sixty pumps were rushed to Birmingham from London and other areas in readiness. Yet, as so often during the war, the Luftwaffe failed to follow up its advantage, and on the night of 23 November its attack shifted to Southampton.' Extract from *Birmingham 1939–70* by Anthony Sutcliffe and Roger Smith.

flares, KGr 100 by means of X-Verfahren and III/KG26 with Y-Verfahren — started numerous fires, many of which quickly gained hold to light the way for the rest of the bomber force. In consequence a high degree of concentration was achieved in the attack and damage was extremely heavy. Indeed, the attack — which lasted precisely eleven hours — was the worst yet experienced by the city, the centre of which bore the brunt of the bombing. Public utilities were badly hit, as were the railway and telephone systems, and there were the usual subsequent communications problems. Casualties were initially placed at 300 dead and 500 seriously injured, but it was thought that the actual figures could have been higher. Such was the scale of the fires that reinforcements were sent in from five other Regions and at daybreak a further 250 firemen were sent from other cities including Manchester, Bristol and Cardiff. However, the city's factories fared remarkably well, with more than 70 per cent of those hit sustaining only slight damage. The attack was heaviest between 1830 and 2000 hours and by 1920 some 300 fires were burning. A serious problem was occasioned by the presence of delayed action or unexploded bombs and a great many people had to be evacuated and roads closed.

Elsewhere bombs fell at Liverpool (where a ship was sunk in the Mersey and some damage to the docks occurred), Portsmouth (IBs reported on the Naval Barracks), Wolverhampton, Stafford, Chester, Oswestry, Bala, Wallasey, Wrexham, Rugby, Coulsdon, Portland, Guildford, Farnborough and in several rural areas.

Fighter Command put up 103 night fighters of Nos. 10, 11, 12 and 13 Groups (36 Blenheims, 11 Beaufighters, 33 Hurricanes, 12 Defiants and 11 Gladiators) and although enemy aircraft were sighted on two occasions, no combats ensued. AA Command achieved a similar lack of success for the expenditure of nearly 11,000 rounds by HAA guns, with batteries in action at Bristol, in the IAZ, the Solent, Gloucester, Birmingham, Slough, Portland, Tyne, Cardiff, Coventry, Thames and Medway South, Brooklands, Derby, Mersey and Holton Heath.

Only one aircraft was lost by the Luftwaffe over Great Britain:

4/KG2 Dornier Do 17Z-1 (3272). Shot down by three Hurricanes of No. 253 Squadron and crashed at Tarring Neville, Newhaven, East Sussex 12.20 p.m. A bomb exploded one hour after the crash, destroying the wreckage. Fw. W. Pleitz, Uffz. K. Treffert and Fw. G. Otterbeck killed. Uffz. G. Weinhold baled out and was taken prisoner. Aircraft U5+CM destroyed.

These pictures actually show earlier damage: to the Market Hall *(left)* and *(right)* the Grapes and Futurist Cinema in Hill Street.

FOLKESTONE

The night of November 18, 1940 saw the heaviest loss of life and casualties in the town of Folkestone when two parachute mines exploded shortly after 4.00 a.m., the first in the congested area near the fish market. Several public houses were wiped out, little cafes and restaurants destroyed, and what was once a baker's shop was now just a heap of rubble. It was from this heap of rubble that the baker and his wife crawled to safety, both severely injured. A large public house was still standing, its gaunt walls cracked and rooms bared to the public view.

Remarkable escape stories were commonplace but a police constable, who had been awarded the George Medal for bravery in another air raid, had probably the most miraculous escape of all. He had just left a police box and was walking away from it when he saw the raider in the moonlight.

'It was only about 400 to 500 feet up and I saw it bank,' said PC William Spain, of the Folkestone Borough Police Force. 'Almost immediately there was a terrific flash and explosion. Something seemed to give me a fearful push in the chest and I was knocked out. When I came round I was in the entrance of a pub! I heard voices inside and on entering found three people trapped at the foot of the stairs. I rescued a little girl and brought her out. I carried her away from the scene of devastation but on my way to the police station I collapsed.'

The parachute mine which had struck Beach Street caused so much damage that the area was never rebuilt after the war. It is now a car park. Eight public houses were eventually demolished, some of them had been in existence for over 200 years, and many had had smuggling associations which were fully documented in the town's archives.

The second mine landed in Rossendale Road, almost simultaneously with that which dropped at Beach Street.

SAVAGE ATTACK ON S.E. COAST TOWN

On the night of Monday 18th November, 1940, a large number of people were buried under the wreckage of shops and homes. Some had remarkable escapes and were either rescued alive or managed to crawl out of the debris unassisted, but others were found dead, many hours later. Rescue squads were assisted by men of the Pioneer Corps and worked untiringly for hours searching among the rubble. Townspeople were stunned at the senseless destruction. The spirit of the people was reflected in the words of a housewife, who after her home had been levelled to the ground, said to Lord Knollys, the Deputy Regional Commissioner, who visited the town just a few hours later, 'I had a wonderful stroke of luck this afternoon, I found my three Christmas puddings!'

FOLKESTONE HERALD, NOVEMBER 23, 1940

Total casualties exceeded 70, including 9 fatalities at Beach Street. Sixty-eight-year-old Alfred Colegate was trapped for eleven hours but died the following day; his wife Sophia was found dead in the rubble at 16 Beach Street. William Maskell, the 71-year-old licensee of the Wonder Tavern, a well-known personality in the fish market, was also dead when the rescuers reached him. Other fatalities included Gladys Aino, Ronald Early, Rose and Charles Rainsford, George Saunders, Charles Stubbington and Walter Tame of Tame's cafe. In all, fourteen people were killed and 60 injured, and the damage was widespread; 56 shops and houses were either completely or partially demolished, and more than 800 damaged, with a further 700 seriously affected.

ROY HUMPHREYS, 1988

Southampton: another concentrated attack during a fortnight which caused well over fifty per cent of all the casualties suffered by the city in 1940. Tom Harrisson of Mass-Observation declared that 'the city was, in the psychological sense, unprepared for what happened in November 1940', and that 'Southampton proved to be typical of the local authorities' inability to cope'. So, we are told, the Minister of Home Security, Mr Herbert Morrison, was infuriated by the Mass-Observation reports, prepared for their main 'client', the Home Intelligence division of the Ministry of Information, which included mention of the fact that RAF officers had had to take control of the main evacuation centre to produce order out of chaos as they 'were absolutely disgusted with the official handling of the evacuation.' *Above and below:* **This is the courtyard behind the police block of the Civic Centre — yesterday and today.**

SATURDAY, NOVEMBER 23-24

Sunset: 1700 Sunrise: 0835
Moon: 0154 — Dawn (Last Qtr+1)

Major attack on Southampton. Minor attacks on London and the south-eastern counties, with long-range fighter patrols over RAF airfields in eastern England. Minelaying off Milford Haven, Lands End, Harwich and in the Thames Estuary, the mouth of the Humber and off the Northumberland and Durham coasts.

UK — Fine in the South-East at first but poor visibility. Lowering cloud moved eastwards with occasional drizzle. Elsewhere little cloud except on western coasts and in northern England; some rain and hail in heavy showers on north-west coasts. Winds light to moderate west to south-west, but fresh on coasts and gale force in Scotland.

The Continent — Fine generally with little cloud but poor visibility.

During the day three fighter-bomber attacks on London were largely frustrated by Fighter Command. Among the enemy aircraft claimed shot down were several Fiat CR-42s of the CAI, some of which were said to be carrying bombs, and four Bf 109s. Only one small formation succeeded in reaching London and a few bombs fell elsewhere in the South-East.

Night operations commenced at 1815 hours with several streams of enemy aircraft converging on Southampton. They belonged to Luftflotte 3 and of the 123 long-range bombers dispatched, 120 reached and claimed to have bombed their targets; two crews aborted and another bombed an alternative target. No aircraft of Luftflotte 3 were reported missing.

In the course of the attack, which lasted from 1820 to 2255 hours, 150 tonnes of HE and Flammbomben (including six of the heaviest bombs) and 464 BSK (16,704 IBs) were claimed dropped on Southampton in its second attack since the widening of the night offensive in the middle of the month. Observation of results was at first hindered by mist, but later on it was possible for crews to check their bombing accuracy and the many fires which resulted. Indeed, within 1½ hours of the first bombs fires were visible from as far away as Cherbourg. At 1850 hours numerous explosions accompanied by a yellow/red glow were seen in the north-west and north-east districts of the town and large fires started. Three fires were also seen in Woolston, where the Spitfire-producing Supermarine factory was located, together with a large fire in the town centre. Two large fire areas were also reported north-east of the power station and assembly works of the General Motors Company, with another

Architecture — then and now. Back in Leicester, damage to the ornate sports pavilion in Victoria Park was being assessed.

major fire to the west of the power station. Some 20 large fires were also seen elsewhere in the town area.

Bomber crews reported seeing three night fighters over the target, but no attacks were made; flak was mainly strong but variable and only partly well directed. There were also reports of numerous searchlights and barrage balloons.

The overall results were clearly good, but in a subsidiary attack on London thick mist prevented an assessment and only after midnight was it possible for some crews to bomb visually. Here, as usual, the Concentration Points were centred on the City and Government offices area where three large and two smaller fires were reported by three crews. Defensive AA fire was strong and well directed with much searchlight activity, but two night fighters seen to the east of London failed to attack.

German records do not indicate which units attacked London, but Luftflotte 3 documents show that the attack on Southampton was carried out by:

I and III/LG1: 14 Ju 88, 2109-2235
I/KG27: 17 He 111, 2002-2110
III/KG27: 11 He 111, 1920-2132
KGr100: 11 He 111, 1850-1945 (follow-up Firelighters)
II/KG51: 3 Ju 88, 2155-2223
I/KG55: 10 He 111, 1915-1955
II/KG55: 14 He 111, 1820-1912 (opened attack using flares for target illumination)
III/KG55: 11 He 111, 2013-2048
Stab/KG55: 3 He 111, 2010-2035
KG76: 6 Ju 88, 1840-1920
KG26: 15 He 111, 1950-2047

Although no aircraft of Lfl 3 were lost due to British action, a Ju 88 of KG76 crashed just before landing at Saint-André following engine and instrument failures.

Fourteen long-range night-fighters were dispatched to patrol Bomber Command airfields and aircraft of IX Fliegerkorps laid mines off the coasts of Northumberland and Durham, in the mouth of the Humber, off Harwich and in the Thames Estuary, off Milford Haven, and between the Lizard and Land's End.

In the attack on Southampton no significant damage was done to the docks although a hospital ship was set on fire, according to Ministry of Home Security Operations Bulletin No. 21. In fact, though, it is known that the tug *Bonaparte* was sunk and the *Llandovery Castle* (10,640 tons) and *Duchess of Cornwall*, berthed at the Royal Pier, were damaged. Damage was also caused to many houses, shops and commercial premises, but damage to war-important installations was negligible. Unfortunately, damage to water mains, particularly in the eastern part of the city, created a serious water shortage and firefighting was severely hampered. In consequence many private and municipal buildings were lost. Casualties totalled more than 70 killed and over 130 seriously injured.

Bombing was also reported in the following places: Bexhill, Tangmere, Tilbury, Stapleford Abbotts, Basingstoke, Skegness, Sleaford, near Hull, Portsmouth, near Bawtry, Cheltenham, Ledbury, Evesham, Wincanton, Marlborough, Andover, Wells and Didcot.

In opposition to the raiders Fighter Command flew patrols by 51 night fighters of Nos. 10, 11, 12, 13 and 14 Groups and it was reported that two aircraft of No. 56 Squadron collided north of Andover at 2015 hours. One Defiant crew saw an enemy aircraft, which jettisoned its bombs, but no raiders were claimed destroyed, either by fighters or the gunners of AA Command. However, an enemy aircraft machine-gunned a Beaufighter as it came in to land at Digby, but caused no damage.

Guns of AA Command were in action at Southampton, Tyne, Tees, Pembroke, Falmouth, Bristol, Chatham, Mersey and the London Inner Artillery Zone, where only 242 rounds were fired at the ten or so aircraft that entered. Countrywide some 4,000 rounds were used, but to little effect.

This night the long-range night fighter unit I/NJG2 lost two Junkers Ju 88Cs over the North Sea, one of which was being flown by the Gruppe Kommandeur, Major Karl-Heinrich Heyse. A Junkers Ju 88 of 5/KG30 also went missing. Two aircraft came down in Britain during the day:

11/JG51 Messerschmitt Bf 109E-1 (3868). Damaged by Squadron Leader D. O. Finlay in a Spitfire of No. 41 Squadron. Pilot made a good forced landing at Ivychurch near New Romney 9.30 a.m. Obergefr. G. Loppach taken prisoner. Aircraft Black 3+ captured damaged.

5/JG53 Messerschmitt Bf 109E-1 (4010). Damaged by Sergeant H. W. Pettit in a Hurricane of No. 605 Squadron. Pilot attempted a forced landing but hit trees and the aircraft was wrecked at Smeeth Railway Station, Kent 4.20 p.m. Lt. O. Zauner taken prisoner. Aircraft Blue 12+ wrecked.

From pav to lav — courtesy of the Luftwaffe! Subsequently it was completely demolished to be replaced by this rather utilitarian toilet block.

SUNDAY, NOVEMBER 24-25

Sunset: 1659 Sunrise: 0836
Moon: 0312 — Dawn (Last Qtr+2)

Major attack on Bristol. Minor attacks on RAF airfields, with minelaying off the Yorkshire coast, between Flamborough Head and the Tyne, and in the Thames Estuary.

UK — Varying amounts of cloud at 2-3,000ft with moderate to good visibility. Little or no cloud over inland and eastern districts where widespread fog developed during the night. Winds south-westerly, light inland but moderate on coasts.

The Continent — Extensive cloud with good visibility, but some fog inland.

Fog in northern France severely restricted German daylight operations and apart from an afternoon raid in the Faversham area, intrusions were limited to overland and shipping reconnaissance flights by single aircraft. The weather over England was fine, however, with only small amounts of low cloud, and by late afternoon improving conditions on the Continent permitted night operations to proceed as planned. Nevertheless, with the threat of fog returning to Continental airfields it was considered desirable to restrict operations to the first half of the night so that the bomber force was back on the ground shortly after midnight.

Of the 214 long-range bombers operating, 148 were ordered to Bristol, an important port and centre of the aircraft industry. It was the city's first major attack and extensive damage was caused by the 134 crews, all of whom belonged to Luftflotte 3, which reached and bombed the target. They dropped 160 tonnes of HE (including five SC 1800, nine SD 1400 and 18 SC 1000) and 333 BSK (11,578 IBs of the B1 El type and 938 B1 El.ZA explosive incendiaries), in an attack lasting from 1830 to 2300 hours. The Concentration Point was centred on the built-up areas on both sides of the city centre docks with the intention of eliminating Bristol as an importing port supplying much of the Midlands and the south of England. Initially, because of broken high cloud, some bombing was by radio and DR methods, but as the attack progressed it became possible to bomb visually, guided by fires. Of the bomber force dispatched, 12 aircraft aborted, one attacked an alternative target, and two were lost.

The attack was opened by II/KG55, dropping flares and bombing visually with some of the heaviest bombs in the German inventory. They produced many small and 18 large, developing fires, of which three were in the vicinity of the works of the Bristol Gas Company and elsewhere in the city docks area. One gasholder was seen to explode with an enormous sheet of flame. An immediate follow-up by the Firelighters of III/KG26 and KGr100 produced more fires and several large conflagrations resulted; indeed, so great was the fire glare that subsequent crews had difficulty in observing the flashes from their own bombs and, with the attack only one hour old, 45 large fires were burning. Whole blocks of buildings were reported on fire, and one jet of flame, which crews estimated shot up to 400 metres, produced a fire which was visible from 250 kilometres distant.

Can this possibly be the same street? It just seems impossible to comprehend the level of destruction wrought in Wine Street, Bristol, in Sunday's big raid, the heaviest attack on the city to date.

The view from the opposite direction from the High Street. The photographer is standing in the ruin of the Olde Dutch House which stood on the corner.

According to returning crews the results were akin to those achieved at Coventry. Flak over Bristol was reported as strong and well aimed, supported by numerous searchlights, and between 20 and 30 barrage balloons were observed. Eight night fighters were seen over the city and two more over the Isle of Wight where, according to some crews, an aircraft was seen to crash into the sea in flames following an explosion in the air. This, it is now known, was an He 111 of II/KG55 on its return flight from Bristol. The other aircraft lost in this attack was a Do 17 of KüFlGr606 (KGr606).

The attack was carried out by the following units of Luftflotte 3:

LG1: 20 Ju 88, 1933-2020
I/KG27: 15 He 111, 2005-2100
III/KG27: 13 He 111, 2100-2200
KGr100: 11 He 111, 1858-1937
(X-Verfahren guided attack in a Fire-lighter rôle)
KGr606: 4 Do 17, 2135-2200
I/KG51: 8 Ju 88, 2110-2235
II/KG51: 10 Ju 88, 2139-2220
III/KG51: 7 Ju 88, 2210-2300
I/KG55: 8 He 111, 2020-2108
II/KG55: 14 He 111, 1830-1915
(opened attack, illuminating target area with flares)
III/KG55: 9 He 111, 1930-2014
Stab/KG55: 2 He 111, 1915-1925
KG1: 9 He 111, 2049-2200
III/KG26: 4 He 111, 1847-1951 (Y-Verfahren guided bombing)

Attacks were now following an established pattern with II/KG55, KGr100 and III/KG26 opening attacks with flares, very heavy HEs (intended, among other things, to shatter water mains and disrupt firefighting supplies), and incendiary bombs. The fires which these tactics produced served to guide other units, less well equipped or less experienced in night operations, to the target cities. And on this occasion it worked well. Much of the centre of the city was destroyed and there was widespread damage in the suburbs. Certain war-important factories and installations were hit, but little lasting damage was caused and the docks escaped surprisingly lightly. Public buildings, churches, shops, schools and private residences suffered badly, however, and there were some 50 casualties when a public air raid shelter was hit. Initial estimates put the casualty list at 106 killed and 153 seriously injured, but this eventually finalised at 200 killed, 163 seriously injured and 526 slightly hurt.

As had been the case at both Birmingham and Southampton, fires were well handled by a Fire Service augmented by outside help from other Brigades, but a water shortage again created problems. Bristol's ARP Services were also supported by units brought in from elsewhere, some of which, together with firefighters, were positioned to the Bristol area before the raid started. There is no doubt, therefore, that there was prior knowledge of the attack, presumably by the interception and decyphering of Luftwaffe Enigma-coded operations messages and/or by the measurement by No. 80 Wing of the VHF navigational beams which intersected over the city.

Unexploded bombs again presented grave difficulties and, with the large number of houses destroyed or rendered uninhabitable, made necessary the evacuation of large numbers of people to 32 hostels. Water supplies were also seriously affected and arrangements had to be made to supply drinking water from tanks and carts brought into the city the next day by the Military

One of the city's characteristic pre-war landmarks, it is believed the house, which bore the date 1676, was originally built in Holland and later dismantled and re-erected in Bristol after being brought to the city by ship. In 1908 the ground floor was cut away to permit the pavement to pass under the first floor. This picture was taken by the renowned local photographer, Reece Winstone, in April 1935, one of a series prepared for 'the generations of the future'.

The Dutch House was so badly damaged that the Army had to move in to demolish what was left of it — amid a great hue and cry over its loss. These pictures taken from the Council House are over forty years apart.

According to the official Civil Defence historian, this raid on Bristol was 'a conspicuous example of "area bombing".' It certainly looked that way with most of the central area of Broadmead flattened. This is another view of the High Street.

Authorities, who also helped with debris clearance and the demolition of unsafe buildings. While there was a good concentration on Bristol, bombs also fell in many surrounding districts of Somerset and Gloucester. In the London area bomb incidents were reported at Dollis Hill, Croydon, Kensington, Enfield and Romford; elsewhere bombs fell at Colchester, Felixstowe, Whitstable, Sittingbourne, West Wittering, Worth Matravers, Portland, Abbotsbury and Bath.

In a bid to counter the attack Fighter Command flew patrols by 29 fighters of Nos. 10, 11, 12, 13 and 14 Groups, comprising nine Blenheims, 13 Hurricanes, one Defiant, two Beaufighters and three Spitfires. No raiders were claimed destroyed, but a Hurricane (P2829, LK-G) of No. 87 Squadron inconclusively engaged an He 111 illuminated by searchlights over Bristol.

HAA guns of AA Command fired some 6,000 rounds during the night, with three Batteries claiming enemy aircraft destroyed. Confirmation, however, went only to the Portsmouth guns, which shot down a He 111 into the sea off St Catherine's Point, Isle of Wight. At various times during the night guns were in action at Bristol, Tyne, Portland, Portsmouth, Plymouth, the London IAZ, Cardiff, Yeovil, Southampton, Falmouth and Thames and Medway (North and South).

One of the aircraft engaged in the attack on Bristol was a Do 17Z2 (7T+TH) of 1/Küstenfliegergruppe 606 flown by Obergefreiter Albert Hoferichter and a crew of three including a naval officer, Leutnant zur See Martin Saueracker. Take off from Lanveoc-Poulmic was at about 2000 hours, with a bomb load of ten 50kg bombs intended for a power station in the city centre. There was no moon, but it was a clear night, apart from a little cloud at 1,500ft, and although Knickebein was available navigation was conducted visually and by means of DR. However, by mid-Channel navigation was no problem whatsoever, for the Do 17's crew could see a distant red glow on the clouds over a burning Bristol.

Upon reaching the Bristol Channel Hoferichter made a wide 180 degree turn to the right to approach Bristol from the north-east and the bombing run was commenced at 13,000ft. The bombs were dropped into the fire area raging below and the aircraft again turned right onto a westerly heading. There was considerable searchlight activity, but with little or no flak it was assumed that night fighters were in the vicinity. The 7T+TH continued westwards and flew over South Wales for a short while before turning southwards towards the Saint-Malo radio beacon and thence direct to Lanveoc-Poulmic, but from hereon there was some confusion. Reflecting on the mission some 40 years later, Martin Saueracker is still not sure what happened, but a reconstruction of the flight leaves little doubt that, as navigator, he made a simple error in calculating the flight time since leaving the target area. It would appear that he overlooked the 20 or so minutes over the Bristol Channel/South Wales area and a descent to cross the French coast below 1,000 metres was initiated too soon. A good signal was received from the Saint-Malo beacon but when a coastline was crossed during the 'homing', together with a bearing of 330 degrees to St Malo, Saurecker assumed that they had overshot the Brest Peninsula and ordered Hoferichter to turn back on to a north-westerly heading. While doing so they encountered the cable of a Plymouth barrage balloon.

Almost certainly, in addition to the navigator's error, an 80 Wing Meaconed beacon was responsible for the plight in which the German crew found themselves. All four managed to bale out safely — one was rescued from the sea at Cawsand and the others were captured in the vicinity of Millbrook. Their aircraft crashed and burnt out at Penlee Point near Plymouth.

Lennards Corner, Queen's Road, should perhaps now be known as Maples Corner.

Two days later when reconnaissance aircraft returned to photograph the damage, fires were still burning north of the river. This is an enlarged section from the cover flown at 4.15 p.m. (German time).

Activity was focused upon the West Country, the following aircraft being lost during the day:

3(F)/123 Junkers Ju 88A-5 (0451). Shot down during a reconnaissance mission to Coventry by Wing Commander Oliver and Sergeant M. Parafinski in Hurricanes of No. 308 Squadron. Crashed at Manor House, Coates, Gloucestershire 4.55 p.m. Lt. H. Hollstein, Fw. H. Schwingshakl, Gefr. H. Gran and Uffz. G. Koch all killed. Aircraft 4U+HL burnt out.

Small pieces gathered from the site by the Severnside Aviation Society include parachute release buckle.

5/KG3 Dornier Do 17Z-2 (4193). Believed crashed into the sea off Portreath, Cornwall 12.30 p.m. Obergefr. G. Limbeck killed. Oblt. H. Kühler, Uffz. T. Muller and Gefr. K. Rauck missing. Aircraft 5K+LN sank in sea.

Aufkl.Gr.Ob.d.L. Dornier Do 215 (0057). Crashed into the sea half a mile off Kynance, Cornwall 12.55 p.m. Returning from a reconnaissance of the Irish coast, shot down by Squadron Leader M. V. Blake and Pilot Officer E. B. Mortimer-Rose in Spitfires of No. 234 Squadron. Lt. O. Bobal and Uffz. F. Redmann missing. Uffz. W. Schmitz killed. Uffz. H. Stangassinger admitted to Helston hospital. Aircraft VB+KR lost.

At night the Luftwaffe lost the following aircraft:

5/KG55 Heinkel He 111H-4 (3092). Hit by AA fire and exploded on a mission to Bristol. Believed crashed into the sea off Isle of Wight 7.40 p.m. SdFr. E Weihmüller, Lt. G. Heiland, Oberfw. W. Müller, Fw. H. Gailk and St.Fw. H. Haidt missing. Aircraft G1+KN lost.

1/Küstenfliegergruppe 606 Dornier Do 17Z (2796). Flew into balloon barrage site 64/11 at Plymouth Harbour after becoming lost due to British 'Meacon' countermeasures. Crashed on Penlee Point, Cornwall 10.40 p.m. Lt. zur See M. Saueracker, Obergefr. A. Hoferichter, Uffz. H. Weiss and Uffz. K. Eiselt all baled out and captured. Aircraft 7T+TH burnt out.

Fortunately one of Bristol's important historical buildings — Ye Llandoger Trow in King Street — narrowly escaped. Built in 1664, it is reputed to be the inn where Alexander Selkirk was told the story which prompted him to write *Robinson Crusoe*, as well as the place on which Stevenson based the ale house in *Treasure Island*.

Nice comparison by the Severnside Aviation Society of the photo-reconnaissance Ju 88 crash at Coates Manor — or what was left of it.

MONDAY, NOVEMBER 25-26

Sunset: 1658 Sunrise: 0838
Moon: 0430 — Dawn (Last Qtr+3)

Minor attack on Bristol/Avonmouth. No other activity.

UK — Extensive cloud with rain and drizzle in many places. Visibility moderate to good in areas with no precipitation.

The Continent — Low cloud with rain and drizzle in most areas except north-western France where visibility was moderate to good.

Fog was widespread by dawn and persisted in some areas for much of the day, restricting German activity to a few reconnaissance missions. There was no improvement after nightfall, but with Vannes airfield one of the few remaining open in Western Europe, an attack was flown against Bristol's Avonmouth docks by nine He 111s of Kampfgruppe 100. These were the only enemy aircraft operating that night.

Using X-Verfahren, the raiders dropped 72 SC 50s and 6,480 B1 El incendiaries in an attack lasting from 1845 to 1911 hours. The beams were aligned on the silos and Cold Storage Depot in the Royal Edward Dock, Avonmouth, and three large and several small fires were subsequently seen by participating crew members. However, thick cloud prevented an assessment of the attack being made. The cloud also rendered the searchlights ineffective, but flak was said to have been variable but generally well aimed. No losses were sustained and all nine aircraft successfully reached their targets, according to the Luftflotte 3 report on the operation.

Two buildings of the National Smelting Company were severely damaged in the attack and elsewhere in Avonmouth part of a factory, two churches, a bank and several houses were damaged, but none of the assigned targets were hit. Nineteen people were injured. Bombs also fell in two districts of Bristol and a number of small fires resulted, but no serious damage occurred.

AA Command had a quiet night, firing only about 1,000 rounds of HAA ammunition, and only ten night fighters were operating. By 1930 hours most activity had ceased. The night was notable, however, for the excellent W/T communications monitoring by the RAF's 'Y' Service, which was able to report in some detail on the call-signs and operating procedures of KGr100 and its ground control station. Beam transmissions were also successfully monitored by the counter-measures organisation.

The only aircraft lost during the day was the following:

2/906 Blohm und Voss BV 138A-1. (0381). Crashed into the sea near Great Blasket Island, County Kerry, Eire. Oblt. zur See K. Neymeyr, Uffz. W. Krupp, Uffz. E. Sack, Fw. H. Biegel and Obergefr. E. Kalkowski interned. Aircraft 8L+CK sank in sea.

Just as Bristolians were trying to comprehend the blow which had struck them, the sirens sounded again: at 4.07 in the afternoon, the Red Warning lasting 21 minutes, and then again at 6.28 p.m. Fortunately there was a sigh of relief throughout the city when the All Clear came quite soon at 7.31. This is Park Street, looking south.

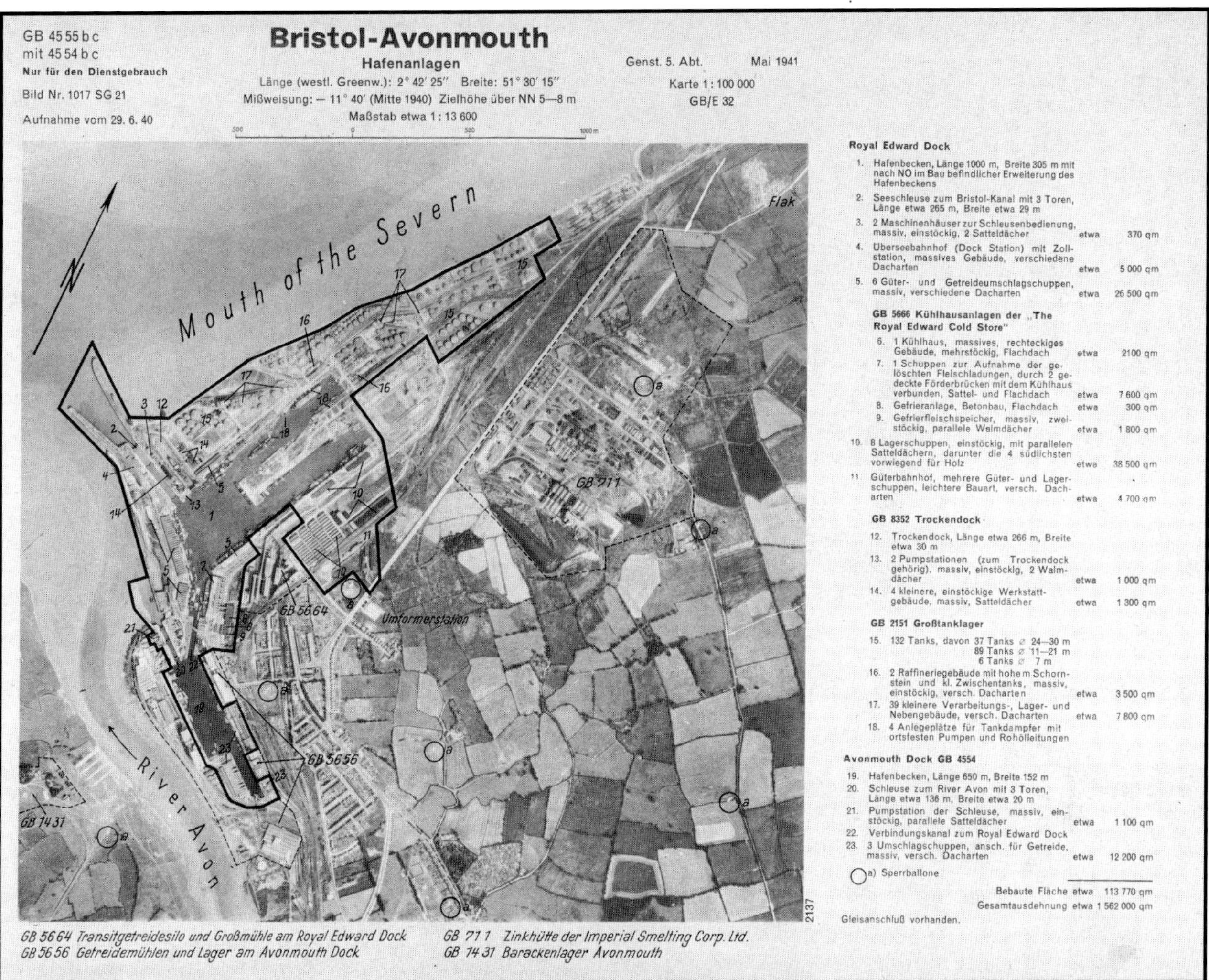

Bristol lies eight miles up river from its port of Avonmouth which received an attack on Tuesday night. This map of Target 45 54/55 is based on a picture taken in June although with the overprint updated to May 1941. The Concentration Point, invisibly marked by X-Verfahren navigational radio beams, was the Royal Edward Cold Store (6, 8 and 9) and the Transit Grain Silo which was important enough to have its own individual target designation: GB 56 64. The small circles denote barrage balloons.

TUESDAY, NOVEMBER 26-27

Sunset: 1657 Sunrise: 0839
Moon: 0550 — Dawn (New −2)

Minor attack on Bristol/Avonmouth. Little other activity.

UK — Fair, becoming increasingly cloudy with freshening winds.
The Continent — Variable amounts of cloud, some rain or drizzle. Visibility moderate to poor, with fog in many districts.

German activity during the day consisted of reconnaissance of south-eastern coastal areas and south-west England, together with attacks on convoys. Nightfall again brought fog to France and the Low Countries and what activity there was came from airfields in Brittany where conditions were appreciably better. Even so, only 29 German bombers were operating including 12 minelayers of IX Fliegerkorps. The remaining 17 aircraft of Luftflotte 3 were engaged in attacks on Bristol/Avonmouth and London.

The Avonmouth attack was conducted by nine He 111s of KGr100, but four crews aborted and one bombed an alternative target. The four that reached their primary targets dropped 24 SC 50s, 2,640 B1 Els and 528 B1 El.ZAs between 1832 and 1848 hours. On this occasion the Firelighter Gruppe's X-beams were set up over two objectives — the Transit Grain Silo and granary of the Co-operative Wholesale Society, and the Royal Edward Cold Store in the Royal Edward Dock. One large fire, several smaller fires and a large explosion were seen, with the subsequent fire glow still visible to returning crews as they crossed the English coast. A lone He 111 of III/KG26 claimed to have bombed Frome as an alternative target and here, too, a fire was discerned.

Three medium sized fires were started in London, according to the crews of six Do 17s of KGr606. In an attack which commenced at 1852 and finished at 1935 hours they dropped 60 SC 50s and 360 B1 Els by means of Knickebein and DR navigation. One of their number aborted.

In fact little damage was caused in Avonmouth; the raiders missed their targets by a narrow margin and also narrowly missed the National Smelting Company's works. A decoy fire was lit, however, and no doubt it was this which the German crews saw through the breaks in the cloud and on their homeward flight. Frome, claimed bombed by the He 111 of III/KG26 also escaped, but bombs were reported at nearby Shepton Mallet where superficial damage was done to farm buildings. In London, too, there was little damage of consequence, despite German claims to the contrary.

AA Command claimed an enemy aircraft 'damaged' but no claims were made by the 34 night fighters on patrol. One Blenheim of No. 604 Squadron was lost when it crashed on Danebury Hill, Wiltshire.

A Messerschmitt Bf 109 of 10/JG51 and a Messerschmitt Bf 110 of III/ZG26 were lost on operations during the day but did not come down over Great Britain.

WEDNESDAY, NOVEMBER 27-28

Sunset: 1656 Sunrise: 0841
Moon: 0708 — Dawn (New −1)

Major attack on Plymouth and a heavy attack on London. A few aircraft laid mines in the Thames Estuary.

UK — Mainly cloudless. A few showers in Scotland and in north-western coastal areas. Good visibility, moderate in inland areas. Winds, light to moderate in inland areas, squally on some coasts and gale force at times in Scotland.
The Continent — Variable cloud, some low in western areas. Visibility moderate to poor with some mist in Holland.

Daytime activity was slight and took the form of reconnaissance flights seeking shipping and a few fighter and fighter-bomber intrusions over south-east England. Nightfall, however, brought forth operations by 191 long-range bombers of Luftflotten 2 and 3 and four of the CAI, with Plymouth and London the principal targets.

Luftflotte 3 dispatched 112 aircraft to Plymouth and the crews of 107 claimed to have reached and bombed the important naval dockyard town. Units of I, IV and V Fliegerkorps were involved and the designated Concentration Points lay in the town and dock area. Five aircraft aborted, but

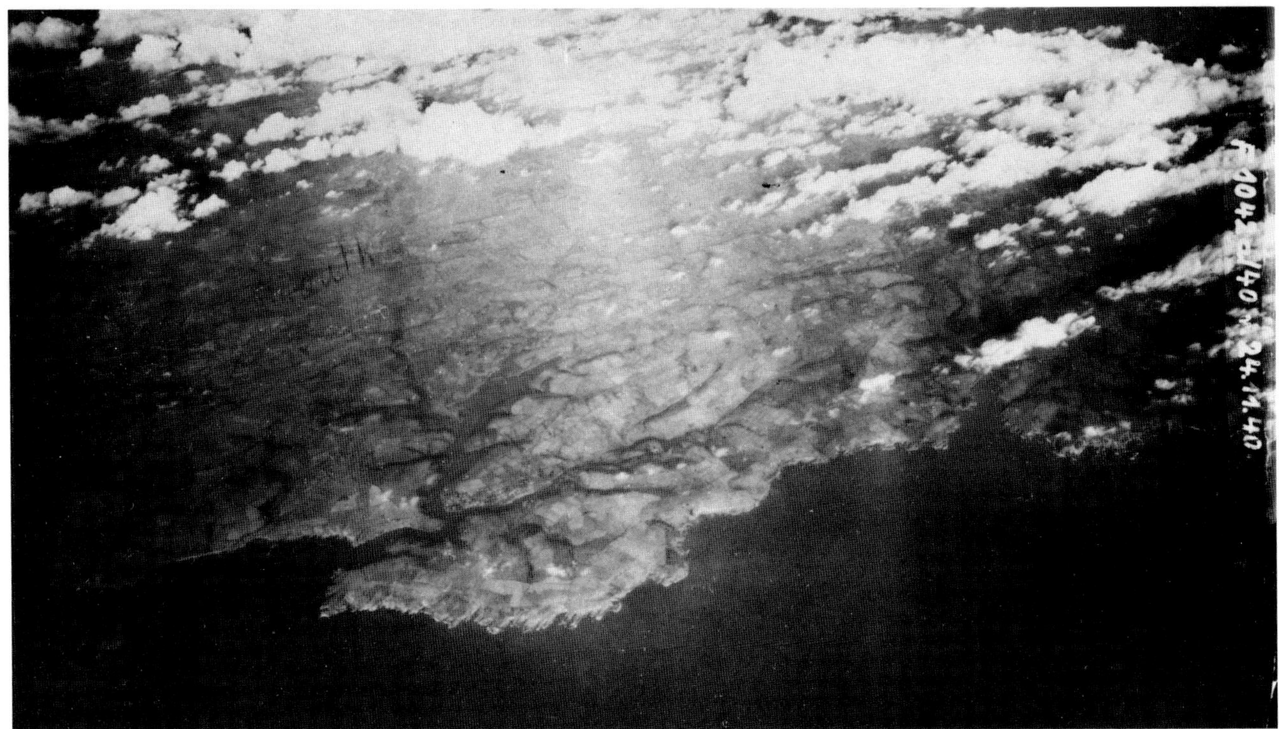

Of all the towns and cities of Britain, if one thinks of invasion there is but one that stands supreme: Plymouth. For centuries when the Royal Navy was the country's only protection, the town has been synonymous with sea power . . . ever since that game of bowls was played out in 1588. Now Drake is overshadowed by the Navy's own memorial, erected four centuries later, to those 'who laid down their lives in the defence of the Empire and have no other grave than the sea'. To the same city in 1940 came another armada from across the sea with sophisticated means of waging war — this time from the air. However, the poor quality of this pre-strike picture taken on November 24 hardly lives up to the claims of the new technology. Plymouth lies over to the left with the rivers Yealm, centre, and Erme, right.

none were lost. Weather conditions were good and most crews were able to bomb visually although there were a few isolated cases of DR bombing. In the course of the attack, which lasted from 1830 to 0210 hours, 109.45 tonnes of HE (comprising one SD 1400, nine SC 1000, 49 SC 500, one LZZ 500, five Flam 500, 153 SC 250, 35 LZZ 250, seven Flam 250 and 466 SC 50) and 170 BSK (6,124 B1 Els) were dropped.

German crews reported many fires and explosions, especially in the north and north-west districts of the town, and a large jet of flame followed an explosion in the south part. In Devonport a large explosion and fire area were seen. The attack was considered to have achieved good results, with the major part of the bombs falling in the designated target areas. Only one night fighter was seen and flak, for the most part, was said to have been weak but was well directed. Flak from ships in the port was apparently strong but poorly aimed and searchlight activity was only slight. The general impression was that the defences were weaker than experienced elsewhere of late, and two decoy fires were clearly not genuine.

The participating units, with bombing times, were:

KG1: 15 He 111 and 8 Ju 88, 1930-2210
III/KG26: 7 He 111, 2120-2208
KG77: 9 Ju 88, 0055-0210
II and III/LG1: 13 Ju 88, 2233-0032
III/KG27: 13 He 111, 1851-2047
II/KG27: 16 He 111, 1840-1920
KGr606: 8 Do 17, 1830-1856
I/KG54: 7 Ju 88, 2123-2220
II/KG54: 5 Ju 88, 2222-2335
KGr806: 6 Ju 88, 1945-2020

Although the Luftwaffe's daily operations report states that no aircraft were lost, the Luftflotte 3 account of the night's operations records that a Ju 88 of KG77 was destroyed when its crew baled out following an engine failure shortly after take off.

One of the targets hit on the night of the 28th was the oil tank store at Mount Batten — Plymouth's seaplane base facing The Hoe. The tanks blazed for several days, presenting a massive signpost by day or night, but rather surprisingly the Luftwaffe failed to take advantage of it. Coincidentally, at exactly the same time the editor of *Der Adler* was putting to bed his next issue in Berlin with dramatic photographs of another oil fire — the massive conflagration at Pembroke Dock earlier that August — the longest-burning individual fire of the war, which was fought for 20 days with over 650 firemen attending from 22 brigades. During the three weeks the fire had been burning with flames up to 1,000 feet high, five firemen had lost their lives when they were engulfed by a fireball and of the 17 tanks at the Llanreath depot only 6 were saved. *Left:* This is the picture published by *Der Adler* on December 3. Vernon Scott, who researched the incident in detail for the 40th anniversary in 1980, says that bearing in mind the size of the fire, the Ministry of Home Security report on August 19 *(see Volume 1, page 218)* must be one of the major understatements of the war!

The same blaze but this time photographed by the RAF. The tank farm had bund walls and a surrounding moat to contain any spillage, which saved many lives from 'boil overs'.

The subsidiary attack on London was undertaken by 65 aircraft, of which 57 reached the target to drop 60 tonnes of HE. The attack was made in three waves (from 1927 to 2253, from 0005 to 0107 and from 0357 to 0655 hours), no doubt with the intention of causing the maximum disruption. During the first part of the night, bombing was carried out visually but later, because of some isolated rain showers, DR bombing was necessary at times. Observation of the results was similarly hindered. Participating units are not recorded in German records, but three aircraft of the Stab Flight of X Fliegerkorps claimed a minor attack on Glasgow with three SC 1000s and four SC 250s. Three fires were started in an attack lasting from 1840 to 1903 hours.

No details are to be found of the CAI operation, but it is fairly safe to assume that the four Italian BR-20s involved were engaged in an operation against one or more of their usual East Coast targets.

Despite the absence of moonlight, the combination of clear skies, moderate to good visibility and a coastal location ensured that participating crews would be able to find and bomb Plymouth successfully. Nevertheless, although an amount of damage was caused some of the bombing went astray and the scale of destruction was reduced accordingly. Many bombs fell on rural areas and others in the sea, and casualties were light, with only ten or so killed and a few seriously injured. London, too, escaped with surprisingly little damage and few casualties.

Forty-one night fighters of Nos. 10, 11, 12 and 13 Groups (12 Blenheims, four Hurricanes, 13 Gladiators, five Defiants and four Beaufighters) flew patrols but no combats were reported. Nor were any enemy aircraft claimed destroyed by AA Command, which expended 2,462 rounds of HAA ammunition. AA guns were in action at Plymouth, Harwich, Cardiff, Portland and the London Inner Artillery Zone, and bombs actually fell at Plymouth, Ripley, near Reading, East Lothian and in the London area at Lambeth, Southwark, Dartford, Woolwich, Edmonton, Tottenham and Purley. Minelaying was observed off the Thames Estuary.

The fog which had restricted operations on November 25 persisted on November 26, but cleared this day allowing several fighter sweeps over Kent. All told, six Messerschmitt Bf 109s were lost, including Gefr. W. Heidorn and Uffz. H. Dhein, both from 2/JG51, who were reported missing after an operation to the Dover area. Those that came down in Britain were as follows:

2/JG51 Messerschmitt Bf 109E-4 (4101). Following fighter action pilot made a forced landing at Manston Airfield 3.40 p.m. Lt. W. Teumer taken prisoner. Aircraft Black 12+ repaired and flown by RAF Enemy Aircraft Flight as DG200.

Aircraft now preserved in Battle of Britain Museum, Hendon.

3/JG51 Messerschmitt Bf 109E-1 (6218). Shot down in combat with Spitfires of No. 41 and No. 74 Squadrons 3.35 p.m. Believed that which crashed at Sarnden Farm, Iden Green, Kent. Gefr. J. Hergefeld missing. Aircraft Brown 2+ destroyed.

Parts of the aircraft recovered by Steve Vizard and the site was subsequently re-excavated by the Brenzett Aeronautical Museum in September 1978. During this recovery acknowledged expert on the Me 109, Peter Foote, found a piece of airframe bearing what was believed to have been a large figure '2' in a brown or very dark yellow colour. This provided a clue to the identity of the pilot who was buried as an unknown airman in Benenden Churchyard. Later the body was exhumed and reinterred at Cannock Chase, still as unknown (Block 1 Grave 82).

3/JG51 Messerschmitt Bf 109E-4 (1634). Shot down in combat with Spitfires of No. 41 and No. 74 Squadrons. Crashed at Crundale House Farm, Crundale, Kent 3.35 p.m. Uffz. A. Benzinger missing presumed killed. Aircraft Brown 6+ destroyed.

Parts recovered by Tony Graves and John Tickner of the London Air Museum and now in the Tangmere Museum. Included are several sheep's ear tags dated 1939 from sheep's carcases which were used to fill the impact crater.

3/JG51 Messerschmitt Bf 109E-4 (1653). Following combat with Spitfires of No. 41 and No. 74 Squadrons aircraft made a forced landing with only slight damage at Horton Court, Monks Horton 3.37 p.m. Fw. W. Erdniss taken prisoner. Aircraft Brown 5+ captured.

Aircraft shipped to New Zealand for exhibition and scrapped 1948.

The loss during the night which was to leave British Intelligence baffled for some time was the following:

6/KG77 Junkers Ju 88A-5 (7116). Hit power cables and broke up at Blindley Heath, South Godstone, Surrey 1.35 a.m. No trace of the crew was found but from hurriedly written notes on the cover of a book found in the wreckage it appeared that the aircraft had been in difficulties. One read, 'I must have a DF bearing'. Another read, 'Pass round — bale out'. The crew baled out over Reims, France, and the aircraft flew from France to Britain unmanned. Aircraft 3Z+EP destroyed.

The few remaining fragments were recovered by the Halstead War Museum. A box of matches removed from the wreck at the time of the crash is in the possession of John Ellis.

Forty years later. The five Cardiff firemen were killed about 200 yards to the left of the white-painted tank. In the foreground the former Pennar Barracks — now Pennar Park holiday complex. These remaining tanks were taken down in 1985.

One of the greatest mysteries of the Blitz — like the aircraft it concerns — comes in two parts! At 0130 hours on the 28th a Ju 88 crashed near Blindley Heath, Surrey. Although its tail unit broke away as it struck an overhead cable, the aircraft remained mainly intact and proved to be a good specimen for examination by AI1(g) and other branches of Air Intelligence. Examination of the wreckage revealed the markings 3Z+EP, identifying it with 6/KG77, and a study of maps and other documents found on board indicated that its base was Reims. Also revealed were the positions of the Knickebein III and V transmitters and other large scale maps showed targets in London and Coventry. Finally there was a list of 12 airfields available for emergency use with details of their runways, Lorenz beam approach frequencies, etc. Strange to relate, however, no trace was found of the German crew.

THURSDAY, NOVEMBER 28-29

Sunset: 1655 Sunrise: 0842
Moon: None (New Moon)

Major attack on Liverpool/Birkenhead. Extensive minelaying covering the Thames Estuary, mouth of the Humber, Liverpool Bay, the Bristol Channel and the Norfolk coast.

UK — Mainly fair in all districts.
The Continent — Rain, hail and thunder locally. Mist inland in some areas later in the night.

Daylight operations were centred on reconnaissance flights, fighter sweeps over Kent and attacks on shipping off the Isle of Wight. Weather conditions were good throughout the day and about 270 German sorties were flown.

Night activity began at 1730 hours, Liverpool/Birkenhead being the principal target for both Luftflotten 2 and 3. In total, 439 long-range bombers were operating, with 324 crews reaching and bombing their Merseyside targets and 21 bombing London. Luftflotte 3 also sent nine aircraft to Bristol, six to Southampton, four to Birmingham, three to Portsmouth and one each to Plymouth, Portland and Cardiff. About 50 aircraft of IX Fliegerkorps laid mines.

The attack on Liverpool/Birkenhead, the most important port on the West Coast, was centred on the east bank of the Mersey where port installations extended in an unbroken line for some 10 kilometres. The Schwerpunkt also encompassed adjoining parts of the city with its many warehouses, gas works and power stations, and included a three kilometres stretch of the Birkenhead side of the river wherein lay the administrative offices, mills, granaries, power station, gas works, wet dock, cattle yard, dry docks, lock gates and other important targets of the port system. During the attack, which started at 1915 and went on to 0315 hours, both towns were severely hit, the attackers dropping 356 tonnes of HE (including 151 'very heavy' bombs) and Flambo and 860 BSK (30,960 incendiaries). On the Birkenhead side many explosions were observed in the docks area and in the town, among goods sheds and in the immediate vicinity of the gas works and power station. On the Liverpool bank it was a similar story, with many large fires and explosions.

Cloud cover of the Target Area was variable throughout the night and bombing by visual means was possible only at times; most of the aiming was done on the glow of fires visible through the overcast or by means of DR navigation. Few crews were able to report on the results of their attack and it was considered that assessment could best be made after a daylight reconnaissance sortie. From the fire glow visible on both banks of the Mersey, however, there was every possibility that a successful attack had been made.

Details of Luftflotte 2's part in the operation are not available, except that 132 aircraft of this Air Fleet bombed their Merseyside targets. Luftflotte 3 dispatched 261 aircraft; of this number 192 crews claimed to have bombed Liverpool/Birkenhead, 48 attacked alternative targets and 18 aircraft aborted. One aircraft was listed as missing, one crashed shortly after take off, and a third crashed in home territory upon returning. Of the three aircraft sent to Glasgow two bombed alternative targets.

Participating units of Luftflotte 3 over Liverpool were as follows:

LG1: 19 Ju 88, 2237-0055
I/KG27: 14 He 111, 2135-2245
II/KG27: 8 He 111, 2058-2145
III/KG27: 8 He 111, 2250-0050
KGr100: 8 He 111, 1955-2040
KGr606: 7 Do 17, 0115-0158
I/KG51: 6 Ju 88, 2240-0050
II/KG51: 9 Ju 88, 0050-0208
III/KG51: 5 Ju 88, 0045-0100
I/KG54: 12 Ju 88, 2222-2350
II/KG54: 1 Ju 88, 2200
III/KG54 (officially still KGr 806): 8 Ju 88, 2220-2355
Stab/KG55: 3 He 111, 2035-2045
I/KG55: 8 He 111, 2025-2106
II/KG55: 8 He 111, 1915-2025 (opened attack, dropping flares to illuminate the Target Area)
III/KG55: 12 He 111, 2050-2140
KG1: 6 He 111 and 5 Ju 88, 2030-2312
KG76: 7 Ju 88, 2005-2132
KG77: 16 Ju 88, 2040-2230
I and II/KG26: 19 He 111, 2035-2300
III/KG26: 3 He 111, 2012-2055

The subsidiary raid on London started at 1840 and terminated at 0045 hours, with 21 aircraft dropping 22 tonnes of HE and Flambo and 44 BSK (1,584 IBs). The CP was centred on the City and Government offices

More than 130 miles away, near Reims, there was another mystery. Following engine trouble the four members of the crew of a Ju 88A5 of 6/KG77 baled out. All landed safely, but no trace could be found of their aircraft, which carried the markings 3Z+EP. Ken Wakefield adds that 'Even Fido in the picture above couldn't work out what had happened and the "mysteries" of that night remained unsolved for the remainder of the war. Only by comparing German and British records for the period under review was it revealed that, unguided by human hand, the Ju 88 had flown on for a considerable time until, presumably, it ran out of fuel and came gliding out of the night sky for a landing in Surrey.'

One of the outstanding German fighter aces of the period, lauded in almost every issue of *Der Adler*, was Helmut Wick. He was Geschwader Kommodore with JG2 — the Richthofen Geschwader. Read what he wrote on returning from a sortie over the Southampton area on November 6: 'We then met a crowd of Hurricanes flying lower than ourselves. Just as I was about to start the attack, I saw something above me and immediately called on the intercom "Achtung! Spitfires ahead". The Spitfires were sufficiently far off that I could still launch the attack on the lower-flying Hurricanes. Just then the Hurricanes made a turn which proved to be their ruin. We shot down four of this group almost at once, one of which fell to me. The remaining Hurricanes turned away but began to climb again and during the climb I caught one of them flying on the right-hand side of the formation. The Hurricanes then dived steeply. I cannot fully explain my next experience, perhaps I was not quite fit or my nerves were frayed, but after my second Englishman went down, I wanted only to fly home. I still had fuel for a few more minutes of action, but the desire to return suddenly became too powerful. When we had completed our turn towards France, I spotted in front of me three Spitfires coming in from the sea. I saw them first and reached them quickly and the first one fell immediately. Now I said to myself, we must get them all. If we let them get away today they will probably kill some of my comrades tomorrow, now away with them! I set my teeth and started the next attack. The second Spitfire fell after a few bursts leaving only one whom I was determined would not return home to report his defeat. I fired at him with my machine guns and soon white smoke poured from him. The pilot appeared to be hit because the aircraft went down out of control, but suddenly it recovered and I was forced to attack it again. The Spitfire slowly turned over and crashed to the ground. Now it really was time to fly home. When I arrived back over my airfield, I did not perform the usual stunts to indicate my victories as my fuel was almost exhausted. When I jumped out of the plane, I hugged the first person who came across to me, who by chance turned out to be an old friend from my training days and who was now a Stuka pilot. I have now scored fifty-three victories and need only one more to draw level with my old instructor, Oberstleutnant Mölders.'

quarter, where a large fire was reported. Another large fire was seen in the area of the Royal Victoria Dock, but cloud and mist made it impossible for crews to assess the effectiveness of the attack.

Crews failing to find their main targets in London and Liverpool/Birkenhead bombed a number of alternatives including, it was claimed, objectives in Bournemouth, Exmouth, Brighton, Chichester and elsewhere.

Although bomb reports showed an obvious and very heavy concentration on Merseyside, incidents were also reported from many other places in the Midlands, Home Counties, the South, South-West and Scotland. Among the places bombed were Bromley, Benfleet, Watford, Shoreham, Selsey, Bognor, Gosport, Stockbury, Ringwould, Aylesbury district, Stamford, Grantham, Matlock, Birmingham, Doncaster, Runcorn, Nantwich, Portsmouth, Exeter, Yeovil, Edinburgh, Ardrossan, and near Dumfries. Except in the Merseyside area, however, where damage and casualties were heavy, no serious consequences occurred. Initial casualty figures for Liverpool/Birkenhead were 264 killed and 62 seriously injured but, as usual, these Ministry of Home Security figures increased as more bodies or injured survivors were found among the rubble of bombed buildings. Four people were killed in Exeter.

Most of the damage in Merseyside occurred on the Liverpool side of the river and many districts of the city were affected. Serious fires were caused and there was a considerable amount of damage to private property. Water and gas mains, telephone communications, underground electric cables, sewers and overhead tram wires also suffered extensively, but there were only two cases of critical damage to industrial premises important to the war effort. The dock area was little affected and overall the attack achieved little of military value. Casualties would have been fewer but for a direct hit on a large public air raid shelter.

Defensive patrols were flown by 48 night fighters of Nos. 10, 11, 12 and 13 Groups but no enemy aircraft were shot down. The only British night fighter casualty this day was Beaufighter R2140 of No. 29 Squadron which crashed at Potterhanworth, Lincolnshire, following an engine failure; the pilot was unable to maintain height on one engine and the crew baled out.

On a night in which AA Command used about 15,000 rounds, only one enemy aircraft was claimed destroyed (by the Mersey guns) while another was claimed 'probably destroyed' over Gloucester. Batteries engaging the enemy that night were in the IAZ, at Slough, Fareham, Newport, Cardiff, Gloucester, Chatham, Merseyside, Thames and Medway North, Manchester, Bristol, Leeds, Birmingham, Bramley, Portland, Holton Heath, Yeovil, Plymouth, Swansea, Humber, Forth and Crewe.

Again daylight sweeps by Messerschmitt Bf 109s were carried out over Kent and one near the Isle of Wight which resulted in the loss of a Messerschmitt Bf 110 of 3(F)/31. A further Messerschmitt Bf 109 of 1/JG26 flown by Fw. W. Karminski is believed to have crashed off the Kent coast. The following came down in the vicinity of Great Britain:

The German air historian Heinz Nowarra comments that 'Wick's report of these events reflects the severe strain on the nerves which the fighter pilots were undergoing. On November 28 he made another sortie with Oberleutnants Leie, Pflanz and Leutnant Fiby. North-east of the Isle of Wight, they met a Spitfire squadron which they attacked immediately and Wick scored his fifty-fifth victory. Shortly afterwards, Leie spotted a lone Spitfire that was attacking Fiby and, at about 3,000 metres, shot it down into the sea for his eleventh victory. On the afternoon of the same day these four flew a second sortie and, approaching the Isle of Wight, they spotted a British formation heading towards Bournemouth. An attack was immediately launched and Wick destroyed another Spitfire while Leie and Pflanz unsuccessfully attacked two others which had remained above the formation. During this fight they lost Wick and before they had time to search for him they were attacked by another high-flying group of Spitfires and only escaped with difficulty. Leie and Fiby returned home safely. Pflanz emerged from the dog-fight at around 3,000 metres and saw about five kilometres ahead of him two aircraft heading towards France. Suddenly he noticed that the second aircraft was firing at the first, and this, a Bf 109, suddenly crashed into the sea. Pflanz had by now drawn up behind the British aircraft and shot it down into the sea close to its recent victim. Although the German rescue service was alerted, neither Major Wick nor the British pilot were ever found and the last entry against Wick's name was "28.11.40, one Spitfire shot down over Bournemouth 5.13 p.m." This was his fifty-sixth and last victory.' The man who finally got the better of the German ace, but who lost his own life in the process seconds later, was Flight Lieutenant John Dundas of No. 609 Squadron.

Stab/JG2 Messerschmitt Bf 109E-4 (5344). Shot down by Flight Lieutenant J. C. Dundas DFC in a Spitfire of No. 609 Squadron. Crashed into the sea south-west of the Isle of Wight. Major Helmut Wick (Geschwader Kommodore) missing. Aircraft lost.

2/JG26 Messerschmitt Bf 109E-3 (1289). Due to fuel shortage pilot made a good forced landing at Udimore, Sussex 4.00 p.m. Uffz. H. Wolf taken prisoner. Aircraft Black 2+ captured.

Aircraft now in the Saxonwold Museum, Johannesburg, South Africa. Maker's plate found by Steve Vizard in 1984 amongst the remains of the RAF Air Intelligence 1(g) collection found at Kenley.

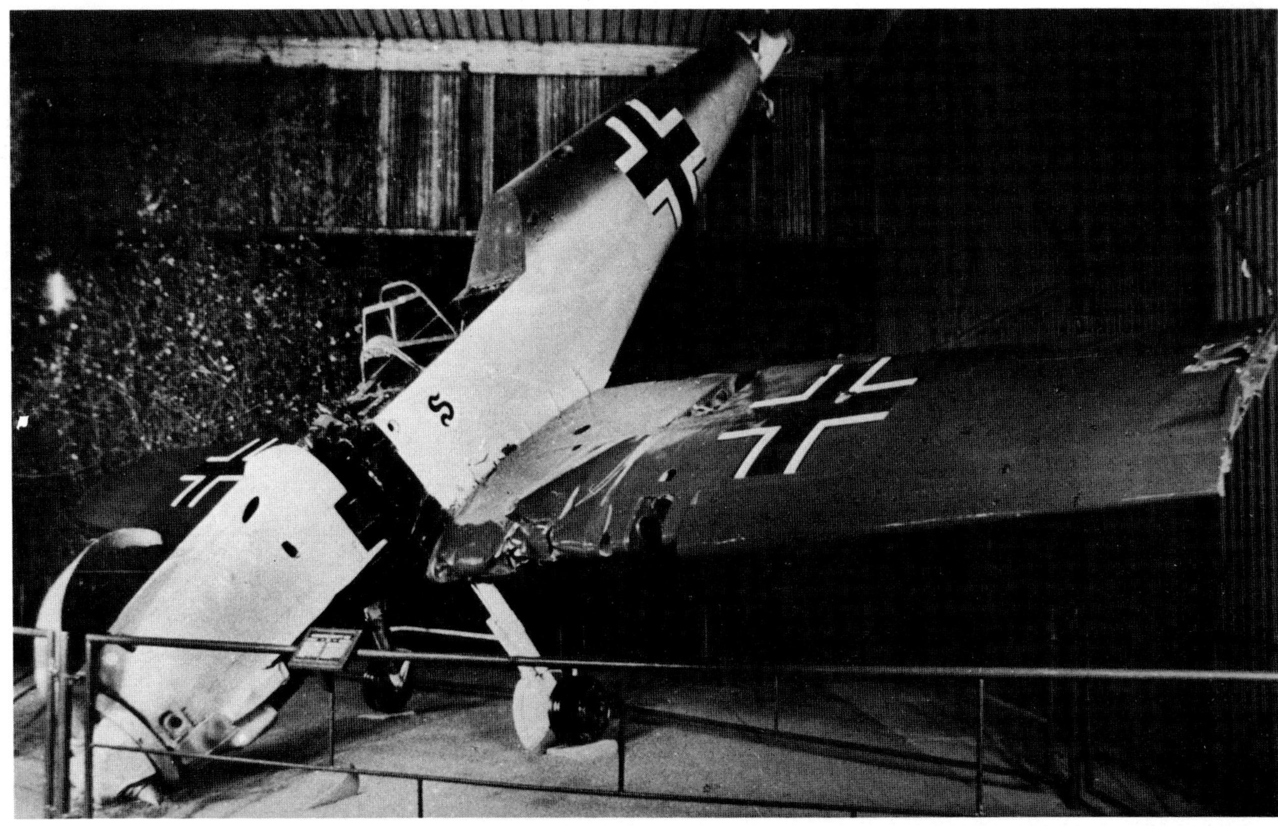

Apart from Mölders and his famed JG51, the other rival in Jagdfliegerführer 2 operating from north-eastern France at this time was the 'Schlageter' Geschwader, No. 26. They also lost an aircraft on the 28th, Unteroffizier Heinz Wolf's Bf 109, which touched down at Udimore. Today that machine is on display in its original condition at the National Museum of Military History having been shipped to South Africa about 1942 to be displayed in a 'Liberty Cavalcade' as part of a drive for war bonds.

FRIDAY, NOVEMBER 29-30

Sunset: 1654 Sunrise: 0844
Moon: Dusk — 1732 (New +1)

Major attack on London. Minor operations by Italian bombers against Ipswich, Great Yarmouth and Lowestoft, with a few long-range night fighters on offensive patrols over RAF airfields. Minelaying in the Thames Estuary.

UK — Cloudy in Scotland with rain showers on the western coasts of England and Wales. Elsewhere mainly cloudless with widespread mist and fog developing inland. Winds calm to light and variable, but fresh in the North.

The Continent — Generally fair in all areas but fog developing later in night.

German operations during the day took the form of extensive reconnaissance and shipping attacks in the English Channel, the Thames Estuary and the Irish Sea. Attacks on ships off the East Coast also materialised and there were the usual fighter and fighter-bomber sweeps against London and the South-East, but all to little avail. Some 200 enemy aircraft were involved, but little serious damage was caused on a day which was fair with local showers in coastal areas.

From 1720 hours incoming raids were plotted in the vicinity of the Scheldt Estuary, but none of these crossed the coast until 1840 hours and it was assumed that the initial raiders were intent on minelaying in the Thames Estuary. Once the main force started crossing in, however, activity was intense and concentrated on the London area. Altogether 371 long-range Luftwaffe bombers, nine CAI bombers and four Luftwaffe night fighters were involved in offensive operations. Of these, the crews of 335 aircraft claimed to have bombed London while the nine Italian aircraft attacked Ipswich, Great Yarmouth and Lowestoft. Minelaying was also completed satisfactorily and long-range intruding night fighters of I/NJG2 patrolled the vicinity of airfields in the eastern half of the country.

In the attack on London, which lasted from 1820 to 0130 hours, 380 tonnes of HE (including 17 'very heavy' weapons) and Flambo were dropped, together with 820 BSK (29,520 IBs). Again, the Concentration Point was the area encompassing the City and Government offices quarter. As usual, the attack was opened by II/KG55's flare-dropping He 111s; KGr100 did not arrive on the scene until some 40 minutes after the first aircraft of II/KG55 had bombed while III/KG26, the third Beleuchtergruppe, was sandwiched between the two.

Cloud cover decreased during the night and permitted visual bomb aiming, but a thickening ground mist — in evidence from the outset and adversely affecting the value of II/KG55's flares — hindered precise observation of the attack. Nevertheless, two large fires were discerned to the west and north-west of the 'S-Bend' of the Thames, with ten large fires in the city centre. One covered an area of some 200×300 metres and some 15 smaller fires were seen in the City where most of the 12 SC 1000s fell. In the Government quarter 11 large fires were reported, with many large explosions.

Luftflotte 3's participation in the attack was as follows:

KG1: 20 He 111 and Ju 88, 1855-2125
KG76: 10 He 111, 1900-1956
KG77: 17 Ju 88, 1853-2254
I and II/KG26: 19 He 111, 1945-2355
III/KG26: 4 He 111, 1840-1945
LG1: 25 Ju 88, 1920-2102
I/KG27: 19 He 111, 1945-2245
II/KG27: 8 He 111, 2107-2145
III/KG27: 14 He 111, 2212-2330
KGr100: 10 He 111, 1900-1949
KGr606: 2 Do 17, 2315-2345
Stab/KG55: 3 He 111, 2115-2122
I/KG55: 11 He 111, 1902-1955
II/KG55: 12 He 111, 1820-1925 (opened attack with flares and 16 very heavy HE bombs)
III/KG55: 11 He 111, 1954-2047
I/KG51: 10 Ju 88, 1942-2208
II/KG51: 7 Ju 88, 2244-2300
III/KG51: 3 Ju 88, 2312-2335
I/KG54: 8 Ju 88, 2308-2340
II/KG54: 6 Ju 88, 2350-0020
KGr806 (operating as III/KG54): 7 Ju 88, 0007-0040

One tiny piece — highly significant — remains in the UK — the plate giving model type and serial number which was found on Kenley airfield in 1984. (See page 101.)

Although there is no precise date with the photograph other than November 1940, it makes a nice comparison with the Watling Street as was. Tangye's City of London office stood on the corner with Queen Victoria Street which has since disappeared at this point when the Legal and General Assurance Company building was erected between 1953 and 1958.

One He 111 of II/KG27 was reported overdue and an aircraft of the same type belonging to KG1 crashed on its return to Saint-André.

Although heavy, the attack on London was of comparatively short duration and damage was mainly confined to a limited area in the eastern, southern and western districts of the capital. Some industrial damage was done and the railway system suffered. Reports of 131 people killed and 267 seriously injured were recorded by the Ministry of Home Security, which also recorded three killed in East Anglia. Some factories in London were hit but damage was negligible in all cases except one, when machinery was expected to take some days to repair. Several Civil Defence premises were damaged, however, including an AFS Station, ARP stores, two Wardens' Posts, a First Aid Post and a Report Centre. The Civic Centre at Dagenham and Richmond Town Hall were also severely damaged. Bombs intended for London also fell in various parts of the Home Counties, particularly in Surrey, and several fires were started in Brighton. Incidents were also recorded at Brentford, Digby, Kingston, Barking, Erith, and in rural districts of Essex and Sussex.

Plots of inbound hostile aircraft started as early as 1720 hours, from the direction of the Scheldt, but these early arrivals were engaged in minelaying in the Thames Estuary and involved some 30 aircraft of IX Fliegerkorps. At 1800 hours the Hampden Patrol, which had been laid on by Fighter Command during the afternoon in anticipation of the attack, was cancelled and the guns of the Inner Artillery Zone were given full reign to engage enemy aircraft, most of which were flying at heights between 12,000 and 20,000 feet. Within the IAZ the HAA guns fired 6,256 rounds, but no illuminations were obtained by searchlights. Many of the flares dropped, however, were engaged, with varying success, by small arms fire. Countrywide in excess of 9,000 HAA rounds were fired by AA Command, without success, with guns in action in the Solent area, at Bramley, Cardiff and Plymouth in addition to the IAZ.

Two incidents involving night fighters occurred on the 29th, resulting in damage to one and the destruction of the other. The aircraft written off was a Defiant (N1564) of No. 141 Squadron which, following an operational patrol, was attempting to land at Gravesend in poor visibility at 2000 hours. Its undercarriage failed to lock down and the aircraft was damaged beyond repair in the subsequent belly landing. The other accident involved Beaufighter R2141 of No. 29 Squadron; while making a flapless landing at Wellingore a heavy touch-down caused the undercarrige to collapse. Altogether 22 night fighters were operating, without success, although a Beaufighter from Tangmere established visual contact with an enemy aircraft near Beachy Head but was unable to engage before it was lost to sight. The absence of moonlight was no doubt a contributing factor.

A limited number of daylight reconnaissance operations resulted in a single loss.

Stab/StG1 Messerschmitt Bf 110 (2301). Brought down into the sea east of Ramsgate, Kent by the combined actions of nine pilots of No. 603 Squadron. Body of Oblt. R. Pytlik recovered from sea. Oblt. T. Fryer missing. Aircraft A5+AA lost.

The appearance of Aufklärungs aircraft on Friday afternoon in a last-minute recce boded no good for Southampton — the target for tonight. Since last weekend's big raid the city had been left to lick its wounds; now she was to undergo another double hit on Saturday and Sunday nights.

Another picture without an accurate date (it was not released until late 1941), showing the junction of Bernard Street and Below Bar, Southampton. On the right, just out of the photo, stands Holyrood Church, destroyed on Saturday night.

SATURDAY, NOVEMBER 30-DECEMBER 1

Sunset: 1653 Sunrise: 0845
Moon: Dusk — 1827 (New +2)

Major attack on Southampton. Limited minelaying between Plymouth and Lands End, off Milford Haven and between Cardiff and Weston-super-Mare.

UK — Cloudy in Scotland, northern England and Wales with occasional light rain in places. Widespread fog in inland districts of England and Wales, otherwise visibility moderate to good. Winds light to moderate in west, south-west and northern England, but gales at times in Scotland; elsewhere light or calm.

The Continent — Cloudy with generally poor visibility.

During the day fighter airfields in Nos. 11 and 12 Groups were fogbound, thereby reducing the RAF's ability to counter German operations, which included two attacks on London and the South-East and one in the Weymouth-Wareham area. Fighter-bombers comprised the bulk of the enemy raiders, some of which dropped bombs in Piccadilly and Westminster. Some 185 hostile aircraft penetrated inland in the course of the day while 242 were engaged in coastal anti-shipping operations.

Night activity started at 1800 hours and was largely confined to the Southampton area. Of 147 bombers operating the crews of 128 claimed to have bombed their primary targets there and four aborted; four crews were dispatched to London and the remainder were engaged in minelaying.

In the attack on Southampton, which took place between 1818 and 0055 hours, 152 tonnes of HE and Flambo and 598 BSK (21,528 IBs) were delivered and, with well broken cloud over the target, bombing was mostly visual. The attack was again opened by the 'Pathfinding' II/KG55 who, in their customary manner of first illuminating the target with LC 50 flares, dropped some of the heaviest HEs available, including two SC 1800s, two SC 1700s, six SD 1400s and six SD 1000s. By the time the last aircraft of the Gruppe had bombed at 1900 hours, 38 fires were in evidence, some of them very large, including a major conflagration in an oil or

Must have started about five past or ten past seven, and it just went on and on and on, not so much terrifying as stupefying. Ten o'clock, still bombers after bombers, the swish, whistle, whine or rushing roar of bombs on the way down . . .

There wasn't much said in our shelter, what could be said? But our mother suffered so, and around eleven she couldn't help crying out almost in disbelief 'When is it going to stop, is there to be no end to this?' It hurt me in knowing how it affected my mother, she had enough to bear as it was with three sons in the Army and a daughter in the WAAF.

At about one o'clock in the morning there was an ominous thud near the shelter. Father dived out to look, gave a shout about an incendiary and went into action to tackle it. My elder sister on leave from the WAAF dived out to help. As they were trying to put it and its fire out our local warden, Mr Lee, leaned over the fence and told my father and sister that they mustn't put water on it as it would be a calcium carbide bomb. My father was the last one to take advice so went on doing what he was doing, putting soil, vegetation and water on it until it was well and truly out.

A bit later when I dived out to the toilet at the back of the house I was struck by the eerie temporary silence between attacks. Of course there were sounds, like distant and not-so-distant gunfire and the faint crackling of fires and thuds as buildings collapsed, but even so it sounded like silence after those many hours of such noise.

The all-clear went about half past six but it did not mean we could sleep then, nerves too shattered after that lot. Someone tried the gas stove for those vital cuppas but it only partly worked and was abandoned, it being very dangerous of course with the gas mains blown up. We were lucky, because we had a good old kitchen range so we got out hot drinks and cooked food. Our local baker, Mr Hoare, threw his baking ovens open for the use of people who had no means to cook.

Unbeknown to us children, father disappeared that morning to make arrangements for us to go with our mother to her sister at Middle Wallop for a break from the raids. We were told near mid-day and caught the mid-afternoon train to Stockbridge. Found when we arrived we were only one field away from very large air base. We had jumped from one great noise to another — but we were thankful for freedom from bombs raining down.

FREDERICK GOODRIDGE, 1977

gas holder complex near Southampton power station. This produced dark red flames and dense black smoke billowing up to 1,000 metres (3,300ft). An hour later and the fires were visible from the French coast; more than 60 fires were raging and the glow was even visible from the French coast south of Jersey. Among other observations participating crews reported two ships on fire in their berths, and the general impression was that the attack was in the same category as those on Coventry and Bristol. Almost incredibly, at 1000 hours the next day observers at Cherbourg could see a yellow cloud of smoke on the horizon, indicating the whereabouts of the stricken city.

The attack, wholly conducted by Luftflotte 3, was carried out by the following units of Fliegerkorps I, IV and V:

I/LG1: 5 Ju 88, 1855-2000
III/LG1: 6 Ju 88, 1858-2017
II/KG27: 7 He 111, 2015-2047
III/KG27: 14 He 111, 2100-2210
KGr100: 9 He 111, 1855-1910 (X-Verfahren bombing as follow-up Firelighters)
I/KG51: 7 Ju 88, 0005-0055
II/KG51: 10 Ju 88, 2316-2355
III/KG51: 2 Ju 88, 2324-2326
Stab/KG55: 3 He 111, 2200-2212
I/KG55: 7 He 111, 2256-2343
II/KG55: 12 He 111, 1818-1900 (opened attack with LC 50 flares and 16 very heavy bombs)
III/KG55: 9 He 111, 2225-2350
KG77: 9 Ju 88, 1910-2108
I and II/KG26: 24 He 111, 1855-2045
III/KG26: 4 He 111, 1820-1920 (Y-Verfahren bombing as back-up Firelighters)

As reported by the German bomber crews, considerable damage was done in Southampton by fire. Serious fires were started in a large timber yard, at the Pirelli works, in a power station, in the South Hants Hospital and in Southampton telephone exchange. All telephone lines linking the city to the outside world were cut and communication was only possible by means of dispatch rider. A shortage of water and fire appliances added to the difficulties. Many fires raged unattended and much of High Street was gutted. Many bombs fell on the central districts of the city, where something like two thirds of the main shopping centre was destroyed and where many of the casualties (70 killed and 120 seriously injured) were caused. On the whole, damage to important factories and the port was slight and there might well have been many more casualties with the fairly well concentrated bombing that was achieved. Outside of Southampton bombs were reported in several parts of the New Forest, at Wootton in the Isle of Wight, Beddington (Surrey), Weymouth, Harrow and Hampstead Heath.

With ground visibility at or below 1,000 yards in many areas, no night fighter patrols were flown, but two raiders were claimed damaged by the Plymouth AA guns. Elsewhere guns opened fire at Yeovil, Portland, Holton Heath, the Solent, Falmouth, Cardiff and the IAZ. Over the entire Command some 6,000 rounds were fired, 2,000 of them by guns in the Southampton area.

The routine daytime fighter sweeps claimed four aircraft, a pilot of 9/JG53 forced to ditch into the Channel being later rescued.

2/JG27 Messerschmitt Bf 109E-1 (6313). Suffered engine failure when several front pistons went through the water jacket. Made forced landing at Woodyhyde Farm, Worth Matravers, Dorset 1.15 p.m. Uffz. P. Wacker taken prisoner. Aircraft ▲+G captured damaged.

5/JG53 Messerschmitt Bf 109E-4 (1145). Shot down by Flight Lieutenant J. C. Mungo-Park DFC and Pilot Officer H. M. Stephen DFC of No. 74 Squadron. Crashed at Ruckinge, near Ham Street, Kent 2.30 p.m. Uffz. F. Wägelein baled out but his parachute was holed and he died on December 3 of injuries received on landing. Aircraft Grey 3+ destroyed.
Famous for being acclaimed as Biggin Hill's 600th kill. Major recovery by Mike Llewellyn of the Kent Battle of Britain Museum revealed many items including control column, Revi gunsight, first aid kit and the aircraft manufacturer's plate which confirmed the identity of the wreck.

6/JG53 Messerschmitt Bf 109E-1 (4900). Aircraft made a forced landing at Wheelsgate Farm, Old Romney 11.00 a.m. cause uncertain. Fw. H. Schmidt taken prisoner. Aircraft White 11+ captured damaged.

As a symbol of the city's worst weekend of the war, when 137 people died — 96 through direct hits on shelters — and a further 471 were seriously injured, the 'sailor's' church has been left unrepaired as a memorial, dedicated especially to those of the Merchant Navy. (In 1972 a further plaque was added; moved from its original site in Cemetery Road, The Common, it remembers the crew, stewards, sailors and firemen from Southampton who lost their lives on April 15, 1912 on the SS *Titanic*.)

ZWISCHEN DEN KÄMPFEN

Freizeitgestaltung bei einer Kampfstaffel

Entre los combates

The December 3 issue of *Der Adler* laid emphasis on the continuing Tiefangriff against Britain. The 'Boy's Own' style of cover illustration was contrasted on the back with scenes of airmen relaxing between sorties.

DECEMBER 1940

Beaufighter delivery delays and the continued lack of success obtained by the Blenheim and other fighters led to the search for an alternative twin-engined aircraft for use as a night fighter and the choice soon fell on the Douglas DB-7 high performance light bomber. Known as the Boston, the type was already on order for the RAF, but an early version of the American-built aircraft arrived in Britain in advance of the British order when aircraft destined for France and Belgium were diverted when those countries were overrun by the Germans. These early DB-7s proved unsuitable for operational use but were used for pilot conversion training until the British specification Bostons, suitably modified as night fighters, became available.

Modification of the Boston to night fighter configuration was undertaken at Burtonwood, near Warrington, and two versions emerged. Both were known as the Havoc Mk 1 but one featured a 'solid' nose containing eight ·303-inch machine guns and was equipped with AI radar; the second version retained the transparent nose of the Boston and was, in effect, a night fighter-bomber intended for offensive patrols over German bomber bases in occupied Europe. Accordingly, in the interests of secrecy, this version was not fitted with AI radar but had an augmented armament which included four fixed machine guns in the nose. The first squadron to receive the AI-equipped Havoc was No. 85; training commenced in December, but operations did not get under way until February 1941. The second version was earmarked for No. 23 Squadron but complete re-equipment took some time, despite the unit receiving its first Havoc in October 1940.

Although well trained in general flying, RAF night fighter pilots were left to develop their own techniques and tactics during the early months of the night air war over Britain for, at that time, there were no night fighter Operational Training Units teaching what was to become a very specialised form of air combat. There was in existence, however, the Night Fighting Flight of the Fighter Interception Unit (FIU) at Tangmere, a small unit initially equipped with AI-fitted Blenheims and engaged in the development of night fighting techniques and procedures. In due course the experience of the FIU and its Night Fighting Flight, together with practical experience gained by the operational squadrons, was used to formulate methods which formed the basis of instructional courses at the specialist Night Fighter Operational Training Units. These taught crews the stealthy AI approach from behind and below with the operator directing his pilot with a running commentary on range and position until the pilot was able to see the enemy aircraft and open fire. The first night fighter OTU, No. 54, opened at Church Fenton in December and thereafter provided a supply of well trained pilots and AI operators to meet the needs of an expanding night fighter force.

An analysis of German ground/air communications by the 'Y' Service produced some valuable intelligence on the methods used by the Luftwaffe in carrying out major night attacks. Normally, specific aircraft of KGr100 or II/KG55 were required to send back weather reports to their control station by W/T; usually this took place as they crossed the British coast and upon arrival in the target area. Occasionally, other reports were transmitted when unusual or unexpected weather conditions were experienced and included reports of icing conditions. In the case of KGr100, the first aircraft to take off normally used the W/T callsign 'F4GA', the second aircraft 'F4GB', and so on — at one time British Air Intelligence was under the impression that the F4GA was the aircraft of KGr100's Kommandeur, Hauptmann (later Major) Kurd Aschenbrenner, but this was not so; it was merely the first aircraft in the 'stream'.

Having carried out its attack and reported on the weather over the target, this first 'Firelighter' aircraft often left the target area for a while, only to return to report on fire developments. This procedure was sometimes repeated several times, the bomber cruising around for quite a long time before setting course on its return flight.

As it gained experience in night bombing on a large scale, the Luftwaffe developed and modified its tactics, although basically its operations were very much influenced by the phase of the moon and forecast weather conditions, factors which often dictated the choice of target within the offensive's broad strategic plan. Visual navigation and bomb aiming — still preferable to DR/radio assisted methods — were only really feasible in conditions of little or no cloud and when the moon was between first and last quarters. Thus, for about 14 nights of each period of a month visual bombing was difficult because of insufficient light and during the remainder of the month only about four nights either side of full moon provided ideal conditions. It follows then that in any one moon period only about eight nights were likely to provide sufficient moonlight. And to expect good weather to coincide with the moon's best phase for eight consecutive nights was asking too much in wintertime over the British Isles. With these factors in mind, the Führungsstab usually chose inland targets during the full moon period; less difficult-to-find targets were selected when just outside this period (from approximately four nights either side of the optimum full moon period), with easy to find targets, such as those on coasts or major rivers, reserved for nights of little or no moonlight. However, in wintertime in Northern Europe good, clear nights are likely to produce mist or fog by the early hours and for this reason it was often necessary for the bombers to be back at their bases before visibility became impaired. On cloudy nights, while target finding was more difficult, the prospects of a safe return were infinitely better.

Ideally, then, clear conditions over the target were desired, with the moon at or near full and with medium cloud over the bomber bases, but such an ideal arrangement was seldom met during the winter of 1940-41. Nevertheless, following the success of the full moon attacks in November similar large scale operations were now envisaged for the same period each month. They were to be known as Moonlight Serenades (Mondscheinserenade), with each target city given a code name in the same manner that Korn had indicated Coventry. Examples were Loge for London, Bruder for Bristol, Liebe for Liverpool, Süden for Southampton and Pinie for Plymouth.

German offensive operations in December followed the pattern established in the second half of November but with a target list expanded to include Sheffield, Portsmouth and Manchester. There were 16 serious attacks, eleven of which came into the major category and five classed as heavy; minelaying was undertaken on six nights. Weather conditions could be described as typical for December and no offensive operations at all were possible on eight nights. On only four nights was there little or no cloud over Britain.

London remained the principal target with three major attacks while Manchester and Liverpool received two each. Birmingham (one major and two heavy raids) also suffered badly, as did Bristol and Sheffield (one major and one heavy attack each). A major attack was also launched against Southampton while Portsmouth underwent an attack classed as heavy. Again, as had been the case in November, particularly unpleasant for the civilian population were attacks on two successive nights against the cities of Birmingham, Liverpool, Birkenhead and Manchester.

German long-range bombers flew 3,979 night sorties during the month while long-range night fighters flew 66; in a minor supportive role the CAI flew 33 night sorties, all of them directed at Harwich but with little effect.

Daylight operations by the Luftwaffe in December remained relatively insignificant and for the most part consisted of coastal and overland reconnaissance flights, fighter sweeps over south-east England and fighter-bomber raids on the London area. There were also a number of 'pirate' operations by single bombers on days when cloud cover enabled attempts on specific targets, such as aircraft factories, but they achieved little.

Despite a series of depressions that

Der Geleitzug ist in heillose Verwirrung geraten. Verschiedene Schiffe treiben, lodernden Riesenfackeln gleich, auf dem Meer. Ein Zerstörer, der vergeblich den Angriff abzuwehren versucht hat, geht mit schwerer Schlagseite langsam in die Tiefe

El convoy está en desesperada confusión. Diferentes barcos van a la deriva como giganteceas antorchas. Un destructor que procuró en vano defenderse del ataque va hundiéndose lentamente de costado

ritmo de hundimientos de barcos el precario abastecimiento de Inglaterra. Inglaterra es una isla que no puede vivir ni morir más que por el mar. Los aviadores alemanes realizan en sus audaces ataques verdaderas proezas en el aire. No hace mucho, un aparato Heinkel He 111 pudo dispersar un convoy a pesar de ir escoltado por veinte destructores y una serie de submarinos. El primer objetivo que se asignó la valerosa tripulación fué un destructor que quedó inmovilizado inclinándose cada vez más por efecto de las ocho bombas recibidas. Barco por barco fué bombardeando después el avión los otros causando enormes incendios y averías en tres grandes cargos. Aunque el He 111 recibió casi veinte blancos del intenso fuego de defensa regresó felizmente a su base después este golpe de audacia

Zeichnungen: Wilhelm Beitz (3)

Wo das Kampfflugzeug He 111 auftaucht, jagt es dem „meerbeherrschenden England" panischen Schrecken ein

Aufn. Scherl-Bilderdienst

Donde aparece el He 111 siembra el pánico en la "dominadora del mar" en Inglaterra

Ein Gigant geht in die Tiefe

El hundimiento de un gigante

Ein deutsches schweres Kampfflugzeug griff am 26. Oktober 1940 in einem kühnen Tiefflug das stark geschützte britische Transportschiff „Empress of Britain" an und versetzte ihm mit zwei schweren Bomben den Todesstoß. In wenigen Minuten bildete der Koloß ein einziges Flammenmeer. Das brennende Wrack wurde am nächsten Tage, als britische Kriegsschiffe es in einen Hafen einschleppen wollten, vollends vernichtet und in den Grund gebohrt

El 26 de octubre de 1940 atacó un avión alemán pesado de combate en audaz vuelo bajo al barco de transporte inglés fuertemente protegido "Empress of Britain" y le asestó con dos bombas pesadas el golpe de muerte. En pocos minutos se convirtió el coloso en un mar de llamas. Los restos ardiendo se fueron al fondo completamente destruidos cuando querían remolcarle a un puerto barcos de guerra británicos

Mit ihren 42 000 BRT war die „Empress of Britain" das zehntgrößte Schiff der Welt. Sein Verlust bedeutet für England einen empfindlichen Schlag. Unsere Bilder, die von einem Besatzungsmitglied des deutschen Kampfflugzeuges während des Angriffs mit einer einfachen Kamera aufgenommen wurden, zeigen die verheerende Wirkung der Bombentreffer. Hoffnungslos den verzehrenden Flammen preisgegeben, sucht das Schiff sich weiteren Angriffen zu entziehen, doch ist das Vernichtungswerk bereits getan

Aufnahmen Luftwaffe (5), Scherl-Bilderdienst (1)

El "Empress of Britain" con sus 42.000 toneladas era el décimo barco del mundo por su tamaño. Su pérdida es un grave golpe para Inglaterra. Nuestras fotografías, tomadas durante el ataque con una sencilla cámara por un miembro de la tripulación del avión alemán, muestran el destructor efecto de las bombas. Desesperadamente, abandonado a las llamas aniquiladoras, intenta el barco sustraerse a otros ataques, pero la obra de destrucción está ya hecha

7

Also portrayed — the attacks on British convoys and featuring the sinking of the 42,000-ton Canadian Pacific liner *Empress of Britain*. In actual fact the famous pre-war cruise ship was sunk by a U-boat while under tow on October 28 north-west of Eire, having been bombed by the Luftwaffe two days before. George Larkin, a Liverpool fireman, was one of those aboard: 'The first I heard was machine gun fire. A moment later a bomb struck the ship. We were trapped, and we had to go right forward again through black choking smoke and fumes. Two men collapsed from suffocation before we reached safety by climbing to the upper deck.' A crewman explained how 'the ship caught fire within a few minutes as the result of hits by incendiary bombs. If it had not been for the fires we would never have had to leave the ship.' An engine room officer told how they kept the engines running for about three-quarters of an hour and a man who was among the last party to leave the forecastle said: 'By the time we left, the foremast was red-hot and the paint was falling off like strips of canvas.'

adversely affected conditions over Britain and over their Continental bases, the German Air Force was able to maintain its offensive during the first two weeks of the month by ringing the changes in target selection and by shortening the length of some attacks. During the third week, however, conditions were prohibitive but on the four nights preceding Christmas the Luftwaffe resumed its bombing in force. However, an unofficial truce covered the Christmas period with no German raids whatsoever for three nights; similarly RAF bombers refrained from attacks on Germany on Christmas Eve and Christmas Day. This followed notification by Germany through Washington that they would cease operations provided the British reciprocated. The German temporary 'truce' offer is recorded in an RAF Intelligence Report although no mention of this is made in the official war history, which ascribes the lull to 'probably on account of the weather'. Two major attacks on London after the holiday brought to an end a month — and indeed a year — in which a great deal of damage had been caused in many historical and industrially important British cities.

DISTRIBUTION OF BOMB LOADS DECEMBER (GERMAN FIGURES)

Target	No. of Attacks Major	Other Heavy	Tonnes of HE	IB Cannisters
London	3	—	625	4,129
Liverpool/Birkenhead	2	—	485	1,701
Manchester	2	—	467	1,925
Sheffield	1	1	435	1,057
Birmingham	1	2	409	1,317
Bristol	1	1	198	773
Southampton	1	—	147	586
Portsmouth	—	1	88	148
Totals	11	5	2,854	11,636

The British night defences continued to offer little effective resistance to the onslaught and German bomber losses remained minimal. Accidents accounted for most aircraft casualties, which amounted to 53 machines of the long-range bomber type missing or lost on operational flights (by day and night) and another 64 damaged in varying degrees. Fighters claimed the destruction of only four German bombers at night while the AA guns claimed another ten for the expenditure of nearly 70,000 rounds of heavy ammunition. Indeed, in the last 61 nights of 1940 in which they were in operation, the AA guns fired just over 500,000 shells for a claimed 39 enemy aircraft destroyed. Fighter Command lost five night fighters during the month.

The small number of German aircraft shot down over Britain produced only twelve PoWs, while the bodies of 16 enemy airmen were recovered from crash sites or coastal waters. British Intelligence suffered in consequence, but the interrogation of one prisoner in particular led to a contretemps between the Prime Minister and the Air Staff, with Professor Frederick Lindemann, Churchill's close friend and scientific adviser the cause of the friction.

In late October Lindemann (later, Lord Cherwell) had written to the Prime Minister complaining that Fighter Command was not doing all it might to counter the German radio navigational beams. He also expressed the view that decoy fires should be lit around likely primary targets. Churchill subsequently passed Lindemann's note to Sir Charles Portal, the Chief of the Air Staff, who tersely replied to the effect that beam information was always passed to Fighter Command whose AOC-in-C could be relied upon to take the appropriate action. Portal went on to stress that a great deal had already been accomplished in setting up decoy fires — 27 were already in use, mainly located near RAF stations, and others were being constructed. Until now decoys had been employed only after the commencement of an attack but from hereon, Portal agreed, they would be used as direct decoys. On the other hand he strongly refuted Lindemann's suggestion that insufficient attention was being paid to the German beam systems. Everything possible *was* being done, he assured the Prime Minister, adding that the beams in the 30.0 and 31.5 m/c band (Knickebein) were being jammed successfully; those on 74 m/c (X-Verfahren) were exceptionally difficult to counter, he stated, but the point had been reached where success was to be expected in the immediate future.

It would appear that Dr R. V. Jones of the Air Ministry's Directorate of Intelligence, was passing to Lindemann some of the Intelligence matter he was producing for the RAF and seemingly Lindemann did not hesitate to use this material to his own advantage. On December 3 Lindemann again wrote to the Prime Minister, stating there was good reason to believe that Wolverhampton was soon to be bombed on the same scale as Coventry. It was to be hoped, Lindemann wrote, that proper arrangements had been placed in hand to light decoy fires and that the Ministry of Home Security had been advised (for the purpose of augmenting the town's firefighting services). The date could not yet be predicted but two hours notice should be possible following the switching on of the beams, Lindemann concluded. Again, Churchill passed his scientific adviser's note to Portal who, in turn, passed it for comment to his Deputy Chief of the Air Staff, Air Vice-Marshal Arthur (later Sir Arthur) Harris. The following day a clearly wrathful Harris replied to Portal, stating that Lindemann's information regarding a possible attack on Wolverhampton was based solely on remarks made by a PoW while under interrogation. So far as decoy fires were concerned, Harris wrote, these were well in hand; decoys were being built at Sheffield, Birmingham, Derby, Wolverhampton, Crewe, Middlesbrough and Manchester, in that order of priority, and to disturb this order would, in Harris's view, be most unwise. Wolverhampton could have a decoy fire in four instead of the expected seven days but Harris was sure that the existing priority was best left alone. The Hampden Patrol was available to cover any attack on Coventry, Harris continued, but he went on to dispute Lindemann's assertion about two hours notice of an impending attack, pointing out in some detail the problems of beam monitoring and stressing the great part that pure luck and conjecture played in the proceedings. Harris concluded his reply with: 'Lindemann's note appears to be based entirely upon information leaking out of D of I's [Directorate of Intelligence] Department through Dr Jones, but naturally we get it all sooner than he (Lindemann) does. Our work is made none the easier by the continual necessity of leaving it in order to write papers and answers to meet the naive queries of outside busybodies who peddle second hand information in the guise of esoteric knowledge until it finally boomerangs back to us in the guise of a bogey or a new discovery. I would therefore suggest a reply to the effect that Lindemann's knowledge emanates from this Department, and that action was taken in this matter long before he heard of it.'

The next day, December 5, Portal dealt with Lindemann's note in his reply to the Prime Minister, but he prudently toned down the clearly irate but justified comments of his forthright deputy. He made it clear to Churchill, however, that he was already well aware of the information being relayed by Lindemann. He went on to state that large decoy fires were already in hand to cover the Midlands, that one for Wolverhampton would be completed as soon as possible and that, contrary to Lindemann's assertion, particular notice of an impending attack could not be guaranteed.

On December 8, in his first Night Interception Report since becoming AOC-in-C Fighter Command, Air Marshal Sholto Douglas conceded that since his predecessor's Report of November 17 no great success had been achieved. Dismal weather and moonless nights had no doubt played their part but, in the course of nearly 100 night fighter sorties, only 31 enemy aircraft had been sighted. Beaufighters and Blenheims made 28 AI contacts that resulted in 23 sightings, but enemy aircraft were actually engaged on only six occasions. Pilots of 'cat's eyes' Hurricanes, Defiants and Gladiators reported seeing eight enemy bombers, seven of which were illuminated by searchlights, but they were able to engage only two. Defiants had also been sent to patrol the French coast, hoping to catch

Luftkampf

Combate aéreo

Den Kriegsberichtern der Luftwaffe Speer und Theyer ist es gelungen, während eines Luftkampfes einzelne Kampfphasen aufzunehmen. In diesen Bildern haben wir das Ergebnis einer hervorragenden Leistung vor uns, deren Voraussetzungen Kaltblütigkeit und Unerschrockenheit sind

Los reporters de guerra de la aviación Speer y Theyer consiguieron durante un combate aéreo fotografiar diferentes fases de la lucha. En las subsiguientes ilustraciones vemos el resultado de una excelente performance, cuyas condiciones previas son la sangre fria y el valor

Aufn. PK Speer-Theyer (7)

1 Zwei englische Jäger nach dem ersten Angriff. Sie haben den deutschen Aufklärer, von dem aus die Aufnahmen gemacht wurden, angegriffen und ziehen nun an ihm vorbei, um zu neuem Anlauf anzusetzen

Dos cazas ingleses después del primer ataque. Han atacado al avión de reconocimiento aleman desde el cual se han sacado las fotografias, y pasan ahora de largo para volver a arremeter de nuevo

3 Immer wieder stoßen die Engländer auf die deutschen Aufklärer hinunter, ohne entscheidende Treffer zu landen. Blick auf den britischen Jäger durch das Kabinenfenster

Los ingleses no cejan en sus arremetidas contra el observador alemán, sin conseguir empero colocar ningùn blanco. El caza inglés visto a través del cristal de la cabina

2 Eine Spitfire, die durch die Rasanz ihres Anfluges an dem deutschen Flugzeug vorbeigetragen wird und nun durch das MG-Feuer des Heckschützen muß. Im Bilde rechts unten sind die Propellernabe und ein Teil des Motors des deutschen Aufklärungsflugzeugs zu erkennen

Un Spitfire, que por lo ceñido de su vuelo pasa al costado del avión alemán y que tiene que atravesar ahora el cono de fuego del metrallero de cola. En la foto inferior de la derecha puede apreciarse el cabezal de la hélice y una parte del motor del aparato de reconocimiento alemán

4 Unbeirrt durch feindliche Angriffsversuche, zieht die Do 17, der „fliegende Bleistift", ihre Bahn. Ihre Schnelligkeit und eine überlegene Bewaffnung machen sie zu einer gefürchteten Waffe. Die britische Spitfire kurvt nach einem ergebnislosen Angriff nach unten weg

Sin inmutarse por los intentos de ataque del enemigo sigue el Do 17, llamado "el lapicero del aire", su camino. Su rapidez y su armamento superior le convierten en un arma temida. El Spitfire inglés desciende evolucionando después de un ataque malogrado

7 Während die Aufklärer unbehindert ihre Bahn ziehen, fliegt über ihnen ein Kampfflugzeug aus der gleichen Waffenschmiede über England, um seine Bomben in die Ziele zu bringen

Mientras los aviones de reconocimiento siguen su camino sin inmutarse, vuela por encima de ellos un aparato de bombardeo procedente de la misma fábrica, para dejar caer sus bombas sobre el objetivo en Inglaterra

5 Auch der nächste Angreifer wird mit Erfolg abgewehrt. Das gut liegende Feuer des Heckschützen zwang ihn, nach unten abzudrehen

También el siguiente agresor es rechazado con éxito. El fuego certero del tirador de cola le ha obligado a torcer hacia abajo

6 Schließlich muß auch der letzte Angreifer ohne Erfolg abdrehen. Zum Verständnis der Bildfolge sei bemerkt, daß in den beiden Aufklärungsmaschinen je ein Bildberichter der Luftwaffe mitflog, die so gegenseitig die britischen Angriffe photographieren konnten

Por fin tiene que torcer también el último agresor sin haber obtenido resultado alguno; para mejor comprensión del reportaje gráfico sea dicho, que en cada uno de los aparatos de reconocimiento iba un reporter de guerra de la aviación, pudiendo así fijar sobre las placas recíprocamente los ataques británicos

8 9

A double-page spread features an assortment of dubious combat pictures — one of which we have commented on before. The 'Englische Jäger' is a Curtiss Hawk used by the French Air Force and later by the Luftwaffe as trainers. Most probably these (and those on page 96) are posed shots, GX and GK being codes allocated by the Germans to captured aircraft.

enemy bombers displaying navigation lights over their own territory, but to no avail. Certain changes had been implemented, however, reported Douglas; following a recommendation by General Pile there had been a revision in the layout of GL sets with the aim of improving overland tracking of German aircraft and to provide an accurate assessment of their height. The new scheme provided a 'carpet' of GL sets along a belt extending from Kent to Bristol, but to achieve this it was necessary to break up the close GL grouping in the Kenley Sector which lay on the prime approach route to London. Clearly, with the impending introduction of the new GCI stations there would be a degree of GCI/GL carpet overlap, but when the GCI stations had been proved it would be possible to reconsider the GL position.

Douglas also agreed to a proposal by General Pile to reposition searchlights throughout the country to work in 'bunches' of three. Such bunches were to be used as pointers to indicate the presence of enemy aircraft to patrolling fighters on clear nights. This indication, plus the height information now expected from the new GL carpet arrangement, or by GCI sets, should appreciably aid visual interceptions.

In addition to these changes Douglas was anxious to increase the number of night fighter squadrons and to improve their airfield facilities. In early December there were still only six AI-equipped squadrons, flying Blenheims and Beaufighters, supported by five 'cat's eyes' squadrons (two with Defiants and three with Hurricanes, with one of the latter converting to Defiants). The AOC-in-C wished to increase this establishment to at least 20 specialist night fighter squadrons of which 12 should be twin-engined AI-equipped (Beaufighters or DB-7s). There was, Douglas knew, a Coastal Command demand for the Beaufighter, but there were a large number of DB-7 Boston variants in the country, few of which had yet reached Fighter Command.

Douglas's demand for more and better equipped aerodromes met with an immediate response from the Air Ministry, for on December 9 he was promised 12 specialist night fighter airfields. He also sought special training for his crews and by the end of the month this, too, was forthcoming; instrument approach courses were started at Watchfield, near Swindon, for Beaufighter pilots flying Standard Beam Approach (SBA) equipped aircraft.

Anxious to try anything to combat the night raider, Douglas continued to urge further experimental work with towed flares, flares dropped from fighters and the use of star shells. Moves were also afoot to expand No. 420 Flight, which was retitled No. 93 Squadron on December 7, into a unit with 12 DB-7s for dropping Long Aerial Mines and six Wellingtons for towing mines in the path of the enemy.

Meanwhile, following complaints of obstructed vision, a new windscreen and cockpit canopy had been evolved for the Beaufighter which significantly improved the final part of an AI controlled interception.

On December 14 all Hampden defensive operations (Hampden Patrol) were permanently cancelled when the decision was made to introduce concentrated fighter patrols stepped up in layers over certain target cities. These patrols were to consist of at least six single-engined fighters using, if necessary, aircraft of day squadrons (flown by selected pilots) in addition to night squadrons. Individual aircraft were to be not less than 1,000 feet apart vertically, with normally 2,000 feet separation, stepped up from 10,000 to 20,000 feet. Pilots were to maintain their patrol area by the use of marker flares on the ground, and the operation was to be cancelled if visual contact with the flares was lost through cloud or other weather conditions. The time allocated for the operation was to be one hour and, if desired, it could be carried out more than once in any one night. The operation was to be code-named 'Fighter Night' and for the period it was in force AA guns were to cease firing and searchlights were to be doused in the patrol area. Operation Fighter Night, it was confidently predicted, offered greater prospects than the almost totally ineffective Hampden Patrol. It also released Hampdens for offensive operations which, after all, was the rôle for which they were better suited.

A B C der Luftwaffe

A B C de la aviación

Besuch in einer Fliegerschützenschule

Visita a una escuela de tiradores de aviación

Nice piece on the training of air gunners at a Fliegerschützenschüle. For defensive armament German bombers relied on the MG15 which had been introduced in 1932 by Rheinmetall-Borsig A.G. specifically for aircraft use — a muzzle booster allowing the rate of fire to increase to 1,000 rounds per minute. It was basically a modification of the MG30 which was a product of the Solothurn Waffenfabrik, nominally a Swiss company but, since 1929, under German control in one of many subterfuges to get round the restrictions of the Versailles Treaty. It was common knowledge in arms circles at the time that parts were being made in Austria and Hungary for assembly in Switzerland although, seemingly, Western governments turned a blind eye.

December 1940 was certainly a month of innovation for Fighter Command, for yet another new venture was tried on the night of 21-22nd, when the first long-range night fighter patrols were flown over German bomber bases on the Continent. These patrols, which were code-named 'Operation Intruder', had their origins in certain earlier activities of Fighter Command and Bomber Command's No. 2 Group. With the fall of France in the summer of 1940, No. 2 Group instituted a series of attacks on German airfields, both by day and night. They were briefly joined in this activity by the Blenheims of No. 604 Squadron, but the need to use No. 2 Group aircraft for attacks on possible invasion ports, and a defensive requirement for No. 604 Squadron, resulted in a cessation of these operations. However, in the autumn the night bomber threat saw a further change in policy and No. 2 Group was again allocated airfield targets in France and the Low Countries. In principle, however, it was felt that the responsibility for such operations should pass to Fighter Command and there followed a valuable interchange between the Staffs of No. 2 Group and Fighter Command. Subsequently in mid-December No. 23 Squadron, Fighter Command, which was then equipped with AI Blenheims, was assigned to the task now named Intruder. Navigators were posted to the squadron and the AI, the capture of which by the enemy could not be risked, was removed from its aircraft. In addition, crews were sent to Wattisham to learn all they could from their No. 2 Group colleagues.

It was proposed that each night one or more of the 'beats' into which enemy occupied territory had been divided, would be assigned to No. 23 Squadron as its exclusive preserve. The aircraft were to carry small bombs and their primary aim was to destroy and harass German bombers as they were landing or taking off or while on the ground. Two more operations were flown during the month, following their introduction on the night of December 21-22, with a total of 14 sorties. Seven enemy aircraft were seen but it was not until March of 1941, by which time the squadron was re-equipping with Havocs, that the first enemy aircraft was claimed destroyed.

The launching of yet another innovation, a 'free balloon barrage', on the night of December 27-28 required the release of a large number of balloons in the path of German aircraft approaching London, with each balloon trailing a length of wire to which was attached a cannister containing explosives. An aircraft flying into a cable would, it was expected, be destroyed, either by the cable itself or by drawing up the explosive device until contact was made. A number of Release Fronts were nominated, to allow for various wind directions, and on December 27, with a north-westerly wind, Release Front No. 13 (along the Hatfield-Hertford road) was employed. However, the launching of the barrage, 'Operation Pegasus', presented some difficulties and was completely unsuccessful — an insufficient number of balloons, unsatisfactory communications and the excessive height reached by the balloons were all contributing factors. No contacts were made with enemy aircraft but many explosions on the ground were reported between the Hatfield-Hertford area and the region bounded by Edenbridge, Hever and Beachy Head.

From as far back as June 1940, when the first German night raids were flown over Britain on a small scale, decoy fires had drawn a good number of bombs. Controlled by a department of the Air Ministry led by Colonel John Turner who specialised in deception of various kinds, the decoys were expanded and took various forms including dummy flarepaths and other false airfield lights. Subsequently large oil-burning decoy fires materialised, intended to resemble a burning built-up area. These were given the code-name 'Starfish', and at a meeting held on December 10 it was decided that executive control of such decoys should be vested in No. 80 Wing Headquarters. Accordingly, an officer of the unique 'Colonel Turner's Department' was attached to No. 80 Wing as

Fire Control Officer to co-ordinate the lighting of decoys with the foreknowledge of impending attacks now regularly available to the radio countermeasures organisation.

Ministry of Home Security reports show that while extensive damage was done in all the major cities that were attacked in December it was, in the main, centred on residential and commercial areas. Industrial damage, too, was extensive, but nowhere did it have a serious, lasting effect and there was no large scale military damage. The Civil Defence and Fire Services successfully dealt with many difficult fire situations and helped enormously to reduce the harm that might have resulted. Civilian morale was officially reported to be very high in all the raided areas, a situation enhanced by British and Greek military successes during the month (although these were to be short-lived). This stimulus was all the more valuable as it came at a time when the spirit of the public, although high, had been subjected to much severe and cumulative strain. The absence of German bombers over the Christmas period was also of enormous benefit although there was, of course, no general previous knowledge of their intended absence. No suggestion of a truce had come from official quarters, but the welcome break certainly gave the ever resilient British public good heart to face the New Year with no less courage than they had shown in 1940. Londoners, however, were to see much of the old City destroyed in the second Great Fire of London on the night of December 29-30. And events this night were to expedite new regulations to deal with the firebomb menace. Countrywide, civilian casualties for the month totalled 3,793 killed and 5,044 seriously injured.

The pattern of the German attacks — flares, followed by incendiary bombs and high-explosives — was by now well established and early in the month Fighter Command issued an Operational Instruction (No. 54) which outlined certain counter-tactics. The instruction pointed out that specialist Luftwaffe bomber units (but thought to be KGr100 only at this time) were being used to carry out the leading attacks with the object of starting fires on which the main force could bomb. These leading raids, the Instruction continued, frequently approached the English coasts at dusk, using directional beams to find and bomb their targets. It was, therefore, intended to take all practical steps to intercept and destroy these special aircraft by (a) searching for them out to sea in the afterglow of sunset, (b) by intercepting them either at sea or over land by normal methods, and (c) by dispatching fighters to locate them in their very limited cone of approach to the target. Any information obtained by Fighter Command Headquarters, either preceding or during an attack, was to be telephoned by the Duty Night Operations Staff Officer to Group Controllers, who were to pass on the information to all Sectors over whose areas the enemy aircraft were expected to pass. This information was based on (1) warnings from 'Y' Service intercepts of preliminary orders to German units; (2) particulars of the bearings of approach beams and the target as shown by beam intersections; (3) indications as to the identity of these particular aircraft among the earlier tracks appearing in the RDF plots during their approach to the coast; and (4) fixes from any W/T transmissions which might establish the definite identity of the special aircraft sought. Clearly, from now on, Kampfgruppe 100 was a marked unit; equally clearly the Instruction reveals the extent of British foreknowledge of German intentions and yet, despite all this, the assault on Britain was to continue with little hindrance.

The month brought no expansion of the night fighter force, but there were several squadron movements as Fighter Command tried to make the most efficient use of its resources. No. 87 Squadron, formerly operating with Flights at Exeter and Bibury, was united for the first time in nearly six months when the unit was moved to Colerne, but operations were also flown from nearby Charmy Down. Another Hurricane squadron, No. 85 at Debden and Kirton-in-Lindsey, moved south to Gravesend, where it joined No. 141 Squadron, while the Defiants of No. 264 moved northwards from Rochford to Debden. No. 29 Squadron, with Sections at Digby and Wittering, now became unified at Digby, which was subsequently vacated by No. 151 Squadron for operations from Bramcote and Wittering.

On the German side perhaps the most significant factor affecting their Order of Battle was the decision to establish the Luftwaffe in the Mediterranean area of operations in support of their ailing Italian allies. In consequence X Fliegerkorps was ordered to Sicily where a Headquarters was established in Taormina under the command of General der Flieger Hans Ferdinand Geisler, a move monitored by British Air Intelligence following intercepts and the decyphering of Enigma-coded operations orders. Similar sleuthing also revealed the imminent departures of II/KG26 and II/LG1 from North-West Europe, while from mid-December a cessation of operations by II/KG1 led to the correct belief that the Gruppe had returned to Germany with elements of KG76. Another change in mid-December was the temporary transfer of KGr126 to IV Fliegerkorps (from IX Fliegerkorps) with the first known operations under its new command being flown on the night of 19-20th. Another development, but not known to British Air Intelligence until Boxing Day, was the existence of a German long-range night fighter unit (I/NJG2) based at Gilze-Rijen in Holland for offensive patrols over British airfields. This came to light when a Ju 88 of this unit was shot down on December 21 while attacking Manby airfield from a height of 200 feet. Finally, on December 29 another Enigma decrypt revealed that VIII Fliegerkorps had been subordinated to Luftflotte 4 and allocated a base in Rumania.

In addition to the movements to the Mediterranean and base changes in North-West Europe, there were several other changes affecting German Air Force operations over Britain. In target selections ports were assuming an importance equal to that of industrial war production centres, with the bomb load for the month more or less equally distributed between both types of target. The attack on Sheffield on the night of December 12-13 — repeated on a much smaller scale the next night — also introduced a shift towards the use of very large numbers of incendiary bombs in preference to high explosives. This was also a feature of the attack on London on the 29th and resulted in an appeal for the guarding of empty premises at night and at weekends to deal with IBs before they could take a firm hold. This 'Fire Watcher' appeal was made by Home Secretary Herbert Morrison during a broadcast on the evening of December 31. At the same time he informed listeners of his intention to make 'fire-watching' compulsory at a later date. It met with a good response, but to cover eventualities legislation was prepared to safeguard all commercial and private premises otherwise left unattended.

A further development on the German side was the introduction of a new heavy bomb, the SC 2500 of 5,500 pounds (2500kg). Announced to Luftflotte 3 units in the West in a memo from the RLM in Berlin dated December 17, the new bomb was cleared to be carried externally by He 111H-5 and He 111H-6 aircraft. According to the memo the new bomb was painted the pale blue (RLM 65 Hellblau) of the undersurfaces of German aircraft and accordingly, when carried at night, it was to receive a coat of the matt black distemper applied to night bombers' undersurfaces. The destructive capability of the new weapon was enormous by then current standards, but its effect on the handling qualities and performance of the He 111, particularly on take-off, initial climb and at high altitudes, restricted its carriage to selected pilots. At the time of its introduction only five Gruppen were equipped with He 111H-5 or H-6 aircraft and of these one was in Sicily (II/KG26) and two were engaged in minelaying (I/KG4 and KGr126). Of the remaining two, I and III/KG26, the latter was clearly favourite to receive the first SC 2500s for use in conjunction with its highly accurate and secret Y-Verfahren beam bombing system.

Since setting up its headquarters at Espinette, Brussels, on October 22 the Corpo Aereo Italiano had contributed little of note towards the bombing offensive against Britain. Up to the end of December its bomber element, KG13 and KG43 (formerly the 13° and 43° Stormo), had flown 97 bomber sorties for the loss of three aircraft. In night operations, totalling 77 sorties, the aircraft of the CAI had dropped 44.87 tonnes of bombs, with most of them intended for Harwich and, to a lesser degree, Ipswich.

DAILY EXPRESS Monday, December 2, 1940

BLACK-OUT
ZERO
HOUR
TO NIGHT
UNTIL 8.18 A.M.
MOON RISES
MOON SETS

Daily Express

No. 12,645 Monday, December 2, 1940 One Penny

Port fights biggest raid as bombs hit churches, hospital, convent

LONDON BLITZ SWITCHED ON SOUTHAMPTON

Nazis claim to have raided it two nights running

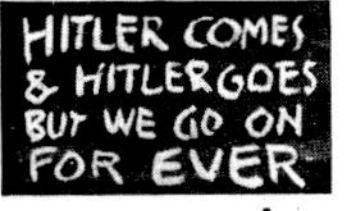

HITLER COMES
& HITLER GOES
BUT WE GO ON
FOR EVER

SPIRIT OF SOUTHAMPTON Poster chalked up by a newsagent in bombed Southampton yesterday.

HITLER, who switched his night blitz from London to Coventry, Birmingham and Liverpool, and then back to London again, turned its power on to Southampton on Saturday night, and last night again attacked a south coast town.

The Germans said this raid, too, was on Southampton, and that they were attacking with bombs of all calibres. One Nazi plane swooped to machine-gun streets.

Saturday night's attack on Southampton was a seven-hour fire-raid. Loads of incendiaries were scattered by waves of bombers in a deliberate raid on the city centre. Then explosives were aimed at the fires.

At the height of the raid the countryside around was lit by the glare of the flames. Several churches, a convent, a theatre, and a newspaper office were burned down; a shopping street was almost laid in ruins. Thousands of people in the city have now been made homeless.

London had two alerts last night. During the first, which was short, three bombs fell—one in a cemetery, two in streets.

Houses were damaged, and about a dozen people were hurt, but not seriously.

Lone raiders came over at long intervals doing the second alert. A single raider was fired at over Merseyside, where a few incendiaries fell without causing damage.

The only daylight bombs reported in England yesterday fell at a point on the southern outskirts of London.

Two housese were wrecked and three people were hurt.

DAILY EXPRESS STAFF REPORTER BERNARD HALL TELEPHONED THIS STORY FROM SOUTHAMPTON LAST NIGHT:—

AS I watched the flames race across Southampton on Saturday night, while bombs rocked the city, it seemed that only a miracle could stop the fires.

Yet when dawn came most of them were under control.

Firemen, wardens, rescue squads, and ordinary men and women stood up to the blitz and made this possible.

Some paid with their lives. Early in the raid four A.R.P. workers were killed by a bomb near their post. A police sergeant was another victim.

LEAP IN DARK

The attack started when people were still in the streets. Several mothers who were wheeling perambulators took their children into a shelter under a building.

I have just seen what is left of the perambulators—charred by a bomb as they stood outside the shelter. But mothers and children inside were unhurt.

One of the shelterers said to me: "Fires were blazing all round. We were in an absolute ring of flame. It was magnificent the way the women and children stood up to it."

A fire bomb fell on a hospital roof. It was seen by a porter named Wilkinson.

He jumped eight feet across a deep gap to the roof, scooped up the bomb with his bare hands, and threw it on to open ground.

The hospital was saved, though other bombs burned down the nurses' quarters.

Girl ambulance drivers in the city carried on their work while bombs fell all round.

One girl's ambulance was blown on to the pavement by blast.

She jumped out to see what damage had been done, and saw three injured men lying in the road.

With no one to help her she got

BACK PAGE, COL. FIVE

GUNS ANSWER
As Nazis use their flares-and-fires technique

A German official communique claims that 36,000 incendiary bombs and flares were dropped on London during Friday night. This vivid Daily Express picture, taken by gun-flash light during the raid, shows an A.A. battery shooting at the raiders. Flares dropped by a Nazi plane can be seen in the top corner.

Crack Nazi flier lost

BERLIN, Sunday.

MAJOR HELMUTH WIECK, commander of the Richthofen Squadron, is missing, the official German News Agency reports tonight. The agency says:—

"Major Helmuth Wieck, who has been awarded a knight's insignia of the Iron Cross, with oak leaves, the highest military decoration in Germany, did not return on November 28 from a flight against the enemy in which he shot down his fifty-sixth enemy plane. He has been missing since then."—Reuter.

[The Richthofen Squadron is named after the famous German ace of the last war.]

Did Hitler say 'No' to Duce's cry for help?

Daily Express Staff Reporter

NEW YORK, Sunday.

MESSAGES reaching Washington tonight said that Mussolini has made urgent requests to Hitler for help in Greece.

According to these reports the Duce's requests have been repeatedly turned down in the last few days.

The appeals are said to have been made by Mussolini on the telephone, and also in person by ex-Ambassador Dino Grandi, who has recently visited Berlin.

Hitler explained that he could not move in Greece at present without risking war with Russia, Jugo-Slavia, Turkey and Bulgaria. He therefore asked Mussolini to hold out and wait.

FIVE TOMMIES ESCAPE FROM FRANCE

"Missing" seven months

Daily Express Staff Reporter

FIVE British soldiers, reported "missing" more than seven months ago, have escaped from France, and are now on their way home to relatives and friends who had refused to give them up as dead.

They are Pte. Albert Martin, whose home is in Elmers End, Kent; Pte. Arthur (Dick) Sutton, of Featherstone, near Pontefract, Yorks; Signaller John Christie, of Hardgate, Aberdeen; Walter Young, of Edinburgh, and Philip Lindsay, of Dundee.

Last night Mrs. Martin, her faith rewarded, waited happily by her parlour fire, expecting any moment to hear a knock at the door announcing the return of her "dead" husband.

She does not know exactly when he will be home, but three days ago—on her birthday—she received a telegram from him saying he had escaped and would soon be with her.

'If any man could—'

"It was the most wonderful telegram I have ever had," she said. "He was posted missing on April 22, but I never gave up hope all the time, although it is over seven months ago.

"I knew that if any man could escape, it would be Albert, and I have had the house re-papered twice so that it would be spick-and-span for him."

Crossing to a cupboard, she produced a bottle of his favourite beer. "I have had this ready for him—I know he will like it."

Private Martin's widowed mother will be there to welcome him, too. She said: "I could hardly believe he would come back, but Nan, his wife, would not let me lose heart.

"A few weeks ago the Germans dropped a bomb near my house. When they did not kill me, I somehow knew that they could not kill my son."

Signaller Christie will return to the home of his married sister, Mrs. [illegible], of Hardgate, Aberdeen. He is twenty-one and was a pre-war Territorial.

He was reported missing on June 4. Some time later a French girl wrote to his home expressing the belief that he had been captured. This—and his escape—was confirmed recently.

KENNEDY WILL NOT RETURN

WASHINGTON, Sunday.

MR. JOSEPH KENNEDY, United States Ambassador to Britain for nearly three years, will not return to London, it was announced in Washington tonight after he had an interview with President Roosevelt.

The announcement reveals that he tendered his resignation on November 6—the day after the Presidential election.

At their meeting today Mr. Roosevelt accepted it.

Mr. Kennedy told President Roosevelt that he felt he could render greater service to the United States by staying at home and working to keep the nation out of the war.

Soon after his return to America in October, Mr. Kennedy was quoted by a New York newspaper as saying that democracy in Britain was "finished."

He declared in reply that his remarks were made "off the record" and that they had been misinterpreted by the newspaper.—B.U.P.

Greeks advance everywhere

Daily Express Correspondent

ATHENS, Sunday midnight.

THE Greek war communiqué issued tonight announced: "A considerable advance has been made all along the front. Positions of exceptional importance for the development of operations have been captured.

"In the Premeti region more than 150 prisoners have been taken. Much war material has fallen into our hands."

The significance of the communiqué seems to be in the reference—for the first time by G.H.Q.—to Premeti. This town is fifteen miles [illegible] the main road [illegible] Tepelent and the coast.

If the Greeks can drive further along this road they may trap the Italians in a pocket from which there would be no retreat except by sea.

Italians shelled from sea—and map.

—Back Page.

STOP PRESS

GREEKS REACH COAST NORTH OF CORFU

BUDAPEST, Sunday.—Greek forces in western sector have reached coast north of Corfu, says Greek radio report picked up in Budapest tonight.—B.U.P.

LORD WILLINGDON IN ARGENTINE

BUENOS AIRES, Sunday.—High British and Argentine officials greeted Lord Willingdon when he arrived here today at head of British commercial mission.—A.P.

Bomb plot to kill Jugo-Slav chiefs

AS PRINCE PAUL WARNS AXIS

Daily Express Staff Reporter C. V. R. THOMPSON

NEW YORK, Sunday.

CABLES from Belgrade tonight revealed an attempted assassination of Jugo-Slavia's Vice-Premier, Josef Machek, and other officials of the Government, on the twenty-second anniversary of the State's foundation.

A series of bomb blasts rocked Machek's home, three bombs exploded in the home of the Governor at Zagreb, and another bomb went off in the residence of the secretary of the Croat Agrarian Party.

Damage was described as small and no casualties were reported.

That was all the news of the attempt that leaked through a dozen different censorships to New York, but even that indicated that the revolutionary hand of Adolf Hitler is not finished yet with what used to be called the powderkeg of Europe.

The bombings gave added significance to a speech last night by Jugo-Slavia's Senior Regent, Prince Paul, in which he gave this clear warning to the Axis: "We are prepared to defend to the utmost the integrity and independence of our State."

Rumania quiet

Although even Berlin was unable to maintain contact with correspondents in Bucharest those messages which did come through indicated, perhaps on purpose, that Rumania was quieter.

It seemed that the general revolution which was expected to be touched off by the official funeral of Codreanu, "martyr" of the Iron Guard, had for the time being been prevented.

Rumania's Foreign Minister, M. Sturzda, returned to Bucharest today from Berlin where he had conferred with Nazi officials. He took a message to Antonescu saying that Antonescu must bring the Iron Guard into control immediately.

From Budapest it was again reported that the Iron Guards had assassinated ex-Ministers Gigurtu and George Bratianu last night—similar reports proved untrue two days ago—and that King Michael is hiding in the countryside.

Sugar prices going DOWN

AFTER December 16 sugar will be a penny a pound cheaper. Here are the new prices:—

Granulated, 4d. a lb.; cubes, 4½d.; refiners' castor, 4½d.; soft brown, 3¾d.; preserving, 4½d.; grocery West Indian, 4½d.

Wholesale prices will be cut to correspond with the new retail prices. This reduction will operate from today to give retailers an opportunity of disposing of stocks already purchased before the retail prices are reduced.

The prices of sugar sold for manufacturing will not be cut.

'Aussies' must train as sprinters

To catch Italians

Daily Express Correspondent

MELBOURNE, Sunday.—Opening the first athletic championships of the Australian fighting forces, Mr. Menzies, Australia's Premier, said yesterday:—

"It is appropriate that these contests should be held as our men are going abroad to fight.

"We do not know where they will fight yet, but as they may have a fair chance of meeting the Italians I would say that our boys will need to be in their best sprinting form to catch them up.

"You might have wondered why we have modified the marathon to twelve miles instead of the recognised twenty-six.

"The Italians, in their retreat, are getting so close to the Albanian coast that it is considered there would be no need to run twenty-six miles to catch them."

[See also Pocket Cartoon: Page 2.]

Savings—£16,106,479

The Little Man ended the first year's savings campaign with a £16,106,479 spurt. Since last November he has saved £479,989,925.

Submarine Triad presumed lost

Sank Nazi ship at Oslo

The loss of the British submarine Triad—"overdue and presumed lost"—was announced by the Admiralty last night. Next-of-kin have been told.

Triad, one of the Triton Class, to which the Thetis belonged, penetrated Oslo Fiord on April 2 and sank a German supply ship with a torpedo. Nine days later two more of her torpedoes found their mark when she attacked a convoy of enemy supply ships.

Her commander, Lieut.-Commander G. S. Salt, R.N., usually had with him a crew of fifty-three.

Britain giving black-list of ships to U.S.

IT is understood that Mr. Hugh Dalton, Minister of Economic Warfare, is to send a black-list of neutral ships to America.

For the last three months agents of the Ministry of Economic Warfare in all parts of the world have watched the suspicious behaviour of certain neutral ships. They fly all sorts of flags—Turkey, Jugo-Slavia, Panama, Portugal and Brazil.

A favourite trick of skippers of these ships to overcome the British blockade is to have two sets of papers.

One purports to prove that their cargoes are for friendly neutrals. Towards the end of their voyages, after they have passed British controls, they divert their ships to enemy ports.

Mr. Dalton suggests to United States authorities that American cargoes should in future be withheld from these ships.

SPITFIRE ACES DOWN FOUR MORE

SPITFIRES from the fighter station which on Saturday claimed its 600th victim carried on into their seventh century yesterday. One squadron shot down four Messerschmitt 109's, without loss, out of the day's bag of eight—all destroyed near the south-east coast.

About 100 Messerschmitt 109's and 110's crossed the Channel during the afternoon. They were in small groups and as usual had the advantage of height when first seen.

Although one squadron had to climb 32,000 feet to intercept a number of Messerschmitt 109's, the Germans promptly headed for home—all but one, who dived on a Spitfire. As he did so a Polish pilot dived on the Messerschmitt and sent him crashing into the sea.

A flight commander who has just been awarded a bar to his D.F.C. fired at one Messerschmitt and saw it blow up in the air. It was his fourteenth success. Five of our aircraft were lost, but all the pilots are safe.

British planes and A.A. defences (apart from the Navy and Fleet Air Arm) shot down 288 "Axis" planes in November.

In the same month the R.A.F. lost 119 planes, but twenty-eight pilots were saved to fight again.

Mussolini lost seventy-nine aircraft from his much-vaunted, multi-coloured regina aeronitaca (not counting his losses in the Greek war).

Hitler lost 201 planes over Britain—97 bombers, 103 fighters and fighter-bombers, and one flying-boat. Eight more of his Luftwaffe were shot down over his own territory.

599 | 1—Kitty for Two—Page Five.

Ingersoll's 'Story Behind the Blitz'—Page Four

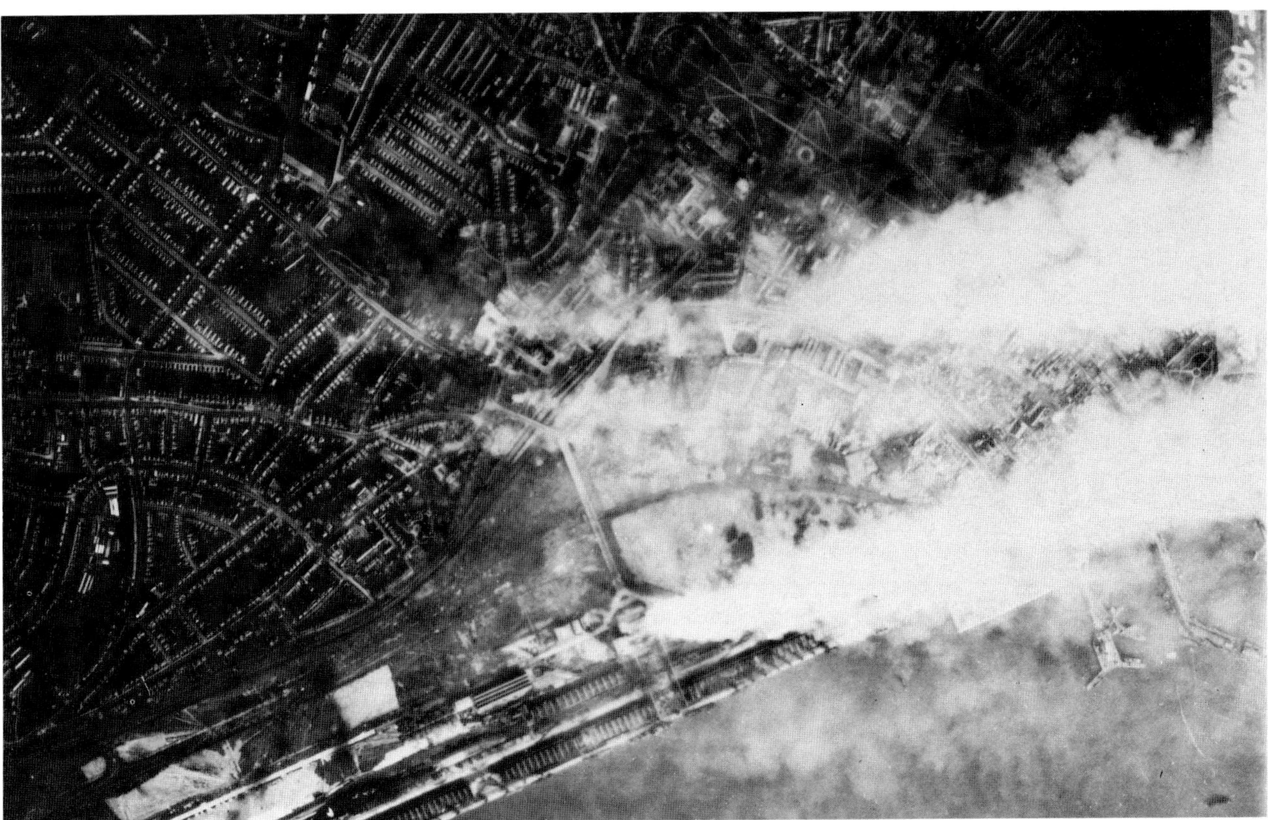

Saturday night and then again on Sunday; by the time the fourth mass attack had struck Southampton the local historian recorded that 'it was as though the town had been the victim of a savage and brutal assassination . . . everything bore the appearance of ruin and decay . . .' On Monday afternoon Luftwaffe reconnaissance cameras were clicking away as the burning city was photographed from end to end.

SUNDAY, DECEMBER 1

Sunset: 1653 Sunrise: 0847
Moon: Dusk — 1928 (New +3)

Major attack on Southampton. Subsidiary harassing attack on London and minelaying off Plymouth, Falmouth, Cardiff and Milford Haven.

UK — Small amounts of low cloud in east and south-east England but poor visibility with extensive fog. Elsewhere moderate to good visibility, with fog patches in the South. Low cloud with rain, continuous at times, spreading slowly southwards from Scotland and northern England.

The Continent — Fog in Holland; elsewhere fair, but fog later in the night in many areas.

German activity during the day was concentrated over south-east England and the Kent coast, with sea and overland reconnaissance the main preoccupation. Widespread fog was in evidence over much of the south of England and the Midlands. Despite the poor conditions — and disregarding the threat of fog on the Continent later in the night — night operations got under way at 1800 hours with an assault on Southampton for the second night running. However, in view of the expected fog, operations were concentrated in time and the country was clear of raiders by 0030 hours.

The attack was carried out by Luftflotte 3 and of the 129 aircraft participating the crews of 123 claimed to have reached and bombed their objectives. Three more bombers of Luftflotte 3 were sent to London, and one each to Birmingham and Liverpool. Of the six crews which failed to attack Southampton, five aborted and one bombed an alternative. No aircraft were reported missing.

Southampton was bombed from 1815 to 2255 hours with 147 tonnes of HE (two SC 1800, two SC 1700, four SC 1400, 30 SC 1000, one Flam 500, 66 SC 500, 13 Flam 250,

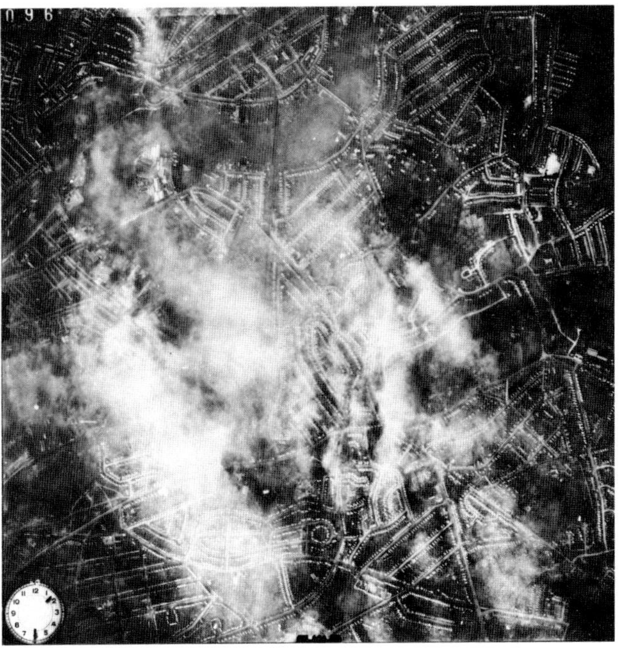

1. *'Morale' in Southampton has distinctly deteriorated.*

2. *This seems to be largely because so little has been done to provide interest and rally local feeling within the town. But it is accentuated by the extent of the ruins and the paucity of human population.*

3. *The public utilities are still seriously affected, and unrepaired structural damage of a minor nature is still immense. Thousands of homes have broken windows and leaking roofs which make them extremely unpleasant, if not uninhabitable. Many more people have gone than a fortnight ago — e.g. out of seven houses whose larders were examined then, six are now deserted.*

4. *The local food situation has much improved. The high price of candles, only form of lighting in many parts, seriously affects the poor.*

5. *Nine-tenths of all talk heard was* **still** *about the damage and the raids of a fortnight ago. This topic remains an obsession, and among many people is becoming dangerously near neurosis. There are apparently* **no** *official attempts to provide any antidote or to make any attempt to extrovert these feelings.*

6. *The only touch of gaiety found in Southampton was a pub which had a pianist and a singer. This pub was congested and did a roaring trade and had a higher degree of cheerful conversation than any other pub — most of the others were practically empty.*

7. *The alleged dis-organization of the authorities and the failure of the local authorities to keep their heads has now become a subject of comment in the surrounding countryside. The notice urging* ***The People of Southampton*** *to return to work was displayed all over the countryside as well as in the town. Removed from its Southampton context, it created a considerably different and even alarming impression.*

8. *No major grumbles seemed to dominate Southampton, and, as previously noted, the shelters are generally regarded as reasonably satisfactory.*

MASS-OBSERVATION REPORT
DECEMBER 19, 1940

In part, so we are told, because the Minister of Home Security was infuriated by the negative attitude portrayed by the Mass-Observation organisation, which conflicted with the reassuring views he was receiving from the local administration, Herbert Morrison sent the Inspector General of Air Raid Precautions to Southampton to report on the situation there. When Wing Commander E. J. Hodsoll presented his findings on December 5, the reality did not make attractive reading. He declared that the Town Clerk was entirely unsuitable for his key post as ARP Controller and that the local authority was unfit to take over; and that the sole concern of the Mayor was that he should not miss his 3.00 p.m. train out of the city each day. The Regional Commissioner also spent three days on a fact-finding visit and reported back to Whitehall that the local authority was incapable of dealing with the emergency. Although the Commissioner had discussed with Hodsoll the possibility of sacking the Town Clerk, they could find no authority or precedent under which it could be done, and the Minister was reluctant to overrule any duly elected or appointed official. The Deputy Commissioner was then drafted in to take over.

With the Hodsoll report hidden away in Home Security files, and local journalists unable to print what they knew, the situation was papered over and few Sotonians were any the wiser. One can therefore imagine the shock when, thirty years later, the whole messy business was revealed in a carefully contrived double press release. With the Hodsoll report due to be declassified in 1973, the Press Association's Special Reporting Unit first released details of the revealing Mass-Observation report which hit the headlines in the city on February 14. No sooner had the arguments and counter arguments begun to abate when the whole thing blew up again on the release of the Hodsoll report the following month. The depth to which the charges were refuted knew no bounds and for a month the civic storm rolled on as a spate of letters and statements rose to the city's defence. A wartime mayor, Rex Stranger, joined the battle from retirement in Jersey 'against those who besmirched the proud name of Southampton,' proposing a committee to answer the wartime accusations in detail. The result was the formation of the 'Defence of Southampton Committee' which produced its own findings suggesting that the Inspector

28 LZZ 50, 90 SC 250 and 757 SC 50) and 586 BSK (21,096 IBs). First over the target was III/KG26, in a Y-Verfahren guided attack, closely followed by the target illuminating aircraft of II/KG55 dropping flares and very heavy HEs and incendiaries and making use of fires still burning from the previous night's attack. The third unit to commence bombing was KGr100, using X-Verfahren and a bomb load predominantly made up of incendiary bombs. The three Firelighter Gruppen succeeded in starting many fires and most follow-up crews had little difficulty in finding the target and bombing it visually; only a few crews reported bombing by DR.

Ten large fires still burning from the previous night were soon joined by many more in the north and west of the town and explosions were reported in the docks and among warehouses. Crews were under the impression that fires covered the entire Target Area and three very large explosions and numerous conflagrations with much smoke were observed. Defensive AA fire appeared to be variable and irregular, but numerous balloons were reported. Five night fighters were also seen, but no attacks resulted.

Participating units, with their bombing times, were as follows:

I/LG1: 8 Ju 88 and 1 He 111, 1939-2116
II/LG1: 8 Ju 88, 1837-1937
I/KG27: 17 He 111, 2025-2132
III/KG27: 10 He 111, 2100-2147
KGr100: 10 He 111, 1827-1904 (X-Verfahren guided attack as Firelighters)
I/KG51: 8 Ju 88, 2155-2308
II/KG51: 4 Ju 88, 2317-0000
I/KG55: 8 He 111, 2200-2225
II/KG55: 11 He 111, 1820-1902 (operating as target illuminators, dropping flares)
III/KG55: 11 He 111, 2215-2255
II/KG76: 8 Ju 88, 1930-2000
II and III/KG77: 14 Ju 88, 1904-2015
III/KG26: 5 He 111, 1815-1950 (opened attack using Y-Verfahren method)

The subsidiary attack on London was made by 17 aircraft (14 from Luftflotte 2 and three from Luftflotte 3) between 1910 and 2335 hours. Bombing was mainly by DR, as cloud and mist obscured the city, making it impossible to assess the results, though the glow of fires could be discerned. The attackers dropped 31 tonnes of HE (27 SC 1000, six SC 500, two SC 250 and a Flam 250). No night fighters were encountered but flak was said to be of medium strength and moderately accurate.

Damage in London was slight and mainly confined to the outer suburbs, but Southampton's second consecutive assault produced a very serious fire situation although damage to industry was not extensive. Casualties were estimated at 40 killed and over 100 seriously injured. Commercial and residential premises suffered badly but the railway system, although damaged, remained open. Roads, on the other hand, were badly hit and all routes in and out of the city were closed to all but essential traffic. Hospitals suffered, too, and several Civil Defence premises were damaged. The paddle steamer *Her Majesty*, of 235 tons, was sunk but damage to the important docks was slight. The war effort was most affected by fires at the Thorneycroft and Supermarine Woolston factories and at the Rank Flour Mills.

In addition to Southampton bombs were reported at Derby, Nottingham, Wokingham, Ascot and Blackwater. In the London/south-east England area bombs fell at Ealing, Southgate, Poplar, Woolwich, Watford, Edmonton, Chigwell, Barnet, Mortlake and Richmond; no industrial damage was reported.

Weather conditions permitted only one night fighter of No. 10 Group to operate, but AA guns were in action at Plymouth, Cardiff, the IAZ, Derby, Merseyside and Falmouth, in addition to the Southampton area. Nearly 4,000 rounds were fired, 1,092 of them in the London IAZ, and three enemy aircraft were claimed either damaged or probably destroyed.

Messerschmitt Bf 109s made several daylight sweeps over Kent and Sussex. RAF claims were eight aircraft destroyed, two probables and six damaged. Two aircraft and pilots were actually lost, only one within sight of Britain, the other being Uffz. W. Misalla of 9/JG51 who was killed when his aircraft crashed into the Channel.

6/JG53 Messerschmitt Bf 109E-4 (0885). Shot down by Flying Officer P. McD. Hartas in a Spitfire of No. 421 Flight. Believed crashed into the sea off Dymchurch, Kent 12.40 p.m. Oberfw. B. Seufert missing. Aircraft Yellow 9+ lost.

General [since deceased and unable to answer back] had been insufficiently informed, perhaps even misled, and had produced a panic report which took no account of the way the local administration had been taxed. In March 1975, in an unprecedented move, the then Home Secretary agreed to have the new report included in the wartime file at the Public Record Office as 'rebuttal evidence'. Even the visit to Southampton of King George VI (seen *above* flanked by the Town Clerk and Mayor) was not free of controversy when one of the wartime M-O observers commented how 'glossifying had gathered enchantment with the passing years'. Anonymous like all Mass-Observation workers, the lady living in Southampton wrote that 'No one has mentioned this, but I remember when I first came to Southampton in 1951, someone told me that "After the big raid, when Southampton's High Street was left in ruins, and most of the centre of the town, the King came on a flying visit. As they went down the High Street, people booed. But we were not booing the King. It was all the town's top brass who were with them. Everybody knew that they got out of Southampton every night and only came back to meet the King".'

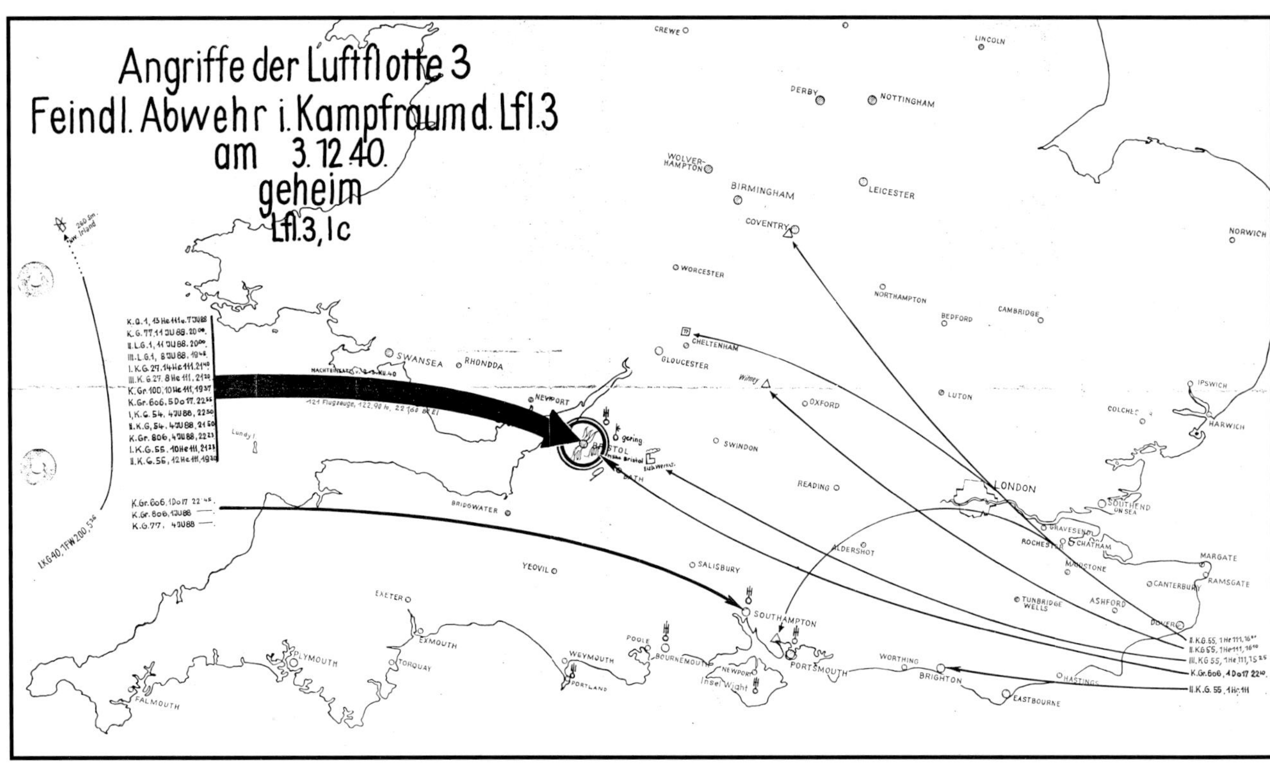

MONDAY, DECEMBER 2-3

Sunset: 1652 Sunrise: 0848
Moon: Dusk — 2033 (New +4)

Major attack on Bristol. Limited minelaying off Plymouth, Falmouth, St Alban's Head and Harwich.

UK — Widespread fog in the Midlands, east and south-east England and locally in Scotland. Cloudless in eastern England but lowering cloud in the West and South, with occasional rain and drizzle, affecting Wales and west England late in the night. Winds mainly light and variable, moderate to fresh in the West.

The Continent — Fair at first, but fog later in all areas.

A fighter sweep by 70 Bf 109s took place over the South-East during the morning and low altitude patrols were maintained in the Straits, but no bombs were reported. Sea and overland reconnaissance missions were also undertaken in mainly good but slowly deteriorating weather conditions. The first night raiders were plotted at 1717 hours coming from the direction of the Somme and others, from Cherbourg, were tracked to Bristol where, as was the case the previous night, the attack was compressed in time to permit a return to base before the onset of widespread fog on the Continent.

The assault on Bristol was made entirely by units of Luftflotte 3 and of the 132 crews dispatched 121 reported over the target. They dropped 122 tonnes of HE (three SC 1800, one SC 1700, one SC 1400, 26 SC 1000, four Flam 500, 40 SC 500, eight Flam 250, 38 LZZ 250, 92 SC 250, and 608 SC 50) and 615 BSK (22,140 incendiaries). Eight aircraft bombed alternative targets, two aborted and one crashed shortly after take off; no other aircraft were lost on this operation.

At the beginning of the attack there was 10/10ths cloud cover in two layers, the lower with a base at about 1,000 feet extending up to 3,000 feet and the upper, some 1,500 feet thick, at 8,000 feet. Underneath, surface visibility was bad and down to 1,000 yards in the Bristol area, with the result that initial bombing was by radio navigation and DR methods. Later, isolated breaks occurred in the cloud enabling some crews to bomb visually but an accurate assessment of the success of the attack was not possible, although numerous large fires could be made out with more of a smaller nature.

Although the first aircraft to actually bomb was an isolated aircraft of KG1, the attack, following standard practice, followed target marking He 111s of II/KG55, closely followed by KGr100. The third Firelighter Gruppe, III/KG26, was not operating on this occasion. Immediately after the bombing by II/KG55, Oberleutnant Otto-Bernard Harms, an He 111 Kommandant and Staffelkapitän of 4/KG55, dived through both layers of cloud to check on the accuracy of the Gruppe's target marking fires, totally disregarding the barrage balloons and AA defences and coming down to less than 1,000 feet. Despite the poor visibility he was able to confirm the accuracy which his Gruppe had achieved using Knickebein and DR,

The local Ministry of Health estimated that Bristol's population had increased with the influx of Britain's equivalent of the Continental war refugee — the Blitz evacuee — by some 200,000 during September and October. Its population was thus over twice that of Southampton; moreover, during the winter of 1940–41 it received about 50 per cent greater tonnage of bombs. Why morale did not crack like its South Coast counterpart was studied with interest by Mass-Observation. After the city's second big raid on the night of December 2–3, M-O's blitz team noted that 'damage in Bristol is considerably less from the civilian and town (centre) destruction point of view, than in Coventry and Southampton.' Professor Harrisson commented in 1976 that 'public utilities, for instance, were working well, the telephone system practically normal. "There is" [M-O wrote in December 1940] "*nothing like* the dislocation of everyday life and the *multiplied personal discomfort* which still dominates the whole of life in Southampton." Hot meals for the homeless were quickly available, for the first time in a provincial blitz. And it was with some surprise that one found a "remarkably low degree of private evacuation and desertion . . . The working classes, in particular, have overwhelmingly 'stayed put' — unlike Southampton or Coventry".'

Tell-tale clues of success for the photo-interpreters in France when they pored over the results of the raid — roofless buildings in the town centre.

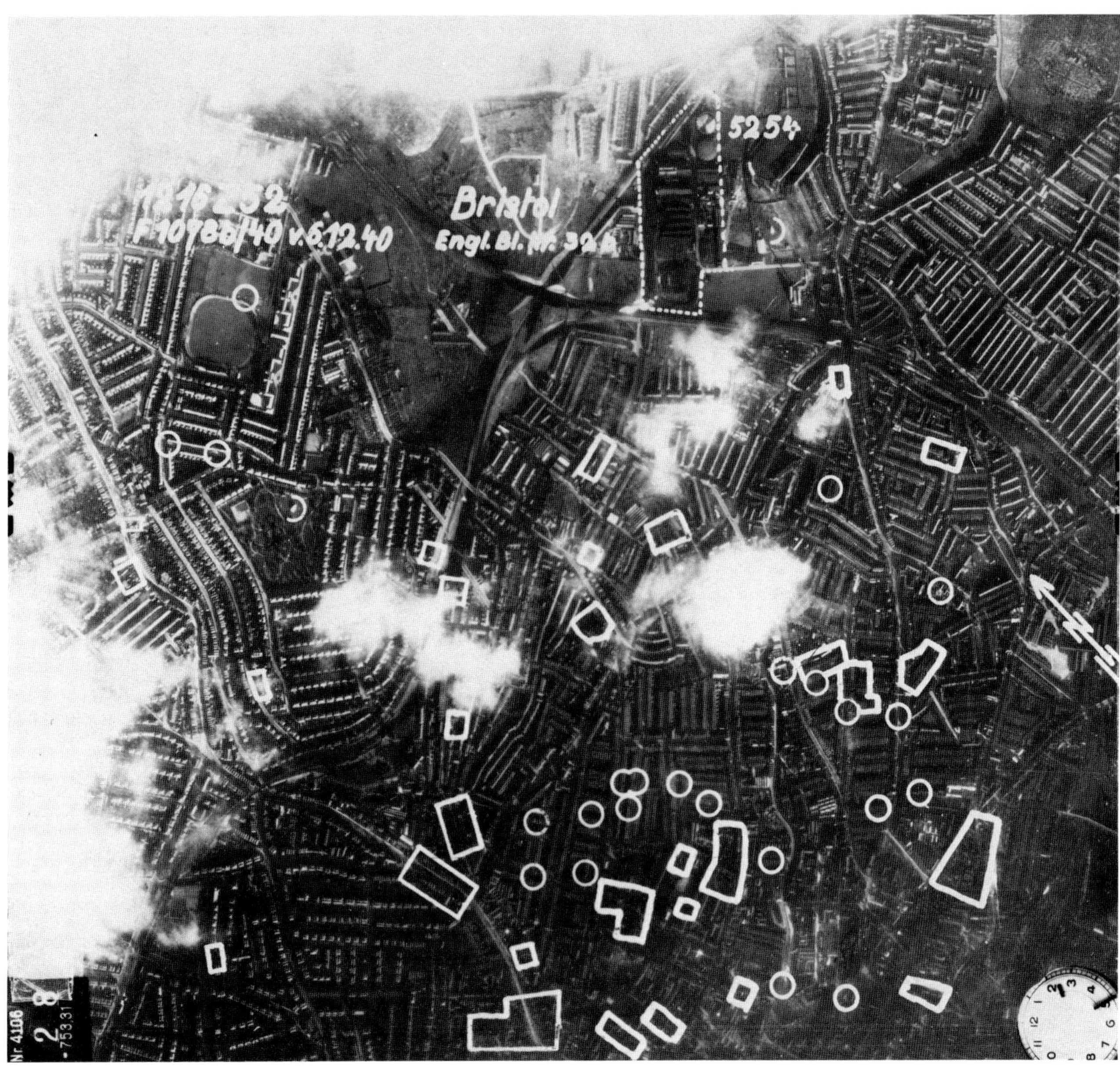

Annotated versions were prepared for submission to higher command, this particular picture being taken on December 6. Although we have included several Operations Maps in this volume (like that opposite), it is important to bear in mind that these cover Luftflotte 3 ops only, the Luftflotte 2 equivalents not having survived. They are purely schematic and serve only to show the targets attacked, not the actual routes flown. Only one version was prepared for each period so discrepancies occur with the text which is based on the Daily Situation (Führungsabteilung Gruppe Ic) Reports which were updated and revised — sometimes as much as eight times — on the day following the raid. Also the bombing times on the maps are according to German time, whereas our text gives British time (BST or DBST as appropriate). Nevertheless the maps are useful in indicating targets claimed bombed by crews attacking alternative or secondary targets.

aided by flares. Harms survived both the Battle of Britain and the Night Blitz only to lose his life in Russia during an attack on Moscow on July 21, 1941.

There were no reports of night fighter interceptions but the flak was said to be both strong and well aimed, both en route and over the target. The thick cloud rendered searchlights ineffective but many balloons were seen, as were decoy fires to the south, south-east and north of Bristol, with another near Weymouth.

The units involved, with their bombing times, were:

KG1: 13 He 111 and 7 Ju 88, 1828-1922
KG77: 11 Ju 88, 1943-2051
II/LG1: 11 Ju 88, 1900-1935
III/LG1: 8 Ju 88, 1848-1940
I/KG27: 14 He 111, 2040-2145
III/KG27: 8 He 111, 2020-2052
KGr100: 10 He 111, 1837-1906 (X-Verfahren bombing as Beleuchter Firelighting Gruppe)
KGr606: 5 Do 17, 2155-2215
I/KG54: 4 Ju 88, 2150-2230
II/KG54: 4 Ju 88, 2050-2143
KGr806: 4 Ju 88, 2123-2204
I/KG55: 10 He 111, 2028-2108
II/KG55: 12 He 111, 1830-1955 (Flare-dropping target illuminators; bombs included three SC 1800s, one SC 1700, an SD 1400 and three SC 1000)

Bristol suffered its most widespread raid yet, with bombs falling in many districts of the city. Private property and public buildings again bore the brunt of the bombing, with damage to a large granary, a cinema, the university, the Bishop's Palace, several churches, a biscuit factory and a timber yard. An electric transformer station was also hit and the railway between Filton and Avonmouth was blocked. Casualties — 31 killed and 131 seriously injured — might well have been higher when the Bristol Children's Hospital was hit. Elsewhere bombs fell at Norwich, Hereford and Rochester.

Fog over much of Britain again reduced the night fighter effort to a single patrol which proved fruitless. The Bristol AA guns, in action from 1820 to 2250 hours, fired 4,530 of the 5,500 rounds expended during the night. Other gun sites in action were those at Fareham, Plymouth, Holton Heath, Cardiff, Falmouth and Gloucester.

The night was notable for the first operational use of a Starfish decoy fire site. In fact, two sites were in operation near Bristol and between them drew 66 HE bombs, a most satisfactory result.

Two aircraft were lost during daylight operations only, one being the Messerschmitt Bf 109 of Fhr. W. Haufe of 1/JG53 who was rescued after landing in the Channel, and the following:

1/JG53 Messerschmitt Bf 109E-4 (5328). Believed to be the aircraft which crashed into Chichester Harbour 1.30 p.m. Lt. S. Fischer missing. Aircraft White 8+ lost.

The traditional inter-war British 'semi' in a typical British suburban street. The repair to No. 14 Roseberry Gardens, Dartford, damaged on December 3, visible today, patched roofs still being a sure-fire sign of war damage.

TUESDAY, DECEMBER 3-4

Sunset: 1652 Sunrise: 0848
Moon: Dusk — 2130 (First Qtr−3)

Heavy attack on Birmingham with a secondary raid on London. Limited mine-laying off Harwich and in the Thames Estuary.

UK — Cloudy with very low cloud in the Midlands and southern England in occasional rain and drizzle; cloud lifting and decreasing from the West after midnight. Visibility moderate to good in the West and South-West, moderate to poor elsewhere with fog patches. Light winds, south-west to westerly.

The Continent — Low cloud with poor visibility in Holland. Fair at first in France and Belgium with some cloud and rain. Local fog in many inland areas, particularly after midnight.

Yet again widespread fog and mist restricted daylight operations and only some 60 German aircraft were operating, mainly on nuisance raids and shipping reconnaissance. Night operations commenced with raiders crossing the coast at Shoreham less than 40 minutes after sunset and only some ten minutes after full darkness.

The attack on Birmingham was undertaken by 69 aircraft of Luftflotte 3, with the crews of 51 claiming to have reached and bombed the city. Between 1825 and 2200 hours they delivered 59.45 tonnes of HE (two SC 1800, one SC 1700, two SC 1000, eight SC 500, seven Flam 250, 48 SC 250 and 238 SC 50) and 448 BSK (16,128 IBs), partly visually and partly by means of DR and radio navigation. Nine large fires resulted with two particularly big ones visible from some 100 kilometres away. Another 25 to 30 fires were seen covering most of the town area, with one large fire area to 'the north of a stadium'. No night fighters were met but the flak and searchlights were very active. Of the attacking force which failed to reach Bir-

AFTER THE RAID

WHEN YOU HAVE been in the front line and taken it extra hard the country wants to look after you. For you have suffered in the national interest as well as in your own in the fight against Hitler. If your home is damaged there is a great deal of help ready for you.

You will want to know where this help can be found and whom to ask about it. Here are some hints about how you stand. Remember, in reading them, that conditions are different in different areas and the services may not always be quite the same.

HAVE YOUR PLANS READY

YOU SHOULD TRY to make plans *now* to go and stay with friends or relations living near, but not too near, *in case your house is destroyed.* They should also arrange *now* to come to you if their house is knocked out.

If you have to go and stay with them until you can make more permanent arrangements the Government will pay them a lodging allowance of 5s. per week for each adult and 3s. for each child. Your host should enquire at the Town Hall or Council offices about this.

Your local authority will be setting up an Administrative Centre where your questions can be answered. Look out for posters telling you where this centre is or ask the police or wardens for the address. In the meantime, in case of emergency, find out from the police or wardens where the offices are at which the local authority and the Assistance Board are doing their work for people who have been bombed.

1

FOOD AND SHELTER

IF YOU HAVE NOT been able to make arrangements with friends or relatives and have *nowhere to sleep and eat* after your house has been destroyed, the best thing to do is to go to an emergency *Rest Centre.* The wardens and policemen will tell you where this is. You will get food and shelter there until you can go home or make other arrangements. You will also find at the Rest Centre an officer whose job it is to help you with your problems. He will tell you how to get *clothes* if you've lost your own, *money*—if you are in need—a new ration book, a new identity card, a new gas mask, etc. Nurses will be there, too, to help with children and anybody who is suffering from shock.

NEW HOMES FOR THE HOMELESS

A HOME WILL BE FOUND for you, if you cannot make your own arrangements. If you are still earning your normal wages you may have to pay rent.

If you have had to leave your home and can make arrangements to go and stay with friends or relatives you will be given a free travel voucher, if you cannot get to them without help. Enquire about this at the Rest Centre or Administrative Centre (or if there is no Administrative Centre, at the Town Hall or Council offices).

TRACING FRIENDS AND RELATIVES

TO KEEP IN TOUCH with your friends and relatives you should, if you find your own accommodation, send your new address to the Secretary, London Council of Social Service,

2

7, Bayley Street, Bedford Square, London, W.C.1. Of course, also tell your friends and relatives where you are.

Anyone who is homeless and has been provided with accommodation can be found through the Town Halls, the Council offices and the Citizens' Advice Bureaux, since records are kept. If you have got sons or daughters in the Army, Navy, R.A.F., or the Auxiliary Services, they can find you, too, through their Commanding Officer, wherever you may be—whether you have gone to the country, are in hospital or are with friends. In the London area through the local authorities and through the Citizens' Advice Bureaux the Director of Welfare in the London and Eastern Commands is helping men and women serving in the Forces to maintain contact with their relations who may have had to move.

FURNITURE AND OTHER BELONGINGS

(1) *If your income is below a certain amount* you can apply to the Assistance Board for :—

(*a*) a grant to replace *essential* furniture* and *essential* household articles ;

(*b*) a grant to replace your clothes† or those of your family ;

(*c*) a grant to replace *tools*† essential to your work.

You also have a claim for your other belongings, but these do not come under the Assistance Board's scheme, and you should make your claim on Form V.O.W.1.‡

* The household income must be normally £400 a year or less (*i.e.*, nearly £8 0s. 0*d.* per week or less).
† Your income in this case must be normally £250 a year or less (*i.e.*, nearly £5 0s. 0*d.* per week or less) or £400 a year or less if you have dependants.
‡ You can get this form at your Town Hall or the offices of your Council.

3

mingham 11 aircraft bombed alternative targets and seven aborted. Three He 111s of I/KG1 were also dispatched, with London as their primary target, while the following were assigned to Birmingham:

I/KG1: 6 He 111, 1825-1924
III/KG26: 2 He 111, 1826-1928 (Y-Verfahren bombing)
II/LG1: 5 Ju 88, 1910-1942
III/LG1: 4 Ju 88, 1845-1945
I/KG27: 8 He 111, 2112-2200
II/KG27: 5 He 111, 2020-2040
KGr100: 9 He 111, 1848-1920 (X-Verfahren bombing)
I/KG55: 7 He 111, 2050-2130
II/KG55: 5 He 111, 1900-1930

The harassing attack was made on London in two phases — from 1825 to 2200 and then from 0024 to 0628 hours. Conditions varied throughout the night and while some of the 22 crews which found London bombed visually, others used DR and radio aids. The attackers (three aircraft of Luftflotte 3 and 19 of Luftflotte 2) dropped 21 tonnes of HE and 52 BSK (1,872 IBs) and reported large fires and explosions in Zielräum 'Otto' and Zielräum 'Nanni', the areas encompassing the City, Westminster and Whitehall, and adjacent districts along the Thames. Cloud conditions hindered the searchlights and the flak was described as feeble but well directed.

Damage in Birmingham was mainly to houses and shops but seven factories, including that of Joseph Lucas Ltd, and a gas works were also hit. Many fires were started in a band running north-south across the city and measuring some three miles in length and half a mile wide, an area no doubt delineated by the X-Verfahren beams set up to guide the fireraising He 111s of KGr100. Public services were also hit and there was some damage to railway installations, but casualties were quite light, with initial reports giving 25 killed and 60 seriously injured.

In the London attack an air raid shelter at Hammersmith received a direct hit but no important industrial plants or other factories were seriously damaged. Bombs also fell in Kensington, Fulham and seven outlying districts, with more incidents in the Home Counties at Ilford, Chertsey, Chatham, Hornchurch, East Grinstead, Epsom, near Dunstable, near Wargrave, Shoreham, Gravesend and Chesham.

Other places reporting bomb incidents were Boston, Warwick, Stratford-on-Avon, Worcester and near Pershore, Swindon, Salisbury, Netheravon, Ringwood, near Christchurch, near Cardiff, Bristol and Newnham.

Adverse weather conditions were confirmed by a single Beaufighter dispatched by No. 10 Group on a weather test and no other night fighter sorties were flown. A decision to operate the Hampden Patrol was also cancelled, but one Hampden was dispatched at 2255 hours to report on the prospects of guidance of enemy aircraft by fires. Subsequently the British crew reported seeing one large fire from 11-12,000 feet but nothing else owing to the blanket of cloud, some 3,000 feet thick, which covered the Midlands.

The Birmingham guns engaged enemy aircraft at heights between 10-22,000 feet from 1850 to 2225 hours, but made no claims of success. Other guns were in action at Portland, the Solent, London's IAZ, Slough, Coventry, Cardiff, Newport, Holton Heath, Plymouth, Gloucester and Bristol, with some 5,500 rounds fired countrywide.

4. Temporary Want or Need

If apart from the loss of furniture and personal belongings referred to above you are in need as a result of air raids, you should explain your case to the Assistance Board Officer mentioned above who, if possible, will help you.

5. Houses Affected by War Damage

(*a*) **Government Insurance Scheme**—Notification of damage should be made to the War Damage Commission within thirty days of the bombing. Owners should apply at the Information Centre, Town Hall, for Form C.1 and explanatory pamphlet C.1.A which explains the provisions of the War Damage Act, 1941, in regard to land and buildings.

(*b*) **Repairs**—Immediately after air raids the Council will proceed to carry out temporary repairs (known as "first aid" repairs) in all cases in which the owner fails to do so. This would normally include the replacing of doors, covering of windows, repair of roofs and gutters and generally such urgent repairs as appear expedient for avoiding danger to health.

In due course the Council will proceed to carry out other repairs in appropriate cases for preventing the deterioration of the building (known as "protective repairs"). With regard to more extensive repairs which the Council have power to carry out subject to certain conditions, the Council will proceed to put this work in hand as and when circumstances permit them to do so.

The owner or occupier need not claim for "first aid" or "protective" repairs done by the Council who will not make any charge against the property in respect thereof. Where any repairs are carried out by the owner or occupier the Council are unable to reimburse the cost or pay the builders' account. The correct procedure is for the owner or occupier to make an application

6

to the War Damage Commission for a "Cost of Works Payment," Form C.2, obtainable from the War Damage Commission.

Enquiries relating to repairs being carried out by the Council should be made at Room 24 (third floor), Town Hall.

(*c*) **Mortgages**—Notice of any damage and of its extent must be given to mortgagees as soon as practicable after it has become known in accordance with the Landlord and Tenant (War Damage) Act, 1939, and the mortgagees must be permitted to enter for purposes of inspection and repair.

Mortgagors will continue to be liable for payments under the mortgage, but the mortgagees' right of recovery is restricted by the Courts (Emergency Powers) Act, 1939. Where an obligation to do repairs is imposed on any person, such obligation does not extend to making good war damage.

(*d*) **Tenancies and Leases**—Tenants and lessees must give similar notices to those referred to above under the heading of "Mortgages," but the liability to repair depends upon the extent of the damage and whether the tenant retains or disclaims his lease or agreement (see Landlord and Tenant (War Damage) Act 1939).

These provisions do not, however, apply in the case of short tenancies, which include weekly, monthly and quarterly tenancies but not tenancies for longer periods. In these cases the Landlord and Tenant (War Damage) Amendment Act 1941, makes special provisions for the cessation of rent when premises are rendered unfit and are not occupied by the tenant wholely or in part. Where a part only of the premises is unfit the rent is to be apportioned in accordance with the provisions of the Act.

6. Personal Injuries, Allowances and Pensions

If you are normally dependent on your wages

7

Home Security pamphlets informed people how to get help; local authorities — this is the Borough of Camberwell — issued more detailed instructions.

(2) *If your income is above certain limits*, you do not come under the Assistance Board's scheme and should make out a claim for all your belongings on Form V.O.W.1.*

The time at which payment can be made for belongings not covered by the Assistance Board's scheme will be settled shortly, when Parliament has passed the War Damage Bill.

(3) If bombing has left you without any *ready cash*, because you have lost your job or cannot get to work to be paid or because you have been hurt, you can apply to the Assistance Board.

COMPENSATION
FOR DAMAGE TO HOUSES

IF YOU *own your house* or hold it on a long lease and it is damaged or destroyed, whatever your income, you should, as soon as possible, make a claim on Form V.O.W.1.* The amount of your compensation and the time of paying it will depend on the passing of the War Damage Bill now before Parliament.

REPAIRS

IF YOUR HOUSE can be made fit to live in with a few simple repairs the local authority (apply to the Borough or Council Engineer) will put it right if the landlord is not able to do it. But how quickly the local authority can do this depends on local conditions.

FOOD

If your gas is cut off, or your kitchen range is out of action, then you may be able to get hot meals at the Londoners' Meals Service restaurants in the London County Council area or at the community kitchens outside that area. A meat dish can be obtained for about 4*d.* to 6*d.* and "afters" for about 2*d.* to 3*d.*, tea for a penny, and children's portions half price. Find out now where these are from the Town Hall, Council offices or the Citizens' Advice Bureau in case of emergency.

* You can get this form at your Town Hall or the offices of your Council.

4

THE INJURED

IF YOU are injured, treatment will be given at First Aid Posts and Hospitals, and :—

(*a*) If your doctor says you are unable to work as a result of a "war injury" you will be eligible to receive an *injury allowance*. Application should be made immediately to the local office of the Assistance Board and you should take with you, or send, a medical certificate from a doctor or a hospital.

b) If you are afterwards found to be suffering from a serious and prolonged disablement, your case will be considered for a disability pension.

c) Widows of workers and Civil Defence Volunteers killed on duty will receive £2 10*s.* 0*d.* a week for ten weeks, after which a widow's pension will become payable. Pensions for orphans and dependent parents are also provided.

Ask at the Post Office for the address of the local branch of the Ministry of Pensions if you want to apply for a pension.

KEEP THIS AND DO WHAT IT TELLS YOU. HELP IS WAITING FOR YOU. THE GOVERNMENT, YOUR FELLOW CITIZENS AND YOUR NEIGHBOURS WILL SEE THAT "FRONT LINE" FIGHTERS ARE LOOKED AFTER!

Issued by the Ministry of Home Security in co-operation with the following Departments: The Treasury, the Ministry of Health, the Ministry of Pensions, the Ministry of Food and the Assistance Board

5

51—8415 (7) F.K.

AFTER
THE
RAID

ISSUED BY THE MINISTRY OF HOME SECURITY
LONDON REGION EDITION DECEMBER [illegible]

WAR DAMAGE CONTRIBUTION. 27 NOV 1941

INSTALMENT DUE AND PAYABLE ON 1 JULY, 1941.

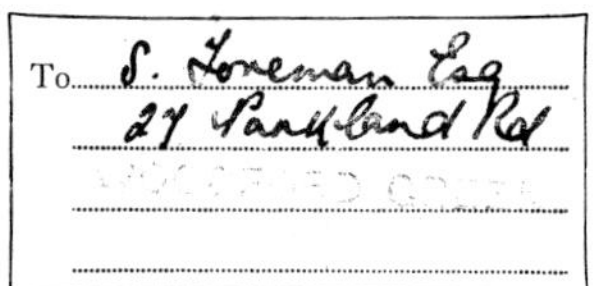

To S. Foreman Esq
27 Parkland Rd

An assessment of the instalment of War Damage Contribution, **due on 1 July, 1941,** has been made in respect of the property described herein; particulars of the assessment are shown below.

Special attention is directed to the Notes enclosed herewith.

If any further explanation in regard to the assessment is desired, application may be made to me.

The instalment of Contribution should be paid to the Collector of Taxes whose address is given on the enclosed economy label.

L. W. SMITH,
STRATFORD 3rd DISTRICT,
DEANERY ROAD,
STRATFORD, E.15.

44095

.... Date.

Reference Numbers	*Description and Situation of Property (if not as above)	Contributory Value: Amount on which Inst. payable at 2/- in the £ (£)	(s.)	Amount on which Inst. payable at 6d. in the £ (£)	(s.)	INSTALMENT PAYABLE (£)	(s.)	(d.)
5/W.D. 90394		27	/	—	-	2	14	-
		—	-					
	Total amount payable on 1 July, 1941							

*Where the instalment applied for relates to more than one property, see details appended.

For further directions as to payment, see overleaf.

W.D.5. 21018 Wt. 11748/9. 6487/8. 5/41. M^cC. & Co. Ltd., Ldn. T51-338.

CO-OPERATIVE PERMANENT BUILDING SOCIETY

London Headquarters: 142, High Holborn, W.C.1 Telephone, HOL 2302/3

Telephone Naphill 130

Please reply to CHILTERN HOUSE HUGHENDEN VALLEY HIGH WYCOMBE, BUCKS.

28th November, 1941.

CH.JEC/WDC/3.

S. Foreman, Esq.,
27, Parkland Road,
WOODFORD GREEN,
Essex.

Dear Sir,

re WAR DAMAGE CONTRIBUTION. Account No.. 44095a

I thank you for forwarding to me your War damage contribution receipt and I have pleasure in confirming that the Society is liable to indemnify you to the extent of .. one-third of the contribution i.e. 18/-d.....

It has been arranged to credit your mortgage account with this amount, and it will be in order for you to deduct this sum from your next mortgage repayment should you wish to do so.

I have pleasure in returning to you enclosed your contribution receipt.

Yours faithfully,

C. F. Dalzline
Secretary.

It feels over-simplistic to point out that in spite of the hardship of life at the time, things had to go on, but it is important to remember that even war did not give an excuse to avoid one's obligations — like building society payments or tax demands!

The War Damage Act of 1941 brought in a property tax to finance compensation for those affected by losses from enemy action, the average cost of repairs then being estimated to be costing £50 per house.

WEDNESDAY, DECEMBER 4-5

Sunset: 1651 Sunrise: 0851
Moon: Dusk — 2245 (First Qtr−2)

Heavy attacks on Birmingham and London. Minelaying off the Pembrokeshire coast, Plymouth, Lands End and between Lowestoft and Harwich. Minor attacks on Southampton.

UK — Low cloud, rain and poor visibility in many areas, improving from the West to give showers and moderate to good visibility after 0100 hours. Surface winds west to north-westerly, strong or gale force locally.

The Continent — Much low cloud with poor visibility. Wind increasing to gale force but conditions slowly improving.

There was little air activity on a day of local mist, fog patches and generally poor visibility. Only 15 enemy aircraft crossed British coasts, but some 60 aircraft were employed on anti-shipping operations and sea reconnaissance. Night operations commenced with hostile aircraft crossing the Kent and Sussex coasts at 1730 hours.

Birmingham was bombed by 62 of the 88 aircraft ordered to the city by Luftflotte 3. Between 1815 and 2300 hours they dropped 77 tonnes of HE (five SC 1800, one SC 1500, 16 SC 1000, eight Flam 500, 20 SC 250, nine Flam 250, eight LZZ 250, 91 SC 250 and 180 SC 50) and 184 BSK (6,624 IBs), all by radio navigation or DR methods. The glow of a large fire, explosions and several small fires were all seen. Flak was of varying strength and, in general, well directed, but two night fighters which were seen did not attack. Units involved, with bombing times, were:

I/LG1: 3 Ju 88, 1923-2142
III/LG1: 5 Ju 88, 1944-2023
I/KG27: 7 He 111, 2126-2225

WAR DAMAGE CONTRIBUTION

See notes overleaf as to recovery of part of an instalment from a landlord, tenant, or mortgagee; for the purpose of such recovery this Receipt should be preserved in case it may be required as evidence of the payment.

Date on which Instalment due	Parish, etc., and Assessment Nos. and District	Contributory Value (£)	(s.)	Description and Situation of Property	Paid by Cheque, Money Order or Postal Order (£)	(s.)	(d.)	Paid by Cash (£)	(s.)	(d.)
1-7-44	5/90394 Woodford.	27	-	27, Parkland Road.	2	14	-			

RECEIVED the above payment.

.... Collector.

Date Stamp

WD—AA 762490

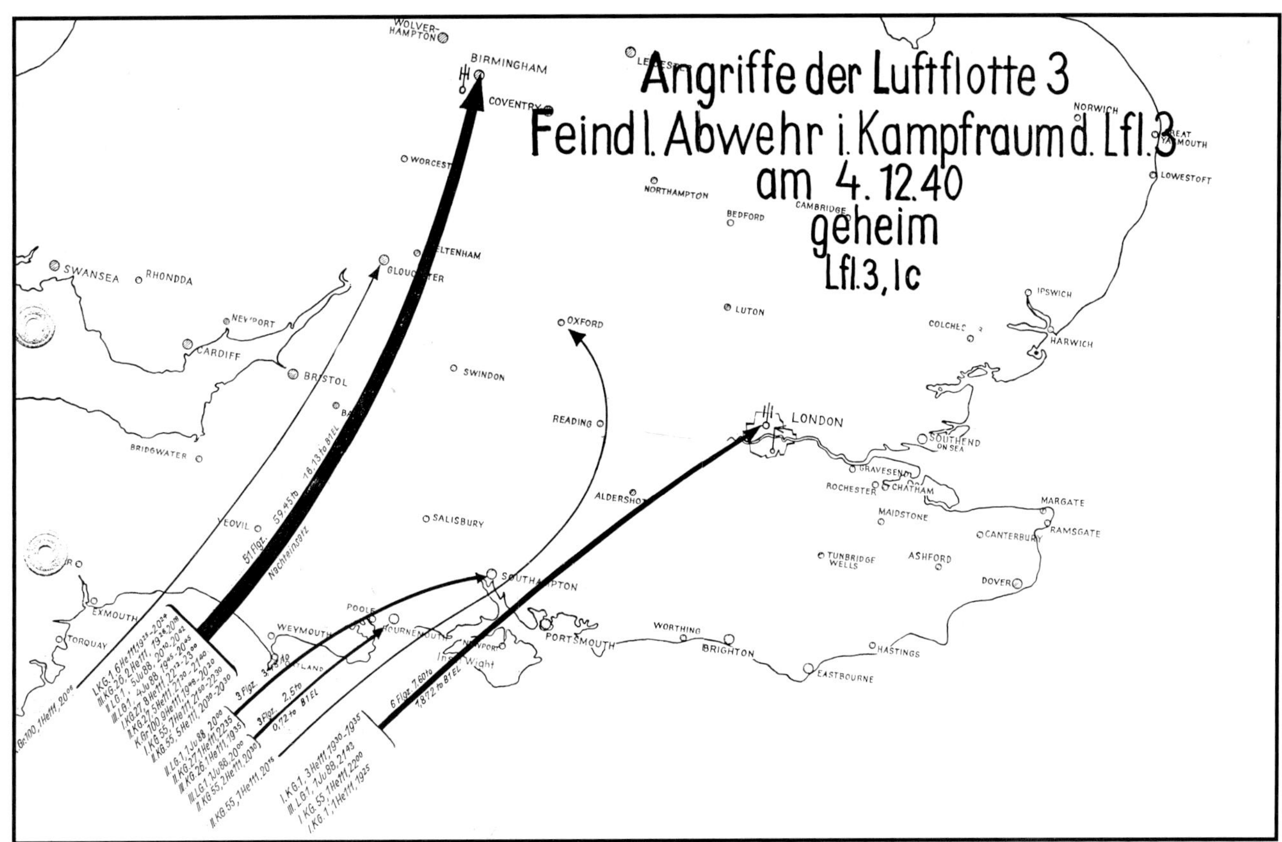

II/KG27: 6 He 111, 2025-2300
I/KG51: 7 Ju 88, 1850-1935
II/KG51: 3 Ju 88, 1925-1953
III/KG51: 4 Ju 88, 2005-2203
I/KG54: 3 Ju 88, 2155-2215
II/KG54: 2 Ju 88, 2139-2150
KG1: 3 He 111, 2010-2030
KG26: 14 He 111, 1925-2020
III/KG26: 5 He 111, 1815-2100 (Y-Verfahren bombing, operating in Fire-lighter rôle)

Seventeen aircraft bombed alternative targets, five aborted and reports from two crews were not received when the Operations Report was compiled by Luftflotte 3. A Ju 88 of I/LG1 was lost on its return flight and an He 111 of III/KG26 crashed near Aumale killing its crew of four.

The attack on London was carried out by 42 of the 48 aircraft dispatched. Bombing between 1820 and 2329 hours they dropped 48 tonnes of HE (18 SC 1000, 24 SC 500, 23 SC 250, five Flam 250 and 226 SC/SD 50) and 39 BSK (1,404 IBs). Bombing was partly visual but most crews used radio and DR methods, their primary target being Zielraum 'Otto', where, in spite of extensive cloud, single fires could be seen. Crews reported that both flak and searchlights were weak and ineffective. Most of the attackers were attached to Luftflotte 2, but Luftflotte 3 participation included aircraft from II/KG27, III/KG51, II/KG54 and KG26.

Seven aircraft of Luftflotte 3 also attacked Southampton as their primary target, dropping 8 tonnes of HE (two SC 1000, three SC 500, nine SC 250, two Flam 250 and 24 SC 50) and 20 BSK (720 IBs) between 1859 and 2145 hours. The participants were single aircraft from III/LG1, I/KG27, II/KG27, II/KG51, III/KG51 and two aircraft from KG26. Bombs were dropped entirely by radio and DR navigation and only isolated fires were discernible through the cloud which covered the area. Flak was assessed as weak.

From bomb incident reports it was difficult for the British to determine the main target — bombing was widespread, with no damage of any real significance, but clearly centred on the counties of Leicestershire, Northamptonshire, Warwickshire and Nottinghamshire, with Coventry, Birmingham, Nuneaton and Leicester the most likely targets. In Birmingham a number of houses were damaged, but the most serious incident was at Witton Tram Depot where 24 vehicles were rendered unusable. Some damage was also done to railway lines within the city but everywhere casualties were light. Countrywide bombs fell at Birmingham, Coventry, Derby, Nuneaton, Northampton, Peterborough, Grantham, Wittering, Kettering, Oundle, Chipping Norton, Slough, Tunbridge Wells and Sheerness, but with little effect.

The raiders were opposed by AA gunfire from the London IAZ, the Solent, Yeovil, Plymouth, Slough, Thames and Medway (North and South), Coventry, Birmingham and Wythall. Birmingham's guns fired 280 rounds between 1910 and 2103 hours, engaging targets flying at heights between 15,000 and 20,000 feet, and AA Command in all used 3,500 rounds for three enemy aircraft claimed destroyed.

Nos. 10, 11 and 13 Groups put up a total of nine night fighters and one Defiant caught a brief sight of, and managed to fire off 35 rounds at, an unidentified enemy aircraft, but the engagement appeared to be ineffective.

THURSDAY, DECEMBER 5-6

Sunset: 1651 Sunrise: 0852
Moon: Dusk — 2351 (First Qtr−1)

Heavy attack on Portsmouth. Minor raid on London, airfield patrols by long-range night fighter-bombers and minelaying by IX Fliegerkorps in the Thames Estuary, off Harwich, in the mouth of the Humber, off Flamborough Head and in the mouth of the Tees.

UK — Continuous rain with low cloud and poor visibility in east and south-east England at first, rapidly moving eastwards. Fair conditions with showers and moderate to good visibility general by 0200 hours. Snow showers in Scotland. Winds west to north-westerly, fresh with gales on western coasts.

The Continent — Rain and low cloud with strong south-westerly winds, improving from the West later in the night.

Two sweeps by German fighter-bombers and shipping reconnaissance occupied the Luftwaffe during the day, but conditions deteriorated to give rain and mist in the afternoon. By evening a gale was blowing, but night operations started shortly after nightfall with aircraft tracking in to Portsmouth.

From 1810 to 2034 Portsmouth was bombed by 74 of the 79 aircraft dispatched by Luftflotte 3. The attack was possible only by DR and radio navigation methods because of cloud cover over the target, but the glow of fires could be seen through the overcast and, through isolated breaks in the cloud, several fires were seen in the town centre. The raiders dropped 88 tonnes of HE (31 SC 1000, 11 Flam 500, 32 SC 500, five Flam 250, 28 LZZ 250, 72 SC 250 and 176 SC 50) and 148 BSK (5,328 IBs). No night fighters were seen; flak was generally slight to moderate in strength and searchlights were hindered by the weather.

Precise details of operating units are not available in German records, but from the RAF's 'Y' Service intercepts and Air Intelligence Summaries it appears that the following units were engaged on operations this night: III/KG27, I/LG1, II/KG54, II/KG51, III/KG51, I/KG77, I/KG26, III/KG26, II/KG53, I/KG4, II/KG4. Some of these units were engaged on minelaying and the precise area of operations for the others is not known. Of those engaged in the Portsmouth attack four aircraft are known to have aborted and one — an He 111 of III/KG27 — was lost when it crashed near Lorient at 2200 hours.

In a subsidiary attack on London only 29 of the 48 participating aircraft reported over the target and again weather conditions prevented an assessment of bombing. The Concentration Point lay in Target Area

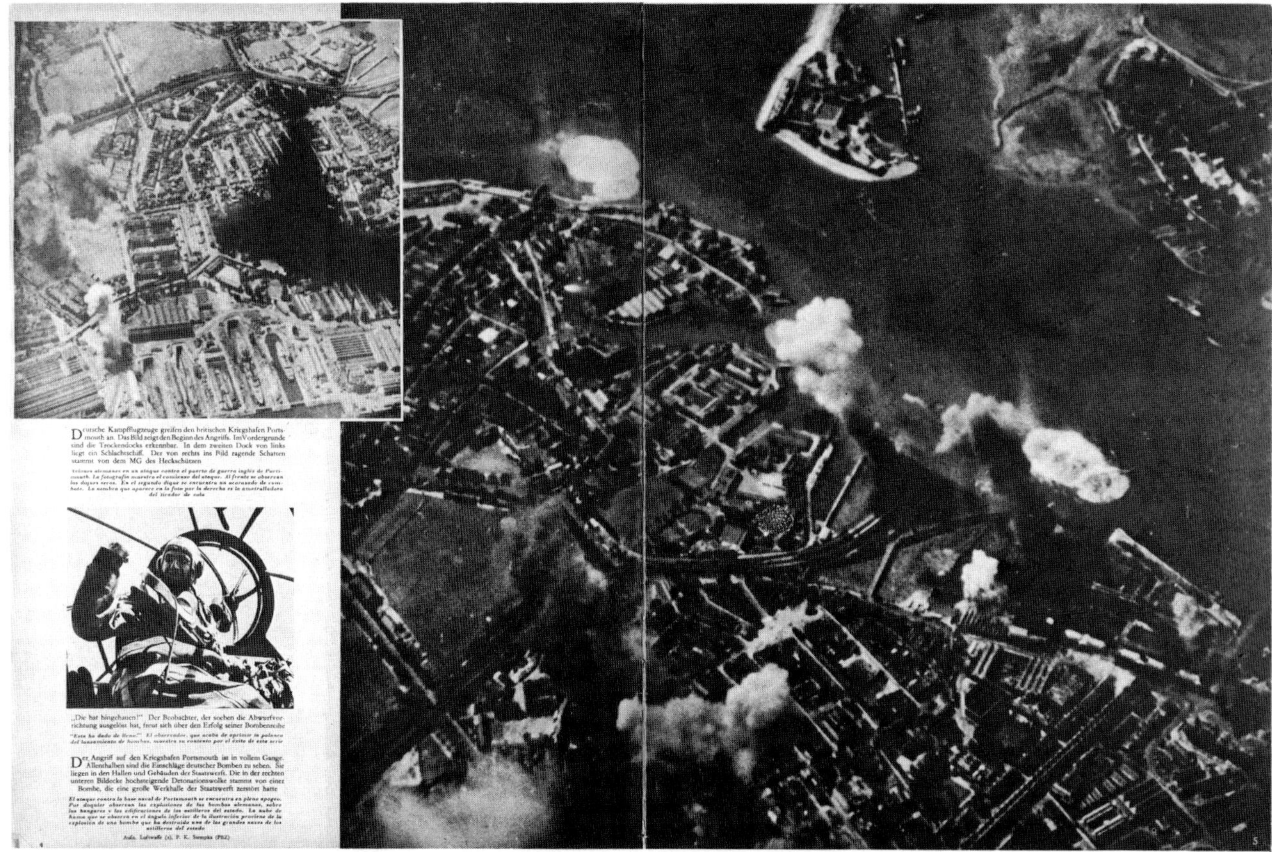

Deutsche Kampfflugzeuge greifen den britischen Kriegshafen Portsmouth an. Das Bild zeigt den Beginn des Angriffs. Im Vordergrunde sind die Trockendocks erkennbar. In dem zweiten Dock von links liegt ein Schlachtschiff. Der von rechts ins Bild ragende Schatten stammt von dem MG des Heckschützen

Aviones alemanes en un ataque contra el puerto de guerra inglés de Portsmouth. La fotografía muestra el comienzo del ataque. Al frente se observan los diques secos. En el segundo dique se encuentra un acorazado de combate. La sombra que aparece en la foto por la derecha es la ametralladora del tirador de cola

„Die hat hingehauen!" Der Beobachter, der soeben die Abwurfvorrichtung ausgelöst hat, freut sich über den Erfolg seiner Bombenreihe

"Esta ha dado de lleno!" El observador, que acaba de oprimir la palanca del lanzamiento de bombas, muestra su contento por el éxito de esta serie

Der Angriff auf den Kriegshafen Portsmouth ist in vollem Gange. Allenthalben sind die Einschläge deutscher Bomben zu sehen. Sie liegen in den Hallen und Gebäuden der Staatswerft. Die in der rechten unteren Bildecke hochsteigende Detonationswolke stammt von einer Bombe, die eine große Werkhalle der Staatswerft zerstört hatte

El ataque contra la base naval de Portsmouth se encuentra en pleno apogeo. Por doquier observan las explosiones de las bombas alemanas, sobre los hangares y las edificaciones de los astilleros del estado. La nube de humo que se observa en el ángulo inferior de la ilustración proviene de la explosión de una bomba que ha destruido una de las grandes naves de los astilleros del estado

Aufn. Luftwaffe (2), P. K. Stempka (PBZ)

In spite of its importance militarily as a target, the bombing of Portsmouth received scant coverage in the pages of *Der Adler* during the period when the air attack on England was topical. The most dramatic coverage had appeared in the September 3 edition — possibly taken on the big raid on August 24. *(See also Volume 1, page 237.)* Portsmouth's night blitz effectively began on December 5 but it was one of the few provincial targets which did not receive the 'doubling' treatment, its next big raid not coming until January 10–11. (Coventry of course was the other industrial anomaly as, after November, it did not receive its next attack until April 1941.) According to Mass-Observation, city dwellers had followed the Southampton cycle of trek and evacuation, the surrounding villages were crowded, with consequent strain on transport, food, health services and rural goodwill, over a half-circle 10–15 miles along the coast east and west.

'Otto', where 33 tonnes of HE (ten SC 1000, three LZZ 1000, 21 SC 500, two SC 250, four LZZ 250 and 160 SC 50) were claimed deposited by radio and DR navigation methods. This was the first known occasion when time fuzes were fitted to give a delayed action with 1,000kg bombs; previous UXBs of this size were almost certainly the result of faulty normal fuzes.

Several large fires were, in fact, started in the Portsmouth dock area, in surrounding residential areas, and at Gosport. High explosives and fires damaged the Royal Marines' Barracks, the Vernon Naval Establishment, two hospitals and a cinema and there was a fire of considerable proportions at a timber yard. Gas and water mains suffered, but not to a serious degree. About 30 people were killed and 60 seriously injured.

No major damage was caused elsewhere although bomb reports were received from Ryde, Havant, Hayling Island and country areas around Portsmouth; in the London area bombs fell at Woolwich, Barking, Chigwell, Ilford and Croydon, with further incidents at Cliffe, Sheerness, Queenborough, Seaford, Lowestoft, Hornchurch, Canvey Island, Clavering, Louth, Raithby, Driffield, Catfoss and several rural areas. A few bombs also landed on Hornchurch airfield but exploded harmlessly and caused no damage to aircraft or injuries to personnel.

Five night fighters of No. 11 Group were sent up but no combats ensued. Overall, AA Command used approximately 2,000 rounds of heavy ammunition, with the Portsmouth guns, which were in action from 1843 to 2040 hours, firing 514. Other sites engaging were the Solent, IAZ and Harwich.

Two Messerschmitt Bf 109s were lost on the two daylight fighter sweeps made over Kent: Lt. H. Heinemann of 1/JG26 and Oblt. H. Vogeler, Staffelkapitän of 4/LG2, both of whom were reported missing. RAF fighters made fourteen claims. The only loss over Great Britain was the following:

3(F)/31 Dornier Do 17 (4094). Shot down into the sea off Portloe Cove, Cornwall 2.55 p.m. by Pilot Officer M. C. B. Boddington in a Spitfire of No. 234 Squadron. Fw. R. Lang killed. Oberlt. F. Scheimer and Fw. H. Bold missing. Aircraft 5D+DL sank in sea.

FRIDAY, DECEMBER 6-7

Sunset: 1650 Sunrise: 0853
Moon: Dusk — 0054 (First Quarter)

Heavy attack on Bristol. Little other activity.

UK — Showers in Scotland and western districts of England and Wales with local thunder, spreading eastwards. Visibility mainly good except in rain. Winds mainly north to north-west, moderate to gale force in some areas, increasing everywhere.

The Continent — Wintry showers with generally good visibility except in rain or snow showers. Strong west to north-west winds.

Of 62 Luftwaffe aircraft operating during the day only a dozen or so crossed the coast. The rest were engaged on patrols and reconnaissance of the English Channel, but gale force winds restricted their activity. The strong winds also rendered inoperative 12 British CHL radar stations during the morning, it being necessary to tie up their aerials as a precaution against possible damage. Damage caused by the wind also put many Observer Corps Posts out of action.

Despite the wintry weather, night operations started at 1735 hours but were to be on a restricted scale with the country clear of enemy aircraft by midnight. Nevertheless, significant damage was done to Bristol.

Eighty aircraft of Luftflotte 3 were involved in the operation and this was the sum total of German bomber activity during the hours of darkness. Of this force, the crews of 67 reported bombing their primary target, seven bombed alternatives and three aborted. One aircraft, an He 111 of II/KG27, failed to return and two crashed in German-occupied territory upon their return.

The attack was opened as usual by flare dropping He 111s of II/KG55 and bombing took place between 1920 and 2245 hours with the delivery of 78 tonnes of HE (two SC 1800, one SC 1700, four SD 1400, 19 SC 1000, 43 SC 500, two Flam 250, seven LZZ 250, 21 SC 250 and 227 SC 50) and 158 BSK (5,688 IBs). The good visibility and broken cloud permitted visual bombing and the attack was assessed as successful. Among the observed results were explosions on the city water works and in two dry docks in the Floating Harbour (the city docks). All crews reported seeing extensive fires over the entire town area. Night fighters were seen over Bristol, but no attacks were reported, and flak was feeble — only guns in the south-east of the city were observed firing. There was, however, strong searchlight activity and balloons were reported at a height of 2,000 metres (6,500 feet). There were also reports of large decoy fires to the west, east and north-east of Bristol.

The units engaged in the attack were:

I/LG1: 3 Ju 88, 2000-2010
II/LG1: 5 Ju 88, 2000-2018
II/KG27: 7 He 111, 1950-2025
I/KG51: 8 Ju 88, 2145-2245
II/KG51: 7 Ju 88, 2050-2135
I/KG55: 8 He 111, 2030-2100
II/KG55: 9 He 111, 1920-2010 (opened attack with flares and two SC 1800s, one SC 1700, four SD 1000s, 28 smaller HEs and 1,920; IBs. Large fires resulted)
III/KG55: 9 He 111, 1950-2020
KG77: 11 Ju 88, 1920-2110

Attacks by aircraft of RAF Bomber and Coastal Commands against a number of German airfields in France and the Low Countries, defensive patrols by 36 night fighters and the employment of the Hampden Patrol, all failed to prevent a damaging attack on the important West Coast port. Several major fires were started and extensive damage was done to houses, churches and public buildings, including the main post office. Electricity and gas supplies were badly affected and although a number of factories were set on fire, the damage was not serious. The railways, however, were considerably disrupted; two trains received direct hits, Temple Meads Station was damaged and several lines were blocked. Communications, too, were badly disorganised, but the water supplies were only affected in some districts. Bombs, both HEs and IBs, were also reported in surrounding areas of Somerset and Gloucestershire. Bristol's casualties were put at 76 dead and 76 injured.

Bombs at Portsmouth did slight damage to the docks but dwelling houses also suffered and in one incident at least eight people were killed by a direct hit on an Anderson shelter. Bombing was also recorded at Crawley, near Lingfield, Hambledon, Bramdean, Gloucester, Worcester, Chipping Sodbury, Filton, South Cerney, Sharpness, Wareham, Wincanton, Stroud and Port Eynon.

Thirty-six night fighters of Nos. 10 and 11 Groups flew patrols and a Blenheim of No. 604 Squadron fired at a Ju 88 flying at 17,000 feet between Wells and Radstock. Momentarily illuminated by searchlights, the German aircraft switched on its navigation lights, presumably to deceive the defenders, but when attacked from behind by the Blenheim it took evasive action and was not seen again.

Earlier, at 1845 hours, a single Hampden had carried out a weather reconnaissance of the Bristol and Coventry areas and, acting on this, a patrol of 20 Hampdens was ordered to Bristol. However, no contacts were made with enemy aircraft and the improvised night fighters were recalled to base at 0120 hours owing to a lack of incoming raids.

Bristol's searchlights illuminated four aircraft during the attack and the city's guns, in action from 1826 to 2245 hours, fired 1,008 rounds. Elsewhere HAA guns engaged raiders at Brooklands, the Solent, Newport, Holton Heath, Bramley and Yeovil, using some 2,000 rounds in the process.

SATURDAY, DECEMBER 7-8

Sunset: 1650 Sunrise: 0854
Moon: Dusk — 0157 (First Qtr+1)

No German night bomber operations; limited long-range fighter intrusions over eastern England.

UK — Small amounts of medium cloud with showers in most districts. Very cold with good to moderate visibility. Gales in eastern coastal districts.

The Continent — Extensive low cloud with snow in many areas. Severe icing conditions in cloud. Mainly fine conditions inland with good visibility. Much of North-West Europe snow covered.

A quiet day, with only a few inland penetrations by German aircraft, was followed by a largely uneventful night. No German long-range bomber operations were undertaken because of the poor weather conditions existing over much of the Continent with the risk of severe icing. However, five sorties were carried out over eastern England by long-range night fighters of the Nachtjägerdivision, mixing with aircraft of RAF Bomber Command returning from attacks on Düsseldorf, airfields and the Channel ports. There was some confusion, however, as about 3 per cent of the returning British bombers did not show IFF while some 35 aircraft did not show IFF until within 20 to 30 miles of the coast. In consequence, 52 British night fighters were dispatched to meet a possible but non-existent threat. (There was a belief among many RAF bomber crews that German night fighters were able to use IFF transmissions to effect interceptions and there was, therefore, a reluctance to switch on the equipment until approaching the English coast.) No bombing was reported anywhere in the UK during the hours of darkness. One RAF night fighter was lost.

Operations during the day were limited to reconnaissance and only one aircraft was brought down in Britain:

4(F)/122 Junkers Ju 88A-5 (0438). Attacked by three Spitfires of No. 611 Squadron and damaged during shipping reconnaissance. Pilot attempted a forced landing but the aircraft crashed heavily at Jackson's Farm, Skidbrooke, near Somercotes, Lincolnshire 12.45 p.m. Lt. B. Tietzen, Fw. W. Bäuerle, Uffz. W. Pinn and Gefr. W. Schenk taken prisoner. Aircraft F6+HM wrecked.

The *Adler* editor made up for his omission with a double-page spread of Bristol showing acres of burnt-out buildings taken, he said, from a reconnaissance aircraft on December 12, which would make it the day after the picture on page 318.

So sieht Bristol aus

Tal es el aspecto de Bristol

Dieses am 12. Dezember 1940 von einem deutschen Aufklärer aufgenommene Luftbild des Stadtkerns von Bristol ist ein überzeugender Beweis von der Wirkung der vernichtenden Schläge, die unsere Kampfverbände auf diese wichtige Hafen- und Industriestadt im Südwesten der britischen Insel haben niedersausen lassen. In der Tiefe unter uns sehen wir den Floating Harbour, das Hafenviertel mit vielen Speicheranlagen. Von wenigen Gebäuden abgesehen, die wahrscheinlich durch spätere Angriffe ebenfalls vernichtet worden sind, ist fast die ganze Hafengegend zerstört. Bei genauer Betrachtung kann man feststellen, daß von den meisten Häusern nur noch die Mauern stehen. Sie sind restlos ausgebrannt, und der Blick des Fliegers dringt durch bis auf den Boden

Esta fotografía aérea del centro de la ciudad de Bristol, tomada el 12 de diciembre de 1940 por un piloto de reconocimiento alemán, es prueba evidente de los efectos de los mortales golpes que nuestras unidades de bombardeo han asestado sobre este importante centro industrial y marítimo del litoral sudoeste de la Isla británica. Al fondo, a nuestros pies, distinguimos el Floating Harbour, el barrio del puerto con sus innumerables depósitos. Quitando unos pocos edificios, que seguramente han sido igualmente destruidos en ataques posteriores, toda esta parte del puerto está devastada. Si se observa más detenidamente puede apreciarse que de la mayoría de las casas no quedan más que los carbonizados paredones exteriores

Tottenham Court Road in the aftermath of London's first major raid for two months, a reprisal attack for an RAF strike against Düsseldorf. Prominent in the centre is Jay's the jewellers which survived the war only to become a household word in April 1947 when it was the target of young thugs in a daring daylight armed robbery. A passer-by, Alec de Antiquis, who tried to stop the gang with his motor cycle, was gunned down; the successful tracking down of the murderers, Geraghty, Jenkins and Rolt, becoming one of the classic cases of 'Fabian of the Yard'. A vital clue to the crime was found in No. 191 further up the road.

SUNDAY, DECEMBER 8-9

Sunset: 1650 Sunrise: 0855
Moon: Dusk — 0300 (First Qtr+2)

Major attack on London. Attacks on airfields in East Anglia and limited minelaying.

UK — A belt of rain with low and medium cloud moved eastwards across the country to reach the East Coast at 0400 hours; clear weather behind the front. Poor visibility in the rain, good behind the clearance. Winds light westerly at first, increasing to strong in West.

The Continent — Fair at first, rain and lowering cloud spreading from the West.

The weather again restricted Luftwaffe operations and only six raiders were plotted over land; 65 were engaged on shipping reconnaissance. At dusk an improvement enabled night operations to commence on a large scale, but cloud was already thickening up from the West again as another front approached from an unsettled Atlantic.

With the exception of three fighter-bombers of I/NJG2 and about a dozen minelayers of IX Fliegerkorps, all units of Luftflotten 2 and 3 operating were given London as their primary target with the City and Government offices area (Zielraum 'Otto') as the Schwerpunkt. Subsequently the crews of 413 aircraft reported over the target (332 from Luftflotte 3 and 81 from Luftflotte 2), dropping 387 tonnes of HE (four SC 1800, 14 SC 1400, 123 SC 1000, two Flam 500, 154 SC 500, 17 Flam 250, 132 LZZ 250, 320 SC 250 and 847 SC 50) and 114,768 incendiaries. The attack, which lasted from 1812 to 0635 hours, was the biggest yet made on the capital and was notable for the massive number of incendiary bombs dropped.

II/KG55 opened the attack with flares and their customary rain of very heavy HEs mixed with incendiaries, but weather conditions made it difficult for some crews to bomb visually. Nevertheless, fires were started and the Luftflotte 2 crews immediately following used these to aim their bombs; aircraft from Luftflotte 3 operated mainly in the later stages of the attack as the weather, improving from the West, cleared their bases. However, bombing throughout was almost entirely by visually aiming at the glow of fires visible through cloud, by DR or radio navigation, or by merely releasing bombs within the flak 'girdle' which so clearly gave away the city's location. The results of bombing could not be seen, except when fires ensued, but some crews were able to report several very large sheets of flame (presumed to be from gas works or petrol installations in the City area), three enormous explosions, 12 very large fires in the loop of the Thames and four large fires in the Government district where the Houses of Parliament were thought to be alight. Altogether there were ten large area fires and more than 40 fires of serious but variable proportions, with the glow on the clouds visible to crews crossing the Channel on their return flights.

Further details of Luftflotte 2's participation are not known, but Luftflotte 3's effort consisted of 373 aircraft dispatched to London, with 332 reaching the target, 30 aborting and seven bombing alternatives. Three aircraft failed to return and another crashed on take off. The poor weather conditions which some crews found upon their return brought about a number of diversions; I/KG55, for example, had several diversions to Chartres because of impossible conditions at Dreux.

Participating units of Luftflotte 3 were:

I/LG1: 10 Ju 88, 2325-2353
II/LG1: 14 Ju 88, 0000-0030
III/LG1: 12 Ju 88, 2326-0035
I/KG27: 17 He 111, 0155-0325
II/KG27: 14 He 111, 0100-0210
III/KG27: 16 He 111, 0026-0157
KGr126:17 He 111, 2205-2315 (operating on this occasion under the control of Lfl 3. Bomb load comprised 34 LM parachute mines)
KGr100: 16 He 111, 2237-2307 (X-Verfahren bombing. No interference to beam signals)
KGr606: 8 Do 17, 0240-0315
KG1: 29 He 111, 2200-0355
KG77: 25 Ju 88, 2305-0205
I/KG26: 26 He 111, 2308-0200
III/KG26: 10 He 111, 2207-0057 (visual bombing. Y-Verfahren not used on this occasion)
I/KG51: 13 Ju 88, 0200-0302
II/KG51: 18 Ju 88, 2150-0155
III/KG51: 6 Ju 88, 0248-0409
I/KG54: 11 Ju 88, 0550-0655
II/KG54: 2 Ju 88, 0450-0505
KGr806: 11 Ju 88, 0335-0440
Stab/KG55: 4 He 111, 2310-2318
I/KG55: 19 He 111, 2155-2300
II/KG55: 18 He 111, 1812-1925 (initiated attack with flares for target illumination)
III/KG55: 16 He 111, 2325-0030

Considerable damage was caused in London, mostly to the docks and riverside targets. The House of Commons, as indicated by some bomber crews, was badly damaged by fire, as were Port of London Authority buildings, Surrey Commercial Docks, Marylebone Station, the Army and Navy Stores and many public and private buildings. Parachute mines brought havoc to Shoreditch (where there were more than 100 casualties), Harold Wood, Orpington and Central London where Broadcasting House was damaged with 50 casualties. War important factories which were damaged in varying degrees included the Siemens works, Airscrews Ltd, Henley Cable Works, Mills Equipment Ltd, and the Imperial Paper Mills. Badly hit districts were Marylebone, Westminster, Lambeth, Southwark, Finsbury, Battersea, Wandsworth, Tottenham, Camberwell, Millwall, Stepney and Wanstead. Farther out from the city centre there was bombing at Croydon, Gravesend, Carshalton, Lewisham, Slough, Ealing, Northfleet, Purfleet, Dagenham, Woodford and Cobham.

It was London's largest and heaviest raid for two months and some 250 people were killed and more than 630 seriously injured. More than 1,700 fires were reported and again hospitals, schools and dwelling houses shared the fate of such well known buildings as Westminster Abbey, the Royal Mint and the Royal Naval College.

December, 1940

I haven't been flying for eight weeks now. Is it because our operational plans have got mixed up? It is quite puzzling.

But getting to know Paris, which isn't far away and is surely the finest city in the world, has been an unexpected present. A gala performance for the Luftwaffe has been given at the Trocadero; including Schiller's 'Kabale und Liebe' [Intrigue and Love] with Heinrich George, Horst Kaspar and other first class actors. This was a wonderful experience.

At last things begin to happen again. On December 8, our squadron commander took me with him on a night flight. For the first time as an observer. We had to darken the beautiful blue undersurface of our plane structure with some kind of carbon black. Does this mean mainly night flights in future?

So now I am sitting in front in the cockpit next to the boss himself, and intend to navigate as if the Devil were after me, and keeping my eyes skinned so as not to do anything wrong. And it's working out well. No mistakes either over decoy fires, to my Chief's evident satisfaction.

They seem to have more confidence in me. One day a new pilot came to join our squadron. Cool-headed and reliable, but very wide awake and as strong as an ox. Ten years older than me and a typical East Prussian, inwardly and outwardly. And said to be a good pilot. I was attached to him as a navigator-observer. He greeted me cordially and took me so to speak under his wing, as someone so much younger than himself . . .

We have stopped continually blackening the undersurfaces of our planes for night-flying operations and then washing them off again with lead benzine for daylight raids. The planes will stay black. Daylight raids cannot be maintained as losses are too heavy. The number of enemy fighters is not getting any less and we can only take advantage of the range of our bombers at night.

We were told the following:

In the first place we have to destroy the British ports on the east and west coasts; and at the same time, in parallel with our U-boats, cripple the supply situation of the British and thus put their defence capabilities in danger.

Secondly, we must hit their northern industrial centres, which have so far remained intact.

There is some talk of new types of navigational aids consisting of directional beams which we only have to follow in order to get exactly over the target. We were also informed that Pfadfindergruppen [pathfinder units] with special training have even better kinds of special instruments for finding any required target, and illuminate it for the combat squadrons following behind.

ROBERT GÖTZ

Outside of London bombs fell at Grimsby, Castle Acre, near Bircham Newton, Dover, Southampton, Bury St Edmunds, Waterbeach, near St Ives (Hunts) and near Hornchurch. One HE fell on Kenley airfield, but only a gun pit was damaged.

To oppose the onslaught Fighter Command's No. 11 Group operated night fighters continuously from dusk until weather conditions rendered airfields non-operational. Numerous dusk patrols were sent to intercept incoming raids and a Do 17 was claimed probably destroyed by a Hurricane over the Thames Estuary; night patrols were flown by five aircraft of No. 10 Group, 29 of No. 11 Group, and one of No. 12 Group. The Hampden Patrol was also activated and after take off at 1850 hours circled Abingdon awaiting instructions but was recalled at 2120 hours.

AA Command claimed two enemy aircraft destroyed for 8,136 rounds fired by the HAA guns of the London Inner Artillery Zone. Nearly 9,000 rounds were used in total with other batteries in action at Thames and Medway (North and South), Slough and Brooklands.

A massive crater blown in the roadway in Mepham Street outside Waterloo Station.

One of the most descriptive accounts to come out of the Blitz from someone who miraculously survived the near blast of a bomb — or, in this case, a parachute mine exploding just a few feet away — occurred on Sunday night in Langham Place although the narrator was not identified by the BBC when they later broadcast the interview. The Langham Hotel *above* had also previously been hit in September, the repaired damage being visible on the third and fourth floors on the left.

On the night of December 8th, 1940, I left the B.B.C. shortly after ten forty-five and accompanied by a colleague, Mr Sibbick, went to the cycle-shed in Chapel Mews. The customary nightly air-raid was in progress, and as we left the cycle shed we could hear the distant sound of aircraft and A.A. gun-fire. We were just entering Hallam Street from the mews when I heard the shrieking whistling noise like a large bomb falling. This noise continued for about three seconds, and then abruptly ceased as if in mid-air. There was no thud, explosion or vibration. I particularly remember this, as I'd heard this happen once before, and was curious as to what caused it and why it stopped. Then came the sound of something clattering down the roof of a building in the direction of Broadcasting House. I looked up thinking that it might be incendiaries, but this was not so. We slowly walked round to the entrance of Broadcasting House, and I estimate that we took about three and a half minutes in doing so. My colleague went inside, returned the cycle shed keys, cycled off towards Oxford Circus. I remained outside the entrance, talking to two policemen, and enquiring about possible diversions on my route home. Their names were Vaughan and Clarke. A saloon car was parked alongside the curb some distance round from the entrance, and I could see to the left of the car the lamp-post in the middle of the road opposite the Langham Hotel. The policemen had their backs to this, so did not observe what followed. Whilst we were conversing I noticed a large, dark, shiny object approach the lamp-post and then recede. I concluded that it was a taxi parking. It made no noise. The night was clear, with a few small clouds. There was moonlight from a westerly direction, but Portland Place was mainly shadow. All three of us were wearing our steel helmets; my chinstrap was round the back of my head, as I had been advised to wear it so shortly after I was issued with the helmet.

A few seconds later I saw what seemed to be a very large tarpaulin of a drab or khaki colour fall on the same spot; the highest part of it was about ten or twelve feet above the road when I first saw it, and it seemed to be about twenty-five feet across. It fell at about the speed of a pocket handkerchief when dropped, and made no noise. Repair work was being carried out on Broadcasting House and I, not unnaturally, concluded that it was a tarpaulin which had become detached and had fallen from the building into the roadway. There were no other warnings of any imminent danger. I drew the attention of the policemen to it. They turned round and could see nothing. It had collapsed, and from where we were it was partly screened by the car, and the roadway at that point was in shadow. They told me that they could not see anything. Then followed some banter, but I persisted in saying that I had seen something fall in the road. They then decided to go to investigate. A third policeman, Mortimer, had meanwhile approached us — he was about to conduct a lady across that part of the road. But after hearing that I'd seen something he told me that he was taking her inside the building while they found out what it was. Vaughan drew ahead of Clarke, who stopped at the curb to ask me just exactly where it had dropped. I went over towards him, calling out that I would show him it. It was about a minute since I'd seen the dark object. I went towards the tarpaulin and had reached a spot to the left of Clarke about six feet from the curb, and twenty-five to thirty feet from 'the thing', when Vaughan came running towards me at high speed. He shouted something which I did not hear. At that moment there was a very loud swishing noise, as if a plane were diving with engine cut off — or like a gigantic fuse burning. It lasted about three or four seconds; it did not come from the lamp-post end of 'the thing' but it may have come from the other end.

Vaughan passed me on my left and Clarke, who apparently had understood the shout, also ran towards the building. Realising that I would have to turn right about before I could start running, I crouched down in what is known as prone-falling position number one. Even at that moment I did not imagine that there was any danger in the road, and thought that it was coming from above, up Portland Place. My head was up watching, and before I could reach position number two and lie down flat the thing in the road exploded. I had a momentary glimpse of a large ball of blinding, wild, white light and two concentric rings of colour, the inner one lavender and the outer one violet, as I ducked my head. The ball seemed to be ten to twenty feet high, and was near the lamp-post. Several things happened simultaneously. My head was jerked

back due to a heavy blow on the dome and rim of the back of my steel helmet, but I do not remember this, for, as my head went back, I received a severe blow on my forehead and the bridge of my nose. The blast bent up the front rim of my helmet and knocked it off my head. The explosion made an indescribable noise — something like a colossal growl — and was accompanied by a veritable tornado of air blast. I felt an excruciating pain in my ears, and all sounds were replaced by a very loud singing noise, which I was told later was when I lost my hearing and had my eardrums perforated. I felt that consciousness was slipping from me, and that moment I heard a clear loud voice shouting: 'Don't let yourself go, face up to it — hold on'. It rallied me, and summoning all my will-power and energy I succeeded in forcing myself down into a crouching position with my knees on the ground and my feet against the curb behind me and my hands covering my face.

I remember having to move them over my ears because of the pain in them, doubtless due to the blast. This seemed to ease the pain. Then I received another hit on the forehead and felt weaker. The blast seemed to come in successive waves, accompanied by vibrations from the ground. I felt as if it were trying to spin me and clear me away from the curb. Then I received a very heavy blow just in front of the right temple which knocked me down flat on my side, in the gutter. Later, in our first-aid post, they removed what they described as a piece of bomb from that wound. Whilst in the gutter I clung on to the curb with both hands and with my feet against it. I was again hit in the right chest, and later found that my double-breasted overcoat, my coat, leather comb-case and papers had been cut through, and the watch in the top right-hand pocket of my waist-coat had the back dented in and its works broken.

Just as I felt that I could not hold out much longer, I realised that the blast pressure was decreasing and a shower of dust, dirt and rubble swept past me. Pieces penetrated my face, some skin was blown off, and something pierced my left thumbnail and my knuckles were cut, causing me involuntarily to let go my hold on the curb. Instantly, although the blast was dying down, I felt myself being slowly blown across the pavement towards the wall of the building. I tried to hold on but there was nothing to hold on to. Twice I tried to rise but seemed held down. Eventually I staggered to my feet. I looked around and it seemed like a scene from Dante's Inferno. *The front of the building was lit by a reddish-yellow light; the saloon car was on fire to the left of me, and the flames from it were stretching out towards the building, and not upwards; pieces of brick, masonry and glass seemed to appear on the pavement, making, to me, no sound; a few dark huddled bodies were round about, and right in front of me were two soldiers; one, some feet from a breach in the wall of the building where a fire seemed to be raging, was propped up against the wall with his arms dangling by him, like a rag doll.*

The other was nearer, about twelve feet from the burning car; he was sitting up with his knees drawn up and supporting himself by his arms — his trousers had been blown off him. I could see that his legs were bare and that he was wearing short grey underpants. He was alive and conscious.

I told him to hang on to an upright at the entrance and to shout like hell for assistance should he see or hear anyone approaching. I went back to look at the other soldier. He was still in the same posture and I fear that he was dead. I looked around. There was a long, dark body lying prone, face downwards close to the curb in front of the building — it may have been Vaughan. There appeared to be one or two dark, huddled bodies by the wall of the building. I had not the strength to lift any of them. I wondered where the water was coming from which I felt dripping down my face, and soon discovered that it was blood from my head wounds. I could see no movement anywhere, and thought I would look round for my steel helmet and gas mask, which I had slung round me at the time of the explosion. I soon found the gas mask and picked up a steel helmet which was not my own.

I was then joined by my colleague who had returned, and went with him to the entrance where I shouted for assistance for those outside, and for someone to bring fire-fighting appliances to put out the car fire, as I was afraid the glare would bring down more bombs.

I walked down to our First Aid Post, where I was treated, and then to Listening Hall 1 where I rested until I was taken away by the stretcher party and sent to the Middlesex Hospital. Here I received every possible attention and kindness. Later on I was told that 'the thing' had been a land mine, and that its explosion or blast had lasted for nine seconds.

The effect of the blast on my clothes is possibly of interest, I was wearing bicycle clips round the bottoms of my trousers at the time; after the blast was over my double-breasted overcoat was slit up the back and torn in several places, but was being held together by the belt. My trousers and underpants were pitted with small cuts about an inch long, but presumably the bicycle clips had prevented the draught getting up my trousers and tearing them off. A woollen scarf, which was knotted round my neck, undoubtedly saved my neck and chest from small fragments such as were removed from my face, which was not covered.

BBC RECORDING, 1940

'We walked round to the entrance of Broadcasting House . . . I could see the lamp-post in the middle of the road opposite the Langham Hotel. . . . '

During daylight weather limited operations to the occasional reconnaissance sortie over the coast and one aircraft was lost:

4(F)/14 Messerschmitt Bf 110C-5 (2256). Shot down during reconnaissance mission by Flight Lieutenant C. G. C. Olive DFC in a Spitfire of No. 65 Squadron. Crashed into the sea off Portsmouth 1.30 p.m. Fw. O. Mercier and Oberfw. A. Schönewald missing. Aircraft 5F+DM lost.

The two aircraft brought down by AA fire during the night were:

8/KG77 Junkers Ju 88A-5 (3191). Hit by AA fire and crashed at North Stifford, near West Thurrock, Essex 2.15 a.m. Lt. H. Guhre, Uffz. E. Knöller, Uffz. W. Hassdenteufel and Uffz. J. Kleiber killed. Aircraft 3Z+ES destroyed.

Site investigated by John Ellis and representative pieces found.

As the day-by-day record shows, so far not one of the December night raiders had been brought down — the days being devoid of the aircraft incidents which peppered our earlier pages. One can therefore imagine the jubilation of the gunners of London's Inner Artillery Zone on the night of December 8–9 when they shot down two Ju 88s in the space of less than two hours. The first, an aircraft of II/LG1 flown by Unteroffizier Max Jappsen, crashed at 0045 hours near Waltham Abbey, Essex, killing all four crew members. The wreckage was strewn over a wide area and identification proved difficult; only a letter 'K' could be deciphered of its markings, together with a red and black crest painted on a piece of the fuselage, but it was in fact L1+KP, a Henschel-built Ju 88A-1. The actual point of impact was close to the Wake Arms public house on the road to Epping. Local funeral directors Poulton and Sons of Epping were called to the scene to remove odd pieces of human remains, which were buried in a single grave at Chingford Mount Cemetery.

6/LG1 Junkers Ju 88A-1 (2206). Hit by AA fire and crashed near the Wake Arms public house in Epping Forest, Essex 12.45 a.m. Uffz. M. Jappsen, Gefr. A. Dornauer, Fw. E. Leipold and Gefr. F. Weber all killed. Aircraft L1+KP destroyed.

Major recovery by the London Air Museum in July 1976 revealed both engines, undercarriage leg, propeller blade, parachutes, oxygen bottles and bomb fins. Majority of items, including engine, propeller blade, oxygen bottle, ammunition drums, parachute and bomb fins, now in the After the Battle collection. Later excavated in April 1979 by a Territorial Army bomb disposal team as bombs were suspected to be on site and two SC500s were successfully defuzed.

Forty years later a TA bomb disposal team searches for reputed UXBs: the thumbs-up from the digger driver indicates success.

Another hectic night. First call after the Alert was to Sewardstonebury where I/B's had fallen. Report had it that Carrolls Farm had caught it, so took the car out and picking up Jess and Walter, went to see. Farm quite OK but bombs all across West Essex Golf Club, some of them the explosive type.

Returning from Sewardstonebury reports arrived of Incendiaries at Volunteer and Honey Lane, so took Chapman out to investigate. Had heard that much larger I/B's had been used, but traces were of the normal type. While at Skilletts Hill Farm Jerry came over again, and put down more Incendiaries over towards Sewardstone. Could hear them swishing down and the popping cracks as they went off. The glare seemed quite close, so back we went to Sewardstone to Eddie Davies only to find that they were just out of our District.

Back again to the Volunteer to find Charlie Parish who took us to see the reputed 2 kilo bombs. Out in the middle of a field when a flare dropped towards the east just the other side of Woodredon Hill. The pale white glare outshone the watery moon, and gave quite an eerie light behind the clouds. Returned home and at 12.30 'phone rang to say that a Jerry 'plane had been brought down in the forest near the Wake Arms, but it was pouring with rain, and I'd had about enough. At 3.30 a.m. 'phone went again, with an urgent call for assistance for the Wardens out at Upshire, where scores of Incendiaries had fallen, setting fire to the Potteries. Gathered together some Wardens in A/G clothing (because of the rain) and set out in the pitch darkness, the moon having gone. All bombs out by the time we got there, and the Potteries blaze well doused. And so to bed again at 4.30.

Up early again the next morning and out to the scene of the crash. An awful muddy mess of clay and water and bits and pieces, smelling of oil and burning material. Lumps of metal strewn all over the place. Brought home a parachute, badly burned, of one of the unlucky ones.

Then went down to the Potteries, and had a look round where the bombs had fallen and discovered quite a number unignited, duly bringing them home to be 'doctored'

Then just to round things off, went up to Scotland Yard to argue with the P/W about warning sirens! Particularly sirens that sounded the Raiders Passed, when they were definitely ***not*** *passed!*

E. J. CARTER, CHIEF WARDEN
URBAN DISTRICT OF WALTHAM HOLY CROSS
DECEMBER 8, 1940

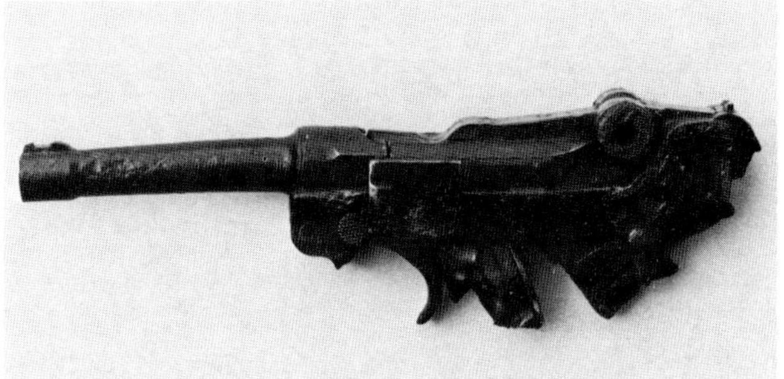

Items recovered from the crash site. ***Left:*** **Part of a seat harness, distorted with the force of the impact as it threw its wearer forward.** ***Right:*** **Even the barrel is twisted on this piece of a smashed Luger Parabellum now in the** ***After the Battle*** **collection.**

MONDAY, DECEMBER 9-10

Sunset: 1649 Sunrise: 0856
Moon: Dusk — 0402 (First Qtr+3)

No German night bombing operations.

UK — Cloud generally 8/10ths to 10/10ths at 1-2,000ft with high winds and rain in the East and South-East. Visibility moderate, with fog patches in some places. Frontal rain belt spreading rapidly from west to east across the country after midnight.

The Continent — Extensive cloud, lowering as rain spread eastwards during the night with moderate to poor visibility.

Daylight operations consisted of only five inland penetrations by German aircraft, with about 30 operating in coastal areas. All German night operations were cancelled because of bad weather conditions although three unidentified aircraft were plotted by Fighter Command as suspected 'hostiles' and 16 night fighters were sent up on patrol. No incidents were reported.

The second aircraft was also blown to pieces when it dived into the ground at high speed near North Stifford, Essex ***(left).*** **Little could be discovered from the wreckage although a list of emergency airfields available to aircraft of I Fliegerkorps was of interest to AI1(k) Branch intelligence officers.**

TUESDAY, DECEMBER 10-11

Sunset: 1649 Sunrise: 0857
Moon: Dusk — 0504 (Full −4)

The miserable scene on an unnamed French airfield, typical of the conditions on Monday and Tuesday which temporarily suspended all operations. Here a mechanic is seen tending the external battery cart (a 'trolley acc' in RAF parlance) as the Ju 88A-5 pilot starts its engine.

No night bombing operations by the Luftwaffe. Minor activity over eastern England by long-range night fighters.

UK — Poor conditions in West and in western coastal districts, but generally fine elsewhere with a little cloud above 3,000ft and good visibility.

The Continent — Extensive low cloud with poor visibility, improving later.

Little daylight activity was followed by a complete suspension of night bomber operations by the German Air Force, but night fighter intrusions were made over eastern England by eight aircraft of I/NJG2. British night fighter response was limited to one Blenheim and a Beaufighter of No. 12 Group. A few bombs were reported in East Anglia only, and the few aircraft that entered the London IAZ were flying out of range of the guns and searchlights at 26,000ft and in consequence were not engaged. One RAF night fighter was reported lost.

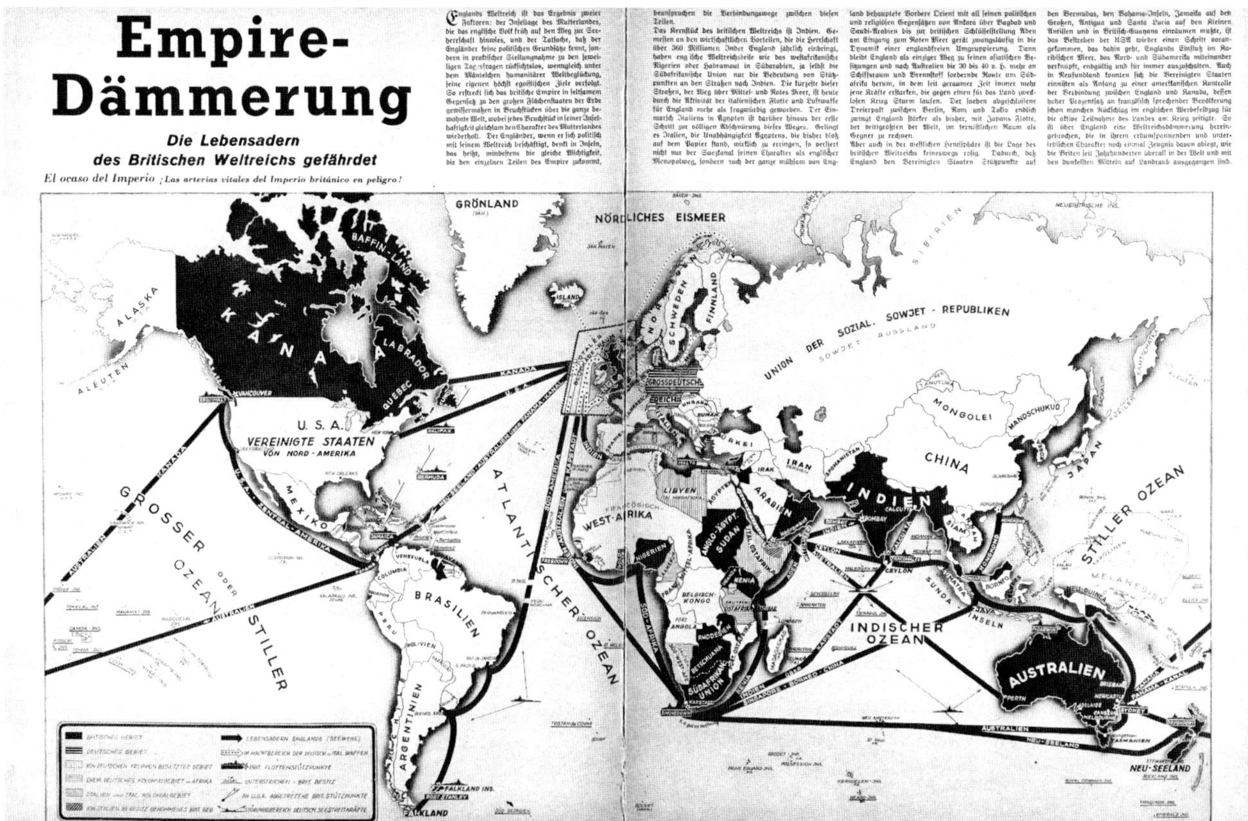

Empire-Dämmerung

Die Lebensadern des Britischen Weltreichs gefährdet

El ocaso del Imperio ¡Las arterias vitales del Imperio británico en peligro!

On December 10, while crews were languishing on their bases enjoying the well-earned rest, Hitler was addressing arms workers in a factory in Berlin when he explained what the loss of the war would mean to Germany. He justified the night raids by saying that while he did not want them, Churchill 'had the idea of starting unlimited warfare at night'. While the British had not smashed a single arms factory, they had hit families and hospitals 'so this kind of warfare had to be waged and it is being waged and it is being waged now. It is being waged with all the determination, all the material and with all the courage which are at our disposal and when the hour of final reckoning comes, this reckoning will come too.'

We are in the middle of a conflagration which is not just a struggle between two countries. It is a struggle of two different worlds. There is no way for these two worlds to exist side by side. One of them must perish. Should we be broken it would mean that the German nation would be broken.

Forty-six million Englishmen rule and own 15,000,000 square miles of the world; 37,000,000 Frenchmen rule 4,000,000 square miles; 45,000,000 Italians have only 200,000 square miles at their disposal, while 85,000,000 Germans have only some 231,000 square miles as their Lebensraum, and this only owing to their own enterprise.

While Britain was building up her giant Empire, Germany was hampered by internal discord and by a number of small States. Italy also shared the same fate while other nations divided the world. Thus two strong nations were deprived of their rights. I saw that there were two ways to remedy this situation. One was by appealing to reason and the second was a resort to force. I appealed to the reason of other countries to avoid bloodshed. . . .

I stand up against the world as the representative of the 'have nots'. I want to see the white masses so organised that the whole German culture flourishes. Britain is governed by quite a thin upper class which always sends its sons to its own educational institutions. They have Eton College, we have the Adolf Hitler schools, the National Socialist Education Institute and the National Political Schools. They are two worlds. In one of them are the sons of the people; in the other, only the sons of a stupid aristocracy and financial magnates. There, only men who come from these schools play a rôle in the State, while here, the men who play a rôle come from the people. These are two worlds, and I admit one of these worlds has to perish. . . .

I am not a man to stop at half measures. When I have to defend myself I defend myself with unbounded fanaticism. There are madmen who maintain that I had a feeling of inferiority towards the British. They are crazy. I never had any such feeling. . . .

Where a German soldier stands no other soldier will ever set his feet . . . and now I can say no power in the world will be able to dislodge us from this territory against our will. . . . This fact is due to the valour of the German Army and to the efforts of the armament workers.

Today we are prepared for any contingency. Britain may do what she likes — she will get heavier blows with every weapon. Should she attempt to gain a foothold somewhere on the Continent she will meet us again; and I hope for just one thing — that we have not forgotten anything and the British have not learned anything.

ADOLF HITLER,
DECEMBER 10, 1940

I'm sorry, but I don't want to be an emperor. That is not my business. I don't want to rule or to conquer anyone. I should like to help everyone, if that were possible — Jew and Gentile, black and white.

We should all want to help one another. We should want to live by each other's happiness, not by each other's misery. But greed has poisoned men's souls and has barricaded the world with hate. It has goose-stepped us into misery and bloodshed.

We think too much. We feel too little. More than machinery we need humanity. More than cleverness we need kindness and gentleness. Without these qualities, life will be violence, and all will be lost.

The aeroplane and the radio have brought us closer together. They cry out for universal brotherhood. Even now my voice is reaching millions throughout the world; millions of despairing men and women and little children, victims of a system that imprisons and tortures the innocent.

To those who can hear me I say: Do not despair. The misery that is upon us is but the passing of the greed and the bitterness of men who fear the way of human progress. Hate will pass away, dictators will die, and the power they took from the people will return to the people.

The riposte came from Charlie Chaplin, alias Adenoid Hynkel, dictator of Ptomania, in the closing scene of his new film *The Great Dictator*, first shown to the King and Queen and the Princesses, the Cabinet and representatives of the Dutch, Free French and Greek allies on December 14.

So long as men will die for liberty, liberty will never perish.

Soldiers, do not give yourselves to those brutes who despise you, enslave you, tell you what to do, what to think, and what to feel, who drill you, diet you, treat you like cattle and use you as cannon fodder.

You people have the power to make this life free and beautiful. Then, in the name of democracy, let us use that power. Let us all unite. Let us fight for a new world, a decent world that will give men the chance to work, that will give youth a future and old-age security.

By promising these things brutes have risen to power. But they lied. They don't fulfil their promises. They never will. The dictators freed themselves but they enslaved their people.

Now, let us fight to free the world: to do away with national barriers, to do away with greed, with hate and intolerance.

Soldiers, in the name of democracy, let us unite.

CHARLIE CHAPLIN,
THE GREAT DICTATOR,
RELEASED DECEMBER 14, 1940

Nice shot of a Stab III/KG51 Ju 88A-5 coded 9K+GD. Although it is not possible to trace actual operations undertaken by individual aircraft in German records, KG51 were on the Birmingham run on Wednesday night.

WEDNESDAY, DECEMBER 11-12

Sunset: 1649 Sunrise: 0858
Moon: Dusk — 0607 (Full −3)

Major attack on Birmingham. Widespread minor attacks elsewhere with targets mainly seaports and airfields.

UK — Little or no cloud inland, showers or rain or hail on South, West and East Coasts. Visibility moderate to poor inland in some areas. Wind north-west to north, moderate to fresh.

The Continent — Some snow or sleet showers with visibility moderate to good but poor in precipitation.

Operations were again on a small scale during the day and consisted mainly of a fighter sweep in the morning and attacks on, and reconnaissance of, shipping. The first night raiders were plotted near Dieppe at 1720 hours, others approaching Harwich at 1740 and more in the Fécamp and Cherbourg areas at 1810, with all four streams converging on the Midlands.

Of the 384 aircraft of Luftflotten 2 and 3 ordered to Birmingham, 278 reached and bombed the city in two phases — from 1805 to 0105 hours and from 0248 to 0715. They dropped 277 tonnes of HE (19 SC 1800, 72 SC 1000, 76 SC 500, one Flam 250, 12 LZZ 250, 391 SC 250 and 646 SC 50) and 24,660 incendiaries. Crews reported a bad weather zone with rain and snow showers between the south-east coast of England and the target and 3/10ths to 6/10ths cloud over southern England and the Midlands, but over Birmingham it was predominantly clear with only temporary areas of layer cloud at 12,500 feet. Good moonlight helped with target location — making rail and waterways particularly easy to recognise — and those crews that got through to Birmingham had no difficulty in bombing visually; in only very few cases was recourse taken to DR or radio navigation, so that a very large proportion of the bombs fell in the town centre as intended. Explosions were also reported in the south of the city and to the north hits were reported on rail and industrial installations. One especially large explosion, followed by a huge yellow-red sheet of flame, was thought to have been the destruction of a gas works. Many large fire areas were seen, with numerous medium and small fires covering the entire town. Several crews reported seeing night fighters; flak and searchlights were said to be of little consequence, but after midnight there was the occasional burst of greater activity.

The brunt of the attack was borne by Luftflotte 3, which dispatched 290 aircraft, 219 of which succeeded in reaching Birmingham; 42 bombed alternatives, 25 crews aborted and three aircraft were lost. Another aircraft, an He 111 of II/KG27, was lost near Moinville, France, following a double engine failure. Aircraft of Luftflotte 3 attacked other targets during the night including London (10 aircraft), Portsmouth (three aircraft), Southampton (11) and Brighton (seven aircraft).

Those attacking Birmingham were:

KG1: 9 Ju 88 and 14 He 111, from 1850 (cessation times not available)
KG77: 14 Ju 88, 2315
I and II/KG26: 21 He 111, 2100
III/KG26: 6 He 111, 1950
I/LG1: 6 Ju 88, 2200
II/LG1: 6 Ju 88, 2200
III/LG1: 5 Ju 88, 2150
I/KG27: 19 He 111, 2020
II/KG27: 17 He 111, 1947
III/KG27: 10 He 111, 2105
KGr126: 17 He 111, 2310
KGr100: 14 He 111, 1930
KGr606: 12 Do 17, 1945
I/KG51: 3 Ju 88, 2125
II/KG51: 11 Ju 88, 2038
III/KG51: 6 Ju 88, 2149
I/KG54: 5 Ju 88, 2250
KGr806: 8 Ju 88, 2235
Stab/KG55: 3 He 111, 1949
III/KG55: 13 He 111, 1905

Although much of the bombing was centred on Birmingham there were many reports of minor attacks from the south and east of England as well as Merseyside. The Birmingham attack was the longest the city had yet experienced and although residential areas were badly hit, there were many incidents in the industrial districts. Nevertheless, little serious damage was done to installations of national importance, but rail communications were dislocated and road traffic in and out of the city suffered a degree of interference. Ten schools, six churches, two cinemas and many houses were destroyed or damaged severely. Casualties were 95 killed and 235 seriously injured.

Cheltenham (where 19 people were killed and 13 injured) and Bristol were also bombed, but not heavily, and elsewhere incidents were reported at Newhaven (where 11 people died), Southend, London, Milstead, Northfleet, Southminster, Kidderminster, Hull, Southampton, Whitstable, Detling, Grain, Brighton, Widnes, Southsea, Portsmouth, Gloucester, Redditch, Stoke-on-Trent and at several points in Worcestershire.

German aircraft were engaged by HAA guns at Birmingham, Bromley, Gloucester, Bristol, Newport, Manchester, Leeds, Slough, Brooklands, the London IAZ, the Solent and Mersey, using 10,000 rounds in the process. One raider was claimed destroyed over the Thames Estuary.

Another enemy aircraft, an He 111, was claimed probably destroyed by two Hurricanes of No. 145 Squadron on dusk patrol south of Shoreham, but no claims were submitted by any of the 126 night fighters operating although several contacts were made and two opened fire on raiders. Also unsuccessful was the Hampden Patrol, operating with 22 aircraft over Birmingham

Some 300 separate fires were reported by Home Security with 14 factories hit, also 10 schools, 6 churches, 2 cinemas and a hospital. Serious damage was caused to the James Cycle Company and the Fisher and Ludlow works. At W. & T. Avery's, the management took this remarkable series of comparisons illustrating the reconstruction of the factory. *Top:* **The scene of utter devastation 12 hours after the raid.** *Centre:* **Almost unbelievable, this is the same view just** ***7 days*** **later, and** ***bottom*** **after 3 months. Such speed could not be publicised for fear of inspiring the Luftwaffe to even greater efforts and publication of these pictures was still being denied in 1943, by which time the factory had been struck again!**

between 1915 and 2315 hours; several Hampden pilots saw enemy aircraft, but lost sight of them before they could turn and close in. No night fighter casualties were formally listed by Fighter Command, but it is known that Defiant N1806 of No. 141 Squadron was written off when it struck some trees on take off from Gravesend at 2109 hours, injuring one of its crew. A second Defiant (N3367 of No. 264 Squadron operating from Debden) was damaged when its pilot, unable to find his base after a night patrol, attempted a forced landing at 2305 hours near Boxford, Suffolk. The Defiant's undercarriage collapsed and the aircraft was subsequently written off.

During a comparatively uneventful day, one fighter failed to return.

StabII/LG2 Messerschmitt Bf 109E-7 (5941). Shot down by Flying Officer H. R. Allen in a Spitfire of No. 66 Squadron. Crashed at Forge Farm, Badlesmere, Kent 11.00 a.m. Oblt. V. Kraft baled out wounded and was taken prisoner. Aircraft Green D+ wrecked.

A major recovery by Mike Llewellyn of the Kent Battle of Britain Museum revealed the control column and major components. Viktor Kraft visited an exhibition featuring pieces of his aircraft in 1975. Site later re-excavated by Steve Vizard and the remaining parts including the bomb rack and balance weight found.

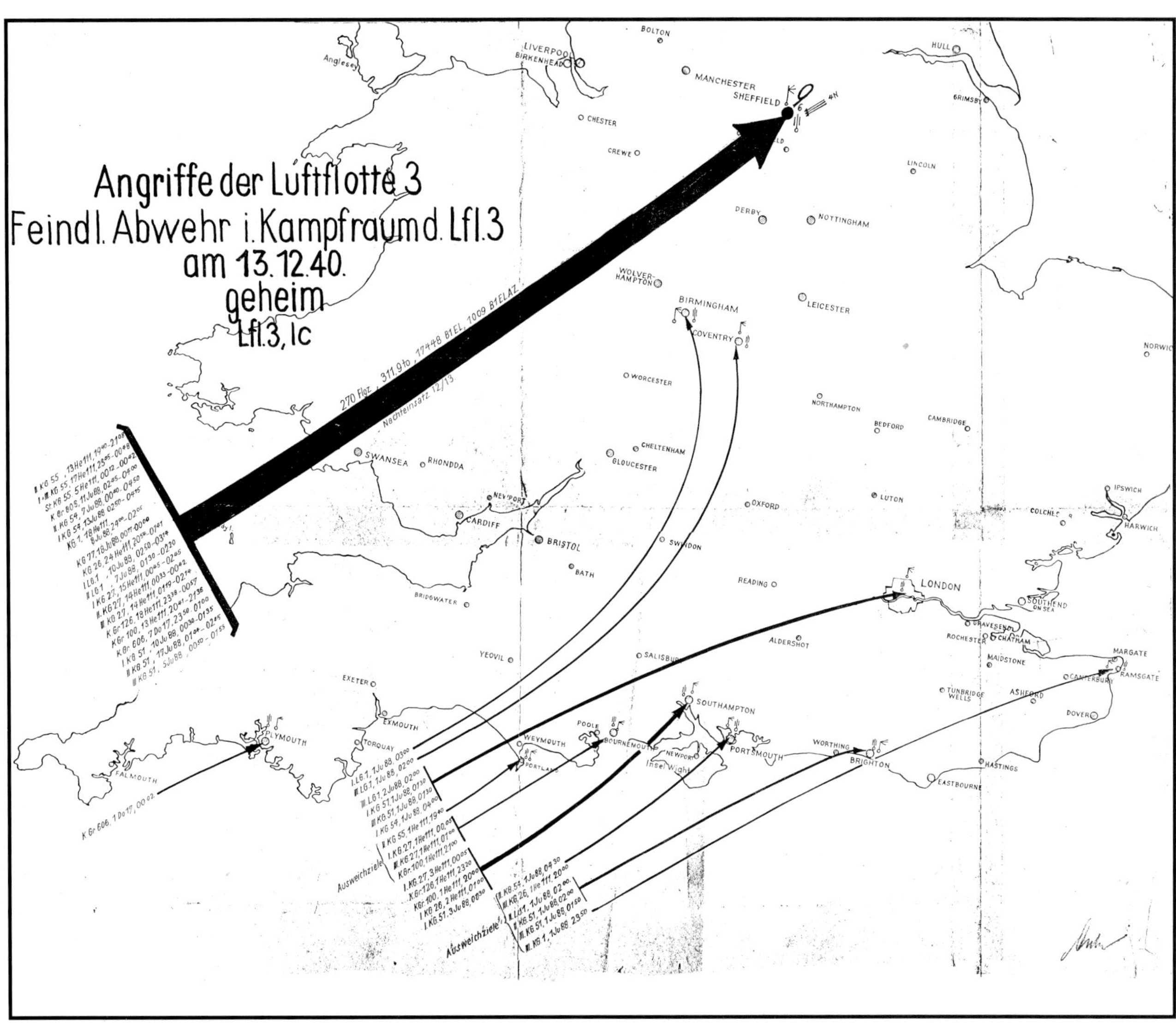

THURSDAY, DECEMBER 12-13

Sunset: 1649 Sunrise: 0859
Moon: Dusk — 0707 (Full −2)

Major attack on Sheffield. Widespread light attacks elsewhere including South Yorkshire, the Midlands, Home Counties and East Anglia, with minelaying in the Thames Estuary.

UK — Occasional rain or drizzle in south-western England, widespread mist or fog in other inland areas. Winds south-easterly on western coasts, fresh or strong locally, but calm or light and variable elsewhere.

The Continent — Considerable cloud with snow in some districts. Poor to moderate visibility.

A morning fighter sweep over Kent and sea reconnaissance up to 1600 hours was the limit of German Air Force operations on a day which was mainly fine and clear. At 1650 hours, however, the Duty Air Commodore at Fighter Command was able to inform all Groups and other essential services that the target for the coming night was Sheffield.

Code named 'Schmelztiefel' (Crucible), Sheffield was described to participating German bomber crews as the centre of the British iron and steel industry and their CP was to be the industrial agglomeration in the north-eastern part of the town. Luftflotten 2 and 3 dispatched 406 aircraft to attack the city and the crews of 336 claimed to have done so, dropping 355 tonnes of HE (15 SC 1800, 120 SC 1000, three Flam 500, 113 SC 500, four Flam 250, 58 LZZ 250, 398 SC 250 and 698 SC 50) and 457 BSK cannisters (16,452 IBs). The first bombs fell at 1840 hours and the attack terminated at 0300, between which times crews observed many large explosions, jets of flame and numerous large, medium and small fires, especially in the central and north-east districts of the town. Nearly all crews in the Target Area at the time reported seeing an extraordinarily big explosion at 2235 hours and presumed it to be the destruction of a gas works. The weather was mainly clear over mid-England, with only occasional patches of cloud, and bomb aiming was almost entirely visual.

Four night fighters were encountered over Sheffield (with three thought to have been Defiants) and all attacked from below and to one side. Flak was medium to strong and well directed; crews flying at about 5,000 metres (16,500 feet) found it particularly accurate.

Again, Luftflotte 3 aircraft predominated — 270 bombed Sheffield, 26 went to alternative targets, 15 aborted and three aircraft attacked Southampton as ordered. No bombers of this air fleet were lost. Those attacking Sheffield were:

KG1: 18 He 111 and 8 Ju 88, 2300-0105
KG77: 18 Ju 88, 2317-0000
KG26: 24 He 111, 1954-0041
I/LG1: 10 Ju 88, 0150-0214
II/LG1: 7 Ju 88, 0030-0125
III/LG1: 6 Ju 88, 0030-0120
I/KG27: 15 He 111, 2345-0145
II/KG27: 14 He 111, 2333-2342
III/KG27: 14 He 111, 0019-0114
KGr126: 18 He 111, 2238-2357 (operating under FlKps IV. Dropped 36 LMB 1000 parachute mines with one, at 2325 hrs, producing an enormous explosion, possibly at a gas works)
KGr100: 13 He 111, 1941-2046 (some crews bombed visually, others with X-Verfahren)
KGr606: 7 Do 17, 2250-0000
I/KG51: 10 Ju 88, 2330-0035
II/KG51: 17 Ju 88, 0044-0145
III/KG51: 5 Ju 88, 2350-0055
I/KG54: 13 Ju 88, 0150-0315
II/KG54: 7 Ju 88, 2340-0350
KGr806: 11 Ju 88, 0145-0300
Stab/KG55: 5 He 111, 2312-2342
I and III/KG55: 17 He 111, 2245-2348
II/KG55: 13 He 111, 1840-2008 (opened attack as target illuminators, dropping flares and heavy HEs. Visual and DR bombing)

Damage in Sheffield was most extensive in the city centre, but all of the many fires which were started were brought under control by 0615 hours. Industrial, commercial and private premises were all badly hit, and there was extensive damage to gas, electricity and water services, but much of the industrial damage, largely caused by fire,

Up until the night of December 12 the war had barely touched Sheffield — the home of Britain's steel-making industry and therefore, one would have thought, a prime target. On Thursday all that changed when the city was singled out for coventration.

As the first enemy aircraft began penetrating the country's defences, like ripples in a pond the warnings travelled both across the country and upwards in ascending scale. The Yellow was received in Sheffield at 6.15 p.m., followed by the Purple 30 minutes later. Even when the Red Warning set the sirens to wail 'Raiders Approach' across the city at 7.00 p.m., no one knew that it was the opening fanfare to the now-familiar Luftwaffe Doppelgänger — the double hit — and that the nine-hour raid that Thursday would be followed up with a three-hour repeat performance on Sunday. Although there was no chance of the Press and Censorship Bureau approving publication of a picture such as that above, a year after the raid the local paper submitted it with the following caption: 'This view from the roof of the *Telegraph & Independent* building in the early morning of Friday, December 13th, 1940, will revive vivid and terrible memories for many of our readers. At the bottom of High Street great tongues of flame from the blazing building near Marples Hotel are licking the line of trams in the roadway. The C. & A. building looks like an iced-cake melting in the heat.' Nevertheless, publication was still refused.

Most of Britain's badly-bombed cities have since spawned local histories, varying in depth, quality and style, on their particular Blitz. Seldom do they come up to the standard of the end-of-war publications produced by many boroughs, some of which even name the entire ARP and Civil Defence personnel as well as listing chronologically all local incidents. Sheffield, however, had the foresight to commission a record while the events of the two December raids were still fresh in everyone's mind, and in February 1941 the Emergency Committee gave the job to the City Librarian, Mr Joseph Lamb, who was also Secretary of the Information Committee. Mr Lamb delegated much of the interviewing and research to one of his librarians, Mary Walton, although as the extent of the destruction of Sheffield was to be kept from the Germans, the report was only circulated on a restricted basis when completed in July 1942. Having lain dormant for over thirty years, in 1980 the Director of Libraries decided to publish the document virtually unaltered under the title *Raiders over Sheffield*. As a contemporary account of two individual raids, it stands supreme.

If there is one thing that stands out more than anything in the pictures taken during Sheffield's December Blitz it is the tramcars, all of which in the city centre were damaged to some degree. The number destroyed is given by the history as 31 but this only covers 'those hideously twisted and burnt-out wrecks whose appearance had so shocked the public on the first morning.' *Top:* The High Street; *above:* the junction with Angel Street.

The first essential on Friday morning was to clear the roads, but no sooner had men of the Transport Department reported to the Queen's Road Depôt than an unexploded bomb went off, killing one of the repairmen. After this unfortunate setback, noted Mary Walton, '. . . they began by clearing West Bar and Snig Hill . . . and The Wicker, where they found a tram cut in two, its upper deck lying upside down beside the track, and another squashed to bits against the wall under the arches. The work here was carried out in an enveloping smell of gas and an embarrassing crowd of onlookers. The trams were lifted on to the track and moved into Tenter Street by a "crab", a marvellous contraption with a crane and a motor which had been hired from a Leeds firm. Afterwards, Commercial Street, Pinstone Street, Ecclesall Road, Abbey Lane, Crookes, and other places where there were stretches of undamaged track well out of the way of the town centre, were used as temporary parking places. Where the tram rails were damaged, the cars were lifted from the track, dragged past the damage, and lifted on to the track again. The trams which appeared to the public to be welded into the rails by molten metal were not, of course, quite so securely fixed, and sharp blows were sufficent to release them. In many cases, however, the axles were found to have seized, and when the towing was in progress they slithered reluctantly on locked wheels.'

The worst incident that night was described by Mr Lamb: 'In only one case was there a tragedy on a major scale. At about a quarter to twelve, a very heavy bomb struck Marples's Hotel at the corner of Fitzalan Square and High Street. The building was seven storeys high, and the whole of it fell into the unstrengthened cellar in which about seventy-five people, some of them already wounded, were sheltering. In the bottling store adjoining the main cellar, a portion of the ceiling remained intact, and although the building burnt fiercely all night, seven people were rescued alive from this store next day.'

proved to be superficial. Only four cases of substantial damage to factories were reported. Transport, however, was badly affected, with main line railways blocked, overhead tram wires destroyed, many vehicles damaged or destroyed, and many roads closed. Casualties, expected to prove heavy, took some time to establish.

The situation in Sheffield could have been much worse, for many crews were clearly unable to find their target and bombs fell widely around the Leeds/South Yorkshire area, over the Midlands, the Home Counties and East Anglia. Indeed, at the height of the attack raids were plotted over almost every part of the country south and east of a line through Scarborough, Blackburn, Wolverhampton and Bournemouth, and bombing was reported from Bolton, near Alfreton, West Ham, Southampton, Birmingham, Nuneaton, Wimborne, Acklington, Bushey, near Derby, Wakefield, Rotherham, Chesterfield, Scarborough, Dewsbury, Bridlington, Huddersfield, Wolverhampton and Nottingham.

Fighter Command put up 39 night fighters from Nos. 10, 11 and 12 Groups, and two Beaufighters (of No. 604 Squadron) engaged enemy aircraft, claiming damage to a Ju 88 and an He 111. A Hurricane on patrol near Wittering also engaged an unidentified enemy aircraft. On the debit side two night fighters were damaged; at Wittering a Beaufighter (R2082) of No. 25 Squadron overshot the flarepath in ground mist and at Middle Wallop a pilot of No. 604 Squadron, making his first night solo flight on a Beaufighter (R2145), overran the airfield on landing, causing the undercarriage to collapse.

Of some 16,000 rounds fired during the night by AA Command the Sheffield guns fired 3,700. Another 4,031 were fired by the IAZ, mainly as aircraft transitted London, and elsewhere HAA guns were in action at Thames and Medway South, Birmingham, Leeds, Dover, Solent, Holton Heath, Cardiff, Portland, Yeovil, Bristol, Gloucester, Newport, Tyne and Tees. Two enemy aircraft were claimed destroyed and another damaged.

At midday a fighter sweep was made over Kent. One aircraft fell on land and is listed below; the second, the 1/JG53 Messerschmitt Bf 109 flown by Uffz. R. Müller, is believed to have been brought down near Barrow Deep, in the Thames Estuary. No other aircraft were lost.

7/JG26 Messerschmitt Bf 109E (3708). Shot down by Flying Officer V. M. Bright and Pilot Officer R. E. Bary in Hurricanes of No. 229 Squadron. Crashed at Abbey Farm, Leeds Castle Estate, Kent 12.10 p.m. Uffz. R. Lendemann baled out wounded and taken prisoner. Aircraft White 2+ destroyed.

Engine recovered by Mike Llewellyn of the Kent Battle of Britain Museum. Site later re-excavated by Steve Vizard and a 20mm MGFF cannon unearthed.

Mary Walton explained that: 'The Marples disaster particularly attracted attention. A rescue squad had been sent to the site during the night, but in the darkness they were unable even to make a plan for getting to work on so formidable an operation, so they returned to their control, to be employed on work which would yield a more immediate return. Next morning work was started, and by 2 p.m. the seven survivors had been rescued; but the grim search for bodies went on for twelve days, and its details, reported with embroidery, gained for the incident a natural but distinctly ghoulish prominence in the public imagination. Sixty-four bodies were finally identified, and a few fragments brought the total number of dead to about seventy.'

Bomb disposal July 12, 1942. Dealing with a UXB dropped on Newcastle Street on December 12, 1940.

Well, there we were, watching everyone knocking off at dinner time to go home for the weekend, when in comes Captain Bowen.

'Corporal Jennings,' he says, 'it looks as if there could be a bomb up in Sheffield. We're just waiting to confirm it.' 'Sheffield,' says Sapper Paul Hulmes, 'that's north of Watford and my passport's out of date. I can't go . . . alright Sir, we'll get the kit ready.'

After a half hour wait the final word comes in. It looked as if it was a 500lb one, near Sheffield United's football ground. So off we set to Sheffield.

Travelling up the motorway with a blue light flashing and two-tone horns blaring must be the quickest way to travel — also the most dangerous with some of the idiots on the road. The weather didn't help much either, by the time we got there the lighting tower looked like a mobile snowball.

When we got to Bramhall Lane it was utter chaos. It was a toss up as to who was looking after the site — the police or the Council. Our first job was to make sure the equipment was working after the long journey, which proved to be a problem as everything had frozen up. Corporal Dave Milnes worked through the night, with the help of a blow torch, to get it working. A sight I won't forget is seeing him at 4.00 a.m., with ice on the bottom of his coveralls, saying 'Hey up Chuck, it's freezing out here.'

A quick look at the bomb and it was obvious it was a 1000kg (Hermann). The next task was to find the fuze. The worst possible place would be underneath. Bets were taken as to where it would be found. After 1½ hours of gentle digging we came across it . . . not quite underneath, but still a problem. A bit of gentle cleaning with a light brush and water and we could see it had a cap on it, meaning it couldn't be identified. The language at this point can well be imagined — even the police took it up and wandered around swearing! After looking at it for half an hour or so — trying to will the cap off — it was decided to drill it off with a trepanner, a dodgy process as the cap was only 3mm thick. A touch too deep and we would be into the fuze and the bomb would go off.

Finally we got the cap off. The fuze turned out to be an ECR, which is an impact fuze using an electrical capacitor. It is only recently that the EOD School has decided that any electrical charge that the capacitor held would have gone, so the only problem would be with picric acid crystals, which are highly volatile. To get rid of the acid we drilled into the side of the fuze and injected a solution. Now it was time for a rest while we waited for the solution to dissolve the picric crystals.

While we waited, it was time for everyone to pose for the Press — or try to hide from them. While Captain Bowen dealt with their questions, the rest of us had a quick discussion as to how we were going to do the next stages. We decided that we would cut holes into the side of the bomb while it was still in the hole, then lift 'Hermann' out and put it in a prepared trench to steam out the explosive.

With the help of a Muirhill borrowed from 106 Squadron (TA), and a Poclain excavator from the Council, everything went smoothly — except that our steamer kept on freezing up. Corporal Milnes and Sapper Danny Christian both had ice hanging off them. There were no other words for it except it was 'bloody cold!'

With the explosives steamed out, the next stage was to remove the fuze pocket. We had a couple of options open to us. One was to cut the fuze pocket, using explosive to detonate the explosives in the pocket, but this would destroy the bomb. The other was to cut the fuze pocket out using the trepanner. We decided to use the trepanner, and this method gave us hardly any problems.

The bomb case was now safe. The last thing left to do was to burn the explosives, and to make sure that where we had steamed the explosives out we left no trace behind. This was done with two controlled explosions, one for the fuze pocket and one for the hole. The only damage was two cracked windows — not bad considering there were 650kgs of explosives in the bomb.

We then checked the site. Once satisfied all was safe we headed back to Chatham with our bomb, the whole operation taking 60 hours from door to door.

CORPORAL G. JENNINGS,
THE SAPPER, APRIL 1985

Sequel in 1985: Captain Paddy Bowen with Sapper Carnie, left, and Corporal Jennings . . . and 'Hermann'.

Running true to form, the Luftwaffe was back on Sunday after a brief 48-hour respite, it being noted by Civil Defence that the Germans deliberately chose Sunday nights, when they hoped the country's defences would be least prepared, for their follow-up fire raids. This time the raid lasted for just over three hours, the All Clear sounding at 10.17 p.m. Two hours later Mr J. S. Bristow took this picture of the city ablaze again, yet the people's mood was surprisingly buoyant: 'We know the worst that Hitler can do now' declared a young woman. 'We are not afraid of him any more.'

FRIDAY, DECEMBER 13-14

Sunset: 1649 Sunrise: 0900
Moon: Dusk — 0805 (Full −1)

No major attack. Operations limited to minelaying in the Thames Estuary and patrolling Bomber Command airfields.

UK — Extensive cloud with moderate to poor visibility.
The Continent — Fog or low cloud with mist in most areas.

During the day activity was slight, with only ten enemy aircraft tracked over land and some 25 operating over adjacent sea areas.

At 1700 hours No. 11 Group sent a Beaufighter 40 miles out to sea off Beachy Head in the hope of intercepting the first approaching bombers, but the first raider did not appear until 1845 and operations were restricted to minelaying in the Thames Estuary. Seven aircraft of I/NJG2 were also operating over eastern England in the hope of catching aircraft of Bomber Command taking off or landing, but no encounters were reported. The Humber AA guns were in action for a short while but there was nothing further of note to report except the loss of a Beaufighter of No. 604 Squadron which retracted its undercarriage too quickly on take off from Middle Wallop.

SATURDAY, DECEMBER 14-15

Sunset: 1649 Sunrise: 0901
Moon: 1713-0805 (Full Moon)

No major attack. Very little activity.

UK — Fog or mist with low cloud in most areas. Gales in Scotland.
The Continent — Low cloud with snow or sleet and strong but decreasing winds. Poor visibility.

Weather conditions continued to limit Luftwaffe daylight operations, with only some 40 aircraft operating, most of them over sea areas. At 1657 hours No. 11 Group's AA guns were given permission for unrestricted firing and at 1712 the first night raiders were plotted approaching from Holland, but they turned back south of Wittering and the country was clear of raiders by 2020 hours. Such was the weather over the UK that all Fighter Command Groups were declared non-operational at 1730 hours.

'Y' Service intercepts show that some of the 37 long-range bombers operating in the early evening, and approaching from the direction of Calais-Boulogne, belonged to KG2. Also operating were eleven BR 20s of the CAI which attempted to bomb Harwich, and five minelayers of IX Fliegerkorps. Two night fighters were sent up later on — a little activity was resumed after 0400 hours — when two raiders entered the London IAZ, but no bombs were dropped. One Beaufighter chased but then lost an enemy aircraft near Hastings, and another raider was claimed damaged by AA fire.

SUNDAY, DECEMBER 15-16

Sunset: 1649 Sunrise: 0902
Moon: 1805 — Dawn (Full +1)

Heavy attack on Sheffield. Slight activity elsewhere.

UK — Mainly cloudy with fog patches. Elsewhere moderate visibility.
The Continent — Variable amounts of cloud. Locally poor visibility and fog in some areas.

Poor weather conditions again restricted day operations and rendered No. 12 Group non-operational. The usual anti-shipping operations were flown by a few aircraft, however, and one aircraft penetrated to the Midlands on reconnaissance. Attempts to intercept this intruder by No. 10 Group were unsuccessful.

Night activity started at 1730 with raids plotted coming in from the Channel Islands direction to cross the Hampshire and Dorset coasts followed by a stream from Cherbourg. Subsequent raids came in from the direction of Cherbourg, Fécamp and Cap Gris Nez, with the last ten attackers approaching from Brest to coast in between Plymouth and Start Point.

Sheffield was the target for 135 aircraft of Luftflotten 2 and 3 but because of deteriorating visibility and the expectation of fog at their bases, two Gruppen were instructed by W/T while en route to attack less distant alternative targets. In consequence only 94 aircraft reached Sheffield where, as on the night of December 12-13, the CP was the north-east and central districts of the town. Between 1900 and 2158 hours the raiders delivered 80 tonnes of HE (four SC 1800, 36 SC 1000, four SC 500, 16 LZZ 250, 91 SC 250 and 150 SC 50) and 600 BSK (21,600 IBs). Over the south and south-east of England there were thickening layers of cloud, but in the north a thinning out with breaks from time to time produced a mixture of visual, DR and radio-aided bombing. Several large and numerous smaller fires were seen, with many joining to form major conflagrations. Several crews reported two particularly violent explosions between 2037 and 2040 hours, followed after some ten seconds by prolonged jets of flame. No night fighters were seen but crews were unanimous about the accuracy of the strong heavy and light flak they experienced. Some 20 to 30 balloons were seen at various heights, with those over the town up to 2,000 metres (6,500 feet). Also observed was a decoy fire to the north of Sheffield.

Left: **Exchange Street with the gutted Brightside and Carbrook Co-operative Society building. The two raids resulted in the destruction of 1,218 commercial and business premises with 1,000 houses and another 2,000 badly damaged.** ***Right:*** **An open air market now occupies the site of the Co-op building.**

Seventeen aircraft of Luftflotte 2 bombed Sheffield, but little else is known of this Air Fleet's participation. However, KG2 was identified on operations by the 'Y' Service and could well have been involved. Units of Luftflotte 3 engaged in the attack were:

KGr126: 17 He 111, 1943-2035 (dropped 34 LM mines)
I/KG27: 16 He 111, 2000-2103
II/KG27: 6 He 111, 1930-2016
III/KG27: 11 He 111, 1937-2205
KGr100: 16 He 111, 1900-1950 (opened attack as Firelighters, dropping 11,520 IBs. Bombing visually and with X-Verfahren)
KGr606: 11 Do 17, 2035-2158

Of the 94 bombers dispatched by Luftflotte 3, 77 reached Sheffield, three bombed Bristol, another three attacked Southampton, seven aborted and single aircraft bombed Plymouth and Dover. In the Dover attack an He 111 of KGr126 dropped two parachute LM 1000s. No aircraft of Luftflotte 3 were lost.

Although the attack was less severe than on the night of the 12th, damage and casualties in Sheffield were again of serious proportions. Industrial and residential areas again suffered, and the railway between Sheffield and York was blocked. In addition the adjacent towns of Rotherham, Leeds, Barnsley, Tadcaster, Batley, Penistone and Saltburn also received bombs no doubt intended for Sheffield. Fire again caused most damage in Sheffield, though all were under control by 0230 hours, but between 6,000 and 7,000 people were rendered homeless. Damage to factory premises was greater than on the previous occasion, but public utility services were not so badly hit. In the two attacks 589 people were killed and 488 seriously injured.

The Sheffield guns again put up a spirited defence, firing over 3,000 rounds, while the London IAZ guns' contribution was 1,303. Over the country as a whole 9,000 rounds were expended by batteries at Cardiff, Harwich, Gloucester, Dover, Leeds, Manchester, Yeovil and Swansea. Night fighters, of which 17 were operating, filed no claims although a Blenheim sighted an enemy aircraft over Mansfield.

In addition to places already mentioned, bombs fell during the night at Corby, Great Dalby, Grantham, near Grimsby, Mablethorpe, Coventry, Wolverhampton, London and six south-east area districts, Epsom, Peaslake, Canvey Island, the Isle of Sheppey, Arundel, Plymouth, Leighterton, Swindon, Tetbury and Redwick Camp.

Mary Walton wrote at the time that 'the visit of the King and Queen on January 5 greatly pleased and heartened everybody. The homeless proudly displayed the extent of the havoc which had not broken their spirits or interrupted their work to the sovereign who throughout those months of testing had become a symbol of the stubborn resistance of Britain.'

However, the reckoning was harsh: when the final count was made the total of killed and missing was 760 — nearly half as many deaths again as those in Coventry a month before. After careful examination of unidentified fragments, it was judged that they represented 47 persons out of the 92 people who were never seen again. As Joseph Lamb wrote in 1941, 'ARP staff, barely out of their teens . . . saw death in forms as horrible as any on the battlefields of the First World War . . . there is no need to dwell on the details, but they were among the realities of the night of which those who escaped such experiences should be aware.' Three-quarters of the relatives chose to have their loved ones buried in family graves, the remainder being laid to rest in two mass burials by the Corporation — the first on December 20. On July 7, 1952 a memorial garden was laid out on the spot designed by the Parks Department manager, Mr E. O. Sadler. On the face of the dwarf granite wall were cut the names of 134 dead with the immortal words from Deuteronomy 33, verse 27: 'The Eternal God is thy refuge, and underneath are the everlasting arms.'

MONDAY, DECEMBER 16-17

Sunset: 1649 Sunrise: 0903
Moon: 1904 — Dawn (Full +2)

No significant activity, but a few aircraft penetrated to Manchester and Nottingham.

UK — Cloudy with poor visibility in the South-East but improving.
The Continent — Some low cloud at first but worsening weather with rain spreading in later.

Of 44 German aircraft plotted during the day by Fighter Command, 19 progressed inland with most bent on reconnaissance. Visibility throughout the day was poor, but the cloudbase lifted in most areas from below 1,000 feet to between 1,500 to 3,000 feet.

Night operations by 32 long-range bombers and four long-range night fighter-bombers were opposed by five RAF night fighters but no interceptions were reported. The Manchester and Nottingham areas received many of the bombs, most of which fell some distance from the town centres, but there were also incidents at Stoke-on-Trent, elsewhere in South Lancashire and Midlands areas, London, East Anglia and Yorkshire. Ten people were killed in Manchester, with more casualties at Stoke, but there was no serious damage outside of these centres. The attack was carried out by Do 17Zs of KG3 and upon their return some landed at Le Culot and others at Saint-Trond instead of their normal base at Lille, presumably because of bad weather. Several aircraft aborted with engine failures and one made a forced landing at La Salles, but none were reported lost.

German records state that unfavourable weather conditions — particularly over their bomber bases — reduced operations to harassing attacks only, mainly directed against Birmingham where the CP lay in the north-east part of Zielraum 'B'. Of the 32 aircraft which started out for Birmingham only 20 succeeded in reaching the city. They claimed to have dropped 10 tonnes of HE (94 SC 50 and 94 SD 50) and 12 BSK (432 IBs), various crews using visual, DR and radio methods. Several fires resulted and a factory was clearly seen to be on fire. London, Newmarket and Manchester were also claimed bombed, with no results visible in the first two but fires were sighted at Manchester.

One of the night fighter-bombers claimed an attack on Scampton airfield; another claimed an attack on a Hampden (intercepted over the same airfield and seen to crash) and then went on to bomb Lincoln and Grimsby from a height of 150 feet, starting fires. A third aircraft of the Nachtjägddivision claimed to have shot down a Hurricane in flames over the coast to the north of The Wash, and then dropped 30 incendiary bombs on Waddington airfield, starting several small fires.

The devastation in Ordnance Street, Chatham, was caused by a mine which exploded around 6.30 p.m. on December 14 — a day of little activity yet one which brought to the town its highest death toll of the war. A gap six houses wide was blown in the terrace, and in each house there were fatalities: Fireman George Kennard in No. 18, Alan Herbert in 20, Rosa Woolven in 22, the Zedgitt family in 24, the Thorns in 26 and Ivy Douglas and daughter Vera in 28.

The second mine — Luftmines were invariably dropped in pairs — blasted the Fort Row and Caroline Street area — now the site of the Sir John Fisher School. The whole devastation is stated to have covered an area of 250 square yards, damaging in some way or another 700 homes, killing a total of 15, with 20 seriously injured and 103 slightly hurt. Hundreds were made homeless and the local historian Andrew Rootes records that 240 people had to be evacuated and even a week after the incident workmen still had over 500 roofs to cover with tarpaulins.

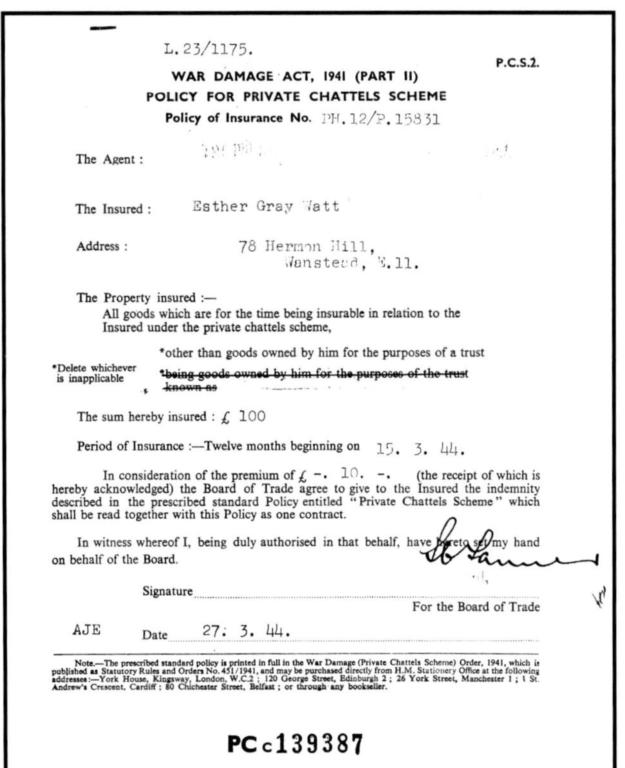

L. 23/1175.

P.C.S.2.

WAR DAMAGE ACT, 1941 (PART II)
POLICY FOR PRIVATE CHATTELS SCHEME
Policy of Insurance No. PH.12/P.15831

The Agent :

The Insured : Esther Gray Watt

Address : 78 Hermon Hill, Wanstead, E.11.

The Property insured :—
All goods which are for the time being insurable in relation to the Insured under the private chattels scheme,

*other than goods owned by him for the purposes of a trust

*Delete whichever is inapplicable ~~*being goods owned by him for the purposes of the trust known as~~

The sum hereby insured : £ 100

Period of Insurance :—Twelve months beginning on 15. 3. 44.

In consideration of the premium of £ -. 10. -. (the receipt of which is hereby acknowledged) the Board of Trade agree to give to the Insured the indemnity described in the prescribed standard Policy entitled "Private Chattels Scheme" which shall be read together with this Policy as one contract.

In witness whereof I, being duly authorised in that behalf, have hereto set my hand on behalf of the Board.

Signature ....
For the Board of Trade

AJE Date 27. 3. 44.

Note.—The prescribed standard policy is printed in full in the War Damage (Private Chattels Scheme) Order, 1941, which is published as Statutory Rules and Orders No. 451/1941, and may be purchased directly from H.M. Stationery Office at the following addresses:—York House, Kingsway, London, W.C.2; 120 George Street, Edinburgh 2; 26 York Street, Manchester 1; 1 St. Andrew's Crescent, Cardiff; 80 Chichester Street, Belfast; or through any bookseller.

PC c139387

Miss E.G. Watt.

QS. 4. No. 20387

DEATH AND INJURY ARISING FROM ANY ACCIDENT

THIS INSURANCE ALSO COVERS WAR & INVASION
including
Air Raids, Gas, Mines, Explosives, Projectiles, etc.

Three Months Cover Effective from 3 - AUG 1944 ***Noon***

This is to Certify *that we have effected with LLOYD'S UNDERWRITERS an insurance whereby in the event of the Assured sustaining any bodily injury by violent external and visible means (including such bodily injury directly caused by WAR) as shall cause his death or disablement within THREE CALENDAR MONTHS thereof, compensation in accordance with the following Schedule will be paid to the Assured, his Executors, Administrators or Assigns subject to the terms clauses and conditions of the Contract policy held by us.*

SCHEDULE OF COMPENSATION

1. Death ... or ... } **£1000**
2. Loss of one or two eyes ... or ...
3. Loss of one or two limbs ... or ...
4. Permanent Total Disablement or ...
5. Temporary Total Disablement (as over) ... **£10.0.0 per week** Limited to 50 weeks

NOTE: In addition to any compensation payable on any admitted claim under item No. 5, any Doctor's charges incurred by the Assured will be paid by the Underwriters up to but not exceeding 15% of the total amount of any such claim as admitted.

PREMIUM - £2.10.0

STEWART, SMITH & Co. LTD.

Issued by H. Leyborne Arbuckle & Co. Ltd. ... Street ... Insurance Brokers

DIRECTOR.

This Certificate must be completed overleaf by the Assured's signature and issued not later than 31st August, 1944.

Just one week earlier the Prime Minister had voiced his concern over the speedy repair of houses only slightly damaged in no uncertain terms. His memo to the Minister of Works, John Reith, on December 9 ran as follows: 'Sometimes I see a whole row of houses whose windows are blown out, but are not otherwise damaged, standing for weeks deserted and neglected. Active measures should be taken to replace the tiles and to close up the windows with fabric, with one small pane for light, and to make such repairs as make the houses fit for habitation. In dealing with house casualties, the least serious should claim priority. You ought to have a regular corps of workmen who would get this job done so that the people may get back into their homes, which are unlikely to be hit a second time. Branches of this corps should exist in all the great cities.' Four weeks later, with no action apparent, Churchill lambasted Reith: 'I continue to see great numbers of houses where the walls and roofs are all right but the windows have not been repaired, and which are consequently uninhabitable. At present I regard this as your No. 1 task.' We have already touched on the plans being made by the Government to compensate the public for damage to their homes. When Sir Kingsley Wood, the Chancellor of the Exchequer, explained the details to Parliament this same month, he said that the proposed War Damage Act would introduce a charge on property under Schedule A assessment, payable for five years no matter how long the war lasted, at 2s. in the pound (see Mr Foreman's demand, page 322), and for plant and machinery at 30s. per cent. In announcing the new measures, Sir Kingsley said that 'No country would proceed with these proposals unless it was confident of victory and, in particular, of the defeat of the enemy in the air.' Nevertheless he admitted that claims could not be met in full during the war but would be limited to £500. Normally, of course, a private 'All Risks' insurance policy excludes war risks, but these interesting documents which have come to light demonstrate that Miss Watt covered £100 of furniture for 10s. (50p) and her personal accident cover for £1,000 has resulted in a premium of £2.10s.0d. per *quarter*. From her subsequent renewal notes it is apparent that the rate changed every three months, introducing a nice twist for the actuaries when they came to estimate the risk involved.

TUESDAY, DECEMBER 17-18

Sunset: 1650 Sunrise: 0904
Moon: 2008 — Dawn (Full +3)

No German night bombing operations.

UK — Widespread fog over England and Wales, except for the extreme West and South-West.

The Continent — Extensive low cloud and fog.

Daylight activity by the Luftwaffe was slight and all night bomber operations were cancelled because of the very bad weather. However, Fighter Command plotted eight enemy aircraft during the hours of darkness — presumably weather reconnaissance flights — and two night fighters were scrambled. No bombs were dropped anywhere in Britain.

WEDNESDAY, DECEMBER 18-19

Sunset: 1650 Sunrise: 0904
Moon: 2118 — Dawn (Last Qtr −3)

No German night bombing operations.

UK — Visibility poor in south and south-eastern districts, improving during the night. Widespread cloud and occasional rain in most areas.

The Continent — Similar to the British Isles.

German daylight activity was restricted to a small number of reconnaissance and coastal patrols, with an attack on shipping in the Irish Sea. Worsening weather conditions precluded any night bombing, but Fighter Command reported plots of four reconnaissance aircraft. Uneventful patrols were flown by two RAF night fighters. No bombs were reported.

THURSDAY, DECEMBER 19-20

Sunset: 1650 Sunrise: 0905
Moon: 2229 — Dawn (Last Qtr −2)

Minor activity only, widely spread.

UK — Cloudy with rain in many places. Some fog in other areas.

The Continent — Much cloud with rain, sleet or snow showers.

Shipping patrols occupied the Luftwaffe during the day and no bombs were reported on land.

Activity was also only slight at night when most of the 51 long-range bombers operating confined themselves to the south-eastern counties. Weather conditions were unfavourable for night fighters and only one was sent up, without avail. Within the London IAZ 693 rounds of ammunition were fired at nine aircraft which entered the Zone, but searchlights did not expose. The raiders were flying at average heights of 17,000 feet. The only other reported bombing was at Swindon where eight houses were destroyed.

Although not reported in German records, it seems likely that some minelaying was also carried out as aircraft of KGr126 are known to have been operating. On this occasion the minelayers, which normally operated under IX Fliegerkorps as part of Luftflotte 2 (although based at Nantes in Luftwaffe 3's territory), came under the control of IV Fliegerkorps, which had its Headquartes at Sevres and a forward HQ at Dinard as part of Luftflotte 3.

German documentation does reveal, however, an intended harassing attack on London's government offices and City districts, where 49 crews claimed the delivery of 40 tonnes of HE (three SC 1800, seven SC 1000, 13 SC 250, two LZZ 250 and 470 SC/SD 50) and 36 BSK (1,296 incendiaries). All of the bombing, it was conceded, was by DR and radio navigation and, because of the dense cloud, only a few bomb detonations were seen.

An interesting speculation: was the Luftwaffe planning a 'Dams raid' all of its own over two years before No. 617 Squadron mounted its own famous Dambusters operation? On December 17 German reconnaissance of the Midlands area particularly included this picture of the twin dams 'südostwärts Manchester'. It was an ironic choice as the dams on the River Derwent were the very ones on which the squadron practised in 1943! The Derwent Dam is top left; Howden Dam bottom right.

FRIDAY, DECEMBER 20-21

Sunset: 1650 Sunrise: 0905
Moon: 2343 — Dawn (Last Qtr −1)

Major attack on Liverpool/Birkenhead. Minelaying in Liverpool Bay and Belfast Lough.

UK — In the southern half of England cloudy, becoming fair by midnight except in the South-West, with moderate visibility improving to good. Elsewhere fine but the weather deteriorated from 2130 hours in the Liverpool area. Winds generally easterly, fresh to moderate on coasts.

The Continent — Clear, frost with haze in Holland. Overcast with squally snow and sleet showers in Belgium and France, clearing from the North.

Of a total of 55 German aircraft plotted during the day 45 were engaged on anti-shipping operations and only ten crossed inland. Yet again there was much low cloud and drizzle, except in the North and South-West where it was cloudy but improving to fine later in the day with moderate visibility. With nightfall the activity became intense with raiders converging on Liverpool in eight main streams; those approaching from the direction of the Channel Islands crossed the coast at St Alban's Head at 1740 hours, followed by streams from Dieppe and Fécamp, the first bomber arriving overhead Liverpool at 1836. The main attack lasted until 2130 hours, but activity continued in the Target Area until 0300.

In favourable weather conditions 205 crews from Luftflotten 2 and 3 attacked Liverpool/Birkenhead with 205 tonnes of HE (12 SC 1800, two SC 1700, 61 SC 1000, 109 SC 500, six LZZ 500, 149 SC 250, 35 LZZ 250 and 320 SC 50) and 761 BSK (27,396 IBs). Bombing took place between 1928 and 0303 hours and was carried out for the most part with visual sight of the ground. With the attack only one hour old a massive fire was developing in the city centre, surrounded by another six to eight large and 50 to 60 smaller fires. Follow-up bombing produced further large fires and explosions and by midnight a dense cloud of smoke blanketed the city, rising to some 13,000 feet. In addition to the fires in the city centre, more were seen in the northern part of the town and in the docks. In the eastern part of Birkenhead three large and six or seven medium fires appeared to merge, creating an even greater conflagration than that on the other side of the river, with up to 30 fires visible from up to 100 kilometres away as the attack drew to a close. Overall the attack on both centres was assessed a great success.

Luftflotte 3 contributed 143 aircraft to the attack, with 122 reaching the target, ten bombing alternatives and nine aborting. One aircraft crashed on take off (an He 111 of III/KG26), and a Ju 88 of I/KG51 was reported missing. Two aircraft were destroyed on their return flights (an He 111 of I/KG27 crashing and catching fire on landing and a Ju 88 of KG77 crashing 30 kilometres north-west of Amiens) according to a Luftwaffe 3 operations report, but these incidents do not readily relate to details given in the Luftwaffe Quartermaster returns on losses.

Luftflotte 3 aircraft which reached and bombed Merseyside were as follows:

I/KG27: 11 He 111, 2030-2230
II/KG27: 8 He 111, 1955-2055
III/KG27: 9 He 111, 2016-2042
KGr100: 18 He 111, 1935-2050 (Firelighters; bombload 14,832 IBs and 16 SC 50. Six large and 10-12 smaller fires started in Birkenhead target area)
KGr606: 16 Do 17, 2020-2050
I/KG51: 2 Ju 88, 0150
II/KG51: 3 Ju 88, 0255 and 0303
III/KG51: 5 Ju 88, 2345-0140
Stab/KG55: 2 He 111, 2250
II/KG55: 8 He 111, 1928-2110 (opened attack with flares; seven SC 1000s included in bombload. Eight fires reported)
I and II/KG77: 17 Ju 88, 2307-0100
III/KG77: 7 Ju 88, 1945-2045
I and II/KG26: 11 He 111, 2316-0015
III/KG26: 5 He 111, 2335-0115

Liverpool's dock area received a large number of bombs and numerous fires were started, the most serious involving warehouses and timber yards. About a dozen major fires were reported by the Chief Fire Officer, with many less serious, but all were dealt with by the Liverpool Fire Brigade without outside assistance. There was the usual tally of damage to schools, shops, commercial premises, churches and dwellings; in Bootle and Wallasey there was considerable damage to private property, but bombing was widespread over both Birkenhead and Liverpool. Generally, however, the working of the port was not seriously affected, but there was considerable delay and dislocation of traffic.

Forty-four night fighters of all Groups except No. 14 were sent on patrol and although two Beaufighters of No. 12 Group made contact with enemy aircraft none were claimed shot down. One Blenheim crashed during the night.

AA Command guns opened fire at Plymouth, in the London IAZ, Thames and Medway (North and South), Yeovil, Holton Heath, Solent, Dover, Portland, Cardiff, Swansea, Duxford, Harwich, Bristol, Birmingham, Derby, Humber, Leeds, Sheffield, Manchester, Bramley and Glasgow. They fired 20,000 shells into the night sky, the IAZ using 2,333 rounds and Merseyside between 5,000 and 6,000, but only one raider was claimed damaged (over Wormwood Scrubbs by the IAZ).

In addition to the attack on Liverpool/Birkenhead some 40 German aircraft

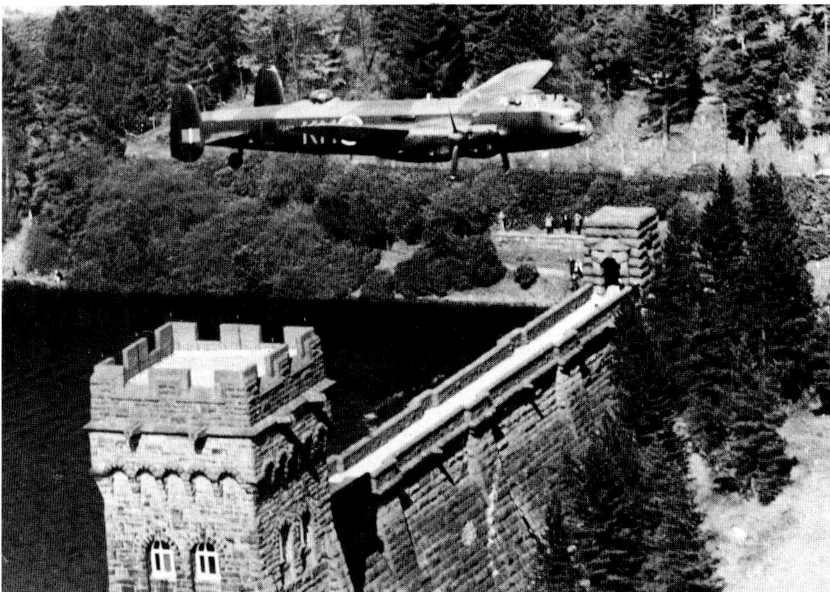

In May 1977 — the 34th anniversary of the Bomber Command raid — the RAF restaged the attack with the Ladybower reservoir dam, whose twin towers simulated those on the Möhne dam in the Rühr, as the target.

appeared to roam all parts of the British Isles including the Isle of Man and Dublin in the Irish Republic. Some of these were undoubtedly minelayers but not all, for bombs were sewn apparently indiscriminately at Sheffield, Workington, Leeds, Glasgow, Mesowen, Whalley, Manchester, Burnley, Fort William, near Dawley, near Wellington, near Brigg, Warsop, Llanddulas, near Grimsby, Lincoln, Chesterfield, Bradford and 28 smaller places.

About an hour before sunrise on the 21st, a Ju 88C-2 (R4+KL) of I/NJG2 was shot down by LAA machine gun fire as it carried out a low level attack on Manby airfield. The German night fighter-bomber was flying at 150-200ft when it was hit and its petrol tanks exploded as it struck the ground, killing Oberleutnant Ulrich Meyer and two crew members. Little could be gleaned from the wreckage beyond the fact that the aircraft was a night fighter version of the Ju 88, but AI1(k) was able to establish that Meyer was the Staffelkapitän of NJG2's 3 Staffel. One of the crew was carrying his pay-book and this, too, provided some useful intelligence, as did a map which revealed several tracks from Schiphol and Gilze-Rijen airfields to target airfields in eastern England. The map was sent to AI3(b) for further analysis, for it also showed marked-in patrol areas. Other captured documents gave the German code letters for 19 RAF airfields, the frequencies of the Lorenz beam approach transmitters at 17 German-occupied airfields, and various radio beacon frequencies. All material relating to radio or W/T matters was passed on to AI1(e) for appropriate analysis and action as necessary. All in all, this was another excellent example of British Air Intelligence at its best; from an almost totally destroyed aircraft with no survivors, a substantial amount of useful intelligence came to light. Above all, perhaps, was the confirmation of the existence and activities of an enemy long-range night fighter/intruder unit, with details of its areas of operation and the target airfields in those areas. German records show that the R4+KL had been operating in Raum (Area) 'B', the central region stretching from the Wash to the Humber. Raum 'A' lay to the south, from the Wash to the Thames Estuary, with Raum 'C' extending northwards from the Humber towards the Firth of Forth and westwards to the Lancashire coast near Fleetwood. Intruder type operations over Britain had commenced on August 17, since when there had been a constant succession of attacks on Bomber Command airfields and against both operational and training aircraft over the Eastern Counties. The first known victim was an Armstrong Whitworth Whitley of No. 58 Squadron, shot down near Thornaby on September 21, but others followed over the next few months. Indeed, I/NJG2 was achieving over Britain what the British Intruder's of No. 23 Squadron were to attempt from this night onwards. Unlike their German counterpart, however, the British long-range fighters were to achieve little success until better aircraft came their way.

On December 16, for the first time, the RAF carried out an operation specifically designed to bring about the 'maximum possible destruction in a selected German town'. Until now the War Cabinet had held back; now, in the face of Coventry, Bristol, Southampton, etcetera, Sheffield became the last straw, and, under the code-name Operation Abigail, a *deliberate* out and out attack was authorised to try to wipe out a whole area. Three possible targets were chosen: Bremen (code-named Jezebel); Düsseldorf (Delilah) and Mannheim (Rachel). A last minute change led to a switch from Delilah to Rachel with the general aiming point 1,500 yards south of the Motorenwerke-Mannheim. Taking a leaf out of the book of the Luftwaffe's firelighter units, KGr100 and II/KG55, fourteen of the most experienced of the Wellington crews were to act as 'pathfinders' to light the target with incendiaries on which the following aircraft would drop an assortment of heavy bombs, mines, and more incendiaries. The RAF claimed that upwards of 80 aircraft had successfully bombed Mannheim but German records show only 100 bombs and 1,000 incendiaries over the whole of Mannheim and neighbouring Ludwigshafen. German casualties were 34 killed and 80-odd injured — less than a tenth of what the Germans had achieved in their mass city attacks. After a lull due to adverse weather conditions over Britain, on the night of the 20th/21st the Luftwaffe was back with a vengeance over Liverpool. Athough undated, this print shows great Charlotte Street with H. Samuel's 'Everite' clock marking the location of their burnt out store.

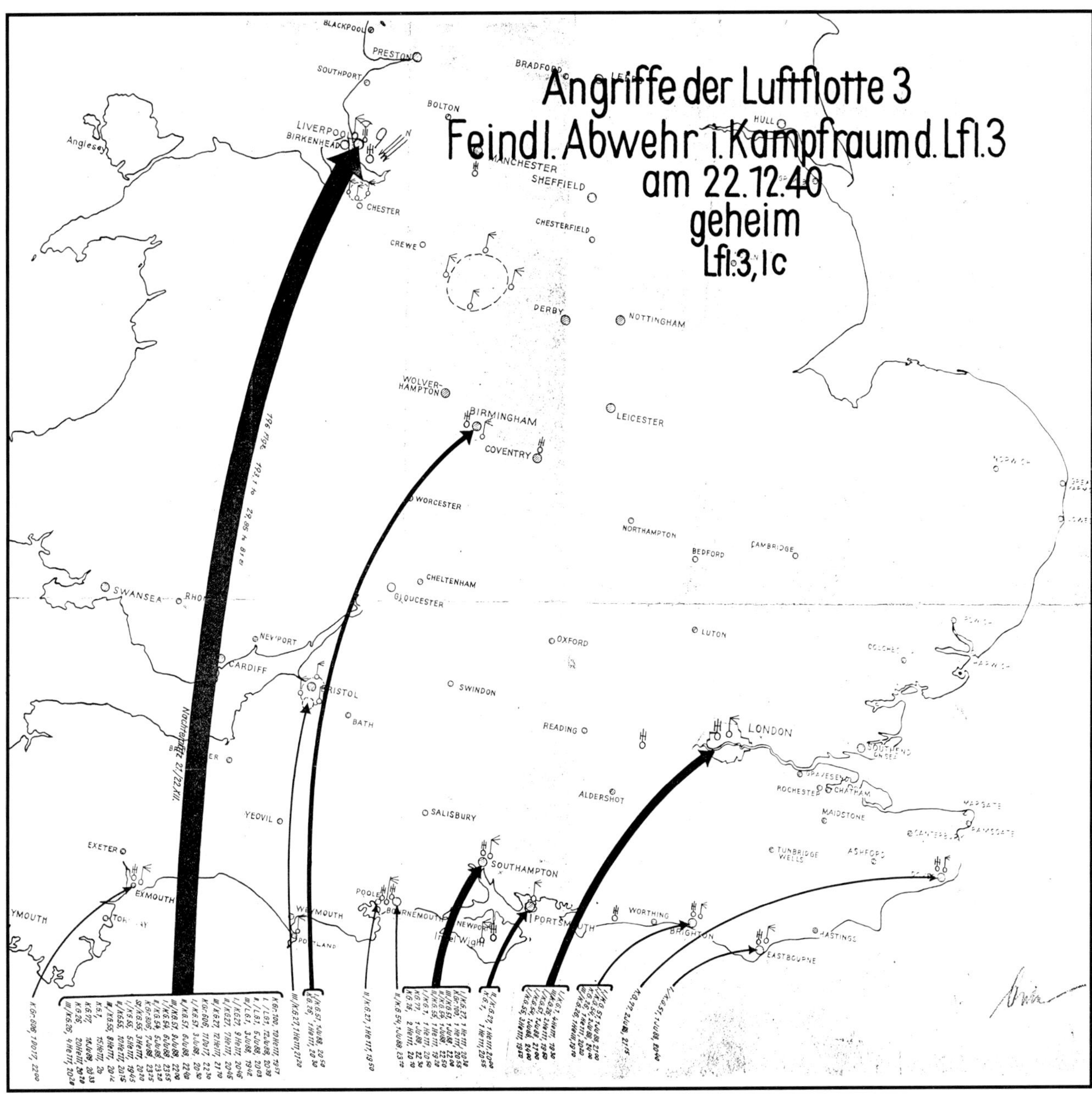

SATURDAY, DECEMBER 21-22

Sunset: 1651 Sunrise: 0906
Moon: 0058 — Dawn (Last Qtr)

Major attack on Liverpool/Birkenhead. Minelaying in Liverpool Bay, off Plymouth, Cromer and in the mouth of the Humber. Night fighter-bomber patrols of RAF airfields in eastern England and a small scale operation against East Coast ports by the CAI.

UK — Little or no cloud at first but increasing in most areas around midnight and becoming 7/10ths to 10/10ths at 2–3,000 feet except on West Coasts. Visibility moderate, poor locally. Winds easterly, light to moderate, fresh locally on East and West Coasts.

The Continent — Generally cloudless with mist in some areas. Very cold with frost in Holland.

In conditions of little or no cloud there was more Luftwaffe activity than of late during the day, but no major operations developed. Night activity started at 1710 hours and for the second night in succession Liverpool was the main target.

The Doppelgänger came the next night, one of the tragedies of the raid being an air raid shelter in Blackstock Street which took a direct hit. When the final count was made by the Medical Officer of Health, over the two days 218 had been killed with 173 seriously injured and another 444 people receiving slight wounds.

The 299 aircraft of Luftflotten 2 and 3 which bombed the twin-city Target Area of Liverpool/Birkenhead dropped 280 tonnes of HE (16 SC 1800, two SC 1700, 61 SC 1000, one LZZ 1000, 142 SC 500, three Flam 500, two LZZ 500, 241 SC 250, one Flam 250, 50 LZZ 250 and 728 SC 50) and 940 BSK (33,840 IBs). The attack, which lasted from 1945 to 0420 hours, was made in good weather conditions and only a few crews were unable to bomb visually. In consequence the results achieved were, to quote participating crews, similar to those achieved at Coventry. Within half an hour eight major and some 20 smaller fires were raging and with the attack 4 to 5 hours old an entire district of Liverpool was a sea of flames with major conflagrations also visible in the dock area stretching from the Canada Docks to the Waterloo Docks. Nelson and Stanley Docks were also seen to be ablaze. On the Birkenhead side the results were just as spectacular with huge fires around the West Float, where tank installations were hit, and in the western area of the docks. By midnight crews inbound to the target could see the glow of fires from 250 kilometres away.

Crews of 103 Luftflotte 2 aircraft claimed to have bombed their targets on Merseyside but no other details are known. Luftflotte 3 had 249 crews operating with 196 bombing Liverpool/Birkenhead and 31 attacking alternative targets; 19 aircraft aborted, two crashed in occupied territory and one was reported missing (a Do 17 of KGr606). Six aircraft bombed London during the night including two He 111s of III/KG26 on a special Y-Verfahren mission. Precisely what the target was is not specified in German records, but for the first time, so far as can be determined, an SC 2500 was dropped on a British target. The other aircraft of the unit dropped an SC 1000 and 576 B1 El. incendiaries.

Luftflotte 3 participants in the attack on Liverpool/Birkenhead were:

KGr100: 10 He 111, 1951-2042 (operating as a Firelighter Gruppe: dropped 7,488 IBs)
I/LG1: 12 Ju 88, 2039-2119

While Liverpool was being pounded for the second successive night 175 miles to the north, literally an earth-shattering event took place in central London which heard for the first time the thunderclap explosion of the first SC 2500 to be dropped on Britain. Although small by the later RAF standards of the 12,000lb 'Tallboy' or the 22,000lb 'Grand Slam', 'Max', which weighed in at 2½ tons, was the largest bomb dropped during the Blitz by the Luftwaffe. Only III/KG26 was authorised to carry it: here 'Max' is hitched underneath a 'Lowën' He 111H-5y, the 'y' (pronounced 'oopsilon' in German) denoting that it is a Y-Verfahren-equipped machine.

II/LG1: 5 Ju 88, 2003-2128
III/LG1: 3 Ju 88, 1942-2007
I/KG27: 9 He 111, 2046-2153
II/KG27: 7 He 111, 2045-2158
III/KG27: 12 He 111, 2110-2210
KGr606: 11 Do 17, 2230-2330
I/KG51: 3 Ju 88, 2030-2205
II/KG51: 6 Ju 88, 2240-2317
III/KG51: 9 Ju 88, 2200-2330
I/KG54: 6 Ju 88, 2355-0025
II/KG54: 5 Ju 88, 2320-2335
KGr806: 7 Ju 88, 2325-0043
Stab/KG55: 3 He 111, 2020-2045
I/KG55: 5 He 111, 1945-2015
II/KG55: 10 He 111, 2015-2040
III/KG55: 8 He 111, 2012-2049
KG1: 8 Ju 88 and 15 He 111, 2020-2135
KG77: 18 Ju 88, 2033-2337
KG26: 20 He 111, 2020-0014
III/KG26: 4 He 111, 2020-2302 (Y-Verfahren guided attacks)

Crews reported strong, well directed flak most of the way from the South Coast to the Target Area, especially in the vicinity of the Isle of Wight, Southampton, Birmingham, Coventry, London, Manchester, and between Brighton and Portsmouth. There were also reports of 'parachute flak' over the target, with lively searchlight activity along the Knickebein approach beams and on the coast, over Bristol and in the Midlands. Several night fighters were seen and a few carried out unsuccessful attacks.

The damage in Liverpool was greater than that suffered the previous night. About 180 fires were started with many of major proportions, but a plentiful supply of water — for only a few mains on the outskirts of the city were ruptured — greatly aided the Fire Services. Casualties, however, were heavy. There was also considerable dislocation of road and rail traffic, but generally speaking the port was not seriously affected although one ship, the SS *Silvio* of 1,293 tons, was sunk.

In London, Victoria Station was hit by 'either a very heavy bomb or mine', to quote the Home Security Operations Bulletin, and this was almost certainly the SC 2500 'Max' dropped by an He 111 of III/KG26 under Y-Verfahren guidance. The Central Signal Box was demolished and the lines so damaged that closure of the station was necessary, but suburban services were resumed on the 24th, in daylight hours, by means of hand signalling.

From elsewhere there were reports of bombs at Harwich, several places in Sussex, Ipswich, Finningley, Grimsby, Crewkerne, Portsmouth, Northampton and Shotley.

From a Fighter Command point of view the night was notable for the dispatch of six Blenheims of No. 23 Squadron on 'Intruder' missions over airfields in occupied France. Bombs were dropped on lights seen on airfields at Poix, Montdidier, Abbeville and Amiens/Glisy. Lisieux, Cherbourg, Evreux and St-André were also visited and several targets of opportunity, such as railway stations, were attacked, but it was difficult to assess the results; while several German aircraft were briefly seen in the vicinity of airfields, none were attacked.

Defensive patrols were conducted by 92 night fighters of Nos. 9, 10, 11, 12 and 13 Groups, but to no avail. However, 'Y'

As Y-Verfahren was capable of pin-point accuracy, we must assume that the bomb was dropped with Victoria Station as its target. It missed by a couple of hundred yards, the edge of the track receiving a nasty dent.

Home Security reported on the explosion the following day: 'In London there was one major incident at Victoria Station where the central signal box was demolished and lines blocked. 57 serious casualties are reported as having been caused. At the same time an L.C.C. Rest Centre at Ebury Bridge and a Warden's Post at Fountain Court were damaged.'

Service W/T intercepts indicated that during the night seven enemy aircraft reported engine trouble and several of these failed to make base safely. Earlier Signals Intelligence work had revealed (at 1645 hours) that the Cherbourg 'River' beam (X-Verfahren) was transmitting and was set up for Liverpool docks. 'Pegasus', called for earlier in the day, had been cancelled by nightfall, presumably with the confirmation of the target-for-the-night.

AA Command had an extremely busy night, firing nearly 29,000 rounds of HAA ammunition and claiming two enemy aircraft destroyed, one probably destroyed and another damaged. In addition to the Mersey guns, batteries were in action at Chatham, Thames and Medway South, the IAZ, Brooklands, Swansea, Portland, Solent, Holton Heath, Yeovil, Bromley, Slough, Coventry, Birmingham, Cardiff, Gloucester, Leeds, Humber, Sheffield and Derby.

In addition to the Dornier 17 lost by Küstenfliegergruppe 606, the following aircraft came down over Britain:

3/NJG2 Junkers Ju 88C-2 (0272). Hit by AA fire from RAF Manby and crashed at Mill Hill, South Cockerington near Louth, Lincolnshire 8.15 a.m. Swastika from tail recovered as a trophy for the gunners. Oblt. U. Meyer (Staffelkapitän), Fw. F. Schöttke and Obergefr. W. Schneider killed. Aircraft R4+KL destroyed.

5/KG2 Dornier Do 17Z-3 (2636). Shot down by Spitfires of No. 64 and No. 611 Squadrons after having been chased from Maidstone. Crashed into the sea off Eastbourne 1.00 p.m. Bodies of Lt. P. Krings and Fw. J. Butz found washed up near Hastings. Obergefr. H. Adler killed. Uffz. G. Mache missing. Aircraft U5+DN lost.

Top: **This is the signal gantry which was blown from the line into Hugh Street, which has since disappeared with post-war high density housing** *above.*

And now . . . Manchester . . . which was about to receive its two most devastating attacks. This picture is without doubt one of the most dramatic symbols of the Blitz, being more reminiscent of Stalingrad than one of Britain's cities.

SUNDAY, DECEMBER 22-23

Sunset: 1651 Sunrise: 0906
Moon: 0213 — Dawn (Last Qtr +1)

Major attack on Manchester. Minelaying in Liverpool Bay, off the Norfolk coast and in the Thames Estuary. Small scale operations by the CAI and Luftwaffe night fighter-bombers.

UK — Variable cloud cover over much of the country but cloudless in western coastal districts. Occasional light rain or sleet in the Midlands. Visibility moderate to good, poor locally in south-eastern England. Winds mainly easterly, moderate to fresh in the South, light to moderate in the North.

The Continent — Cloudless with local mist and frost in Holland.

Daylight activity was slight, with most German aircraft engaged on coastal and shipping reconnaissance. Other incidents included a low level attack by a Ju 88 on the British Aluminium Company's works at Fort William (which did no damage), a Bf 109 attack on the Dover balloon barrage, and an attack on a ship off Rathlin Head. Cloud was mainly 8-10/10ths with occasional light rain, except in Scotland where it was clear locally.

Night activity started at 1715 hours and for the first time Manchester was selected for a major attack. The raid came as no surprise, however, for 'Y' Service W/T intercepts, interpreted by GC and CS at Bletchley, revealed in advance that Manchester was to be attacked by KG51, KG54 and KG55. In fact, many more units were involved, the following being those from Luftflotte 3:

KGr100: 11 He 111, 1955-2033 (Beleuchtergruppe operation dropping 9,576 IBs by means of X-Verfahren)
I/LG1: 9 Ju 88, 2025-2115
I/KG27: 6 He 111, 2120-2210
II/KG27: 7 He 111, 2130-2217
III/KG27: 9 He 111, 2121-2255
KGr606: 5 Do 17, 2110-2150
I/KG51: 1 Ju 88, 2125
II/KG51: 4 Ju 88, 2155-2215
III/KG51: 5 Ju 88, 2202-2310
I/KG54: 5 Ju 88, 2257-2342
II/KG54: 4 Ju 88, 2335-0032
KGr806: 6 Ju 88, 0040-0120
Stab/KG55: 2 He 111, 2025-2035
I/KG55: 5 He 111, 1945-2015
II/KG55: 12 He 111, 2000-2031 (target illuminating with flares. Visual and Knickebein bombing with heavy HEs and IBs)
III/KG55: 6 He 111, 2025-2053
KG1: 12 He 111, 9 Ju 88, 2045-2200
KG26: 11 He 111, 2105-0034
KG77: 15 Ju 88, 2040-2350
III/KG26: 5 He 111, 2009-2220 (Y-Verfahren bombing with mixed loads of heavy HEs and IBs)

Thus Hitler changed the face of England. Piccadiily Gardens, now dominated by the towering Hotel Piccadilly.

In addition to these 149 aircraft of Luftflotte 3, 121 of Luftflotte 2 also took part, the total of 270 crews claiming to have dropped 272 tonnes of HE (eight SC 1800, one SC 1400, 88 SC 1000, 136 SC 500, six Flam 500, 219 SC 250, 49 LZZ 250 and 598 SC 50) and 1,032 BSK (37,152 incendiary bombs) on the city in an attack lasting from 1945 to 0120 hours and again from 0200 to 0655.

At their briefing crews were told that Manchester, lying at the east end of the Ship Canal, was an adjunct to the port of Liverpool and was the world centre of the wool industry. Its importance was further heightened, they were told, by the armaments and other industrial plants which the city contained. Accordingly, their Concentration Point was to be the town centre.

Most crews bombed visually while others used radio aids (including Knickebein, X-Verfahren, Y-Verfahren and radio beacon direction finding) and DR navigation. The initial raiders — and this included all three Beleuchtergruppen — succeeded in lighting up the target for following crews and shortly after the attack commenced four large and 15 small fires were visible. Subsequent bombing was mainly on the west side of the city, the docks and the industrial area, and within two hours the fires had reached the size of those seen in Liverpool the previous night. Whole streets and entire blocks of buildings were seen to be engulfed in flames, with their glare visible by crews passing over London on their way home.

Luftflotte 3 also sent six aircraft to London and five to Southampton, the total effort resulting in 149 aircraft over Manchester, with 23 bombing alternatives, eleven aborts, two over Bristol, two over Southampton and two over London. An He 111 of I/KG55 failed to return and probably this was the aircraft other crews reported seeing shot down near Hastings at 1902 hours.

In addition to all the normal night activity there was a dusk low level attack by five FW 200 Condors of KG40 against shipping in Loch Sunari, some 45 kilometres south-west of Fort William, at 1850 hours. The attack resulted in claims of one ship of 12,000 tons and two smaller vessels being hit. Another four ships were attacked but the results could not be ascertained.

German expectations were largely realised at Manchester where 400 fires were started, 100 of them serious. Guidance to the Target Area was assisted by fires still burning in Liverpool and Birkenhead from the previous night and these places, too, drew bombs yet again. The very large number of incendiary bombs dropped on Manchester, particularly before 0300 hours, presented many problems and although there was no shortage of water, it was not possible to extinguish them all before nightfall the following day. Many parts of the city and surrounding areas were badly hit, but the greatest concentration was in the central district and to the north-east, with the industrial Trafford Park area particularly affected. The main bus depot and both of the city's main railway stations were hit, as were many houses, schools and churches.

Bombs also fell at Prestwick, Wallasey, Huddersfield, Rochdale, Liverpool, Cuddington, Stockport, Wakefield, Dagenham, Orpington, Leicester, Poole, Portsmouth, Ealing, Brentford, Potters Bar, Oxted, Filton and Ripley.

Counter action by Fighter Command consisted of Intruder missions by seven Blenheims of No. 23 Squadron and defensive patrols by 55 night fighters of Nos. 9, 10, 11 and 12 Groups. Two enemy aircraft were claimed destroyed — one by a Defiant near Beachy Head and the other by a Hurricane 20 miles west of Blackpool — and several other interceptions were reported. One Intruder Blenheim (L6686) of No. 23 Squadron crashed into the sea off the Isle of Wight killing two crew members but the pilot was reported to be safe. The other Intruders again attacked various airfields, causing flare paths to be extinguished at some, but no German aircraft were encountered.

Piccadilly as seen from the gardens — a picture from the files of the *Manchester Evening News* where a long-forgotten retoucher has been at work adding a ghostly crew to the vehicle in the foreground.

For the second night in succession AA Command fired some 29,000 HAA shells, but without apparent success. The Manchester guns used 6,000 rounds and the London IAZ fired 3,747 at the 62 raiders plotted passing through the Zone. Elsewhere guns were in action at Birmingham, Coventry, Leeds, Grantham, Humber, Derby, Horsham St Faith and Sheffield.

At 1805 hours on December 22 a German bomber fell to a Defiant at night for the first time. The Defiant belonged to No. 141 Squadron and was flown by Pilot Officer James Benson with Sergeant F. Blain air gunner. Their victim was an He 111P-4, the G1+PL of I/KG55, which had taken off from Dreux at 1700 hours bound for Manchester flown by Unteroffizier Bruno Zimmermann and three crew members. After crossing the Channel at 17,000 feet, the Heinkel was attacked by the Defiant and its starboard engine was set on fire. It subsequently crashed at Etchingham, Sussex, and was largely destroyed. However, several items of interest were discovered by AI1(g) officers including a large PVC 1006L external bomb rack, several MG 15 machine guns, a tail-mounted grenade ejector tube, new-type bomb rack fittings and engines fitted with an unusual type of blower. Two bodies were found in the wreckage and another, that of Zimmermann, was found at Grandturzel Farm, Burwash, the next day, together with a damaged parachute. The only survivor, who also baled out, was the bomb-aimer, Feldwebel Walter Richter.

The single aircraft lost was:

3/KG55 Heinkel He 111P-4 (3107). Shot down during a sortie to Manchester by Pilot Officer J. G. Benson and Sergeant F. Blain of No. 141 Squadron in a Defiant. Crashed at Underwood House, Etchingham, East Sussex 6.05 p.m. Uffz. B. Zimmermann, Gefr. A. Waibel and Gefr. A. Wroblewski killed. Fw. W. Richter baled out and gave himself up at Burwash. Aircraft G1+PL destroyed.

Oxygen mask removed at the time was donated to the Robertsbridge Aviation Museum.

MONDAY, DECEMBER 23-24

Sunset: 1652 Sunrise: 0907
Moon: 0330 — Dawn (Last Qtr +2)

Major attack on Manchester. Small scale operation by long-range fighter-bombers.

UK — Extensive cloud over the eastern half of England with occasional light rain, drizzle, sleet or snow. Moderate to poor visibility with fog at first in the South-East. In the Manchester-Merseyside area visibility was moderate to good but poor with local fog at first. Wind north to north-east light to moderate, fresh at times.

The Continent — Low cloud with local snow; visibility poor to moderate. Freezing at surface.

Cloudy and hazy conditions prevailed during the day and German operations were confined mainly to shipping or weather reconnaissance, and of the 109 aircraft operating, only 11 crossed the British coasts. At 1700 hours, night fighters of I/NJG2 attempted to intercept outbound RAF night bombers near Cromer and the first inbound German bombers crossed the English coast at 1736. All Groups were advised by the Duty Air Commodore at Fighter Command that the target for the night was believed to be Manchester, for the second night running, and this proved to be correct.

Again the town centre was the CP for the attack, which on this occasion was made by 171 aircraft entirely drawn from units of Luftflotte 3. Between 1915 and 0000 hours they delivered 195 tonnes of HE and 893 BSK (7,020 IBs), some crews bombing visually, some by DR and others simply by aiming at fires seen through the cloud which at times completely covered the city. One especially large fire was discerned in the industrial and docks area besides numerous smaller fires elsewhere. Participating units were:

Stab/KG55: 1 He 111, 2015 hours
I/KG55: 8 He 111, 1950-2015
II/KG55: 12 He 111, 2133-2155
III/KG55: 8 He 111, 2005-2045
I/KG28: 18 He 111, 2214-2327 (operating on temporary detachment to FlKps IV from Lfl 2)
I/LG1: 9 Ju 88, 1 He 111, 1930-2014
I/KG27: 14 He 111, 2030-2232
II/KG27: 3 He 111, 2109-2130
III/KG27: 8 He 111, 2046-2226
KGr100: 10 He 111, 1915-2009 (opened attack as Beleuchtergruppe with 9,642 IBs. X-Verfahren subjected to interference and bombing subsequently scattered but five fires started)
KGr606: 4 Do 17, 2015-2030
I/KG51: 2 Ju 88, 2030-2055
II/KG51: 3 Ju 88, 2115-2140
III/KG51: 2 Ju 88, 2125-2215
I/KG54: 7 Ju 88, 2315-0000
II/KG54: 8 Ju 88, 2206-2310
KGr806: 7 Ju 88, 2130-2305
KG1: 11 He 111, 6 Ju 88, 1928-2125
KG77: 9 Ju 88, 1930-2101
I and II/KG26: 13 He 111, 1952-2117
III/KG26: 7 He 111, 1933-2050

Altogether 171 aircraft bombed Manchester, 19 attacked alternative targets, eight aborted, one carried out a special operation against Portsmouth and one was reported missing (an He 111 of KG1). The special mission against an unspecified target in Portsmouth was carried out by an He 111 of III/KG26, using X-Verfahren and dropping an SC 2500 'Max' at 1849 hours. This was the second known occasion on which this enormous type of high explosive bomb was dropped on the UK. Huge explosions rocked Manchester, too, where each of the He 111s of I/KG28 participating dropped two LM 1000 parachute mines. This is revealed in the Luftflotte 3 report on the operation, although the Luftwaffe Daily Summary of operations states that the unit dropped 36 of 'the heaviest bombs'.

In a subsidiary attack on London, which lasted from 2012 to 2150 hours, 28 aircraft dropped 11 tonnes of HE (224 SC 50) and 56 BSK (2,016 incendiaries) with their Schwerpunkt in the City and government offices quarter. Complete cloud cover required bombing by DR navigation and radio guidance and consequently results were not seen. However, the glow of a large fire was visible through the cloud. Similarly at Portsmouth all that was seen of the attack with the SC 2500 was the flash of its detonation, seen through the dense cloud.

Up to the night of the 22nd, Manchester had escaped lightly, but the twin attacks cost the city dear with 376 fatalities — more than a third of its total for the entire war. This view shows a near escape for the cathedral.

In almost a re-run of the Liverpool double, on Manchester's second night III/KG26 dropped its second 'Max', only this time it was Portsmouth on the receiving end. Initially, only two pilots were authorised to drop the bomb, one being Oberfeldwebel Herbert Rose. At the end of the war, as his home was in East Germany, he lost all his possessions, photographs and records so it is not possible to clarify who dropped which Max. He also lost his liberty, being imprisoned for the next seven years for belonging to what the Soviets judged to be a criminal organisation. When Ken Wakefield tracked him down in West Germany unfortunately he could no longer recall the name of the other authorised pilot, save that he was an officer. If with the Portsmouth bomb one assumes that the Royal Naval Dockyard was the intended target, the accuracy of the single weapon again came within a couple of hundred yards of the aiming point, landing in Conway Street, blowing a massive crater.

Manchester's second major attack brought the casualty list for the two nights to 376 people killed and a rather larger number seriously injured. Damage was again extensive and caused, in the main, by fire. Factories and other commercial premises sustained serious damage. However, damage to public utilities was not severe (electricity and sewerage works being practically unaffected) but the strain on the Civil Defence services was great, with extensive damage to houses rendering 6,000 people homeless in Manchester, 5,000 in Salford and 4,000 in Stretford, by the end of the second attack. Rest Centres were able to cope at all three centres, however, with meals being supplied by Mobile Canteens.

Early in the evening a large number of IBs fell at Morton, a small Lincolnshire village, and other bombs fell at Linton-on-Ouse, Cuffley, Buckfastleigh, Hailsham, Dartford, Deptford, Chislehurst, Kensington, Lambeth, West Ham, Willesden, Henley and Cranage. The Ministry of Home Security reports say nothing, however, of the single very heavy bomb claimed dropped on Portsmouth, but five ships were struck and at least three of them seriously damaged in an attack on shipping in the Firth of Lorne off Oban. Variously reported as one and then two FW 200s, the attacker(s) came down to mast-head height to carry out the bombing after previously dropping flares shortly after 1800 hours.

Unfavourable weather precluded Intruder missions but defensive night patrols were flown by 22 fighters of Nos. 10, 11 and 12 Groups of Fighter Command, resulting in the claimed destruction of an He 111 by a Beaufighter of No. 604 Squadron 50 miles south of Lulworth.

At 1655 hours an He 111H-2 (6N+DL) of 3/KGr100 had taken off from Vannes to attack Manchester. One of the first German bombers to take off, it arrived over Lyme Bay before full darkness had settled and was seen from some distance away by Flight Lieutenant John Cunningham on dusk patrol in a Beaufighter of No. 604 Squadron with Sergeant John Phillipson, AI operator. Cunningham carefully stalked the Heinkel in the afterglow of sunset and finally closed in from behind and below. Upon opening fire a large flash was seen in the belly of the German machine which seemed to disintegrate as it poured out sparks and flames. It slowly rolled over and went down into the clouds below; no one was seen to bale out. Cunningham subsequently claimed the enemy aircraft as 'destroyed' — a fair assumption — but in fact the German pilot, Feldwebel Georg Deininger, managed to regain control of his machine while his crew extinguished the flames and jettisoned a load of burning incendiary bombs.

Deininger and his crew assumed that they had been hit by AA fire from a flak ship. The He 111's starboard engine had failed immediately they were hit, the port engine lost power rapidly and the nose of the aircraft was shattered. Deininger was unhurt, but his three crew members were all slightly wounded by splinters. At the time of the incident the bomber was at 19,500 feet (6,400m) and although the flying controls were damaged — the rudder and ailerons were still working but there was no pitch control through the elevators — Deininger was able to control the aircraft longitudinally by extremely delicate movements of the elevator trimmer. After a short while the port engine also failed completely, but Deininger managed to maintain a southerly course back towards the French coast where he succeeded in making a brilliantly executed 'dead-stick' landing. Ploughing through a wood the He 111's fuselage broke in two and the port wing was torn off, but apart from an injury to the pilot's forehead no further injuries were sustained by the crew. Deininger spent Christmas in hospital at Caen, but received a special commendation from Generalleutnant Kurt Pflugbeil, commanding IV Fliegerkorps, in recognition of his fine airmanship and extraordinary skill. In fact, he had experienced his second brush with the British defences, for only three weeks previously he had successfully landed his flak-damaged aircraft on one wheel.

Some 10,000 rounds were fired by the heavy guns of AA Command at Manchester, the London IAZ, Slough, Brooklands, Birmingham, Bromley, Swansea, Cardiff, Bristol, Portland, Holton Heath, Yeovil, Gloucester, the Solent and Thames and Medway (North and South). Busiest were the guns at Manchester (2,775 rounds) and the IAZ (2,530 rounds against the 43 aircraft which entered the Zone), but no successes were claimed anywhere.

The blast broke windows up to a mile away. Nearly 500 people were rendered homeless and hundreds of private and business premises were damaged. Depending on which account one consults, the death toll was either 13, 18 or 100! Speculation was rife as to the cause of the huge explosion, one rumour being that a plane had crashed with its bomb load aboard. Today this entire area has been cleared and incorporated within the expanded perimeter of the naval base.

The unofficial Christmas truce. In World War I it was a game of football, but a quarter of a century later it was snowballs for the Flak soldiers of the Luftwaffe. Herr Direktor von Boehmer of *Der Adler* loved his montaged covers, this one celebrating 'War Christmas' being by Dr Strache. Very little has appeared in print on the truce, Churchill making no reference to the proposal by Germany. In England on Christmas Day the King broadcast his traditional message: 'This time we are all in the front line and the danger together', adding that 'we have surmounted a grave crisis.'

TUESDAY, DECEMBER 24-25

Sunset: 1653 Sunrise: 0907
Moon: 0447 — Dawn (Last Qtr +3)

No German night bombing operations.

UK — Extensive cloud, base 1-2,000ft. Occasional rain in the East.
The Continent — Similar to the British Isles.

Word reached the British Government via the German Embassy in Washington that attacks on Britain would be suspended over Christmas provided the RAF also refrained from carrying out raids on Germany. No formal agreement was made, but no bomber operations were flown by either side from Christmas Eve until Boxing Day, when the RAF bombed a number of airfields in France. The Luftwaffe retaliated on the night of December 27 with a short but sharp attack on London.

At 1701 hours on Christmas Eve No. 80 Wing's Headache Control reported that there was no indication of impending enemy action, but nevertheless three defensive patrols were flown by Beaufighters. Four tracks of enemy aircraft were plotted by Fighter Command during the night, but the intruders were presumed engaged on weather reconnaissance. No bombs fell anywhere in the UK.

Christmas Eve, December 24, 1940

Jurak, the East Prussian, has confidence in me. On Sunday we were already together 'over there' for the second time. We had started out very early, at 18.33 hours, heading for Manchester, and approached the enemy coast with mixed feelings as it was quite light. But nothing happened, and it was not until we were over London that we were subjected to regular anti-aircraft fire exploding beneath, and were caught twice by the searchlights. But Jurak managed to work his way out as usual.

And yesterday, at about the same time of day, we took off for Manchester again (once more it was still unpleasantly light over the French coast). As we were taxi-ing at the start we had to brake sharply. Aircraft 'K' from 3 Staffel taxied in between us and then took off in our place. We swore loudly at them. During the debriefing after our return from the mission, Jurak complained to the commander that other squadrons had upset the take-off sequence ordered. The commander's terse reply was: 'The "K" aircraft from 3 Staffel which pushed in front of you during taxi-ing was caught in the directional beam while still over the Channel in the dusk, and was shot down by three fighters.' We stood there feeling absolutely stunned. We knew that if that plane had not pushed itself into our place, it would have been us whose number was up. We too had seen these three fighters but we had taken them to be ours . . .

Furthermore, radio navigation over England had become completely impossible. The system was thoroughly jammed. We continued to receive incorrect bearings, often about 90 degrees out. On our return flight, as this had made me uncertain, Jurak said with complete calm: 'We'll soon be landing somewhere in England . . . 'Naturally I protested vigorously, and thought to myself: 'Our dead-reckoning checks can't be completely wrong; to hell with all these doubtful bearings'. And just as we reached the French coast the bearings were again precisely correct . . . For an inexperienced and possibly rather careless crew, it would have been a very dangerous situation.

There was a story going round about the young crew of a Ju 88 which had landed on an illuminated airfield with air traffic in progress. Its navigation lights were switched on, and it rolled to a stop. Suddenly the crew noticed that one of the doors of a hangar had large lettering on it in English. They realised what had happened, rushed frantically across the airfield and took off again. This time they really landed in France. Something similar could have happened to many of our planes which had gone missing without trace.

It is Christmas Eve. We have managed to get hold of a small pine tree and it will be placed on our table this evening, decorated with lighted candles; almost like at home, but only 'almost'. I wonder if my people at home have yet received my long letter?

ROBERT GÖTZ

WEDNESDAY, DECEMBER 25-26

Sunset: 1653 Sunrise: 0907
Moon: 0600 — Dawn (New −3)

No German night bombing operations.

UK — Considerable cloud at 2-4,000ft with light rain in eastern, western and northern coastal areas. Moderate or poor visibility.
The Continent — Extensive cloud with rain in some areas. Visibility moderate to poor inland, good on coasts.

All German offensive operations were suspended in accordance with the unofficial truce.

Reduced operations in observance of the Christmas 'truce' saw only twenty Luftwaffe reconnaissance sorties. One aircraft was shot down by the Fleet Air Arm.

3(F)/22 Junkers Ju 88A (0535). Attacked by Lieutenant L. V. Carver and Sub-Lieutenant T. R. U. Parke in Martlets of No. 804 Squadron Fleet Air Arm during a reconnaissance of Scapa Flow. Made forced landing at Sandwick, Loch Skaie, Orkneys 2.05 p.m. Lt. K. Schipp, Fw. H. Schreiber, Uffz. J. Spörtl and Obergefr. K. Rotter all taken prisoner. Aircraft 4N+AL captured damaged.

THURSDAY, DECEMBER 26-27

Sunset: 1654 Sunrise: 0907
Moon: 0710 — Dawn (New −2)

No German night bombing operations.

UK — Occasional rain in the East with variable amounts of cloud over the entire country at 2-3,000ft.
The Continent — Cloudy, with rain in places.

The lull in German activity continued, but British counter-measures activity continued during the day. At 1015 hours the free balloon barrage (Pegasus) was ordered to operate that night, but cancellation followed. Mutton, too, was required to stand by and subsequently cancelled, as was 'PV One' (a code-name which has not been positively identified, but is believed to refer to the use of flash flares or star shells to illuminate enemy aircraft) which was alerted for the period 2200-0200 hours. In the event two sea reconnaissance flights only were plotted by Fighter Command during the night and two 'special defensive patrols' (presumably in connection with 'PV One') had nothing to report.

In the Christmas issue Herr von Boehmer was seen distributing prizes for the best essay competition, first prize going to Fluglehrer Wilhelm Pachmann of Vienna. The same issue also included a mystery picture — the only clue given was that 'it is not London'. Anyway, even if someone does recognise it, it's too late to enter now!

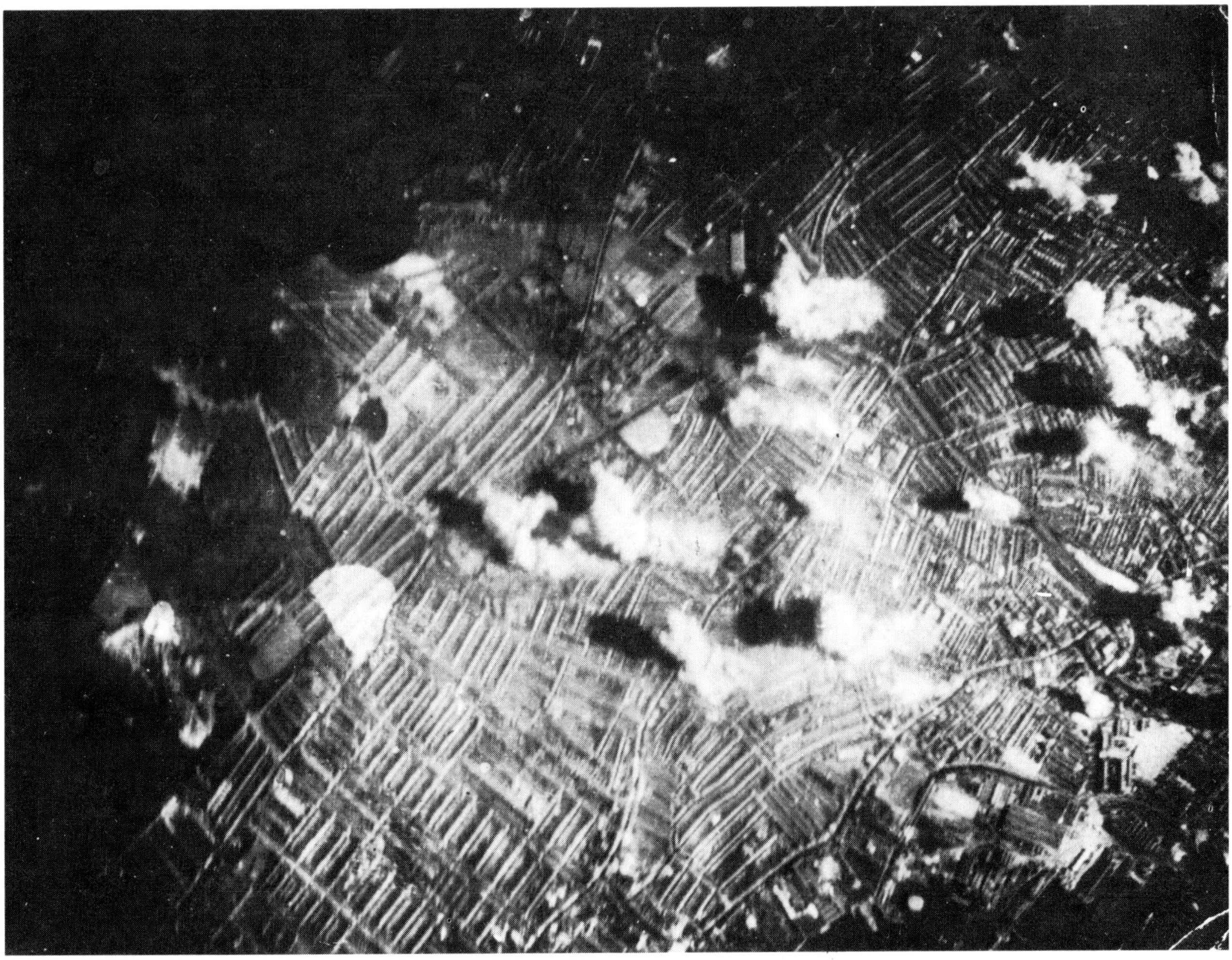

When hostilities resumed after the Christmas break the wheels were set in motion for another Doppelgänger raid . . . and this time the target was London. The Friday attack was spearheaded by Luftflotte 2 with I/KG28 causing particular havoc with mines. Salisbury Square House, home of the London office of the *New York Times*, was damaged in the first raid and finished off in the second.

FRIDAY, DECEMBER 27-28

Sunset: 1655 Sunrise: 0908
Moon: 0812 — Dawn (New −1)

Major attack on London. Small scale night fighter-bomber operations. Minelaying in the Thames Estuary and off Harwich.

UK — Little or no cloud in Scotland, northern England, Wales and south-west England. Elsewhere cloudy, base 2,000-3,000 feet. Visibility moderate to poor inland in England and Wales, good on western and south-western coasts. Winds mainly light, between north and north-west.

The Continent — Low cloud with poor visibility in Holland and Belgium. Variable cloud with moderate visibility in France.

German activity was on a small scale during the day. At 1127 hours, 'Mutton' was instructed to operate between 1900 and 2300 hours, in anticipation of forthcoming enemy night operations, but was cancelled during the afternoon. 'PV One' was also ordered to operate (initially from 2000 to 2130 but later extended to 2230 hours) with 'one aircraft carrying flares, one aircraft bombs'. From this, quoted from the Operations Record Book of Fighter Command, it would appear that the intention was to illuminate and then attempt to 'bomb' the enemy aircraft. 'Pegasus', the free balloon barrage, was also alerted for the night's expected raid which, it was correctly anticipated, was to be made on London.

From 1845 to 2232 hours London was bombed by 108 aircraft of Luftflotten 2 and 3 with, yet again, the Concentration Point in the City and government offices districts. They delivered 111 tonnes of HE (34 SC 1000, 67 SC 500, 116 SC 250, eight LZZ 250 and 254 SC 50) and 328 BSK (11,808 IBs). The first aircraft to bomb was an He 111 of KGr100 using X-Verfahren but visual bombing was carried out by most of the early arrivals of other units. In the course of the attack, however, worsening weather made bombing by DR and radio navigation necessary. Few results could be perceived through the thickening cloud, but a large fire in the East End, another in the west of the City and four along the Thames (thought to be 'in the India Docks') were reported. A large fire area was also made out to the east of Hyde Park with numerous smaller fires elsewhere and, in general, the attack was believed to have been at least moderately successful.

Unusually, Luftflotte 2 played the major rôle, with 60 of its crews reporting over the target against 48 from Luftflotte 3. The latter comprised:

I/KG27: 12 He 111, 2002-2205
I/KG28: 18 He 111, 1926-2010
KGr100 10 He 111, 1845-2005 (opened attack as Beleuchtergrup using X-Verfahren to drop 8,496 B1 El incendiary bombs)
KGr806: 8 Ju 88, 2020-2040

Luftflotte 3 had only 49 aircraft operating because of inclement weather over its bases and of these 48 bombed London and one used Brighton as an alternative. All returned safely but, as expected, bad weather reached western France in the small hours to make landing conditions difficult.

Damage in London and the South-East was unusually serious in proportion to the comparatively small size of the attacking force, with transport and transport depots particulary badly affected. Many buses were damaged in garages at Chelsea, Dalston and Nunhead, as were trams in a depot at New Cross. Railways were damaged at Surrey Docks, Lambeth, Beckenham and Hendon and service mains were particularly badly disrupted at Lambeth. A considerable number of fires resulted and parachute mines, dropped by I/KG28, caused havoc with their tremendous blast effect. The initial casualty list was 141 killed and 455 seriously injured, leaving Londoners in no doubt that the Christmas lull was over; one hit on a shelter in Southwark caused some 50 casualties alone. Altogether some 30 London districts reported incidents and bombs also fell in parts of Kent, Essex and widely over the South-East.

'Pegasus', the free balloon barrage, was launched at 1830 hours to cover an area bounded by Bishop's Stortford – Chatham – Hastings – Tangmere – Reading – Luton – Bishop's Stortford and, in due course, many explosions occurred within this boundary and outside of it. Investigations later showed these to be the explosive devices fitted to Pegasus balloons, a so-called safety device failing to work in very many cases and causing more damage and alarm to the civil population than to the German Air Force. The guns of the IAZ fired 2,975 rounds of HAA ammunition at the 32 Raids plotted within the Zone and countrywide AA Command reported the expenditure of 3,500 rounds. Other sites in action were those at Brooklands, Datchet, Thames and Medway (North and South), Fareham and Harwich. No successes were claimed.

The operation of the free balloon barrage restricted night fighter action to patrols by only nine aircraft, with a further four sent out at dusk. No offensive Intruder patrols were undertaken because of the weather situation and Pegasus was finally concluded at 0440 hours, by which time visibility was poor everywhere with fog in many areas.

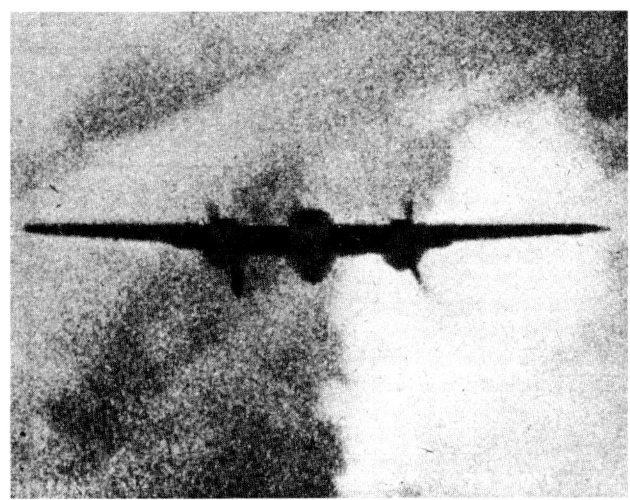

SATURDAY, DECEMBER 28-29

Sunset: 1656 Sunrise: 0908
Moon: None (New Moon)

No major attack but a short raid was made on Plymouth

UK — Fine at first but cloud increasing and lowering in many areas. Visibility mainly good.
The Continent — Low cloud with strong winds but moderate visibility in Holland. Good visibility in France at first, but deteriorating.

Overland and sea reconnaissance flights were carried out during the day by 25 German aircraft. Interception was prevented by widespread fog and cloud but night activity began soon after 1700 hours. The attacking units, comprising KGr100, KG55 and III/KG26, were all correctly identified by the RAF's 'Y' Service which was monitoring German W/T communications with increasing success.
A short, sharp attack was made on Plymouth by 21 of the 24 aircraft sent out by Luftflotte 3. Three crews aborted and the remainder, which attacked the town area between 1837 and 1927 hours, delivered 17 tonnes of HE (one SC 1800, 12 SC 1000, one SC 500 and 12 SC 250) and 347 BSK (12,492 incendiaries). Some crews bombed visually, others by DR and radio navigation, and three large and several smaller fires were started. Good results were anticipated. Taking part were:

KGr100: 9 He 111, 1837-1927 (opened attack, some aircraft using X-Verfahren and others Knickebein)
II/KG55: 9 He 111, 1850-1915 (visual bombing aided by flares)
III/KG26: 3 He 111, 1841-1853 (bombing by Y-Verfahren)

From the foregoing it can be seen that the attack was made by the three night-bombing Beleuchter or Firelighting 'pathfinder' units, with each practicing its own specialist method of attack. Prevailing weather conditions no doubt brought about the decision to use only the three 'crack' units, with the result that never before had so much night attack expertise been brought to bear in an attack concentrated into only 50 minutes. Three crews aborted but all returned safely to their bases. Two night fighters were seen over the English Channel and crews stated that they had met flak of all calibres over Plymouth, but that searchlight activity was trivial and rendered useless by the weather.
Although many fires were started in Plymouth very little damage was done to military or naval installations, but a number of houses, shops, two hospitals and an institution were hit. Casualties were listed as eleven killed and 34 seriously injured. All the fires were extinguished or under control by midnight.
Three night fighters patrolled and two contacts were made with German aircraft but no claims were filed. AA Command ammunition expenditure for the night totalled only some 1,000 rounds and the country was clear of Raids by 2220 hours.

After the impressive victory of David over Goliath in the daylight battles which marked the battle for the command of the air (see page 9), the RAF were agonising over their impotence to counter the Luftwaffe night raids. Except for the odd lucky break, night after night the enemy force had little to fear from British night fighters with only slightly increased odds against being hit by flak. General Pile, commander of AA Command, called the whole period of the night attacks 'essentially a gun battle' and in the last six months of the year the gunners claimed 102 enemy machines destroyed against 35 by night fighters. As reference to this work will show, even these figures were over the top but the ratio of gun kills to those by aircraft continued at the same 3 to 1 ratio during January and February 1941. As if to mitigate the dearth of victories by the RAF, about this time the Air Ministry released a batch of pictures 'enlarged from the film records of recent combats'. These camera gun frames streaked with tracer were almost certainly taken earlier in the summer. Spitfires were equipped with the G42B cine camera gun on a bracket attached to a rib close to the root on the port wing, with exposures being made through a hole in the leading edge. A special sponge rubber ring sealed the gap to prevent the entry of air currents to the wing. The camera was aligned with the gun sights and a combined footage indicator and exposure control mounted in the cockpit.

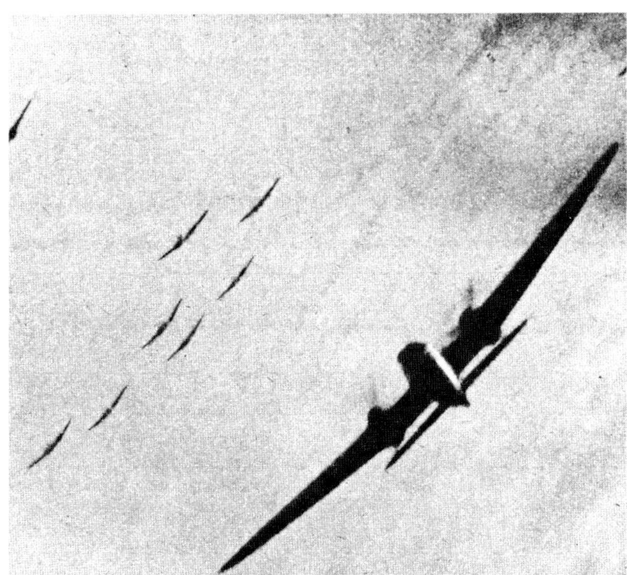

FIRE-STORM!

The most famous picture of all time, used a thousand times to portray the Blitz. Taken by Herbert Mason from the roof of the *Daily Mail*, it is sometimes cropped on the left to centralise St Paul's, thereby losing the spire of St Augustine's — today the entrance to St Paul's Choir School.

Christmas 1940 passed quietly but on December 29 a large raiding-force appeared over London shortly after six o'clock and showered the City — the square mile — with fire bombs and high explosive. All fire stations in the area were swamped with calls and reinforcements were mobilised from the whole of the London Region.

Fires were joining up in the vicinity of St Paul's Cathedral and further serious fires were raging in Gresham Street, St Martin's le Grand, Moorgate and Queen Victoria Street. A fire involving the great warehouses in the Minories was out of hand owing to shortage of water and the famous London Guildhall and the Wren Church of St Lawrence Jewry, nearby, were well alight.

The Thames tide was at an abnormally low ebb when the raid began, making pumping from the river very difficult. Fireboats pulled as close to the banks as possible, their crews wading ashore through thick mud, dragging hose lines to supply the land pumps with water. Many street mains, as usual, had been fractured and with the great demands being made on those still carrying water, supplies were inadequate to control the great fires that were spreading through the heart of London.

The area around St Paul's was among the worst affected and the Prime Minister, appreciating what the cathedral meant to the nation, sent out an instruction that St Paul's, at all costs, was to be saved.

The great jumble of multi-storeyed buildings in the area bounded by Warwick Lane, Newgate Street, Paternoster Square and Ludgate Hill, separated in some places only by narrow alleys, received a deluge of fire bombs. Over three hundred incendiaries a minute were being showered on the City, and the area around St Paul's rapidly became an inferno, with flames bridging the streets in both directions. Debris cascaded into the narrow streets as high explosive bombs ripped buildings apart, exposing the flammable contents to surrounding fire and the non-stop flood of incendiaries. Roads became choked with debris as a deadly barrage of roof tiles, bricks and slabs of masonry rained down, halting the advance of branchmen. They were fighting a losing battle and it became doubtful if firemen, even with unlimited water, could make an impression on the conflagration.

And water was far from unlimited. The mains system was able to provide only a fraction of the water required for firefighting that night, and bombs had reduced that quantity to a trickle. Firemen were forced to rely mainly on water relayed by hose lines from the Thames, a time consuming and laborious operation. The relay teams heaved and sweated, coupling up sections of fire hose and running their fifty-foot lengths along City streets, spurred to superhuman effort by the spectacle of the dome of St Paul's outlined against a background of flame and wreathing smoke.

The flow of precious water came gushing all too slowly into the portable emergency dam that had been erected in St Paul's Churchyard at the top of Cheapside. Pump operators waited impatiently for sufficient depth of water to collect before commencing to pump vital fire streams. Even less patient branchmen, facing a sea of flame with dry branchpipes, were yelling unjustified abuse at members of a relay team who had run themselves to a standstill in providing a link with the Thames and who stood taking a breather before returning to the riverside to do it all over again.

It was a desperate situation calling for skilful placing of the few available jets to make the best use of the water and it was only after long hours of slogging effort that the fiery advance on St Paul's was halted as the flames neared the cathedral threshold.

Picture a fire pump arriving at the job. The officer indicates the area of operations:

'We'll try to stop it there, lads.'

I remember only too well the night of the 29th December, a Sunday night. Shortly after the alert it was obvious that the City was the target for the night. It wasn't long before incendiaries were coming down like rain. Within an hour or so the whole of the City seemed to be lighting up. In the near foreground buildings were blazing furiously and it wasn't long before the Wren church of St Bride's was a mass of flames. The famous wedding-cake steeple was being licked. In the distance through the smoke you could see the fires increasing, and as the evening wore on an artificial wind sprang through the heat caused by the fires, parted the clouds, the buildings in the foreground collapsed, and there revealed in all its majesty was St Paul's, a hauntingly beautiful picture which no artist could recapture. Down below in the street I went towards Ludgate Hill, which was carpeted in hose pipes, a scampering rat here and there, a reeling bird in the flames. The heat became intense as I approached St Paul's Churchyard. Firemen were fighting a losing battle. Pathetically little water was coming from their hoses. Suddenly a fresh supply would come and a hose running riot would lash out and knock firemen from their feet. The heat was so intense that embers were falling like rain and clattering on your helmet. Cheapside was a mass of flames, leaping from one side of the road to the other.

Back at my vantage point on top of the ***Daily Mail*** *building, where I was, I could see that this night I was going to obtain the picture which would for ever record the Battle of Britain. After waiting a few hours the smoke parted like the curtain of a theatre and there before me was this wonderful vista, more like a dream, not frightening — there were very few high explosives. It was obvious that this was going to be the second Great Fire of London. The tragedy of this second great fire of London was the fact that there were so few fire-watchers. Single handed I could have prevented thousands of pounds' worth of damage being done, but the buildings were locked, there was nobody present to force an entry. There were so few people. It was pathetic.*

HERBERT MASON
DECEMBER 1940

The multitude of narrow streets and alleys of the City, just as in 1666, served to hamper efforts at firefighting and hasten the spread of the flames in the Second Great Fire of London. This is Amen Court close to St Paul's Churchyard.

The pump is set in to a street fire hydrant and the operator crosses his fingers and prays that the mains will hold out, at least until the inevitable water relay arrives. The crew run out a line of hose along the street and two firemen work their way towards the target, clambering over heaps of debris and slithering on fragments of plate-glass from shattered windows. As they proceed they splash their jet about, dousing smaller areas of flame as they advance shoulder to shoulder, arms linked as they share the strain of the kicking branch. Their heads are bowed to protect faces from the blistering heat and stinging sparks, searing embers and hot ash swirling about the street, driven by the fierce winds that always accompany a conflagration. A crew mate lends a hand, easing the cumbersome line of hose over the debris, avoiding snags and kinks.

The thump of falling incendiaries impels them to hunch their shoulders in the hope of reducing the target area of their bodies, for the eyewitness account of the screaming fireman in Pennington Street, Shadwell, with an incendiary bomb embedded in his back, is vivid in their minds. Despite the heat they take a quick squint aloft, on the lookout for collapsing walls or falling coping stones. They know that their officer will keep an eye open for such hazards but he now has several crews to watch over and a large area to supervise. What was it they taught us in the drill class? 'One hand for yourself and one for the ship. Keep your eyes peeled.'

They cry out with pain as glowing embers, driven by the mini-cyclone, fly under the brim of their steel helmets and settle on an ear, the neck or in an eye. But most stick it out unless badly injured, for they know that the fire will engulf them if they let up and few reserves are available if they quit.

Many were the deeds of heroism performed that night. Brave deeds observed were reported and rewarded but there were many that escaped notice in the widespread horror and destruction. It was a battle for the city and for personal survival.

As men fought the fires the enemy made the most of a well-lit target. Incendiary and high explosive bombs fell without pause; the heat was intense and buildings across wide streets were ignited by radiated heat from fires opposite.

The Moorgate area presented a fearsome spectacle. Flames roared from buildings on a broken front extending over hundreds of yards, reaching westward along Fore Street and threatening to join up with fire raging around Whitbread's brewery, between Chiswell and Redcross Streets.

Fire crews early on the scene found water available in the mains and their jets were soon at work, checking the spread. But pressure began to drop as more and more pumps were set in and the jets lost their punch. The issue was decided when vital mains carrying water to the hydrants were shattered by HE bombs.

It was a situation akin to an infantry

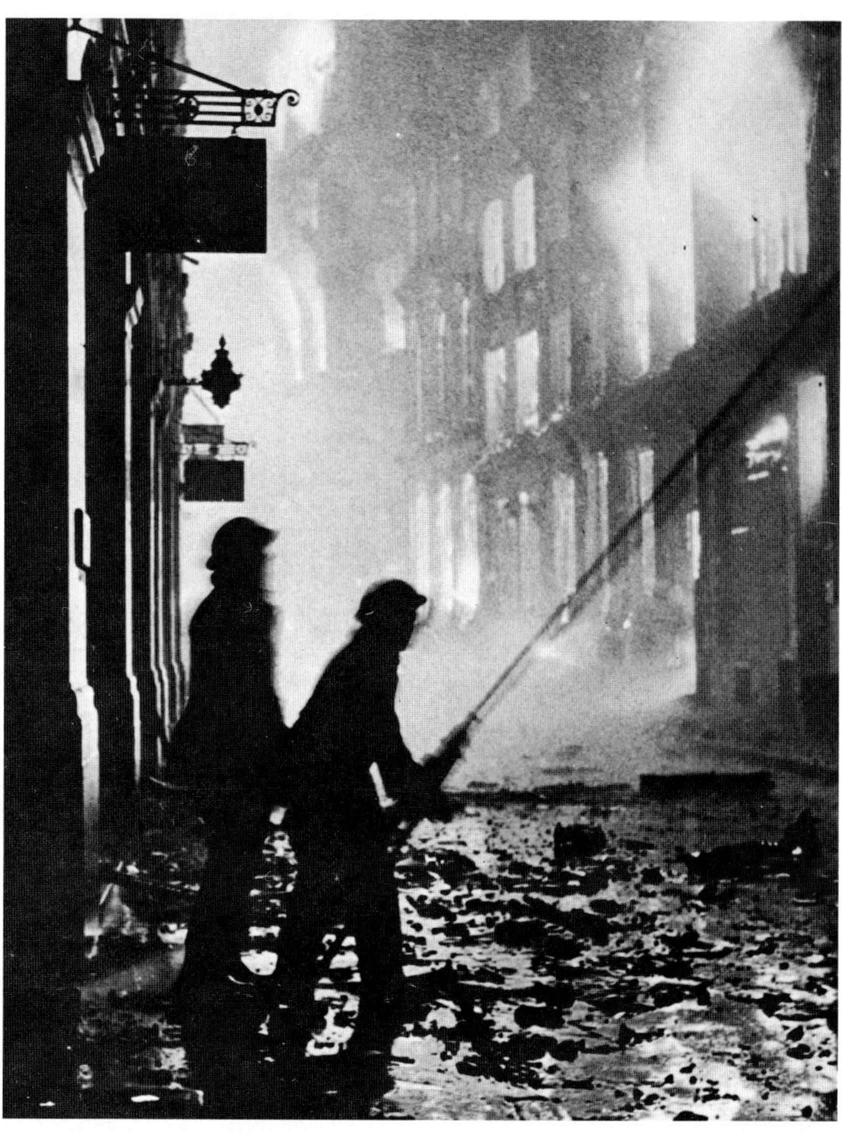

Ave-Maria Lane: how totally inadequate the firefighters must have felt when faced with walls of flame against which their pathetic jets could make no impression.

Purged in fire and flame: out of the old cometh forth the new.

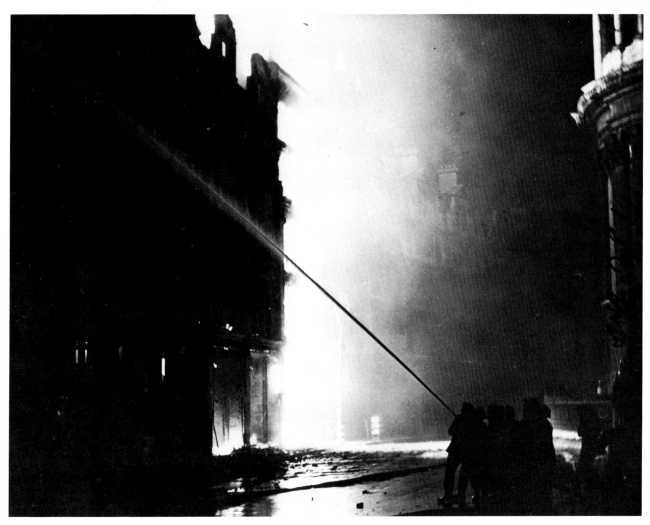

Old Change as seen from St Paul's Churchyard. The cathedral is visible in the reflected glare on the right.

battalion running out of ammunition in the midst of a heavy enemy attack. There was only one course of action to be taken in such circumstances: retreat. Firemen watched helplessly, impatiently awaiting the arrival of water relay crews as flames clawed out unhindered to embrace adjoining buildings.

The atmosphere was stifling. A shrivelling blast carried sparks and glowing embers to every corner of the street, sweeping them high into the air as the fire wind gathered strength. Firemen, deprived of the protection of their jets, found breathing painfully difficult and were forced back to positions where the air temperature permitted them to fill their lungs freely without searing the air passages.

St Giles Church, Cripplegate, enveloped in flames, threatened Redcross Street Fire Station from across the street. The whole of Jewin Street adjoining the church and the buildings beyond, reaching back to Aldersgate Street, were doomed. Nothing could be done to save them, for great heaps of debris blocked access to the stricken area even if sufficient water had been available to enable firemen to force entry between the blazing office blocks.

Men in Whitecross Street faced a formidable task. Flames leapt from building to building, racing past fire crews whose puny jets were absorbed and turned to steam as they strove to cut off the spread. A difficult fire situation became an impossible one and the men, with no other escape route available, were forced to abandon their fire appliances and flee for their lives, escaping to safety through an underground railway tunnel.

West Ham, for a change, had been by-passed, but the local firemen did not expect to be given a night off. The pattern of operations was the familiar one, only the venue was changed. The Luftwaffe's radio navigational beam was not intersected over the Royal

The second most famous picture of the Blitz, also of — or rather from — St Paul's. The view is looking north-west with Paternoster Square in the foreground. To the German bomber crews the scene below resembled 'bubbling pea soup' as each new load of bombs and incendiaries fuelled the spreading conflagration.

Docks, where it had been aimed almost continuously for nearly three months, but over the City, five miles to the west.

Eric Earl, officer in charge of Stratford Fire Station, had been standing by fully rigged since the moment the red alert had been received. It was his experience that there would be but a short pause between the wall of the sirens and the scream of falling bombs. But tonight there was an uneasy wait before the alarm bells shrilled and a firewoman came running with the attendance slip.

'Come on, me lads,' shouted Eric to the crew. 'We're ordered to Whitechapel Fire Control.'

The pump was quickly on its way along Stratford High Street towards the fires that were lighting up the western sky. An anti-aircraft battery in Victoria Park opened up at the invisible enemy as the pump reached Bow Church, the shells bursting directly overhead. The crew firmed their helmets and the driver crouched a little lower over his wheel as the shrapnel came whanging down, rattling on roofs and pavements and striking sparks from granite kerbs.

The Mile End Road loomed ahead, illuminated in patches by fires on both sides of the road and by incendiaries burning harmlessly on the surface. A warning jangle on the bell as they overtake a Civil Defence rescue squad on their errand of mercy, to dig some unfortunate family from the ruins of its home.

At Whitechapel Fire Control they were ordered on to Leadenhall Street to deal with fires burning on the upper floors of office blocks. All West Ham fire appliances were equipped with hose reels, supplied initially with water from an inbuilt sixty gallon tank. It is surprising what can be done with such a relatively small quantity of water in the hands of an experienced crew and Station Officer Earl and his men extinguished several fires, forcing entrance doors and racing up flights of stairs as they progressed along Leadenhall Street. There was no water in the street mains but the crew replenished the hose reel tank from emergency dams in the district. Around eight o'clock they were busy filling the tank from the emergency dam on the forecourt of Adelaide House, a large office block on the northern approach to London Bridge. A number of trailer pumps were at work and one glance told the station officer that water was being taken from the dam faster than it was being put in by pumps lifting water from the river at Freshwater Quay, where the Thames had been dredged to allow coastal steamers to berth at all stages of the tide. This was one of the few situations from which pumps could be set into the river that night.

Earl ran down the steps leading to Fish Street Hill to do what he could to improve the situation. He spotted two trailer pumps and directed their crews to the quay. The suctions were quickly connected and lowered into the murky stream whilst other members of the crew laid lines of hose to be hoisted up over the London Bridge balustrade. The new supply came gushing into the dam and the surface of the water began to rise.

A motor cycle came screeching to a halt and a London Fire Brigade Superintendent stepped from the pillion seat.

'Pump and crew from Stratford, sir, Station Officer Earl in charge.'

'My name's Dann,' replied the Super. 'Where are you pumping to?'

'Anywhere there's a fire, sir.'

'Good man. Tell you what I want you to do. We've got a serious situation in Moorgate and a shortage of water. Get a relay working along King William Street and I'll organise it from there. I'll keep in touch.'

'Very good, sir,' replied Earl as the Super mounted his pillion seat and roared off.

At that moment another West Ham pump drew up, Station Officer Percy Smither in charge.

'Just the bloke I'm looking for,' said Earl. 'We've got to get a relay working to Moorgate, Perce. You lay a twin line along King William Street, over there, and I'll supply you from this dam.'

'Right,' replied Smither and the officers ran off to detail their crews. Four more pumps would be required to complete the relay to Moorgate; Superintendent Dann would be supervising

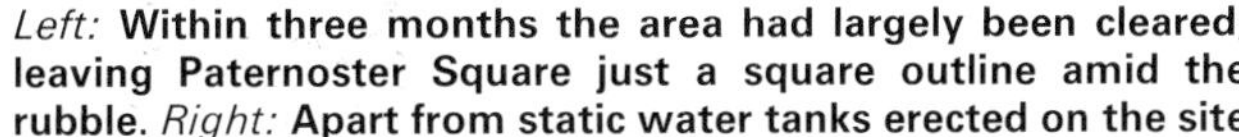

Left: **Within three months the area had largely been cleared, leaving Paternoster Square just a square outline amid the rubble.** *Right:* **Apart from static water tanks erected on the site later in 1941, the square remained 'open plan' until redeveloped with the sprawling £9 million development completed in 1964. The square itself is now elevated, with a car park below.**

Left: **September 1929;** *right:* **January 1941. The ancient thoroughfare of Paternoster Row, named after the Pater Nosters — the makers of rosary beads — who were originally based there before the Reformation, disappeared in the rebuilding.**

the work, spacing the pumps the regulation seven hundred feet apart. Earl and Smither soon had the hose laying under way and good progress was made despite the rough going created by the debris-strewn streets.

With the centre of London in danger of becoming a huge conflagration with two thousand pumps and some nine thousand firemen at work, the firefighters were dumbfounded but delighted to hear the All Clear sound before midnight. They could not believe that the Nazis would fail to make the most of such a prominent target; indeed, it was their intention to do so. That they did not was due to fog on the Channel Coast, grounding their aircraft.

The All-Clear brought relief from the bombardment but no diminution of the urgency of the situation. Fires were still spreading and much more water would be required to surround the conflagration area. None of the firefighters could relax.

'Keep it going,' yelled Superintendent Dann from his motor cycle. 'We're well past the Bank.'

And so the work continued throughout the night. More pumps on the streets supplying more lines of hose; more pumps at the riverside feeding the dam until twelve lines of hose carried water to the pumps fighting the Moorgate conflagration from this single point. And a small boost to the firemen's morale; the tide was coming in, allowing more pumps to gain access to water from the riverside.

But not all the water from the Adelaide House dam was being pumped to Moorgate. Several trailer pumps were supplying water for fighting smaller outbreaks in Gracechurch Street, Eastcheap and Lower Thames Street, where tenacious crews laboured to prevent isolated fires from merging to reach major proportions.

Dawn was breaking as a canteen van arrived at Adelaide House and never was a cup of tea and a biscuit more gratefully accepted by grimy, weary and smoke-dried firemen, now becoming painfully aware of their inflamed eyes and the burns, cuts and bruises accumulated during the night's action. Some sat on the kerbside, emptying water from

The view looking in the opposite direction, December 30, 1940. By August 1943 it was just another typical City bomb-site.

While all around is a smoking ruin, the Scales of Justice stand out almost symbolically on the dome of the Central Criminal Court. The following day when Churchill visited the City he was met with the cry: 'When are we going to give it back to them?'

their fireboots and nursing blistered feet, chafed and raw after hours of clambering over heaps of masonry.

The usual Monday morning trek of commuters across London Bridge began. The laconic BBC broadcast, of course, gave no hint of the target nor of the damage done. Listeners to the early morning news heard the by now familiar bulletin:

'Enemy aircraft attacked towns in the south of England during the night causing some damage. Fires were started and casualties have been reported.'

The crowds of city workers emerging from London Bridge railway station saw evidence of the night's activity in the station precincts and the buildings around Guy's Hospital but they were unprepared for the sight that met their eyes as they crossed the bridge. Many were moved to tears as they gazed at the scene of destruction, with its background of flame and smoke rising, it seemed, from the whole of the city. They picked their way through streets littered with debris and jagged fragments of plate glass; squeezed past bomb craters and stepped over a tangle of fire hoses only to find a heap of smoking rubble instead of the office building they expected to occupy. Others were unable to approach their workplace, for firemen were still heavily engaged in putting out the flames. But those that could set to work clearing broken glass and tidying furniture tossed about by bomb blast before attending to the day's correspondence, miraculously delivered by the GPO.

Some of the workers were so affected by the plight of the firemen that they took sandwiches from their cases and offered them to the exhausted men in the only practical gesture of support they could make.

Considering the weight of the attack, the number of buildings demolished and the rapid spread of fire stoked by the thousands of incendiary bombs dropped by the enemy, it is not surprising that casualties were heavy. One hundred and sixty civilians were killed, five hundred were injured. Sixteen firemen died, more than two hundred and fifty were seriously injured and many others with minor injuries were allowed home after treatment.

CYRIL DEMARNE, 1986

SUNDAY, DECEMBER 29-30

Sunset: 1657 Sunrise: 0908
Moon: Dusk — 1811 (New +1)

All the paraphernalia of the night's battle greeted office workers as they made their way to their desks on Monday morning. This is Farringdon Street with trailer pumps working from an emergency 5,000 gallon capacity tank being constantly topped up with water pumped from the Thames at Blackfriars.

Major attack on London.

UK — Fair, becoming cloudy in the London area by dawn. Visibility moderate to poor.

The Continent — Fresh to strong westerly wind with lowering cloud bringing rain and drizzle. Visibility poor to moderate.

German daylight activity was almost exclusively reserved for attacks on shipping but no damage was caused. During the day 'Mutton' was laid on for operation between 1900 and 2100 hours with 'PV One' required between 2000 and 2230. London seemed the likely target and this was confirmed shortly after enemy night activity started at 1720 with the first Raids tracking in to the Capital from the direction of the Channel Islands and Cherbourg.

Between 1817 and 2130 hours 136 bombers (107 of Luftflotte 3 and 29 of Luftflotte 2) attacked the City and government area of London with 127 tonnes of HE (32 SC 1000, two Flam 500, 65 SC 250, 36 LZZ 250 and 280 SC 50) and 613 BSK (22,068 IBs). Throughout the attack — which was compressed to ensure that aircraft were back at base before the arrival of bad landing conditions — large breaks in the cloud permitted many crews to bomb visually and few had to make use of DR or radio navigation methods. In some cases crews were able to make use of existing fires as aiming points.

The attack was opened by KGr100, using X-Verfahren to place 10,470 incendiaries into the City with astonishing results. By the time the last KGr100 crew bombed at 1850 hours they could see 54 fires, 17 of them very large, along both banks of the Thames in Target Area 'Otto', their assigned objective. Towards the end of the attack more than 100

'The whole bloody town's lit up!' were the words of one fireman on duty on the night of Sunday, December 29 who viewed the inferno engulfing the City from the vantage point of his turntable ladder over the Barbican. This is Wood Street as seen from London Wall on Monday morning as firemen negotiate a sea of rubble which hindered further their efforts to clear up. The only common identifying feature which is immediately recognisable in both photographs is the tower of St Alban's Church, which survives on an island site in the middle of the road.

Naturally the Press made great play of the destruction wrought to the City's historic buildings, especially to its Wren churches of which eight were destroyed or badly damaged. ***Above:*** **Of St Vedast in Foster Lane only the steeple survived, the interior being left a charred ruin** ***(below)*****. During the rebuilding a replacement reredos was found, which once adorned the long-demolished St Christopher-le-Stocks; a font came from St Anne and St Agnes, which itself suffered in the raid; the pulpit was the one which formerly stood in All Hallows, Bread Street, demolished in 1876, and an organ from another extinct City church, St Bartholomew-by-the-Exchange.**

continuously expanding fire areas could be seen, with thick black smoke obstructing vision to the extent that the explosions of bombs could no longer be made out. Especially good results were anticipated, with crews little troubled by ineffective flak and feeble searchlight activity. Only one night fighter was seen and that failed to attack. Luftflotte 3's participating units were:

III/KG27: 10 He 111, 1914-1955
I/KG28: 7 He 111, 1843-1919 (bombload given as 14 'heaviest bombs' but almost certainly 14 LMB parachute mines)
KGr100: 10 He 111, 1817-1850 (Beleuchtergruppe operation to mark Target Area with fires)
KGr606: 9 Do 17, 1835-1850
I/KG51: 8 Ju 88, 1830-1935
II/KG51: 9 Ju 88, 1853-1935
III/KG51: 9 Ju 88, 1931-1950
I/KG54: 7 Ju 88, 1952-2032
II/KG54: 6 Ju 88, 2036-2126
KGr806: 6 Ju 88, 1945-2045
KG1: 11 He 111, 8 Ju 88, 1820-1915
III/KG26: 7 He 111, 1853-1945

Two aircraft of Luftflotte 3 aborted and a Ju 88 of II/KG51 crashed on landing.

This is Wallbrook with, on the left, St Stephen's — another of Wren's great masterpieces with its experimental dome.

St Mary-le-Bow — the Bow Bells church — (see page 83), an empty shell after the raid, was rebuilt between 1956 and 1964.

St Mary Aldermanbury stood on the corner of Love Lane and Aldermanbury. A church of this name had existed here since the twelfth century up until 1965 when the ruined shell was dismantled stone by stone and transported for re-erection at Westminster College, Fulton, Missouri, as a memorial to Churchill and his historic speech there in 1946. The site, now an open space, still contains the bases of the original twelve Corinthian columns, and part of the lower courses.

St Lawrence Jewry, seen here in 1946. When it caught fire, sparks and embers showered across and set the Guildhall ablaze.

'The Great Fire of London. The Hun Sky Vandal does his job! Another famous Wren church, St Bride's, Fleet Street, blazing furiously — a study by the light of fire.' Original caption as passed by the censor — but ironically not until May 8, 1941, just two days before the City was devastated again.

This night's attack, one of the most spectacular of the war, was to become known as The Second Great Fire of London but it was, in fact, a holocaust on a much greater scale than that which 'fired much of the City of London' in the reign of King Charles II. Six enormous conflagrations engulfed most of this ancient square-mile, destroying the Guildhall and eight Wren Churches. Many historic buildings disappeared in the course of a few hours and the catalogue of destruction was breathtaking. Guy's Hospital had to be evacuated and eight other hospitals were damaged; the Central Telegraph Office was

The 'Wedding Cake' church (it is believed that the tiering was adopted by a Ludgate Hill baker in the eighteenth century, beginning a tradition which continues to this day) was restored to the designs of Godfrey Allen.

In Queen Victoria Street, the seventh of Wren's creations struck that night, St Andrew's-by-the-Wardrobe, lay derelict until it was restored by Marshall Sisson in the late 1950s. These pictures from 1956 and 1988.

Unlike Berlin, which has adopted as its permanent reminder of its wartime dead the ruined Gedächtniskirche on the Kurfürstendamm, London has no monument or memorial to remember the thousands killed in the Blitz. Nearly half of all those who lost their lives in enemy bombing in Britain did so in the Capital — almost 30,000. To our way of thinking, Christ Church, at the junction of Newgate Street and Holborn Viaduct, abandoned since 1940, should be our memorial. We commend the idea to our City fathers, who purchased it in 1962.

demolished and the modern Wood Street telephone exchange building was burnt out, inflicting the worst blow of the war on a telecommunications establishment. With the Thames at a low ebb, fire boats could do little to help the shore-based firemen and many riverside fires had to be abandoned. Railway and Underground traffic was greatly disrupted and the closing of five rail termini and 16 Underground system stations added to the difficulties. Some of the dock installations were also seriously damaged and for some time the working of the Port of London was affected. Casualties were 163 persons killed and 509 injured, many of these occurring as a result of incidents in the East End, where extensive damage was caused to houses, and the Millwall, Victoria and London Docks. Almost beyond belief, St Paul's Cathedral, although ringed by fire, escaped virtually unscathed.

In addition to the bombs on many districts of London, further incidents were reported from Romford, near Chelmsford, Tunbridge Wells, Bromley and Croydon.

The most grievous blow — materially — took place right alongside the church in Newgate Street when the GPO's Central Telegraph Office received a direct hit. Not only that but three City telephone exchanges in the new building in Wood Street were knocked out. It was the worst blow to Britain's telecommunications network during the war as the Headquarters of the PABX, and the hundreds of repeaters for circuits passing through Faraday Building, were also lost.

The building was linked by an overhead bridge across Angel Street with GPO North — the building further down St Martin's-le-Grand which housed various departments of the Postmaster General. ***Left:*** **This shot was taken in 1935 with the building decorated for the Jubilee celebrations for King George V.** ***Right:*** **After December 29, 1940 the top four floors were dismantled and a temporary roof added.**

Speculation was rife at the time that the Luftwaffe was inclined to launch its major attacks on Sunday nights when the military and Civil Defence services might well be less alert and when, almost certainly, the central districts of the big cities would be devoid of their normal weekday working population. Thus, fires started in the depopulated districts were more likely to gain hold. No evidence has been found to substantiate this supposition, but it is certainly true that major attacks were made on six of the seven Sunday nights that had passed since the Night Blitz opened on November 14. And on the seventh of them, the attack had failed to reach the 'major' classification (100 tonnes of HE) by a mere six tonnes (against Sheffield on the night of December 15-16). Certainly the experience of this latest attack, and that gained in several other recent attacks, led to a review of existing firefighting methods and stressed the need to have all premises guarded against the possibility of firebomb attacks at all times.

The by now famous 'London Barrage' — music to the ears of Londoners even if no great threat to the Luftwaffe — was in action from 1812 to 2200 hours and again, firing at individual aircraft, from 2320 to 2335. In all, the guns of the IAZ fired 2,800 rounds at targets flying from 9,000 to 25,000 feet. Other sites engaging enemy aircraft were those at Thames and Medway (North and South), Slough, the Solent, Portsmouth and the Isle of Wight. Altogether 4,000 rounds were fired but no enemy aircraft were claimed destroyed.

Further repairs took place soon after the war and the remaining two stories — one of central London's most war-torn buildings — combined to serve as the Central Telegraph Office until 1967. A new £16 million building was erected for British Telecom on the site in the early 1980s. ***(See also Volume 1, page 105.)***

And the most historic building to be struck that night must be the Guildhall. Built between 1411–30, it was damaged in the first Great Fire and restored partly by Sir Christopher Wren. In the second fire it lost its roof, the picture on the *right* being taken in February 1941 after the debris had been cleared.

From 1941 to 1953 it was covered by a temporary roof of steel and asphalt slabs until Sir Giles Scott carried out his proposals to build a new roof with the stone arches strengthened with hidden steel. The Justice Rooms (on the left in the 1940 picture) were demolished in 1969 to enlarge Guildhall Yard, whilst the Art Gallery (on the right), also badly damaged in the 1940 raid, still remains today as it was then; neglected but with no firm decision as to its future.

Twenty-nine fighters flew patrols, including a 'Mutton' aircraft of No. 93 Squadron (which took off from Middle Wallop but was recalled at 1946 hours) and a Blenheim Intruder. The latter returned to Ford at 2023 hours having seen nothing over northern France where the cloud was solid between 5,000 and 8,000 feet with very poor, deteriorating visibility underneath. The problems of the night fighters (eleven of which patrolled over the east side of London) were compounded on this occasion by a breakdown of communications which put the radar stations at Dover, Rye, Dunkirk and Pevensey out of service. Some came back into operation before the attack ended, using public telephone lines, but the 'black-out' on a main approach line to London created even more difficulties for the hard pressed and frustrated defenders. Several contacts were made by night fighters, but no combats ensued.

MONDAY, DECEMBER 30-31

Sunset: 1657 Sunrise: 0908
Moon: Dusk — 1918 (New +2)

No German night bombing operations.

UK — Extensive cloud at 1,500-2,500ft, lowering to 1,000ft in precipitation. Moderate visibility.
The Continent — Low cloud with particularly poor visibility in northern France.

All operations were cancelled because of the generally adverse weather conditions, particularly on the Continent. No enemy aircraft were plotted by Fighter Command, but No. 10 Group ordered two night fighters to patrol for part of the night.

I am a neutral reporter. I have watched the people of London live and die ever since death in its most ghastly garb began to come here as a nightly visitor. I have watched them stand by their homes. I have seen them made homeless. I have seen them move to new homes. And I can assure you that there is no panic, no fear, no despair in London town; there is nothing but determination, confidence and high courage among the people of Churchill's Island.

It is true that the Nazis will be over again tomorrow night and the night after that and every night. They will drop thousands of bombs and they'll destroy hundreds of buildings and they'll kill thousands of people. But a bomb has its limitations. It can only destroy buildings and kill people. It cannot kill the unconquerable spirit and courage of the people of London.

London can take it!

QUENTIN REYNOLDS
LONDON CAN TAKE IT
CROWN FILM UNIT, 1940

HEAVY RESCUE

The Town Clerk, Arthur Roche, was appointed Air Raid Precautions Officer for the City of London and established his headquarters in the Guildhall. The Rescue, Shoring and Demolition Section, later renamed the Heavy Rescue Squad, came under the City Engineer, to whom I was responsible. None of us had much idea what was expected of us in the early days but the picture became clearer when the Home Office Civil Defence Training Syllabus was issued and we commenced training.

We had been allocated five depots in the City; my headquarters were set up in the basement at Ibex House in the Minories. We had ample tools and equipment, distributed at the various depots, and our labour force consisted of ten gangs of eight men and a leader. The men had been drawn mainly from building labourers in the East End, a rough and ready lot but nearly all good and loyal workers. We worked alternate shifts of twenty-four hours on duty and twenty-four off. None knew when the air raids would start so the training periods were hectic until the specific subjects had been dealt with. Then it was practise, practise and more practise until we felt confident of being able to face up to anything necessary in our particular field.

The City Corporation had equipped the Heavy Rescue Squad with a number of old Albion chain-drive lorries which proved ideal for demolition work. We just ran a steel cable round the masonry and hitched it up to the lorry. The specialist carpenters attached to our section cut shores, usually timber joists 9in by 3in, according to the requirements of the particular building, on site, and we supported weakened floors of buildings with 'Acrows' — adjustable metal supports.

We read newspaper reports of the air raids on Warsaw and Rotterdam and realised what we had let ourselves in for; at least, we thought we did, but nobody can possibly imagine what it's like to be bombed until he's actually heard the bombs screaming down all around and come face to face with the results.

The worst night of the war, so far as the City is concerned, came on the night of December 29, 1940, when about 300 German bombers delivered a heavy attack on the 'Square Mile'. Some high explosive bombs were dropped but it was mainly incendiaries that rained down without pause for about five hours. Everywhere there were raging fires; six floor office blocks and warehouses, blazing from top to bottom. Walls and coping stones were crashing down, filling the narrow streets with debris. Firemen were shouting warnings to each other — 'Watch that wall!' or 'Look out over there!' There were some hoses working but many water mains had been hit and the pumps were taking what water there was from the emergency dams. There was nowhere near enough water to deal with all those fires, and still the fire bombs showered over the City.

Even after the Luftwaffe had returned to their bases, the explosions continued to reverberate across the City as Royal Engineers' demolition squads began work. Here a 40lb charge of guncotton drops an unsafe building in Newgate Street.

I was called to a serious incident at the rear of the *Daily Express* building in Fleet Street. A group of large buildings were blazing and one had collapsed, burying eight firemen under a great heap of debris. The Rescue Squad leader was faced with a terrible problem. It was obvious that it would take hours of work by several gangs to make any impression on that enormous pile of rubble and the men would be in constant danger from other collapsing buildings as they worked. I could not imagine that any of those firemen could possibly be alive under that pile of bricks and mortar so I told the leader to call off his men. It was a very difficult decision to make but there was no point in risking further casualties.

I decided to report this serious incident to Control. No telephones were working so I set out to walk to the Guildhall, normally about a fifteen minute journey but it took me an hour. Many of the streets were impassable due to fires, debris and bomb craters and I had to make several detours. When I reached the Guildhall, I saw that it, too, was alight and surrounded by fires including St Lawrence Jewry and the Church of St Mary the Virgin in Love Lane, both built by Sir Christopher Wren after the Great Fire of London in 1666. The Guildhall Control had been evacuated and the staff transferred to the Secondary Control in the basement of the City Police HQ in Old Jewry. I reported the *Daily Express* incident and set out to do what I could elsewhere.

We had a depot in the City of London Boys' School where I was told that seven separate showers of incendiaries had fallen on Sion College, The Temple and on buildings in the vicinity of John Carpenter Street. The All Clear sounded before midnight, much to our relief for we thought the raid would continue throughout the night; what the outcome would have been if it had I just can't imagine. Although the bombers had gone there was still plenty for us to do and we were kept busy for several days demolishing dangerous walls and shoring up others, clearing debris to open up streets to pedestrians and traffic and, of course, searching heaps of debris for persons reported missing.

HARRY ANDERSON, 1984

More Of A Pal Than Ever

SHERLEY'S
TONIC AND CONDITION POWDERS

Daily Mail

FOR KING AND EMPIRE

LATE WAR NEWS SPECIAL

Cycle Accessories LIGHTWEIGHT FEATHERWEIGHT NOWEIGHT Bluemel's

NO. 13,941 TUESDAY, DECEMBER 31, 1940 ONE PENNY

Hitler Planned Monday Swoop

London was to Blaze First

By NOEL MONKS, Daily Mail Air Correspondent

HITLER meant to start the second Great Fire of London as the prelude to an invasion.

This was the belief held in well-informed quarters in London yesterday.

WAR'S GREATEST PICTURE: St. Paul's Stands Unharmed in the Midst of the Burning City

America Moves

BIG ARMS FLOW HAS BEGUN

From Daily Mail Correspondent

New York, Monday.

THE United States Defence Commission announced to-day that they had approved arms contracts worth £1,000,000,000.

Monthly production had now risen to 2,400 aircraft engines, 700 warplanes, 100 tanks, and 10,000 automatic rifles.

LATEST

MORE U.S. AID FOR GREECE

ADMIRAL LEAHY REACHES EUROPE

HAVOC COULD HAVE BEEN SAVED

By Daily Mail Reporter

MANY of Sunday night's fires in the City of London could have been avoided if fire-watching regulations had been properly observed.

That is the opinion of Commander A. N. G. Firebrace, the London Fire Brigade chief, who has just been transferred to the Home Office to help in organising local brigade duties through the country.

Even on Sundays

'Spain to Fortify Canary Islands'

Berlin Radio Went 'All Quiet'

Four Raiders in Pacific'

100 to 1 Backing for Roosevelt

From Daily Mail Correspondent

WASHINGTON, Monday.

PRESIDENT ROOSEVELT is "tremendously pleased" at the reaction to his speech, in which he pledged more aid to Britain and declared that the Axis could not win the war.

End of Hitler

China Seeks U.S. Planes

500 Were Killed in Manchester

Churchill Sees London's Ruins

Morrison on Radio To-night

Nummer 4 23. Januar 1941

Berliner Illustrierte Zeitung

50. Jahrgang Preis 20 Pfennig

Copyright 1941 by Deutscher Verlag, Berlin

Die City von London brennt!

Rund um die St. Pauls Kathedrale prasseln die Flammen zum nächtlichen Winterhimmel empor. F. F. Bauer

Dicke Rauchwolken verhüllen die ungeheuren Zerstörungen, die der Angriff der Luftwaffe auf die City in der Nacht zum 30. Dezember anrichtete. Es war die größte Feuersbrunst, die London seit dem vernichtenden Brand der City im Jahre 1666 erlebte. Von den Bauten, die nicht unter der Wucht der Bomben einstürzten, blieb fast bei allen nur die äußere Schale übrig. Das Weiß der Kuppeln und Türme war am nächsten Morgen geschwärzt von Rauch und Ruß. Tage nach dem Angriff noch mußten Pioniere und Feuerwehrmänner die Mauerreste sprengen und so die Einsturzgefahr bannen. Die City, der Sitz der britischen Hochfinanz, brennt nieder.

TUESDAY, DEC. 31–JANUARY 1

Sunset: 1659 Sunrise: 0908
Moon: Dusk — 2025 (New +3)

No German night bombing operations.

UK — Generally cloudy with snow in central and eastern districts. Visibility moderate, poor in snow.

The Continent — Much low cloud with snow in many areas.

Adverse weather conditions on both sides of the Channel effectively halted all air activity over Britain.

***To date,* the 'war's greatest picture'. So said the *Mail* in their Tuesday morning edition; Berliners had to wait until January 23 to see the same photograph in their 'local' on their Früstück tables. Meanwhile on the bases, snow led to further operations being temporarily abandoned.**

A rather remarkable comparison to end a remarkable year in Britain's history. *Above:* **Taken by the City of London Police from Apothecary Street; we are looking north towards Ludgate Hill on which the double deckers are running. Although undated, it is most probably later in the war as the flooding of basements to provide emergency water supplies came a little later.** *Below:* **Except for the give-away motor cars, a foreground almost unchanged in 45 years!**

1548

THE HAVOC OF THE VANDALS IN LONDON

At dusk on the evening of Sunday, December 29, the Nazis launched their most vicious attack on the City of London. There was no pretence that a single target was of any military importance. Ten thousand incendiary bombs were rained down on the City in a deliberate attempt to set fire to it. Some of the City's proudest possessions were destroyed, including the historic Guildhall part of which survived the last fire of London in 1666. Nine churches were burnt out or damaged. Hospitals were set on fire, business premises and homes were destroyed. The picture above was taken while the fires were raging. Above the smoke and flame rises the noble dome and cross of St. Pauls, symbol of our faith that the forces of evil will yet be overcome.

This gaunt and blackened skeleton is all that remains of the Guildhall, for many years the seat of London's government. This was the famous Banqueting Hall. The statues of Wellington and Nelson have survived the vandals.

Among the heroes of this awful night in London were the gallant and hard-worked firemen. Surrounded by burning and crashing buildings, with still more fire bombs descending in showers upon them, they fought the flames until gradually they subdued them. Many were injured; some were killed.

The ruins of St. Bride's, one of Wren's finest churches. For more than 200 years the graceful steeple of this church has looked out on to Fleet Street. Now only these columns and charred beams are left. Six other Wren churches were damaged or destroyed.

Seen through different eyes: the outlook for 1941. ***Left:*** **From the Luftwaffe the way to a victorious New Year;** ***right:*** **from England the hope that the forces of evil will yet be overcome.**

JANUARY 1941

In January 1941 the German bomber offensive was hampered by adverse weather conditions over Britain and, even more restricting, by conditions on the Continent. No bomber operations were possible on 13 nights, but significant attacks were completed on the same number of nights, with a dual raid a feature on one occasion (9-10th) when simultaneous attacks were made on London and Manchester. Eight of the month's attacks were directed at ports (with two against Avonmouth), four on London and only one against a purely industrial target (Derby). By German reckoning, seven attacks were classed as major and an identical number in the heavy category. In the course of the month minelayers of IX Fliegerkorps were active on 13 nights, visiting a variety of coastal areas.

During the first week of the month North-West Europe was dominated by an anti-cyclone centred over the North Sea with a ridge of high pressure extending south-westwards over Britain. This brought bitterly cold north-easterly winds to much of the country with considerable snowfalls over eastern coastal districts. Snow also penetrated to most other regions and at night, with clearing skies in many areas, temperatures fell to well below freezing level.

The first heavy attacks of the New Year, against Cardiff and Bristol, revealed an excellent response by the public to the call for vigorous action against incendiary bombs. Also revealed was the equally good reaction to the restated need to maintain 'Firewatcher' guard over empty premises (including premises vacated only at night and during weekends, such as shops), for many incipient fires were promptly extinguished in both cities.

From January 6 low cloud with snow, sleet or rain interfered with Luftwaffe attacks on Britain until an improvement on the night of 9-10th permitted the double assault against London and Manchester. Other attacks followed against Portsmouth, London, Plymouth, Derby, Bristol/Avonmouth, Swansea and Southampton, but the third week in the month again brought extremely poor weather and there were no major attacks from the 20th onwards. Widespread snow did much to disrupt transport and life in general in Britain, as on the Continent, and impossible conditions during the last week resulted in less German Air Force activity than at any time since intensive raiding began the previous summer.

The German concentration on ports seemed to indicate an increasing emphasis on the blockade aspect of the offensive rather than a direct assault on the industrial war effort. Since the Sheffield raids in mid-December, heavy attacks had for the most part been directed at dock facilities, storage installations and the commercial quarters of London, Liverpool, Manchester, Cardiff, Bristol, Southampton and, to a lesser degree, Plymouth, and this policy was to continue with the addition of other ports including Swansea and Hull. The bomb loads for January, according to German records (significant attacks only), were as indicated in the table. Total civilian air raid casualties for the month were officially stated to be 922 killed and 1,927 seriously injured.

To counter the German offensive, RAF Fighter Command flew 486 defensive night-fighter sorties, but only three enemy aircraft were claimed destroyed. AA Command, on the other hand, claimed 12 destroyed at night for an expenditure of 49,044 heavy AA shells, an average of 4,087 rounds per victim. Actual German casualties (aircraft of long-range bomber type only) for January — most of which occurred by night

Target	No. of Attacks		HE (Tonnes)	IBs
	Major	Heavy		(Cannisters)
London	2	3	490	1,987
Bristol/Avonmouth	2	1	360	3,720
Portsmouth	1	—	148	1,409
Cardiff	1	—	115	392
Manchester	1	—	111	735
Swansea	—	1	89	901
Derby	—	1	59	41
Southampton	—	1	57	325

In December Mr Herbert Morrison had advised the War Cabinet that although 'the men and women of the civil defence organisation have stood their ground splendidly . . . there are gaps in the ranks — gaps that are dangerous in "blitz" conditions.' He therefore asked that his colleagues in the Cabinet work out a firm plan so that these deficiencies could be made up permanently. Then came December 29 when the damage possible from the little incendiary was brought home with a vengeance. On December 31 he announced that compulsory air raid precautions service for men would be introduced and, at the same time, he called for volunteers on a large scale to form street firefighting parties. Morrison did not mince his words: 'Some of you lately, in more cities than one, have failed your country. This must never happen again. We need a Home Guard — a Civil Defence Home Guard. It is your duty to yourself, to your neighbours and friends, to your city and your country, to guard your own homes, business or factory from fire bombs. You cannot stop a high explosive bomb from bursting, but you can stop a fire bomb from starting a fire. We must leave the fire brigades and auxiliary fire services free to fight big fires, while fire parties must be formed to see that not a single incendiary, wherever it falls, has the chance to get a firm hold.' While the Home Secretary said that he would apply compulsion to everyone — managers, office staffs and manual workers — he called on the country to tackle the job at once and not wait for the legislation. Householders, he said, should form themselves into parties of neighbours to take turns during raids to watch for falling fire bombs. 'Not one single house or building in our towns must be left uncared for' said Morrison. 'Every group of houses and business premises must have its fire party; every party must guard its own group of buildings. Each household must, if possible, provide at least one member, man or woman, for its party; businesses must act in accordance with their size, but even the smallest must act. See your warden at once. Fall in the fire-bomb fighters!'

Beat
'FIREBOMB
FRITZ'
BRITAIN
SHALL NOT
BURN
BRITAIN'S FIRE GUARD IS BRITAIN'S DEFENCE

— were 28 destroyed or missing and 37 damaged. Many of the latter were the results of take-offs and landings in unfavourable weather conditions or the consequences of operating from waterlogged, frozen or snowbound airfields.

German aircraft of all types shot down by day and night over Britain and its coastal waters produced only 18 prisoners-of-war. The bodies of 35 airmen were also recovered and another four bodies, recovered from the sea, were crew members of aircraft shot down in November and December. The morale of the PoWs, as assessed by the interrogating officers of AI1(k) Branch, was on the whole higher than observed in the two previous months and an Air Intelligence explanation for this claimed that, with the exception of two men from KG53, the captured airmen were 'from rather special units and included a large proportion of highly trained or specialist personnel'. Nine of the PoWs (50 per cent of the total for the month) were from several aircraft of III/KG30 brought down towards the end of the month and their interrogation produced a great deal of information about this unit's operations over the last three months.

Despite every effort the defences could claim no significant improvement in their performance. In December the AOC-in-C Fighter Command had stressed the need to implement Fighter Night operations as soon as possible and in January these took place on three occasions — over Bristol on 3-4th, at Portsmouth on 10-11th and at Bristol again on 16-17th. Subsequently No. 10 Group HQ reported that the first was not a success because of the delay in passing instructions, the excessively prolonged intervals between the take-offs of participating fighters, and the consequent irregular termination of patrols. Steps were taken to improve this ragged performance, but the three Fighter Night operations of January produced claims of only one enemy aircraft destroyed and another damaged. This was most disappointing, and there were other problems; the absence of AA gunfire while fighters were patrolling over Bristol had caused widespread comment and discontentment among the city's population and a similar reaction could be expected elsewhere. Nor, indeed, was this feature of Fighter Nights accepted by the AOC No. 11 Group who proposed, at a meeting held at Fighter Command Headquarters, that the guns should be permitted to fire but restricted in height to 2,000 feet below the lowest patrolling fighter. This was rejected by the AOC-in-C, however, who felt there was little probability of enemy bombers coming below 10,000 feet over a Target Area. There was, too, the risk of mistakes on the part of gunners. Douglas also had reservations about a No. 10 Group proposal that fighters might patrol outside the gun zone in an outer fighter

CORPORATION OF LONDON

FIRE GUARD

WILL BE FOUND AT:—

LLOYD'S

No. 12

LEADENHALL STREET

AREA C3 ZONE A1

It was estimated that apart from voluntary fire-watchers, the Fire Service needed an additional 10,000 men and the police forces another 10,000 — and this was apart from the extra hands needed in the rescue, casualty and other segments of the civil defence organisation. However, when it was announced that men over 30 registering for military service could opt for full-time service in the Police War Reserve, the Auxiliary Fire Service or First Aid Parties, the response was poor, only 400 choosing these options at the following two registrations on Saturdays 11th and 18th. Therefore the Government had little alternative but to press ahead with compulsory measures which were enshrined in the National Service Act which received the Royal Assent on April 10. As a result all three bodies received recruits but still never as many as required. ***Above left:*** **When the City of London was organised into Sectors, Areas and Blocks for fire prevention purposes, Lloyd's became the headquarters of Area C3, covering the triangle bounded by Leadenhall Street, Fenchurch Street and Gracechurch Street. This notice appeared at each entrance.** ***Right:*** **Evening returns were prepared by every Block listing the number of fire guards on duty.**

ring', with searchlights defining the safe areas, but after due deliberation he finally agreed to his SASO's suggestion to undertake a trial over Plymouth.

During the month there were a number of changes to both the British and German Orders of Battle, with developments on the British side probably of greater importance. On January 10 the first five Defiants of No. 307 (Polish) Squadron arrived at Blackpool (Squires Gate) from Jurby, Isle of Man, to participate in the night defence of the North-West. Shortly afterwards they were joined by the rest of the squadron which, since December, had been engaged predominantly in daylight convoy patrols over the Irish Sea. The arrival of No. 307 Squadron released the night-flying Hurricanes of No. 96 Squadron to return to Cranage (from where they were on temporary detachment), the last aircraft departing Squires Gate on December 21. Another move involved the Defiants of No. 264 Squadron, 'A' Flight leaving Gravesend — never a satisfactory night-flying base — for Biggin Hill on January 12.

Heavy snowfalls, followed by slush and waterlogging, rendered unuseable many airfields normally available to night fighters and this situation persisted for much of the month. Typically, on January 21 Ford, Charmy Down, Edinburgh (Turnhouse), Liverpool (Speke), Wittering, Ternhill, Southend (Rochford) and Shoreham were all reported unfit for use at night.

An extremely important development during the month was the opening of new GCI stations at Waldringfield, Orby, Durrington and Willesborough, augmenting that already in use at Sopley. Siting problems and early teething troubles arose, but they were quickly overcome, with everyone concerned eager to prove the GCI/AI combination the biggest threat yet to the night bomber.

January also brought improvements and further development of the radio counter-measures activities of No. 80 Wing. On the 9th the Bromide at Alcester was moved to Shipham, Somerset, to counter the X-Verfahren signals in the Bristol area and three days later another of Shipham's transmitters was moved to Porlock to disrupt beam transmissions from Morlaix. On the same day a new Aspirin anti-Knickebein transmitter was installed at Scole.

By late December evidence was accumulating to indicate that a new German single-beam radio aid was in use. Confirmation was obtained by a Whitley of No. 109 Squadron (formed on December 10 from the Wireless Intelligence Development Unit) which found signals on 43 megacycles emanating from Poix, the base of III/KG26. From other W/T intercepts and the decoding of Enigma signals it was established that the Luftwaffe was in possession of a third beam system, now code-named 'Benito' by No. 80 Wing, and steps were immediately taken to devise counter-measures. It was clearly a very complex system, but by the end of January the scientists at the Telecommunications Research Establishment had assessed its method of operation. Within two months of discovering the system — the Luftwaffe's Y-Verfahren — a counter-measure, called 'Domino', was available.

Domino took the form of a receiving station at the BBC site in Swains Lane, Hampstead, which picked up the ranging signal 'triggered' back by the aircraft of III/KG26. This signal was relayed by an existing landline to the pre-war BBC television transmitter at nearby Alexandra Palace. This powerful transmitter was suitably modified to the Y-Verfahren ground station frequency in order to re-radiate the ranging signal from the aircraft. This caused ambiguity in the signals received by the German ground control station and prevented accurate measurement of the aircraft's distance from the controller. In theory, this would prevent the ground controller passing the bomb release instruction at the appropriate time and from its inception this subtle counter-measure proved effective on a number of occasions. Confident of impending success, No. 80 Wing immediately made plans for a second Domino station which, when set up on Beacon Hill, near Salisbury, was expected to give a complete coverage of southern England. However, effective as Domino was to be against Benito (or Y-Verfahren), it was by no means always effective and the British claim of near complete and immediate success (as indicated in various publications including the official war history series of books) conflicts with the German view. More than satisfied with Y-Verfahren, which they had been using over Britain unhindered since September, the Luftwaffe had made plans to extend the system and three stations were quickly introduced. These were station 'Anton' on the Cap de la Hague (Cherbourg), 'Berta' at Cassel, near Calais, and 'Cicero' at Palvel-Conteville, near Fécamp. Anton, the first to become available, was first used in an attack on Portland in late September and by the end of the year it was possible for the He 111s of III/KG26 to be taken all the way to the target automatically — a further Wotan II beam transmitter at Poix was arranged to provide track guidance to an intersection with the 'target' beam at a position over the Channel, thereby providing automatic navigation from Poix airfield to the bomb release point.

No. 80 Wing was not devoting all its time to Y-Verfahren, however, and by mid-January every major city in the southern half of the country was provided with an X-Verfahren jammer to cover its approach from the direction of Cherbourg. Further, on the 18th a new Meacon came into operation at Mintlaw, but from then until the end of the month there was little enemy activity to counter. It was at this time, too, that the code-names given to individual X-beam stations were changed by the RAF, the surnames of members of the Nazi hierarchy replacing the names of rivers, as had previously been the case. Thus, the beam stations with the German code-names Weser, Elbe, Rhein, Isar, Oder and Spree, until now also adopted by the British, became known to the RAF as Göring, Hitler, Himmler, Ribbentrop, Hess and Schirach. Fittingly, the collective name for the stations in the system was changed from Rivers to Ruffians.

Other changes introduced by No. 80 Wing during the month included the installation of a new Aspirin at Shipham on the 20th, the transfer of an Aspirin from Glastonbury to Templecombe on the 22nd, the removal of a similar transmitter from Upavon, the installation of a new Aspirin at Mow Cop and the introduction of a new Meacon at Reston. As the month drew to a close, the Bromide at Birdlip was moved to Porlock, another Aspirin appeared at Frodsham and yet another at Coalville. Finally, the Aspirin at Addington was removed for modifications to facilitate its operation in the 40 to 50 mc/s band. All in all, despite the reduced scale of enemy operations, it had been a busy month for the Wing, but now, with all the expansion and redeployment that had taken place, it was better equipped to deal with an expected renewed onslaught.

January also brought changes on the other side of the Channel and the North Sea. These resulted in an overall reduction in the long-range bomber strength available, and of this force more than formerly were henceforth to concentrate on anti-shipping operations although, when the need arose, they remained available for use as night bombers.

At the end of December, 2/KG4 had been transferred to X Fliegerkorps and by early January it was operating from Sicily as a sea-mining Staffel. The departure of this unit was closely followed by the move southwards of II/LG1, III/LG1 and II/KG26 — nominally about 100 aircraft — so that by the end of the month some 120 long-range bombers were based in the Mediterranean area. A move in the opposite direction was completed by I/KG26 which departed Beauvais for Aalborg, in Denmark, but it continued to operate against Britain as formerly.

The movement of units to the Mediterranean was also accompanied by the redeployment of the CAI from Belgium and by January 14 all the bombers of this force were back on Italian bases.

The reduction of the Axis bomber force in the West was quickly detected by British Signals Intelligence, but the RAF appreciated the extreme mobility of the Luftwaffe and it was accepted that the departed units could just as quickly be repositioned northwards,

No. 11

THE MIDNIGHT WATCH

BROADSHEET OF BRITAIN'S FIRE GUARD AND CIVIL DEFENCE WORKERS

SCIENTISTS TEST NEW NAZI EXPLOSIVE FIRE BOMB AND FIND EFFICIENT METHOD OF ATTACKING IT

Detailed Pictures of How the Bomb Works

GERMAN BOMB B2·2 EI-Z (ANTI PERSONNEL INCENDIARY BOMB)

TAIL UNIT · ARMING WIRE · INCENDIARY UNIT · INFLAMMABLE ALLOY CASE · MAIN INCENDIARY FILLING · CAP (PRIMER) · DETONATOR · SAFETY PIN · FUZE BODY · TIME FUZE · DETONATOR · MAIN EXPLOSIVE CHARGE · DELAYED ACTION EXPLOSIVE UNIT · STEEL EXPLOSIVE CONTAINER · NOSE COVER

You Can Throw Water At It When A Stirrup Pump Is Not Handy

MINISTRY of Home Security scientific research workers have been working night and day on the new German anti-personnel explosive fire bomb so that Fire Guards throughout Britain will know how to deal with it. Preliminary details of this bomb have already been published.

Since these were issued further extensive experiments have been made by these scientists personally with the co-operation of men and women who volunteered to assist them. They have discovered that this bomb can be tackled rapidly and successfully. The results of their work are printed here. They should be studied closely by Fire Guard Street Captains, Party Leaders, Wardens and members of other Civil Defence Services who should pass on this information to householders at once. In business premises occupiers should see that the urgent attention of Fire Guards is drawn to this vital information.

THE enemy are now using a more powerful type of explosive incendiary bomb. Many of the incendiaries that they are dropping are of the old kinds but any incendiary bomb may be one of the new explosive ones. All incendiary bombs must therefore in future be attacked in the following way :—

(1) Bombs falling where they may start a fire.

(2) The use of cover in attacking bombs.

(3) Bombs falling where they will do no harm should be left to burn themselves out.

(4) The fire, not the bomb, should first be attacked by the stirrup pump team.

(5) Bombs lodging in roofs.

(6) All floors should be searched for bombs.

ATTACK FROM BEHIND COVER LET HARMLESS BOMBS BURN OUT

SAFE COVER

THROWING WATER

WHERE THE BOMB MAY LODGE

IN AWKWARD CORNERS

Compulsory Training Will Teach You All These Jobs

THIS BROADSHEET MUST NOT BE EXHIBITED IN ANY PUBLIC PLACE

'Fall in the Fire-bomb Fighters. Still more auxiliaries are being recruited to keep ready additional first-line pumps. But apart from these a new army has come into being — the army of the fire-bomb fighters. These thousands of roof spotters and private fire-fighting parties are of inestimable value. Previously many fires could have been prevented from assuming grave proportions by the prompt action of a man on the spot. Now there are men and women on the spot. By law, all commercial premises throughout London must be watched during air raids. Incendiaries can thus be dealt with as they fall, though maybe some will always elude detection. In addition to this army commanded by law, there are thousands of civilians who regard it as their job to watch their own streets and their own roofs. This is a voluntary duty, but there are few streets in London without their fire parties. No longer will these people see their homes ablaze because incendiaries have worked unseen in dark attics screened from the street by windowless roofs. Men and women are on the alert to hear them drop and mark their position. Only so can they attack the fire germ before it takes hold and infects a whole dwelling. These people saw their homes burning and they were angry. They rose to the suggestion of private fire-fighting and fire-watching and worked out their own salvation. Their weapons are stirrup pumps, shovels and sand: water is kept ready to hand in buckets so that little tax is put upon the mains. The only organisation is a rota system whereby the strain of fire fighting above their normal daily work is equally borne.' *Fire over London, 1940–41.*

should the need arise. Also noted by the British was the return to Châteaudun of elements of II/KG76, a former Do 17 Gruppe which had gone to Giebelstadt and Ansbach in October 1940 to train and re-equip with the Ju 88. January also saw the formation of a new III/KG4, the original unit so designated having been absorbed into KG30 the previous October. The new III Gruppe was based at Leeuwarden, equipped with He 111s, but its first operations were not carried out until February.

Other movements during the month were II/KG77 from Jouvincourt to Reims, II/KG54 to Wittmundhafen from Saint-André, II/KG2 to Merville and III/KG30 to Amsterdam/Schiphol.

WEDNESDAY, JANUARY 1-2

Sunset: 1659 Sunrise: 0908
Moon: Dusk — 2133 (New +4)

No major night attack. Minor activity over London, the Midlands and north-western England, with small scale attacks on airfields in eastern England. Limited minelaying.

UK — Frequent falls of snow over eastern England. Light snow with strong winds over western districts.
The Continent — Extensive cloud with snow in many areas.

Unfavourable weather restricted German operations by day to small scale shipping attacks and reconnaissance flights. After nightfall the continued adverse conditions resulted in the dispatch of only 52 long-range bombers and six long-range night fighters, but their activities were dispersed over a wide area and consequently placed many important towns under a Red Alert for much of the night. Parachute mines were reported to have caused damage and casualties in London, Birmingham and Manchester while conventional bombs killed five people in Cumberland.

As was deduced by the RAF's 'Y' Service, aircraft of II and IX Fliegerkorps were involved, but in addition six night fighters of I/NJG2 were sent to attack airfields in Lincolnshire after mingling with returning British bombers (not all of which were showing IFF and thereby adding to the difficulties of identification). Defensive patrols were flown by 41 night fighters, but no combats ensued with the raiders, ten of which were suspected of minelaying. A Harrow of No. 93 Squadron was airborne for a short time on a Mutton patrol, but was forced to return to Middle Wallop with R/T trouble. Seven dusk patrols were also flown, but again without success. One night fighter was lost.

Following a heavy raid, the first priority was to assess the extent of the damage so that the various bodies responsible for restitution and reconstruction could be made aware of the problems they faced at the outset. Therefore on the morning after, a team of officials from the local authority and central government departments would make a tour of the area and a speedy appreciation produced for the Regional Commissioner's daily conference. In London over 13,000 troops had been on permanent standby since October, and the civilian force of workmen available was 27,000 for road and public utility services and 17,000 on debris clearance and salvage. In the big December raid the headquarters of the City of London Police 'A' Division in Moor Lane was badly damaged by a mine which exploded on the roof of premises opposite. Twelve officers were injured, Police Constable Joseph Gorton having a miraculous escape when two heavy doors were blown off their hinges only to form a 'tent' beneath which he was shielded from falling debris. As the station was virtually a write-off, the work of the headquarters was transferred to temporary premises in St-Martin's-le-Grand, and later to No. 39 King Street. After 1945, 'A' Division was dissolved and its responsibilities devolved to the surviving 'B', 'C' and 'D' Divisions. Nevertheless, there is still an Old Moor Lane Association which meets in September each year at Wood Street police station.

THURSDAY, JANUARY 2-3

Sunset: 1701 Sunrise: 0908
Moon: Dusk — 2239 (1st Qtr −3)

Cardiff's biggest raid of the war on January 2 was also hailed as one of the best examples of a well prepared and effective civil defence, especially so as the towns of South Wales contained a proportionately greater number of volunteers than other parts of the country. Nevertheless the raid caused 167 casualties.

Major night attack on Cardiff, coastal reconnaissnce and minelaying. Bombs also fell at Portland, Weymouth, and in Kent, Sussex, Gloucestershire and Essex.

UK — Little or no cloud in western districts with moderate to poor visibility. Snow showers over north-east and eastern coasts extending into northern England and the Midlands. Winds mainly north-easterly, light to moderate.

The Continent — Almost cloudless inland but heavy, broken cloud with frequent snow showers near coasts and adjacent sea areas. Visibility moderate, poor in showers. Fresh or strong north-easterly winds.

There was very little Luftwaffe offensive activity during the day with only five raiders plotted overland by Fighter Command. In the afternoon, in anticipation of operations that night, Mutton and Albino instructions were issued but Albino was subsequently cancelled.

Night operations commenced shortly after sunset and were directed mainly at Cardiff where 111 bombers (61 of Luftflotte 2 and 50 of Luftflotte 3) dropped 115 tonnes of HE (comprising 3 SC 1800, 53 SC 1000, 39 SC 500, 20 LZZ 250, 79 SC 250, 254 SC 50) and 392 BSK (14,112 IBs) in two phases — from 1843 to 2354 hours and again from 0321 to 0421. Minelaying between St David's Head and Carnsore Point was undertaken by aircraft of IX Fliegerkorps while on the other side of the country four Fiat BR 20s of the CAI attempted to bomb Ipswich in what was the last operation by the Italian Air Force over England.

German reports reveal that the attack on Cardiff was opened by He 111s of KGr100 using X-Verfahren and the Concentration Point was centred on the docks and large steelworks in the south-east part of the city. The units known to have participated were as follows:

Luftflotte 2
61 aircraft over the target. Units not known,

The Ministry of Information included 'one small episode of the raid' in its wartime publication *Front Line 1940–1941* 'because it so faithfully exhibits the spirit of the Welsh cities under bombing and the roots of that spirit. When a rescue party set to work to see who might be buried in the debris of a demolished house, they were warned of life to be saved and guided to their mark by the notes of "God Save the King" sung at the top of his voice by a little boy of six. It turned out that he was trapped under the staircase, where he had to stay for six hours until rescued. He was singing most of the time. His rescuers asked him why. He told them — "My father was a collier, and he always said that when the men were caught and buried underground they would keep singing and singing and they were always got out in time".' *Above:* Cardiff's housing stock suffered worst of all; this is the corner of Deburgh and Neville Streets. Here the bombed properties have been replaced in character with those destroyed. The ruin on the right was the Riverside Conservative Club, built in 1899 and rebuilt in 1954.

PORTSMOUTH : the Guildhall is in the background.

SOUTHAMPTON : near the city centre.

SWANSEA : Goat Street.

CARDIFF : Llandaff Cathedral.

PLYMOUTH : from the Guildhall towe

LIVERPOOL : Lord Street ; South Castle Street ; Customs House in the background.

CLYDESIDE : Dellingburn St., Greenock.

BELFAST : a burning church.

HULL : Newbridge Road.

except for III/KG2, but the British 'Y' Service reported activity by KG2, KG3, KG4, KG30 and KG53.

Luftflotte 3
57 aircraft dispatched to Cardiff; 50 reported over the target, 3 bombed alternatives, 3 aborted and a Ju 88 of III/KG1 was listed 'overdue'.

***Front Line The Official Story of the Civil Defence of Britain* — was published in 1942 price two shillings — the equivalent of about £2 today. As the usual price of a second hand copy is now around £1 it can be considered very good value. Its story must obviously be read in the context of the period; although the Blitz was over for the time being, it was written at a time when Britain's fortunes generally were at a low ebb and, more importantly, when the writers had no idea of the eventual outcome of the war. The attack on Cardiff was described as the 'Luftwaffe's New Year gift' with a picture of Llandaff Cathedral included in a pictorial round up to illustrate attacks on Britain's ports . . .**

COVENTRY : the city centre.

BIRMINGHAM : corner of New Street and High Street.

BRISTOL : Park Street.

SHEFFIELD : High Street.

MANCHESTER : corner of Portland Street.

. . . with a similar montage of pictures depicting raids on the 'arms towns'.

Those over Cardiff were as follows:

I/LG1: 7 Ju 88, 2323-2354
I/KG27: 11 He 111, 2217-2331
III/KG27: 7 He 111, 2220-2328
KGr100: 8 He 111, 1843-1918
II/KG55: 9 He 111, 1944-1950
III/KG26: 3 He 111, 1857-1914
III/KG1: 6 Ju 88, 0321-0401

The clear weather permitted visual bombing for most of the attack and good results were anticipated. Numerous fires were reported and aided the approach to the target by succeeding crews. Later in the attack the fires were visible from 100 kilometres distant and one large explosion in the docks area was seen to send a sheet of flame some 2,000 metres into the night sky. The AA defences were described as 'lively, with well-aimed heavy and light flak', and the searchlights were 'very active'. Numbers of balloons were seen and night fighters were encountered over the Channel and on the approach to

Cardiff, where three engagements occurred. In one of them two crew members of a Do 17 of 8/KG2 were wounded. One Ju 88 of Luftflotte 3 failed to return and an He 111 of III/KG26 made an emergency landing near Le Havre on its return flight and was slightly damaged.

The Ministry of Home Security reports state that bombs fell in most districts of Cardiff and to the south-west, towards Penarth and Barry, with no particular concentration. (A Starfish site at Leckwith, to the south-west of Cardiff, might well have attracted bombing in this direction.)

Residential and commercial areas suffered but no serious damage was caused in the docks. Some factories were affected, but mostly indirectly through UXBs or loss of utility services. A good deal of delay and dislocation was also inflicted on the railway system, although damage was mainly of short duration and dislocation largely the result of UXBs. Public buildings and service establishments were also hit, as were Llandaff Cathedral and Llandough Hospital. Initial estimates put the number of casualties at 103 killed and 168 seriously injured. There were reports of parachute mines causing considerable damage but it was mainly fires — 12 of which were classed as major — that wreaked havoc in the main shopping centre. Nevertheless, in the main the fires were promptly handled and most of them were extinguished by midnight. Ninety-five houses were destroyed, 233 badly damaged and 426 made uninhabitable in the attack, which was later officially assessed as moderately successful.

The clear up in Cardiff — the modern comparison reveals that this is the corner of Croft and Rose Streets.

A total of 48 fighters from Nos. 9, 10 and 11 Groups flew dusk and night patrols. In addition six Blenheims of No. 23 Squadron flew Intruder patrols over German bomber bases in northern France. However, at 1900 hours No. 11 Group recalled all its fighters, except those of No. 219 Squadron and the Blenheim Intruders of 23 Squadron, because of snowstorms and thunderstorms. At 1915 hours the single Mutton Harrow returned for the second night in succession with R/T trouble; it took off again later, only to return once more with the same problem at 2020.

Two enemy aircraft were claimed probably destroyed — one, an He 111, by a Beaufighter of No. 604 Squadron 10 miles south of Lyme Regis and the other, also an He 111, by an Intruder Blenheim of 23 Squadron in the vicinity of Dreux airfield. Another enemy aircraft was claimed damaged by a Hurricane of No. 87 Squadron south-west of Bristol. No night fighters were lost.

The heavy guns of AA Command expended some 5,500 rounds during the night, with the Cardiff guns claiming one enemy aircraft destroyed. Other guns in action were those at Yeovil, Bristol, Brooklands, Bramley, Portland, the London IAZ, Solent and Humber.

FRIDAY, JANUARY 3-4

Sunset: 1702 Sunrise: 0908
Moon: Dusk — 2343 (1st Qtr −2)

Major attack on Bristol and minelaying off Flamborough Head and the Norfolk and Suffolk coasts. Minor activity over the London area, the Midlands and north-western England.

UK — Mist with small amounts of cloud in western districts. Elsewhere variable cloud with snow showers. Fog in the Forth Valley, Clydeside, Tyneside and Merseyside. Winds north-easterly, light to moderate in the West. Very cold in all regions.

The Continent — Cloudy with snow showers. Squally north-easterly winds. Visibility moderate but poor in snow.

Luftwaffe activity during the day was confined to reconnaissance and anti-shipping patrols and only ten German aircraft were plotted overland, but 'Y' Service wireless intercepts indicated that a night attack was planned against Bristol. German navigational beams, it was learned, were to operate from 1700 hours and the first raid was expected to reach Bristol at 1830 hours, flying at 20,000 feet on a beam bearing of 335°. With this foreknowledge of the impending attack — and with due consideration of prevailing and anticipated weather conditions — a Fighter Night operation was ordered, with a Zero Time of 1855 hours. Mutton was to operate between 1900 and 2100 hours.

The attack developed as forecast but, according to plots maintained by Fighter Command, many German aircraft 'appeared to meander about after crossing the coast' and some early arrivals circled the Bristol area without bombing until the arrival of other aircraft from the direction of the Channel Islands. It was later discovered that the aircraft of KGr100 were late departing Vannes because of weather conditions there and several aircraft of other units awaited their arrival before bombing.

Crews of 178 bombers claimed to have bombed Bristol in two phases, from 1835 to 0038 hours and from 0140 to 0551. The Schwerpunkt was the town centre on both sides of the River Avon and 154 tonnes of HE (comprising 14 SC 1800, 5 SC 1700, 53 SC 1000, 4 Flam 500, 41 SC 500, 21 LZZ 250, 71 SC 250 and 393 SC 50) and 1,488 BSK (53,568 IBs) were dropped.

It was a cloudless night in the Target Area and with snow-covered ground and a moon nearly in its First Quarter, the city and the River Avon running through it were clearly recognised. Cloud amounts increased during the night and while breaks still permitted a degree of visual bombing, recourse to radio and DR bombing was at times necessary until fires had sufficiently developed to be used as aiming points. Such fires were eventually visible to approaching crews from 150-170 kilometres distant, but from the outset numerous small fires were observed to be joining to form large fire areas. Good results were also expected of HE bombs, but it was difficult to assess their effect because of the combination of fire glare and increasing cloud cover. Known participating units were as follows:

Luftflotte 2
77 aircraft dispatched; 10 bombed alternative targets or aborted and 67 bombed Bristol. Units not known, but the 'Y' Service reported activity by KG2, KG3, KG4 and KG30.

Luftflotte 3
125 aircraft dispatched; 5 bombed alternatives, 8 aborted and one attacked Bournemouth. No losses sustained.

The tragedy of Berkeley Square. No nightingales were singing in Bristol on Friday morning as local folk stood stunned at the direct hit on the Young Women's Christian Association Hostel where 24 people were trapped. The Warden and 11 residents were killed.

Those over Bristol were:

I/LG1: 4 Ju 88, 2325-0110
I/KG27: 14 He 111, 2150-2308
II/KG27: 9 He 111, 2155-2330
KGr100: 9 He 111, 1920-1940
I/KG54: 7 Ju 88, 2040-2235
II/KG54: 6 Ju 88, 2104-2145
I/KG55: 3 He 111, 2014-2021
II/KG55: 9 He 111, 1905-1943
III/KG55: 5 He 111, 1945-2010
I/KG1: 10 He 111, 3 Ju 88, 1835-2010
KG77: 19 Ju 88, 1855-2035
I/KG26: 9 He 111, 1920-2000
III/KG26: 4 He 111, 1935-2006

From the foregoing it can be seen that the attack was opened by I/KG1 followed by some aircraft of KG77; flares were dropped by II/KG55 from 1905 hours — preceding four SC 1800s and five SD 1400s — and it was not until 1920 that KGr100, using X-beams that were reported free from interference, joined the attack, with nine He 111s dropping 10,368 IBs in only 20 minutes. III/KG26 bombed visually and not by means of their usual Y-Verfahren.

Participating crews reported good results. Only slight flak was reported (presumably because of the Fighter Night tactics adopted by the defenders) but searchlight activity was described as 'lively', as was the flak at Portland. Three night fighters were seen in the Target Area, as were balloons, and another fighter was reported between the Isle of Wight and the target. A good number of decoy fires, light beacons and airfield lights were also seen by crews, some of whom stated the biggest fires were in the city docks area between targets GB 52 51 (the Floating Harbour) and GB 56 51 (Cumberland Basin).

As claimed in the German reports, damage in Bristol was extensive, with fires in the city centre and at Temple Meads railway station, the General Hospital and a rope works. Most damage, however, was to be found in commercial and residential areas, but all fires were rapidly brought under control. Incendiaries were also promptly dealt with at Bath, Wells and in country districts of Somerset. In the course of the all-night raid 192 incidents were reported in Bristol, but the general working of the docks was not impaired, despite the loss of a granary in the City Docks containing 8,000 tons of grain. About 2,500 houses were damaged, 149 people killed, 133 seriously injured and 218 slightly hurt.

The night was bitterly cold and the ARP and Fire Services had to contend with frost as well as fire — jets of water from hoses formed huge icicles on buildings and pumps and formed massive sheets of ice underfoot, while spray froze on firemens' uniforms and helmets. Benumbed and frostbitten, with high-explosives raining down upon them, they fought the fires for hours on end, for it was Bristol's longest attack to date.

Damage to utility services was lighter than

Hauptmann Krahl

Hauptmann Adolph

Hauptmann Storp

Leutnant Schnell

Leutnant Illg

Oberst Angerstein
Aufn. Scherl-Bilderdienst (5), PBZ (1)

Wie sie das Ritterkreuz erwarben

Meanwhile in Germany it was New Year's Honours for the Luftwaffe as the latest awards for gallantry were announced. On September 1, 1939, Hitler had revived the old Prussian Iron Cross decoration as an Order in four classes; the Grand Cross being awarded just once to Göring on the fall of France in July 1940. The Ritterkreuz or Knight's Cross — the second highest class — was itself divided into five levels: with golden oakleaves, swords and diamonds (also awarded just once, to Oberstleutnant Hans-Ulrich Rudel in December 1944); with oakleaves, swords and diamonds (27 awards); with oakleaves and swords (160 awards); and just oakleaves (882 awards). Those announced and illustrated here are for the simple Ritterkreuz.

in previous raids on the city and in a comparatively short time most supplies were back to normal. Railway services were dislocated but road transport was well maintained. Other buildings damaged included the Guildhall, Royal Exchange, Central Police Station, the Chamber of Commerce, three hospitals and several schools and churches.

The Bristol AA guns were in action from 1845 to 1855 hours but then ceased firing for nearly two hours as fighters patrolled the city in accordance with the Fighter Night directive. Firing was resumed at 2041 and did not finally cease until 0604 the next morning. Other heavy guns in action were those at Cardiff, Yeovil, Portland, Bramley, Brooklands, Holton Heath, Slough, the Solent, the London IAZ and Thames and Medway South, firing some 4,000 rounds. No enemy aircraft were claimed destroyed.

The German operations were also opposed by 76 aircraft of Fighter Command, comprising 48 of No. 10 Group, 25 of No. 11 Group (including six Intruder patrols over France) and three aircraft of No. 12 Group. A Mutton Harrow of No. 93 Squadron was also sent on patrol, but the only success of the night went to a Hurricane of No. 87 Squadron that claimed damage to a Ju 88 over Bristol at 21,000 feet. A Blenheim Mk IF of No. 23 Squadron which failed to return from an Intruder patrol over France, was Fighter Command's only loss of the night.

In addition to the bombing of Bristol and elsewhere already mentioned, there were four bomb incidents in London and minor bombing was also reported at Poole, Warminster, Weymouth, Emsworth, Bentley, Lewisham, Ashby-de-la-Zouch, Bilhorne, Huyton, Newton-le-Willows, St Helens and near Bescot and Warrington.

SATURDAY, JANUARY 4-5

Sunset: 1703 Sunrise: 0907
Moon: Dusk — 0046 (1st Qtr −1)

Heavy attack on Bristol/Avonmouth, with subsidiary operations over eastern England, the East Midlands, South Wales and the London area. Minelaying in the Bristol Channel.

UK — Cloud over Scotland, eastern and southern England and the southern Midlands, lowering to 1,000 feet in occasional slight snow in south-eastern England; visibility moderate or good, poor in snow. Elsewhere conditions fair to fine with moderate visibility but fog or mist patches developing in industrial areas. Very cold in all regions.

The Continent — Similar to southern England with more general snow in some areas.

German daylight offensive operations were similar to the previous day and were mainly confined to reconnaissance and minor attacks on shipping off the East Coast. In anticipation of the forthcoming night's operations, Albino was laid on but was cancelled at 1350 hours. At 1645 hours the 'Y' Service advised Fighter Command that there were no indications from W/T intercepts of a heavy attack that night, but by 1800 hours a multiplicity of radar plots disproved this. Then, at 1845, the 'Y' Service reported that the Kleve Knickebein was believed to be aligned over the Thames Estuary.

Avonmouth was the primary target with the CP centred on the docks and industrial installations situated in the west and north-west part of the town. The crews of 103 German aircraft claimed to have bombed their primary targets, dropping 82 tonnes of HE (three SC 1800, 30 SC 1000, 29 SC 500, three Flam 500, 47 SC 250, 10 LZZ 250 and 325 SC/SD 50) and 752 BSK (27,072 IBs) between 1835 and 0615 hours. However, because of cloud and poor visibility at Avonmouth, 21 aircraft bombed Bristol (between 2343 and 0427 hours, dropping one SC 1800, 12 SC 1000, six SC 500, five SC 250, 88 SC 50 and two BSK), where explosions and fires were seen. Other alternative targets bombed by single aircraft were Cardiff, Newport, Portishead, Hastings and various flak and searchlight sites. Two aircraft bombed Bournemouth while three, ordered elsewhere, attacked Bristol as an alternative. London was bombed by 17 aircraft whose crews were unable to locate their primary objectives at Bristol/Avonmouth (dropping two SC 1800, 16 SC 1000, four SC 500, 13 SC 250, and 10 SD/SC 50).

The Avonmouth attack was opened by Ju 88s of I/KG51, joined shortly afterwards by the first He 111s of KGr100; in the main aircraft of Luftflotte 3 took part in the first part of the attack, with those of Luftflotte 2 participating in the later stages. Early arrivals found weather conditions that permitted bombing with sight of the ground, but as the attack progressed bombing was principally by DR and radio-navigation or by the use of fires visible through the cloud. Increasing cloud made it difficult to assess the results of the bombing and only after midnight could fires be discerned. Flak over the target was reported to be of moderate strength but was generally aimed too low; at other times the flak was lively, but without effect. The searchlights, too, were active, but were hindered by cloud. Single night fighters were seen over the Channel coast and in the Target Area, but only one attack was reported, this by an He 111 of KGr100 which subsequently aborted. However, as no interceptions were made by Fighter Command that night it seems likely that it was mistakenly fired upon by another German bomber.

Oberst Schwartzkopff

Hauptmann Dürbeck

Hauptmann Kowalewski

Hauptmann Helbig

Hauptmann Groth

Oberleutnant Frhr. v. Gravenreuth

Oberleutnant Richter
Aufn. Scherl-Bilderdienst (7)

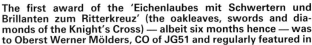

The first award of the 'Eichenlaubes mit Schwertern und Brillanten zum Ritterkreuz' (the oakleaves, swords and diamonds of the Knight's Cross) — albeit six months hence — was to Oberst Werner Mölders, CO of JG51 and regularly featured in *Der Adler*. Readers will recall that his brother was now a prisoner in England (see pages 166–167) but they were never again to meet as Werner was killed in a plane crash in November 1941 on the Eastern Front.

Participating aircraft were as follows:

Luftflotte 2
78 aircraft dispatched to Bristol, with the crews of 49 reporting over the target; 21 bombed alternatives (17 attacking London), 9 aborted and 1 ordered to London. Nine aircraft engaged on mining the Bristol Channel near Cardiff. Units not known, but the 'Y' Service reported activity by KG2, KG3, KG4 and KG30.

Luftflotte 3
87 aircraft dispatched, with 75 over Avonmouth; 7 bombed alternatives and 5 aborted.

I/KG27: 11 He 111, 2140-2225
II/KG27: 10 He 111, 2143-2243
KGr100: 6 He 111, 1857-1905
I/KG51: 4 Ju 88, 1835-1900
II/KG51: 2 Ju 88, 1910-1915
III/KG51: 1 Ju 88, 1925
I/KG54: 3 Ju 88, 2010-2025
II/KG54: 3 Ju 88, 2010-2108
KG77: 25 Ju 88, 2225-0009
I/KG26: 10 He 111, 2228-0020

From the foregoing it can be seen that only one of the three 'Firelighter' units participated (Kampfgruppe 100) and unfortunately for the attackers three aircraft of this Gruppe aborted, reducing the guidance force by one third.

The Ministry of Home Security reported that fires started in Avonmouth and Bristol were quickly brought under control and all were extinguished by 2200 hours. Many IBs fell on and around Avonmouth Docks, but surprisingly little damage resulted and casualties were light with only 23 people killed. This was unlike the previous night, when serious damage and heavy casualties were caused in the area. Prompt firefighting and unfavourable weather clearly did much to alleviate the attack, which lacked concentration. In fact, after 2200 hours a fire which started at Weston-super-Mare attracted more bombs and from then on the Somerset coastal town was inadvertently attacked by a number of aircraft.

In addition to bombing in the Bristol/Avonmouth area there were reports of incidents at Cheddar, Exmouth, Thrapston, Letchworth, Barnet, Richmond (Middlesex), Bermondsey, Rotherhithe, Gilfach Goch, near Rhonnda, Swansea, Cardiff, Marshfield and Peterstone. During a dusk attack by units operating from Holland bombs had fallen at Grimsby, Malton, Market Rasen, York, Norwich and near Linton-on-Ouse airfield.

To counter the German effort of 174 bombers and nine night fighters, Fighter Command flew 61 sorties including two dusk patrols, but no interceptions were made. The Bristol AA guns were active from 1816 to 0600 hours and heavy guns were also in action at Portland, Cardiff, the Solent, Thames and Medway South, the London IAZ, Gloucester (where an enemy aircraft was claimed damaged at 0208 hours), Harwich, Bramley, Holton Heath, Yeovil, Brooklands, Slough, Thames and Medway North and Dover. Nearly 6,000 rounds were fired during the night.

The only loss occurred during the afternoon of the 4th:

Wekusta 26 Dornier Do 17Z (2643). Crashed into the sea south-west of the Shambles, Portland, Dorset 2.00 p.m.. Last radio message received from the aircraft stated that it was under fighter attack. Shot down by Pilot Officer E. S. Marrs DFC in a Spitfire of No. 152 Squadron. Reg.Rat. a.Kr.Dr. S. Russ and Gefr. W. Seurig killed. Obergefr. B. Altmann and Uffz. S. Schwän missing. Aircraft 5Z+I destroyed.

SUNDAY, JANUARY 5-6

Sunset: 1704 Sunrise: 0907
Moon: Dusk — 0148 (1st Qtr)

No major attack, but London was the centre of activity. Minor raids were also made on the Midlands and the North-East Coast.

UK — Snow, sleet and drizzle with poor visibility in most areas south of the Humber. The Continent — Low cloud with snow or sleet in some areas. Poor to moderate visibility.

During the day about 45 German aircraft were operating and incidents were reported in the West Country, London and the Home Counties. The poor weather conditions prevented fighter interceptions and at one time unseen fire was permitted in No. 11 Group territory. Little bomb damage occurred.

In anticipation of night operations by the German Air Force, Albino was called for but cancellation followed in the early afternoon. At 1645 hours the 'Y' Service reported that there was no indication of a mass attack but two hours later No. 80 Wing advised that Knickebein beams from Kleve were suspected over the Thames Estuary. In due course enemy activity commenced from the direction of the Scheldt and Belgium with London as the main target, but activity had ceased by midnight.

Fighter Command plotted 36 bombers in the London IAZ where 1,639 rounds of HAA ammunition were fired; searchlights did not expose, because of the weather conditions, and for the same reason night fighters did not operate. Over the country as a whole some 4,000 rounds of heavy AA ammunition were expended for two enemy aircraft claimed probably destroyed.

With French airfields closed through

With the weather curtailing large-scale activities, Britain received a brief respite from night raiding from January 6–8. One of the few bombs dropped on the Monday struck the ancient 12th Century parish church of St Mary Magdalene in East Ham. Although the church had been restored by 1945, a later generation has allowed the churchyard to revert to nature.

weather, operations were limited to 66 bombers of II and IX Fliegerkorps and five long-range night fighters of I/NJG2, operating from bases in Belgium and Holland.

According to a Ministry of Home Security report, a number of parachute mines were dropped on London; fires were started by IBs, but the central districts of the capital were little affected. As was becoming general everywhere, the fires were promptly dealt with and damage was thereby restricted. Twenty-eight people were killed and 124 seriously injured.

Some damage was also reported in County Durham and elsewhere on the north-east coast. Manchester and South Lancashire also received bombs, but no serious damage was done.

MONDAY, JANUARY 6-7

Sunset: 1705 Sunrise: 0907
Moon: Dusk — 0250 (1st Qtr +1)

No German offensive night operations.

UK — Low cloud with poor visibility. Freezing drizzle or snow in many areas.
The Continent — Low cloud with snow or fog in many regions.

During the day, in conditions of very low cloud, limited operations were flown by single German aircraft. In one instance the streets of Croydon were machine-gunned and bomb incidents were reported at East and West Ham, various parts of Essex, East Anglia and the Home Counties.

At 1635 hours No. 80 Wing reported that Knickebein beams from Dieppe and Haarlem were intersecting over London, but all German night operations were cancelled because of the poor weather conditions.

TUESDAY, JANUARY 7-8

Sunset: 1707 Sunrise: 0906
Moon: Dusk — 0352 (1st Qtr +2)

No German night operations over Britain.

UK — Extensive low cloud (base 500-1,000 feet) with rain in south-eastern England. Poor visibility.
The Continent — Low cloud with rain in places. Poor visibility.

In poor to moderate visibility daylight attacks were made on London and airfields in the Home Counties. No. 11 Group was unable to operate fighters and therefore permission for unseen fire was given. Bombs were also reported in East Anglia and Coventry, making this the most extensive daylight raiding for some weeks.

In anticipation of forthcoming night operations, Mutton was provisionally prepared, but was cancelled at 1638 hours. At 1850 hours No. 80 Wing reported that Knickebein beams were intersecting over London, but all German night operations were cancelled because of the weather. Nevertheless, Fighter Command reported a single unidentified aircraft off Ardrossan during the night and at 2322 hours the Barr HAA guns (Thames and Medway North) engaged and claimed to have probably destroyed an enemy aircraft flying at 14,800 feet. No other incidents were reported and no bombs were dropped during the hours of darkness.

WEDNESDAY, JANUARY 8-9

Sunset: 1708 Sunrise: 0906
Moon: Dusk — 0453 (1st Qtr +3)

No operations by the Luftwaffe over Britain by night.

UK — Extensive low cloud with rain and poor visibility in most areas.
The Continent — Low cloud. Poor visibility with rain in places.

German activity was only slight during the day; 50 aircraft were plotted by Fighter Command but only six penetrated inland, with bombing reported at Ipswich during the morning and Coventry in the afternoon. Damage and casualties were light. Continuing bad weather resulted in the cancellation of all night operations except for a little activity off the British coasts two hours before sunrise.

THURSDAY, JANUARY 9-10

Sunset: 1709 Sunrise: 0906
Moon: Dusk — 0552 (1st Qtr +4)

Major attack on Manchester with a secondary attack on London. Minelaying in the Thames Estuary, off Worthing, Harwich, the Norfolk coast, the Humber and Liverpool Bay.

UK — Cloudy with occasional rain in the East; snow or sleet in the South-East after a cloudless early evening. Moderate visibility after fog in the London area at first. Almost cloudless in the West initially, but cloudy with local rain after midnight. Fog on Merseyside and the Forth and Clyde areas. Winds north to north-east, mainly light to moderate.
The Continent — Increasing cloud at 3,000 feet near Dutch and Belgian coasts. Cloudless elsewhere with good visibility. Moderate easterly winds but stronger in the West with gales locally on the coast of Brittany.

With improved weather conditions German aircraft were active during the day, but bombs were reported at only one place in Kent, where they fell on open ground. Albino was alerted but subsequently cancelled, while Mutton was reported inoperable until January 16.

Widespread night activity started at 1735 hours with the approach of the first of 346 German aircraft operating. Subsequently the crews of 143 claimed to have bombed Manchester, attacking between 1942 and 0005 hours with 111 tonnes of HE and 'Flambo' (comprising one SC 1800, six SC 1400, 20 SC 1000, 54 SC 500, two Flam 250, 25 LZZ 250, 1,000 SC 250 and 465 SC 50) and 735 BSK (26,460 IBs). The CP was the town itself and in the early stages of the attack crews were in visual contact with the ground for the last 40 kilometres of the approach to the target. Bombing was mainly visual at first, but before long increasing cloud made bombing possible only by means of DR or radio navigation and it was difficult to determine results. About 30 minutes after the attack started one crew of KGr100 came below cloud to check on the location and extent of fires, but in general the cloud and poor visibility hindered observation of results.

In the secondary attack on London bombing was in two phases, from 1915-1921 and 2154-0135 hours, and 62 aircraft dropped 65 tonnes of HE and oil bombs (30 SC 1000, 19 SC 500, two Flam 250, 13 LZZ 250, 75 SC 250 and 72 SC/SD 50) and 470 BSK (16,920 IBs). Prior to 2300 hours bombing was by DR and radio navigation, with the CP in the city, but without observed results. Later, seven crews found it possible to bomb visually through holes in the cloud cover and explosions were seen on the north side of the Thames U-bend, together with several small fires and one large one. Five aircraft, unable to find London, bombed alternative targets.

The London attack was wholly carried out by Luftflotte 3, the participating units and their bombing times being as follows:

I/LG1: 4 Ju 88, 2200-0057
I/KG27: 2 He 111, 2303-2320
II/KG27: 5 He 111, 2242-2317
III/KG27: 6 He 111, 2329-0103
Stab/KG55: 5 He 111, 0002-0005
I/KG55: 5 He 111, 2348-0018
II/KG55: 1 He 111, 1942

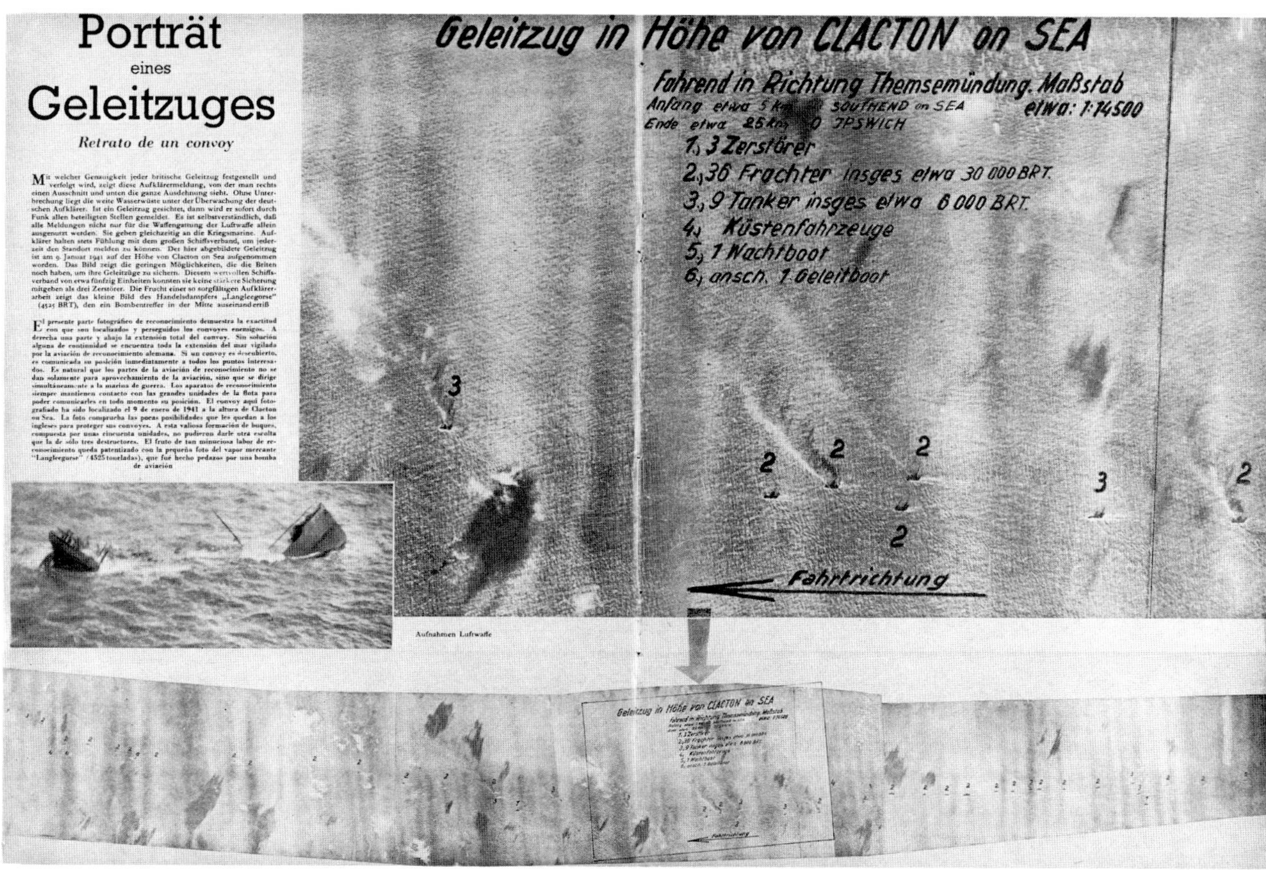

Porträt eines Geleitzuges

Retrato de un convoy

Mit welcher Genauigkeit jeder britische Geleitzug festgestellt und verfolgt wird, zeigt diese Aufklärermeldung, von der man rechts einen Ausschnitt und unten die ganze Ausdehnung sieht. Ohne Unterbrechung liegt die weite Wasserwüste unter der Überwachung der deutschen Aufklärer. Ist ein Geleitzug gesichtet, dann wird er sofort durch Funk allen beteiligten Stellen gemeldet. Es ist selbstverständlich, daß alle Meldungen nicht nur für die Waffengattung der Luftwaffe allein ausgenutzt werden. Sie geben gleichzeitig an die Kriegsmarine. Aufklärer halten stets Fühlung mit dem großen Schiffsverband, um jederzeit den Standort melden zu können. Der hier abgebildete Geleitzug ist am 9. Januar 1941 auf der Höhe von Clacton on Sea aufgenommen worden. Das Bild zeigt die geringen Möglichkeiten, die die Briten noch haben, um ihre Geleitzüge zu sichern. Diesem wertvollen Schiffsverband von etwa fünfzig Einheiten konnten sie keine stärkere Sicherung mitgeben als drei Zerstörer. Die Frucht einer so sorgfältigen Aufklärerarbeit zeigt das kleine Bild des Handelsdampfers „Langleegorse" (4525 BRT), den ein Bombentreffer in der Mitte auseinanderriß

El presente parte fotográfico de reconocimiento demuestra la exactitud con que son localizados y perseguidos los convoyes enemigos. A derecha una parte y abajo la extensión total del convoy. Sin solución alguna de continuidad se encuentra toda la extensión del mar vigilada por la aviación de reconocimiento alemana. Si un convoy es descubierto, es comunicada su posición inmediatamente a todos los puntos interesados. Es natural que los partes de la aviación de reconocimiento no se dan solamente para aprovechamiento de la aviación, sino que se dirige simultáneamente a la marina de guerra. Los aparatos de reconocimiento siempre mantienen contacto con las grandes unidades de la flota para poder comunicarles en todo momento su posición. El convoy aquí fotografiado ha sido localizado el 9 de enero de 1941 a la altura de Clacton on Sea. La foto comprueba las pocas posibilidades que les quedan a los ingleses para proteger sus convoyes. A esta valiosa formación de buques, compuesta por unas cincuenta unidades, no pudieron darle otra escolta que la de sólo tres destructores. El fruto de tan minuciosa labor de reconocimiento queda patentizado con la pequeña foto del vapor mercante "Langleegorse" (4525 toneladas), que fué hecho pedazos por una bomba de aviación

Aufnahmen Luftwaffe

While the Blitz on the cities has absorbed all our attention, we must not lose sight of the fact that the Luftwaffe was still keeping an eye on — and attacking — shipping. This convoy, photographed on January 9, was strung out over twenty kilometres down the East Coast, and the smaller picture claimed to show the end of the steamer *Langleegorse*.

KGr806: 1 Ju 88, 2250
KG1: 5 He 111, 1 Ju 88, 2154-2318
KG77: 14 Ju 88, 2115-0057
I/KG26: 10 He 111, 2300-0135
III/KG26: 3 He 111, 1915-1921 (alternative target, visual bombing)

Manchester was attacked by units of both Luftflotten 2 and 3 as follows:

Luftflotte 2
55 aircraft reported having bombed Manchester. No further details known.

Luftflotte 3
88 aircraft reported over the target, as follows:
I/LG1: 3 Ju 88, 2159-2215
I/KG27: 4 He 111, 2233-2315
II/KG27: 3 He 111, 2317-2325
KGr100: 6 He 111, 2004-2020
I/KG54: 1 Ju 88, 2347
II/KG54: 5 Ju 88, 2253-2348
I/KG55: 3 He 111, 1942-2155
II/KG55: 8 He 111, 1942-2155
III/KG55: 10 He 111, 2200-2250
KGr806: 1 Ju 88, 2250
KG1: 10 He 111, 12 Ju 88, 2205-2310
KG77: 13 Ju 88, 2205-0005
I/KG26: 2 He 111, 2210-2330

Forty-eight aircraft of both Luftflotten 2 and 3 were unable to find their primary targets and attacked alternatives, with nine going to Southampton, three each to Birmingham and Bristol, six to Portsmouth, four each to Liverpool and Bournemouth and one to Portland and elsewhere. Eleven more aircraft aborted for various reasons, mainly through icing or technical failures, and Luftflotte 3 reported one aircraft (a He 111 of II/KG27) missing.

Crews attacking both Manchester and London subsequently reported medium to strong well directed flak and searchlights; six night fighters were seen, but no attacks were carried out.

In fact, bombs fell widely over much of Britain south of Preston, with little concentration on the intended German targets. According to MHS reports, flares were dropped over Leicester, Sheffield, Rugby, Cardiff and, later, over Bristol and London, but after an initial concentration on Coventry the main targets appeared to be Liverpool, Birmingham, Rugby and Northampton. However, bombs were also reported at Portsmouth, Gosport, Poole, Dorchester, Cheltenham, Egham, Grantham, Nottingham, Runcorn, Wigan, Birkenhead, Stoke-on-Trent, Newcastle-under-Lyme, Burslem, Burton, Southampton, Surbiton, Hendon, various points in the West Country and South Hampshire, Llandudno, Plymouth, Bournemouth, Gloucester, Ludgershall, Builth, Guildford, Marham, Yarmouth and in the Eastern Counties from Cambridgeshire to Yorkshire. Casualties were caused in many places, with 27 people killed in Liverpool; over the entire country 73 were killed and 114 seriously injured. Fires were started in Liverpool, Southampton and Bristol, but in London there was no concentration of bombs and incendiaries that fell in dock areas were quickly extinguished. Only one factory of importance was hit, but there was no damage to plant or machinery. By 0230 hours the country was free of enemy aircraft.

Fighter Command flew a record 118 night fighter patrols, including two offensive sorties, but met with little success. One Ju 88 was claimed damaged by a Defiant of No. 264 Squadron, but Blenheim L1226 of No. 23 Squadron failed to return from an Intruder mission. Over the country as a whole some 12,000 HAA rounds were fired, 4,579 of them in the London IAZ, and three enemy aircraft were claimed destroyed. Searchlights in the Southampton area claimed three illuminations but no claims were registered by local AA gun sites. However, 'Y' Service intercepts of German aircraft W/T traffic indicated that three, possibly four, bombers may have forced landed. AA guns were in action at Portsmouth, Gloucester, Manchester, Birmingham, Coventry, Cardiff, Swansea, Merseyside, Dover, Bromley, Plymouth, Bristol and in the London IAZ.

JANUARY, 1941—(*Contd.*)							
19	BONNINGTON COURT	M.	4,909	275° 9.5 cables from Sunk L.V.	A.C.	B.	
20	FLORIAN	S.	3,174	North Atlantic	S.M.*	—	
20	STANPARK	S.	5,103	09°27′S. 03°00′W.	Raider	—	" Admiral Scheer "
21	TEMPLE MEAD ...	S.	4,427	54°14′N. 14°30′W.	A.C.	B.	
21	ENGLISHMAN* ...	Tug	487	40m. W. of Tory Island	A.C.	B.	
23	LURIGETHAN ...	S.	3,564	53°46′N. 16°00′W.	A.C.	B.	
23	LANGLEEGORSE ...	S.	4,524	53°19′N. 13°11′W.	A.C.	B.	
23	MOSTYN	S.	1,859	54°30′N. 14°52′W.	A.C.	B.	

She was actually bombed and sent to the bottom on the 23rd as shown by this extract from the official Admiralty list of merchant vessels lost during the war. The January total of merchant shipping lost from all causes — mines, submarines, aircraft and surface raiders — was, at 208,567 GRT, the lowest since the air attacks on England began in June 1940.

The 51-year-old Guildhall in Portsmouth, set alight in the city's great fire blitz on the night of January 10, burned all next day, flames leaping out from the tower, which looked like a giant 200-foot-high torch. A high-explosive bomb brought the roof down and it was some days before the interior had cooled sufficiently to allow entry. With even the panelling burned from the walls, virtually everything was lost; all except the Corporation plate, some dating from 1525, and 17th Century Mace which had fortunately escaped by being stored in the Muniments Room under the tower.

FRIDAY, JANUARY 10-11

Sunset: 1711 Sunrise: 0905
Moon: Dusk — 0648 (Full −3)

Major attack on Portsmouth. Minor harassing attacks and minelaying in Liverpool Bay.

UK — Extensive low cloud with rain in most parts. Cloudy but fair in Scotland, western Wales and along the southern coast of England at first (low cloud and rain here after 2300 hours).

The Continent — Cloudy with some coastal drizzle in the Low Countries; visibility moderate but poor in drizzle. In northern France mainly fair with moderate to good visibility; broken cloud near coast. Light to moderate N-NE winds in all districts.

German Air Force activity during daylight hours was limited to mainly defensive fighter patrols over the English Channel and only two minor bombing incidents were reported (in Kent).

During the day 'Y' Service intercepts of German ground-to-ground W/T traffic revealed that a heavy night attack was planned against Manchester, but later on the target was changed to Portsmouth, almost certainly because of adverse weather conditions in the North. The change in target was also indicated by the monitoring of German VHF beams, which were set up to intersect over Southsea Common, and in anticipation Fighter Night Portsmouth was ordered, with Zero Hour at 1930 hours. Mutton was also ordered to operate in Area 'C' from 1900 to 2300 hours.

Night activity began at 1835 hours with bomber streams approaching Portsmouth from the direction of Le Havre, Dieppe/Abbeville and Cherbourg. Altogether 180 bombers operated during the night, with 155 aircraft of Luftflotte 3 ordered to attack Portsmouth. Of this force 153 crews claimed to have bombed their primary target, delivering some 140 tonnes of HE and oil bombs (two SC 2500, eight SC 1800, seven SD 1400, 31 SC 1000, 75 SC 500, 143 SC 250, 30 LZZ 250, four Flam 250, 290 SC 50 and 50 SD 50) and 1,409 BSK (containing 39,706 B1 E1 and 1,138 B1 El ZA incendiaries). Initially bomb aiming was by visual means, but after 2200 hours weather conditions made it necessary to bomb by DR, radio navigation, or the use of fires already burning. Crews reported especially good results, with two large explosions during the first 38 minutes of the attack. Within a very short time six large and

The view from Russell Street some time later — like so many wartime bomb-sites, now a car park.

Above: **In the suburb of Southsea the popular shopping area in Palmerston Road was virtually wiped out. What was left had to be dynamited to stop the fires spreading along Osborne Road. This is Handley's Corner.**

Below: **The Harbour Central Station the morning after the raid although the picture was not released until 1943. Lack of water led to many fires burning uncontrolled and, in the end, water was relayed a distance of over three miles.**

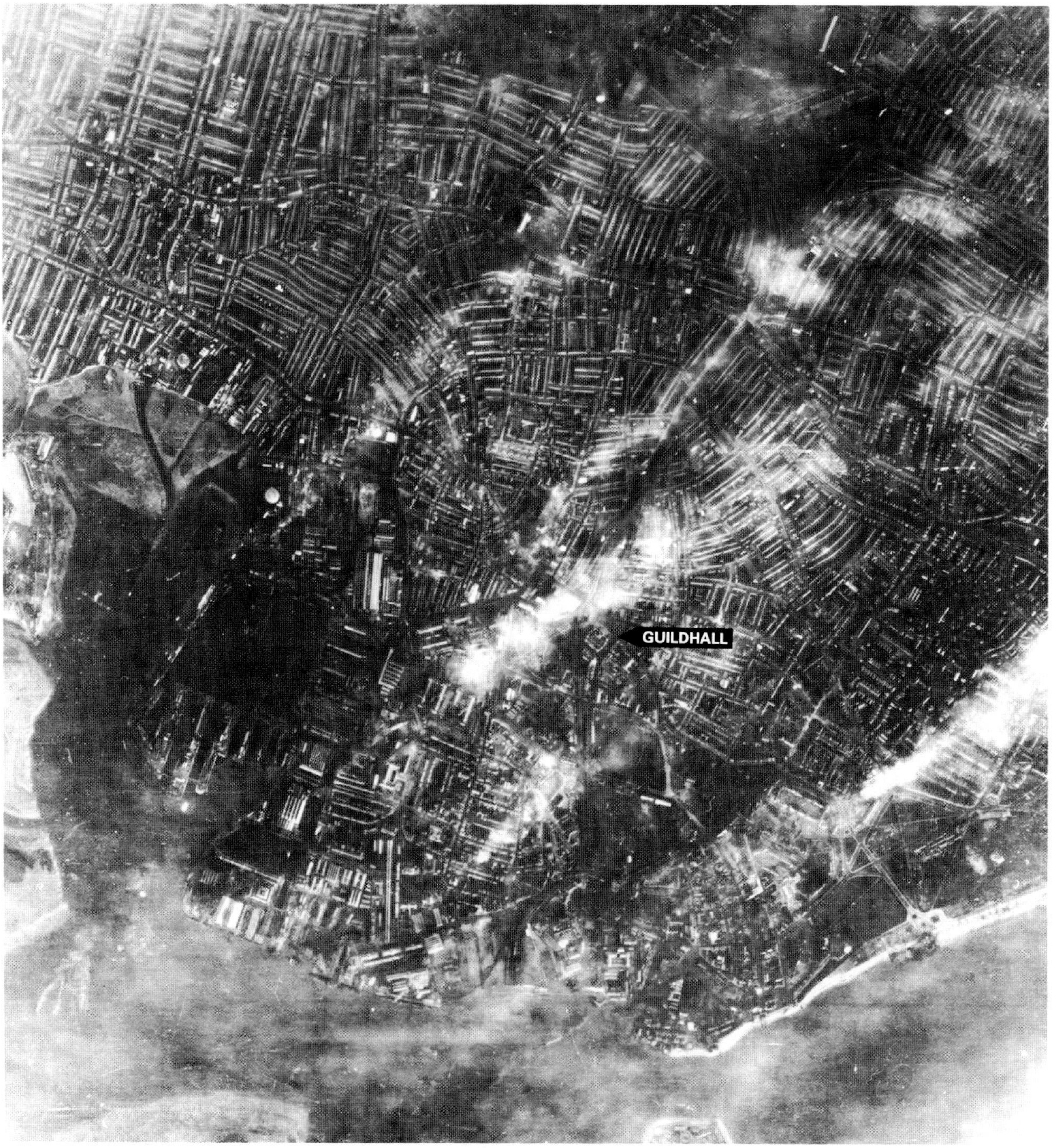

Three days after the attack the fires were still burning when a reconnaissance aircraft crossed the city on Sunday to carry out Mission F19. Although they may well have been unaware of the significance of HMS *Vernon*, the shore station to the west of the city, more by luck than judgement the Luftwaffe had hit the headquarters of the Royal Navy's mine counter-warfare establishment from where the battle was being waged against the German mines. Eight bombs fell in *Vernon*, Building 17 *(left)* being gutted. Fortunately a newly-built blast wall saved the Wardroom from serious blast damage *(right)*.

Although lacking a precise date, this Portsmouth *Evening News* picture, most probably taken by their staff photographer, Mr Victor Stewart, shows St Thomas's Cathedral, one of the few buildings to come through unscathed, from Oyster Street.

20 smaller fires could be seen, distributed over the entire Target Area. The first phase of the attack lasted from 1852 hours — with II/KG55 leading — until 2100, and by this time the glow of fires was visible from the French coast. The second part of the attack started at 2337 and was completed at 0126, by which time fires covered the entire town but were concentrated on the dock area and the south-west district. As some 75 per cent of the aircraft in the first phase bombed visually, accurate bombing and very great damage seemed to have been achieved.

Participating crews found the flak over Portsmouth variable in strength, as indeed it was as required by Operation Fighter Night. Searchlight activity, too, was not particularly lively, but several night fighters were encountered. Overall, however, the defences were reported as 'trivial', with the early effort (which was classed as 'good, but ineffectively aimed') noticeably dwindling as the attack progressed.

Participating units were:

I/KG27: 10 He 111, 2345-0050
II/KG27: 9 He 111, 2337-0005
III/KG27: 10 He 111, 0045-0126
KGr100: 10 He 111, 1900-1930 (X-System bombing with a visual check on accuracy)
KGr606: 11 Do 17, 2350-0010
I/KG51: 6 Ju 88, 1925-1955
II/KG51: 6 Ju 88, 1955-2025
III/KG51: 5 Ju 88, 1955-2008
I/KG54: 12 Ju 88, 2007-2022
KGr806: 10 Ju 88, 2013-2040
II/KG55: 19 He 111, 1852-1945 (opened attack dropping 28 LC 50 flares; bombs included eight SC 1800, seven SD 1400 and seven SC 1000 heavy HEs)
KG1: 13 Ju 88, 14 He 111, 1940-2100
I/KG26: 11 He 111, 2000-2046
III/KG26: 6 He 111, 1858-1957 (visual aiming; bombs included two SC 2500)

In addition three Ju 88s of I/KG51 were dispatched on special 'Störangriffe' or 'destruction' attacks against the aircraft factories at Hucclecote and Yate, and Glasgow West Dry Dock, but because of unfavourable weather alternative targets at Portsmouth, Bristol and Brighton were claimed bombed instead. Two aircraft bound for Portsmouth also bombed alternatives and three aborted. No aircraft were lost by Luftflotte 3 units.

MHS reports confirm that extensive damage was caused in Portsmouth and Gosport, with particularly serious fires in the former where the business centre was badly hit. Extensive damage also occurred in Southsea and fires were started in timber yards and warehouses; major damage was also done to public utilities but damage to important dockyard installations was less serious. The working of the Gosport Gas Works was interrupted by an unexploded bomb and both detonated bombs and UXBs brought about interference to railway services; for a time all traffic in Portsmouth was stopped, trains terminating at Havant and Cosham. The Guildhall was gutted by fire and three AFS stations, two hospitals, several churches, many houses, commercial premises and schools also suffered. Casualties were officially put at 68 killed and 161 seriously injured. Elsewhere in the country bombs fell at Worthing, near Hereford, Selsey Bill and Romney Marshes.

The Fighter Night operation achieved little, but one of the three Spitfires of No. 65 Squadron on patrol intercepted and claimed the destruction of an He 111 over Gosport. Including five fighters on dusk patrols, Fighter Command flew 24 sorties; in addition, a single Harrow was sent up on a Mutton patrol, but there was a lack of enemy aircraft in the Middle Wallop Sector and no aerial mines were released. HAA guns were in action at Swansea, Bristol, Cardiff, Portland, Plymouth and Falmouth, in addition to the Solent guns which engaged the enemy between 1800 and 2240 hours and again from 2330 to 0130, claiming one enemy aircraft destroyed. Countrywide nearly 4,000 rounds were fired by HAA batteries.

In addition to the concentration on the Portsmouth area, some 25 aircraft were tracked from Lyme Bay to Liverpool Bay with some routing via Cardiff and Colwyn Bay while others went as far north as Whitehaven. Almost certainly all were engaged on sea mining and most probably belonged to I/KG28. The country was clear of all enemy aircraft by 0130 hours.

Only the occasional aircraft crossed the British coast during daylight hours, with a small number continuing maritime patrols. Losses were as follows:

2(F)/123 Junkers Ju 88A-5 (0358). Whilst on a reconnaissance mission to Manchester crashed into the sea off Newquay, Cornwall. Exact cause of crash unknown. Fw. H. Herold killed, his body being found at Newquay. Oberlt. H-J von Sydow, Oberfw. E. Steiner, Fw. R. Löffel all missing. Aircraft 4U+FK lost.

Stab I/KG40 Focke-Wulf FW 200C-3 (0035). Shot down by Mr Reilly, Mate of ocean-going tug *Seaman*, with a Lewis gun during an attack on the ship 200 miles north-west of Ireland at 1.50 p.m. Oberlt. F. W. Burmeister, Ob.Ing. B. Gumbert and Uffz. R. Steinmeyer captured. Oberfw. W. Lebe, Uffz. H. Kittner and Lt. H. John killed. Aircraft F8+AB sank in sea.

Coming hard on the heels of the December raids which had already severely shaken morale, the fire raid of January 10 led Mass-Observation to closely monitor local reaction — with mixed results. A middle-aged woman, nervous and depressed, said: 'I feel stunned — like — seem to 'ave lost all me power of concentration. It all seems difficult — people can put up with a lot, but there's a limit. I'd make any sacrifice if the war could be over' and a woman of 26, haggard and strained, who had four children under four to look after, and a husband at sea: 'I don't know how I ever stood it. My God, I never knew how I stood it!' The other side of the picture came from a charwoman, wiry, energetic and talkative, who remarked: 'Old 'Itler's not going to drive me out of my 'ome! Everything's ready in *my* shelter! Blast wall, electric lights and all snug! But people ought to be more prepared.'

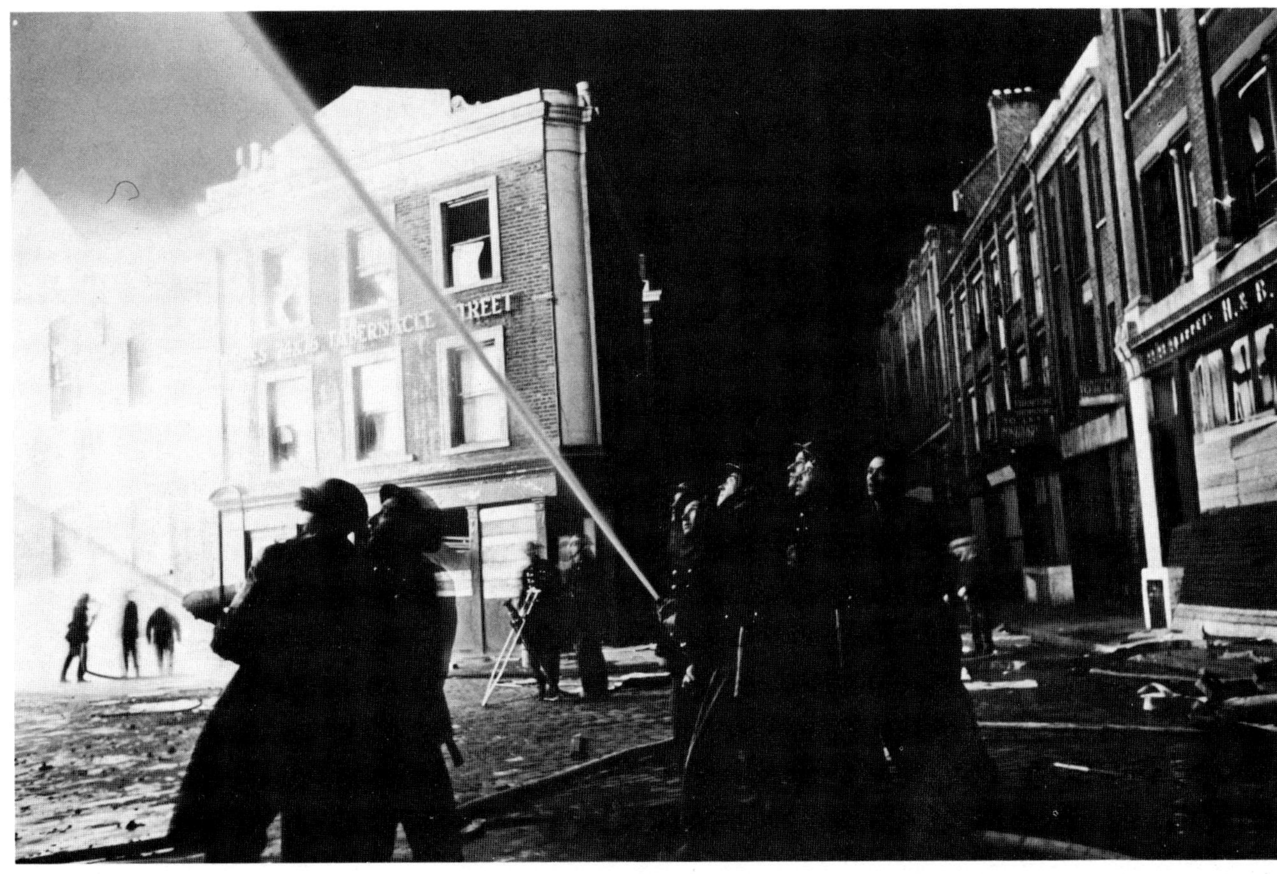

SATURDAY, JANUARY 11-12

Sunset: 1712 Sunrise: 0904
Moon: Dusk — 0740 (Full −2)

Major attack on London. Minelaying in Liverpool Bay, the Bristol Channel and at various points off the West Coast.

UK — Mainly cloudy with poor visibility but with fine intervals and improving.
The Continent — Cloud at 1,000-2,000ft over the Low Countries, mainly fair in northern France. Visibility poor in northern France and the Low Countries, with mist or fog patches developing, but moderate to good elsewhere.

Bad weather with low cloud reduced German activity to a very low level during the day and only nine inland penetrations were plotted. A few bombs were dropped in the South-East and two people were killed.

Night activity started just after 1800 hours with the approach of the first raiders from the direction of Cap Gris Nez. The early start — and the concentration in time of the ensuing attack — was almost certainly due to fog expected over the bomber bases in northern France and the Low Countries by midnight. Accordingly, in an attack on London lasting only from 1825 to 2130 hours, 137 long-range bombers of Luftflotte 3 dropped some 144 tonnes of HE (comprising ten SC 1800, four SC 1400, 55 SC 1000, 85 SC 500, 23 LZZ 250, 39 SC 250 and 148 SC 50) and 598 BSK (21,528 IBs). Except for a few isolated cases, bombing was conducted without sight of the ground, using DR and radio navigation methods, and the thick cloud over the capital made observation of the results extremely difficult. Only the glow of three

Not often can one find such striking comparisons as these . . . where right in the middle of a heavily blitzed area so little has changed in over 40 years. These fine studies of firefighters in action were taken in Tabernacle Street on the night of January 11 (see also frontispiece). Normally one man could just hold a branch working at 70 pounds per square inch but, as he would need help moving it, it was usual to have two men working together. Sometimes the pump feeding the hose would be turned up to 100 psi to 'knock out' a fire. The fireman in the background has a branch holder to assist him.

large fires could be discerned, but a number of smaller fires were apparent at times through the cloud deck. Flak was met in variable strength, but in general was described as 'moderate'. Searchlights were unable to penetrate the cloud, but several balloons were seen. There were numerous reports of night fighters with, in some cases, 'stubborn but unsuccessful attacks'; nevertheless, one attacked Ju 88 was forced to jettison its load of two SC 500s some 50 kilometres south of London. As usual, aircraft of IX Fliegerkorps carried out the mining of Liverpool Bay.

Of the 145 bombers dispatched to London the crews of 137 claimed to have bombed their primary target; seven aircraft aborted and one bombed an alternative.

The participating units (all of Luftflotte 3) and their bombing times were as follows:

I/LG1: 11 Ju 88, 2058-2131
I/KG27: 13 He 111, 1936-2055
III/KG27: 12 He 111, 1930-2037
KGr100: 11 He 111, 1905-1945
I/KG51: 6 Ju 88, 1920-1950
II/KG51: 6 Ju 88, 2050-2115
III/KG51: 7 Ju 88, 2055-2130
II/KG54: 7 Ju 88, 1955-2032
KGr806: 6 Ju 88, 2034-2052
I and II/KG55: 16 He 111, 1850-1922
KG77: 27 Ju 88, 1825-2046
I/KG26: 15 He 111, 1945-2018

Luftflottenkommando 3 reported no losses from the operation, but reported that prevailing conditions made an assessment of the attack impossible.

From the British point of view the attack was officially classed as 'neither a success nor failure'. East and South London, the City and the West End received many incendiary bombs, accompanied by HEs in seemingly greater numbers than of late, but the most serious damage was the result of fires in the City, South London, Finsbury and Kensington, despite the valiant efforts of firewatchers. Some damage was also caused in the docks and there were serious incidents with many casualties at Liverpool Street and Bank Stations. Five factories of importance were hit but damage was negligible, mainly owing to rapid firefighting at all but one of them. Sixteen hits were reported on the railway system, causing considerable disruption to services. Of 105 people killed, 35 were killed at Bank Station, six at Green Park Station and 43 at Liverpool Street, most of them waiting passengers. Seven people also died at Lambeth Hospital, with three more deaths at a nursing home in the same district. Utility services were relatively slightly damaged and by the next day few consumers were without gas or electricity supplies.

However the pictures were withheld by the censor for four months and only released on May 8. Because their release coincided within a couple of days with the massive attack on London of May 10-11, after they were published it was only natural for them to be used thereafter to depict an incident in *that* raid.

Where the young men of another age now park their Japanese motor cycles, their fathers once fought a war for survival.

While the attack on London was in progress about 30 aircraft, believed to have been minelayers of I/KG28, were tracked from the direction of Brest-Morlaix to various points off the West Coast including St David's Head, Milford Haven, Liverpool Bay, Caernarvon Bay and the Bristol Channel.

Outside of the London area bombs fell at Horton Kirby, Chobham, Bletchingley, Orpington, Withyham and Banstead.

Meteorological conditions, including surface and upper winds, were favourable for the release of a Free Balloon Barrage over the London area but although successfully launched — and in spite of the number of enemy aircraft concentrated over the city —

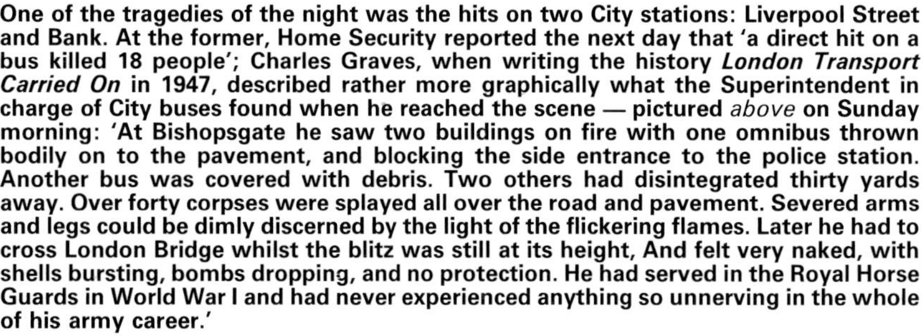

One of the tragedies of the night was the hits on two City stations: Liverpool Street and Bank. At the former, Home Security reported the next day that 'a direct hit on a bus killed 18 people'; Charles Graves, when writing the history *London Transport Carried On* in 1947, described rather more graphically what the Superintendent in charge of City buses found when he reached the scene — pictured *above* on Sunday morning: 'At Bishopsgate he saw two buildings on fire with one omnibus thrown bodily on to the pavement, and blocking the side entrance to the police station. Another bus was covered with debris. Two others had disintegrated thirty yards away. Over forty corpses were splayed all over the road and pavement. Severed arms and legs could be dimly discerned by the light of the flickering flames. Later he had to cross London Bridge whilst the blitz was still at its height, And felt very naked, with shells bursting, bombs dropping, and no protection. He had served in the Royal Horse Guards in World War I and had never experienced anything so unnerving in the whole of his army career.'

The force of the blast etched into the wall of Bishopsgate Police Station; well prepared against air attack. The police recorded the explosion on No. 135 opposite at 8.20 p.m. The London Passenger Transport Board reported that 'fifteen central buses were damaged, four of them severely; these four buses were in Bishopsgate; two drivers and one conductor were killed and one driver and two conductors injured and, as far as is at present known twenty-two passengers were killed and others injured. The remaining buses sustained minor damage.'

no successes were registered. Nor were casualties claimed by the AA gunners, despite the 3,775 rounds fired within the London IAZ. Only nine night fighters were operating, because of the low cloud and poor visibility over England, but apart from a sighting of an He 111 by a Hurricane pilot no interceptions were effected. One Blenheim took off on an Intruder operation, but was forced to turn back at the French coast because of the weather. Countrywide some 4,100 rounds of HAA ammunition were expended during the night, with guns in action at Portsmouth, Plymouth, Falmouth, Merseyside, Cardiff, and the Solent in addition to those in the IAZ, at Thames and Medway North and Thames and Medway South.

SUNDAY, JANUARY 12-13

Sunset: 1713 Sunrise: 0904
Moon: Dusk — 0826 (Full −1)

Major attack on London. Minelaying in Liverpool Bay, the Bristol Channel and off Plymouth.

UK — Cloudy, but with fine intervals and improving in the West. Elsewhere visibility poor with occasional rain and showers.

The Continent — Mainly fair, becoming cloudy in the Low Countries with some coastal showers later. Visibility poor generally with local fog patches inland. Light variable wind but light to moderate westerly in Holland and northern Belgium.

Only ten German aircraft crossed the British coast during the day because of the unfavourable weather. Patrols were flown over adjacent sea areas, but no bombs fell on land.

London was the target for the second night in succession and again the attack was of comparatively short duration, activity starting shortly after 1830 hours with the country clear of all enemy aircraft by 2230. The attacking force comprised 141 bombers of Luftflotte 3 and they dropped 155 tonnes of HE (three SC 1800, 61 SC 1000, four SD 1000, 53 SC 500, 81 SC 250, 72 LZZ 250, 406 SC 50) and 823 BSK (29,628 incendiaries) between 1837 and 2205 hours. The Concentration Point for the attack was the docks to the west and east of the Thames U-bend

Ministry of Home Security Appreciation No. 223 for the period 0600 hours 11th January to 0600 hours 12th January 1941; Special Damage Report by Night, London: 'The worst single incident occurred at the BANK STATION in the City, which suffered a direct hit with an H.E. bomb causing booking hall and circular gallery to cave in. Estimated casualties are more than 50 dead, and 6 of the station staff are missing.' Closure of roads to the City's vital seven-way interchange, as well as the Underground station below serving three lines, brought life to a standstill on Monday morning when this picture was taken.

including dock installations within the loop of the river north of Greenwich, but extensive cloud hindered crews in the early stages. The weather in the Target Area improved later, as was forecast, but full advantage could not be taken of this — fog was expected to form on the Continent later in the night and it was necessary to have the bombers back on the ground well before midnight. All bombing was carried out by DR or radio navigation methods for the first couple of hours or so, but towards the end of the attack visual bomb aiming, and the observation of results, were possible. Various large fires were then seen in the built-up areas north and south of the Thames loop, with one very large fire in South-East London. There was also considerable smoke, thought to be emanating from an oil fire, and about an hour after the attack started a very large explosion was reported. The visual observations reported led Luftflottenkommando 3 to believe that, in general, good results had been achieved.

German crews considered that the defences were of the usual strength but largely ineffective although the flak was well aimed; searchlights were of little use for most of the time, because of cloud, but about 20 balloons were reported flying at heights up to about 6,000 feet. Night fighters were encountered on the approach to and over London and one attack, by a Blenheim, produced four strikes on an attacking bomber. However, no losses were sustained by Luftflotte 3 and of the 144 bombers dispatched the crews of 141 claimed to have bombed London, the other three bombing Portsmouth, Brighton and Eastbourne as alternatives. In total 167 bombers were operating, including aircraft of IX Fliegerkorps which laid mines in Liverpool Bay, off Anglesey, in the Bristol Channel and off Plymouth.

The London attack was carried out by the following units:

I/LG1: 10 Ju 88, 1930-2010
II/KG27: 14 He 111, 2105-2205
KGr100: 10 He 111, 1903-1930
KGr606: 14 Do 17, 1955-2050
I/KG51: 6 Ju 88, 1845-1910
II/KG51: 6 Ju 88, 2045-2105
III/KG51: 6 Ju 88, 2115-2130
I/KG54: 15 Ju 88, 2007-2041
Stab/KG55: 3 He 111, 2005-2025
I/KG55: 4 He 111, 1950-2008
III/KG55: 10 He 111, 1905-2020
KG77: 31 Ju 88, 1837-2100
I/KG26: 12 He 111, 1932-2035

A typical Monday morning forty years later. According to the official Civil Defence history, 38 people were killed but this must be incorrect as 55 names are recorded in the Civilian War Dead Roll. However, even this number cannot be taken as an accurate total as some of the injured may well have died in hospitals outside the City, their names being thereby recorded in another borough. Suffice it to say that nothing remains at Bank today to mark one of the most horrific wartime occurrences.

The bomb had exploded in the booking hall a few feet beneath the roadway, the blast travelling down the escalator shaft which 'collapsed like a pack of cards'. All the lights went out, the only light being provided by the flickering oil lamps and torches carried by the rescue party which reached the spot from Liverpool Street. There they found a terrible scene. Several people had been blown onto the track just as a train had entered the station. The blast blew the driver's hands from the controls and, although the automatic brake came into operation, it was too late to stop some of those blown off the platform being run over. With no way out to the surface, the survivors made their way along the track and after about three hours the whole station had been cleared of dead and injured, save for those buried under the escalators. Royal Engineers were soon helping City engineers remove the rubble and steelwork from the booking hall to enable a start to be made on throwing a temporary bridge across the yawning gap to get the traffic moving.

From the foregoing it is of interest to note that aircraft of KG77 were the first to commence bombing, nearly 30 minutes before the arrival of the first He 111 of KGr100; all ten aircraft of this Beleuchtergruppe bombed by DR and not by the more usual use of X-Verfahren. The other normal lead Gruppen, II/KG55 and III/KG26, did not operate.

The Ministry of Home Security reported that the attack, although heavy, was not as serious as that of the previous night. Most damage occurred in East and South-East London and along the Thames Estuary, with fires at Woolwich Arsenal, Erith, Victoria and Albert Docks, Crayford (where Vickers Armstrong premises were affected), and at Purfleet (the Anglo-American and Shell-Mex depots). Bombs were also dropped at Corringham, where three HEs hit the Thames Oil Works, and at Brentwood, Chelmsford, Southend, Rainham, East and West Ham, Leyton, Barking, Greenwich, Plumstead, Chislehurst, Orpington, Bromley, Walthamstow, Tottenham, Paddington, Lambeth, Oxted, Godalming, Hounslow, Tilbury, Hornchurch and Shoeburyness. Outside of the Greater London/Thames Estuary region, bombs fell at Plymouth, Milford Haven and Lynton, Devon, where three people were killed. Casualties in the south-east London area totalled 46 dead and 102 seriously injured.

To counter German operations Fighter Command flew 32 defensive night fighter

By February 1 what was called the 'largest crater in London' had been cleared and the bridge was beginning to nose out from the western side towards Cheapside.

The bridge was completed by Monday, February 3 when it was opened by the Lord Mayor, after which the men of No. 691 General Construction Coy, R.E., had the honour of being the first across.

sorties and three Intruder patrols by Blenheims of No. 23 Squadron from Ford. One of the latter bombed Chartres airfield, which was clearly visible although the ground was snow-covered; another went to Beauvais, but cloud cover prevented an attack, while the third aborted because of deteriorating weather. The only encounter involved a Beaufighter of No. 604 Squadron and an He 111 about five miles off the South Coast. The German bomber was claimed damaged.

In addition to the London IAZ, HAA guns were in action at Southampton, Merseyside, Swansea, Bristol, Portland, Thames and Medway North and South, Fareham, Plymouth, Falmouth, Cardiff, Pembroke Dock, Yeovil and Dover. One raider was claimed destroyed and two probably destroyed. Within the IAZ 4,258 rounds of ammunition were expended with a nationwide total of nearly 7,000.

MONDAY, JANUARY 13-14

Sunset: 1715 Sunrise: 0903
Moon: 1754 — Dawn (Full Moon)

Sharp attack on Plymouth/Devonport. Minelaying in Liverpool Bay and the Bristol Channel, and anti-shipping patrols.

UK — Generally fair with 4 to 8/10ths cloud at 2,000-3,000ft in occasional showers. Moderate visibility, reduced in precipitation.

The Continent — Visibility moderate to good on coasts, but local mist or fog inland in the Low Countries and northern France. Over western areas of northern France variable cloud with freshening westerly wind.

During daylight there was much fog in the South and consequently there was little German activity and no reports of bombing. In view of a possible clearance, however, Mutton was alerted to operate in the usual Area 'C' between 1900 and 2100 hours.

This model of the 691 bridge was made by one of the sappers who worked on the real one and was displayed later that year at the School of Military Engineering at Chatham.

The station was back in action by March 17 and by May the roadway had been repaired and the bridge taken out.

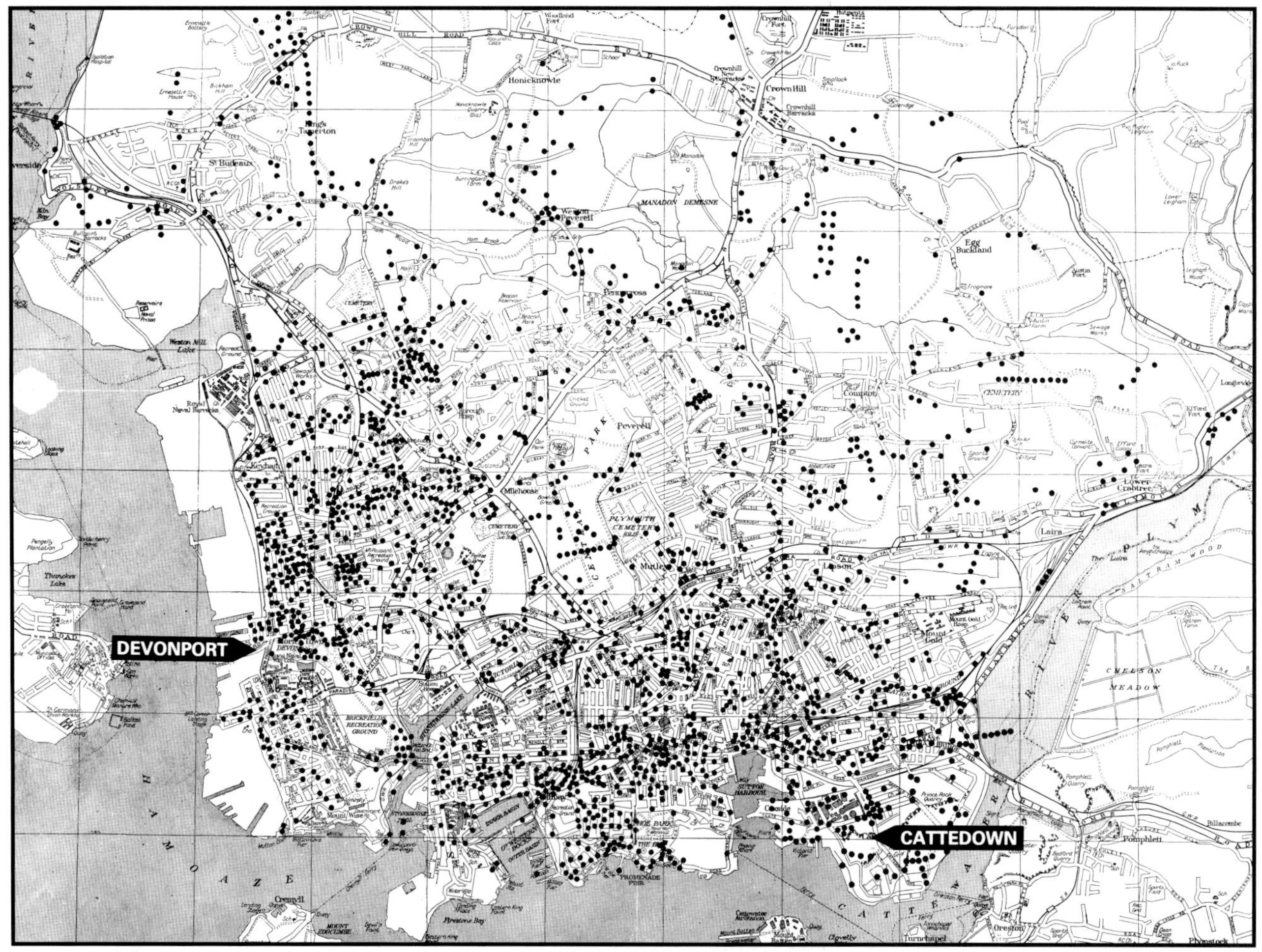

After the two-night attack on London at the weekend, on Monday the Luftwaffe switched their attention to Plymouth. Although the Schwerpunkt had been laid down as Devonport dockyard in the south-western corner of the city, bombing went awry and the majority of hits were scored to the south-east in the Prince Rock–Cattedown districts. This map has been taken from the publication *The Blitz of Plymouth 1940–44*, produced to commemorate the fortieth anniversary of the most severe air raids in April 1941, and shows the overall bomb plot three years later.

From 1801 hours, with the commencement of enemy activity, permission was given for unseen fire in all areas of No. 11 Group, but most of the incoming Raids were heading for the Plymouth area in No. 10 Group's territory. The Luftwaffe report on operations this night again emphasised the requirement to confine the attack to a short period in the early evening because of the threat of fog later on. The meteorological assessment also indicated the better weather prospects for the West of England and hence the choice of Plymouth/Devonport for the main target. In passing, as expected by the Wetterdienst, the fog forecast for the previous night had materialised and by the early hours fog or lifted fog covered most airfields north of the Seine.

The attack on Plymouth/Devonport lasted from 1843 to 2250 hours and was carried out by 50 aircraft of the 63 operating that night. They dropped 21 tonnes of HE (comprising one SC 1000, two SC 500, four LZZ 250, 23 SC 250 and 236 SC 50) and 749 BSK (26,964 IBs). The CP lay over the docks and dockyard installations, with their associated support plants, in the west and south-west of the town. Bomb aiming was visual throughout and the conditions permitted observation of the results — explosions and fires were seen in the docks and in the town and it was claimed that bombing was accurate and mainly in the ordered Target Area.

The AA defences appeared to be normal — the flak was described as 'variable, well directed at times', but the searchlight activity was said to be trivial. Some 20 balloons were seen, as were several night fighters although no attacks were made. Decoy fires were also reported at several points around Plymouth.

One aircraft on anti-shipping patrol over the Bristol Channel bombed Plymouth when no ships were found; another dropped an SC 1000 on Swansea, where a large explosion was seen in the dock area, and en route to this target attacked a tanker in Pembroke Dock with four SC 250s, but without success. Crews of the entire force of 49 bombers sent to Plymouth by Luftflotte 3 bombed their primary targets, with no attacks on alternatives, no aborts and no losses. Participating units were:

I/KG27: 16 He 111, 1908-2025
III/KG27: 10 He 111, 1900-2015
KGr100: 11 He 111, 1843-1907
KGr606: 12 Do 17, 2028-2050

Kampfgruppe 100, leading the attack, dropped 11,520 B1 Els and 1,152 B1 El ZAs in the space of 24 minutes and crews were able to confirm the accuracy of their bombing (on dock installations and the southern part of the town) by visual observation.

MHS reports confirm the German reports of fires and damage, but contrary to the Luftwaffe's assessment they were mainly centred on residential areas in the south-eastern part of the city. Electricity and gas supplies were badly hit, however, but the water system escaped remarkably lightly. Two hospitals were also damaged, but little damage of importance was recorded. Nevertheless, although of short duration it was a sharp attack in which 18 people were killed and 15 seriously injured.

A Harrow of No. 93 Squadron took off on a Mutton operation at 1900 hours, but because of an absence of enemy aircraft in the Middle Wallop Sector it returned to base at 2115. Thirty-three night fighters were also on patrol during the night, but despite the full moon no combats with enemy aircraft ensued. The gunners of Anti-Aircraft Command fared no better; about 3,000 rounds were fired during the night by various batteries including those at Merseyside where enemy aircraft were engaged at heights between 500 and 10,000 feet. Like other aircraft in the Bristol Channel area, these were engaged in minelaying.

TUESDAY, JANUARY 14-15

Sunset: 1716 Sunrise: 0902
Moon: 1903 — Dawn (Full +1)

No German night operations over Britain.

UK — Fog in south-eastern England. Cloudy elsewhere with occasional rain, but snow in the North.

The Continent — Extensive cloud with snow in the North and in coastal areas.

Daylight operations by the Germans were restricted to a few reconnaissance missions and no bombing was reported. Mutton was ordered to operate in Area 'C' (Middle Wallop Sector) from 1900 to 2300 and a Harrow of No. 93 Squadron took off at 1810 hours to comply. However, it returned to Warmwell 20 minutes later because of the bad weather. Three night fighters were also sent on patrol, but all German night operations had been cancelled.

JOHNSON, Pilot Offr. ALFRED OWEN, 67596. R.A.F. 221 Sqdn. 22nd June, 1941. Age 28. Son of Robert Cooper Johnson and Agnes Johnson, of Beverley, Yorkshire; husband of Dorothy Amelia Johnson, of Beverley. Panel 33.

JOHNSON, First Offr. AMY V., C.B.E. Air Tpt. Aux. 5th January, 1941. Age 37. Daughter of John William and Amy Johnson, of Beverley, Yorkshire. B.A., A.R.Ae.S., F.R.G.S., F.S.E., M.W.E.S. President's gold medal from Society of Engineers, 1931; Egyptian gold medal for valour, 1930; League of Aviators', Women's Trophy, 1930; Segrave Trophy, 1932; Royal Aero Club's gold medal, 1936. Panel 287.

JOHNSON, Sgt. ARROL, 1595131. R.A.F. (V.R.). 619 Sqdn. 5th January 1945. Age 25. Son of

Tuesday morning, the 500th day of the war, and the nation wept as a memorial service was held in St Martin's-in-the-Fields for one of Britain's heroes of the air, that courageous lady, Amy Johnson. Amy's name had become a household word ever since she became the first woman to win the King's Cup — the Aerial Derby instituted by King George V in 1922 — beating 88 starters to the finishing line at Hanworth Air Park in 1930. Her long distance flights were legendary and by 1940 her log book had built up to some 2,300 hours. Even so she had to undergo a test in May before the RAF would accept her as a ferry pilot in the Air Transport Auxiliary. Then came Sunday, January 5, a bleak day of snow and low cloud, yet First Officer Amy set off to ferry an Airspeed Oxford down from Blackpool. Lost above cloud, the aircraft ran out of fuel over the Thames Estuary and she took to her parachute. Amy was spotted by the crew of the naval trawler *Haslemere* and Lieutenant Commander Walter Fletcher lost his life in a rescue attempt. However the sea was rough with a heavy swell and Amy was sucked down by the stern. Her body was never recovered and today under her maiden name (she had married the famous airman Jim Mollison in 1932) she is remembered on Panel 287 of the RAF Memorial to the Missing at Runnymede.

WEDNESDAY, JANUARY 15-16

Sunset: 1718 Sunrise: 0901
Moon: 2017 — Dawn (Full +2)

Medium weight attack on Derby. RAF airfields in eastern England attacked by a small force of long-range night fighters. Scattered bombing at other points including London and the Midlands. Minelaying between Harwich and Scarborough.

UK — Variable cloud with snow showers, particularly heavy in northern Scotland and on coasts. Visibility generally good, but poor in snow showers and in industrial areas. Winds north to north-east.

The Continent — Cloudy with snow showers, particularly in northern areas of France and the Low Countries.

A somewhat amazing innovation introduced on Wednesday was the return of the Stuka dive-bomber — only this time at night! The Ju 87 had been withdrawn from the battle the previous August after horrendous losses in spite of a three to one fighter escort *(see Volume 1, Pages 214–216)* and only reintroduced for attacks against shipping in the Channel where it could be given adequate fighter cover. Now two machines ventured as far as London to make dive-bombing attacks under cover of darkness. It was a short-lived experiment with a second attack on Friday night and then again on Sunday. After the following spell of bad weather brought ops to a halt, it failed to appear again at night until February 11-12.

On Wednesday night Derby received its heaviest raid of the entire war, although mild when compared with some of the punishment then being meted out by the Luftwaffe elsewhere. The lack of heavy bombing on the town is somewhat surprising considering that Derby is an important industrial centre: the home of the vitally important Rolls-Royce factory, then in production of the Merlin aircraft engine. The local historians Clive Hardy and Russ Brown speculate in *Derby at War* that this was possibly due to the Luftwaffe basing their target information on an outdated Ordnance Survey map which showed several features incorrectly described or located. Another reason, the authors feel, might be that the town was difficult to find and often hidden by fog or a very effective smoke-screen (see February 4–5 page 422, also page 602). This picture they included to illustrate an impromptu concert in the Abbey Street shelter on Christmas Eve.

Luftwaffe activity during daytime was restricted in extent but started in a spectacular fashion when a Ju 88 flew at low level down the Caledonian Canal to Fort William to drop a heavy HE bomb near the lock gates. No damage was caused. Elsewhere bombs fell in Kent, but again caused no damage or casualties. Only six German aircraft flew overland while 36 were engaged in coastal reconnaissance and anti-shipping patrols in very poor weather conditions.

Night activity started at 1826 when German aircraft were located off the Dutch Islands heading in the direction of Birmingham and crossing the coast between Harwich and Flamborough Head. The principal target was, in fact, Derby, which was claimed attacked by the crews of 49 aircraft. Between 2000 and 2233 hours, at 2320 hours, and again between 0200 and 0400, they dropped 59 tonnes of HE (four SC 1800, 26 SC 1000, 25 SC 500, 26 SC 250, three LZZ 250, and 115 SC 50) and 41 BSK (1,476 IBs), with the Concentration Point in south-east Derby, the location of the Rolls-Royce aero engine works. However, the factories could not be seen because of thick cloud and poor visibility, although one crew, some 1½ hours after the attack started, reported a detonation in the works. Several other crews reported fires and explosions in the general Target Area including possibly serious damage to a gasworks by an SC 1000.

An unusual feature of the night was a dive-bombing attack on London by two Ju 87 Stukas, each carrying an SC 1000 and diving from 4,500 to 2,000 metres. The first attacked Deptford at 0023 and the crew of the second believed they bombed Kidbrooke. Both claimed hits on large blocks of buildings. Another Stuka, diving from 4,600 to 800 metres, attacked Dover with an SC 1000 and although the bomb was believed to have hit the target, further results could not be determined because of avoiding action necessitated by the port's barrage balloons.

Finally, in the early hours, single long-range night fighters, 15 of which were operating, attacked Feltwell and Marham airfields. Two Blenheim aircraft were claimed shot down over eastern England by one of these German night fighters of I/NJG2. Other German units operating are not indicated in Luftwaffe records, but according to the RAF's 'Y' Service operations were conducted by KGs 2, 3, 4, 27, 30 and 51. German records do reveal, however, that 129 bombers (including minelayers) were operating besides the 15 night fighters.

According to Ministry of Home Security records, the bombing was widespread, both over the Midlands and London, but no serious damage was done. In Derbyshire and the North Midlands 26 people were killed and 37 lost their lives when a lodging house was hit in Westminster Bridge Road, London. Bombs were also reported in Yorkshire and Kent, but probably the most serious damage was caused in the West Midlands, where many houses and a gasworks were set on fire. Most districts of London experienced bombing, as did Derby, Nottingham, York, Grantham, Sheffield, Mansfield, Stoke-on-Trent, near Walsall, Seagrave, Ramsgate, Dover and Burton. At Church Fenton airfield three aircraft were attacked and the raider dropped some 80-90 incendiary bombs on the airfield, but no damage was done.

Fighter Command flew 43 night defensive sorties, but no Intruder operations were undertaken, presumably because of the generally poor weather over northern France. Conditions in the London area, however, were quite good for much of the night and condensation trails from German aircraft were clearly visible in the bright moonlight. Within the London IAZ searchlights engaged but no illuminations were reported; 24 Raids entered the Zone — aircraft returning from the Midlands — flying at heights between 10,000 and 25,000 feet and mainly out of searchlight range. Illuminations were obtained, however, by the 2nd AA Division.

The variety of tracks plotted by Fighter Command during the night made it difficult to assess the Luftwaffe's primary target, but 34 enemy aircraft were plotted operating between Scarborough and Harwich where, it was assumed, they were engaged on mine-laying.

The attacks by night fighters of I/NJG2 achieved a measure of success. Between 0200 and 0500 hours nine different plots were tracked to airfields at Church Fenton, Kirton-in-Lindsey, Leconfield, Driffield and Finningley, and three of five aircraft engaged on night training at Church Fenton (the home of No. 54 Operational Training Unit) came under attack. The three aircraft, a

'Laurel Bank' in Derby Lane, its roofs torn off by a near miss in the raid. It was estimated that fifty high explosive bombs straddled Derby on Wednesday night, bombs also falling in Litchurch Street, Canal Street, and on the Meadows. The bandstand in the Arboretum was demolished completely, and No. 4 Platform on the railway station hit by two bombs. The Bliss factory was hit, but Rolls-Royce escaped.

The corner of Offerton Avenue and Kenilworth Avenue. The raid cost the lives of 20 people with another 48 injured, yet the night ended on a high note for the RAF when Pilot Officer Richard Stevens returned to base having brought down not one but two of the raiders.

Blenheim and two Defiants, were forced to make crash landings, but there were no casualties. The airfield defences were unable to engage because of the presence of other friendly aircraft.

More than 1,000 rounds of HAA ammunition were fired during the night, with guns in action at Derby, Thames and Medway North, the IAZ, Harwich and Humberside, but no enemy aircraft were claimed destroyed. Fighter Command, on the other hand, had a comparatively successful night, with No. 151 Squadron in particular distinguishing itself with claims of two destroyed and two damaged. Another 'probable' went to a Beaufighter of No. 25 Squadron.

The night was particularly noteworthy for the destruction of two enemy aircraft by Pilot Officer Richard P. Stevens of No. 151 Squadron. Flying Hurricane V6934 he shot down his first victim, a Do 17 of 4/KG3, near Brentwood, Essex; his second, an He 111 of 2/KG53, came down near Canvey Island. They were the first night victories achieved by No. 151 Squadron since the unit's change to night fighting in November. They were also the first victories of Richard Stevens, but by no means were they to be his last.

A former civilian pilot, Stevens already had considerable night flying experience when he joined the RAF in 1939 at the age of 32, the maximum acceptable upper age limit. Shortly after his first successful night — during which he earned the DFC and became only the third pilot to destroy two enemy aircraft in one night — he was taken off flying with ear trouble, but he returned to the fray to claim two more He 111s on April 8 and a Ju 88 and another He 111 two nights later. This was followed by an He 111 on the 19th and two more on May 7, another and a 'probable' on the 10th and yet another destroyed on June 13. With his score standing at 14 enemy aircraft destroyed, Stevens was awarded the DSO on December 12, to add to his DFC and Bar, but just three nights later the inevitable happened and he was killed while engaged on a night intruder patrol. By this time he was a Flight Commander with No. 253 Squadron and the RAF's top scoring night fighter pilot.

4/KG3 Dornier Do 17Z-2 (3456). Shot down by Pilot Officer R. P. Stevens DFC in Hurricane V6934 of No. 151 Squadron 1.36 a.m. Crashed at Hartswood near Brentwood. Uffz. M. Schindler, Uffz. J. Sanktjohanser, Gefr. W. Teichmann and Uffz. L. Winkler killed. Aircraft 5K+DM destroyed.

Recovered by local ATC unit and subsequently re-excavated July 1982 by enthusiast Malcolm Pettit. Items recovered including crew identity disc now in the Tangmere Military Aviation Museum. Crash site in parkland landscaped by the recovery team.

2/KG53 Heinkel He 111H-5 (3638). Shot down by Pilot Officer R. P. Stevens DFC in Hurricane V6934 No. 151 Squadron 5.20 a.m. Aircraft hit barge and crashed in the sea near Spit Buoy off Holehaven, Canvey Island. Lt. G. Möhring, Gefr. T. Lübking, Gefr. E. Henduck all baled out and taken prisoner. Uffz. H. Graf killed. Aircraft A1+JK lost.

What a fine trophy this would have been to have given to Britain's top scoring night-fighter ace — the Spanish Cross belonging to one of the crew of the Brentwood Dornier. However, this only came to light when the crash was investigated in 1982, by which time Richard Playne Stevens had been dead for forty years, having fought his last battle on December 15, 1941. His grave can now be found in Bergen-op-Zoom war cemetery in the Netherlands.

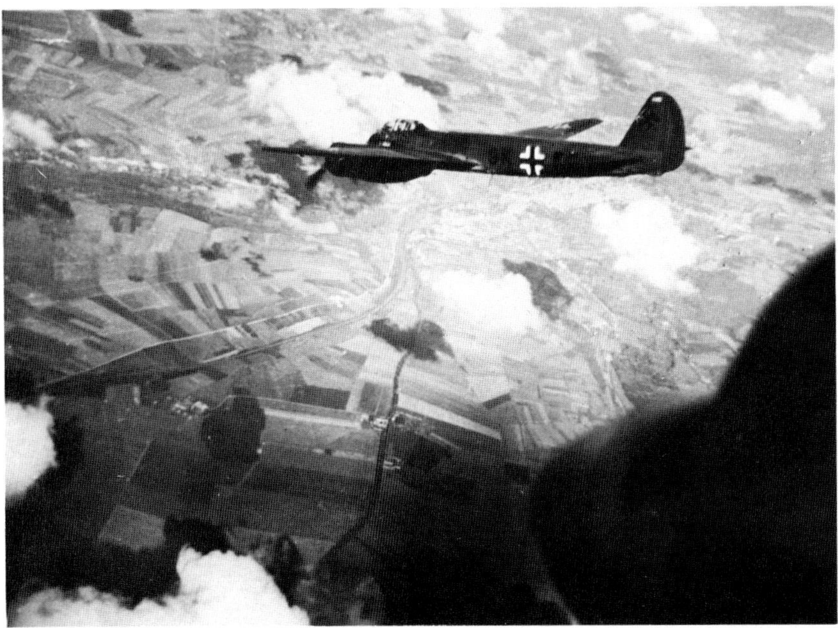

Cause and effect No. 1. Although these illustrations are not specific to the night's raid, they do show a Ju 88A-5 of Stab III/KG51 which despatched three aircraft to Avonmouth. For obvious reasons, shots of aircraft on night raids do not exist and Ken Wakefield comments that these uncaptioned pictures from French archives in Paris might even have been taken over the Balkans, which had become a battlefront in October 1940 with the Italian invasion of Greece.

THURSDAY, JANUARY 16-17

Sunset: 1720 Sunrise: 0900
Moon: 2132 — Dawn (Full +3)

Major attack on Bristol/Avonmouth. Minelaying off south-western coasts.

UK — Cloudless with local mist or fog patches except in Wales and the West of England where there were frequent snow showers and increasing cloud. Visibility moderate to good in the West, but poor in snow showers.

The Continent — Cloudy over the Dutch coast but lifting and breaking inland and in northern France. Visibility moderate but with local fog patches. Winds light, west to south-west.

Most of the German activity during daylight was directed at shipping reconnaissance and Channel patrols and only two inland penetrations were recorded. No bombs were dropped.

Night activity started at 1835 hours with the first of a stream of enemy aircraft coming from the Dieppe/Somme area approaching Hastings. Another stream — led by the first aircraft to reach the Target Area — came from the direction of the Channel Islands to cross the coast between Portland and Swanage. Both streams, as anticipated by Fighter Command, converged on the Bristol area where the main objectives were at Avonmouth docks.

The initial German Operations Order called for an attack by both Luftflotten 2 and 3 on Avonmouth, but in the event only Luftflotte 3 participated, sending 177 aircraft. Of this number the crews of 126 claimed to have found and bombed their targets as ordered while 44 attacked alternatives, seven aborted and two were lost. The attack on Avonmouth was centred on the town and the northern half of the docks area and its industrial installations. The attackers dropped 124 tonnes of HE (four SC 1800, 12 SD 1400, 29 SC 1000, 32 SC 500, 135 SC 250, 429 SC 50; and four SD 50) and 1,480 BSK (53,280 B1 El incendiaries) between 1930 and 0508 hours.

Initially cloud and poor visibility made target identification difficult and some crews were forced to bomb by DR or radio navigation procedures, including those of KGr100 who were the first to arrive. X-Verfahren beams were aligned over Avonmouth but a signal failure and winds stronger than forecast made their bombing uncertain. Ten minutes after the attack opened the first of six He 111s of III/KG26 joined in the target illumination phase, using Y-Verfahren, and shortly afterwards the third Firelighter unit, II/KG55, commenced bombing visually. With improving weather crews were able to see explosions and fires in granaries, warehouses and other dock installations, with a large fire area to the north of the transit silo. One aircraft dived down to 1,200 metres at about 2300 hours and the crew were able to confirm that there was a very large fire in the designated Target Area. Towards the end of the attack between five and eight large fires were visible with more to the south-east, but their exact location could not be determined because of the dense smoke which now covered the Target Area. Nevertheless, further hits were claimed on a lock gate and on oil tanks. Overall assessment of the results of the attack was difficult, however.

According to German crew reports the flak over the target was variable in strength and poorly directed. Numerous searchlights were encountered but they, too, proved ineffective. Two night fighter attacks over Bristol were also reported, but neither was successful. Decoy fires were seen to the south and west of Bristol and to the west of Avonmouth.

Forty-four crews bombed alternative targets, including two sent to attack aircraft factories at Gloucester and Yate (near Bristol). Their targets were the city of Bristol (15 aircraft), flak sites near Avonmouth (12), Southampton and Plymouth (six crews to each), while single aircraft attacked Bournemouth, Portland, Portsmouth, the Isle of Wight and two unspecified places on the South Coast.

Reported successful bombing of Avonmouth was made by the following:

III/KG26: 6 He 111, 1940-2230
I/KG51: 1 Ju 88, 2250
II/KG51: 4 Ju 88, 2355-0044
III/KG51: 3 Ju 88, 2341-0014
I/KG54: 2 Ju 88, 0020-0120
II/KG54: 7 Ju 88, 0130-0225
KGr806: 2 Ju 88, 0155-0243
I/KG55: 3 He 111, 2245-2330
I and II/KG55: 17 He 111, 1948-2015
III/KG55: 6 He 111, 2155-2300
Stab/KG55: 4 He 111, 2230-2340
I/LG1: 9 Ju 88, 0405-0508
I/KG27: 13 He 111, 0212-0325
II/KG27: 19 He 111, 0203-0355
III/KG27: 11 He 111, 0220-0347
KGr100: 19 He 111, 1930-2020

Two participating aircraft failed to return. One, an He 111 of KGr100, reported at 2046 that it was estimating radio beacon 'Max' (near Caen) in ten minutes; the other, a Ju 88 of I/LG1, made a W/T transmission at 0521 hours to advise that it was on its return flight. Nothing was seen or heard again of either aircraft.

As the German crews observed, there were many fires in Avonmouth, but contrary to their belief damage was not serious in the docks and, in fact, the fire services were not fully extended. Small quantities of feeding

The aircraft seen is 9K+GD or CD.

Cause and effect No. 2. Again although not brought about as a direct result of Thursday's attack, nevertheless an everyday occurrence in every town in the country after a night raid: road closed. This incident actually took place on January 10 in Mount Road, Chatham, where 13-year-old Neville Cate and Mrs Anna Perkins were struck down at No. 24. Chatham, home of the Royal Navy in Kent until recent times, suffered some fifty deaths during the war, the majority in Ordnance Street in December. Civilian casualties at HM Dockyard totalled 10 during the war: Fred Amey, Bob Blakey, Charlie Brown, Bert Burfoot, Bill Grant, Alf Hedges, Bill Higgins, Fred New, Andrew Sang and Bernard Tranah.

stuff and oil were destroyed and several food installations were damaged by fire and HEs, but there was little other damage in the dock area and only six people were killed. In Bristol itself there was also some damage, but the attack lacked the concentration and severity of previous raids on the city. Casualties were again surprisingly light, with only two people killed. Elsewhere bombs were reported at Exeter, Weymouth, Poole, Folkestone, Cheltenham and Pembroke Dock. Three minor incidents occurred in London, with others at a number of places in Sussex and the Isle of Wight.

To counter the attack Fighter Command dispatched 62 aircraft, including six on dusk patrols. Two interceptions were effected but without result. A Fighter Night operation was flown over Bristol by 12 Hurricanes of Nos. 87 and 501 Squadrons but the Mutton patrol with one Harrow, which had been pre-alerted to operate in Area 'C' between 1900 and 2300 hours, was unable to participate because of aircraft unserviceability.

Intruder patrols were also ordered over German airfields and five Blenheims of No. 23 Squadron took off from Ford during the night. However, four returned without completing their missions because of adverse weather, but the fifth patrolled Poix for about 35 minutes and dropped four bombs on the airfield from 4,000 feet.

The Bristol guns were in action from 1925 to 0535 hours, firing 3,000 rounds, and AA guns were also in action at Plymouth, Portland, Brooklands, Bramley, Yeovil, Cardiff (where one enemy aircraft was claimed destroyed), Slough, Gloucester, Portsmouth, Pembroke Dock, Holton Heath, and in the London IAZ. Altogether some 5,000 rounds of HAA ammunition were fired.

With its customary skill, the RAF's 'Y' Service discovered, through W/T message intercepts, that two German bombers were missing and two other aircraft damaged. It was also determined that 33 aircraft were engaged on minelaying operations (off Milford Haven, Falmouth, Plymouth and in St Bride's Bay) although German records show that only 21 aircraft of Luftflotte 2 (IX Fliegerkorps) were so employed. Altogether 200 bombers and four night fighters were involved in the night's operations.

Two aircraft failed to return. The Cardiff AA guns claimed one aircraft destroyed but records do not establish which one.

3/KGr100 Heinkel He 111H-2 (5441). Missing following an attack on Avonmouth. Fw. E. Schül, Uffz. H. Bolle, Fw. E. Buck and Gefr. K-H Kayser all missing. Aircraft 6N+CL lost.

2/LG1 Junkers Ju 88A-5 (6183). Missing following an attack on Avonmouth. Lt. M. Zodrow missing. Uffz E. Lipps, Fw. B. Gülzow and Uffz. B. Finke all killed. Aircraft L1+LK lost.

FRIDAY, JANUARY 17-18

Sunset: 1721 Sunrise: 0859
Moon: 2247 — Dawn (Last Qtr −3)

Heavy attack on Swansea. Scattered minor bombing in the South, South-East, Midlands and south-west England. Limited minelaying in western coastal areas.

UK — Thickening and lowering cloud with snow and sleet spreading rapidly into South Wales and south-western England after 2100 hours and affecting most southern districts during the night. Much fog or mist in eastern England and scattered snow showers in Scotland and northern England.

The Continent — Cloudy or fair at first with occasional snow, sleet or rain in northern France and the Low Countries. Visibility moderate, becoming poor inland, with moderate southerly winds.

During daylight hours German air activity was not extensive and of the 90 or so aircraft operating most were engaged on patrols in the Cap Gris Nez area. Late in the afternoon — on a day of frequent snow showers in the West — advance warning was given by the 'Y' Service that KGr100 was to operate that night against targets in Swansea and Avonmouth. A further warning was passed to Fighter Command by No. 80 Wing that the Cherbourg Knickebein was transmitting and was aligned over Swansea. Acting on these valuable pointers three Groups dispatched dusk patrols — three fighters of No. 10 Group patrolled Swansea while two more were sent to patrol the sea approaches, No. 11 Group sent fighters to patrol off Beachy Head and Selsey Bill, and No. 13 Group provided further support. Two Intruder Blenheims of No. 23 Squadron were also operating, with instructions to patrol the German bomber base at Poix.

Of the 142 German bombers operating, 120 were dispatched to Swansea and of this number the crews of 88 reported having reached and bombed their target. Between 1943 and 0324 hours they dropped 89 tonnes of HE (one Max, six SC 1800, 12 SC 1400, 24 SC 1000, 36 SC 500, 30 SC 250 and 192 SC 50) and 901 BSK (32,436 IBs) with their Concentration Point the southern part of the town, wherein lay the docks, industrial installations and railway centre. Subsequently the crews of KGr100 (the first unit to reach the target) reported that their bombs fell on the town and docks area as ordered and that six large and several smaller fires were started to guide the follow-up attackers. An hour after the attack opened a very large explosion was seen in the docks, where four big and 10 small fires were reported, and an hour later 15 serious fires were apparent. A ship, too, was seen to be on fire and a large conflagration followed the detonation of the SC 2500 Max dropped by an He 111 of III/KG26 under Y-Verfahren guidance. As the attack progressed visibility worsened, but the glow of numerous fires could be seen even in the closing stages although increasing cloud prevented the last nine crews observing the results of their bombing. There was no doubt, however, in view of the observations made during the early part of the attack, that a good measure of success had been attained. Nevertheless, 29 crews failed to find Swansea and bombed alternative targets instead and three crews aborted for technical reasons. Those claiming to have bombed Swansea were as follows:

I/KG26: 18 He 111, 2044-2233
III/KG26: 5 He 111, 2144-2238 (Y-Verfahren attack, dropping one SC 2500 Max and four SC 1000)
III/KG27: 8 He 111, 2236-2336
KGr100: 16 He 111, 1943-2030 (opened

Flügzeüge als Schachfigüren

Aviones como figuras de ajedrez

Startbereit zum Einsatz gegen die britische Insel. Der Ernst der Wirklichkeit wird hier zum unterhaltsamen Spiel. Jäger, Stukas, Kampf- und Aufklärungsflugzeuge der deutschen Luftwaffe erscheinen als Schachfiguren, von geschickten Fliegerhänden gebastelt. Sinnvoll stellt das Schachbrett auf dem Grund der Karte von England das Einsatzgebiet der Originale dar, denen diese bunte Luftflotte nachgebildet ist

Listos para despegar contra la Isla Británica. La gravedad de la realidad se convierte aquí en holgado pasatiempo. Esculpidos por las manos hábiles de muchachos aviadores, aparecen aquí los cazas, Stukas y los aviones de bombardeo y de reconocimiento en forma de figuras de ajedrez. La tabla del juego ostenta en su fondo un mapa de Inglaterra, campo de operación de los originales en la realidad, en este caso curiosa copia

Links: Do 215 auf D 5 schlägt Me 110 auf F 7. Ein Bomber „schießt" einen Jäger ab, diesmal ausnahmsweise im harmlosen Kampf auf dem Schachbrett

Izquierda: El Do 215 sobre el campo D 5 bate al Me 110 sobre el campo F 7. Un bombardero "derriba" a un caza. Pero en este caso se trata de una lucha sin consecuencias sobre la tabla de ajedrez

Aufnahmen: PK Kling (Scherl) 4, PK Scholz (Scherl) 1

Rechts: Das zierliche Modell einer Do 215, eine der liebevoll-sorgfältig geschnitzten Schachfiguren

Derecha: El estilizado modelo de un Do 215, figura de ajedrez labrada con esmero y habilidad

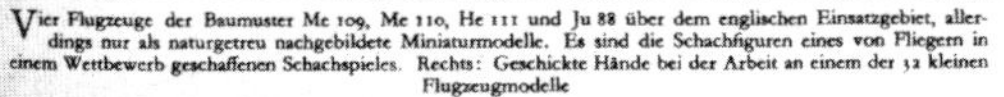

Vier Flugzeuge der Baumuster Me 109, Me 110, He 111 und Ju 88 über dem englischen Einsatzgebiet, allerdings nur als naturgetreu nachgebildete Miniaturmodelle. Es sind die Schachfiguren eines von Fliegern in einem Wettbewerb geschaffenen Schachspieles. Rechts: Geschickte Hände bei der Arbeit an einem der 32 kleinen Flugzeugmodelle

Cuatro aviones del tipo Me 109, Me 110, He 111 y Ju 88 sobre los campos de operaciones ingleses, como modelos de miniatura fielmente copiados del original. Son las figuras de ajedrez hábilmente labradas por aviadores aficionados a dicho juego, a raíz de un concurso. Derecha: Hábiles manos confeccionando uno de los 32 pequeños modelos

The latest game in the crew rooms of the Luftwaffe: aviation chess . . . played out on the map of Britain! With a close-up of a check-mate situation over South Wales, it was no game to the people of Swansea on Friday night, on the receiving end of their first major raid.

To the caption writers of the *Western Mail* it was reality: 'private property wrecked by Nazi raiders'. Swansea was spared a follow-up attack — that was to come with a vengeance four weeks later.

For a second night that week, the odd phenomenon of Stukas dive-bombing at night was a feature of 'the game' although this time no points were scored. We checked with the local records at both Croydon and West Ham but no incidents at all were recorded in either borough on January 17-18. Indeed no casualties were reported anywhere in London on that night. The principle of dive-bombing had been enthusiastically pursued by the Luftwaffe ever since the RLM engineer, Ernst Udet, had seen the Curtiss Helldiver in action in the United States, and tests showed dive bombers to be 40 per cent more accurate than conventional horizontal bombers. On the Ju 87, the psychological effect of the howl of the engine turning at high speed during the dive was accentuated by fitting sirens to the starboard undercarriage leg although these were seen to have outlived their purpose by 1941 and were removed.

attack as Firelighters with 32 SC 50s and 17,280 B1 El)
KGr606: 6 Do 17, 2225-2235
II/KG51: 1 Ju 88, 0250
III/KG51: 3 Ju 88, 0240-0324
I/KG54: 8 Ju 88, 0010-0025
II/KG54: 2 Ju 88, 0110-0148
III/KG54 (KGr806): 3 Ju 88, 0055-0107
I and II/KG55: 17 He 111, 1950-2055 (II Gruppe operating as target illuminators, dropping 28 LC50 flares. Bombs included 12 SD 1400 and three SC 1000)
KG1: 1 Ju 88, 1955

The attack was exclusive to Luftflotte 3 and alternative targets included Portland, Plymouth, Bristol, Southampton, Portsmouth and Aldershot. Over Swansea, flak was reported to be variable in accuracy and intensity with the searchlights weak and ineffective. Balloons, seen to be flying at heights between 1,000 and 2,000 metres, also gave no problems. Two night fighters were seen over Swansea but no attacks were made; other fighters were seen in the Aldershot area, both on the way to and returning from the target.

An unusual event during the night was an attack by three dive-bombers of an unknown Stukageschwader on Croydon Airport and another unrecorded objective in London. Each single-engined Ju 87 carried an SC 1000 and all three crews reported explosions but were unable to observe further results. The first crew bombed a block of buildings at West Ham at 2115 hours, following a dive from 3,200 to 2,500 metres, the second bombed Woolwich at 2148, diving from 4,700 to 1,500 metres in the process, and the third crew dropped their bomb in the Croydon area at 2243 hours following a dive from 4,000 to 3,000 metres. Almost certainly the aircraft belonged to StG1.

The damage at Swansea was mainly in the commercial and residential areas, but some damage occurred in the docks, where hydraulic and electrical power systems were affected. The Prince of Wales Dry Dock was hit and some stores were gutted. Some small workshops in another dry dock were also hit and damage to plant and machinery was considerable. The casualty list included 54 fatalities. Outside of the main Target Area the most serious damage was caused in Devon, where eleven people were killed. In addition bombs were reported at Yeovil, Weymouth, Brixham, Littlehampton, Christchurch, near Dorchester, in rural districts of Somerset, Ramsgate, near Kidderminster, near Nottingham, in various parts of Glamorgan, and at Exmouth. Contrary to the German dive-bomber claims, British records mention that only 'one enemy aircraft flew over Central London and dropped bombs in the St Pancras district'. RAF records also show that minelaying was suspected off St David's Head, between Portland and St Alban's Head, off Plymouth, in Lyme Bay and to the south-west of the Isle of Wight, with 12 aircraft participating.

Between dusk and dawn 47 RAF night fighters flew patrols and although several enemy aircraft were sighted, and a few engaged, only one 'probably destroyed' claim was filed, this by a Blenheim of No. 23 Squadron on an Intruder operation over Poix airfield. One Beaufighter, R2087 of No. 604 Squadron, was lost when it crashed near Stratford-upon-Avon following an engine failure, but the crew baled out safely. Two Gladiators and a Hurricane were themselves attacked by enemy aircraft as they were landing, but no damage or casualties occurred. Anti-Aircraft Command claimed two raiders destroyed — one in the sea off Sully Island, near Barry, and the other outside Swansea Docks — and another probably destroyed in the Yeovil area. The Command's heavy guns used nearly 5,000 rounds during the night, of which 1,304 were fired by the 5th AA Division.

Clearly, with only about 73 per cent of the force sent to Swansea managing to find the target — despite the use of Knickebein, X- and Y-Verfahren — crews must have experienced navigational difficulties occasioned by the deteriorating weather and this is supported by Fighter Command plots of the tracks flown by the raiders. Enemy aircraft were seen to be flying on irregular courses and clearly had difficulty in locating their primary objective. A few aircraft penetrated to mid-Wales and others were tracked to Birmingham, Wolverhampton, Kidderminster, Northampton and elsewhere. Nevertheless, most of the activity was confined to the southern counties of England and AA guns were in action at Portland, Bristol, Yeovil, Bramley, Brooklands, Holton Heath, Falmouth, Chatham, Plymouth, Solent and Gloucester, in addition to Swansea and Cardiff.

One aircraft was lost, the other, an He 111 of III/KG26, being damaged.

Wetterek St.Ob.d.L Heinkel He 111H-2 (2645). Shot down during weather reconnaissance mission over the Shetlands by Pilot Officer G. Berry in a Hurricane of No. 3 Squadron 11.02 a.m. Force landed on Fair Isle and burnt out. Wetterdienst Insp.a.Kr. L. Gburek and Gefr. G. Nentwig killed. Lt. K-H Thurz, Fw. J. Wohlfahrt and Uffz. B. Lüking captured. Aircraft T5+EU destroyed.

SATURDAY, JANUARY 18-19

Sunset: 1723 Sunrise: 0858
Moon: 0003 — Dawn (Last Qtr −2)

No German night operations over Britain.

UK — Much low cloud with poor visibility. Snow in some northern areas and the Midlands with rain in the South.

The Continent — Low cloud with rain or drizzle; fog in places.

With snow in all areas, except the North, daylight activity was slight and confined to shipping reconnaissance and limited attacks on aerodromes in East Anglia. In the South the snow gave way to rain, but conditions prohibited night operations.

SUNDAY, JANUARY 19-20

Sunset: 1724: Sunrise: 0857
Moon: 0118 — Dawn (Last Qtr −1)

Heavy attacks on Southampton and London. Minelaying in the Thames Estuary and off Harwich.

UK — Extensive cloud at about 1,000 feet with rain or snow at times. Visibility moderate, poor in precipitation. Heavy snow with gale force winds north of the Humber.

The Continent — Much low cloud with intermittent rain at first in northern France, becoming continuous. Visibility moderate or poor. Occasional rain with moderate southwesterly winds in the Low Countries.

During the day 79 enemy aircraft were plotted by Fighter Command, mainly over coastal districts with shipping the main targets. Weather conditions were poor but in spite of this Signals Intelligence intercepts showed that night operations were planned, with KGr100 expected over Plymouth at 1800 hours, probably operating at 15,000 feet on a beam bearing 350°. This, in fact, proved not to be the case, but in anticipation of the expected attack, Mutton was laid on to operate in area 'C' from 1900 hours.

It is possible that existing weather conditions changed German plans, for instead of the anticipated attack on Plymouth the Luftwaffe carried out a dual assault on London and Southampton. In total 183 bombers were dispatched, with two Stukas and 54 long-range bombers of Luftflotten 2 and 3 attacking London and 62 bombers of Luftflotte 3 attacking Southampton.

The London operation commenced at 1825 when the first of two Ju 87s carried out an attack on Greenwich, dropping an SC 1000 following a dive attack from 4,300 to 2,500 metres. The second Ju 87 carried out its attack at 1839 hours over central London, diving from 3,500 to 2,900 metres and again dropping an SC 1000. In Greenwich, an explosion and subsequent fire was reported, but no results were seen following the second attack. Next, at 1914 and 1917 hours, two He 111s of III/KG26 carried out Y-Verfahren attacks on the Beckton Gasworks, dropping two SC 2500 Max bombs; huge explosions were seen but no further results could be determined. Then, at 1945 the main attack got under way and continued until 0204 hours. In total, the two Stukas and 54 bombers that attacked the capital dropped 48 tonnes of HE (two Max, seven SC 1800, one SC 1700, ten SC 1000, 16 SC 250, six LZZ 250 and 254 SC/SD 50) and 160 BSK (5,760 IBs). At around 2100 hours four crews bombed visually but otherwise bombing was entirely by radio aids or DR navigation and cloud and poor visibility precluded an assessment of the success or failure of the attack. However, the glow of three large and numerous small fires could be seen, together with many explosions.

Una base de campaña en un lugar cualquiera de Francia, dos stukas dispuestos a despegar, pilotos en pleno equipo con caras curtidas por el temporal, voces, órdenes ...

En realidad nos encontramos sobre el terreno de la Ufa en Babelsberg, donde se está rodando una nueva cinta. El film será el poema épico de nuestra aviación y un monumento de inquebrantable camaradería. Verídico y sin mistificación de autenticidad hará revivir la lucha y la victoria de los pilotos alemanes en Francia. Hoy en día hay en Alemania un realizador que, además de su capacidad artística, es el más indicado para rodar este film: el oficial de aviación de tiempos de la Gran Guerra Profesor Karl Ritter. Está compenetrado como pocos con los comienzos de la aviación alemana. Presenció su destrucción después de la Guerra Mundial así como su renacimiento bajo la dirección del Mariscal del Reich Hermann Göring y ahora se encuentra de nuevo en primera línea. Poder volar, este es el resorte secreto de su vida extraordinariamente rica en emociones y acontecimientos.

"En realidad soy un águila vieja", dice en perfecto dialecto wurzburgués al comenzar la descripción de su pasado. "Ya de chico estaba predestinado a ser soldado. Entré en un cuartel, fui cadete y más tarde teniente de zapadores. En 1909 me casé y me incorporé al arma aérea. Por cierto que esto no era tan fácil como hoy. Quien quería volar tenía que proporcionarse el

Oberleutnant Hans Wilde, Staffelkapitän der 7. Staffel. Sein „Steckbrief" im Drehbuch lautet: Großer Flieger. Freude am Kampf. Rauher Spötter. Haßt Sentimentalität. Liebt „schräge" Musik. Raucht Pfeife. Inhaber des Spanienkreuzes. Sein Name im Zivilleben: Hannes Stelzer

Teniente Hans Wilde, capitán de la 7.a escuadrilla. Su papel en el film dice: Formidable piloto. Espíritu de combate. Sarcasmo. Odia sentimentalismo. Le gusta la música "alegre". Fuma en pipa. Es portador de la Cruz de España. Su nombre civil es: Hannes Stelzer

Unten: Stabsfeldwebel Niederegger, die wahre „Staffelmutter". Er ist streng und energisch, aber stets gerecht und hilfsbereit. Er kennt die Gewohnheiten eines jeden und ist immer besorgt, daß es „seinen" Offizieren und Leuten gut geht. — Darsteller: Lutz Götz

Abajo. **Brigada Niederegger, verdadera "madre de la escuadrilla". Severo y enérgico, pero siempre justo y presto a la ayuda. Conoce las costumbres de todos y cuida siempre de "sus" oficiales y subordinados. Artista: Lutz Goetz**

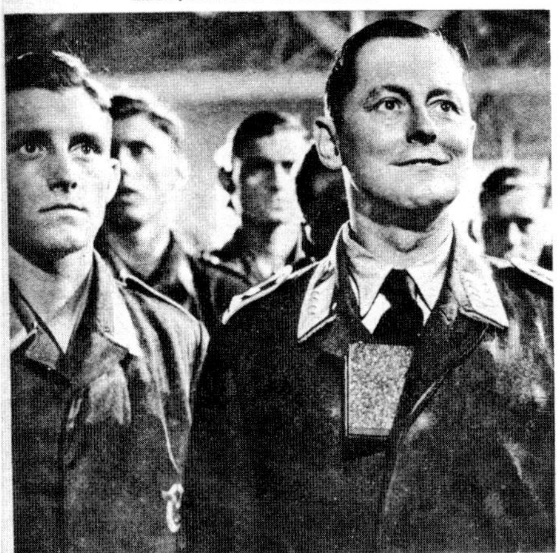

Der Spielleiter des Stuka-Films, Prof. Karl Ritter, zeigt seinem jüngsten Darsteller Johannes Schutz, wie er eine Szene spielen soll

El realizador de la pelicula Stuka, Profesor Karl Ritter, enseña a su más joven actor Johannes Schütz como debe representar la escena

And then again on Sunday Stukas opened the night attack. Perhaps it was really just a pre-publicity stunt for Professor Karl Ritter's new film about to be released in Germany!

The attack on Southampton by Luftflotte 3 lasted from 2130 to 2300 hours, the 62 crews who reported over the target dropping 57 tonnes of HE (29 SC 1000, 40 SC 500, 46 SC 250, 23 LZZ 250 and 16 SC 50) and 325 BSK (11,700 IBs). Here, too, bombing was predominantly by DR and radio navigation and results were impossible to ascertain although the glow of many fires and explosions could be seen through the overcast. Altogether Luftflotte 3 dispatched 75 aircraft, two of which bombed alternative targets, two aborted, four went to London, two attacked the Beckton Gasworks, three were reported missing (one after reporting over London), and the remainder bombed Southampton as follows:

KG1: 14 He 111, 17 Ju 88, 2030-2153
KG77: 25 Ju 88, 2120-0000
III/KG26: 6 He 111, 2045-2215 (X-Verfahren bombing)

The losses comprised one He 111 of III/KG26 and two He 111s of KG1, while a Ju 88 of KG77 came to grief at Compiègne. Also noteworthy was the fact that the two aircraft which aborted did so because of icing. Among the alternatives bombed by aircraft of Luftflotte 3 were Dover, London (by a new crew of III/KG26 who became lost while trying to find Southampton) and Brighton.

Only relatively light damage was, in fact, caused in London and this was mainly confined to riverside boroughs. At Beckton Gasworks, the target of III/KG26, a gasholder and a retort house were damaged but had little effect on supplies to consumers. And this was the only industrial damage worthy of note. In Southampton 14 fires were started and one person was killed, but yet again residential and commercial premises suffered, rather than industrial and port installations. The only reported industrial damage here was at the Southern Railway Locomotive Works at Eastleigh. Bombs also fell widely over surrounding areas of Hampshire, at Portsmouth and on the Isle of Wight. In the London area bombs fell at Deptford, Beckenham, Eltham, Lambeth, Greenwich and Heston, with further bombing widely scattered over Kent and Sussex.

The generally poor weather conditions restricted Fighter Command's operations and only 18 night fighters flew patrols. No interceptions were made and the Mutton Harrow, which took off from Middle Wallop at 1822 hours, returned at 2016 because of a snowstorm and lack of hostile aircraft. Only Nos. 10 and 11 Groups were able to operate. AA Command, on the other hand, claimed

Ein neuer Film
von
Prof. Karl Ritter

Nuevo Film del profesor Karl Ritter

Der Kommandeur der Stuka-Gruppe, Hauptmann Bork, am Bombenzielgerät. Er verkörpert den Typ des deutschen Fliegeroffiziers, einfach, unpathetisch, ein vorbildlicher Führer seiner Mannschaft. Stets ist er der erste am Feind. In der Rolle: Carl Raddatz

El Comandante del Grupo Stuka, Capitán Bork, junto al dispositivo de localizacion del blanco Encarna el prototipo del oficial de aviación alemán, sencillo, un jefe ejemplar de sus hombres Siempre es el primero en enfrentarse con el enemigo. — Artista: Carl Raddatz

aparato. Empecé construyéndome, un avión. Para terminarlo lo más rápidamente posible me dirigi a mis superiores con la súplica de que pusieran a mi disposición un mecánico, un carpintero y un local apropiado. La respuesta del comandante del regimiento fué categórica: "Este hombre se ha vuelto loco." Pero triunfó mi voluntad y el armatoste voló. No sé si la juventud de hoy dia puede comprender la importancia que esto tenia para mi en aquel entonces. De todas formas raras veces he aterrizado normalmente, siempre se rompia algo. Pero inmediatamente después lo reparaba y despegaba de nuevo. Por fin me destinaron a la escuela aeronáutica. Entonces mi divisa continuó siendo la misma que ha regido mis actos durante toda mi vida: estudio. En 1911 hice los exámenes de piloto con un monoplano construído por mí mismo y recibí el carnet de la Fédération Aéronautique Internationale con el número 121."
A partir de este día el teniente Ritter del III batallón de Baviera no tuvo ni un momento de tranquilidad. Con todas sus energias fomentó el Arma Aérea dentro del Ejército bávaro. Cuando estalló la Guerra Mundial manifestó el expreso deseo de entrar en la aviación. Cierto que fué al frente como oficial de zapadores pero poco después fué trasladado a las Fuerzas Aéreas. Realizó numerosas

sigue pág. 122

Deutsche Infanterie wird von feindlichen Tanks bedrängt. Stukas greifen ein und vernichten den Gegner

Infantería alemana es acosada por tanques adversarios. Stukas atacan y aniquilan al enemigo

Zum Bilde unten: Am Schluß kehren Kameraden, die vermißt waren, zur Staffel zurück Und alle sind wieder beisammen zum Kampf gegen England

Abajo: Al final regresan a la escuadrilla algunos camaradas que habían desaparecido. Y todos están de nuevo juntos para la lucha contra Inglaterra

Although the machine may have been shot out of the daylight skies over England, it had certainly not lost its punch overseas — as 'audiences' in the Mediterranean were finding out.

four enemy aircraft destroyed and several damaged or probably destroyed. Guns were in action in the IAZ, at Dover, the Solent, Thames and Medway (North and South), Harwich, Bramley, Brooklands, Slough and Chatham, using some 3,000 rounds.

Various attacks on Southampton resulted in the loss of three aircraft. The crew of a II/KG77 Junkers Ju 88 were forced to bale out near Compiègne.

1/KG1 Heinkel He 111H-3 (3325). Crashed at Wyckham Farm, Steyning, West Sussex 8.09 p.m. Hit by AA fire over Shoreham. Hptmn. G-F. Graf zu-Castell-Castell (Staffelkapitän) killed, body returned to Germany after the war. Oberfw. H. Schubert, Oberfw. G. Janson, St.Fw. X. Kroiss and Gefr. G. Lenning all killed. Aircraft V4+FH wrecked.

2/KG1 Heinkel He 111H-3 (6941). Believed shot down by AA fire one and a half miles off Selsey Bill 9.00 p.m. Oberfw. F. Ralfs killed. Lt. G. Bockhorn, Uffz. Jänicke and Uffz. H. Kaiser missing. Aircraft V4+FK lost.

III/KG26 Heinkel He 111H-5 (3602). Brought down by AA fire. Fell at Allington Manor Farm, Eastleigh, Hampshire 8.20 p.m. Uffz. K. Lindhorst, Fw. H. Radke, Gefr. E. Krause, Obergefr. P. Karzel and Fw. W. Enslin all killed. Aircraft 1H+FT destroyed.

A 3.7-inch shell case inscribed 'Heinkel 111 19 Jan 1941 near Eastleigh 310 H.A.A. Bty. GPO 2/Lt B. T. Young' now owned by Nigel Parker who also identified site and recovered representative pieces.

Only the previous week a massed attack by Junkers Ju 87s heralded the beginning of a new phase in the intensified air attacks on Malta which was, alongside Britain, then experiencing daily bombing raids from the Luftwaffe. The previous autumn the Stukas had been flown by Italian pilots; in January all that changed with the arrival of Fliegerkorps X which opened operations with a heavy attack on a Malta-bound convoy on January 16 — what was called locally the *Illustrious* blitz after the escorting aircraft carrier of that name was hit six times before limping into Grand Harbour, Valletta . . . but that's another story.

Not that the Germans were having it all their own way. Of the formations which battered Southampton again on Sunday night, three aircraft were brought down, although AA Command claimed a total of four. At 8.20 p.m., an He 111H-5 (1H+FT) of III/KG26 crashed and was totally destroyed near Eastleigh. Although there is a time discrepancy, this aircraft was almost certainly that claimed destroyed over the Solent at 2041 hours by HAA guns at Holton Heath. The Heinkel was flying at 14,600 feet and, after being hit, broke up in the air; one wing and the tail unit landed about two miles from the main wreckage, much of which was burnt out. Little could be gleaned from the remains and, unfortunately for the AI1(g) Branch investigators, there was no sign of the Y-Gerät with which the aircraft was fitted. There was evidence, however, of the aircraft striking a barrage balloon as it crashed. The German pilot, Unteroffizier Karl Lindhorst, and his entire crew were killed, four being found in the wreckage while the fifth was killed when his parachute failed to open. The 3·7in shell case, fired to bring the Heinkel down, has survived and is now owned by Nigel Parker. These pitiful harness buckles were found by him at the crash site.

MONDAY, JANUARY 20-21

Sunset: 1726 Sunrise: 0856
Moon: 0233 — Dawn (Last Quarter)

No German night operations over Britain.

UK — Cloudy with moderate visibility in some areas, but fog patches inland.
The Continent — Cloudy with snow or rain over northern areas.

Daylight activity was mainly restricted to oversea and general reconnaissance flights, but a few bombs were dropped in Norfolk, Kent and Cambridgeshire. Worsening weather resulted in the cancellation of all offensive night operations.

TUESDAY, JANUARY 21-22

Sunset: 1727 Sunrise: 0855
Moon: 0347 — Dawn (Last Qtr +1)

No German night activity over Britain.

UK — Low cloud with poor visibility in rain and fog.
The Continent — Similar to the UK in most areas.,

Anti-shipping and reconnaissance flights occupied a small number of German aircraft during the day, but 16 penetrated inland and bombs were dropped in London, Kent and East Anglia, mainly damaging houses. All night operations were cancelled because of prevailing weather conditions.

Limited activity due to poor weather conditions resulted in a single loss in unknown circumstances.

4/KG53 Heinkel He 111H-2 (2783). Crashed into the sea off Dover. Body of Gefr. F. Ahrer washed ashore at Hastings February 1. Fw. H. Sticht, Uffz. H. J. Schwarz, Uffz. B. Lang and Uffz. H. Schenk missing. Aircraft A1+FM lost.

WEDNESDAY, JANUARY 22-23

Sunset: 1729 Sunrise: 0854
Moon: 0456 — Dawn (Last Qtr +2)

Minor activity with minelaying in the Bristol Channel.

UK — Extensive cloud with poor visibility in all areas. Rain with hill and coastal fog in many districts during the night.
The Continent — Low cloud with rain and poor visibility affecting many areas of northern France and the Low Countries.

During daylight hours German aircraft were mainly engaged in attacks on shipping and reconnaissance, but of the 80 or so aircraft plotted by Fighter Command only ten penetrated inland.
Night operations were on a very small scale and involved only 12 enemy aircraft, most of which were engaged on minelaying in the Bristol Channel, but a few made a shallow penetration of the East Coast before returning. A Mutton patrol was flown by a Harrow of No. 93 Squadron, but an absence of raiders resulted in it landing back at Middle Wallop at 2005 hours. There were no reports of bombs anywhere in the British Isles.

Operations were confined to coastal activities and again a single casualty was sustained. A Heinkel He 111 of 6/KG53 was also slightly damaged over Southampton.

9/KG1 Junkers Ju 88A-5 (0578). Believed shot down off Great Yarmouth by three Hurricanes of No. 242 Squadron 3.10 p.m. Lt. W. Lademann, Uffz. E. Plasa, Uffz. G. Reber and Gefr. E. Fink missing. Aircraft V4+HT lost.

THURSDAY, JANUARY 23-24

Sunset: 1731 Sunrise: 0852
Moon: 0456 — Dawn (Last Qtr +3)

No night activity over Britain.

UK — Low cloud with widespread drizzle, fog or mist.
The Continent — Similar to the UK in most parts.

German Air Force daylight activity was on a small scale and limited to shipping reconnaissance. All night operations were cancelled because of the very poor weather conditions prevailing over much of northern Europe.

FRIDAY, JANUARY 24-25

Sunset: 1733 Sunrise: 0851
Moon: 0655 — Dawn (New Moon −3)

No night activity over Britain.

UK — 5/10ths cloud at 1,500ft in southwest England; elsewhere widespread fog with occasional rain or drizzle.
The Continent — Extensive low cloud with drizzle and poor visibility in many areas.

There was slight German daylight activity, mostly confined to reconnaissance, but one aircraft bombed Edinburgh and machine-gunned the streets. All night operations were cancelled, again because of the weather situation.

SATURDAY, JANUARY 25-26

Sunset: 1734 Sunrise: 0850
Moon: 0742 — Dawn (New −2)

Minor operation over Cornwall.

UK — Low cloud with sleet, rain or drizzle in most areas. Poor visibility in the South.
The Continent — Low cloud with sleet or rain in many districts of northern France and the Low Countries.

Weather conditions were poor during the day and Luftwaffe operations were on a small scale and confined to anti-shipping patrols.
During the hours of darkness only seven German bomber aircraft were dispatched, of which three were to attack St Eval and two St Merryn. At St Eval airfield one of seven SC 250s hit a shelter, killing 21, but St Merryn escaped. Bombs also fell at St Ives, causing a few casualties, and a house and two bungalows were destroyed.
RAF 'Y' Service W/T intercepts revealed that the unit responsible was KGr126, normally a minelaying Gruppe but operating on this occasion as a normal long-range bomber unit, as it did from time to time. While reporting this, a Fighter Command Intelligence Summary also advised, quite correctly, that henceforward this unit was to be known as I/KG28.

However, something of a mystery surrounds the loss of the second aircraft engaged in the attack on Southampton on the 19th–20th. At about 8.00 p.m. the German ground control station serving I Gruppe of KG1 received a message from V4+FH, an He 111H-3 flown by Hauptmann Graf zu Castell, the Staffelkapitän of 1/KG1, stating 'starboard engine on fire, landing in England'. Nothing further was heard and nine minutes later Graf zu Castell's aircraft crashed at Steyning, Sussex, with the loss of all four crew members. According to one account, the Heinkel circled the area several times — the glow of a fire could be discerned — with the crew firing signal flares, before it burst into flames and crashed. The burial of two of the airmen in Steyning Churchyard inspired Mrs Hannah Hunt to pen these lines back in 1942. Perhaps we can forgive her poetic licence in the first line: unless of course the wheat grew a little faster in those days!

The country was clear of raiders by 2155 hours and no further activity was reported until 0738 when a reconnaissance aircraft appeared off Cromer.

SUNDAY, JANUARY 26-27

Sunset: 1736 Sunrise: 0848
Moon: 0742 — Dawn (New Moon −1)

No German night operations over Britain.

UK — Except in parts of the North there was extensive low cloud with mainly poor visibility in occasional snow, sleet, rain or drizzle.
The Continent — Much low cloud with snow, sleet or drizzle. Poor visibility in all areas.

Several attacks were made on single ships and convoys off the East Coast during the day. Of six attacking aircraft, three were claimed shot down by ships' guns. There was no activity after 1925 hours because of deteriorating weather conditions.

An attack was launched on shipping near the Thames Estuary, the three aircraft lost are detailed below.

8/KG30 Junkers Ju 88A-5 (0634). Attacked HM Trawler *Galvani* and crashed through masts and rigging. Landed on marsh at Somerton Holmes, Great Yarmouth 9.05 a.m. Crew dragged dinghy towards coast but surrendered upon being confronted by two unarmed local residents. Fw. W. Guttmann, Uffz. J. Schmalze, Uffz. S. Gaber and Uffz. F. Martin taken prisoner. Aircraft 4D+LS burnt out.

8/KG30 Junkers Ju 88A-5 (7198). Believed crashed in the Thames Estuary. Oberlt. E. Gaul, Gefr. J. Eibert and Uffz. W. Reindfleisch missing. Obergefr. E. Stölzel killed. Aircraft 4D+GS lost.

8/KG30 Junkers Ju 88A-5 (3261). Shot down by HMS *Wallace*, *Reids* and *Fisher Boy* off Brightlingsea 4.00 p.m. Oberlt. I. Kraft, Fw. R-E Kollmeyer and Uffz. H. Müllerstein killed. Oberfw. K. Fröhlig captured. Aircraft 4D+AS sank in sea.

MONDAY, JANUARY 27-28

Sunset: 1738 Sunrise: 0847
Moon: None (New Moon)

No German night operations over Britain.

UK — Very low cloud with continuous rain and poor visibility in most regions.
The Continent — Similar to the UK in many areas.

HARVEST

He lay among the ripening wheat
As if asleep, one brown hand pressed
Against his chest — we did not speak,
The golden wings shone on his breast.
Looking upon his handsome, ruffled head,
Old Jarvis sighed, 'A bloody shame he's dead.'
Bob spat, 'Remember Jimmy and young Joe,
Killed at Dunkirk?'
Jarvis said, 'Yes, I know.
This Hun's so like it seems he's home again.'
He shook his fist towards the crumpled 'plane,
''Taint right, why don't the swine
That make the wars go fight?
This here's a coward's game,
Kids killing kids, a bloody shame!'
'I'd like to get my hands on them,' says Joe.
'By God there'll come an awful reckoning day,
When all the men who've lost their lads, like me,
Britons and Huns maybe, will set men free,
From blackguard power and greed and cruelty!'
'God rest his soul,' they said, and bared their heads,
Over the German dead.

HANNAH M. HUNT, 1942

One of the great losses to London during the December–January period was the 'Toc H' church of All Hallows, Barking, where the Reverend Philip Clayton carried on memories of Talbot House which had been established during the First World War in the Belgian town of Poperinghe by the Reverend Neville Talbot. Toc H — army slang for TH — was named after his brother Gilbert who had been killed in July 1915, and the club he formed for 'Everyman' became a haven of relaxation from the horrors of the Front. After the war, 'Tubby' Clayton continued the Toc H movement whereby young men could pledge themselves to a life of fellowship and service (11,500 men being ordained through his ministry), and the Lamp of Maintenance *(left)* was lit in All Hallows by the Prince of Wales in 1920.

Twelve hostile aircraft were reported during the day. Some damage was done in an attack on a shipyard near Newcastle and 15 people were killed at Grantham, where a Ju 88 was destroyed by AA fire. Night operations were not possible because of the weather conditions.

Once again bad weather limited the scale of Luftwaffe activities to coastal areas, resulting in only one casualty.

9/KG30 Junkers Ju 88A-5 (2280). Damaged by AA fire during attack on Grantham and made a forced landing at Tilley's Lane, near Boston, Lincolnshire 3.30 p.m. Oberlt. F. Rinck (Staffelkapitän) Obergefr. E. Stiller, Oberfw. W. Reuter and Uffz. F. Wissing all captured. Aircraft 4D+CT set on fire by crew and destroyed.

TUESDAY, JANUARY 28-29

Sunset: 1740 Sunrise: 0846
Moon: Dusk — 1915 (New Moon +1)

Limited minelaying in the Bristol Channel. No other night operations over Britain.

UK — Much low cloud with rain, sleet or snow. Visibility mainly moderate, but poor in precipitation.
The Continent — Mainly similar to the UK.

During the day — and in the afternoon in particular — 'tip and run' attacks were made by 13 aircraft, flying low and taking advantage of the low cloud cover. Bombs fell in London and elsewhere, but only one fatal casualty was reported and damage was slight.
Eleven hostile aircraft were plotted during the night by Fighter Command, but the weather over the UK prevented night fighters operating. Unseen fire was authorised by AA Command from 1805 hours.

Nine of the raids were tracked in over Lyme Bay to the Bristol Channel where, according to German records, seven aircraft of I/KG28 laid mines. Of this number three were damaged or destroyed on returning to base, presumably because of the poor weather, a fact which no doubt caused the Luftwaffe's Operations Staff to reflect upon the wisdom of ordering even limited operations in really bad weather conditions.

WEDNESDAY, JANUARY 29-30

Sunset: 1742 Sunrise: 0844
Moon: Dusk — 2022 (New +2)

Heavy attack on London. Long-range

The church had already survived a devastating explosion of 27 barrels of gunpowder in a nearby ship chandler's in 1650, and the Great Fire in 1666, but not Hitler's war three hundred years later. On December 8, 1940 a bomb severely damaged the east wall and incendiaries completed the almost total destruction by fire on Holy Innocents' Day, December 28.

On July 19, 1948 Her Majesty Queen Elizabeth laid the foundation stone for the rebuilding, materials for which came from Australia, Canada, Rhodesia, New Zealand and the United States of America. When the church was rededicated by the Bishop of London in July 1957 the Toc H flame was relit in the original lamp which had been saved from the fire. Because the name has caused much confusion over the years — the church is some seven miles west of Barking — it is now referred to as All Hallows-by-the-Tower and is united with St Dunstan's-in-the-East.

night fighter-bomber patrols over bomber airfields in eastern England intended, but London bombed as an alternative target.

UK — Low cloud with rain, sleet or drizzle in many areas. Visibility moderate to poor.
The Continent — Generally similar to the UK.

Only 17 enemy aircraft were plotted during the day, with two of them flying inland. At 1715 hours night raids to the London area were plotted coming from the Dutch Islands, but only 37 bombers and seven night fighters were employed. The greatest activity occurred between 1840 and 2100 hours, with most bombs falling on East London. With No. 11 Group declared non-operational on account of the weather, the guns were allowed to engage unseen targets and those of the IAZ fired 929 rounds. After 2130 hours there was no activity. There were also reports of bombs in the West of England, but no damage or casualties were caused; elsewhere incidents occurred at Hunsdon, Chigwell, near Chelmsford, Bexley, Walthamstow, Greenwich, Sidcup, Hendon, Dagenham, Ilford, Staines, Edmonton, East Ham, West Ham and Hampstead.

In addition to the IAZ, guns were in action at Gloucester, Harwich, Thames and Medway (North and South), Slough and Brooklands. Nearly 2,000 rounds were fired.

According to the German report on the night's operations the London attack was made in two waves. The first wave comprised the seven long-range night fighter-bombers which, in the absence of RAF Bomber Command airfield activity, attacked London as an alternative target at dusk, dropping 50 SC 50s and 120 IBs but without observed results. They did claim, however, the destruction of seven barrage balloons, all of which went down in flames.

The main assault, by regular bombers, occurred between 1928 and 2129 hours with 36 aircraft dropping 58 tonnes of HE (five SC 1800, 36 SC 1000, 24 SC 500 and five SC 250) and 72 BSK (2,592 IBs). The CP for the attack was the port of London, but visual bombing was not possible and no results were observed except for one fire glow, bomb explosions and the glare of burning incendiary bombs.

THURSDAY, JANUARY 30-31

Sunset: 1743 Sunrise: 0843
Moon: Dusk — 2128 (New Moon +3)

No German night activity over Britain.

UK — Much low cloud and poor visibility in the South and southern Midlands. Visibility moderate elsewhere, but rain spreading from the South-West during the night with lowering cloud and reduced visibility.
The Continent — Extensive low cloud with moderate to poor visibility. Rain moving progressively eastwards during the night.

During the morning there was a trial release of the free balloon 'minefield' (Albino) from Cardington, from which, presumably, some lessons were learned. German daylight activity by single aircraft was continuous over the south-east of England. Houses were damaged in London and there was further bombing and some machine-gunning in East Anglia, Kent and southern England. Altogether some 40-50 enemy aircraft were involved and activity was scattered east of a line from the Isle of Wight to the Humber. A Ju 88 crashed near Clacton. Minelaying by IX Fliegerkorps took place during the afternoon, but all night operations were cancelled because weather conditions, already bad, were forecast to deteriorate further.

The aircraft which was destroyed was:

2/KG30 Junkers Ju 88A-5 (6053). Brought down by AA fire at Whyers Hall Farm, St Osyth 1.45 p.m. Fw. W. Muth, Gefr. W. Schütze Uffz. E. Kretschmann and Gefr. J. Polaschek all killed. Aircraft 4D+CK destroyed.

FRIDAY, JANUARY 31-FEBRUARY 1

Sunset: 1745 Sunrise: 0841
Moon: Dusk — 2232 (New Moon +4)

No night operations over Britain.

UK — 10/10ths cloud below 1,000 feet and visibility less than 1,000 yards in England and Wales. 8/10ths cloud in Scotland with two miles visibility.
The Continent — Extensive low cloud with moderate to poor visibility.

During the hours of daylight some 95 German aircraft were plotted by Fighter Command. Attacks were made on London, airfields and against shipping in the Thames Estuary and three enemy aircraft were claimed destroyed or probably destroyed; one crashed on Plumpton Racecourse. More casualties were caused in London than on any day during daylight since October 25 (including 28 killed) and a large fire was started in Southwark. Three hospitals, houses and a barracks were also hit and outside of London incidents were reported in East Anglia, Hampshire and Sussex.

Mines were laid during the day by IX Fliegerkorps but all night operations were cancelled except for a few overseas reconnaissance missions.

Again low cloud permitted limited operations. Two aircraft were lost and a Dornier Do 17 of 7/KG3 was damaged by AA fire at Wattisham.

1/KG28 Heinkel He 111H-5 (3757). Shot down by fire from a naval patrol boat after machine gunning fishing vessels. Crashed into the sea 4 miles off Treen, Cornwall during a mission to Falmouth 8.05 a.m. Hptmn. R. Gottschalck (Staffelkapitän) Fw. H. Külpmann and Uffz. H. Teske missing. Fw. R. Hille killed and buried at Penzance. Aircraft 1T+LH lost.

2/KG53 Heinkel He 111H-5 (3750). Crashed at Wales Farm, Plumpton, East Sussex 4.40 p.m. Aircraft, flying low in bad visibility, hit anti-landing wires during attack on London. Lt. W. Helm, Gefr. G. Hensel, Fw. R. Taesler, Uffz. H. Schäfer and Gefr. W. Wagner killed. Aircraft A1+GK wrecked.

Weather forecasts were an essential part of pre-raid planning and, because the prevailing winds in Western Europe bring most of Britain's weather in from the Atlantic, the Luftwaffe was at a distinct disadvantage when trying to predict the conditions over the country. Long flights by the Wettererkundungs Staffel skirting round the Shetlands attempted to gather data to produce a forecast. Here one of the unit's Dorniers returns from a nine-hour flight to Fair Isle on July 31, 1940. Observer: H. Dohrmann, left; pilot Karl Heinz Thurz, right, on his second recce mission.

FAIR ISLE INCIDENT

Fair Isle is a small island situated between the Orkney and Shetland groups off the north coast of Scotland. Most widely known for its knitwear and the distinctive 'Fair Isle' patterns, it is also renowned amongst ornithologists as one of the premier bird observatories in Europe. Its isolation in the North Sea and relatively small size (being only 3 miles long and 1 mile across) has meant that it has always been a welcome refuge for both man and bird on their journeys; a shelter from the inhospitable sea, together with fresh water and a chance to rest up without too much disturbance. The Vikings knew it as Fridarey, 'The island of peace' and on a fine summer's day it is very easy to appreciate their words. However, during one of the frequent storms, one need only look down from the top of the sheer cliffs that ring most of the island to temper this with the power of the elements; a chart reveals a multitude of wrecks littering the surrounding water, from Spanish galleons to Russian trawlers.

The present community is a thriving one, with natives and 'incomers' helping to create a healthy and vibrant atmosphere which is tangible in the warm welcome they give everyone who braves the four-hour crossing from Shetland on *The Good Shepherd* — the ferry and lifeline with the outside world. More recently a scheduled air service has created a quicker entrance and exit route although still not immune to the unpredictable and swift-changing climate. For it is the weather that commands the island; its position, at the junction of the Atlantic, the North Sea and the Gulf Stream means that it is one of the melting-pots from which arise new twists in the weather-patterns of the area.

However important weather forecasting is in peacetime, it becomes doubly so in war and the collection of data for compiling long-range forecasts is a vital operation which must be carried out regularly to ensure accuracy. As the path of the western hemisphere's weather is predominantly eastward, accurate European forecasting is primarily concerned with the formation of patterns out in the Atlantic; thus Germany's position in central-eastern Europe was not ideal as a base for weather-reconnaissance aircraft. At the outbreak of war, with no Atlantic coastline from which to operate, the most valuable route, avoiding concentrations of enemy defences, was via the North Sea around the top of the British Isles. This area around the Orkney and Shetland Isles soon became well known to the Luftwaffe; as their early raids tended to concentrate there, thus avoiding attacking mainland Britain itself. These arduous flights, usually lasting nine hours or more, were carried out by Wettererkundungs Staffel Ob.d.L. (the long-range weather reconnaissance unit of the Luftwaffe High Command) which flew missions daily from its base at Oldenburg, near Bremen, to the Faroes. Each flight carried a meteorologist, and readings were taken at regular intervals for later analysis. The general

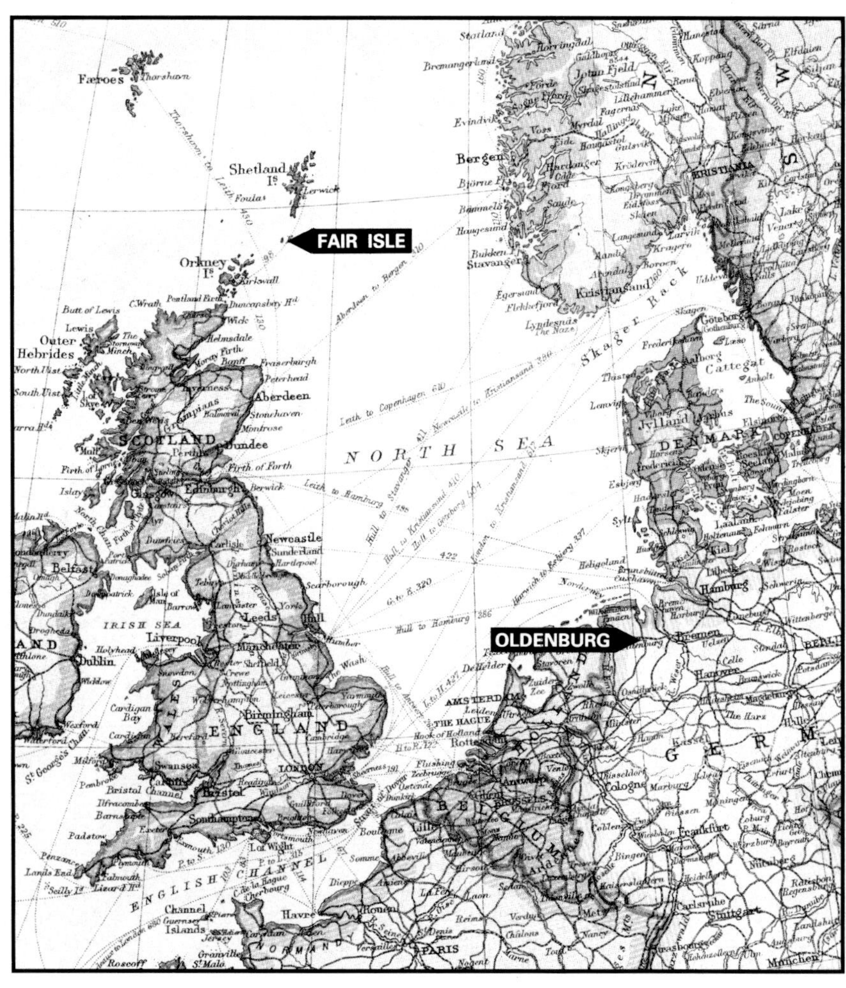

Fair Isle, midway between Orkneys and Shetlands, was a common landmark and the island was incorporated by Wetterstaffel 1 on their shield — seen *left* outside their quarters at Oldenburg. *Right:* Fair Isle in reality — a speck in a stormy sea.

flight plan was to stay as low as possible throughout their time under British radar surveillance to avoid detection. Upon reaching the turn-around point, a climbing turn would be executed to take readings of air temperature, etc., at heights between sea-level and 7000 metres (22,000 feet). The information was then transmitted back to base, and the flight-path retraced. When a proposal for the creation of a Staffel insignia was aired, the design accepted was that of a silhouette of Fair Isle, with a lighthouse prominent, one of the principal landfalls of their route, together with a rainbow arcing above to signify the Staffel's weather reconnaissance rôle.

These operations continued throughout 1940; the fall of France meant that Atlantic coastal bases became available, but the 'Northern Route' continued, and the local population came to know the aircraft as 'The Weather Willie'. Obviously the purpose of these flights did not escape the attention of the defending forces in the area and, as the number and range of radar installations increased, a more concerted effort was made to stop them. In addition, the threat of attack from the east became more prominent with the occupation of Norway, and increased enemy air activity by long-range maritime patrol aircraft, such as the FW 200 Condor, began to pose a problem to Allied shipping. The primary airfield on Shetland was at Sumburgh, at the far eastern tip of the mainland; as the base grew in importance the runways were extended, and facilities for aircraft and personnel increased. However, it was still an inhospitable place to operate from, particularly as the climate did not lend itself to operational flying for most of the year; accounts of full 45-gallon oil drums being picked up by the wind and sent tumbling across the field, and of trolley acc's smashing into parked aircraft of their own accord, are not to be queried if you have ever witnessed a full Shetland gale — wind speeds of 130 mph plus are not unheard of.

In the winter of 1940, the coldest since 1881, the decision was taken to send a flight of Hurricanes to the area to intercept enemy patrols. No. 3 Squadron, then based at Castletown near Wick, were chosen, sending flights to Sumburgh as well as to Skaebrae in the Orkneys. In the period from January 2 to March 29, 1941, 'A' Flight was dispatched to Sumburgh, whilst 'B' Flight went to Skaebrae, where snow, a rarity amongst the isles in winter, cancelled most operational flying. Upon arrival, 'A' Flight, together with its 60 or so ground staff, tried to contend as best as possible with the prevailing conditions; luckily, sharing residency with a Fleet Air Arm detachment ensured a copious supply of rum with which to combat the numbing cold! The isolation of their locality also gave rise to supply problems; in one case repairs had to be effected on a Hurricane fuselage with wood from a beach-combed orange box (wood being scarce on Shetland, due to the lack of trees)! Soon after arrival, problems were encountered with the Rotol wooden-bladed propellers fitted to the planes; stones would be drawn up from the pebble-covered runway and severely splinter them, rendering them unairworthy. Replacement metal props were soon despatched to cure this ailment, but unfortunately matching spinners never arrived, so throughout their stay the Hurricanes were flown without them.

Despite all of the above, 'A' Flight did manage to carry out effective operational sorties, with their first encounter on January 12 resulting in the destruction of a Dornier 215. Three days later a Junkers Ju 88 was found 10 miles north of Fair Isle and attacked, although without definite results. The sudden appearance of these swift adversaries, so far from known enemy concentrations, must have come as an unwelcome surprise to the German crews, with the added hostility of the elements and distance from friendly coasts. The average survival time in these waters began to be measured in minutes rather than hours.

January 17 was typical of the area in

By making a low approach it was hoped to avoid being detected by British radar in the Orkneys (ostensibly guarding Scapa Flow) — the closest CH station in mid-1940 being at Netherbutton with a CHL at Gaitnip *(see Volume 1, pages 124–137)*. Another photo by Wetterstaffel 1.

winter; sleet and snow showers from sea-level upwards driven by a persistent north-westerly wind. Approaching from the south-east, three hours into its flight, was 'Weather Willie', in reality a Heinkel 111 H-2, designated T5+EU, aiming to pass over the Fair Isle channel and out into the Atlantic. The crew consisted of Wetterdienst Insp. A. Kr Leo Gburek, the meteorologist; the 1st Wireless Operator, Feldwebel Josef Wohlfahrt; the 2nd W/O, George Nentwig; the engineer, Unteroffizier Bernard Lüking; and the pilot, Leutnant Karl Heinz Thurz who I had the privilege to interview on his return to Fair Isle, 46 years after these events. It was his 25th combat sortie.

Approaching the channel, conditions at sea-level became so inhospitable that they were forced to climb to 2600 metres (8,000 feet) to avoid them. 'Soon after', recalls Karl Heinz Thurz, 'through a gap in the clouds, I saw Fair Isle.'

Karl Heinz Thurz at the controls, a Wetterstaffel Heinkel He 111H-2.

Undoubtedly gaining height had placed the Heinkel onto the radar screens and at 10.45 a.m. Red Section were ordered to scramble, the five aircraft splitting into two groups; one of these, consisting of Pilot Officer 'Eddie' Berry, a New Zealander, and Flying Officer R. C. Watson, a Canadian, flew off in the direction of Fair Isle. Both pilots were relatively new to the squadron, having joined during the previous autumn. After ten to fifteen minutes of climbing through cloud they entered a patch of clear airspace, and spotted the Heinkel above them. The German aircraft must have entered the same clear patch about the same time, and seeing the Hurricanes climbing to intercept, attempted to gain the safety of the clouds. But too soon the Hurricanes drew level, and started their attack. Berry made the first run, his fusillade running the length of the fuselage, wounding the gunner, Unteroffizer Lüking, with shots through both legs, and Gefreiter Nentwig with severe side injuries. Then Flying Officer Watson began his attack; in an effort to avoid further strikes Leutnant Thurz slewed the Heinkel, but Watson's rounds hit home in the engines. After a third attack the clouds were reached and the pursuit ended, with the Hurricanes being unable to follow. It then broke the clouds with smoking engines and, diving towards land, managed to make a forced landing at Vaasetter.

The last moments of the Heinkel had not gone unnoticed on the island, and from the naval base at North Haven and the anti-aircraft positions on Ward Hill men were running to the crash site. Jimmy Stout had been nearby as the plane came over, and with his brother Jerry had dived behind a convenient wall for cover. 'There were three Germans sitting on the grass about 60 yards away when the petrol tanks exploded', recalls Jimmy. 'Then all the flares went off and the machine gun bullets started to stutter. I went on the motorcycle to fetch a stretcher from the nurse's house for one of the Germans, who was wounded.' Soon afterwards, the military arrived, and the crew were taken into custody. A search for the missing crew members found them 600 feet behind the main wreckage, dead. The lower rear portion of the aircraft had

We took off at 8.00 a.m. from our base at Oldenburg [30 km west of Bremen]. Our orders were weather reconnaissance on a flight-path to the Faroes via the Fair Isle channel, avoiding enemy contact (fighting!). We headed north-west across the North Sea through heavy snow flurries at 30–50 feet above sea level, occasionally climbing to 3–400 metres to avoid the worst patches but encountering higher winds in the process. After three hours, as we were approaching the Northern Scottish Islands, the snow showers became so intense that I was forced to climb to about 2600 metres to avoid them. Shortly after that, through a hole in the clouds, I saw Fair Isle. After passing through a further cloud-bank we flew into a clear patch, and soon after spotted two Hurricanes climbing up towards us at about four o'clock. I tried to make for the clouds, but they were too far away and soon the first Hurricane came up and attacked from behind. His bullets raked the plane from tail to nose. The second Hurricane came in and I slewed the aircraft to one side to try and get away but he hit us too, in the engine. After the third attack we managed to get into the clouds, where the Hurricanes couldn't follow, so I was lost for a while. Our Gunner (mechanic Bernhard Lüking) was wounded with shots through the legs and our Wireless Operator (George Nentwig) was badly shot in his side. Leo Gburek, our Meteorologist, went to the rear from the cockpit to bandage Nentwig, and Lüking came up to take his place.

The plane was a mess; the only instruments left working were a small magnetic compass, the airspeed indicator and altimeter. My first plan was to head for Norway, so I turned east. Shortly after this the starboard engine started to pour oily black smoke, so I closed it down, and from that moment I knew we couldn't get home, because the wheels also dropped down. So I thought what now was to be done and thought about jumping, but that depended where we were! Next the port engine started to smoke so I shut it down too. Not long after we came out of the clouds and saw Fair Isle just right on the wing 2000 metres below, and I decided to land there. In order to avoid more fighter attacks I dived down to lose height and gain speed. I came in from the north-east past North Haven (?) and touched down, but the plane jumped in the air again, as we were too fast. So I glided over my intended landing point. The plane wouldn't go down so I forced it down using the rudder and crashed it down; the plane skidded along the ground, going through a stone wall and catching fire.

As we came to a halt the first man to get out was the mechanic with his wounded legs — he just crawled through the remains of the Plexiglas nose! The W/O jumped through a hole in the side of the fuselage which had appeared during the crash. The plane was beginning to burn fiercely so I unhooked my belts, opened the sliding hatch above my head, and pulled myself out. I was slightly burned about my face and wrists in the process. Then the flares (?) and ammunition started to explode, we sat down on the grass and had time to think. The Meteorologist and 2nd Wireless Operator were found 200 metres behind the main wreckage — both dead. It was a pity as Gburek was not injured until the impact; the Wireless Operator was very badly injured and I am not sure whether he would have survived anyway.

LEUTNANT KARL HEINZ THURZ, 1987

Gunner Tom Flyn and Gunner Ed Morgan inspect the wreckage of T5+EU on Fair Isle at Vaasetter.

borne the brunt of the impact during the crash, and it seems they were thrown out and killed as the plane disintegrated. The bodies were attended to by the islanders.

Meanwhile, Berry and Watson returned to Sumburgh, landing at 11.20 a.m. No. 3 Squadron records state:

17/1/41 Sumburgh — Red Section of 'A' Flight at Sumburgh were ordered to scramble at 10.45 hours and intercepted and shot down a Heinkel He 111. The enemy aircraft crashed on Fair Island.' *(sic)*

The surviving German crew were taken to the Pund, which was being used as barracks by the Navy, and held there whilst a boat could be arranged to take them to Lerwick. Their wounds were attended to and they were given a bed. Being such a small detachment, there was no separate dormitory or room in which to place the prisoners, so they shared the servicemen's rooms; on such a small island security was not as tight and formal as could be the case elsewhere. For all parties it was the first glimpse of 'the enemy', so natural curiosity overcame any inhibitions which may have been present. Luckily Karl Heinz Thurz was fluent in English, and so could act as interpreter. 'There was a young Londoner whose parents had lost their home in a raid the week before — he was most kind to me, and we played draughts that evening.' The next morning Heinz was left alone in the barracks with a radio for company; it was tuned to the Home Service. 'I noticed that Radio Bremen was not far away on the dial, so I retuned it and caught the end of the news, which told of my aircraft being missing!'

As soon as the report of the crash reached Mainland an RAF launch was dispatched from Lerwick; this was *HSL 117*, under the command of Flight Lieutenant Dainty. It arrived at the south harbour on the southern tip of the island, and lay offshore as it was found it could not berth due to the force of the sea. In the evening the wind shifted, and it was decided to attempt a landing in the north of the island so the launch made its way round. The possible landing places in the north are created by the rocky outcrop of Burness being attached to the rest of the island by a spit some 25 feet high, forming two small Havens, North and South. Into the South Haven came *HSL 117*. Driven by the following sea, she was swept straight onto Mare Rock, where she was badly holed, forcing the crew to beach her. A trawler, dispatched from Lerwick to pull her off, arrived next morning. However, in an effort to get in as close as possible to secure a line, it too went aground. 'The Germans made such an awful lot of expense', recalled Willie Eunson, one of the islanders involved with getting the airmen off the island. That night the trawler managed to extract itself at high water, using its winch, and a further attempt was made to refloat the launch by the supply boat for the naval camp but the tow-rope parted. Finally the Lerwick lifeboat was sent for, entering the North Haven on Sunday morning, January 19, and the

Today this remains the largest known piece of German bomber wreckage still to be seen on its original crash position in the United Kingdom. Although somewhat depleted over the years, let us hope that its remote location keeps the remainder intact as a unique relic of the Blitz.

three airmen and two accompanying Marines were rowed out by Willie Eunson and his colleagues and put on board. It was Karl Heinz's 21st birthday, and his lasting memory of it was being violently seasick throughout the journey, together with his crew-mates and the Marines!

So what was the fate of the participants in this five-minute encounter? For the surviving German crew it was three days in Lerwick, in jail and hospital, where Bernhard Lüking's wounds were attended to more thoroughly, and thence transport to London via a series of hops in aircraft, motor cars and trains. Their first leg was by Handley-Page Harrow from Sumburgh, and there they met Berry and Watson. Thurz recalls them as being very shy: 'I don't know why; it was not I who had harmed them — they had shot at me!' After interrogation at Cockfosters he was sent to No. 1 PoW Camp at Grizedale Hall, Cumberland *(see Volume 1, pages 114–115)*. Ultimately he was shipped to Canada, spending four years at Camp 20 at Gravenhurst, 100 miles north of Toronto, before being returned to Britain. He was released on January 19, 1946. During this time he met a colleague, who told him that a passing German aircraft had been 'listening in' on the British R/T, and thought he had been shot down near the Orkney island of Burray, as he heard that he 'had been shot down by Berry'! As Karl Heinz Thurz remarked when he revisited the island, he was not entirely unhappy about being shot down as he couldn't envisage surviving the whole war with the rate of attrition his Staffel had suffered.

As for Pilot Officer A. E. Berry, he stayed with No. 3 Squadron, was awarded the DFC in March 1942 and became a Squadron Leader in May. He was killed whilst leading the Squadron into attack against ground positions at Dieppe on August 19, 1942.

Today the remains of the Heinkel are probably the largest pieces of a German aircraft still to remain above ground where it crashed. A section of the tail and fuselage and the two deteriorating

In 1987 we tracked down Herr Thurz in West Germany and our researcher Chris Barker — a devotee of the island and its habitat — made arrangements to meet him on Fair Isle. After a tramp across the inhospitable landscape in pouring rain they reached the spot where 46 years before Leutnant Thurz ended his war. Out came his camera.

Junkers Jumo 211A–3s still lie amid other small items scattered across the bald patch in the grass which marks the spot where the plane burned. The high winter winds have spread the lighter pieces over the surrounding fields and into the small stream that runs down to the old mill. Sacrificial electrolysis has left some parts as clean and bright as new, whilst others crumble at a touch. Over the years parts have been put to practical use, such as exhaust pipes for tractors, etc., owing to the scarcity of materials locally. One of the elevators was said to have ended up on the island of Yell, to be used as a wind-vane on a windmill. The pilot's seat-armour was converted directly into ploughshares, although it had to be sent away to Lerwick, being too hard for any local cutting machinery.

The two dead crew members, George Nentwig and Leo Gburek, were buried in the small parish churchyard at the southern end of the island, to share it with generations of islanders and past victims of the sea. As the burial service proceeded, two Hurricanes flew overhead, performing aerobatics, One wonders if this was Berry and Watson? We may never know.

CHRISTOPHER BARKER, 1987

The two dead crewmen lay buried on the island until they were exhumed and reinterred in the German War Cemetery at Cannock Chase (Block 3, Graves 291 and 292). This picture was taken by John Tupham in 1957.

FEBRUARY 1941

Impossible weather for much of February severely hampered Luftwaffe offensive operations and for the first time in many months no major attacks were carried out. However, operations were completely cancelled on only five nights and Swansea suffered badly in the course of three sharp attacks on successive nights. London, Derby, Liverpool and Chatham received lesser attacks and more attention than formerly was paid to RAF airfields, particularly in the eastern half of the country. Minelaying was carried out on 12 nights. Altogether German long-range bombers flew 1,644 night sorties over Britain while long-range night fighters completed 25 offensive sorties.

In response to the reduced German offensive RAF Fighter Command flew 421 single-engined night fighter sorties (producing 33 visual sightings and nine combats) and 147 by twin-engine aircraft (which resulted in 25 AI detections and four combats). Night fighters of both classes claimed four enemy aircraft destroyed and AA Command eight. No night fighters were lost as a result of enemy action in combat, but there were a number of accidents while engaged in operations and on training.

During the month there were numerous moves affecting night fighter squadrons, together with an expansion of the night fighter force. No. 264 Squadron was transferred from Gravesend to Biggin Hill, No. 85 Squadron left Gravesend for Debden and No. 307 Squadron was declared fully operational at Squires Gate. No. 256 Squadron, reformed as a night fighter unit on November 23 at Catterick, was declared partly operational in February with a detachment at Middle Wallop although the squadron did not gain full operational status until April 1. Equipment changes, too, were in evidence as more Beaufighter and Havoc aircraft became available to replace the Blenheim Mk IF in the twin-engine squadrons.

Although only two of the three attacks on Swansea came into the heavy classification by German reckoning, the third was close behind in terms of bomb weight and damage caused. The cumulative effect of three successive attacks on the town was extremely harassing for the civil population and the Civil Defence authorities alike, but the raids were borne with the same fortitude that other cities had shown. Although extensive damage resulted, less purely military or war important damage was caused than experienced elsewhere in heavy attacks of this nature. The attacks — directed mainly at the dock facilities — followed the expected course of the air blockade and added weight to the argument to improve the defences of Britain's ports where possible, even, if need be, at the expense of industrial centres.

February also brought a great deal of sea mining with more than the usual activity in evidence off the east and north-east coasts although west and south-west coastal areas were also mined. Civilian casualties for the month were 789 killed and 1,068 seriously injured.

Mit dem Führer vorwärts!

Von Generalfeldmarschall Keitel

Chef des Oberkommandos der Wehrmacht

Unbeugsam in seinem Willen, unerschütterlich in der Zuversicht des Sieges, stark im Glauben, den Blick auf den Führer gerichtet, so geht das deutsche Volk über die Schwelle des neuen Jahres. Die Soldaten der Großdeutschen Wehrmacht aber erfüllt in diesen Tagen nur das eine Gelöbnis, das scharfe Schwert ihres Obersten Befehlshabers zu sein bis zum Siege. Mit Gelassenheit und Sicherheit stehen sie bereit und warten auf den Befehl, wann immer er kommen, wohin immer er sie rufen wird. Wer im Kampf zur See und in der Luft eingesetzt ist, bleibt dem Feind hart an der Klinge. Die übrigen exerzieren und üben, bis der Einsatz kommt. Sie sorgen, daß der weite Raum, welchen die deutsche Wehrmacht besetzt hält, ein Kraftfeld deutschen politischen Wollens ist, dessen Energien dem Führer für sein Handeln zur Verfügung stehen.

Großes ist in dem jetzt abgelaufenen Jahre 1940 geleistet worden. Als wir an seinem Anfang standen, verkündeten die feindlichen Staatsmänner der Welt mit lauten Worten, ihre Armeen würden dank ihrer überlegenen Kampfkraft und durch ihre bessere Moral die deutsche Wehrmacht schlagen und dann unser Land aufspalten und vernichten. Von den skandinavischen Ländern her gedachten sie, das Reich wirksam anzugreifen und zu blockieren. Im Westen lagen Rhein und Ruhr im Blickfeld ihrer Pläne. Die ihnen nach dem Polnischen Feldzug vom Führer gebotenen Friedensmöglichkeiten hatten sie mit überheblicher Geste ausgeschlagen. So mußten die Waffen entscheiden.

Die Entscheidung, welche das deutsche Schwert erzwang, war eindeutig und einmalig. Norwegen wurde in wenigen Wochen erobert und der Engländer vertrieben. Fliehend erreichten seine Truppen die rettenden Schiffe; der lange vorbereitete Plan, Norwegen zur englischen Operationsbasis zu machen, war endgültig zerschlagen. Es folgte im Mai und Juni die gewaltige Auseinandersetzung auf den Schlachtfeldern des Westens. Sie endete nach 6 Wochen mit einem Sieg der deutschen Waffen, dessen Ruhm nie verblassen wird. Holland, Belgien und Frankreich kapitulierten. Das englische Expeditionsheer aber, dessen Vormarsch laut Tagesbefehl seines Oberbefehlshabers noch Mitte Mai unaufhaltsam war, wurde durch die überlegene Kraft der deutschen Waffen gestellt, bezwungen, zum Rückzug genötigt und mußte zuletzt das Festland räumen. Nur unter Verlust ihrer gesamten Ausrüstung erreichten seine geschlagenen Truppen die heimatliche Insel.

Diese und ihre Verbindungen aber, werden seit 4 Monaten von den heldenmütigen Soldaten unserer Luftwaffe und unserer Kriegsmarine Tag und Nacht angegriffen; England kämpft nach dem Eingeständnis seines für die Entfesselung dieses Krieges verantwortlichen Staatsmannes Churchill um sein Leben.

Es ist eine stolze Bilanz, welche das deutsche Volk am Jahresende im Hinblick auf die erreichten Ziele ziehen kann. Sie wurden erreicht durch die Meisterschaft der Führung, die politisch und militärisch in der Hand des Führers und Obersten Befehlshabers liegt. Die geeinte Kraft des deutschen Volkes in Waffen, das sich unauflöslich mit seinem Führer verbunden weiß und wie ein Mann zu ihm steht, die enge Verbundenheit zwischen Heimat und Wehrmacht, der Fleiß und die Zuverlässigkeit des deutschen Menschen daheim, die entschlossene Haltung der deutschen Frauen und Mütter, vor allem aber die todesmutige Tapferkeit der deutschen Soldaten waren die Garanten des Sieges.

Sie sind es erst recht in der Zukunft. Blickt das deutsche Volk ein Jahrzehnt zurück und denkt es an die verzweifelten Sorgen, die damals wie Bergelast auf ihm lagen, so liegt eine Zeit des Aufstiegs hinter ihm von so überwältigender Größe, wie sie wohl nie in der Geschichte einem Volk beschieden gewesen ist. Eine zerstörte Wirtschaft, ein zerrissenes und zerklüftetes Volk, völlige politische und militärische Ohnmacht waren damals die Kennzeichen einer deutschen Lage, aus der es keinen Ausweg zu geben schien. Da wurde uns der Führer geschenkt. Sein bergeversetzender Glaube erreichte, was vorher unmöglich schien. Er schuf ein neues Volk und führte es wieder zu Freiheit, Ehre und Größe.

Aufgaben von geschichtlicher Größe liegen vor uns und harren der Lösung. Wenn der Urheber dieses Krieges, England, bezwungen ist, eröffnet die Fülle dieser Aufgaben allen Deutschen ein Leben, erfüllt von frohem Schaffen und großem Gestalten. Ein wehrhaftes Leben, denn das ist die Bestimmung des Deutschen und entspricht dem Kern seines Wesens, sich Freiheit und Leben durch immer neuen Einsatz zu erobern.

So stehen wir bereit, des Befehls gewärtig. Die Parole lautet: Mit dem Führer vorwärts für Großdeutschland!

2

Although February was a month of reduced activity, No. 80 Wing did not relax its efforts to counter German radio navigation systems. Nor, for its part, did the Luftwaffe allow matters to rest, for it now introduced the use of the maximum number of frequencies available — in a bid to swamp the 80 Wing monitors — and at the same time ordered greatly reduced W/T communications between aircraft in flight and their control stations. It became common practice from hereon to maintain complete W/T silence until the first wave of aircraft had completed their attacks. 'Phoney' targets were also introduced, with X-Verfahren and Knickebein beam intersections set up over places not scheduled for attack that night. Rapid frequency changes while the attack was actually in progress were also introduced towards the end of the month, but No. 80 Wing had anticipated such a move and the appropriate Bromide transmitters followed suit within a few minutes. The first Domino station to counter the Y-Verfahren was also brought into service and appeared to have been most successful against certain aircraft of III/KG26. Others of the same unit which had not received the Domino treatment had, it was reported, bombed with considerable precision, so the importance of the new counter-measures transmitter at Alexandra Palace was not in doubt and apparently more than justified the use of a second Domino just about to come into service to counter the Cherbourg group of transmitters. The number of high powered Meacon transmitters was also increased during February with one new site at Mundesley, near Cromer, coming into operation and two others, at Louth and Filey, under construction. Almost certainly on account of 'meaconing', one German aircraft that was seemingly lost and low on fuel came down on a British airfield during the month and was captured; two others which landed realised their mistake in time and managed to take off again, according to an 80 Wing report.

Starfish sites were lit on four occasions during the month — three times at Swansea and once at Cardiff — and drew bombs on two occasions, but the general lack of Luftwaffe activity prevented greater use of this ruse.

While the number of PoWs taken in February was too low for any definite conclusions to be drawn by the ever cautious AI1(k) Branch, there was apparently no falling off in the average ages and experience levels of German Air Force personnel. The morale of the 23 prisoners taken (43 bodies were also recovered) was, on the whole, very good, but was more difficult to assess than of late because they appeared to be particularly security conscious. A useful amount of intelligence matter was nevertheless obtained, including the fact that from the third week in February, the whole of 4/KG2, and possibly aircraft from other Staffeln in II Gruppe, had gone over to attacks on RAF night flying airfields. In this activity they were not alone, for I/NJG2 had been so engaged, mainly against Bomber Command airfields and aircraft, since the previous summer.

The German Order of Battle in the West did not change significantly during the month although there were a few unit moves and changes in rôle. On February 11, I/KG55 left Dreux on a temporary transfer to Le Bourget and later in the month I/KG27, while still available for normal night operations, was forthwith to concentrate on anti-shipping operations. On February 2 III/KG26 had moved to Grevillers while an asphalt runway was laid at Poix, their permanent base, but a further move to Le Bourget took place on the 19th. Early in the month, too, I/LG1 left the wintry north-west Europe scene for Rumania to join VIII Fliegerkorps for operations in the Balkans.

He 111H-2, H-3 and P-2	
8×50kg bombs	400kg
2×250kg bombs	500kg
576 B1 El bombs	576kg
	1476kg
Ju 88 (Load/Equipment State 'B')	
4×250kg bombs	1000kg
10×50kg bombs	500kg
	1500kg
For attacks against especially important port and industrial targets:	
5×50kg bombs	250kg
180 B1 El bombs	180kg
1×500kg bomb	500kg
	930kg

He 111H-4, H-5 and P-4	
4×50kg bombs	200kg
1×250kg bomb	250kg
288 B1 El bombs	288kg
1×500kg bomb (externally)	500kg
	1238kg
Ju 88 (Load/Equipment State 'C'	
4×250kg bombs	1000kg
OR	
3×250kg bombs and 1×500kg	1250kg
For use only against port and industrial targets where 500kg bombs would be especially effective:	
2×250kg bombs	500kg
2×500kg bombs	1000kg
	1500kg

Despite the advent of the new and heavier HE bombs now available, the SC 50, SC 250 and SC 500 continued to predominate together with the B1 El incendiary. Indeed, bombs of heavier weight were only to be used when so ordered by the appropriate Fliegerkorps HQ, according to an operational instruction issued by Luftflottenkommando 3 on February 22, 1941. An exception to this was the unrestricted use of heavier weapons by III/KG26. The instruction went on to state the ratio of HEs to be carried by He 111s and Ju 88s for night attacks against ports and industrial centres when the range/fuel load situation permitted bomb loads of approximately 1,500kg. The laid-down bomb loads were as shown in the table.

The same operational instruction laid down that all Luftflotte 3 units flying He 111H-4s, H-5s and P-4s were to ensure that two aircraft in each Staffel were fitted with external PVC carriers beneath their bomb doors so that heavy bombs could be carried when so ordered against special targets.

In February 1941, III/KG4 reformed with the H-5 and H-6 models of the Heinkel III. Shown to advantage here are the two centre-section external bomb carriers of the H-5 variant to which armourers are hoisting an SC1000 with Kopfring. The winch-launch cable attachment point for Schleuderstart assisted take-offs can also be seen, to the right of the Lotfc 7c bombsight periscope. Unfortunately this picture from German archives comes devoid of a precise caption. It has appeared elsewhere in the belief that it shows KG53 in 1940 but Ken Wakefield points out that according to unit aircraft and crew strength returns, this Geschwader was not equipped with H-5s.

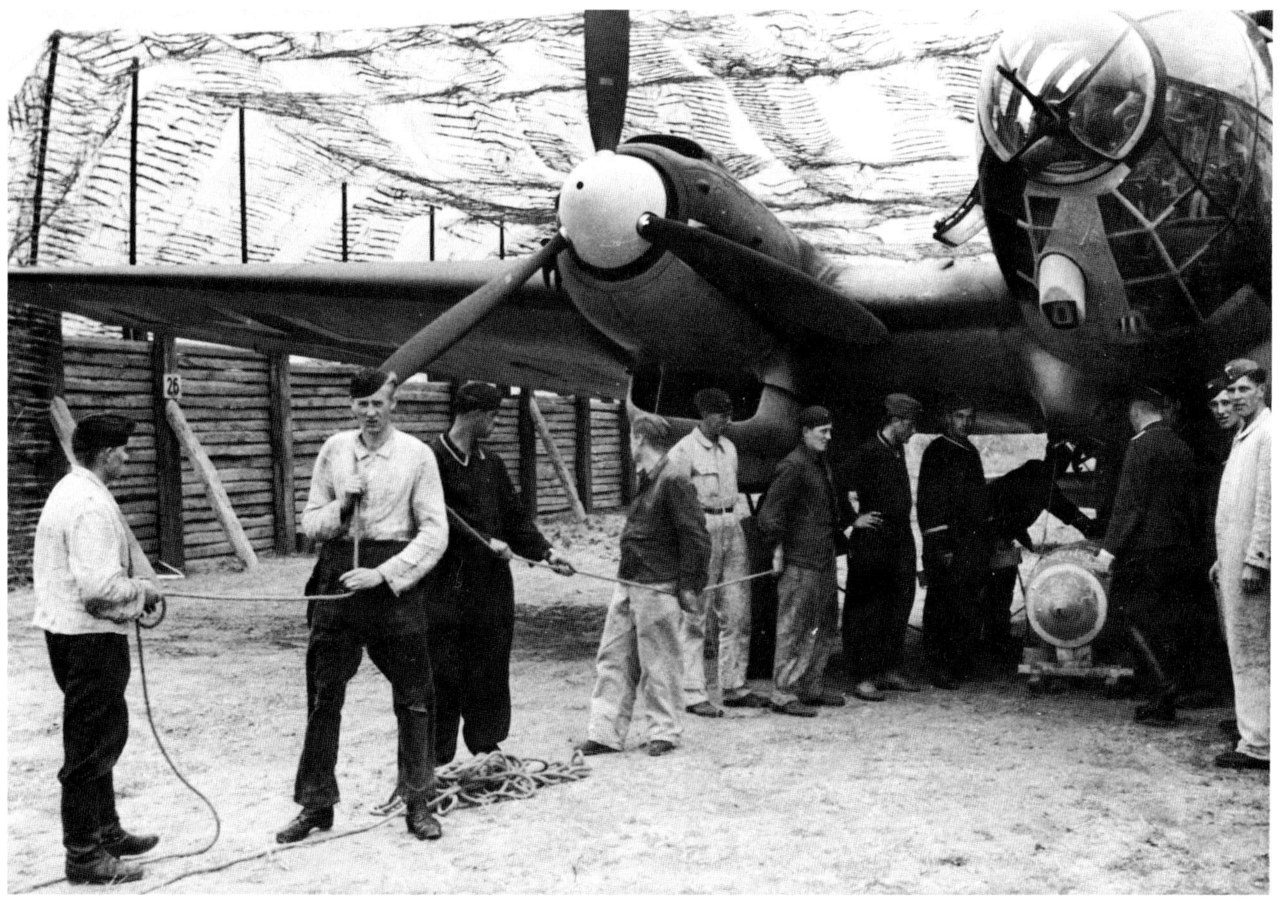

SATURDAY, FEBRUARY 1-2

Sunset: 1747 Sunrise: 0840
Moon: Dusk — 2336 (First Qtr −3)

No significant activity.

UK — Low cloud, strong winds and snow in many areas. Visibility poor.
The Continent — Similar to UK in northern France and the Low Countries.

Only three German aircraft operated during the night, after a day of little activity. A few night fighter patrols were flown and one aircraft, a Beaufighter of No. 604 Squadron from Middle Wallop, crashed on landing.

SUNDAY, FEBRUARY 2-3

Sunset: 1749 Sunrise: 0838
Moon: Dusk — 0038 (First Qtr −2)

No German night bomber operations.

UK — Extensive low cloud with rain or snow in many areas. Generally poor visibility.
The Continent — Mainly similar to the UK.

Small scale weather and shipping reconnaissance flights were undertaken by the Luftwaffe during the day and a few bombs fell in East Anglia and on the Kent coast. All night operations were cancelled on account of the weather.

MONDAY, FEBRUARY 3-4

Sunset: 1751 Sunrise: 0836
Moon: Dusk — 0140 (First Qtr −1)

Minor activity over the London area and Home Counties.

UK — Low cloud with light to moderate snow in many districts. Visibility poor, particularly in precipitation.
The Continent — Similar to UK over much of northern France and the Low Countries

Single enemy aircraft dropped bombs on several places in London, Kent and East Anglia during the day, but operations were on a small scale. Anti-shipping patrols and reconnaissance were also carried out by a few aircraft.

During the night 15 German aircraft were operating, mainly over London where a few fires were started by incendiary bombs. A few HEs and some IBs also fell in East Anglia and Lincolnshire.

Operations were restricted to mining in coastal areas and single aircraft bombing sorties. Two aircraft were lost. A Messerschmitt Bf 110 of 1/Erprobungsgruppe 210 failed to return, its crew being missing.

5/KG53 Heinkel He 111H-2 (5517). Shot down by Pilot Officer A. C. Bartley, DFC, in a cannon armed Spitfire V. of No. 92 Squadron 3.50 p.m. Crashed in the Thames Estuary near Southend. Lt. M. Petry and Gefr. E. Kaiser killed. Fw. H. Bock, Uffz. H. Wordelmann and Gefr. R. Massarsch missing. Aircraft A1+AN lost.

TUESDAY, FEBRUARY 4-5

Sunset: 1753 Sunrise: 0835
Moon: Dusk — 0241 (First Quarter)

Small scale night attack on Derby. Minelaying in several coastal areas.

UK — Little or no cloud in many districts but mist or fog developed in some areas during the night. Winds mainly light northwesterly.
The Continent — Variable cloud. Visibility moderate to poor, with mist inland.

Daylight hours produced more German activity than of late and comprised fighter sweeps, shipping and weather reconnaissance and a few inland penetrations. Bombs fell on the East Coast and some damage and casualties resulted.

During the night, when 159 bombers were operating, bombs fell on London, the East Midlands and in various eastern counties. Fog in northern France grounded many units, but Luftflotte 2 mounted an attack against the Rolls-Royce factories at Derby. Between 1945 and 2155 hours the crews of 40 aircraft claimed to have reached and bombed Derby, dropping 28 tonnes of HE (one SC 1800, six SC 1000, one SC 500, nine SC 250, eight LZZ 250 and 308 SC 50) and 96 BSK (3,456 IBs). Initially visual bombing, aided by radio navigation, was possible, but many crews were obliged to bomb using DR and radio navigation because of increasing cloud and decreasing surface visibility. For the first part of the attack the light of the moon in its first quarter and a snow-covered landscape aided navigation, but the worsening weather prevented observation of the effects of the bombing and only one fire was seen in the south of Derby. No great success was therefore anticipated, and this proved to be the case, for bombing was in fact widely scattered. One factory was badly damaged but casualties and damage in general were light except in Southend where a heavy HE bomb fell in the centre of the town. At Hull, too, many people were rendered homeless by two HEs.

Sixty night fighter patrols were flown by Fighter Command for one enemy aircraft destroyed, but less than 1,000 rounds of HAA ammunition were fired by AA Command.

The two aircraft listed below both came down during the day on February 4.

2/Erprobungsgruppe 210 Messerschmitt Bf 110E-1/N (3849). Believed shot down by two Hurricanes of No. 249 Squadron and crashed into the sea near Kentish Knock Light Vessel. Uffz. G. Drews and Uffz. R. Steindal both missing. Aircraft S9+PK lost.

4/KG2 Dornier Do 17Z-2 (1132). Shot down by No. 158 Light AA Battery and Pilot Officer Barnes and Sergeant V. Brejcha of No. 257 Squadron. Landed on the sea half

At the beginning of 1941, while the German armed forces were being exhorted by OKW chief Generalfeldmarschall Keitel to 'go forward with the Führer', the British leader was involved in the opening moves in the introduction of a new immensely powerful weapon of war, and one which would eventually bring victory — lend-lease. After the First World War, America was almost united in its determination not to suffer the horror of war again and in 1935 enacted the Neutrality Acts designed to cut the United States off from any nations involved in war anywhere else in the world. Up until 1940 this isolationist standpoint was supported by over three-quarters of Americans. Asia, where Japan was fighting China; North Africa, where Italy was extending its territory, and Europe, where Germany was knocking off countries one by one, were thousands of miles away — even though President Roosevelt warned in 1937: 'Let no one imagine that America will escape.' Limited steps to help Britain were taken in the summer of 1940 with the supply of small arms (see page 93), field guns and destroyers but, with Roosevelt facing re-election in November, these deals had to be confined strictly to a friendly seller basis. Although Roosevelt may have wished to do more, not until his presidency was assured could he begin to turn American foreign policy towards more active assistance for Britain. By that time, however, Britain was nearly bankrupt; having placed orders with America in December, January and February totalling $1,000 million, she had barely half this sum left in gold and dollar reserves. With all Britain's funds in the US exhausted by Christmas, Roosevelt arranged for an American warship to go to South Africa to collect £50 millions of British gold held there, yet such a move was really a cosmetic exercise to demonstrate to the American public how little money Britain had left to purchase war stores. All Britain's reserves had been shipped across the Atlantic after France fell and stored in a vault christened the United Kingdom Security Deposit in the lower basement of the Sun Life Assurance Company building in Montreal.

a mile off Corton, Lowestoft 9.30 a.m. during a raid on Mildenhall. Fw. H. Ablonski and Gefr. F. Müller baled out but died when their parachutes failed to open and they fell into the sea. Fw. W. Blaschyk captured slightly injured. Lt. F. Heilmann taken to hospital but died there. Aircraft U5+LM sank in sea.

During the night of February 4-5, in addition to the loss below a Dornier Do 17 of 2/NJG2 failed to return from an intruder sortie. Another Dornier Do 17 of I/KG2 crashed on take-off at Epinoy and was destroyed but its crew saved.

7/KG2 Dornier Do 17Z-3 (2907). Shot down by Sergeant H. E. Bodien and Sergeant D. E. C. Jonas of No. 151 Squadron in a Defiant during an attack on Derby. Dived into ground and exploded at Cowthick Lodge, Weldon, Northants. 9.30 p.m. Oberlt. H. Krisch, Fw. H. Bahr, Uffz. H. Kliem and Fw. H. Uehlemann killed. Aircraft U5+AR destroyed.
Site investigated by Philippa Hodgkiss and found to have vanished in an open cast mine.

WEDNESDAY, FEBRUARY 5-6

Sunset: 1754 Sunrise: 0833
Moon: Dusk — 0341 (First Qtr +1)

Minor attack on Chatham and other targets including airfields. Minelaying in several coastal areas.

UK — Extensive cloud with moderate to poor visibility in all areas.
The Continent — Similar to the UK in northern France and the Low Countries.

During the day Luftwaffe operations were on a small scale and largely confined to anti-shipping operations although bombs were reported in north-east Scotland and Kent. Night operations were also affected by the weather and only 141 German aircraft were dispatched, including seven night fighters sent to harass RAF Bomber Command operations. Chatham was the target for 26 aircraft, but good results were not anticipated by the Luftwaffe — only at the commencement of the attack was visual bombing possible and thick cloud and bad visibility prevented an assessment of the results. Bombing took place between 1932 and 2120 hours, and 17 tonnes of HE (three SC 1800, two SC 1000, one SC 500, 12 SC 250 and 114 SC/SD 50) were claimed delivered, together with 103 BSK (3,708 IBs). Explosions were observed from time to time, as were several small fires, seen through breaks in the cloud, and shortly after 2000 hours a large fire area was seen to develop in what crews took to be the town centre.
Many crews were unable to find Chatham, where naval installations (including the arsenal, shipyards and the personnel training depot) were encompassed in the laid-down Schwerpunkt, and sought alternative targets instead. Often, in practice, this meant dumping bombs almost anywhere if a suitable target of opportunity did not present itself, for few crews were prepared to risk a landing at night, often in difficult weather conditions, with a load of bombs still on board.
No doubt because of the weather conditions bombing was in fact widely scattered, with a number of incidents in East Anglia, Kent and London. At Southend there was considerable damage and 15 people were killed. Several small fires were started at Tilbury Docks and damage was inflicted in eight boroughs of London, but only five people were killed.
A few night fighters managed to operate, without success, but, unusually, one enemy aircraft was claimed destroyed by Balloon Command. About 1,000 rounds were fired during the night by the heavy guns of AA Command, but again without success.

President Roosevelt's long awaited initiative came in a press conference on December 17. At it he proposed that the United States should take over Britain's munitions orders and 'enter into some kind of arrangement for their use by the British on the grounds that it was the best thing for American defence, with the understanding that when the show was over, we should get repaid something in kind, thereby leaving out the dollar mark . . . substituting it for a gentleman's obligation to repay in kind.' By way of further explanation for the gathered newsmen, he gave them an example with his homily about the garden hose. He said that if his neighbour wanted to borrow his hose to put out a fire, he would not say 'Neighbour, my garden hose cost me $15; you have to pay me $15 for it.' It was not the $15 he wanted, but my 'garden hose back after the fire is over'. On the day of the devastating raid on the City of London, the President broadcast to the people of America in his annual end-of-the-year Fireside Chat. In this he pointed out that '. . . we cannot escape danger by crawling into bed and pulling the covers over our heads. We must be the great arsenal of democracy.' The Act was formally born eight days later when Roosevelt addressed Congress (*above*). In his State of the Union address, he called for legislation to implement the Lend-Lease Bill promising the Democracies that 'we shall send you, in ever-increasing numbers, ships, aeroplanes, tanks and guns'.

In addition to those below, a Do 17 of 8/KG2 was shot down off Boulogne.

2/StG1 Junkers Ju 87B-1 (5225). Shot down by Pilot Officer R. H. Fokes of No. 92 Squadron 9.50 a.m. after it had attacked HM Trawler *Tourmaline* which was subsequently sunk by a second Junkers Ju 87. Dived into the ground at Cheeseman's Farm, Minster. Lt. E. Schimmelpfennig and Obergefr. H. Kaden both killed. Aircraft J9+BK wrecked.
Site excavated by local enthusiast Nigel Douglas in 1983. Minor items recovered.

1/KG40 Focke-Wulf FW 200C-3 (0042). Crashed on hillside between Durrus and Schull, County Cork, Eire 8.00 a.m. Shot down by gun-fire from SS *Major C.* Oberlt. P. Gömmer, Oberfw. W. Doose, Fw. W. Clasen, Oberfw. W. Albrecht and Reg.Rat.Dr. E. Herrström (Meteorologe) all killed. Fw. M. Hohaus injured. Aircraft F8+AH destroyed.

Our most useful rôle is to act as an arsenal for them as well as for ourselves. They do not need manpower; they do need billions of dollars' worth of weapons of defence. The time is near when they will not be able to pay for them in ready cash. We cannot, and will not, tell them that they must surrender because of their present inability to pay for weapons which we know they must have. . . . Let us say to the Democracies: 'We Americans are vitally concerned in your defence of freedom. We are putting forth our energies, resources and organising powers to give you strength to regain and maintain a free world. We shall send you, in ever-increasing numbers, ships, aeroplanes, tanks and guns. This is our purpose and our pledge.
We look forward to a world founded upon the four essential human freedoms. The first is freedom of speech and expression — everywhere in the world. The second is freedom of every person to worship God in his own way —everywhere in the world. The third is freedom from want — which means economic understandings which will secure to every nation a healthy peacetime life for its inhabitants — everywhere in the world. The fourth is freedom from fear — which means a worldwide reduction of armaments to such a point and in such a thorough fashion that no nation will be in a position to commit an act of physical aggression against any neighbour — everywhere in the world. This was no vision of a distant millennium; it was a definite base for a kind of world attainable in our own time and generation.

PRESIDENT F. D. ROOSEVELT,
JANUARY 6, 1941

However, the January 6 address was only the beginning; there followed three months bitter argument and debate, in which the 'America First' campaign attempted to block the proposal, but on March 11 the Act was passed by Congress with a large majority. In the meantime, Roosevelt sent his emissary, Harry Hopkins, to Britain to smooth the waters and establish just what Britain required to win the war. Hopkins arrived on January 8 and stayed for a month, during which time he saw first hand what England was suffering. On Friday, January 31 he accompanied Churchill to visit the south coast ports which had been hit particularly badly. With the party which included Mrs Churchill was the Prime Minister's Principal Private Secretary, Eric Seal who described the visit later in a letter to his wife: 'On Friday we went off to Southampton and Portsmouth, to look at the damage. It is a dismal sight, particularly at Portsmouth, where one whole street we went along has just ceased to exist. . . . We did not see anything quite so bad at Southampton; but they say that it is even worse there in places.' ***Above:*** **Churchill and Hopkins, right, with the Regional Commissioner, Mr Harold Butler, and Admiral Sir William James, C-in-C Portsmouth.**

THURSDAY, FEBRUARY 6-7

Sunset: 1756 Sunrise: 0831
Moon: Dusk — 0438 (First Qtr +2)

Very little activity. Limited minelaying.

UK — Low cloud and poor visibility in many areas, mist or fog elsewhere.
The Continent — Low cloud with mist or fog in many parts.

There was very little to report during the hours of daylight and at night only eleven German aircraft were operating, with most of them engaged in minelaying. No bombs fell anywhere in the UK.

FRIDAY, FEBRUARY 7-8

Sunset: 1758 Sunrise: 0830
Moon: Dusk — 0531 (First Qtr +3)

No German bomber aircraft activity.

UK — Much low cloud with very poor visibility in all areas.
The Continent — similar to the UK.

Despite the near impossible weather conditions, a few German aircraft managed to operate during the day and several bombs fell on the coasts of north-east Scotland and East Anglia. At Fraserburgh a low level raider hit a gas holder, which caught fire, and during the afternoon eight people were killed at Lowestoft where damage was done to buildings in the harbour. All night operations were cancelled.

In Southampton with, on the left, Churchill's personal bodyguard, Detective-Inspector Bill Thompson of the Special Branch. Thompson wrote in 1951 that 'if Mr Churchill had to walk about in the open amongst crowds, I would usually keep my revolver in my overcoat pocket with a hand ready on the butt.' There is some confusion as to exactly what weapon Thompson carried, he himself telling the Editor in 1977 that his pistol at this time was a .32 Webley and Scott but Churchill's post-war bodyguard, Detective-Sergeant Roy Astley Richards, declared that he had loaned Thompson his 7.65mm Menta semi-automatic.

Hard on the heels of the Prime Minister came the King and Queen, seen here (*left*) in Portsmouth on February 6. At the ruins of the Guildhall, *right*, their Majesties were shown the muniment room where the civic plate had been spared.

Directions for operations against the English war economy

1. The effect of our operations against England to date:

(a) Contrary to our former view the heaviest effect of our operations against the English war economy has lain in the high losses in merchant shipping inflicted by sea and air warfare. This effect has been increased by the destruction of port installations, the elimination of large quantities of supplies, and by the diminished use of ships when compelled to sail in convoy. A further considerable increase is to be expected in the course of this year by the wider employment of submarines, and this can bring about the collapse of English resistance within the foreseeable future.

(b) The effect of direct air attacks against the English armaments industry is difficult to estimate. But the destruction of many factories and the consequent disorganisation of the armaments industry must lead to a considerable fall in production.

(c) The least effect of all (as far as we can see) has been made upon the morale and will to resist of the English people.

2. Consequences for our own future operations.

In the course of the next few months the effectiveness of our naval operations against enemy merchant shipping may be expected to increase thanks to the wider use of submarines and surface ships. On the other hand, we are unable to maintain the scope of our air attacks, as the demands of other theatres of war compel us to withdraw increasingly large air forces from operations against the British Isles.

It will therefore be desirable in future to concentrate air attacks more closely and to deliver them chiefly against targets whose destruction supplements our naval war. Only by these means can we expect a decisive end to the war within the foreseeable future.

3. It must therefore be the aim of our further operations against the English homeland to concentrate all weapons of air and sea warfare against enemy imports, as well as to hold down the English aircraft industry and, where possible, to inflict still further damage on it.

For this purpose it will be necessary:

(a) To destroy the most important English harbours for imports, particularly port installations, and ships lying in them or building.

(b) To attack shipping, especially when homeward bound, by all methods.

(c) Systematically to destroy the key points of the aircraft industry, including factories producing anti-aircraft equipment and explosives.

These duties must still be carried out by such forces as remain available for operations against England even should a large proportion of the Luftwaffe and a smaller proportion of naval forces be withdrawn in the course of the year for employment in other theatres.

4. For the execution of these tasks, it should be noted:

(a) The sinking of merchantmen is more important than attack on enemy warships.
The same is true of the use of aerial torpedoes.
By reducing the available enemy tonnage not only will the blockade, which is decisive to the war, be intensified, but enemy operations in Europe or Africa will be impeded.

(b) When attacks against ports or aircraft factories have obviously been successful they will be repeated again and again.

(c) By continuous laying of minefields the enemy's feelings of uncertainty and losses will be increased.

(d) After attacking the large import-harbours, efforts will be made, as far as the range of aircraft allows, to prevent the transfer of supplies to smaller ports.

Only when the weather or other conditions prevent attack on the targets designated in paragraph 3 will attacks be made on other armaments plants, towns of particular importance to the war economy, and dumps in the interior of the country, and transport centres.

No decisive success can be expected from terror attacks on residential areas or from attacks on coastal defences.

5. Until the beginning of the regrouping of forces for 'Barbarossa', efforts will be made to intensify the effect of air and sea warfare, not only in order to inflict the heaviest possible losses on England, but also in order to give the impression that an attack on the British Isles is planned for this year.

6. Special orders will be issued for cooperation between naval and air forces in reconnaissance over the sea.

7. Directive No. 9 of 29th November 1939, the amplification of Directive No. 9 of 26th May 1940, and Directive No. 17 of 1st August 1940 are no longer valid.

ADOLF HITLER, DIRECTIVE No. 23,
FEBRUARY 6, 1941

SATURDAY, FEBRUARY 8-9

Sunset: 1800 Sunrise: 0828
Moon: Dusk — 0620 (First Qtr +4)

Very little activity.

UK and the Continent — Continuing very poor conditions with low cloud, drizzle and mist or fog in all areas.

A few anti-shipping and reconnaissance missions were undertaken by the German Air Force in daylight and there were several reports of bombs in coastal areas. Little damage was caused. Night operations were confined to sorties by seven minelayers and four night fighter-bombers.

Apart from those detailed below, a Heinkel He 111 of Wekusta 2 Ob.d.L. engaged on a weather reconnaissance flight crashed near Brest killing the crew.

5/LG2 Messerschmitt Bf 109E-7 (6410). Hit by ground defences at RAF Hawkinge during attack on airfield 3.15 p.m. Fell at Arpinge Farm, Newington, Kent. Lt. W. Schlather killed. Aircraft ▲+T disintegrated.
Excavated by Brenzett Aeronautical Museum September 1973. Surviving remains recovered.

5/196 Arado Ar 196 (0129). Crashed into the sea 3 miles south-east of Dodman Point, Cornwall 9.50 a.m. Shot down by Pilot Officer K. A. G. Graham in No. 263 Squadron Whirlwind P6969 (which was itself believed to have crashed into the sea as a result of the combat — pilot missing). Oberlt. A. Berger (Staffelkapitän) and Lt. zur See H-E. Hirtz killed. Aircraft 6W+ON lost.

Pilots of 92 Squadron pick over the remains of the Ju 87 which they have just brought down on the north-western outskirts of Manston aerodrome. In the background the No. 1 School of Technical Training hangar with Brambletye Cottage on the left and Cheeseman's farm on the right. Forty-two years later Nigel Douglas pinpointed the spot beside the B2050 by small fragments in the soil.

On Saturday, February 8, a Messerschmitt 109 of LG2 based at Calais-Marck dived out of cloud on RAF Hawkinge, Kent, where No. 421 Flight's Spitfires had formed into No. 91 Squadron. The attacker, Leutnant Werner Schlather, flying a red-nosed machine with a yellow tail, tried to defy the airfield defences with what amounted to a cheeky aerobatic display. However, hit by the blast of an AA shell as it stall-turned, the port wing started to fall, the undercarriage dropped, and, out of control and followed by more shell bursts, it spun into a field near Arpinge Farm.

SUNDAY, FEBRUARY 9-10

Sunset: 1802 Sunrise: 0826
Moon: Dusk — 0703 (Full −3)

UK — Low cloud with mist in many districts. Visibility poor in the South, moderate to poor in the north of England and Scotland.
The Continent — Variable cloud with generally poor visibility.

There was slight German Air Force activity during the day, but no bombs fell on land. After dark 71 German aircraft were dispatched to attack airfields and various industrial targets in different parts of the Home Counties, East Anglia, Scotland and elsewhere. They achieved little beyond destroying two houses in Campbeltown, Argyllshire, where two people were killed. Some 25 British night fighters flew patrols and AA Command's guns fired nearly 1,000 rounds for the claimed destruction of two enemy aircraft.

MONDAY, FEBRUARY 10-11

Sunset: 1804 Sunrise: 0824
Moon: Dusk — 0741 (Full −2)

Slight activity over east and south-east England. Limited minelaying.

UK — In most areas 5/10ths cloud, but mainly poor visibility.
The Continent — Variable cloud, mist or fog in some districts.

The usual weather and shipping reconnaissance flights were carried out by the Luftwaffe during the day, but still on only a small scale. Night operations involved more aircraft than of late, with 102 bombers operating (including minelayers). Most of the activity was centred over east and south-east England and bombs at Ipswich caused two deaths. No serious damage was reported.
Approximately 1,000 rounds were fired by the heavy guns of AA Command during the night and Fighter Command flew about 75 sorties. Two enemy aircraft were claimed probably destroyed by No. 255 Squadron's Defiants, and another was claimed destroyed by the Humber guns.

TUESDAY, FEBRUARY 11-12

Sunset: 1806 Sunrise: 0822
Moon: Dusk — 0814 (Full −1)

Minor activity over east and south-east England.

UK — Extensive low cloud with poor visibility in many areas.
The Continent — Similar to the UK.

There was very little activity of note during the day and at night only eight German aircraft operated over the UK. Only a few bombs fell and no significant damage ensued.

StG1 continued its experiment in night dive-bombing using Stukas which had begun with the sorties on the night of January 17-18.

5/StG1 Junkers Ju 87B-2 (0528). Presumed crashed into the sea off Brightlingsea during experimental night bombing of Chatham. Shot down by HMS *Eager* 4.00 a.m. Fw. K. von Cramm killed. Uffz. P. Träger missing. Aircraft J9+DL lost.

WEDNESDAY, FEBRUARY 12-13

Sunset: 1808 Sunrise: 0820
Moon: 1908 — Dawn (Full Moon)

Minor activity, mainly over south-west England and south Wales.

UK — Extensive low cloud with poor visibility in many areas.
The Continent — Similar to the UK in northern France and Holland.

Anti-shipping and reconnaissance missions occupied most of the small number of German aircraft operating in daylight. During the night 19 bombers and a single reconnaissance aircraft were engaged on operations; bombs fell at several points in the South-West and Wales, killing several people but doing little damage.

The only loss to the Luftwaffe occurred due to bad weather conditions which hampered air activity.

1(F)/120 Junkers Ju 88A-1 (0482). Aircraft hit ground in low cloud during a sortie to Kinnairds Head, Aberdeenshire. Crashed in Pittairie Wood, near Monifieth, Angus 10.20 a.m. Fw. W. Presia, Fw. W. Wilken, Gefr. B. Endres and Fw. W. Schnee all killed. Aircraft A6+HH wrecked.

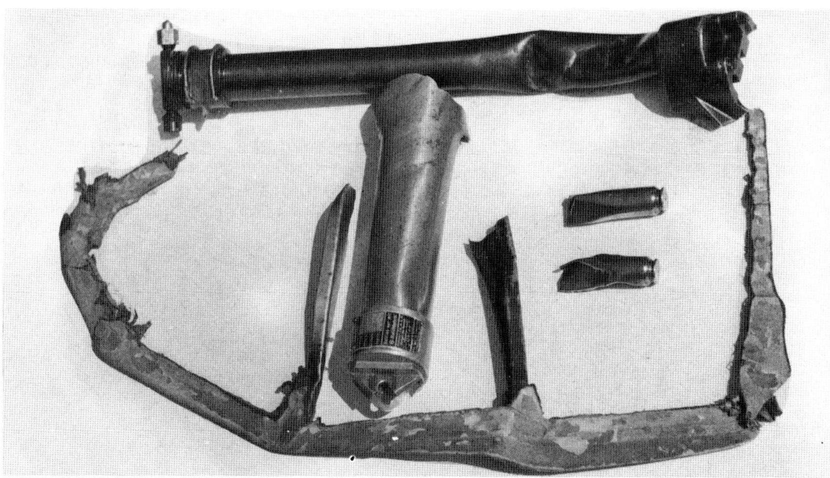

The late LAC Donald V. Elliott, who raced to the scene on the station fire tender with the ambulance in front, wrote: 'When we got there all that was left was part of a wing, the tail and a few odd bits. The rest was in the ground, about 12 feet down, still blazing.' LAC Elliott, who collected relics extensively in the Battle of Britain, brought home on his next leave the following relics from Schlather's fighter: part of the rudder with yellow fabric still adhering; part of the 20mm cannon mechanism, stamped 42858; two spent but twisted 20mm shell cases (after firing these had gone into the empties box in the wing), and undercarriage leg piece with plate inscribed 'Bf. 109' and 'Werk Nr. U 5008'. In May 1941 LAC Elliott volunteered for duty in the Far East leaving his collection of relics in the care of his younger brother Christopher. For the next four years Donald led a charmed life as he just got back to Singapore from up country ahead of the Japanese from where he escaped to Java, being ordered to surrender at Tasik Malaja airfield on March 8, 1942. Towards the end of 1944, the Japanese made the prisoners of Sandakan PoW camp force march 180 miles through virgin jungle: Donald survived the journey only to die in the foothills of Mt Kinabalu at Ranau. Today Christopher cherishes his brother's memory and his collection to which he has added many items of his own as entries on these pages have revealed. (See for example page 233.)

THURSDAY, FEBRUARY 13-14

Sunset: 1809 Sunrise: 0818
Moon: 2027 — Dawn (Full +1)

Minor operations over the Home Counties, the east of England and London.

UK — Cloudy conditions (varying from 2/10ths to 10/10ths cover) with generally poor visibility.
The Continent — Similar to the UK in northern France and the Low Countries.

A single German bomber attacked a factory in Scotland during the day. There was also reconnaissance and anti-shipping activity on a small scale, mainly around the East Coast.

At the time — and indeed right up to the present day — it has been a mystery to the people of Hendon as to precisely what caused the massive damage and loss of life on the night of February 13–14, 1941. People were stunned at the wide area of devastation centred on Ravenstone and Borthwick Roads. Even the Ministry of Home Security were baffled at the cause of so massive an explosion. In their appreciation of the events of the day they reported that 'A single raider dropped one HE, of very heavy calibre, at West Hendon at 2011 hours, just before the alert had been sounded. It fell in a densely populated district, and damage was done over a wide area — windows were broken in the neighbouring borough of Wembley. Public utility services were also affected, but full reports are not yet available. Casualties are reported as 36 killed and 150 seriously injured. In addition there are more bodies to be recovered, and several hundred people slightly injured. 800 people are homeless. The crater made by this bomb was not unusually large — about 40×15 ft. Blast effect is said to have extended for a radius of a mile. The spirit of the people in West Hendon is said to be excellent. All the homeless were got under cover last night, and factory workers from the damaged houses turned up for work this morning as usual. It is not thought that casualty figures (there may be as many as 75 dead) were affected by the absence of public warning. It is said that the people do not go to their Anderson shelters in this district, since they are on clay soil and are mostly flooded.'

Left: **All the public were told when this picture was released on the 14th was simply that members of a rescue squad were 'rescuing an old lady from the wreckage of her house several hours after it had been demolished by a bomb dropped by a lone raider.'** *Right:* **This picture, being more explicit, was banned.**

The Max — still a relatively new weapon in the Luftwaffe's armoury — would not have been deliberately dropped on civilians and the navigation beams would have been locked onto a military target of some importance — most probably the de Havilland plant — Target GB 73 33 in Stag Lane, Edgware. On this occasion the crew of III/KG26 who dropped the SC 2500 (records do not indicate if it was Herbert Rose's aircraft), after a flight of 200 miles from their base at Poix, came within 3,000 yards of hitting their target. This section of a plan from ARP records for the borough for 'Occurrence 21/32' shows the varying degree of damage from the epicentre at the back of Nos. 50 and 52 Ravenstone Road. The statistics indicate the numbers of persons taken to hospital and killed on the upper and lower floors respectively of the properties concerned — quite a feat of compilation bearing in mind the degree of damage: 84 houses totally destroyed; 78 uninhabitable and 84 temporarily so. Over 750 houses were affected in some way and over 600 made homeless from the one bomb.

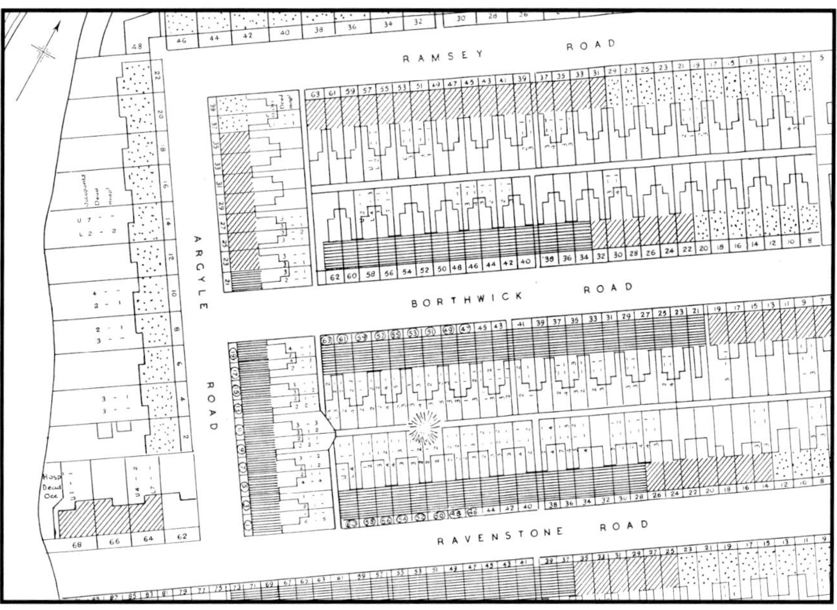

Rescue operations continued non-stop until Sunday evening and on the 23rd a memorial service was held in remembrance of the victims. The photographs were initially passed by the censor but then permission was rescinded until December.

Night operations were flown by 21 bombers including a single He 111 of III/KG26 which attacked London with an SC 2500 Max under Y-Verfahren control. The massive bomb fell at Hendon causing considerable damage and many casualties, its blast effect being in the order of a quarter-mile radius. Bombs also fell in Scotland, where 19 people were killed, and the Eastern Counties.

The enormous destruction at Hendon caused Civil Defence personnel to speculate on the possibility that the Luftwaffe was using a new bomb and fragments were sought for investigation. The weapon destroyed 196 houses, rendered 170 uninhabitable, damaged 400 more and killed 75 people. Another 445 sustained injuries of varying degrees.

In addition to the aircraft detailed, a Junkers Ju 88 of Küstenfliegergruppe 806 landed at Caen with three injured crew after being severely damaged by fighters and a Heinkel He 111 of 3/KG53 was forced to land at Sangatte.

9/StG1 Junkers Ju 87B-1 (0500). Believed crashed into the Thames Estuary, cause uncertain. Fw. F. Lewandowski and Uffz. L. Rener missing. Aircraft J9+LL lost.

The official Civil Defence historian states that 75 persons were killed but the meticulously compiled local records say 80 with 148 hospital cases and 300 slightly injured. Today no memorial cross stands to recall their passing. Argyle Road was completely demolished, the broken spurs of Ramsey, Borthwick and Ravenstone only remaining to mark Hendon's greatest tragedy.

FRIDAY, FEBRUARY 14-15

Sunset: 1811 Sunrise: 0816
Moon: 2145 — Dawn (Full +2)

Minor attack on London. Further attacks on east and north-east England and extensive minelaying by IX Fliegerkorps.

UK — Considerable cloud over much of the country with poor visibility.
The Continent — Similar to UK in France and the Low Countries. Mist or fog in many inland districts.

A German fighter sweep over south-east England constituted the biggest daylight intrusion of British airspace for some time, some 30 aircraft participating. There were also the now usual weather and shipping reconnaissance missions with a few inland penetrations. Bombs fell in several places including north-east Scotland and Kent, but little damage resulted.

During the night, in which 123 bombers were operating, an attack was made against London. Twelve aircraft were so ordered, but they were joined by four more using London as an alternative target. Together, the 16 aircraft dropped 16 tonnes of HE (two SC 1000, seven SC 500, 22 SC 250, six LZZ 250 and 62 SC/SD 50) and 100 BSK (3,600 incendiaries). The attack took place between 1940 and 2210 hours and was a mixture of visual and DR/radio navigation bombing, but no results could be determined because of total cloud cover.

Additionally in the London area five He 111s of III/KG26 independently attacked the aero engine factory at Edgware using Y-Verfahren. One crew reported two fires, but the others saw nothing because of the thick cloud cover.

Various other alternative targets were bombed including Great Yarmouth, by three crews who subsequently reported seeing four small fires in the port district, and Newton, near Kings Lynn.

For the second consecutive night what appeared to be a very heavy bomb was reported by London's Civil Defence Service. This time it fell on open ground at Harrow, some 800 feet from the nearest building, and while no houses were totally destroyed there was extensive damage to a lesser degree over a wide area; casualties were confined to one killed and another person injured.

Fragments of the bomb, together with bits of that dropped at Hendon the previous night, were examined by experts and the Ministry of Home Security subsequently issued a cautiously worded confidential report to Civil Defence Regional Commissioners advising that the incidents 'may possibly have involved a new German HE bomb'. Examination of the fragments did not produce a positive indication of the bomb's weight but, the report stated, 'both from the exceptionally wide area affected by blast and from the nature of the fragments collected, it may be judged that the weapon has a high charge/weight ratio, a thin casing and an impact fuse'.

The British appreciation was quite accurate, for an SC 2500 Max was indeed dropped by one of the He 111s of III/KG26. In addition the five aircraft of this Gruppe dropped four SC 1800s and 64 SD 50s, carrying out individual Y-Verfahren runs starting at 1946 and finishing at 2012 hours.

The use of the SC 2500 was still very restricted but several had been dropped since their introduction in late December. It appears, however, that on previous occasions the damage that resulted was thought to have been caused by parachute 'land mines'. So far III/KG26 was still the only unit to use SC 2500s — presumably they were considered too valuable to trust to non-precision guided units — and even in this Gruppe only two pilots had until then been cleared to carry them. The only other precision bombing unit, KGr100, was equipped with He 111H-3 aircraft (possessing internal bomb racks only) which were incapable of carrying bombs larger than the SC 250.

In London several fires were started but damage was not serious. There were also incidents at various places in east and north-east England, but there was no concentration. Airfields in the eastern half of the country, from Yorkshire to Kent, also came in for some attention, but again no serious damage was caused. Minelaying, which was extensive, was carried out in the mouth of the Humber and off the coasts of Lincolnshire, Yorkshire and Cornwall. Shipping off the Scottish east coast was attacked by five aircraft operating in that area.

About 30 night fighter sorties were flown, without success, and more than 1,000 rounds were fired by the heavy guns of AA Command. One enemy aircraft was claimed shot down by light AA in the Humber area.

As we have seen, compulsory civil defence duties were introduced in January — officially the Defence Regulations 26A, 27A and 27B. Government departments and local authorities were required to make adequate arrangements for detecting and combating fires in business and industrial districts under the Fire Precaution (Business Premises) Order, and men aged between 16 and 60 had to register for part-time fire prevention duties — limited to 48 hours per month. Women and youths were encouraged to play their part voluntarily and steel helmets, and armbands with the initials 'SFP', were issued to these Street Fire Parties. Stirrup pumps and sandbags were given out on a 'free on loan' basis, but parties had to provide their own receptacles for water. It was a shoestring affair, loosely organised, which was never really successful, and was superseded by the Fire Guard service introduced in August 1941. We found this nice series of pictures illustrating the Dead End Kids' SFP down Wapping way, their 'HQ' being an annexe of Watson's Wharf Shelter.

While this series illustrates a practice exercise, there was obviously a propaganda value in releasing pictures showing the dedication of these young lads volunteering to form their own Street Fire Party. *Left:* Here, with their shelter surrounded by buckets and baths, the gang is called out by their leader Patsy Duggan. *Right:* Wapping is in the midst of great change as Docklands undergoes its metamorphosis into the high-tech business centre of the 21st century. We caught this shot of Sampson Street in 1983 — at the chrysalis stage!

Down the road, so the original caption says, 'leader Patsy Duggan hurries two urchins off the streets and down into the shelter'. This is Hermitage Wall with Sampson Street on the right, but what's happened to Patsy's free-on-loan helmet!

SATURDAY, FEBRUARY 15-16

Sunset: 1813 Sunrise: 0814
Moon: 2304 — Dawn (Full +3)

Minor attacks on Liverpool, airfields in East Anglia and other industrial targets. Large scale minelaying.

UK — Extensive but variable amounts of cloud with poor visibility.

The Continent — Cloudy with poor visibility in northern France, moderate to poor visibility in the Low Countries.

Fighter patrols over the Straits, reconnaissance and anti-shipping missions occupied units of the Luftwaffe during the day but operations were not on a big scale despite generally good weather with a cloud base of about 3,000 feet. Bombs fell at several places on the East Coast.

During the night 129 long-range bombers were operating, 45 of them being minelayers of IX Fliegerkorps carrying out their task along the length of the coast from Flamborough Head to St Abbs Head. It was also planned to send 79 bombers of Luftflotte 3 to attack the docks at Liverpool and five to bomb the Hawker Aircraft factory at Langley but, following a weather report from an aircraft previously dispatched to north-west England, 40 aircraft of IV Fliegerkorps already on their way were recalled at 2100 hours. Of the remaining 30 aircraft the crews of twelve (seven Ju 88s and four He 111s of KG1 and a single He 111 of III/KG27) claimed to have bombed Liverpool, dropping 15.4 tonnes of HE and 2,006 IBs. Two crews of III/KG26 dropped 3.6 tonnes of HE on the Langley aircraft factory, another aircraft bombed Southampton and seven attacked alternative targets. Another four aircraft aborted, two aircraft were lost (an He 111 of II/KG27 and a Ju 88 of I/KG1) and a Ju 88 of III/KG77 crashed in occupied territory on its return flight. Long-range night fighter-bombers achieved no success over RAF airfields.

Bombing was in fact very widespread, with incidents reported in every Civil Defence Region except Wales. Several parachute mines were also reported, but nowhere was damage serious although there were a few fatal casualties.

AA Command's heavy guns fired 3,000 rounds during the night, without positive success, but one raider was shot down by a night fighter, 80 of which were on patrol.

At about 1900 hours an incoming German bomber — allocated the identification 'Raid 143' — was plotted approaching the Dorset coast, but as it was too light to cross the coast the raider made three orbits before continuing. Meanwhile, unknown to the German crew, a Beaufighter of No. 604 Squadron, flown by Flight Lieutenant John Cunningham, DFC, with Sergeant Rawnsley, AI operator, was closing in under the control of 'Harlequin', the Sopley GCI Station. John Rawnsley took over the interception once AI contact was firmly established and after a stealthy approach from behind and below in the classical manner, John Cunningham reported visual contact and identified the Raid as an He 111. Just north of St Alban's Head at 13,500ft, Cunningham opened fire and the enemy aircraft caught fire with a large orange flame at 1916 hours.

After it was hit Raid 143 turned westwards, losing height. It jettisoned a load of incendiary bombs, which were seen burning on the ground, and eventually crashed at 2015 hours (according to the AI1(g) report)

'Out of the yard the kids rush with their barrow in which hose, ladder and firefighting gear are piled.' Their depôt was located in Thomas Allen's cartage yard.

'Along the deserted streets, under the dockwall, the gang runs to the fire.'

'Now they are in the street where the fire is. They quickly connect their hose to the nearest hydrant.' Getting his back into turning the key is 15-year-old Oswald Bath.

at Higher Luscombe Farm, Harberton, near Totnes, Devon. Much of the aircraft, an He IIIP-2 (1G+FR) of III/KG27, was destroyed or burnt out and the Observer and aircraft commander, Leutnant Eberhard Beckmann, pilot Oberfeldwebel Max Unselt and two other crew members were killed. Their aircraft, which had been bound for Birmingham, was still burning when Cunningham's Beaufighter landed back at Middle Wallop at 2050 hours. It was the British pilot's third officially credited night victory, a feat widely reported in the press the next day and which led to his 'Cat's Eyes' name tag. Naturally, the secrecy of AI and GCI had to be maintained and so was born the legend of night fighter pilots endowed with extraordinary night vision enhanced by eating carrots. Even the Beaufighter was still on the Secret List and no mention could be made of this type in official communiqués or press reports. However, the Germans were aware of its existence and had more than an inkling of the British early warning RDF or radar system. Airborne AI radar was unknown to them, on the other hand, and it became widely believed by German bomber crews that the increase in the number of night interceptions was occasioned by RAF fighters tracking along the German radio navigation beams.

Some eight hours after the crash of the 1G+FR near Totnes, another German aircraft came down on British soil, but this one was virtually intact and proved a magnificent gift-horse to British Air Intelligence. At 0430 hours an unidentified aircraft displaying its landing light was seen in close proximity to two aircraft, a Blenheim and a Hurricane, circling Steeple Morden landing ground in bright moonlight. When challenged by a signal lamp the unidentified aircraft fired off a red/yellow signal cartridge. It then came in to land, cross-wind and across the flarepath, but after touch-down its starboard landing gear leg collapsed resulting in slight damage to the starboard propeller, engine, radiator, wing tip and tailplane. Upon arrival at the aircraft, RAF personnel recognised it as a Ju 88 and its crew of four were disarmed and taken into custody.

The Ju 88 was an A-5 variant with the markings V4+GS. Belonging to III/KG1 it had been engaged in the attack on Liverpool, flown by Leutnant Herbert Florian and a crew of three. After bombing, a W/T message was transmitted, reporting 'attack carried out and starting on return flight', and then some trouble was experienced with the starboard engine. After approaching Liverpool from the direction of the Irish Sea, Florian had taken the Ju 88 low over the city — into the flak — for the bombing and it is possible, according to crew member Ferdinand Wühr, that the engine was then damaged. Wühr, then an Unteroffizier and the W/T operator, recalls: 'Finally the engine caught fire. We tried to transfer and then jettisoned petrol to maintain height; we were very close to baling out. Suddenly we found ourselves in the middle of a balloon barrage and it was horrible — ghostlike. I still wonder how we got out, but after some dangerous manoeuvring we found ourselves very close to the ground. We managed to gain a little height, but we owe our survival to the moonlight.'

Florian and his crew knew they had no chance of getting back to France and therefore attempted a single engine emergency landing as, once again, the Ju 88 lost height. And they succeeded, their aircraft sustaining only superficial damage. Being immediately captured, they had no opportunity to destroy their aircraft, which later went to the Royal Aircraft Establishment at Farnborough for detailed examination. Subsequently it was used as a source of spares to keep two more Ju 88A-5s flying with the RAF's Enemy Aircraft Flight.

A third German aircraft was lost at 0035 hours (February 16) when an attacking He 111P-4, the 5J+GP of II/KG4, struck a barrage balloon cable at South Shields, causing it to dive steeply into the ground. Upon impact the wreckage caught fire and 20 minutes later a mine which the Heinkel was carrying exploded, blowing the aircraft and the remains of four members of its crew to pieces. A fifth crew member, believed to have been the pilot, Oberfeldwebel Wilhelm Beetz, managed to bale out but was electrocuted when he landed on trolley bus overhead wires. There was clearly some difficulty in identifying the crew and informing the German authorities of their fate through the International Red Cross — Beetz and another crew member were reported killed almost immediately, but Hauptmann Heinz Styra, the aircraft Kommandant and Observer, and another crew member were not shown as killed in German records until January 1942 while the fifth crewman remains listed as missing.

Formal details of the aircraft lost are as follows.

8/KG1 Junkers Ju 88A-5 (6214). Landed at RAF Steeple Morden, Cambridgeshire at 4.30 a.m., after an attack on Liverpool. Lt. H. Florian, Uffz. A. Wassmeier, Uffz. F. Wühr and Gefr. K. Fredrich all taken prisoner. Aircraft V4+GS captured intact save for a collapsed starboard undercarriage and other minor damage.

Dismantled and taken to RAE Farnborough. Later allocated the serial HX360 and used as spares by No. 1426 (Enemy Aircraft) Flight.

6/KG4 Heinkel He 111P-4 (3085). Hit by AA fire, collided with a balloon cable and dived into the ground where it later exploded killing one policeman and three firemen. Crashed at Bents Park, South Shields, Co. Durham 12.35 a.m. Oberfw. W. Beetz baled out but died after landing on trolleybus wires. Hptmn. H. Styra, Uffz. K-G. Brützsam, Gefr. F. Janeschitz and Uffz. H. Jeckstadt all killed. Aircraft 5J+GP destroyed.

7/KG27 Heinkel He 111P-2 (2911). Shot down by Flight Lieutenant J. Cunningham DFC and Sergeant C. F. Rawnsley of No. 604 Squadron during a raid on Birmingham. Crashed at Higher Luscombe Farm, Harberton, Devon 8.15 p.m. Oberlt. E. Beckmann, Oberfw. M. Unseld, Oberfw. M. Bunge and Oberfw. R. Streubel all killed. Aircraft 1G+FR destroyed.

Fighting the fire: left, Oswald's elder brother Graham and Pat Duggan's son Jack. Cyril Demarne, our professional fire chief, points out that the boys are having to use an old-fashioned pre-war copper branch.

Saturday night and Sunday morning . . . and some unwelcome visitors to the shores of England. ***Left:*** **These are the burnt-out remains of 1G+FR of the 7th Staffel of Kampfgeschwader 27 — Cat's Eyes' third night victory. Up till now it was the AA guns which formed the only really effective defence against the raiders, and during January and February the guns claimed 20½ hostile aircraft against seven by night fighters. (Who got the other half, one wonders?) However, in March the figures swung 17 to 22 in favour of the fighters as their Airborne Radar and Ground Controlled Interceptions drastically improved the kill rate.** ***Right:*** **Robin Hood of the Devon Aircraft Research and Recovery Team in the same field on Higher Luscombe Farm.**

SUNDAY, FEBRUARY 16-17

Sunset: 1815 Sunrise: 0812
Moon: 0022 — Dawn (Last Qtr −2)

Small scale minelaying and coastal reconnaissance operations only.

UK — Low cloud with generally poor visibility in most areas.
The Continent — Similar to UK.

Except for a fighter sweep over south-eastern Kent by about six Messerschmitt Bf 109s, only a few single enemy aircraft flew inland during the day. Night bomber operations were cancelled because of the weather conditions, but about ten aircraft laid mines off the East Coast between Clacton and Skegness and two attacks were made on shipping off the east coast of Scotland.

New Zealanders under training with the RAF at Steeple Morden — satellite to Bassingbourn — had an unexpected surprise on Sunday morning when they awoke to find an almost intact Ju 88 sitting on the 'drome. Here it is being inspected by their High Commissioner, the Rt. Hon. W. J. Jordan. It was dismantled and moved to Farnborough on May 7 and given the British serial HX360 before going to the Enemy Aircraft Flight ***(see Volume 1, page 69)*** **in June 1942.**

Left: **Rather less was left of the Heinkel 111 which hit a balloon cable on the North Foreshore at South Shields. In almost a re-run of the incident in April 1940 when a Heinkel came down in Clacton** ***(see Volume 1, pages 79–83),*** **25 minutes after the crash a parachute mine on board went off, breaking windows as far away as Tynemouth and North Shields on the other side of the river. In the explosion Police Constable Lamb was killed and Auxiliary Firemen Purvis, Renwick and Wharton were mortally wounded. Other bombers appeared to use the flames of burning wreckage as a target and within minutes three people had been killed in Brodrick Street.** ***Right:*** **After the explosion little remained to be seen at the spot just off Beach Road.**

MONDAY, FEBRUARY 17-18

Sunset: 1817 Sunrise: 0810
Moon: 0137 — Dawn (Last Qtr −1)

Moderate attack on London. Extensive minelaying and patrols by night fighter-bombers over RAF airfields in East Anglia.

UK — Low cloud with poor visibility in many districts.
The Continent — Similar to the UK.

During the day German offensive operations were on a small scale, with only eight aircraft of the 125 operating penetrating inland. The remainder were engaged on oversea reconnaissance or attacks on shipping. A few bombs fell in east and south-east England and in Scotland, but little damage resulted.

Nightfall brought operations by 148 bombers and 6 night fighters, the biggest force to fly over Britain by night since February 4. A large part of this force was devoted to attacks on airfields in East Anglia, for on this occasion the night fighters of I/NJG2 were joined by Do 17s of I, II and III/KG2, all operating from Merville, and He 111s of I and II/KG53 from Lille/Vendeville. The London attack was made by Luftflotte 3 which sent 43 aircraft, 40 of which, according to their crews, reached and bombed the capital. They were:

KGr606: 10 Do 17, 1935-2050 (bombing by Knickebein)
II/KG76: 6 Ju 88, 2014-2115 (Knickebein and DR bombing)
I and III/KG77: 17 Ju 88, 2120-2300 (7 bombed visually, 10 by means of Knickebein beams)
III/KG26: 6 He 111, 2124-2155 (Y-Verfahren guided attack on the Isle of Dogs/Millwall Docks)

Another Do 17 of KGr606 was believed to have bombed London, but it failed to return. In the course of the attack 42 tonnes of HE (six SC 1800, seven SC 1000, 20 SC 500, three LZZ 250, 100 SC 50 and ten SD 50) were claimed delivered, together with 128 BSK (4,608 IBs). The SC 1800s were dropped by the He 111s of III/KG26, operating independently of the main force in a Y-System precision guided attack on the Isle of Dogs/Millwall Docks. Their crews subsequently reported seven fires in that area, visible up to 50 kilometres distant on their return flight, but little else could be seen owing to the thick cloud and poor visibility which prevailed; in most cases, other units bombed by DR and Knickebein and although bomb detonations and the glow of fires could be discerned, it was not possible to assess the results of the attack. One crew bombed Southampton as an alternative target and two aborted.

Of the participating Luftflotte 2 aircraft approximately 90 were engaged in minelaying between Yarmouth and Flamborough Head and in the Thames Estuary, with ten more He 111s of I/KG28 laying mines off the coast of Cornwall, in the Bristol Channel and in Liverpool Bay. Several mines, no doubt intended to go into the sea, did in fact come down on land but without serious consequences.

Apart from purpose-built shelters, many existing structures — warehouses, basements, even church crypts — were turned into refuges. Massive railway arches gave a semblance of safety yet only a thin crust formed the overhead protection. It was on Monday night that what the authorities feared would happen, did happen — at the Stainer Street shelter under London Bridge Station which received a direct hit at 10.50 p.m. The awful scenes that night were spared the photographer's lens; only after the crushed and mangled remains of the shelterers had been removed was the scene recorded. This is the clear up operation under way in St Thomas Street.

Left: **Initial reports indicated 35 killed and 55 seriously injured but when the tons of masonry and brickwork had finally been cleared the death toll was revised to 90.** *Right:* **Stainer Street is one of three vaulted roads running under the station from which numerous lock-up warehouses operate. Now the southern end where the tragedy occurred has been cut back to allow for the introduction of a vehicle ramp from the concourse above.**

The worst incident of the night occurred in London where a bomb which exploded in an archway shelter at London Bridge station killed some 90 people. Two further fatal casualties were caused by a delayed action bomb which was dropped at the same time, about 60 feet away, but went unnoticed until it exploded five hours later. Several fires were started in the city, but only two assumed serious proportions. Several important factory and railway system targets were hit, but on the whole damage was slight and no significant loss of production occurred — the chief cause of such loss was occasioned by damage to roofs and windows, interrupting night work, but no loss of production was greater than four days. Elsewhere attacks were not severe, but bombs were reported in many parts of the Home Counties and East Anglia. Again, little damage of military or industrial importance was reported.

The heavy guns of AA Command expended approximately 3,000 rounds during the night and claimed four raiders destroyed or damaged. Night fighters were also operating and shot down one enemy aircraft. On the debit side, a Defiant (N3334) of No. 255 Squadron was written-off at Kirton-in-Lindsay when it overran on landing and collided with another Defiant.

The weather at Lanveoc-Poulmic airfield, just south of Brest, was cold and cloudy on February 17 and it was with some reluctance that the crews of 2 Staffel, Kampfgruppe, formerly Küstenfliegergruppe, 606, were roused from their beds in the late morning. Since night operations were planned for that day, breakfast was taken at 11.00 a.m. but during the afternoon some crews were called for 'Storangriffe: London' — harassing attacks by single flying aircraft to keep the British defences busy and, not least, to disturb the entire population.

'It was no big thing that day, only routine,' recalls Gunther Hübner, then a Leutnant and Do 17 pilot with the former naval air unit that had been integrated into the Luftwaffe's bomber force. Before the day was over, however, much was to happen to the 20-year-old native of Hermsdorf.

'I came to 606 in October, 1940', he relates, 'after I had been trained as a bomber pilot in the Luftwaffe. The crews of 606 came at first from the navy, but after the unit's task was changed reinforcements came from the Luftwaffe. The naval officers remained as navigators (Observers), but one by one they were transferred back to the navy to reinforce U-Boat crews. My navigator, too, was a Leutnant zur See — Rolf Dieskau — and the entire crew of four had flown together a long time so we knew each other well. Our spirits were high and we were convinced that we fought for a just cause. We were educated in an idealistic sense and we did our duty. It was a fine crowd.'

Hübner's Do 17Z-3, the 7T+JL, took off from Poulmic at about 1900 hours bound for London. Passing over the Channel Islands, with Cherbourg's flak in action (as always, according to Hübner) to his right, the German pilot set course for Brighton en route to the British capital. 'We saw the big 'U'-bend of the Thames and dropped our bombs', continues the former German pilot. 'We changed course again and suddenly we were attacked from behind. Everything then happened very fast. The cockpit filled with smoke. The starboard engine caught fire. I was unable to hold the aircraft on course and we lost height rapidly. I then saw the night fighter very close to us — it was a Beaufighter. I then told my crew to bale out and tried to follow them, but I was in some difficulty — I could not get free from my seat

Not much left of Leutnant Hübner's Dornier although he probably would have smiled at the papers next day which reported that the pilot had been killed in the crash.

for as soon as I let go the stick the aircraft went out of control. Finally I made it, but the aeroplane came frighteningly near to my parachute. I then landed in a field near the burning plane and broke my ankle. Soon Home Guard men arrived and took my pistol before taking me to the nearest police station.'

The 7T+JL was shot down by Squadron Leader J. H. Little, DFC, flying a Beaufighter of No. 219 Squadron. It crashed at 2030 hours at Oakley Court, near Bray, Berkshire, and was completely destroyed and burnt out, but all four crew members successfully baled out and landed safely to be taken PoW.

Later on, while talking to his naval officer navigator in a PoW Camp, Hübner learned that when the Beaufighter attacked his aircraft no one had been looking out to the rear. While the navigator was at the forward-facing bombsight the flight mechanic, who normally manned the lower rear-facing gun, was trying to dispose of an additional box of some 20 or 30 1kg incendiary bombs through a hatch. He was having some difficulty, however, and accordingly the W/T operator cum upper rear gunner left his position to assist — and at that moment the Beaufighter struck.

In the grey light of dawn on the 18th another German aircraft, an He 111H-3 (A1+CM) of 4/KG53, was shot down, but this time by the less common PAC (parachute and cable) rocket weapon developed for airfield defence against low flying aircraft. Werner Schmoll, then an Unteroffizier and the W/T operator of the A1+CM and now living in Berlin, recalls: 'We were ordered to attack a convoy in the mouth of the Wash at dawn, but the day started badly. On run-up we had a problem with one engine, so had to take another aircraft. We took off at about 0330 hours, but shortly afterwards our transmitter, receiver and D/F radio compass went unserviceable, and although we had standing instructions to return to base in such a situation, we decided to carry on. It was a very cloudy morning with the base almost at ground level and with no vertical visibility, so we had to fly on instruments and navigate by compass and dead reckoning. When we estimated that we were just beyond our target we attempted to descend, but could find no holes in the cloud so decided we must return to our base at Lille. This was about 0700 hours and we turned onto a course of approximately 120°, flying at 1,000 metres. When we estimated that we must have been approaching the Belgian coast we went down to 300 metres and came out of the clouds. In front of us we saw land and almost immediately we crossed the coast. Continuing inland we became aware as dawn broke that we were over an unfamiliar landscape with parks, castles, etc., and then we were fired at by flak positions. There was now no possibility of regaining cloud, so we went down as low as possible to avoid the flak, but we were unlucky enough to cross several air bases and on one of them we dumped our bombs to increase our manoeuvrability. But then we were hit and as the aircraft went out of control we crash landed in a field.'

Schmoll's aircraft, which was piloted by Feldwebel Heinrich Busch and under the command of Oberleutnant Erich Langguth, crashed at 0755 hours some four miles to the north-east of Watton airfield. According to the Watton defences the Heinkel was flying at only some 100ft or so when it was hit by the PAC; one cable was struck by the port wing leading edge and the ensuing gash went back to the main spar, severing the port aileron control rod and jamming the aileron. A second cable cut the port wing eight feet from the tip and a third struck the starboard wing 12 feet from its tip, both cutting through to the main spar. Nevertheless, the German pilot made a good belly landing and the aircraft, despite sliding into a bank, remained fairly intact and provided AI1(g) with some interesting material. The crew of five, two of whom were slightly hurt, were taken prisoner, but in 1946, while detained in Canada, Busch was found guilty of the in-camp murder of a fellow prisoner who had been classed as 'White' (that is, one not sympathetic to Nazi ideology and cleared for repatriation by the Camp authorities) and executed on December 18, 1946.

During the day two Junkers Ju 88s — from 8/KG1 and 6/KG76 — failed to return from attacks over the East Coast and were lost at sea. Only two aircraft fell in Britain as a result of the night's operations; one of them on the evening of the 17th, the other on the morning of the 18th:

3/KGr606 Dornier Do 17Z-3 (3472). Shot down by Squadron Leader J. H. Little DFC and Sergeant S. Austin of No. 219 Squadron in a Beaufighter during an attack on London. Crashed at Oakley Court, Bray, near Windsor 8.30 p.m. Lt. zur See R. Dieskau, Uffz. E. Tietjen, Lt. G. Hübner and Gefr. W. Arnold all baled out and were taken prisoner. Aircraft 7T+JL entirely disintegrated.

Site investigated by Simon Parry and a few fragments recovered from a market garden.

4/KG53 Heinkel He 111H-3 (3349). When flying at 100 feet aircraft hit by Parachute and Cable rocket apparatus from RAF Watton. Crashed at Ovington, Norfolk 7.55 a.m. Fw. H. Busch, Oberlt. E. Langguth, Uffz. W. Schmoll captured unhurt, Uffz. O. Ludwig and Gefr. K. Kammermeier captured slightly wounded. Aircraft A1+CM wrecked.

TUESDAY, FEBRUARY 18-19

Sunset: 1723 Sunrise: 0858
Moon: 0248 — Dawn (Last Quarter)

No German night operations over Britain.

UK — Extensive very low cloud with poor to bad visibility (less than 1,000 yards in many areas).

The Continent — Low cloud, mist or fog in northern France and the Low Countries.

Daylight activity by a few German aircraft produced reports of minor bomb incidents in the South, South-East and East Anglia. The only serious casualties were at Newmarket where seven people were killed and 40 badly injured when several houses and shops were destroyed.

All night operations were cancelled in view of the extremely bad weather existing on both sides of the Channel.

At least the mud had been transformed into a market garden when we took our comparison.

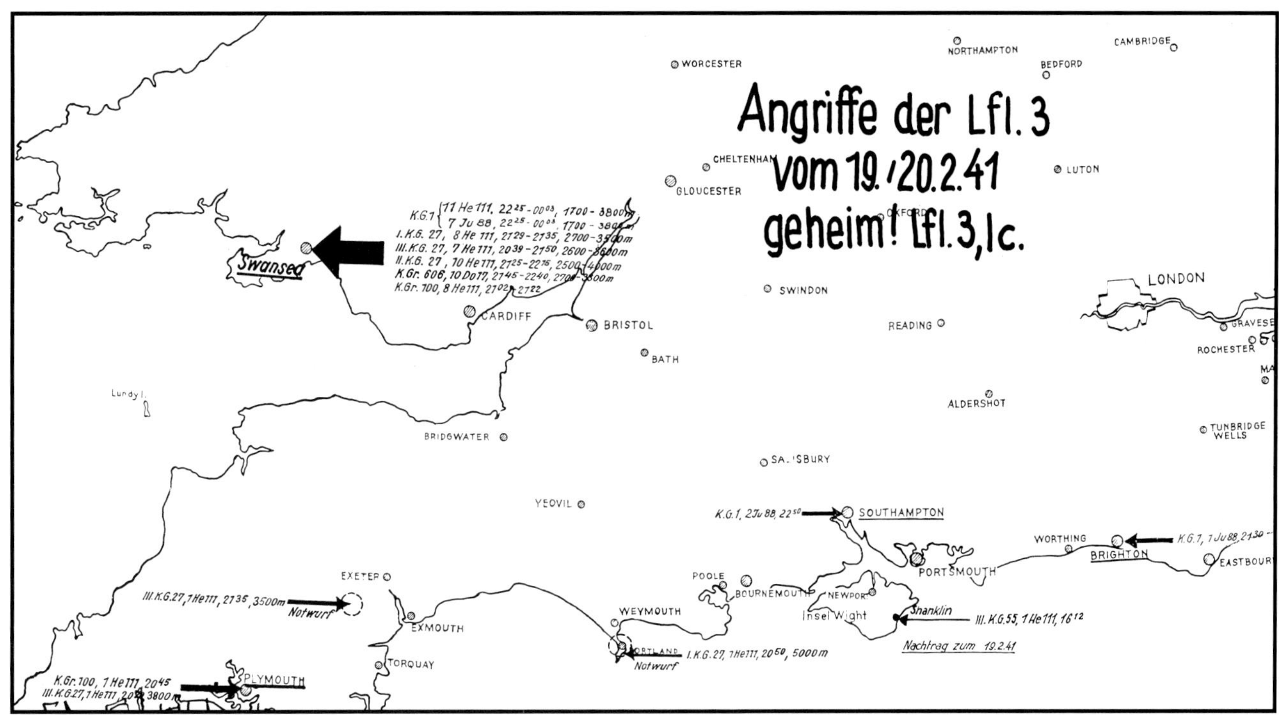

WEDNESDAY, FEBRUARY 19-20

Sunset: 1820 Sunrise: 0806
Moon: 0353 — Dawn (Last Qtr +1)

Serious attack on Swansea with minor attacks on London and Chatham. Limited minelaying activity.

UK — Extensive low cloud with poor visibility and sleet or snow in many areas. Broken cloud and wintry showers with mainly good visibility in southern Wales and south-western England.

The Continent — Broken cloud with snow showers and moderate to good visibility in France and the Low Countries. More frequent snow in Holland.

Daylight operations continued on a small scale with mainly reconnaissance and anti-shipping sorties. A few German aircraft penetrated inland, flying singly, and there were reports of bombs on the coasts of north-east Scotland, East Anglia and Yorkshire.

An improvement in the weather in the West was expected and while not good enough to permit a major operation, enabled a sharp attack to be made on Swansea by 61 aircraft of Luftflotte 3. Between 1937 and 2305 hours they dropped 54 tonnes of HE (four SC 1000, ten SC 500, 34 LZZ 250, 80 SC 250 and 334 SC 50) and 537 BSK (19,332 IBs). Cloud over the target was often 10/10ths and never less than 6/10ths, according to German crew reports, with the result that most of the bombing was by DR or radio navigation methods and observation of the results was made difficult. Nevertheless, three large, two medium and several smaller fires were seen. No aircraft of Luftflotte 3 were lost, but seven of the force of 71 ordered to Swansea bombed alternative targets and three aborted. Those reporting over the target were:

I/KG27: 8 He 111, 2029-2035
II/KG27: 10 He 111, 2025-2115
III/KG27: 7 He 111, 1937-2050
KGr100: 8 He 111, 2002-2022 (X-Verfahren bombing)
KGr606: 10 Do 17, 2045-2140
KG1: 11 He 111, 7 Ju 88, 2125-2305

Of the other 36 bombers operating during the night, 17 attacked London between 2110 and 2205 hours, dropping one Flam 250, an SC 250, 207 SC 50s and 108 incendiary bombs. Their target was dock installations but visual bombing was not possible and it was difficult to assess the results although a large fire glow was seen through the cloud. A further attack was planned against naval installations at Chatham, but only three crews reached there, to drop one Flam 250, ten SC/SD 50s and 20 LMB parachute mines. Again, thick cloud and poor visibility interfered with the attack, but explosions were seen in the Target Area.

According to the official RAF historians, 'the Blitz was split into three phases: September 7 to November 13; November 14 to February 19; and the third phase up to May 12.' However, they admit that whereas the first and second phases began dramatically with massive attacks on London and Coventry respectively, the choice of February 19–20 as the beginning of the third phase 'is a little arbitrary, although it marks a period in which the Germans endeavoured more strenuously to put towns out of action by raids on successive nights, marks a distinctly greater emphasis on the western and south-western ports and a decline in the number of raids carried out on industrial cities of the provinces.' In the compilation of the table on page 9 we have adopted the viewpoint of Dr Karl Klee, who gave the German view in his book *Decisive Battles of World War II*, in that there was no division of Stage III into two phases. However, whatever line one chooses to accept, February 19–20 certainly marked a traumatic beginning for the people of Swansea, who were to be subjected to three nights of heavy bombing.

At Swansea damage was done to residential and commercial premises, the town centre receiving the main weight of bombing, but a factory of Imperial Chemical Industries was damaged. A few bombs also fell in the docks but little damage was caused. Schools, a hospital and a railway station were also hit, but comparatively little industrial damage occurred. Road and rail services were temporarily but seriously affected, however, and water and gas supplies were interrupted. Unexploded or delayed action bombs caused many diversions and evacuations and one, exploding two days after the attack, killed six soldiers of a bomb disposal unit. Civilian casualties in the attack were 48 killed and 79 seriously injured.

In the attack on London the most serious incident was at St Stephen's Hospital, Fulham Road, where 19 people were killed. A large fire was started at Paddington and bombing also took place at Wandsworth, Battersea, Chelsea, Hayes, Marylebone, Hampstead, St Pancras and Richmond. Bombs also fell at Sunbury, Windsor, Uxbridge, Falmouth and Plymouth, and attacks were made on ships off Kinnairds Head, south-west of Montrose and in Lunan Bay. Nowhere, however, was any significant damage done to military, naval or industrial objectives.

Dusk and dawn patrols were flown by 11 fighters of Nos. 13 and 14 Groups, but only six night fighters of Nos. 10 and 11 Groups took off and bad weather prevented interceptions. Heavy guns of AA Command engaged Raids at Plymouth, Portland, Cardiff, the IAZ, Dover, Thames and Medway (North and South), Brooklands, Slough, Falmouth, Portsmouth, Southampton and Swansea. They fired approximately 2,000 rounds for the claim of one enemy aircraft probably damaged.

Fighter Command was at this time operating under extremely difficult airfield conditions: snow, slush and waterlogging affecting the serviceability of Cranage, Squires Gate, Charmy Down, St Eval and Middle Wallop, all airfields used by night fighters. The Luftwaffe faced similar difficulties, of course, and in addition on this particular night, bad weather over their normal bases made it necessary for returning aircraft of III/KG27 to divert to Avord while most aircraft of KGr100 diverted from Vannes to Dinard. Three aircraft, a Do 17 of KGr606 and two He 111s of KGr100, were subsequently damaged on landing or while taxiing, but sustained no crew casualties.

During the day a Heinkel He 111 of I/KG26 caught fire in the air whilst off the Scottish coast and disappeared into the North Sea. A Dornier Do 17 of 8/KG3 was damaged by fighters near Great Yarmouth and two of its crew injured. A Junkers Ju 88 of 3(F)/121 landed at Morlaix with two injured crewmen again as a result of fighter action. None came down over Great Britain.

THURSDAY, FEBRUARY 20-21

Sunset: 1822 Sunrise: 0804
Moon: 0449 — Dawn (Last Qtr +2)

No major operation but a serious attack was made on Swansea with a secondary raid on Chatham. Minelaying operations completed on a small scale.

UK — Low cloud with snow and poor visibility over the eastern half of the country. In the West, little or no cloud except in scattered wintry showers in coastal districts, with moderate to good visibility.

The Continent — Scattered showers of sleet or hail with mainly good visibility in northern France. Low cloud with sleet, rain or snow in the Low Countries with fresh south-westerly winds

In daylight the usual German reconnaissance and anti-shipping operations were carried out by a small number of aircraft and a few bombs fell on East Anglia. Improving weather conditions in the West favoured night operations in this region on a moderate scale and for the second night in succession Swansea suffered a sharp attack. Chatham, too, was selected for a second attack, while minelaying was undertaken by five aircraft of I/KG28 near Lands End and The Lizard. In total 150 long-range bombers took part in the night's programme and activity was continuous from 1800 to 0630 hours.

Luftflotte 3 sent 88 aircraft to Swansea, but the crews of only 64 reached and reported over the city where their Concentration Point was centred on the port and adjacent industrial installations. Between 2000 and 2345 hours the attackers dropped 58 tonnes of HE (two SC 1800, 26 SC 500, 93 SC 250, 30 LZZ 250 and 253 SC 50) and 554 BSK (19,944 IBs). With the exception of eleven He 111s of KGr100, which dropped 12,672 incendiaries at the beginning of the

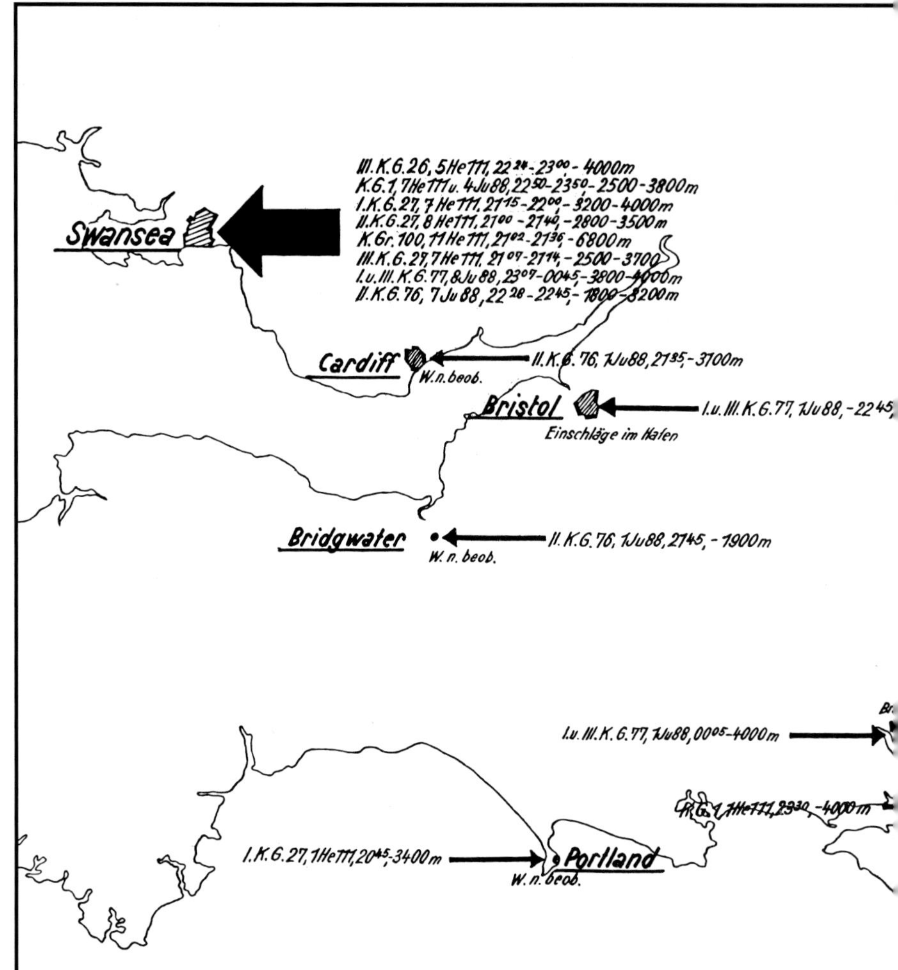

With its brief caption 'Damage caused by Nazi raiders at Swansea' one cannot say precisely when this picture was taken . . .

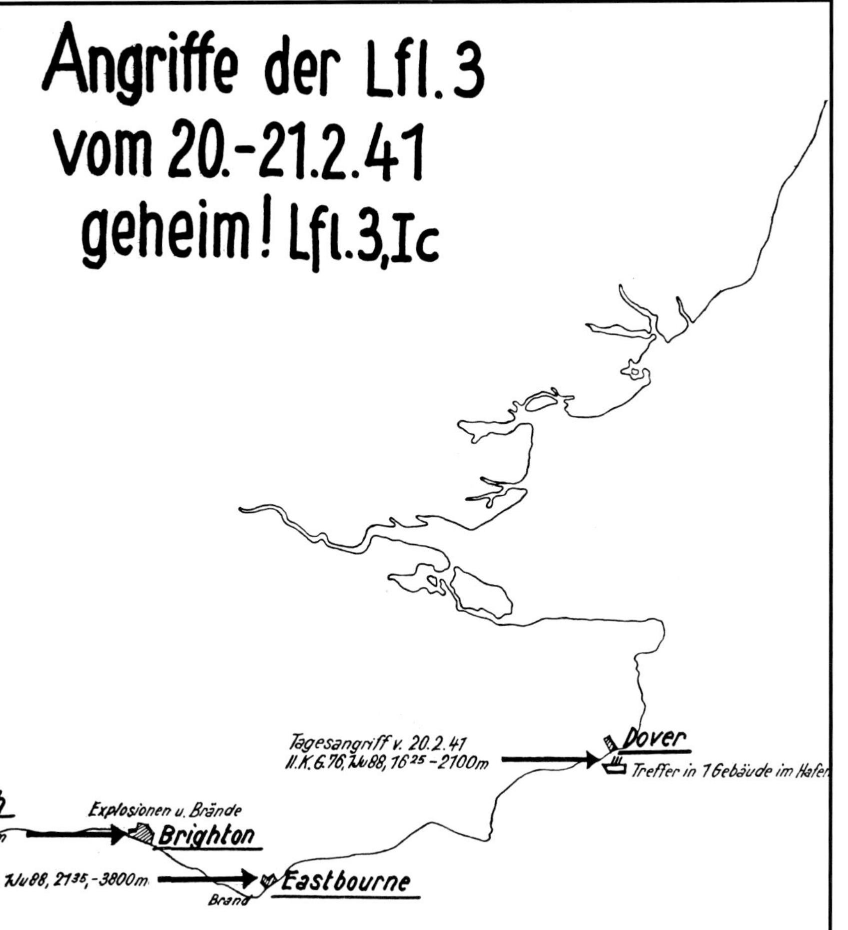

attack under X-Verfahren guidance, and five He 111s of III/KG26 using the Y-Verfahren, bombing was almost entirely visual and a good result was anticipated. Explosions and fires were reported near flour mills, in the vicinity of the gas works, by a magnesium works and in the town centre. Hits on the docks were claimed and over the Target Area as a whole crews reported five large and eight smaller fires. Flak over Swansea was comparatively light and several decoy fires were observed and seemingly avoided by most crews. The units which succeeded in reaching Swansea were:

I/KG27: 7 He 111, 2015-2100
II/KG27: 8 He 111, 2000-2040
III/KG27: 7 He 111, 2007-2014
KGr100: 11 He 111, 2002-2036 (X-Verfahren bombing from 6,800 metres with 10,560 B1 El and 2,112 B1 El ZA)
KG1: 7 He 111, 4 Ju 88, 2150-2250
II/KG76: 7 Ju 88, 2128-2145
I and III/KG77: 8 Ju 88, 2207-2345
III/KG26: 5 He 111, 2124-2208 (Y-Verfahren bombing from 4,000 metres)

Two aircraft were lost — an He 111 of III/KG27 crashed shortly before landing and a similar aircraft of I/KG27 crashed in occupied territory after its crew baled out. Eight aircraft bombed alternative targets and 16 aborted.

The attack on Chatham was made by 34 aircraft in two phases, from 0115 to 0300 hours and again from 0353 to 0605. Their CP was the naval dockyard and associated installations and it was claimed that 44 tonnes of HE (six SC 500, three LZZ 500, four LZZ 250, 156 SC 50 and 14 Luftminen 'B') were dropped visually, aided by the light of flares. Explosions were seen in the middle basin, but without fires developing. In other basin areas one medium and several small fires were reported, with considerable thick smoke ensuing.

. . . except that it certainly shows the gutted David Evans store on Goat Street — now called Kingsway.

The ancient ruins of Swansea Castle seen from the ruins newly-created by the German Air Force.

Among the targets bombed as alternatives were London (by five aircraft), Portland, Eastbourne, Brighton, Cardiff, Bridgwater, Bristol and Southampton.

Once more, considerable damage was done to Swansea town centre and commercial and residential premises suffered badly. Road and rail communications were also affected and public utilities were again interrupted. Several factories were also hit and there was some damage in the dock area, but no serious industrial or port damage was reported.

Chatham, attacked by KG4 aircraft more usually employed in minelaying and by elements of II and III/KG2, also received some damage but except for damage to a gas works it was again without serious effect. Elsewhere bombs were reported at Pontypool, Brecon and Port Talbot, no doubt dropped by aircraft engaged in the Swansea attack, while in Kent and Sussex incidents occurred at Framfield, Gillingham, Rochester, East Hoathly, Southwick and Littlehampton. London, too, received a few bombs, including an incident at West Hendon.

Fighter Command dispatched 55 aircraft during the night, including two offensive patrols over north-eastern France by No. 23 Squadron. Three raiders were detected, but no engagements resulted. One Intruder Blenheim, however, attacked Poix airfield, but snow storms and heavy cumulus cloud caused the other to return to base. Three AI contacts were made by two Beaufighters of No. 604 Squadron, but on each occasion contact was lost before the enemy aircraft could be engaged.

AA Command received reports of gun sites engaging German aircraft at Falmouth, Swansea (where 986 rounds were fired between 1954 and 2346 hours), Plymouth, Cardiff, Brooklands, Slough, Thames and Medway (North and South), Portland and the London IAZ. In total approximately 3,000 rounds were fired, without apparent success.

A Defiant night fighter was lost at 2130 hours when N3446 of No. 256 Squadron, operating from Colerne, struck trees and a stone wall at Bannerdown, near Batheaston, killing a crew member.

The experimental flight development wing, Erprobungsgruppe 210, lost one aircraft:

3/ErproGr 210 Messerschmitt Bf 110E-1 (3474). Crashed into the sea off Harwich during a raid on that town 11.25 a.m. Shot down by AA fire from HM Minesweeper *Bramble*. Lt. F. Heunich and Gefr. R. Gärtner both missing. Aircraft S9+PK lost.

FRIDAY, FEBRUARY 21-22

Sunset: 1824 Sunrise: 0802
Moon: 0538 — Dawn (Last Qtr +3)

Damaging attack on Swansea. Minor operations over London and some Eastern Counties. Limited minelaying.

UK — Small amounts of cloud and good visibility in most areas.

The Continent — Mainly fair in northern France. Cloudy on coasts of the Low Countries, breaking inland. Visibility mainly moderate, becoming poor inland.

German daylight operations were on a modest scale and largely confined to overwater activity around the East and South-East Coasts although a few bombs fell, without significant effect, in Scotland and East Anglia.

Nightfall brought another attack on Swansea, for the third night in succession, carried out by 59 of the 68 aircraft Luftflotte 3 dispatched to the Welsh port. They dropped 47.6 tonnes of HE (19 SC 500, 79 SC 250, nine LZZ 250, and 322 SC 50) and 567 BSK (containing 17,671 B1 El incendiaries and 2,765 explosive incendiaries) in an attack lasting from 1950 to 2249 hours. The units involved were:

I/KG27: 8 He 111, 1950-2130
II/KG27: 7 He 111, 2012-2115
III/KG27: 8 He 111, 2010-2105
KGr100: 12 He 111, 2028-2102 (dropped 11,059 B1 El and 2,765 B1 El ZA by means of X-beams from a height of 6,800 metres/22,300 feet)
KGr606: 7 Do 17, 2111-2135
KG1: 6 He 111, 5 Ju 88, 2155-0000
II/KG26: 6 He 111, 2147-2249 (using Y-Verfahren and bombing from 3,800-4,000 metres/12,400-13,100 feet)

One particularly large explosion, followed by fire, was seen in the town centre, together with seven large fire areas in the west of the town. Numerous small fires were also reported and as most of the bombing was carried out visually good results were anticipated. Two aircraft bombed alternative targets and seven aborted. Two He 111s of II/KG27 crashed on their return flights, one near Valognes, slightly injuring one crew member, and the other to the south-west of Caen, killing one and injuring four crewmen.

Small scale operations over London and Essex were carried out by Ju 88s of II/KG30 and the long-range night fighter unit I/NJG2, both operating from Gilze-Rijen in Holland.

Although there were bombs in London, Essex and the South-West, no serious attack developed outside the Swansea area and even here the docks and other targets important to the war effort escaped lightly. Damage was extensive in the town centre and residential areas, however, and firefighting was hampered to some extent by low water pressure. At one time about 200 fires were burning, but water was pumped from the docks and all were brought under control before 0600 hours.

By Saturday, February 22 — after three successive nights of bombing — 14 Rest Centres had been opened to accommodate more than 2,000 homeless people, but it was estimated by the Ministry of Home Security that an additional 2,000 to 3,000 people were making their way out of Swansea every night to find accommodation at Mumbles and on the Gower Peninsula to escape the bombing. Some went as far as Aberdare, where a Rest Centre was opened; others slept wherever accommodation could be found. Nevertheless, on the whole the population had stood up to their ordeal very well and were not, according to the Ministry of Home Security 'disheartened'. In the three nights 219 were killed and 260 seriously injured, with the worst casualties (98 killed and 78 seriously injured) on the 21-22nd.

Elsewhere bombs caused damage at Cardiff, where the Cardiff-Newport railway line was closed and the city centre suffered, Sunderland (where an electricity sub-station was hit), Hepburn, Durham, Morpeth, Bristol, Weston-super-Mare and in rural districts of East Anglia, the South and South-West. Bombs fell in the vicinity of several airfields but did no harm.

Night fighter patrols were flown by 120 aircraft including six offensive patrols of the Intruder type over northern France. Several contacts were made with enemy aircraft and Intruders claimed one probably destroyed and another damaged. Contacts were also made by a Beaufighter of No. 29 Squadron near Cromer, by a Hurricane of No. 87 Squadron over Bristol, by two Hurricanes of No. 615 Squadron in the Beachy Head area, and by a 219 Squadron Beaufighter from Tangmere, but no claims were made of enemy aircraft destroyed.

More than 1,000 rounds were fired by the heavy guns of AA Command during the night but the Swansea guns ceased firing at 2015 hours to permit night fighter operations over the town. Elsewhere guns were in action at Cardiff, Newport, Bristol, Holton Heath, Gloucester, Tyne, Tees, Humber, the IAZ, Thames and Medway North and South, Portsmouth, Datchet and Brooklands. One raider was claimed shot down.

In addition to the aircraft listed below, I/KG26 lost another of its aircraft in unexplained circumstances off the Scottish coast. Also a Junkers Ju 88 of Küstenfliegergruppe 106 crashed at Nord Wijerhout killing all four crew.

3/KG26 Heinkel He 111H-5 (3737). Crashed into the sea off the Faroe Isles. Remains of aircraft recovered March 9 by SS *Lamerick* and brought into Leith. Fw. H. Much, Oberlt. H. Rönau, Fw. J. Thaler and Fw. K. Roick all missing. Aircraft 1H+KL wrecked.

An interesting appraisal was issued for internal consumption by the Ministry of Home Security on February 21 listing the damage which had occurred to domestic housing throughout the country. It must have been a formidable task for whoever produced the report, for by stating that the figures were correct 'up to 15th February, 1941', one must assume therefore that this is a cumulative total since the beginning of the war. The number of houses which had been affected to that date was stated in the report as:

Destroyed and damaged beyond repair	
In London	**33,575**
Elsewhere (excluding Scotland)	**60,290**
Seriously damaged but repairable	
In London	**123,395**
Elsewhere (excl. Scotland)	**175,520**
Slightly damaged but repairable	
In London	**379,140**
Elsewhere (excl. Scotland)	**715,050**

Therefore, at the values quoted by the Ministry of £750 for rebuilding destroyed houses, £100 for repairing severely damaged and £30 for repairing the slightly damaged, the bill comes to £113,115,950.

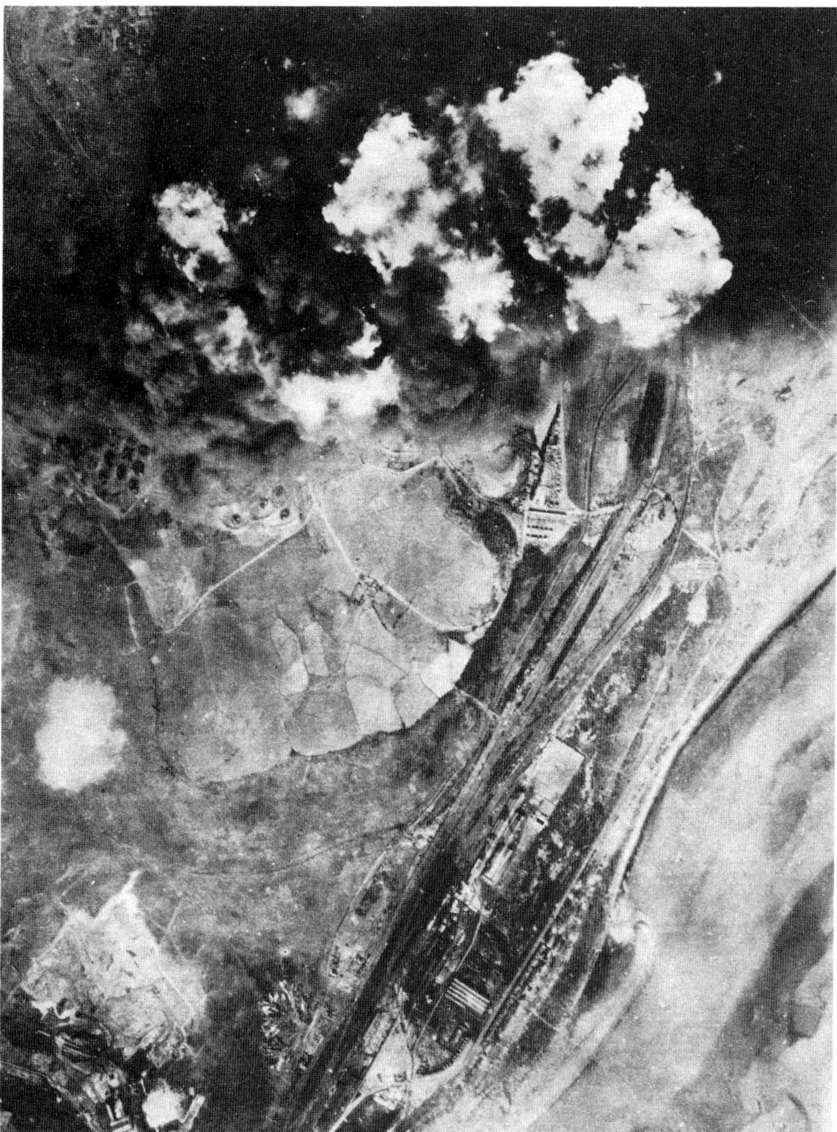

As far as the Luftwaffe was concerned, they gave little publicity to the big Swansea attacks, the only coverage of the area included in their house magazine being this old shot of the raid on the night of September 1–2 on the tank farm at Llandarcy when six 10,000-ton oil tanks were hit.

To bring this up to date with the devalued pound of the 1980s, one should multiply by a least a factor of 20, giving a present-day debit account of over £2½ thousand million. *Above:* **Shall we say about £10,000-worth for work done by the Luftwaffe in Lynemouth, Northumberland, during February?**

Unfortunately no date appears on this recce picture of Hull, singled out for treatment on Saturday night. Apart from the operational targets '2' and '6', the circles numbered '1' indicate barrage balloons.

SATURDAY, FEBRUARY 22-23

Sunset: 1826 Sunrise: 0800
Moon: 0619 — Dawn (Last Qtr +4)

Minor attack on Hull. Minelaying off the south-west coast of England.

UK — Low cloud with rain giving way to clear skies during the night. Mist or fog developing in many districts.
The Continent — Similar to the UK in northern France and the Low Countries.

Inland penetrations by a few single aircraft, taking advantage of the low cloud, accompanied the usual daylight reconnaissance activity in eastern and south-eastern coastal areas. Bombs dropped caused only slight damage and few casualties.

Weather conditions over German bomber bases restricted night operations to 21 aircraft of Luftflotte 2. Their main objective was Hull, but the participating aircraft of KG4 and KG30 — both of which were normally used as minelayers — achieved little success.

The crews of 17 aircraft claimed to have reached and bombed the docks and industrial installations at Hull, dropping 32 tonnes of HE (15 SC 1000, one SC 250, 16 LMB and one LMA). Most crews bombed or dropped their mines on the target visually with only a few using DR/radio navigation, but poor surface visibility prevented assessment of the results. In one case, however, a large fire followed the detonation of a Type 'B' mine (LMB), and one crew reported seeing a large explosion and subsequent fire in the Target Area half an hour after the attack.

During the evening aircraft of IX Fliegerkorps (almost certainly I/KG28) laid mines off the south-west coast.

Less than 1,000 rounds were fired during the night by the heavy guns of AA Command and only 12 night fighters flew patrols. One enemy aircraft was claimed destroyed, by AA Command, and at dusk an He 115 seaplane was claimed damaged off Peterhead by three Spitfires of No. 111 Squadron.

Bombs were reported in Scotland, but the main concentration was on Hull and the North-East generally. In Hull four people were killed and a large UXB, believed to be a 1,800 kilogramme bomb, caused road closure problems. Bombs also fell in various parts of Lincolnshire, but did little harm. Strangely, only five parachute mines were reported in the North-Eastern Region whereas German records indicate that 17 were dropped altogether.

Despite the high level of activity, with fighter sweeps and reconnaissance operations, only two aircraft were lost in the vicinity of the UK:

2(F)/122 Messerschmitt Bf 110 (22602). Shot down by fighters over convoy north-east of Whitstable 10.25 a.m. Oberfw. G. Bodenschatz and Uffz. H. Tonssaiet missing. Aircraft F6+WK lost.

4/KG27 Heinkel He 111H-3 (3247). Brought down by 3.7-inch AA guns of 'B' troop, 236 Battery, 76 Anti-Aircraft Regiment, Portishead. Crashed 2.10 p.m. on the water's edge between Avonmouth and St George's Wharf, Portbury. Lt. B. Rusche baled out and became a prisoner of war. Fw. A. Hanke and Uffz. H. De Wall killed; Fw. G. Jankowiak and Gefr. E. Steinbach missing. Aircraft 1G+GM destroyed.

Parts recovered from deep mud by the South West Aircraft Recovery Group

On Saturday afternoon members of the Gordano gunsite at the mouth of the Avon were at action stations, peering out into the mist; one of the gunners being Sid Phipps of 'B' Troop. 'One round only was fired,' recalled Mr Phipps in 1978, 'and there was a big explosion in the air 1,000 feet up. On Sunday morning the battery commander rounded up a salvage party and they duly arrived at the crash site and found the wreckage was well out of reach. Their rowing boat was grounded because the tide was right out. A local boatman came on the scene and said: "If you wait for the tide the wreck will be under water. So just put the boat on the soft mud, get your oars in and row." This did the trick and a couple of hundred yards later they were surveying the bits of a Heinkel 111. On the door of the plane was the "Missions Accomplished" record neatly painted with the falling bombs in drill formation. There were only four raids — the last one simply said Bournemouth with just one bomb symbol. The loaded boat was very slow to lift as the tide came in. The salvage party struggled back to shore through the slippery mud, leaving one reliable old soldier in charge of the loot.'

SUNDAY, FEBRUARY 23-24

Sunset: 1828 Sunrise: 0758
Moon: 0654 — Dawn (New −3)

Minor attacks on Humber area. Night fighter activity over eastern England.

UK — Variable cloud but moderate to poor visibility in all areas.
The Continent — As for UK in Low Countries and northern France.

There was only slight German daylight activity, mainly off the eastern and south-eastern coasts and no bombs fell on land. During the night 68 bombers and six night fighters were operating, with reports of bomb incidents in the London area, Hull and at scattered points on the North-East and East Coasts but nowhere was much damage caused and casualties were light. Among the units operating were I/NJG2, I/KG30, I/KG53, II/KG53 and III/KG26, while Luftflotte 3 records show that eight aircraft of that Air Fleet attacked the Hawker Aircraft factory at Langley and London dock installations. Almost certainly these were He 111s of III/KG26 using Y-Verfahren.

The docks at Hull were claimed attacked by 49 crews who between 1930 and 2015 hours dropped 60 tonnes of HE (19 SC 1000, 15 SC 500, 17 LMB and seven LMA) and 128 BSK (4,608 IBs) in the light of 20 LC 50 parachute flares. Their Concentration Point was the Victoria and Alexandra Dock, but because of cloud and poor visibility few crews managed to bomb visually — the cloud, in fact, rendered the flares useless and their glare, reflected on the cloud, made their task even more difficult. In consequence, most of the bombs or mines were released on DR or by means of radio navigation; other crews used the presence of searchlights and barrage balloons as indications that they were in the Target Area. Two strongly burning fires were seen through the cloud, with more fires following the explosion of one of the heavier bombs or mines.

The attack on the Hawker factory at Langley was claimed by three crews. They bombed between 2019 and 2127 hours, dropping three SC 500s and 48 SC 50s from a height of 4,500 metres (14,800 feet). Five more crews bombed, as alternative targets, dock installations in the East End of London with two SC 1000s, four SC 500s and 60 SC 50s, all by DR/radio methods without observed results.

In the Humber area 14 people were killed and some damage resulted. In Lincolnshire, too, there were a number of incidents and further damage was caused in several places in Kent and South Buckinghamshire.

Countrywide AA Command used about 1,000 rounds of heavy ammunition and ten night fighters were operating, but to no avail.

A Defiant (N3388) of No. 151 Squadron, Wittering, was destroyed at 2130 hours when abandoned short of fuel near Watton, Norfolk. One crew member was killed.

In addition to the He 111 below, a second loss was a Heinkel He 115 of 3/506 which failed to return from a sortie to the east coast of Scotland.

8/KG27 Heinkel He 111P-2 (1605). Shot down by Lewis gun fire from trawlers *Grackle* and *Dandara*. Crashed into the sea off Kenmare Bay, Eire 9.55 p.m. Fw. W. Segner and Fw. A. Pütz missing. Oberlt. K. Häfele killed. Fw. F. Schütz killed and body washed up in Kenmare Bay. Aircraft 1G+LS lost.

Not till George Morley of the South West Aircraft Recovery Group began to delve into the incident was the identity of the mystery boatman — seen here in the seaman's cap and waders — established. He was Bert Rice of Pill, an experienced local mariner, for many years connected with the Pill-Shirehampton ferry.

In February there was still much talk of invasion, spurred on by a statement made by the US Secretary to the Navy to the Senate Committee at the beginning of the month. It was reported that he had been informed authoritatively that the Germans were studying weather conditions with the object of seizing the first available fine spell in which to attack. All the signs were that the crisis would occur within 60 to 90 days (i.e. March or April) and there were indications that the Nazis might use gas on a large scale. Although Churchill was aware, via Enigma, that certain changes in German Air Force dispositions in Belgium and Northern France during January indicated no immediate cause for concern, a German broadcast in February added to the war of nerves when the announcer spoke of the special training of Nebeltruppe (fog troops) equipped with 'fog shrapnel' and 'fog grenades'. Fuel was added to the speculation when Hugh Slater, ex-Chief of Operations in the International Brigade in Spain in 1938, published his handbook *Homeguard for Victory* illustrating seven invasion possibilities. PLAN 1 — Encirclement, with vast numbers of landings by troop carriers and strong naval forces.

MONDAY, FEBRUARY 24-25

Sunset: 1830 Sunrise: 0756
Moon: 0724 — Dawn (New −2)

No major attack. Minelaying off the western and south-western coasts.

UK — Cloudy with moderate to poor visibility. Calm with fog in many districts.
The Continent — Generally poor conditions with mist or fog in parts of northern France and the Low Countries.

No damage or casualties were caused by the few bombs which fell on northern Scotland during the day, and elsewhere activity by the Luftwaffe was on a very small scale.
Nightfall brought little more activity. Of the 42 bombers operating some were engaged in minelaying (I/KG28 from Nantes) off the western and south-western coasts of England. What few inland penetrations occurred were made by aircraft of I, II and III/KG2 operating from Merville. Apparently few other German-occupied airfields were operational because of the weather conditions, but a few HE and incendiary bombs fell widely scattered during the night, mainly in East Anglia.
AA Command used less than 1,000 rounds and only a few patrols were flown by night fighters. No German aircraft were claimed destroyed but Fighter Command lost a Blenheim (L1326 of No. 600 Squadron) when it hit HT cables during a night take off from Prestwick.

TUESDAY, FEBRUARY 25-26

Sunset: 1832 Sunrise: 0754
Moon: 0750 — Dawn (New −1)

No major attack. Some minelaying and slight activity by night fighters. Minor attack intended on Hull.

UK — Largely cloudless but mist or fog forming in many areas.
The Continent — Similar to UK.

No bombs fell on land during a day on which most German air activity was centred on weather and shipping reconnaissance.
During the night aircraft of Luftflotte 2 carried out operations on a small scale only with 60 bombers and four night fighters. The units employed were:

II and III/KG2: (operating from Merville)
I, II and III/KG53 (from Lille/Vendeville)
II/KG30: (from Amsterdam/Schiphol; engaged on mining)
II/KG3: (from Amsterdam/Schiphol)
I/NJG2: (from Gilze-Rijen; night fighter patrols of RAF airfields)

The principal target (claimed bombed by 25 crews) was Hull, attacked from 1955 to 2320 hours with 25 tonnes of HE (five SC 1000, four SC 500, 33 SC 250, nine LMB and one LMA) and 3,888 incendiary bombs. Bombing was mainly visual and several small fires were seen in the docks area (wherein lay the CP) and another large one in the eastern part of the town. Attacks were also recorded on a number of night-flying airfields, including Sutton Bridge where a large explosion was seen among the hangars and adjacent buildings.
There was some damage to houses and a few casualties in Hull, together with a number of incidents in Yorkshire's East Riding, Lincolnshire and elsewhere in East Anglia, where three people were killed. There were also fires, but no casualties, in Folkestone, but three people were also killed in Hampshire.
Some 40 night fighters were operating but the guns of AA Command expended only about 500 rounds during the night. One enemy aircraft was claimed destroyed — by a Hurricane of No. 85 Squadron — and another claimed damaged by an Intruder Blenheim of No. 23 Squadron near Merville airfield.

Better weather gave rise to several small scale raids. One raider, that detailed below, was lost over Great Britain.

4/KG2 Dornier Do 17Z-2 (1134). Shot down by Squadron Leader P. W. Townsend DFC and Bar in a Hurricane of No. 85 Squadron 9.25 p.m. during a raid on London. Aircraft dived into the ground and exploded at Little Waldingfield, near Lavenham, Suffolk. Uffz. P. Schmidt baled out but was killed when his parachute failed to open. Lt. H. Patscheider, Oberfw. M. Mummert and Fw. A. Beysiegel baled out and were taken prisoner. Aircraft U5+PM destroyed.

WEDNESDAY, FEBRUARY 26-27

Sunset: 1833 Sunrise: 0752
Moon: None (New Moon)

No major attack but operations were on a fairly extensive scale over much of Southern England and South Wales, with London and Cardiff the principal targets. Minelaying and small scale night fighter activity.

UK — Cloudy but moderate to good visibility.
The Continent — Mainly fair.

Although daylight activity was slight and largely confined to coastal districts of Kent and East Anglia, improving conditions permitted the operation of 144 long-range bombers and three long-range night fighters during the hours of darkness. The principal targets were London, attacked by 53 aircraft, and Cardiff (58 aircraft).
The London attack, carried out between 1935 and 2233 hours, was marred by thick mist and much of the bombing was by DR and radio navigation. Bomb explosions and a few fires were seen by participating crews, but little else and it was impossible to assess the results. It was claimed that 73 tonnes of HE were delivered (comprising 18 SC 1000, 13 SC 500, 52 SC 250, 180 SC/SD 50 and 30 parachute mines in the form of 23 LMB and seven LMA), together with 1,692 IBs. Extensive use was made of parachute flares, a total of 60 LC 50s being dropped to offset the absence of moonlight.
Cardiff was the target for 68 aircraft of Luftflotte 3, but seven crews bombed alternatives and three aborted. The remainder comprised:

I/KG27: 4 He 111, 2010-2110
II/KG27: 5 He 111, 2045-2057
III/KG27: 6 He 111, 2035-2110

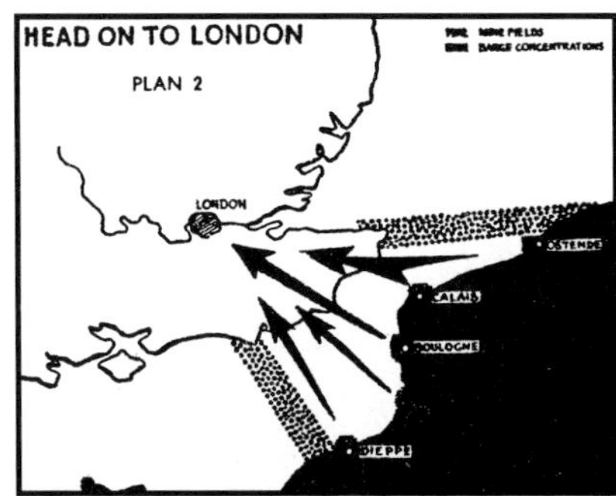

PLAN 2 — A concentrated drive against Dover; thick minefields laid against our Navy from Ostend to the North Foreland, from Dieppe to Eastbourne, leaving a channel from Calais, Dunkirk, and Boulogne across to the East Sussex and Kent coast.

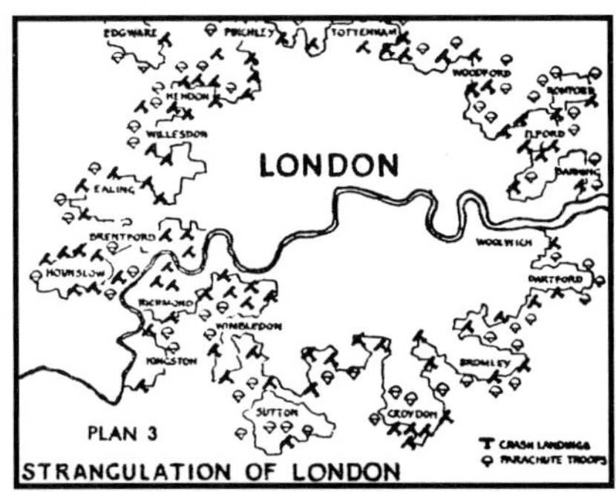

PLAN 3 — Great numbers of parachutists, combined with crash-landings, in a ring around London's inner suburbs, to disrupt our brain-centre and neutralise our preponderance of tanks and mechanised forces by compelling us to fight in streets and groups of buildings.

PLAN 4 — Many widely dispersed landings from troopships and barges, combined with close air-landings round the south, east and west coasts, to feel for footholds which could be exploited where most successful.

KGr100: 15 He 111, 2025-2100 (X-Verfahren bombing)
KG1: 4 He 111, 7 Ju 88, 2005-2058
I/KG77: 9 Ju 88, 2035-2059
III/KG26: 8 He 111, 2045-2121 (Y-Verfahren bombing)

Again, because of the absence of moonlight, parachute flares were used in abundance to illuminate the ground, with 50 LC 50s being used. In their light many crews were able to bomb visually and good results were anticipated; about six medium sized fires were reported, with many of a smaller size. It was claimed that 47.6 tonnes of HE hit the target (consisting of 14 SC 500, 103 SC 250, ten LZZ 250 and 197 SC 50) and 22,392 incendiaries including 2,880 of the explosive B1 El ZA type. Several night fighters were seen by the attackers, but they did not engage, and flak was described as accurate but without effect. Numerous decoy fires were also seen and reported. One returning bomber, about to land at Rosieres, was attacked by a fighter but was undamaged and landed safely. Luftflotte 3 sustained no losses, but in the attack on London one aircraft of Luftflotte 2 was lost, this being a Do 17 of 4/KG2.

Attacks were also claimed during the night against six airfields (West Raynham, Mildenhall, Tuddenham, Stradishall, Upwood and Wattisham), all with the aid of LC 50 parachute flares, and explosions and fires were seen to develop in most cases.

Bombs fell in many parts of Britain but the most serious incident occurred in London where a military hospital canteen was demolished by a parachute mine, killing 30 people. Altogether 21 fires were started in the capital, where eastern districts were worst hit. Elsewhere there was damage at Bristol (with one fatal casualty), Cardiff (ten fatalities) and in Monmouthshire six people were killed. Bombs also fell in east, south and south-west England, but with little effect.

AA Command used more than 3,000 rounds of heavy ammunition for one raider claimed destroyed. Fighter Command, which put up about 50 patrols, lost a Defiant

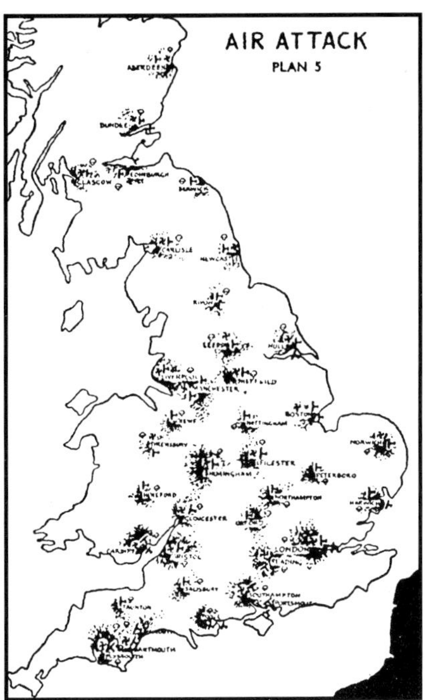

PLAN 5 — Establishing innumerable occupied points by parachutists and airborne troops widely dotted throughout the country; on aerodromes and landing-grounds, particularly close to towns.

(N3520 of No. 256 Squadron) and scored no successes. The Defiant crashed while making an attempted forced landing, short of fuel, at West Collingbourne near Upavon, Wiltshire, at 2110 hours. The air gunner baled out successfully, but the pilot was killed.

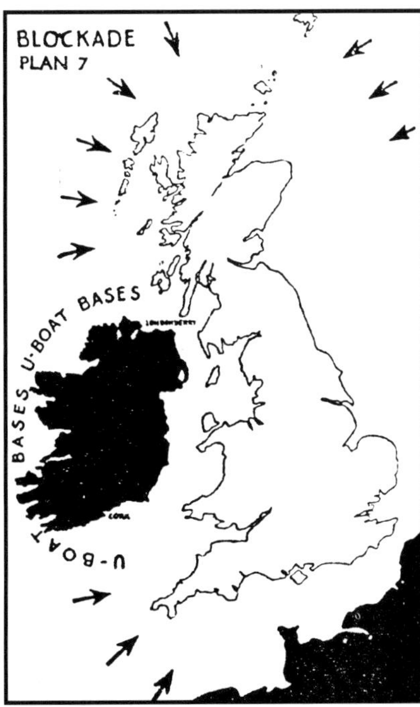

PLAN 7 — An attempt to occupy Ireland completely by air and naval landings and blockade the British Isles throughout the winter, taking advantage of bad weather to interrupt and disrupt our counter-attack. Any or all of these plans, Mr Slater added, may be tried; or, more likely, a combination of two or more at the same time. The Home Guard, he said, was the only possible tactical counter to *attack in depth* as distinct from the old frontal attack.

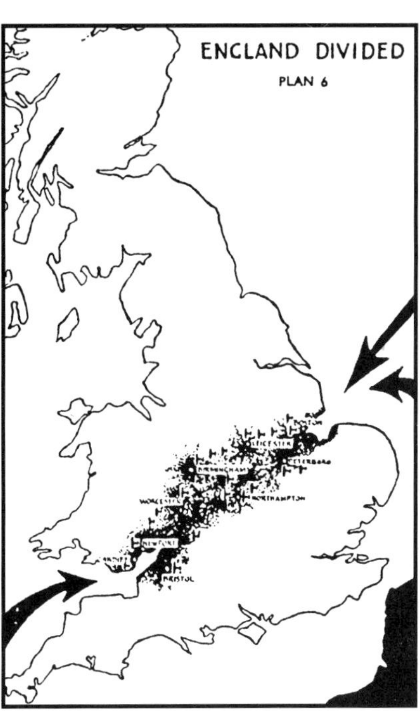

PLAN 6 — Establishing a belt of these 'expanding blots' right across the centre of England from Wash to Severn Estuary by air-descents combined with concentrated naval landings in Bristol and Norfolk areas.

In addition to the aircraft detailed, IV/JG51 lost its Gruppenkommandeur Oblt. Hans Keitel when his Bf 109 was shot down into the English Channel.

3(F)/121 Junkers Ju 88A-5 (0667). Presumed shot down by AA fire from South Wales and crashed into the Bristol Channel. Lt. H. Schmidt, Oberlt. K. von Sichartshoff, Uffz. F. Abtmaier and Obergefr. B. Müller all missing. Aircraft 7A+AL lost.

THURSDAY, FEBRUARY 27-28

Sunset: 1835 Sunrise: 0750
Moon: Dusk — 2018 (New +1)

No German bomber operations.

UK — Extensive low cloud with only moderate visibility.
The Continent — Similar to UK in most areas.

German daylight operations were restricted to minor weather and shipping reconnaissance and a few inland penetrations by single aircraft taking advantage of cloud cover. One such attacker caused heavy casualties at the aircraft factory at Yate, and 15 people were killed in a raid on Grantham. A further deterioration in the weather led to a cancellation of night operations.

FRIDAY, FEBRUARY 28-MARCH 1

Sunset: 1837 Sunrise: 0747
Moon: Dusk — 2122 (New +2)

No significant night attacks.

UK — Extensive low cloud with only moderate visibility.
The Continent — Similar to UK.

Activity during the day was slight but a few bombs were dropped at Dover, causing little damage and no casualties. At night only three aircraft operated over Britain, dropping bombs on London, the Home Counties and in East Anglia, but to little effect.

Der Adler
Portugal Esc. 1.50
España Pts. 1.—
HERAUSGEGEBEN UNTER MITWIRKUNG DES REICHS-LUFTFAHRTMINISTERIUMS
Der Schöpfer der deutschen Luftwaffe, die am 1. März auf ein ruhmreiches sechsjähriges Bestehen zurückblicken kann, im Gespräch mit einem jungen Fliegeroffizier an der Westfront
Aufn. PK Eitel Lange
El creador del Ejército del Aire Alemán, que el 1.º de marzo cuenta seis años de gloriosa existencia, conversando con un joven oficial de aviación en el frente occidental

MARCH 1941

The policy of concentrating on one target centre for several nights in succession was accentuated at the beginning of March when there were three attacks on Cardiff in a week. In good weather conditions, and in the light of a moon approaching its First Quarter, the city suffered badly. Sustained fair to good weather around the full moon period also aided damaging attacks on Liverpool, Clydebank, Hull, Glasgow and Southampton, and a continuation of favourable conditions into the moon's Last Quarter facilitated heavy assaults on London, Bristol and Plymouth. Almost everywhere it was a return to heavy bombing, with consequences equalling anything experienced since the Blitz started. The worst night was March 19-20, when there were 479 bombers over London, but repeated attacks on Portsmouth (five nights in one week), Glasgow and Plymouth caused extensive damage and many casualties. However, indifferent or bad weather over German bomber bases in France and the Low Countries — always more of a deterrent than conditions over Britain — caused a marked decline in operations for the last week of the month although attacks on shipping and minelaying continued unabated, mainly from Norwegian bases.

During the month German long-range bombers flew 4,372 night sorties, backed by an additional 46 sorties by long-range night fighters. There were also 48 night sorties by light bombers, a new feature of the Blitz involving the use of Messerschmitt Bf 110 fighter-bombers and Junkers Ju 87 dive-bombers, types normally used in daylight only.

The main weight of bombs again fell on ports, with only two industrial centres (Birmingham and Sheffield) receiving attention. Twelve of the attacks were classed as major and six heavy; minelaying was carried out on ten nights but adverse weather caused the cancellation of attacks on seven nights. Civilian casualties were 4,259 killed and 5,557 seriously injured.

The March attacks served to confirm certain conclusions already becoming apparent — despite more than six months of heavy attacks damage to vital war production was not serious, but the direct and indirect effects on less essential production were significant. Public morale, always difficult to assess, appeared to remain very high although a temporary lowering was apparent from time to time, particularly where attacks on successive nights led to nightly treks out of the probable target cities by large numbers of people. But the populations of the target cities had suffered greatly; up to the end of March total civilian casualties since the start of bombing reached 28,859 killed and 40,166 injured and detained in hospital. Some 550 soldiers had also been killed.

To counter the March raids, Fighter Command put up 735 single engine night fighter sorties which produced 34 sightings and 25 combats; twin engine night fighters flew 270 sorties resulting in 95 AI and 20 visual contacts which led to 21 AI and 10 purely visual combats. Twenty-two enemy aircraft were claimed destroyed by night fighters while the guns of AA Command claimed seventeen. This was a big increase in numbers, but still amounted to only 0.8 per cent of the attacking force, a loss rate which the Luftwaffe could sustain almost indefinitely. Morale among night fighter crews and gunners alike was lifted, however, by the vastly improved results.

Morale in the German bomber force was also at a high level and this was confirmed to some degree during the interrogation of 47 PoWs captured in March; their morale, according to the RAF's AI1(k) Branch, was well up to average. None of them showed signs of discontent, nor were they particularly glad to be out of the war. It was noticed, however, that they were very security conscious and adhered strictly to the specific instructions they had been given regarding their conduct if taken prisoner. The bodies of 53 German airmen were also recovered during the month and, with the 47 prisoners, enabled the RAF to deduce that the average age of operational German aircrew showed an increase, if anything, over recent months. The length of service figure was maintained or showed a slight increase, but it was recognised that the total numbers from which the averages were calculated were too small to provide a conclusive guide to the Luftwaffe in general. One captured observer was only 18½ years old, but had already attained the rank of Feldwebel and had seen considerable service. A wireless operator of 19 was also shot down during the month. Once again, using all methods available to it, AI1(k) arrived at a mass of intelligence material relating to German Air Force operations and personnel. Most of its work was extremely serious, but at times it had its lighter moments — like the time when it was discovered that four of the five men crewing a shot-down He 111 of 2/KG27 were named Müller, clearly a surname as common as Smith in England!

The German concentration on British ports — and particularly the West Coast ports which handled most of the essential war material and food imports from the USA — was the cause for some concern and on March 9 Air Marshal Douglas was notified by the Air Ministry that henceforth his primary task was the defence of these vulnerable targets. Accordingly, after consultation with

General Pile, Douglas issued instructions on March 11 for the withdrawal of 58 HAA guns from mainly industrial centres for reallocation to ports. The guns were taken from Birmingham and Coventry (24), Sheffield (8), Scapa Flow (8), Brockworth (4), Weston-super-Mare (4), Daventry (4), Leighton Buzzard (4), and Acklington (2). These were redistributed, with another 23 from the production lines, as shown in the table.

Port	1939 Scale	1940 Scale	Strength 27.2.41	Additions 28.2–12.3	New Scale 21.3.41	Strength 21.3.41	Additions Sanctioned 21.3.41
Clyde	80	120	67	19	144	88	56
Mersey	104	104	84	12	112	96	16
Bristol/ Avonmouth	56	80	36	28	80	68	12
Swansea/ Port Talbot/ Llanelly	32	48	18	18	48	36	12
Barry/ Cardiff/ Newport	48	64	52	4	64	56	8

There was, of course, an element of chance involved in robbing one target group in favour of another, but the shortage of HAA guns left Douglas with no alternative. Even a new AA rocket weapon that was quick and cheap to produce was slower to materialise than anticipated; known as 'UP's (Unrotating Projectiles) to protect their secrecy, the new weapons showed great promise and although the 8,400 projectors allocated to General Pile were arriving on schedule, a shortage of associated rockets prevented their widespread use for some time to come. Cardiff was the first recipient, but by the end of March AA Command was able to deploy only 840 projectors with ten rounds apiece and, with the Admiralty accorded top priority, the immediate future offered little hope of further expansion. Eventually the UPs went into action, and when they did it was in a spectacular fashion — the projectors were laid out in groups of 64 in what were known as Z-Batteries, and their simultaneous firing was a most impressive sight.

Searchlight expansion was limited not by shortages of equipment but by manpower problems and in view of this — and a similar shortage in other sections of his Command — General Pile pressed for the use of women of the Auxiliary Territorial Service (ATS) to perform certain duties on gunsites. Four months were to pass, however, before the first mixed battery went into action at Richmond Park, Surrey, but ultimately the use of ATS girls released 28,000 soldiers for other duties.

While the increase in the number of night fighter interceptions in March was seen as a most welcome trend, Fighter Command did not relax its efforts to master the night menace in full. Scientific aids to interception were largely responsible for the improvement and the AOC-in-C was anxious to see an expansion of both GCI stations and AI-equipped night fighter squadrons. As an immediate step in this direction he wished to re-equip two Defiant squadrons with Beaufighters or Havocs and an approach along these lines was made in writing to the Air Ministry, but both Coastal and Bomber Commands were also seeking variants of these aircraft.

Intruder operations by Blenheims of No. 23 Squadron were improving in effectiveness as experience was gained. On many occasions bombs were dropped on flare paths, runways and hangars, and a number of enemy aircraft were claimed damaged on the ground.

At the beginning of March, readers of *Der Adler* were treated to a glimpse of Dr Ernst Heinkel in his office at Rostock-Marienehe. However, 'eine nutzlose Waffe' (a useless weapon) was the almost universal verdict of bomber crews flying He 111s fitted with the fixed tail-mounted MG 17 machine gun seen here. Equally useless was a tail-mounted tube device installed as an alternative to the MG 17 in some He 111s and intended to eject explosive canisters into the path of pursuing fighters. Neither of these ill-conceived defensive measures could be aimed and they were seldom used. The whitewall tailwheel tyre, incidentally, was a standard fitting on most Heinkels in the early part of the war.

Dr Dornier was also shown with his chief test pilot flying the latest development from his stable — stated in the article as being the Do 215.

In the first three months of 1941 three German aircraft were also claimed shot down, four probably destroyed and three damaged. Two intruders were lost. It had been hoped that No. 23 Squadron's Blenheims would be entirely superceded by Havoc aircraft by March, but delivery of the new type remained slower than anticipated.

Fighter Night operations were carried out on several occasions and one enemy aircraft was claimed destroyed over Cardiff on the night of March 3-4. More effective, however, were GCI interceptions, with five of the planned stations now in full and successful operation at Sopley, Waldringfield, Orby, Durrington and Willesborough. Another station at Avebury was moved to Exminster, to cover the approaches to the Welsh ports, and by the end of the month another one was opened at Sturminster. An eighth was expected to open a few weeks hence at Langtoft. Meanwhile, as a result of experiments at Sopley, an improved height reading system was introduced which drastically improved the GCI/AI interception rate. The fitting of Mk IIG IFF to night fighters was also of enormous benefit; the new IFF, which responded to the GCI frequency, greatly facilitated identification of the fighter and thereby eased the task of the GCI Controller.

Another development was the conversion, though still not complete, of No. 93 (LAM) Squadron to DB-7s (Havocs/Bostons) and Wellingtons. However, experiments with a Wellington equipped for mine-towing were disappointing, the speed and altitude achieved being unacceptably low. No air mining (Mutton) operations at all had been carried out in February, but when resumed by a single Harrow on March 13-14 an enemy aircraft was claimed as probably destroyed. It is clear though that Douglas, who had opposed Mutton operations from the beginning, still considered them largely a waste of time and effort.

Like Mutton, there had been no Albino (free balloon barrage) operations in February, but on the night of March 10-11 some 1,200 balloons were launched from South-East London on a south-easterly wind to cross the German bomber streams approaching the Midlands. No results were claimed, as had been the case the previous night when about 1,000 balloons were released from the Kidbrooke area, although explosions were subsequently reported in the Winchester district.

Albino had been deployed in the London area on ten occasions in February, but releases were subsequently cancelled because of the lack of suitable enemy activity. Further, on no less than 14 occasions in six weeks, Albino had to be cancelled owing to adverse winds. There were also failures of the self-destruct apparatus and, all things considered, Douglas felt that the enormous effort involved was not justified. He continued to support the experiments with Flash Flares being conducted by the Royal Aircraft Establishment, but was not hopeful of much success with Star Shells fired by 4.5-inch AA guns. During experiments, the shells burst well below the patrolling Defiants, dazzling their crews and thereby serving no useful purpose. A new development, seen by Douglas as more acceptable, was the installation of a nose-mounted searchlight in Havocs equipped either with AI or an infra-red detector being developed by Frazer-Nash.

There were few changes affecting the night fighter Order of Battle in March, but No. 68 Squadron (Blenheim Mk IFs), which had reformed for night fighting on January 7 at Catterick, was declared operational during the month. During March, too, No. 307 Squadron moved its Defiants from Squires Gate to Colerne, No. 600 Squadron (Blenheims and Beaufighters) at Catterick with a detachment at Drem, moved to the latter base and then operated a detachment at Prestwick, while the partly operational No. 256 Squadron (Defiants and Hurricanes) departed Colerne for Squires Gate. From Catterick, with an operational detachment at Middle Wallop, No. 256 had taken up residence at Pembrey in January, but in February was moved to Colerne, still with its operational detachment at Middle Wallop. At Squires Gate it was to become fully operational for the first time, serving in the defence of the North-West as a complete squadron.

Good progress was maintained throughout March by both the 'Y' Service and No. 80 Wing, while an acceleration in the decrypt of Enigma-coded Luftwaffe W/T transmissions resulted in the prior knowledge of impending attacks to an ever increasing degree. The Germans continued attempts to nullify the X-Verfahren

Stiftungsurkunde.

Als sichtbares Zeichen der Anerkennung für Bewährung beim Fronteinsatz in der Luft, zugleich als Ansporn zu höchster Pflichterfüllung vor dem Feind genehmige ich die Einführung der

Frontflug-Spange

für fliegendes Personal.

Space was also given to publicise the introduction of the Frontflugspange which had been introduced at the end of January to be awarded to mark specific numbers of operational sorties carried out. Separate badges were designed for reconnaissance, fighter and bomber crews with the bronze being given for 20 operational flights (Frontflügen); the silver for 60, and the gold for the completion of 110 missions.

A fascinating insight into standing orders governing the behaviour of airmen from II/KG53 when on leave in Paris was picked up by RAF Air Intelligence around this time. The document stated that: 1. Visits to Paris were permitted only by personnel having service reasons for going there. 2. Curfew in Paris for Unteroffiziere and other ranks was 2300 hours and for Feldwebel 2400 hours. 3. Travel on the Metro was free and all members of the Forces were entitled to First Class seating. 4. Personnel were to remain aloof from the French civilian population. 5. Prohibited were: dancing, absolutely; smoking in the streets, on the Metro or in cars; sitting on bar stools; taking French women in service cars or walking arm-in-arm with persons of the opposite sex. 6. Good manners were expected in cars and buses. While paragraph 1 applied to KG53, based at Lille, possibly the unit depicted *above*, this restriction did not apply to units based in the Paris area. For instance, it is known that personnel of KG55 (Robert Gotz's unit) spent much of their free time in Paris where they frequented night clubs and other places of entertainment where, in addition, they could hardly comply with the limitations imposed by paragraphs 4 and 5!

counter-measures of No. 80 Wing by (a) using a large number of frequencies to exhaust available Bromide transmitters, (b) delaying the switching on of X-beam transmitters until just prior to the attack, (c) changes in the cross beam arrangement, (d) the use of an unmodulated signal on one occasion, (e) one or more frequency changes during all operations, and (f) using additional frequencies immediately prior to the arrival of aircraft over the target. Nevertheless, No. 80 Wing was quick in every case to follow these moves, but the results were not as good as believed and KGr100 continued, in the main, to use X-Verfahren. With the Y-Verfahren (used by III/KG26) No. 80 Wing appears to have had more success — up to mid-March only 18 out of 89 aircraft monitored appeared to receive the bomb release signal. After March 13, normal Domino action was not so successful, so carefully applied jamming was adopted and appeared to have some effect. Jamming action and the interjection of false beams was also applied to counter Knickebein transmissions whenever these were in evidence. Meaconing of German beacons was also maintained and to increase the effectiveness of Aircraft D/F Meaconing (the cunning response to German aircraft requesting D/F bearings), the stations at Henfield and Harpenden were moved to Flimwell and Mundesley. From their new locations they were able to 'assist' German aircraft over a wider area.

March also saw some excellent results from the use of Starfish sites. Seventeen sites were lit during the month, with two outstanding successes at Cardiff on March 4-5 and at Bristol on 16-17. The average 'draw' per lighting was 16 HE and 130 to 140 incendiary bombs.

There were many German bomber unit movements in March, most of them of a temporary nature enforced by airfield unserviceability. Many airfields were still without hard surface runways or taxiways and the heavy rains and thawing snow resulted in much waterlogging. Of a more permanent nature was the removal of several bomber Gruppen for anticipated use in the Balkans, although as a first step they were transferred to bases in Austria. In this category, Stab, I and III/KG2 were moved to Zwölfaxing, III/KG3 to Münchendorf and, on the last day of the month, Stab, I and III/KG51 to Wiener-Neustadt, where they were to be joined by II/KG51 in mid-April. Also by the end of the month II and III/KG27 were at Brest to reinforce I Gruppe in anti-shipping operations. A further move to boost air attacks on shipping involved I/KG1, released from operations in mid-March for training in its new role and subsequent employment at Quimper where it was redesignated III/KG40.

In order to control and co-ordinate the expanding maritime strike force, a new Command was established under Oberstleutnant Martin Harlinghausen, an officer with extensive experience in anti-shipping warfare. Harlinghausen, formerly the commander of X Fliegerkorps in the Mediterranean, set up his new Command, to be known as Fliegerführer Atlantik, with its headquarters at Lannion. Several more bomber Gruppen were due to come under his control in the near future, but at all times the anti-shipping units were available to Luftflotte 3 for normal bomber operations when so required. This flexibility was soon to become apparent to British Air Intelligence, which was also quick to learn of the new Command's existence. It was also appreciated that even bombers based in Germany, Austria, the Mediterranean and, later on, the Balkans, could be recalled at short notice for operations requiring maximum effort.

By the third week in March the German bomber force in the West was back to the strength it enjoyed at the end of 1940, but this state of affairs was to be short-lived. The remaining non-operational elements of II/KG76 at Giebelstadt returned to Châteaudun to

Between operations, we roam around the peaceful little town of Dreux, lying to the south of Paris; on the outskirts of which we are installed in a former boarding school for girls. There are bars and small cafes, and fantastic pastries of a kind we have never come across. Absolutely all the nice things that have been unobtainable at home for a long time are to be found. Wine and all other kinds of alcohol, which have disappeared in Germany, can be had in any quantities, and lead to many uproarious drinking sessions ending in huge hangovers . . .

Hauptmann Rudolf Kiel, the squadron commander — he has the Ritterkreuz since the French campaign — and the squadron officers have once taken me to Paris with them to 'Korniloff', a famous Russian restaurant with cooking and elaborate menus which I wouldn't have believed possible. Kiel has asked me if I would like to become an officer. I was dumbfounded, but despite having passed my school-leaving exams rejected the idea. I am not ready for this yet, I'm far too young and wouldn't have confidence in myself. It seems to me somehow more normal, and more appropriate at this early stage, for me to serve as an ordinary private under command in the front line. Haven't I even so scarcely trusted myself to come through our flights against the enemy with due calm? Old Kiel shrugged his shoulders, and won't try to insist for the present.

ROBERT GÖTZ

Although one cannot be certain, this photo most probably depicts a Do 217 of KG2, first issued to the unit in March 1941 for evaluation prior to its use in the later Baedeker raids and subsequent attacks. In the foreground with their yellow stripes are two SC 500s.

resume active service with their new Ju 88s; Kampfgeschwader 51, 54 and 55 (after some two months of rest or greatly reduced activity) had resumed full operational strength, and I and II/KG53 were also back in France. In addition, the whole of KG76 had returned from Germany to complete the replacement of the four long-range bomber Gruppen transferred to the Mediterranean and Rumania at the beginning of the year, but almost at once came the moves to Austrian bases in preparation for the Balkans offensive.

Meanwhile, II/KG2, still in France, received a few of the new Dornier Do 217E-1s for initial conversion training and operational evaluation, but some time was to elapse before they were used on operations. Also non-operational as a training and reserve unit but, in fact, available for operations if so required, was IV/KG55, expanded from an Ergänzungsstaffel to a full Gruppe at Landsberg and moved to Dijon on March 21.

Other unit movements during the month were as follows:

March 1-12 — I and III/KG76 to Chateaudun, III/KG26 to Le Bourget, II/KG77 to Beauvais

By March 15 — I/KG3 to Amsterdam/Schiphol, I/KG4 to Soesterberg, 3/106 to Amsterdam; Temporary transfers: III/KG1 to Rosieres and Amiens, II and III/KG3 to Schiphol (joining I/KG3), II/KG4 to Soesterberg and Eindhoven, III/KG4 to Leeuwarden, I and II/KG53 to Wittmundhafen and Leeuwarden, I and II/KG54 to Caen, I/KG77 to Jouvincourt

By March 18 — II/KG1 to Rosieres, I and II/KG53 and I/KG54 to their normal bases at Vitry, Lille/Vendeville and Evreux; temporary transfers: II/KG51 to Bretigny, I/KG55 to Villacoublay, II/KG77 to several bases in Holland

By March 21 — Temporary transfers: III/KG51 to Bretigny (joining II/KG51), I and II/KG54 to Evreux

By March 25 — II/KG54 to Evreux/Fauville, I/KG2 using Merville for night operations.

The month was also marked by the first use of light bombers at night, the Messerschmitt Bf 110s of Erprobungsgruppe 210 operating at first from Ursel, near Bruges, and then from Courtrai/Wevelghem in Belgium.

Although the Dornier Do 17Z was past its prime, it was still in use with those odd units which had not yet been transferred out to the Balkans.

Mission F37II to Southampton — hit again on the night of March 1–2. The dotted areas correspond with specific numbered targets; the circles show bomb craters, with areas more heavily damaged enclosed with a line. Half-circles indicate barrage balloons while single numbers (i.e. 4) probably show AA positions.

SATURDAY, MARCH 1-2

Sunset: 1839 Sunrise: 0745
Moon: Dusk — 2225 (New +3)

No major attack. Minor operations against Hull, Southampton, Bristol, Newport and Cardiff, with minelaying off the North-East Coast.

UK — Extensive cloud with poor to moderate visibility in many areas.
The Continent — Similar to UK.

Only seven German aircraft crossed the coasts of Britain on a day when activity was largely confined to fighter sweeps over the Channel and weather/shipping reconnaissance.

Night operations were flown by 100 long-range bombers and six long-range Nachtjäger but without concentration on any one target. Instead, Hull was selected for the attention of Luftflotte 2 while Luftflotte 3 was allocated Cardiff. For the latter attack 37 aircraft were dispatched, but the crews of only 15 reached their primary objective; 18 crews bombed alternative targets, three aborted and one aircraft (a Ju 88 of III/KG77) failed to return. Crews claiming to have bombed Cardiff were as follows:

III/KG27: 2 He 111, 2030-2040 (Knickebein and DR bombing)
III/KG1: 4 Ju 88, 2020-2030 (visual bombing)
III/KG77: 9 Ju 88, 2004-2110 (visual)

Southampton, as an alternative to Cardiff, was bombed by:

I/KG27: 6 He 111, 2045-2055
II/KG27: 5 He 111, 2048-2145
III/KG27: 2 He 111, 2130-2145
III/KG1: 4 Ju 88, 2021-2035
In addition a single He 111 of II/KG27 bombed Bristol.

The attack on Cardiff, in which 17 tonnes of He (56 SC 250 and 52 SC 50) and 24 BSK (864 IBs) were aimed at dock installations, was a mixture of Knickebein and DR bombing with a few crews managing to bomb visually through holes in the almost continuous cloud cover. Accordingly no great success was anticipated, although two or three small fires were seen. Similar results were obtained at Southampton.

At Hull, attacked by 24 aircraft of Luftflotte 2 between 2027 and 2135 hours, there was a similar lack of observed results except for bomb detonations and three small fires in the ordered Target Area (docks and industrial installations). The attackers dropped 29 tonnes of HE (13 SC 1000, two SC 500, two SC 250, six SD 50, 13 LMB and three LMA) and 24 BSK (864 IBs). The units involved were II/KG3, I and II/KG4.

Aircraft of I/NJG2 and all three Gruppen

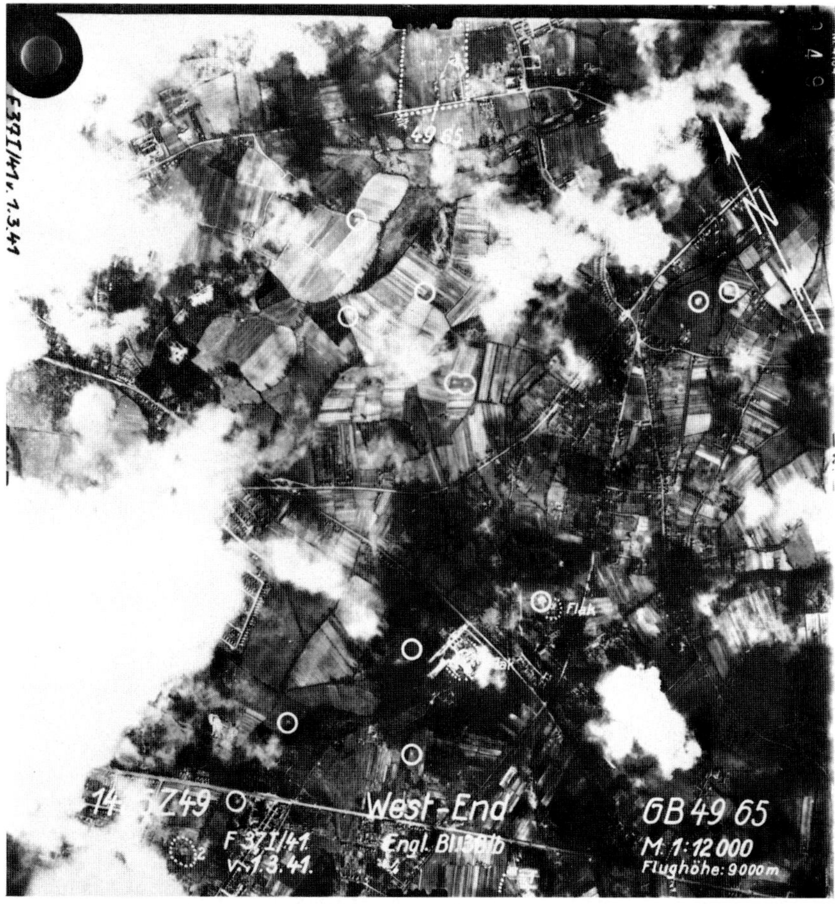

The associated Mission F37l brought back this picture of target GB 49 65 — the radio station at West End east of the city.

of KG2 patrolled East Anglian airfields and off the East Coast in a bid to counter the activities of RAF Bomber Command. Several airfields were claimed attacked including Wattisham and Oulton.

A dusk patrol by three Spitfires of No. 145 Squadron claimed the destruction of a Ju 88 off Selsey Bill but no successes were achieved by the 25 or so night fighters which operated. AA Command, whose heavy guns expended about 1,000 rounds countrywide, fared no better; an He 111 believed to have crashed into the sea off Melrose Head, Banffshire, was allocated to 'other causes'.

Bombing was widespread and affected several areas in the East, South and South-West. Parachute mines were dropped in Hull, where four people were killed, and minor damage occurred in Yarmouth, Southampton and London. Three people were killed at Exmouth and in South Wales slight damage was done at Newport; considerable minor bombing occurred in many areas south of a line joining the Humber and the Severn and one person was killed at Cruden Bay, Scotland.

The two aircraft lost off the shores of Britain were as follows:

2/KG26 Heinkel He 111H-5 (3774). Crashed into the sea after engine failure 1 mile off Whitehills, Melrose Head, Banff 7.57 p.m. Salvage attempted but aircraft broke loose and sank in 10 fathoms. Oblt. H. Kühn, Uffz. F. Grossardt, Gefr. M. Hänel and Uffz. F. Männling captured. Aircraft 1H+BK sank in sea.

Jumo 211 engine caught in trawler's nets and landed at Whitehills in 1976. Scotland West Aircraft Investigation Group and the Aberdeen Sub-Aqua Club recovered the engine and the propeller which are now at the Strathallan Aviation Museum.

7/KG77 Junkers Ju 88A-5 (5147). Believed crashed into the sea off St Catherine's Point, Isle of Wight 7.15 p.m. during a raid on Cardiff. Oblt. W. Fick killed. Uffz. P. Langmesser, Fw. G. König and Fw. H. Schwarz missing. Aircraft 3Z+DR lost.

SUNDAY, MARCH 2-3

Sunset: 1841 Sunrise: 0743
Moon: Dusk — 2327 (First Qtr −4)

Negligible activity. Limited minelaying.

UK — Cloudy with moderate visibility.
The Continent — Poor visibility with mist or fog in many inland areas.

Daylight activity was on a very minor scale and mainly confined to shipping patrols and reconnaissance; only seven enemy aircraft flew over land.

Non-operational weather over German bomber bases permitted only 10 aircraft to fly during the night. Most of these were He 111s of I/KG28 engaged in minelaying off Falmouth, although some damage and a few casualties were reported in south-western, eastern and south-eastern England. Three people were killed at Teignmouth.

MONDAY, MARCH 3-4

Sunset: 1842 Sunrise: 0741
Moon: Dusk — 0028 (First Qtr −3)

Concentrated attack on Cardiff, minelaying and attacks on airfields in eastern England.

UK — Fair with not more than 5/10ths cloud and moderate to good visibility in many districts.
The Continent — Mainly cloudy with occasional showers, becoming clear at times. Gusty westerly winds on coasts; good visibility.

There was more daylight activity than of late — a reflection on the improved weather conditions — involving about 180 German fighters and approximately 50 long-range bombers and reconnaissance aircraft. Some 70 raids were plotted over land, but most of the activity was over the English Channel and adjacent coastal areas. Only Ramsgate was bombed and damage here was confined to houses; two people were killed.

Nightfall brought an attack on Cardiff, reached and bombed by 47 of the 68 aircraft dispatched by Luftflotte 3. Fifteen crews bombed alternative targets, five aborted and one aircraft failed to return. Almost without exception bombing was visual and good results were apparently obtained by the 52 tonnes of HE (12 SC 500, 79 SC/SD 250 and 286 SC/SD 50) and 406 BSK (14,616 incendiaries) that were aimed at the docks and adjoining industrial installations. The attack lasted from 2005 to 0050 hours and produced three large fires north of the docks and in the town centre with additional fires and explosions in and around the Dowlais steelworks in the east part of the docks area. Other dock installations were claimed hit, including the Channel Dry Dock. Participating units were:

KGr100: 7 He 111, 2005-2051 (opened attack as Firelighters with 8,064 IBs. Three aircraft used X-Verfahren, four bombed visually)
III/KG27: 3 He 111, 2115-2130
I/KG1: 8 He 111, 2207-2300
III/KG1: 7 He 111, 2219-2250
II/KG76: 8 Ju 88, 2215-2315
I/KG77: 4 Ju 88, 2305-0050
III/KG77: 4 Ju 88, 2210-2300
III/KG26: 6 He 111, 2201-2308 (used Y-Verfahren, bombing from 4,000-6,000 metres altitude)

Fourteen aircraft bombed Southampton as an alternative target and the fifteenth attacked Plymouth. Reported missing was an He 111 of III/KG26.

Aircraft of Luftflotte 2 were further engaged in attacks on industrial installations on the Tyne Estuary and at Newcastle; 22 bombers (of which two acted as firelighters or pathfinders) took part, dropping 18 tonnes of HE (one SC 1800, 11 SC 500, 34 SD 250 and 48 SD 50), 83 BSK (2,988 IBs) and 56 LC 50 parachute flares between 2008 and 2105 hours. The CP was on the banks of the Tyne at Newcastle but also earmarked for attack were armaments and industrial plants, workshops, dockyards and dock installations at the mouth of the Tyne. For the most part bombing was carried out visually and bomb explosions and resulting fires were in evidence. Increasing cloud cover and decreasing visibility prevented an accurate assessment of results, however.

Further aircraft were allocated various night flying airfields in eastern England, including Mildenhall, and minelaying was carried out between the Tees and the Tay.

German records do not indicate which units of Luftflotte 2 were operating, but according to the British 'Y' Service these were:

I/KG53: 18 aircraft; operating from Vitry-en-Artois
II/KG53: 12 aircraft; from Lille/Vendeville
II/KG3: 7+ aircraft; from Amsterdam/Schiphol
I or II/KG4: 20 aircraft; from Soesterberg

In addition, I/KG26, with six aircraft from Stavanger, Norway, was operating in coastal areas between Kinnaird's Head and Dundee. Engaged in airfield attacks and patrols against British bomber aircraft off the East Coast were I, II and III/KG2 and I/NJG2.

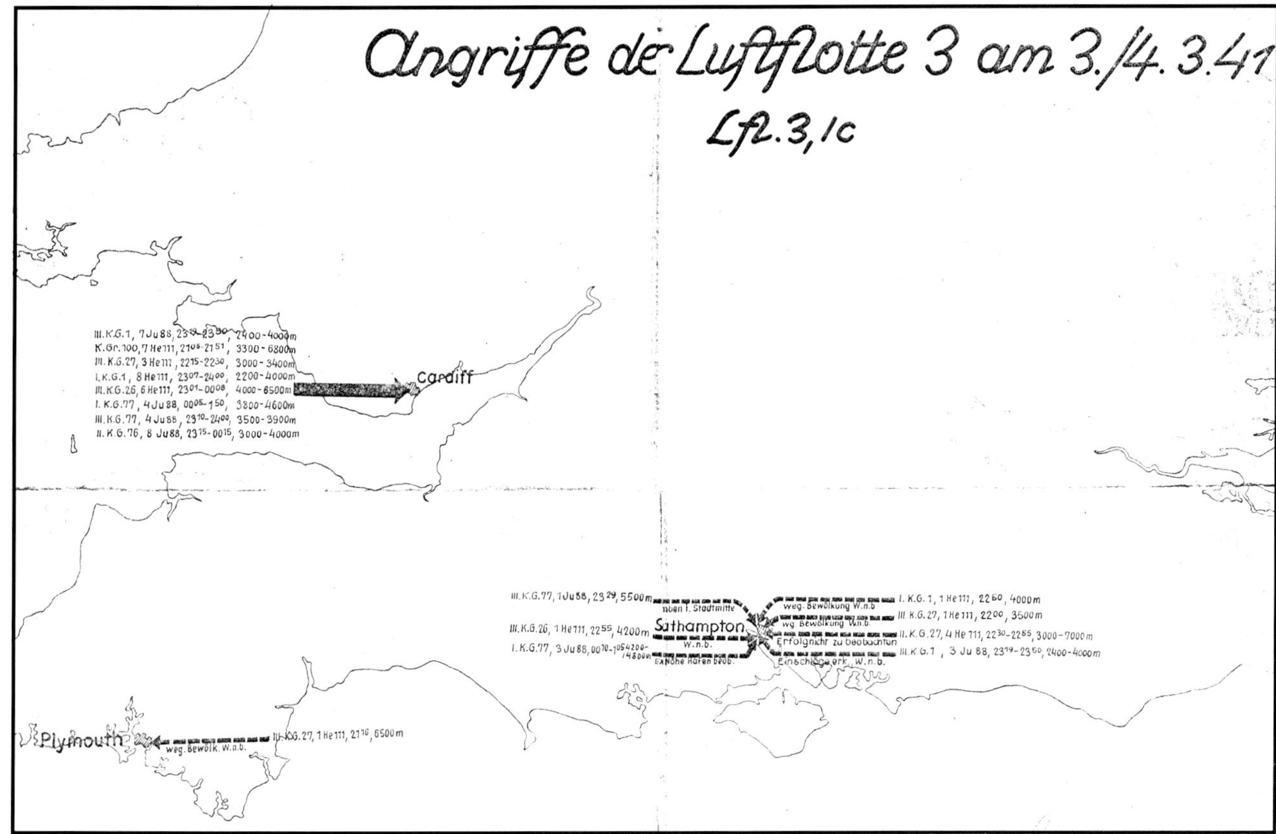

Bombing in the North-East was not concentrated and incidents were reported in many districts; Northumberland, Durham, East Anglia, London, the South and South-Western Regions all reported bombing. More serious was the attack on Cardiff where fires, some of them serious, were started. The city centre was most affected and a number of public buildings, St David's Cathedral among them, were damaged. Initial casualty lists showed 48 people killed and 97 seriously injured. Two people were also killed in East Lothian.

Night patrols were flown by 120 aircraft of Fighter Command including six on Intruder offensive operations over France, but only claims of one enemy aircraft probably destroyed and one damaged were made. AA guns were in action at Cardiff, Newport, Bristol, Holton Heath, Gloucester, Tyne, Tees, Humber, the IAZ, Thames and Medway (North and South), Portsmouth, Datchet and Brooklands. They fired more than 5,000 rounds, of which 3,600 were by the Cardiff and Newport gunners, who were in action from 2013 to 0019 hours and claimed one enemy aircraft destroyed.

Aircraft lost during the day around Britain were the following.

3/JG51 Messerschmitt Bf 109E (2035). Shot down by Pilot Officer A. R. McL. Campbell of No. 54 Squadron. Crashed at Brenzett 4.00 p.m. Lt. M. Ottmer baled out but killed when parachute failed. Aircraft TG+GW destroyed.

3/KG27 Heinkel He 111H-5 (3911). Last radio message, 'Fighters — landing in sea near Scilly Isles — engine failure'. Landed on Lundy Island 3.20 p.m. due to engine failure. Fw. H. Scharrschuch, Uffz. E. Böttcher, Fw. H. Bongers, Fw. H. Ludwig and Gefr. P. Timmermann taken prisoner. Aircraft 1G+AL completely burnt out by crew.

Site investigated by the South West Aircraft Recovery Group who found an area of burnt earth and small fragments.

3/KG27 Heinkel He 111H-5 (3664). Damaged by fighters over Irish Sea. Made a forced landing at Lackenshane, Co. Wexford, Eire. Uffz. G. Rister killed. Lt. A. Heinzel, Fw. A. Voigt, Fw. R. Hengst and Gefr. M. Galler taken prisoner. Aircraft 1G+HL wrecked.

The only casualty during the night was incurred during an attack on Cardiff.

7/KG26 Heinkel He 111H-5 (3601). Presumed crashed into the sea off South Wales 10.08 p.m. Fw. W. Rudiger, Lt. O. Friton, Uffz. F. Jäger, Uffz. O. Frühwald and Gefr. F. Bürgel missing. Aircraft 1H+GR lost.

Attacked on Saturday and again tonight: Cardiff, with Southampton and Plymouth as alternatives. In Cardiff 21 serious fires were reported by Home Security, a feature of the raid being 'the large percentage of explosive incendiary bombs employed'. The Royal Infirmary had to be evacuated; the Institute for the Blind burnt out, and more than 600 were made homeless. Home Security deduced that 'the enemy appears to have used the same tactics against Cardiff as he has done on many other occasions, notably in the recent raids on Swansea where he attacked the centre of the town, first with flares and incendiary bombs and then with HE'.

With the improved weather earlier in the day, during the afternoon a number of aircraft crossed the south-east coast, dropping 26 bombs on Ramsgate. The fighters were brought to battle, one Bf 109 being hit by Pilot Officer Campbell. The pilot, Leutnant Martin Ottmer, baled out but too late and his parachute failed to operate. He was found lying dead at Ivychurch. His machine hit the ground at speed here at Brenzett, leaving little on the surface to mark its passing.

On Monday and Tuesday nights it was back to Cardiff after a brief respite — it makes one wonder just how the Luftwaffe wheel of misfortune was operated to pick the daily target. Was it a sophisticted process with committees and analysts predicting the ins and outs . . . or was it more like a game of roulette or a blind man selecting objectives with a pin? On the worst night, the 3rd–4th, 57 citizens died, with the shopping and business areas in the centre badly hit. At the Royal Infirmary, a patient was on the operating table, receiving emergency treatment for an injury caused earlier from an explosive incendiary, when a bomb fell between the pathology block and the nurses' homes. The theatre window was blown across the room but there were no casualties and the operation was completed with the light of a torch in the anaesthetic room. *Left:* Nurses trying to salve anything undamaged in the dispensary, and *right* from their homes in Newport Road.

TUESDAY, MARCH 4-5

Sunset: 1844 Sunrise: 0738
Moon: Dusk — 0128 (First Qtr −2)

Concentrated attack on Cardiff. Minor attacks on London and Southampton, patrols over airfields in eastern England and minelaying.

UK — Cloudy with moderate to poor visibility (mist or fog in many areas). Winds light or calm.

The Continent — Mainly cloudy with occasional rain. Moderate to poor visibility; light variable winds.

Fighter sweeps (including some sorties by fighter-bombers), anti-shipping patrols and reconnaissance (weather and general) occupied the Luftwaffe during the day, but not more than 170 aircraft were involved in total and no bombs fell on land.

During the night Luftflotte 3 attacked Cardiff for the second successive night, this time dispatching 68 aircraft with the crews of 61 claiming to have bombed their primary targets (the port and industrial installations). They dropped 48.3 tonnes of HE (12 SC 500, 108 SC 250, 11 LZZ 250 and 251 SC 50), 17,196 B1 El incendiaries and 3,082 B1 El ZA explosive incendiaries between 2043 and 0035 hours. Target illumination was provided by the light of 36 LC 50 parachute flares and most of the bombing was carried out visually. Participating units were:

I/KG27: 4 He 111, 2045-2104 (visual)
II/KG27: 7 He 111, 2050-2130 (visual)
III/KG27: 9 He 111, 2043-2300 (visual)
KGr100: 16 He 111, 2049-2119 (11 a/c with X-Verfahren, 5 visual)
I/KG77: 6 Ju 88, 2235-2315 (visual)
II/KG77: 8 Ju 88, 2235-0000
III/KG77: 4 Ju 88, 0015-0035 (visual)
III/KG26: 7 He 111, 2223-2342 (Y-Verfahren, accuracy checked visually with 28 LC 50s)

After 2300 hours worsening visibility made target location difficult, but earlier in the attack bombs were seen to hit the docks and industrial area and fires were clearly discerned there and in the town to the north of the Dowlais steel works. Good results were expected.

Four Cardiff-bound aircraft seeking an alternative target joined two more ordered to bomb Southampton, two aircraft aborted and one, a Ju 88 of III/KG77, was reported overdue.

London was attacked by nine aircraft, their targets being Tilbury and other docks on the Thames, and fires were seen here and at Southampton. Minelaying was carried out off the East and South-West Coasts (including the Bristol Channel) and a ship was attacked some 40 miles south-west of Milford Haven.

The British defences continued to give little concern to German crews, but, over Cardiff the flak was said to be 'moderate and, to a degree, well aimed'.

The Cardiff attack — the third suffered by the city in a week — was not as intensive as that of the previous night and fires, which were mostly small, were all under control by 2200 hours. Nearby Penarth received many of the bombs intended for Cardiff, however, and here there were more than 20 fires, several of them of medium proportions. Public buildings sustained a good deal of damage, as did commercial and residential property. In Cardiff itself there were a few fires in the dock area but damage was neither extensive nor serious. The Public Health Clinic, the University Students' Union and St Martin's Church and numerous other buildings were damaged or destroyed, adding to a growing list which, from the previous night's attack, included the main Post Office, the Royal Infirmary, the Institute for the Blind,

And schools. This is Marlborough Road School in Roath Park.

the Central Hall and the Law Courts. At Penarth three churches, a school and the Public Library were damaged.

Elsewhere bombs were reported at Sidcup, Woolwich, Orpington, Upminster, Chislehurst, East Tilbury, Walton-on-the-Naze, Thameshaven, Portsmouth, Newport (Isle of Wight) and near Andover.

Guns of AA Command were in action at Thames and Medway (North and South), the London IAZ, Holton Heath, Portland, Cardiff (firing 2,500 rounds between 2028 and 0034 hours), Southampton, Harwich, Portsmouth and Gloucester. Countrywide some 4,000 rounds were fired for four enemy aircraft claimed destroyed. Fighter Command dispatched 75 aircraft including 28 on dusk patrols and two on Intruder operations over northern France. One He 111 was claimed destroyed by a Beaufighter of No. 604 Squadron.

Maritime sorties continued to be the main feature of daylight activity.

1(F)/120 Junkers Ju 88A (0683). Lost on reconnaissance of Scapa Flow. Crashed into the sea 1 mile east of Westray Island, Orkneys 2.35 p.m. after combat with three Hurricanes of No. 253 Squadron. Fw. J. Mischke, Fw. H. Schmidt, Uffz. C. Ingwersen and Gefr. R. Priebsch all missing. Aircraft A6+LH lost.

For the second night running, on the night of March 4-5, a raid was launched upon Cardiff. In addition to the losses shown an aircraft of 8/KG77 also failed to return.

1/KG28 Heinkel He 111H-5 (3561). Shot down by Squadron Leader M. F. Anderson in a Beaufighter of No. 604 Squadron. Crashed into the sea off Beer Head, Devon 9.58 p.m. Lt. zur See O. von Hanffstengel, Fw. W. Ernst, Uffz. O. Hinrichs and Gefr. H. Kura killed. Aircraft 1T+BH lost.

1/KG28 Heinkel He 111H-4 (3293). Shot down by Barry AA Batteries at Cardiff. Crashed half a mile off Nell's Point, Barry at 9.09 p.m. Major Dr R. Auernig (Staffelkapitän), Uffz. A. Dries, Uffz. H. Hartisch and Gefr. H. Felten all killed. Aircraft 1T+AH lost.

And homes. The indignity of having one's house disembowelled, with treasured possessions bared for all to see, perhaps ruined by water or, even worse, consumed without trace by fire. Yet blast was a funny thing, sometimes sweeping through sparing things like this clock resting on its mantlepiece, the mirror unbroken . . . This is 226 Newport Road, Cardiff.

Angriff auf das Flugzeugwerk Bristol Aeroplane in Filton

Oblt. Hollinde

Obfw. Libuda

Uffz. Weber

Gefr. Schillig

Gefr. Schwarz

Ein Kampfflugzeug unter der Führung von Oberleutnant ***Hollinde*** mit der Besatzung Obfw. *Libuda*, Uffz. *Weber*, Gefr. *Schillig*, Gefr. *Schwarz*, griff am 6. 3. 41 das Flugrüstungswerk Bristol Aeroplane in Filton aus 300 m Höhe nach Erdsicht an. Nach Bombeneinschlag in der Mitte des Zieles waren starke Rauchwolken zu beobachten. Außerdem wurden 5 bis 6 abgestellte Feindflugzeuge vom Muster Bristol „Blenheim" unter MG.-Feuer genommen und Treffer in den Flugzeugen beobachtet.

(Diese Leistung wurde unter Nennung der Besatzung im Bericht des Oberkommandos der Wehrmacht vom 7. 3. 41 besonders erwähnt.)

WEDNESDAY, MARCH 5-6

Sunset: 1846 Sunrise: 0736
Moon: Dusk — 0225 (First Qtr −1)

No significant activity.

UK — Extensive cloud with mist in many areas.
The Continent — Low cloud, mist or fog in northern France and the Low Countries.

Only eight German aircraft flew inland during a day of unfavourable weather conditions and no bombs were reported. During the evening, five aircraft, operating singly, approached the south coast and three bombs were dropped at Vospers Ltd, Portsmouth, causing some damage. All night operations were cancelled.

The only loss suffered near Britain was from I/KG27, their third loss over the Irish Sea in as many days. Two crew members of another I/KG27 aircraft were injured, again over the Irish Sea.

2/KG27 Heinkel He 111H-5 (3734). Shot down by Sunderland 'J' of No. 10 Squadron RAAF. Crashed into the sea off Stone Head, Eire 12.06 p.m. Oberfw. T. Böhner killed. Lt. H. Brodski, Fw. W. Korell and Fw. F. Alter missing. Aircraft 1G+EK sank in sea.

And the Germans also had their air heroes. In Britain the bombing exploits of Cheshire, Gibson and Pickard have gone down as brave exploits, but do we look equally on the single-minded attacks of Hollinde and Lohmann or Rudolph and Knauth? Exponents of the Seeräuberangriffen — disparaged by the British as 'hit and run' attacks — these are some of the operations they carried out in March as seen through the German eyes of *Frontnachrichtenblatt der Luftwaffe*. Oberleutnant Hollinde's attack on the Bristol factory at Filton was later described by the Italian journalist Carlo d'Ongaro in *Giornale d'Italia*: 'This was one of the most difficult raids carried out by the Luftwaffe on England, on account of the exceptional defences at the Filton works designed to keep off dive bombers. Two rows of balloons were placed round the installations like two concentric circles, and each balloon was very close to the next. They were flying at a height of over 1,200 metres, and their diameter was such that they formed a sort of well into which no pilot in his senses would think of going. Oberleutnant Hollinde was aware of the difficulties and for several days he practised aerobatics and worked out the best method of attack. Finally he selected a suitable day with bands of clouds moving across the sky. The buildings at Filton are camouflaged and not easily identified, but the balloon barrage was clearly visible and was useful for locating the target. Hollinde dived down vertically from 3,000 metres and released all the bombs he was carrying: but, although the entry into the balloon well was a practically normal manoeuvre for a pilot of his class, entailing only courage and skill, to get out again was another matter. In view of the speed of his aircraft he could not keep on a straight course inside the balloons and, circling round, he tried to gain height. He was flying so low that he could see the faces of the AA gunners, and his gunner fired on the gun crews and on the balloons in turn, but his fire was not sufficient either to silence the guns or to open a way through the balloons. Hollinde then decided to try a dangerous manoeuvre and he went into a sideslip and slipped between the balloon cables. Even then he was only inside the second circle, where the balloons were still closer, but he had no time to waste as the daylight was going and he would not have been able to see the cables. Fortunately his manoeuvre again succeeded . . . ' In reality Hollinde's attack was a failure, the bombs falling two miles away on a housing estate at Southmead, killing Albert Brown and injuring 15. At the time the factory was heavily engaged in the production of the Beaufighter; had the attack succeeded it could well have dealt a massive blow to British counter-measures against the night bomber,

THURSDAY, MARCH 6-7

Sunset: 1848 Sunrise: 0734
Moon: Dusk — 0319 (First Quarter)

Minor activity with a little minelaying off the East Coast.

UK — Cloudy with moderate to poor visibility.
The Continent — Similar to UK in northern France and the Low Countries.

Taking advantage of the low cloud base and poor visibility several German aircraft penetrated inland during the day and there were many bomb incidents in the East and South-East. Damage and casualties were caused at Sheringham and Great Yarmouth, and at Lowestoft, which was attacked three times, and where considerable damage was done to public buildings and two people were killed. Another aircraft machine-gunned Cambridge and in London houses were damaged and several people injured at Woolwich. Although, of course, it was not realised at the time, this was the last occasion that bombs were to fall on London in daylight until July 17, 1942.

Night operations were limited to sorties by 29 aircraft, including minelayers which were active off the East Coast. At dusk a few bombs fell on Bristol, where one person was killed, and in the North-East two mines, probably intended for the sea, fell on land.

FRIDAY, MARCH 7-8

Sunset: 1850 Sunrise: 0732
Moon: Dusk — 0409 (First Qtr +1)

No major operations.

UK — Extensive cloud with generally poor visibility in all areas. Drizzle and hill fog in the West.
The Continent — Similar to the UK in northern France and the Low Countries. Fog in many inland districts.

German daylight operations were flown by 70 long-range bombers and 19 fighter-bombers and bombing incidents were widespread; a factory at Newark was attacked, killing 36 people, the railway was damaged at Skegness and there were many incidents in East Anglia. Low-level bombing and machine gun attacks accounted for most of the damage, carried out by single aircraft taking advantage of cloud cover — known in the Luftwaffe as Seeräuberangriffen (pirate attacks), but better known to the British public as 'hit-and-run' raids — and some penetrated to RAF stations in the Midlands and near Manchester. Also attacked were an Infantry Training Centre in Devon, and the Parnall Aircraft factory at Yate, near Bristol.

A further deterioration in the weather led to a cancellation of night attacks, but one long-range bomber operated, according to German records. No bombs fell on Britain during the night.

The following aircraft were lost:

2/Erprobungsgruppe 210 Messerschmitt Bf 110 (3827). Presumed shot down by HMS *Guillemot* during a raid on Harwich. Crashed into the sea off Harwich. Fw. C. Fleischmann and Fw. G. Helling killed. Aircraft S9+IK lost.

Oberleutnant Hermann Lohmann, who successfully hit the factory at Yate causing extensive damage and killing three people, was no stranger to Parnall's as it was he who had struck a devastating blow there just a week earlier in one of the most successful single-aircraft attacks of the period. At 2.30 p.m. on February 27, 52 had been killed, many from a delayed action bomb which exploded 10 minutes later.

Angriff auf das Flugzeugzellenwerk Parnall Aircraft Co. in Yate

Oblt. Lohmann

Obfw. Beckmann

Stabsfw. Köster

Stabsfw. Trageser

Gefr. Hey

Am 7. 3. 41 führte ein Kampfflugzeug unter der Führung von **Oberleutnant *Lohmann*** als Beobachter und Kommandant mit der Besatzung Obfw. *Beckmann*, Flugzeugführer, Stabsfw. *Köster*, Bordfunker, Stabsfw. *Trageser*, Bordmechaniker, Gefr. *Hey*, Heckschütze, einen Zerstörangriff gegen die Flugzeugzellenfabrik der Parnall Aircraft Co. in Yate erfolgreich durch. Es wurden Treffer in Fabrikhallen, Baracken und Nebengebäuden erzielt. Die Besatzung konnte gleichzeitig als Wirkung ihres ersten, am 27. 2. 41 gegen dasselbe Werk durchgeführten Angriffs feststellen, daß der Mittelteil des Werkes, aus Montagehallen bestehend, zerstört und ausgebrannt war und auch die übrigen Teile der Fabrikanlagen schwere Beschädigungen aufwiesen. Da der am 7. 3. 1941 durchgeführte Angriff vermutlich ebenso wirksam war wie der erste, kann angenommen werden, daß dieses wichtige Werk der britischen Flugrüstungsindustrie schwer beschädigt worden ist.

(Diese Leistung wurde unter Nennung der Besatzung im Bericht des Oberkommandos der Wehrmacht vom 9. 3. 41 besonders erwähnt.)

Angriff auf die Kugellagerfabrik Newark

Lt. Rudolph

Lt. Metzmacher

Uff. Gröper

Uffz. Hahn

Am 7. 3. 41 erzielte ein Kampfflugzeug unter der Führung von Leutnant ***Rudolph*** als Flugzeugführer und Kommandant mit der Besatzung *Lt. Metzmacher,* Beobachter, Uffz. *Gröper,* Funker, Uffz. *Hahn,* Mechaniker, bei einem Tiefangriff auf das Kugellagerwerk Newark Treffer in Gebäuden in der Mitte des Werkes. Die Besatzung beobachtete eine sehr starke Detonation und stellte besonders starke Wirkung des Bombenabwurfs im Westteil des Zieles fest.

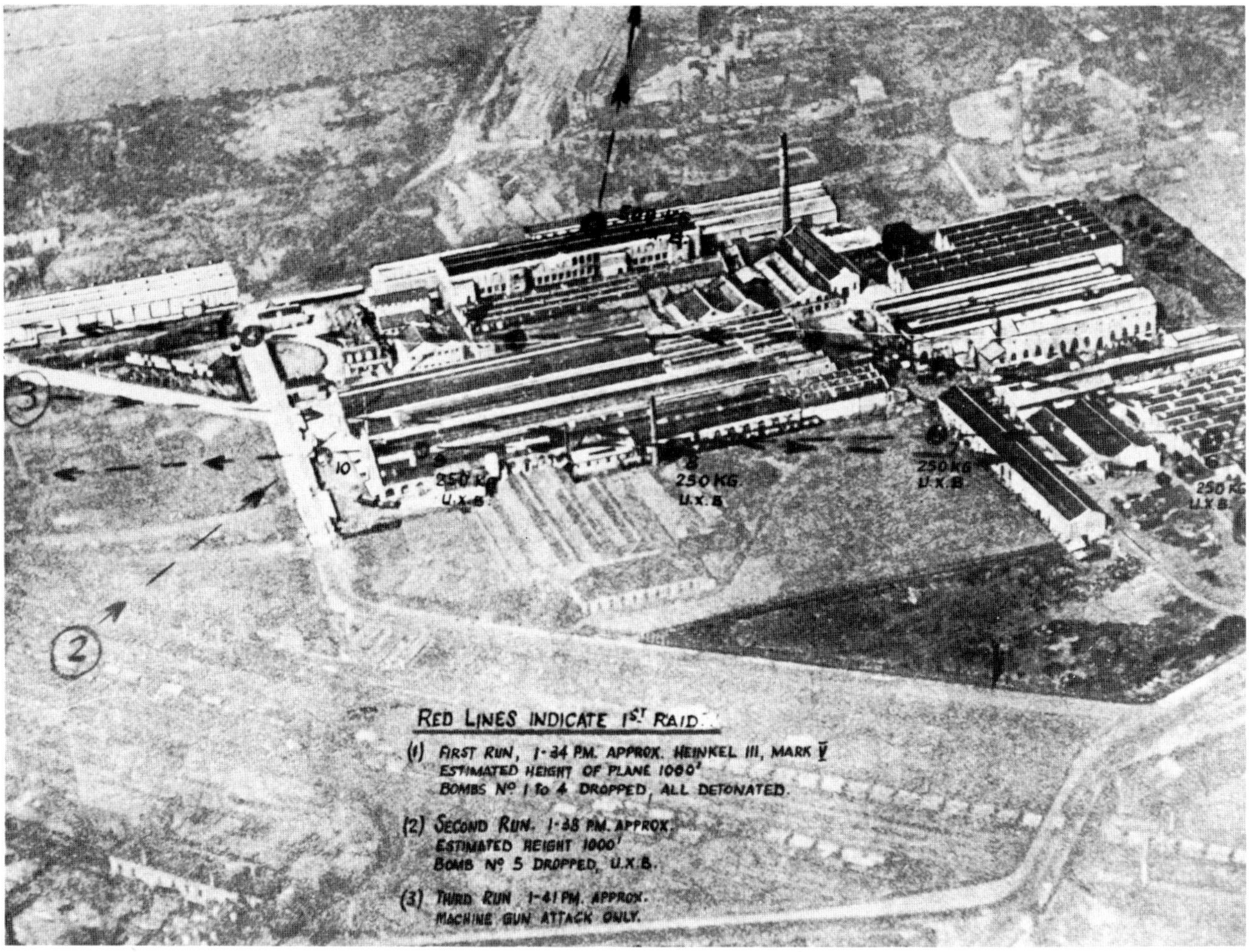

The same day a pin-point attack by Leutnant Rudolph and his crew caused severe damage to the Ransome and Marles works at Newark — one of the vital ball-bearing factories which were seen by the strategic planners of both sides as important economic targets as their output, or lack of it, would have a drastic effect on the production of all kinds of vehicles, tanks and aircraft, all dependent on ball or roller bearings. As this post-raid picture shows, the aircraft made three passes over the factory, 36 workers losing their lives and another 42 being severely injured. It was Newark's blackest day.

2/KG3 Dornier Do 17Z-2 (3391). Ditched in the sea off Gorleston, near Great Yarmouth during a sortie over the Thames Estuary 7.35 a.m. cause unknown but credited to the Hopton AA battery. Fw. W. Ophoff killed. Oblt. E. Kunst, Oberfw. H. Vendland and Uffz. H. Ockinghaus taken prisoner. Aircraft 5K+MK sank in the sea.

1/KG26 Heinkel He 111H-5 (3650). During a sortie to Kinnairds Head aircraft hit the mast of a ship it was attacking and crashed into the River Tay off Buddon, Angus 8.06 p.m. Uffz. K. Seeland killed. Uffz. F. Beckmann, Gefr. W. Gabriel and Uffz. H. Rettstadt all missing. Aircraft 1H+HH wrecked.

SATURDAY, MARCH 8-9

Sunset: 1851 Sunrise: 0729
Moon: Dusk — 0454 (First Qtr +2)

Major attack on London. Minelaying off the East Coast and attacks on airfields.

UK — Largely cloudless (2/10ths cloud in the London area) but poor visibility with mist or fog in many districts.
The Continent — Rain in Holland but dry elsewhere with low cloud and moderate to poor visibility. Mist and fog forming later.

Minor incidents were reported in Norfolk, the North and North-East during the day. Damage and casualties were also reported at Lowestoft and at Lopness, Orkney.

Nightfall brought the first major attack on London since January 12. Of the 153 long-range bombers operating, 125 bombed London, dropping a claimed 130 tonnes of HE (28 SC 500, 289 SC 250, 15 LZZ 250 and 802 SC 50) and 693 BSK (24,948 IBs) between 2010 and 2325 hours. Despite the poor visibility bombing was for the most part carried out visually, but crews were generally unable to assess their accuracy. Nevertheless, on both sides of the Thames, from the famous U-bend to the Tower, eight large and numerous smaller fires were seen and at 2105 hours a large explosion occurred. Another six to eight fires were in evidence on the south side of the same stretch of the river with ten more large fires in the docks on the north bank to the east of the bend. Further huge fire glows were made out in the loop of the river and in the West India Docks. Overall, good results were anticipated.

The attackers comprised 32 aircraft of Luftflotte 2 and 93 of the 97 dispatched by Luftflotte 3 (four crews aborted). The Luftflotte 3 contribution was as follows:

II/KG27: 15 He 111, 2120-2200
I/KG1: 12 He 111, 2024-2115
III/KG1: 14 Ju 88, 2010-2052
II/KG76: 15 Ju 88, 2040-2145
I/KG77: 8 Ju 88, 2108-2158
II/KG77: 9 Ju 88, 2010-2040
III/KG77: 9 Ju 88, 2023-2112
III/KG26: 11 He 111, 2015-2210 (8 aircraft used Y-Verfahren, 3 bombed visually)

Luftflotte 3 dispatched 126 aircraft to London but the crews of 29, unable to locate their primary target, bombed Portsmouth, their designated first alternative. These aircraft were:

II/KG27: 12 He 111, 2055-2120 (visual bombing)
III/KG27: 1 He 111, 2055 (visual bombing)
KGr806: 6 Ju 88 0018-0320 (DR bombing only)
I/KG1: 4 He 111, 2208-2325 (visual bombing)
II/KG76: 3 Ju 88, 2135-2219 (visual bombing).
III/KG26: 3 He 111, 2145-2150 (unable to bomb London due to failure of X-system)

Another aircraft, a Ju 88 of III/KG1,

The raid on London on Saturday night was marked by two notable incidents. The first was when the Palace was bombed, the North Lodge receiving a direct hit. Fortunately their Majesties were not in residence at the time.

The scene recorded from outside the walls *(top)* and within the walls *(above)* by gracious permission of Her Majesty the Queen.

attacked a convoy off Dover at 2315 hours and its crew claimed to have set fire to one ship. Two more crews aborted and an He 111 of II/KG27 failed to return.

Fifty boroughs of London reported bombing and many fires resulted including some in the docks. Losses were slight, however, but the railway system was affected — three

On Saturday, March 8, Londoners emerged from the longest raid-free period since the Blitz began on another Saturday just six months previously, breaking nearly six weeks of respite with an incident of particular tragedy — the bombing of the Café de Paris. Located below the Rialto Cinema in Coventry Street, Leicester Square, in what had been in an earlier age of barbarity a bear-baiting pit, the restaurant had been fashioned on the design of the ballroom of the liner *Titanic* (both being in course of construction at the same time) with two sweeping staircases leading down from the 'bridge' enclosing the bandstand area.

The resident musicians were Ken (short for Kenrick) Johnson's Carribean jazz band, the man himself being known to the public as 'Snakehips'. He lived in London and had arrived early with the greeting: 'Man, it's terrible outside — just terrible.'

Being underground the Café de Paris was advertised as the safest restaurant in town and being Saturday, was full. The patrons were largely uniformed officers with their ladies, the 'quality' of the customers being noted upon by one of those present, Lady Betty Baldwin, daughter of the former Prime Minister. The men that evening seemed extraordinarily handsome; the young women in their long evening gowns very beautiful, the evening having been described as almost comparable to the Duchess of Richmond's ball before Quatre Bras.

Snakehips had just begun the second chorus of *Oh Johnny* when two 50kg bombs struck the Rialto and, without going off, penetrated the floor — the roof of the restaurant — and smashed into the ballroom below. One exploded just in front and to the right of the band, killing Ken Johnson and another member of his band, Charles the head waiter and the manager who had been standing on the balcony, and thirty of the diners. The second bomb failed to go off although the case split when it hit, scattering the contents about the floor. Home Security reported another 80 taken to hospital but due to an incorrect message being relayed to the Westminster Report Centre, and due to the nearest Warden's Post being somewhat depleted, some of the most seriously injured had to wait nearly an hour for a place in an ambulance.

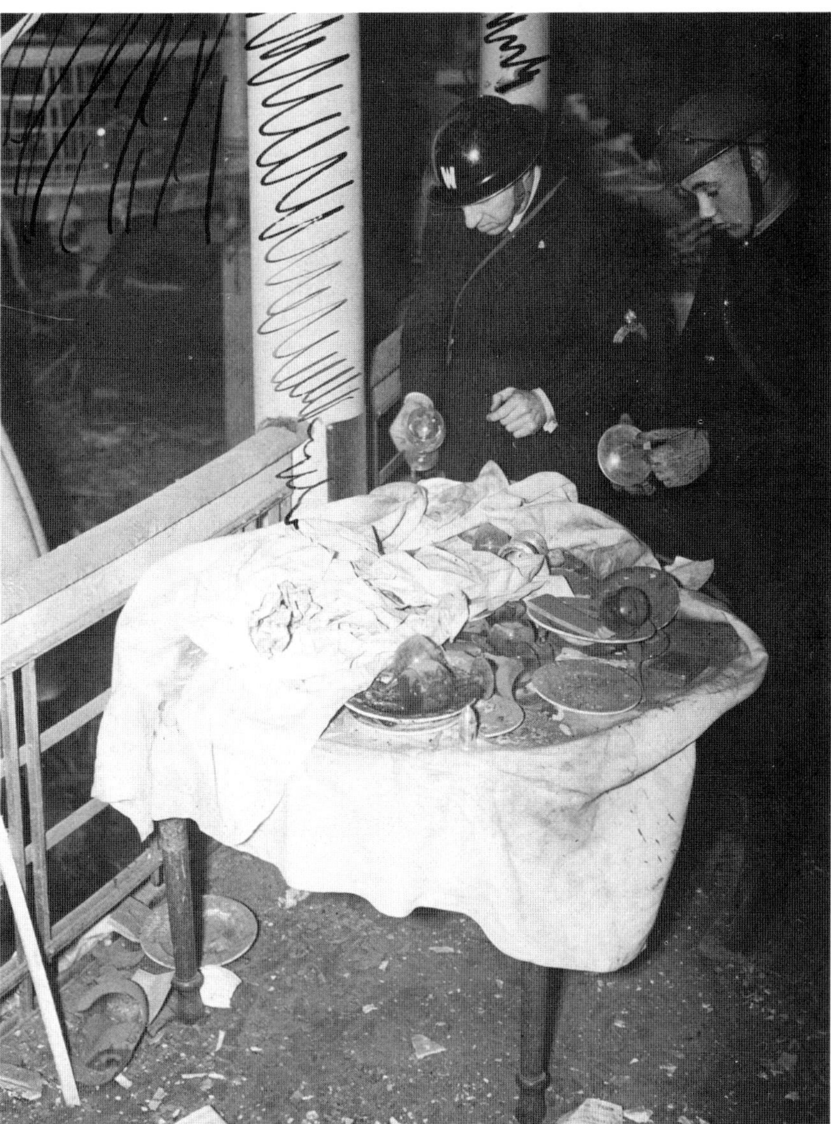

main line termini were hit and there was some dislocation of traffic, but none of the damage was irreparable and disruption was of a temporary nature. Only at Bermondsey were gas supplies seriously affected and other utilities fared better than in most previous attacks. One important factory was hit but numerous public buildings were damaged including St Bartholomew's Hospital and a Salvation Army Hostel. Casualty figures were enlarged by two serious incidents; at the Café de Paris in Coventry Street 34 people were killed and about 80 injured, and at a North London public house 14 were killed. Five HEs fell near Buckingham Palace, where the North Lodge was hit and two casualties caused. One person was killed in an East London shelter and there were also casualties in a North-West London block of flats.

Damage was also reported in Portsmouth and elsewhere in the South, South-East and Eastern Regions including Norwich, Cardington, Swaffham, Bassingbourn, Swindon, Oxford, Brough, Thirsk, Harrow, near Guildford, Lewes, Cuckfield, Ditchling, Cowden, Halstead, Farnham Common, Stanstead, Wilmington, East Wittering, Bognor Regis, Southend, Meopham, Chislehurst, Enfield, Croydon, Horley and Godstone.

AA Command's ammunition expenditure for the night totalled some 4,000 rounds, with the IAZ accounting for 1,081 rounds of 4.5-inch, 1,340 rounds of 3.7-inch and 121 3-inch shells. Elsewhere batteries were in action at Portsmouth, Slough, Thames and Medway (North and South), Brooklands, Harwich, Dover and Fareham. Sixty night fighters flew patrols, nine of them on Intruder missions, and two enemy aircraft were claimed damaged. One Defiant (N3478 of No. 264 Squadron) was written off on the 8th when it collided with another Defiant from Biggin Hill. The second aircraft, N3332, landed safely.

Two aircraft were lost close to the British mainland:

4(F)/122 Junkers Ju 88A-5 (0404). Shot down by Flying Officer Ferris and Sergeant van Schaick in Spitfires of No. 266 Squadron. (Ferris was killed when his Spitfire crashed during the combat.) Crashed into the sea off Skegness 10.13 a.m. Lt. G. Neumann, Oberfw. F. Benker, Uffz. A. Schuler and Uffz. K. Lessmöllmann all killed. Aircraft F6+BM lost.

4/KG30 Junkers Ju 88A-5 (2220). Shot down by fire from No. 158 Light AA Battery during a sortie to Newcastle. Crashed into the sea off Lowestoft 11.20 a.m. Hptmn. K. Schneider (Staffelkapitän) killed. Fw. A. Ewald, Uffz. K. Kirchner and Gefr. K. Oetsch missing. Aircraft 4D+FM lost.

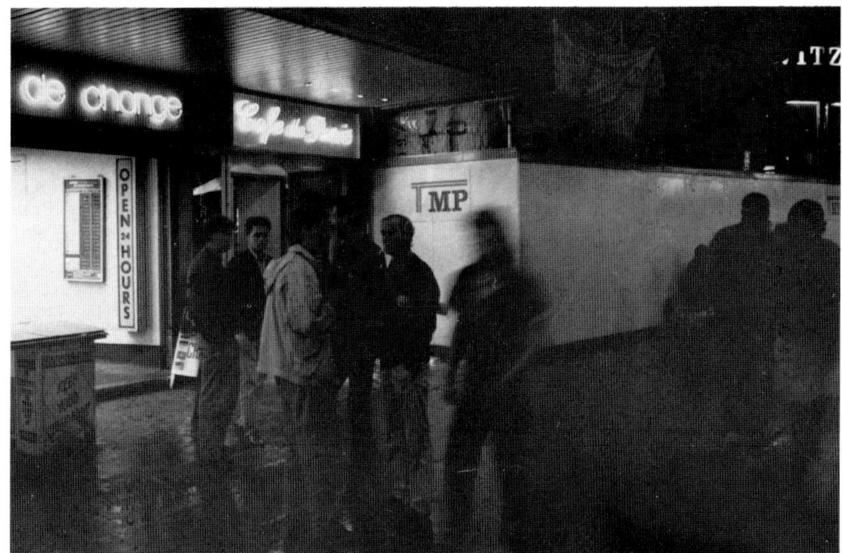

Others were evacuated in taxis and a First Aid Post was set up in the hotel across the road. Anthony Jacobs, a well-known actor on the wireless of the pre-war period, was on leave in London that night: 'I was in a milk bar in Leicester Square. . . . Suddenly the milk bar shook, and there was obviously a bomb somewhere near. Well, a few moments later I strolled out towards Piccadilly Circus and there in Coventry Street there was a crowd round the entrance to the Café de Paris. I think the entrance was brightly lit, in spite of the blackout, and injured people in evening dress were coming up the stairs now and again, being helped up, staggering, they really were staggering, and the crowd began to grow. . . .' *Above:* But do they remember today?

We have previously discussed the problems faced after many of the early surface shelters were found to have been constructed of an incorrect mix of mortar (pages 116-117), and in March 1941 the Ministry of Home Security decided that all such shelters must be closed or demolished. Those constructed with lime-cement mortar were to be examined and closed or demolished as necessary. The closing of so many places of shelter which, at first sight, seemed quite safe led to widespread criticism from the public. In a new design of shelter, prepared by the Research and Experiments Department of the Home Office in December 1940, the walls were constructed of hollow concrete blocks, bricks or ferro-concrete with the steel reinforcing rods tied into the floor and roof. A damp-proof course was incorporated and a roof overhang to help keep it dry. This 'colony' of the new dormitory shelters complete with central canteen and medical block was built outside Cardiff.

SUNDAY, MARCH 9-10

Sunset: 1853 Sunrise: 0727
Moon: Dusk — 0534 (First Qtr +3)

Heavy attack on London. Secondary attack on Portsmouth with further operations over East Anglia and against shipping. Minelaying in Liverpool Bay and in Lyme Bay.

UK — Fair in the South but cloud thickening and lowering after midnight. Moderate visibility, slowly worsening. Elsewhere, extensive low cloud with rain, sleet or snow and moderate to poor visibility.

The Continent — Much medium cloud, variable low cloud. Visibility moderate to good. Fog patches later in some districts of northern France and the Low Countries.

During a day of limited German activity bombs fell near Sleaford, killing five people, at several points in Kent, and in East Anglia. Damage and injuries were also caused in Sheringham and at Rochford an empty wing of the Municipal Hospital was hit. Attacks on airfields were also attempted and reported incidents included one from Kent.

Including one aircraft that attacked the capital as an alternative target, a total of 94 bombers reached London in a raid which lasted from 2021 to 0230 hours. They dropped a claimed 97 tonnes of HE (nine SC 1000, 22 SC 500, 11 LZZ 250 and 299 SC/SD 50) and 464 BSK (16,074 incendiaries), entirely by DR or radio navigation due to total cloud cover over London which effectively cut off all sight of the ground. Nevertheless, around 2055 hours a large explosion, followed by a spreading fire glow, penetrated the cloud, but the exact position could not be determined. Bombing accuracy could not be verified and it was impossible to assess the effectiveness of the attack. All the attackers belonged to Luftflotte 3 and comprised:

II/KG27: 2 He 111, 2040-2049
III/KG27: 6 He 111, 2040-2200
KGr100: 4 He 111, 2021-2050 (opened attack using X-Verfahren)
I/KG1: 8 He 111, 2130-2305
III/KG1: 14 Ju 88, 2115-2305
II/KG76: 15 Ju 88, 2125-2315
I/KG77: 11 Ju 88, 2103-2147
II/KG77: 8 Ju 88, 2132-2212
III/KG77: 8 Ju 88, 2200-2236
III/KG26: 11 He 111, 2112-2224 (bombing by means of Y-Verfahren)
KGr806: 6 Ju 88, 0020-0231

On this occasion 22 London boroughs reported bombing but most of it was on the north-east side of the city. Among the buildings damaged were St Pancras Church, St Pancras Hospital, a school at Dagenham and the Custom House School at West Ham. Again, utility services suffered, as did residential and commercial premises, telephone, road and rail communications, but no serious damage was caused to military establishments or factories. There was also widespread bombing in East Anglia, with five people killed in Essex and nine more in Portsmouth, where damage was not severe. Bombs also fell in surrounding districts including the Isle of Wight; two people were also killed in Brighton and two more near Worthing. There was also some minor bombing in Scotland. Only at Portsmouth, however, were there any fires of note (in the barracks and in the dockyard), but they were quickly brought under control and no serious consequences resulted.

Free balloon barrages were released during the night from Kidbrooke and from Chigwell and it was optimistically reported that one enemy aircraft 'may have encountered the barrage at 0114 hours near Winchester' — three explosions were reported by the Observer Corps and the raider was said to have changed course and immediately recrossed the coast. Forty-two night fighters flew uneventful patrols and the guns of AA Command fired about 6,000 rounds, also without success. Within the IAZ the guns were in action from 2004 to 0245 hours, using 1,269 rounds of 4.5-inch, 1,366 rounds of 3.7-inch and 40 rounds of 3-inch ammunition. HAA guns were also in action at Portsmouth, Thames and Medway (North and South), Holton Heath, Slough, Dover, Brooklands, Gloucester, North Weald, Plymouth, Mersey, and Weston-super-Mare.

MONDAY, MARCH 10-11

Sunset: 1855 Sunrise: 0725
Moon: Dusk — 0609 (Full −3)

Major attack on Portsmouth. Widespread minor activity and minelaying.

UK — Little or no cloud in the South with visibility moderate to good but poor locally inland. Some showers in the South-West. Low cloud with drizzle and considerable fog patches in the North-East, eventually affecting much of eastern England except the South-East.

There was a resident caretaker and each shelter could accommodate 48 people.

The Continent — Well broken cloud but local thundery showers, particularly in Brittany. Moderate to good visibility, deteriorating generally with local mist in inland areas of northern France and the Low Countries.

German daylight activity was mainly confined to the English Channel and South-East England, where three bomb incidents were reported. Some damage was done in Chichester but elsewhere damage was negligible.

Nightfall brought with it the heaviest attack by the Luftwaffe since the raid on Manchester on December 22. Portsmouth was the target for 244 aircraft of Luftflotten 2 and 3 with 238 crews claiming to have reached and bombed the important naval base and city. Bombing was almost exclusively visual and because of this the attack was assessed as very successful. The claimed bomb load consisted of 193 tonnes of HE (12 SC 1000, two SD 1000, 52 SC 500, four SD 500, 389 SC 250, 52 LZZ 250, 673 SC 50 and 222 SD 50) and 1,291 BSK (46,476 IBs). Observed results included a particularly big and developing fire area and several smaller fires in the vicinity of Basins 1 and 2 of the shipyard and the Vosper works. Numerous fires covered the entire Target Area before the attack, which began at 2000 hours, ended at 0245.

Luftflotte 3's contribution was 178 aircraft, 175 of which reached Portsmouth while only three aborted. The attackers comprised:

I/KG27: 10 He 111, 2016-2057
II/KG27: 18 He 111, 2014-2120
III/KG27: 9 He 111, 2020-2114
KGr100: 11 He 111, 2005-2040
KGr806: 15 Ju 88, 0000-0245
Stab/KG55: 5 He 111, 0105-0122
III/KG55: 16 He 111, 0005-0058
I/KG1: 12 He 111, 2335-0055
III/KG1: 14 Ju 88, 2350-0015
II/KG76: 10 Ju 88, 0005-0150
II/KG76: 3 Ju 88, 2008-2020 Dive-bomb attacks (4,000 metres to 2,000 metres) on west part of target GB 12 32 — Dry Docks in Basin No. 3 and in Target Area 'b'
I/KG77: 14 Ju 88, 0050-0146
II/KG77: 13 Ju 88, 2327-0142
III/KG77: 8 Ju 88, 0004-0043
III/KG26: 4 He 111, 2020-2130 (Y-Verfahren bombing)
III/KG26: 13 He 111, 2349-0124 (Y-Verfahren bombing)

Two aircraft of Luftflotte 3 were lost after reporting over the target, a Ju 88 of III/KG1 failing to return and an He 111 of I/KG1 crashing near its base killing the crew of four.

Serious fires were started at both Portsmouth and Gosport where public buildings, residential property and commercial premises were damaged or destroyed. At Portsmouth more than 30 people were killed and another 17 lost their lives in incidents at Gosport. Fires and damage from HEs were also reported at Fareham. Utility services — and particularly the electricity system — were damaged, but road and railway communications were not seriously affected. The Roman Catholic Cathedral, St Luke's School and the Coliseum Theatre were among the buildings damaged. A number of neighbouring towns were also involved including Southampton, Hamble, Selsey, Littlehampton and the Isle of Wight, but the most serious damage occurred at Portsmouth where fires involved the petrol and oil storage tanks, the Naval Dockyard and the Royal Naval Barracks.

Minor bombing was also reported on a number of towns, aerodromes and rural districts in Norfolk, Lincolnshire and Yorkshire while at Crewe a power station was machine-gunned but without apparent damage. Bombs also fell at Minster (Sheppey), in the Scilly Isles and at Langley.

Although built of bricks, this shelter in Middlesborough, built with the correct mix of cement just six weeks previously, stood the test of a bomb dropping just five feet away. All those sheltering inside were unharmed. 'In this way', the 1941 caption writer claimed, 'we are defeating the bombs and the morale is unshaken.'

The Portsmouth and Southampton guns, in action from 2001 to 0355 hours, fired 3,300 rounds; countrywide some 6,000 rounds were used for the claimed destruction of four enemy aircraft. Night fighter patrols were flown by 114 aircraft, including five Intruder missions by Blenheims of No. 23 Squadron and Fighter Night patrols (between Selsey Bill and Beachy Head) by aircraft of Nos. 264, 610 and 616 Squadrons. One Spitfire of 610 Squadron intercepted an He 111 at 13,000 feet and after an attack, in which the fighter closed to 30 yards range, the enemy aircraft was seen to dive into the sea. In addition a Ju 88 was destroyed off Linney Head and another aircraft of the same type forced landed near Sutton Bridge.

One aircraft was lost during the day:

3(F)/123 Messerschmitt Bf 110E-3 (2316). During action in the Channel aircraft believed to have crashed into the sea off Portsmouth. St.Fw. H. Ziegenbalk missing. Fw. W. Ruschenburg killed. Aircraft 4U+XL lost.

Although several large raids appeared over Britain at night, only two aircraft were lost, one of which was a night intruder in search of RAF bombers.

9/KG1 Junkers Ju 88A-5 (3354). Presumed shot down by AA fire during a raid on Portsmouth. Crashed into the sea off Ryde, Isle of Wight 12.58 a.m. Uffz. W. Benne killed. Uffz. E. Hofmann, Uffz. J. Stöcklein and Uffz. K. Kugler missing. Aircraft V4+IT destroyed.

1/NJG2 Junkers Ju 88C-2 (0343). On intruder sortie aircraft suffered engine failure and made a belly landing at Hay Green, Terrington St Clement, Norfolk 11.30 p.m. Oblt. K. Hermann, Uffz. E. Bottner and Fw. W. Rüppel taken prisoner. Aircraft R4+CH captured damaged and transported to Farnborough.

Following Government advice, surface shelters, trenches and reinforced basements had been provided extensively in shops, offices and factories. In May 1941 Defence Regulation 23AA empowered local authorities to close any unsafe or unhygienic shelters in private premises. Although many of the commercial shelters had qualified for a Government grant, no further money was made available for improving defective shelters although the Inland Revenue agreed to look on such expenses as allowable expenditure for relief against income tax. Here a reinforced concrete shelter in Quin and Axten's in Brixton has withstood a direct hit on the store.

TUESDAY, MARCH 11-12

Sunset: 1856 Sunrise: 0723
Moon: Dusk — 0641 (Full −2)

Major attack on Birmingham. Secondary attack on Southampton and minor operations against airfields and other targets, including shipping. Night reconnaissance.

UK — Low cloud with moderate to poor visibility in eastern England. Elsewhere variable cloud, fine locally, but with thundery showers in extreme South-West. Deteriorating conditions spreading westwards from the East with local mist or fog developing inland.

The Continent — Low cloud over Holland with moderate to poor visibility. Variable broken cloud over northern France, thundery in the North-West, but low cloud with mist or fog spreading into northern France later.

Minor daylight activity resulted in a few bombs in West Suffolk and Essex soon after sunrise, but no other incidents were reported.

Ringing the changes with a switch from port to industrial targets, the Luftwaffe carried out a major night attack on Birmingham with 135 aircraft of Luftflotten 2 and 3. They dropped 122 tonnes of HE (two SC 1800, 22 SC 1000, 50 SC 500, 216 SC 250, 23 LZZ 250 and 236 SC 50) and 830 BSK (29,880 incendiaries) between 2030 and 2357 hours. No specific target was laid down for most participating crews — the town itself being their objective — but some, almost certainly including III/KG26 using Y-Verfahren, were given a Concentration Point in north-west Birmingham between the railway and a canal where industrial plants were situated.

Some crews were able to bomb visually through breaks in the cloud, but most of the attackers were obliged to fall back on radio navigation and DR. The observation of results was also hindered but a large fire in east Birmingham and burning oil tanks or gas holders in the west were reported, together with two very large conflagrations in the industrial area to the north-east of the city centre. Numerous small fires covered the entire built-up area. However, as an attack on an industrial centre the raid was considered moderately successful only.

Luftflotte 3 bore the main weight of the attack, dispatching 177 crews but only 113 reported over the city. Sixty crews went to alternative targets and four aborted. Five more crews were sent to attack airfields (Boscombe Down, Plymouth/Roborough, Abingdon, Harwell and the Hawker Aircraft factory at Langley), eight were sent on shipping armed reconnaissance and one on a night reconnaissance mission to Portsmouth and Cardiff, using flares to illuminate both cities. No losses were sustained by Luftflotte 3 and the following units reported bombing Birmingham between the times stated:

I/KG27: 7 He 111, 2155-2250
II/KG27: 4 He 111, 2115-2153
III/KG27: 2 He 111, 2114-2135
KGr100: 9 He 111, 2105-2150 (6 aircraft bombed visually, 3 by means of X-Verfahren)
KGr806: 12 Ju 88, 2030-2330
Stab/KG55: 2 He 111, 2205-2225
III/KG55: 11 He 111, 2155-2255
II/KG76: 22 Ju 88, 2055-2258
I/KG77: 11 Ju 88, 2123-2347
II/KG77: 14 Ju 88, 2148-2302
III/KG77: 5 Ju 88, 2300-2333
III/KG26: 14 He 111, 2100-2238 (bombing by Y-Verfahren)

As a designated alternative Southampton was attacked by the following aircraft of Luftflotte 3:

I/KG27: 5 He 111, 2016-2305 (all new, inexperienced crews)
II/KG27: 16 He 111, 2125-2202 (all diverted to Southampton by order of the Gruppenkommandeur)
III/KG27: 5 He 111, 2032-2230
KGr100: 4 He 111, 2214-2258 (diverted to Southampton following X-System failure)
KGr806: 6 Ju 88, 2025-2225
III/KG55: 3 He 111, 2145-2245
II/KG76: 5 Ju 88, 2135-2258
I/KG77: 1 Ju 88, 2210
II/KG77: 1 Ju 88, 2219
III/KG77: 1 Ju 88, 2337
III/KG26: 2 He 111, 2237 and 2255 (Y-Verfahren faulty over Birmingham)

A looming threat to Britain in March — apart from the renewed spring offensive by the Luftwaffe — was that posed to the Atlantic convoys, now even more important than ever with the passing of the Lend-Lease Bill on Tuesday by the House of Representatives by 317 votes to 71. Here at home, during the heavy raid on Birmingham, bombs fell in Priory Road, Edgbaston, just a few hundred yards from the family home of one of the city's greatest statesmen: Neville Chamberlain, who had died four months earlier after a long illness.

1. *We must take the offensive against the U-boat and the Focke-Wulf wherever we can and whenever we can. The U-boat at sea must be hunted, the U-boat in the building yard or in dock must be bombed. The Focke-Wulf and other bombers employed against our shipping must be attacked in the air and in their nests.*
3. *All the measures approved and now in train for the concentration of the main strength of the Coastal Command upon the North-Western approaches, and their assistance on the East Coast by Fighter and Bomber Commands, will be pressed forward . . . All the more important is that the Focke-Wulf and, if it comes, the Junkers 88, should be effectively grappled with.*
6. *The Admiralty will have the first claim on all short-range AA guns and other weapons that they can mount upon suitable merchant ships plying in the danger zone . . .*
7. *We must be ready to meet concentrated air attacks on the ports on which we specially rely (Mersey, Clyde and Bristol Channel). They must therefore be provided with a maximum defence . . .*

WINSTON CHURCHILL
MARCH 6, 1941

Although, as we have seen, January's total of shipping sunk (76 ships) was the lowest for over six months, when the February figures reached Churchill the news was bad: 403,393 tons (of which over 300,000 tons were British merchantmen) lost from a combination of mines, aircraft, surface ships and U-Boats. Churchill revealed that the Atlantic was now his greatest worry a 'mortal danger to our life-lines' which 'gnawed my bowels'. As a result on March 6 the Prime Minister altered course from the bombing of Germany to give absolute priority to the 'Battle of the Atlantic'. His directive launching the attack was a lengthy document from which the above is but a brief extract yet its message was clear: for the next four months Bomber Command must aim its main effort against those targets which were, either directly or indirectly, the cause of the shipping losses. The Air Ministry passed the orders to Bomber Command on March 9 and a special 'Battle of the Atlantic Committee', under Churchill's chairmanship, sat from March to October to oversee the crisis. However the losses continued to mount: 139 ships in March (GRT 529,706) and 195 in April (GRT 687,901). In May, when continuous air cover was achieved right across the Atlantic for the first time, the total dropped slightly to 511,042 GRT. We now know that at this stage the Kriegsmarine had only 30 U-Boats deployed in the Atlantic, and that the real reason for their outstanding success was the decryption of the British Naval Cipher and the British and Allied Merchant Shipping code.

The four stages of the Bull Ring metamorphoses: pre-war, wartime, under construction in 1959 and completion in 1967 as illustrated by Anthony Sutcliffe and Roger Smith in *Birmingham 1939-1970*. The fire depicted in 1941 is most probably that of April 9-10 or the following night.

All claimed to have bombed the docks and industrial installations at Southampton, dropping 38 tonnes of HE (one SC 1000, 16 SC 500, 79 SC 250, 16 LZZ 250 and 98 SC 50) and 196 BSK (7,056 IBs). With cloudless skies for much of the time bombing was mainly visual and numerous explosions and fires were seen, particularly between the Inner Dock and the gas works and also on a new test quay. Several particularly large explosions were reported in the town and on dock installations at the mouth of the River Itchen.

Another seven aircraft bombed Portsmouth and single aircraft attacked Plymouth, Bristol, Stoke and Worthing. Shipping was attacked in the vicinity of Falmouth, the Isle of Man and elsewhere.

Bombs fell very widely during the night with incidents reported in the North-East, in East Anglia, south-east England, the West and in Wales, but some concentration was achieved in the Manchester, Birmingham, Southampton-Portsmouth and London areas. Nine people were killed in Portsmouth and 17 in Southampton where some 20 fires were started; neighbouring districts were also affected and one person was killed in Newport, Isle of Wight. In the Midlands bombing was scattered and good firefighting did much to reduce the amount of damage caused; six people were killed in this Region. The worst hit area was Manchester, where a number of fires were started. Thirteen people were killed in Manchester, five in Salford and one at Hyde, but unlike the December raids on Manchester the city centre was not greatly involved — most of the damage occurred in industrial and suburban districts. Six important factory installations were hit but five suffered only slight damage. London's damage and casualties were not heavy. Other places reporting bombs included Southfleet, Brighton, near Bournemouth, Basingstoke, Barnet, Harrow, Truro, Plymouth, Nottingham, Coventry, Burton-on-Trent, West Bromwich, Moseley, Redditch, Witton, Erdington, Swinton, Stretford, Leek, Congleton, Sutton Coldfield, Boston and at various points in Caernarvon, Kent and Sussex.

The Birmingham guns were in action from 2000 to 0030 hours and fired 5,127 rounds of 3.7-inch and 90 rounds of 4.5-inch ammunition. AA Command as a whole expended nearly 7,000 rounds, with batteries engaging the enemy at Fareham, Brooklands, Slough, Plymouth, Thames and Medway (North), Bristol, Manchester, Mersey, Gloucester, Crewe, Portland, Newport, Dover, Harwich and Holton Heath.

Forty-one night fighters were operating, including two on Intruder patrols over northern France, and a number of inconclusive contacts were reported. A free balloon barrage was released at 2043 hours but no successes were claimed.

Besides that listed below, a Heinkel He 111 from the Geschwader Stab KG26 went missing from a sortie to the west coast of Scotland and a Heinkel He 59 fell to the guns of a No. 220 Squadron Hudson off Esbjerg. In addition, a Messerschmitt Bf 110 of 5(F)/122 was lost during a reconnaissance mission to Portsmouth.

3(F)/123 Messerschmitt Bf 110C-5 (2309). Shot down by 3 Spitfires of No. 234 Squadron. Crashed into the sea 20 miles south-west of Portland 5.40 p.m. Lt. W. Gössmann and Uffz. G. Hippe missing. Aircraft 4U+SL lost.

WEDNESDAY, MARCH 12-13

Sunset: 1858 Sunrise: 0720
Moon: Dusk — 0712 (Full −1)

Major attack on Liverpool/Birkenhead, minor attacks on many other areas, minelaying off the East Coast and attacks on shipping.

UK — Mainly cloudless, but moderate to poor visibility with mist or fog in some districts later in the night.

The Continent — Cloudless in north-eastern France and the Low Countries with good visibility. In north-western France lowering cloud with occasional rain and strong winds reaching gale force on coasts. Visibility good but poor in rain.

Apart from a few fighter and fighter-bomber sweeps over Ashford, Folkestone and Dover, and a machine gun attack on Hawkinge airfield when two bombs were also dropped, there was little activity during daylight hours. The Luftwaffe made up for this after dark, however, when 373 aircraft were sent over Britain with 316 of them attacking Merseyside.

The main objective on Merseyside was Birkenhead where the Schwerpunkt was centred on the docks, shipyards and granaries. Another CP, allocated to other units, lay on the most southerly of the oil cake mills adjacent to the soap factory and whale oil store on Bromborough Docks. Favourable weather enabled all participating crews to bomb visually and good results were anticipated. Only the most southerly targets (an

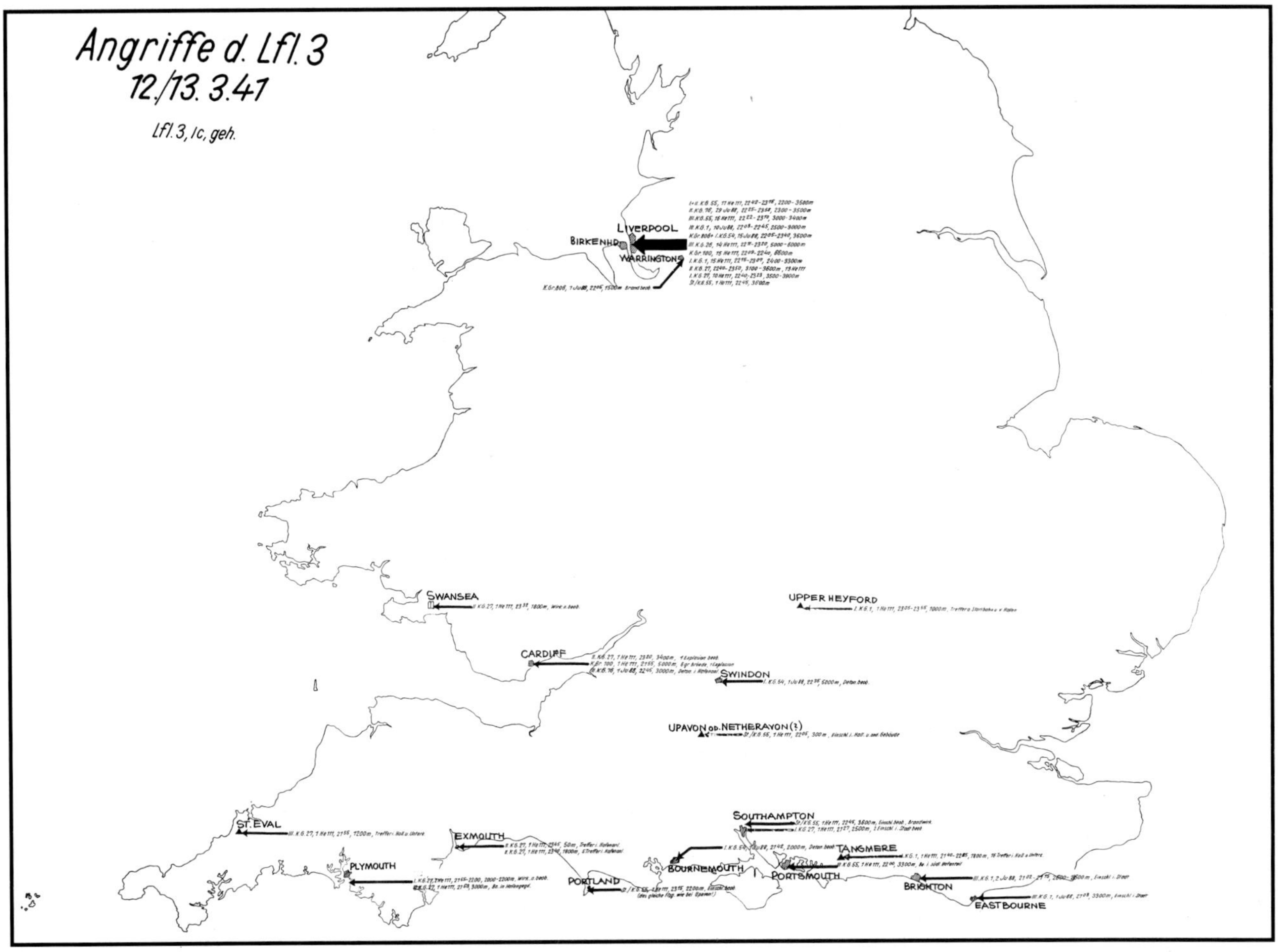

Angriffe d. Lfl. 3
12./13.3.41
Lfl. 3, Ic, geh.

LIVERPOOL
BIRKENHEAD
WARRINGTON
SWANSEA
CARDIFF
SWINDON
UPPER HEYFORD
UPAVON od. NETHERAVON (?)
ST. EVAL
PLYMOUTH
EXMOUTH
PORTLAND
BOURNEMOUTH
SOUTHAMPTON
PORTSMOUTH
TANGMERE
BRIGHTON
EASTBOURNE

oil cake mill and margarine factory on the banks of the Mersey) could not be precisely located, because of mist, and crews allocated these objectives bombed other targets in Birkenhead. Crews subsequently reported hits on shipyards, mills and granaries, cattle yards, cold stores and the slaughter house. Oil storage tanks at the west end of the West Float, the power station and the gas works to the west of the Camell Laird shipyards were also claimed showered with incendiary bombs. Numerous fires in and around the ordered target areas were discerned, particularly in the docks area.

The attack lasted from 2100 to 0309 hours and the raiders, drawn from both Luftflotten 2 and 3, dropped 303 tonnes of HE, 1,782 BSK (64,152 incendiaries) and 40 LC 50 parachute flares. Unusually the aircraft of Luftflotte 2 outnumbered those of Luftflotte 3, the former air fleet putting 170 bombers over the target. Luftflotte 3 dispatched 169 aircraft, of which 146 reached the target, 11 bombed alternative targets, six aborted and six failed to return. Another aircraft, an He 111 of III/KG26, crashed and burnt out near Amiens airfield. Crews reporting over the target were:

I/KG27: 10 He 111, 2140-2223
II/KG27: 10 He 111, 2140-2250
KGr100: 15 He 111, 2109-2140 (visual bombing; out of X-Verfahren range)
I and II/KG55: 11 He 111, 2142-2216 (flare assisted visual bombing)

The crew of Ju 88 F1+BT of the 9th Staffel of KG76 pictured shortly before their last and final mission — to Liverpool on Wednesday night. L-R: Feldwebel Meier, observer; Feldwebel Unger, pilot; Oberfeldwebel Dirk, flight engineer, and Unteroffizier Bergmann, the wireless operator/gunner. Just as their bombs were released the aircraft was hit. . . .

KGr806: 15 Ju 88, 2105-2240
III/KG55: 16 He 111, 2122-2210
Stab/KG55: 1 He 111, 2145
I/KG51: 15 He 111, 2115-2207
III/KG51: 10 He 111, 2103-2145
II/KG76: 29 Ju 88, 2125-2258 (allocated Camell Laird shipyard, Clover, Clayton & Co shipyard, cattle unloading dock, slaughter yards and cold storage depot)
III/KG26: 14 He 111, 2111-2220 (Y-Verfahren bombing from between 5,000 and 6,000 metres. Beam accuracy checked visually; 4 direct hits on docks target)

I looked round and saw a small but very bright glow on the cowling immediately behind the starboard engine. The metal was actually burning, which meant that there must have been intense heat, probably from a fire inside the nacelle. At first the visible spot of fire was very small; but it grew rapidly and flames began to trail behind the aircraft. I could see there was no hope of our getting home so I ordered the crew to bale out. The flight engineer opened the escape hatch at the rear of the cabin and jumped, followed by the radio operator. As they left I turned the bomber until it was pointing out to sea, so that when it crashed there would be nothing for the enemy to find. As I left my seat the observer dropped out of the hatch. The Junkers was flying properly trimmed, flying straight and level perfectly well on two engines. For a moment I considered trying to get home alone, but a further glance at the blaze made it clear that this would have been impossible; I clambered to the rear, and followed my crew out of the hatch.

GÜNTHER UNGER, 1976

Crews reported seeing four night fighters and flak over the target was strong and well directed; searchlight activity was said to be trivial. One aircraft of II/KG76 was attacked by a night fighter over the South Coast but succeeded in escaping. Those less fortunate and which failed to return included two He 111s of KG55, two more aircraft of the same type belonging to II/KG27 and III/KG26, and a Ju 88 of II/KG76.

In addition to the main raid on Merseyside other aircraft of Luftflotte 3 attacked the airfields at Boscombe Down, Upavon, Tangmere, Upper Heyford, St Athan, St Eval and Exeter (one aircraft visiting each); single aircraft were also sent to Cardiff, Southampton and Yeovil, where the Westland Aircraft factory was the target. Finally, four aircraft were dispatched on sea reconnaissance missions.

Evening Despatch picture of the Junkers 88 which crashed last night in a West Midland village. The crew baled out some miles away from the scene.

Having trimmed his aircraft to fly westwards out over the Irish Sea where he hoped it would come down without trace, Günther Unger was amazed to receive a letter forty years later from the Warplane Wreck Investigation Group telling him that far from disappearing at sea, his Junkers had performed an about turn and flown another 100 miles before crashing in this field at Wychbold, Worcestershire. (Out of interest we have left on the original wartime caption.)

It seemed to Unger to be almost untrue until he returned to the spot and was shown a serial plate found on the crash site which corresponded with the number of his aircraft given in German records. At The Croft (*left*) he met Squadron Leader Harry Newton who presented him with a Luftwaffe dress dagger in memory of the day when they had met briefly as adversaries on August 18, 1940 when each shot the other down during the 9/KG76 attack on Kenley. (The loss is not listed in Volume 1 because the Dornier came down in the Channel and the crew were rescued by the Kriegsmarine.)

Willi Weisse, Karl Brüning, Konrad Steiger and Alexander Düssel, with their Heinkel of the 5th Staffel of KG55 decorated up to celebrate its 100th mission.

My story is one which ended with the deaths of my three friends, Düssel, Weisse and Steiger, and brought me six and a half years of captivity. The Lord God may know why all this happened to me. It was March 12, 1941. My last flight over enemy territory had been in November the previous year. At Christmas and New Year I was in the Homeland. From January until March we flew no more sorties due to the rain which had made the runways at our base of Chartres very muddy. The day before we had left for Avord, south of Chartres, from where we could use the hard runways and start with a load of bombs. As only a few sorties were foreseen from Avord we only took the most important things, but with our ground crew, technical equipment, spares and our own kit the aircraft was fully laden. On the 12th our first mission started. The target was Birkenhead. My observer, Oberleutnant von Dem Hagen, had been detained at Chartres for administrative duties. So I took Feldwebel Alexander Düssel. Feldwebel Konrad Steiger was the wireless operator and Oberfeldwebel Willi Weisse the flight mechanic.

At 2100 hours we left in our He III G1+GN, which had replaced the G1+GN lost on August 26, 1940. We crossed the English coast at 5,000 metres. The weather was good, with few clouds, excellent visibility and moonlight. I suppose it was perfect for nightfighter operations. There was no flak and no searchlights. On account of my experiences, I felt we could expect fighters, so I put my crew on the alert. Then, without them noticing anything, all hell was let loose.

We were surprised with many direct hits and the aeroplane caught fire. Both engines were hit and stopped at once. The oil temperature shot up and the speed fell. The aircraft lost height and I was completely preoccupied with trying to control the machine. Through the intercom I heard the screaming and groaning of Steiger and Weisse, both of whom seemed to be seriously wounded. My left hand on the throttle and left ankle were injured, being outside the protection of the 8mm armour plate behind me, but I felt only light blows and no pain. Düssel seemed unhurt, so I told him to go back and see to Steiger and Weisse and throw them out after preparing their parachutes. I could see no other chance of hanging on to life. There was no way I could bring the aeroplane down as the situation was desperate. Hopeless! Düssel came back and said he could not reach them as the gangway was ablaze. Steiger and Weisse, if they were still alive, would have to take their own destiny into their hands. They were on their own now. I couldn't tell if they could hear me, but I called 'Ready to Jump'. Düssel jumped immediately through the side hatch. On the order 'Jump' he had already gone. I think he jumped without a parachute. I don't know why, but perhaps his pack was in the fire and maybe he preferred to die that way rather than be burnt or die in a crash. Poor Alexander.

I trimmed the machine carefully in order to be able to jump out well myself. Good old G1+GN still responded! I examined my parachute carefully as it was my only means of escape. Then I opened the sliding roof to jump from my seat but realised I would be jumping into the fire, so I decided to go from the side hatch. As I left my seat I saw the night fighter in front of my cockpit, and only 10 to 20 metres away. He was making a left turn in order to pull away to the rear to start a new attack. I had to jump quickly!

As I was afraid of falling into the tail unit I tried to jump forwards, with hands and feet pulled in tight but I couldn't overcome the slipstream. I lost my strength and let go and was thrown about turbulently in the air. Several seconds must have passed before I opened the parachute. It cracked open and with rushing lurching movements I fell earthwards. Below me I saw the aeroplane spiralling earthwards in flames. At about 2,000 metres I saw it impact and explode violently.

I made a soft landing in a clump of bushes and managed to free myself from the parachute and harness. I was in a daze and the previous twenty minutes went before me slowly, in detail, like a movie. Despite my wounds I felt nothing of them. After a while I began to shout and then, in the bright moonlight, I saw two people approaching me. They called 'Hands up'. I did not understand and went closer to them when they were able to see that I did not intend to harm them and, indeed, needed help. I waved and they hesitantly came nearer. I soon realised that they were kindly disposed towards me and I gave the man my pistol and holster and made him understand that he could keep them as souvenirs and that I would say later I had possessed no weapons. In exchange an offer of cigarettes took place. The woman with this man saw my bleeding hand and wanted to bandage it with her own handkerchief. I indicated my front pocket from where she took out my two packets of field dressings. She said something, and 'very good', which I understood. She bandaged my hand carefully and in a kindly, caring way. I was surprised, especially when she made me understand 'Evacuated from London'. This is still in my memory today. If I could only see those two people again I would be very glad to meet them. I would be really grateful.

Slowly we walked together and came to a Home Guard post where I was handed over. At the outpost I was treated well and hospitably; they gave me tea and cigarettes. My foot was now hurting so I took my boot off. It was badly injured and bleeding and from then I could not walk properly on it. Shortly afterwards a truck came with soldiers and took me to a bigger place. Here, I was made to strip naked and this is not easy with one hand and standing on one foot! They took away all my belongings, then took me, naked, to an interrogation room. There I was interrogated until morning. I laid the wounded leg on a wooden stool and it was not long before the blood was flowing freely onto the floor. Sometimes the stool was kicked away from me. I shall not go further into this interrogation or the ones that

Thursday morning down on Dene Farm, Ockley.

Plater 35 left Tangmere at 1945 hours and was vectored from Beachy Head to the Inner Artillery Zone. No contact was made with enemy aircraft so returned to Beachy Head and orbited. Was then vectored on to a second raid and after a second and third vector Sgt. Gash picked up a bandit at 800 yards, about 700 feet above and flying on a parallel course on the port beam. The enemy was approached under the starboard wing and identified as a He III. Enemy Aircraft was then engaged from 50 yards from this position with a series of one second bursts. First burst started a small fire in the starboard engine whilst the next two bursts set the engine thoroughly on fire. At this juncture, the reflector sight went out. Carrying on with night tracer Sgt. Gash transferred his attention to the cabin and fired several more one second bursts. The de-Wilde ammunition could be seen bursting in the cabin, which forthwith filled with flames. The bandit then fell off in a left hand spiral dive and plunged to earth where the bomb load exploded. The position of the aircraft has now been traced to Oakwood Hill, south of Dorking, and it turns out that one of the crew baled out and is now at Horsham. Another member of the crew baled out but his parachute did not open. The new ammunition was extremely good and the controller reports this was partly a C.L. interception. My gunner fired with his perspex closed. I landed at Biggin Hill at 2125 hours having expended 1000 rounds.

COMBAT REPORT, DEFIANT N1801, MARCH 12, 1941

As for the attacking aircraft which Karl Brüning (*left*) had glimpsed briefly through the perspex whilst on the point of baling out, this is easy to identify as being a Defiant of No. 264 Squadron from Biggin Hill. Defiant N1801, PS-B, departed from Tangmere at 7.45 p.m. for a defensive patrol flown by Flying Officer F. Hughes and his gunner, Sergeant F. Gash, both experienced night fighters. Their report ties in well with the known facts of the Ockley crash and the account of Karl Brüning, though the time discrepancy can be attributed to the different clock time in use on either side of the Channel.

followed, which sometimes went beyond the limits of what was permitted. Then they showed me a cigarette case, which I identified as Düssel's. He was dead they said, so were the others. So, I was the only survivor. To keep me going through the night they gave me meat broth and tea, with some cigarettes.

It was a dreadful time that night, but in the morning I was dressed and taken for medical attention at Horsham Hospital. I found that my Iron Cross had been stolen from my tunic, which made me sad, but I was alive. At the hospital I was operated on immediately. On waking from the anaesthetic I found myself in a single room, a soldier with a pistol sitting by my bed. A friendly nursing sister brought me a glass of milk and yet more cigarettes! Soon I was taken away by an officer, despite much protest from the doctor. I was sent to an interrogation camp and was kept in isolation for a week and almost constantly questioned. I had to clean handcuffs and rub down shovel handles with glass paper almost non-stop. The only joy in the day was the visit from the doctor and medical orderlies who often managed to get me a 'fag'. After a week I went by rail to Bury PoW camp to begin my long imprisonment. This ended in July 1947 when I came home to Rheine and my family. Later I joined the post-war Luftwaffe, and left the service in 1976. On my last day as a serving airman my thoughts turned to Steiger, Weisse and Düssel. What would they have made of this old man, their Karl, in Luftwaffe uniform more than thirty years on? I had had some luck; theirs ran out on March 12, 1941.

KARL BRÜNING, AUGUST 1978

In 1978 plans were laid by the Air Historical Group to investigate the crash of G1+GN which had scattered wreckage across four fields. The excavation of the impact point unearthed a quantity of wreckage including parts of the ventral gondola with its armour plating showing signs of bullet strikes. Amongst the wreckage a maker's plate confirming 2994 was discovered, together with a small quantity of human bones. (These could only have originated from the bodies of Steiger and Weisse, both of whom were officially recovered from the wreckage, identified and buried in Horsham Cemetery in 1941. Interred beside them was the body of their colleague, Alexander Düssel, having been found lying dead in Lintotts Field, Holbrook Park, near Fivens Green to the north-west of Horsham. All three have since been moved and reburied at Cannock Chase Soldatenfriedhof.) Then a green-painted triangle of steel plate was unearthed, painted with a broad yellow stripe, which was immediately identified as the fin from an SC 500 and, as a result, the Army bomb disposal team were called in: No. 49 Explosive Ordnance Disposal Squadron from Chattenden in Kent under Major Barry Birch (who had also defuzed one of the bombs uncovered in Epping Forest from the Ju 88 which crashed there on the night of December 8-9 — see page 330). A single 500kg was located at a depth of several feet and examination revealed that the weapon, originally bound for Merseyside, was still in pristine condition, allowing Major Birch and his team to carry out a textbook neutralising operation.

When the first raids took place on Merseyside in August 1940 the area's fighter defences by night were virtually non existent and, to provide at least a semblance of protection, No. 96 Squadron was formed on December 18 from No. 422 Flight formerly at Shoreham. Its aircraft were Hurricanes and its CO Squadron Leader R. G. Kellett. Their base was at Cranage, just north of Byley in mid-Cheshire, ideally placed, it was hoped, to catch enemy raiders to Manchester and Liverpool.

Bombs fell on every Civil Defence Region during the night, but Merseyside bore the brunt of the onslaught with particularly heavy attacks on Birkenhead and Wallasey. The attack was mainly concentrated on the dock area and in Birkenhead, where residential areas were also badly hit, many fires were started and serious damage resulted. Residential property in Wallasey was also extensively damaged while a number of fires, some of them of major proportions, broke out in both Liverpool and Bootle. Initial casualty figures were 264 killed in Birkenhead, 198 in Wallasey and 49 in Liverpool. The widespread damage to houses caused many accommodation problems and when four out of twelve Rest Centres were damaged the situation became acute. A large number of people left the district on subsequent nights but overcrowding of the larger shelters remained a difficulty. Fortunately considerable help was provided by the military, who helped with firefighting, first aid, rescue work and the evacuation of the homeless and those whose homes were threatened by the many UXBs which littered the area. Dockside installations and equipment suffered considerably in this attack and fires broke out in warehouses, sheds, timber yards and offices. Utility services, too, were seriously affected, as was the railway system. The University, the Cotton Exchange and St Anne's School were damaged and in Birkenhead three hospitals and the art school were damaged.

Bombs also fell during the night on Warrington, Bolton, Runcorn, Ormskirk, Barrow-in-Furness, Anglesey, Southampton, Eastbourne, Dagenham and many other districts of the North, North-East, South, West, the Midlands and Scotland. Two people were killed in Swansea, six in East Anglia and a few elsewhere, but outside of the Mersey area casualties and damage were generally light.

The Mersey AA defences were in action from 2048 to 0305 hours, firing 3,100 rounds at raiders flying between 6,500 and 22,000 feet. Over the country as a whole 12,000 rounds were used by HAA guns at Brooklands, Portsmouth, Southampton, Thames and Medway (North and South), the London IAZ, Gloucester, Slough, Bristol, Portland, Plymouth, Birmingham, Manchester, Humber, St Eval, Falmouth, Derby, Crewe, Sheffield, Swansea, Leeds, Dover, Tyne, Cardiff, Nottingham, Acklington, Tees and Harwich.

A record number of 261 fighters flew dusk, night and dawn patrols and, in the light of a moon only one night off full and in almost cloudless conditions, made a number of interceptions. Claims were duly made of four enemy aircraft destroyed, four probably destroyed and three damaged to augment AA Command claims of three destroyed, one probably destroyed and five damaged. Fighter Command detailed six Blenheims to carry out Intruder patrols over northern France and several German-occupied airfields were attacked. Only one of the large number of fighters operating was lost.

At 1945 hours a Defiant of No. 264 Squadron took off from Tangmere, flown by Flying Officer Frederick D. Hughes with air gunner Sergeant F. Gash, and headed for Beachy Head. From here the Defiant was vectored towards an enemy aircraft, but after approaching the IAZ, and without having made contact, the night fighter returned to Beachy Head and took up an orbit. After a while Hughes was directed after a second raider and after three vectors his gunner caught sight of an aircraft some 800 yards ahead and about 700 feet above. The other aircraft was identified as an He 111 and after closing in to 50 yards Gash opened fire with a

Today the aerodrome has disappeared almost without trace as the M6 motorway carves its way across the north-eastern corner.

Pilots identified in this February-March shot at a rather muddy Cranage are Flying Officer V. Vesely (left) and Flying Officer J. Kloboucnik, two of several Czechs serving with the squadron.

series of one second bursts from his four machine guns. Almost immediately the enemy aircraft's starboard engine caught fire and it spiralled down to crash at 2105 hours near Ockley, Surrey.

The German aircraft, an He 111P-4 of II/KG55, had taken off from Avord and was bound for Liverpool. Its pilot, Stabsfeldwebel Karl Brüning, was wounded in the hand and ankle but he managed to bale out and was taken prisoner. The other three members of his crew were killed.

Both Gash and Hughes also survived the war, the former Defiant pilot remaining in the post-war RAF to become an Air Vice-Marshal with the CB, CBE, DSO, DFC and two Bars, and AFC.

A second He 111 of II/KG55 was shot down on the night of March 12-13. Shortly after the G1+OP of 6 Staffel had bombed the docks at Birkenhead it was attacked from the rear by a Hurricane of No. 96 Squadron flown by Sergeant McNair. Both engines of the Heinkel failed and three members of its crew including the pilot, Oberfeldwebel Karl Single, and the observer/aircraft commander, Hauptmann Wolfgang Berlin, baled out. As the aircraft came down it struck a balloon cable and slewed around to crash into the ICI Recreation Field, Widnes, at 2210 hours.

The German aircraft had taken off from Avord at 1923 hours and on the way to Birkenhead, Wolfgang Berlin remembers, there was only a little AA fire and not much searchlight activity. 'The weather was fine and clear and a bright moon was lighting up all of southern England', Berlin continued. 'If I remember correctly we were flying at about 3,000 metres. After the attack on the docks at Birkenhead we turned for home and shortly afterwards our wireless operator/gunner, Unteroffizier Xaver Diem, reported on the interphone that a night fighter was coming up from the lower rear. Only seconds later bullets ripped through the Heinkel; this first burst killed our gunner, Feldwebel Heinrich Ludwinski, and flight mechanic/gunner Feldwebel Leonhard Kutznik. The second and third bursts put both our engines out of action so I ordered the radio operator to bale out. However, he was unable to open either of the two rear exits because of damage inflicted by the fighter so he had to crawl forward along the narrow passage between the bomb bay chutes to reach the cockpit. I opened the front emergency exit but by this time we were down to about 1,000 metres and rapidly getting lower. We remaining three — pilot, radio operator and me — then got out. As I descended by parachute I could see below me fenced meadows in the bright moonlight and men running in the direction of my point of landing which was in the middle of a field near a farmhouse. As soon as I landed the men arrived, shouting "Hands up!" They were members of the Home Guard, but I don't know how many. Then they guided me to the farmhouse and I was led into the living room where a homely fire was burning. It was very peaceful. The farmer then brought me a piece of buttered toast, so I knew I really was in England! My deep regret is that my schoolboy English was so poor, for I responded with "Thank you so much, madame"! Only the armed guard standing at the door reminded me that a war was going on.'

After a little while Hauptmann Berlin was escorted away by the police and then transferred under military escort for interrogation by AI1(k) at Cockfosters before proceeding to a PoW Camp. He was later sent to Canada and was repatriated to Germany in 1947.

In addition to the aircraft stated below two of the Luftwaffe losses included a Heinkel He 111 of Stab III/KG26 and a Heinkel He 111 of Stab KG27 which landed at St Malo with four injured crew after being attacked by a fighter.

4/KG27 Heinkel He 111H-4 (2705). Believed shot down by Flying Officer T. Welsh DFC and Sergeant H. Hayden DFM of No. 264 Squadron in a Defiant during a raid on Birkenhead. Crashed into the sea 15 miles south of Hastings 11.45 p.m. Lt. H. Robrahn, Oblt. H. von Jeinssen, Oberfw. E. Behrens and Oberfw. A. Welge all missing. Aircraft 1G+DM lost.

5/KG55 Heinkel He 111P-4 (2994). Shot down by Flying Officer F. D. Hughes and Sergeant F. Gash in a Defiant of No. 264 Squadron during a raid on Liverpool. Aircraft caught fire in air and exploded before hitting ground 9.30 p.m. at Dene Farm, Ockley, Surrey. St.Fw. K. Brüning baled out wounded and taken prisoner. Fw. A. Düssel baled out but killed when parachute failed. Fw. K. Steiger and Oberfw. W. Weisse killed. Aircraft G1+GN wrecked.

Site excavated by Simon Parry in 1977. Unexploded SC 500 bomb rendered safe by EOD team. Iron Cross made by Karl Brüning whilst in captivity presented to Andy Saunders.

Although the squadron began to convert to the Boulton-Paul Defiant in March most operational patrols were still being flown in the Hurricane. Some of the frustrations of the Czechs in their anxiety to get to grips with the enemy are revealed in their operational diary for March 14-15: 'It appears a great disadvantage that the squadron is not equipped with AI for locating the enemy as are the Beaufighters of another squadron which have achieved such great successes during the last three nights. The Defiant pilot has no guns of his own and must always manoeuvre the aircraft so that the gunner can open fire. The Operations Room can give the pilot only an approximate course towards the enemy and is unable to provide an approximate height. Often there is no visual contact. 'A' Flight is short of pilots and we have been at readiness for the last six days. The aircraft have a very small radius of action and the whole flight is made on a weak mixture. Many times we have landed with only a few gallons of fuel in the tanks.' Here Flying Officer Kloboucnik waits at readiness with trolley acc attached.

The squadron's first successful interception took place on the night of March 12-13 when Sergeant McNair in V7752 successfully intercepted a Heinkel over Liverpool. He was circling the fires at 12,000 feet when he spotted the bomber flying in a southerly direction. Closing to about 75 yards he opened his attack with two bursts of four seconds each. Oil from the bomber covered his windscreen but he pressed home several more attacks until it plunged to the ground at Widnes on what is now the sports field of the Fisher and More High School in Milton Road. He just scraped back to Cranage with tanks almost dry having been airborne for 2 hours 40 minutes.

6/KG55 Heinkel He 111P-4 (2989). Shot down by Sergeant McNair in a Hurricane of No. 96 Squadron during a raid on Liverpool. Crashed at Widnes, Lancashire. 10.10 p.m. Hptmn. W. Berlin, Oberfw. K. Single and Uffz. X. Diem baled out and taken prisoner. Fw. L. Kutznik and Fw. H. Ludwinski killed. Aircraft G1+OP burnt-out.

Site investigated by the Warplane Wreck Investigation Group but the area found to be in use as a rugby pitch.

6/KG76 Junkers Ju 88A-5 (6236). Shot down during a raid on Portsmouth by Flying Officer K. I. Geddes and Sergeant A. C. Cannon in a Beaufighter of No. 604 Squadron. Crashed at Kingston Deverill, Wilts. 10.45 p.m. Fw. K. Berger baled out and taken prisoner. Hptmn. H. Herrmann, Fw. J. Raue and Oberfw. H. Busch killed. Aircraft F1+OP destroyed.

9/KG76 Junkers Ju 88A-5 (7188). Damaged by Sergeant Jankowiak in a No. 307 Squadron Defiant and AA fire during a raid on Liverpool. Crew baled out over Merseyside and aircraft flew on to crash into trees and houses at The Croft, Wychbold, Worcestershire 10.20 p.m. Fw. G. Unger, Uffz. F. Bergmann, Fw. A. Meier and Oberfw. W. Dirk all baled out and were taken prisoner. Aircraft F1+BT destroyed.

Site investigated by Warplane Wreck Investigation Group. Pieces in Fort Perch Rock Museum and Hodgkiss Collection. Site revisited by surviving aircrew in 1980.

THURSDAY, MARCH 13-14

Sunset: 1900 Sunrise: 0718
Moon: 1919 — Dawn (Full Moon)

Major attack on Glasgow and Clydeside, heavy attack on Liverpool/Birkenhead and a lesser attack on Hull. Widely scattered minor bombing elsewhere including attacks on airfields, industrial works and dock installations. Minelaying and anti-shipping operations.

UK — Fair or fine with little cloud except in south-western England and south-west Wales where it was cloudy with rain locally. Visibility generally good but poor in rain in the South-West and in the lee of some large towns elsewhere. Winds variable in direction, light to moderate.

The Continent — Cloudy with rain locally in north-western France, elsewhere fair or fine with moderate to good visibility.

German daylight activity was of a very minor nature, with only a few bombs reported in the north of Scotland, but improved weather conditions resulted in night operations on a massive scale, with 431 long-range bombers and 15 light bombers engaged in widespread operations against multiple targets.

For the first time Glasgow and Clydeside received a major attack. From 2130 hours until 0547 the next morning the docks and industrial objectives in Glasgow and similar installations and shipyards along the Clyde were attacked by 236 aircraft of Luftflotten 2 and 3. They dropped 272 tonnes of HE and 1,650 BSK (59,400 IBs) in favourable weather conditions, all crews bombing visually. The ordered Target Areas were picked out with ease and were claimed effectively bombed without interference by the defences. In consequence the length of the Clyde reflected the light of numerous large fires, with more than 100 visible in Glasgow alone. Particularly large fire areas were seen on the north bank of the Clyde between Yoker and Dalmuir and from Scotstoun to the dock basin, with huge fires raging among warehouses in the docks on the south bank. One large ship was claimed hit and two more were reported on fire. It was also believed that the dense black smoke produced over west Glasgow came from oil tank installations located there, but so great was the mass of fires that identification of individual targets became impossible. In short, extremely good results were anticipated — and it was rare that the Führungsstab Intelligence IC Section made such an assessment.

The second heaviest attack of the night was directed at Liverpool/Birkenhead, where 65 aircraft of Luftflotte 3 dropped 58 tonnes of HE and 122 BSK (4,392 incendiaries) between 2100 and 2303 hours. Their targets were as on the previous night and, in good visibility, good results were claimed. Fires were seen in the cattle unloading docks, in the mills and granaries in the East Float and at Wallasey power station. Large explosions were also seen in the northerly part of Wallasey and in the southerly part of Birkenhead.

The third heavy attack was made on Hull, where 78 aircraft dropped 39 tonnes of HE

The Heinkel was from 6/KG55 and the three survivors later revealed that their target had been Birkenhead Docks. Immediately after the bombs had been released, they were attacked three times by a night fighter and both engines were put out of action. Three of the crew — the pilot, observer, and wireless operator — baled out at between 3 and 4,000 feet. The aircraft flew on for a short while then hit a balloon cable and crashed, killing the flight engineer and gunner who were still on board. Local folklore has it that the pilot was almost lynched by irate civilians but rescued by the police!

and 125 BSK (4,500 IBs) between 2201 and 0225 hours. Again, bombing was entirely visual on a CP — industrial and dock installations on the north side of the river — that was easily discernible in the good visibility and bright moonlight. Indeed, to improve their bombing accuracy, many crews made multiple runs over the target, dropping one bomb at a time instead of the more usual long 'stick' or salvo. Two large and many medium or small sized fires were started in the centre and south part of the target area, and thick smoke was thought to be emanating from an oil cake mill or granary.

Luftflotte 2's contribution to the night's operations is not known in detail, but Luftflotte 3 dispatched 137 aircraft to Glasgow (of which 129 reached and bombed their targets) and 81 to Liverpool (65 successfully). Overall, 13 crews attacked alternative targets and five aborted. Four aircraft were reported missing, three made forced landings in their own territory and one crashed on landing. In addition, three aircraft were sent to Southampton (with two reaching the target and one failing to return), one to Yeovil, and four on Channel reconnaissance and attacks on airfields. Those participating in the major raids were:

Glasgow:
III/KG26: 12 He 111, 2330-2355
II/KG55: 9 He 111, 2247-2340
II/KG27: 5 He 111, 2213-2225
I/KG1: 12 He 111, 2227-2330
I/KG27: 9 He 111, 2205-2232
I/KG27: 4 He 111, 2134-2150
III/KG1: 7 Ju 88, 2250-2317
KG77: 28 Ju 88, 2255-0254
III/KG1: 4 Ju 88, 0250
II/KG76: 15 Ju 88, 0222-0310
I/KG54: 12 Ju 88, 2148-2255
KGr100: 12 He 111, 2154-2225

Liverpool:
III/KG55: 12 He 111, 2100-2220
II/KG54: 6 Ju 88, 2146-2245
I/KG51: 2 Ju 88, 2125
II/KG51: 1 Ju 88, 2110
III/KG51: 4 Ju 88, 2117-2149
II/KG27: 7 He 111, 2207-2234
Stab/KG55: 1 He 111, 2305
I/KG55: 7 He 111, 2145-2203
II/KG76: 15 Ju 88, 2125-2215
III/KG27: 8 He 111, 2110-2150
I/KG27: 2 He 111, 2138

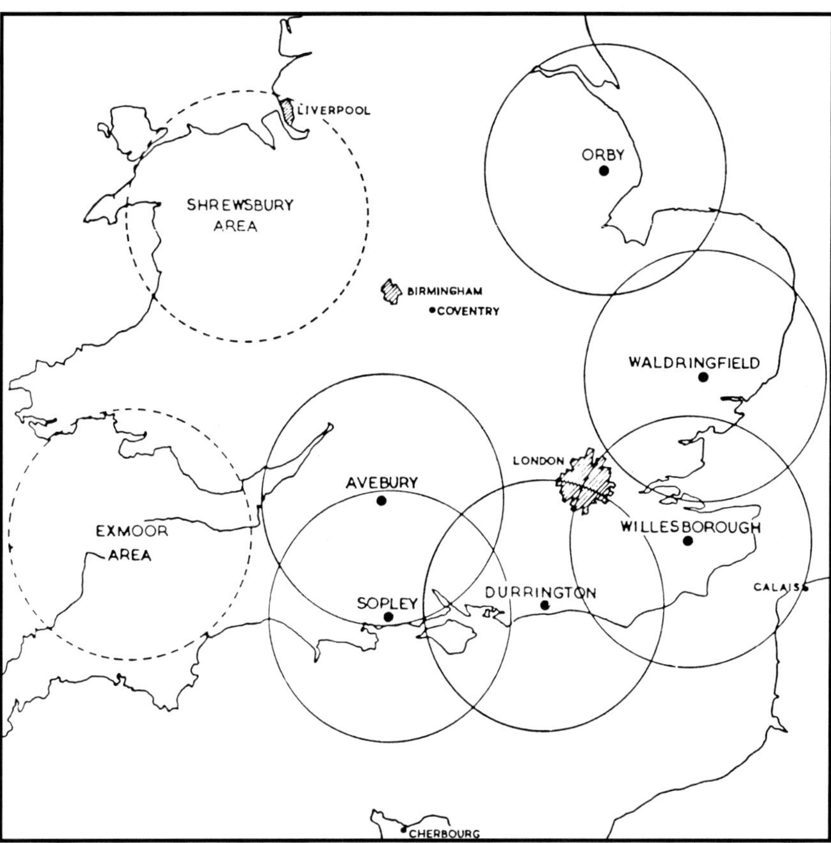

Following an agonising few months for the RAF, as impotent against the night raider as they had been successful with the daylight bomber, the night of March 12-13 was an occasion of justified jubilation. With five of the enemy knocked down within a couple of hours perhaps this was at last the turning point. Central to this success was Ground Controlled Interception. At the beginning of the year, of the 47 GCI stations planned by June, just six were operational. (Projected cover in the Shrewsbury and Exmoor areas shown dotted.)

The air fleet's casualties were seven He 111s and two Ju 88s. Flak over Liverpool was said to be strong with that over Glasgow weak. Returning crews reported having seen 14 night fighters, seven of which carried out attacks.

The districts in Glasgow which suffered most were those to the west and north-west, while at Clydebank, which was very heavily hit, riverside areas sustained severe damage. A serious shelter incident took place at one shipyard when some 80 workers were killed; some Clydeside docks suffered severely and all other docks received a certain amount of damage. The centre of Glasgow itself received surprisingly little damage and utility

The first installations were of the fully mobile type which could be erected and dismantled in twelve hours. All the equipment was wheeled and could be installed and set up by the actual crew of the station. The mobile stations were an emergency stopgap and the original six had many limitations, especially in height finding, an essential for successful night interception.

Meanwhile experimental modifications were carried out to the mobile station at Sopley to try to improve the performance. The movement of the initial aerials was confined to a short sweep back and forth over a small arc which effectively limited its use to one bomber at a time but the modifications allowed continuous rotation of the aerials.

The aerial operated on 209 megacycles and was known as a 'Split 10' array using the same four bays of eight dipoles for transmitting as well as receiving. Peak power was 150 kilowatts giving an effective range of around 45 miles up to 45,000 feet although some detections had been made up to 80 miles from the station. Against low-flying aircraft the range dropped to 30 miles at 5,000 feet and 16 miles at 1,000 feet.

services were not badly affected. However, communications both in Clydebank and Glasgow were seriously interrupted. Damage to public buildings was not extensive but among those hit were Glasgow University, Garscadden Hospital and Bankhead School. In the Merseyside area most of the bombs fell on Wallasey but damage was not serious and casualties were comparatively light with only 12 killed. Damage and casualties were also caused at Southport. Outside of the Clyde area the most severe bombing took place at Hull, where fires were started and 29 people killed. Bombing was very widespread, however, with many Civil Defence Regions reporting incidents from Alton in Hampshire (where five people were killed) to northern Scotland. In attacks on RAF airfields slight damage was reported at Kirton-in-Lindsey, Tangmere and Boscombe Down.

In the course of dusk, night and dawn patrols Fighter Command dispatched 299 aircraft. These included five Intruders, some of which claimed successful attacks on German airfields. Altogether nine enemy aircraft were claimed destroyed, including one by a Harrow of No. 93 Squadron on a Mutton patrol over the Isle of Wight. A Fighter Night operation was flown over Glasgow by five Hurricanes of No. 43 Squadron and four Spitfires of No. 602 Squadron, but only one Spitfire engaged an enemy aircraft and this without apparent success. One night fighter, Beaufighter R2158 of No. 600 Squadron, was lost when it crashed into the sea off Prestwick following

Once wooden huts were erected the mobile equipment, save for the aerial trailer, could be driven away leaving what was officially called 'a GCI 'Intermediate' Mobile Station'. Total operational personnel comprised one squadron leader and three flight lieutenants as controllers, with one sergeant, nine aircraftmen, three WAAF corporals and 13 aircraftwomen as operators. With the addition of technical and service staff, clerks, drivers, cooks, medical and security personnel, the total strength of the GCI Station was 53 RAF and 30 WAAFs. If one can assume from this picture taken in the Reporting and Operations Room that the station concerned is central on the map on the wall, this must show Sopley GCI.

fuel mismanagement which produced an engine failure.

The Clydeside guns, in action from 2124 to 0630 hours, fired 4,000 rounds; those at Merseyside were engaging enemy aircraft from 2055 to 0155 while the Humber guns fired 1,026 rounds between 2144 and 0300 hours. AA Command used some 14,000 rounds in total for one raider claimed destroyed.

Limited activity continued during the day, the main forces being marshalled for the coming night attack. A Heinkel He 111 of III/KG26 was forced to land in the sea off Cherbourg after being damaged by fighters and the following were lost near the British mainland.

II/JG54 Messerschmitt Bf 109E-4 (3911). Presumed hit by AA fire. Aircraft caught fire and crashed into the sea off Folkestone 7.02 a.m. Uffz. S. Helmberger missing. Aircraft White 8 lost.

4(F)/121 Junkers Ju 88A-5 (0419). Believed shot down by three Hurricanes of No. 302 Squadron off Worthing. Crashed in mid-Channel 4.40 p.m. Lt. G. Fabricius, Uffz. E. Schmidt, Uffz. L. Walter and Uffz. E. Junker all missing. Aircraft 7A+LM lost.

A total of nine aircraft were lost during the night. In addition to those listed below, a Heinkel He 111 from the Geschwader Stab KG55 went down in the Channel, all but one of the crew being rescued and two more of the unit's aircraft returned with damage. Another Heinkel He 111 of 3/KGr100 crashed in Europe and one from 6/KG27 failed to return from Glasgow.

Stab/KG2 Dornier Do 17Z-2 (4248). Shot down by Flying Officer J. R. D. Braham DFC and Sergeant Ross of No. 29 Squadron in a Beaufighter during a raid on Hull. Crashed into the sea south-east of Skegness Pier 9.45 p.m. Oblt. H. von Keiser and Fw. B. Rücker missing. Fw. H. Genähr and Lt. B. Meyer killed. Aircraft U5+DA sank in sea.

7/KG26 Heinkel He 111H-5 (3610). Shot down by Sergeant J. A. Clandillion and Sergeant Dodgie in a Beaufighter of No. 219 Squadron during a raid on Southampton. Crashed at Smokehall Farm, Shipley, Sussex 8.35 p.m. Uffz. E. Herrmann, Uffz. F. Graf Calice, Gefr. L. Schmid and Obergefr. W. Kallert all killed. Aircraft 1H+IR wrecked.

On April 7 the first of a limited batch of 12 'Intermediate Transportable' Stations with rotating aerials was opened at Langtoft in the Wittering Sector. It had been manufactured by the Royal Aircraft Establishment at Farnborough and the whole station could be transported using six prime movers and six trailers. However once at the site the gantry and aerial had to be erected on ground foundations, an operation which employed ten men and took three days to complete. These stations, like the Mobile GCIs, were termed Air Ministry Experimental Stations (AMES) Type 8. (The fixed stations under construction but yet to come on stream were similar in style to CHLs — *see Volume 1 page 133* — would be designated AMES Type 7.)

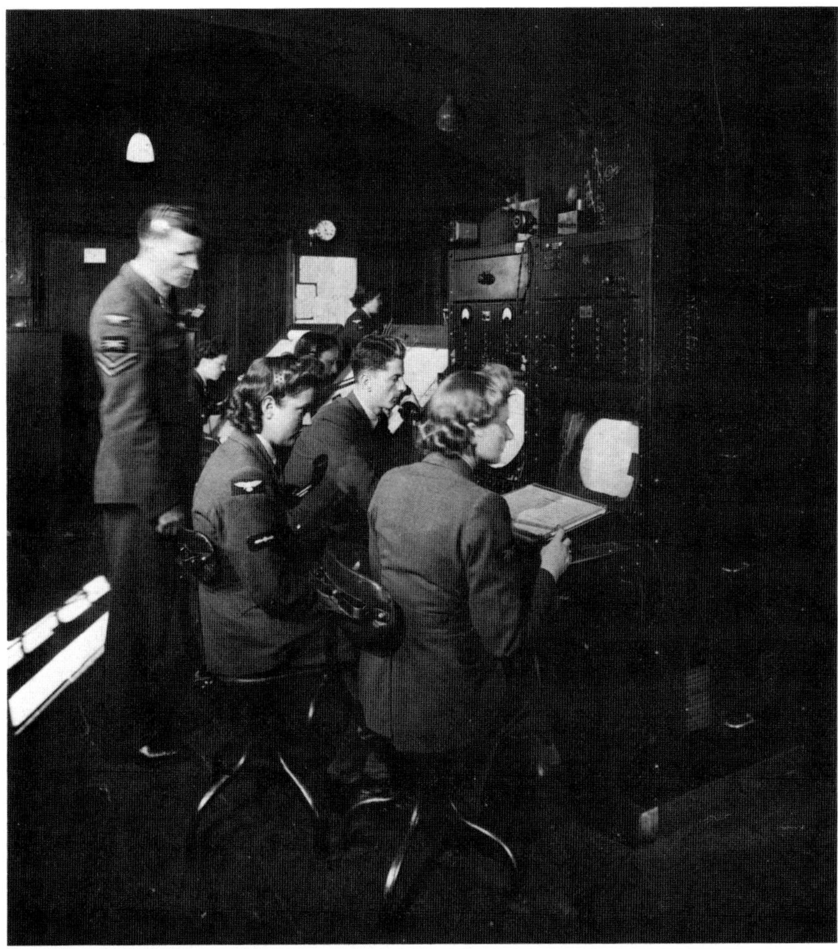

The aerial — a 'Split 10' as at the mobile stations — had an additional aerial about 35 feet high, the array having the ability to rotate at two rounds per minute, inch, or reverse. Height finding operated between one and a half and eleven degrees up to 50,000 feet plus, and out to 90 miles, while the range at 1,000 feet was improved to 35 miles. Here in the ops room the blonde WAAF on the right is operating the height and range receiver while the brunette sits in front of the PPI — the Plan Position Indicator.

German aircrews' fear of of being stalked in the darkness was compounded by their belief that the real reason for increasing RAF successes at night was because fighters and guns were being concentrated along their own X and Y beams. It was a logical explanation and in fact a method which had already been tried by fighters 'hunting the beam' but without success. Nevertheless the psychological seed had been sown that the spate of fighter attacks were somehow connected with the invisible, yet easily detectable, pathway to their targets. Here are the results of a Beaufighter versus Heinkel duel after Sergeants Clandillion and Dodgie brought down one of Thursday evening's raiders to Southampton.

7/KG55 Heinkel He 111P-2 (2806). Shot down by Pilot Officer A. J. Hodgkinson and Sergeant B. E. Dye in a Beaufighter of No. 219 Squadron during a raid on Glasgow. Crashed at Wood Farm, Bramdean, Hampshire 8.40 p.m. Oblt. W. Hesse and Fw. G. Groschopf baled out and taken prisoner. Oberfw. B. Manek and Fw. H. Klein killed. Aircraft G1+MR destroyed.

1/KGr100 Heinkel He 111H-3 (3352). Shot down by Pilot Officer G. A. Denby and Pilot Officer Guest of No. 600 Squadron in a Blenheim during a raid on Glasgow. Crashed at Drumshang Farm, Dunure, Ayrshire 10.25 p.m. Oblt. W. Schultz, Oberfw. B. Boyungs, Oberfw. R. Pölkemann and Oberfw. H. Ungethum (injured) all baled out and taken prisoner. Aircraft 6N+AH disintegrated.

3/Küstenfliegergruppe106 Junkers Ju 88A-5 (2234). Believed that shot down by Flight Lieutenant D. Sheen in a Spitfire of No. 72 Squadron. Crashed into the sea off Amble, Northumberland 10.25 p.m. Lt. zur See R. Dietze, Obergefr. W. Wesseres and Obergefr. H. Vandanne missing. Body of Oblt. H. Voigtländer-Tetzner recovered from the sea and buried at Thornaby-on-Tees under the date April 27, 1941. Aircraft M2+JL sank in sea.

4/NJG2 Junkers Ju 88C-4 (0604). On intruder sortie shot down by Wing Commander S. C. Widdows and Sergeant B. Ryall of No. 29 Squadron in a Beaufighter. Aircraft broke up in air and crashed at Smith's Farm, Dovendale, Lincolnshire. 3.30 a.m. Gefr. H. Körner, Gefr. K. H. Spangenberg and Uffz. W. Gesshardt killed. Aircraft R4+GM destroyed.

FRIDAY, MARCH 14-15

Sunset: 1902 Sunrise: 0716
Moon: 2040 — Dawn (Full +1)

Major attack on Glasgow/Clydeside and a heavy secondary attack on Sheffield. Elsewhere, minor attacks on airfields and other targets, minelaying and anti-shipping patrols.

UK — Small amounts of low cloud in south-western and north-eastern England, elsewhere only high or medium cloud (with about half cover in Scotland). Visibility moderate at first, becoming poor in many places in the early hours. Winds light and variable.

The Continent — Little or no cloud, moderate visibility.

Little use for parachutes at Smokehall Farm, Shipley, as all four crewmen were killed in the crash.

One large piece landed on the roof . . .

. . . while a bullet-holed wing ended up in a poultry farm.

There was little daylight activity of note, with no reports of bombing, but nightfall again brought operations on a massive scale with 451 long-range bombers, 14 light bombers and 18 long-range fighters engaged in attacks on British targets.

The principal target was again Glasgow/Clydeside, attacked by 203 aircraft between 2100 and 0200 hours. In addition to the specific objectives of the previous night, some units were ordered to bomb the Rolls-Royce factory at Hillington. As on the previous night, the weather conditions permitted crews to find their target with no difficulty, only the later attackers having any problems in pin-pointing their allocated Concentration Points as smoke from fires started by earlier arrivals interfered with visibility. Especially big conflagrations were seen to develop in oil tank installations near Dalmuir (where a large explosion and large fires sent smoke billowing up to over 3,000 feet), and in the vicinity of the Princes Dock at Govan on the south bank of the Clyde. Further big fires were reported in or near the gas works at Eglinton railway station, by the Phoenix tube works north of Rutherglen, in the town north of the dock area and in the large power station at Yoker. Three ships were seen to be on fire in Rothesay Dock with more sheds ablaze at Yoker. In the Hillington Rolls-Royce works fires were started following the detonation of numerous bombs. The general impression of the last attacking crews was of a success even greater than that achieved the previous night. It was, in the view of some crews, the best results obtained in any attack to date, with most of the 231 tonnes of HE and 782 BSK (28,152 incendiaries) landing in the designated Target Areas.

At Sheffield, with a TA encompassing the town centre and extending north-eastwards to include the industrial area, 83 tonnes of HE and 328 BSK (11,808 incendiary bombs) were dropped by 117 aircraft between 2120 and 0320 hours. Here, unlike Glasgow, visibility decreasing during the night resulted in about half the participating crews bombing by the use of radio aids or by DR navigation and results were not so conclusive. Nevertheless, it appeared that satisfactory results were obtained in the Templeborough works group of steel- and rolling-mills, at the armaments factory on the River Don and in the Atlas steel works. Large fires and explosions were discerned and at one time 30 to 50 fires were raging; especially numerous were fires in the city centre industrial area. All in all, it was reckoned that a large part of the bomb load

Although Bomber Command's main emphasis had been switched to the U-Boat threat, nevertheless, a proportion of the force was still carrying out Operation Abigail — the reprisal counter-bombing programme instituted some weeks earlier (see page 346). On Tuesday the Luftwaffe had hit Birmingham; on Wednesday the RAF retaliated against Hamburg, Bremen and Berlin. When the Luftwaffe attacked Liverpool on Wednesday, the RAF bombed Hamburg again on Thursday. As the Germans' response that night was a two-night attack on Clydeside, the British tit-for-tat was to visit Düsseldorf two nights in a row . . . and so it went on. At least when Churchill telegraphed the Foreign Secretary, then in Cairo, on Friday evening, he was able to claim that 'we have begun to claw the Huns down, in the moonlight to some purpose'.

England's green and pleasant land at peace after the violence of yesterday: this is Shipley with Broomers Cottage in the background.

March 14/15, 1941

Take-off 20.37 hours. Target: Glasgow, Scotland; industrial, and particularly dock installations; 2000 kilometres there and back.

Our radio beam system was again being interfered with. So we flew low along the British west coast in a northerly direction to enable us to identify the boundary between land and sea. Below us were snow-covered hills. It was a long flight over seemingly dead country of a peculiarly rugged aspect.

We glanced here and there, circling continuously above the dark earth — and in order to find landmarks then under the starry sky — to ensure we were not surprised by a night fighter; looking at our instruments and engines, and at their exhaust flames. The fact is that our engines are not absolutely reliable. Our industry has problems with its materials. The valves are a particular headache. Occasionally they melt or give out loud reports like cannon shots during take-off. Many a take-off in France, which could not be aborted in time, has ended in disaster. If a valve is not precisely fitted into its seat, the small blue exhaust flame will develop into a long, yellow trail . . . and we don't want that at all.

On several occasions we have had to turn back owing to engine breakdowns. Once in mid-October (I happened not to be flying at that time), my crew were forced to bale out while still over France because of engine damage.

In short, we always look at our two engines with mixed feelings during these long flights and mentally give them a pat when they keep throbbing quietly and reliably without spitting and spluttering.

In the far distance the sky has already turned red. This means that our pathfinders have already reached the target area. Three times we circle above flames and haze until we are able to get an overall picture of where the harbour installations are — and drop our bombs.

The oil-containers appear to be burning. From the biggest of these oil fires, a blood-area with jagged outlines is sending up a huge wall of smoke which is reaching a height of a good 3000 metres. (When we got back to our base I learnt that this explosion had been caused by a bomb released by my friend Willi Amman — the theology student. He was scared stiff when he realised what he had done.)

At last we veered away, rose to a height of 4000 metres as a precaution, and flew southwards again over seemingly endless distances.

There now — practically no fuel left in the outside wing tank, as we try to pump out from it. What has gone wrong?

This means that we can't get home and will be forced to stay in England. Feeling somewhat desperate, I make some calculations. If we fly at an economical speed, we might reach the middle of the Channel. Should we take the risk? The others were also frantically trying to think how the fuel could have disappeared. Would it help if we continued flying on one engine? Jurak was already throttling back the engines. But this meant we would still be over enemy territory in the morning. What wretched luck! Is this the end for us? At best, we might become prisoners of war. We descended to a lower level at which the engines would use less fuel. Higher up, the outside temperature had been −30 degrees. For some time we continued to fly in sombre silence, and in a warmer layer of air — at a height of about 2000 metres. Then suddenly, the fuel supply came back.

What a crazy situation! Either the pumping system had broken down or the fuel gauge reading had been incorrect on account of frost. We all feel that a huge weight has been lifted from our hearts.

Under all this pressure my attention had slipped, and we found ourselves over the centre of Liverpool; with its entire Flak making a furious onslaught on us — the solitary, hapless target. The well-aimed fire drew far from complimentary remarks from the crew in the rear concerning myself.

On the other hand, the Flak did have its advantages. One could always rely on the anti-aircraft gunners in Liverpool, Manchester, Birmingham, London, etc., as they fired at our planes so punctually each night; regularly and with complete dependability. What would we have done without these Flak fireworks? In pitch-black darkness, they have been our only reliable navigational aid over the whole extent of the British Isles. We know them very well and have become increasingly confident in them. The fact that they strain our nerves when we are flying over our target, and particularly those of the rear crew, usually nearest to the fire, is another matter.

At long last the coast comes into view again. Frozen stiff and very sleepy, we are drooping in our seats. Suddenly, to keep us awake, a strange shape — an enemy night fighter — is flying close past us on an opposite course. We shake him off. He has gone and we see no more of him. If it had been a bit lighter there might have been a lot of trouble.

We landed at Le Bourget at 03.30, with our fuel gauge registering zero. I jumped out of the plane, and couldn't believe my eyes. The heavy 500-kilo bomb we had been carrying was still there below the fuselage. I was stunned. Our flight to Scotland had taken nearly seven hours, and we had left only our smaller bombs up there. Was it my fault or had there been a defect in the bomb-release mechanism? I shall try to forget it . . .

ROBERT GÖTZ

was successfully dropped on the ordered TA, despite the deteriorating visibility which, it was believed, was partly accentuated by an artificial smoke screen coming from a group of factories in north-east Sheffield.

Plymouth also figured in the night's target list and was attacked by eleven aircraft of Luftflotte 3 between 2115 and 2310, while eight aircraft bombed Southampton, where the flak defences were said to be good. Over Glasgow the flak was weak, but strong and well aimed at times and at Sheffield, too, it was well directed and very strong at times. Crews of Luftflotte 3 reported seeing 11 night fighters and also said that many decoy fires were in evidence.

Existing records of Luftflotte 3 reveal that this night it dispatched 132 aircraft to Glasgow (of which 112 reached their target), 70 to Sheffield (reached by 49), 16 to Plymouth (bombed by 12) and eight to Southampton (found by all eight). Eight crews aborted, 35 bombed alternative targets, 16 were engaged in attacks on 'Zerstörziele' (harassing or 'destructor' raids on specific factories, mainly in the aircraft industry), three in attacks on airfields and two on reconnaissance. Two failed to return and a Ju 88 of III/KG51 made an emergency landing near Trouville.

Luftflotte 3 aircraft reaching their primary targets were:

Glasgow:
I/KG27: 7 He 111, 2130-2225
II/KG51: 1 Ju 88, 2214
I/KG51: 1 Ju 88, 2208
I/KG27: 6 He 111, 2207-2235
III/KG1: 6 Ju 88, 2220-2333
II/KG27: 13 He 111, 2205-2245
III/KG51: 3 Ju 88, 2145-2155
III/KG26: 5 He 111, 2312-0150
I/KG1: 12 He 111, 2223-2340
II/KG76: 14 Ju 88, 2145-2230
KG77: 10 Ju 88, 2215-2246
KGr806: 10 Ju 88, 2250-2305
KGr100: 7 He 111, 2215-2300
I/KG55: 9 He 111, 2230-2310
II/KG55: 8 He 111, 2240-2310

Sheffield:
II/KG55: 5 He 111, 2210-2237
II/KG76: 18 Ju 88, 2315-0040
II/KG51: 1 Ju 88, 2130
III/KG26: 1 He 111, 2126
III/KG1: 1 Ju 88, 2130
II/KG1: 9 Ju 88, 0035-0113
I/KG54: 7 Ju 88, 2202-0035
Stab/KG55: 1 He 111, 2200
III/KG27: 5 He 111, 2120-2258
I/KG55: 1 He 111, 2255

Plymouth:
I/KG27: 5 He 111, 2115-2145
I/KG51: 1 Ju 88, 2125
III/KG51: 1 Ju 88, 2207
Stab/KG55: 1 He 111, 2200
II/KG55: 2 He 111, 2240-2310
III/KG55: 1 He 111, 2240
III/KG26: 1 He 111, 2128

Southampton:
I/KG1: 2 He 111, 2107-2215
III/KG1: 1 Ju 88, 2127
I/KG77: 5 Ju 88, 2115-2200
In addition, 12 aircraft attacked Southampton as an alternative target.

Clydeside again sustained heavy damage and many casualties. The most serious incident occurred in Glasgow when three blocks of tenements were destroyed and many deaths and injuries resulted. The industrial situation was by no means a disaster, however, and while damage occurred in the dock areas it was not irreparable. Rest Centres and feeding arrangements proved inadequate, on the other hand, and many people had to be evacuated to Rest Centres in surrounding districts. It took some time to

establish true casualty figures but the initial list showed totals, for the two nights, of 327 killed in Glasgow and 214 in Clydebank. In the surrounding areas, which also suffered extensively, 59 were reported killed in Dumbartonshire.

The attack on Sheffield was, in fact, widely dispersed. Many fires were started in Leeds, where 52 people were killed, and damage was extensive with nearly 2,000 made homeless. In Sheffield six people were killed, five in Wakefield and a further seven in various parts of what was then the West Riding of Yorkshire. Incidents in the Midlands and East Anglia included damage at Tupton, where 11 people were killed, and at Grays, where there were two fatalities. Four people were killed in Southampton, where the firefighting capabilities of the Fire Services and the public did much to contain the situation; damage and casualties were also reported at Portsmouth. Fires, two of them serious, and five deaths were reported from Plymouth and another four people lost their lives at Tunstall, Stoke-on-Trent. At Merseyside bombs were dropped but no serious damage occurred.

In addition to the places mentioned bombs fell at Paisley, Renfrew, Maryhill, Dumbarton, Sunderland, Yarmouth, Nottingham, Huddersfield and Lowestoft. Damage was also reported at Wittering aerodrome.

The heavy guns of AA Command fired 16,000 rounds during the night, with the Clyde guns firing 4,025 between 2101 and 0200 hours. One enemy aircraft was claimed destroyed. Three raiders were claimed destroyed by night fighters and another was claimed destroyed on the ground by an Intruder aircraft. On this occasion two Hurricanes of No. 87 Squadron joined four Blenheims of No. 23 Squadron on patrols over northern France and it was one of the Hurricanes which claimed the destruction of an enemy aircraft on the ground (a Do 17 at Caen). Altogether 226 fighters flew dusk, night and dawn patrols.

Above left: **The first marker incendiaries in the Clydebank area in Thursday's attack fell on the timber yard belonging to the Singer Manufacturing Company (on the left) in Kilbowie Road.** *Above right:* **Although the factory has now been replaced by the Clydebank Business Park, the old La Scala on the right came through and also survived the intervening years under passive attack from television.**

The collapse of many of the tall tenement blocks added greatly to the death toll, this picture which has since become symbolic of the Clydeside Blitz being taken close by in Radnor Street.

The wholesale destruction of the area during the war led likewise to wholesale redevelopment after the war. This is the linking shot picturing the corner of Crown Avenue (the cinema is on the left), with Radnor Street the first turning up the road.

Death and destruction on the Dumbarton Road, *above* at the tram terminus and *right* looking east towards the town hall. Near here lies Jellicoe Street down by the canal where at No. 78, a mortal blow was struck when 15 members of the Rocks perished. It was the most grievous tragedy to befall one family in the whole Clydeside Blitz, if not during the entire night Blitz on Britain. Back in November (see page 224) we illustrated the difficulty faced when releasing accurate reports of the number of casualties and extent of the damage as words such as 'slight' or 'serious', being relative terms, have little meaning by themselves. With regard to the heavy attacks on Scotland on Thursday and Friday, the official communiqué broadcast by the BBC stated that though the attacks had been heavy, the casualties, though serious, were not expected to be numerous. To all those in Glasgow and along the Clyde this was plain Sassenach nonsense as it was obvious that many hundreds of people had been killed, and the immediate impression was that London was attempting to conceal the true facts. When on March 18 the Ministry of Home Security reluctantly gave casualty figures of 'about 500' the Minister, Herbert Morrison, was accused of making misleading statements and was told in no uncertain terms that the figures had caused incredulity and great resentment on Clydeside.

AA batteries in action were those at Portsmouth, Brooklands, Portland, the IAZ, Tyne, Dover, Gloucester, Harwich, Manchester, Birmingham, Thames and Medway (North and South), Acklington, Mersey, Chatham, Plymouth, Holton Heath, Humber, Leeds, Sheffield, Datchet, Nottingham, Forth, Tees, Grantham, Clyde, Crewe, Barrow, Blackpool and Coventry.

Apart from the aircraft listed opposite, a Heinkel He 111 from 6/KG55 was damaged, two Junkers Ju 88s of KG30 returned to Eindhoven with damage and a Junkers Ju 88 of 3(F)/123 crashed near Jersey killing its crew.

The whole matter was raised at the Duty Room Conference on the morning of March 20 at the Ministry of Information at which it was pointed out that it was impossible for the Duty Officer to provide an accurate estimate of casualties during the night in time for the BBC's eight o'clock news. His task was made even worse on big raids when lines of communication were disrupted. However, it was pointed out that 'no subject gave rise to more criticism with the public than this question of communiqués about air raid casualties'. To try to avoid understatements in future, which would only further reduce the general public's confidence in the official news presented to them, a solution was worked out on March 26 whereby the eight o'clock news would 'let the listener know at least what part of the country the main raids were in'. This early statement could then be followed up at noon with fuller details in time for the one o'clock news. A second full report would then be issued at 8.00 p.m. which would catch the 9.00 p.m. broadcast. The Ministry of Home Security also memoed the Chief Press Censor, Rear-Admiral Thomson, on April 2 to try to avoid well-worn phrases in future communiqués. It was pointed out that there was some doubt 'whether the German bombing policy is really affected by our statements as (a) they do not necessarily believe them (habitual liars rarely recognise the veracity of others) and (b) post-raid reconnaissance will usually enable them to verify the facts for themselves.' Meanwhile thousands of people were leaving the Clydeside area. This queue of refugees was formed up in Glasgow Road to await special buses laid on by Glasgow Corporation.

2/KG1 Heinkel He 111H-3 (5683). Shot down by Flight Lieutenant G. P. Gibson DFC and Sergeant R. H. James in a Beaufighter of No. 29 Squadron during an attack on Glasgow. Crashed into the sea one and a half miles off Ingoldmells Point near Skegness 10.00 p.m. Lt. G. Stugg, Uffz. H. Pauer, Uffz. L. Auer and Uffz. H. Seidel all killed. Aircraft V4+HK lost.

6/KG55 Heinkel He 111P-4 (3096). Shot down by Flying Officer K. I. Geddes and Sergeant A. C. Cannon in a Beaufighter of No. 604 Squadron whilst en route to Glasgow. Crashed at Brinkmarsh Farm, Falfield, Gloucestershire 9.40 p.m. Oblt. E. Henschke, Fw. H. Krüger, Fw. F. Härter and Fw. W. Smolinski killed. Aircraft G1+IP destroyed.

Site investigated by the South West Aircraft Recovery Group and the Severnside Aviation Society. Propeller blade and pitot tube among the relics unearthed.

1/KGr806 Junkers Ju 88A-5 (8200). Shot down by a Beaufighter during a raid on Liverpool. Crashed into the sea off Beachy Head. Fw. S. Helbig and Fw. J. Hafner killed. Body of Gefr. L. Rüdiger found off Newhaven seven weeks later. Uffz. K. Hilke missing. Aircraft M7+EH lost.

With the danger of wildly exaggerated rumours gaining ground should the Government's future pronouncements no longer be relied on, on April 1 Morrison took his Scottish MP colleagues into his confidence, telling them that total casualties for the two raids were actually 1,100 killed and 1,000 seriously injured. However the figures were kept from the public until an article in the *Sunday Post* on the anniversary of the raids in March 1942 slipped past the censor and leaked the truth by referring to 1,200 people having died. Meanwhile on Sunday, March 16, a Department of Health official arrived to supervise the burial of the unclaimed dead.

It was decided that the first 67 bodies from the temporary mortuary in St James's Church hall should be buried without delay the following day in a mass grave which had been dug in Dalnottar Cemetery. Unfortunately it had not been possible to provide coffins and the victims were simply wrapped in white sheets tied with string around the waist and neck. On Tuesday a further 54 casualties were interred in the same grave, Sir Steven Bilsland, the District Commissioner, complaining bitterly to the Department over the indecorous manner in which the burials had taken place.

Angriff auf Hütte und Kraftwerk Lochaber

Oblt. Fidorra

Lt. Mündel

Obfw. Bothe

Uffz. Reiners

In der Nacht zum 13. 3. 41 wurde die Aluminiumhütte mit Wasserkraftwerk Lochaber bei Fort William durch ein Kampfflugzeug unter der Führung von **Oberleutnant *Fidorra*** als Kommandant mit der Besatzung Lt. *Mündel,* Flugzeugführer, Obfw. *Bothe,* Bordfunker, Uffz. *Reiners,* Bordschütze, angegriffen. Größere Brandherde im Werk als Wirkung waren beim Abflug noch bis 50 km Entfernung deutlich sichtbar, so daß das Werk als erheblich beschädigt angesehen werden muß.

After the new outbreak of heavy Luftwaffe attacks, Home Security issued an honest appreciation — secret at the time — as to their deduction of German tactics: 'The late-winter lull in enemy air operations seems now unmistakably to have given way to renewed heavy raiding, in which the blockade of the ports, particularly on the west coast, is likely to play a prominent part. The enemy's night bombing seems to have improved, and the attacks on Merseyside and Southampton, like that on Portsmouth on the night of the 10/11th March, were directed primarily on military objectives, and not on the commercial centres or the morale of the people in the towns involved.' The Ministry also felt that 'the remarkable success of the defences is a timely reply to this renewed offensive'. Although the mass raids grabbed the headlines in Britain, there were individual exploits by German crews that merited equal coverage in Germany. On the afternoon of March 13 Oberleutnant Fidorra and his Ju 88 crew were detailed to knock out the British Aluminium Company plant at Fort William.

SATURDAY, MARCH 15-16

Sunset: 1904 Sunrise: 0713
Moon: 2201 — Dawn (Full +2)

Major attack on London. Secondary attack on Southampton.

UK — Little or no cloud except for low stratus on the East Coast. Widespread fog and mist in many areas by midnight. Winds light and variable, becoming calm.

The Continent — Little or no cloud with fog or mist in many areas except north-western France where visibility remained moderate.

There was little daylight activity by the Luftwaffe and no bombs fell on land. At night, with fog expected to envelop many Luftflotte 2 airfields, operations were largely restricted to Luftflotte 3 which contributed 78 of the 101 aircraft engaged in a raid on London.

The Target Area in London was the area inside and downstream of the loop of the Thames with dock basins the main objectives, but bombing was entirely by DR or radio navigation and observation of the result was made difficult. Through the cloud and mist, however, bomb explosions and several large fires were seen, with one particularly big explosion and fire in the West India Docks. Between 2025 and 2310 hours, 103 tonnes of HE and 397 BSK (14,292 IBs) were claimed delivered, but the attack was assessed as only moderately successful.

In addition to 93 long-range bombers sent to London, of which 78 reached the target, Luftflotte 3 dispatched nine aircraft to Southampton. Of the total force nine bombed alternatives, four aborted and two failed to return (one He 111 of Stab/KG55 and another of III/KG55). Luftflotte 3 aircraft attacking London were:

I/KG51: 3 Ju 88, 2108-2130
II/KG51: 8 Ju 88, 2135-2220

Fort William lies in the western highlands of Scotland at the foot of Ben Nevis, Britain's highest mountain, and the flight and attack on the factory on the shore of the loch was no mean feat. *Der Adler* readers were treated to a rather over dramatised version with Oberleutnant Fidorra planning the raid . . .

. . . diving down the 4,400-foot mountain with workers running in panic for cover. The original German text in *Frontnachrichtenblatt der Luftwaffe* opposite states that the attack took place at night but Home Security say that it was late afternoon. German radio claimed direct hits on the north-west wing and added that fires could be seen at 50 kilometres.

III/KG51: 4 Ju 88, 2133-2158
I/KG54: 9 Ju 88, 2025-2246
II/KG54: 6 Ju 88, 2210-2243
III/KG54 (KGr806): 15 Ju 88, 2048-2310
Stab/KG55: 1 He 111, 0000
I/KG55: 9 He 111, 2125-2257
II/KG55: 12 He 111, 2105-2300
III/KG55: 11 He 111, 2205-2300

With the exception of isolated incidents in the Midlands and the Isle of Wight, bombing was concentrated on London and the Home Counties, with 33 London boroughs reporting incidents. The east and south-east districts of the capital were hardest hit and some damage was caused in the docks. The most serious incident, however, occurred at Southgate, where 42 people were killed and shops and houses demolished. Five more people were killed at Eltham and three at Gravesend. Hospitals featured largely in the list of buildings damaged during the night and included a First Aid Post in Woolwich, Eltham Health Centre and hospitals at Bermondsey and Peckham.

Bombs also fell at Chislehurst, Ashford, East Romford, Southend, Hornchurch, Walthamstow, Chigwell, in rural areas of Kent and Essex, at Beaulieu, Christchurch, Hillhead, Cowes, Marchwood, Cadland, Epsom, Chelsham, Sutton, Kingsdown, Tatsfield, Aldingbourn, Tangmere, Westhampnett, Chenies, Hanslope, Sandy, Broxbourne, Biggleswade, Towcester, Kimbolton and Hunton-on-the-Hill.

AA guns were in action in the London IAZ, at Brooklands, Thames and Medway (North and South), Harwich, Portsmouth, North Weald and Slough, firing some 4,000 rounds. The guns of the IAZ used, 1,144 rounds of 4.5-inch, 1,190 of 3.7-inch and 33 rounds of 3-inch ammunition, engaging raiders flying at heights between 8,000 and 23,000 feet. Night fighter activity was severely curtailed by extensive fog but, including dusk patrols, 20 aircraft operated. No Intruder missions were undertaken.

The only loss during the day was as a result of a fighter skirmish over the Channel.

5/LG2 Messerschmitt Bf 109E-7 (3725). Shot down by three Hurricanes of No. 615 Squadron on convoy escort duties. Crashed into the sea off Dungeness 4.37 p.m. Oberfw. A. Seidel killed and buried at St John's Cemetery, Margate with May 4, 1941 shown as the date of death on his headstone. Aircraft Black L+ lost.

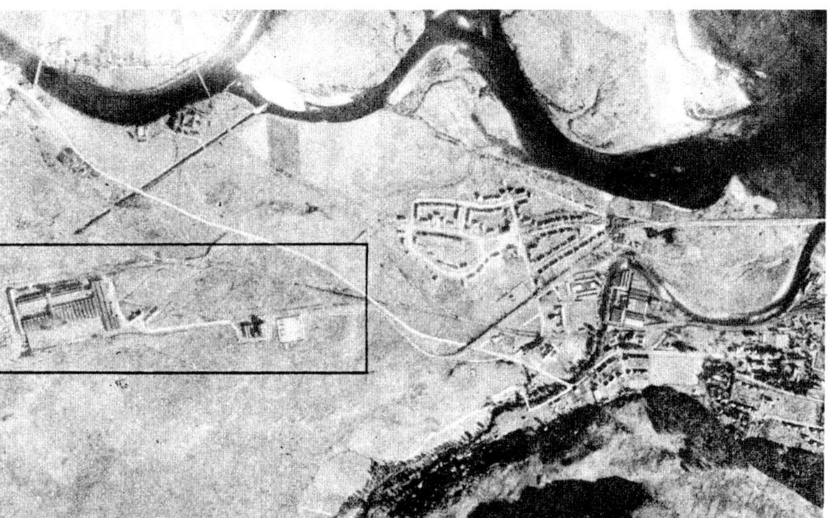

Poor old Fidorra — if only he knew he had returned with egg on his face as the nearest 'hits' were four miles away! The plant is outlined on this original German recce picture — whether it is pre- or post-raid cover they are both the same!

The company merged with the Canadian firm Alcan in 1982 to become British Alcan — still the main producer of aluminium in the UK.

SUNDAY, MARCH 16-17

Sunset: 1905 Sunrise: 0711
Moon: 2321 — Dawn (Full +3)

Major attack on Bristol.

UK — Low stratus in eastern districts and the South Coast of England. Elsewhere cloudless with widespread fog forming through the night. Wind, light easterly or calm.

The Continent — Cloudless in northern France. Widespread fog after dark except in north-west France where fog did not develop until the small hours.

Dense fog in many parts of Britain and the Continent was only slow to clear and severely limited daylight activity. For the forthcoming night a very heavy attack was in the offing, involving both Luftflotten 2 and 3, but fog totally prohibited operations by the former. Nevertheless, 184 bombers of Luftflotte 3 operated, with 108 ordered to bomb Bristol Target Area 'a', (the docks at Avonmouth) and the remaining 76 to attack Bristol Target Area 'c' (the south-west and west central part of the city), where dock installations were also the main objective.

In the event 57 crews reported having bombed Avonmouth, dropping 54.8 tonnes of HE (five SC 1000, 12 SC 500, 110 SC 250, 17 LZZ 250 and 243 SC 50) and 634 BSK (22,824 IBs), with 105 crews bombing Bristol (with 109.85 tonnes of HE comprising four SC 1000, 43 SC 500, 261 SC 250, seven LZZ 250 and 347 SC/SD 50, together with 11,016 incendiaries). At Avonmouth the CP was a rectangle covering the port area, adjacent warehouses and industrial works; bombing was predominantly by radio and DR methods and although numerous bomb explosions were seen it was difficult to ascertain the results. However, three large fires were observed to the east of the Royal Edward Docks with more in the vicinity of the silos, warehouses and cold storage depots around Avonmouth Dock. A 'fire area' was also visible, but no claim was made with regard to its precise location.

Within Bristol itself the Schwerpunkt was centred on the Floating Harbour downstream of Bathurst Basin and here, too, bombing was by DR and radio methods. However, towards the close of the attack intermittent improvements in conditions enabled some crews to bomb visually, but many used the searchlight activity as an indication that they were over the city, sometimes additionally aided by the glow of fires seen through the cloud or mist. Numerous bomb flashes were also seen, but little else was discerned and it was impossible to assess the results of the attack; subsequently, the Führungsstab recorded that 'the attack cannot be judged an outstanding success'. That on Avonmouth was expected to have achieved a greater effect. Six crews unable to bomb either Bristol or Avonmouth bombed Yeovil, Weymouth and Portland as alternatives, ten crews aborted, four attacked airfields and one bombed Portsmouth. Two Ju 88s of I/KG51 failed to return (with one reporting by radio that it was landing in England), another crashed on take off, one crashed near Cherbourg and another ran out of fuel over occupied territory, its crew baling out. Participating in the attack were:

Avonmouth (as the primary target):
II/KG76: 29 Ju 88, 0200-0325
III/KG51: 2 Ju 88, 0018-0037
II/KG51: 3 Ju 88, 0045-0108
I/KG51: 3 Ju 88, 2324-2330

A seven-ton bus overturned by blast in Easton Road after Sunday night's attack on Bristol.

Beckington Road, Knowle, Bristol and a legacy of the 1941 bombing is finally recovered and rendered safe in 1944. Note the windows of all the houses have been opened to reduce blast effect although a 'Satan' going off this close above ground would not have left any of them standing!

Leeds had received its first appreciable attack on March 14-15 but Home Security reported that 'damage was done to private property and telecommunications but casualties were comparatively light'. This is the Town Hall with the Civic Hall opened by George V in 1933 in the background.

III/KG27: 1 He 111, 2345
I/KG54: 2 Ju 88, 0040-0043
KGr100: 5 He 111, 2245-2342 (X-Verfahren bombing)
I/KG27: 14 He 111, 2300-0020
II/KG27: 14 He 111, 2255-0025

Bristol (as primary target):
I/KG51: 6 He 111, 2100-2130
II/KG1: 7 Ju 88, 2035-2050
I/KG77: 5 Ju 88, 2158-2325
II/KG77: 4 Ju 88, 2240-2305
III/KG26: 14 He 111, 2100-2237 (Y-Verfahren used)

Bristol (as an alternative to aircraft ordered to attack Avonmouth):
KGr100: 3 He 111, 2315-2355
II/KG27: 2 He 111, 0020-0028
III/KG27: 7 He 111, 2230-0023
I/KG51: 5 Ju 88, 2345-0006
III/KG55: 1 He 111, 0050
I/KG55: 10 He 111, 0000-0035
III/KG55: 13 He 111, 0040-0122
II/KG55: 12 He 111, 2350-0010
Stab/KG55: 1 He 111, 0045

Bristol (Whitchurch) Airport (alternative to Bristol TA 'c'):
Stab/KG55: 1 He 111, 2225

Bombs were dropped on every ARP Division of Bristol and although numerous fires were caused no major damage was reported in the docks. Residential and shopping districts were mainly affected and the amount of industrial damage was small. There was, however, serious dislocation of utility services, transport and communications. Many railway incidents were reported, road transport was seriously affected and four factories were damaged. Two well known buildings which suffered were the Bristol General Hospital and St Michael's Church. Heavy casualties occurred when two public shelters received direct hits and a further 13 people were killed while sheltering in the crypt of a church; initial casualty assessments put the total killed at 208. Incendiary bombs and fires were tackled with commendable speed and efficiency and the Regional Civil Defence Headquarters reported: 'The police and others were much impressed by the work of the fire-fighting parties in Bristol. In some cases there were not enough bombs to go round.'

The Bristol guns, in action from 2018 to 0400 hours, fired 2,356 of the 4,500 rounds used during the night by AA Command. Elsewhere guns engaged enemy aircraft at Portsmouth, Southampton, Holton Heath, Cardiff, Pembrey, Portland and Weymouth. Only nine night fighters were able to operate, because of unfavourable weather, and no offensive Intruder patrols were flown, but a Beaufighter of No. 604 Squadron intercepted and claimed to have damaged an He 111 over Studland, Dorset.

Outside of Bristol, where a good measure of success was obtained by a Starfish site, bombs fell in mainly rural districts of Somerset, Gloucestershire, Dorset, South Wales, Wiltshire and Hampshire, but no serious damage resulted.

In addition to the single loss sustained during the Bristol raid, three Junkers Ju 88s crashed in Europe and were destroyed, eight crewmen being killed.

2/KG51 Junkers Ju 88A-5 (8124). During a raid on Bristol crashed at RAF Chilmark, Dinton, Wilts. 11.40 p.m. after double engine failure. Last radio call — 'Emergency landing in England'. Lt. E. Arz, Oberfw. O. Reimer, Fw. A. Konrad and Fw. O. Hoferrichter baled out. Three of crew taken prisoner immediately. After two days of intense search for the fourth crew member, Otto Hoferrichter, he was arrested at night at Barford St Martin by Sergeant Warder White who, unarmed, took him prisoner and disarmed him of his pistol. Aircraft 9K+AK disintegrated.

MONDAY, MARCH 17-18

Sunset: 1907 Sunrise: 0709
Moon: 0036 — Dawn (Last Qtr −3)

All night bomber operations cancelled

UK — Mist, fog or low cloud and drizzle over much of England, mainly overcast in Scotland but fair or fine in the extreme north.

The Continent — Low cloud with mist or drizzle in most areas and fog inland.

A few raids were plotted inland during the day, with some penetrating some distance, but no bombs were dropped in England. In Scotland a few bombs fell, causing little damage, and in the South-East the Dover balloon barrage was attacked with machine gun fire.

All night bomber operations were cancelled, but in view of the fact that a few bombs were reported in the North Midlands and East Anglia it seems possible that a very small number of oversea reconnaissance flights took place, with one or two penetrating inland seeking alternative targets.

Beauty and the beast . . . as depicted here by aviation historian Miss Philippa Hodgkiss wrestling with the leg of the remains of the undercarriage of the Junkers which crashed within the perimeter of RAF Chilmark, Wiltshire.

TUESDAY, MARCH 18-19

Sunset: 1909 Sunrise: 0706
Moon: 0415 — Dawn (Last Qtr −2)

Major attack on Hull. Secondary attacks on London, Southampton and elsewhere.

UK — East and south-eastern England cloudless with moderate visibility becoming poor during the night. Elsewhere mainly cloudy with slight rain in the South-West. Winds light and variable.

The Continent — Some cloud on coasts of north-western France and northern Holland, elsewhere little or no cloud. Visibility moderate to good.

A little more daylight activity than of late included fighter patrols over the Channel, anti-shipping patrols, plus general and weather reconnaissance. Some 30 German aircraft penetrated inland and bombs were dropped in Kent and West Suffolk.

Operations were resumed on a very large scale during the night, with 464 long-range bombers and 19 light bombers operating. Hull was the main target — 378 of the 419 aircraft dispatched reaching and claiming to have attacked their primary target. Between 2040 and 0155 hours they delivered 316 tonnes of HE and 77,016 incendiaries in the light of 189 LC 50 flares, the moon not rising until the attack ended. The destruction of the docks and industrial installations was again the intention, but mist made target location difficult at times and recourse was taken to DR/radio bombing by some crews. Numerous decoy fires also led to difficulties, it was readily admitted, but in spite of these problems most crews were able to make out their targets and aim their bombs visually. Numerous fires resulted, mainly in the north-east part of the town, with several, including one large conflagration, in the docks. Here, too, a very large explosion occurred.

Luftflotte 3's contribution was 223 aircraft, with 187 crews reporting over Hull. Another 23 aircraft were sent to Southampton, reached by 17 aircraft which dropped 15 tonnes of HE and 1,440 IBs. Explosions and fires were reported in the town but because of mist — and because new, inexperienced crews gaining operational practice were involved — only moderately successful results were anticipated.

London, ever popular as an alternative target on account of its size, was attacked in this capacity by 33 bombers and 3 light bombers (presumably Bf 110 fighter-bombers of Erprobungsgruppe 210) which dropped 35 tonnes of HE and 2,410 incendiaries. Thick mist hindered bombing, but a fire was observed to the north of the West India Docks. Twenty-nine of the attackers were from Luftflotte 3 and two more aircraft of this air fleet bombed Portsmouth; another 15 attacked Zerstörziele and airfields, nine aborted and two were lost (an He 111 of III/KG55 crashed near Amiens and another aircraft of the same type belonging to I/KG1 crashed nearby).

Luftflotte 3 participation was as follows:

Hull:
I/KG27: 12 He 111, 0125-0353
II/KG27: 13 He 111, 0142-0300
III/KG27: 10 He 111, 0209-0307
KGr100: 12 He 111, 0045-0150
I/KG51: 5 Ju 88, 0225-0310
II/KG51: 2 Ju 88, 0207-0300
III/KG51: 4 Ju 88, 0124-0135
I/KG54: 12 Ju 88, 0050-0240
II/KG54: 7 Ju 88, 0125-0150
KGr806: 10 Ju 88, 0100-0205
I/KG55: 8 He 111, 0130-0245
II/KG55: 10 He 111, 0105-0130
III/KG55: 12 He 111, 0125-0245
I/KG1: 7 He 111, 0130-0220
II/KG1: 7 Ju 88, 0240-0330
III/KG1: 10 Ju 88, 0140-0220
II/KG76: 2 Ju 88, 0320-0330
I/KG77: 13 Ju 88, 0225-0344
II/KG77: 10 Ju 88, 0159-0248
III/KG77: 9 Ju 88, 0136-0235
III/KG26: 12 He 111, 0052-0147

Southampton:
I/KG51: 4 Ju 88, 0212-0235
II/KG51: 2 Ju 88, 0110-0230
III/KG51: 3 Ju 88, 0037-0105
II/KG54: 4 Ju 88, 2020-2035
III/KG55: 1 He 111, 0115
III/KG1: 1 Ju 88, 0105
III/KG26: 2 He 111, 0015-0105

London (as an alternative target):
II/KG51: 2 Ju 88, 0155-0230
I/KG54: 1 Ju 88, 0105
II/KG55: 1 He 111, 0135
KGr806: 3 Ju 88, 0210-0230
I/KG27: 1 He 111, 0010
III/KG27: 1 He 111, 0200
I/KG76: 2 Ju 88, 0225-0300
III/KG76: 2 Ju 88, 0120-0130
III/KG51: 4 Ju 88, 0104-0250
II/KG1: 3 Ju 88, 0140-0300
I/KG51: 1 Ju 88, 0230
II/KG55: 2 He 111, 0103-0207
KGr100: 1 He 111, 0030
III/KG27: 1 He 111, 0510

While we are in Wiltshire a momentary digression to Westbury . . . and into the world of philately. What a fascinating story this envelope could tell of life during the Blitz . . . as it affected both sides. Paul Bookbinder, who showed us this item from his collection, explains how it was still possible to post letters between Germany and England in wartime: 'A postal service between Great Britain and enemy or enemy-occupied lands was handled by Thomas Cook, the travel agents, via Portugal. This envelope is quite intriguing as we see the German Hindenburg stamp plus Berlin postmark adjacent to the George VI stamp with its London postmark. Here the letter addressed to Gerda Huppert was posted in Berlin on January 13, 1941 with the German censor mark on the reverse. It arrived at the P.O. Box 506 address of the Thomas Cook office in Lisbon on January 24 where it was again stamped on the back. It reached London on March 18 where it was censored by Examiner 1975, relabelled, stamped and redirected to Mrs Huppert's new address — possibly she had been bombed out of Clapton or had been evacuated to Wiltshire.'

Another exercise in censorship can also be illustrated on March 18 with the heavy raid on Hull — Number 10 in the overall league table of cities receiving the heaviest totals of bombs during the Blitz (page 28). Always when the word 'Hull' appeared in a wartime caption, the censor turned it into 'a north-east coast town', and it so angered the people of the city never to see their name in print alongside the other major sufferers. In this example after the *Hull Daily Mail* submitted this print, the name has been deleted but right up to May 1942 permission to publish was being withheld for a 1941 raid.

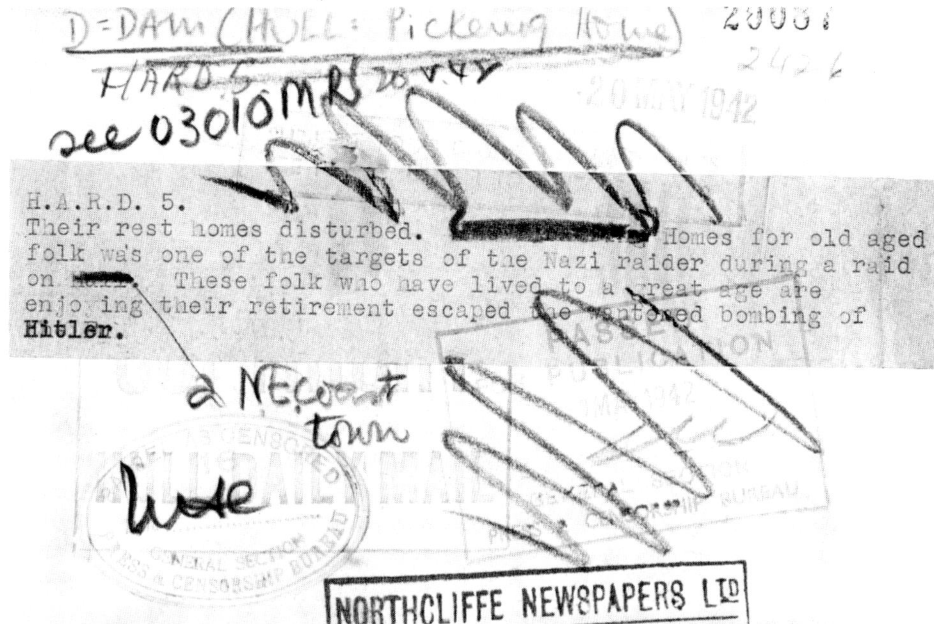

D=DAM (HULL: Pickering Home)

HARD 5

see 03010MR

20 MAY 1942

H.A.R.D. 5.
Their rest homes disturbed. Homes for old aged folk was one of the targets of the Nazi raider during a raid on ~~Hull~~. These folk who have lived to a great age are enjoying their retirement escaped the wantoned bombing of **Hitler**.

a NE coast town

NORTHCLIFFE NEWSPAPERS LTD

I/KG27: 2 He 111, 0422-0440
Stab/KG55: 1 He 111, 0410
III/KG77: 2 Ju 88, 0325-0435

Although bombing was widely dispersed over many parts of the country there was a heavy concentration on Hull where residential and industrial property was severely damaged. Many fires, some of them large, were started but were brought under control very quickly, but public utilities suffered extensively. At first 66 people were reported killed, with another 12 at Scarborough, which was bombed intermittently for about four hours from 2100. Other areas of Yorkshire also reported bombs; casualties and damage were also caused by two parachute mines at Beverley. Four people were killed in the Driffield area.

At Southampton both IBs and HEs fell on the town and also at Calshot, Northam and Woolston, but no serious damage was caused. Elsewhere bombs fell at Dagenham (where damage was done to the Ford Motor Company factory and the docks), Barking, East Ham, Erith, Fulham, Richmond, Wembley and some 20 other locations in Essex, Kent, Middlesex, Surrey and Sussex.

The Humber guns fired 2,500 of nearly 8,500 rounds used by AA Command during the night, with guns also in action at Dover, Portsmouth, Nottingham, Coventry, Gloucester, the IAZ, Bristol, Harwich, Holton Heath, Slough, Thames and Medway (North and South), Brooklands, Tees, Derby, Grantham, Cardiff and Humber. Fighter Command put up 56 aircraft on dusk, night and dawn patrols, but activity was affected by widespread fog. Nevertheless, several contacts were made by Beaufighters of Nos. 219 and 604 Squadrons but no claims were registered.

Portsmouth; Bombed January 10, 1941; photographed specially for Barclays Bank, but not passed for publication until July.

3 A.M. on the Plaistow Road, East End, March 1941 **by Leslie Baker.**

'THE WEDNESDAY'

Luftwaffe attacks during the early months of 1941 were spasmodic, probably affected by bad weather over the coastal regions of France and the Low Countries. But with the approach of better flying conditions, the enemy stepped up his attacks on London and the large provincial cities, mounting a spectacularly heavy raid to mark the opening of the spring offensive on March 19, 'The Wednesday', as it came to be known in the East End of London.

From time to time information was received from official sources of the target for the bombers and one afternoon at about 4.00 p.m. came word that the target that night was to be the Royal Group of docks. There were five auxiliary fire stations within the Group with manpower totalling some one hundred and twenty. Here was a problem. To be warned of the intended target was one thing; to consider whether it would, in fact, be bombed, another. Should all appliances and men be withdrawn or should they be left to take their chance?

West Ham covers such a relatively small area that it was argued that if the men were withdrawn they could only be accommodated in schools, and even near misses of dock targets could result in hits on the augmented stations. So it was decided to take no action other than to direct the officers to arrange for their men to go to the shelters immediately the warning came.

At about 7.30 p.m. the sirens wailed and the sound of anti-aircraft gun-fire was heard. Then the bombers were overhead, the scream of falling bombs mingling with the thump of gun-fire. The skies were lit by clusters of parachute flares, dropped by the raiders to illuminate their target with a cold, hard light that always left me feeling naked and isolated; a sole, prominent target for hundreds of eager marksmen. I had more than a twinge of sympathy for the ostrich; it was my instinct, too, to put my head under cover at such times.

The ack-ack guns opened up at the flares and a number of hits were scored but those that escaped the shells continued to shed their eerie, menacing light on the target area. There was no gradual build-up to the full weight of the attack. It seemed that all the bombers over West Ham responded to a signal to release their cargoes of destruction simultaneously and the skies were soon aglow with the glare of fires.

The German aircraft were readily identifiable to us on the ground by the irregular beat of their unsynchronised engines and many, many bombers were heard overhead that night. Air Marshal Sir Philip Joubert, whose radio talks brought us such comfort during the dark days, always asserted that British and German aircraft were indistinguishable by the sound of their engines alone. With all deference to the great man, I had to differ with him in this respect, unless it happened that British aircraft were showering incendiaries and high explosive on us as we strove to put out the fires or recover our dead and wounded. We had no doubt that the deep-sounding throb of engines, the woom-woom coming from above, was the precursor to the scream of falling bombs and we could not believe that the RAF would treat us this way!

Among the reinforcements arriving at West Ham Control was a contingent from Beckenham, Kent. This small brigade had been singularly unfortunate throughout the Blitz and had suffered casualties proportionately far higher than any other in the Region. This night was to be no exception, for a Beckenham pump, one of a convoy en route to a fire at Silvertown, was obliterated in a land mine explosion in Plaistow Road, with the loss of its entire crew. Their names — Leading Fireman Stan Short and Firemen Charles Drew, Denis Fitzgerald, Fred Moore and Les Palmer — subsequently were added to the Beckenham Fire Service Roll of Honour.

The bombers dropped several parachute mines that night, inflicting numerous casualties on civilians and Civil Defence personnel, including Auxiliary Fireman Roy Huggett of West Ham, killed with his comrades from South London. Yet the Royal Docks escaped, practically unscathed. An auxiliary fire station was hit but the crews had been called out and no one was hurt.

Those responsible for the decision to stand fast breathed a sigh of relief when the All Clear sounded; the signs had been ominous in the early hours of the raid.

CYRIL DEMARNE, 1986

This is the spot that wartime firefighter artist, South African Leslie Baker depicted — where the pump from Beckenham was obliterated by the land mine. Homes on both sides of the road were demolished — the break in the terrace on the left remains as a tell-tale sign of the tragedy.

WEDNESDAY, MARCH 19-20

Sunset: 1910 Sunrise: 0704
Moon: 0245 — Dawn (Last Qtr −1)

Major attack on London. Minor secondary operations, mainly attacks on airfields.

UK — Generally cloudless at first with mist and some fog. Low stratus spread into East Coast areas soon after midnight and local fog became more widespread. Winds light or calm.

The Continent — Low cloud in northern Holland spread into Belgium and extreme north-east France, but elsewhere cloudless. Visibility moderate to good, but poor locally.

Only some 60 German aircraft operated during the day and few of these crossed the coast. No bombs were reported.

After dark a massive assault was made on London by 479 of the 510 aircraft operating (which included 5 long-range night fighters sent to patrol Bomber Command airfields). The London attackers dropped 470 tonnes of HE and 3,397 BSK, the largest number of incendiary bombs (122,292) yet used in any attack on Britain. With no moon until the early hours, use was made of 96 LC 50 parachute flares to illuminate the target which, on this occasion, encompassed dock installations along the length of the Thames

The sirens wailed the Raiders Approach Red Warning over East London at nine minutes past eight, the first bombs screaming down to burst in West Ham shortly before 8.45 p.m. Forty-five minutes into the raid, the first massive thunderclap erupted in Richard Street heralding the arrival of the first mine-carrying aircraft but its twin, floating down to land on John Knights, failed to explode. Amidst the continual crump of bombs, the banging of the AA and crash of falling buildings, the next two mines struck the borough just after ten o'clock, one exploding harmlessly in West Ham Park, the other on St Mathias Shelter. Then at 10.20 p.m. it was the turn of Riles Road with Dale Road (*above*) a few minutes later.

Hitler's aim achieved at last . . . yet this is Dale Road in 1983 when the whole of the area was undergoing redevelopment.

By cross-checking the times that ARP reported mine explosions, allowing say five minutes leeway either side for discrepancies between different warden's posts, it is fairly safe to say that 12 aircraft dropped Luftmines over West Ham on Wednesday night. One can pair up all the incidents save one — the disastrous single hit on Plaistow Road at 1.25 a.m. which killed the fire crew (page 488). ***Above:*** **Rochester Avenue, Upton Park, received its mine at 23 44. There were deaths at several houses: No. 18, 26, 27, 30, 31, 32 and 36. At No. 23A two Russian nationals were killed, Mr and Mrs Morris Koenigsblatt.**

from London Bridge downstream to the beginning of the Thames loop. Included were the St Katherine and London Docks on the north bank, Surrey Commercial Dock on the south side, and the Royal Victoria, Royal Albert and King George V Docks. Throughout the attack, which lasted from 2010 to 0158 hours, bombing was mostly visual although, as fires took a hold, smoke blotted out much of the CP and led some crews to revert to either DR or radio aid bombing; others opted to bomb the fires which were discernible through the enormous pall of smoke. A very great many fires were observed with extensive conflagrations joining up to form massive fire areas with many large explosions erupting from them. Most discernible were two burning gas holders and a huge factory fire. One large ship was also seen to be on fire and at 2357 hours there was an enormous explosion, apparently emanating from the Beckton Gasworks. At one time there were so many fires and explosions occurring that crews found it impossible to assess the numbers. In the opinion of some of the most experienced crews the results were the greatest yet achieved anywhere.

In addition to the main attack a small number of aircraft was sent to attack Bristol (Whitchurch), Hullavington and other airfields.

Luftflotte 3's contribution comprised 303 aircraft to London (of which 295 reported over the target), four to Southampton and three to attack airfields. Seven crews aborted and numerous alternative targets were bombed by crews which failed to reach their primary target. Two aircraft were lost — a Ju 88 of II/KG51 which crashed near Versailles and a Ju 88 of II/KG54 which made an emergency crash landing immediately after take off. Luftflotte 3 aircraft participating in the London attack were:

I/KG27: 13 He 111, 2108-2210
II/KG27: 15 He 111, 2210-2255
III/KG27: 16 He 111, 2055-2208
KGr100: 13 He 111, 2040-2108 (opened attack using X-beams)
I/KG51: 14 Ju 88, 2202-2245
II/KG51: 12 Ju 88, 2144-2220
III/KG51: 10 Ju 88, 2115-2150
I/KG54: 12 Ju 88, 2150-2238
II/KG54: 9 Ju 88, 2043-2130
KGr806: 9 Ju 88, 2128-2143
I/KG55: 12 He 111, 2127-2150
II/KG55: 12 He 111, 2127-2158
III/KG55: 16 He 111, 2120-2150
Stab/KG55: 3 He 111, 2145-2150
I/KG1: 8 He 111, 2122-2230
II/KG1: 13 Ju 88, 2045-2214
III/KG1: 16 Ju 88, 2050-2145
II/KG76: 39 Ju 88, 2100-2215
I/KG77: 15 Ju 88, 2100-2155
II/KG77: 15 Ju 88, 2118-2258
III/KG77: 10 Ju 88, 2235-2310
III/KG26: 13 He 111, 2105-2235 (Y-Verfahren bombing; four SC 2500 Max included in bombload)

Parachute mines rent whole streets asunder. Hudson Road virtually ceased to exist after 11.14 p.m. Now it has totally been expunged.

Luftwaffe records indicate that four III/KG26 Heinkels were armed with SC 2500s. One Max we know, aimed at West India Dock, fell wide of its intended target, blasting a huge area at Poplar. This is Cording Street, north of the Institute on East India Dock Road. But what happened to the other three? Overall, the raid was the heaviest for loss of life since the start of the Blitz. It feels awful to continually compare raid with raid by the number of human lives lost as the figures begin to be meaningless: 430 killed on September 7; a similar number on October 15-16; 554 at Coventry on November 14-15; 450 in Birmingham five days later and so on. Total casualty figures in London for March 19-20 vary, the immediate post-raid figure by Home Security of 356 escalating to 'some 750' in the official Civil Defence history. (Although the Great Fire Raid in December attracted much publicity, it nevertheless yielded few casualties because the City is not a residential area, 'only' 163 persons being killed.)

As claimed by the Germans the bombing of London was severe and there were many fires. Almost all the docks in the capital were damaged to some degree with the eastern and south-eastern boroughs the worst hit. On only one previous occasion (October 15-16) had London experienced so heavy a scale of attack; 1,881 fires were started, of which three were classified as conflagrations, ten as major and 53 as serious. Casualties, too, were at a new high level, with 631 killed. West Ham (where 150 people were killed), Poplar and Stepney were particularly hard hit and in adjacent dock areas sheds, warehouses, wharves, stores and their contents were all destroyed. Handling equipment, docks machinery and railway lines were extensively damaged and of the factories which were hit damage was severe at three and substantial at five others. Utility services suffered widespread damage with gas supplies especially affected. The Town Hall at Leyton, the Ministry of Supply offices at Woolwich, Cumberland Market, Poplar Employment Exchange and the Public Library at Bromley were among the buildings damaged, as were hospitals in Poplar, East Ham, Bethnal Green, Lewisham, Woolwich, Deptford, Dartford and Carshalton. ARP shelters were hit by bombs in several districts of London including one in Poplar (where 44 people were killed), three in Stepney and one at Carshalton.

A number of incidents were reported from the Home Counties and fatal casualties were reported from Rainham (where nine were killed), Meopham, Sutton-at-Hone, and Southampton.

The guns of the London Inner Artillery Zone, in action from 2017 to 0155 hours, fired 4,689 rounds; overall, AA Command used some 7,500 rounds with guns in action at Harwich, Thames and Medway (North and South), Solent, Brooklands, Slough, Dover and Cardiff. Fighter Command despatched 71 aircraft on dusk, night and dawn patrols, including five on Intruder operations, but all without any confirmed success.

At a later date a diary discovered on a PoW from III/KG26 was found to contain a reference to the bombing this night of the West India Dock with an SC 2500 dropped by means of Y-Verfahren in conditions of good visibility. The German airman recorded in his diary that 'the bomb fell right in the middle of the target' which, he said, harboured a warship and a tanker. He also stated that he had been dazzled by the flash which he described as lighting up 'the whole of London'. In fact the bomb fell about one and a quarter miles north of its intended target, demolishing a large Institute in Poplar and causing severe blast damage over a quarter mile radius.

The spirit of the East End! A cuppa amid the destruction in Eric Road, Forest Gate, after 'the Wednesday'.

THURSDAY, MARCH 20-21

Sunset: 1912 Sunrise: 0702
Moon: 0337 — Dawn (Last Quarter)

Major attack on Plymouth/Devonport, with a secondary attack on London. Mine-laying off the East and West Coasts and attacks on airfields.

Westwell Street Plymouth with the tower of the Guildhall on the right. It was to Plymouth on Thursday that the King and Queen came on their first visit to the city to tour the blitzed areas and give encouragement to the people and members of the civil defence organisations. Viscountess Astor, Lady Mayoress, was their hostess and it turned out to be a splendid day; an all-too-short respite with music and dancing on the Hoe. Then, just two hours after she had bade her royal visitors farewell, came the rude awakening when the Luftwaffe arrived in force to mete out one of their infamous double hits. It was Plymouth's worst raid to date, laying waste the whole of the city centre.

UK — Low cloud and rain in Scotland and the North. Elsewhere little or no cloud but extensive fog in the Midlands and the southern half of England. Winds strong to gale force in the North, light and variable in the South.

The Continent — Fair or fine. Visibility moderate at first with much fog in the later part of the night.

German daylight operations were on a small scale but there were three minor attacks in the South-East, where three people were killed and some damage done at Ramsgate.

During the night Plymouth suffered its worst attack so far. Between 1900 hours (before it was fully dark) and 2320, the docks at Plymouth were the objective of 125 aircraft of Luftflotte 3. No doubt because fog was expected by midnight the attack started and finished early; normal practice was to prolong attacks to create the utmost disruption and to extend the defences, but this policy was modified on occasions like this. Even so, the attackers delivered 159 tonnes of HE (17 SC 1000, 63 SC 500, 248 SC 250, 36 LZZ 250, 633 SC 50 and 153 SD 50) and 31,716 incendiaries (881 BSK). The Concentration Point lay in the harbour area between the mouth of the Hamoaze and the dock installations at the east end of the Great Western, and in spite of the absence of moonlight, bombing was almost entirely visual. Accurately placed incendiaries started fires in the Target Area which greatly aided later attacking crews. Indications were that most of the bombs fell on the CP and eastwards towards the docks at Sutton Pool and on the town.

Numerous fires developed, one particularly big one being about 300 metres northwest of the Great Western Docks, and were visible from a great distance. Bombing appeared to be well concentrated and it was reported back that very good results seemed probable. The units which carried out the attack were:

I/KG27: 16 He 111, 2220-2320
II/KG27: 15 He 111, 1900-2212
III/KG27: 8 He 111, 2051-2150
KGr100 16 He 111, 2041-2103 (X-Verfahren bombing from 5,800 metres altitude)
II/KG51: 9 Ju 88, 2200-2225
III/KG51: 12 Ju 88, 2116-2158
I/KG54: 13 Ju 88, 2055-2135
II/KG54: 10 Ju 88, 2158-2235
KGr806: 7 Ju 88, 2103-2112
I/KG55: 13 He 111, 2128-2150
II/KG55: 15 He 111, 2115-2225
III/KG55: 15 He 111, 2115-2140
Stab/KG55: 3 He 111, 2148-2200

Arthur Mee, *The King's England:* 'O dear Plymouth town, O blue Plymouth Sound, O where in the world can your equal be found? She is the mother of cities, and her children are gathered far and wide. They have given her name to forty Plymouths in four corners of the earth. Her fame befits her splendour, for every traveller knows that she is beautiful to see. Her name is on all our tongues, for it belongs to history. Her memory lives with all who have passed this way, for the spectacle of this town with three communities in one, this city that rises on a rock 150 feet above the waves, is one of those few sights of the world that men do not forget. Like the Statue of Liberty, the Pyramids, or the Dome of St Paul's, Nature has made her wonderful to see, and man has made her unforgettable.' Unforgettable indeed was the Luftwaffe's contribution to Plymouth's immortal history in 1941.

Drake's Inferno. The heart of the jewel seen burning here for the second time on the night of April 21-22.

The local firefighters were overwhelmed by the extent of the fires and many blazes just had to be left to burn themselves out. This pitifully small group of firemen are fighting a losing battle in Old Town Street. Even when help arrived from other districts it was found that their equipment would not fit Plymouth's hydrants. The third prong in the brigades' armoury after men and machines was water, often hopelessly inadequate as it was estimated by the Chairman of the Metropolitan Water Board in London that one single raid could lead to a demand for 100 million gallons from the mains.

FRIDAY, MARCH 21-22

Sunset: 1914 Sunrise: 0700
Moon: 0420 — Dawn (Last Qtr +1)

Major attack on Plymouth/Devonport.

UK — Low cloud with occasional rain and moderate visibility in the South and West. Elsewhere variable cloud, cloudless in places with moderate to good visibility. Winds light westerly to north-westerly.

The Continent — Much low cloud with occasional rain or drizzle and poor visibility in north-east France and the Low Countries. Cloudy with occasional rain and moderate visibility in northern France and elsewhere.

Minor daylight activity brought a few bomb reports from Norfolk and the Kent coast but no damage or casualties were caused. During the night, however, Plymouth was subjected to its second major attack in two nights, with 171 of the 179 aircraft operating participating in the assault on the important naval base and dockyard town.

Of the force dispatched, 168 crews claimed to have reached and bombed Plymouth, dropping 187 tonnes of HE (19 SC 1000, 83 SC 500, 331 SC 250, 44 LZZ 250 and 645 SC 50) and 36,108 incendiaries. The attack, which lasted from 2043 to 2340 hours, was centred on the south part of the docks between the mouth of the Hamoaze and the Sutton Pool, but few crews were able to

One Ju 88 of I/KG54 crashed near Lisieux and another, belonging to KGr806 and which had reported over the target, was lost on its return flight.

A secondary attack was made on London by 32 aircraft of Luftflotte 2. They delivered 24 tonnes of HE (seven SC 500, 28 SC 250, 158 SC/SD 50 and six LMB mines) and 134 BSK (4,824 IBs) between 2050 and 2155 hours. Dock installations were again the intended target and a CP was selected which covered an area just inside the loop of the Thames and some distance downstream. However, thick mist over London brought about the release of bombs purely by DR and radio aid methods and it was not possible to check the results, but three large and several smaller fires were seen downstream of the loop. Further attacks were made on St Eval airfield by two aircraft and single aircraft bombed Cardiff and Harwich; minelayers of IX Fliegerkorps were active off the East and West Coasts.

Considerable damage was done in Plymouth, especially in the centre of the city and in the Millbay area where some damage was caused in the docks. Eleven fires were also started in Plymstock, where ten people were killed. All public utility services were badly affected and transport, both road and rail, was severely disorganised. Railway stations were damaged and two trains burnt out.

In the secondary raid on London bombing was not concentrated and damage was of little consequence. Other places reporting bombs were Redruth, Weston-super-Mare, Ilminster, Woolwich, Dartford, Crayford, Bromley, Beckenham, Orpington, Camberwell, Dulwich, Dagenham, Shoreditch, Islington, Hendon, Finchley, Sutton, Horley, Horton Kirby and Stone.

The Plymouth guns were in action from 2035 to 0004 hours and fired 2,483 rounds of 3.7-inch and 310 rounds of 3-inch ammunition. AA Command's total expenditure of ammunition was just over 4,000 rounds with batteries engaging at Falmouth, Solent, the IAZ, Thames and Medway (North and South), Dover, Portland, Bristol and Yeovil.

Fighter Command put up 24 aircraft on dusk, night and dawn patrols, but with no success.

As dawn broke on Friday morning there was little time to assess the situation before the Luftwaffe returned to deliver the knock out blow. These pictures also show Old Town Street — then and now.

'The whole area within a radius of 600 yards from the Guildhall was levelled, a large part of the shopping centre was destroyed by fire as the result of a complete failure of water supplies, over 18,000 houses were destroyed or damaged, 329 persons killed, 283 badly injured and some 5,000 made homeless.' The bald statistics from the Civil Defence historian make chilling reading.

bomb visually, the great majority reverting to DR and radio aids. Leading crews, however, were aided in locating Plymouth by making use of decoy fires, the precise locations of which, relative to Plymouth, had been carefully observed the previous night. In addition, once fires had been started by early arrivals, these were used as aiming points by follow-up crews.

Despite the difficulty in seeing the ground it was possible to make out particularly big fires in the vicinity of the Devonport dockyards, between the Great Western Docks and the mouth of the River Hamoaze and in the southern part of the Plymouth dockyards. Assessing the probable results of the attack, the Führungsstab considered it likely that considerable damage was caused in both the town and the dock installations. Flak over Plymouth was variable in strength but at times was well directed; searchlight activity

Top: The view north from the tower of St Andrew's, the ancient parish church hard by the burned out shell of the Guildhall. *Above:* The rebuilding of the city after the war involved wholesale clearance with the introduction of Royal Parade in the foreground — a broad new double carriageway replacing Union Street.

two nights Plymouth suffered severely. The municipal and commercial centre of the city was largely destroyed by fire, mainly as a result of lack of water occasioned by damaged mains, and the ARP Services were hampered by the destruction of the city's Report Centre. In the two raids more than 300 people were killed and in excess of 5,000 rendered homeless; public buildings damaged included the Guildhall, Municipal Buildings, the old Guildhall, Stonehouse Town Hall, the General Post Office, the County Court, the Food Control Office, Pounds House, the Marine Biological Laboratory, the Lockyar Street YMCA, the Ballard Institute and the Promenade Pier. The Prince of Wales' Hospital, eight churches and six schools were also damaged. Damage was also done in the docks and at Devonport Dockyard and a trawler, HMS *Asama* of 303 tons, was sunk.

The Plymouth guns claimed one enemy aircraft damaged, with AA Command as a whole using nearly 3,000 rounds of heavy ammunition. Fighter action was hampered by adverse weather conditions, but 38 aircraft flew dusk, night and dawn patrols; no enemy aircraft were claimed destroyed.

Above: **Gutted by fire but still standing. Like Coventry Cathedral services were later held under open skies in St Andrew's but it is Charles Church (*right*) which has now become Plymouth's Blitz memorial and a fitting symbol of the city's suffering.**

was slight and generally ineffective, as were five or so attacks by night fighters patrolling over the town.

Units and aircraft engaged in the attack were:

I/KG27: 11 He 111, 2125-2225
II/KG27: 12 He 111, 2105-2153
KGr100: 9 He 111, 2050-2110 (one crew bombed visually, eight by X-Verfahren and Knickebein)
I/KG51: 14 Ju 88, 2108-2232
II/KG51: 9 Ju 88, 2155-2225
III/KG51: 12 Ju 88, 2132-2148
I/KG55: 11 He 111, 2115-2205
II/KG55: 8 He 111, 2115-2147
III/KG55: 16 He 111, 2120-2135
Stab/KG55: 3 He 111, 2110-2133
II/KG76: 16 Ju 88, 2043-2210
I/KG77: 9 Ju 88, 2217-2319
II/KG77: 11 Ju 88, 2155-2250
III/KG77: 11 Ju 88, 2146-2243
III/GK26: 10 He 111, 2140-2340 (bombing by means of Y-Verfahren)

In addition, Luftflotte 3 sent eight aircraft on harassing attacks against a variety of targets. From the entire night's operations four crews bombed alternative targets and four aborted. One aircraft was lost (a Ju 88 of I/KG51) but the crew baled out and landed safely.

In the course of its second major attack in

In 1634 the town had petitioned King Charles for the parish to be split into two and the new Charles Church was completed in 1658. It was regarded as one of the finest post-Reformation churches in the Kingdom but it was completely burned out on the night of March 21-22 and abandoned. After the war the ecclesiastical authorities decided not to rebuild, and in 1957 the ruin was purchased by Plymouth Corporation to be preserved as a memorial to all the civilians of the city who lost their lives during the war from enemy air attacks. It now stands ruined, yet majestic, on a new island site at the eastern end of Royal Parade, the old churchyard covering more than an acre being lost with the construction of the new Exeter Street.

While en route to bomb RAF Leeming in North Yorkshire on Saturday evening, hoping to catch RAF bombers on the ground, Oberleutnant Fritz Danzenberg and his crew from KG4 at Eindhoven entered the balloon barrage over the Humber estuary. They then came under fire as the Heinkel swooped low over the 111th Light AA Battery, Gunner Dick Booth being credited with the kill (and rewarded with the gift of a barrel of beer!). Having jettisoned its bombs on waste land between Immingham Docks and the loco sheds, the Heinkel skimmed the rooftops, with one of the crewmen wrapped around the tail with his parachute. The aircraft made a wheels up landing in a field beside the Immingham–Habrough road. Two of the crew, Stephan and Heisig, survived the crash although one of them — it is not clear which — had broken both his legs. There was a dance at the local school that evening and, when news arrived of the crash, a crowd of dancers rushed up Pelham Road, tramping through gardens to get to the scene. This picture shows 5J+KN passing through Scunthorpe on its Queen Mary transporter.

SATURDAY, MARCH 22-23

Sunset: 1916 Sunrise: 0658
Moon: 0456 — Dawn (Last Qtr +2)

All German night bomber operations cancelled.

UK — Extensive low cloud with drizzle, rain or mist in many areas.
The Continent — Similar to the UK.

Minor daylight activity resulted in some damage in Essex and two people were killed in Brightlingsea. At night slight activity over Lincolnshire and the Shetlands was occasioned by a couple of sea reconnaissance aircraft, but no attacks took place.

5/KG4 Heinkel He 111P-4 (2938). Hit by AA fire during a sortie to RAF Leeming and then flew into a balloon cable. Force-landed west of Immingham, Lincolnshire. 7.45 p.m. Fw. W. Kösling attempted to bale out but killed when parachute caught on tail. Oblt. F. Danzenberg killed in crash. Fw. E. Stephan and Fw. H. Heisig taken prisoner. Aircraft 5J+KN destroyed.
Life jacket in the Humberside Aircraft Preservation Society collection; a housing estate has now been built on the area of the crash site.

SUNDAY, MARCH 23-24

Sunset: 1917 Sunrise: 0655
Moon: 0527 — Dawn (Last Qtr +3)

All German night bomber operations were cancelled.

UK — Extensive low cloud with rain, drizzle or mist in most areas.
The Continent — Similar to the UK.

Three people were killed by bombs which fell on Shanklin in the Isle of Wight during the day and there were also minor incidents in Kent and Scotland but no damage resulted. Continuing very bad weather greatly restricted activity and all night bomber operations were cancelled. However, one or two aircraft crossed the north-east coast, where some slight damage was reported, and one person was killed in Lincolnshire; the intruders were most probably aircraft engaged on armed sea reconnaissance which dumped their bombs on land rather than return to base with them still on board.

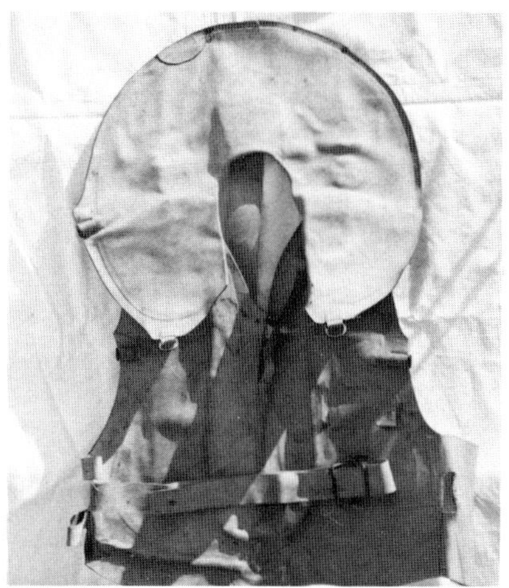

Although the Army were already there, many local people managed to collect souvenirs. One of the items taken from the crewmen that day was this lifejacket — an unusual type, strikingly different from the more bulky kapok version usually worn by bomber crews.

The two dead crewmen were buried in Grimsby's Scartho Road Cemetery, which had itself been attacked on February 27 — a day now known locally as Bloody Thursday — when a Dornier mounted a solo raid on the area. Flares and incendiaries fell on the cemetery but worse was to come when a stick of bombs straddled Cleethorpes Road. Then, at rooftop height, the raider machine-gunned traffic in Scartho Road and Louth Road before disappearing out to sea as quickly as it had appeared. Eleven people were killed, one of whom was Constable Frank Fisher.

Just after midday on Sunday a Junkers was shot down at Poling in Sussex, this rather nice souvenir being signed by the two pilots concerned.

Two aircraft were lost during the day:

4/KG77 Junkers Ju 88A-5 (7103). Damaged by Flight Lieutenant E. J. Morris and Sergeant F. A. Bernard in Hurricanes of No. 238 Squadron. Aircraft attempted to land but hit anti-landing obstacle. Crashed at Parsons Farm, Poling, Sussex 12.30 p.m. Oblt. W. Lode, Uffz. E. Waraczinski and Oberfw. J. Billesfeld taken prisoner. Uffz. F. Wallner killed. Aircraft 3Z+DM wrecked.

Small pieces of aircraft recovered by many individuals over the years.

Stab ZG76 Messerschmitt Bf 110E-2 (3774). Shot down by RN Bofors guns. Crashed just off shore at Sullom Voe, Shetlands 11.35 a.m. Uffz. K. Rüdiger and Gefr. G. Reichel killed. Aircraft M8+WE lost.

MONDAY, MARCH 24-25

Sunset: 1919 Sunrise: 0653
Moon: 0554 — Dawn (New −3)

All night bomber operations were cancelled.

UK — Extensive cloud with moderate to poor visibility in most areas.
The Continent — Similar to the UK.

Minor German daylight activity was largely confined to the Channel and patrols in search of coastal shipping, but a few bombs fell on land killing three people at Hythe and causing damage and casualties at Ipswich. Bombs were also dropped ineffectively in South Wales. Continuing bad weather led to the cancellation of all night bomber operations and no bombs fell anywhere. A lone long-range night fighter-bomber of I/NJG2 flew over the East Coast area, but returned to base after a fruitless patrol.

TUESDAY, MARCH 25-26

Sunset: 1921 Sunrise: 0650
Moon: 0618 — Dawn (New −2)

All German night bomber operations were cancelled.

UK — Extensive cloud with poor visibility affected most areas.
The Continent — Similar to UK.

A slight improvement in the weather brought about a small increase in activity over recent days but only about ten raiders crossed the coasts. Slight damage was done at Evercreech railway junction in Somerset and the gas works at Portslade, Sussex, was hit, but apparently with little effect. A further deterioration in conditions led to a cancellation of all night operations, but at dusk a few bombs fell in East Anglia.

WEDNESDAY, MARCH 26-27

Sunset: 1922 Sunrise: 0648
Moon: 0641 — Dawn (New −1)

All German night bomber operations were cancelled.

UK — Extensive very low cloud with drizzle, rain or mist in many areas.
The Continent — Similar to the UK.

Taking advantage of the low cloud, some 20 German bombers penetrated inland and, flying singly, attacked with bombs and machine gun fire a number of places in south and south-west England. Aircraft factories were the primary targets and the most serious damage occurred at Gloucester (where the railway was hit and five people

A few days later it arrived, courtesy of the ubiquitous Queen Mary, outside the Corn Exchange in Brighton for an exhibition to raise funds during War Weapons Week.

Now it's 'Laser Magic' in Brighton — a town noted for its weekend pleasures.

After the battle. Although few German aircraft were now being recovered compared with 1940, the public were informed with this picture that 'Nazi planes make a substantial contribution to the national scrap metal salvage campaign'.

killed) and Yeovil, where seven were killed and many houses damaged. Fatal casualties were also caused in Hampshire and at Newbury, Berkshire.

All night operations were cancelled because of the weather conditions over German bomber bases, but a few sea reconnaissance flights took place. No bombing was experienced.

The aircraft below was the only one to come down on British soil but a Dornier Do 17 of 5/KG3 crashed near Eindhoven killing the crew and another Dornier Do 17, this time from 2/KG2, was damaged by fighters over the Channel.

6/KG76 Junkers Ju 88A-5 (4259). Aircraft attacked Andover airfield at low level. Hit by fire from Lewis guns. Crashed at Red Rise Farm, Andover 1.30 p.m. Lt. O. Peper, Uffz. E. Meier, Uffz. H. Reuter and Fw. H. Hoppe all killed. Aircraft F1+FP disintegrated.

THURSDAY, MARCH 27-28

Sunset: 1924 Sunrise: 0646
Moon: None (New Moon)

No night bomber operations. Limited minelaying.

UK — Extensive low cloud with moderate to poor visibility.
The Continent — Similar to UK, but mist and drizzle in many areas.

German daylight activity was again on a small scale, but in addition to oversea activity about 30 bombers were engaged in widespread low-level attacks. These Luftwaffe 'pirate' operations were generally unsuccessful but on occasion caused serious damage and heavy casualties. Such an occasion occurred this day when 29 people were killed in Poole. Elsewhere damage was caused in Folkestone and Bournemouth, while bombs also fell without effect in the Shetlands. After dark the only German activity was minelaying off the south-west coast by seven He 111s of KG28.

One aircraft was lost near the UK:

3/KG27 Heinkel He 111H-5 (3747). Shot down by gunfire from HMS *Leith*. Crashed near the Smalls Lighthouse, Milford Haven 9.30 a.m. Lt. J. Crenz, Oberfw. C. Eilers, Oberfw. R. Gebhardt, Fw. E. Jansen and Gefr. W. Koch all taken prisoner. Aircraft 1G+EL destroyed.

FRIDAY, MARCH 28-29

Sunset: 1926 Sunrise: 0643
Moon: Dusk — 2015 (New +1)

No German night bomber operations.

UK — Extensive cloud with moderate to poor visibility.
The Continent — Low cloud with mist or drizzle in many areas and poor visibility.

Apart from a few bombs on Fair Isle, Orkney and Eastbourne, where two people were killed, there was little German daylight activity. At night no German aircraft at all were in operation over Britain or its coastal waters.

In March we are transferred to Le Bourget, one of the Paris aerodromes, and there, a new daily routine begins.

At midday, there is a stand-to for night operations. In the afternoon, this is lifted, and everybody looks forward to going out into the city. Then there is another stand-to. But now the weather is unfavourable — so this is lifted too. Going into Paris is authorised, and we all rush to the Metro. Some theatre or other, or a music-hall. Then I usually go with my friend Faulhaber to 'El Garón', a small bar in one of the galaxy of streets branching off from the Place Pigalle. A Frenchman provides music, and Faulhaber knows a really nice girl there, who is said to be studying political economy. There is chatting in German and French, and the French want to know more than anything whether we shall soon be landing 'over there'.

The wine is cheap, the music makes you feel depressed, and life is like dancing on a tight-rope. My friend Faulhaber, the sober student of mathematics and physics, and a radio operator, says: 'If we soon win the war, it may work out all right. But if we look like losing it, they'll harry us right into the ground. We shan't in any case survive a lost war . . . '

But in view of what the Führer has till now demonstrated to the world, who could have doubts about our victory? No one has any serious doubts. We will probably soon land on that island. But after that I am sceptical.

We, the Luftwaffe, will anyway not manage to sink the entire English fleet if it takes up a position in the Channel.

And suppose we don't land? Will our night attacks, so restricted by navigational factors, be sufficiently effective?

We struggle inwardly to believe — though night by night we discover that most of our bombs are missing their targets in the eternal fog and clouds . . . Only in bright moonlight and otherwise in exceptionally good weather conditions have we any real chance of hitting what we should and are trying to hit. Will that be enough? Or are others more competent than we are?

One question after another. But what have we to do with questions? A soldier's job is not to ask questions, but only to do his duty.

And furthermore:

Our leadership has always, and promptly achieved far more than we and anyone else in the world would have believed possible.

In Poland it was all over in 14 days. Russia was on our side, with no war on two fronts as in 1914–1918. As for France, it was finished almost as quickly there; including the British army on the Continent.

And at this moment there is a special communiqué being issued on the radio, saying: Our comrades are overrunning Serbia and the whole of Greece with unparallelled drive — after the Italians (why must we always be tied up with them?), despite wearisome efforts, have achieved nothing there other than a heavy and culpable defeat . . .

And then there are our U-boats with Dönitz. Suppose they don't bring it off? Our leadership will know how it will all turn out.

ROBERT GÖTZ

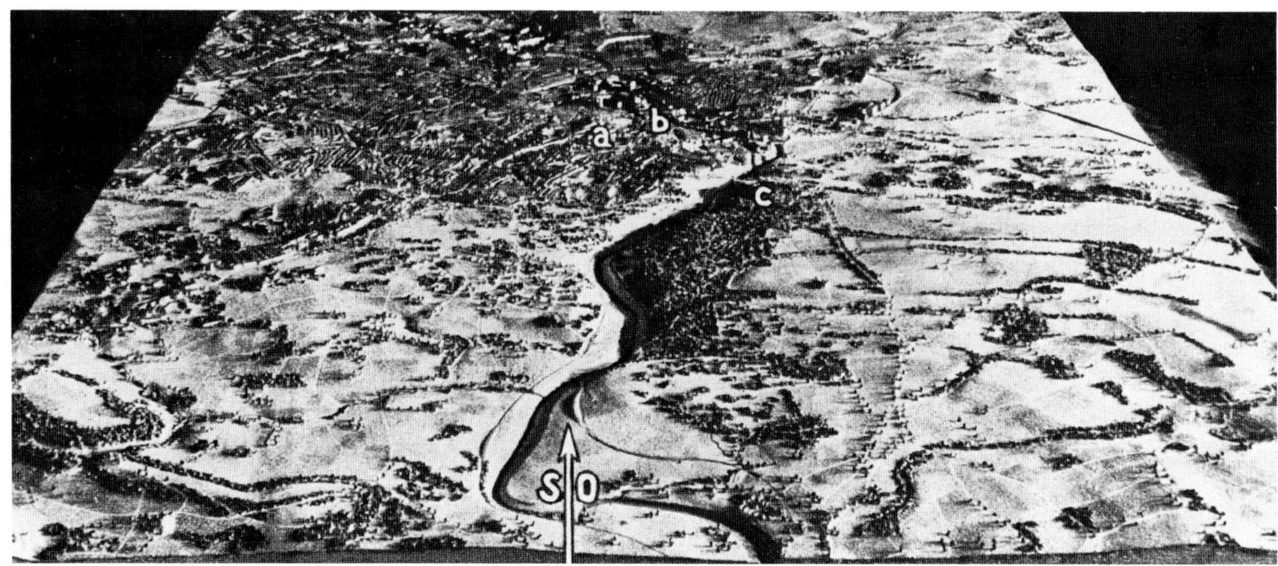

Occasionally the Luftwaffe used models as target locating aids but more often the models were photographed and the end result, suitably annotated, used as part of the crews' briefing documentation. This example of Bristol, target for Saturday night's attack, picks out 'a' the Cabot Tower; 'b' the city docks and 'c' Clifton Suspension Bridge.

SATURDAY, MARCH 29-30

Sunset: 1928 Sunrise: 0641
Moon: Dusk — 2118 (New +2)

Minor attack on Bristol/Avonmouth. Minelaying in coastal areas.

UK — Variable but mainly small amounts of cloud with moderate to good visibility. Mist in some districts.

The Continent — Low cloud with very poor visibility in most areas. Better conditions with moderate to poor visibility in northern France.

Daylight operations continued to be severely limited by weather conditions but a low-level machine gun attack on a train near Norwich killed one person and a considerable amount of damage was caused to property at Walberswick in East Suffolk.

An improvement in the weather over some of the German bomber bases in north-west France late in the day permitted a small scale attack to be made against Bristol's Schwerpunkt 'a', the docks at Avonmouth, and port and industrial installations in Bristol itself.

The Avonmouth attack lasted from 2105 to 2208 hours and in this time 16 aircraft dropped eight tonnes of HE (five SC 500, 95 short time delay SC 50 and eight normal SC 50) together with 11,396 incendiaries. Fires were started in the Target Area and helped to guide following crews who had some difficulty in locating the target. The fires grew into a fire area with marked red glow.

Over Bristol itself, where the CP lay between the east end of the Floating Harbour and the two gas holders situated two kilometres east-north-eastwards, 20 aircraft delivered 25 tonnes of HE (six SC 500, 63 SC 250, five LZZ 250 and 95 SC 50) and 1,692 incendiaries. Only five crews bombed visually, the other 15 using DR and radio methods. One large explosion and a large fire glow were seen, but further observations were not possible because of the cloud and mist. Units involved in the attack were:

Bristol, Target Area 'a' (Avonmouth):
KGr100: 11 He 111, 2105-2153 (seven crews used X-beams, four bombed visually on fires)
III/KG26: 5 He 111, 2138-2208 (Y-Verfahren used; clear signals without interference)

Bristol Target Area 'd' (city docks):
III/KG1: 11 Ju 88, 2110-2145 (7 aircraft bombed by DR, 4 visually)
II/KG76: 8 Ju 88, 2115-2140 (bombing a mixture of DR and radio navigation methods)
KGr100: 1 He 111, 2153 (bombed the city visually)

Two Ju 88s of III/KG1 broke off their attacks, one because of engine trouble and the other, of the same unit, because of radio failure. No aircraft were lost, but upon their return some aircraft of III/KG1 diverted to Beauvais and Orléans/Bricy because of adverse weather conditions at their home base.

Damage in Avonmouth was not extensive and in nearby Shirehampton, where many of the bombs landed, mainly private property suffered. Eleven people were killed, including six in a school shelter in Shirehampton. Most of the fires in Avonmouth were quickly extinguished and although nine important dock objectives were hit, substantial damage was reported in only two. No damage of importance was reported in Bristol.

Elsewhere bombs fell at several points in the South, Wales and the Midlands, but no significant damage was done.

'Raid in the Bristol Channel area.' A somewhat imprecisely-captioned, yet dramatic, picture of an attack on the city in 1941.

That poor 'north-east town'. Even *The Hull Times* reporting on Monday night's raid were forced to use the term when they announced that 'considerable damage and some casualties were reported when the Germans made a sharp raid on a North-East coast town . . .' a rather unnecessary subterfuge by the censor especially in a local paper as he allowed the editor to include the German communiqué for Tuesday which claimed that Hull had been attacked during the night! At least the shake up at the Ministry of Information earlier in the month (see page 480-81) seems to have done some good as the effects of the raid were allowed to be reported in some detail.

SUNDAY, MARCH 30-31

Sunset: 1929 Sunrise: 0639
Moon: Dusk — 2219 (New +3)

No major activity by night.

UK — Extensive cloud with moderate to poor visibility. Rain and sleet in some areas, some snow on high ground and in the North.
The Continent — Much low cloud with snow in many areas.

Daylight operations were largely curtailed by weather conditions but there were reports of bombs in Scotland and in Sussex at Worthing. No damage or casualties resulted.
During the night 40 long-range bombers and three long-range night fighters operated, seeking various targets, with little success, in Scotland, the north Midlands and East Anglia. There were no casualties and little damage.

In the last four days of March, five aircraft were lost on operations to Britain. Only one fell on land, the remaining four crashing into the North Sea or the Channel.

1(F)/123 Junkers Ju 88A (0115). Shot down by Flight Lieutenant A. D. J. Lovel DFC in a Spitfire of No. 41 Squadron during a reconnaissance of Manchester. Aircraft dived into the ground at Wilton Moor, Eston, North Yorkshire 3.50 p.m. Lt. W. Schloth, Lt. O. Meinhold, Fw. W. Schmigale and Uffz. H. Steigerwald all killed. Aircraft 4U+GH destroyed.

MONDAY, MARCH 31-APRIL 1

Sunset: 1930 Sunrise: 0637
Moon: Dusk — 2319 (New +4)

Sharp attack on Hull. Scattered light attacks elsewhere from South Wales to the North-East.

UK — Extensive cloud with moderate visibility in most areas.
The Continent — Mainly similar to the UK, but poor visibility with fog in some districts.

There was little daylight activity apart from fighter skirmishes over the English Channel and ineffective bombing in Huntingdonshire and off Falmouth. During the night, operations were undertaken by 79 bombers and 11 night fighters and although targets in the Humber area were the main objective, bombing was widespread.

The main target was Hull, where dock installations were claimed bombed by 47 aircraft between 2045 and 2253 hours. They dropped 39 tonnes of HE (five SC 1000, six SC 250, and 32 LMB parachute mines) together with 22,688 IBs. The CP lay between the City Docks and the Alexandra Dock, with bomb aiming assisted by means of 74 LC 50 parachute flares. One large fire developed in the north-east district of the town besides numerous large and small fires in the docks area. Further results were difficult to assess because of cloud, light rain and generally poor visibility.
Another 26 aircraft (including two seeking alternative targets to Hull) attacked dock installations at Great Yarmouth with 29 tonnes of HE (14 SC 1000, 20 SC 500, 20 SD 500 and four LMB mines) and 7,956 incendiaries between 2017 and 2300 hours. Visual bombing was attempted, in the light of 40 LC 50 flares, and was seemingly succesful. Crews reported explosions and fires in the Target Area, with one extraordinary large fire on the west bank of the River Yare. A ship was also seen to be on fire.
Night fighters of I/NJG2, sent to patrol airfields, attacked Hemswell and Waddington and as alternatives bombed industrial targets in Leeds and Grimsby and searchlights in the Midlands. Aircraft of IX Fliegerkorps laid mines in coastal waters.
Considerable damage was done in Hull and a number of public buildings were destroyed or damaged. High explosives and land mines fell in almost every section of the city with 200 casualties reported, 50 of them fatal. Upwards of 500 houses were damaged. Damage in the docks was only slight, although police premises and the infirmary were also hit. Bombing was widely scattered over the North-East and East Anglia, but damage and casualties also occurred at Barrow-in-Furness, Portsmouth and Swansea, where three people were killed.

Although the newspaper was allowed to include a photograph of the ARP HQ, which would have been instantly recognisable to readers as the Shell Mex building on the corner of Ferensway and Spring Bank, it was only identified as 'property . . . in a north-east town.' The article in the April 5 edition reported that 'Casualties included a number of deaths, and one of the persons killed was the deputy Medical Officer of Health for the town. He was in an A.R.P. post when the building was demolished by a direct hit. He had just completed a successful campaign for blood donors in the area, in which thousands of people had volunteered to give their blood for the benefit of people badly injured in air raids. . . . Two soldiers who were in an adjacent car park were also killed, and at an A.R.P. post a policeman on duty at the door was killed. The deputy medical officer . . . was in the basement of a building with a number of other people. He was talking to a councillor and another doctor, a colleague who had just arrived in the town to take over the duties of casualty officer. When the bomb fell and exploded, the doctor was standing in a position which caused him to receive the full force of the blast, and he was killed instantly.' The 'bomb' was in fact a land mine — still forbidden to be mentioned as such — and the town's Deputy Medical Officer of Health, Dr David Diamond, who was handing over to the newly-appointed Civil Defence Medical Officer, Dr Wheatley. The policeman, PC Robert Garton, was never seen again.

APRIL 1941

The poor weather conditions of late March continued into early April to give a quiet start to what was to become the month of heaviest bombing yet. There were 16 major and five heavy attacks, and on only three nights were all German operations cancelled. Attacks on coastal shipping were stepped up, but minelaying at night was scaled down to four occasions only. For the first time more than 1,000 tonnes of HE were claimed dropped in one attack — on London by 712 aircraft — and civilian casualties reached an all time high of 6,062 killed and 6,926 seriously injured. Major or heavy attacks were also directed at Bristol/Avonmouth, Glasgow/Clydeside, Liverpool/Birkenhead, Coventry, Birmingham, Tyneside, Belfast, Plymouth/Devonport, Sunderland and Portsmouth as the Luftwaffe continued to ring the changes, with ports again the prime objectives.

Luftwaffe night sorties over Britain totalled 5,451 by long-range bombers, 205 by long-range night fighters and 68 by light bombers; to counter them RAF Fighter Command flew 842 single- and 342 twin-engined night fighter sorties, with the former producing 45 visual contacts which resulted in 39 combats. The twin-engine sorties achieved 117 AI and 10 visual interceptions giving 50 AI and five visual combats. Forty-eight enemy aircraft were claimed destroyed by night fighters of both categories and 39 by AA guns, again breaking all previous records.

The improving night defences gave some satisfaction to Air Marshal Douglas, who was particularly pleased with the better results obtained by 'cats-eyes' units engaged in Fighter Night operations in bright moonlight. Nevertheless, he placed on record, in a report on enemy activity, his firm belief 'that AI assisted by GCI control will prove the primary means of dealing with the night interception problem, although good success may be anticipated with "cats-eyes" fighters on moonlight nights'. For this reason he was concerned at the slow progress being made in the supply of twin-engine night fighters fitted with AI. And understandably so, for the rate of delivery of these aircraft to Fighter Command was so low that his Beaufighter strength decreased slightly, and for this reason he most strongly urged the Air Ministry to either allot a larger proportion of available production to his Command, at the expense of Coastal Command, or increase production of this type.

With the approach of spring and the shortening hours of darkness, Douglas felt that henceforth there would be greater concentration against targets in the southern part of Britain and in anticipation he sanctioned the transfer of No. 600 Squadron from Prestwick and Drem to Colerne, No. 307 Squadron from Colerne to Exeter (with a detachment at Pembrey) and No. 29 Squadron from Digby to West Malling; No. 141 Squadron at Gravesend was to move in the opposite direction, northwards to Ayr, where it was to re-equip with Beaufighters in place of Defiants. From its new base No. 141 Squadron was to work with another recently opened GCI Station — at St Quivox near Ayr — which became fully operational in April, as did another new GCI Station at Langtoft, near Wittering. Other stations at Hack Green, near Shrewsbury, and at Dirleton near Edinburgh, were also due to enter service in the immediate future.

HEFT 6 / BERLIN, 25. MÄRZ 1941
Der Adler
Portugal Esc. 1.50
España Pts. 1.—
HERAUSGEGEBEN UNTER MITWIRKUNG DES REICHS-LUFTFAHRTMINISTERIUMS
„Das hat mal wieder hingehauen!"
Oberleutnant Baumbach, dessen jüngster Kampfbericht in diesem Heft enthalten ist, im Gespräch mit einem Kameraden unmittelbar nach Rückkehr von seinem erfolgreichen Angriffsflug
"¡Otra vez hemos tenido éxito!"
El teniente Baumbach, cuyo informe de combate publicamos en este número, conversando con un camarada inmediatamente después de haber regresado de su brillante acción contra el enemigo

Dive-bombing exponent extraordinaire. Oberleutnant Werner Baumbach of the Eagle Geschwader — KG 30 — appropriately featured on the current issue of *Der Adler*. Well on his way to his Knight's Cross (it was awarded in May), it was claimed that as the unit's 'Schiffs-Experten', he had sunk 200,000 tons of merchant shipping. The actual magazine article featured him carrying out an attack on a convoy off Harwich in February.

Fighter Night patrols were in operation during the month over Bristol, Coventry, Birmingham, London and the Thames Estuary and in every case gunfire was permitted below the lowest fighter patrol height in accordance with the new policy. From all points of view, this was a major improvement in the system and was to continue thus, but only when good moonlight was accompanied by clear weather over a point of concentrated attack.

Intruder patrols by No. 23 Squadron continued through April, but slow delivery of Havocs meant the continued use of obsolescent Blenheim Mk Is. The few Havocs in service were being used to determine range and performance characteristics before their wider adoption, but No. 93 Squadron's Havocs were by now fully operational on Mutton mine-dropping operations. Previously, when using Harrows, Mutton patrols had been confined to defined areas notified as hazardous to other RAF Commands, but from April onwards Mutton minelaying aircraft were cleared to operate in any area where enemy aircraft were to be found. Another activity of No. 93 Squadron was proving unacceptable — further trials with the mine-towing Wellington revealed a ceiling of less than 10,000 feet and a speed of only 120 mph. Douglas therefore recommended that this project be abandoned, a view subsequently accepted by the Air Ministry. Further discussions also took place regarding the use of the Albino free balloon barrage; no releases were made in April, but it was agreed that further trials should be undertaken with Admiralty co-operation after May 15, when it was hoped to launch a massive 10,000 balloons in the Liverpool area.

Trials also continued with the special Flash Flares (achieving a measure of success which led to a production order) and with the airborne searchlight ('Turbinlite') intended for use by AI-equipped Havocs and attendant satellite Hurricanes. There were some initial difficulties, however, and it took a little time to evolve operating procedures, but Douglas was optimistic about the eventual outcome of the Turbinlite Havoc/Hurricane combination. His optimism was misplaced, however, for despite extended trials and operational use, it failed to achieve the success anticipated.

Douglas agreed to continue with Star Shell experiments to illuminate enemy aircraft, but bad weather in the moonless period of April — and it was in the darkness of no moon periods that the Star Shells were expected to be most effective — did little to help the trials.

By now several 'Z' Batteries had been established, equipped with UP (rocket) projectors, and on the night of April 7-8 the first such site, at Cardiff, claimed the destruction of an enemy aircraft. Although intended originally for use against low flying aircraft, the adoption of these projectors as weapons for use against aircraft at medium and high altitudes proved to be an excellent move.

Also effective, but less easy to measure by reason of their passive nature, were two methods of obscuring targets from enemy eyes. The first was the use of smoke generators as used, for example, at Liverpool to obscure the docks. Secondly, industrial 'smog' or haze was deliberately increased in certain areas by encouraging factories to emit more smoke than normal peacetime restriction regulations allowed. Smoke screens were in fact used throughout April at Derby and Nottingham, and for ten days from April 4 at Accrington, Cheltenham, Coventry, Luton, Newcastle, Gloucester, Wolverhampton and eleven other places, but nothing is known of the German reaction.

Although British night fighter losses had not been serious, there was some disquiet concerning the number of accidents, particularly at Operational Training Units. In the first quarter of 1941, Fighter Command aircraft were involved in 89 fatal accidents resulting in 106 deaths. There were 16 air collisions and 11 pilots were killed by flying into high ground in bad weather; most of these involved inexperienced squadron or OTU pilots, and in a letter from Fighter Command to all Group Commanders stress was laid on the vital necessity to take all possible steps to reduce the accident rate. An improvement did materialise in due course, but the very nature of the task offered little hope of a significant reduction. However, improved communications and other technical innovations helped,

Einer von vielen

Uno de muchos

Hace algunas semanas, echó a pique un avión de gran bombardeo de la aviación alemana el vapor inglés "Lighthouse Service" a quince grados de longitud oeste de Irlanda. De las seis bombas de 250 kilogramos arrojadas dieron cuatro sobre cubierta. Las fotografías, obtenidas por un miembro de la tripulación momentos después del ataque, dan una impresión convincente de sus efectos

Die „Lighthouse Service" ist schwer getroffen. Der weiße Rauch aus dem Schornstein des Dampfers läßt auf eine Kesselexplosion schließen. Sämtliche Aufbauten des Schiffes sind zerstört

El "Lighthouse Service" ha sido alcanzado de lleno. El vapor blanco que sale a borbotones de la chimenea hace suponer la explosión de la caldera. Todas las construcciones sobre cubierta del barco han quedado destruidas

Bilder rechts und unten: Im Abflug zeigt sich der Besatzung das sinkende Schiff noch einmal. Ungeheure Rauchwolken ziehen über die See Aufn. Luftwaffe (4)

Derecha y abajo: En el momento de emprender el vuelo de regreso observa la tripulación por última vez al buque antes de hundirse. Enormes nubarrones de humo se extienden sobre el mar

Die Aufnahme links zeigt das Schiff über den Bug. An Backbord ist ein Rettungsboot zu Wasser gelassen

La foto de la izquierda presenta al buque desde proa. A babor ha sido bajado al agua un bote de salvamento

192

Although not credited to Baumbach, this sequence shows an undated attack on a ship called 'Lighthouse Service'. In fact the picture shows the *Isolda*, an Irish Lights tender on December 19, 1940 after she was bombed off Saltee, County Wexford. She had just served the Coningbeg lightship when she was attacked, killing the chief steward, the coxswain, two firemen, a greaser and an able seaman.

for not all the development work was directed against the enemy.

The Luftwaffe continued its efforts to establish technical superiority over the opposition, but met with no particular success. To counter the radio countermeasures of No. 80 Wing the Germans adopted a number of changes including, from April 1, frequent frequency and call-sign changes of their impressive array of radio aids. As previously, however, No. 80 Wing was quick to respond. Interference to the X- and Y-Verfahren transmissions was also pursued by the RAF, but KGr100 was still able to make use of their X-beams. III/KG26, on the other hand, appears to have been more adversely affected by British counter-measures; according to 'Y' Service and No. 80 Wing monitors, the bomb release signal was received by more than 25 per cent of participating aircraft of this unit on only two occasions during the month. An increase in the number of aircraft of III/KG26 that were operating over the country each night — as determined by W/T intercepts — led British Air Intelligence to believe that this unit was replacing KGr100 as the leading 'Firelighter' unit, but this was not strictly the case. The effectiveness of British countermeasures was, of course, difficult for No. 80 Wing to assess, but information gleaned from PoWs and other sources led to the acceptance of a success rate which is not supported by German records. The interference to X-Verfahren remained more of a nuisance that was largely overcome until later on; that to Y-Verfahren was variable but could, on the whole, be described as moderately successful, as was the interference to Elektra. Knickebein, on the other hand, was very successfully countered, but still the most successful of all British action was the Meaconing of radio beacons and the passing of false bearings to enemy aircraft by RAF aircraft Meaconing stations masquerading as German D/F stations. Four of the latter were now in operation: those

Englands Flotte verkriecht sich

La flota inglesa se esconde

Nur höchst selten treten größere Einheiten der britischen Flotte auf hoher See in Erscheinung. Daß die edlen Lords sich ähnlich wie im Weltkrieg irgendwo verkrochen haben, war längst bekannt. Aber wo ihre stolze Flotte steckt, das haben deutsche Aufklärer festgestellt: in den äußersten Schlupfwinkeln der zerklüfteten Westküste des nördlichen Schottland. Unser Luftbild zeigt drei Einheiten der britischen Kriegsmarine im Loch Alsh, ostwärts der Hebriden. Höher hinauf ging's nicht mehr. Im Weltkrieg hatten die Briten ihre Grand Fleet in ähnlichen Mauselöchern versteckt. Damals war sie dort außerhalb des Aktionsbereichs der deutschen Flieger in völliger Sicherheit. Das ist heute anders geworden, und die Briten werden das eines Tages noch zu spüren bekommen

Rara es la vez que operan en alta mar las unidades mayores de la armada británica. De sobras se sabía que los honorables lores habrían de esconderse en algún lado siguiendo la costumbre de la Gran Guerra. Pero los observadores alemanes han sabido localizar el escondite de tan arrogante flota: nada menos que en los escarpados acantilados de la costa oeste del norte de Escocia. Nuestra fotografía aérea muestra tres unidades de la marina de guerra inglesa en Alsh, al este de la Hébridas. Más arriba ya no podía ser. En la Gran Guerra supieron los ingleses esconder su Grand Fleet en ratoneras análogas. En aquel entonces se encontraba por cierto sobre seguro fuera del radio de acción de los aviadores alemanes. Pero hoy ha cambiado la cosa, y los ingleses no dejarán de darse exacta cuenta de ello en su día

Aufnahmen Luftwaffe (4)

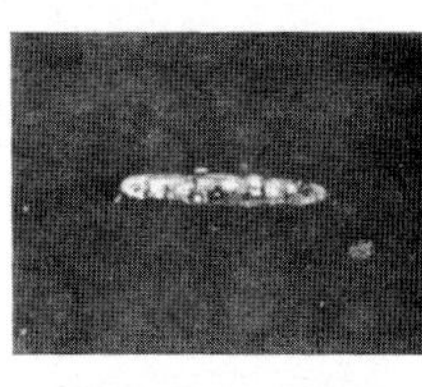

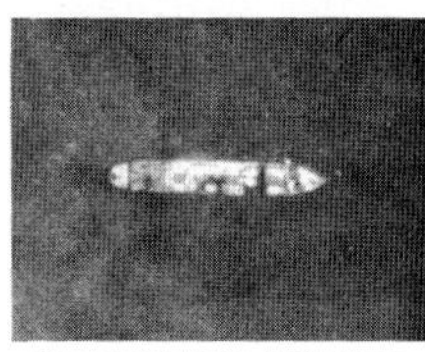

Es sind ganz ansehnliche Pötte, die sich in dieser zerklüfteten Felsenlandschaft versteckt halten. Bei den oberen Schiffen handelt es sich um große Frachter von etwa 8 bis 10 000 BRT, die wahrscheinlich als Hilfskreuzer Verwendung finden, während der untere Dampfer ein Kriegsschiff darstellt, das weit vor dem Ufer vor Anker gegangen ist und auf irgendeine Order wartet

Por cierto que son navíos singulares los que han intentado ocultarse al abrigo de tan escabrosos peñascales. Los buques superiores son mercantes de 8 a 10.000 toneladas, los que al parecer son empleados como cruceros auxiliares, mientras que el buque inferior es una unidad de guerra que ha echado anclas a cierta distancia de la costa, quizás en espera de alguna orden

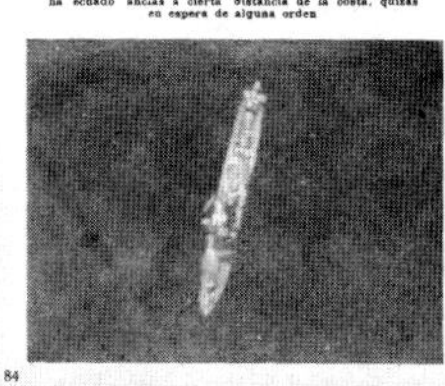

84

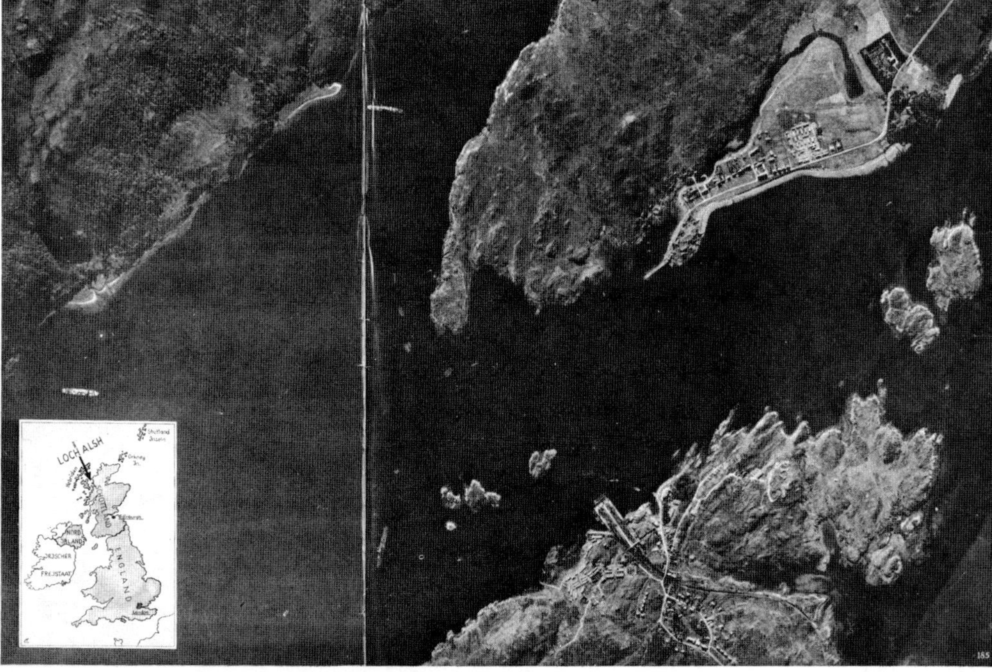

185

Maintaining the emphasis on shipping under observation by Aufklärungs units, illustrated in recent issues, were these shots taken *above* at Loch Alsh in the extreme north and *opposite* at the other end of the country off Southend Pier.

at Mundesley, Flimwell and Honiton being joined in April by a new station at Louth. Further D/F stations of this type were under construction, together with an HF station intended for the same purpose.

Seventeen Starfish decoy fires were lit in April and all but six succeeded in drawing bombs intended for nearby targets. Especially successful was the Portsmouth (Sinach Common) Starfish, which drew 170 HE bombs, 32 parachute mines and about 5,000 IBs on the night of April 17.

Anti-aircraft guns had increased in numbers at a steady rate and by the end of the month General Pile was able to deploy 1,691 heavy and 940 light guns, with most of the HAA guns working under GL control. The night fighter force had also expanded and by the end of the month Douglas was able to boast seventeen squadrons towards his stated requirement of twenty. He was by no means satisfied, however, with the ratio of twin- to single-engine squadrons, but a later mark of AI equipment now being introduced augured well for the immediate future. At last, it seemed, the tide could be turning.

Despite their greater losses, morale in the Luftwaffe remained very high, a feature borne out during the interrogation of PoWs by AI1(k) Branch. During April 97 prisoners were taken and the bodies of 93 German airmen were recovered. Investigation revealed an average age of 24½ years for bomber pilots (as against 26 for the 25 bomber pilots shot down in March); the youngest PoW was a Bordmechaniker aged 18½ and there were cases of both observers and W/T operators aged 19. The youngest pilot was 21 and the oldest 34, but almost without exception the captured airmen showed a confidence indicative of excellent morale. There were, however, several instances of men being glad to be out of the war and security discipline was less in evidence than in recent months. It was felt that German successes in the Middle East and in the Balkans were responsible for a marked buoyancy among both newly captured and existing PoWs — indeed there were cases, noted by postal censors, of Luftwaffe PoWs advising their relatives not to send any more letters or parcels to England as they would be home in the near future.

The German offensive in the Balkans, which opened on April 6 with the advance into Greece and Yugoslavia, met with accustomed success. Nevertheless, it occasioned the withdrawal of valuable bomber units from the strategic bombing of Britain and by the end of April there were more than 1,000 German aircraft of all types operating in the Balkans under Luftflotte 4. To offset the reduction in bomber strength, many crews in North-West Europe were now obliged to carry out two and sometimes three missions in one night on short-range flights such as attacks on London, often using forward bases for refuelling and re-arming. The effect on crews was to be damaging, but a sustained, high level of operations was necessary, indeed essential, to camouflage German plans for the assault on Soviet Russia, now due to be launched in the early summer of 1941. This plan was opposed by several senior officers who dreaded a war on two fronts — and with Britain still unvanquished, and now with the war in the Balkans and a Middle East involvement, they were faced with the prospects of war on three or more fronts. The basic plan, however, still called for a continued assault on Britain's war economy, industrial capacity and importing docks, while imposing a strict submarine and air blockade. Russia, it was confidently expected, would be crushed before the onset of winter, when a return of the Luftwaffe bomber arm to the West was planned. Meanwhile the offensive against Britain was to be maintained throughout the summer by a token, mainly anti-shipping, bomber force. Another full winter of bombing could then be undertaken, if necessary, to force Britain to capitulate, but expectations were that Churchill might well come to terms in the meantime. However, if all else failed, an invasion of England would be carried out at the time best suited to the Germans. Naturally, none of this was known to the British, although intelligence reports began to indicate the course of events long before they in fact occurred. For instance, despite German efforts to conceal movements to the Balkans (and shortly afterwards farther eastwards towards the Russian border), the RAF's 'Y' Service was not fooled by 'spoof' W/T transmissions and was well aware of events. Thus the departure of

II/KG51 to Austria, en route to the Balkans, was noted on April 12, followed by the transfers of Stab I and III/KG2 (accompanied by II Gruppe's 6 Staffel) and II/KG4, all bound for the Balkans. Of a more local nature was the transfer of I/KG55 from Dreux to Melun/Villaroche, on April 14, and the move of I/KG76 from Chateaudun to Beaumont-le-Roger. Not immediately known to the RAF, however, was the formation on April 1 of a new light bomber unit from elements of the former Erprobungsgruppe 210. Under the command of Major Walter Storp, formerly the Kommandeur of II/KG76, the new Bf 110-equipped unit was designated Schnellkampfgeschwader (Fast Bomber Wing) 210 (abbreviated to SKG210) and initially comprised I Gruppe with a Stab and an Ergänzungsstaffel. Storp took up his new command on April 24 and, an experienced day and night bomber pilot himself, set about the task of training his crews, many of whom had flown day fighter-bomber sorties only, for both day and night attacks on land and shipping targets. Eventually, the unit was to re-equip with the new Messerschmitt Me 210 fighter-bomber, but production delays followed problems with the prototype aircraft and the future of the type was in doubt.

Other German Air Force movements in April included III/KG3 to the Balkans, III/KG76 to Soesterberg, III/KG1 to Roye/Amy, II/KG54 to Bretigny/Le Plessis-Pate, I/KG77 to Laon/Athies and I/KG3 from Le Culot to Wunstorf in Germany. Another return to Germany involved II/KG3 which left its base at Antwerp/Deurne for Bremen/Oldenburg, while 3/906 departed from Aalborg for Tromsö/Skattora, Norway.

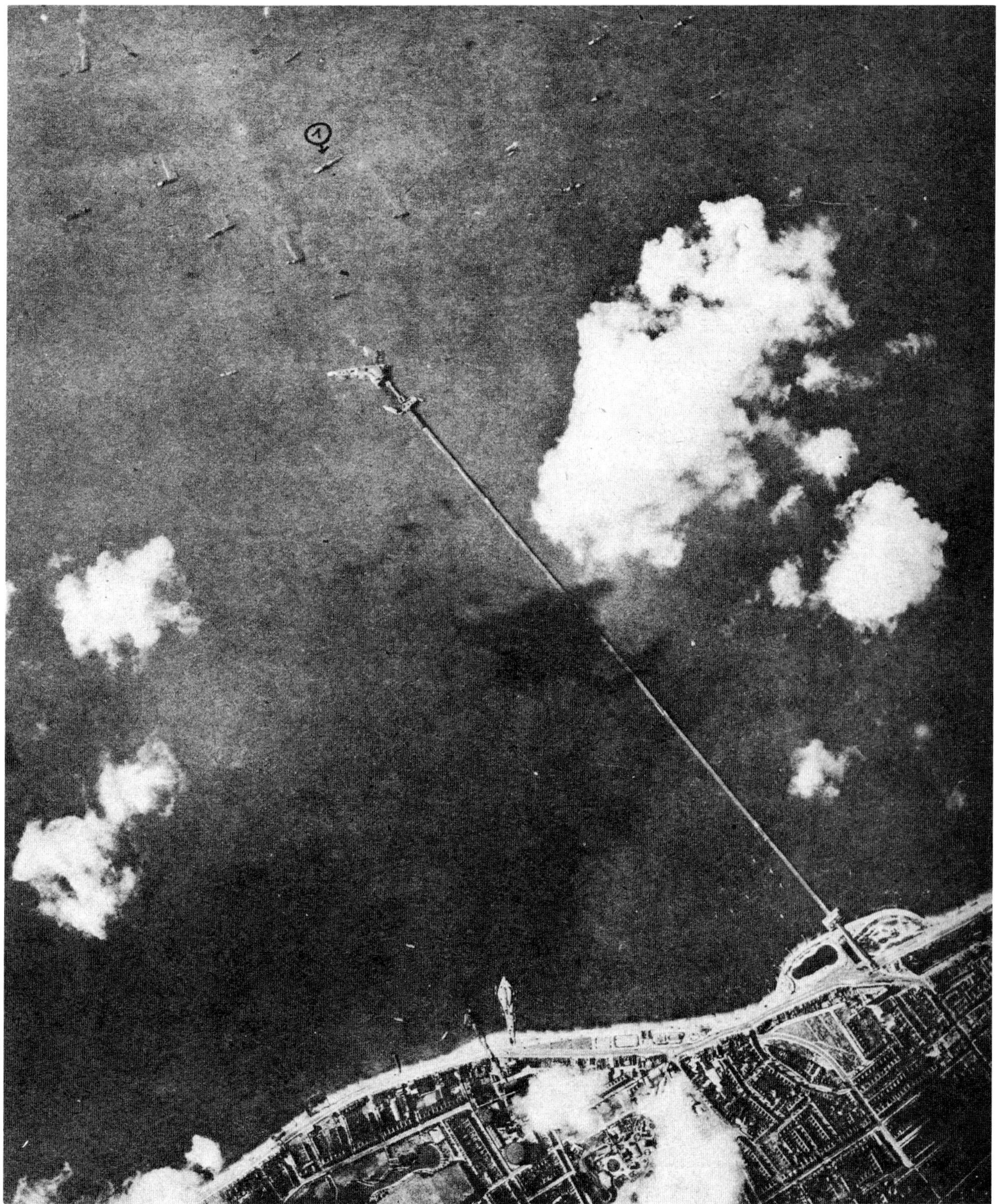

TUESDAY, APRIL 1-2

Sunset: 1932 Sunrise: 0635
Moon: Dusk — 0017 (First Qtr −4)

No German night bomber operations.

UK — Extensive cloud with moderate to poor visibility and rain in most areas. Strong to gale force winds in many districts.
The Continent — Similar to the UK.

During the day single, low flying 'Pirate' raiders dropped bombs in various parts of the country. Leeming and Warmwell airfields were attacked and St Eval came in for attention at dusk. Bombs also fell harmlessly in East Anglia but extensive damage was done to property at Seaford, Sussex, where one person was killed. In Scotland the Bell Rock lighthouse was machine-gunned and there was some dislocation of railway traffic near Berwick.
Night bomber operations were cancelled because of poor weather over German bases.

Although activity was on a limited scale, five aircraft were lost all of which are listed below. A Heinkel He 111 from 3/KG4 returned to Soesterberg with one man injured after being attacked by fighters.

8/KG1 Junkers Ju 88A-5 (6245). Flew into a hill in bad visibility during a raid on Birmingham. Crashed at 'The Wicket', Brown Clee Hill, Shropshire 9.45 a.m. Uffz. H. Ewald, Uffz. H. Prochnow, Uffz. W. Lehnhardt and Fw. E. Wels all killed. Aircraft V4+BS disintegrated.
Site investigated by Philippa Hodgkiss and the Warplane Wreck Investigation Group. Iron Cross, NCO's cap badge, Walther Signal Pistol and numerous airframe parts in the Hodgkiss Collection.

1/KG27 Heinkel He 111H-5 (3635). Crash landed after combat with Pilot Officer B. Anders and Flying Officer A. Gabszewicz in Hurricanes of No. 316 Squadron at Ballyristeen, County Wexford, Eire 5.18 p.m. Lt. H. Grau, Oberfw. E. Lorra, Uffz. E. Gensen, Uffz. O. Jäger and Lt. G. Flieshmann all interned in Eire. Aircraft 1G+LH wrecked.

3/KG27 Heinkel He 111H-5 (3837). Suffered engine failure over the Bristol Channel. Attempted to land on Lundy Island but crashed into a cliff 75 feet from the top 5.45 p.m. Uffz. G. Nikolai and Uffz. H. Kunze killed. Uffz. H. Kroker, Uffz. F. Keuchel and Gefr. A. Hohenbaum taken prisoner. Aircraft 1G+FL destroyed.

3/KG27 Heinkel He 111H-4 (6993). Shot down by Flight Lieutenant Haysom DFC in a Hurricane of No. 79 Squadron. Crashed into the sea 5 miles west of St. David's Head, Pembrokeshire 6.05 p.m.

Oh, to be in England, now that April is here! The dubious pleasure of being the month's first long-stay visitor fell to a Ju 88 of KG1. Post-war relics from Shropshire *below*.

Fw. H. Hegemann, Fw. W. Eckold and Gefr. H. Dahmen killed. Oberfw. R. Bör and Fw. A. Ullmann taken prisoner. Aircraft 1G+HL lost.

5/KG77 Junkers Ju 88A-5 (0614). Shot down by Squadron Leader W. P. F. Treacy and Flying Officer R. D. Grassick in Hurricanes of No. 242 Squadron. Dived into the ground at Basey Fisher Farm, Hulver, Suffolk 5.25 p.m. Lt. P. Meyer and Uffz. H. Richmann killed. Uffz. C. Petermann and Uffz. H. Heidrich baled out and taken prisoner. Aircraft 3Z+LN totally destroyed.
Small pieces obtained from the crash site in the Norfolk and Suffolk Aviation Museum collection.

April 1941 — a month in which London was about to earn the dubious distinction of being the first city to receive 1,000 tonnes of high explosive in one attack. . . .

WEDNESDAY, APRIL 2-3

Sunset: 1933 Sunrise: 0633
Moon: Dusk — 0112 (First Qtr −3)

No German night bomber operations.

UK — Extensive low cloud with rain in many areas. Visibility moderate to poor.
The Continent — Similar to the UK in most areas.

Only ten German aircraft were over Britain during the day and, apart from an attack on Catfoss airfield, there was little to report. As a result of the weather all night operations were cancelled.

One aircraft came down near Britain and a Junkers Ju 88 of 3/806 also failed to return. A Junkers Ju 88 of 3(F)/121 landed at Dinard after being severely damaged by fighters.

7/KG55 Heinkel He 111P-2 (2137). Shot down by Flight Lieutenant P. T. Parsons in a Hurricane of No. 504 Squadron. Crashed into the sea off Budleigh Salterton, Devon 7.30 a.m. Body of Oblt. H. L. Wolff recovered from the sea and buried at Exeter. Uffz. H. Wagner, Uffz. K. Papadik, Oberfw. W. Bürkle and Uffz. R. Ehlers all killed. Aircraft G1+LR lost.

THURSDAY, APRIL 3-4

Sunset: 1935 Sunrise: 0631
Moon: Dusk — 0202 (First Qtr −2)

Heavy attack on Bristol/Avonmouth, subsidiary attack on Hull and minelaying.

UK — Showers and local thunderstorms in the South, low cloud and rain in the North. Visibility moderate to good, but poor inland.
The Continent — Fair inland, but showers on the coasts. Visibility moderate to good.

Daylight activity remained slight with only 15 German bombers flying over Britain. A few bombs were reported, with some railway damage at Newhaven, but there were no serious consequences.

After nightfall, taking advantage of the generally improved weather conditions with the passage of a cold front, a heavy attack was made on Bristol/Avonmouth by units of Luftflotte 3. Of 94 aircraft dispatched, the crews of 76 reported over the main target area, but instead of bombing the port and industrial installations at Avonmouth, 27 crews attacked Bristol City Docks and industrial areas. The other 49 crews who succeeded in locating their Avonmouth CP dropped 50 tonnes of HE (five SC 1000, 26 SC 500, 67 SC 250, 11 LZZ 250 and 256 SC 50) and 7,786 IBs. Some crews bombed visually, but the majority used DR and radio aids. One large and two small fires were subsequently observed but, except for bomb detonations, little else was seen. The attack opened at 2116 and the last aircraft bombed at 2335 hours.

The 27 aircraft bombing the Floating Harbour and industrial area of Bristol dropped 29 tonnes of HE (ten SC 500, one LZZ 500, 81 SC 250, ten LZZ 250 and ten SC 50) and 1,152 IBs between 2135 and 0045 hours. Bombing was entirely by DR/radio methods and total cloud cover prevented crews assessing the results; at best, therefore, only a moderate success was anticipated by the Luftwaffe Intelligence Section.

The units and aircraft involved were:

Avonmouth
KGr100: 13 He 111, 2122-2205 (X-Verfahren bombing)
II/KG27: 11 He 111, 2130-2300
KGr806: 5 Ju 88, 2202-2245
I/KG54: 5 Ju 88, 2116-2325
II/KG54: 9 Ju 88, 2308-2335
III/KG26: 6 He 111, 2140-2234 (4 aircraft by Y-Verfahren, 2 visually)

Bristol:
KGr100: 1 He 111, 2205
II/KG1: 11 Ju 88, 2330-0010
III/KG1: 5 Ju 88, 2310-0045
II/KG76: 10 Ju 88, 2135-2230

Eleven crews of Luftflotte 3 bombed other alternative targets including Bournemouth, Portsmouth, Southampton and Poole; earlier in the evening three aircraft made low level attacks on Exeter airfield and single aircraft attacked Thirsk and another airfield north of Bournemouth. One Ju 88 of III/KG1 failed to return.

In a subsidiary raid, Luftflotte 2 aircraft attacked Hull between 2120 and 2230 hours, with a CP on the docks and industrial installations. Nine aircraft reached and bombed the Target Area, delivering five SC 1000, 12 SC 250 and 3,672 incendiaries by means of DR and radio navigation. Again, because of total cloud cover, the bombing accuracy and results could not be ascertained.

At Avonmouth most of the bombs fell in the docks area and it was here that most of the damage was done. Nevertheless, the working of the port was not seriously disrupted but surrounding districts were badly hit. In Bristol, too, residential and commercial premises suffered, but damage to public buildings was less severe than in previous attacks on the city, and public transport and utility services were less seriously interrupted. Some 30 fires were reported in Bristol but firefighting was rapid and effective; factories and other installations were damaged, but with no serious consequences, and casualties were not heavy although 15 people were killed. There were also military casualties when an AA site in Somerset was hit.

Several places were bombed in the North, where Hull was the main objective; fires were started but none were of serious proportions. Further south there was a serious incident near Slough, where houses were damaged and eight people were killed. Bombs also fell in Cardiff, Monmouth, York, Corsley, Barton-on-Humber, Catfoss, Beccles, Poole, Washbourne and near Pevensey.

Anti-aircraft batteries engaging enemy aircraft during the night were those within the IAZ, at Thames and Medway (North and South), on Humberside and at numerous other sites. Guns in the Bristol area were in action from 2112 to 0050 hours, firing 3,327

. . . and Plymouth which was to be annihilated in concentrated bombing in five nights out of seven. The retrieval of UXBs in the city after the two-nighter in March suffered a grievous blow as the ARP Control Room including all the maps, reports and records of local unexploded bombs had been destroyed, and the work of these silent heroes was not achieved without loss of life. *Top:* SC 50s fitted with screamers awaiting delivery and *above* the Plymouth collection service. But for these men. . . .

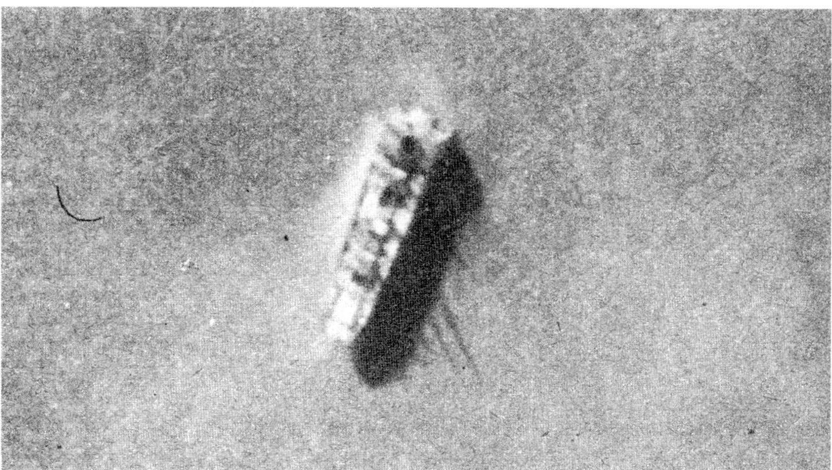

An important aspect of bomber warfare on both sides was the conventional use of mines in enemy waters against shipping, and on most days the Luftwaffe was active in the Western Approaches where effective mining could cripple the convoy routes from North America. Although equal efforts were made to sweep any mines laid, it was still a very effective method of passive war as these two pictures go to show but therein lies a story. They appeared in *Der Adler* in April 1941 with the following caption: 'Nothing escapes the German air reconnaissance. Even before the German Luftwaffe was about to launch its last big attacks on Swansea, a large British freighter met its fate in the Bristol Channel. Severely damaged, the ship was just able to reach the safety of smooth waters near the coast; but then broke up there under the action of the wind and waves. The British could not accept the loss of the many tons of valuable metal represented by leaving the ship to disintegrate. If the vessel was no longer usable as such, at least its potential scrap-metal had to be recovered. But the attempts to salvage the ship were only partially successful. While its stern section resisted all the efforts made, it proved possible to tow away the bow half of the ship. And this was brought into dry dock at Swansea, a harbour on the north bank of the Bristol Channel. In the photograph below, designated with an arrow, the front portion of the ship can be clearly seen in the drained dock. Both photos are outstanding examples of German long-range reconnaissance, and once again prove how closely all developments in the British Isles are kept under observation'.

rounds of ammunition at raiders flying between 6,000 and 15,000 feet. Countrywide some 5,000 rounds were used and two enemy aircraft claimed damaged.

Dusk, night and dawn patrols were flown by 73 aircraft of Fighter Command and included one Intruder operation over northern France by a Blenheim of No. 23 Squadron. One He 111 was claimed destroyed over the Channel following an AI interception by a Beaufighter of No. 604 Squadron from Middle Wallop, and several other sightings were reported.

The pilot and gunner of Defiant T3913 of No. 141 Squadron were killed when they crashed near their base at Gravesend at 0025 hours upon returning from an operational patrol. Another accident occurred at Burghley Park, near Wittering, when Beaufighter X7541 of No. 25 Squadron was destroyed following a spin induced during a descending turn.

Two aircraft were lost, both engaged in coastal operations during daylight. A Heinkel He 111 of 2/KG26 landed at Stavanger with damage.

5/KG1 Junkers Ju 88A-5 (7208). Shot down by Flight Lieutenant Morris and Sergeant Ballard in Spitfires of No. 610 Squadron. Believed crashed into the sea 3 miles off Seaford Head, Sussex 6.57 a.m. Oblt. H. Speh and Uffz. J. Gassen missing. Fw. R. Twartz and Fw. J. Mania killed. Aircraft V4+KV lost.

1/KG27 Heinkel He 111H-5 (4014). Shot down by Squadron Leader M. Rook and Pilot Officer H. N. Hunt in Hurricanes of No. 504 Squadron. Crashed into the sea 3 miles north of Stepper Point, Padstow, Cornwall 5.25 p.m. Lt. F. Huhle, Uffz. A. Eggert, Fw. R. Ahrenholz, Gefr. P. Bienieck and Gefr. E. Borschick all taken prisoner. Aircraft 1G+MH lost.

During the attack on Bristol a single aircraft was lost. A Junkers Ju 88 of II/KG76 made a forced landing at Amiens after being damaged by fighters.

7/KG1 Junkers Ju 88A-5 (4224). Believed that shot down by Flight Lieutenant J. Cunningham and Sergeant C. F. Rawnsley in a Beaufighter of No. 604 Squadron. Aircraft disintegrated and pieces hit the Beaufighter. Crashed into the sea south of the Needles, Isle of Wight 12.50 a.m. Lt. E. Menge, Uffz. R. König, Uffz. W. Hahn and Uffz. W. Schreiber all missing. Aircraft V4+AR lost.

FRIDAY, APRIL 4-5

Sunset: 1937 Sunrise: 0628
Moon: Dusk — 0248 (First Qtr −1)

Heavy attack on Bristol/Avonmouth; minor attacks on airfields, Southampton and elsewhere. Extensive minelaying.

UK — Much low cloud and drizzle. Thundery rain in places. Visibility moderate to poor.

The Continent — Mainly cloudy, dispersing inland, with moderate to poor visibility. Fog patches forming and becoming extensive.

German daylight activity was on a larger scale than of late but most of the aircraft were engaged on anti-shipping, mining or reconnaissance duties and only 16 flew inland. No bombs were dropped.

For the second consecutive night a sharp attack was made on the Bristol area with the docks and industrial area of Avonmouth the primary target. Luftflotte 3 dispatched 105 long-range bombers, of which 83 claimed

Almost correct . . . but not quite. When Mervyn Amundson saw the pictures and researched the story he found that they show the *Protesilaus* which broke in two after hitting a mine over a *year* before — on January 21, 1940. One half was beached on the Mumbles, the other towed to Swansea dry dock for rebuilding. However the damage was deemed to be too extensive and she remained high and dry until she was broken up in 1942.

attacks on Avonmouth, two bombed Bristol, 18 attacked other alternative targets, one aborted and one was lost (an He 111 of III/KG26 which crashed in France on its return flight).

Avonmouth received 80 tonnes of HE (49 SC 500, 171 SC 250, 29 LZZ 250, 54 SC 50 and 64 SC 50mV with short-delay fuzes) and 19,656 incendiaries between 2115 and 0130 hours. Bombing was predominantly visual and only a small proportion of crews found it necessary to use DR or radio navigation. The TA was visible for much of the attack and at times was very clearly seen in the moonlight. Numerous medium and small fires covered the entire TA, with one of very large proportions in the zinc factory north of Avonmouth town. Good results were anticipated.

Crews reported flak of varying intensity and accuracy, backed by active, well directed searchlights. Numerous night fighters were seen and some attacks were experienced. Crews also commented on decoy fires seen to the south-west, west and north of Avonmouth, with one very large one between Avonmouth and Bristol. Two crews experienced double attacks by night fighters causing one, a Ju 88 of II/KG54, to abort when just south of Bristol. The other, a Ju 88 of II/KG77, also aborted but then bombed Southampton.

The units attacking Avonmouth were:

II/KG27: 12 He 111, 2115-2204
KGr100: 10 He 111, 2117-2144 (bombing by means of X-Verfahren)
I/KG54: 7 Ju 88, 2156-2305
II/KG54: 12 Ju 88, 2254-0023
KGr806: 3 Ju 88, 2206-2220
I/KG77: 14 Ju 88, 2248-2355
II/KG77: 9 Ju 88, 2300-0030
III/KG77: 5 Ju 88, 0040-0130
III/KG26: 11 He 111, 2157-2311 (8 crews bombed using Y-Verfahren, 4 visually)

A further attack was made on the docks at Great Yarmouth by 18 aircraft of Luftflotte 2. The weather situation here was less favourable than in the Bristol area and results were difficult to assess. Nevertheless, 12 crews aimed their bombs visually, aided by the light of sixteen LC 50 flares, but later crews adopted DR/radio methods. Fourteen SC 1000 and five SC 250 HE bombs were dropped, together with 9,756 incendiaries.

At Bristol bombs actually fell over a wide area and damage was thereby lessened, but at Avonmouth fires were started and took some time to bring under control. Eleven fires were also started in Bristol but the last was well in hand by 0200 hours; only one was in the serious category. Industrial damage was more or less confined to the docks at Avonmouth, but the working of the port was not significantly affected.

Elsewhere minor incidents were reported in Huntingdonshire, Norfolk and Blackburn. Fires and casualties occurred at Great Yarmouth and one person was killed in the Isle of Wight. Mines no doubt intended for the Thames Estuary fell on land on either side, but without serious consequences. Further bomb damage occurred at Penzance where there were also a few casualties.

AA Command returns show that heavy guns were in action at Bristol, Thames and Medway (North and South), Humber, Cardiff, Harwich, Gloucester, Portland, Portsmouth, St Eval, Plymouth and Falmouth. In all approximately 8,000 rounds were expended, the Bristol guns accounting for 6,450 fired between 2055 and 0200 hours at targets in the height band 8,000-18,000 feet. Several raiders were claimed damaged and two destroyed.

Including an Intruder operation by a Blenheim of No. 23 Squadron, Fighter Command dispatched 125 aircraft on dusk, night and dawn patrols. Several contacts were made and one He 111 was claimed destroyed by a Beaufighter of No. 604 Squadron.

Morning in Westbury on Trym, which suffered in the spill over from the raid on Bristol on Thursday night.

Although the He 111H-5 was fitted, as standard, with a cable attachment 'hook' for winch-assisted take-offs, it appears that only III/KG26 adopted this procedure operationally. Known as a 'Schleuderstart' this take-off procedure made use of a powerful Maybach winch which, by means of a cable attached to the hook mounted on the lower nose position of the He 111H-5, provided rapid acceleration and appreciably shortened the bomber's take-off. Having manoeuvred the aircraft into position at the start of the take-off run the cable was attached and, while holding against the brakes (aided by a powerful electro-magnet attached to the rear fuselage) the engines were opened up to take-off power. The winch took up the cable 'slack' and, as the brakes and retarding electro-magnet were released, hauled the bomber rapidly up to take-off speed. The cable was released as the aircraft passed some 50 to 100 feet above the winch, the landing gear was then retracted, normal climb power selected and the flight from thereon continued as after a normal take-off. The Schleuderstart, viewed by many crews as a rather dangerous procedure, enabled a heavily laden aircraft (such as an He 111 carrying an SC 1000 or heavier bomb externally) to take off from airfields of limited dimensions. And it was in just these circumstances that III/KG26 found itself following a move to Le Bourget (after a short period at Grevillers) while a hard surfaced runway was laid at Poix, their normal base.

On the evening of May 4 Oberfeldwebel Herbert Rose carried out a Schleuderstart from Le Bourget in the 1H+ED, an He 111H-5 of the Stab/KG26. Slung below the Heinkel's fuselage was an SC 500; its internal bomb chutes contained a full load of 16 incendiary bomb cannisters. However, on previous occasions this aircraft had carried SC 2500s, for Herbert Rose was one of the few pilots cleared for missions with these enormous weapons. On this occasion Rose was bound for the docks at Avonmouth where the attack was to be carried out under the control of the Y-Verfahren station located near Calais.

Course was set to intercept the Y-beam but upon reaching the vicinity of this turning

Now the memory is fading but here at Cheriton Place in darker days a life was lost — Theo McDowall.

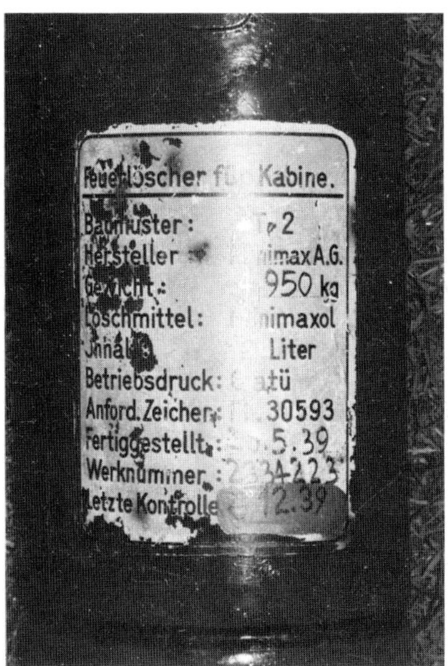

Souvenir of the last flight of the 'Max' expert. It was on the night of April 4-5 that Herbert Rose and his crew were knocked out of the fight after their pioneering mission with the SC 2500. This pristine fire extinguisher was recovered by the Severnside Aviation Society during their investigation at Hewish.

point no signals were received, so Rose and his observer, Feldwebel Georg Fietzek, concluded that the transmitter was unserviceable. Nevertheless, they continued towards Bristol, flying at 15,000 feet to carry out a visual attack on Avonmouth Docks, if possible. Some two hours after take-off the German crew could see fires ahead and Fietzek left his collapsible seat beside the pilot to take up a prone position in the nose to operate his Lofte 7c bombsight. The time was nearly 2220 hours.

Some 90 minutes earlier Beaufighter R2252 of No. 604 Squadron had taken off from Middle Wallop with Flying Officer Edward Crew at the controls and Sergeant Norman Guthrie in the AI operator's position. After initially working with the Middle Wallop Sector Controller, Crew was handed over to the Sopley GCI Controller who vectored the Beaufighter after an incoming 'Raid' until AI contact was established. After a lengthy, cautious pursuit under 'Gus' Guthrie's guidance, four tiny points of light — the Heinkel's exhausts — were seen. Closing in, the raider was identified as an He 111, and as the silhouette of the German bomber slid gently into the centre of his dimmed reflector sight, Crew pressed the firing button. Almost immediately a small fire appeared in the forward fuselage of the enemy aircraft, its starboard wheel came down and it turned sharply to the right, towards the moon. In no time at all it became a ball of fire and after a while was seen to hit the ground on what appeared to be marshy land to the west of Bristol. The weather, Crew reported, was fine with no cloud and a bright half-moon.

The attack came without warning for Herbert Rose and his crew, one of whom, gunner Gefreiter Mathias van Kaldenkerken, died immediately with a bullet through the head. The other four members of the crew baled out, but the parachute of Oberfeldwebel Erich Blüher, the W/T operator, failed to open and he fell to his death. Their aircraft crashed at West Hewish, between Bristol and Weston-super-Mare, and was totally destroyed; during salvage operations it was ascertained by RAF crash investigators that the aircraft was fitted with a tail 'grenade' or explosive cannister tube (installed for defence against attacking fighters but rarely used in practice, most crews viewing it as a useless device). The assisted take-off hook was also found, together with the external bomb racks, suggesting that the Heinkel had been carrying a heavy load, but no trace was discovered of the special receivers and other equipment with which it was equipped for Y-Verfahren bombing.

One Heinkel failed to return and two Junkers Ju 88s from II/KG54 were damaged during the Bristol attack.

Stab III/KG26 Heinkel He 111H-5 (3595). Shot down by Flying Officer E. D. Crew and Sergeant N. Guthrie in a Beaufighter of No. 604 Squadron. Crashed at West Hewish, Weston-super-Mare 10.25 p.m. Oberfw. E. Blüher and Gefr. M. van Kaldenkerken killed. Oberfw. H. Rose, Fw. G. Fietzek and Uffz. E. Groschle baled out and taken prisoner. Aircraft 1H+ED destroyed.

Parts excavated by Malcolm Pettit included first aid kit, propeller blade, oxygen bottles and numerous other relics.

SATURDAY, APRIL 5-6

Sunset: 1939 Sunrise: 0626
Moon: Dusk — 0328 (First Quarter)

No German night bomber operations.

UK — Extensive low cloud with moderate to poor visibility.
The Continent — Similar to the UK.

Small scale daytime German activity was largely confined to over-water operations and only ten aircraft penetrated inland. Attempted attacks on airfields were unsuccessful, but four workers were killed when a factory at Fraserburgh was hit. Bell Rock lighthouse was again machine-gunned, yet once more the light survived. Deteriorating weather led to the cancellation of night bomber operations but a few bombs were reported in Cornwall and Devon, where two people were killed, presumably dropped by one of the small number of maritime reconnaissance aircraft which were operating.

A few night fighter patrols were sent up and one aircraft, Beaufighter R2259 of No. 604 Squadron, was lost. Low on fuel and with fog closing all airfields within range the crew baled out; their aircraft was totally destroyed when it crashed near Hungerford.

SUNDAY, APRIL 6-7

Sunset: 1940 Sunrise: 0624
Moon: Dusk — 0404 (First Qtr +1)

No major attack. Extensive minelaying and attacks on shipping. Airfield patrols.

UK — Extensive cloud but mainly moderate visibility.
The Continent — Cloud with poor visibility in many areas.

There was very little German activity during daylight hours and the only bombs to fall damaged houses in Worthing. There were no casualties.

During the night, when 57 German aircraft were operating, mines were laid in Liverpool Bay, off Milford Haven and off the Northumberland coast. A few aircraft patrolled airfields in East Anglia, Lincolnshire and South Yorkshire but apart from attacks on shipping, several unexploded bombs at Barrow and some slight damage in Aberdeen Harbour, there was little to record.

On Saturday morning Churchill was sent a copy of a new Air Ministry publication. Although in the midst of the Balkan crises he found time to read it and drop a note to the author, Hilary St George Saunders. Complimenting him on the 'admirable' booklet, he was critical that 'Sir Hugh Dowding, the Commander-in-Chief in this great battle, is not mentioned in it'. The following Friday — Good Friday — the PM fired a broadside at Sir Archibald Sinclair, the Air Minister: 'The jealousies and cliquism which have led the committing of this offence are a discredit to the Air Ministry, and I do not think any other Service Department would have been guilty of such a piece of work. What would have been said if the War Office had produced the story of the Battle of Libya and had managed to exclude General Wavell's name, or if the Admiralty had told the tale of Trafalgar and left Lord Nelson out of it! It grieves me very much that you should associate yourself with such behaviour. I am sure you were not consulted beforehand on the point, and your natural loyalty to everything done in your Department can alone have led you to condone what nine out of ten men would unhesitatingly condemn.'

Nachtangriff gegen England. Destined for Britain, an SC 1000 lies ready as blacked out Ju 88s are prepared for the night's attack.

MONDAY, APRIL 7-8

Sunset: 1942 Sunrise: 0621
Moon: Dusk — 0437 (First Qtr +2)

Major attack on Glasgow/Clydeside with a heavy attack on Liverpool/Birkenhead. Widespread bombing elsewhere. Long-range night fighter patrols over RAF airfields.

UK — Extensive cloud cover except in western districts where cloud was broken. Scattered wintry showers in eastern England. Visibility mainly good.

The Continent — Broken cloud over north-western France; elsewhere continuous cloud with wintry showers. Visibility mainly good.

Daylight activity by the Luftwaffe was mainly directed at shipping, with attacks developing off Falmouth, Plymouth, Orfordness and Clacton. Only ten raiders penetrated inland and no bombs were reported.

During the night operations were flown on a massive scale by 478 long-range bombers, 15 light bombers and 24 long-range night fighters. The main undertaking, code-named "Mondscheinsonate" (Moonlight Sonata), was to be against Glasgow/Clydeside with Greenock, Dumbarton and Hillington the designated target areas, but a large number of aircraft ordered to these objectives failed to reach them and bombed alternative targets instead. In the event, only 179 crews claimed to have bombed the Clydeside area, delivering 204 tonnes of HE and 722 BSK (25,992 IBs), and in Luftflotte 3 alone 109 crews bombed alternative targets. At Greenock, attacked by 97 aircraft, 102 tonnes of HE (one SC 1000, 34 SC 500, 268 SC 250, 23 LZZ 250 and 214 SC/SD 50) were dropped, accompanied by 9,828 incendiaries. Fifteen small fires were claimed.

Dumbarton, attacked by 30 aircraft, received some 30 tonnes of HE (seven LMB parachute mines, 32 LMA mines, seven SC 1000 and one SC 500) and 6,912 incendiaries. More explosions and fires were seen, as was the case at Hillington where the bomb load intended for the Rolls-Royce works consisted of 72 tonnes of HE (nine LMB mines, five LMA mines, 13 SC 1000, four SC 500, 138 SC 250, 11 LZZ 250 and 173 SC/SD 50) and 9,240 IBs, delivered by 52 aircraft.

Detailed Luftflotte 3 records show that 213 aircraft were sent to Greenock (97 of which reached the TA), 51 were ordered to attack Liverpool (reached by 41 crews) and 20 were sent to Bristol (with all reporting over the target). To some extent the attacks on Liverpool and Bristol were augmented by some of the 109 aircraft that bombed alternatives to Clydeside targets, but more than twenty other places were also bombed. The Dumbarton and Hillington attacks were the responsibility of Luftflotte 2.

Luftflotte 3's principal operations were carried out by the following:

Greenock:
II/KG55: 5 He 111, 2335-0035
KGr100: 3 He 111, 2326-2332
KG77: 12 Ju 88, 2345-0125
KGr806: 4 Ju 88, 2310-0010
II/KG27: 9 He 111, 2310-0010
I/KG27: 6 He 111, 0040-0108
III/KG26: 6 He 111, 2335-0224
KG76 and III/KG1: 22 Ju 88, 2215-2314
II/KG54: 7 Ju 88, 2225-0053
I/KG54: 12 Ju 88, 2225-0053
I/KG55: 11 He 111, 2325-0030

Glasgow:
III/KG1: 7 He 111, 2240-2315
KGr100: 3 He 111, 2326-2332
KG76 and III/KG1: 18 Ju 88, 2230-2350
II/KG55: 1 He 111, 2336
II/KG1: 7 Ju 88, 2340-0040

Liverpool:
I/KG54: 3 Ju 88, 2310-0000
II/KG54: 3 Ju 88, 2210-2250
I/KG55: 2 He 111, 0020-0035
III/KG27: 16 He 111, 2240-0100
Stab/KG55: 4 He 111, 0020-0046
II/KG55: 1 He 111, 2345
I/KG54: 4 Ju 88, 2240-2310
II/KG55: 2 He 111, 0040-0100
II/KG1: 4 Ju 88, 2245-2350
III/KG55: 14 He 111, 0105-0130
III/KG54: 1 Ju 88, 2200
KG77: 4 Ju 88, 2246-0128
KGr806: 1 Ju 88, 2200
II/KG27: 4 He 111, 2230-0032
KGr100: 1 He 111, 2240
KGr100: 2 He 111, 0100-0110
III/KG26: 1 He 111, 0224
I/KG27: 2 He 111, 0020-0100

Bristol:
KGr100: 1 He 111, 2125
KGr806: 2 Ju 88, 2113-2125
III/KG1: 1 Ju 88, 0220
III/KG27: 2 He 111, 2228-2230
II/KG55: 2 He 111, 2220-2230
KGr100: 1 He 111, 0050
I/KG54: 1 Ju 88, 2125
III/KG55: 5 He 111, 0040-0117
II/KG1: 6 Ju 88, 2305-0000
III/KG55: 1 He 111, 0045
I/KG54: 1 Ju 88, 2220
I/KG27: 1 He 111, 0042

Luftflotte 3 listed two He 111s (of I/KG55 and III/KG26) and a Ju 88 (of II/KG54) missing; two Ju 88s (of I/KG76 and II/KG54) crashed over occupied territory, but both crews managed to bale out. In addition, 12 aircraft of Luftflotte 3 aborted. Nine more aircraft were sent to attack airfields.

Bomb loads claimed dropped in subsidiary attacks were as follows: Bristol — 32 tonnes of HE and 6,442 IBs. (DR and radio navigation bombing); Liverpool — 65 tonnes HE, 13,556 IBs (DR bombing); Great Yarmouth — 3,212 IBs (partly visual bombing).

Every Civil Defence Region in Britain reported bombing during the night and for a considerable period nearly every area of the UK was under the air raid alert. In the Clydeside area many of the districts badly hit in the raids of March 13 and 14 again suffered; 4,000 were made homeless in Glasgow but most of the many fires started were quickly brought under control. Some 20 deaths were reported, with more at Gretna. Damage and casualties also occurred at Leith, but Clydebank took the main weight of the bombing. Eight important installations, including shipyards, were hit, but damage was mainly slight. Inevitably, rail

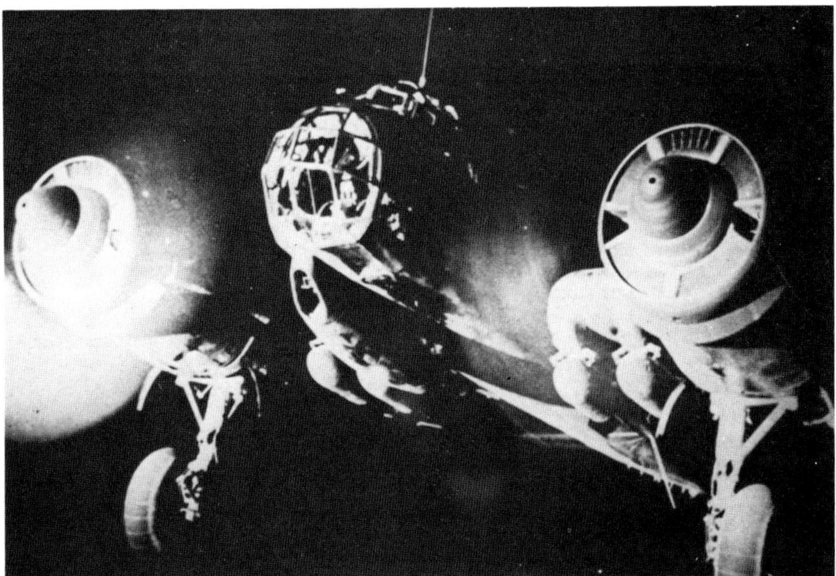

On Monday the main weight of the attack was to be aimed at Clydeside but we must not forget that while it is inevitable that we have highlighted the major raids on the large cities, dozens of other towns and villages were facing a nightly threat. April 7-8 is a good example as at one time every part of the country was under alert.

There were serious incidents in all parts of the country but for the first time an East Anglian town came in for sustained rough treatment with a succession of mines, incendiaries and bombs on Great Yarmouth. By the standards of the big city attacks the incidents would be looked on most probably as run-of-the-mill but for the Suffolk coastal town it was a traumatic experience. Recalling Monday night, the then Town Clerk wrote that 'I shall never forget the appalling sight that Yarmouth presented and, with the additional fires that continually broke out, it seemed that nothing could prevent the destruction of the town and South Quay'. In all there were 65 large fires into which KG53 dropped two more mines, wrecking Blackfriars Road and Queen's Road, where five special constables lost their lives, and Middlegate Street. Three rescue parties had to be sent in from Norwich and overall casualties would have been much higher than 17 had not almost half the town been evacuated.

and road communications were badly hit, as were utility services.

Little success was achieved by the Luftwaffe at either Tyneside/Tees area, nor at Bristol and Plymouth. Yarmouth, however, suffered substantial civilian damage and 20 fatal casualties. Other places bombed were Ipswich, the Thames Estuary area, Crewe (which sustained some damage to the railway system), Birmingham and Merseyside (with little damage at either place). In Belfast about a dozen fires were started and both mines and bombs fell on London for the first time since March 20. Aerodromes in the East, South and Scotland were also attacked, but with little success. Altogether only some 130 people were killed countrywide, a comparatively small number in view of the size of the bomber force operating. A serious fire at John Brown's Clydeside shipyard, fires at the Short Brothers aircraft factory at Rochester and a timber yard fire in Belfast were perhaps the most important German successes of the night.

The AA defences were very active, firing some 16,000 rounds of heavy ammunition by the guns at Thames and Medway (North and South), Bristol, Fareham, Tyne, Portland, Swansea, Tees, Cardiff, Humber, Forth, Clyde, Mersey, Linton, Gloucester, Barrow, Plymouth, Brooklands, Slough, Belfast, Dover, Coventry, Manchester, Crewe, Orkney and the London IAZ.

During the night Fighter Command dispatched 260 aircraft on dusk, night and dawn patrols, including 12 on offensive operations (six Blenheims and a Havoc of No. 23 Squadron and five Defiants of No. 141 Squadron which patrolled off the North Coast of France). Numerous AI and visual contacts were reported and five enemy aircraft were claimed destroyed. At 2345 hours Defiant N1694 of No. 256 Squadron was lost near Southport but the crew, one of whom was injured, successfully baled out. Another Defiant was lost at 0450 hours (8th) when N3424 of No. 256 Squadron lost height on take-off from Squire's Gate and crashed near Blackpool, killing its crew of two.

The Duke of Kent visited Yarmouth on April 25, here seen conversing with the town's Mayor and Chief Constable in Middlegate Street.

A mine on Rochester, dropped with Short's Aircraft Works as its target, blasted the St William's Way area. Eleven died including four members of the White family at Nos. 29 and 31 Wickham Street.

Three raiders were brought down over Britain and the crew of a returning II/KG54 Junkers Ju 88 were forced to abandon their aircraft near Rouen after running short of fuel.

9/KG26 Heinkel He 111H-5 (3603). Shot down by Flight Lieutenant D. H. Ward in a Hurricane of No. 87 Squadron. Also claimed by Squadron Leader J. Cunningham and Sergeant C. F. Rawnsley in a Beaufighter of No. 604 Squadron. Aircraft crashed into the sea off Branscombe, Devon 9.45 p.m. Lt. E. Hartmann, Uffz. R. Lortz, Uffz. F. Grochowski and Gefr. H. Hackel all killed. Body of Uffz. W. Belser washed up at Beer on May 5. Aircraft 1H+GT sank in sea.

5/KG54 Junkers Ju 88A-5 (8138). Shot down by Flight Lieutenant D. R. West and Sergeant Adams in a Defiant of No. 256 Squadron during a raid on Dumbarton. Crashed at Banks Marsh, near Southport, Lancashire. 11.59 p.m. Oblt. G. Klemm and Lt. H. Cöster baled out and taken prisoner. Fw. A. Hofmann and Fw. H. Ilse killed. Aircraft B3+IN entirely disintegrated.

An inner tube and main wheel tyre on display in the Warplane Wreck Investigation Group Museum are believed to have originated from this aircraft.

1/KG55 Heinkel He 111P-4 (2976). Shot down by Pilot Officer A. J. Hodgkinson and Sergeant B. E. Dye in a Beaufighter of No. 219 Squadron during an attack on Greenock. Crashed into the sea off Worthing 1.37 a.m. Oberfw. H. Schwiering, Fw. W. Letzius and Fw. W. Erlich all killed. Body of Fw. E. Nottmeier found on the beach at Shoreham April 18. Aircraft G1+KH lost.

TUESDAY, APRIL 8-9

Sunset: 1944 Sunrise: 0619
Moon: Dusk — 0508 (First Qtr +3)

Major attack on Coventry. Minor attacks elsewhere including Portsmouth and sorties against airfields.

And Belfast — a target for bombers then as now. This is the Police Court in Chichester Street, where the barricade of 1941 has been replaced with the wire netting and vehicle traps of 1981. The city received its first raid on Monday night causing fires in McCue's timber yard, Harland and Wolff's shipyard and damaging Rank's Flour Mills.

The apparent change of tactics by the Luftwaffe from mounting all-out attacks on one specific city to more widespread bombing over the whole country was seen by Home Security to be a possible attempt to counter Britain's new-found ability to bring down the night raiders in greater numbers. Casualties needless to say in Coventry after Tuesday's raid were grave: initial MHS reports of 152 swelling to in excess of 280. The following day the figures were released of the number of British civilian deaths from air attack since the war began: 29,856. Did the country but know it, she had now almost reached the half-way stage in the total civilian death toll she was to suffer for the whole war. At least with the latest attack on Coventry four of the bombers were brought down — a four-fold increase over the first raid. This actual aircraft was one of them: a Y-Verfahren-equipped Heinkel He 111 of III/KG26 which was brought down near Hitchin.

Flashback to Coventry — smashed again like this negative exposed in November.

UK — Variable cloud with moderate to good visibility. Low cloud with rain in western Scotland.
The Continent — Much layer cloud. Moderate to good visibility.

German fighters flew a number of sweeps over East Kent during the day and attacks on coastal shipping continued. Reconnaissance aircraft were also busy and some 45 penetrations were tracked over land, but no bombs were dropped.

It was another busy night for the Luftwaffe, with 341 long-range bombers, six light bombers and 17 long-range fighters participating. Luftflotte 3 sent 282 aircraft to Coventry and 237 crews subsequently claimed to have reached and bombed their targets. Many crews bombed visually, others by means of DR and radio aids, and between 2135 and 0350 hours they delivered 315 tonnes of HE (11 SC 1000, 214 SC 500, 513 SC 250, 66 LZZ 250 and 1,053 SC 50) with 23,552 incendiaries. Important plants of the aircraft and motor industries were the main objectives and good results were claimed; in the city centre, and to the south and north, numerous large and small fires were reported.

In a subsidiary attack, 43 aircraft (including a number bound for Coventry seeking alternative targets) bombed Portsmouth between 2145 and 0245 hours with 40 tonnes of HE (20 SC 500, seven LZZ 250, 99 SC 250 and 76 SC 50) and 12,536 incendiaries and fires were started here and in the neighbourhood of the food office. Altogether 30 aircraft of Luftflotte 3 bombed alternative targets, 11 aborted, 15 attacked Zerstörziele and five were reported missing (He 111s of I/KG27, II/KG1, III/KG26 and I/KG55, and a Ju 88 of II/KG1).

The attack on Coventry, where the flak was reported to be of variable strength and accuracy, was carried out by the following:

I/KG27: 10 He 111, 0130-0315
II/KG27: 13 He 111, 0040-0140
III/KG27: 16 He 111, 0052-0155
KGr100: 12 He 111, 2200-2240 (7 crews with X-Verfahren, 5 visually)
II/KG1: 14 Ju 88, 0130-0230
III/KG1: 9 Ju 88, 0032-0139
KG76: 35 Ju 88, 2135-0255
KG77: 48 Ju 88, 0055-0350
III/KG26: 11 He 111, 2204-2252 (some crews with Y-Verfahren, others visually)
I/KG54: 12 Ju 88, 0043-0200
II/KG54: 4 Ju 88, 0114-0130
KGr806: 9 Ju 88, 0000-0045
Stab/KG55: 2 He 111, 0140-0155
I/KG55: 14 He 111, 0123-0204
II/KG55: 13 He 111, 0110-0140 (mixed Knickebein and visual bombing using flares)
III/KG55: 15 He 111, 0100-0218

Many alternative targets were attacked including Portland, Southampton, Norwich and Brighton. Airfields attacked (unsuccessfully) included Tangmere, Ford, Shoreham and Middle Wallop.

In contrast with the previous night, bombing was well concentrated and Coventry suffered badly in consequence. Determined firefighting helped to alleviate the situation, however, and only two fires reached really major proportions. Residential, commercial and public buildings were all badly hit, as were three important factories, but fire-watchers and night-shift workers saved one factory from certain destruction by fire. Casualties were heavy, with 281 killed in what was the worst attack experienced by the city since the night of November 14; transport and utility services also suffered.

Other than Coventry the most serious attack was on Portsmouth but no major damage was inflicted and only eight people

By April life was still hard but rubble had been cleared and a brave attempt made to reopen shops in makeshift premises.

And so to today. Holy Trinity, which survived both the bombing and subsequent rebuilding, enhances this three-way comparison.

were killed. Bombs also fell in Great Yarmouth, Brighton (where ten people were killed), Bexhill, Falmouth, Daventry, Hatfield, Leicester, near Leeds, Doncaster and near Norwich.

Heavy guns of AA Command were in action at Derby, Slough, Solent, Brooklands, the IAZ, Nottingham, Coventry, Crewe, Thames and Medway (North and South), Portland, Harwich, Bristol, Gloucester, Grantham, Holton Heath and Cardiff, using nearly 8,000 rounds.

Patrols were flown by 251 fighters at dusk, during the night and at dawn, and included four sent on Intruder missions over northern France. A Fighter Night operation over Coventry by nine Hurricanes and Defiants of No. 151 Squadron produced claims of four enemy aircraft destroyed and one damaged; overall, Fighter Command claimed six raiders destroyed, one of them being an He 111P-4 of the Gruppenkommandeur of I/KG55, Hauptmann Otto Bodemayer, who was taken prisoner when his aircraft crashed at Peckleton, Leicestershire.

At 2020 hours on April 8 Squadron Leader A. T. D. Sanders took-off from Biggin Hill in a Defiant of No. 264 Squadron and after

The same Hitchin Heinkel 1H+ET we saw on page 513. No doubt the photographer could not believe his luck as a Tiger flew over just as he was about to picture the smouldering remains.

What a pity the tail unit was incomplete — we could have had a nice comparison with the next frame on the roll showing 3628 in France, for when the fitters blacked out the insignia, they left the Werke Nummer visible.

The proverbial Heinkel on the lawn. Having left their base at Dreux, the crew of G1+DL of the 3rd Staffel of KG55 bound for Coventry crashed instead at Desford, Leicestershire, 30 miles from their target. Two members of the crew baled out before she went down but the other two remained on board and miraculously survived the impact. It was another feather in the cap for Richard Stevens (see page 403) as Otto Bodemayer — Robert Götz's Gruppenkommandeur — was an experienced veteran of the Spanish Civil War.

gaining height over Beachy Head was vectored towards an inbound raider by the Kenley Sector Controller. The enemy aircraft was flying at 16,000 feet and after a long chase, and upon approaching the IAZ, some very accurate AA fire 'boxed' the night fighter. After requesting that the guns should cease firing, Sanders and his gunner, Pilot Officer Sutton, caught sight of the enemy aircraft some 500 yards ahead. The Defiant closed in to 350 yards and at this range Sutton fired a two seconds burst into the fuselage of the raider. There was no return fire and as the German bomber took no evasive action, Squadron Leader Sanders was able to formate on it, positioning below and at a range of 50 yards. From this position Pilot Officer Sutton gave it two more bursts and the bomber turned over and went straight down.

The raider was not positively identified by the Defiant's crew but it was, in fact, an He 111H-5 and belonged to III/KG26. Flown by Leutnant Julius Tengler it was en route for Coventry when intercepted and shot down. It crashed near Bendish, Hitchin, and only one crew member escaped unhurt; of the remainder three were badly wounded and the other killed.

Previously Julius Tengler had made 25 operational flights over Britain, his first being against Plymouth on December 5, 1940. Since then he had taken part in attacks on London, Sheffield, Liverpool, Manchester, Swansea, Southampton, Derby, Chatham, Cardiff, Birmingham, Portsmouth, Glasgow, Hull, Bristol and Plymouth, and he is therefore well qualified to speak of the events of that period. Many of his operational flights were Y-Verfahren guided and, he later recalled, he never once failed to receive the bomb release signal. Nor indeed was he aware of any radio countermeasures success apart from the well known (in the Luftwaffe) British interference with radio beacons and Knickebein. Like other crew members of III/KG26 questioned by the writer, Tengler thought most highly of the Y-System and does not accept the counter-measures claims of No. 80 Wing.

His 9 Staffel, he said, did not make use of Schleuderstart winched take-offs although the other two Staffeln (7 and 8) of III/KG26 regularly did so. In his view the assisted take-off procedure was infinitely more dangerous than flying over Britain by night! Generally speaking, he thought that most crews had few worries about night operations, apart from what might be termed the 'natural' hazards of flying, and flak was regarded as being no problem at all. Shortly before he was shot down, however, losses had increased and there were signs of an increased respect for British night fighters.

Apart from the one listed below, another Heinkel He 111 of 1/KG26 suffered engine failure whilst on a sortie to Kinnairds Head and failed to return.

III/KG40 Heinkel He 111 (3175). Believed that shot down by Squadron Leader J. W. C. Simpson DFC in a Hurricane of No. 245 Squadron. Crashed into the Irish Sea. Lt. H. Förster, Uffz. G. Guthschmidt, Oberfw. H. Niemeyer and Gefr. W. Göpfarth all missing. Aircraft V4+GL lost.

This was one of a series of pictures taken by the Ministry of Information and given to Lieutenant Colonel J. Baxter, a local Home Guard officer and the first military man on the scene.

We are indebted to Delwyn Griffith for sending us his comparison which he had taken of Roe's Rest Farm virtually unchanged in 1979.

Four aircraft fell on British soil during the raid on Coventry and a fifth, a Junkers Ju 88 of 2/KG30 is believed to have crashed in the North Sea. I/KG76 lost two Junkers Ju 88s in Europe when their crews were forced to bale out, one after combat with fighters, the second after being hit by their own AA fire.

9/KG26 Heinkel He 111H-5 (3628). Shot down by Squadron Leader A. T. D. Sanders and Pilot Officer Sutton in a Defiant of No. 264 Squadron. Crashed at Vickers Farm, Bendish, near Hitchin, Hertfordshire 10.12 p.m. Lt. J. Tengler, Uffz. H. Faber, Uffz. H. Zender and Gefr. F. Reitmeyer baled out and captured. Gefr. W. Euerl killed. Aircraft 1H+ET broke up in the air.
Surface relics, discovered during taking of comparison photographs, in the After the Battle collection.

2/KG27 Heinkel He 111H-5 (4018). Shot down by Pilot Officer R. P. Stevens DFC. in a Hurricane of No. 151 Squadron. Crashed at Little Hill Farm, Wellesbourne, Warwickshire 1.15 a.m. Oberfw. H. Müller, Fw. H. Müller and Fw. G. Schäfer all baled out and captured. Oblt. H. Müller baled out but died when his parachute failed and Sd.Fr. W-D. Müller died in the crash. Aircraft 1G+FK destroyed.
Subject of a joint recovery by the Stratford-on-Avon Militaria Enthusiasts and Wellesbourne Aviation Group 1981. Major parts of airframe recovered.

3/KG55 Heinkel He 111P-4 (2962). Shot down by Pilot Officer R. P. Stevens DFC in a Hurricane of No. 151 Squadron, his second combat that night. Crashed at Roe's Rest Farm, Desford, Leicestershire 1.45 a.m. Hptmn. O. Bodemayer (Gruppenkommandeur), Oberfw. H. Söllner, Fw. H. Link (injured) and Fw. H. Kaufhold taken prisoner. Aircraft G1+DL disintegrated.

8/KG55 Heinkel He 111P-4 (2908). Aircraft's destruction credited to Flight Lieutenant D. F. W. Darling and Pilot Officer J. S. Davidson in a Defiant of No. 151 Squadron and also to AA fire. Crashed at Fernhill Cross Roads, Windsor Great Park 2.30 a.m. Oblt. J. Bartens (Staffelkapitän) and Oberfw. F. Vonier killed. Fw F. Pons and Fw. H. Hübler baled out and taken prisoner. Aircraft G1+LS destroyed.
Site investigated by Paul Kiddel and a few fragments unearthed.

And what a night Pilot Officer Stevens was having! For the second time since his double success on January 15-16, he had brought down two machines in one night, the first already a smoking pile of scrap metal scattered over two fields at Wellesbourne. Although the RAF shied away from attributing the accolade 'ace' to its pilots, when it came to night fighting Richard Playne Stevens was just that. The citation to his DFC awarded in January said that he had done 'outstanding work and showed the utmost keenness and determination for operations in all conditions of weather', yet an early medical report nearly rejected him as 'too excitable to fly'. A combination of all these talents led him to use anti-aircraft fire as a signpost to find the enemy which he stalked right within the barrage.

Today the two fields at Little Hill Farm have been blended into one although the trees and bushes of the hedgerow maintain some continuity with the intervening years.

. . . and then there were four. This time it was our old friend with the Doppel MG — G1+LS of KG55's 8th Staffel; the same aircraft which had caused such havoc on the South Coast in October (see page 170). These pictures show Pons's unique invention before they ended up smashed to pieces on the ground at Windsor.

View of the Bull Ring Birmingham as it was after the raid of April 9-10.

WEDNESDAY, APRIL 9-10

Sunset: 1945 Sunrise: 0617
Moon: Dusk — 0537 (Full −2)

Major attacks on Birmingham and Tyneside. Secondary raids on Bristol/Avonmouth, Lowestoft, Ipswich and Plymouth. Anti-shipping and airfield patrols, minelaying and scattered harassing attacks.

UK — Variable but mainly small amounts of cloud. Some wintry showers in East Coast areas. Moderate visibility.

The Continent — A little broken cloud over the Low Countries, with increasing amounts over France and slight rain in the extreme West. Visibility moderate to good.

Although some 200 sorties were flown by the GAF during the day, most were concerned with fighter sweeps, anti-shipping patrols, minelaying or weather and general reconnaissance. Only ten aircraft penetrated inland but no bombing was reported.

The night offensive continued with sorties by 450 long-range bombers, 15 light bombers and 16 long-range night fighters. The principal target was Birmingham, attacked by 237 bombers which dropped 285 tonnes of HE and 40,000 incendiaries between 2145 and 0205 hours. The Schwerpunkt covered the town centre and adjacent districts to the east, north-east and south-east, wherein lay many important industrial premises. Most crews were able to bomb visually and good results were reported. Many fires, large and small, developed, and it appeared that particularly important targets were hit, including the Saltley waggon works, the Midland Railway, Birmingham East goods station, the Rover Motor Company, the large gas holders at Saltley and Nechells and the Windsor Street gas works.

Luftflotte 3 carried out the attack alone (leaving Luftflotte 2 to concentrate on other targets and minelaying), dispatching 282 aircraft to Birmingham of which the following 237 claimed to have reached and bombed the city:

Stab/KG55: 2 He 111, 0010-0035
II/KG27: 10 He 111, 0055-0130
II/KG27: 2 He 111, 0105-0110
II/KG55: 12 He 111, 2355-0100
II/KG1: 12 Ju 88, 0040-0205
KGr100: 13 He 111, 2154-2250
III/KG1: 7 Ju 88, 0015-0050
KGr806: 6 Ju 88, 2345-0012
KG76: 46 Ju 88, 2145-0140
III/KG26: 11 He 111, 2215-2343
I/KG55: 17 He 111, 0032-0107
KG77: 41 Ju 88, 2231-0140
I/KG54: 14 Ju 88, 0007-0050
I/KG27: 7 Ju 88, 0046-0128
II/KG54: 6 Ju 88, 0003-0100
III/KG27: 15 He 111, 0031-0140
III/KG55: 18 He 111, 0030-0105

In addition Luftflotte 3 sent ten aircraft to Southampton (reached by seven crews); in all, 35 aircraft bombed alternative targets, 13 aborted, two bombed Zerstörziele and four attacked airfields. Six aircraft were lost.

Luftflotte 2's contribution included a heavy attack on docks, dockyards and industrial installations on the river downstream from Newcastle between Tynemouth and South Shields. Between 2320 and 0426 hours the 116 aircraft that reached the Target Area dropped 152 tonnes of HE and 50,280 incendiary bombs and again, with many explosions and fires in evidence, good results were anticipated. It is known that KG53 participated in this attack. In addition, moonlight attacks against shipping were carried out by I/KG1 and I/KG27 (which was by now devoting much of its time to such tasks) off the Lizard, I/KG30 and II/KG76 off the East Coast, and I/KG26 off the north-east coast of Scotland. Minelaying, as usual, was carried out by I/KG4 in eastern coastal waters and I/KG28 in western, with long-range night fighters of I/NJG2 engaged in offensive patrols off the East Coast and over eastern airfields on the lookout for RAF bombers.

Birmingham experienced an extremely serious fire situation, aggravated by a shortage of water, and much damage resulted in the city centre. Also badly affected were the districts of Nechells, Aston, Stechford, Small Heath and King's Heath; seven churches, the cathedral and many public and commercial buildings were damaged or destroyed, as were many houses. Damage to gas, electricity and water mains was extensive and, in addition to direct damage, resulted in lost production in many factories.

The attack on Tyneside was scattered, with bombing reported at Tynemouth, Wallsend and Whitley Bay on the north side of the river, and on South Shields, Gateshead, Jarrow, Hebburn, Bolden and Sunderland to the south. Fires and damage were also caused in Newcastle where, as in other places in the area, military targets of some importance were hit. Casualties were comparatively light, only some 40 people being killed, but many of these occurred in Tynemouth. Hull was also affected, as was Lowestoft, where 22 were killed, and Ipswich, where damage included major fires in the docks. At Bristol/Avonmouth a few casualties occurred, as was the case at Holyhead and Ramsgate.

HAA batteries which engaged the enemy during the night were located at Coventry, Birmingham, Mersey, Bristol, Falmouth, Gloucester, Portland, Cardiff, Swansea, Plymouth, Harwich, Portsmouth, Slough, Thames and Medway (North and South), the IAZ, Brooklands, Derby, Leeds, Humber, Grantham, Tyne and Tees. They used 8,000 rounds, including 3,133 by the Tyne guns, 2,210 at Birmingham and 700 at Coventry.

A total of 297 fighters flew dusk, night and dawn patrols, with six of them taking part in offensive operations over northern France. Fighter Night patrols were maintained over Birmingham by Spitfires of No. 266 Squadron and Hurricanes and Defiants of No. 151 Squadron. Other special patrols were flown over Tyneside and another likely, but unspecified, Target Area. Subsequently eight enemy aircraft were claimed destroyed, five probably destroyed and six damaged. One of the 'probables' was claimed by an aircraft of No. 93 Squadron on an LAM patrol 10 miles south-east of Portland. A Hurricane of No. 257 Squadron was lost and its pilot, Sergeant Truman, killed after shooting down a Ju 88 off Lowestoft.

At 2000 hours on April 9 Ju 88C-2 (R4+CM) of 4/NGJ2 departed Gilze-Rijen to carry out an intruder-type night fighter-bomber patrol over RAF airfields. However, at about 2210 hours it was itself intercepted by a British night fighter patrolling between Lowestoft and Leicester and shot down. The German pilot, Gefreiter Franz Brotz, was killed and the flight mechanic was badly injured, but the W/T operator, Unteroffizier Willi Lindner, was only slightly hurt and landed safely by parachute in a field. Lindner buried his W/T notebook and, despite having lost his boots during his parachute descent, started walking towards the nearest town, which happened to be Langham, near Oakham, in Rutland. Still wearing his flying overalls and in his stockinged feet, he was passed by a soldier who wished him goodnight; a railway signalman then opened some level crossing gates for him, and other people passed by but took no notice. Eventually, after asking the way to the police station in broken English, he was asked to wait a moment while a member of the Home Guard was sought. Finally, accompanied by the Home Guard, he was taken to the police. Lindner's note book was later discovered and was carefully examined by British Air Intelligence.

The R4+CM was shot down by a Beaufighter of No. 25 Squadron, flown by Sergeant Bennett, following an AI interception. It crashed on the Burley-Langham road, part of the aircraft lying in a deep crater and the rest spread over two fields. It was not possible to learn much from the wreckage but AI1(g) examining officers deduced that it was probably a night fighter version of the Ju 88 from the remains of its armament and armour plating.

Daylight sorties claimed two victims. A Messerschmitt Bf 110 of 3/ErproGr 210 going missing on a sortie to the East Coast.

III/KG40 Heinkel He 111H-3 (6840). Shot down by Squadron Leader J. H. Heyworth in a Hurricane of No. 79 Squadron. Crashed into the sea two and a half miles south-west of St. David's Head, Pembrokeshire 9.45 a.m. Oberfw. H. Knäbel and Oberfw. E. Winroth missing. Oberfw. H. Salzsieder killed. Body of Fw. K. Bucek found washed up along the Pembroke coast. Aircraft V4+HH lost.

Eight aircraft were lost during the Birmingham and Coventry raids. Two further Heinkel He 111's from III/KG40 and Stab/KG27 are believed to have been shot down south of the Isle of Wight. Four aircraft of KG27 and one of II/KG54 were damaged by fighters.

II/KG1 Junkers Ju 88A-5 (0157). Shot down by AA fire and fighters during a raid on Coventry. Crashed at Preston Hill Farm, Whitwell, Hertfordshire 2.00 a.m. Oberfw. F. Rüdig, Uffz. K. Neumerkel, Fw. E. Zimmert and Fw. C. Frehe baled out and taken prisoner. Aircraft V4+JV destroyed.

II/KG1 Heinkel He 111H-2 (3148). Crashed into the English Channel. Exact cause unknown but believed to have fallen victim to a night fighter. Lt. K. Martin, Fw. W. Leisegang and Uffz. K. Pauly missing. The body of Fw. W. Such found on the Goodwin Sands June 22 and buried at sea. Aircraft V4+DJ lost.

4/KG27 Heinkel He 111P (1555). Shot down by fire from a Defiant, then hit a balloon cable and fell on houses, 213-218 Hales Lane, Smethwick, Staffordshire 1.45 a.m. Fw. E. Grolig and Fw. H. Häcke killed. Uffz. R. Müller and Fw. W. Strecke baled out and taken prisoner. Aircraft 1G+KM destroyed.

Aircraft manufacturer's plate bearing the number '1555' now in the possession of Colin Prately.

5/KG55 Heinkel He 111P-2 (1423). Shot down by Flight Sergeant E. R. Thorn DFM and Sergeant F. J. Barker DFM in a Defiant of No. 264 Squadron. Crashed at Shepards Hangar, Busbridge, Surrey 11.55 p.m. Uffz. A. Müller, Gefr. R. Langhans and Uffz. G. Neumann killed. Gefr H. Berg (injured) taken prisoner. Aircraft G1+DN wrecked.

One wonders if it had not been for Hitler's war, would the centre of Birmingham still have been transformed to look like this?

3/KG77 Junkers Ju 88A-5 (2170). Shot down by Flight Lieutenant D. A. P. McMullen DFC and Sergeant S. J. Fairweather DFM in a Defiant of No. 151 Squadron during an attack on Birmingham. Crashed near RAF Bramcote, Warwickshire 11.35 p.m. Fw. K. Jähner killed. Hptmn. F. von Schrötter, Oberfw. F. Ruff and Oberfw. K. Hundertmark baled out and taken prisoner. Aircraft 3Z+AL totally destroyed.
Site now under a caravan park.

2/KGr100 Heinkel He 111H-3 (3181). Shot down by Flying Officer R. Chisholm and Sergeant W. G. Ripley in a Beaufighter of No. 604 Squadron. Tail came off in air and aircraft crashed at Boveridge Farm, Cranborne, Dorset 9.05 p.m. Oberfw. W. Lorentzen baled out and captured. Oblt. H. Vander, Fw. B. Lenz and Uffz. R. Kramer killed. Gefr. O. Kohl baled out but his parachute failed and he was killed. Aircraft 6N+BK completely burnt out.
Instruments, Junkers Jumo 211D engine plate, badge and sundry engine parts recovered by Peter Foote and Philippa Hodgkiss 1984

4/NJG2 Junkers Ju 88C-4 (0776). Shot down by Sergeant S. Bennett and Sergeant Curtiss in a Beaufighter of No. 25 Squadron. Crashed at Oakham, Rutland 10.10 p.m. Gefr. F. Brotz killed. Uffz. W. Lindner and Gefr. E. Gorlt baled out and taken prisoner. Aircraft R4+CM destroyed.
Small parts in the Derbyshire Historical Aviation Society Collection.

The demise of one of the Brum raiders; another nice comparison by Del Griffith. Delwyn writes that this Heinkel was fittingly shot down by a Brummie, Flight Lieutenant E. C. Deansley. Nevertheless it was a Pyrrhic victory bought with the lives of seven residents who had abandoned their Anderson shelter because it had flooded. It is said that either Müller or Strecke landed on a rooftop and was subsequently beaten up by his rescuers although by the time the story was reported in the newspapers he had 'fallen off a roof'! Although the houses were rebuilt to the same design, after the war this section of Hales Lane was renamed: thus Nos. 281 and 283 have now become 23 and 25 St Mark's Rise.

THURSDAY, APRIL 10-11

Sunset: 1947 Sunrise: 0615
Moon: Dusk — 0607 (Full −1)

Major attack on Birmingham; minor attacks elsewhere including Nottingham, Rugby and Southampton, minelaying operations and attacks on airfields.

UK — Generally fair in the South but much rain and drizzle with low cloud moving southwards from the North-West. Visibility generally good at first, except in the lee of large towns, but patches of mist developing in the South. Winds moderate in the North, light and variable in the South.

The Continent — Little cloud with generally good visibility but mist patches forming later in the night. Winds light and variable.

During the day there were a number of fighter sweeps over Kent, but no bombs were reported. Anti-shipping and reconnaissance aircraft were also active on what was one of the busiest days for some time.

For the second consecutive night Birmingham was the principal target and on this occasion it was a joint effort by Luftflotten 2 and 3, with the former contributing 40 aircraft. Luftflotte 3 dispatched 280 aircraft, of which 206 claimed success in reaching their objective, and the combined attacking force dropped 246 tonnes of HE and 42,608 IBs between 2200 and 0400 hours. The Concentration Point lay along a line from the city centre towards Castle Bromwich airfield, wherein were situated, according to German Air Force Intelligence, many important factories of the aircraft industry. Most crews bombed visually and several large and numerous smaller fires resulted within the laid down Target Area. Two explosions and a fire were seen in the works of the Dunlop Rubber Company and a very big explosion, followed by dense black smoke, was perceived in the north-west part of the CP. By the close of the attack the entire town area was covered with fires of various dimensions and crews were confident that their bombing had achieved good results. Luftflotte 3's participation was as follows:

III/KG1: 6 Ju 88, 2200-0026
II/KG1: 11 Ju 88, 2240-0145
III/KG54: 5 Ju 88, 0128-0210
KG76: 41 Ju 88, 2140-0240
I/KG54: 8 Ju 88, 0149-0250
III/KG27: 12 He 111, 0025-0150
II/KG54: 7 Ju 88, 0115-0220
Stab/KG55: 1 He 111, 0215
II/KG55: 2 He 111, 2345-2355
II/KG54: 1 Ju 88, 2355
II/KG55: 10 He 111, 0050-0150
I/KG55: 14 He 111, 0143-0255
II/KG27: 2 He 111, 0045-0105
I/KG27: 8 He 111, 0005-0120
II/KG27: 12 He 111, 0020-0140
KGr100: 9 He 111, 2219-2316 (X-Verfahren bombing by all crews)
III/KG55: 12 He 111, 0130-0300
KG77: 37 Ju 88, 2220-0250
III/KG26: 13 He 111, 2223-0005 (bombing partly visual, partly with Y-Verfahren)

Luftflotte 3 also sent seven aircraft to Portsmouth, all of which reported over the target, and 15 to airfield and Zerstörziele targets. In total, 67 aircraft failed to reach their primary targets and bombed alternatives, nine crews aborted, one aircraft crashed on take-off (a Ju 88 of KG77), one ditched in the sea near Trouville (an He 111 of I/KG55) and nine failed to return (two He 111s of III/KG26, two of III/KG55, single He 111s of I/KG55 and KGr100, and Ju 88s of II/KG1, III/KG1 and I/KG54). Two of these reported over the target and were lost on their return flights.

A secondary attack on Nottingham was carried out by 28 aircraft of Luftflotte 2 between 0205 and 0335 hours. They delivered 27 tonnes of HE and 9,924 IBs, most crews bombing visually, but thick mist hindered late arrivals. A cloud layer moved in, too, and while some crews bombed fires which were still visible, a large number diverted to alternative targets. Among the latter were crews who searched for some

We shall remember them. Here in Birmingham's City Cemetery at Witton, a quiet corner for contemplation and meditation.

time to find their primary target, even descending to 800 metres (2,600ft), but to no avail. Several small and medium fires were seen before the weather closed in, but their precise position could not be determined.

Aborting and diverting aircraft bombed a large number of targets of opportunity, but concentration on three ports — Yarmouth, Southampton and Portsmouth (earmarked, anyway, for attack as a primary target for seven aircraft) — produced what amounted to sharp raids. At Southampton, bombed by 32 aircraft between 0152 and 0320 hours, 47 tonnes of HE and 288 IBs were claimed to have started fires in the docks area and in industrial installations. Great Yarmouth, attacked by 12 Ju 88s of KG77, KG76 and II/KG1 between 2200 and 0250, suffered a lighter attack, but Portsmouth received attention from the following:

I/KG27: 1 He 111, 0050 hours (diverted because of radio failure)
III/KG27: 2 He 111, 0000-0150 (one with engine trouble, one D/F failure)
I/KG54: 7 Ju 88, 0135-0325 (5 weather diversions, 1 engine failure and one aircraft after night fighter attack)

In the two raids on the city about 350 people lost their lives amongst them those killed in the crash at Smethwick: Mr Alfred Smart and his 2-year-old son Malcolm together with his sister-in-law Doris and her two children Albert, 13, and Brian, 8, and also Mrs Amy Hanson from next door and her 24-year-old daughter Doreen.

The changing face of New Street. ***Left:*** **An early shot with Marshall & Snellgrove's steel-framed building on the left.** ***Right:*** **The corner with High Street — note the building on the right.**

III/KG54: 2 Ju 88, 0138-0140 (1 weather diversion, 1 with fuel pump failure)
I/KG55: 4 He 111, 0216-0340 (2 weather diversions, 2 with engine trouble)
II/KG55: 2 He 111, 0210-0245 (weather diversions)
III/KG55: 5 He 111, 0200-0220 (all weather diversions)
II/KG1: 2 Ju 88, 2355-0235 (weather diversions)
III/KG1: 4 Ju 88, 2340-0025 (new crews on 'milk run' introductory operation to gain experience)
III/KG26: 3 He 111, 2123-2245 (two new crews gaining operational experience one aircraft with engine trouble. Bombing partly with Y-Verfahren, partly visual)

Other targets bombed as alternatives were Eastbourne, Bournemouth, Weymouth, Poole, and Portland. Airfields attacked included those at Harwell, Reading, Chichester and Upper Heyford.

In the Birmingham raid fires were started in many districts, those principally affected being Halls Green, Acocks Green, Erdington and Solihull, but damage was considered largely superficial. Casualties were less than the previous night, but the two attacks caused nearly 350 fatalities. Much damage was also done in Coventry, undoubtedly as a result of faulty navigation; here many important buildings which had escaped earlier raids were hit, including the head Post Office, which was destroyed by fire, and the Council House. Rescue Parties were called to 80 incidents and 126 people were reported killed.

Damage was widespread in other parts of the country and among the places affected were Bridlington, Nottingham, Rugby, Derby, Great Yarmouth, Cromer, London and Thameshaven, where the oil tanks were attacked three times during the night. Parachute mines, HEs and IBs were also reported on the South Coast where the greatest damage occurred at Southampton, killing 13 people. Bournemouth, Cosham and Poole also had fatalities, as did Ryde in the Isle of Wight. Other incidents occurred at Cheltenham, Plymouth, Oxford, Hull, Gosport, near Stratford-on-Avon, Harwell and Andover.

Heavy AA guns were in action at Thames and Medway (North and South), Solent, Brooklands, Humber, Slough, Portland, Harwich, the IAZ, Derby, Falmouth, Bristol, Plymouth, Coventry, Gloucester, Cardiff, Mersey, Manchester, Crewe, Birmingham, Nottingham and Grantham, expending 9,000 rounds.

Dusk, night and dawn patrols were flown by 158 aircraft of Fighter Command and included special patrols over likely target areas. Ten enemy aircraft were claimed destroyed, four probably destroyed and three damaged, one of the 'probables' again going to a Havoc of No. 93 Squadron on an aerial mining operation. A Defiant was lost when N3460 of No. 256 Squadron crashed near Cannock at 0300 hours; while on an operational patrol its crew became lost and, running low on petrol, they baled out.

An He 111H-5 (1H+FS) of III/KG26 was on its return flight from an attack on the Morris Motors factory at Castle Bromwich when it was intercepted and shot down near Kineton, Warwickshire. According to surviving crew members, the Heinkel was shot down by a Spitfire, but almost certainly its assailant was a Defiant of No. 256 Squadron flown by Flight Lieutenant Deansley. However, there is a slight element of doubt because of uncertainties in time; Deansley claimed an He 111 destroyed near Birmingham at 2300 hours, the AI1(g) report gives a crash time of 2235 hours, and an Air Ministry Intelligence Summary quotes 2315 hours.

The interception occurred at 13,000ft and

Looking back down the street, the same building casts a windowless shadow over the ruins.

The old juxtaposed with the new . . . in New Street today.

after one engine was set alight the He 111 was abandoned by its crew. It then partially broke up in mid-air but was still on fire when it hit the ground, spreading wreckage over a large area. Subsequent examination of the wreckage by the RAF failed to discover that the aircraft was equipped for Y-Verfahren bombing and no identification markings could be discerned apart from a large 'F' in white on the fuselage, a red 'F' on the top surface of the wing, 'FS' in yellow on the rudder, and green painted spinners. It was also learned that the aircraft had been built under licence by the Junkers company in 1939 and that its works number was 3623, as painted on the fin.

The He 111's pilot, Feldwebel Alfons Schmid, and the Bordfunker, Unteroffizier Herbert Puschmann, survived but were injured; the other two crew members were killed.

A fighter sweep over Kent during the day resulted in the loss of a Messerschmitt Bf 109 and maritime reconnaissance sorties claimed two other aircraft.

3(F)/121 Junkers Ju 88A-5 (0665). Crashed into the sea off Anglesey whilst engaged on a reconnaissance sortie of the Irish Sea, exact cause unknown. Bodies of Lt. H. Stech and Uffz. H. Koch found washed up at Hell's Mouth, Pwllheli. Obergefr. H. Gebbe and Lt. E. Teschke killed. Aircraft 7A+CL lost.

3(F)/122 Junkers Ju 88A-5 (0529). Shot down by Sergeant Casey and Sergeant Prytherch in Spifires of No. 72 Squadron during a reconnaissance of Newcastle. Crashed at Alnmouth, Northumberland 7.40 p.m. Lt. R. Bräose, Uffz. E. Helmert and Fw. K. Däux missing. Body of Fw. O. Gräobke found at Amble. Aircraft F6+NL lost.

II/JG51 Messerschmitt Bf 109E (5670). Shot down during a raid on Canterbury by Pilot Officer P. Chesters in a Spitfire of No. 74 Squadron. Crashed at Frost Farm, St. Nicholas-at-Wade, Kent 5.00 p.m. Fw. F. Mäoller killed. Aircraft Black 8+ destroyed.

Following the combat Pilot Officer Chesters performed a victory roll over RAF Manston but spun into the Barrack Square and was killed in Spitfire P7854. Parts of Daimler-Benz DB601 engine recovered by the Brenzett Aeronautical Museum in June 1973.

In addition to those listed below KG55 lost three further Heinkel He 111s and a Junkers Ju 88 of Stab II/KG76 failed to return. A Junkers Ju 88 of II/KG77 crashed on take off from Haarlem killing its four crew, and two Heinkel He 111s of I/KG27 and II/KG55 were damaged by fighters.

II/KG1 Junkers Ju 88A-5 (4203). Shot down by Pilot Officer R. P. Stevens DFC in a Hurricane of No. 151 Squadron during an attack on Birmingham. Crashed at Murcott, Oxfordshire 11.05 p.m. Fw. W. John, Uffz. E. Sadegor, Fw. J. Berger and Uffz. H. Schmid all killed. Aircraft V4+FV destroyed.

Small components unearthed by Nigel Parker.

StabIII/KG1 Junkers Ju 88A-5 (3207). Believed crashed into the sea near the Nab Tower off Selsey Bill 12.20 a.m. Hptmn. H. Fischer (Gruppenkommandeur), Oblt. G. Sommer, Uffz. E. Schreiber and Obergefr. O. Schindler all missing. Aircraft V4+AD lost.

StabIII/KG26 Heinkel He 111H-5 (3592). Crashed and burnt out at Blatchington Golf Course, Seaford, Sussex 10.00 p.m. Shot down by Flying Officer E. G. Barwell DFC and Sergeant A. Martin in a Defiant of No. 264 Squadron. Uffz. K. Schwarzer, Gefr. W. Eckardt and Sd.Fr.K A. Richter baled out and taken prisoner. Oberfw. H. Platt baled out but parachute failed and he was killed. Lt. K. Conrad landed the aircraft amongst anti-invasion wires and was captured. Aircraft 1H+JD wrecked.

8/KG26 Heinkel He 111H-5 (3623). Shot down by Flight Lieutenant E. C. Deansley and Sergeant W. J. Scott in a Defiant of No. 256 Squadron. Broke up in the air near Radway, Warwickshire 10.35 p.m. Fw. A. Schmid and Uffz. H. Puschmann baled out and taken prisoner. Fw. S. Kiehl and Uffz. F. Lösekann killed. Aircraft 1H+FS disintegrated.

Site on the Civil War battlefield of Edge Hill (1642) investigated by Philippa Hodgkiss in visits between 1956 and 1984.

1/KG54 Junkers Ju 88A-5 (2185). Believed crashed into the sea off St Aldhelm's Head, near Swanage, Dorset 1.45 a.m. after being engaged by a Beaufighter of No. 604 Squadron. Oblt. H. Wickert and Fw. J. Blottenberg killed. Gefr. R. Schild and Oberfw. A. Lohmann missing. Aircraft B3+PH lost.

A hit on Wednesday night creates utter chaos in Temple Row. Appearances created by a few photographs can be deceiving as contemporary observers have recorded that even in the central area the 'amount of serious damage was relatively small' and that 'damage in Birmingham was never immediately obvious to strangers and had to be look for.' The detailed Civil Defence records record a total of 5,129 high explosive bombs were dropped on the city during the war of which 930 failed to explode — an amazing figure of nearly 20 per cent! If one can assume a similar number of bombs dropped over the entire country failed to go off, civilian casualties were therefore probably over 10,000 less than they might have been had the German armaments industry been able to produce a totally reliable fuzing mechanism.

9/KG55 Heinkel He 111P-2 (2827). Shot down by Pilot Officer R. P. Stevens DFC in a Hurricane of No. 151 Squadron. Crashed and exploded at Rothwell Lodge, Kettering, Northamptonshire 2.50 a.m. Fw. W. Schelle, Uffz. K. Roick and Uffz. F. Schober killed. Lt. G. Buse baled out and taken prisoner. Fw. W. Kanera baled out and died in captivity June 5, 1942. Aircraft G1+AT disintegrated.

3/KGr100 Heinkel He 111H-3 (6929). Shot down by Flight Lieutenant G. O. Budd and Sergeant Evans in a Beaufighter of No. 604 Squadron. Broke up in the air near The Hermitage, Chale Green, Isle of Wight 11.28 p.m. Fw. O. Kuntze, Lt H. Tretow, Obergefr. H. Kiersch and Oblt. H. Klingenfuss killed. Fw. H. Hauk baled out and taken prisoner. Aircraft 6N+HL totally disintegrated.

FRIDAY, APRIL 11-12 Good Friday

Sunset: 1949 Sunrise: 0612
Moon: Dusk — Dawn (Full Moon)

Major attack on Bristol/Avonmouth. Secondary attack on Portsmouth.

UK — Extensive medium level and variable lower level cloud over much of the country, but much low cloud with rain or drizzle and poor visibility in extreme eastern England and the western coasts of England and Wales. Away from extreme east and west coastal areas, moderate visibility but poor locally.

The Continent — Low cloud and poor visibility in Holland, elsewhere much medium cloud with moderate visibility, poor locally. Low cloud over the western coast of Brittany.

There was little German daylight activity and only five aircraft crossed inland. No bombing occurred.

Night operations were carried out by 219 long-range bombers, with Luftflotte 3 dispatching 164 to Bristol. Portsmouth was attacked by aircraft of Luftflotte 2, joined by some of Luftflotte 3 which failed to find Bristol, and airfields were sought by both air fleets. Luftflotten 2 and 3 also flew anti-shipping and sea mining operations off Milford Haven, in the Bristol Channel and as far north as Anglesey.

Crews of 153 aircraft reported having found and bombed their targets in Bristol, where the docks and industrial installations in the city (TA's 'c' and 'd'), Avonmouth (Bristol TA 'a') and Portishead (Bristol TA 'b') constituted four Concentration Points. The town CP was bombed by 98 aircraft from 2214 to 0300 hours; they dropped 133 tonnes of HE and 20,016 IBs, mainly with visual reference but from time to time thick cloud required crews to revert to DR or radio assisted bombing. Explosions were seen in the dry docks in the Floating Harbour, in the vicinity of Bathurst Basin and on the south side of the river where a strikingly large and rapidly expanding fire took a hold. At 0210 hours a particularly big explosion occurred adjacent to a large granary or warehouse in the Floating Harbour district, where timber yards and saw mills appeared to be ablaze.

Avonmouth (TA 'a') was attacked between 2215 and 0315 hours, 38 aircraft delivering 48 tonnes of HE and 9,644 IBs allegedly onto docks and industrial plants at Avonmouth Dock and the Royal Edward Dock. Again, bombing was mostly visual and big fires were claimed in a transit silo, large flour mill, sheds, and the cold store in Avonmouth Dock. Lock gates were also claimed to have been hit and fires of various sizes covered the Target Area.

Portishead was bombed entirely by visual reference, 17 aircraft attacking between 2210 and 0225 hours with 12 tonnes of HE and 5,228 IBs and producing fires and considerable smoke in the dock basin area. The actual bomb loads claimed dropped on each TA were:

Bristol
1 SC 1800, 25 SC 1000, 55 SC 500, 257 SC 250, 18 LZZ 250, 236 SC/SD 50, 21,016 B1 El.

Avonmouth
25 SC 1000, 2 SC 500, 49 SC 250, 8 LZZ 250, 114 SC 50, 32 SC 50mV, 9,644 B1 El

Portishead
4 SC 500, 27 SC 250, 3 LZZ 250, 24 SC 50, 32 SD 50mV, 5,228 B1 El

Participants in the attacks on Bristol TA's 'a', 'b', 'c' and 'd' were:

II/KG1: 5 Ju 88, 0145-0230
III/KG1: 5 Ju 88, 0120-0140
III/KG26: 5 He 111, 2214-2250 (3 aircraft with Y-Verfahren, 2 visually)
I/KG27: 3 He 111, 0115-0220
II/KG27: 12 He 111, 0145-0230
III/KG27: 7 He 111, 0125-0225 also 6 He 111, 0130-0215
KGr100: 8 He 111, 2215-2309 (6 aircraft with X-Verfahren, 2 visually) also 4 He 111, 2210-0031 (visual bombing)
I/KG54: 14 Ju 88, 0030-0141
II/KG54: 10 Ju 88, 0020-0130
III/KG54: 7 Ju 88, 0006-0110
I/KG55: 14 He 111, 0142-0300

Another night of triumph for Pilot Officer Stevens with a third double victory, and his fourth night raider destroyed in three days. At the time this sketch was made by Eric Kennington, 'Steve' as he was known to his fellow pilots, was at the height of his short-lived career.

On Tuesday, with Easter approaching, Churchill issued instructions to ensure that Ministers would not presume that the war would take a holiday over the weekend and that they would take a break in rotation and be available on the telephone at the shortest notice. 'Easter is a very good time for invasion', he added. As far as he was concerned, he planned a visit to Bristol and South Wales and to kill two birds with one stone. Firstly he could see for himself how people were standing up to the bombardment, and secondly, as Chancellor of the University, he was to present honorary degrees to the American Ambassador and Australian Prime Minister. Both John Winant and Robert Menzies were with Churchill and his wife and daughter when they left London by special train on the evening of Good Friday — the very day the Luftwaffe had planned their own trip to Bristol. Although the bombing woke Churchill and his party, no harm befell their train although the danger was still there. This is what happened to one hit at South Shields the day before.

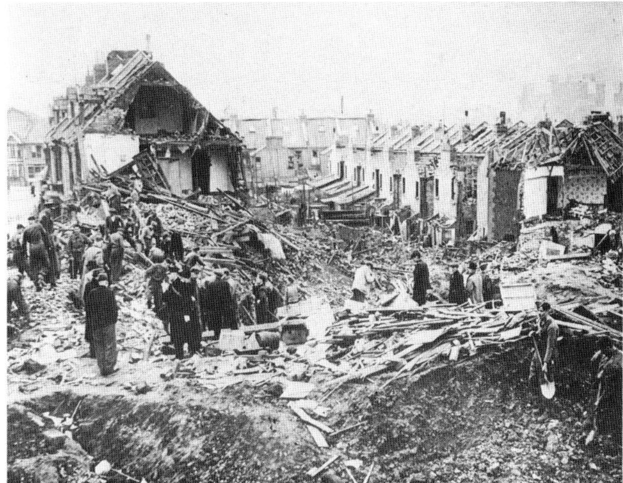

Winston Churchill: 'Our train lay for the night in a siding in the open country, but we could see and hear the heavy air raid on the city of Bristol. We pulled into the station early in the morning and went straight to the hotel. There I met a number of dignitaries, and almost immediately started on a tour of the most stricken parts of the town. The Air Raid Services were feverishly at work and people were still being dug out of the ruins.' ***Left:*** **St Francis Church, North Street, Ashton.** ***Right:*** **Palmyra Road, Bedminster.**

II/KG55: 9 He 111, 0145-0225
III/KG55: 16 He 111, 0121-0145
Stab/KG55: 1 He 111, 0110

Crew reports stated that flak was 'medium to strong and well directed' over Bristol and 'moderate' over Avonmouth, while both searchlight and night fighter activity in the area was said to be 'lively'. Four aircraft were lost — one He 111 of III/KG27 and a Ju 88 of II/KG54 failed to return, an He 111 of III/KG55 was believed to have ditched in the sea north of Cherbourg, and a Ju 88 of III/KG1 crashed near Abbeville on its return.

The secondary attack on Portsmouth was directed against dock installations, shipyards and other important military targets and good results were claimed by the 26 crews participating. They dropped 21 tonnes of HE and 12,168 IBs in an attack lasting from 2225 to 0245 hours; bomb aimbing was carried out visually in conditions of very good visibility and hits were claimed in the town, on and around the dockyards, around two barracks, on a large power station and on the west side of the river in the vicinity of a main supply depot. Explosions and large fires were seen in Basins 1 and 2 of the dockyard, which were hit by heavy calibre bombs. Returning crews could still see the fires of Portsmouth from far out to sea, and good results were anticipated. The bomb load delivered consisted of one SC 1800, 25 SC 1000, two SC 500, four SD 250, 36 SD 50 and 12,168 B1 El.

Harassing attacks were made on several places including Plymouth, Cardiff and Southampton, and against a number of airfields including St Eval (low-level attack) and one north of Bournemouth.

The attacks on Bristol, which came in two phases and affected different districts, caused much serious damage. In the first phase bombing was mainly along a line running from the city centre towards Horfield; after midnight, the second phase produced bombing of a more random nature over the southern districts of the city. The destruction of an important bridge adjacent to a power station serving the tram system was a serious feature of the raid. Many fires were started and casualties included more than 140 killed, but effective firefighting by both fire-watchers and the Fire Service brought many potentially major fires under control very quickly. Bombs also fell in Avonmouth and other places in the area including Bath, Yeovil and Frome, but the only significant war-important damage was in Bristol docks. UXBs and damage to rail and roadways disrupted communications, but nowhere was lasting damage done.

Churchill: 'The ordeal had been severe, but the spirit of the citizens was invincible. At one of the rest centres a number of old women whose homes had been wrecked and who still seemed stunned were sitting there, the picture of dejection. When I came in they wiped away their tears and cheered wildly for King and Country.'

'The ceremony went forward as planned,' wrote Churchill later. 'I spent an hour driving round the worst hit places, and then repaired to the University. Everything proceeded with strict formality, but the large building next to the University was still burning and the bright academic robes of some of the principal actors did not conceal the soaked and grimy uniforms of their night's toil. The whole scene was moving. "Many of those here to-day," Churchill said in his address, "have been all night at their posts, and all have been under the fire of the enemy in heavy and protracted bombardment. That you should gather in this way is a mark of fortitude and phlegm, of a courage and detachment from material affairs, worthy of all that we have learned to believe of ancient Rome or of modern Greece." ' On the left: Australian Prime Minister Robert Menzies with the United States Ambassador John G. Winant. A Doctorate of Law was also conferred on Dr J. B. Conant, President of Harvard University.

Bull's Eye! The bomb that put Bristol's trams out of action — for all time. Although the building in the background, the power station serving the tram system and listed by the Luftwaffe as Target GB 50 50, was not badly damaged, the main power supply cable in St Philip's Bridge was. After this, trams never again ran anywhere in Bristol.

The attack on Portsmouth achieved little that might have affected the war effort but numerous fires were started, four of them serious. The Southsea and Portsea districts were most affected but there was some damage in the dockyard and in naval establishments. Only four civilians were killed.

Also in the South four people were killed at Portland, one in Paignton and three in Bognor. In attacks on airfields slight damage was done at St Eval and Portreath; at Filton, where no damage was reported, two airmen were killed. There were also incidents at Kingswear, Falmouth and Bournemouth.

The Bristol guns were in action from 2143 to 0330 hours, firing 5,781 rounds of 3.7-inch and 934 rounds of 3-inch ammunition; other guns to engage the enemy were those at Plymouth, Solent, Cardiff, Falmouth, Holton Heath, Portland and Gloucester; overall some 9,000 rounds were fired.

During the night, and including dusk and dawn patrols, Fighter Command dispatched 39 fighters and claims resulted of two enemy aircraft destroyed, three probably destroyed and one damaged. Two more were claimed destroyed by AA Command.

> *I go about the country whenever I can escape for a few hours or for a day from my duty at headquarters, and I see the damage done by the enemy attacks; but I also see side by side with the devastation and amid the ruins quiet, confident, bright and smiling eyes, beaming with a consciousness of being associated with a cause far higher and wider than any human or personal issue. I see the spirit of an unconquerable people. I see a spirit bred in freedom, nursed in a tradition which has come down to us through the centuries, and which will surely at this moment, this turning-point in the history of the world, enable us to bear our part in such a way that none of our race who come after us will have any reason to cast reproach upon their sires.*
>
> WINSTON CHURCHILL, APRIL 12, 1941

The night operations resulted in the loss of five aircraft. three Heinkel He 111s of Stab II/KG26, III/KG40 and 8/KG55 and a Junkers Ju 88 of 5/KG54. The fifth was as follows.

9/KG27 Heinkel He 111P-2 (2002). Crashed and exploded at Prowers Farm, Lydlinch, Dorset 1.35 a.m. Shot down by Sergeant F. O. Jankowiak and Sergeant J. Lipinski in a Defiant of No. 307 Squadron en route to target. Also claimed by Squadron Leader J. Cunningham and Sergeant C. F. Rawnsley in a Beaufighter of No. 604 Squadron. Uffz. L. Röth, Oberfw. W. Franke, Uffz. F. Unterieser and Uffz. W. Rüggeberg all killed. Aircraft 1G+HT blown to pieces.

Major recovery by Simon Parry in July 1982. One engine and propeller blade in the Tangmere Military Aviation Museum.

Churchill toured the streets sitting on the hood of an open tourer. Raising and twirling his 'John Bull' hat on his cane caused amazement but was a gesture people loved. On Saturday afternoon he went on into South Wales to Swansea.

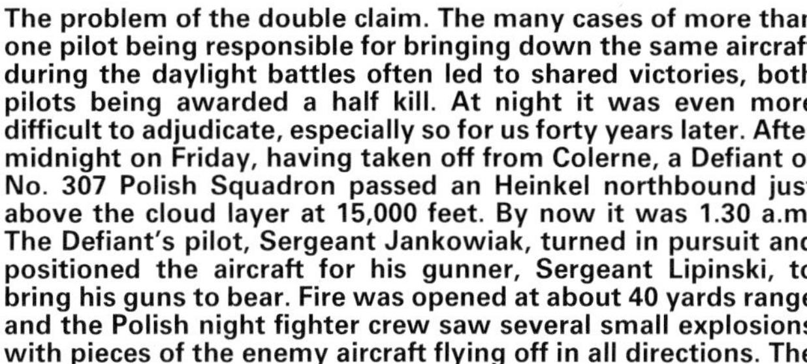

The problem of the double claim. The many cases of more than one pilot being responsible for bringing down the same aircraft during the daylight battles often led to shared victories, both pilots being awarded a half kill. At night it was even more difficult to adjudicate, especially so for us forty years later. After midnight on Friday, having taken off from Colerne, a Defiant of No. 307 Polish Squadron passed an Heinkel northbound just above the cloud layer at 15,000 feet. By now it was 1.30 a.m. The Defiant's pilot, Sergeant Jankowiak, turned in pursuit and positioned the aircraft for his gunner, Sergeant Lipinski, to bring his guns to bear. Fire was opened at about 40 yards range and the Polish night fighter crew saw several small explosions with pieces of the enemy aircraft flying off in all directions. The raider then went into a steep dive and was duly claimed destroyed, its crash being confirmed by the Observer Corps. However, at about the same time a Beaufighter of No. 604 Squadron, working under Sopley GCI, intercepted a northbound raid near Shaftesbury at 11,000 feet. Following a final AI approach directed by Sergeant 'Jimmy' Rawnsley, the Beaufighter closed in for Squadron Leader John Cunningham to identify the aircraft as an He 111 and shoot it down. The time, according to the Fighter Command Combat and Casualty Return was 0108, but No. 604 Squadron records put it at 0130 hours. ***Left:*** **Sergeant Jankowiak with Sergeant Lipinski on the right.** ***Right:*** **Sergeant Rawnsley and Squadron Leader Cunningham.**

SATURDAY, APRIL 12-13

Sunset: 1950 Sunrise: 0610
Moon: 2053 — Dawn (Full +1)

No significant activity.

UK — Fair or fine at first but becoming cloudy and deteriorating generally. Moderate visibility.
The Continent — Extensive low cloud with poor visibility in most areas.

What little daylight activity materialised was mainly concerned with anti-shipping patrols and weather reconnaissance. Shipping in the Bristol Channel was attacked, almost certainly by aircraft of I/KG27 now specialising in this type of operation around the West Coast, but only five inland penetrations were made. No bombs fell on land.

During the night only 17 German aircraft were operating, most of them minelayers, but Boscombe Down and Exeter aerodromes were attacked and night reconnaissances were made over the West Country and coastal areas of East Anglia. Earlier, a dusk attack was made on a ship west of Bude and in the early morning hours of the 13th shipping was attacked off Milford Haven. The few bombs which fell did little damage and caused no casualties; places affected were Southampton, Barry and Par Harbour, Cornwall.

SUNDAY, APRIL 13-14 Easter Day

Sunset: 1952 Sunrise: 0608
Moon: 2213 — Dawn (Full +2)

No significant German attacks.

UK — Generally cloudy but moderate to good visibility.
The Continent — Extensive low cloud with mist and generally poor visibility in many areas.

There was considerable early morning activity against shipping but poor weather conditions over Luftwaffe bases restricted operations later in the day and not more than 15 aircraft flew inland over Britain. Apart from a few bombs which fell ineffectively in East Anglia there was little to record.

Thirty aircraft flew night operations, with minelaying the main occupation and some employed on anti-shipping patrols. Units operating were all three Gruppen of KG27, I/KG53, II/KG55 and KGr106, but little bombing was recorded although there was an attack on Exeter airfield. Often, if their search for shipping proved unsuccessful, aircraft dispatched on armed sea reconnaissance attacked briefed alternative land targets on their return flights and this might well have been the case with the attack on Exeter. Barrow-in-Furness was also attacked twice during the night and a factory, public buildings and houses were damaged; 19 people were killed.

However, only one enemy aircraft crashed in the Shaftesbury area, where both combats are believed to have taken place, and this was at 1.35 a.m. (according to an AI1(g) crash report) when an He 111 totally disintegrated upon striking the ground at Lydlinch, Dorset. It is not certain beyond doubt, therefore, whether 1G+HT was the victim of the Defiant or the Beaufighter although, with its combat location confirmed by Sopley GCI, it seems more likely to have been the latter. ***Below:*** **Not much left at Lydlinch then . . . or now!**

The following aircraft were lost:

1/906 Heinkel He 115 (3256). Damaged by AA fire during a reconnaissance of the south coast of Eire. Landed in the sea 10 to 12 miles off St. David's Head, Pembrokeshire and towed into Pembroke Dock. OberFhr. O. Kuzora, Uffz. E. Schwarzer and Obergefr. J. Pätzel all taken prisoner. Aircraft BL+CH captured.

Wekusta 51 Heinkel He 111H-3 (5722). Shot down during a mission to St. George's Channel by Sergeants Brooker and Short in Spitfires of No. 152 Squadron. Landed in the sea off Falmouth 11.14 a.m. Oberfw. W. Decker, Reg.Rat. G. Gründel, Oberfw. F. Zahn and Gefr. H. Steinbrecht missing. Oberfw. F. Ehlers killed. Aircraft 4T+FH sank in sea.

3/KG28 Heinkel He 111H-5 (3803). Flew into Llwytmor Mountain, near Aber, Snowdonia during a sortie to Barrow 5.30 a.m. Lt. L. Horras, Oberfw. B. Perzanowski and Gefr. K. Schlender taken prisoner. Gefr. J. Brüninghausen killed. Aircraft 1T+EL wrecked.

Junkers Jumo 211 engine flown off mountain by helicopter in 1970. Given to Bill Hamblin and Peter Foote and now on display in the Brenzett Aeronautical Museum in Kent.

In the more remote corners of Britain evidence of wartime battles can still be found by ardent walkers and climbers, like this Jumo engine on a Snowdonian mountainside, although this particular example from 1T+El now reposes in the Brenzett Aeronautical Museum in Kent!

The Lyndhurst Hotel in Alfred Road, Cromer — closed for Easter by the Luftwaffe on the night of April 11.

MONDAY, APRIL 14-15
Easter Monday

Sunset: 1954 Sunrise: 0606
Moon: 2328 — Dawn (Full +3)

No significant activity but serious casualties in two minor incidents.

UK — Extensive cloud but moderate to good visibility and becoming fair in most districts.

The Continent — Low cloud and rain with poor visibility in most areas.

Extensive sea patrols were flown by the German Air Force during the day, particularly between Lands End and Start Point, and two small ships off the East Anglian coast were attacked, but only 12 aircraft flew inland. Incidents occurred at Manchester, where a factory was damaged but without casualties, and at Digby, Lincolnshire, where one person was killed. Minor damage was caused at several points in East Anglia, in the Isle of Wight and at Par in Cornwall where a signal box was damaged.

The weather over Luftwaffe bases limited night operations to 15 long-range bombers, two of which attacked South Shields and a foundry at Elswick. Portland was also bombed, killing 15 people and starting a fire at the naval base, and almost certainly this attack was made by one of 12 aircraft which operated off Pembroke Dock and in the Bristol Channel between 0200 and 0400 hours in search of shipping. Another attack, also most probably by an anti-shipping aircraft, was made on Carew Cheriton airfield where a sick bay was hit, killing 11 airmen. Almost certainly this attack was the work of an He 111 of III/KG27; that on Portland was by an aircraft of II/KG55 and the units which bombed South Shields were I/KG4 and the reconnaissance Staffel 1(F)/122.

The enigma of Belfast. After the lull in operations over Easter, caused more by the poor weather conditions than any feelings of peace and goodwill, the Luftwaffe's next priority was Belfast — 'the most unprotected major city in the United Kingdom'. Because there was a general belief that aircraft would never fly the 1,000 miles from France and risk crossing the coastline perhaps six times on one raid, few precautions had been taken by either civilians or the authorities. Belfast had the lowest provision of air raid shelters per head of the population than any other city, caused probably by wranglings between the central government in Westminster and the Unionist government in Northern Ireland as to which party was to foot the bill. Only 24 heavy and 12 light anti-aircraft guns were available to guard the whole province; there were no searchlights, no night fighters, no effective Observer Corps and only one small balloon barrage over the Docks. The sharp raid on April 7-8 had woken up everyone to the fact that, in spite of its remote location, the city was as eligible as any other as a target and eminently more vulnerable. By now of course it was too late to remedy the deficiences and on Tuesday night the city lay naked, at the mercy of a tried and tested foe. But the biggest controversy at stake over the Belfast attack is the number of deaths. Naturally when casualty totals were first reported by Home Security they were subject to upward revision, and the first estimate of 200 in the Daily Summary (reproduced here) has been increased in an unknown hand to 758, confirmed later as 310 men, 237 women, 148 children, and unclassified 163 (although our addition makes that 853!). However on April 22 the Ministry of Public Security in Northern Ireland backtracked and reduced the total to 500. The *Ulster Handbook* for 1947 published by HMSO states 'at least 700'. Amazingly the raid is completely ignored by Terence O'Brien in the 1955 Civil Defence history but local historians writing in 1984 increase the total to 'almost 900'. The Civilian War Dead Roll lists 675 dead in the city itself.

HOME SECURITY. SECRET.

APPRECIATION NO.317 FOR THE PERIOD 0600 HOURS TUESDAY 15th APRIL to 0600 HOURS WEDNESDAY 16th APRIL, 1941.

PART I - GENERAL.

(a) By Day.

Flying conditions and visibility were good. 44 enemy aircraft crossed the coast, but of these some 41 were engaged in brief fighter sweeps over Kent. Single aircraft visited Lancashire, Devon and Lincolnshire. No bombs were dropped.

(b) By Night.

Weather conditions were favourable and enemy activity was on a heavy scale, and very widespread, the main concentration being in Liverpool Bay and Belfast area.

Some 300 enemy aircraft were in operation. Of these 60 raided Belfast, 40 Liverpool Bay area, some 100 were on the North East Coast and 50 minelaying. Many incidents were also reported from Hants, Dorset, Somerset and Devon.

(c) Civilian Casualties (Approx.).

By Night Only.	Killed.	Injured. Seriously.	Injured. Slightly.
LONDON:	-	8	5
BELFAST:	~~about 200~~ 758	454	~~unknown~~ 1038.
ELSEWHERE:	~~93~~ 185	~~139~~ 175	~~221~~ 462

(d) Enemy Aircraft Casualties.

By Day: 3 destroyed.

By Night: 6 destroyed; ~~2 probable.~~

PART II - WARNINGS.

See Appendix A.

PART III - SPECIAL DAMAGE. (All by night.).

TUESDAY, APRIL 15-16

Sunset: 1956 Sunrise: 0603
Moon: 0035 — Dawn (Last Qtr −3)

Major attack on Belfast with secondary attacks on Liverpool, Portland, Bristol, Plymouth, Sunderland and Tyneside. Widely scattered minor attacks elsewhere, minelaying and offensive patrols by long-range night fighters.

UK — Variable cloud at first with local showers in northern and eastern England, becoming fine generally but cloud persisting in northern England and on coasts. Visibility generally good but moderate in the North becoming poor locally.

The Continent — Variable cloud in the Low Countries with showers or rain. Elsewhere, cloudy at first, becoming mainly fine with moderate to good visibility.

No bombs were reported during the day but reconnaissance flights were made over much of Yorkshire, Lancashire and the North Midlands. Other aircraft were engaged in fighter sweeps and reconnaissance.

At night the first major attack was made on Belfast, Luftflotten 2 and 3 combining to put 180 aircraft over the target. They dropped 203 tonnes of HE (one SC 1800, 25 SC 1000, 65 'B' mines, 11 'A' mines, 29 SC 500, 271 SC 250, 28 LZZ 250 and 320 SC 50) and 29,091 incendiaries. Severe as the attack was, it could have been very much worse; 327 long-range bombers were dispatched but of this force 147 bombed alternative targets, with 51 of them attacking Liverpool.

Most of the aircraft which failed to reach Belfast diverted because of weather conditions. Until 2200 hours Northern Ireland was more or less free of cloud, but from then on conditions deteriorated with complete cloud cover, according to German crew reports, until late in the night when conditions again improved. Thus early and late arrivals had little difficulty and were able to bomb visually but other crews were obliged to bomb blindly on DR or divert to targets in England, which was predominantly clear in the South and West.

Three Concentration Points were nominated in the Belfast Target Area, namely the north-west part of the docks (where explosions and fires were reported on and around a granary, warehouses and silos), the east part of the docks (wherein lay the Harland and Wolff shipyards and the Short and Harland aircraft works and where 30 to 40 good size fires were started), and the town itself (where two large and several smaller fires were seen).

Details of Luftflotte 2's contribution are lacking, but it is known that the following units participated: I/KG28, I/KG53, I/KG30 and II/KG30. Luftflotte 3 units were:

II/KG27: 8 He 111, 0055-0158
Stab/KG55: 1 He 111, 0035
I/KG77: 4 Ju 88, 0136-0230
II/KG76: 11 Ju 88, 0045-0145
II and III/KG77: 17 Ju 88, 0030-0225
II/KG54: 5 Ju 88, 0135-0200
I/KG27: 8 He 111, 0100-0145
II/KG1: 8 Ju 88, 0213-0250
III/KG1: 7 Ju 88, 0145-0345
III/KG27: 5 He 111, 0205-0226
III/KG26: 8 He 111, 0200-0329
I/KG54: 2 Ju 88, 0140-0145
III/KG54: 3 Ju 88, 0115-0145
I/KG55: 7 He 111, 0027-0117
II/KG55: 9 He 111, 0037-0120
I and III/KG76: 5 Ju 88, 0005-0016
III/KG55: 10 He 111, 0015-0225

The 51 aircraft of Luftflotte 3 which attacked Liverpool as an alternative to Belfast were as follows:

II/KG55: 2 He 111, 0035-0130
I/KG55: 5 He 111, 0025-0050
I/KG54: 8 Ju 88, 0042-0150
III/KG1: 4 Ju 88, 0209-0305
KGr806: 1 Ju 88, 0047
II/KG27: 3 He 111, 0030-0205
Stab/KG55: 1 He 111, 0035
II and III/KG77: 5 Ju 88, 0150-0241
I/KG77: 2 Ju 88, 0123-0145
II/KG54: 3 Ju 88, 0048-0259
KGr100: 2 He 111, 0020-0040
I/KG27: 1 He 111, 0200
II/KG1: 8 Ju 88, 0220-0310
III/KG27: 3 He 111, 0209-0220
III/KG55: 3 He 111, 0000-0110

Complete and utter devastation in Annadale Street off the Antrim Road close to the shipyards, one of the Schwerpunkts for the operation, which led to the surrounding streets being virtually razed to the ground.

Between 0123 and 0310 hours they dropped 49.45 tonnes of HE (five SC 1000, four SC 500, 135 SC 250, four SD 250, 12 LZZ 250 and 94 SC 50) and 8,433 IBs.

Bombing was visual throughout and numerous fires were seen in the docks area, with more, including one of large dimensions, in the northern part of the town. Across the river more fires were visible in Birkenhead, probably following hits on oil tanks.

Independent of the attack on Belfast, Luftflotte 2 made a secondary raid on Sunderland and Tyneside (covering Newcastle, Hebburn and South Shields), with 38 aircraft delivering 38 tonnes of HE (one SC 1000, four SC 500, 30 SC 250, 26 LMB and three LMA) and 4,200 incendiaries. Most of the bombing was carried out visually and the usual explosions and fires were claimed in eastern districts of Newcastle, in dock installations at Hebburn, and in South Shields, where the CP was centred on the docks and shipyards. Similar results were claimed at Sunderland where the docks were also the objective.

A further independent attack was made by units of Luftflotte 3 against Portland, where explosions and fires were seen in and adjacent to the dockyard and torpedo factory. This attack was made by 28 aircraft which dropped 33 tonnes of HE (three SC 1000, nine SC 500, 74 SC 250, five LZZ 250 and 111 SC 50) and 2,682 IBs. All crews bombed visually and explosions were followed by fires, one large one being in the torpedo factory. Units taking part in this attack were:

I/KG54: 3 Ju 88, 2200-2215
KGr806: 4 Ju 88, 2130-2230
II/KG55: 2 He 111, 2235-2240
II/KG27: 1 He 111, 0220
II and III/KG77: 1 Ju 88, 2345
KGr100: 4 He 111, 2159-2229
I/KG27: 2 He 111, 2340-0020
II/KG1: 2 Ju 88, 0025-0200
III/KG1: 1 Ju 88, 0215
III/KG26: 3 He 111, 0120-0145
II/KG55: 1 He 111, 2333
I/KG76: 3 Ju 88, 0010-0050

To summarise, then, Luftflotte 3 had 270 long-range bombers operating, with 118 over Belfast, 51 over Liverpool and 28 against Portland; numerous alternative targets were attacked, including Manchester (by two aircraft), Hull (11 aircraft), Bristol/Avonmouth (9 aircraft), Plymouth (6 aircraft) and Portsmouth (five aircraft). Single aircraft attacked other places and five were dispatched to airfield targets. Three aircraft were lost (a Ju 88 of II/KG54 and two He 111s belonging to II and III/KG55) and a Ju 88 of II/KG76 crashed over German-occupied territory.

Considerable damage was done in Belfast, where many fires required all available reinforcements to be called in. Communications broke down and all utility services were

Now this is the not-so-famous New Lodge part of the city where danger still hangs oppressively over the empty, graffiti-plastered streets.

badly hit. Residential and commercial property suffered badly and about 20,000 people were made homeless, but docks and industrial premises were also damaged in varying degrees. Immediately after the raid an initial casualty tally showed 323 people killed and 329 seriously injured, but this was expected to rise as rescue work continued. Many of the fires were still burning the next afternoon and it was thought some would still be alight after nightfall. Outside Belfast the most serious incident occurred at Londonderry, where 12 people were killed.

The bombing of Merseyside caused casualties and industrial damage at Birkenhead, Seaforth, Everton, Bootle, Liverpool (where more than 20 people were killed), Waterloo and Litherland. It was a serious attack in many ways, also affecting Salford, Barrow, Southport and Kendal, where 11 people died.

In other parts of the country mines, HE bombs or IBs caused damage in Tynemouth, Sunderland (where 14 people were killed), Middlesbrough, Whitley Bay (ten killed), Masham (five killed), Thornaby, Loftus, Hull (where 38 were killed and a hospital, commercial and other buildings damaged) and Great Yarmouth. Incidents also occurred in Weymouth and at Avonmouth, where IBs were quickly dealt with and fires quickly suppressed. There were also incidents in Scotland, with some damage caused on the Clyde; at Greenock seven people were killed. Bombs also fell at Newark, Louth, Sheffield and Plymouth and on airfields at Feltwell, Hemswell, Cottesmore, Binbrook and Driffield, but without causing significant damage.

AA Command's guns expended over 12,000 rounds during the night, claiming three raiders destroyed and three probably destroyed. Fighter Command put up 225 aircraft on dusk, night and dawn patrols, with three of them engaged on offensive patrols over Luftwaffe airfields in northern France. Fighters duly claimed a score of six enemy aircraft destroyed, one probably destroyed and one damaged.

At 2255 hours on April 15, Squadron Leader John Cunningham in a Beaufighter of No. 604 Squadron intercepted an He 111 while on a 'free-lance' patrol over the Bristol Channel. Both engines of the enemy aircraft were put out of action and the aircraft was set on fire as it crossed the coast of South Wales at 16,000ft. The German pilot ordered his crew to bale out and subsequently three were captured between Lydney and Coleford in the Forest of Dean. One of them, the observer, spent the night hanging by his parachute from a tree but no trace was found of either the aircraft or the fourth member of the crew, pilot Unteroffizier Walter Költzsch. Both, it was presumed, had fallen into the sea.

One of the survivors, former Obergefreiter Heinrich Schmidt, the flight mechanic, recalls that they had been held by searchlights for much of the time since crossing the English coast. They were flying at 5,000 metres on the prescribed route to Belfast and, in view of searchlight activity, he urged his pilot to alter course for the west coast and an alternative track up the Irish coast, but Költzsch would not concur. 'It was possible to read a newspaper in the aircraft because of those searchlights', Schmidt remembers, 'but apart from the drone of the engines, it was uncannily quiet. Then came a tremendous lurch and we had flames all around us'. A quick check on the intercom revealed that no one was injured, but then came the order to bale out. In fact, the pilot had called 'Bomben raus!' — the command to jettison the bomb load — but the three crew members heard only '. . . raus!' or 'get out'. And out they went. However, the German pilot managed to retain control of his badly damaged aircraft, an He 111P-2 (W.Nr. 2812), G1+DS of 8/KG55, and attempted to re-establish intercom contact with his crew. Eventually he realised that they had baled out so, without the aid of a navigator, wireless operator or flight mechanic, he

Only the church on St George's Circus has survived the changing years on Eglington Street off the Crumlin Road, redeveloped once since Göring's men swept through the area, with the post-war replacements themselves awaiting demolition when photographed by Andrew Hyde in 1981.

The junction of Bridge Street and High Street, with the Albert Memorial in the background.

attempted the return flight to France. And he succeeded, belly-landing at Caen airfield some hours later. Shortly afterwards he was promoted to the rank of Feldwebel and, in recognition of his magnificent feat, was sent on leave by General von Greim, the officer commanding V Fliegerkorps.

At 2145 hours on the same night a Ju 88A5 B3+DC (W.Nr. 4280) took off from Saint-André with other aircraft of II/KG54 to bomb Liverpool docks. Just over an hour later it lay scattered over a wide area at Holcombe Burnell, near Exeter, after disintegrating in flight.

The German bomber was intercepted at about 15,000ft, shortly after crossing the Devon coast, by Flight Lieutenant Gomm in a Beaufighter of No. 604 Squadron crewed by Pilot Officer Curnow, AI operator. The interception had been controlled by Exminster GCI and following an AI approach, Gomm opened fire, setting alight the Ju 88's port engine. The German pilot, Unteroffizier Albert Barth, dived away steeply in an attempt to extinguish the flames, but these rapidly spread to the cabin. Two of the crew, though badly wounded, managed to bale out, but Barth and his gunner were killed, either in the air or when their aircraft crashed at 2255 hours.

Four aircraft of 3/KG53 took off from Vitry-en-Artois at 2200 hours on April 15 to attack Belfast. Altogether 12 He 111s of the Gruppe were participating in the raid and their allocated Target Areas included electrical and aircraft factories on the north side of the Lough and dock installations to the south. One machine, the A1+AL, was commanded by the 3 Staffelkapitän, Hauptmann Werner Höring, flying on this occasion as Observer; his pilot was Feldwebel Karl Menzel.

The A1+AL flew towards the Humber at 10,000ft, carrying a 1,000kg bomb and sixteen BSK 36 incendiary bomb containers.

Landfall was made near Flamborough Head, but as the Heinkel approached Kirby Stephen on its flight across England, the oil pressure on the starboard engine fell to zero. There had been no AA gun-fire or fighter attack, so mechanical failure was suspected. The decision was made to return to base, but it proved impossible to maintain height on one engine. However, approaching Ripon, the starboard engine burst into flames, whereupon the large HE bomb was jettisoned and the crew baled out. All five crew members landed safely and were taken prisoner; their aircraft, an He 111H-5 (W.Nr. 9370), crashed at Huby, Yorkshire, at 0200 hours.

Another raider fell victim to a Beaufighter of No. 604 Squadron when an He 111P-2, the G1+ES of III/KG55, was shot down over Southampton at 0200 hours on the 16th. And again, Squadron Leader John Cunningham and Sergeant Rawnsley were the team responsible, claiming three aircraft destroyed this night.

Apparently the Heinkel was flying south on its return flight, after failing to find its target, when there was an explosion on board which the crew attributed to AA fire. The aircraft went out of control and the cabin caught fire. Bombs were instantly jettisoned and the crew ordered to bale out by the pilot and aircraft commander, Oberleutnant Günther von Siedlitz. However, the pilot's parachute did not open properly and the Observer's was torn off, apparently by a balloon cable, and both were

It was also a night of shared suffering. At the climax of the raid, with all Belfast's 200 pumps committed, the firemen were battling against a monster for which they were ill-prepared. To this end the Police Commissioner, Mr R. D. Harrison, advised John McDermott, the Minister of Public Security, to contact Dublin and ask if they could send help. In spite of their publically-declared neutrality, the Irish Free State responded immediately and within two hours 13 brigades were despatched to the North. The willingness to help a neighbour in distress was marked only by the crews unpreparedness and they were withdrawn as night fell on Wednesday for fear a second raid might produce casualties, compounding a difficult position for the Irish Government. The weekend following the raid saw the first mass burials of the unclaimed and unidentified dead. The larger plot lies in the City Cemetery and includes others from the May 4-5 raid for which a total of 149 are listed in the Civilian War Dead Roll. It was dedicated on October 22, 1951 'In sad remembrance of 123 citizens of Belfast, men, women and children, killed in an air-raid by German bombers on the night of Easter Tuesday, April 15th, 1941, and whom no one was at the time able to identify, and 31 such so killed on May 4th, 1941. They are buried in this plot. "Since by man came death, by man came also the resurrection of the dead. We sorrow not, even as others which have no hope".'

killed. The other two crew members escaped although one, already wounded, broke his leg on landing. Upon crashing, the Heinkel struck a house in Padwell Road, Portswood, and most of it was burnt out. Oberleutnant von Seidlitz was formerly the Adjutant of I/KG55, but since transferring to operational duties in December he had completed about 15 missions.

Early in the evening a Dornier Do 215B of 2/Aufklarungsgruppe Ob.d.L. had been lost on a reconnaissance sortie, possibly in preparation for the coming night's attack. During operations, three crewmen of a III/KG55 Heinkel He 111 baled out after their aircraft was hit by fire from a No. 604 Squadron Beaufighter. All were posted missing but the pilot returned the aircraft safely to Caen. The crew of a II/KG76 Junkers Ju 88 abandoned their aircraft over Europe and a 1/KGr100 Heinkel He 111 was damaged by fighters over the Bristol Channel.

3/KG53 Heinkel He 111H-5 (9370). After starboard engine failure, aircraft dived into the ground at Bull Lane Bridge, Huby, Yorkshire 2.00 a.m. Fw. K. Menzel, Hptmn. W. Höring (Staffelkapitän), Oberfw. R. Lackner, Uffz. O. Seltmann and Fw. A. Wächter all baled out and captured. Aircraft A1+AL destroyed.

StabII/KG54 Junkers Ju 88A-5 (4280). Shot down by Flight Lieutenant Gomm and Pilot Officer Curnow in a Beaufighter of No. 604 Squadron during an attack on Liverpool. Fell at Rughouse Farm, Holcombe Burnell, Devon 10.45 p.m. Uffz. A. Barth and Gefr. H. Otto killed. Obergefr. H. Pengel and Gefr. L. Rauhhoff baled out and taken prisoner. Aircraft B3+DC broke up in the air.

Manufacturers' labels and parts of the oxygen equipment in the Hodgkiss Collection.

StabII/KG55 Heinkel He 111P-4 (3094). Believed that shot down by Flight Lieutenant Gomm and Pilot Officer Curnow in a Beaufighter of No. 604 Squadron, their second combat that night. Crashed in flames off Portland Bill 2.30 a.m. Oberfw. W. Frädrich killed. Oblt. E. Pawlak, Oberfw. A. Burschik and Oberfw. H. Volg missing. Aircraft G1+AC lost.

8/KG55 Heinkel He 111P-2 (2857). Shot down by Squadron Leader J. Cunningham and Sergeant C. F. Rawnsley in a Beaufighter of No. 604 Squadron. Crashed at Padwell Road, Southampton 2.00 a.m. Uffz. H. Sauer and Uffz. H. Rosenberg baled out and captured. Oblt. G. von Seidlitz and Fw. F. Hümmer baled out but killed. Aircraft G1+ES destroyed.

Commemoration to the Roman Catholic dead in Milltown Cemetery. On the morning after the attack, plans were immediately set in motion to evacuate the city in the face of the 40,000 who were homeless. More than 100,000 people dispersed to other parts of Northern and Southern Ireland and trekkers, called 'ditchers' in the Province, began a nightly exodus into the surrounding countryside. The tragedy had been overwhelming yet history has done Ulster a grave dis-service in failing to acknowledge the scale of the raid of Easter Tuesday.

Throughout these pages we have seen many dramatic pictures taken in the midst of raids, for photographers have always been willing to chance their lives on occasions to get that special shot. It is invidious to compare bravery — like the pitifully small group of firefighters shown here — or the talents of those who risked danger to picture them. It must have been particularly galling for the *Daily Mirror* photographer who took this shot on the Wednesday night to find it blocked under the '28-day & 2nd Raid rules' which had been instituted by the Press and Censorship Bureau in December to delay publication of recognisable locations linked with specific raids which might help the enemy determine the accuracy of his bombing.

Early next morning a *Daily Sketch* photographer pictured Wallis's store having burnt itself out. The *Sketch's* caption which stated 'last night's raid' was adjusted by the censor to 'a recent raid' — but also subject to the 28-day embargo.

Then along came Associated Press, by which time part of the 'building block in the centre of London' had collapsed.

WEDNESDAY, APRIL 16-17

Sunset: 1957: Sunrise: 0601
Moon: 0132 — Dawn (Last Qtr −2)

Major attack on London. Minor attack on Chatham by light bombers. Anti-shipping patrols.

UK — Fine, but with high and medium level cloud spreading in from the West. In the North, low cloud with intermittent rain. Visibility good, moderate in precipitation. Winds light in the South, moderate to fresh in the North.

The Continent — Little or no cloud with good visibility.

There was a marked increase in German activity with fighter sweeps by eight small formations during the day. High altitude penetrations were made over Sussex, Kent and the Thames Estuary, but they did not intrude far inland and no bombs were dropped. Anti-shipping aircraft were also active and weather and general reconnaissance flights were undertaken.

The cover of darkness brought with it the heaviest attack yet made on Britain, with 685 bombers attacking London in a raid which lasted from 2050 hours to 0518. Many crews made two trips during the night, and some three, delivering 890 tonnes of HE and 151,230 incendiary bombs. Favourable weather enabled crews to find the Target Area with little difficulty, but ground mist prevented them locating specific targets within the TA; initially, bomb aiming was assisted by the use of LC 50 parachute flares but later arrivals were able to locate their Target Area by the many fires started by earlier crews.

The laid down Concentration Point covered the dock and industrial installations along the banks of the Thames downstream from the Tower of London and a great number of fires, many of enormous size, resulted in this area. Especially noteworthy were two huge explosions and sheets of flame which, it was believed, emanated from the gas holders of the South Metropolitan Gas Works at Rotherhithe. Further very big explosions were claimed in the Surrey Commercial Docks, near Stepney power station, among the large granaries opposite the Tower, within the loop of the Thames and in Southwark, Bermondsey and Deptford. One of the last attacking crews observed 80 major conflagrations but found it impossible to count the lesser fires because there were so many. So great was the fire and smoke towards the end that crews were quite unable

Forty years later Andrew Hyde completes the story with his picture of Holborn Circus and the Sir Owen Williams/Anderson Forster and Wilcox replacement built for the International Printing Corporation in 1958-60. The Prince Consort, of course, who has been doffing his hat and riding his horse since 1874, has seen it all before!

Just to complete the story, this is the view looking eastwards with Charterhouse Street on the left — though strictly speaking this is cheating as the fire pictured here was on May 10.

to make out the flash of their own bombs exploding. Subsequently, the Luftwaffe Intelligence Section was able to claim the attack as 'the most fully effective on London since the beginning of the war'.

During the night sorties were flown by 728 long-range bombers, 11 light bombers and 20 long-range night fighters and all available units were involved with the exception of I/KG3 and II/KG53. Again, precise details of Luftflotte 2's contribution are not available, but London was attacked by the following units of Luftflotte 3:

First Sorties:
I/KG54: 18 Ju 88, 2123-2320
II/KG54: 15 Ju 88, 2210-2247
III/KG54: 14 Ju 88, 2100-2218
Stab/KG55: 5 He 111, 2155-0327
I/KG55: 17 He 111, 2125-2235
II/KG55: 15 He 111, 2050-2215 (opened attack, using LC 50 parachute flares)
III/KG55: 15 He 111, 2125-2227
I/KG27: 14 He 111, 2105-2300
II/KG27: 13 He 111, 2215-2303
III/KG27: 14 He 111, 2133-2210
KGr100: 18 He 111, 2150-2233
II/KG1: 20 Ju 88, 2145-2325
III/KG1: 12 Ju 88, 2150-2310
I/KG76: 14 Ju 88, 2140-2312
II/KG76: 14 Ju 88, 2125-2239
III/KG76: 14 Ju 88, 2130-0030
I/KG77: 15 Ju 88, 2210-2300
II/KG77: 18 Ju 88, 2215-2300
III/KG77: 15 Ju 88, 2221-2302
III/KG26: 15 He 111, 2130-2257

Second Sorties:
I/KG54: 9 Ju 88, 0045-0220
II/KG54: 13 Ju 88, 0300-0330
III/KG54: 9 Ju 88, 0002-0110
I/KG55: 14 He 111, 0230-0345
II/KG55: 12 He 111, 0115-0245
III/KG55: 18 He 111, 0040-0340
I/KG27: 12 He 111, 0153-0231
II/KG27: 12 He 111, 0141-0345
III/KG26: 6 He 111, 0125-0230
KGr100: 16 He 111, 0230-0340
II/KG1: 17 Ju 88, 0120-0410
III/KG1: 7 Ju 88, 0020-0240
I/KG76: 4 Ju 88, 0145-0350
II/KG76: 12 Ju 88, 0100-0251
III/KG76: 11 Ju 88, 0330-0400
I/KG77: 11 Ju 88, 0313-0418
II/KG77: 18 Ju 88, 0150-0340
III/KG77: 10 Ju 88, 0230-0345

Third Sorties:
III/KG1: 2 Ju 88, 0315-0330

In a separate attack five light bombers, Messerschmitt Bf 110s of I/SKG 210, bombed the dockyard at Chatham, dropping 12 SC 500 and 24 SD 50 HEs between 0335 and 0410 hours. Some crews claimed their bombs hit the target, but the results could not be determined because of mist.

Armed reconnaissance of the South Coast was carried out by three aircraft, one of which attacked two ships of some 1,500 tons which were located off Start Point at 0330 hours, but the result of the attacks could not be established.

Opposite a pitiful scene of the City Temple and St Andrew's Church side by side in their ordeal by fire. The Temple was fired a second time on May 10 but was the first to rise again, the foundation stone being laid by the Lord Mayor of London, Sir Seymour Howard, on the anniversary of the raid in 1955. Six years later St Andrew's, a Wren church dating from 1687, was restored.

The four phases in the life . . . and death . . . of another Wren masterpiece. A church had stood here as far back as 1223 but in 1066 the Great Fire swept up Bread Street . . . St Mildred's was rebuilt by Sir Christopher about 1682 and it was one of the few churches left in the City with original panelling and pews, being also the location of the Memorial to the first Governor of Australia, Admiral Arthur Phillip. The attack on April 16-17 left it a shattered ruin.

After the site was cleared the tower remained a forlorn relic of wartime London . . . just another weed-strewn bomb site with broken walls and empty windows . . . until 1971 when the site was sold for redevelopment for the Credit Lyonnais bank.

Above: **Puzzle picture. A well known square — known the world over and a firm favourite of every visitor to London — but does anyone recognise it on a Thursday morning in 1941?** *Below:* **As a further clue, the building on fire had been known as 'xxxx' Corner ever since R. E. Jones took over the building in 1919 but before that it was the Hotel de Provence — in Victorian times not quite the place a gentleman would go for an evening out with his wife.**

As the smoke dies down and we see the art nouveau facade of the Warner Cinema it becomes clearer. Of course . . . it's . . .

In this, the heaviest raid of the war to date, more fires were started and more casualties caused than in any previous attack. Bombing was apparently indiscriminate and widespread, involving 66 Boroughs, and 2,251 fires were started with eight of them major and 41 serious. Residential, commercial and industrial premises suffered extensively, with the worst effects apparent inside the area bounded by Willesden, Hackney, Barnes and Lewisham. Many important buildings, 18 hospitals and 13 churches were destroyed or damaged and initial casualty lists were 1,179 killed and 2,233 seriously injured. London Transport and the Southern Railway were badly affected and road damage disrupted transport in the City, West End and many areas south of the river. Utility services were not too badly hit nor, surprisingly, were the docks. More serious were a number of hits on gas works. Over 60 public buildings were damaged in varying degrees including the Admiralty, the Houses of Parliament and the Law Courts. St Pauls received a direct hit but luckily survived. Less fortunate were the occupants of air raid shelters at Holborn, Camberwell, Ealing, Lambeth and Leicester Square. Damage outside of London was mostly of a minor nature though there was a fire at Purfleet and railway damage at Dagenham. Damage and casualties (four killed) were also caused at Margate, and seven died in an incident at Warlingham, Surrey. In the West bombs were again dropped near Exeter and elsewhere at Maidstone, Hastings, Grimsby, Thameshaven, Sevenoaks, Newhaven, Shoreham-by-Sea, Kirton-in-Lindsey, Bircham Newton, Yarmouth and Bury St Edmunds. Bombs also fell on or near airfields at Langham, Digby and Exeter but damage was caused only at Langham.

Countrywide, heavy guns of AA Command used 9,000 rounds, with London's IAZ firing 2,629 4.5-inch shells, 2,610 3.7-inch and 177 3-inch shells between 2115 and 0440 hours.

. . . Leicester Square! The basement of Leicester Corner was subsequently flooded, as were many bombed buildings, to provide emergency water supplies. Further down on the left lies the Rialto and Café de Paris (see page 460-461).

Referring back to the Café de Paris incident, this is a good opportunity to lay to rest several previously published accounts which have stated that Al Bowlly, considered at the time to be the country's finest jazz singer, was killed there on March 8-9. This is incorrect. Al, a South African of Greek descent, came to Britain in 1928 as a vocalist and banjoist to join Fred Elizalde's Band at the Savoy. He joined Roy Fox and his orchestra at the Monseigneur Restaurant in 1931 and rode to world fame with great recordings which Ray Noble was making with the New Mayfair Orchestra. A trip to America followed and from 1934 to 1937 he was one of the leading singers in the States but he grew homesick and returned to record with top class bands including Geraldo, Sydney Lipton, Mantovani, Lew Stone, Maurice Winnick and Oscar Rabin although, as was customary, his name rarely appeared on the record label itself. He was a sport lover, compulsive gambler and a ladies man. In March 1941 he was playing a theatre date in the Midlands when he received a letter from a lady fan 'MM of Scunthorpe' that she had dreamed that she had seen him talking to a Negro and suddenly he had been blown to pieces. The same day he received the news that one of his closest friends, Ken Johnson, had been killed at the Café de Paris. Al was of a superstitious nature and the coincidence worried him greatly and he confided to a friend that it was a warning to him. The week before he died he was performing at the Rex Theatre in High Wycombe; on Wednesday night he was reading in bed in his flat in Duke's Court, Duke Street, when he was killed. 'Concentrating as he did, in later years on variety work,' wrote Stanley Nelson in one obituary, 'present-day swing fans probably only knew him as a singer of pop songs. But to the older fans . . . he will always be one of the brightest features in the small British constellation which had a very real place in the world firmament of jazz'.

Duke Street is a side turning off Oxford Street; little did these office and shop girls know as they marched bravely to work that morning that their heart throb lay dead just a couple of hundred yards away. The news of his death was 'flashed' out by the Press Association late on Thursday afternoon; by Friday the whole world knew.

And what of the landmarks? Selfridge's famed Palm Court — a sorry sight on April 18, 1941 — now Top of the Shop.

The very last record broadcast by the BBC was of Al Bowlly with Ken Johnson's band. 'Say don't you remember they called me Al . . .' said the headlines using words from his signature tune *Buddy Can You Spare a Dime*? as his epitaph, but what proportion of those hustling and bustling along London's premier shopping street recall the darkness of April 1941?

A near escape in Trafalgar Square for one of Sir Edwin Landseer's four beasts . . .

. . . and an even closer shave for St Paul's where a bomb penetrated the roof in the north transept and broke through the floor into the crypt. Visitors were allowed to inspect the damage for the first time on Whit Monday.

'Would the office still be there?' were the thoughts as one turned the last corner. This is Southampton Row.

John Adam Street near the Adelphi.

Enter at your peril — the story then as now in Kirby Street in Hatton Garden.

Not much left in Jermyn Street.

Since the beginning of the Blitz, Deutschlandsender radio in Hamburg had been using the powerful Hilversum transmitter in Holland to beam its English language news broadcasts to Britain. The *Germany Calling* programmes, and the clever prophecies of the statements made by its presenter, led many people to believe his threats; that there would be 'reprisals for the crimes perpetrated against non-combatants in Berlin, Hamburg and other German cities'. The well-spoken German announcer had first been picked up by Leslie Pratt working at the radio station at Cherkley, Surrey, and he described the intonation to Sidney Smith in charge of the reporting team as 'a proper Haw-Haw voice'. Smith, later Squadron Leader Sydney Smith, wrote a news story which appeared in the *Daily Express* dubbing the announcer 'Lord Haw-Haw' and the name became an instant household word. Picking on the proverb 'An eye for an eye, and a tooth for a tooth', Lord Haw-Haw boasted that 'for every microscopic part of enamel England rubs off a German tooth, England will lose a complete set of her own.' With hindsight, up to May 1941 this was a perfectly true statement as the Luftwaffe was meting out ten, twenty and thirty-fold the punishment being inflicted on German towns by the RAF where nearly 50 per cent of British bombs were falling in open countryside. With so much speculation in the British press as to just who the well-spoken newsreader was, on April 3, 1941, listeners were surprised to hear Lord Haw-Haw reveal his identity for the first time: 'I, William Joyce, left England because I would not fight for Jewry against Adolf Hitler and National Socialism. I left England because I thought that victory which would preserve existing conditions would be more damaging to Britain than defeat.' When the RAF bombed Berlin on the night of April 9-10, hitting the State Opera House, Haw-Haw's 'There's *go*ing to *be* a *bombing*' came horribly true in Hitler's retaliation on London on April 16-17.

'There's going to be a bombing'. There certainly was down at Bromley where St Peter and Paul's had stood since the 15th century. Hazel Kissick, an 18-year-old firewatcher on duty in the parish church, was fatally injured in the blast.

The church was rebuilt under the guidance of Mr D. H. Harold Gibbons, set a little further back from the road though retaining the restored tower. The foundation stone was laid by the then-Princess Elizabeth in October 1949.

The Ministry of Home Security were very concerned lest the extent of the bombing crack the morale of a sorely-tried population. In their immediate post-raid analysis, it was noted that 'Though the spirit of the public on the morning after the raid appeared admirable, there is no doubt that an attack of greater intensity than any so far experienced caused some alarm at the time. An example is reported from Lewisham of minor panic on the Downham Housing Estate, where 100 people who were not homeless betook themselves to a Rest Centre.' When all the facts and figures were examined after the war, the raid did in fact prove to be the heaviest in terms of the weight of bombs dropped; the most costly as to the number of casualties inflicted; and the largest with regard to the number of fires caused. At the final count, there had been over 2,250 fires, 1,180 people had been killed and 2,230 badly injured. One of the worst incidents was here in Pancras Square where a land mine killed 77 and injured 52 out of the 200 people occupying a surface shelter.

The square off Pancras Road as it was at the end of the war. Platt Street disappeared completely — now replaced by The Chenies.

The grey garb of war-torn London. *Above:* Sutherland Terrace, Pimlico and the Monster pub — both now lost for ever. *Below:* Featherstone Buildings, High Holborn — all except the one on the left replaced by the massive bulk of State House.

The raid produced two spectacular crashes in the London area, the first during the early evening, undoubtedly from the first wave of KG76. Steel helmets, with the sides hammered out so that they would fit over flying helmets with earphones, were a practical precaution not often photographed. This is Oberleutnant Moll (second from left) and his men from the 3rd Staffel.

Three enemy aircraft were claimed destroyed by pilots of Fighter Command, 164 of whose aircraft flew dusk, night and dawn patrols including five sent to northern France to patrol enemy airfields. One night fighter was destroyed when it was abandoned by its crew (who became lost following radio failure) while flying in the Crowborough area. The aircraft, Defiant N3369 of No. 264 Squadron, Biggin Hill, was possibly previously hit by British AA fire.

Their Ju 88 came down in Wimbledon making rather a mess of the back garden of No. 15 Denmark Hill. It had taken off from Beaumont-le-Roger and was approaching the Capital — where its target was the dock installations in the U-bend of the Thames — from the south-west at about 12,000 feet, when its crew saw an approaching fighter. Moll at the controls took evasive action and the fighter was not seen again, but shortly afterwards his aircraft was momentarily held by searchlights and then hit. The Ju 88 caught fire, the bombs were jettisoned, and the crew baled out. The W/T operator was killed — one report mentions that this was owing to a burnt parachute — but the other three members of the crew landed safely.

Shortly after two o'clock a Ju 88A-5, of III/KG77 crashed in the Observatory Gardens, Campden Hill Road, Kensington, after striking the roof of a house in a shallow dive and disintegrating, scattering debris widely over adjoining houses and gardens. Some hours previously — at about 2100 hours — this aircraft had left Jouvincourt, carrying a 1,000kg HE and several IB cannisters, bound for London. Its pilot, Leutnant Günther Sissimato (who, despite his un-Germanic surname was born in Berlin), attempted to bomb a railway triangle near Bethnal Green Junction which he approached from the Isle of Dogs at about 12,000 feet. However, because of poor visibility, the bombs were finally dropped near two large red fires which were seen in east London, and the aircraft landed back at base at Jouvincourt not long after midnight.

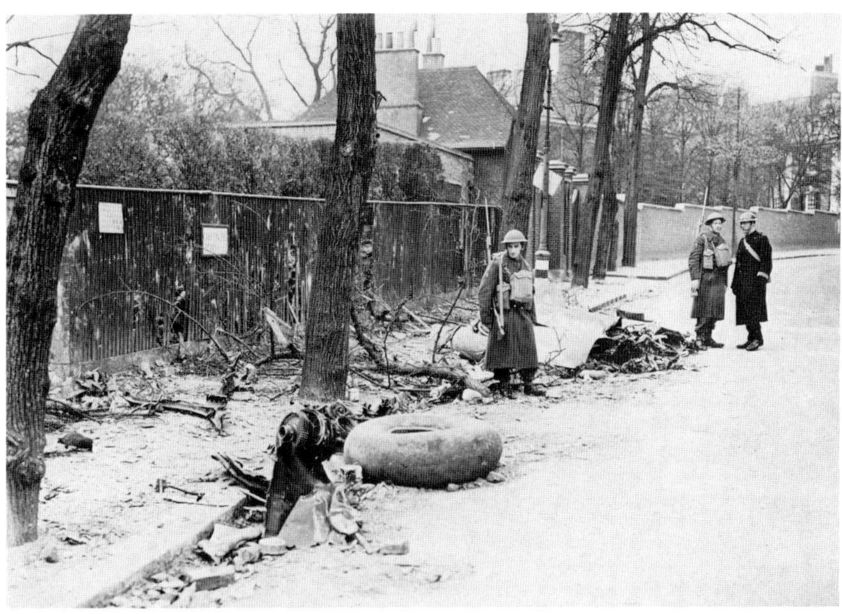

It was then refuelled and re-armed for a second sortie and at 0045 hours the 3Z+BS took off once more, this time carrying two 500kg HEs and more incendiaries intended for the West End of London. The two HEs were dropped on a fire in the target area from 13,500 feet and the IBs released a little later with the intention of starting a new fire. Its second mission completed, the Ju 88 turned westwards to start its return flight when a sudden impact was followed by a fire behind the W/T operator's position. The crew did not know whether this was due to AA fire or a night fighter, but almost certainly it was the former. All four crew members baled out and landed safely to be taken prisoner.

In addition to those detailed below a Junkers Ju 88 of 3/KG77 went missing.

4/KG1 Junkers Ju 88A-5 (4300). Shot down by Wing Commander T. G. Pike and Sergeant W. T. Clark in a Beaufighter of No. 219 Squadron. Dived into the ground at Thorns Flush, Cranleigh, Surrey 1.35 a.m. Oblt. E. Schlecht (Staffelkapitän), Oberfw. F. Hermann, Oberfw. H. Friesen and Oberfw. R. Gerleid all killed. Aircraft V4+MU destroyed.
Recovered by Tony Graves and John Tickner of the London Air Museum and subsequently investigated by Simon Parry. Parts now in the Tangmere Military Aviation Museum collection.

2/KG28 Heinkel He 111H-5 (3573). Shot down by Wing Commander T. G. Pike and Sergeant W. T. Clark in a Beaufighter of No. 219 Squadron, their second combat this night. Broke up in the air over Petworth Road, Wormley, Surrey 2.30 a.m. Uffz. T. Hammer and Oberfw. A. Engel baled out and taken prisoner. Gefr. W. Schüller and Gefr. R. Mattern killed. Aircraft 1T+EK disintegrated.
Site investigated by Simon Parry but nothing of consequence found. Propeller blade retained by the late Marshal of the Royal Air Force, Sir Thomas Pike KCB CBE DFC.

3/KG76 Junkers Ju 88A-5 (7172). Shot down by Flight Lieutenant Dotteridge and Sergeant Williams in a Beaufighter of No. 219 Squadron. Crashed into the garden of a private house, 15 Denmark Hill, Wimbledon 9.34 p.m. Oblt. E. Moll, Fw. K. Brähler and Fw. E. Franke baled out and taken prisoner. Fw. O. Staude baled out but his parachute failed and he was killed. Aircraft F1+DL totally destroyed.
Site investigated by Simon Parry and a few small fragments recovered from beneath a lawn. Airframe components, found by current owner of No. 15, donated to After the Battle collection.

3/KG77 Junkers Ju 88A-5 (8212). Aircraft crashed into trees at Sheldwich, Faversham, Kent 4.00 a.m. Uffz. K-H Praetorius, Uffz. L. Heindl, Uffz. T. Warnke and Uffz. E. Schwartner all killed. Aircraft 3Z+GL destroyed.

8/KG77 Junkers Ju 88A-5 (5131). Hit by AA fire during action over London. Aircraft hit roof of house in a shallow dive and disintegrated 2.05 a.m. Parts widely spread amongst houses and gardens at Observatory Gardens, Campden Hill Road, Kensington. Lt. G. Sissimato, Gefr. P. Schumann, Uffz. W. Meissler and Uffz. G. Abell all baled out and taken prisoner. Aircraft 3Z+BS disintegrated.

The corner shop — part of the British way of life. This is Southsea on Friday, April 18. In the night raiders have been over Portsmouth and this was the result of one bomb. Just an ordinary bomb . . . just one of the hundreds dropped that night . . . and just one of the many incidents. Nothing out of the ordinary except that here a poor widow died . . . Mrs Ethel Burch . . . now united with her Tom at last.

THURSDAY, APRIL 17-18

Sunset: 1959 Sunrise: 0559
Moon: 0219 — Dawn (Last Qtr −1)

Major attack on Portsmouth. Anti-shipping and airfield patrols.

UK — Extensive cloud with rain in the North and North-West. Heavier rain spreading in from the West. Visibility moderate, poor in rain.

The Continent — Cloud and heavy rain over extreme north-western France. Elsewhere variable cloud. Visibility generally moderate except in rain; fog in some inland areas towards dawn.

The usual fighter sweeps, armed sea reconnaissance and weather reconnaissance missions occupied the Luftwaffe during the day, but only seven aircraft penetrated inland and the only incident occurred at Fraserburgh where some damage was done and seven people killed.

During the night operations were flown by 258 long-range bombers, eight light bombers and 24 long-range night fighters. Portsmouth was the target for attack by 249 aircraft of Luftflotten 2 and 3 which between 2235 and 0415 hours delivered 346 tonnes of HE (36 SC 1000, 140 SC 500, 236 SC 250, 31 LZZ 250, 90 SC 50, 54 Type 'A' mines and 142 'B' mines) and 46,280 IBs. The CP encompassed the western side of Portsmouth and the eastern edge of Gosport, wherein German Intelligence placed the most important naval installations. Bombing was mainly visual, but some crews used DR or radio methods while others aimed at fires visible through the cloud. Explosions and fires were claimed in the designated TA and towards the end of the attack 17 large and about 100 smaller fires covered the area between the dockyard and the barracks.

Participating units of Luftflotte 2 were I and II/KG53, which opened the attack, followed by elements of KG3, KG4 and KG30, many of which were carrying Luftminen 'A' and 'B' parachute mines. The second phase of the attack was undertaken by the following units of Luftflotte 3:

II/KG1: 15 Ju 88, 0300-0410
III/KG1: 10 Ju 88, 0250-0323
II/KG77: 11 Ju 88, 0300-0415
III/KG77: 3 Ju 88, 0310-0318
III/KG26: 6 He 111, 0101-0308
II/KG27: 15 He 111, 0225-0335
I/KG54: 14 Ju 88, 0157-0224
II/KG54: 13 Ju 88, 0210-0247
KGr806: 13 Ju 88, 0209-0255

On this occasion Luftflotte 3 achieved a very good ratio of aircraft which reached the target to those dispatched — 100 and 106 respectively. One aircraft bombed an alternative target, three aborted and two were reported missing (Ju 88s of I/KG54 and III/KG77).

Portsmouth and neighbouring districts of Hampshire took the brunt of the bombing and in addition to damage in the city, naval establishments were hit, causing a number of casualties. Relatively few civilians were killed despite the damage inflicted on residential areas and there was only limited dislocation of utility services; important, though, was the failure of electricity supplies to the dockyard, but every effort was made to remedy this.

Activity elsewhere was limited and the only serious incidents occurred at Great Yarmouth. An attempt to bomb Bawdsey radar station came in the early hours.

The Solent guns, in action from 2135 to 0445 hours, fired 2,200 rounds and across the country as a whole AA Command used just under 4,000 rounds. Fighter Command dispatched 93 aircraft on dusk, night and dawn patrols including a single offensive patrol over northern France, but no claims were made of enemy aircraft destroyed.

The censor tried his damndest to stop anyone finding the location by scrubbing out the name but after a little effort we found it; on the corner of Pretoria and Haslemere Roads.

St Cuthbert's, Hayling Avenue, had already been damaged after having been straddled by a stick of five bombs on November 10, 1940. Even greater damage was caused on Thursday from a land mine which exploded at 11.45 p.m. The church was partially restored in 1949 when the nave was rebuilt but it was not until 1958 that the new east end was completed.

Two aircraft were lost during the day:

3(F)/123 Messerschmitt Bf 110E-3 (2328). Shot down by Squadron Leader R. F. Boyd DFC and bar, and Flying Officer E. F. J. Charles in Spitfires of No. 54 Squadron. Crashed into the sea off Ramsgate 11.00 a.m. Lt. J. Schnieder missing. Uffz. O. Neumann killed. Aircraft 4U+SL lost.

1/KG40 Focke-Wulf Fw 200C-3 (0051). Crashed into the sea off the Shetland Isles in unknown circumstances. Oblt. Kalus, Uffz. Bittner, Fw. Heidrich and Obergefr. Greschenz missing. Oberfw. Schulze killed. Body of Uffz. W. Zeller recovered from the sea on May 21 and buried in the Shetland Isles. Aircraft F8+FH lost.

The two aircraft lost during the night raid are detailed below. Additionally a Junkers Ju 88C of I/NJG2 crashed at Gilze-Rijen killing its three crew and another of this unit's aircraft was damaged after a night intruder sortie to Britain.

2/KG54 Junkers Ju 88A-5 (6025). Hit by AA fire during an attack on Portsmouth. Crashed on Thorney Island airfield near Portsmouth 2.00 a.m. Oberfw. H. Meier, Uffz. W. Dietzel, Uffz. R. Rothenspieler and Oberfw. G. Hocke all killed. Aircraft B3+GK disintegrated.

7/KG77 Junkers Ju 88A-5 (6260). Crashed into the sea off Nab Tower during an attack on Portsmouth 2.07 a.m. Lt. K. Höflinger, Oberfw. K. Odelga, Oberfw. K. Vogelhuber and Fw. K. Herfort all missing. Aircraft 3Z+JR lost.

4/NJG2 Junkers Ju 88C-4 (0345). Said to have been shot down by another enemy aircraft. Dived vertically into ground at Gothic House Farm, Thorney, Peterborough 9.23 p.m. Obergefr. W. Beetz, Gefr. R. Kronika and Gefr. J. Mittag killed. Aircraft R4+BM totally destroyed.

Major recovery by the Wealden Aviation Archaeological Group led to the identification and subsequent burial of all three crew members at Cannock Chase with full military honours. Engine donated to the Fenland Aircraft Preservation Society. Other items including tail wheel, propeller blade and dinghy now in the Tangmere Military Aviation Museum collection.

Hitler may have changed the face of Portsmouth but these pictures prove the reverse of the old adage in that what goes down must go up! Langport Road captured on film and illustrating the changing fortunes of the Connaught Drill Hall.

This is a battlefront! Once again the Lincolnshire flatlands echo to the sound of throbbing motors as the experten of the Wealden Aviation Archaeological Group move in to investigate the wreck of the second Junkers Ju 88C night fighter which crashed in Britain on April 17, 1941.

BEATING THE EXPERTS

The dictionary defines 'archaeology' as the 'study of human antiquities usually by excavation.' The discovery of past events, the detection of clues to piece together an unknown jigsaw, and the knowledge that one is being allowed a glimpse back in time, are all aspects which have spurred men to look into the happenings of former generations. The examination of wartime aircraft wreckage buried deep in the soil of the United Kingdom by a new young breed of investigators has gained momentum during the past twenty years, coining a new term in the process: wreckology. The dedication of the many loose-knit groups which have been formed in some cases borders on the fanatic: an additional challenge being provided by the opportunity to try to 'beat the experts' — the RAF Intelligence Officers — whose job it was to record the details at the time of the crash. Their work was hampered by the number of crashes, wartime expediency and lack of mechanical aids, yet to them the trail was hot. More than two score years later time and nature have combined to cover the traces, yet detailed examination and comparison of the written records of both sides now help enormously to establish the true facts.

The families of many aircrews, formerly listed as missing, have been greatly comforted by the results of painstaking research which often leads to a former husband, son or brother being rescued from his undignified tomb to be accorded a decent burial.

Such is the case of the Gedney Hill Junkers 88, one of the earliest night fighters to crash in England during the war, something, one would have thought, that the authorities at the time would have spent much effort to try to establish the details. In this instance they did not, leaving a forty-year-old mystery to be unravelled.

The Air Intelligence Report contained in the Public Record Office file Air 22/267 is enough to excite the interest of most aviation archaeologists, as it records the loss of the Junkers 88 which crashed at Hurns Farm, just off French Drove at Gedney Hill near Peterborough and reads as follows:

'Junkers 88. Crashed on 17.4.41 at 21.23 hours at Hurns Farm, Thorney, near Ely. Map reference F.7828. No markings were visible and no plates were found, but one rubber cover of a petrol tank bore the date 1.11.40. The

The first of the new mark of aircraft had landed in England more or less intact five weeks before (see page 463) and been completely removed by the RAF at the time. Thus the investigation of this second machine, also intact but all below ground, promised to be fruitful. The 'battle' began on the morning of October 7, 1978.

Virtually everything was there . . . from wheels to prop blades!

cause of the crash is unknown; no fighter action appears to have taken place in the area and the aircraft is not claimed by AA. It appears to have been on fire in the air. The aircraft dived vertically into soft clay, is almost entirely buried and the crater is full of water. Pieces of an MG.15 were found and a few bits of armour, but no details possible. Crew; presumed 4, believed all killed in crash.'

In actual fact, the statement by the RAF Intelligence Officer that four crew were killed was incorrect. No doubt this presumption was based on the belief that the aircraft was the usual type of Ju 88, a bomber carrying four men. However, during 1977, in a letter to the Wealden Aviation Archaeological Group who had become interested in the site, the Deutsche Dienststelle (WASt), the German records centre in Berlin, suggested that the aeroplane involved could well have been a Junkers Ju 88 C variant of the 4th Staffel/NJG2, lost with its crew of three on April 17, 1941. Subsequent investigations and an excavation indeed proved this to be the case, although the significance of its arrival on British soil had clearly been lost on RAF Intelligence during 1941. It was, in fact, one of the first Ju 88 night fighters to fall on land over the United Kingdom, the first intact example coming down more or less intact near King's Lynn on March 10, 1941. The Gedney Hill Junkers would probably have revealed considerably less in the way of technical detail than its Norfolk counterpart, although the eventual excavation in 1978 did locate some items which would have been of interest to the RAF in 1941!

Following difficult negotiations for permission to excavate which involved the tenant farmer, Mr Ernest Hurn, the land agent and Trinity College, Cambridge which owns the land, an investigation and metal detector survey was made of the field on Saturday, September 16, 1978. At the end of an all day search tiny fragments of the aircraft were found close to the road — a long way from the area of the crash which had been indicated by eyewitnesses. Despite the shortage of firm evidence, and only faint metal detector readings, an excavation was organised for the weekend of October 7/8, 1978, employing the local plant hire firm of Messrs. Thory's — the only operator in the area having a Hymac 580c with an extended 35-foot boom. From eyewitness and official reports, together with an assessment of the very soft soil type, it was felt that a mechanical excavator with a deep reach would be needed.

The first few feet of the excavation revealed nothing, and barely any sign of soil disturbance. Then, at about seven

This is the dinghy and one of the parachutes.

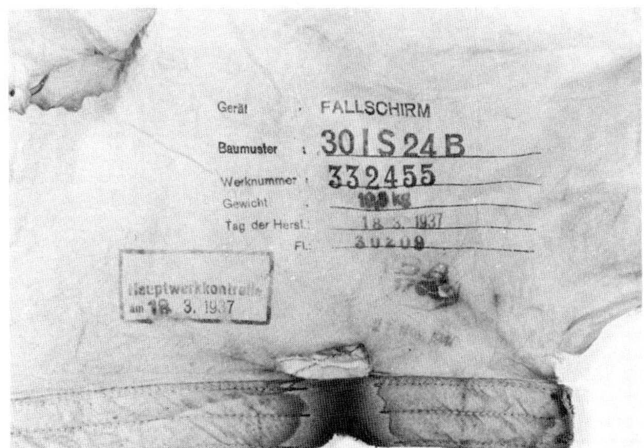

Although pieces of wreckage, like this acceptance stamp on the parachute, give interesting pointers, it is the personal belongings that mark it above all else, a human tragedy.

feet, a large timber railway sleeper was unearthed. Beneath it could be seen the glint of aluminium — in fact, a Luftwaffe NCO's belt buckle! At this depth there were clear signs of aircraft wreckage, and a pungent reek of fuel and oil. Following the trail downwards a mass of wreckage was unearthed throughout the day, including propellers, undercarriage assemblies, the tail wheel, oxygen cylinders and a crankshaft and pistons from one shattered engine. The quantity of wreckage recovered, it would be true to say, overwhelmed the recovery team. Clearly little had been salvaged in 1941 and almost the entire aeroplane, tail wheel forward, had gone into the ground. Sorting of the wreckage revealed smaller, more interesting objects, including cockpit items, flares, a dinghy and also some firm evidence that the crew were still in the aeroplane. Remains of flying clothing indicated beyond doubt that three men had died, this proven by the remains of three pairs of flying boots. Further examination revealed fragmentary human remains, and consequently the Peterborough City Police were notified. They removed from the crash site the remains of three airmen and a quantity of ammunition which had been uncovered.

Detailed examination of the items taken away by the Wealden Group revealed a quantity of interesting paperwork, including some documents which would have been welcomed by Intelligence at the time. One document listed RAF airfields in East Anglia, together with corresponding code letters. Also, the strap from the first aid kit confirmed the Werke Nummer (0345) and a handkerchief bore the initials RK. Undoubtedly, then, this was the suspected aeroplane of 4/NJG2. Not only did the Werke Nummer correspond, but the initials RK would probably indicate its owner to have been Rudolf Kronika, the wireless operator. No identity discs or papers were found, and nothing to firmly establish the identities of the other two crewmen. By deduction, however, they were obviously the pilot, Obergefreiter Wilhelm Beetz, and the gunner, Johann Mittag. He, like Kronika, held the rank of Gefreiter.

This information was communicated to the Coroner's Officer of Peterborough City Police and, simultaneously, to the German War Graves Commission by the Wealden Group. However, on October 11, 1978, Superintendent Les Braithwaite of the Peterborough Police announced that the Coroner did not propose to hold an inquest and by November 4 the remains had been handed to the German authorities for burial at Cannock Chase. By this time the Germans had accepted the evidence presented to them (they had also been sent the initialled handkerchief) and the three airmen were named and buried in Block 8 of the German Military Cemetery. The remains were buried in a single grave, beneath a headstone bearing the three names.

Official efforts in Germany to trace relatives of the three men only succeeded in locating the family of Wilhelm Beetz, who still had a brother and sister living in Heide, West Germany. Attempts to trace the families of Kronika and Mittag failed, and it was concluded that they were deceased or living in East Germany. Even an article in the popular national German newspaper *Bild* raised no response from anyone who was related to, or who knew, Mittag and Kronika. However, Günter Meier writing from Celle revealed that he had learnt to fly before the war with 'Willi' Beetz, at Fliegerschule 52 at Halberstadt. Writing in December 1978 he recalled how he shared a room with Willi and a Theo Gentsch for two years before they completed their training and were posted to operational units. Gentsch and Meier were luckier than their colleague Beetz, both of them surviving the war, with Meier becoming a post-war gliding champion in Lower Saxony. In his letter he enquired if Beetz's gold signet ring had been found. This he described as being plain gold, with no

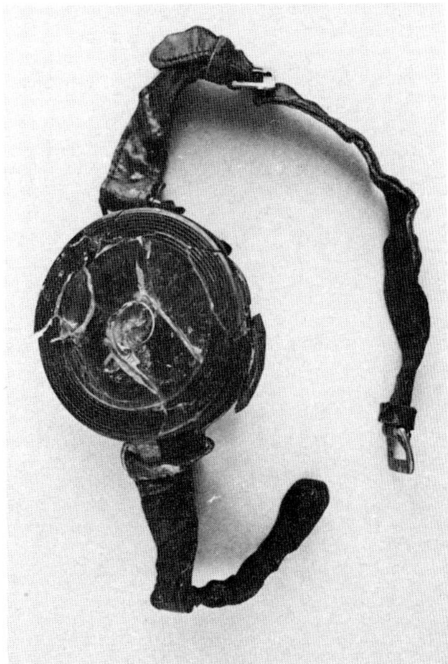

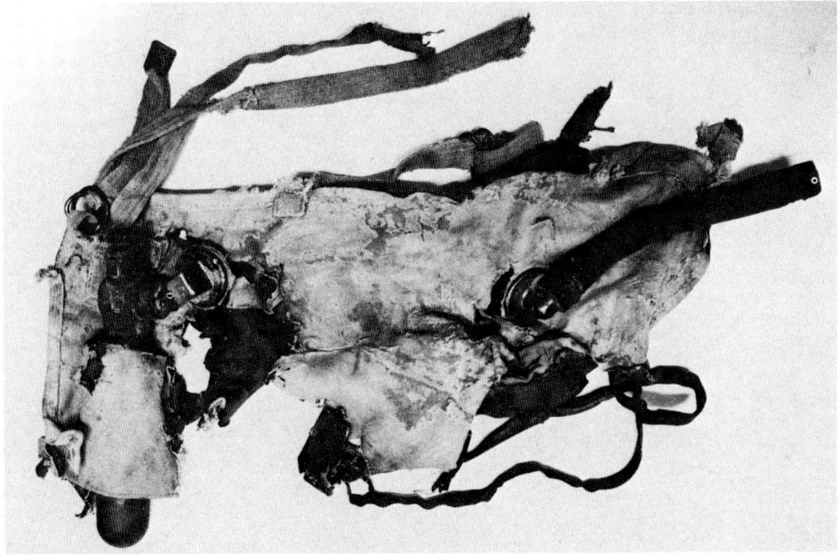

A wrist compass and the lower part of a lifejacket with inflation bottle.

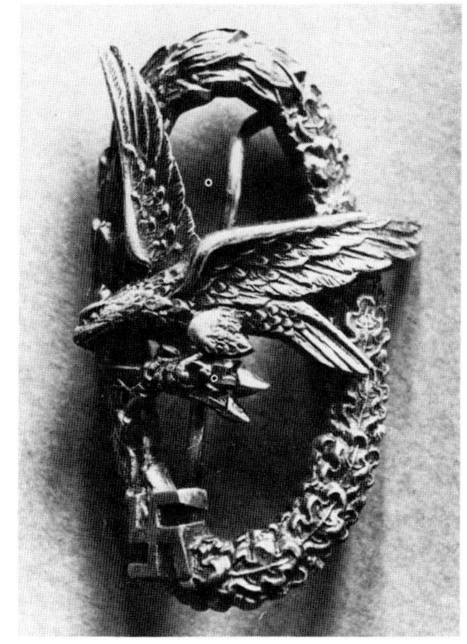

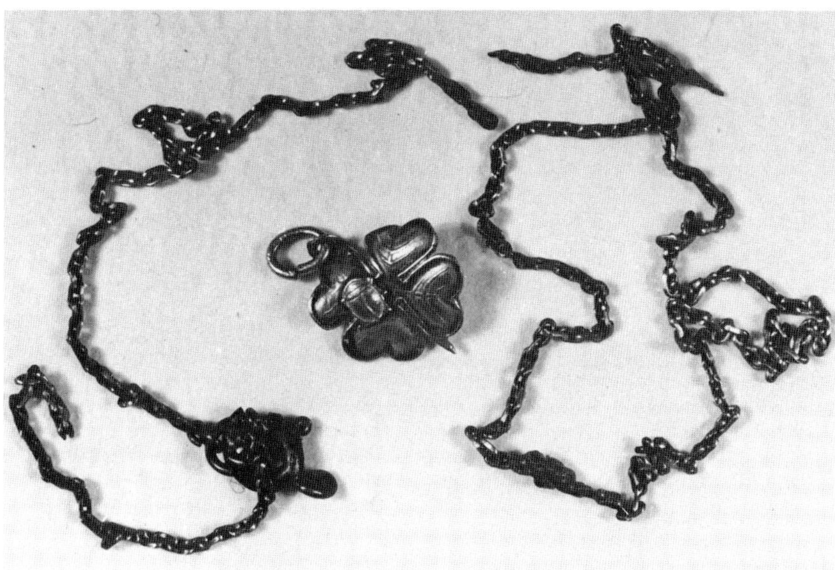

initials engraved on it. It is believed that he wore this following his engagement on April 1, 1940, to a 'Fraulein Erika'. Little is known of Miss Erika by Willi's brother, Rudolf, or his sister, Anni Bukowski, except that she was the daughter of a police officer. Neither of them had met her, nor did the family have any contact with her after Willi's death. Sadly, the gold ring was never found during the excavation, but a leather purse, believed to be Willi's, did come to light. It contained a few coins, a locker key, a train ticket to Breda (his unit was stationed at Gilze-Rijen in the Netherlands) and an aircraft manufacturer's plate obviously taken from an aeroplane by the owner of the purse. Perhaps his first solo.

The significance of this maker's label will probably remain unknown, just as will the exact reason or cause of the loss of the Ju 88, which could well have been through some failure or accident, rather than by hits from British defences. Witnesses to this incident were few in this remote and sparsely populated area on the Lincolnshire/Cambridgeshire border, but all speak of the aircraft being on fire in the air. This was clearly recalled by the farmer, Mr Ernest Hurn, and 75-year-old Mr Horace Watson of Gedney Hill, who was interviewed at the time of the excavation. He still lived at his home in Chesnut Cottages from where he witnessed the crash.

'It was about 9.30,' recalled Mr Watson, 'and I had just left the house on my bike when I heard a shrill whistling noise in the air. I saw some sparks, then there was a great explosion across the fields, followed by a great blaze. I rushed over, but there was nothing anyone could do. There was still a fire, with just a great hole in the earth and fragments scattered in all directions. I saw somebody in the road pick up what I thought was an incendiary bomb, so I grabbed it and threw it in the ditch. Nothing was ever got out. They just filled in the hole and left it — men and all. I think they tried to get something out, but abandoned it after very little effort.'

Last word must go to the family in Germany who were pleased and touched that, at long last, their brother Willi had been found and buried. Writing in January 1979, his brother Rudolf said that 'the news of the discovery has touched me deeply and occupied me a lot. I have thought long and hard with melancholy and sadness about the best sons of our land who sacrificed themselves in good faith. Those terrible years took away so many young men, amongst them our Willi. Both my sister and I have been pleased to know, after so long, what happened to our dear brother. Now we are happy that before we die we may go to see his last resting place and thank you for your efforts. I am sure that this is what Willi and his comrades would have wanted.'

ANDY SAUNDERS, 1986

Whatever the ebb and flow of the battle in the Balkans and the Middle East, the real issue remains to be decided over Great Britain and the English Channel.

This continuation of the Battle of Britain, the first round of which was won last autumn, will be fought chiefly in the air. Soon the enemy will be making desperate efforts to end it, spurred on by the knowledge of our growing strength reinforced by the might of the United States.

The whole strategy of the war is bound up in these air operations. . . .

Germany has brought up her bomber strength in France to at least the equal of what it was there last September. This has been done by calling on reserves from Germany. The whole operational heavy night-bomber strength of the Luftwaffe in the West was concentrated against London on Wednesday night. The fact that the raid was not followed up the next night may be an indication of the extent of the forces used, the exhaustion that the effort caused, and the careful planning necessary to prepare so much concentration of effort for one night only.

however attractive as a balm for personal suffering, are dangerous at this stage for two reasons. First, we have so many vital military objectives to attend to that our bomber strength is not yet strong enough to allow a diversion to large-scale reprisal bombing without leaving important and even vital military targets untouched. Secondly, the enemy has more bombers on nearer bases than we have, so that at present he must be in a position to counter reprisals with even more ferocious reprisals on us.

Our recent heavy attack on Kiel has been quoted as being the exact opposite. That is utterly misleading. Kiel is close (380 miles to Berlin's 620 miles); it is an important manufacturing town; it is a shipbuilding base and an invasion port. Kiel is an ideal target, combining many important objectives. It is an isolated instance on which generalisations cannot be based.

The job of the Bomber Command is to strike the German war effort and the German will-to-war in the most powerful, the most concentrated, and the most effective manner possible. That aim is best gained by bombing with

We have already discussed at length the dislocation caused to communication and services by UXBs. The UXPM was a bigger, yet easier, problem as in nine cases out of ten it remained lying on the surface, plain for all to see. This Luftmine B on Hungerford Bridge was a left over from Wednesday's raid. Regardless of whether its inertness was caused by fault or design, just imagine the risk the photographer was taking by approaching this close to 1,000 kilogrammes of HE. The chip in the stonework where it clonked the abutment still remains to be seen.

In the present stage of the war to spread false hopes of coming victories is just as pernicious and just as dangerous to morale as to assume that the present German advantage in weight and numbers will persist. Long-term faith is needed, for this is to be a long-term war. . . .

German anxiety about our mounting production at home causes him to turn aside periodically from his supreme preoccupation of cutting our Atlantic supply line in an effort to interfere with output by destroying some of the services on which production must depend. In this the Luftwaffe remains faithful to its old ham-handed system of trying to smash the areas in which munitions are built rather than the individual objectives themselves.

That scheme fails when it comes up against a place as big as London. The vast extent of London's contribution to war production must inevitably force the enemy to target bombing if he is to obtain results. That is just the thing the Luftwaffe has shown itself incapable of doing by night — or even by day when hampered by fighter opposition.

Thus London stands in a class by itself. In that class the Coventry methods are ineffectual. London can take it by virtue of its very size.

Wednesday's vicious attack on London again demonstrated this fact. All the available bomber strength was concentrated on the one large objective in indiscriminate fury. The German claim that it was a reprisal raid for our attack on Berlin was doubtless true. The German raid on London was dictated by the force of public opinion.

Here again we must accept the long-term view. Reprisals, discrimination those objectives known to be vital links in the chain of Germany's war effort.

We all know how ineffectual the indiscriminate bombing of cities can be. We cannot afford to waste our bombs, as the Germans waste their bombs, on non-military objectives. Tit-for-tat, bombing, in which personal feelings overcome strategic necessity, can never prove effective.

Unfortunately part of our effort must be diverted to the so-called invasion ports. That is necessary. Those who say that they welcome invasion do a grave disservice to our cause. An invasion cannot be anything but a grim and bloody struggle. It would certainly involve a large portion of the country even if it were beaten back quickly.

It is likely that a landing will be attempted, and possible that it could be made. Those troop-carrying gliders and tank-carrying aeroplanes are no fable, and are not easy to counter at night. Above all, the defence of the fighter aerodrome against surprise parachute attack is of the utmost importance.

Germany may attempt an invasion soon. That invasion will be repelled, and again in daylight the Luftwaffe will suffer decisive defeat. Yet let us acknowledge the problems with which we are confronted, and not underrate either the enemy or ourselves. The air defence on four fronts this summer will pave the way to concerted attack on one front next summer. That front will be Germany itself and the whole German war machine.

SUNDAY TIMES, APRIL 20, 1941

'Der Tausand Tonne Geschenk!' Göring's birthday present to Hitler was to mount the 'Thousand Ton Raid' — the one and only time during the Blitz that the Luftwaffe was able to drop 1,000 tonnes of high explosive on a single target on a single night. Londoner's still dazed after the Wednesday attack, were just beginning to pick up the pieces — these residents of flats in the West End are waiting to be evacuated from Jermyn Street.

FRIDAY, APRIL 18-19

Sunset: 2001 Sunrise: 0557
Moon: 0258 — Dawn (Last Quarter)

Minor activity only.

UK — Extensive cloud with rain and poor visibility in many areas.
The Continent — Similar to the UK.

Daylight activity was on a small scale and consisted primarily of armed sea reconnaissance missions. Three ships were attacked off the coast of Scotland between Wick and Aberdeen during the night and a large tanker was damaged off St Anne's Head, but few bombs fell on land. Only 27 aircraft operated after nightfall and ten of these were engaged in minelaying.

I/KG40 lost its third Focke-Wulf Fw 200 in as many days and a Junkers Ju 88 of 3(F)/123 returned to Brest after being damaged by fighters.

3/KG40 Focke-Wulf Fw 200C-5 (0053). Crashed into the sea off Schull, Co. Cork, Eire. Oblt. E. Müller, Fw. K. Macht, Fw. G. Siegl, Gefr. E. Sächel, Uffz. W. Salbenblätt and Reg. Rat. W. Habich all landed by boat in Eire and interned. Aircraft F8+GL sank in sea.

SATURDAY, APRIL 19-20

Sunset: 2002 Sunrise: 0555
Moon: 0331 — Dawn (Last Qtr +1)

Major attack on London. Minelaying, airfield patrols and armed sea reconnaissance.

UK — Fair to fine conditions in the South, rain and low cloud in the North clearing eastwards. Visibility moderate to good, poor in rain.
The Continent — Low cloud with rain giving way to broken cloud and good visibility.

> *The German people, fully confident of victory are celebrating in earnest mood and high spirits the 52nd birthday of the Führer. The hearts of all Germans go out to the defender of German honour and freedom and the guarantor of the German future, in unchangeable and unextinguishable gratitude.*
> *We look back on the uninterrupted chain of fruitful victories which could only have been achieved under the leadership of one who is not only a statesman and a soldier but also a leader and a man of the people.*
> REICHSMARSCHALL HERMANN GÖRING, APRIL 20, 1941

Daylight operations were not on a big scale but anti-shipping patrols, weather reconnaissance and general reconnaissance occupied several units including I/SKG 210, I/KG40 and 1(F)/122. Seven aircraft came inland but bombs were dropped only at Whitby, without effective result.

During the night the Luftwaffe launched what was to be the heaviest attack of the war on a British target centre, with the crews of 712 aircraft claiming to have bombed London. For the first and only time, too, more than 1,000 tonnes of high explosives were dropped in one raid. In total, 783 bomber and two night fighter sorties were flown — many crews engaged in the attack on London flying two, and some three, missions.

The CP in the capital was that stretch of the Thames from Tower Bridge downstream to a position south of Beckton, extending on both banks to cover the granaries and port installations, and it was over this target that 1,026 tonnes of HE (four SC 2500, ten SC 1800, 271 SC 1000, 306 SC 500, 1,014 SC 250, 76 LZZ 250, 534 SC/SD 50, six LMA and 247 LMB) were claimed dropped, together with no less than 153,096 incendiaries. Also dropped in the early stages to aid target location were 12 LC 50 parachute flares.

For much of the attack, which lasted from 2115 to 0415 hours, a layer of cloud covered London and many crews bombed without sight of the ground using DR and radio methods, aiming at the glow of fires visible through the overcast, or using the bursting flak shells and searchlights as target location 'indicators'. Some crews managed to bomb visually, however, through occasional breaks in the cloud, and reported seeing many large fires.

From 0300 hours the cloud began to break, but mist continued to hamper sight of the ground. Nevertheless, enormous fires were visible in and around the Royal Victoria

One of those thousand tons landed here in East Ham. Casualties from the parachute mine were three members of the Stockwell family, Eliza, Grace and Sidney, Ken Fage and Harry Nightingale. On the 23rd the King and Queen came to the borough and down to Caledon Road.

Dock, the East and West India Docks, in large granaries in Millwall Docks, in the vicinity of the Greenwich power station and along the north bank of the Thames and over adjacent districts of the town.

Luftflotte 2 flew 208 sorties over London, using every available unit except KG3. Luftflotte 3 dispatched 540 sorties, with 504 crews reaching the target area; two aircraft bombed alternative targets, 32 aborted and four aircraft were lost (two after bombing).

Units involved were:

I/KG27: 12 He 111, 2157-2327 + 10 He 111, 0214-0330
II/KG27: 15 He 111, 2143-2240 + 10 He 111, 0030-0330 + 2 He 111, 0315-0353
III/KG27: 16 He 111, 2145-2223 + 13 He 111, 0200-0335
KGr100: 17 He 111, 2209-2241 + 17 He 111, 0115-0347 + 1 He 111 at 0350
II/KG1: 16 Ju 88, 2125-2240 + 7 Ju 88, 0053-0305
III/KG1: 12 Ju 88, 2130-2240 + 8 Ju 88, 0002-0035 + 1 Ju 88 at 0215

I/KG76: 11 Ju 88, 2150-2225 + 4 Ju 88, 0315-0415
II/KG76: 16 Ju 88, 2150-2255 + 11 JU 88, 0050-0255
III/KG76: 15 Ju 88, 2130-2210
I/KG77: 14 Ju 88,. 2220-2259 + 10 Ju 88, 0220-0345
II/KG77: 15 Ju 88, 2155-2235 + 12 Ju 88, 0015-0312 + 1 Ju 88 at 0300
III/KG77: 10 Ju 88, 2218-2320 + 5 Ju 88, 0137-0315
III/KG26: 13 He 111, 2115-2300 + 9 He 111, 0150-0320 (opened attack)
III/KG40: 6 He 111, 2150-2225 + 5 He 111, 0210-0240
I/KG54: 15 Ju 88, 2140-2225 + 7 Ju 88, 0108-0145 (one BM 1000 dropped by an aircraft in the first attack)
II/KG54: 18 Ju 88, 2138-2218 + 10 Ju 88, 0215-0320
III/KG54: 17 Ju 88, 2140-2215 + 12 Ju 88, 2357-0120 + 6 Ju 88, 0205-0329
Stab/KG55: 2 He 111, 2214-2340 + 2 He 111, 0124-0133 + 1 He 111 at 0340
I/KG55: 20 He 111, 2200-2245 + 15 He 111, 0202-0345
II/KG55: 13 He 111, 2205-2230 + 11 He 111, 0102-0205
III/KG55: 17 He 111, 2210-2300 + 18 He 111, 0122-0245 + 6 He 111, 0355-0415

The aircraft lost on this operation — all Ju 88s — belonged to I/KG76, II/KG76 (two aircraft, one after bombing and the other crashed on its return), and II/KG77 (crashed after take-off).

London again suffered badly although the first phase of the attack produced fairly scattered bombing. The second part of the attack produced more concentration in the dock areas, however, and caused considerable damage in the East End. Altogether 1,460 fires were started, more than 1,200 people were killed and more than 1,000 seriously injured. Considerable damage was done to warehouses, sheds, silos, timber yards, barges, a variety of dock installations, the Royal Naval College at Greenwich. St Peter's Hospital and many other buildings including hospitals, churches and museums were also damaged or destroyed. A very bad incident occurred at Nuttall Street, Shoreditch, where three blocks of LCC flats and an underground shelter were destroyed, producing an initial casualty list of 46 killed and another 46 missing.

There were also many incidents in the Home Counties, particularly in Essex and Kent; 14 people were killed in Romford, with more damage and casualties at Southend, Hornchurch, Rochester, Dartford, Reigate, Otford and Darenth.

In action from 2123 to 0420 hours against raiders flying at heights between 6,200 and 20,000 feet, the guns of the Inner Artillery Zone fired approximately 9,000 of the 13,000 rounds used countrywide during the night. Fighter Command dispatched 101 aircraft on dusk, night and dawn patrols, but they were severely hampered by unfavourable weather and only one enemy aircraft was claimed destroyed. Another was credited to AA Command.

While making its second sortie of the night, an He 111H-5 (5J+JR) of 7/KG4 based at Leeuwarden, Holland, was shot down on its approach to London by a Hurricane of No. 151 Squadron flown by Pilot Officer Stevens. The Heinkel's W/T operator returned the fire, without having actually seen the fighter, but both engines of the bomber were put out of action and the bombs were jettisoned. In fact, it seems more than likely that a mine was being carried in addition to bombs, for KG4 often carried these weapons. However, confirmation is lacking although later examination of the wreckage revealed four vertical bomb chutes and a PVC 1006L external rack (for large bombs or mines). Having disposed of his load, the German pilot, Oberleutnant Josef Baierl, attempted a forced landing, but crashed on the Detling–Sittingbourne road at Whitstable's Meadow, Stockbury, at 0430 hours (April 20). Baierl and his Bordfunker were seriously injured and the other two members of the crew were killed in the crash.

The wreckage of this aircraft held special interest for the technical officers of AI1(g) Branch, for it was found to have fittings for an anti-barrage balloon fender although the fender itself was not installed. This was in accord with several previous reports of fender-equipped aircraft; on April 9 one was seen and reported by the Navy during a low level attack on Holyhead, and on April 16 military sources reported a searchlight-illuminated low-flying raider with what appeared to be an attachment in front of its wings which was probably an anti-balloon device.

The East End suffered grievously with wildly scattered bombing due to crews being unable to bomb visually. Their Majesties visited the scene of another incident during their Royal Tour in Freemasons Road near Victoria Docks. Here eight died.

And Ladlow's still survives, albeit in rebuilt premises beside Coolfin Road.

Four aircraft were lost on sorties to London, those not detailed here being a Heinkel He 111 of 3/KG4 and Junkers Ju 88 of 4/KG76. A second II/KG76 machine crashed upon its return. KG77 lost a Junkers Ju 88 and its crew in a crash on the Continent and a II/KG53 Heinkel He 111 crashed at Brugge, Begium, killing three and injuring two of its crew.

7/KG4 Heinkel He 111H-5 (3924). Shot down by Pilot Officer R. P. Stevens DFC in a Hurricane of No. 151 Squadron. Made a forced landing but hit a bank and broke in two at Whitstable's Meadow, Stockbury, Kent 4.30 a.m. Oblt. J. Baierl and Gefr. W. Mrozeck injured and taken prisoner. Uffz. G. Schumann and Oberfw. T. Völker killed. Aircraft 5J+JR wrecked.
Manufacturer's plate bearing '3924' in the Colin Pratley collection.

1/KG76 Junkers Ju 88A-5 (5151). Shot down by Brooklands AA guns. Crashed at Slaughter Bridge, Slinfold, Sussex 10.30 p.m. Fw. H. Burkart, Obergefr. B. Kalmus, Obergefr. R. Scheithauer and Oberfw. W. Haselsteiner all killed. Aircraft F1+GH destroyed.
Major recovery by the Wealden Aviation Archaeological Group produced a dinghy, propellers and other parts.

SUNDAY, APRIL 20-21

Sunset: 2004 Sunrise: 0553
Moon: 0359 — Dawn (Last Qtr +2)

No significant activity.

UK — Variable amounts of cloud, mainly moderate visibility but poor in places.
The Continent — Similar to the UK.

Daylight activity by the Luftwaffe was on the biggest scale for some time with numerous fighter sweeps, reconnaissance flights and anti-shipping operations. About 70 aircraft flew inland but mainly without deep penetration. Bombs fell at Aberdeen, killing one person, and once again damage and casualties were inflicted at Fraserburgh. Several attacks were attempted on ships including one on an anti-submarine trawler off Orfordness by two Bf 110s of SKG210 (both of which were claimed destroyed by the trawler).

Despite reasonable weather conditions, both over the UK and on the Continent, only four long-range bombers and 12 long-range fighters operated during the night. A few bombs fell in East Anglia and in Cornwall. British Air Intelligence believed that the Luftwaffe was conserving resources in preparation for another massive assault.

Eight hundred miles away across Europe, in a pleasant wooded valley in the land of his birthplace, Hitler was celebrating his 52nd birthday at his headquarters, code-named Führerhauptquartier Frülingssturm, located in his train 'Amerika' standing at the little station of Mönichkirchen (*left*), 70 kilometres south-west of Vienna. *Right:* It remains today much as it was that day in 1941.

It was a day of celebration — things were going well for Germany. Three days earlier Yugoslavia had capitulated and tomorrow the Greek army would surrender. In Africa Rommel was pushing back the British with ease while plans were nearly complete to launch a massive attack on the Soviet Union.

Against Britain Göring could justifiably claim an intensification of the air attacks which might just tip the balance before much of the Luftwaffe in the West would have to be withdrawn to participate in the campaign in the East and Berlin had been avenged with the biggest raid on London yet. No wonder it was smiles all round that Sunday.

It was to the last resting place of one of England's greatest warrior kings, King Harold, struck down while attempting to repel the Norman invasion, that nine centuries later another would-be invader arrived . . . but this time with stealth under cover of darkness. King Harold had been buried in Waltham Abbey in October 1066; in April 1941 a parachute mine exploded a few dozen yards from his reputed grave.

Saturday April 19th.

'Alert' sounded soon after nine. Although officially 'off' thought I would turn out. Walked over to A.3 and then on to Control, and heard two very heavy bangs that I thought might be H/E's over towards High Beech. Visited A.2 and got annoyed with the merry-makers coming in and out of the Drill Hall opposite, while Jerry was overhead and a heavy barrage going. After calling for my cycle went down to see A.8, by which time the procession of 'planes indicated that London was getting it again. Sat talking to Elledge when a very loud wallop indicated that something was really near; a second or two after came the most appalling crash ever, and an awful sound of crashing glass and roof tiles. Post seemed to wobble in concert. Went outside where someone was yelling frantically for brandy, and the local residents were running into the shelters. Burst had appeared to be north of the Post, and I wondered if Sun Street had caught it. Tried to 'phone 2084 but was told that the line had 'just gone out of order'! Got on cycle to see what the trouble was, but had to walk before getting very far owing to the great quantities of broken glass all over the road. Met Windle in Market Square who didn't know where bomb was but told me his place was half down, and he 'couldn't get in to 5 Church Street'. Awful thoughts in my mind as I turned into Church Street. Church appeared to be O.K. and scrunching all over broken glass etc., found the family all present and correct, though somewhat draughty owing to lack of windows.

On then to Control where exact location of bomb was not known, but was told that it was at the back of the Romeland. Went down to investigate and found bricks, tiles, slates, glass, timber and rubbish all over everywhere. The shelter was filled with an excited noisy crowd, some of them pot-black from dust and soot. Prowled round to find the exact site of bomb, and decided from the large quantities of black mud thrown up, and the wide area affected, that a paramine was either in the Abbey Stream or the watercress beds. Too dark and too awful underfoot to see exactly, but as the river seemed to be flowing normally came to the conclusion that it was watercress beds.

Looking in at the Shelter again, found that several of the occupants would have to go to Rest Centre, and while back in Control the Vicar came in to see what arrangements were being made. Offered to drive him in his car to make arrangements. First of all, however, gave him a hand in moving some stuff from the Vicarage (which was rather the worse for wear) to the Church. Took him up to Honeylands then, while the 'Raiders Passed' and the 'Alert' sounded again in quick succession, and picking up Mrs. Courtney went back to Rest Centre (another cup of tea!) and via A.4, to Control. A final visit to the Rest Centre, and then back to A.9, with Jerries still around, although the 'Raiders Passed' had gone. Then a little job to do in Control for a sailor delayed from rejoining his ship owing to the bombing, and then home to bed but not to sleep. Barrage was louder than ever again, and the absence of windows added to the noise. Turned out again at 5 a.m. to see what was going to happen about the clearing up. In the half-light of morning, the mess at the bottom of the Romeland looked eerie.

Sunday April 20th 1941.

Morning. First trip was round the house to see what damage we had got. Mainly front door, windows blinds, frames, curtains etc. Arriving at the incident found that P/M was in watercress beds, and tons of wet black mud strewn everywhere. Severe damage to houses in Romeland particularly Abbey Cottages. The old Abbey Gateway had caught a packet, and was amazed that it had got off so lightly. Then it was 'pick and shovel' work for all Wardens available. Helped clear out Windle's shop first, and shifted loads of glass from Church Street.

Went into the Church and found horrible mess all over. Nearly all the black-outs down, and practically all the stained glass on the north side completely destroyed. Dust everywhere and lumps of masonry all over the floor. A very bad crack between the main structure and the ceiling of the north aisle where the whole roof had been drawn out about a foot. Vestry badly damaged through roof and ceiling and altogether a very sorry picture.

Took my camera up on top of Tower and got some shots of the damage and found that the roof of the Nave, Lady Chapel and Tower were all affected. Then a spot of work fixing a duty rota of Wardens to stand-by at Incident, and then some breakfast.

An odd thing happened during the night. After all the folk had been cleared away, the Warden on duty heard footsteps, and investigating found an elderly man searching in the ruins. Said that he had come for his eggs, which he had left in the copper! As the copper was in the most damaged house of the lot, the result of his search was problematical. Oddly enough the eggs were found and were not even cracked!

E. J. CARTER, CHIEF WARDEN
URBAN DISTRICT OF WALTHAM HOLY CROSS

Sunday morning in Chigwell, on the other side of Epping Forest, one of Essex's worst incidents had just occurred in the Prince of Wales. A darts match was in full swing on Saturday evening when a ton of explosive silently floated down to burst on the little pub in Manor Road. It was a terrible sight which greeted rescue workers with dismembered bodies and parts of bodies being festooned all around. People say it took over a week to clear up and even then many of the victims could not be identified . . . besides regulars, just casual customers who suddenly one night failed to come home. They were buried together in this corner of Chigwell churchyard. Yet is the overgrown state of the grave a symbol of how much we care?

MONDAY, APRIL 21-22

Sunset: 2006 Sunrise: 0551
Moon: 0424 — Dawn (Last Qtr +3)

Major attack on Plymouth/Devonport.

UK — Small amounts of cloud except on the East Coast. Visibility good at first, but mist and fog in many areas after midnight.

The Continent — Little cloud except in the Low Countries. Visibility good at first, but mist and fog forming in many places later.

Daylight operations by the Luftwaffe were on a small scale and followed the now well established pattern. No bombs fell on land anywhere in Britain.

'Simple murder' was how Lieutenant Colonel J. T. C. Moore-Brabazon, the Minister of Transport, described damage and deaths caused in his own Merseyside constituency of Wallasey, adding that 'attacks of such magnitude on a residential area are simple murder with no excuse or military object.' This picture taken on April 21 shows the clear-up in Church Road. 'The people of Wallasey have borne raids nobly and the Civil Defence workers have been an example to the whole country.'

On the opposite side of Britain, Suffolk was now bearing the brunt of enemy activity against East Anglia. During an incendiary raid on Lowestoft on Monday, the thatch-roofed church at Pakefield caught fire but gallant efforts by the Rector and parishioners and firemen were all to no avail.

With widespread fog forecast over their bomber bases, the Luftwaffe was restricted to targets in the south of England (thus permitting the attackers to be back on the ground by the early hours) and Plymouth was so selected. In an attack lasting from 2140 to 0140 hours, 120 aircraft of the 133 dispatched to the target by Luftflotte 3 delivered 139 tonnes of HE (31 SC 1000, 49 SC 500, 224 SC 250, 38 LZZ 250 and 361 SC 50) and 35,996 IBs. Excellent weather conditions enabled crews to locate their Target Area without difficulty and, bombing visually, several large and many smaller fires were started in the shipyards on the east bank of the river Hamoaze, in the dockyard on the south side of the town, at Sutton Pool and in the town area. Six particularly big explosions were reported, two of them in the dockyard area, with one enormous blast and subsequent fire in the gas works. Flak over Plymouth was described as medium to strong in intensity and, in part, well directed. Several night fighters were seen, but the searchlights were ineffective.

Units participating in the attack were:

II/KG1: 13 Ju 88, 2345-0027
III/KG1: 12 Ju 88, 0042-0140
KG77: 14 Ju 88, 0025-0135
III/KG26: 8 He 111, 2239-2326 (bombing with Y-Verfahren)
I/KG27: 10 He 111, 2145-2318
III/KG27: 10 He 111, 2146-2230
KGr100: 9 He 111, 2139-2155 (bombing with X-Verfahren)
Stab/KG55: 1 He 111, 2215
I/KG55: 18 He 111, 2200-2245
II/KG55: 8 He 111, 2200-2220
III/KG55: 17 He 111, 2230-2250

In addition three aircraft bombed Portsmouth and Salcombe as alternative targets, and three aborted. Five more aircraft were sent on armed sea reconnaissance and two were dispatched to the airfields at Warmwell and Exeter.

On the other side of the country 13 aircraft of Luftflotte 2 carried out an attack on Great Yarmouth, delivering 15 tonnes of HE (nine SC 1000, five SC 500 and 74 SD 50) and 6,336 IBs between 2135 and 2250 hours. Thick mist hindered the identification of individual targets, but five fires were claimed started in the vicinity of the docks.

The most serious fires and damage occurred in the dockyard area of Plymouth, but the centre of the city was also considerably affected. Many fires were reported, but all were brought under control by early morning, including those at naval establishments. Some 6,000 houses were damaged in varying degrees, but commercial premises were also badly hit; some 30 large fires were started, some of which broke out again the following day, after it was thought they had been contained. Utility services were disrupted but the railways were not badly affected. Elsewhere during the night bombs fell at Norwich, Exeter, Yarmouth, Lowestoft and Swanage.

Plymouth's AA guns, in action from 2136 to 0254, fired 3,281 rounds of 3.7-inch and 36 of 3-inch ammunition; AA Command's total expenditure was little more than this, but two enemy aircraft were claimed destroyed. Two more raiders were credited to Fighter Command, which dispatched 78 aircraft on dusk, night and dawn patrols, with ten operating over northern France.

On Monday, Plymouth. The Red Warning sounded at 9.31 p.m. and within three minutes a lethal mixture of high explosive and fire bombs assaulted the sorely-tried city. This time the naval facilities in Devonport suffered severely with Area Combined HQ a total loss and fires in the Naval Exchange, Royal Naval Barracks, South Raglan Barracks, Army Gun Wharf, Royal William Yard, South Yard, Keyham Quarry, Marine Barracks, Millbay and Millbay Dock. In the civil area the telephone exchange was hit, the failure in telephone communications adding to the difficulties being faced by the authorities.

The corner of George Street today, transformed out of all recognition yet Derry's clock incredulously survived — a symbol which in latter years came to signify the determination of the citizens to rebuild a better Plymouth.

On Tuesday Plymouth. As one day's bombing followed another, whether a particular picture was taken after this raid or that raid was irrelevant. Overall the city was doomed. The main concern of the authorities on Tuesday was to get the fires damped down — some broke out again during the day — so that none would be visible to the enemy by nightfall. The Royal Engineers sent in ten rescue parties and an infantry working party of 200 was due to arrive on Wednesday.

TUESDAY, APRIL 22-23

Sunset: 2007 Sunrise: 0549
Moon: 0447 — Dawn (Last Qtr +4)

Major attack on Plymouth/Devonport. Minor subsidiary attack on Portsmouth.

UK — Extensive cloud in the East spreading to all areas except South Wales and south-western England. Visibility moderate to good with local fog patches in the South-West.

The Continent — Little cloud over north and north-western France, fair becoming cloudy elsewhere. Visibility moderate to good at first but fog or mist patches developing late in the night.

During a day of limited activity only 15 German aircraft crossed British coasts. Channel fighter sweeps, reconnaissance and anti-shipping patrols were again the order of the day and no bombs fell on land.

For the second consecutive night Plymouth, and particularly Devonport, received the attention of the Luftwaffe; crews of 125 of the 132 aircraft dispatched by Luftflotte 3 claimed to have reached and bombed the important naval port, delivering 146 tonnes of HE (one SC 1800, 28 SC 1000, 42 SC 500, 242 SC 250, 31 LZZ 250, two SD 250 and 529 SC 50) and 35,796 incendiaries between 2143 and 0358 hours. Bomb aiming was almost entirely visual, only a few crews adopting DR methods.

The CP covered dock installations and that part of the town where the power station, gas works and main food offices were situated, and in this area it was claimed that numerous large fires were started. Further fires covered the entire town and at 2230 hours a very large explosion was seen. Both light and heavy flak were experienced over the target and crews reported that it was well aimed. Seven night fighters were also seen.

Crews reporting over the target were as follows:

I/KG27: 8 He 111, 2143-2217
III/KG27: 12 He 111, 2145-2240
KGr100: 9 He 111, 2150-2219 (8 used X-Verfahren, one bombed visually)
Stab/KG55: 1 He 111, 2224
II/KG55: 11 He 111, 2230-2255
I/KG55: 17 He 111, 2210-2305
III/KG55: 19 He 111, 2200-2320
II/KG1: 10 Ju 88, 0025-0100
III/KG1: 7 Ju 88, 0005-0055
I/KG77: 12 Ju 88, 2239-0158
II/KG77: 11 Ju 88, 0010-0050
III/KG26: 8 He 111, 2235-2350 (some crews used Y-Verfahren, others bombed visually)

Four aircraft aborted, one bombed Portsmouth as an alternative and four were lost (one after bombing) including two He 111s of I/KG55 (with the crew of one baling out over their own territory) and a Ju 88 of II/KG77 which crashed on landing. In addition, Luftflotte 3 dispatched six aircraft on armed sea reconnaissance and attacks on airfields.

In a secondary attack 13 aircraft of Luftflotte 2 (II/KG53 according to the RAF's 'Y' Service) bombed Portsmouth with 26 tonnes of HE (13 SC 1000 and 52 SC 250) in a visually conducted attack which lasted from 2123 to 2157 hours. Bomb explosions were seen in the docks area, but the effectiveness could not be judged. Shipping off Kinnaird Head, north of Montrose and east of Berwick was also attacked with minelaying in Liverpool Bay and the mouth of the Tyne.

April 22/23, 1941
Take-off Villaroche, 21.28 hours

The objective for my 30th operational flight is Plymouth, that sorely-tried city. Well-aimed bomb drops are possible. But then we are shown aerial photographs for the first time, and see that the city is in fact destroyed down to its foundations . . . Have the inhabitants been evacuated? Surely. We also convince ourselves that the Londoners must undoubtedly have been evacuated. Anything else would indeed be unimaginable.

But Plymouth, the seaport in the south, has in fact been attacked more than all the other towns. Did that really have to be so?

ROBERT GÖTZ

Barely had the citizens of Plymouth recovered from the major assault of the previous night when they were subjected to another four hours of devastation. Fires and damage were again extensive, both in the town and the dockyard, and nearby places including Torpoint and Torquay also suffered.

The raid on Portsmouth was a minor one by comparison but nine people were killed and some damage done; a few HE bombs also fell on Southsea where a public shelter was destroyed, killing 20 people. Elsewhere minor bombing occurred at Kidderminster, Aberdeen, Torquay, Newbury, Banbury and in rural areas of Dorset, Glamorganshire, and on Hayling and Brownsea Islands.

Engaging attackers flying at heights between 6,000 and 20,000 feet, the Plymouth AA defences fired 2,479 rounds of 3.7-inch ammunition and 166 3-inch shells. Across the country as a whole AA Command's guns used under 4,000 rounds.

Dusk, night and dawn patrols were flown by 48 aircraft of Fighter Command but no enemy aircraft were claimed shot down.

WEDNESDAY, APRIL 23-24

Sunset: 2009 Sunrise: 0547
Moon: 0510 — Dawn (New −3)

Major attack on Plymouth/Devonport. Minor subsidiary attack on Portsmouth.

UK — Generally little or no cloud. Visibility mainly good.

The Continent — Variable amounts of cloud with good visibility.

Although nearly 300 German aircraft of all types were operating during the day most were engaged in Channel fighter sweeps, reconnaissance and anti-shipping work and only a few penetrated inland. The few bombs which landed in East Anglia and the South-East did little damage and caused no casualties.

Yet again, for the third successive night, the Luftwaffe concentrated on Plymouth.

22.4.41

Air Ministry and Ministry of Home Security Communiqué.
Enemy aircraft attacked the South-West of England
last night. The raid did not last long but
in one town, which was the main target, a
number of fires were started, some of them large.
The fire situation was under control before daylight
and reports indicate that, although the raid was
severe, neither damage nor casualties were as serious
as in previous attacks on this area.
Bombs were also dropped in one or two other
districts, mainly in East Anglia. These caused little
damage but among the few casualties were a
small number killed.

0725.

After so much, the greatest insult to the suffering of the people of the city came, not from Hitler, but from the Ministry of Information. The original communiqué drafted for the Monday raid is reproduced above — a masterly understatement. To those at the sharp end in Plymouth it could have been describing another planet, their own part of this one looking more and more like the face of the moon. Lady Astor was incensed; putting it bluntly it was a kick in the proverbials and she let the Ministry of 'Inflammation' as she called it, know precisely how she felt. The men at the Ministry, true to form, lived up to their reputation for never ever admitting a mistake in their internal memo dated April 25: 'Our communiqué was justified by the facts and I think we must be concerned to give a balanced picture to the country as a whole without paying undue attention to the sensibilities of the unfortunate inhabitants of the town attacked. It is quite clear that any objective statement however carefully worded would sound thin and perhaps callous to people who have suffered heavy raiding on three successive nights. In point of fact the words employed were not as quoted. Our communiqué read "A town in the South West of England was raided but the attack though severe was not on the heavy scale of previous raids. It ceased shortly after midnight and though damage was done the situation was always well under control". In the circumstances this appears to be a very reasonable statement.' Such was the notice taken of the lesson learned from Clydeside (pages 480-81).

And again on Wednesday. By now the exhausted firefighters had been unable to kill the fires by nightfall and, attracted like moths to a flame, the bombers had no difficulty in stoking the blaze. Houses . . . shops . . . factories . . . it was all the same.

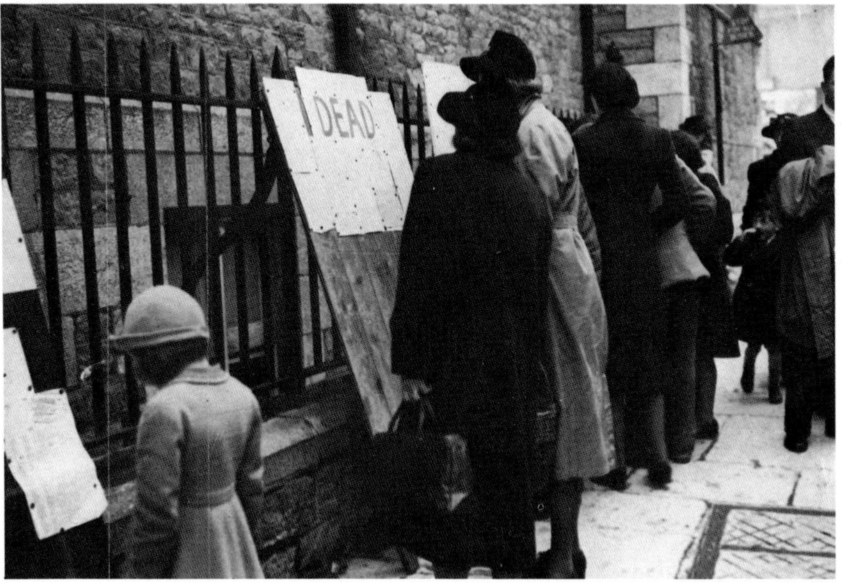

Strictly 'not to be published.' Fortunately casualties were lighter — some 478 dead from the three raids — than might have been expected, largely helped by the trekking which gathered ever-increasing momentum as the week wore on. Following Lady Astor's fury at the way Plymouth was being treated by the BBC, the position became so serious that a lengthy report was prepared on May 2 following the Regional Information Officer's investigation. It is reproduced in full on these pages.

The R.I.O. visited Plymouth personally after the heavy blitzes, inspected the damage to civilian and public property, met large bodies of citizens, and watched all the ameliorative services in action. After over 20 years residence in the city and continuous association with its public life, he naturally is familiar with its problems and difficulties. Though he has been in the Bristol area for all the raids and worked upon all its post-blitz efforts, the experiences at Plymouth were a shock and acutely distressing.

Damage is more intense at Plymouth than at Bristol. The Germans obviously used heavier bombs and obtained better concentration. Though the defence is very good and more German planes were hit, these factors added to the strain of those who had to endure five out of nine nights of agony, with only brief respites. Civilians had to survive about 20 hours fierce battle in which casualties were high and danger never absent.

The R.I.O. has had the opportunity of reading full translations from the monitoring service of all the German broadcasts. They are faulty in regard to naval losses and characteristically blatant about their achievements, but obviously their reconnaissance has not revealed the actual devastation. They claim that the fires could be seen out in the English Channel. Actually the fires were so intense that the glow could be seen beyond Dartmoor, which rises to 1700 feet, by people in North Devon and in the smaller towns beyond the Exe estuary in East Devon.

An unexpected development which is naturally receiving the closest attention is the weakening of the morale of the volunteer firemen. This, of course, is no concern of ours. The underlying cause is the terrible strain and steady casualties among volunteer and unpaid men who have to work all day and battle all night and feel that there are thousands of troops outside the city, bored stiff with nothing to do, who ought to be trained to assist in this fighting of one of the principal battles of the war.

What is happening is that these volunteer firemen are quietly absenting themselves, and when the assistance came from neighbouring brigades who have had the same experience, the police had to control the road to ensure that they kept to the shortest route and arrived swiftly. As the R.I.O. left Plymouth, London Metropolitan paid firemen were arriving.

Incidentally, Plymouth is one of the blitzed cities where the fire chief is also head of the police and in control of the traffic. Now that the city has been lost they are appointing a fire chief. The Commissioner estimates that 9/10ths of the damage was caused by fire. The centres of both Plymouth and Devonport have been totally destroyed and the damage is in millions. All the drapery establishments have gone, the banks, insurance offices, the principal traders: every section, indeed, of trade and commerce, and the stocks and buildings as well. In this connection it must be remembered that Plymouth was the shopping and commercial centre of a rich countryside. Before the Great War there were three towns which united to form the modern Plymouth. Each had its town hall or guildhall and civic centres. These have gone, along with the historic churches and edifices of other denominations. Tens of thousands of dwelling-houses will have to be scheduled for repair or demolition, but a high proportion may be rendered habitable. Compared with Bristol, however, fires and damage to civilian dwelling-houses are more serious and are due to the massing of small properties in endless rows near the Royal Dockyard and the heavy concentration of large bombs that was made on the naval establishments. Nevertheless, as at Bristol, the enemy has not seriously or adversely affected the war issue. The commercial docks, though surrounded by devastation and without warehouse accommodation, can still be worked at pressure. The Admiralty have closed down rigidly and resolutely in regard to damage in the dockyard and naval establishments. It is obvious, however, from bereavements and funerals that the workers must have suffered, and as the Royal Naval Barracks had to admit the loss of 75% of its kitchen equipment, there must have been extensive damage. The German radio claimed the sinking of several vessels in harbour. All that the civilians know is that above the din of battle could be heard the shrieking S.O.S. of ships' hooters.

Plymouth and the surrounding countryside, indeed, the whole West Country, is agitated with rumours that hundreds of dockyard men and naval ratings were killed, that the terrace of the official residences, including that of the Admiral Superintendent, were demolished and one of the big dockyards rendered unusable.

In civilian official circles it is believed, however, that the number of dead in the dockyard is not more than 200. The Admiralty will no doubt pursue the policy of refusing to disclose any information concerning either damage or casualties. It would help in the restoration of shaken morale and facilitate recovery among a stunned people if something were revealed for word-of-mouth dissemination, emphasising that the naval war effort has not been seriously impaired. Any such statement would have to ring true and avoid the falsity and shortcomings of the early statements issued by the Air Ministry and Ministry of Home Security.

Lady Astor, one of the Plymouth M.Ps. who is also Lady Mayoress, was savage and distressed when she publicly criticised the Ministry of Information, which she described as the "Ministry of Inflammation". Her indignation was due entirely to the references in the B.B.C. bulletin to a short and sharp attack which by implication falsified the casualties and damage. The R.I.O. immediately replied in the local press. The evening paper gave his short explanation a front page panel and the morning paper also issued it. It was to the effect that her ladyship's criticism was misdirected and did not apply to the M. of I. She was criticising the communique of the Air Ministry and the Ministry of Home Security, and the M. of I. and the B.B.C. were merely channels of communication.

A curious phenomenon was the way these communiques and the M.P's criticism were linked in animated discussion about our Director General's broadcast. The R.I.O. heard in Plymouth from important people the statement 'Monckton told us the M.O.I. told the truth, yet here we know the ghastly truth and had to listen to the lies of the official statements. How can we believe the B.B.C., the M.O.I. or the Government after this exposure'.

It must be admitted frankly that while her ladyship misdirected the criticism, she accurately reflected public indignation among sorely stricken people, and the R.I.O's prompt action was taken simply to make certain that the M.O.I. was not made a wrong target. Though no doubt their feelings are due to the shock of their experiences, the feeling exists strongly, and it is such a pity when the communique could so easily, without revealing anything to the enemy, have stimulated and comforted as well as informed the people. The R.I.O. was, before the war, the editor-in-chief of English daily newspapers and if such a report had been given and passed by members of his staff he would have instantly dismissed those concerned for falsifying news of grave public importance.

Such a concentrated blitz for five terrible nights has created new aspects of old problems for the Regional organisation of the Ministry of Information. When air attacks develop in this way, with heavy casualties in homes and among firewatchers and fighters, and when damage is incalculable and there is wide distress and shortages, the public for a few days are unable and unwilling to listen or comprehend official pronouncements from loudspeakers or to read typewritten or printed directions and statements. Therefore, at Plymouth we evolved on the spot, with the cooperation of the W.V.S. and the social services, a scheme whereby experienced ladies and students went round the worst areas from door to door explaining, comforting and helping.

Another improvisation following the belated decision to evacuate children, aged and others, as well as the hospitals, was to send out experienced broadcasters with loudspeaker vans into neighbouring towns and villages with patriotic appeals to citizens to immediately improvise arrangements to receive evacuees.

The effort was essential though the prospects were poor because all the areas already are saturated with evacuees, voluntary and otherwise, from London, Bristol, even Southampton and Portsmouth. In passing, it is vitally important to have quickly in a blitzed area an experienced and responsible officer from M.O.I. Regional headquarters for consultation with high authority, with the power to make immediate decisions and sanction expenditure. Telephonic and other communication with headquarters are futile for days.

Another difference between isolated and continuous blitzes is that rest and feeding centres are apt to disappear and the usual routes to the new ones are devious, due to closed roadways consequent on debris and unexploded bombs. Improvised signposts are therefore imperative. An innovation we made, the idea of the press department and carried out by Mr. Hawkins, was to have one printed on the lines of 'Follow the M.O.I. green (or blue) line to the Rest and Feeding Centres', with a big arrow for direction. As evidence of the dislocation which does occur, one of our vans discovered a district where people had been without food for two days, and we were able to search out a mobile canteen.

This brings the R.I.O. to the point mentioned in previous reports, that after these heavy raids throughout the hours of darkness the local organisations of firefighting and civic administration are apt temporarily to collapse. There is consequently great need of such information services as we can create. Post-blitz rumours, especially about casualties, and other distortions may not be started by enemy agents but by the work merely of neurotic people, but the effect on public confidence is the same, and as the war months lengthen the necessity for dealing with these problems may become even more acute. The lowering of the morale of the volunteer firemen is a symptom which should not be ignored because only a few weeks ago these people were keen and enthusiastic and proud of their training and the opportunity of service.

The R.I.O. found a feeling in Plymouth that the Ministry of Health's decision to evacuate children and the aged was a panic one and the result of press agitation under big headlines. He therefore arranged at once a press conference for the representatives of the national and local press, the Regional Officer of the Ministry of Health being present and answering a barrage of questions. He is an able and experienced officer and a great improvement upon a pompous predecessor, but his admission that evacuation was a new sidelight in their work created an unhappy impression. We talked the pressmen out of their first desire to let the story run upon the lines that this was another indication of how the Government was unprepared for the realities of the war on the home front.

During the height of the pressure of the successive raids, the R.I.O. was impressed with the obvious evidence of how the office of the M.O.I. becomes a focal point for the blitzed people overcome by the difficulties. As an instance, a man came in and quietly asked what he was to do because he thought he could make a room or two in his battered home habitable if the authorities could arrange to remove a bus upon his roof. The huge fires evidently enabled the German airmen to pick out the bus depot and they rained bombs on it, so that the station was wrecked and many buses damaged or obliterated. One was hurled high into the air and fell across the depot roof, one of several to do this. For days afterwards dented and damaged buses, without windows or with jagged fragments of glass could be seen in the streets, crowded with cheering passengers.

For the present Plymouth as a business and commercial centre of a prosperous countryside has ceased to exist. The children from 2/3rds of it, and the aged and infirm, and the great army of pensioners who always live in the dockyard towns and naval ports will dwell in the countryside around. Given a few weeks all will recover their poise and the absence of further continuous raids will enable the city to improvise arrangements and resume its shaken life. Deep-rooted, however, is the realisation that there is no adequate protection for life and property against concentrated night attack. It would be wrong to assume that the people are broken. Equally it would be suicidal to ignore the implications and symptoms of the actual state of affairs, and to avoid probing the disturbing causes of the aftermath of the fiercest raid upon a provincial centre.

Strength should be added to any efforts Regional Commissioners may make to ensure that local authorities provide better mortuary accommodation and obviate the distressing incidents which did occur at Bristol and Plymouth. One incident will suffice. A youth at Plymouth had to identify a family consisting of father, mother and daughter. When he arrived at the improvised mortuary he found bodies stacked on slabs in three tiers and the attendant said that there were 200 there.

MoI REPORT, MAY 2, 1941

The pain and the sorrow in Efford Cemetery. Stacked coffins for the mass burials in the services attended by Lady Astor.

This time the dockyard and port installations were targets for 120 Luftflotte 3 bombers, and of this force 110 crews claimed to have achieved their mission. They dropped 118 tonnes of HE (seven SC 1000, 72 SC 500, 232 SC 250, 30 LZZ 250, and 196 SC/SD 50) and 18,484 IBs, commencing at 2146 and finishing at 0051 hours. Their CP was the dockyard on the west side of the town and dock installations immediately to the south-east.

The approach to the target was simplified for early arrivals because two large fires started the previous night were still burning in the south-west part of the town. These were soon joined by more, in and around the dockyards, with what appeared to be a big oil fire producing volumes of dense black smoke. At 2328 hours crews reported seeing a particularly big explosion, followed by a succession of smaller ones, and a ship was seen to be on fire in one of the docks. Fires covered much of the town, too, and good overall results were anticipated by participating crews. Taking part were:

I/KG27: 9 He 111, 2350-0051
III/KG27: 12 He 111, 2315-0000
KGr100: 9 He 111, 2146-2230 (8 used X-Verfahren, 1 bombed visually)
II/KG54: 11 Ju 88, 2300-0005
II/KG54: 15 Ju 88, 2305-0005
III/KG54: 12 Ju 88, 2239-0020
II/KG1: 14 Ju 88, 2206-2302
III/KG1: 9 Ju 88, 2205-2236
I/KG77: 11 Ju 88, 2242-2313
III/KG26: 7 He 111, 2245-1130 (Y-Verfahren and visual bombing)

Crews saw several night fighters and reported that the flak was mainly well aimed. Three aircraft bombed alternative targets, two aborted, three failed to return and two crashed in German-occupied territory. Additional operations were flown by one aircraft against Boscombe Down airfield and five He 111s of III/KG40 (operating under the command of Fliegerführer Atlantik) engaged in armed reconnaissance of the Bristol Channel and St George's Channel. Finding no shipping targets they bombed Lands End instead with 24 SC 250s but no results were seen. One aircraft of III/KG40 was reported missing and another crashed in France. Other casualties were two He 111s of III/KG26 and a Ju 88 of II/KG54 which crashed on fire near Evreux.

As on the previous night another subsidiary attack was made on Portsmouth by nine aircraft of Luftflotte 2 between 2144 and 2218 hours. Aiming visually they dropped nine SC 1000, 28 SC 250 and 1,152 incendiaries and crews claimed that all landed in the designated TA, the dockyard and barracks area, where explosions and fires occurred.

The attack on Plymouth/Devonport was a little less severe than on the previous two nights and came in two phases, the first lasting about an hour and the second an hour and a quarter. Altogether 29 fires were reported, but despite the serious water situation brought about by the previous raids, all except one fire in the town centre were brought under control by 0145 hours. Casualties and damage were again serious and the cumulative effect of the raids on utility services was creating many problems. Interference to the railway system was also significant but of a temporary nature. Three serious shelter incidents occurred and once more residential and commericial premises were badly hit and at least four churches were damaged or destroyed. More than 400 civilians had been killed in the three consecutive raids and 256 seriously injured.

The subsidiary raid on Portsmouth was a minor affair with no casualties; elsewhere bombs were reported at various places in Scotland, the North and North-East of England and in Wales, but all were without serious damage or casualties. Places reporting bombs included Saffron Walden, Ipswich, Wells, Pennar, Hull, Pocklington, Gorleston, Yarmouth and near Grantham.

The Plymouth guns fired 2,000 rounds of 3.7-inch and 183 rounds of 3-inch ammunition and were in action from 2145 to 0113 hours. Only 3,000 rounds were used in total by AA Command during the night. Fighter Command dispatched 125 aircraft on dusk, night and dawn patrols, with one engaged on an Intruder mission over France, and two enemy aircraft were claimed destroyed.

Ministry of Information
Tavistock Road, Plymouth.

Sir,

Criticism by Lady Astor, M.P., of the Ministry of Information, concerning the B.B.C. bulletin of an air raid on Plymouth is misdirected.

The announcement to which her ladyship refers was a communiqué prepared by the Air Ministry and the Ministry of Home Security.

The Ministry of Information and the B.B.C. were merely the channels of communication.

The attention of the authorities in London has been called to the facts of which complaint has been made.

The Regional Officer

The final straw. Rubbing salt in the wounds as well as passing the buck, a letter to the local *Western Evening Herald* published on April 30.

At least the canine fraternity came in for extra rations . . . and ready cooked at that! Dogs in Britain actually received their call-up papers the following month when the War Office invited certain breeds 'with natural qualifications of a high order' to register for National Service. Those acceptable were 'Airedales, Collies (both rough and smooth), Hill Collies, Crossbreds, Lurchers and Retrievers (Labrador and Golden) and members of other breeds provided that their intelligence and natural ability were of a superior standard.' It was hoped that friendly aliens, such as the Alsatian, would not be turned down through prejudice! The Army announced that accepted candidates would be given an intensive course of training at Willems Barracks, Aldershot. Successful dogs would serve for the duration of the war, and receive skilled care and attention, but those which failed to pass the tests would immediately return home.

A composite print, roughly joined together by the unknown photographer in 1941, to show, as he called it, 'Dante's Inferno'.

THURSDAY, APRIL 24-25

Sunset: 2011 Sunrise: 0545
Moon: 0533 — Dawn (New −2)

No major attacks. Minelaying, long-range fighter operations and anti-shipping patrols. Minor attack on Portsmouth.

UK — Extensive cloud with moderate visibility.
The Continent — Variable cloud. Moderate to poor visibility.

In the course of daylight fighter sweeps and fighter-bomber operations in the Channel and over the South-East there were minor bomb incidents at Dover, Hythe and elsewhere in Kent.

Night operations involved 72 long-range bombers and 11 long-range night fighters and the main target, although on a small scale, was Portsmouth. Here, 21 aircraft of Luftflotte 2 claimed 21 tonnes of HE (17 SC 1000, one SC 500, 12 SC 250 and four SD 50) and 10,368 IB fell on the Target Area between 2115 and 2250 hours. Bomb aiming was entirely visual and crews reported nearly all their bombs fell on the dockyards/barracks area, with flames shooting up to 1,500 metres (4,800 feet). There were also many smaller fires and the overall fire glow could be seen from 80 kilometres (50 miles) away by returning crews. The results were expected to be good.

One of the patrolling German night fighters of I/NJG2 attacked a training aircraft near Church Fenton airfield and eight HE bombs were dropped on the airfield. Anti-shipping patrols were flown, as on most nights, by He 111s of I/KG26 and minelaying was continued by elements of I and II/KG30 and by two Gruppen of KG4.

Despite German expectations the attack on Portsmouth was a complete failure. Many bombs fell on the Isle of Wight, however, where it seems that Newport and Cowes were mistaken for Portsmouth, which experienced no bombing. Four medium fires were started in Newport and one in Cowes, but many bombs fell on open land. The only casualties, including one person killed, occurred in Cowes.

One British night fighter was destroyed when Defiant N3391 of No. 307 Squadron, on an operational patrol from Colerne, suffered an engine failure. Abandoned by its crew, the Defiant crashed near Carlton Musgrove at 2230 hours.

2/JG52 Messerschmitt Bf 109E-7 (5895). Shot down by Squadron Leader J. E. Rankin and Flight Lieutenant Brunier in Spitfire Mk.Vb's of No. 92 Squadron. Crashed at Black House Farm, Camber, Kent 9.02 a.m. Oberfw. G. Struck baled out and taken prisoner. Aircraft Black 6+ destroyed.

During captivity in Canada April-May 1944 Günter Struck feigned mental illness and was released as incurably ill, he returned to Germany via New York and Spain to become a test pilot for the Messerschmitt company. Complete remains of the aircraft recovered by the Brenzett Aeronautical Museum in 1974. Items unearthed included the control column, first aid kit, engine, maps, throttle levers with flying glove trapped in them, bomb rack, undercarriage and tail fin bearing yellow rudder and swastika together with tail wheel.

It transpired to have been taken here in Dante Road, Lambeth, and it showed the aftermath of the night of April 17 when eight people died here in a shelter. Once bomb sites were cleared of debris, they became the location for 'pre-fabs' — prefabricated houses of several different types designed to provide temporary accommodation for the homeless for ten years. Thirty years after that period should have expired, modernised versions of the wartime pre-fab still stand in Dante Road. After the traumas of the early part of the week, Thursday turned out an anti-climax, uncannily quiet with the Luftwaffe's declared raid on Portsmouth going strangely awry on the 24th-25th. Then a German news flash on the 25th claimed that Ipswich had experienced a fierce attack in which a factory was hit but no bombs at all fell in the Ipswich area that night!

FRIDAY, APRIL 25-26

Sunset: 2012 Sunrise: 0543
Moon: None (New −1)

Heavy attack on Sunderland. Minelaying and long-range night fighter patrols.

UK — Extensive cloud with moderate to poor visibility in many areas. Strong to gale force winds on coasts, strong elsewhere.
The Continent — Similar to the UK.

Daylight operations followed the established pattern with little of importance reported. At Lancing, Sussex, houses and railway property were damaged and the Dover balloon barrage was machine-gunned by German fighters.

On Saturday morning German radio claimed that the main attack of the previous night's raid was the 'Sunderland flying boat works at Sunderland'. In fact this was another bungled raid by the Luftwaffe as no bombs at all fell on the city. With two spurious German claims running, Home Security could only deduce that inexperienced crews were being employed. They felt that the large number of parachute mines exploding in Tyneside, (i.e. north of the river) was believed explained by the north-east wind which had blown them inland during sea mining operations. This was the result: 35 killed in Guildford Place alone including six members of the Angus family; five of the Robsons; four of the Hagons and the Snowdons; and three members each from the Parks and Reeds. It was Newcastle's greatest tragedy.

Night operations were undertaken very largely by units of Luftflotte 2, with Sunderland the principal target. In an attack lasting from 2155 to 2310, 57 aircraft dropped 80 tonnes of HE (12 SC 1000, 42 SC 250, 70 SC 50, 20 Luftminen 'A' and 44 Luftminen 'B') and 9,480 incendiaries, their CP being the dockyards and industrial installations alongside the river. In the absence of moonlight, 62 LC 50 parachute flares were used and most crews bombed visually. Explosions were claimed in the Hudson and Hendon Docks and in the north-west part of the Thompson shipyards. Five large and medium fires were started, with more of a smaller nature, both in the CP and in the town area.

On publication of *Front Line 1940-41* (see page 381-82), Mr S. E. Sterk, writing in his resumé for the *Newcastle Evening Chronicle*, commented that 'the North-East gets small mention . . . but though its ordeal has been less concentrated, and cannot point to great areas of devastation, the North-East can show many hundreds of scars, the result of "drip" bombing over a long period such as has not been experienced in most other parts of Britain. . . . On Tyneside alone nearly 400 people were killed between July 1940 and December 1941. . . . To that total can be added many more in other North-East towns.' One of the very first to be killed in Newcastle was Mary Mackay at the School House *(right)* at Heaton Secondary Girls' School on the night of July 28-29, 1940. The school was bombed a second time during the night of September 16-17 but causing no damage save the destruction of an empty house adjoining the school. Sunderland's most memorable night was September 5 when a Heinkel was shot down in Suffolk Street *(See Volume 1, page 311).*

More fires were seen outside the ordered Target Area, but their precise location could not be determined because of cloud.

The fires were visible from a great distance and were even reported upon by an aircraft not engaged in the attack. This was an aircraft of the Generalstab der Luftwaffe attached to the Oberkommando der Marine and engaged in an armed reconnaissance of the Firth of Forth in search of shipping.

Three aircraft, unable to bomb their primary target at Sunderland, attacked Hull instead, dropping five 'B' type parachute mines and 612 IBs. One large and several smaller fires were claimed. Minelaying was carried out between Flamborough Head and the Tyne, in the mouth of the Humber and in Liverpool Bay.

Newcastle-upon-Tyne suffered most in the North-East where, on Tyneside in particular, firefighting was extremely effective. Houses and other property sustained damage at Wallsend, where seven people were killed, and there were also fatal casualties at Seghill and Shiremoor. Tynemouth also received some damage, as did Cullercoats, South Shields (seven killed), Jarrow and Hebburn. There were also fires and casualties at Gateshead, but the night's attacks hardly constituted what the Luftwaffe called a heavy attack on Sunderland. To the south severe damage was done in Hull, however, parachute mines also killing seven people, but in an attack on Barrow-in-Furness the few bombs dropped failed to explode. Bombs also fell in Blyth, Whitby, near Market Rasen, Louth, near Kings Lynn, Yarmouth and near Royston.

During the night the heavy guns of AA Command fired only about 1,000 rounds, with those on the Tyne accounting for 809 (482 4.5-inch, 251 3.7-inch and 76 3-inch). Fighter Command dispatched 130 aircraft on dusk, night and dawn patrols, but no claims against enemy aircraft were submitted.

At 0200 hours Defiant N1568 of No. 54 Operational Training Unit, Church Fenton, was attacked by an enemy aircraft while on a training flight. While taking evasive action the Defiant struck a tree about five miles from Church Fenton and crashed, killing its crew of two.

Not that Sunderland did not suffer on other occasions. This is the end of the famed Winter Gardens (and its parrots) in Mowbray Park. Stage 1: April 15, 1941.

Stage 2: November 1961, replaced by a new library and social amenities centre.

SATURDAY, APRIL 26-27

Sunset: 2014 Sunrise: 0541
Moon: None (New Moon)

Major attack on Liverpool/Birkenhead. Various other places bombed as alternative targets. Anti-shipping and airfield patrols.

UK — Mainly cloudy, but good visibility in many districts.
The Continent — Variable cloud with moderate visibility, poor in some areas.

Casualties and damage were reported at Folkestone but nowhere else did bombs fall on Britain on a day of limited German activity.

During the night 92 aircraft of Luftflotten 2 and 3 attacked the port of Liverpool between 2230 and 0053 hours, delivering 113 tonnes of HE (nine SC 1000, 15 SC 500, 154 SC 250, 20 SD 50, 16 LMA and 49 LMB) and 15,336 IBs. Bombing was by DR and radio methods, but eleven LC 50 flares were also dropped in a bid to provide target illumination. The weather was unfavourable for such tactics, however, but crews of one unit reported six to eight large fires, seen through breaks in the almost continuous cloud cover. Others claimed explosions in the dock installations and reported the glow of fires discerned through the thick cloud.

Luftflotte 3's contribution consisted of 52 aircraft, and the crews of 37 reported over the target; eleven aircraft bombed alternatives and four aborted. No aircraft were lost and the following completed their mission:

II/KG1: 1 Ju 88, 2312
III/KG1: 3 Ju 88, 2245-2310
KG76: 11 Ju 88, 2230-2325
KG77: 16 Ju 88, 2305-2350
III/KG26: 6 He 111, 2255-0053

Apart from the fact that 55 crews reached the target, nothing more is known of Luftflotte 2's participation.

This was not one of the Luftwaffe's more successful attacks on Merseyside, although a fair amount of damage was done at Formby, Southport, Wheelock and, well outside the Target Area, at Ainsdale, where three of the five fatal casualties in the area occurred. Residential property suffered most, but some railway damage was caused and there

Churchill's grand tour of Merseyside. A weekend out of the office and into the streets of Liverpool, Manchester and Merseyside. It was almost uncanny the way the Luftwaffe followed him around the country of late — at Bristol a fortnight before and now in Liverpool. With the Prime Minister on the tour were two of President Roosevelt's envoys, Averell Harriman and James Forrestal, as Churchill intended to show the Americans the facilities in the Mersey, so important to the North-Western Approaches. On Sunday evening he broadcast to the nation.

I was asked last week whether I was aware of some uneasiness which, it was said, existed in the country on account of the gravity, as it was described, of the war situation. So I thought it would be a good thing to go and see for myself what this uneasiness amounted to. And I went to some of our great cities, seaports which had been most heavily bombed.

I have come back not only reassured but refreshed. To leave the offices in Whitehall, with their ceaseless hum of activity and stress, and to go out to the front, by which I mean the streets and wharves of London or Liverpool, Manchester, Cardiff, Swansea or Bristol, is like going out of a hothouse on to the bridge of a fighting ship. It is a tonic which I should recommend any who are suffering from fretfulness to take in strong doses when they have need of it.

It is quite true that I have seen many painful scenes of havoc and of fine buildings and acres of cottage homes blasted into rubble heaps of ruins, but it is just in those very places where the malice of the savage enemy has done its worst and where the ordeal of the men, women and children has been most severe that I found their morale most high and splendid. Indeed, I feel comforted by an exaltation of spirit in the people which seemed to lift mankind above the level of material facts into the joyous serenity we think belongs to a better world than this.

Of their kindness to me I cannot speak, because I have never sought it or dreamed of it and can never deserve it. I can only assure you that I and my colleagues, or comrades rather, for that is what they are, who deal with every scrap of life and strength, according to the lot granted to us, shall not fail these people or be wholly unworthy of their faithful and generous regard.

What a triumph the life of these battered cities is over the worst which fire and bombs can do. What a vindication of the civilized and decent way of living we have been trying to work for and work towards in our island.

This ordeal by fire has, in a certain sense, even exhilarated the manhood and womanhood of Britain. The sublime but also terribly sombre experiences and emotions of the battlefield, which for centuries have been reserved for the soldiers and sailors, are now shared for good or ill by the entire population. All our crowds have been proud of being under fire of the enemy — old men, little children, the crippled, the veterans of former wars, aged women, and the ordinary hard-pressed citizen or subject of the King, as he likes to call himself, the sturdy workman who swings a hammer or loads a ship, the skilful craftsman, the members of every kind of A.R.P. service, are proud to feel that they stand in the line together with our fighting men when one of the greatest causes is being fought out — and fought out it will be to the end. This, indeed, is the great heroic period of our history and the light of glory shines on all.

WINSTON CHURCHILL, APRIL 27, 1941

was some interruption to gas, electricity and water supplies. No serious damage was done to any important port, industrial or military target.

Away from Merseyside, Portsmouth was the target for a subsidiary attack which was completely ineffective and there were also a few isolated incidents in Wales and the West. In addition 21 people were killed in a public house at Horning, Norfolk.

Of the 6,000 or so rounds of heavy AA ammunition used during the night, 2,507 were fired by the Mersey guns, but nowhere were any successes claimed.

Dusk, night and dawn patrols were carried out by 134 aircraft of Fighter Command and while several contacts were made with enemy aircraft, none were claimed destroyed.

A Heinkel He 111 of II/KG53 crashed on landing at Vendeville.

SUNDAY, APRIL 27-28

Sunset: 2015 Sunrise: 0539
Moon: Dusk — 2112 (New +1)

Heavy attack on Portsmouth. Minor attacks elsewhere.

UK — Mainly fair. Mist in some parts of the Midlands and North-West England late in the night.

The Continent — Rain and low cloud in the Low Countries and northern France. Elsewhere cloudy with moderate to poor visibility.

A Saturday evening at the local — but an evening which turned out to be their last for 21 visitors to the picturesque Ferry Inn at Horning, Norfolk. A mecca for Broads visitors, then as now, Home Security in their 'Most Secret' Daily Appreciation reported that 'two direct hits were made, the inn was demolished and there were 20 *(sic)* people killed, three of whom were service personnel.' The picture was not released until December 1944.

In 1956 the rebuilt Horning Ferry Hotel was opened by Bob Stanford Tuck representing the many airmen from Coltishall who frequented the inn during the war, but in 1965 it was burnt down in a disastrous fire on March 31. The present Ferry Inn was built in 1966.

No bombs fell on Britain during a day of slight German activity, but after nightfall another attack was made on Portsmouth where, yet again, the CP lay over the dockyard and barracks area. From 2150 to 2333 hours 38 aircraft dropped 69 tonnes of HE (16 SC 1000, 52 SC 250, four Flam 250, four Type 'A' and 37 Type 'B' mines) and 7,108 incendiaries, visually and with good sight of the ground. Crews claimed five bombs in the No. 1 Basin of the dockyard, followed by fires, and four bombs in No. 3 Basin, also with subsequent fires. The gas works, too, was claimed hit by four bombs and five more large and numerous small fires were seen.

After two ineffective attacks, Portsmouth was more efficiently bombed on this occasion and considerable damage was done. Thirty-eight fires were started in Portsmouth, two of them major and four of a serious nature, but all were brought under control by 0150 hours. Damage was inflicted on military and naval targets as well as residential and

commercial property and the railway system was dislocated. At least 85 civilians were killed; service casualties are not known but, according to the Ministry of Home Security report, appeared not to be heavy. In Gosport there were six fires; a cinema and the railway station were set alight and six people were killed. Three Portsmouth hospitals were damaged and some disruption was caused to public utility services.

The AA guns defending Portsmouth were in action from 2153 to 2337 and again from 0544 to 0551 hours, in total firing 584 rounds; elsewhere, few batteries were in action and the Command's expenditure for the night was less than 1,000 rounds. Between dusk and dawn Fighter Command dispatched 119 aircraft with two engaged in offensive patrols over France and one over Holland. One enemy aircraft was subsequently claimed destroyed and another damaged. A Defiant (N3389 of No. 96 Squadron, Cranage) was destroyed and the two crew members killed when it flew into high ground near Wellingore airfield at 2310 hours.

Two aircraft were lost whilst engaged on coastal work.

4(F)/122 Junkers Ju 88A-1 (0294). Shot down by Pilot Officer D. O. Hobbis in a Beaufighter of No. 219 Squadron. Crashed into the Solent. Lt. H. Berger, Fw. G. Klier, Fw. A. Reicherzer and Gefr. W. Paulke all killed. Aircraft F6+AM lost.

1/KG26 Heinkel He 111H-5 (3677). Shot down by AA fire from Fighter Catapult Ship *Patia* which later sank due to damage caused in the attack. Its captain, Commander D. M. B. Baker went down with the ship. Aircraft crashed into the sea 35 miles off the River Tyne 9.30 p.m. Oberfw. E. Fenchel, Gefr. R. Klamand and Uffz. S. Warko baled out and taken prisoner. Gefr. J. Schürgel killed. Aircraft 1H+MH sank in sea.

Other casualties at night included a Junkers Ju 88D-2 of 1(F)/122 which went missing in unknown circumstances. Two crew of a I/KG1 Junkers Ju 88 baled out before their aircraft crashed near Rouen killing the remaining two crewmen. Two Heinkel He 111s of I/KG26 and a Junkers Ju 88 of I/KG77 were damaged.

6/KG27 Heinkel He 111H-3 (5660). Shot down by AA fire during an attack on Portsmouth. Crashed into the sea off Lyme Regis. Oblt. H. Brandenburg, Oblt. R. Lange, Fw. G. Feindt and Fw. G. Bohnekamp killed. Aircraft 1G+CP lost.

By the end of April 1941 much of Cornwall Street, Portsmouth, was burnt out; forty years later much has gone completely.

In Commercial Road the Royal Portsmouth Hospital, already hit twice on previous occasions, was blasted again on Sunday night. Although patients had been evacuated, several members of staff were killed. Twenty-four-year-old Dr James Salwey was buried for three hours; he was extricated mortally wounded and died next day in Queen Alexandra Hospital.

Those of Portsmouth's civilian dead buried communally lie in Kingston Cemetery where the inscriptions on twin memorials facing each other in a walled garden recall the dark days of 1941: 'Erected to the memory of those men, women and children both known and unknown who died as a result of enemy bombing in this city and whose last resting place is near this spot. Out of the depths of sorrow and sacrifice will be born again the glory of mankind.'

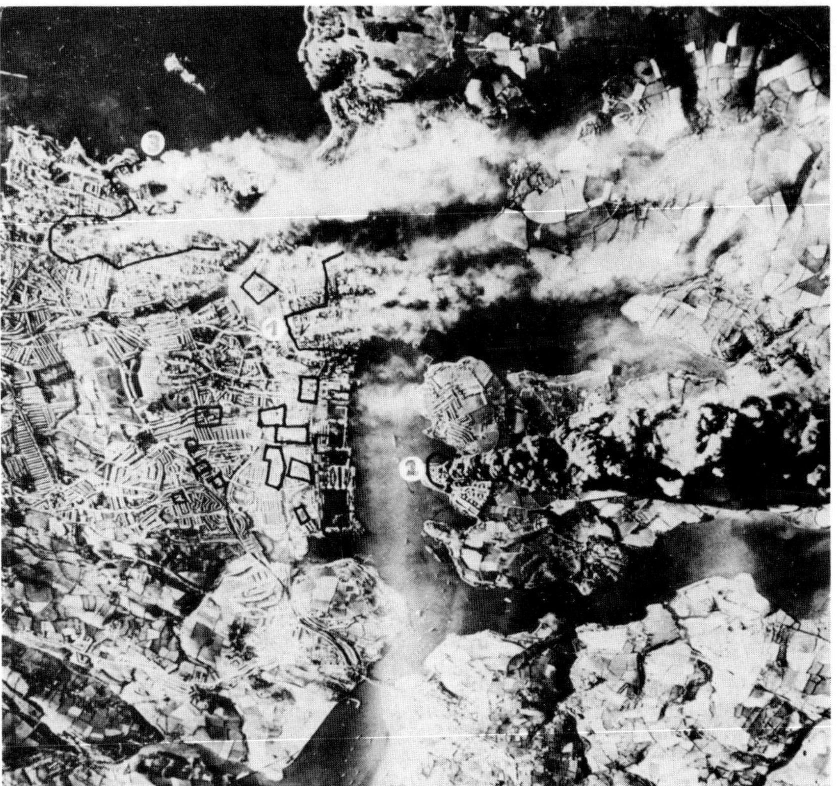

Just how much could one take? After an all-too-short respite to lick its many wounds, that other great south coast naval city, grievously bleeding from the previous week's attacks, now came in for more punishment. Ministry of Home Security April 30: 'Plymouth is an accessible target to the G.A.F., who may hope by these heavy attacks to further Germany's success in the battle of the Atlantic. The enemy may have been led by the reports of these heavy raids to suppose that he could get the population "on the run" and deprive the dockyards of labour. If he is changing his strategy, and intends to try to put single towns out of commission one by one by repeated bombardment, urgent consideration will have to be given to the arrangements for maintaining the community's life and work in the face of such attack. A valuable respite will be secured for the development of these arrangements by the increased hours of daylight, but the problems nevertheless are many and pressing. It should not be forgotten that the need for a change of tactics on the enemy's part is in itself an encouraging sign, and the courage and resolution of Plymouth have been finely maintained through these heavy attacks.'

MONDAY, APRIL 28-29

Sunset: 2017 Sunrise: 0537
Moon: Dusk — 2211 (New +2)

Major attack on Plymouth/Devonport. Minor bombing elsewhere.

UK — Cloudy in the East, mainly fair or fine in the West. Visibility moderate, poor locally near industrial areas. Light winds.

The Continent — Variable low cloud with rain locally. Visibility moderate, poor in some areas.

German daylight activity was on a larger scale than of late with machine gun attacks by low flying aircraft at several places in Scotland, where a few bombs also fell at Newburgh. Slight damage was caused at Great Yarmouth and there was a report of damage and casualties in a factory in the north of England. Most German activity, however, took the form of fighter sweeps off and over the Kent coast.

The main feature of the night was a major assault on Plymouth by 124 aircraft of Luftflotte 3. Between 2205 and 0240 hours they delivered 159 tonnes of HE (two SC 1800, 31 SC 1000, 38 SC 500, 295 SC 250, 43 LZZ 250, 336 SC 50 and 76 SD 50) and 29,580 IBs. The CP covered the southern part of Plymouth and the western area of Devonport, with dock installations and the dockyard the objectives, and most crews claimed to have bombed this area visually and with good effect. Numerous fires resulted, both in the CP and in the town centre; one very big explosion occurred in the gas works and another in a north-west district of the town. As the raid progressed, many small fires linked to form a large fire area. Flak, according to participating crews, was strong and partly well aimed, but the searchlights were ineffective. Crews also reported seeing two aircraft shot down — one on fire over the target at 2308 hours and the other about 30 miles south-east of Plymouth at 2225. Night fighters were seen both over Plymouth and to the south, but no returned crews reported attacks.

Luftflotte 3 dispatched 145 aircraft during the night, 124 bombing Plymouth, one attacking Portsmouth as an alternative and six breaking off their missions. Two aircraft were lost — a He 111 of II/KG27 failed to return and a Ju 88 of III/KG1 crashed after its crew baled out near Rouen. There were also attacks on airfields by 12 aircraft; St Eval was attacked by a single He 111 of III/KG55 and St Athan, near Barry, was attacked by seven He 111s of KGr100 (between 2352 and 0017 hours, using X-Verfahren and bombing from heights of 6,100 to 7,100 metres) and four similar aircraft of III/KG27 (between 2315 and 0057 hours from 400 to 950 metres). Explosions and several fires resulted with three described as large.

The units which bombed Plymouth were:

II/KG1: 14 Ju 88, 2205-2243
III/KG1: 7 Ju 88, 2243-2309
III/KG26: 10 He 111, 2230-0012 (visual and Y-Verfahren bombing)
KG77: 20 Ju 88, 2211-2315
II/KG27: 9 He 111, 2210-2255
III/KG27: 6 He 111, 2212-2236 also 2 He 111, 0138-0210
KGr100: 7 He 111, 2201-2216 (X-Verfahren bombing) also 3 He 111, 2340-0047 (visual bombing)
Stab/KG55: 2 He 111, 2240-2255 also 1 He 111, 0035
I/KG55: 18 He 111, 2215-2315
II/KG55: 8 He 111, 2240-2317
III/KG55: 17 He 111, 2230-2300

Once again the dockyard suffered badly, but on this occasion the city centre escaped comparatively lightly. However, water and gas mains were badly hit and supplies were disrupted for some time. Among adjacent areas which suffered was Saltash, where 40 houses were burnt out and four people killed. Bombs also fell at Foxhole, Cornwall, at St Athan airfield, Ipswich, Hove, Cardiff and Aldeburgh in East Anglia. Only at Plymouth did serious damage and heavy casualties occur, however.

Approximately 3,000 rounds of heavy AA ammunition were used during the night, mostly in the Plymouth area, and four of the attackers were claimed shot down and another damaged. Fighter Command flew dusk, night and dawn patrols with 100 aircraft and claimed one enemy aircraft destroyed (by a Beaufighter of No. 604 Squadron off Lyme Regis) and another probably destroyed by a Havoc of No. 93 Squadron.

TUESDAY, APRIL 29-30

Sunset: 2018 Sunrise: 0535
Moon: Dusk — 2317 (New +3)

Major attack on Plymouth/Devonport. Minor attacks on Cardiff and elsewhere.

UK — A little medium cloud at first, followed by low cloud increasing in the South-West with rain. Extensive cloud elsewhere. Visibility moderate to good, poor in rain.

The Continent — Fair or fine in north-eastern France. Elsewhere extensive low cloud with rain in many places.

Small scale German daylight activity developed but no bombs fell on land until after dark when, for the second consecutive night, Plymouth suffered another major attack.

Between 2150 and 0040 hours the docks and shipyards of the Devonshire naval base constituted the Concentration Point for 162 bombers of Luftflotten 2 and 3. For the most part aiming visually, they dropped 210 tonnes of HE (58 SC 1000, 100 SC 500, 295 SC 250, 29 LZZ 250, four Flam 250 and 422 SC 50) and 19,124 incendiaries. Several large and some 50 medium and small fires were seen within the confines of the CP, with two very large explosions in the docks and gas

April 28, 1941

The target is again Plymouth. Does it really make sense to drop so much on the south coast, just because it lies nearest to us?

ROBERT GÖTZ

works. Flak was medium to strong in intensity and, in part, well directed, but searchlight activity was described as trivial. One night fighter carried out three attacks on one of the attackers. Several crews reported seeing an aircraft going down in flames over Plymouth at 2330 hours.

Luftflotte 2 contributed 32 aircraft to the attack, joining 130 of Luftflotte 3; two aircraft of the latter air fleet aborted, six were sent to attack Exeter airfield, one to Andover airfield and six on armed sea reconnaissance. One Luftflotte 3 aircraft, an He 111 of III/KG26, which reported over its target failed to return. The following were those units of Luftflotte 3 to reach and bomb Plymouth:

II/KG1: 14 Ju 88, 2215-2248
III/KG1: 12 Ju 88, 2253-0038
KG77: 22 Ju 88, 2215-2310
III/KG26: 8 He 111, 2220-2330 (Y-Verfahren and visual bombing)
I/KG27: 10 He 111, 2210-2250
III/KG27: 5 He 111, 2213-2220
KGr100: 7 He 111, 2154-2215 (6 by X-Verfahren, one bombed visually; opened attack with 8,064 IBs)
I/KG54: 13 Ju 88, 2315-0020
II/KG54: 16 Ju 88, 2320-0010
III/KG54: 13 Ju 88, 2240-0015

For the fifth time in nine nights Plymouth received a heavy attack and this was the heaviest yet. Initially inaccurate bombing resulted in many HEs and incendiaries falling in open country to the north of the city, but crews eventually found their Target Area. The main weight of the attack fell on Keyham and Milehouse, between Plymouth and Devonport, and before long about 20 fires were burning in Milehouse, Devonport and Torpoint. Residential and shopping areas of Plymouth again suffered, with Beacon Park and Hartley the worst hit areas. The city's resources, and probably the morale of its people, were now stretched to the limit — after this latest attack only some 10 per cent of the city's food distribution facilities remained and about 40,000 people were homeless. Looking after so many people was a major problem and every large building not already in use as a hospital or feeding centre was pressed into use as a rest or accommodation centre. Nearly 600 people had been killed and another 450 seriously injured. Little remained of the city's shopping centre, more than 20,000 houses had been damaged or destroyed in the last three attacks, and the dockyards had been seriously hit (with the Devonport dockyards especially so). Fortunately, both for the people of Plymouth and the Royal Navy, the Luftwaffe subsequently turned to other targets.

The secondary attack on Cardiff did little damage but four fires were started and there were 117 casualties, five of them fatal. Bombing was widespread over many parts of Glamorgan and 18 people were killed at Pentre and four at Barry. Bombs also fell in the West Country, and at Norwich several fires occurred with three factories and many houses damaged. Places reporting bombs included Tynemouth, Lincoln, Newark, near Lowestoft, Penzance and the Scillies.

Of the 5,000 rounds fired during the night by AA Command, Plymouth's contribution was 2,783 (2,533 3.7-inch and 250 3-inch) with the guns in action from 2153 to 0138 hours. Five enemy aircraft were claimed destroyed and more damaged.

Fighter Command dispatched 139 aircraft on dusk, night and dawn patrols and claimed three enemy aircraft destroyed — an He 111 by a Beaufighter of No. 604 Squadron, an unidentified enemy aircraft by a Havoc of No. 93 (LAM) Squadron, and a Bf 110 by an Intruder Havoc of No. 93 Squadron over Rosieres airfield in northern France.

Destroyed in an instant; a lifetime's work for Dame Agnes Weston, affectionately known to two generations of sailors as 'Aggie'. She had begun her mission to cater for the welfare of the Navy ashore at Devonport in 1873 by latching onto the growing temperance movement to provide an alcohol-free environment for those sailors who did not want, or were not able to, spend every evening propping up a bar. Her first premises near the dockyard gates soon outgrew itself and eventually she ended up founding the huge Royal Sailors Rest, more popularly known as 'Aggie Westons', on Fore Street with accommodation for 1,000. Created a Dame by Queen Victoria for her work, she died in December 1918 and became the first woman to be accorded a naval funeral. The building was gutted during the attack and was subsequently demolished and not rebuilt. After the war the outer perimeter wall of the Naval Dockyard was extended to encompass almost the whole of Fore Street, the original entrance (on the right) now standing rather superfluously inside the base.

An unusual occurrence this day was the arrival of a Bücker Bu 131B GD+EG which landed at Somerford, Hampshire after being stolen from Caen by Messieurs Heberd and Bergerac, two ex Armée de l'Air pilots and was put on display during War Weapons Week in London. A 1(F)/120 Junkers Ju 88 made a forced landing at Sola and a III/KG26 Heinkel He 111 crashed near Evreux killing three of its crew.

1/KG40 Focke-Wulf Fw 200C-3 (0054). Crashed into the sea off the Shetland Isles cause unknown. Oblt. R. Schelcher and Obergefr. R. Renntrop killed. Oberfw. O. Verpahl and Uffz. J. Niklas missing. Bodies of Uffz. J. Obergaulinger and Gefr. E. Sengbusch recovered from the sea and buried in the Shetlands but now moved to Cannock Chase. Aircraft F8+HH lost.

WEDNESDAY, APRIL 30-MAY 1

Sunset: 2020 Sunrise: 0533
Moon: Dusk — 2359 (New +4)

No significant activity.

UK — Extensive low cloud with rain in many areas. Moderate to poor visibility.

The Continent — Similar to the UK in many areas.

No bombs fell on Britain on a day of little activity. Continued bad weather resulted in the cancellation of night operations in strength and only ten long-range bombers and five long-range night fighters were over Britain after dark. Bombs were reported in Yorkshire, East Anglia and in Lincolnshire where slight damage was caused at an RAF station.

A Defiant (N3376) of No. 96 Squadron, Squire's Gate, crashed in Gatley, Cheshire, while on an operational patrol. Following engine failure it was abandoned by its crew at 2255 hours.

Another loss this day in addition to that below was a Heinkel He 111 of 3/KG4 which failed to return from a sortie to Plymouth.

1/506 Junkers Ju 88A-1 (0715). Believed shot down by Spitfires of No. 72 Squadron during a sortie to Whitley Bay, Yorkshire and crashed into the sea off Farne Islands 3.00 p.m. Lt. H. Jark, Fw. K. Pahnke and Uffz. J. Schaare killed. Body of Obergefr. J. Schumacher recovered from the sea and buried at Brandesburton. Aircraft S4+JH lost.

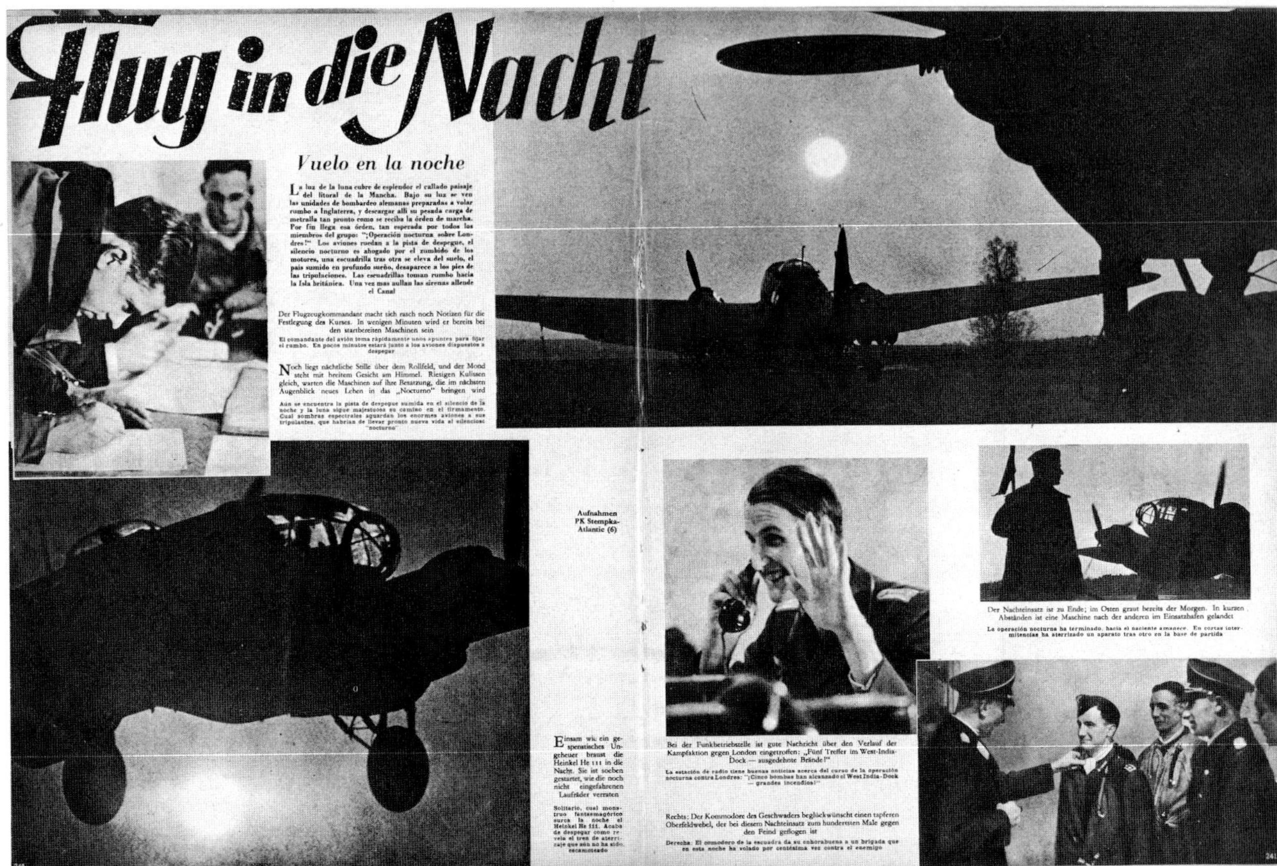

'Fünf Treffer im West-India-Dock . . .' Night flight feature in the latest *Der Adler*.

MAY 1941

Although they did not realise it, the end of the Blitz was in sight for the British people, but before the end they were still to undergo some highly destructive attacks with heavy casualties.

Following a devastating concentration on Plymouth at the end of April, the Germans turned to Merseyside where a series of attacks resulted in the deaths of some 1,900 people and seriously injured 1,450. Glasgow and Clydeside also suffered a double assault and on the 10th London, a target to the end, was attacked by more than 500 bombers in one of the worst raids of the entire offensive. Finally, on the night of May 16-17 the Luftwaffe turned to Birmingham. From then on it was preoccupied with the forthcoming invasion of Russia and operations on other fronts. True, air raids on Britain continued for the next three years or so — and at times they were severe — but the heavy and sustained night bombing of Britain was over. On the night of the 17-18th only some 50 German aircraft were over Britain; about the same number came the next night and again on May 19-20, but from then on the numbers fell away, with only five raiders over the country on the 25-26th, and so on.

Up to and including the night of May 16-17 there were eleven major and four heavy attacks, with no significant operations thereafter. Up to the 25-26th Luftwaffe offensive night sorties totalled 4,385 by long-range bombers and 215 by night fighters. An innovation on the night of May 11-12 was the use by night of 63 single-engine day fighters, but whether or not they were carrying bombs is not clear. In reply the RAF flew 1,345 single-engine and 643 twin-engine night fighter sorties during the entire month. Ninety-six German aircraft were claimed destroyed by fighters while AA guns claimed 31½; 10½ enemy aircraft were destroyed by 'other methods'. These were results which gave enormous satisfaction to both Douglas and Pile but both also felt a sense of frustration; just as the defences were about to gain the upper hand they were deprived of the victory that assuredly was about to be theirs. Their frustration was tempered, however, by thankfulness that the ordeal of the civil population was seemingly at an end. In the last few weeks of the offensive 5,394 people lost their lives and 5,181 were badly injured. During the month the RAF lost 16 fighters in night operations.

The increased effectiveness of the defences produced a record number of German Air Force PoWs, 135 falling into British hands during the month. The bodies of another 174 Luftwaffe personnel were also recovered, but there were many others listed as missing who fell into the sea or crashed on their return to the Continent. Enough evidence was available, however, for AI1(k) to draw some useful conclusions and obtain some valuable data. For example, a German aircrew 'life expectancy' ratio of 44 per cent compared less favourably with the 51 per cent obtained the previous month, yet only three out of 19 gunners brought down were killed. This gave a life expectancy figure for gunners of 84.21 per cent, the highest ever recorded. At no time before had gunners a higher life expectancy than other crew members. The average age of bomber pilots was also the highest ever recorded (at 26.85 years), and they had an average of almost five years service. From this it is clear that even at the end of the campaign, the Luftwaffe was still using, in the main, very experienced pilots. Against this, however, the average age of observers was 23.35 years, the lowest yet recorded although again they averaged above five years service. The youngest crew member brought down was a gunner aged 18½, and the oldest a major of the General Staff aged 53.

British suspicions of the impending attack on Russia were confirmed to some extent by mid-May when the Intelligence decrypt of German W/T traffic intercepted by the 'Y' Service revealed the subordination of II Fliegerkorps to Luftflotte 2. It was already known that this air fleet was connected with a build-up in the East and further Enigma decoded messages, together with aircraft and ground control station W/T messages, revealed the eastward movement of several Gruppen of Luftflotten 2 and 3. On May 23 it was known to Air Intelligence that an attack on Russia — or an attempt to intimidate her — was likely. A month later only 299 bombers remained in the West, including those primarily employed on anti-shipping work, with only about half of these serviceable. The whole of Luftflotte 2, with many units formerly under Luftflotte 3, was now in action on the Eastern Front.

THURSDAY, MAY 1-2

Sunset: 2022 Sunrise: 0532
Moon: Dusk — 0046 (First Qtr −3)

Sharp attack on Liverpool/Birkenhead.

UK — Cloud increasing and lowering in the East, partly cloudy in the West. Visibility mainly moderate, some fog in the East.

The Continent — Extensive low cloud with rain at times. Visibility moderate in north-west France, poor elsewhere.

Sea reconnaissance covered all coastal areas during the day but there were few inland penetrations with only one of note. This involved a Ju 88 which approached the coast at Lyme Bay during the morning, bent on a pirate raid on Portland where it damaged a factory, starting fires and killing two people. Flying very low, it was engaged by LAA fire and claimed damaged.

During the night Liverpool/Birkenhead was attacked by 43 of the 59 aircraft ordered to the target by Luftflotte 3. Of the remainder eight bombed alternative targets, six aborted and two were lost (an He 111 of II/KG27 and a Ju 88 of I/KG54 which ditched in the Channel). The attackers comprised:

KGr100: 8 He 111, 2317-2334 (visual bomb aiming)
I/KG27: 9 He 111, 2315-2350
II/KG27: 9 He 111, 2325-0008
I/KG54: 11 Ju 88, 2250-2335
II/KG54: 6 Ju 88, 2312-2330

Bombing between 2250 and 0008 hours the raiders delivered 48 tonnes of HE (13 SC 500, 86 SC 250, 19 SC 250mV, 13 LZZ 250, 226 SC 50 and ten SD 50) and 4,032 IBs. The Schwerpunkt was centred on the mid-portion of the docks complex between the Pier Head and Sandon Docks and that part of the town containing warehouses and industrial installations. Bombing was visual, in conditions of good visibility, and one large, five medium and numerous small fires developed in the prescribed Target Area. In spite of the small size of the force used, good results were anticipated.

In fact most of the damage in Liverpool was done in the centre of the city but neither the docks, industry or private property suffered extensively and not more than 13 people were killed. At Birkenhead there were about 30 small fires and ten fatalities. Railways were affected, there was one large fire in the docks, and a factory at Bromborough was slightly damaged. Bombs were also dropped in many widely scattered areas including Crosby, near Bristol, Southport, near Preston and in the vicinity of Leyland, Manchester, Blackpool, Kinnaird's Head, Tangmere and Yeovil.

AA Command used 6,000 rounds of heavy ammunition during the night including 1,654 by the Mersey batteries which were in action from 2246 to 0008 hours.

Dusk, night and dawn patrols were undertaken by 103 aircraft of Fighter Command for claims of one He 111 destroyed and two damaged (one by a No. 93 Squadron Havoc following the release of its mines 10 miles west of Portland Bill).

During the day 2/KG26 lost an He 111 and two aircraft failed to return at night, that not detailed below being from I/KG54.

4/KG27 Heinkel He 111P (2604). Shot down by Pilot Officer A. J. Hodgkinson and Sergeant B. E. Dye in a Beaufighter of No. 219 Squadron. Crashed into the sea off Shoreham 10.45 p.m. Lt. H. Ballauf and Fw. F. Förster killed. Uffz. R. Averberg killed and buried at sea July 14. Fw. H. Platt killed and washed up at Shoreham June 19. Aircraft 1G+HM lost.

For almost a year now Churchill had shouldered the awesome burden of responsibility for conducting a war whose boundaries increased almost daily against inadequate resources which shrank almost hourly. With record sinkings of nearly 700,000 tons by the German Navy in April; with the mother country steadily being pounded into the ground by the German Air Force, and with the German Army victorious in the Balkans their was little to smile about on the first day of May when Churchill travelled westward through the night to Plymouth. Intelligence reports indicated an imminent attack against Crete and the build up to a massive assault on the Soviet Union. Iraqi troops attacking British forces on April 30, coupled with news of a successful U-Boat attack on an escorted convoy in daylight, was the last straw. The problems on all fronts seemed insurmountable and a lesser man would have cracked long ago; at Plymouth Churchill nearly did after he returned from a day spent touring the Devonport Dockyard and the city areas in which scarcely a house appeared habitable. He was very depressed on returning to Chequers, where bad news from other fronts cast him, as John Colville, his private secretary wrote, into 'the worst gloom that I have ever seen him in . . . I think it is largely Plymouth that has caused him such melancholy — he keeps on repeating "I've never seen the like." '

FRIDAY, MAY 2-3

Sunset: 2023 Sunrise: 0530
Moon: Dusk — 0127 (First Qtr −2)

Major attack on Liverpool/Birkenhead.

UK — Low cloud with rain in the extreme south-west of England. Elsewhere little or no cloud with moderate to good visibility. Winds NE to E, light to moderate.

The Continent — Fair or fine with little cloud and moderate to good visibility.

Armed sea reconnaissance, particularly off the coasts of Devon and Cornwall, and fighter sweeps over the Channel and the South-East occupied the Luftwaffe during the day and no bombs fell on land.

With nightfall came the second consecutive attack on Liverpool/Birkenhead, but this time Luftwaffe 2 carried out the major share of the bombing. Between 2158 and 0015 hours 65 aircraft (51 of Luftflotte 2 and 14 of Luftflotte 3) dropped 105 tonnes of HE (15 SC 1000, 73 SC 250, 24 Flam 250, 125 SC 50, 13 LMA and 53 LMB) and 6,042 IBs. Under almost cloudless skies, with good visibility, the TA was readily discerned and visual bombing was concentrated on the ordered CP which, on this occasion, was centred on dock installations on the east bank of the Mersey. A large fire started in the north part of the docks between Gladstone and Huskisson Docks, with another developing later between Sandon Docks and the Pier Head. Explosions and fires were also reported between the Pier Head and Herculaneum Dock with further fires, one of them very big, on the Birkenhead bank of the Mersey. All in all, good results were anticipated. Little is known of Luftflotte 2's participation, but the following units of Luftflotte 3 took part:

III/KG76: 11 Ju 88, 2158-2324
III/KG77: 3 Ju 88, 2340-0000

From this small Luftflotte 3 force two Ju 88s, both of III/KG77, were lost. Other aircraft flew armed reconnaissance missions off the East Coast in search of shipping.

Actual damage in Liverpool was widespread, and casualties were reported in many parts of Merseyside. Several serious fires were started but all were brought under

Whereas night fighter victories had slipped a little of late, during the first week of May the score began to mount again. On Night One of the Mersey raids only one bomber failed to return; on Night Two it was five, this being one of them wallowing in a watery grave off Weybourne beach in Norfolk.

control by dawn. A number of public shelters were hit and altogether more than 110 people were killed including fatalities in Birkenhead, Bootle and the Stretford district of Manchester. The rail and tramway systems suffered but although a number of fires were started in the docks damage was not severe. However, the public gas, water and electricity services in Liverpool suffered considerable damage.

All districts of Liverpool reported bombs and elsewhere they fell at Warrington, on the Wirral, in Cheshire and in various districts of East Anglia. Parachute mines were reported at Lowestoft.

The country's HAA batteries fired 7,000 rounds (of which those on Merseyside accounted for 4,639 while in action between 2229 and 0236 hours) for three raiders claimed destroyed. Between dusk and dawn 177 aircraft of Fighter Command flew patrols including five over northern France. Three enemy aircraft were claimed destroyed, one of them over Vitry airfield by a Havoc of No. 23 Squadron on an Intruder patrol.

A Junkers Ju 88 of 1/506 was lost during the day, the following at night.

1/KG30 Junkers Ju 88A-5 (8180). Shot down by Pilot Officer Guy A. Edmison and Sergeant A. G. Beale of No. 151 Squadron in a Defiant. Aircraft made a good belly landing just off shore at Weybourne, Norfolk 3.30 a.m. Major W. Seeburg, Fw. E. Geiger, Fw. H. Laser and Fw. R. Altmayer all captured. Aircraft 4D+BH captured damaged.

3/KG40 Heinkel He 111H-5 (4021). Crashed into the sea off St. Agnes Head, Cornwall during an attack on Bristol. Cause unknown. Lt. A. Loose, Oberfw. A. Pickart, Oberfw. H. Burvam and Fw. F. Schwarz all killed. Aircraft V4+JL lost.

8/KG77 Junkers Ju 88A-6 (2368). Shot down by Flight Lieutenant G. O. Budd and Sergeant G. J. Evans in a Beaufighter of No. 604 Squadron. Crashed at Little Oaks, Highland Water, near Lyndhurst, Hampshire 10.30 p.m. Fw. F. Beckmann killed. Fw. W. Winkler, Uffz. F. Pohl and Uffz. A. Mayer baled out and taken prisoner. Aircraft 3Z+DS destroyed.

Site originally investigated by David Sommersby who recovered some cockpit components, parachute release buckle and oxygen bottles. Subsequently re-excavated by Malcolm Pettit but little significant wreckage discovered.

9/KG77 Junkers Ju 88A-5 (5105). Shot down by AA fire from Brooklands and crashed at Fairmile Common, Cobham, Surrey 1.00 a.m. Oblt. H. Hempel, Fw. H. Rösch, Fw. H. Höchersteiger and Fw. O. Schulle all baled out and taken prisoner. Aircraft 3Z+AT burnt out.

Site now obliterated due to the construction of the A3 Esher Bypass in 1977. Small item from this aircraft in the Guy Smith Collection.

Thirty miles away at Lowestoft the police station received a surprise on Saturday when a 250kg bomb landed outside the front door — on the precise spot where a bomb had struck on February 19! The station had been heavily sandbagged and there were no casualties. (The censor approved publication with the tell-tale signs deleted.)

SATURDAY, MAY 3-4

Sunset: 2025 BST Sunrise: 0628 DBST
Moon: Dusk — 0304 DBST (First Qtr −1)
(All times in Double British Summer Time from hereon)

The infamous 'May Week' raids began on Thursday night, but the destruction of local records at Liverpool including the 'Bomb Census' for the Air Ministry (initially maintained only for London, Birmingham and Liverpool) makes it difficult to apportion the damage to particular nights though it is thought that nearly half the deaths were inflicted on May 3-4. Here the old Bryant & May factory at Bootle burns bright like its matches while timber for future production can be seen stacked outside.

Major attack on Liverpool/Birkenhead. Minor attacks on Hartlepool, Barrow-in-Furness and numerous other places. Armed coastal reconnaissance.

UK — Mainly cloudless. Good visibility becoming poor locally near large towns.
The Continent — Similar to the UK in all areas.

German daylight operations were greatly intensified, with fighter sweeps over the Channel and south-east England, and weather, general, and coastal reconnaissance flights in many areas. There were several cases of machine-gunning but bombs fell only at one point in the south-east of England.

During the night a very heavy raid was made on Liverpool/Birkenhead. In total, night operations were flown by 441 bombers and 11 fighters, with Merseyside claimed bombed by 298 aircraft. In an attack lasting from 2200 to 0340 hours DBST (there was a change from British Summer Time to Double British Summer Time during the night), the raiders delivered 363 tonnes of HE and 49,706 incendiaries. Their CP was centred on the docks and warehouses on the east bank of the Mersey and with visual bombing possible throughout the attack very good results were expected. Numerous large, medium and small fires were started, many linking to form vast conflagrations over the entire area of the town including the docks. Large explosions were also observed near the Pier Head and northwards to Gladstone Dock. At 0044 hours an especially large explosion sent a surge of flame up to approximately 500 metres (1,600 feet). Hits were also claimed on the granary and oil mills near Waterloo Dock, in installations of the Queen's Dock, south of the Pier Head and in the vicinity of Clarence Dock where, following the detonation of an SC 1000, a fire with a dark red glow developed. Towards the end of the onslaught the dock installations along the east bank of the river appeared to be engulfed in one large fire area some 6 kilometres in length.

A further attack was made against Hartlepool by 20 aircraft which dropped 32 tonnes of HE (13 SC 1000, six SC 500 and 65 SC 250) and 2,160 IBs between 2320 and 0225 hours. Their CP covered the 12 kilometres stretch between Hartlepool and West Hartlepool, to the north of Middlesbrough, where docks and industrial installations were situated. Here too the Target Area was easily picked out by crews and visual bombing followed. However, mist prevented a detailed assessment of the results although numerous explosions, mostly in the TA, were seen. Two small fires were started, but they were quickly extinguished.

A further subsidiary attack was made on Barrow-in-Furness by 14 aircraft which bombed between 2356 and 0050 hours, releasing 27 tonnes of HE (one SD 1400, three SC 1000, nine SD 250, three LZZ 250 and 20 Type 'B' mines) and 576 IBs. Incendiaries were seen to fall in the town centre and in the vicinity of the Haematit Iron and Steel Works. Most of the HEs appeared to fall in the dockyards of Vickers Armstrong with individual bombs exploding in the town area.

Further targets — some of them alternatives to the previous mentioned attacks — included Portsmouth, Great Yarmouth, Bristol, Plymouth, the Rotol Airscrew Company at Cheltenham, the torpedo factory at

May 3/4, 1941
Take-off Villaroche 21.40 hours

Liverpool. Being made a marker-plane is an honour for us. But hadn't they any better observer than me, the youngest lad they have? In order to place the flares exactly, we attack at a height of only 1000 metres. The first rounds of Flak immediately burst thickly on the left. We saw the puffs of the explosions and at first took them for planes . . . So far, so good. It's burning over a wide area down there. The town itself must have suffered immense hits . . .

Frozen to the bone, tired and stiff as we are suspended in our seats, after a long flight we get ready to land at Villaroche at about 3.30 hours. While we are still at a height of two hundred metres, the landing gear is let down. The jolt brings us down a little lower.

At this moment, whole clusters of sparks fly over us and disappear, exactly following the line from which we had jolted down. There is an English night fighter behind us. He has his finger on the trigger of his weapons. But thank God is dazzled by the cone of fire of his tracer bullets.

We put out our landing light, then the other lights; retract the landing flaps, pull up the landing gear again, and fly away very close indeed to the ground. We seem to have come through safe and sound. Now the airfield lighting is also being switched off. Air raid alert! The airfield is unavailable to us. We fly on towards Villacoublay, and look for hits. But can't find anything. But then we hear the 'All Clear', and at once head for Villaroche again. There we find that with those bursts of fire intended for us 'Tommy' has nevertheless damaged some planes and shot a soldier through his bottom!

ROBERT GÖTZ

Endeavouring to detect any change in tactics by the Luftwaffe, Home Security noted after Thursday night's raid that 'this is the third occasion within two weeks that enemy aircraft have visited Merseyside by night, the former occasion being on the night of 15/16th April and 26/27th April. It may be that the comparatively small results achieved in the present case were due to weather conditions; alternatively these three operations may be regarded as a reconnaissance in force, in preparation for major raiding. In any case the occurrences point to the probability of heavy attacks on this area, which must be made within the next three weeks if the enemy is to take advantage of the hours of darkness. The vital importance of the western ports suggests that all possible steps should be taken to minimise the dislocation that will be caused by a "blitz" on the Liverpool area.' Then after the following night's return visit: 'There is no indication that the enemy was attempting to attack any specific target: the results, which were widespread and apparently indiscriminate, give the impression that the raid was more in the nature of a prelude to further and more systematic attacks. The recent examples of Clydeside and Plymouth taken in conjunction with the vital importance of our Western ports would suggest that Merseyside may now be scheduled for similar treatment, to be followed by the ports on the Bristol Channel.' *Above:* We have often read in the reports by crews of huge explosions on the ground during an attack, most probably caused where gasholders exploded. This is the result of one such hit at the Linacre works.

Portland and the airfields at St Athan, Warmwell, Drayton-St Leonard and Harwell. Bombs also fell at Lowestoft, York, Harwich, Hull, Avonmouth, Weymouth, Reading and Lands End, and offensive night fighter patrols were flown over eastern England.

A detailed breakdown of Luftflotte 2's operation is not available, but it is known that Luftflotte 3 dispatched 293 aircraft, 218 of which bombed Liverpool while 24 attacked Portsmouth, 25 bombed alternatives, five sought airfields, 11 aborted, two attacked Zerstörziele (Cheltenham and Portland) and one searched for shipping. Seven Luftflotte 3 aircraft were lost (three He 111s of III/KG26, one He 111 of III/KG27 and three Ju 88s belonging to KG77, II/KG54 and III/KG54). Aircraft of this air fleet that participated in the Liverpool attack were:

I/KG27: 10 He 111, 2320-0015 (all times here in BST)
II/KG27: 8 He 111, 2334-0005
III/KG27: 18 He 111, 2320-0048
KGr100: 17 He 111, 2331-0010
I/KG54: 11 Ju 88, 2250-2345
II/KG54: 11 Ju 88, 2310-0032
III/KG54: 10 Ju 88, 2312-2340
Stab/KG54: 3 He 111, 2330-2335
I/KG55: 11 He 111, 2327-0008
II/KG55: 13 He 111, 2330-0050
III/KG55: 19 He 111, 2310-2340
II/KG1: 17 Ju 88, 0002-0135
III/KG1: 9 Ju 88, 2337-2358
II/KG77: 17 Ju 88, 2317-0110
I and III/KG77: 8 Ju 88, 2355-0030
III/KG26: 9 He 111, 2328-0105 (bomb load included two BM 1000).
KG76: 22 Ju 88, 2255-0013

Extensive damage was caused in Liverpool and the fire situation became very serious, particularly in Bootle. There were major fires in the docks and several ships were sunk including the *Europa* of 10,224 tons and the *Elstree Grange* of 6,598 tons. A tug, six barges and another steamship, the *Malakand* of 7,649 tons, were also sunk and other ships

Ruined properties in Drury Lane next to the India Offices.

were set on fire or seriously damaged. Rail traffic and utility services were also badly affected, telecommunications severely interrupted and the telegraph service completely stopped. The Corn Exchange and two hospitals were among the many buildings damaged, but Wallasey and Birkenhead received less attention on this occasion with no really serious incidents. A total of 406 people were killed in Liverpool, 57 in Bootle and 16 in Litherland.

Considerable damage was also caused in Barrow-in-Furness, with ten people killed and some 2,000 rendered homeless, and at Tyneside there was more extensive damage and heavy casualties. Casualties were particularly heavy at Tynemouth where a public shelter received a direct hit with some 76 casualties. Fires were also started in Sunderland, where 18 people were killed, but industrial damage in this area was slight. In West Hartlepool there was damage to the railway system, and two people were killed, but only little damage occurred in Gateshead and Newcastle.

At the same time, Herbert Morrison, the Minister for Home Security, was really worried about the effect of the provincial raids on morale. At a Civil Defence Committee on May 7, the Minister 'underlined the fact that people cannot stand this intensive bombing indefinitely and that sooner or later the morale of other towns will go, even as Plymouth's has gone.' With Merseyside undergoing heavy attacks for seven nights in a row, that next town might well be Liverpool.

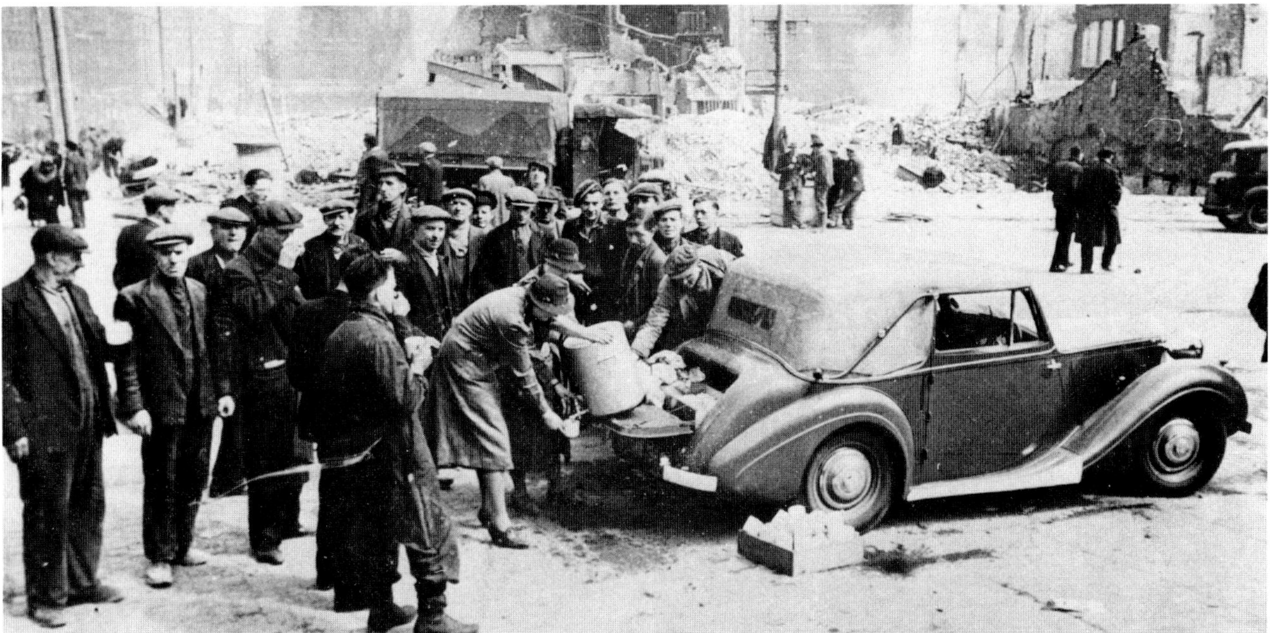

'The general feeling — it is difficult exactly to express it, but residents spoken to felt it too — that there was no power or drive left in Liverpool.' So wrote Mass-Observation in May 1941, groping for words to describe reactions on Merseyside. Tom Harrisson writes of 'a sense of damp defeat' lying across the scarred city with little being done 'to put people back on their feet after the worst continuous battering any people yet had.' Speaking of the failure of the authorities to cope with the situation, Professor Harrisson said it 'closely resembled Southampton's, but on a much larger scale (nearly ten times the population). Liverpool's dissatisfaction in May reached a level of 'vehemence' (our word at the time) unmatched elsewhere. (In Southampton and in other cities criticism of the authorities had been slight and slow to grow.)'

The casualties had been high — 1,900 dead and 1,450 badly injured — and in Liverpool, for the first time in any blitzed town, there were publicly-expressed signs of disgruntlement moving towards a willingness to surrender. The presence of the Army and police and their act of closing the city centre to vehicles and anyone without specific reasons for being there — a normal occurrence elsewhere to enable the clearance of debris from unsafe buildings and to extract any unexploded bombs — appears to have triggered off a belief that martial law had been declared in the city. *Above:* **Here the Army have sealed off Paradise Street at the junction with Lord and Church Streets.**

Twenty people lost their lives at Portsmouth and Gosport (where several small fires were started) and service casualties occurred in the dockyard. Most of the damage in this area, however, was done to private property. At Weymouth 15 fires were started, the railway was dislocated and three people were killed, but no important military or naval establishments were affected.

Bombs also fell at Hull, Plymouth, Hastings, Nottingham, Newark, Grantham and Derby.

Some 10,000 rounds of heavy AA ammunition were used during the night, many of them by the Mersey guns but the actual figure is not available as 20 sites did not make reports. Those that did report fired 2,240 rounds and were in action from 2243 to 0400 hours. Countrywide the guns claimed three enemy aircraft destroyed and a number damaged.

Fighter Command dispatched no less than 286 aircraft on dusk, night and dawn patrols, including six over northern France, and claimed a very satisfactory 10 enemy aircraft destroyed over Britain, two over northern France, five probably destroyed and two damaged. Special patrols were maintained over and on the approaches to the Liverpool area and Beaufighters, Havocs and Defiants all shared in the successes of the night. Two fighters were lost; one of them a Spitfire of No. 222 Squadron whose pilot, Pilot Officer Klee, was killed.

A Ju 88 that crashed at Lostock Green near Northwich, Cheshire, at 2345 hours was of particular interest to crash investigators of AI1(g), for a manufacturer's identification label showed it to be an A-6 variant. This was the first time a Ju 88A-6 had been encountered, but as the aircraft — B3+EC of Stab II/KG54 — had dived into the ground, entirely disintegrated and then burnt out, little else was discovered.

B3+EC had left Bretigny at about 2100 hours, bound for the Liverpool docks, and was carrying one 500kg and three 250kg bombs. The flight to the target and the attack were carried out with no problems, but very soon afterwards the Ju 88's left engine failed

The lack of any explanation from the authorities — it being said at the time that there was an 'almost complete divorce' between the politicians and officers at the top with the sufferers at the bottom — added fuel to the rumour which rip-roared across the country after the last big raid on May 7. Within hours it had reached London with a responsible MP and a BBC spokesman, amongst others, all confirming that a peace demonstration had taken place and that as a result Liverpool was under martial law. The lack of any official information, and the inability of editors to be able to confirm the situation by telephone, all added to an already confused situation which was still unclear late in May. ***Below:*** **This is the Paradise Street area photographed in June.**

and height was rapidly lost. Leutnant Hans Glänzinger, the pilot, gave the order to bale out and shortly afterwards his aircraft caught fire.

Feldwebel Hans Richter, the flight mechanic, and Unteroffizier Hans Stettwieser, the observer, successfully baled out, but their pilot, Glänzinger, and W/T operator, Unteroffizier Gerhard Harmgart, were killed. Glänzinger's parachute failed to open and Harmgart baled out without fastening his parachute harness. There is a difference of opinion between the two survivors as to what caused the engine to fail, but it seems likely that flak — which was described as intense over the target — was responsible. However, Richter, who was not a regular member of the crew and who was making his first operational flight, recalls that they were also attacked by what he thought was a Spitfire. They were flying at 3,600 metres at the time and had just left the Target Area. Glänzinger then put the Ju 88 into a steep dive and the British fighter was lost to view. And it was then that the engine failed.

Richter landed unhurt but Stettwieser injured his knee as he baled out. To add to his troubles he landed in what he thought was the River Mersey and being in full flying kit had some difficulty in struggling to the bank. In fact he had alighted in a stretch of water known locally as a 'Flash' — flood water from an old salt mine — near Northwich. The observer (now Dr Hans Stettwieser, a veterinary specialist) was on his 80th war flight over Britain.

Hans Richter had a second narrow escape that night. While being guarded by a rather nervous member of the Home Guard a rifle was accidentally discharged and the bullet narrowly missed the German airman.

After taking off from Colerne at 2200 hours, Beaufighter T4632 of No. 600 Squadron came under the control of Exminster GCI but with the 'moon rising to its best and brightest quarter and with the Hun over in force', to quote the Squadron Operations Record Book, control of the Beaufighter was passed to the GL Carpet. Before long the night fighter, being flown by Flying Officer

Ranelagh Street as seen from Lime Street with the ruins of Lewis's department store on the left. After Saturday night's raid, Home Security feared that 'quite apart from the loss of material in air raid attacks, continuous harassing of the transport and dock working communities must have its effect on the human element, unless provision is made for adequate rest to maintain physical and moral power. This could probably be achieved by their organized removal to quieter areas at night within such a distance that they can return to work by day.'

Woodward with Sergeant Lipscombe, AI operator, was vectored onto an incoming raid and following an AI contact and subsequent visual sighting, the enemy aircraft was shot down.

The German bomber, Ju 88A-5 M7+AH of Küstenfliegergruppe 806, was bound for Liverpool and flying at 12,000 feet when attacked. Its port engine caught fire and the pilot, Oberfeldwebel Fritz Schäfer, ordered his crew to bale out. Among them was Leutnant Gottwald Gerlach, who was slightly wounded, and W/T operator Helmut Soland, making his 80th operational flight. All four members of the crew landed safely, with flight mechanic Feldwebel Walter Krämer also slightly wounded. Their aircraft crashed at Stoke St Michael, near Shepton Mallet, Somerset, still with its bomb load on board, and exploded on impact, scattering wreckage over two or three fields.

By this time KüFlGr806 was listed in many German records (Abteilung 6 returns, for example) as Kampfgruppe (KGr) 806, but the precise date of re-designation is not known. Certainly, according to Helmut Soland, his unit was KüFlGr806 and not KGr806 when he was shot down, but the correct designation is open to some doubt. In April the unit had been attached to KG1 (to replace I/KG1 which had been transferred to Quimper as an anti-shipping unit and re-designated III/KG40), but earlier in the year it had operated under the auspices of KG54. Later in May it left Caen for eventual operations on the Eastern Front, and by this time was certainly designated KGr806.

The following aircraft were shot down.

Stab III/KG26 Heinkel He 111H-5 (3620). Shot down by Flight Lieutenant Speke in a Beaufighter of No. 604 Squadron. Crashed at Rexton Gorse, Crowcombe, near Taunton, Somerset 1.00 a.m. Oberfw. R. Gemar, Fw. H. Kopp and Uffz. W. Ditz killed. Uffz. H. Müller baled out and taken prisoner. Aircraft 1H+BD destroyed.

8/KG26 Heinkel He 111H-5 (4064). Shot down by Flight Lieutenant Dotteridge and Sergeant Williams in a Beaufighter of No. 219 Squadron. Aircraft broke up in air and crashed at Keynor Farm, Sidlesham, Chichester 10.35 p.m. Uffz. G. Macher and Gefr. B. Winterscheid baled out and taken prisoner. Uffz. O. Kaminski and Gefr. B. Möllers killed. Aircraft 1H+DS disintegrated.

9/KG26 Heinkel He 111H-5 (3626). Intercepted and shot down by a Beaufighter, possibly that of Wing Commander T. Pike of No. 219 Squadron. Crashed at Eastergate Corporation Scrap Yard, Arundel 10.50 p.m. Lt. H. Loos, Fw. R. Lekscha and Obergefr. H. Dieterle killed. Uffz. E. Cerlach and Uffz. A. Heublein baled out and taken prisoner. Aircraft 1H+AT disintegrated.

9/KG27 Heinkel He 111P-2 (1482). Shot down by Squadron Leader J. Cunningham DSO DFC and Sergeant C. F. Rawnsley DFM in a Beaufighter of No. 604 Squadron. Crashed at Wheatsheaf Farm, Corton Denham, Somerset 10.45 p.m. Oblt. H. Zöllner, Uffz. E. Ehlers and Uffz. F. Pichota baled out and taken prisoner. Fw. A. Amode killed. Aircraft 1G+IT destroyed.

Excavated by Perry Adams in December 1985 when small pieces of badly burnt airframe were unearthed. A manufacturer's plate bearing Wn.1482 was also discovered to confirm the aircraft's identity.

2/KG53 Heinkel He 111H (3975). Believed to have hit balloon cable. Crashed into the river Mersey 12.01 a.m. Lt. K. Baller, Uffz. L. Palubicki, Uffz. K. Fliechmann, Uffz. G. Stolper and Gefr. E. Donner all killed. Aircraft A1+EK lost.

3/KG53 Heinkel He 111H-4 (3235). Shot down by Pilot Officer Bodien and Sergeant Wrampling in a Defiant of No. 151 Squadron. Aircraft made forced landing and fired by crew at Sharrington, Norfolk 1.04 a.m. Gefr. B. Kauhardt killed. Lt. A. Plank von Bachfelden, Gefr. B. Reynat and Uffz. W. Richter captured. Aircraft A1+LL destroyed.

StabII/KG54 Junkers Ju 88A-6 (3381). Shot down by fire from a Defiant and crashed at Field's Farm, Lostock Green, Lostock Gralam, Cheshire 10.45 p.m. Lt. H. Glänzinger and Uffz. G. Harmgart baled out but both killed due to parachute failure. Uffz. H. Stettwieser and Fw. H. Richter baled out and taken prisoner. Aircraft B3+EC disintegrated.

Site investigated by Warplane Wreck Investigation Group. Shattered engine and sundry small items recovered.

3/KG77 Junkers Ju 88A-5 (4269). Suffered engine failure and made a forced landing at Welney Wash, near Downham Market, Norfolk 4.00 a.m. Lt. J. Wreschnick, Uffz. F. Podlech, Uffz. R. Siekmann and Gefr. H. Pix all taken prisoner. Aircraft 3Z+CL captured damaged.

A manufacturer's plate bearing Wn.4269 in the Colin Pratley collection.

1/806 Junkers Ju 88A-5 (8161). Shot down by Flying Officer Woodward and Sergeant Lipscombe in a Beaufighter of No. 600 Squadron. Crashed at Moons Hill Farm, Stoke St. Michael, Somerset 11.30 p.m. Lt. G. Gerlach, Oberfw. F. Schäfer, Fw. H. Soland and Fw. W. Krämer all baled out and taken prisoner. Aircraft M7+AH totally disintegrated.

Small pieces in the Hodgkiss Collection.

The boarded-up windows of the *Telegraph* offices in Royal Avenue, Belfast, main target for Sunday night's maximum effort.

SUNDAY, MAY 4-5

Sunset: 2127 Sunrise: 0626
Moon: Dusk — 0337 (First Quarter)

Major attack on Belfast. Secondary but heavy attacks on Barrow-in-Furness and Liverpool/Birkenhead. Numerous minor attacks elsewhere.

UK — Fine generally but cloudy in the East later. Local fog in the Midlands and near industrial towns towards dawn. Winds light and variable.
The Continent — Fine but low cloud and rain near German border regions. Elsewhere good visibility but some fog patches late in the night.

A few bombs fell ineffectively in Suffolk during the morning but there was little else to report on a day of limited German activity. Night operations, however, were conducted by 450 bombers and 21 fighter-bombers, with three principal target centres.

The main weight of the offensive fell on Belfast where 204 aircraft dropped 237 tonnes of HE and 95,992 IBs in a raid lasting from 2122 to 0335 hours. The CP was the north-east part of the town where bombs, aimed entirely visually, were intended for dock installations east of the Victoria Channel, the Harland and Wolff shipyard, the Short and Harland aircraft factory and adjoining installations. Numerous fires resulted, with many joining to form large fire areas. Very good results were anticipated.

A further attack was made on Liverpool/Birkenhead — the fourth in a row — with 55 aircraft delivering 55 tonnes of HE and 11,560 IBs. Large fires were still burning from the previous night and to these more were added, all crews bombing visually. Explosions covered the area between the Pier Head and the Waterloo Dock, to the north of the dry docks in Langton Dock and

May 4, 1941
Take-off at Villaroche,
21.51 hours

We are bound for Belfast — in Ireland.

Highly unenjoyable navigation. Absolutely no sight of the ground. Not even the coastline can be seen. There is total interference with the radio-navigation system. Since last December, the precision of our target-finding has suffered extremely from the British radio-jamming. Even the way in which the much-prized directional beams operate is still a puzzle to us. Deflectable? Is that at all possible?

Unremitting dead-reckoning is all that remains to us. But what if the wind reported differs just a little from the weather forecasts — as in 50 per cent of these cases? For the weather comes from the west, and we don't get any news from that direction. One thing is now clear: it is only in conditions of clear air and bright moonlight that we can really expect to find and hit our targets. But how often do these two things coincide? It seems to me that our commanders don't want to accept this, and that our officers don't pass this upwards clearly and loudly enough . . .

Today has again been a catastrophe. Our transmitter, which is getting further from me as I fly towards the Isle of Man, is suddenly giving a bearing which is 100 degrees out over England. Is Tommy now deflecting it, or am I myself reading it wrongly? It makes you sick! The directional beam is functioning just as badly. As usual, we are therefore flying lower than almost ever before when we are heading northwards — contrary to express orders. It only needs a very little moonlight for us to be able to make out the coastline on the west coast, in both directions, and compare it with the map. But today there is only mist and clouds at all heights. After hours, we circle in to where we imagine the Isle of Man to be, in the Irish Sea; as the radio operator announces a message saying: 'Switch target to attack on Liverpool harbour'.

What's all this now? Shaking our heads, we turn away; thinking that we were already seeing the Belfast Flak flashing around us.

The Liverpool Flak welcomes us as usual, so then we at least know exactly where we are. We try to recognize the coastline and drop our bombs. We land at 04.45 hours.

ROBERT GÖTZ

Corporation Street. With the continuing attacks against the Mersey port, and now the re-introduction of Belfast docks as a target, Home Security had little doubt that the 'enemy's intention is to render our ports unworkable.'

A German war correspondent, Dr Hermann Weninger, accompanied the raid: 'We stared silently into a sea of flame such as none of us had seen before. In Belfast there was not a large number of conflagrations but just one enormous conflagration which spread over the entire harbour and industrial area. . . .' Thus it was on the night of May 4-5 over Belfast.

in the town. Numerous fires were seen in the middle of the dock installations and over the entire city and, as in the case of Belfast, good results were almost certainly achieved.

The third main operation was centred on Barrow-in-Furness, attacked by 55 aircraft from 0010 to 0312 hours with 81 tonnes of HE and 11,266 IBs. However, thick cloud and mist severely hampered crews, but by descending through the overcast or by taking advantage of the occasional gaps in the cloud, most crews were able to bomb visually. Their assigned CP covered the shipyards and adjacent iron works and explosions and fires were seen in this area, but the poor visibility precluded an assessment of the results.

On the other side of the country an attack was made on dock installations at Hartlepool by 17 aircraft. Single fires were started in an attack which lasted from 0020 to 0245 hours, but bad weather conditions made it impossible to ascertain their precise whereabouts. At the same time Middlesbrough was attacked, in similar weather, the bomb load on both centres totalling 28 tonnes of HE (14 SC 1000, seven SC 500, 33 SC 250 and 48 SC 50) and 5,616 incendiaries.

Other places claimed attacked, mostly as alternative targets, were Plymouth, Swansea, Portland, Greenock, Portsmouth, Shoreham, Falmouth, Poole, Exeter, Cardiff, Weymouth, Great Yarmouth, Newhaven and Witney airfield.

Luftflotte 3 played a major rôle in the night's activity, dispatching 270 aircraft, of which 167 bombed Belfast as follows:

I/KG27: 9 He 111, 0125-0200
II/KG27: 11 He 111, 0215-0255
III/KG27: 12 He 111, 0113-0308
KGr100: 16 He 111, 0113-0155
I/KG54: 5 Ju 88, 0120-0153
II/KG54: 10 Ju 88, 0123-0200
III/KG54: 11 Ju 88, 0117-0205
I/KG55: 7 He 111, 2122-2150
II/KG55: 6 He 111, 0057-0220
III/KG55: 13 He 111, 0105-0145
Stab/KG55: 2 He 111, 0115-0123
II/KG1: 17 Ju 88, 0120-0245
III/KG1: 5 Ju 88, 0105-0215
KG76: 21 Ju 88, 0100-0210
KG77: 20 Ju 88, 0104-0217
III/KG26: 2 He 111, 0148-0207 (bomb load included one BM 1000)

The following Luftflotte 3 crews attacked Liverpool as their primary target:

I/KG27: 1 He 111, 0118
I/KG54: 3 Ju 88, 0112-0125
III/KG54: 1 Ju 88, 0040
II/KG55: 1 He 111, 0110
I/KG55: 1 He 111, 0120
II/KG55: 2 He 111, 0115-0145

The following attacked Liverpool as an alternative target:

II/KG27: 1 He 111, 0330
I/KG54: 5 Ju 88, 2325-0138
II/KG54: 1 Ju 88, 0100

I/KG55: 5 He 111, 0110-0135
II/KG55: 6 He 111, 0105-0248
III/KG55: 4 He 111, 0115-0223
II/KG1: 3 Ju 88, 0140-0338
III/KG1: 4 Ju 88, 0055-0210
KG76: 2 Ju 88, 0040-0120
KG77: 3 Ju 88, 0030-0135

Four Ju 88s of Luftflotte 3 failed to return (two of KG77 and others of II/KG54 and III/KG1) and another of III/KG1 made an emergency crash landing in France, injuring four crew members.

The damage actually sustained in Liverpool was less than on the previous night, but again fires were started in the docks. More serious here though, was the increased railway dislocation; many roads too were blocked and transport generally was seriously disorganised. Several fires were started in the city and damage to homes, shops, schools, etc., was again experienced. Much worse was the damage inflicted on Belfast where large fires were started all over the city and in the docks; public utilities were also badly disrupted and casualties included 56 killed.

In Barrow-in-Furness there was considerable damage to residential and other private property and this attack brought the total homeless to about 5,000. Some damage and four fatal casualties also occurred at Portsmouth and five people were killed at Torquay. Elsewhere, damage was done in the North-East and in East Anglia, with five people killed at Ipswich. Bombs also fell at Hull, Weymouth, Portland, Ipswich, Broadstairs, Lowestoft, Manchester and Rugby. Attacks on airfields included two evening strikes against Manston (in which buildings were machine gunned and three aircraft damaged), Martlesham (superficial damage only), Coltishall (negligible damage but one killed and five injured), Tangmere (no damage), Debden (one killed but negligible damage) and Exeter (where the runways were damaged and a landing Defiant — N1769 of No. 307 Squadron — crashed after its crew successfully baled out). At Duxford a German night fighter shot down a Hurricane of No. 257 Squadron which was about to land, killing the pilot, Sergeant R. Parrott.

It was a very busy night for the gunners of AA Command who used 16,000 rounds; the figures for Belfast are not available, but the Mersey guns fired 4,800 rounds, those at Barrow 1,667, and on Clydeside 441. Three raiders were claimed destroyed.

Fighter Command dispatched 269 aircraft between dusk and dawn, including five which visited northern France on Intruder missions. A large number of AI and visual contacts were made which resulted in claims of two raiders destroyed, four probably destroyed and six damaged.

In addition to those listed below, two other Junkers Ju 88s of 4/KG30, and 2/106 were lost during the night operations.

8/KG1 Junkers Ju 88A-5 (3358). Shot down by Wing Commander D. F. W. Atcherley and Flight Lieutenant J. Hunter-Tod in a Beaufighter of No. 25 Squadron during an attack on Belfast. Dived vertically into a building and became buried in rubble at Butcher's Arms public house, Eastgate, near Bourne, Lincolnshire 11.45 p.m. Four civilians, including the licensee and his wife, together with three soldiers were killed and six more injured. Uffz. A. Becker, Gefr. R. Kitzelmann and Gefr. K. Focke killed. Gefr. R. Dachshel baled out and taken prisoner. Aircraft V4+BS totally destroyed.

The remains of the building were demolished and the site cleared, but during excavations for a garage being built in 1964 some wreckage and a 500kg bomb were discovered.

6/KG54 Junkers Ju 88A-5 (6142). Shot down by Pilot Officer P. F. Jackson DFM and Sergeant S. N. Hawke in a Beaufighter of No. 604 Squadron during an attack on Torquay. Attempted a belly landing but hit an earth embankment near the Seven Stars Inn, East Burton, Dorset 11.30 p.m. Fw. W. Jeruschke, Fw. K. Weise, Fw. W. Dickschen and Oberfw. G. Scholz all captured. Aircraft B3+AP wrecked.

Stab II/KG77 Junkers Ju 88A-5 (6027). Suffered engine failure and fuel shortage on a sortie to Belfast. Attempted a forced landing at Waxham, Norfolk 4.12 a.m. but hit a sand dune. Uffz. J. Simon killed. Lt. K. Obenhack, Gefr. H. Rose and Uffz. W. von Mohrendorf taken prisoner. Aircraft 3Z+EC wrecked.

6/KG77 Junkers Ju 88A-5 (7117). Landed on the sea off Bridlington, Yorkshire 00.15 a.m. following engine failure. Oblt. M. Baumann, Fw. W. Hopfer and Oberfw. K. Auernhammer killed. Oberfw. E. Schieting rescued by a passing ship and captured. Aircraft 3Z+FP sank in sea.

2/106 Junkers Ju 88A-5 (0656). Shot down by a night fighter and dived into houses at 13-15 High Street, Idle, Bradford 12.45 a.m. Two civilians killed, two later died of injuries and two injured. Oblt. zur See R. Metzger, Oblt. E. Jürgens, Oberfw. H. Beeck and Fw. H. Jänicken all baled out and taken prisoner. Aircraft M2+DK wrecked.

Drogue parachute, removed by a local policeman at the time of the crash, now in the After the Battle collection.

Proud of the results achieved, *Der Adler's* editor devoted a complete page to the post-raid appreciation: 'Figure 1 shows the built-up Belfast harbour area . . . around 100,000 square metres destroyed, including the silos indicated by Figure 2. Figure 3, the big British Harland and Wolff shipyard . . . completely destroyed. On the slipways, three ships have undoubtedly suffered devastation and damage. These consist of a tanker of some 10,000 tons BRT (point 'a'), and merchant ships of about 10,000 and 7,000 BRT (points 'b' and 'c'). Point 4 indicates an oil depot at Conns Water. The aircraft factory indicated at point 5 shows hits and damage leaving it severely affected. Point 6 indicates a power station, and point 7 Belfast airport.'

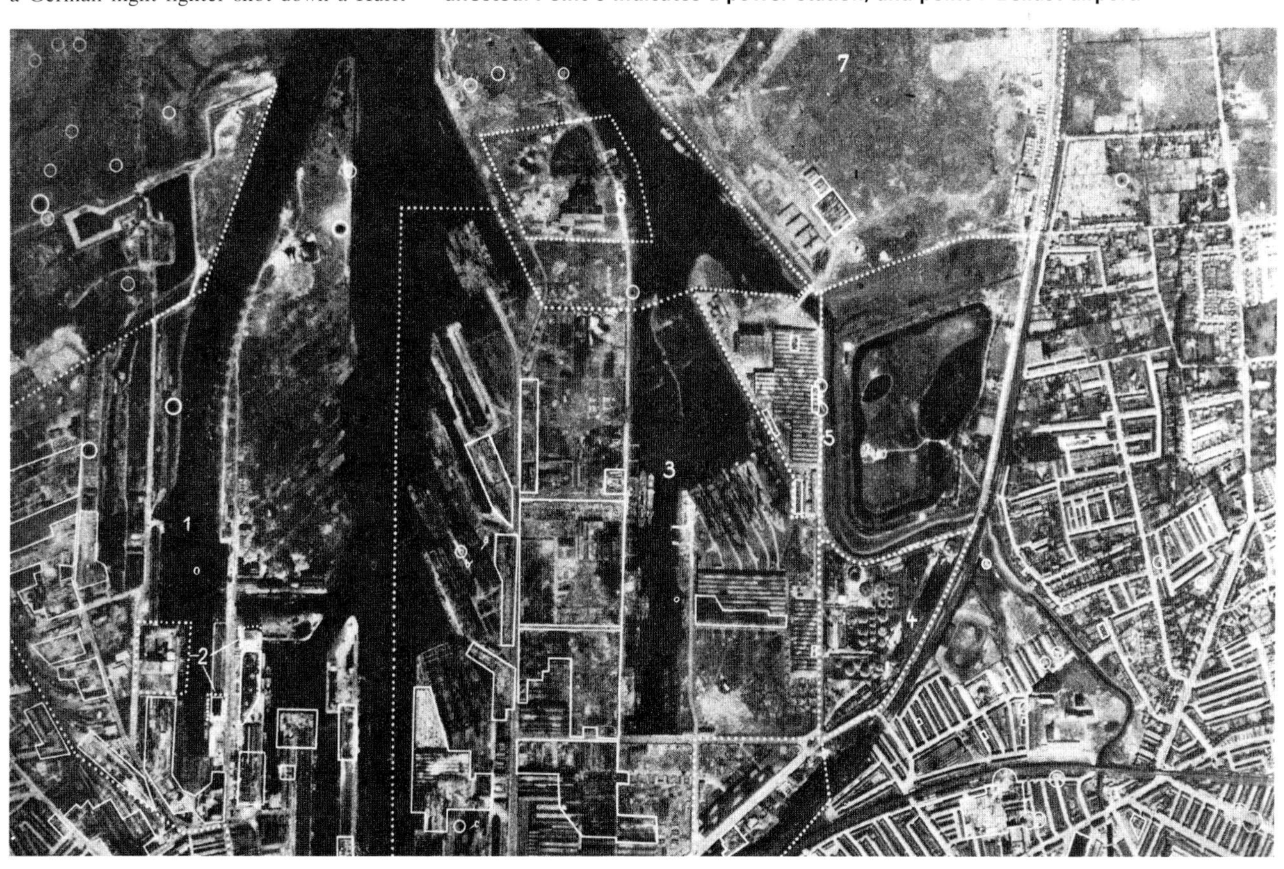

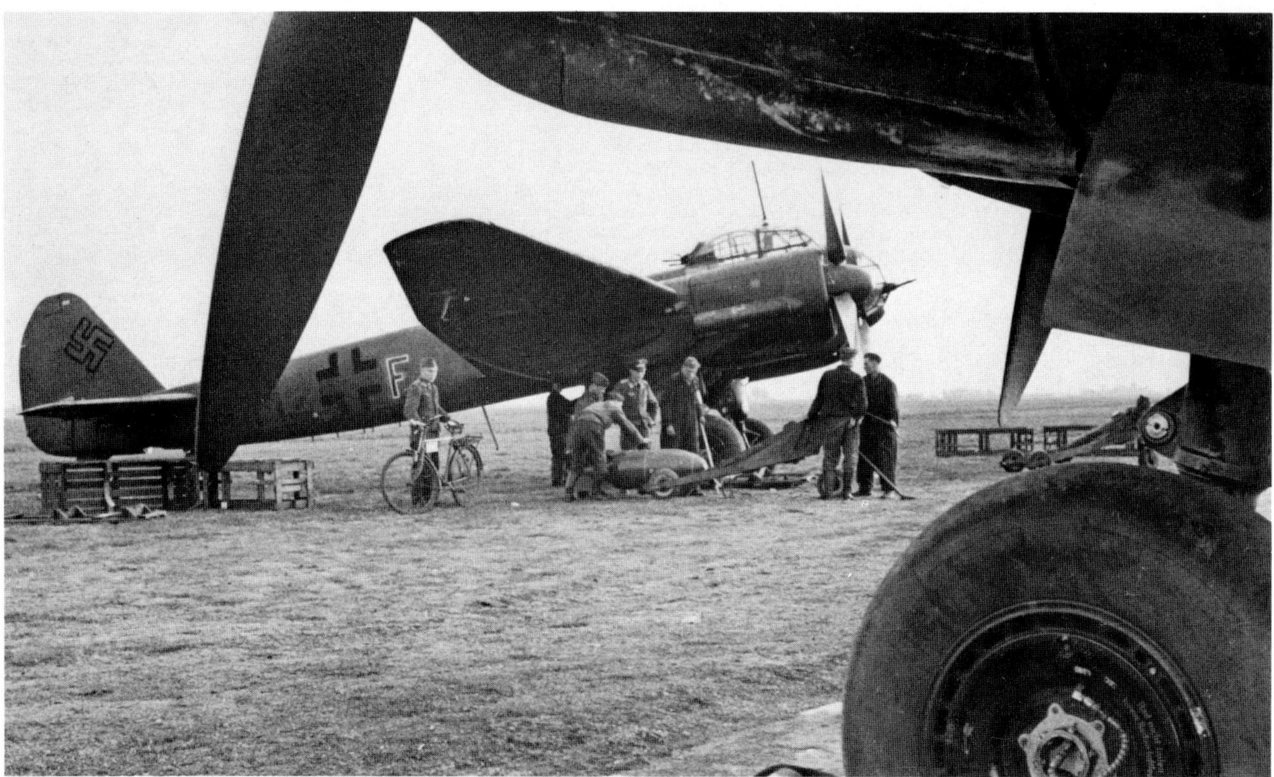

For the first few months of the night Blitz, Gruppe 106 (a peculiar coastal unit which did not normally use the KG, KGr or KüFlGr prefixes but only a Staffel number prefix such as 2/106) was converting from Heinkel He 115 seaplanes to Junkers Ju 88s. Having done so, while remaining primarily an anti-shipping unit, it also joined in the night bombing offensive with its new aircraft and took part in the major attacks on Belfast and Glasgow.

MONDAY, MAY 5-6

Sunset: 2128 Sunrise: 0624
Moon: Dusk — 0407 (First Qtr +1)

Major attack on Glasgow/Clydeside. Secondary attacks on Merseyside, Tyneside, Plymouth and Hull. Minor bombing elsewhere, mining, armed sea reconnaissance and attacks on airfields.

UK — Broken cloud with scattered showers in the East, little or no cloud in the West. Visibility mainly moderate to good, but some smoke or mist near industrial centres.

The Continent — Little or no cloud with moderate to good visibility in France and Belgium. Much cloud in Holland and north-west Germany with showers on coasts.

German fighter sweeps over the Channel and Kent, together with armed sea reconnaissance, took place throughout the day and there were several attacks on airfields in the South-East, but all to little effect.

Night operations were conducted by 460 long-range bombers and five night fighters with Glasgow/Clydeside the main Target Area, but encompassing Greenock and Dumbarton.

Between 0025 and 0340 hours the shipyards and industrial districts of Glasgow were attacked by 103 aircraft. Their Target Area, in fact, stretched along the Clyde from Rutherglen to Dalmuir, and in this area they dropped 130 tons of HE and 1,872 incendiaries. Most of the bombing was carried out visually and good results were apparently obtained; explosions and fires were reported in the Rothesay Docks in Yoker, and in the John Brown yards at Clydebank, in the Renfrew district and on dock land and shipyards between the central station and Scotstoun. Four large and several smaller fires were also seen between Yoker and Dalmuir, with many more in the town itself.

Greenock was the target for 80 aircraft which, attacking between 0117 and 0240 hours, delivered 112 tonnes of HE and 8,064 IBs. Here, too, visual bomb aiming was possible and good results, with explosions and many fires, were seen among shipyards and docks on the south bank of the Clyde. One of these fires was alleged to be in the Scott and Greenock shipyards.

On the north bank of the Clyde, dock installations and the Deny Brothers factory were claimed hit by some of the 103 aircraft which were allocated Dumbarton as a Concentration Point. In an attack which started at 0030 and finished at 0300 hours they dropped 109 tonnes of HE and 36,880 IB, with results similar to those obtained at Greenock and Glasgow. At one time five large and several smaller fires were raging and at 0240 hours there were two big explosions.

On the east coast of Scotland, Leith was bombed by ten aircraft between 0005 and 0155 hours. They dropped 20 tonnes of HE and 1,440 IBs on a CP which covered the docks, shipyards and dry docks and, once again, good results were claimed with explosions and isolated fires in the Target Area. Eight crews, unable to find Leith, attacked Edinburgh with nine tonnes of HE and 576 IBs and once more it was the familiar story of fires and explosions.

Another minor but sharp attack took place at Liverpool, where 27 aircraft dropped 34 tonnes of HE and 6,228 IBs between 0025 and 0215 hours. Cloud over this TA was quite thick, but most crews were able to bomb visually through gaps and further observed explosions and fires in the docks

When the Luftwaffe returned to Scotland in May, the target area was extended from the City of Glasgow itself out along the Clyde to Greenock (*above*).

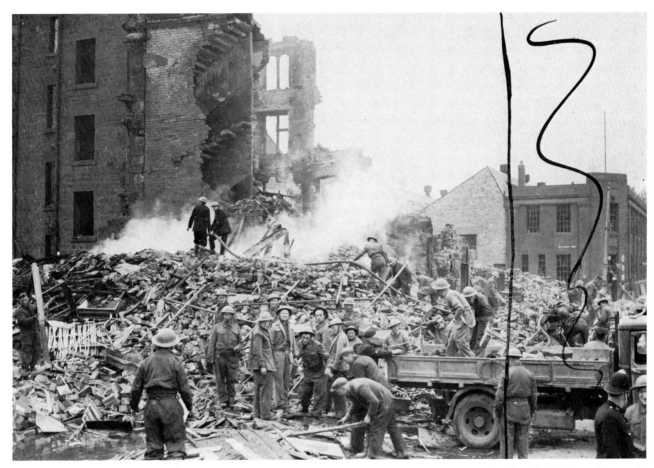

A tenement has collapsed in Rue End Street opposite Victoria Harbour, Greenock, with little hope for those crushed beneath the mound of rubble. Permission granted for publication by *The Times* once the bus garage had been deleted.

area and in the town. The glow of fires from the previous night's attack served to guide the first arrivals.

On the South Coast 15 aircraft attacked the docks and shipyards at Plymouth with 16 tonnes of HE and 1,296 IBs. Bombing took place between midnight and 0215 hours and fires resulted in both the dockyards and in the town.

Minor attacks, with 12 aircraft involved in each, also took place at Newcastle and Hull. At the former 14 tonnes of HE and 1,728 IBs were claimed dropped on the shipyards to the east of the town in an attack lasting from midnight to 0300; some crews bombed through gaps in the cloud, but others descended to make low altitude attacks from below the cloud base. At Hull, where bombing took place between 2341 and 0205 hours, 14 tonnes of HE were dropped, some by DR and some aimed visually.

Elsewhere attacks were made on shipping, airfields and a variety of alternative targets. Luftflotte 2 statistics are not available, but it is known that Luftflotte 3 dispatched 276 aircraft with 72 attacking Glasgow, 54 over Greenock, 49 over Dumbarton, 27 over Liverpool, five to airfields, five on shipping patrols and one on a Zerstörer attack on the Birmingham-Longbridge aircraft factory. In addition 15 new, inexperienced crews were sent to Plymouth and 12, in the same category, to Hull, both targets being classed as comparatively easy to find. Six Luftflotte 3 aircraft were lost (two He 111s of III/KG40, a Ju 88 of II/KG54 and another He 111 of I/KG55; another aircraft of this unit ditched in the Channel, and an He 111 of I/KG27 crashed in France following an engine failure). Further details of actual unit participation are not available.

The attack on Clydeside succeeded in inflicting considerable damage. Both sides of the river suffered and damage was heavy at Greenock, Paisley, Dumbarton and elsewhere in Renfrewshire, but damage to the docks was very slight. The working of the docks, however, was somewhat retarded by disruption to the railways. As usual, public utilities suffered, but worst hit were residential areas; industry was also badly affected. There were also fires, and five people killed, in Edinburgh.

The further raid on Liverpool again produced a serious fire situation, owing to a lack of water. The city centre again took the main weight of the bombing but numerous fires were also started in Birkenhead. On Tyneside damage was not so extensive, but ten people were killed in Tynemouth and two in Newcastle. Some damage was also done in the docks at Hull and there were three fatal casualties at Plymouth and slight damage at several points in South Wales.

The Clyde guns were in action from 0020 to 0357 hours and fired some 3,000 rounds; countrywide nearly 14,000 rounds were used for one enemy aircraft claimed destroyed and several damaged. Fighter Command's contribution of patrols by 245 aircraft between dusk and dawn resulted in claims of eight enemy aircraft destroyed including one over an airfield in northern France. Three LAM Havocs of No. 93 Squadron operated but did not drop their mines and a Fighter

A second carriageway added since the war now runs through the spot.

Night operation was carried out over Glasgow by three Defiants and six Hurricanes of No. 141 Squadron, stepped up from 12,000 to 20,000 feet at 1,000 feet intervals.

The following crashed near Britain.

1/KG4 Heinkel He 111H-5 (3520). Shot down by night fighter during an attack on Greenock and crashed at Whorlton Park, near Newcastle 3.00 a.m. Obergefr. W. Koch killed. Hptmn. E. Eichler, Fw. F. Olsson and Gefr. H. Schiedlinski captured. Aircraft 5J+IH destroyed.

III/KG40 Heinkel He 111H-5 (4063). Crashed into the sea near the Blackwater Lightship, County Wexford, Eire during a sortie to the Bristol Channel. Oblt. W. Hollborn and Uffz. E. Joseph interned in Eire. Fw. W. Franke and Oberfw. E. Seyfried killed. Aircraft V4+DK lost.

4/KG54 Junkers Ju 88A-5 (6321). Shot down by Flying Officer I. K. S. Joll and Sergeant R. W. Dalton in a Beaufighter of No. 604 Squadron during an attack on Dumbarton. Crashed at Stone Farm, Hiddons Wood, Chawleigh, Devon 12.30 a.m. Obergefr. F. Eisvogel baled out and taken prisoner. Gefr. G. Cavelius and Gefr. H. Beutel killed. Fw. H. Menke baled out but his parachute failed to open and he was killed. Aircraft B3+BM destroyed.
A major recovery by Perry Adams in May 1985 revealed one Jumo 211G-1 engine with its propeller boss and much other wreckage.

Two nights hence, the RAF claimed to have brought down 23 enemy bombers and this picture was said to be one of them. Because it showed an aircraft in close up it had to be approved for release by the AI6 Air Adviser who indicated that the department had no objection to its publication by *The Times* provided the Geschwader badge was deleted — not from any security aspect at home but because it would have helped enemy intelligence establish its identity. Fortunately your Editor's intelligence experts immediately identified the shield as KG4 but no losses on May 7-8 could be found to fit the location. As the original caption states 'one member of crew killed, two escaped, without injury, and one was wounded', it would appear to show one of the Greenock raiders of *Monday* night: 5J+IH down at Whorlton Park, Newcastle.

TUESDAY, MAY 6-7

Sunset: 2130 Sunrise: 0622
Moon: Dusk — 0436 (First Qtr +2)

Major attack on Glasgow/Clydeside. Minor attacks on Liverpool, Plymouth, Newcastle and elsewhere. Attacks on airfields and shipping. Minelaying.

UK — Fair to cloudy in southern Scotland and eastern England; fair or fine elsewhere and cloudless over many areas. Visibility moderate to good, becoming poor locally towards dawn.

The Continent — Fair or fine. Good visibility; some mist later.

Some damage and minor casualties were caused at Lowestoft and Margate, and attacks were made on Manston airfield and the Dover balloon barrage, but little else of consequence occurred during a day in which over-sea activity was the main preoccupation of the Luftwaffe.

Nightfall again brought widespread attacks but, as on the previous night, the main concentration was on Glasgow/Clydeside which was bombed by 232 of the 387 long-range bombers operating. Also over Britain, concentrating on airfields in the East, were 13 long-range night fighters of I/NJG2.

The Clyde area between Greenock and Dumbarton was attacked by 155 aircraft of Luftflotten 2 and 3 between 0010 and 0245 hours. Aiming visually, they dropped 174 tonnes of HE and 38,750 IBs and many fires were started, with one massive explosion in Greenock Gasworks. Glasgow, bombed between 0045 and 0320 hours, received 97 tonnes of HE and 2,304 IBs, delivered visually by 77 aircraft. Better results were obtained, crews claimed, than on the previous night — large fires being seen in the vicinity of shipyards, at a large power station and in an armaments factory; very big explosions also occurred in the south-east part of the town.

Docks and industrial targets were also claimed destroyed by 28 crews sent to Tyneside; again, large fires were started in dock installations at Newcastle, Hebburn and Wallsend in an attack lasting from midnight to 0200. Numerous fires were also reported at Liverpool, attacked by 27 aircraft between 0010 and 0135 hours, while at Plymouth 30 aircraft claimed hits in the docks and in the south part of the town in a raid which started at 2326 and terminated at 0400 hours. Ipswich, Canterbury and Manston airfield were also claimed attacked, as were numerous alternative targets and shipping.

No detailed information is available for Luftflotte 2's contribution, but records show that Luftflotte 3 dispatched 235 aircraft, of which 54 bombed Glasgow, 49 Greenock, 35 Dumbarton, 27 Liverpool, 30 Plymouth, 12 Newcastle and one attacked shipping. Fourteen aircraft bombed alternative targets, nine aborted and three failed to return (an He 111 of III/KG27 and Ju 88s of I/KG76 and I/KG54). Further details of unit participation are not known.

Actual damage at Clydeside was heavy and was especially severe at Greenock where fires were started and casualties were high. A serious fire also developed at Ardeer, and at many places along the Clyde industry and

At the end of the first Clydeside double-attack (March 13-15), of the 12,000 tenements in Clydebank it was stated that only seven remained wholly undamaged. Now it was Greenock's turn. It had earlier been suggested, rather jokingly, that Greenock would never be bombed because of its foul weather where 'it always rains except when it's snowing'. Although this picture is only identified as 'Clydeside', it was taken looking from Serpentine Walk towards Belville Street, an area now totally redeveloped.

A scene more reminiscent of Blitzkrieg in Belgium in 1940 rather than Blitz on Britain in 1941. This is St Andrew's, Carnock Street, Greenock.

private property suffered badly. The heaviest casualties occurred at Greenock, Paisley and in Renfrewshire and for the two consecutive attacks a total of 306 people were killed.

The Merseyside attack was less intense and rather spasmodic in nature. Most of the bombs fell on Liverpool, and the Customs House and the Oxford Street Heart Hospital were both damaged in this raid, in which 32 people were killed. As usual, residential areas were subjected to much bombing.

No serious damage was done at Tyneside, but the Tees area was more severely hit, especially Middlesbrough and West Hartlepool. Industrial damage was not heavy, however. Elsewhere nine people were killed at Aylesham, Kent, and damage to railways occurred at Weymouth. Bombs also fell at several points in East Anglia and South Wales and a power station was damaged at Newton Abbot.

The Clyde guns, in action from 0029 to 0325 hours, fired 3,559 rounds while AA Command in total used nearly 14,000 for two German bombers claimed destroyed.

Including offensive patrols over northern France, Fighter Night layer patrols over Target Areas and 'special interception patrols' by No. 93 Squadron, Fighter Command dispatched 300 aircraft between dusk and dawn. Subsequently 12 enemy aircraft were claimed destroyed, five probably destroyed and seven damaged. At 0110 hours (7th) a Defiant, N3500 of No. 256 Squadron, was shot down by a Ju 88 near Widnes, but the crew of two successfully baled out.

Early on May 6, a Heinkel He 115 taxied into Broadstairs Harbour its crew of four Dutchmen waving a white flag. The following were lost over Britain.

7/KG27 Heinkel He 111H-5 (2513). Shot down by Squadron Leader Pritchard and Sergeant Gledhill in a Beaufighter of No. 600 Squadron which was damaged by return fire. Crashed at Foxwell Farm, Oborne, near Sherborne, Dorset 3.45 a.m. Lt. E. Wullenweber baled out and taken prisoner. Fw. E. Ebert, Oberfw. T. Kowolik and Fw. H. Ottlik killed. Aircraft 1G+BR broke up in air.

A few pathetic belongings salvaged on the corner of Woodhall Terrace in Port Glasgow — neighbour of Greenock on the south bank of the Clyde — where an air raid shelter has received a direct hit.

All this time Liverpool was suffering its 'May Week' raids — night after night in the most prolonged provincial attack — which had begun to have a serious effect. Virtually half the berths were put out of action at one stage or another. Road and rail access to the docks was blocked and tonnages landed fell by three-quarters. Over 66,000 houses were destroyed or damaged. Churchill concluded that 'had the enemy persisted [with the attacks] the Battle of the Atlantic would have been even more closely run than it was'. This is the South Huskisson Branch Dock where the ammunition ship, the *Malakand*, received a direct hit on May 3, the resulting explosion devastating the dock.

5/KG30 Junkers Ju 88A-5 (7177). Shot down by Flying Officer Day in a Defiant of No. 141 Squadron. Made forced landing on the north side of Holy Island, Northumberland 4.00 a.m. Uffz. H. Schaber, Gefr. H. Nöske, Fw. P. Graupner and Gefr. W. Arndt all captured. Aircraft 4D+EN burnt by crew.

2/KG53 Heinkel He 111H-5 (3550). Crashed at the St George's Mental Hospital, Morpeth, Northumberland 11.59 p.m. cause uncertain. Uffz. K. Rassloff, Gefr. E. Lernbass, Uffz. K. Simon, Gefr. W. Schmidt and Gefr. H. Wittenbaum all taken prisoner. Aircraft A1+CK destroyed.

2/106 Junkers Ju 88A-5 (0662). Shot down by Squadron Leader E. C. Wolfe and Sergeant A. E. Ashcroft in a Defiant of No. 141 Squadron. Aircraft dived into the ground and exploded at Newlands, Lennoxtown, Stirlingshire 2.00 a.m. Hptmn. G. Hansmann (Staffelkapitän) and Oblt. W. Coenen killed. Oberfw. E. Langanki and Fw. W. Müller baled out and taken prisoner. Aircraft M2+CK totally disintegrated.

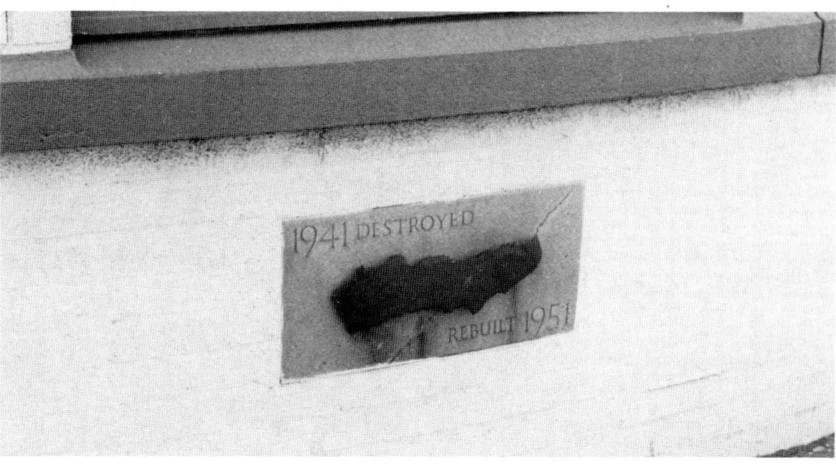

A sense of history in Birkenhead. Dave Smith spotted this interesting relic of 1941 — a piece of bomb casing — set in a wall of a factory on the corner of Cleveland Street and Duke Street.

WEDNESDAY, MAY 7-8

Sunset: 2132 Sunrise: 0620
Moon: Dusk — 0504 (First Qtr +3)

Major attacks on Liverpool/Birkenhead and Hull. Minor bombing elsewhere, armed sea reconnaissance, minelaying and attacks on airfields.

UK — Mainly fair or fine with little or no cloud in some places. Visibility moderate to good, some industrial haze later.
The Continent — Similar to UK.

There was little German activity during the day and no bombs fell on land. During the night there was again widespread bombing with major attacks on both the East and West Coasts. A total of 346 bombers was engaged, backed by 18 night fighters, with 166 crews reporting over Liverpool and 72 over Hull.

The attack on port installations at Liverpool started at 0010 and terminated at 0340, the raiders dropping 232 tonnes of HE (44

The South Huskisson dock was filled in, burying the remains of the *Malakand*. With the removal of the overhead dock railway, the vantage point for Stewart Bale in 1941, we had to make do with a panorama from a little lower down.

On Thursday night the Luftwaffe finally left Liverpool alone to deal with Hull but on Wednesday the final big attack went in. On the left the telephone exchange with the back of Woodhouse's Lord Street premises on the right. In the distance the Queen Victoria memorial and the National Bank.

SC 1000, 47 SC 500, 446 SC/SD 250, nine LZZ 250, six Flam, 547 SC/SD 50, eight Type 'A' and 18 Type 'B' mines) and 29,064 incendiaries. Initially, participating crews had some difficulty in bombing visually, but an improvement in the weather quickly remedied the situation. Very good results were obtained and very big fires were reported at Bootle, in warehouses at Stanley Dock, near Waterloo Dock and in Alexandra Dock where a very large explosion also occurred. At Clarence Dock another big explosion, followed by an oil fire, followed the dropping of an LMB parachute mine.

The same heartrending scenes that we have seen performed at the other badly-hit cities were enacted at Anfield Cemetery, where a final total of 554 unclaimed and unidentified victims were buried in this long communal grave.

Kingston-upon-Hull received their softening up on Wednesday, somewhat by accident as a result of aircraft en route for Liverpool being diverted to the secondary target because of poor conditions over the primary. Those photographs which survive, taken by the *Hull Daily Mail*, are not segregated between this first raid or the follow up, but we know that almost the whole of the riverside was razed by fire. This is Eagle Mills — then and now.

Hull's industrial and dock installations received 110 tonnes of HE (18 SC 1000, seven SC 500, 62 SC 250, one LZZ 250, 18 Flam 250, 139 SC/SD 50, ten LMA and 56 LMB) and 9,648 IBs in an attack lasting from 0035 to 0241 hours. Part of the force bound for Liverpool was ordered to attack Hull instead (by W/T while en route) because of the poor conditions reported over Merseyside by the first attackers. Nevertheless, despite the rather impromptu nature of the attack, very good results were obtained; visual bomb aiming was carried out by most crews and very large fires were reported in installations and the timber yard adjacent to the Victoria Docks. An extensive fire area was also seen to the west of the docks and near three large mills situated on the river. Some 20 to 30 fires were also seen in the town.

Docks and industrial installations were also claimed bombed at Hartlepool (by five aircraft), West Hartlepool (nine aircraft), Middlesbrough and the large chemical works at Billingham (by five aircraft), Barrow-in-Furness (by eight aircraft allocated the Vickers-Armstrongs dockyard as a CP), Plymouth (by ten aircraft) and Bristol (16 aircraft). Further, as alternatives, other crews bombed Great Yarmouth, Ipswich, Exmouth, Falmouth and airfields in the vicinity of Dorchester and Lincoln, while in a Zerstörziele-type attack a lone aircraft attempted to destroy the entrance lock-gates to the Manchester Ship Canal at Eastham with two Type 'B' parachute mines dropped visually from a height of 2,200 metres (7,200 feet).

Returning crews reported considerable night fighter activity over the East and South Coasts, over the Bristol Channel area near Cardiff and Bristol, over Hull, Liverpool and Plymouth and on the approach routes to Merseyside. This, it was felt, explained the heavy losses sustained — Luftflotte 3 alone reported nine aircraft missing (four He 111s of I/KG55, single He 111s of I/KG27, II/KG27, III/KG27, KGr100 and II/KG55, and a Ju 88 of III/KG76).

Luftflotte 3's participation in the attack on Liverpool was as follows:

I/KG27: 8 He 111, 0053-0155
II/KG27: 8 He 111, 0105-0145
III/KG55: 15 He 111, 0030-0140
KGr100: 7 He 111, 0054-0132
KG76: 17 Ju 88, 0030-0150
I/KG77: 3 Ju 88, 0105-0115
II and III/KG77: 13 Ju 88, 0025-0157
I/KG54: 11 Ju 88, 0120-0230

II/KG54: 10 Ju 88, 0223-0340
III/KG54: 6 Ju 88, 0047-0135
I/KG55: 14 He 111, 0125-0220 (large fires followed detonation of a BM 1000 at 0210 hours)
II/KG55: 10 He 111, 0147-0215
III/KG55: 15 He 111, 0055-0130
Stab/KG55: 3 He 111, 0100-0210

As claimed by the Luftwaffe, considerable damage was caused in this, the seventh consecutive raid on Merseyside. Bootle was particularly badly hit on this occasion and not until 1700 hours on May 8 was the fire situation reasonably in hand. Some 14,000 houses were damaged, between 4,000 and 5,000 destroyed and an estimated 20,000 people rendered homeless; with 11 out of 12 rest centres put out of action the difficulties of accommodating the homeless were enormous. Fires and damage covered a wide area and all parts of the docks were affected; the railway system was badly disorganised and with many blocked roads transportation became a major problem. In the seven consecutive nights of bombing the Liverpool/Birkenhead area had suffered terribly; at one stage 70 out of 144 berths were put out of action and blocked road and rail facilities brought all movements in and out of the

The statue of Andrew Marvel, local 17th century poet, satirist and diplomat, stands supreme amid the blazing junction of Jameson and Bond Streets. Having survived the Blitz when all around him disappeared, he too has now gone from the scene having been moved to Hull Grammar School in 1963.

The junction of Jameson with King Street. Half the shops in the city centre were destroyed, including five department stores.

docks to a virtual standstill. For a period the actual tonnage landed was only 25 per cent of normal and total casualties for the seven nights were 1,900 killed and 1,450 seriously injured. Homeless people eventually totalled more than 70,000; 66,000 houses were destroyed or damaged, ten hospitals were hit and utilities very badly affected.

The attack on Hull produced extensive residential and commercial damage but industry, on the whole, was not seriously affected. The main weight of bombs fell on the town centre and damage in the docks was not severe; no shipping suffered damage although UXBs, damage to roads and the dislocation of the railway system interfered with dock working. Communications and public utilities suffered severely and the Paragon Station was closed for a while. Some 10,000 people were made homeless, with 32,000 houses damaged or destroyed, and the Royal Infirmary was among the buildings hit. Fires were numerous, with 150 burning at one time, but all were reported to be well in hand by 0655 hours.

At Manchester most of the bombing occurred at Stretford and Trafford Park and many fires were started, many of them in commercial premises. Serious fires broke out at Eccles and Ashton-under-Lyne.

Other incidents occurred at Altrincham, where Government property was damaged, at Bromborough, Cheshire, where a maternity home was hit, and at Barrow-in-Furness, where industry and private property were affected.

In the two attacks of Wednesday and Thursday nearly 450 were killed and ten per cent of the population made homeless. Trekking began in earnest and Mass-Observation estimated that a third of the population had quit the city by mid-May. As such a sight would for the bystanders at any disaster, the 'watch tower' beside the collapsed Prudential building at the junction of King Edward and Paragon Streets provided a focus of attention on Thursday; later it had to be demolished.

Comparisons like this almost make one wonder if one is dreaming. Could the forecourt of the City Hall really be the same place?

Damping down the flames on Thursday morning. Then Chapel Street was just a side turning off Jameson Street but in the post-war reconstruction it doubled its width with the completion of Queen's House in 1952.

Between May 15–20, a photographic survey was carried out on the instructions of the Chief Engineer of Hull Docks to illustrate the damage caused by both attacks. *Left:* **Riverside Quay and** *right:* **Alexandra Dock.**

In Bristol 82 incidents involved damage to both industrial premises and private property. The railway system suffered and while many fires resulted, all were under control by 0500 hours. Many well known public buildings were damaged, including the Merchants Hall, and three hospitals were hit. Two important factories were hit but damage to utilities was not serious. Some 20 people were killed.

Fires which were started in Plymouth were soon mastered, but at Teignmouth 11 people were killed and at Shieldhall, Glasgow, a serious fire resulted. In attacks on a number of airfields in the North and North Midlands, no serious damage was inflicted. At Stockport the Fairey Aviation works sustained some damage but a fire there was quickly brought under control. Bombs also fell on Great Yarmouth and Cleethorpes.

AA guns were in action on many sites during the night and nearly 12,000 rounds of ammunition were expended for six raiders claimed destroyed. Fighter Command put up 339 aircraft on dusk, night and dawn patrols and set a new claims record of 21 enemy aircraft destroyed, four probably destroyed and 13 damaged. A Fighter Night Layer patrol of 12 aircraft was maintained over Liverpool and resulted in the claimed destruction of three German aircraft. Two night fighters were lost, one of them a Beaufighter of No. 604 Squadron which was hit by return fire from an enemy aircraft destroyed off The Needles. The pilot, Sergeant Wright, was wounded in the encounter.

'The most spectacular ruins in Hull are along the banks of the river Hull (a small tributary of the Humber) — particularly the east side. Here one sees the still smouldering remains of the tall flour mills and stores. Ranks, the largest of all, Spillers, Gilboys, Rishworth, Ingleby and Lofthouse are completely destroyed. Only the CWS and Paul's remain undamaged. The workers from the ruined plants now work in these two. Further east and north-east, the industrial and working-class residential areas have suffered heavily. The huge Reckitts works (blue, starch, polish) are almost completely burnt out, and a large power-station is almost unrecognizable. The gasworks looks almost untouched, but Hull was without gas for six weeks after the May raids. Whole streets of working-class houses are down. One of the most impressive bomb-holes is on the Holderness Road. There, there is a crater almost 20 yards across, filled with greenish water, in which planks and barrels are floating. By the side of the crater stands the remainder of the Ritz cinema.' Mass-Observation visitor to Hull in May 1941.

Although of necessity this book has had to concentrate on the major events — and Liverpool, Belfast and Clydeside have occupied our thoughts since the beginning of May — we must not forget that the Luftwaffe still had the strength to be able to bomb targets at the same time throughout Britain. For example while we were preoccupied with Liverpool on May 3-4, bombs fell on Sunderland, three large HEs straddling Fulwell, destroying Redby School. In Duke Street (*above*) shelters were no match for the power of the bomb and Mr and Mrs Anthony Storey were killed with their daughters Audrey 4 and Edith 13 months. Mr and Mrs Frederick Forster were also victims while 200 yards away in Westcott Terrace nine lay dead. . . .

A total of thirteen aircraft were lost.

Stab I/KG4 Heinkel He 111H-5 (3987). Believed that shot down by Flying Officer R. P. Stevens in a Hurricane of No. 151 Squadron. Made a forced landing on the beach at Withernsea, Yorkshire 3.00 a.m. Oblt. zur See P. Tholen and Oberfw. H. Schröder taken prisoner. Fw. W. Schreiber and Oberfw. A. Hoffmann killed. Aircraft 5J+ZB wrecked.

Geschwader Stab/KG27 Heinkel He 111P (1647). Shot down by Flying Officer Howden of No. 600 Squadron in a Beaufighter. Crashed at Stock Lane, Langford, Weston-super-Mare 12.12 a.m. Oblt. J. Maron, Oberfw. H. Ronge, Fw. H. Dietrich, Uffz. H. Eggert and Gefr. H. Hilger all baled out and taken prisoner. Aircraft 1G+NA destroyed.

Several relics, including Heinz Dietrich's named flying Helmet taken at the time of the crash held by Ken Wakefield.

Stab II/KG27 Heinkel He 111P (2862). Shot down by Flying Officer R. S. Woodward in a Beaufighter of No. 600 Squadron. Crashed at Farringford Farm, Freshwater, Isle of Wight 1.40 a.m. Oberfw. W. Range, Uffz. K. Dillinger and Uffz. A. Habesreiter killed. Oberfw. H. Laube baled out and taken prisoner. Aircraft 1G+CC wrecked.

A major excavation mounted by Steve Vizard in 1982 recovered both Daimler-Benz DB601 engines, one undercarriage leg with tyre along with many other items now on display in the Tangmere Aviation Museum.

7/KG27 Heinkel He 111H-5 (1639). Shot down by Squadron Leader J. Cunningham and Sergeant Rawnsley in a Beaufighter of No. 604 Squadron. Crashed at Andersea Farm, Weston Zoyland, Somerset 11.30 p.m. Oberfw. H. Laschinski and Fw. O. Willrich baled out and taken prisoner. Fw. H. Schier and Fw. F. Klemm killed. Aircraft 1G+DR destroyed.

Investigated by the South West Aircraft Recovery Group and Severnside Aviation Society. A manufacturer's plate bearing Wn.1639 and other parts found.

Stab/KG53 Heinkel He 111H-3 (3210). Shot down by Sergeant Johnson and Sergeant Aitchison in a Defiant of No. 255 Squadron. Bombs exploded destroying the aircraft at Scrooby, near Bawtry, Nottinghamshire 12.30 a.m. Hptmn. E Kölmel killed, Fw. G. Merten, Gefr. E Schönberger, Fw. H. Müller and Gefr. O. Wilfingseder baled out and taken prisoner. Aircraft A1+BA totally destroyed.

1/KG55 Heinkel He 111P-4 (1724). Failed to return from attack on Liverpool, precise cause unknown. Lt. G. Becker, Uffz. E. Faulhaber, Oberfw. G. Lunz, Uffz. E. Vierser captured. Aircraft G1+GH lost.

1/KG55 Heinkel He 111P-4 (2871). Shot down by Flight Lieutenant E. C. Deansley and Sergeant W. J. Scott in a Defiant of No. 256 Squadron. Crashed at Hazel Grove, Stockport 1.20 a.m. Oblt. A. Knörringer, Oberfw. K. Kohlhepp, Uffz. L. Rathsam and Oberfw. A. Kloss baled out and taken prisoner. Aircraft G1+LH totally disintegrated.

3/KG55 Heinkel He 111P-4 (2951). Crashed into the sea off Portland 12.40 a.m. Believed shot down by Sergeant Wright and Sergeant Vaughan in a Beaufighter of No. 604 Squadron. Lt. A. Wolff, Uffz. W. Amann, Uffz. E. Ante, Fw. P. Tibusch and Flg. C Mildenberger all killed. Aircraft G1+KL lost.

On return from patrol, when 15 miles from Bournemouth, the Beaufighter caught fire. Wright and Vaughan baled out and were picked up from the sea.

3/KG55 Heinkel He 111P-4 (2874). Shot down by Pilot Officer D. Toone and Flying Officer R. L. Lamb in a Defiant of No. 256 Squadron. Crashed near Bagillt police station, river Dee Marshes, Flintshire 1.40 a.m. Lt. H. Dunkerbeck and Fw. F. Kitzing taken prisoner. Uffz. A. Gentzsch and Uffz. J. Salm killed. Aircraft G1+LL destroyed.

6/KG55 Heinkel He 111P-4 (2908). Shot down by Flight Lieutenant D. R. West and Sergeant Adams in a Defiant of No. 256 Squadron. Only one of the Defiant's four Brownings would fire but the pilot was determined to bring down one of the enemy aircraft 'even if it meant throwing the control column at it'. Crashed at Llwyn Knottia Farm, Wrexham 2.00 a.m. Oberfw. W. Hottenrott, Uffz. P. Götze, Oberfw. K. Gerstle and Oberfw. H. Reese all killed. Aircraft G1+HP exploded in air.

Site excavated by Wartime Aircraft Recovery Group. Armour plate and various items recovered.

StabIII/KG76 Junkers Ju 88A-5 (6213). Believed damaged by fighter. After flying low with engine failure hit hillside at Goldsitch Moss, Moss End Farm, Gradbach, Staffordshire 1.00 a.m. Major D. H. von Ziehlberg, Oblt. W. Lemke, Oberfw. R. Schwalbe and Fw. G. Mahl all killed. Aircraft F1+AD burnt out.

Site investigated by Moorland Aircraft Recovery Group 1976 and Derbyshire Historical Aircraft Society 1970. Numerous items recovered.

3/KGr100 Heinkel He 111H-2 (2432). Shot down by fire from a Defiant. Broke up in air and crashed at Egerton Hall Farm, Malpas, Cheshire 1.30 a.m. Uffz. K. Schmidt and Gefr. O. Schimmeyer baled out and taken prisoner. Gefr. O. Rittershaus and Uffz. E. Hirnschall killed. Aircraft 6N+FL disintegrated.

Small fragments gathered from the site by the Warplane Wreck Investigation Group.

May 8, 1941

'. . . where have you gone to?
the wind howls,
the waves are foaming and,
moving on their way . . .'
HEINRICH HEINE

Now I have lost the desire to write about flying.

We have been to Liverpool, and have had a disturbed night of it. The deviating directional beam, remarkably, appeared not to have been interfered with. But very soon we received a radio message: 'Stop using the directional beam. Night fighters have got on to it!'

For once at last on a good course, for which dead-reckoning and radio navigation had given the same result, we were quite simply most reluctant to make an uncertain change of course. Let them first of all find us, in the pitch darkness! And we were fortunate. We landed again at Villaroche at about 04.00 hours, unmolested.

There are four of the crews in our Gruppe missing; two of them from our No. 1 Staffel. And who were among them? With Oberleutnant Knörringer, my friend Rathsam. With Leutnant Becker, my friend Edgar Faulhaber. With Leutnant Wolff, my Willi Amann.

I cannot believe that it is true, though they are indeed not the first ones. Schwering and my friend Ehrlich, from No. 1 Staffel, have been missing since the Greenock flight. And in mid-April even the Gruppe Commander did not return.

A night and a day pass by. No news.

Yesterday I had spent the whole afternoon with Edgar Faulhaber in the park around the château, talking about God and the world. I had talked about not having any hope of surviving. But he was far from having any thoughts about death. Jurak, my pilot, came across us and all three of us were photographed together.

Even on the runway Edgar came over to me for a minute, and we didn't leave each other until the engines were started up. At Glasgow he was still reporting release of the bombs and engine damage. From the others, nothing. But couldn't a search be made for them?

Leutnant Wolff, with Amann as his observer, had orders to destroy sluice-gates at Liverpool with a low-level attack. Rathsam had just celebrated his twentieth birthday and quite by chance was not flying with his usual crew. Shortly before the flight briefing, already in my flying suit, I dropped in with a bunch of flowers, to congratulate him. What will his girl say?

And then there is my great friend Willi Amann, whom I have so much admired. He wanted to be a priest. I hope he is still alive. When I think how in Poland, in Cracow in the barracks dormitory, we used to spend the whole night discussing indefinable problems that were beyond our reach . . . I had never been able to talk to anybody like that. And is the fact that he and the others are no longer here irrevocable? God help them and me.

As I wander through the little town, and can't look at anyone any more without bursting into tears, our old radio Oberfeldwebel, a soldier from the pre-war days, is coming towards me on the other side of the street. We have never liked each other much. But today the old Oberfeldwebel makes a point of greeting me as 'My young lad' from afar; before I myself can greet him as his rank requires . . . This is his way of trying to show me that he shares my sadness at the death of my best friends.

ROBERT GÖTZ

2/NJG2 Dornier Do 17Z-10 (2843). Shot down whilst on night intruder sortie by Pilot Officer D. W. Thompson and Pilot Officer L. D. Britain in a Beaufighter of No. 25 Squadron. Crashed at Carrington, near Boston, Lincolnshire 12.30 a.m. Uffz. G. Herden and Uffz. H. Thomas (injured) baled out and taken prisoner. Fw. W. Lettenmeier baled out too low and killed. Aircraft R4+GK destroyed.

Major recovery by the Lincolnshire Aircraft Recovery Group in 1984 unearthed both engines and undercarriages, tail wheel, and numerous other items.

. . . but the grief was not all one sided. As we have seen the RAF claimed 21 victories that night but in fact only 13 German aircraft failed to return. of these, three were from KG55 — Robert Götz's unit. Fortunately his colleague Ludwig Rathsam turned out to be a prisoner, but Willibald Amann, 'my Willi' was dead.

This smoking crater at Hazel Grove, Stockport, might have been the last resting place of four more men from his unit, Oberleutnant Knörringer and his crew, had they not safely baled out before it disintegrated.

The widening of the air offensive by the Luftwaffe on Wednesday to include inland targets led Home Security to make a special note of the addition of industrial targets in the Manchester area. 'In this connection', wrote the Duty Officer, 'it may be interesting to note that a review of his scale of effort at night since September 1940 shows that if the level of the past five nights can be maintained for a further two, it would exceed his previous maximum for any one week by rather over 400 aircraft. While he will presumably take the fullest possible advantage of the present moonlight period, it is open to doubt whether he can sustain for much longer without a break the present weight of attack.' These firemen are pictured on Thursday morning on the corner of Miller Street and Rochdale Road.

THURSDAY, MAY 8-9

Sunset: 2133 Sunrise: 0619
Moon: Dusk — 0534 (Full −3)

Major attacks on Hull and Nottingham. Heavy attack on Sheffield with minor attacks elsewhere. Anti-shipping patrols, attacks on airfields and long-range night fighter operations. Minelaying.

UK — Broken cloud dispersing during the night with moderate to good visibility; some mist later. Much cloud with rain or drizzle in Scotland.

The Continent — Little or no cloud. Visibility mainly good. Broken cloud with a few scattered showers over Holland and north-west Germany.

German daylight operations were again of little consequence with only ineffective machine-gunning at Hythe and Deal reported, but nightfall brought on widespread attacks carried out by 389 long-range and light bombers and 27 long-range night fighters. The pattern was again one of multiple attacks, with three centres — Hull, Nottingham and Sheffield — bearing the brunt of the bombing.

Nottingham, attacked between 0030 and 0238 hours by 95 aircraft of Luftflotte 3, received 137 tonnes of HE and 6,804 IBs. The Schwerpunkt centred on an arms factory immediately to the north-east of the railway workshops and, bombing visually, crews reported about ten large fires in this area and to the east of it. At 0100 hours several large explosions seemed to indicate the successful destruction of the nearby gasworks. With most of the bombs falling in the designated TA, good results were anticipated. Participating were:

KG1: 19 Ju 88, 0042-0140
KG76: 31 Ju 88, 0043-0205
KG77: 7 Ju 88, 0115-0143
KG77 and KG1: 26 Ju 88, 0100-0238
III/KG26: 5 He 111, 0047-0112 (Y-Verfahren and visual bombing)
II/KG27: 7 He 111, 0030-0115

Nottingham was reached by 95 of the 107 crews dispatched but seven crews then continued to Derby which they also attacked with part of their bomb load. Altogether, then, Derby was attacked by 23 aircraft, all from Luftflotte 3, with the Rolls Royce factory and a group of works (two rolling mills and a machine factory) their objectives. They dropped 14 tonnes of HE and 18,432 IBs on this area, aiming visually, and crews saw large fires in the TA, in the town centre and in the Midland Waggon works. The units involved in this attack were:

I/KG27: 7 He 111, 0025-0115
II/KG27: 2 He 111, 0110-0220
III/KG27: 12 He 111, 0145-0215
KGr100: 2 He 111, 0020-0038

During target selection 44 aircraft were earmarked for the Derby attack, but many aborted or bombed alternative targets. Sheffield was the intended main target of the night but when early arrivals found weather conditions unsuitable the majority of the force was ordered by W/T to divert to Hull. Nevertheless, 34 crews claimed to have found and bombed Sheffield where their CP extended from the town centre to the north-east along a string of steel works in the direction of Rotherham. With 8/10ths to 10/10ths cloud, visual bombing was extremely difficult and led to the many diversions, but it was claimed that 53 tonnes of HE and

When taking this comparison for us, Alex King drew our attention to one of the hand-operated public fire alarms (on the right-hand kerb in the 1941 photograph) which could then be found all over Manchester. The ornate columns once supported the tram wires of Route 51 which ceased running in 1940. In the present day view Victoria Station can be seen in the background.

28,880 IBs were successfully delivered. Individual targets could not be recognised but it appeared that large fires were started in or around the Tinsley steel works and in that general area, but a truly damaging attack did not seem probable. Units claiming to have bombed Sheffield were:

I/KG54: 9 Ju 88, 0047-0140
III/KG54: 2 Ju 88, 0110-0125
II/KG55: 1 He 111, 0115
III/KG55: 5 He 111, 0035-0105
Stab/KG55: 1 He 111, 0040

Although not planned to be attacked, Hull actually received the heaviest raid of the night, carried out by 120 aircraft that had been ordered to other targets initially, with most of them bound for Sheffield. Upon arrival over Hull diverted crews found favourable weather and all bombed visually. Between 0008 and 0340 hours they dropped 167 tonnes of HE and 19,467 IBs, allegedly over the industrial area in the eastern and north-eastern districts of the town. Numerous large fires duly erupted over the entire city with the biggest in the vicinity of the Albert and William Wright Docks and among factories along the river. Explosions and fires were also reported in the gasworks and, overall, very good results were expected. The attackers comprised 71 aircraft from Luftflotte 2 and, as follows, 49 from Luftflotte 3:

KG76: 2 Ju 88, 0055-0210
KG77: 2 Ju 88, 0055-0100
III/KG27: 1 He 111, 0144
KGr100: 4 He 111, 0045-0107
II/KG54: 7 Ju 88, 0200-0304
III/KG54: 6 Ju 88, 0117-0134
I/KG55: 8 He 111, 0050-0140
II/KG55: 7 He 111, 0120-0340
III/KG55: 11 He 111, 0045-0130
Stab/KG55: 1 He 111, 0055

Altogether 88 aircraft of Luftflotte 3 failed to reach their designated primary targets and of the 224 dispatched, six were lost (one Ju 88 of II/KG1 and He 111s of III/KG40, I/KG27, II/KG55 and II/KG54, with two aircraft of the latter unit crashing in France).

Various other operations were carried out during the night including attacks by single aircraft on various Zerstörziele including the torpedo factory at Portland, the shipyard at Plymouth, the High Duty Alloys factory at Slough (attacked by two aircraft from a low height) and the Westland Aircraft factory at Yeovil. Barrow-in-Furness was also bombed by a number of aircraft, as was Plymouth in a second attack by ten aircraft, while light bombers struck at a number of targets including one by two aircraft on a factory at Chelmsford at 0215 hours, dropping two SC 500s from 200 metres (650 feet).

Damage actually inflicted on Hull was

For the second night running, weather conditions caused Hull to be upgraded from secondary to primary target — a good illustration how the hand of fate was inexorably tied up with the hand of Nature. Kingston-upon-Hull's easy approach across the North Sea meant that it was an ideal target and Herbert Morrison considered that it was the town which had suffered most — 'night after night Hull had no peace'. In the event, forces were split fairly evenly on Thursday between it and Nottingham, which suffered its first heavy raid of the war. The *Nottingham Guardian* published this shot of damage in Friar Lane, in their 'Review of the Blitz' in June.

The caretaker of Moot Hall was missing after the blast; his body was found later in Burton's window on the opposite side of the road where he had lain unnoticed among the tailor's dummies.

Almost a German goal at the Notts County ground in Meadow Lane.

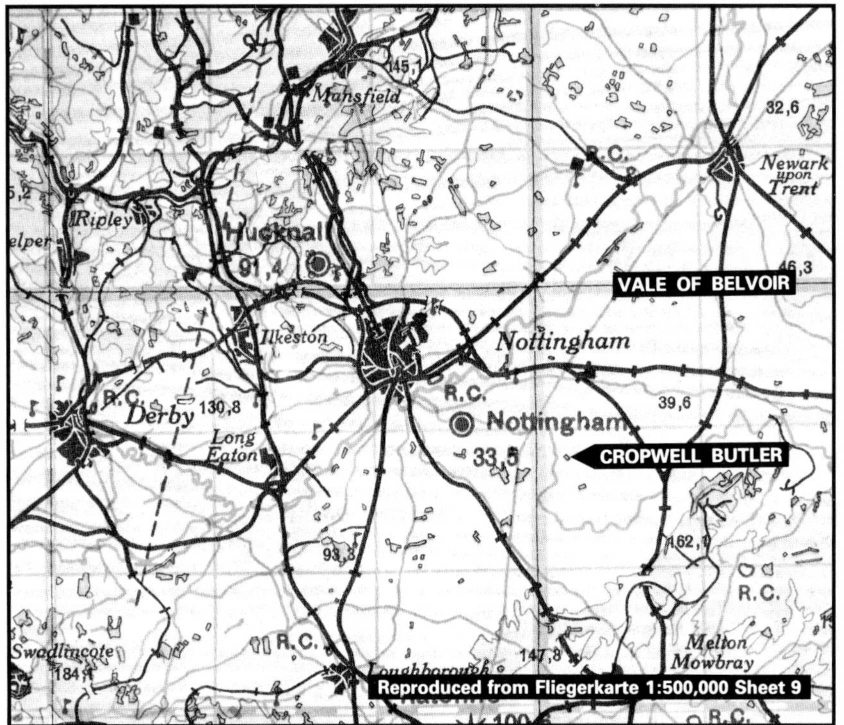

In his account of *The Second World War* published in 1950, Churchill uses the raid as an instance of British success at interrupting the Luftwaffe's navigational beams: 'During 1941 we went on deflecting the German beams despite their various improvements. An example may be cited. On the night of May 8 the Germans planned two attacks, the first upon the Rolls-Royce works at Derby and the second on Nottingham. Through our interference with their beams, which were set upon Derby, they bombed instead Nottingham, where small fires were still burning from the previous night. Their original error then carried their second attack to the Vale of Belvoir, about as far from Nottingham as Nottingham is from Derby. The German communiqué claimed the destruction of the Rolls-Royce works at Derby, which they never got near. Two hundred and thirty high-explosive bombs and a large number of incendiaries were however unloaded in the open country. The total casualties there were two chickens.' Exactly the same example was also cited by Basil Collier seven years later in the official history *The Defence of the United Kingdom*. Bombs certainly fell north-east of Derby and east of Nottingham, the authors of *Derby at War* (who have been quoted before) stating that 'Nottingham would have been hit more heavily had it not been for the lighting of a Starfish site at Cropwell Butler on the same bearing and distance from Nottingham as Nottingham is from Derby.' Ken Wakefield adds that, as far as German records are concerned, there is no proof to substantiate the claims either way. As Starfish sites were under the control of 80 Wing (*see Volume 1, pages 223-229*), the Derby/Nottingham affair could be a demonstration of the effect of electronic and physical counter-measures at their very best.

heavier than on the previous night with 200 incidents reported. Damage was particularly heavy in east Hull where fires were intense and concentrated. Casualties were heavy and in the two nights were in excess of 440 killed; some 30,000 people were rendered homeless. There were extensive fires in the city centre and in the docks, the working of which was seriously affected by the dislocation caused to the railway. Utility services, on the other hand, escaped lightly and the water supply was maintained.

At Nottingham the city centre and Leenside area were most affected; 209 incidents were reported and included one serious, 22 medium and 22 small fires, all of which were in hand by 0530. The Shire Hall and two schools were set on fire and a convent was damaged, but residential and commercial premises bore the brunt of the attack. There were two serious shelter incidents and total casualties in Nottingham were in excess of 150 killed. Nearby at West Bridgeford another 40 were killed and several more at Beeston. Elsewhere in the North another 1,000 people were made homeless at Barrow, sixteen people were killed at Doncaster and casualties also occurred in Sheffield.

In the South a few incidents and casualties occurred in London, and at Great Yarmouth there were seven fatalities when an isolation hospital was hit. At Chelmsford, where the

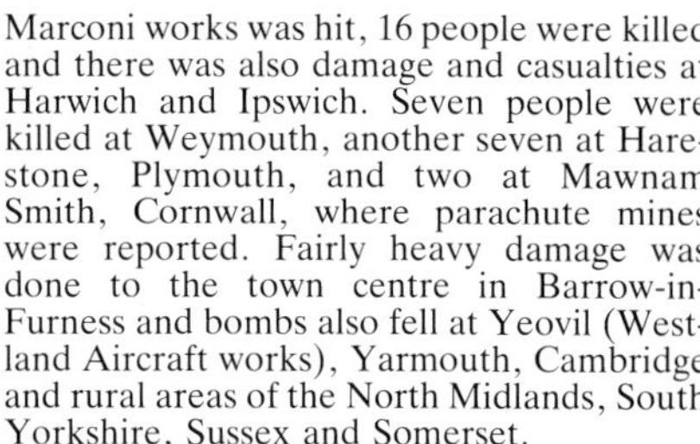

Marconi works was hit, 16 people were killed and there was also damage and casualties at Harwich and Ipswich. Seven people were killed at Weymouth, another seven at Harestone, Plymouth, and two at Mawnam Smith, Cornwall, where parachute mines were reported. Fairly heavy damage was done to the town centre in Barrow-in-Furness and bombs also fell at Yeovil (Westland Aircraft works), Yarmouth, Cambridge and rural areas of the North Midlands, South Yorkshire, Sussex and Somerset.

Just under 8,000 rounds of heavy AA ammunition were used during the night, including 254 at Nottingham and 210 at Sheffield, for three enemy aircraft claimed destroyed.

Fighter Command dispatched 324 aircraft on patrols between dusk and dawn. These included offensive patrols over enemy airfields, layer patrols over Target Areas and aerial mining sorties by No. 93 Squadron. Twelve enemy aircraft were claimed destroyed, two probably destroyed and five damaged. Fighter Night patrols were flown over Hull by 15 Defiants of No. 255 Squadron, two Spitfires of No. 65 Squadron and two Hurricanes of No. 401 Squadron, with No. 255 Squadron claiming six raiders destroyed. Over Derby patrols were flown by six Hurricanes of No. 402 Squadron and nine Spitfires of No. 66 Squadron, with four Hurricanes of No. 256 Squadron employed over Barrow. A Defiant of No. 256 Squadron was lost in a combat with an enemy aircraft near St Helens, but the crew escaped.

During the day, JG3 were involved in a combat off Deal and lost four Messerschmitt Bf 109s. Two were shot down into the Channel. Later an aircraft flown by Lt. J. Pfeiffer of 4/JG53 was shot down whilst engaged in the search for the previous aircraft.

1(F)/123 Junkers Ju 88A-5 (0444). Believed that which crashed into the mouth of the river Tay 4.00 p.m. Body of Fw. G. Knappe recovered from the sea. Fw. J. Hauberg, Oberfw. L. Knoch and Uffz. K. Hoffmann all killed. Aircraft 4U+KH lost.

Some sources suggest that this could have been the aircraft claimed the previous day by pilots of No. 43 Squadron and that the date of the loss according to Luftwaffe records is wrong.

Never was the saying 'One man's meat, another man's poison' more true than on Thursday night. Churchill's succinct account fails to mention that Derby's lucky escape ended up killing 156 in Nottingham, which received nearly 90 per cent of all its wartime bombs on that single night. One fell on the University College in Shakespeare Street — now beautifully repaired and part of Trent Polytechnic.

1/JG3 Messerschmitt Bf 109F-2 (5467). Shot down by fire from Hurricanes of No. 302 Squadron and broke up in air. Crashed at Tenterden, Kent 12.45 p.m. Lt. G. Pöpel baled out and taken prisoner. Aircraft 3+ totally destroyed.

Losses at night close to Britain were as follows.

2/KG27 Heinkel He 111H-5 (4019). Shot down by Flying Officer Braham and Sergeant Ross in a Beaufighter of No. 29 Squadron. Crashed on Wimbledon Common, South West London 12.10 a.m. Lt. D. Stähle, Obergefr. F. Senft, Gefr. H. Berner and Obergefr. A. Weitz all killed. Aircraft 1G+MK wrecked.

III/KG40 Heinkel He 111H-3 (3333). During a sortie over St George's Channel, crashed into the sea off South Stack, Holyhead, Anglesey. Cause unknown. Oblt. H. Waldvogel and Oberfw. H. Lehmann killed. Bodies of Oberfw. K. Raub and Oberfw. F. Resch found washed up at Holyhead. Aircraft V4+BH lost.

4/KG53 Heinkel He 111H-5 (4006). Shot down by a Defiant of No. 255 Squadron. Crashed at Sunk Island Road, Patrington, near Hull 2.00 a.m. Uffz. F. Magie baled out and taken prisoner. Uffz. G. Reinelt, Uffz. J. Kalle and Obergefr. R. Lorenz killed. Gefr. H. Wulf missing. Aircraft A1+FM destroyed.

6/KG53 Heinkel He 111H-5 (4042). Shot down by a Defiant of No. 255 Squadron. Crashed at Wellings Farm, Patrington, Hull 1.30 a.m. Uffz. H. Teschke baled out and taken prisoner. Gefr. W. London, Gefr. J. Kaminski, Gefr. H-J. Stieglitz and Gefr. H. Decker killed. Aircraft A1+CW destroyed.

6/KG55 Heinkel He 111P-4 (3000). Damaged by a Defiant from No. 255 Squadron. Made forced landing at Long Riston, Yorkshire 1.40 a.m. Lt. G. Ender and Uffz. B. Schakat killed. Fw. G. Schopf and Fw. H. Muller taken prisoner. Aircraft G1+FP wrecked.

At the Meadow Lane bakery of the Nottingham Co-operative Society night shift workers had gone down to the two basement shelters — one under the bread baking section, the other beneath the confectionary department — when both received direct hits. Fred Kummer, a member of the works fire party, was there: 'It hit the floor of the shelter at an angle and skidded along the floor away from me to a corner. It looked like a dustbin coming through to me. As it hit the ground it shook the building. Then there was a terrific flash. The blast blew me about three yards under a chlorinator which had recently been installed on the wall. I was up to my waist in bricks and fragments of concrete. The blast had torn away my clothes leaving me in my pants and one sock. And the bricks and broken concrete tore pieces out of my leg. They were so hot from the explosion that they cauterised the wounds at the same time and they never bled. I lost my glasses, my hair, my eyebrows, all the flipping lot.' The ceiling of the second shelter collapsed bringing down the machinery above and about a thousand tons of flour. The Rev. Frederick Ralph, vicar of St Christopher's also virtually destroyed in the raid, reached the bakery when the rescue was in full swing. 'They persuaded me not to try to get into the bombed air raid shelter' he recalled in 1973. 'There was nothing I could do . . . the wreckage was all mixed up with marmalade and jam and flour and bodies. It was terrible.' No pictures were taken of the worst tragedy in 'Nottingham's Night of the Blitz' and perhaps that is just as well for today the memory of the 49 employees who lost their lives through enemy action — and one could say, in saving Rolls-Royce — are remembered through one of the finest company memorials in the country. The Co-op did everything in their power for the relatives and in this memorial on their graves in Wilford Hill Cemetery was one outward sign of their concern.

Also at Wilford Hill Cemetery at West Bridgford a pleasant departure from the communal aspect of the other mass Blitz graves: individually named headstones. Set in two rows, one of 17 graves, the other of 25, even those known only to God have their own tribute from the city of Nottingham.

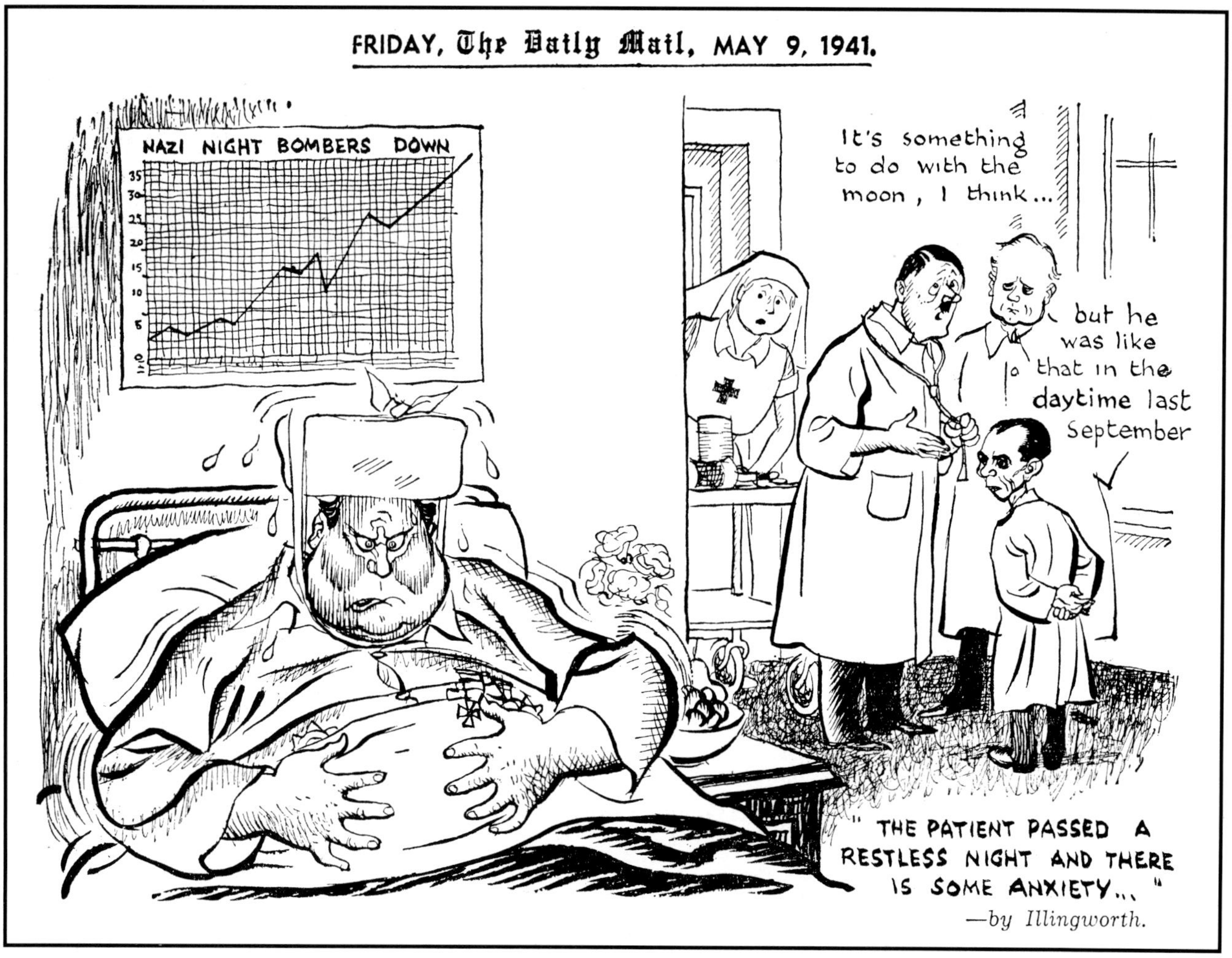

FRIDAY, The Daily Mail, MAY 9, 1941.

NAZI NIGHT BOMBERS DOWN

It's something to do with the moon, I think...

but he was like that in the daytime last September

" THE PATIENT PASSED A RESTLESS NIGHT AND THERE IS SOME ANXIETY... "

—*by Illingworth.*

Over recent weeks, as the number of RAF successes against the night raiders has increased, we have tended to include details of more aircraft coming down in the sea around, yet close, to Britain than we did, say, in September and October when the great daylight combats were at their height. Our rule of only detailing aircraft down on land, or from which prisoners or bodies were recovered, would have tended to paint a false picture once night airborne interceptions began to make themselves felt. One loss which no doubt added to Göring's collywobbles on Friday came down at Wimbledon — rather appropriately just at the same time that this cartoon was running off the presses in Fleet Street.

May 9 — and another Midlands town receives its hour of trial at the hands of the Luftwaffe. The Civilian War Dead Roll tells the story: of the 22 people killed at Doncaster in the six years of war, 16 died on Friday in a land mine incident in the suburb of Balby. The main damage was centred on Weston Road.

FRIDAY, MAY 9-10

Sunset: 2135 Sunrise: 0617
Moon: Dusk — 0606 (Full −2)

Minor but widespread attacks, mostly on airfields. Anti-shipping and minelaying operations.

UK — Cloudy but fair in many places. Moderate to good visibility.
The Continent — Similar to the UK.

German day activity followed the usual pattern of fighter sweeps over south-eastern coastal areas and over the Channel with armed sea reconnaissance and attacks on shipping. Few aircraft crossed the coasts, however, and no bombing was recorded.

During the night there were far ranging attacks in which 89 long-range bombers and 19 long-range fighter-bombers were engaged. In addition to the usual night fighter patrols in the vicinity of RAF Bomber Command airfields, there were attacks on airfields in many other parts of the country, shipping attacks off the East Coast and in the Bristol Channel, where a trawler was sunk, and against industrial installations and dock facilities at Barrow-in-Furness, Nottingham, Peterborough, Rugby, Norwich and Southampton. Luftflotte 3 contributed 46 aircraft with 11 ordered against Zerstörziele, 19 against airfields, 13 on armed sea reconnaissance and three on overland night reconnaissance. Luftflotte 2 embarked on similar activity with 43 bombers and the Nachtjagddivision dispatched 19 aircraft.

Among the airfields target-listed were St Eval (by eight aircraft of III/KG27 and three of KGr100), Exeter (one He 111 of III/ KG55), Warmwell (one Ju 88 of II/KG54) and Upper Heyford (a Ju 88 of II/KG1). Typical Zerstörziele were the Birmetals Aluminium factory at Birmingham (allocated to a He 111 of III/KG55 which, in the course of a low level attack from 100 feet dropped a PC 1400, four SC 250 and ten SD 50 high explosive bombs) and the Ordnance Factory at Nottingham (attacked from 300 feet by a Ju 88 of I/KG76). Attacks on ships were made by aircraft of III/KG27, III/KG54, II/KG55, II/KG1, III/KG1, II/KG77 and III/KG77, all with varying claimed degrees of success. Aircraft unable to find ships bombed a number of land alternative targets including Swansea (by one He 111 of III/KG27), Plymouth (two aircraft), Dundee (one), Holyhead (one), and Dartmouth (one). Luftflotte 3 lost one aircraft, a Ju 88 of III/KG1 which crashed into the Channel on its outward flight.

Aircraft of Luftflotte 2 attacked shipyards at Barrow-in-Furness and in the North-East, but details of units and bomb-loads are not known. Most of the bombs dropped at Barrow-in-Furness landed on residential property but the shipyards were also damaged. The ARP Control Centre was hit, causing additional problems for the Civil Defence personnel, but no serious damage resulted to industry. Casualties included 16 killed.

In the North-East damage was done over a wide area; Scarborough experienced six fires and some damage was caused in the Rugby district. Two fires were started in Nottingham and damage was also reported at Skegness and at Peterborough, where four fires occurred.

In the South ten people were killed in Southampton, where the South Hants Hospital was again damaged.

Another daylight fighter sweep over Kent resulted in a single loss.

Stab/JG53 Messerschmitt Bf 109F-2 (4708). Shot down by Sergeant Bowen-Morris in a Spitfire of No. 92 Squadron during a sortie to the Folkestone area. Crashed at Eastwell Park, Kennington, near Ashford, Kent 6.20 p.m. Lt. J. Heger (injured) baled out and taken prisoner. Aircraft 4+ destroyed.

Site excavated by Alan Brown and Steve Vizard and surviving remains unearthed.

One crashed near Britain at night.

9/KG1 Junkers Ju 88A-5 (3217). Believed shot down by Pilot Officer A. J. Hodgkinson DFC and Sergeant B. E. Dye in a Beaufighter of No. 219 Squadron during a raid on Brighton. Crashed into the sea 2-3 miles east of Selsey 12.12 a.m. Oblt. O. Weickhardt, Fw. P. Schucklies and Oberfw. K. Rogoss missing. Body of Fw. H. Jütte washed ashore at Bognor Regis July 20. Aircraft V4+KT lost.

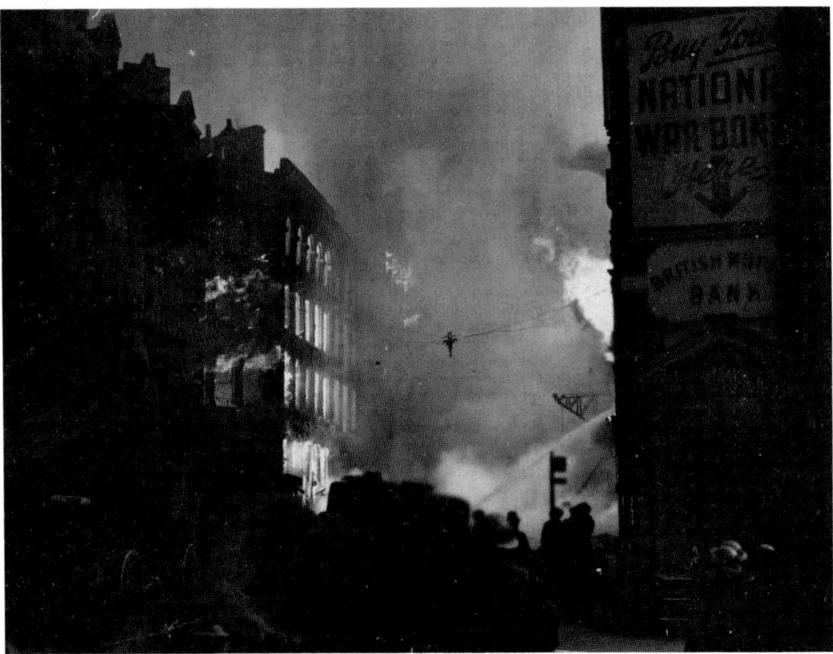

FULL MOON

The most devastating raid on London occurred on May 10, 1941 when a full moon coincided with a very low Thames ebb tide. Firemen knew they were in for a bad night with the odds stacked against them, as hundreds of bombers maintained a shuttle service across the Channel, returning to their bases in northern France to refuel and rearm.

West Ham received its usual greeting from the Luftwaffe early in the raid when several medium-sized fires developed in the Dock area. A more serious outbreak was started in the Temple Mills sidings at Stratford, then one of the largest railway marshalling complexes in the country, but this was a relatively quiet night for West Ham firemen. There were minor falls of incendiaries in various parts of the borough and these were pounced upon by the local lads and lassies if not with glee, then certainly with the speed and efficiency born of long practice. It was a matter of pride for them to deal with a simple fall of fire-bombs without calling the brigade; 'Leave the boys to deal with the big fires, mate.'

The raiders were able to choose their targets by the brilliant light of the moon and, later, by the glare of fires stretching across London from Dagenham to Hammersmith. Street water mains were flowing only in the early stages; demand soon outstripped supply as fresh fires were started; the flow becoming further depleted with the inevitable fracturing of trunk mains. Frustrated firemen who had laboured to bring their jets to bear on blazing buildings watched helplessly as the fire streams faltered and died. Their comrades, meanwhile, sought emergency sources of water not already crowded out by pumps with suction hoses set in. Fireboats lay fifty yards from the Thames banks, running their hose lines ashore over mud flats from what looked like a village stream, so low was the tide. But there were far more pumps seeking water than the fireboats could hope to supply and water officers directed crews to public swimming pools, canals and ponds. Some opportunist pump operators set their appliances into flooded bomb craters, even sewers, in an effort to make use of every possible drop of water available.

Hose lines were laid from the water

Fires were started. These pictures illustrate just two of the 2,000-odd fires which the fire service had to try to contain on Saturday night. It was exactly two weeks after the thousand ton raid that the Luftwaffe turned its attention back to London. With the lighter evenings it was becoming more difficult to reach the long-distance targets under cover of darkness for the whole flight, but with London it was still possible to get in two trips in one night, so doubling the weight of the attack with the prospect of overwhelming the civil defences. Coupled with the full moon — the bomber's moon as it was called — Saturday, May 10 was one of the last good opportunities before the impending withdrawal of forces to the East.

Top: **At ground level crews are hard-pushed to get at the seat of the fire. Meanwhile another blaze bursts out behind them** *Left:* **With a colleague hooked to the ladder with a steel ring, the turntable is trained on the fire. Beside the second fire, a burnt-out building collapses.**

source to the fireground, the men clambering over debris and running themselves into the ground, driven by the urge to provide water for the fires ahead, growing ever larger and more menacing in the absence of extinguishment operations. To many, it seemed a hopeless task as they strove to get their hose lines laid with failing strength and nerves stretched by the unending scream of falling bombs and the ever present fear of being hit or overwhelmed by an unexpected avalanche of masonry.

But there was always something or someone to rally flagging spirits. 'Come on, lads. Don't let them bastards get you down', shouted a fireman, lucky enough to be making use of a decent jet. Lorries, carrying a mile of hose, raised a weak cheer from firemen as they laid twin lines of hose at twenty miles an hour whenever they could find roads clear of debris.

It was one of the most punishing nights London firemen had experienced, and nowhere was it more cruel than in Southwark and Lambeth. It started with a heavy fall of incendiaries and HE in the vicinity of the Elephant and Castle, the famous south London pub at the junction of Old Kent Road and Newington Butts. Freeman, Hardy and Willis's boot and shoe warehouse; Dean's Rag Book factory and Spurgeon's Tabernacle were among the many buildings hit and the area had all the makings of a conflagration from the onset.

The first pumps to arrive set in to a nearby 5,000-gallon emergency dam whilst orders were given for water relays to be put in operation from the Manor Place baths and the converted basement of the old Surrey Music Hall at St George's Circus, each about 800 yards distant. The first jets emptied the 5,000-gallon dam in just five minutes, bringing firefighting to a halt until new water supplies became available.

Meanwhile, fire crews worked frantically to set in their pumps to the swimming pool at Manor Place and to the basement dam at St George's Circus. Weary firemen somehow found reserves of energy and ran their hose lines along the kerbside towards the great raging inferno.

Then disaster struck. A large HE bomb crashed among the cluster of pumps crowding around the old Music Hall dam, killing seventeen firemen and creating such havoc that access to the water supply was completely blocked. The fire was now out of control and rapidly spreading as the enemy pilots, recognising a prime target, set about stoking it up to even greater fury.

More water relays were put in hand from the Thames at London, Waterloo and Westminster Bridges and from the Surrey Canal, over distances ranging from a mile to a mile and a half. Slowly, jets were brought to bear on the fringes of the fire to halt the spread and gradually built up as more hose lines were linked to the Thames.

Nearly two thousand five hundred fires were started in the London Region, adding to the enormous damage caused by high explosive bombs. The British Museum library was an early casualty, where damage included the loss of a quarter of a million books. The House of Commons Chamber was set ablaze and Westminster Abbey was but one of the churches damaged. Five of the city's telephone exchanges were disrupted and thousands of other buildings were demolished or severely damaged including eight of the capital's main line railway terminals. Nearly fifteen hundred Londoners died on that night of terror and many hundreds more were severely injured.

Numerous fires were out of control as dawn broke on the Sunday morning. The exhausted firemen found it hard to raise a cheer when sirens sounded the All Clear and barrage balloons climbed slowly into the clouds of smoke that were obscuring an otherwise clear sky. Vast numbers of Londoners found themselves without water, gas and electricity when they emerged from their shelters but thanked God for their deliverance as they looked around at the devastation and saw smoke and flame still rising from many fires.

But the Nazis didn't have it all their own way. The Fighter Boys claimed thirty-three bombers shot down with the aid of the new radar equipment in this, the last of the major raids on London.

CYRIL DEMARNE, 1986

A post-war survey based on photographic studies of damage in Germany indicated that, ton for ton, incendiaries were nearly five times as effective as high explosive bombs on commercial, industrial and residential areas. However in the opinion of Sir Arthur Harris, C-in-C of RAF Bomber Command, 'the Germans again and again missed their chance . . . of setting our cities ablaze by concentrated attack. . . . But they did do us enough damage to teach us the principle of concentration, the principle of starting so many fires at the same time that no firefighting services, however efficiently and quickly they were reinforced by the fire brigades of other towns, could get them under control.' The battle of firemen versus flame: St Bride Street.

SATURDAY, MAY 10-11

Sunset: 2136 Sunrise: 0615
Moon: Dusk — Dawn (Full −1)

Major attack on London. Night fighter and anti-shipping operations.

UK — Fine with little or no cloud in most districts. Visibility mainly good apart from some haze near large towns in the South and fog patches in the Midlands and the North near dawn.

The Continent — Similar to southern England in France and the Low Countries, but much high and medium cloud in north-west Germany.

Keystone Press Agency: 'At great risk to his life, our cameraman toured the city during the height of the Luftwaffe's fury, dodging fire-bombs, escaping the shrapnel from our own guns, let alone the chance of burial under the debris of falling buildings and envelopment in the blazing inferno. That the old city of London is not entirely laid in ruins is largely due to the bravery of our firemen who fought fearlessly throughout the night the great blanket of flames which enveloped the whole area. Many lost their lives, but this did not deter their comrades from continuing the fight to prevent the fire from spreading. The heroism of London's firemen during this night of terror is clearly illustrated in this photograph.' With their branch visibly short of water, these firefighters are pictured in Shoreditch High Street.

Fighter sweeps, armed sea reconnaissance and weather reconnaissance occupied units of the Luftwaffe during the day, but there were few inland penetrations and no reports of damage or casualties.

During the night 571 sorties were flown by German long-range bombers over Britain, together with 24 by long-range fighters, with most of the bomber effort directed at London. It was a night of maximum effort and some crews flew two, and a few three, sorties over the hard-hit British capital.

Is that a 'V' for Victory . . . no, surely it must be 'V' for Volkswagen!

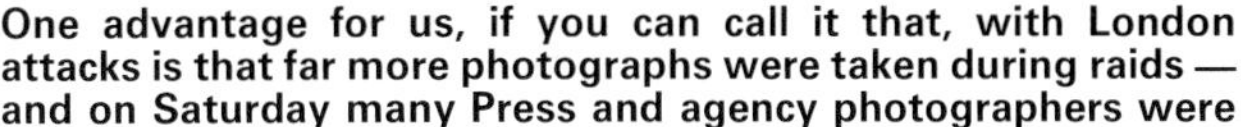

One advantage for us, if you can call it that, with London attacks is that far more photographs were taken during raids — and on Saturday many Press and agency photographers were out on the streets, especially in and around their own patch in Fleet Street. The *Mirror* captured the end of St Clement Danes — the 'oranges and lemons' church — we last saw on page 174.

The bombing started at 2315 and by 0524 hours 507 aircraft had delivered 711 tonnes of HE (seven SC 1700, 111 SC 1000, 366 SC 500, 947 SC/SD 250, nine LZZ 250, 72 Flam 250, 1,492 SC/SD 50, eight LMA and 69 LMB) and 86,173 incendiaries. The ordered Concentration Point covered the 'north side of the Thames from Tower Bridge downstream to, and inclusive of, the loop of the Thames, and the districts of Stepney, West Ham, Bethnal Green and Leyton', to quote the Luftwaffe Führungsstab report. As expected, the weather was very nearly perfect, with no cloud, and visibility was hampered only as dawn approached by a light mist. Accordingly visual bombing and the observation of results was possible without hindrance.

Nearer to base, this shot was taken in Fetter Lane, almost opposite the White Horse pub.

Shoe Lane at the corner with Charterhouse Street by a cameraman from Planet News.

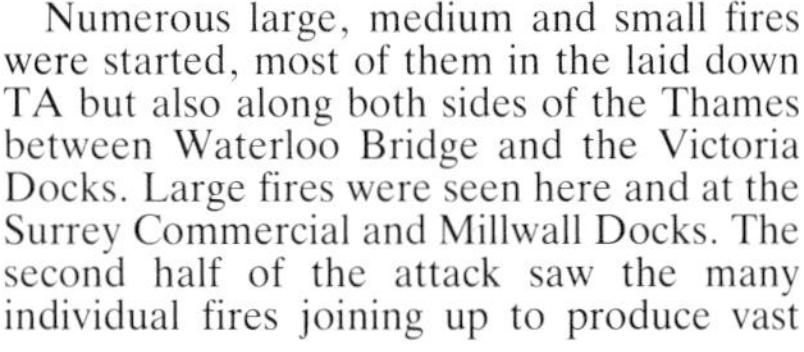

Numerous large, medium and small fires were started, most of them in the laid down TA but also along both sides of the Thames between Waterloo Bridge and the Victoria Docks. Large fires were seen here and at the Surrey Commercial and Millwall Docks. The second half of the attack saw the many individual fires joining up to produce vast areas of fire and huge conflagrations were observed in Stepney, Bow and the west part of the City with smoke rising to 10,000 feet; in the loop of the Thames some 20 fires were perceived, with even more covering the districts north of the London Docks and to the north-west of Hackney Marshes. The reports of crews left the GAF Intelligence Staff in no doubt about the great success achieved.

In addition to the London operation, single aircraft made Zerstörangriffe on the shipyards at Plymouth and the torpedo factory at Portland, while two aircraft made very low level attacks on the High Duty Alloys factory at Slough.

In their communiqué, the German High Command referred to May 10 as a reprisal raid on which 100,000 incendiaries were dropped. In England the disaster of a second great London fire within six months brought to a head the rumblings over the organisation of the fire services, still under the control of each local authority. Even since December the full extent of the risk from incendiary bomb warfare had still not been grasped but after Saturday the Government acted with a speed which amazed some of its critics when three days later the Home Secretary announced sweeping reforms and the creation of a new National Fire Service. Too late though for Fetter Lane, where another aspect was pictured by the *Daily Mail*.

Also by the *Mail* Queen Victoria Street just as dawn was breaking. With the available fire services overwhelmed, whole streets had to be left to burn. On the right, mid-way down and already a blazing shell, is the church of St Nicholas, Cole Abbey.

The London raid was a joint Luftflotten 2 and 3 venture with 149 crews of the former reporting over the target. Luftflotte 3 dispatched 378 aircraft sorties during the night; 371 of them were to London (with 358 crews reporting over their targets there) while two attacked Zerstörziele, four carried out armed sea reconnaissance, four bombed alternative targets, six aborted and ten failed to return. Many Luftflotte 3 crews flew double missions, those engaged in the first attack being:

KG1: 30 Ju 88, 0030-0215
KG76: 41 Ju 88, 0100-0300
II and III/KG77: 21 Ju 88, 0043-0140 (strengthened by part of I/KG1) also 16 Ju 88, 0005-0030 (strengthened by part of I/KG1)
I/KG77: 13 Ju 88, 0005-0110
III/KG26: 10 He 111, 0040-0110
I/KG27: 13 He 111, 0037-0120
II/KG27: 15 He 111, 0047-0150
III/KG27: 16 He 111, 0105-0126
KGr100: 11 He 111, 2354-0006
I/KG54: 22 Ju 88, 2315-0015
II/KG54: 16 Ju 88, 2343-0012
III/KG54: 21 Ju 88, 0025-0105
I/KG55: 13 He 111, 0035-0122
II/KG55: 9 He 111, 0035-0105
III/KG55: 20 He 111, 0015-0200
Stab/KG55: 4 He 111, 0040-0320

In this phase of the attack Luftflotte 3 dispatched 300 aircraft, with 291 reaching the target, three bombing alternatives and three breaking off their missions. Five aircraft were lost, but of these three had reported over the TA. All were He 111s and comprised two of III/KG27, two of I/KG55 (one of them ditching in the Channel, its crew being rescued) and one of II/KG27 (whose crew baled out near Orléans).

Centre: **The gaunt ruin pictured by Central News Illustrations Service on May 27 and** ***right*** **after rebuilding in 1962 under the guidance of Sir Arthur Bailey.**

The hopeless odds faced by London's firemen that night as seen in Ludgate Hill through the lenses of the photographers of the *Evening News* and London News Agency. *Above left:* **This is the premises of Messrs Strakers on the south side near the railway bridge.**

Luftflotte 3's participation in the second part of the attack was:

II/KG1: 6 Ju 88, 0250-0320
II/KG77: 10 Ju 88, 0300-0340
I/KG54: 18 Ju 88, 0144-0404
II/KG54: 9 Ju 88, 0501-0524
III/KG54: 12 Ju 88, 0225-0330
III/KG55: 11 He 111, 0250-0350
Stab/KG55: 1 He 111, 0325

On second missions, Luftflotte 3 dispatched 71 crews, 67 of them reporting over the target with one bombing an alternative; two aborted and three aircraft were lost (three He 111s of III/KG55, one of which ditched in the sea, and a Ju 88 of KG77 which crashed on take-off).

Damage actually sustained in London was extensive and widespread, with incidents in 61 boroughs, but the main weight of the bombing fell on central, eastern and south-eastern areas. A grave fire situation resulted, with 2,154 fires reported, and the central and docks areas were worst hit. Fire services were extended to the full. Although damage in the docks was substantial, the ability of the port to function as a whole was not seriously affected although there was inevitably serious dislocation of road and rail transport and many termini were closed. All routes through the city were closed but utility services stood up to the onslaught reasonably well. Damage to public buildings was extensive and those hit included the Houses of Parliament, Westminster Abbey, the British Museum, the Law Courts, the London Museum, the Mint, the Royal Naval College at Greenwich, the War Office, the Public Record Office, the London Sessions House, the Mansion House, the Guildhall Art Library and the Tower of London. Churches hit included St Clement Danes; St Stephen's, Walbrook; St Mary-le-Bow; Holy Trinity, Sloane Street; and St Columba's, Pont

Left: **With no one available to attend to it, the fire has gained hold on the entire block, giving the LNA photographer a chance to picture a fine study of bravery, their only weapon — water — in pathetically short supply.**

As it begins to get light, with the spire of St Martin's silhouetted against St Paul's, Associated Press pictured the opposite side of the street where Benson's Watches is well alight. There are no firefighters available — Benson's burns . . . the hands on the sole face remaining of their famous triple-clock frozen in time at twenty to eleven.

Literally all hands to the pump. The Wide World photographer appears to have started out rather late in the day; having missed the Benson's fire he caught another incident further up the Hill. The water pressure is now noticably higher.

Above: **Tangle of hoses leading down to the river in this shot of Ludgate Circus from the Paul Popper Agency.** *Below:* **The bombed area on the right around Pilgrim Street remains as a unique piece of blitzed London — but for how long?**

This dramatic view from the cathedral by the LCC Fire Brigade itself looks back down towards the Circus. When Home Security worked out the statistics of Saturday night's raid, they broke down the 2,036 fires into 2 of 'conflagration' level; 8 as 'major' outbreaks; 43 serious, 280 medium and 1,073 small.

Street. Fourteen hospitals were affected, as were many schools, including Westminster. Immediately after the attack casualties were put at more than 1,000 killed and some 2,000 injured, but the final figures exceeded these. Many casualties occurred as a result of direct hits on air raid shelters, seven of which were destroyed or damaged; in one, at Stepney, 20 people were killed, and at Eaton Square the Mayor of Westminster was killed when visiting a trench shelter. The Mayor of Bermondsey was also killed when his Town Hall was hit. Especially large fires developed at Southwark, Shadwell, Mark Lane, Whitechapel, and in Westminster.

The guns of the IAZ were in action from 2250 to 0515 hours, firing 4,510 of the 7,000 or so rounds used by AA Command during the night. Two aircraft flying in the London area were claimed destroyed.

Including offensive patrols over northern France, layer patrols over and on the approach to the London Target Area, and aerial mining patrols, Fighter Command dispatched 325 aircraft. They claimed the destruction of 28 enemy aircraft — the highest number yet — with many of them going to 'Cat's Eye' fighters, 60 of which flew layer patrols over London with more on the approaches to the city. One Hurricane was destroyed, and its pilot killed, and a Beaufighter and another Hurricane badly damaged, all the result of combat.

And this is from *The Times* photographer in Pilgrim Street at ground level: 1941-1988

Eleven aircraft were lost, the four not detailed below being three Heinkel He 111s of KG55 which are presumed to have gone down in the Channel and a Junkers Ju 88 of 3(F)/122 which crashed off the Dutch coast killing its crew. Whilst this attack was in progress, the Deputy Führer, Rudolf Hess, chose to arrive in Scotland by parachute.

7/KG27 Heinkel He 111P-2 (1389). Believed shot down by Pilot Officer Grout and Sergeant Stanton in a Beaufighter of No. 29 Squadron. Crashed into the sea 3 miles south of Seaford, Sussex 2.04 a.m. Hptm. W. Langner, Fw. E. Ortmann, Uffz. K. Beirsack and Uffz. H. Krause all killed. Aircraft 1G+GR lost.

8/KG27 Heinkel He 111P-2 (2657). Shot down by Wing Commander T. G. Pike DFC and Sergeant S. Austin in a Beaufighter of No. 219 Squadron. Crashed and bombs exploded at Great Witheybush, Cranleigh, Surrey 1.10 a.m. Uffz. J. Maihöfer, Uffz. J. Hermann and Uffz. B. Bärwald killed. Uffz. H. Schäfer baled out and taken prisoner. Aircraft 1G+IS disintegrated.

May 11, 1941

Return flight from London.

The moonlight reflections in the Channel are wonderful, fabulous. Through shimmering, grotesquely-shaped mountains of clouds, we follow our lonely course above the glittering reflections from the sea. The attack and its dangers are behind us. These relaxed homeward flights — with the engines rumbling quietly and evenly — lull us into the feeling that nothing more can happen. Any attempt to speak is silenced by the sight of the wide, silvery, dreamlike landscape.

Who could restrain himself from feeling deeply thankful? And when you perhaps see from afar the first lights of Fécamp blazing up on the French coast, that is almost like looking at a Christmas tree.

Somewhere on the coast the flashes thrown up by the German defences can be seen. From our lonely height, everything looks so peaceful and so like a game . . .

Landing at Villaroche at 02.00 hours.

At the operational headquarters, we hear that another crew has 'caught it'; a plane from No. 3 Staffel has ended up in the waters of the Channel. Oberleutnant Karbe, their Kapitän, decides to start out and look for his little 'lambs'. As his own crew has already gone to their billets in the barracks, we offer ourselves and I hasten to find out which command location they themselves have notified from their own navigating records (their SOS came through and was also located by the land-based, direction-finding stations), and which location the air-sea rescue shore stations are working to. What a big difference!

On the strength of my own experience, I propose searching from where they had been located by the shore stations. After going to and fro for a while, Karbe agrees. And at 03.40 we fly off at a low altitude. Every minute is precious. Another pilot from our Staffel had volunteered as well, and had quickly disappeared into the darkness with his crew.

We soon reach the map grid notified, fly systematically over the large stretch of water, and peer down without saying a word. Are they in the rubber dinghy? Are they suspended in their life-jackets? Or have they already been drowned?

Through the dawning light we see the chalk cliffs of Dover shimmering over there; rising to the same height as we are flying at — a damnably unpleasant feeling!

Have the Tommys really still not noticed anything? Or have they recognized the emergency and are letting us search?

It's all the same now.

There they are. The mechanic, who is lying in the turret looking backwards, cries out: 'They are firing flares behind us . . . Let's turn round and go back.' Newly aroused to maximum tension, I push myself right forward in the rounded cockpit.

There again — just in front of us — a flare zooms up, and a small puff of smoke floats over the gently rolling waves. But there is no sign of human beings, or of a rubber dinghy. It's not surprising. It's still only just getting light, and the moon is still casting its own beams onto the water. And over such a gigantic area, a minute boat is just a dot. As we continue to move away, another flare rises high behind us. Let us hope that Tommy, who must also have boats out there, hasn't seen anything.

We call for help on the radio, and decide that come what may we will give our beam call-sign. Suddenly I am amazed to see a plane on the light eastern horizon. Is it Tommy? Karbe tugs the plane round . . . No! It's a Heinkel 111 with the confidence-inspiring identification marks of No. 1 Staffel. It's Oberfeldwebel van Risswyk.

But it has now become almost completely light, and those chalk cliffs . . . There is a joyful shout. Yes, the yellow boat is floating down below there; and apparently with all four men in it. We fire flares over it and make signals . . . They also make signs to us with the paddles, and appear to be unimaginably happy. We stay above them and circle round. Suddenly there is a Schnellboot with the German flag lying alongside them — we hadn't seen it coming. They climb into it . . . All right this time.

On the next evening they are already flying again. But not a word of thanks has come from them, our dour comrades. The road from the third hut to the first seems indeed to have been too long, in the Villaroche park.

ROBERT GÖTZ

The Sport and General photographer looks down the full length of Charterhouse Street towards the East where the dawn really is coming up like thunder.

1/KG28 Heinkel He 111H-5 (3534). Shot down by fire from a night fighter and crashed at Beehive Lane, Galleywood, Chelmsford 12.32 a.m. Lt. O. Krüger, Uffz. K. Schrey, Gefr. Lindenmayer and Uffz. O. Gauernack all baled out and taken prisoner. Aircraft 1T+HH destroyed.

3/KG53 Heinkel He 111H-5 (4002). Shot down by a Defiant. Crashed at Gore Farm, Upchurch, near Gillingham 2.00 a.m. Lt. W. von Sieber and Fw. J. Fischer baled out and taken prisoner. Uffz. A. Schurff, Oberfw. H. Meister and Fw. E. Wylezol killed. Aircraft A1+CL disintegrated.

Wide World, again late on the scene, look back up the street to Holborn Circus. Shoe Lane can be seen on the left by the new bridge.

Queen Victoria Street on Sunday morning by the *News Chronicle* — we are looking in the opposite direction to the opposition's photo on page 611. During the night 'Nobby' Clark, an Auxiliary Fireman with the Benfleet Volunteer Fire Brigade, was in the street and he recalls that at the height of the battle, 'all the jets just dried up'. During the raid, three 42-inch mains were cut; five 36-inch and 34 of 12 inches and over. Pressure was low in most boroughs of the London County Council area with about another hundred smaller mains fractured.

5/KG53 Heinkel He 111H-5 (3976). Damaged by Spitfires of No. 74 Squadron and made forced landing at Kennington, near Ashford, Kent 12.05 a.m. Hptmn. A. Hufenreuther, Fw. R. Führthmann, Uffz. K. Gerhardt, Uffz. J. Berzbach and Gefr. E. Weber all taken prisoner. Aircraft A1+JN captured damaged.

Radio and radio mast on display at the Kent Battle of Britain Museum, Hawkinge.

9/KG55 Heinkel He 111P (1619). Shot down by fire from a night fighter and crashed at Swifts Field, Station Road, Withyham, East Sussex 3.30 a.m. St.Fw. A. Schied baled out but died of injuries. Lt. M. Reiser baled out and taken prisoner. Oberfw. L. Huber and Oberfw. L. Schuderer killed. Aircraft G1+BT destroyed.

Site excavated by many groups and individuals including Steve Vizard and Ken Anscombe.

9/KG55 Heinkel He 111H-8 (3971). Believed hit by fire from the No. 380 Searchlight Battery. Crashed at Rumbush Farm, Earlswood, near Birmingham 12.45 a.m. Oblt. J. Speck (Staffelkapitän), Fw. F. Muhn and Fw. S. Rühle killed. Gefr. R. Budde thrown into a ditch with his clothes on fire but survived to be taken prisoner. Aircraft G1+ET wrecked.

Site visited by Philippa Hodgkiss but little except burnt fragments and perspex found on the surface. Throttle quadrant in the possession of the land owner's grandson.

Messerschmitt Bf 110 (3869). Crashed at Floors Farm, Bonnyton Moor, Glasgow 11.05 p.m. Flown from Augsburg by Deputy Führer, Rudolf Hess, on what is taken to have been a peace mission. Hess baled out and died while in prison at Spandau in August 1987. Aircraft VJ+OQ wrecked.

One DB601 engine on display in the Imperial War Museum, Lambeth. Other wreckage, including rear fuselage bearing code letters, in store at Duxford Airfield. Other DB601 engine held by the RAF Museum, Hendon.

Left: With no water they were helpless to save the Salvation Army headquarters building — it can be seen in the top photo on the right beyond the turntable. *Above:* The replacement building opened by Queen Elizabeth, the Queen Mother, in 1963 lies a little further along, the original building standing nearer to where the post-war ramp was built on the right leading down to the Blackfriars underpass.

Further down Queen Victoria Street, close to the Mansion House, was taken what must be one of the most spectacular pictures of the Blitz. Early morning the Topical Press Agency photographer pictured John Wood & Sons premises at No. 23. At this stage the fire was burning uncontrolled. If we assume the clock further down is still going, the time is nine o'clock Sunday morning.

SUNDAY, MAY 11-12

Sunset: 2138 Sunrise: 0614
Moon: 2202 — Dawn (Full Moon)

Minor attacks on Middlesbrough (Billingham). Anti-shipping and fighter-bomber attacks, minelaying. Attacks on airfields.

UK — Mainly cloudy with moderate visibility. Rain in some areas with moderate to poor visibility, but mainly fair in the South.
The Continent — Cloudy with some rain in the West. Moderate visibility.

There was no daylight activity of note, most German operations being confined to fighter sweeps and armed sea reconnaissance.

The main feature of the night was attacks on airfields, but the large chemical works at Billingham, near Middlesbrough, was attacked by 19 aircraft from 0030 to 0210 hours with 27 tonnes of HE (ten SC 1000, seven SC 500 and eight SC 50) and 1,584 IBs. Visual bombing was carried out and most bombs were claimed dropped in the TA, causing large fires and thick smoke. Dundee and West Hartlepool were attacked by single aircraft as alternative targets.

Luftflotte 3 was mainly concerned with attacks on airfields and 241 aircraft were so employed with the biggest attacks on Exeter (22 aircraft), St Eval and Portsmouth (20 aircraft each), St Athan (12 aircraft), Coningsby and Tangmere (ten aircraft), Sutton Bridge and Marham (eight aircraft each), and Waddington (nine aircraft). Other airfields claimed attacked included Filton (seven aircraft), Warmwell, Boscombe Down, Yeovil, Harwell, Bicester, Feltwell, West Raynham, Manby, Scampton, Hemswell and Armthorpe. Numerous towns and villages were also attacked as alternative targets, stretching from Dartmouth to Grimsby. Luftflotte 3's losses were four Ju 88s (of I/KG54, KG1 and III/KG76) and a He 111 (III/KG55).

A new feature of the night was the use of 63 fighter aircraft which augmented the operations of 505 long-range bombers and 21 long-range night fighter-bombers. It is not clear from German records whether the fighters were carrying bombs or merely operating over the South and South-East in search of RAF aircraft in the light of a full moon, but the latter appears more likely.

Some damage to industry occurred at Hartlepool, where 12 people were killed, in Middlesbrough, Stockton and at two works in Billingham. The County Hall and other buildings suffered at Northallerton and some damage was done to the docks at Hull. In East Anglia damage and casualties were reported at Great Yarmouth, Felixstowe and at Elmsett, Suffolk. Elsewhere bombs fell at Ipswich, Lowestoft, Rochford, Margate,

Fires caused by incendiaries naturally started at the top of a building, working their way down as each floor collapsed dropping embers on the one below. By the time forces were available to deal with this one, the fire had spread down to the shop area. Fortunately all fire crews were clear and no one was hurt when it collapsed — a City policeman is believed to have snapped this shot at the vital moment. Print now at the Guildhall.

So where exactly did No. 23 stand? Give or take an inch or so, where the Temple of Mithras can now be seen. During rebuilding in Walbrook in 1954, the complete foundations of a Mithraic temple were uncovered but commercial considerations dictated that the remains could not be retained so it was dismantled stone by stone, and re-erected a hundred yards east of the original spot.

Another Sunday scene with hoses snaking up New Bridge Street from the Thames at Blackfriars, although it's difficult to understand why the censor has insisted that the *Daily Mail* cut the smoky background of Ludgate Circus.

Guildford, Weymouth and Cardiff, but the heaviest casualties were at Pembroke, where 21 people were killed. In the attack on Exeter airfield Defiant N3439 of No. 307 Squadron was destroyed.

III/KG40 lost a Heinkel He 111 during the day, on a shipping sortie over the St George's Channel.

2/JG51 Messerschmitt Bf 109F-1 (5691). Hit by light AA fire whilst engaged in a low level attack on Rochford airfield, Essex 9.30 p.m. Uffz. A. Ludewig killed. Aircraft Black 3+ hit a building and disintegrated.

In addition to the losses detailed, a Junkers Ju 88 of 4/KG1 engaged on a sortie to Sutton Bridge is believed to have been shot down off the Norfolk coast.

4/KG1 Junkers Ju 88A-5 (7170). Hit by AA fire from RAF Watton during an attack on Sutton Bridge. Crashed at Rectory Farm,

Left: **The *Daily Herald* pictured this action in Old Bailey where a truck has received a direct hit from a high explosive bomb.**

Right: **Fox Photos were a little late on parade and only appeared when all the excitement was over.**

Some photographers arrived back at base to find the office burnt out — like *The Star* in Bouverie Street.

Scoulton, Norfolk 1.45 a.m. Lt. F. Bäumel, Uffz. H. Simon and Oberfw. H. Ausserfeld killed. Uffz. M. König (injured) taken prisoner. Aircraft V4+DM completely destroyed.

1/KG54 Junkers Ju 88A-5 (2388). Shot down by Solent AA fire. Crashed into the sea 200 yards off Egypt Light, Cowes, Isle of Wight 12.25 a.m. Uffz. L. Muth, Gefr. G. Tischendorf and Oberfw. K. Stiebitz missing. Body of Gefr. P. Adomat washed ashore. Aircraft B3+LH sank in sea.

Propeller blades on display in Carisbrook Castle and at the Holmwood Hotel on the sea front at Cowes erroneously identified as being that from a Heinkel He 111. Many parts recovered by divers over the years.

8/KG55 Heinkel He 111P-2 (2858). Briefed to attack Bicester which its crew could not find. Attacked and sunk BOAC flying boat, Short S21 *Maia* G-ADHK composite aircraft in Poole Harbour. Night watchman, Francis Smith, killed in flying boat. Heinkel He 111 hit by light AA fire from harbour shipping and patrol boats. Crashed into Poole Harbour, Dorset 1.28 a.m. Fw. W. Wimmer, Oblt. H. Gündel and Fw. H. Neuber killed. Uffz. K. Scheuringer and Gefr. K. Röhl taken prisoner. Aircraft G1+ES lost.

8/KG76 Junkers Ju 88A-5 (5168). Crashed at Brattleby Lane, near RAF Scampton 1.35 a.m. Hit by airfield defences during low altitude attack. Lt. K. Manning, Gefr. J. Dietrich, Gefr. H. Wimmeder and Uffz. F. Hansen all killed. Gefr. E. H. Reidel believed to have been one of the ground crew appears to have also been on board, although unofficially, and is buried in the same grave as Wimmeder at Scampton. Aircraft F1+BS wrecked.

2/SKG210 Messerschmitt Bf 110E-1N (3459). Bombed Martlesham 1.43 a.m. Hit by AA fire and dived into the sea 1 mile east of Shingle Street, Bawdsey 1.44 a.m. Uffz. H. Engel, Uffz. R. Schilling and Gefr. A. Knoechel all missing. Aircraft S9+CK lost.

Right: **Next to the *Star*, the *News of the World* building also housed the bureaux of United Press of America and the Newspaper Enterprise Association. It had also suffered in the raid and staff had already started to pile furniture outside on the pavement when a gas main exploded on Monday, setting fire to the main building.**

Fires or no fires there was still work to be done. This couple seem to know exactly where they are going as they walk briskly past the fire in St Bride Street which we last saw burning on pages 606-607.

May 11-12, 1941

For my last operational flight to England, the target was the RAF aerodrome at Harwell. It lasted more than four hours, was our first low-level night assignment, and was a failure.

Low-level flight? At least the entire light and medium Flak massed around such a fighter air base will treat us as an easy target. The planes attacking first may come through it. But in the bright moonlight we will be clearly visible at a height of 30 or 100 metres — almost as clearly as in the daytime, when our slow bombers laboriously circle around trying to find the most promising attacking position; and in the process cannot themselves see anything really precisely.

The chances of our slow 'tramp ship' escaping when flying low over airfield Flak are likely to be small. But we have never yet tried this before. Another thing is that almost all the British light Flak is stationed around the south coast.

The preparations for the flight and the flight briefing take place long beforehand. The feeling is one of slight unease. The oldest of our flying personnel, a radio operator still serving since the Spanish war, also has a remarkably rigid, pasty face as he goes past me towards the plane; already in his flying suit and wearing his life-jacket. I realize that even quite old hands are feeling as strange as I am.

And how is it going to be with these barrage balloons? Will they get ripped up if we run into them? Let's hope so. A plane once came home with an enormous hole in the front edge of its right wing. But the wire cable had been torn away on the main spar. To deal with this, 'balloon-defences', in the form of steel cutters, had been fitted to the front of the wings. But these had been given up as they were too heavy.

Once again, my old Jurak is a tower of strength. At 23.45 hours, he pushes the throttle quite calmly forwards — as he has always done. In the Channel, there are mirror-like reflections of the moonlight. At a height of 50 metres, we fly out over the water.

In front of the enemy coast looming up, there is suddenly a thick bunch of flares. Slanting downwards from behind — only just missing us — and from now on behind us . . . We move downwards until we are close above the surface of the water — and we've been lucky. It was in fact an outpost boat that had seen us zooming down on him one second too late . . .

In front of us are the chalk cliffs lit up by the moonlight — tremendous tension — we are past the coast now — nothing — surprise that we have succeeded for the time being. In one dash we are past the first high ground and are flying on course. Right in front, I am lying in the cockpit, my eyes glued to the targets.

At first there is clear moonlight. A thousand eyes must have seen us. As we are approaching at such an unusually low level, they probably think we are RAF bombers returning home. In front of us, from this very unusual angle looking as if they were spurting up from a giant primeval forest, are the Yeovil searchlights. And now we are past them.

Below us is a railway station with jets of smoke spurting up. But now it's the same story all over again. Mist, mist, mist. Where is there as much mist and fog as there is over this island? Again and again, it is driving us mad. The general rule is: over the Continent, clear; over the island, magical obscurity — until there's an exception . . .

We turn — we must be near the target — long after our scheduled time, circling round in the thin, milky mist; trying desperately to find our bearings. Barrage balloons? Sod them! We are searching, searching, searching; but there's nothing, absolutely nothing. And no signs of any Flak.

At last we believe we have identified a landing ground (perhaps camouflaged?); on our right-hand side. We drop our bombs in that direction — with no sign of anything stirring. It's enough to make you cry.

As we withdraw, it soon becomes lighter. And near the coast there is bright light again over the island — 50 metres below us. And we no longer have any fear over an emergency landing — as if we were at a height of 3000 metres. It is also unusually warm down there, in this peaceful landscape still lit up by the moon as well. Nobody fires at us.

We fly low along a road leading to a village tucked into a hollow — a few metres above its white church with a squat tower. And almost automatically my hand reached for the machine gun, as I saw a train entering a small railway station. But it is a passenger train, with passenger coaches.

Now there is already a sparkling, silvery sea in front of us — the Channel. A breakneck leap over the last ridge, past a hay elevator. Then Jurak swooped through a valley from which a road wound down to the beach. Up again and out of it. We are clear of the island. We fly home only a few metres above the still moonlit sea.

No one would have believed that about one and a half months later, on our next operational flight, we would be attacking the airfield at Kiev, the capital of the Ukraine.

ROBERT GÖTZ

No one who was there will forget the sights that Monday morning as they emerged from their station — if their station was in fact open. King's Cross and Liverpool Street were, although damaged, but St Pancras, Broad Street and Fenchurch Street were still closed. The Underground was running except for journeys between Baker Street and Aldgate; Ladbroke Grove to Paddington; South Kensington to Bromley, and Wood Lane to Ealing, but Oxford Circus and Clapham South were shut.

MONDAY, MAY 12-13

Sunset: 2140 Sunrise: 0612
Moon: 2315 — Dawn (Full +1)

Scattered light attacks, minelaying, armed sea reconnaissance and night fighter patrols of RAF airfields.

UK — Cloudy but mainly good visibility.
The Continent — Similar to the UK.

There were few inland intrusions by the Luftwaffe during the day and at night only 66 bombers and four night fighters were over Britain. Several aircraft engaged on armed sea reconnaissance bombed land targets as alternatives, including five which bombed Falmouth with 20 SC 250. Plymouth and Pembroke were similarly attacked by two and single aircraft respectively.

During the night bombs fell on London and at Gorleston, Lowestoft, Plymouth (where an oil tank was fired at Keyham) and Falmouth, where 20 people were killed and a good deal of damage caused.

A Junkers Ju 88 of 3/106 was lost on operations during the night.

TUESDAY, MAY 13-14

Sunset: 2141 Sunrise: 0610
Moon: 0020 — Dawn (Full +2)

Minor activity only.

UK — Extensive cloud with moderate to poor visibility.
The Continent — Similar to the UK.

The day was one of little activity with night operations conducted only by 25 long-range bombers, most of which were engaged on anti-shipping patrols. Again, some of these, failing to find shipping targets, turned their attention landwards and attacks were carried out on Plymouth (by three aircraft), Falmouth, Cardiff and Weymouth (single aircraft).

Bombs fell at only a few places during the night; there was a little damage to property in Weymouth and in Wales the Cardiff to Merthyr road was blocked for a few hours. Incidents were also reported from the mouth of the Tees, where machine-gunning caused one casualty.

The rush hour almost a half-century later. It must have been chilly that Monday — much like the May of 1988!

Perhaps one would arrive at the office to find this: a notice on a pile of rubble advising of an alternative or temporary address. Here Dixons, the advertising agency, have been forcibly evicted from Oxford Street.

WEDNESDAY, MAY 14-15

Sunset: 2143 Sunrise: 0609
Moon: 0113 — Dawn (Full +3)

Minor operations only.

UK — Cloudy with moderate to poor visibility.
The Continent — Similar to the UK in many areas.

During the afternoon a few German aircraft penetrated inland and bombs fell near Nottingham, causing a few casualties, and in Lincolnshire. Some damage and a few casualties were also reported at Swanage, but most Luftwaffe activity was concerned with over-sea patrols and fighter sweeps in the Channel.
At night operations were carried out by 31 aircraft but the only incident occurred at Veryan, Cornwall, where one person was killed.

Losses were as detailed below.

6/KG1 Junkers Ju 88A-5 (6263). Shot down by AA fire from patrol boat *Protective*. Crashed into the sea off Spurn Head, Humber 12.32 a.m. Oblt. K. Schröder and Oberfw. W. Dietzsch killed. Uffz. J. Fridel and St.Fw. E. Wingenfeld taken prisoner. Aircraft V4+GP lost.

1/KG54 Junkers Ju 88A-5 (3201). Hit a balloon cable and crashed into Falmouth Harbour 4.15 a.m. Obergefr. E. Kutzner missing. Oblt. A. Fischer, Gefr. H. Dapp and Uffz. S. Roesner killed. Aircraft B3+HH sank in sea.

THURSDAY, MAY 15-16

Sunset: 2144 Sunrise: 0607
Moon: 0157 — Dawn (Last Qtr −3)

Minor activity only. Some long-range night fighters in operation over eastern England.
UK — Extensive cloud with moderate to poor visibility.
The Continent — Similar to the UK.

The few bombs which fell in Kent and Sussex during the day did no damage and caused no casualties. Small scale German activity occurred over the Channel and over the South-East, but inland penetrations were few.
Night operations were flown by 39 bombers and 14 night fighters and minor attacks were made on the docks at Barrow-in-Furness, Newcastle and Middlesbrough. Yeovil and Plymouth were also attacked, but the only casualties of the entire night occurred at Plymstock, Devon.
I/SKG210 lost a Messerschmitt Bf 110 during an attack on Aldeburgh during the day.

FRIDAY, MAY 16-17

Sunset: 2146 Sunrise: 0606
Moon: 0233 — Dawn (Last Qtr −2)

Major attack on Birmingham. Airfields and other targets attacked elsewhere.

UK — Fine in the South but slight rain in the North-East at first. Visibility generally good, deteriorating towards dawn.

The Continent — Fine in most areas, but cloudy with occasional rain in north-west Germany late in the period.

No bombs fell on Britain on a day in which over-water activity pre-occupied the small German force operating. By night, however, there was an upsurge in activity with 192 long-range bombers and 16 long-range fighters operating, the main target being Birmingham.

The old *Stratton Street Strut* reduced to slow time up the West End for this old dear.

Preliminary figures issued by Home Security on Sunday stated 358 dead and 1,087 seriously injured but these numbers were 'likely to increase very considerably'. By Wednesday latest reports indicated 646 dead, 1,404 seriously injured and 1,384 with slight wounds. In the official account of the Civil Defence forces published in 1955 the final figure was given as 1,436 killed and 1,800 seriously injured. As an anniversary raid to mark a year of victorious war for Germany, it stands supreme for the greatest number of casualties in a single attack on Britain. For London, the raid had historical consequences. Westminster Abbey was hit, with the Deanery destroyed by fire. Here the Dean on the left watches debris being cleared from the High Altar.

Starting and finishing at 0045 and 0357 hours respectively, the Birmingham attack was carried out by 111 aircraft which dropped 160 tonnes of HE (62 SC 1000, 20 SC 500, 158 SC 250, 24 SD 250, 14 Flam 250, two LZZ 250, 92 SC 50, 134 SD 50 and 27 Type 'A' parachute mines) and 2,076 incendiaries. The Concentration Point was an area extending east and north-east from the city centre along two railway lines and including important factories of the aircraft and armaments industries.

Cloud and darkness due to the late moonrise made target recognition difficult and early crews bombed mainly with DR methods or radio assistance. Later crews bombed fires which developed as the attack progressed. In addition 20 LC 50 parachute flares were dropped, but these did little to assist bomb aiming. However, the detonations of many bombs were seen and their location was established within the TA; the many fires claimed started were mainly in the east and north-east districts of the city with ten small fires between the town centre and Castle Bromwich airfield and five more in the south of the city. In view of the weather conditions, however, positive assessment of the bombing was difficult and therefore it was anticipated that the attack was only moderately successful.

Little is known of Luftflotte 2's participation, although 53 aircraft of this air fleet reported over the target. Luftflotte 3 dispatched 79 aircraft with 58 of them reaching the target, but details of only 28 are known. These were:

KG1: 11 Ju 88, 0108-0151
KG76: 11 Ju 88, 0107-0320
KG26: 6 He 111, 0050-0155

Luftflotte 3 also sent 13 aircraft to St Eval airfield (reached and claimed bombed by 12) and one new crew to Plymouth for operational experience. Fourteen aircraft bombed alternative targets, four aborted and four were lost (a He 111 of III/KG55 and Ju 88s of KG1, II/KG76 and III/KG76).

Although Birmingham was the intended target the main weight of the attack fell on Nuneaton in error. A large number of fires broke out and much industrial and other damage was caused and, in view of Nuneaton's limited Civil Defence and Fire Service resources, aid was sent from Coventry. Casualties included 83 people killed.

Industrial damage was also done in Birmingham, including fires at the works of ICI Chemicals, the Dunlop Rubber Company, Wolseley Motors and the Kynoch Works, but nowhere was it classed as serious. More than 30 people were killed, however, and here and at Nuneaton essential utility services were interrupted. In both towns, too, commercial and residential premises were badly hit and again there were a number of shelter incidents. Damage and casualties were also reported from Hinckley, Burbage, Leicester, Tipton, Tettenhall and Kidderminster. Elsewhere bombs fell in Aberdeenshire, Middlesbrough, Harwich, Norwich, Southwold, Plymouth and in the Southampton/Portsmouth area.

Some 3,500 rounds were fired during the night by the heavy guns of AA Command and between dusk and dawn 208 aircraft of Fighter Command flew patrols (including seven over northern France). Layer patrols were flown over Birmingham but without apparent success. Fighters elsewhere claimed three enemy aircraft destroyed with another credited to AA gun-fire at Falmouth. Three night fighters were lost including a Beaufighter of No. 600 Squadron crewed by Squadron Leader Pritchard and Sergeant Gledhill, both of whom were wounded. Another Beaufighter (of No. 25 Squadron) crashed at Langham, Norfolk, after destroying a He 111, but both the pilot and AI operator baled out safely. The third loss was Defiant N3335 of No. 255 Squadron, written off when it ran into a floodlight on take off from Hibaldstow at 0030 hours (17th).

Sorties continued on a comparatively small scale; two Messerschmitt Bf 109s of I/JG3 were shot down into the Channel during the day. This night's attack on Birmingham resulted in the loss of five aircraft, Junkers Ju 88s of 6/KG76, 8/KG76 and 3/106 also going missing.

7/KG1 Junkers Ju 88A-5 (5230). Shot down by Flight Lieutenant A. D. McN. Boyd and Flying Officer A. J. Clegg in a Beaufighter of No. 600 Squadron. Crashed at Danes Mill Farm, Plymtree, Devon 12.12 a.m. Oberfw. F. Preugschat, Uffz. H. Kretschmer, Uffz. G. Feus and Uffz. F. Mitzkath all killed. Aircraft V4+IR totally disintegrated.

Current occupier of Danes Mill has oil tank cap. Crew entry ladder in possession of local aviation enthusiast.

7/KG55 Heinkel He 111P-2 (2801). Shot down by Pilot Officer A. J. Hodgkinson DFC and Sergeant B. E. Dye of No. 219 Squadron in a Beaufighter. Crashed on Downs near Sompting, Sussex 12.02 a.m. Lt. H. Pichler, Fw. B. Abraham, Fw. L. Stöger and Oberfw. K. Seefeld all killed. Aircraft G1+GR broke up in air.

The follow-up raid which might have been expected failed to materialise, Home Security believing that 'the enemy was probably glad to take advantage of imperfect flying conditions to give G.A.F. a rest after their recent very heavy scale of operations.' But time was now running out. After one last effort on Friday against Birmingham, the Luftwaffe began to withdraw to a new war about to break out in the East. On March 30 in the Chancellery in Berlin, Hitler had announced to an assembled audience of senior officers for Barbarossa — the attack on the Soviet Union — that the operation would begin on June 22 — exactly a year after the fall of France.

It is a year almost to a day since, in the crash of the disastrous Battle of France, His Majesty's present Administration was formed. Men of all parties, duly authorized by their parties, joined hands together to fight this business to the end. That was a dark hour, and little did we know what storms and perils lay before us, and little did Herr Hitler know, when in June 1940 he received the total capitulation of France and when he expected to be master of all Europe in a few weeks and the world in a few years, that ten months later, in May 1941, he would be appealing to the much-tried German people to prepare themselves for the war of 1942. When I look back on the perils which have been overcome, upon the great mountain waves through which the gallant ship has driven, when I remember all that has gone wrong, and remember also all that has gone right, I feel sure we have no need to fear the tempest. Let it roar, and let it rage. We shall come through.

WINSTON CHURCHILL,
HOUSE OF COMMONS, MAY 7, 1941

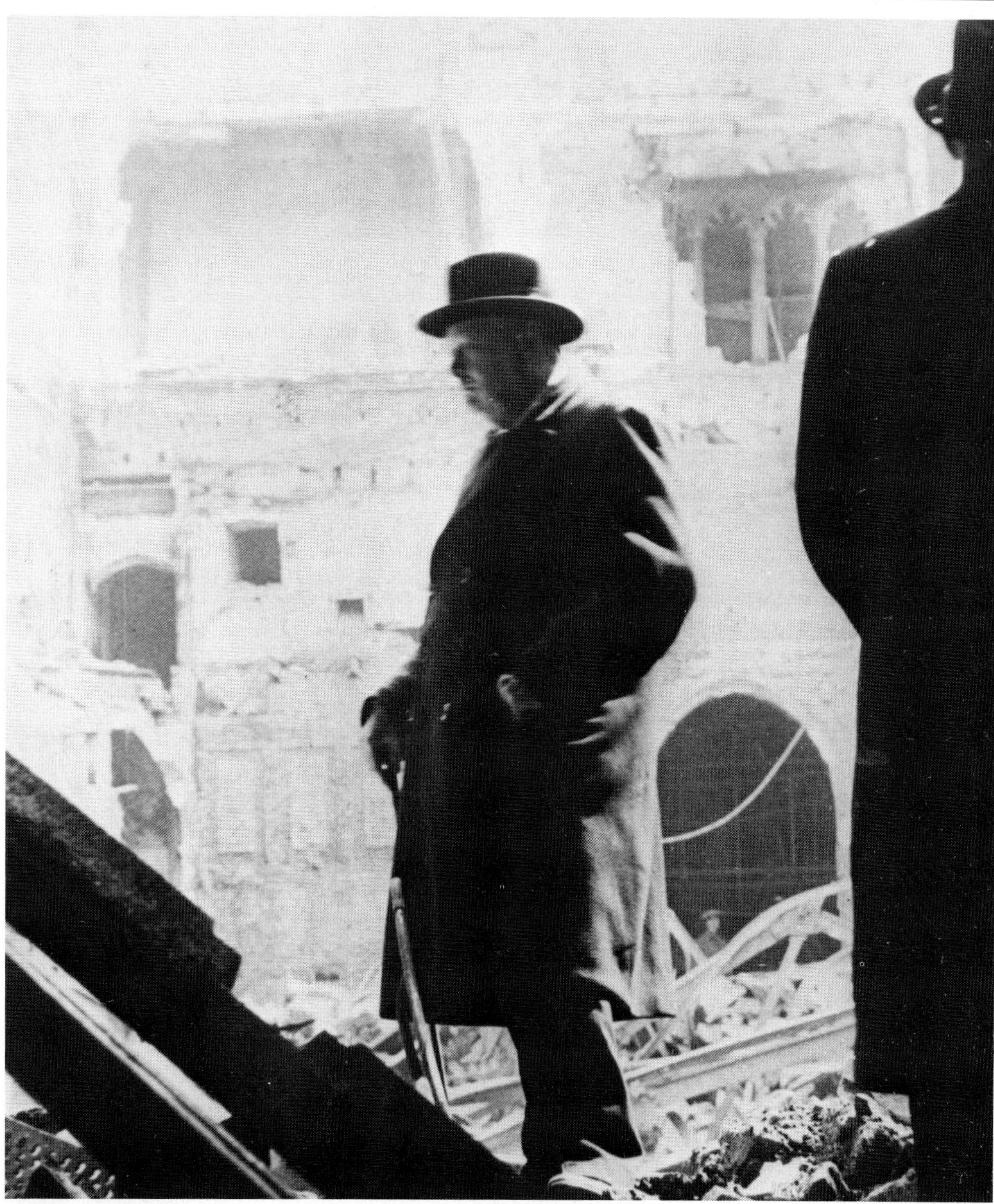

On the Wednesday before the raid, the House of Commons saw one of its most historical sessions when Churchill faced an upsurge of criticism over the fall of Greece and Cyrenaica. His speech to a packed Chamber was followed by a division in which the Government received a vote of confidence of 447 to 3 again. Three days later the same Chamber was a smoking ruin.

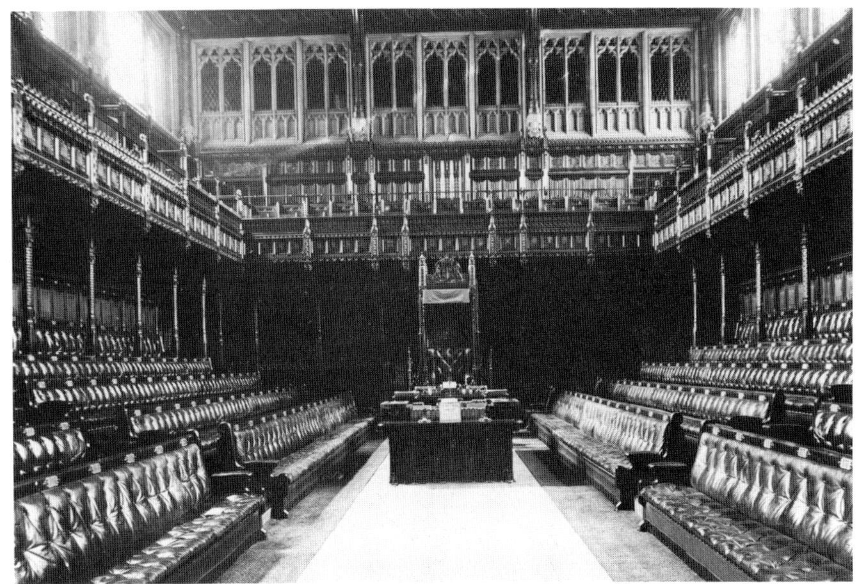

FINALE

Although the night Blitz on Britain had failed to bring about the collapse the Germans had anticipated it had not been unprofitable for them. Most rewarding had been the adverse affect on British aircraft production, which had been seriously impaired by the destruction of factories manufacturing components and ancilliary equipment and by the enforced dispersal of plant. Not until February 1941 did aircraft production reach the level of the previous early autumn. Shipbuilding and the iron and steel industry had also suffered serious setbacks, as had arms manufacture, communications, stocks of oil and food supplies. Further, more than 600,000 men had been tied to the military and civil defence of the country when they might better have been employed in activity against the Axis on other fronts.

The Germans had also inflicted heavy commercial and residential damage on the towns and cities which they attacked. More than one million houses were damaged or destroyed and casualties sustained by the civilian population were nearly 45,000 killed and some 50,000 injured. However, the Blitz was far from being a strategic victory. Widespread as the damage undoubtedly was, its effect on the country's overall production was not serious and in the onslaught on the ports only approximately 70,000 tons of food stocks were destroyed; oil stocks were depleted by less than one half of one per cent. Damage to communications — road, rail and telephone — was serious at times, but in every case repairs were quickly effected. At no stage of the German offensive did it appear that permanent, irreparable damage was being done to industry and that the ability of the country to wage war would be impaired. Nor was there any real likelihood of morale reaching the point where the population would force the Government to sue for peace. It must be conceded, though, that the Germans achieved a considerable amount of damage for an almost insignificant loss rate in aircraft and crews. Wholesale destruction and disruption had been achieved for the loss on night operations of about 600 bomber aircraft or approximately 1.5 per cent of the sorties flown. Thus, the campaign had been conducted at no great expense, but militarily it achieved little more than forcing the Royal Air Force and the Army to retain large numbers of men and equipment in the United Kingdom when they were sorely needed in other parts of the world.

The Blitz taught much to both the British and the Germans, but one thing was particularly clear — truly effective strategic bombing could only be achieved by directing an enormous weight of bombs at vital objectives such as power installations, the aircraft industry and ports. And for much of World War Two this was beyond the capability of any nation. It was certainly beyond the capability of Nazi Germany in the winter of 1940-1941.

Top: **The Chamber before and after May 10, 1941.** *Above left:* **Salvage work began in November, this picture showing completion of the debris removal in June 1942.** *Above right:* **The restored Chamber was completed in 1950 by Sir Giles Scott but the first official picture of the House of Commons in session was not taken until November 12, 1986.**

Glossary

AA Anti Aircraft
AI Airborne Interception (radar)
AI Air Intelligence (British)
AI1(g) Air Intelligence Technical intelligence (all air equipment)
AI1(k) Air Intelligence Interrogation of prisoners of war
Albino Free balloon barrage (originally named **Pegasus**)
Anzündergruppe A flying unit charged with lighting fires in a target area for the guidance of other less well-equipped units. Also known as a Beleuchtergruppe or, later, Pfadfindergruppe
Aspirin British radio jamming device
Aufklärungsgruppe Reconnaissance wing
AZ (Aufschlag Zünder) Impact bomb fuze

Beleuchtergruppe Luftwaffe fire raising unit for target marking (see also **Anzündergruppe**)
Benito The RAF code-name for the Y-Verfahren radio navigation system
Beobachter Observer (navigator/bomb aimer)
Blitz Literally 'Lightning'
Blitzlichtcylindrische Photographic flash bomb
Bombenmine (BM) 1000kg sea-mine adapted to be dropped on land, with or without a parachute, named 'Monika' or 'G' (George) Mine
Bordfunker Wireless Operator/Air Gunner
Bordmechaniker Flight Engineer
Bordschütze Air Gunner
Bromide RAF code-name for jamming X-system navigational radio signals
Brandebombe Incendiary Bomb (IB)
BSK Container holding incendiary bombs
BST British Summer Time

CAI Corpo Aereo Italiano
CP Concentration Point
CWGC Commonwealth War Graves Commission

DA Delayed action bomb
DBST Double British Summer Time
D/F Direction Finding equipment
Domino Jamming of German Y-Verfahren navigational radio beams
DPL Double-Parachute-Link (balloon cable)
DR Dead reckoning method of navigation. Also Dispatch Rider

El.A.Z (Electrische Aufschlag Zünder) Electrical impact bomb fuze
El.Z (Electrische Zünder) Electrical bomb fuze
Elsie Searchlight radar (see also SLC)
Enigma Machine for the encryption of signals traffic
Erprobungsgruppe 210 Experimental flight development wing equipped with the Bf 110 during the Battle of Britain and Blitz periods but later the Me 210
Esau 1000kg armour-piercing bomb

Fallschirmleuchtbombe Parachute flare
Fieseler Fi 103 V1 Flying Bomb
Fighter Night Defensive RAF Fighter patrols from 10,000-20,000ft
FIU Fighter Interception Unit
Flammenbombe (Flam) Fire or oil bomb
Fliegerkorps A command, subsidiary to a Luftflotte, and responsible for a variable number of Geschwader
Flugzeugführer Pilot
Fritz 1400kg armour-piercing bomb
Führungsstab Operations Staff of the Luftwaffe High Command
FTS Flying Training School (RAF)

GAF German Air Force
Geschwader Operational unit, approximately equivalent to a Group in the RAF. Normally comprised three operational Gruppen and a Staff Flight, with a total establishment of approximately 100 aircraft. Prefixed Kampf- (bomber), Jagd- (fighter), Zerstörer- (long-range fighter), etc., to indicate rôle
GC and CS Government Code and Cypher School
GCI Ground Control Interception
GL Gun Laying radar
Grossbritannien (GB) Great Britain
Gruppe (Gr) Operational unit, approximately equivalent to a Wing in the RAF. Normally comprised three Staffeln and a Staff Flight with a total establishment of approximately 30 aircraft. An independent bomber Gruppe was prefixed Kampf-
Gruppenkommandeur Commander of a Gruppe or Wing
GST German Summer Time

HE High Explosive
Headache RAF code-name for Knickebein beams
Heer Germany Army
Hermann 1000kg thin-cased general purpose bomb

IAZ Inner Artillery Zone
IB Incendiary Bomb
IFF Identification Friend or Foe transponder
Intruder Offensive RAF patrol over the Continent
IO Incident Officer

Jagdgeschwader (JG) Fighter Group

Kampfgeschwader (KG) Bomber Group
Kampfgruppe (KGr) Bomber Wing
Kette Flight, usually three bombers or four fighters
Knickebein (Kn) Code-name for German radio navigation beam, literally 'crooked leg'
Kopfring Steel ring fitted to nose of bomb to prevent excessive penetration into ground
Kriegsberichter War Correspondent
Kriegsmarine Navy
Küstenfliegergruppe (KuFlGr) Coastal Reconnaissance Wing

LAM Long Aerial Mine
LC (Leuchtcylindrische) Parachute flare (LC50)
Lehrgeschwader (LG) Instructional/operational development group
Luftflotte Air Fleet
Luftmine Sea mine adapted to be dropped on land by parachute (LMA=500kg, LMB=1000kg)
LZtZ (also LZZ) (Langzeitzunder) Long time delay bomb fuze

Max 2500kg thin-cased general purpose bomb
Meacon Retransmitting of German navigational radio beacons to give false bearings
MHS Ministry of Home Security
Monika 1000kg 'G' (George) Mine
MRC Main Regional Control
MU Maintenance Unit (RAF)
Mutton Air mining by Harrow aircraft
mV (mit Verzögerungszunder) Delayed-action bomb fuze

Nachtjagdgeschwader Night Fighter Group

Oberbefehlshaber Commander-in-Chief
Oberkommando der Luftwaffe (OKL) Air Force High Command
OTU Operational Training Unit (RAF)
oV (ohne Verzögerung) Bomb fuze without time delay

PAC Parachute and Cable airfield defence
PC (Panzerbombe-Cylindrisch) Armour-piercing bomb
Pegasus Free balloon barrage
Phosphorbrandbombe Phosphorus incendiary bomb
PPI Plan Position Indicator

Reichsluftfahrtministerium (RLM) German Air Ministry
Rivers RAF code-name for X-System radio navigational beams. Later re-named **Ruffians**

Satan 1800kg thin-cased general purpose bomb
Sprengbombe-Cylindrisch (SC) Thin-cased general purpose bomb
Sprengbombe-Dickwandig (SD) Thick-cased semi-armour piercing fragmentation bomb
Schleuderstart Winch-assisted method of take-off
Schwerpunkt Aiming point for raid
Seenotflugkommando Air Sea Rescue Service
Seerauberangriff literally 'Pirate' attacks, known to British as 'tip-and-run' or 'scalded-cat' raids
SLC Searchlight Control Radar, also known as 'Elsie'
Splitterbombe Anti-personnel 'Butterfly' bomb
Sprengbombe high-explosive bomb
Sprengbrandbombe Explosive incendiary bomb
Stab Staff
Staffel Squadron, normally nine aircraft
Staffelkapitän Squadron Commander
Starfish Dummy targets lit by fires to draw bombs from the intended target
Störangriffe Harassing attack
Stuka (Sturzkampfflugzeug) Ju 87 dive-bomber

TA Target Area

UP Unrotated Projectile — 'Z' battery anti-aircraft rocket
UXB Unexploded Bomb

Vergeltungswaffe Literally 'Revenge Weapon', i.e. V1 and V2
VHF Very High Frequency

Wehrmacht German Armed Forces as a whole, i.e. Army, Navy and Air Force
Wettererkundungs Weather reconnaissance
WIDU Wireless Intelligence and Development Unit
Wotan I The beam transmitter associated with the X-Verfahren VHF beam precision bombing aid
Wotan II The beam transmitter associated with the Y-Verfahren VHF beam precision bombing aid
W/T Wireless Telegraphy

X-Gerät X-Equipment. The aircraft installation associated with the reception of X-Verfahren signals
X-Verfahren X-System. A VHF multi-beam precision bombing system

Y-Service Wireless interception branch (RAF)
Y-Verfahren Y-System. A VHF single beam/range-measuring precision bombing system

Zerstörer Long-range fighter-bomber
Zerstörziele literally 'destruction' raids or attacks on specific factories
Zielraum Target Area
ZtZ (Zeitzünder) Time bomb fuze
Zunder Bomb fuze

Index to Volume 2

THE INDEX IS SPLIT INTO FOUR SUB-INDEXES: GENERAL, AIRCRAFT, PERSONNEL AND LOCATIONS. NUMBERS IN ITALIC REFER TO PHOTOGRAPHS.

GENERAL

AIRCRAFT

PERSONNEL

LOCATIONS

And this is the comparison to the picture which appeared on page 8 — the St Thomas Street façade of London Bridge station, — scene of the Stainer Street tragedy.

Photograph Credits

Adco Photo Service: 544 centre.
Aerofilms: 158 top.
Air Historical Branch: 468 top.
Air Ministry: 174 bottom.
Associated Newspapers: 189 bottom.
Associated Press: 155 top, 526 bottom.
Belfast Telegraph: 513 top.
Birmingham Libraries: 464 top.
M. Bowyer: 512 top left and centre.
Bundesarchiv: 23 top, 28, 30 top, 51 bottom, 56, 96, 97, 260 bottom, 421, 449 top, 450 top, 500 top.
Central Press: 39, 71 top, 74 top, 76 bottom left, 83 top rigt, 84 top, 107 top left, 128 bottom, 152 top, 153 top, 184 bottom, 267 top, 364 top right, 611 centre.
City of London Police: 85 bottom left, 367 bottom left, 375 top, 396 top right.
Clydebank District Libraries: 480 top.
Coventry Evening Telegraph: 263 top, 264 top, 266 middle left.
J. I. Cross: 528 top.
Daily Mail: 610 bottom left, 611 top.
Daily Mirror: 609 top left, bottom left.
Derby Evening Telegraph: 401 bottom.
ECPA: 29 bottom, 40, 130 top and middle, 136, 138, 174 top, 202 top and bottom, 203 top and bottom, 212 top and bottom, 213 top and bottom, 214 top and bottom, 215, 218, 257, 332, 334, 374, 401, 404 top and bottom, 447, 513 bottom.
Express and Independent: 122 top.
Flight: 163 centre.
Fox: 54 top, 108 top left, 182 top, 436 top, 515 top, 546 middle, 547 bottom left.
Grimsby Evening Telegraph: 497 top.
Guildhall Library: 217, 364 bottom left, 367 centre, 369 bottom right, 413 top left, rear endpaper.
Hull Daily Mail: 501 top, 594 top and bottom left, 595 top and bottom left, 596 top and bottom left, 597 bottom.
Imperial War Museum: 35 both, 36 top and centre, 38 top, 57, 61, 65 top and left, 67 top, 119 top left, bottom left, 132 bottom left, 135 top left, bottom left, 152 bottom, 231 both, 232 top and centre, 233 top left, 237 both, 238 top and centre, 239 top left, 243 bottom, 362 top, 385, 398 both, 417 top, 433 centre, 454 top, 455 top left and bottom, 522 right, 525 centre and bottom, 526 bottom, 570, 577.
H. Jenkins: 239 bottom left.
Keystone: 54 bottom left, 479 centre, 604 top, 608 top.
Liverpool Daily Post: 204 top left, 346.
Liverpool Record Office: 581, 582-583 bottom, 592 top.
London Fire Brigade: 61 bottom, 326 top, 366 bottom, 366 bottom left, 371 top left.
London Transport Museum: 244, 245 top, 247 both, 248.
Victor von Lossberg: 27 both.
Manchester Evening News: 350 top, 351 top, 352 top.
Melody Maker: 460 bottom left, 540 top.
Ministry of Defence: 163 top.
Ian Macrae: 151 bottom.
J. E. Marsh: 581 bottom.
National Monuments Record: 364 top left, 368 bottom left.
Newham Library Service: 58 top left, 59 top, 60 top left, 63 top, 77 both, 78 top left, 79 bottom, 241 top, 489 top, 490 top left, 491 bottom.
New York Times: 20, 21, 64 top.
Paul Popper (Popperfoto): 66 bottom, 68 top, 69 top, 189 top, 358 top, 361 top.
Polish Institute: 163 bottom left.
Portsmouth and Sunderland Newspapers: 195 bottom, 390 top right, 393 top, 553 bottom left, 572 top, 573 top.
Press Association: 340 bottom.
Radio Times Hulton Picture Library: 101 top right, 132 top left, 204 bottom left, 302 bottom, 316, 329 left, 546 bottom, 547 top.
RAF Museum: 239 centre.
Royal Commission on Historical Monuments: 146 top, 175 bottom.
G. Ruppelt: 34.
Schmeelke Collection: 29 top, 99 top.
Sheffield Newspapers: 338 centre left, 339 top and centre, 342 top left.
Solo Syndication and Literary Agency: 86 bottom right.
South Eastern Newspapers Ltd: 194 top, 236 top, 291 top, 343 top and bottom left, 405 top, 512 bottom left.
South Shields Central Library: 433 bottom left.
Southern Newspapers: 241 bottom, 424 bottom.
Southern Railway: 327 bottom left, 391 bottom.
Swains Norwich: 571 top.
Times Newspapers: 55 top, 100 centre, 133 top left and bottom left, 179 top, 266 top, 396 top left, 626.
Ullstein: 201 top.
Ulster Museum: 530 top, 531 top, 533 both.
US National Archives: 18–19, 49, 50, 51 top, 125 top, 131 top right, 135 top, 273 both, 315, 318 bottom, 319.
Via Ken Wakefield: 25 top, 26, 33, 37 bottom.
Western Mail and Echo: 438.
Western Morning News: 492 top, 493, 494 top centre, 495 top, 496 top.
Western Telegraph (Martin Cavaney): 301 bottom.

Additional photos from: Mrs Charlotte Felkin 32, D. J. Smith 37 top and Steve Hall, Alex King, Dennis Knight, the late Wilf Nicoll, Simon Parry, Dr Alfred Price, Andy Saunders, Vernon Scott and Ken Wakefield.